OF TIME AND LAMENTATION

Of Time and Lamentation

REFLECTIONS ON TRANSIENCE

Raymond Tallis

agenda
publishing

For Terry, my time's dearest companion

First published in 2017 by Agenda Publishing
First paperback edition 2019

Agenda Publishing Limited
The Core
Bath Lane
Newcastle Helix
Newcastle upon Tyne
NE4 5TF
www.agendapub.com

ISBN 978-1-78821-174-1

British Library Cataloguing-in-Publication Data
A catalogue record for this book is available from the British Library

Typeset by JS Typesetting Ltd, Porthcawl, Mid Glamorgan

Printed and bound in the UK by TJ International

Contents

Acknowledgements

I owe a debt of gratitude to four individuals who read the present volume in manuscript. Two young polymaths, Joe Boswell and Raja Panjwani, commented on the first part of the book, dealing with the way physics traduces time and the metaphysical claims of certain physicists. They steered me away from certain crass errors. Professor Barry Dainton's generous and very helpful response to the manuscript compounded the debts I had already incurred through reading his beautifully lucid and comprehensive *Time and Space* (Durham: Acumen, 2010). Finally, Professor Sir Roger Scruton read the manuscript (typos and "thinkos" and all) with great care and made many excellent suggestions.

This book was largely conceived and written in solitude. Most of my debts therefore are to strangers whose names and publications appear in the references. Time seems to attract more than its fair share of philosophers who not only write beautifully but have the capacity to keep in view the fundamental questions (and the excitement associated with them). In addition to a (necessarily incomplete) acquaintance with primary sources, I have been guided and inspired by secondary literature, foremost among them being (in addition to Dainton's *Time and Space*), Richard Gale's *The Philosophy of Time: A Collection of Essays* (London: Macmillan, 1968), Robin Le Poidevin's *Travels in Four Dimensions* (Oxford: Oxford University Press, 2003), the mighty *Oxford Handbook of Philosophy of Time* edited by Craig Callender (Oxford: Oxford University Press, 2011), and many authoritative and accessible essays in the *Stanford Encyclopedia of Philosophy*. I have also been happily and fruitfully provoked by frequent disagreements with D. H. Mellor's *Real Time* (Cambridge: Cambridge University Press, 1981) and *Real Time II* (London: Routledge, 1998), which are models to me of philosophical writing, although the reader will see at once that I cannot match his succinctness. Finally, many writers on physics have helped me get the scientific issues in focus and (perhaps not the effect they had looked for) enabled me to see more clearly the baselessness of the claims of physics to provide the answers to metaphysical problems.

I am more indebted than ever to Steven Gerrard who has been a wonderful supporter of my writing for nearly a decade and a publisher who is truly passionate about ideas.

Some of the material in this book has appeared in abbreviated form elsewhere. My regular column in *Philosophy Now* has seen earlier versions of several strands in the argument against the claims of physics to have the last word on the metaphysics of time, against logical fatalism, and on the idea that time began with a bang, and discussions of the nature of causation. The latter also draws on "Causes as (Local) Oomph" published in *Epimethean Imaginings: Philosophical and Other Meditations on Everyday Light* (Durham: Acumen, 2014). Shorter forms of the discussion of mathematics and reality in Chapter 3, of eternity in Chapter 9, and of freedom in Chapter 12 have been published in *The Mystery of Being Human: God, Free Will and the NHS* (London: Notting Hill, 2016).

Raymond Tallis

Overture (mainly polemic): why time?

I wasted time, and now doth time waste me. Shakespeare, *Richard II*

PERSONAL (1)

When I wake up each morning, I am less likely to reflect that a new day has arrived than that yet another day has departed. What we unthinkingly call "the passage of time" tinges the first few minutes with apprehension. I have entered my seventies and, although the end is as invisible as it ever was, my probability of dying in a given year is many times greater than when, as a teenager, I first tried to imagine the extinction of my life, my world, and all those who had shared it with me. My human being is more "begoing" than becoming. As Christopher Hitchens put it, "every day represents more and more subtracted from less and less".[1] The merely probable "not-yet" is shorter than the definite "no-longer"; and "ago" is increasingly measured in decades rather than years. An optimistic calculation puts the number of days I imagine as "lying ahead" of me between a half and a third of the number that lie behind me: I am somewhere between supper-time and midnight in my life's day. Since my last phase may be marked by chaos, confusion, pain and despair, the period in which I may be capable, in particular capable of thought, will most probably be even shorter than the quantity of time that remains to me.

This may be why, in certain moods, an ordinary Tuesday can seem, from the ordinary Wednesday that succeeds it, unreachable, beyond recall, in its own special sunlight; a privileged place merely in virtue of owning more of the future than does this present day. The extra day of "being there" becomes a giant stretch when I think of the fewness of my days of "I am" compared with the days of "I am not", the endless – dateless and data-less – night of my absence which lacks even the quality of darkness.

What's more, the pace seems to be quickening. "I can't believe that a year has gone by since ..." is now replaced by a second order dismay: "I really can't believe a year has gone by since I last said 'I can't believe a year has gone by since ...'". Inflation seems to affect time as surely as it does money. There is an obvious, but probably wrong, explanation for this feeling that the tug towards increasing age is getting stronger; namely that the lengthening contrail of memory makes each successive day a smaller fraction of life so far. This proportionality explanation does not work, of course, because, by the time you were forty, days would be flashing by 80 times as fast as when you were 6 months old. Such an acceleration does not seem to fit with the occasional day that does drag, as when you are ill, listening to the uninvited monologue of a fellow passenger on a long haul flight, or stuck on a slow-moving train late for an appointment.[2] Perhaps the acceleration is due to the diminishing significance or novelty of the events that fills our hours.

Whatever the cause, on each 1 January the number designating the year just past looks less used up than its predecessor. By the time 1960 had arrived, my 1959 was worn out and its replacement overdue. When 2011 was announced, I was still not used to 2010 and even 2009 and 2008 looked scarcely touched. It is hardly surprising that I sometimes feel – as I imagine you, reader, do when yet another day, another week, another summer, another year has melted away – as if I were being swept, log-like, towards a cataract dropping into oblivion.

This feeling of suppressed panic has prompted me to think systematically about time, perhaps in the hope that, by cultivating a special kind of attention to it, I might slow it down or (if the expectation of having such an impact on the universe was unrealistic) slow my own passage to oblivion. An exploration prompted by gathering uneasiness would, you might think, best be addressed through lyric poetry or fiction that endeavours to rescue time lost. I have chosen philosophy not just because the familiar conundrums always yield something new. No; it is because the traditional problems are the visible surface of the invisible mystery of our "time-torn" condition. Granted, it is easy, too easy, to slip from thinking about whatever we have in mind when we feel the need to engage with "time itself" to thinking about the thoughts that others have had about time.

If this is an ever present danger it is because the literature on time – even if you confine yourself to metaphysics and bypass the huge bibliographies on the psychology of time perception, the representation of time in myth, in different cultures, in history, and the various ways time is expressed in narrative – is almost boundless. I am sufficiently aware of the size of that literature to know that no life of normal duration would be adequate to engage with it. And this will be evident in the modest list of references at the end of the book.

In his brilliant *Real Time II*, one of the many books that I have argued with (mainly against) in the last decade or so, D. H. Mellor says that he hopes "that the fewness of my references will not be taken as a sign of ignorance or arrogance"; on the contrary, it is because "I take it that my main points, if disputed, to be so common in the literature as to be by now public property."[3] In my case, arrogance is not an issue; indeed, I am humbled by my awareness of the other failing named by Mellor, namely "ignorance".

Even so, I think I know enough of what is, and has been, thought about time that I can be reasonably sure of not missing the main issues and of not being self-deceived into a fantasy of originality simply because, like Irie in Zadie Smith's *White Teeth*, I was unaware that certain thoughts had been "thunk" before.[4] To elect not to engage with the ideas and arguments of other thinkers, advanced in the millennia since time became a central theme of western philosophy, would be a self-impoverishing and self-defeating ordinance that would result not in intellectual independence and novelty but an unwilled dependence on a muddled version of the half-recalled views of predecessors. While much of *Of Time and Lamentation* is closer than it may appear to being an argument with myself than a work of scholarship, I am aware that an argument that has sufficient merit to be worthy of auditing by a third party, must be enriched by engagement with the work done by others in the philosophy of time, even when the engagement is non-systematic and far from comprehensive.

A first philosophy?

I have written about time as an indirect way of thinking about mortality. If *Of Time and Lamentation*, therefore, has all the appearance of a treatise, and even at places a scholarly one, it is not, as conventional as it appears. Its scope and ambition, for a start, is foolhardy – as befits an attempt to confront my (and your) finitude; of trying to think about a truth that defeats thought because it spans all that I am. Not that the mysteries of time offer an easy approach to otherwise inconceivable mortality: they resist contemplation almost as strongly as death repels it.[5] Most obviously, this is because we seem to have to stand outside of time to be able to see it clearly; to adopt a viewpoint that is not merely outside of some particular inside but outside of all outsides. There is something deeply contradictory about assuming such a position if only because writing, thinking, reading are all located in time.[6]

Of course time-talk is not uniquely disabled in this way.[7] Philosophy is always written in the teeth of its own impossibility if only because it is encircled, and encroached upon, by its objects of study; and the inquiry often rests on the assumptions or materials that are being inspected. Any metaphysical discussion of "Being" has to be conducted by beings, who are minute fragments of Being, the bounded part trying to encompass the boundless whole. The philosophy of language has to be pursued from within language, using words and sentences to rise above words, and examine sentences. Thinkers have to think their way to a position from which they imagine they can think about "thought". Discussions of "the reality of the outside world" have to assume that it is "out there", if only in the form of interlocutors. Anyone who wants to think at a metaphysical level about time – or "consciousness" or "the universe" come to that – therefore faces the Munchausen challenge of lifting one's self by one's own hair. We can sometimes do this, or seem to do so, too easily, commenting in the most automatic even absent-minded, way on, say, "the world", asserting gigantic truths (or falsehoods) in ordinary sentences that hardly have the draught to accommodate the thoughts we echo.

The very existence of the word "time" and the identification of time as a discrete theme for inquiry should therefore surprise us. We should not assume unquestioningly that there is something definite, unified, solid corresponding to a word, even when it has the office of a noun. This assumption does however form a necessary platform from which to launch our inquiry. Here, as elsewhere, to philosophize is to enter a conversation and we have to employ the terms that are used by our interlocutors. Uncertainty about the firmness of this platform, however, explains why the question "(What) Is Time?" is postponed to the final part of the book, where I shall try (among other things) to clarify what remains when we have set aside the almost irresistible metaphors that intervene between our experience of time and our thoughts about it.

Ontology, logic, epistemology have all laid claim to being a starting point for philosophy; and Emmanuel Levinas has even argued that, since responsibility precedes any searching after truth, ethics is the foundational philosophical discipline.[8] Some of the reasons for adding the metaphysics of time to this short list will, I hope, be evident in the chapters that follow. Like any ground floor philosophical inquiry, that into the nature of time reaches into other fundamental philosophical preoccupations – for example, the nature of change, the fundamental stuff of the world, the relationship between discourse and that which it is about, human consciousness (by a long chalk, the most frequent subject of my published philosophical writings), and human freedom. Time entered the history of Western philosophy even before philosophy clearly separated itself from mythology and it has subsequently been a theme of equal concern to philosophers and theologians.

Physics and philosophy

If thinking about time is an indirect way of meditating on our mortality, then we need to focus on time as it is lived. This means rescuing time from the jaws of physics, one of the primary aims of the present volume – and it connects with the fundamental motivation of many of my other books.

For several decades, I have believed that the great intellectual challenge of contemporary thought is to find a way of thinking about ourselves that does not regress to supernatural beliefs or slip into a reductive naturalism. As part of meeting this challenge, we have to deal with the conflict between on the one hand possibly the most profound, and certainly the most practically effective, ways of thinking about the world in which we pass our lives, namely natural science, and on the other our everyday experience of the world, of ourselves, and of each other – the world in which scientists actually live and the rest of us make use of their findings. Science aims towards the most objective view and arrives at us humans – its starting point – last. The humanities and the arts begin from ourselves and reach out to the world; or at least they have done so in recent times in Western cultures though, historically, they have often skipped the world and reached past it to God. The endeavour to find a place at which the scientific and humanistic views of humanity are reconciled, and to examine the relationship between what the American philosopher Wilfrid Sellars characterized as the "manifest" and the "scientific image", and to seek something that encompasses them both, is our real task.[9] This goes deeper than merely making links between art and the sciences – between bad art and pop science.

More importantly, this project begins with a rejection of scientism that sees science (ultimately physical science) as in some sense superseding the view of ourselves explored and elaborated in the arts and humanities. It is an essential part of this project to challenge the increasingly prevalent assumption that physics has the last word on the nature of time. To do so, however, is to risk being classified with the kind of individual who, writing to Professor Einstein from a park bench (with a crayon in one hand and a methylated spirits spritzer in the other), points out the errors in his theory of relativity. So it is important to make clear that *Of Time and Lamentation* does not aim to correct the physics of time but only to say why and how physics has little or nothing to say about much that truly matters about time. In an important sense it "loses" time – something that some physicists might welcome, given that aspects of it seem to have no place in a physical world whose laws seem to be time reversible, or invariant with respect to temporal reversal, and hence indifferent to the unfolding of time.

Several prominent physicists have attacked philosophy as a waste of breath. Notable among them is the Nobel Prize winner Steven Weinberg, who devotes an entire chapter of his *The Theory of Everything* to this topic.[10] Even where "the insights of philosophers have occasionally benefitted physicists", he says, this has been "generally in a negative fashion – by protecting them from the preconceptions of other philosophers".[11] Ouch! And he reports that "I know of *no-one* who has participated actively in the advance of physics in the post-war period whose work has been significantly helped by the work of philosophers."[12]

It is tempting to respond by inviting him to "get out more" or at least to note that in the early part of the twentieth century many of the great physicists (Einstein, Bohr, Schrödinger, and Heisenberg) *were* preoccupied with philosophy and acknowledged the influence of philosophers. Some physicists and philosophers of physics – most notably Lee Smolin – have even argued that the stagnation in particle physics since the Standard Model was completed in 1974, might have something to do with the rejection of the kind of radical reflection on the conceptual framework of science that philosophers indulge in.[13] George Musser notes that while certain physicists think that being seen talking to a philosopher is "like being caught coming out of a pornographic cinema" others do have different views.[14] Musser quotes Carlo Rovelli, a leading figure in the endeavour to reconcile quantum mechanics with the general theory of relativity, who has argued that "the contributions of philosophers to the new understanding of space and time in quantum gravity will be very important".[15]

Rovelli – who, as we shall discuss, believes that time at the fundamental level is unreal – and Smolin are probably in a minority in their belief that physicists need philosophy. The quantitative epidemiology of opinions is an uncertain science: it is possible to mistake loudness for quantity. What is beyond question is the prominence of those for whom mathematical physics is the only way to advance our understanding of time. Foremost among them in the popular mind is Stephen Hawking. He has famously argued that questions such as "How can we understand the world in which we find ourselves? How does the universe behave? What is the nature of reality? Where did all this come from? Did the universe need a creator … ?" – traditionally questions for philosophy – are this no longer. His assertion that "philosophy is dead. Philosophy has not kept up with modern developments in science, particularly physics" attracted wide public attention and a good deal of uncritical agreement.[16] The absurdity of his one-time claim that astrophysics can even answer questions that philosophers usually leave to theologians does not seem to have discredited him in the eyes of many people. M-theory, which unifies (or, we are promised, will one day unify) quantum mechanics and the general theory of relativity, is apparently able to explain how the universe came into being; why there is something rather than nothing.[17]

The dismissal of philosophy by physicists has been made easier by the fact that many philosophers have colluded in the capitulation of metaphysics to physics. The heirs of the Vienna Circle who gave birth to logical positivism and the most scientistic strands of analytical philosophy would have agreed with Weinberg: "The insights of the philosophers I studied seemed murky and inconsequential compared with the dazzling successes of physics and mathematics."[18] The deferential attitude to physics among philosophers has outlived logical positivism and the discrediting of its critique of metaphysics. The philosopher Hilary Putnam was speaking for many when he stated quite baldly that philosophy has little to contribute to our understanding of time: "I do not believe that there are any longer any philosophical problems about Time; there is only the physical problem of determining the exact physical geometry of the four-dimensional continuum that we inhabit".[19]

The conviction that the last word on the ultimate nature of the universe, and even of items in the universe such as you and me, belongs to (mathematical) physics which is approaching by successive approximations a God's eye view is tenacious. The contrary notion that time is inseparable from human consciousness – which would seem to challenge the assumption that physics has the last word on time – does not cut much ice with some. After all, physicalist accounts of consciousness have, until recently, been in the ascendant in philosophy, though there are signs that they are now in retreat.[20] One of the most striking expressions of the belief that metaphysical problems are problems for physicists is an incongruously cheerful philosophical suicide note by James Ladyman and his fellow authors in *Every Thing Must Go*.[21] They embrace scientism as "a badge of honour" and advance what they call the "Principle of Naturalistic Closure":

> Any new metaphysical claim that is to be taken seriously at time t should be motivated by, and only by, the service it would perform, if true, in showing how two or more specific scientific hypotheses, at least one of which is drawn from fundamental physics, jointly explain more than the sum of what is explained by the two hypotheses taken separately.[22]

This is an assertion that quickly runs into all sorts of internal difficulties (as do the conclusions it is used to uphold, such as denying the reality of particular objects located in definite places including, one presumes, Professor Ladyman's own body, in favour of relations or relational structures)[23] but its main deficiency is that it bypasses the essential work of the metaphysician, which transcends Ladyman's claim that it is "the attempt to unify the sciences".[24] What is meant by "unification" here is not clear; after all it is obviously the job of physics, not metaphysics, to unify (say) the laws of electricity and magnetism into those of electromagnetism, to connect thermo-dynamics with the laws governing the movements of atoms, or reconcile quantum mechanics and relativity theory. At any rate, thinking philosophically about the fundamental nature of the world will go beyond adopting the humble under-gardener role of helping current science ("at time t"!) to progress towards its own notion of a Theory of Everything; it will include looking critically at science itself, at the metaphysical assumptions upon which it is founded, and the processes by which its mathematical objects and images become established as either the most faithful or most complete portrait of reality in itself.[25]

It is, of course, entirely proper that we should be willing to sacrifice an intuitively satisfying understanding of the phenomena of everyday life for the sake of mathematical truths that will greatly enhance our predictive and manipulative power through the technology that mathematized science makes possible. To this end, we may embrace an awe-inspiringly effective theory such as quantum mechanics when we try to predict what is happening in the physical world and to create technologies that exploit our mathematized understanding of the nature of material reality. And, as Tim Maudlin has expressed it, "Empirical science has produced more astonishing suggestions about the fundamental structure of the world than philosophers have been able to invent, and we must attend to those suggestions".[26] But we should not accept that the last word on the universe in which we live and on the nature of reality is to be spoken in the language of physics – for the simple reason that the great pioneers from Nils Bohr onwards admitted that quantum mechanics was not only "astonishing" but also unintelligible.

It was Richard Feynman who said "I can safely say no one can understand quantum mechanics" – with the implication that anyone who thought they *did* understand quantum mechanics manifestly did not.[27] As the astrophysicist Jim Al-Khalili has noted:

> [Quantum mechanics] is remarkable for two seemingly contradictory reasons. On the one hand, it is so fundamental to our understanding of the workings of our world that it lies at the very heart of most of the technological advances made in the past half-century. On the other hand, no one seems to know exactly what it means.[28]

And the progress of physics in those areas where it would presume to displace metaphysics has, over the last half-century, been ever deeper into unintelligibility, notwithstanding its increasing mathematical power to make predictions that extend even to previously undiscovered properties of the material universe.

It is an appropriate philosophical task, and an urgent intellectual challenge, to confront the fact that a theory such as quantum mechanics that is entirely unintelligible should also be so powerful, vastly extending our ability to manipulate and predict the world. It makes the chasm between the scientific and everyday or manifest image of the world a kind of scandal. In addressing this, we must bear in mind that the power of physics depends on excluding much of the world, exsanguinating it of phenomenal reality, reducing it to a residual stuff best described mathematically. Weight is reduced to a ratio, and shorn of the sense of heaviness; inertia is characterized without appealing to the experience of effort and labour; colours are combinations of radiations defined in terms of frequency and amplitude; and so on. Physics travels fast and far because it travels light.

There comes a point, after qualities such as warmth, brightness and loudness have been dismissed as merely secondary, when effort and hurry disappear as they are replaced by forces and velocities, and even the idea of definite location is seen as belonging only to the macroscopic realm of approximate truths, when we want to say "stop". This point has been reached when physicists and their philosophical fellow travellers tell us that their understanding trumps all other ways of understanding and, what is more, that one day it will be complete in the sense of encompassing everything, leaving nothing, including ourselves, unexplained. Just as it would be unscientific to accept current scientific theories as the definitive account of space and time, it is unphilosophical to assume that *any* scientific theory would have the last word on what there is and what we are. What is more, as we have already suggested, some of the present difficulties that fundamental physics finds itself in may be due to conceptual confusions which result from failure to pay attention to those things that concern philosophers. At any rate, it seems likely to be true that, as Hans Halvorson has said, "If we put bad metaphysics into our scientific theories, then we can expect to get bad metaphysics out of them".[29]

Mellor deplores the fact that "so many philosophers are absurdly credulous of the wildest speculations of physicists about time".[30] Not all philosophers it seems are so prone to cringe before the authority of science or believe that their role is merely to act as cheerleaders for physical science on the grounds that the immensely powerful, and complex and largely unintelligible discourses of science are not only the latest, but will generate the last, word on metaphysical issues. Numerous writers have assimilated the findings of physicists but have nonetheless continued with their own inquiries, confident that the nature of time is not entirely to be revealed in the world of mathematical physics. They have examined the logic of tenses, puzzled over the nature of becoming, tried to grasp what we mean, or should mean, about the passage of time and the idea of the direction of time, endeavoured to make sense of past and future events, and wondered whether time is inseparable from change, whether it is punctuate or continuous, and whether tensed time, or even time itself, are real – all without deferring to physics.

Those who hunger to make other than mathematical sense of physical theories such as those of quantum mechanics are often rebuffed by physicists. The truth is in the mathematics: this is all ye know and ye need to know. This attitude is encapsulated in David Mermin's famous "Shut up and calculate!"[31] This is unsatisfactory – not the least to those such as myself who are not particularly brilliant at calculation. But that's not the only reason that I, for one, am not going to shut up. The more important reason for opening my mouth – or at least thinking for myself – is that I, too, live in time and inhabit space, and so I am entitled to talk about both. And I am inclined to retort to the physicists: "shut up and get on with your calculations". For I have no problem with those who simply get on with their calculations, so long as they don't think their calculations are metaphysics, or that they render philosophical metaphysics redundant, like a cognitive ox cart in an age of sports cars and jumbo jets.

There are other reasons for not turning to physics for the last word on time. Firstly, physics is itself in something of an impasse, with its two most powerful theories in conflict. As Barry Dainton has put it:

> We know that our current fundamental physical theories are imperfect: quantum theory and general relativity have yet to be fully reconciled. It may well be that the theory that emerges from this eventual marriage will have very different implications for the nature of space and time than those of currently acceptable theories, so it would be very short-sighted to take *current* scientific theories to be the last word on space and time *in our universe*.[32]

Since general relativity treats physical quantities such as velocity and position as having determinate values which quantum mechanics cannot accommodate and quantum mechanics allows influences to be transmitted at faster-than-light speeds not permitted by general relativity, this is not only short-sighted but also contrary to the spirit of science.

But there is a deeper reason that is closest to what has motivated this book. There are many aspects of time – most notably tense, but also other key features of it – that lie beyond the reach of physical science (even where the reality of time is accepted at all). The assumption that what physical science cannot see, or has no use for, is not real or is less real, needs to be questioned. It is an assumption that has allowed the scientism that is so prevalent in contemporary thought to spread unchallenged and for an anti-humanist naturalism to predominate in so many quarters.[33] The case against this scientism – though it must still acknowledge that we are in some respects (minute) parts of the natural world and that living our lives requires us to go with the grain of the natural world – is well founded. We are (a) conscious of the natural world; (b) active explorers of that world who have ever-increasing objective knowledge of it; and (c) true agents whose lives are acted out rather than merely suffered. Making this case will require much preliminary work – including showing how physical science is unable to accommodate the conscious observer that makes physical science possible. That is why it is not until the final chapter of this work that it is addressed head on.

For the present I note that it is not only unscientific but also unphilosophical to assume that *any* findings and theories from objective, quantitative science will settle the nature of time once and for all or that what is lost in physics of our experience and of what makes our world intelligible was well lost because illusory.[34] To say this is not to reject science – how could any sane person deny that it is the greatest collective cognitive achievement of humanity? – but to assign it to its proper place and to rescue time from the jaws of physics and from the dropped jaws of philosophers so awed by physics as to hand over metaphysical inquiry to physicists. And in respect of the latter, physics-savvy philosophers should not succumb to the temptation described by Jean Paul Van Bendegem: "When appealing to findings from empirically well-grounded disciplines, philosophers face a strong temptation to overstate their case – especially if their opponents can be relied upon to be relatively innocent of new developments in the relevant sciences".[35]

Although much of this book amounts to affirmative action for our ordinary experience of time, I don't entirely support the claim that immediate experience and intuition are more significant than rationalism and science for understanding reality.[36] For a start, we need to clarify what we mean by "reality": it is wilfully naïve to confine it to what is present to unmediated and immediate experience or even to the mediated experience of common sense. It is, however, equally culpable to overlook the "there" in the conception of "what is there" (or even what there is). As I shall discuss in Chapter 11, the irruption of viewpoint – that makes what there is be explicitly what is *there* and underpins the emergence of those aspects of time that physics seems to let slip or set aside – has to be taken into account in any fundamental understanding of reality.

And there are many physicists, most notably Einstein, who were unhappy with the impoverished (though immensely powerful) conception of time he had had such a crucial role in developing. He would have sympathized with this question from Paul Davies, physicist and brilliant popularizer of science:

> Should we simply shrug the human experience of time aside as a matter solely for psychology? ... Does our impression of the division of time into past, present and future tell us nothing about what time *is* as opposed to how it merely appears to us muddle-headed humans? ... It seems to me that there is an aspect of time that we have so far overlooked in our description of the physical universe.[37]

It is the role of philosophy to try to bridge – or, if this is too ambitious, to find a way of thinking that accommodates – both of Wilfrid Sellars's epistemic realms and not to reject either in favour of the other. While the emphasis in the present volume (especially in the first part) has been to criticize the assumption that natural science (and in particular physics) will ultimately provide us with all we need to answer metaphysical questions insofar as they are answerable, this is only because *Of Time and Lamentation* is a *corrective*. What is left unaddressed (because I do not know how to address it) i.s the actual contribution physics may make to metaphysics and vice versa or what a unified world picture, beyond a unified science, would look like. In physics (or at least in quantum mechanics under certain interpretations) it may be true that (as Ladyman argues) "every thing" – mountains, trees, tables, and bodies – "must go", we then have to try to understand how it is that we live in a world where things most definitely have stayed and just where they always are: here, there and everywhere. I shall return to the question of the relationship between philosophy and physics at the end of Part I.

PERSONAL (2)

I have come late to thinking about this First Philosophy and to writing about it even later. Though I touched on time in my commentary on Martin Heidegger's *Being and Time*,[38] my focus has been on the philosophy of mind, in the broadest sense, and on the relationship between language and the world. Of all the grand topics of philosophy, time had until recently seemed most alien to me, notwithstanding that nothing else, seemingly, could touch more intimately on the kind of beings we are, on our mode of existence.

I blame this on the first discussions I had about time as a schoolboy. These were dominated by those classmates who, unlike me, had televisions and had watched Hermann Bondi's pioneering series on cosmology, physics – and time. They were able to talk with seeming confidence about relativity, time dilation, and the famous twin paradoxes. The knowingness of those who thought that Einstein had spoken the last word on time both irritated and dispirited me. Even then, I did not believe that the truth of time could be grasped only by those who felt at home with complex mathematics. But while I was genuinely sceptical of the relevance of mathematics and physics to understanding what time meant in everyday life, I had an uneasy feeling that my scepticism may have been at least in part motivated by my limited mathematical abilities. Even so, Lorentz coordinates and the like seemed remote from the time that was expressed in hurry, anxiety, hope, longing, waiting, enduring, planning, promising, joyful expectation, and grief; in short from time as it was manifested in my life and narrated in the thoughts that accompanied that life. Real time was composed of mornings and afternoons and evenings as well as quantities that could be tucked under a denominator or multiplied by themselves and seemed to have little to do with physical systems that evolved according to physical theory in a way that requires complex numbers to be represented.

And so things remained until a few years ago, when a concatenation of events awoke my interest in this theme. The first was retirement after 37 years as a physician. As the dust settled down on a career that had occupied most of my waking consciousness between my early twenties and the age of 60, I had the sense of entering what had once been viewed as the final phase of life, along with the leisure to reflect on this. Another was the accident of coming across, in my own library, and not re-read for 30 years, a remarkable collection of papers about time edited by Richard Gale and accompanied by an equally remarkable introduction and commentary.[39] I read it on a Greek island, in sunlight that seemed especially conducive to thought. I made copious notes that in turn spurred me to further thought. In 2008, my mother, the place of my beginning in time and with whom I had spent much time, especially in the decade after my father's death, died after a long illness. The fact that she and I could no longer talk together seemed at least as strange as it felt sad. We had often talked about the strangeness of death and it was doubly strange now that I could not talk to her about that strangeness. Her going made the mystery of her life visible and demanded that I should think, at a level deeper than I had customarily done so, about mortality and transience, and hence time. All my experiences of her were in the past and it seemed more urgent to examine the nature of past events.

It has often been said that philosophy should teach one how to die. As a doctor I have seen enough of dying to be aware of the distance of most philosophical thought from the final phase of our return to the earth which has supported our singular existence. Nevertheless, I do believe we should use the idea of death to enhance our sense of life and its mystery.[40] Life at its most abundant is life lived in full consciousness of its finitude, in luminous awareness that our hands will grasp and our eyes will see and our hearts will beat for only a while. The art of living is also the art of outliving: to get over those who have "gone before" without becoming shallow. A meditation on time – on the mystery of the past we shared with them, the passage of time that took us past them, the future which seems to lie like a buffer between this moment and death – is an appropriate kind of *memento mori*, a way of getting closer to the unthinkable.

It will now be clear why this book is written in implicit, and frequently explicit, opposition to the domination of scientific accounts of time rooted in mathematical physics. The glory and triumphs of physics are in part the result of our getting ourselves, our parochial perspectives, out of the way; as a consequence, however, it looks straight past our lives. While there is nobility in seeing ourselves as part of a greater whole, and an unsentimental honesty in thinking of ourselves – including our days and hours – as minute physical parts of a boundless physical world, the domination of physics and natural science in our thinking threatens to attenuate our conception of what we and our lives are. And this is most strikingly elevated in its stripping time to the quantitative skeleton of itself. A truly serious inquiry into time, one that is adequate to our death-pervaded lives, should be haunted, as our lives are, by hope, loss, and fear; by joy and lamentation. The story told by caesium clocks and four-dimensional coordinate maps needs to be supplemented by moss on rocks, and tears on faces, and the long narratives of our human journey. Our temporal lives deserve a richer attention than is afforded by equations, diagrams, and numbers. The present work (alas, more argumentative than lyrical) is at least a preface to that kind of attention. The fact that I have avoided the Rolls-Royce of philosophical logic in favour of the sedan chair of ordinary English prose is not merely a reflection of my lack of expertise in this area. I have not tried very hard to amend this because I feel that you can lose contact with any intuitive sense of the issues at stake when formulae take over and you don't seem somehow to arrive at the places they take you to. I believe this feeling may be shared by many of those whom I hope might read this book.

I am not sufficiently capable of magic thought to believe that, by thinking hard about time, and perhaps revising conceptions of it, I can somehow escape the transience that characterizes all of time's children. Or that by showing the notion of "the passage of time" to be ill-formed I can render myself immune from the mortality to which increasing age makes me increasingly vulnerable. The journey from my house to the excellent pubs and cafés where much of this book has been written could still be the scene of a car crash that will mark this day as my last and any publication of *Of Time and Lamentation* that of a posthumous torso. Nothing that I have written or thought will make it a whit more likely that "the block of frozen urine falling towards my head from an overhead 747" (to borrow Nick Hornby's metaphor for the catastrophic event, always expected in general but always unexpected when it happens) will reverse direction and return whence it came.[41] In short, I do not imagine that by unpicking a few conceptual locks, I will escape the prison of transience; or take the benefits of universal change (the most obvious being that it brought me into existence) without paying the price of it (that it will sooner or later bring Raymond Tallis to an end).

Nevertheless, I have to confess that this exploration of lived time *is* in part an attempt to think my way out of the sense of being frogmarched past a succession of "day marks" to the end of myself; an endeavour to row back against the ultimate helplessness, and the inevitable end of purpose, stealing up as we express and deliver on our purposes. If, as I know full well, even this is more than can be hoped for, I still feel that, by re-thinking time, we may elude a form of naturalism that sees us as being at bottom material objects whose nature will ultimately be described by physics. We are more than cogs in the universal clock, forced to collaborate with the very progress that pushes us towards our own midnight. By placing human consciousness at the heart of time, it is possible to crack ajar a door through which a sense of possibility can stream.

And if this still seems like magic thinking, it is nothing compared with the hope of Paul Davies that physics may lead us to a place beyond lamentation, the sunlit uplands of No More Tears:

> And what if science were able to explain away the flow of time? Perhaps we would no longer fret about the future or grieve for the past. Worries about death might become as irrelevant as worries about birth. Expectation and nostalgia might cease to be part of the human vocabulary. Above all, the sense of urgency that attaches to human activity might evaporate.[42]

Rather touching that this hope should flower in what must be the stoniest of soils, in an intellectual landscape dominated by physical science.

While, inevitably, there will be some difficult passages in what follows, it is genuinely addressed to anyone who, like myself, is obsessed by what we are inclined to call "the passage of time" and wants to see it more clearly. I take my cue from the great philosopher Henri Bergson, who once said to a journalist: "There is nothing in philosophy that could not be said in everyday language."[43] This was not always apparent in Bergson's own works but I hope that there will be sufficient everyday language in what follows, given that it deals, however inadequately, with the profoundest every-day concern of us all; that, as Hamlet's mother characterized it, chiding her son for his excessive grief over his father, "all that lives must die / Passing through nature to eternity".[44]

Nor will I pretend to question things that cannot truly be questioned. The picture of time that I offer is descriptive, a set of reminders, not revisionary; for I agree with the great American philosopher C. S. Peirce that we should "not pretend to doubt in philosophy what we do not doubt in our hearts".[45] But I might at the very least feel that I have earned the right to look critically at something I said at the outset of this Overture: that my days are numbered.[46] For our lives are not truly represented as divided into temporal units, even ones that are as informal and homely as days. Or if they are, the numbers do not reach to the heart of our experience of time.

I would like this book not only to intrigue but also at times to console. I have men-tioned my 37 years as a doctor. The physician's habit of trying to "cure, improve, or comfort" is hard to break. I warm to Epicurus:

> Empty are the words of that philosopher who offers no therapy for human suffering. For just as there is no use in medical expertise if it does not give therapy for bodily diseases, so too there is no use in philosophy if he does not expel the suffering of the soul.[47]

In this case, the patient and the physician are one. Join me, fellow sufferers in exam-ining the source of our pain, and our joy, of our limitations and our capabilities, of actuality and possibility: time.

PART I

Killing time

The laws of physics contain a time variable, but it fails to capture key aspects of time as we live it – notably the distinction between past and future. And as researchers try to formulate more fundamental laws, the little "t" [the time variable] evaporates altogether.

Musser, "A Hole at the Heart of Physics", 30

CHAPTER 1

Introduction: seeing time

Ineluctable modality of the visible.   Joyce, *Ulysses*, 45

1.1 VISION: FROM IMPLICIT TO EXPLICIT TIME

Something we call "time" permeates everything that happens and everything we do. Events, processes, experiences, actions, and activities take place at particular times and occupy stretches of time, are composed of constituents that also occupy time, have a temporal order, and are otherwise related in time to each other. Time also seems to be intimated to us from within our own bodies, incarnate in what we may think of anachronistically as "proto-clocks" formed out of recurrent and cyclical events within the cycle of our days: waking and sleeping, rising and settling down, the patterns of hunger and thirst, and, more prominently, the rhythms of breathing and the heartbeat and the tick-tock of walking. But this inherent time of the body does not amount to fully explicit time, even less "timing", since it is not clearly offset from the changes in which it is expressed. The rhythm of my heart is, even when it is noticed, interwoven with the activities or emotions that cause the organ to beat faster and more thickly. The temporality of what is going on is consequently for the most part implicit, woven into what is experienced.

Time as something "in itself", that is available ultimately to be clocked, is most clearly developed in relation to our consciousness of things outside of our bodies, "out there". The immediate presentation of the world around us, unfolding in or over time, is the first step towards opening up the present to an ever more remote past, an ever more distant future. Eventually we locate ourselves in a common past and future flanking a communal present – in a remembered social history and anticipated social future we share with our fellow humans, and a natural history we share with all beings. Ultimately, we come to be aware of our lives as brief episodes in a story that stretches from pre-history to post-history, from the Big Bang to the Big Crunch.

Foremost among the senses that yield an explicit sense of time, though by no means exclusive, is vision.[1] While it is obvious that vision is a revelation of explicit space it is less easy to appreciate its importance in the revelation of explicit time. Even so, it is the case; and it is of fundamental significance not only for the metaphysics of everyday life, but also for the development of the physical sciences that have challenged that metaphysics, and for the relationship between the two. The key role of vision in making time explicit, which predisposes us to spatialize it, lies at the root of the intellectual, cognitive and cultural developments that are examined critically in this book.

Before I argue for the privileged relationship between vision and explicit time, I want to pre-empt a serious misunderstanding. The world we humans live in is not merely a sensory bubble, revealed to individual viewpoints. It is the product of the joint labour of all of us – our predecessors and our contemporaries.[2] Each of us acquires the world in which we live our lives largely "off the shelf" rather than constructing it directly out of sense experience. World-acquisition is overwhelmingly dependent on sign systems, the most elaborate of which (though not by any means the earliest or the most fundamental) is language as conventionally understood. The temporally deep world extends far beyond that which is revealed to vision; and it is available to anyone who can participate in the community of shared consciousness that is humanity. And this of course includes individuals who are congenitally blind. I make this perhaps rather obvious point in order to head off the objection that the initial importance of vision in humanity's development of the intuition of temporal depth would preclude those without sight from full participation in a world saturated in explicit time – something that is manifestly untrue. In some respects, people who have congenital blindness bypass the ground floor of explicit time as presented through vision (as I shall describe) and proceed directly to the higher levels. What is more, they draw on the explicit time made available through other senses – touch, hearing, and the experience of kinesis – which are overshadowed in the experience of the sighted for whom the visual sense dominates in explicit time.

I want, also, to pre-empt another potential misunderstanding. What I will describe is how we come to perceive "the passage of time" as it is conventionally understood. I shall argue in §2.2.3 that there is no such thing as the passage of time. The tendency to use dynamic metaphors is rooted in the fact that time becomes explicit most clearly through a particular, universal form of change, namely motion. Time made explicit through motion is liable to be thought of as being itself in, or a kind of, motion; hence talk of "the flow" or "passage of time".

Let us now examine the special relationship between vision and explicit time. Consider an object moving across your visual field. It occupies a succession of positions, P_1, P_2, P_3, etc., at times t_1, t_2, t_3, etc. The object survives the move, essentially unchanged. But, more importantly, the *positions* occupied by the object outlast the period during which they are occupied by the object. P_1 (composed of the matter that surrounds the object at t_1) is still there at t_2 when the object has moved on to P_2. And P_3, a position the object has not yet reached, is also present and visible at t_2, when the object is at P_2. Because *all three positions are co-present* in my gaze, I can see the past and future locations of the object as well as its present position. By virtue of being the past position of the object, P_1 stands for its past when the object reaches P_2. And by virtue of already being in place when the object is at P_2, P_3 represents the future of the object. More generally, we can say that places typically outlast the events (such as the transit of an object) that have occurred in them; they provide a constant background against which a succession of events can be bound together into the event of succession and the object, which can occupy only one point at one time, can nevertheless trace a trajectory that has both spatial extensity and temporal depth. The position – which is the surviving *relatum* of the relationship between the object and a position, or of the complex object-in-a-position – curates the past of the object.[3]

1.2 THE HEGEMONY OF VISION IN EXPLICIT TIME SENSE

It hardly needs saying that vision is not the exclusive domain of explicit time sense. *Sound* can also yield temporal depth. If I am listening to a sequence of notes, is it not true that I retain the earlier notes while I am listening to the later ones? If this were not the case, how could I ever hear a melody or, indeed, a whole note that occupies more than a notional instant? And speech would not make sense if we did not both hold together and keep apart the beginning and end of utterances.

All of this is true; but it does not challenge the pre-eminent (but not exclusive) role of vision in establishing explicit time because the earlier and later notes of a melody or first and last words of a spoken sentence do not co-exist in the way that the visible successive positions of a moving object do. There is nothing corresponding to P_1 and its successors which would be occupied by the notes and outlast them. These positions – unlike successive notes – are side by side and simultaneous, even though the object can occupy only one of them at a time. In other words, the status of a succession of states or events as a *succession*, marking out a span of time, depends not simply on the retention of the past events or states as memories (as in the case of the successive notes of a melody) or future ones as anticipations. It requires something more and vision supplies this: the still-visible position occupied by the object. This past position is not merely an inner, private memory but an outer, visible, public steward of the past. This is even more striking in the case of the visible positions of our own bodies in relation to other objects. Consider my walking away from a car I have just parked. The parked car gives my occupation of it a posthumous existence after I have vacated it. We may of course imagine *sounds* (say, of a car coming closer) occupying successive "positions", but the translation of this into space and the co-presence of side-by-side past, present, and future, is on the basis of borrowing, or parasitizing a spatial field opened up by vision.[4] So while hearing (music, utterances, and natural sounds such as the babbling of a brook) is manifestly temporal, it does not make *time itself* as explicit as does vision by co-locating the contents of successive moments in space.

There is a possible objection to the notion that sight has a privileged (though not exclusive) role in delivering explicit time. It goes as follows: Surely, to say that we see time in the way I have described it is simply to state the obvious: we see the past (e.g. view P_1 from P_2) because we remember it and the future (e.g. view P_3 from P_2) because we anticipate it. And that is of course true; but, to reiterate the point that I made in relation to hearing a succession of notes, it is only in vision that memory and anticipation are given an *external* (public) location. Past and future are "out there", underwriting memory and anticipation, and providing a springboard for deeper forays into pasts and futures no longer based on direct observation. We have to see the past and future literally in order to conceive of (public, shared) pasts and futures in which we situate memories and anticipations. What is more, our concern here is not with the difference between past and future or between memory and anticipation but their translation into explicit time which includes before-and-after.

Other senses can clearly reach outside of the present. We think we can smell the past in the scent of a musty building, or in a room where a perfumed someone has been; or taste the future in the first mouthful of many to come. But these pasts and futures are not actually present in themselves, side by side with the present. The invisible past and future grows ultimately out of a visible past and future. What about touch? We might be inclined to dismiss this as a source of explicit time – of time "out there", untethered from the implicit corporeal time of heartbeats and coordinated motor activity such as complex manipulations or ambulation, because it is inseparable from the body. It is, however, worth addressing this question because doing so reveals, by contrast, another feature of vision that is central to its key role in the genesis of the sense of explicit time.

When I explore an object entirely by touch, my moving finger and palpating hand pass over unmoving locations that outlive contact with the finger, of the hand but my hands are clearly not experiencing the present, the near-past, and the future locations *at the same time*. My finger *is* where it is and not where it has been or it will be: it is confined to its present position and does not retain the previous position or fore-touch its next position. Admittedly, blind palpation may build up the idea of a three-dimensional object, or indeed a three-dimensional space which that object occupies, that exceeds the surface in contact with the finger pads and even more obviously that part of the surface that is being touched at any one instant. Touch may therefore seem to hold or retain successive positions touched by the fingers. More strikingly, active manipulations may be impregnated with an idea of a future yet to be achieved and a past of what has been completed so far – something that we shall discuss in Chapter 12. Perhaps an even more persuasive example of the co-presence of the past and the future is provided by scratching, where the after-sensation associated with the beginning of the scratch are co-present with those associated with subsequent points on the scratch and, in addition, with the itch in the as yet unscratched part of the body. However, this co-presence is distributed over a severely restricted area. Admittedly, there are larger tactile areas than those available to our fingers; for example the surfaces of our trunk and limbs. Even so, the space that is revealed all at once by, say, the buttocks feeling the pressure of the chair, legs aware of trousers, or torso aware of a shower, is severely constricted compared with that afforded to vision.[5]

Size, however, is not the only issue, or even the most salient one. There are two other important differences – one very straightforward and readily dealt with; the other more complex.

Firstly, vision sees objects at a distance: to use the technical term, the eyes are telereceptors. Sight is not fastened to or contiguous with its object as touch is. It is this that underpins the contrast we have just addressed – that touch is confined to the area defined by the surface of the touching organ. This is just as true when the touching organ is a spread of fingers or, indeed, both hands: there is no touching beyond the actual, that is to say present tense, area of contact of the touching organ. In the case of vision, there is no question of a space of experience being defined by the size of the sensitive surface – in this case the orb or the retina. That is why there is nothing in touch comparable to panning round an array of co-present, indeed co-presented, but still distinct items, whose co-presence is given immediately.

But there is another more important difference: continuity. The tactual area is *patchy*, as is any space we may imagine as being marked out by hearing (and even more so by smell or taste). We may capture this difference saying that vision is the only sense that has a fully developed *field*. The continuum of the visual field is the progenitor of our idea of space, which is continuous. While a succession of glimpses or peerings may seem like a series of distinct probes, the eye – being at a distance from what it sees – retains what it scans, and has both a centre and a peripheral field and the non-foveal penumbra is co-present with the foveal centre of attention.[6] The co-presence of the past, present, and future of a particular movement is thus secured. The privileged connection between vision and explicit time is not therefore surprising. It is rooted in the fact that the visual field is a *space*.

The least we should ask of a space is that it should be continuous and that all its occupants are related to one another. Let us now turn our attention to this continuity.

1.3 THE VISIBLY HIDDEN

What is the basis of the continuity that makes it appropriate to speak of a visual *field* but not of an auditory, tactile, olfactory or proprioceptive field? It is that our gaze sees not only what is visible, but also *that* there are things or parts of things that are *in*visible.[7] Indeed, invisibility is inseparable from visibility. An object that hid nothing, either its own interior or other objects behind it, because it was absolutely transparent, would be invisible. The visual field is dappled, and necessarily dappled, with explicit, indeed *visible, invisibility.* It even has visible limits that indirectly reveal the invisible: things whose surfaces conceal their depths, their interiors, or which are folded over themselves. Beyond this, the curtained window, the bend in the road, the outline of the hill, all visually display that which is not, but might be, seen. The seen without the hidden would be a flat plane of exposure.

Objects, events, processes are therefore visible in virtue of being opaque, revealed through concealment – not only of other objects but of other aspects of themselves

– the back, the underside, and the interior. In the field of sight, the visible and the visibly invisibly, the overt and the hidden, are inextricably intermingled. We see surfaces, and see that we see only surfaces, and yet see objects whose surfaces that they are. We look past what we see. That which is as it were "visually implied" underwrites the continuity of visibility. This is essential to the character of the seen as a *scene* which is continuous and connected.[8]

There is nothing comparable to this in the other senses. Although we sometimes talk of an audible, even a loud, or deafening, silence, this is not meant literally. We do not hear the inaudible as we see the invisible: masking sounds have to be audible to do their work. And while music without silence between the notes would not be music, the silence does not have a primary presence. The untouched is not tangibly untouched. Our hands do not reach into a field of mixed tangibility and feel intangibility. Gloves or numbness may modify touch sensation but they do not deliver a perception of the untouched beyond our fingers. We cannot "foretouch" what we are going to touch or indeed foretouch what is going to happen. In contrast, we may fore*see* it, as we observe two cars heading towards one another and anticipate a collision. Nor can we hind-touch what we are no longer touching. The continuation of a tactile sensation of something we are no longer holding is a property of our body and not the presence of something out there.

Hitherto, I have focused on observed movement as the basis for explicit time. The visibly invisible expands the sense of the past and future beyond that which is yielded by objects moving from one enduring position to another. The past is present in, say, a half-concealed object that was just now entirely visible. The future lies in the possibility of revelation of that which is concealed. When we move or are transported from place to place, we are treated to a visual ballet of revelation and concealment, the sliding panels, informal coordinates, of foreground, middle ground, and background, of the hidden future being revealed and the revealed present becoming a hidden past. The invisible also contains the unexpected, the as-yet-undetermined: the bend in the path not only conceals the future towards which we are travelling but also reveals a place from which the future might come towards us – neither sought out nor, indeed in some cases, yet in place.

The visibly invisible is essential to the continuity and unity of the visual field and of the myriad of distinct items we see at any time connected in a single network of relations, encompassing (say) an object and the successive positions it occupies. It is on this basis that vision gives us a viewpoint: a view is an over-view; *opsis* is *synopsis*. There is no comparable unified auditory or tactile field, in which the audible or tangible are glued together by, respectively, the inaudible and the intangible. Hearing does not give us a hear-point, touch a touch-point, smell a smell-point, or taste a taste-point, commanding a corresponding space. There is no tactile equivalent, for example, of finding a better viewpoint, as when we climb a tree to command more territory. And while there are active and passive modes of both touch and vision, the varieties of active touching – squeezing, groping, palpating – are not equivalent to active seeing – attentive watchfulness, staring, peering, scrutinizing, scanning, instrument-assisted looking.

The visibly invisible takes many forms: the object seen from an angle, the partly clothed body, the half-concealed animal in a thicket, the closed drawer, the unopened envelope. These are just the beginning; but they represent an essential step in our liberation from the prison of the present, from a succession of "nows" that is confined to that which is before us and currently being experienced. Seeing that which is no longer or not yet, and (more importantly) *that* it is no longer or not yet, is the vestibule of a larger past and future: a past which ultimately includes those things that cannot be visited and so will always be unseen (most obviously in the case of the historical past); and a future which may or may not transpire and so for that reason must also always lie beyond the reach of vision.

The special status of the eye among the sense organs is reflected in the manner in which intentionality – or *aboutness* – is most explicit or most developed in visual experience. The experiencer and that which he or she experiences – the object of experience – are most clearly separated in the case of vision. Sight, as we have already noted, is a distance sense and we are aware of its objects as being visibly distinct from us, and consequently as being explicitly other than us, as being "over there" with respect to ourselves who are "over here"; as being "in themselves" other than ourselves.[9] The obverse of the sense of the objectivity of objects is our awareness of being *offset* from the place where we are, where we find ourselves. We confront the world rather than being dissolved in it. To use the expressive verb – we *face* it.

This has many consequences. For example, we not only see objects but we also see that we see them from a certain angle, from a certain distance, in a certain light. We can therefore envisage other angles, other distances, other lights – and viewpoints other than our present one; our own future viewpoints and the viewpoints of others. At a very basic level, we see the object but also see that our view of the object is restricted: we see that we cannot see the inside of the object or the object as it looks from another viewpoint. This is another aspect of the visibility of the invisible in our visual field; of the presence of the not yet and no longer of vision. The temporal depth of the visual field, in other words, is underlined by the sense of past and future viewpoints.

The notion that there are other viewpoints, in particular those assumed by eyes other than our own, is a further visual evidence that there is more to see. This is highlighted when I not only see you seeing but also see that you can see what I cannot see and cannot see what I can see. Looking at you, located in a position I may have occupied in the past or may occupy in the future, correspondingly extends my sense of possible – future and past – visual experience. When you point to something that I cannot see, and I follow your implicit instruction by climbing a tree or going upstairs to get a better view, I express my awareness of the objectivity of the world beyond my experience of it and my sense of the future through seeking future experiences; in short of a world pregnant with possibilities.

Vision is the most public of all our senses and closest to a shared awareness. We lookers are located in a pooled space that we can also see, not the least because we can see each other seeing; or at least looking. We cannot, by contrast, hear each other hearing, though we may infer that sounds are audible to others. And touch is even more private. In the absence of vision, we can be aware only of that which is touching ourself. In a world in which all were blind there would be no compensating public tactual sphere, underpinning a present moment with individual and shared pasts and futures. Explicit time made available through vision is thus open to being shared, to being objectivized and ultimately measured.

Vision, in summary, is of all the senses, the least fastened to a present carnal reality and most liberated from the solitude of the organism. It reveals not only that which is experienced through the senses but also, through this, that which is not, or not yet, or no longer, experienced. The sense of the hidden, of the concealment and possible revelation of the visibly invisible, makes the world of sight more than a temporally flat exposed surface. It is the ground floor of the sense of an objective reality checked against sense experience but transcending it. The name for that transcendent awareness is "knowledge". And so this sense is ripe to open our temporal awareness to minutes, hours, and years.[10]

Our gaze as it were reaches out to the object and alights on it in anticipation of our future direct encounter with it through touch, pressure, grasp and manipulation. This is one of the many respects in which the visible object is the site of future possibilities; of a temporal side-by-side – in this case the present and the future – that gives the visual field temporal, as well as spatial, depth. Sight is fore-sight in virtue of being fore-touch, or the promise of some other direct or indirect engagement.

Vision has other characteristics that assist the embodied subject in extricating time from the immediately experienced rhythms of the body, such as the heartbeat and breathing. We *see* our body in action – our moving limbs, which we experience directly, are also visible to us.[11] We see ourselves in reflective surfaces. And we see our shadows that are, and are not, ourselves – animated by our movements and yet distinct from our bodies. We are items located in the same space as are the items we encounter and engage with at every moment of our lives, though we are not located in the same way, since our relationship to them is asymmetrical: I am related to them but they are not related to me.[12]

1.4 CONCLUSION

The key thought in this chapter is that the sense which makes space explicit is also that which makes time explicit. The coherent unity of the visual field in which everything is manifestly related to everything else makes it a space in the most literal sense; indeed, it is the seeming direct revelation of space. We have examined how this is connected with our sense of temporal depth. The special relationship between the origin of our explicit time sense in the most spatial of senses prepares the ground for the notion of time as a quasi-spatial sense.

What I have advanced in this chapter is not a misconceived *a priori* argument about matters of empirical fact. My thesis does not depend on vision being the *exclusive* source of our explicit time sense, of our sense of time as something in itself.

Clearly, successive sounds, successive positions of our body in coordinated activity, also make time explicit. However, there is a particularly profound connection between on the one hand vision and on the other explicit time, "time out there", time in itself, that sets us on a path towards a spatialization of time. The key point is that when time becomes objectified, externalized, and explicit as something distinct from the time implicit in the unfolding of the world and our experience of our bodies, ripe to be measured and clocked, it is prone to be spatialized. Increasingly, we are persuaded that the reality of time is to be found, on the far side of visualization, as a quasi-spatial entity.

This is crucial to the argument of this book because spatialization is the first step towards losing time, not simply (though importantly) because it places what is considered to be the truth of time outside of ourselves, privileging measured over lived time. Time, as perceived through the most discarnate of senses, starts to be conceived in ways which are ever more remote from our lives as they are lived. Vision abets our alienation from time because it opens the path to seeing the contents of the world as forms. Such forms – foreshadowed in shadows – are amenable to being reduced to pure shapes and magnitudes leading ultimately to the quantitative, numerical world picture that physical science deals in. The spatialization of time, which has its roots in vision, is reinforced by measures of time that use spatial intervals. Seen time becomes clocked time and clocked time takes over our life. While bringing immeasurable benefits, this places over those lives the stranglehold of an ever more constricting matrix of the time table.[13]

And it is to this that we now turn our attention.

Addendum
Human and animal vision and temporal depth

The privileged relationship between our vision and explicit temporality raises a question. Many animals have vision and, in some cases, and in some respects, it is superior to ours. Do they too have a sense of temporal depth? Do they too have a shared history and look forward to a future had in common? If not, why not?

I have elsewhere argued that animal worlds – even those of our nearest primate kin such as chimpanzees – are without past and future or even an explicit present as something located between past and future. I will not rehearse these arguments in detail here, as I have dealt with them *in extenso* in several places.[14] You are, however, entitled to a brief account of some of the reasons for believing this; at the very least some indication of what is special about *human* vision that makes it uniquely the basis of explicit time.

While the first inkling of the sense of the no-longer and the not-yet is rooted in the observation of moving objects that occupy successive positions that outlast their being occupied by those objects, the transformation of that into a developed sense of no-longer and not-yet must depend upon awareness of a world in which the visible conceals the invisible and reveals it as invisible. This is most clearly evident in our apprehension that things "out there" have a definite and explicit existence independent of our experience. Our human world is populated by such items – entities that transcend that which we currently perceive of them. This does not appear to be true of other animals – even of other primates. There is therefore no holding bay for the not-yet and the no-longer.

The best evidence (summarized in my *Michelangelo's Finger*) is that the visual field of our nearest primate kin is one in which consciousness of objects is confined to the experiences that are being had of them. Out of sight is not merely out of mind but out of existence, whereas for us, "out of sight" may be "into mind". The notion of an enduring object that is the subject of change is not part of what Daniel Povinelli has called the "folk physics" of apes. What is more, chimpanzees do not have a sense of the invisible world: what is visibly invisible to us is invisible *tout court*, and hence non-existent, to them.[15]

This difference between our "folk physics" and that of chimpanzees – expressed in many ways, notably a lack of causal sense – has momentous consequences.[16] If the object exists independently of my experiences, as human experience tells me, then (a) behind its appearance is an underlying stuff, with intrinsic properties that are quite different from my consciousness of it; (b) it has aspects additional to those which are exposed to my present viewpoint; and (c) the object, and its aspects, belong to a domain that transcends me – a public domain shared with others. This realm of shared vision, coordinated by joint attention and a sense of others' viewpoints links the past and future of the items in the visual field with my past and my future and, beyond this, my past and future with the past and future of others. In the absence of these intuitions, the vision of non-human animals fails to deliver the temporal depth that opens up in us into the great realms of memory, anticipation, The Past and The Future.

So while animals may have eyesight and perception of movement that is superior to ours, their consciousness does not have the temporal depth that characterizes our consciousness. Their visual sense is placed on an entirely different existential platform, is part of an unimaginably alien *umwelt*. The origin of the ontologically richer human gaze is complex and here is not the place to discuss it – I have done so elsewhere.[17] Essentially, it is rooted in the fact that we are *embodied subjects* and not just organisms; *em*bodied in the way that material objects are not. A pebble is not *em*pebbled. We relate to our bodies as that which we "am" but also in other ways: we possess, use, care for, judge and objectively know, our bodies in a manner that is unique in the animal kingdom.[18] This mode of embodiment underwrites the sustained self-consciousness of the human subject which in turn makes of the seeing eye an "I" that is aware of being located in his or her visual field. This sense of being an enduring self that is more than a succession of experiences is projected into the objects that are revealed in the visual field. We are able to intuit or envisage the objects as enduring beneath their changes (including changes of position). The past and future that are held in the fleeting passage of the object through a succession of positions that remain in place is reinforced by the sense of one's own future: the future position of the objects is the future *for me*; its past participates in *my past*.

Our uniquely complex relationship to our bodies – in which, as already noted, we identify with them as something we "am" and yet are also distant from them, as items we possess, utilize, judge, know and so on – maintains the distance opened up between the time "in here" that we experience through the rhythms of the body – our heartbeat, our breathing, our footsteps – and time as something "out there". It must not be inferred from this that our experience of temporal depth in the world is entirely a product of our sense of our own temporal depth. The relationship is a dialectical one. The initial inkling of temporal depth is based on the synthesis of the successive positions – and hence the successive moments – of the object. This reinforces the sense of our own temporal depth, as embodied subjects, which will in turn deepen our sense of the temporal depth of the world around us. The iterative process is, of course, not enacted simply within the individual but in the evolving community of minds that is the human world.

CHAPTER 2
Time as "the fourth dimension"

> Western scientific tradition takes for granted since Aristotle that Time
> is closely related to motion, and therefore to space. As a consequence
> of this view, we have inherited the idea of an isomorphism between
> time and one-dimensional space.
>
> Prigogine, "The Rediscovery of Time"

The world we see around us is saturated with marks of time. The mossed log, the characterful face, the crumbling wall, the worn shoes and the well-thumbed book, are rich with intimations of the past, with effects broadcasting recent or ancient causes. The baby, the sapling, the dawning day, turn our thoughts to the future, or futures, pregnant with possibilities that beckon us. And the inner world is correspondingly charged with the mementos of time past and time future. "Now", unlike the empty, unextended instants of mathematical time, is informed with an inexpressibly complex past, recalled at will or arriving without summons, bringing regret, nostalgia, satisfaction or joy – or, more practically, information and guidance that take us through projected futures, that are already active, seeming to await us, making us hurried and harried, hopeful and fearful, impatient or resigned, reflective or busy. The humble knotted handkerchief is a present reminder, laid down in a past when this present was future, of a duty whose time has now arrived.

The origins of these pasts and futures are associated, as I have argued, intimately – but of course by no means exclusively – with the most mysterious of our mysterious senses: vision. Without vision, the most spatial of our senses, we would have had a less explicit or immediate sense of being located between a known (though, of necessity, largely forgotten) past and an unknown (but of necessity patchily anticipated) future. But the domination of vision in the immediate presentation of experienced time leads ultimately to a mode of awareness of explicit time that both alienates time from us and yet also makes us able to draw on a deeper and more complex past and reach further into an evermore controlled future, in the service of a present that, while it is enriched in its material possibilities, is, along with the rest of time, conceptually impoverished by the very science that extends our powers.

Time according to this rival sense is spatialized. While it is expanded, it is also reduced – ultimately to a dimension, a pure extensity or magnitude. It is eventually shrivelled to a number, a quantitative variable signified by a letter – "t" – conceived as a one-dimensional topological space that maps on to a line of real numbers. It is this reduction of time to a numerical skeleton that we shall examine in the next three chapters. That this scientific image of time is built on our visual sense and that science itself is one of the most potent agents of our freedom are two connected facts about us. The visual sense, a revelation of the world from a distance, is one of the keys to our collective ability – extended of course to those who (to reiterate) take the world largely off the shelf, including those who are blind from birth – to develop as relatively free subjects in the natural world of which we are a part and from which we are also apart.

It would be of course ridiculous to dismiss the practical value of seeing time as a quasi-spatial dimension, and ultimately as a pure quantity, for the purposes of developing a potent scientific account of the material world. No; my target is the widespread belief, or unspoken assumption, that this portrait of time, most fully developed in physics, reveals its ultimate reality. The spatialization of time will be examined in this chapter. In the next chapter I shall investigate the reduction of space (and hence space-like time) to pure quantity: I regard time and space as being equally traduced when they are seen as dimensions reducible ultimately to pure quantities. In Chapter 4, I shall explore the most obvious manifestation of the reduction of time to a pure quantity: "clocking" that makes of time the value of a variable. This will be connected with a larger inquiry into the nature of physical science and its central conviction that (to quote Galileo's famous aphorism), "the book of nature is written in the language of mathematics".[1] Although "clocking time" is the theme of Chapter 4, I will glance briefly at early clocks in the present chapter because they firmed up and elaborated spatialized conceptions of time originating out of vision.

2.1 FROM MOVING SHADOWS TO THE SCIENCE OF MECHANICS: THE SEDUCTIVE IDEA OF TIME AS SPACE

Objects cast shadows, a visible darkness that presents them as their abstract forms, a half-way house (as we shall see in Chapter 3) to reducing them to numbers. It is an inescapable observation that shadows lengthen towards evening before they unite in the universal shadow that is night, the great hyphen between the days, when, before the invention of artificial light, all were impeded by darkness: work had to stop, and wakefulness was replaced by sleep – a wise move given that dangers were more dangerous for being invisible. Dawn is the image of the primordial beginning. According to Genesis, the universe began with the command that there should be light, so that the void became the world and Chaos was shaped into Cosmos. And nightfall is the primordial image of ending. The cycling of light and darkness marks the most basic division of our lives into units of time.

There are shadows more portable than the universalized shadow of night or the celestial orchestration of daytime shadows by the apparent movement of the sun. The most portable and handy – indeed it is inescapable – is that which is cast by one's own body. It forms the basis of "the peasant's clock" and it is calibrated for each one of us. Your shadow is longer than my shadow but the length of my shadow compared with the length of my body will be the same for each of us at a particular time of day, assuming our separation is on a local rather than a global scale. We can therefore arrange to meet when (say) our shadows are as long as our own bodies: by this means, our activities are coordinated. It is extraordinary to think how we exploit the opacity of our own bodies to coordinate our shared lives but this is but one manifestation of our astonishing self-consciousness as embodied subjects. Our shadows, synchronized in their waxing and waning to the apparent motion of the sun, orchestrate the ballet of our shared lives: they are co-ordered and our paths intersect according to our plans.[2] We converge at appointed times.

Exploitation of our shadows was a significant advance in rendering time as something explicit, out there, shared and objective: shadows are *used* to highlight and collectivize explicit time and ultimately to transform time into "times" at which events are deemed to have happened and to create a network in which they are located and interconnected. The passage from visible object to visible silhouette and from visible silhouette to the length (another abstraction) of the shadow compared with that of our bodies is an early step in the journey from visible time to time as a dimension, as a quantity, as a number.

The peasant's clock gives only locations in time – morning, noon, afternoon, evening – and not quantities of time. Enter the obelisk. An obelisk is a tall, four-sided pillar whose shadow indicates the time of day. Markers round the base of the monument divide the day into equal parts. The obelisk not only separates time-keeping further from the body, and displays it in a public space, but also measures *quantities* of time. Separated time is broken into units and counted. The obelisk is a kind of maypole around which the activities of the citizens are coordinated: a dance to the shadow of time. Fluffy periods such as "evening" or "forenoon" acquire hard edges.

The principle of the obelisk was transferred to a (relatively) pocket device: the sundial which tracks the apparent movement of the sun round the earth by casting the shadow of its style or gnomon on to a surface etched with time divisions. By this means, public or objective time is imported further into the interstices of human life. The sundial's hour hand depends on the earth's rotation round its axis, perceived as the movement of the sun. And its year-hand is based upon the earth's orbit, sweeping out 150 million kilometres a year. We use the earth's gigantic journeying to orchestrate our little movements. What delicious cheek to exploit the relative motion of the earth and the sun to tell us when to have our tea! And human cheek will be extended even further when (as we shall see) the universe itself will be described as giant clockwork mechanism. But clockwork lies ahead. The tick of the sundial is soundless, though it makes time itself visible as the passage of shadows, extracting, so it seems, time itself from the evolution of the day.

Early chronometers – peasant's clocks, obelisks and sundials –reinforce the sense of time as a kind of (visible) space. This remains true when other methods of measuring time are introduced. The water clock represents time as the height of a volume of water and mechanical clocks give intervals of time as distance moved by fingers on a dial and actual times as spatial locations. The hour glass exhibits time as a flow of sand and a "growing" past and a "shrinking" future as an accumulation of sand in one chamber and its depletion from another. The transferred epithet "the sands of time" is an augury of the future conflation of time with the method of measuring it. It is only comparatively recently that clocks have lost their intimate relationship with space and come to represent time purely as numbers – a development that encompasses space as well and whose roots we shall explore in the next chapter.

We seem destined, then, to think of time in spatial terms. Even before time is represented as a quasi-spatial line on graphs (the "abscission" of time), we speak, and presumably think, of "stretches" of time, of "long" times and "short" times, "near" and "distant" times, of times for events getting "close" or being "a long way off", of looking forward (with foresight) to the future that comes close and "looms" ever large in our thoughts and looking backwards (with hindsight) to the "receding" past getting smaller as it is more distant. (Or vice versa in other cultures, as we discussed in the previous chapter.) "Years ago" seems analogous to "miles away". We talk of "a certain space of time". Clocks reinforce this way of thinking by representing the division of time into equal quantities as equal intervals of space. And the circularity of time as represented on the clock can be unfolded when we think of successive circuits as being like a rolling hoop that traces out a straight line.[3]

Clocked time, like space, has both locations and distances; a "when" and a "how much" corresponding to a "where" and a "how big". Duration seems analogous to size or distance between a beginning and an end: for example, the two hour stretch *between* 2 o'clock and 4 o'clock on the same day. And the temporal "at" can seem like a spatial "at": it is (at) 2 o'clock when the fingers of the clock are at the place marked 2 (o'clock). And an interval of time corresponds to the spatial gap between two spatial-temporal "ats". This everyday manner of seeing, talking and thinking about, and marking time prepares the way for the eventual fusion of timelines and spacelines in space–timelines or "world-lines"; for the marriage of time with one, two, or three dimensions of space, so that they together form a single (spatio-temporal) location or interval.

The notion of time as a quasi-spatial dimension is also implicit in the pre-scientific notions of time passing (and passing at subjective different speeds – from "flashing by" to "almost standing still"), as a line that grows at a tip that is the present, into the future, adding to the past, or as an expanding block, or as moving spotlight (corresponding to now) playing successively over different locations, so that they move from the future to the past. One of the simplest and most potent manifestations of spatialization of our conception of time is the image of successive events located on what is called a "timeline", like beads on a string.

The understanding of time as "the fourth dimension", alongside the three of space, was already conventional before it became inescapable through the special theory of relativity which led, via Hermann Minkowski, to the fusion of time and space in a four-dimensional space–time. Though Einstein's revolutionary ideas were at first seen to be counter-intuitive, several millennia of quasi-spatial thought about time lay behind them. The everyday propensity to think of time spatially, however, has been greatly reinforced by the gradual domination of mathematical physics over our conception of the natural world. We may think of several connected processes: (a) making time something in itself, lifted out of the order of things; (b) representing time spatially; and (c) (via the reduction of space to numerical magnitudes – the theme of Chapter 3) the reduction of time to a number, the value of the variable little t.

These processes were irreversibly entrenched in scientific thought when the Galilean–Newtonian revolution of the seventeenth century foregrounded time as a measurable quantity. Galileo was one of the first to represent time by a line and this was supported by Newton's presentation of mathematical time as a continuous straight line. The construction of reliable clocks, representing time spatially, as a result of which time was measured to increasingly high level of agreement between observers, reinforced the sense that it was an independent quasi-spatial quantity. While, as we shall discuss in Chapter 4, there are problems with the simple idea that clocks measure time, or the passage of time, the notion that they captured time itself, gradually took root in our way of thinking. That quantifiable something was confirmed in its status as a *dimension*.

The introduction of time as a quantitative variable (little) "t", which has characterized post-Galilean mechanics, prepared the way, therefore, for placing time on all fours with the three spatial dimensions. The use of graphs to represent motion, in which time assumes coordinate values very similar to those of space, makes spatial and temporal locations and intervals seem deeply analogous. What is more the analogy is one way: a graph is a *spatial* representation: the spatial representation of time is not complemented by a temporal representation of space (whatever that might be). This asymmetry is at least in part a consequence of the fact that the measurements of time are measurements of space, typified in the movement of the fingers on a clock face but present even in the earliest clocks such as obelisks and sundials as already noted.

The inspiration of Newton's *Principia Mathematica*, which showed that the movement of the planets and the movements on earth that fill our daily lives were subject to the same laws made it seem possible, as Pierre-Simon Laplace argued, to understand the universe in terms of the laws of motion: the world we live in is a giant mechanism encompassed by the science of mechanics in which time is simply a dimension alongside those of space. Behind this is the widespread assumption that to understand nature is to understand motion; that the science of mechanics is the key to the real world.

The idea of time as "The Fourth Dimension" received its classic popular exposition in H. G. Wells's *The Time Machine* (which also contains everything one needs to refute the idea of time as a dimension analogous to space):

"Clearly", the Time Traveller proceeded, "any real body must have extension in *four* directions: it must have Length, Breadth, Thickness, and – Duration ... There are really four dimensions, three, which we call the three planes of Space, and a fourth, Time ... *There is no difference between Time and any of the three dimensions of Space except that our consciousness moves along it.*"[4]

There are, of course, many reasons for resisting the idea that time is space-like. I will come to these presently, but it is worth first pausing to head off a misunderstanding. It would be naïve to suggest that contemporary physics – notably that which builds on relativity theory – *inevitably* spatializes time in the sense of turning time into space, although there is much in the literature to suggest that some physicists think it does.[5] What it does is to break down a fundamental difference between space and time and to deny their independence of one another.

To take the most obvious example, relativity theory places time and space on all fours as part of a four-dimensional frame, so much so that separations between events can be described as "time-like" or "space-like" mathematical relations. What is more, time is captured in coordinate systems as a line and moments in time as positions in space. When an event is located in fused space–time its location is presented as values of four variables – x, y, z, and t – and they are treated as deeply comparable. Where only two dimensions can be shown, it is natural to present the relationship between (say) x and t as a line, analogous to that between x and y when mapping a trajectory. As we shall discuss in Chapter 3, when space and time are fused into space–time they are similarly victimized. The denial of the separateness of space and time is the result of reducing all change to measurement of movement and the structure of reality to whatever conserves the laws of motion. Time is a fourth dimension in an unchanging structure.

2.2 AGAINST SPACE-LIKE NOTIONS OF TIME

The "disanalogies" between space and time are numerous, but these are some of the most obvious:

A.   Space has three dimensions, time only one. We could express this difference in another way, suggesting that it is even more profound: that, while space *has* three dimensions, time *is* a single dimension.

B.   There are constraints on the way we move in time that are not evident in space. The obverse of this is that time (apparently) has a directionality that space does not.[6]

C.   There is a prescribed ordering of temporal locations but nothing comparable in the case of space; there is a temporal ordering of visits to the same point in space but not a spatial order of times of visits.

D. There is a propensity to think of time, but not of space, as flowing or (more broadly) "dynamic".

Let's look at each of these differences in turn.

2.2.1 A single dimension

There is no way of reducing the three spatial dimensions to a master-dimension that would encompass up–down, side-to-side, and back-to-front. It may be argued that the three dimensions of space are only artefacts resulting from the way we specify locations in space and the intervals between them. That response should cut no ice. Firstly, these three coordinates seem to be indispensable for the physical description of the world – they are not simply the product of mathematics. Space seems intrinsically voluminous and volumes three-dimensional. Secondly, the trend in recent physics, which attempts to unify its account of the world towards a Theory of Everything, has been to multiply, not reduce the number of spatial dimensions.[7]

The use of a single notion – dimension – to encompass "height", "breadth", "length" and "time" should make us suspicious for several reasons. First of all, "height", "breadth", and "length" are clearly related to each other in the way that the dimension of time is not related to them. "Before–after" (never mind past, present, future) does not sit easily in the company of "up–down", "front–back" and "left–right". The three dimensions of space do seem like a genuine trio whose components are inseparable. Indeed, we can rotate an axis through 90 degrees to change it from being a measure of one to a measure of the other. The same ruler, or kind of rule, is used to measure all three. Trying to use a ruler to record how long it takes me to run 100 yards or a clock to measure the length of a table, on the other hand, would be absurd. And of course we can turn the breadth of an object into its height by rotating it through 90 degrees whereas we cannot change any of its spatial dimensions into time – say height into duration – by a simple manoeuvre.[8]

We could highlight this disanalogy between space and time by asking this question: What could possibly correspond in the realm of time to the 90° angles by which up–down and side-to-side define each other; or to the difference between this 90° angle and the dimensions – up–down and side-to-side – themselves? Nothing. Nor could there be anything in time corresponding to the reference field that makes one spatial dimension (up–down) and defined by gravity and inertia and the other two that are defined by inertia alone.

Time seems to be more substantial than the individual dimensions of space, such as length. Whether or not time exists by or in itself, it is clear that length does not, except as an abstraction that has to be represented by a concrete line; and the latter of course has to have three dimensions to be visible, even though it gives the impression of representing pure length because its length far exceeds its width and depth. (For more on this see §3.4.2). Time seems more the peer of three-dimensional space than of any of the three individual spatial dimensions.[9]

That time does not fit easily into the company of the other three, that it is something of an add-on, is betrayed by our calling it "the fourth dimension". It is never referred to as "the first dimension" or "the second dimension". "Length, breadth, height – and time" is a natural way of ordering the characters, and "height, length, breadth and time" would be equally natural. "Height, time, length and breadth" would seem less natural – a rather clumsy attempt at inclusiveness, at a policy designed to make time feel at home as one of a group of four equals. The natural place of time is, at best, a D'Artagnan to the Three Musketeers of space. We can order x, y, z (the three spatial dimensions) as we wish but t is always an add-on.

It might be argued that time is analogous to space in that it, too, has two aspects: location and quantity; or where and how much. Location in both space and time involve "at" phrases: "It is two o'clock on 12 July 2011" and "We are at 5 Valley Road, Bramhall". Quantity of time and space seem even more closely analogous: we can say of two events that they were three miles or three seconds apart. There is a third apparent analogy: the duration of an event seems equivalent to the spatial size of an object. We can also say that an event occupied 10 seconds or filled 10 seconds or that an object occupied or filled 2 cubic metres. In short, time seems to have all the qualifications for being, or having, a (single) dimension. However, at least two of these seeming analogies wilt on closer inspection.

Firstly, the idea of location. The notion of a something taking place "at" a particular time does not mean occupying that piece of time, whereas "at" of space is space occupancy. This is because that which takes place in time is typically an event – something which *occurs*; whereas that which takes its place in space is typically an object.[10] The difference may be expressed by saying that an object (at any given time) has exclusive occupancy of a patch of space whereas an event does not have exclusive occupancy of the stretch of time in which it takes place.[11]

And how seriously shall we take the analogy between duration (of an object or an event) and the size (of an object or event)? Firstly, it is stretching it a bit to speak of an object having a duration in the way that an event does. We have to decide somewhat arbitrarily when it became itself and when it ceased to be itself. Events differ from objects in another respect. There is no equivalent of the spatial boundaries of an event which are clear-cut and continuous. We can say, quite confidently, that the war between the United Kingdom and Hitler's Germany began in 1939 and ended in 1945, but it would be absurd to try to trace the spatial boundaries of this event in the way that we can speak of its temporal boundaries, which are capable of being settled by fiat. This is because during its course an event will occupy different quantities of space. Consider a running battle in which different parts of space are occupied at different times. What are the spatial boundaries of this event: the sum total of all the spaces occupied during the course of the battle; or the maximum area occupied at any one point in the battle? There is no answer because the idea of the space occupied by an event does not map on to the idea of space occupancy as it is ordinarily understood, as when we apply it to an object. If there is an analogy that holds up, it is between quantity of time and quantity of space – for example, the interval between locations of events (in time) and between locations of objects (in space). But this holds up only because space and time have been reduced to pure quantities stripped of any characteristics.

2.2.2 Constraints on movement

There may be constraints on my movements in space but, in ordinary experience, these do not arise from space itself (unless one thinks of gravitational field as a manifestation of curved space – of which more in §3.5.2). It is not space itself but a brick wall (an object ontologically similar to my body) occupying it that prevents me from continuing in a certain direction. In the absence of obstacles, I can move up or down, from side to side, and from back to front in any direction I please. This freedom is in part the result of something that is captured by the notion that space is multi-dimensional. If it were only one-dimensional, I would not be able to move even in one-dimension, because, as an irreducibly three-dimensional being, any movement allowed me would require three dimensions. Even one-dimensional free movement in time is not possible – something which has been wrongly interpreted to imply that time has an intrinsic direction that we are obliged to conform to. We can choose to remain spatially immobile or to move in any direction, whereas we can neither choose to move a particular direction in time or to remain temporally still. There is no obligation to visit spatial locations in a definite order – they have no intrinsic order – unless they are located on a straight line we are confined to.

The metaphors of movement are inescapable because of the spatial origins of our explicit sense of time; of time as being "out there", the time in which our "in here" is located, the time that belongs to us all and to the natural world beyond our individual and immediate experiences. Behind the metaphors is the notion that events occur in, or objects endure in, time in a way comparable to events taking place in or objects occupying, space that is distinct from them. The major contribution of vision to developing our sense of explicit time, and even more in clocking it, has much to answer for.

2.2.3 The flow of time

It is obvious that space does not have a direction: it is itself the sum total of all directions – and this would be true even if space were not "isotropic" or uniform in all directions. Nor does it move: it is that in which movement takes place, and this is true at least locally even if we think of space relationally rather than as a substance. If space were to flow, what direction would it flow in? After all, having a direction would require privileging (for example) up–down as the direction of movement over left–right or front–back as the background. The two other dimensions might be reluctant to throw in their lot with, or concede sovereignty to the privileged one. And if, say, height were chosen as the direction in which space "pointed" or "moved", then space could move either up or down, or alternate between the two – first up and then down. Height would be divided against itself: it would have to subordinate one of its putative directions to the other as well as subordinating length and thickness to itself. For one half-dimension of space to set a direction for the other two and a half is unthinkable. No wonder we are not inclined to talk about "the passage of height". And what would the dimension flow in? Would it flow in hyperspace? What kind of point of origin or destination would it have?[12]

Of course, if time really *were* a dimension like "up–down" it would not have a direction (of movement), it would *be* a direction or a frame against which a direction could be specified. "Up–down", after all, doesn't have a direction in addition to the dimension it is. (The fact that it would seemingly have two directions cancelling one another out reveals this.) The notion that time has a direction is inseparable from the idea that we progress or it progresses, *from* "earlier" *to* "later". Clearly if "earlier-to-later" *were* a direction, we could just as well go from "later" to "earlier" times or events. The line that confers the possibility of one direction in fact confers the possibility of two directions. You can be faithful to a line by going in either of two directions at 180° to one another.

While this disanalogy between time and space is not contested, the tenacious images of the flow, passage, growth, and so on of time, bear witness to the power of spatialization in our conception of time. Objects can be at different places at different times and those different times are represented as different places on a timeline or different points which a growing timeline has reached. So even where time is not thought of as a quasi-spatial dimension, it is thought of as being like something that is *in* space. When we represent the movement of an object, its trajectory through space is given as a line that grows as the journey moves towards its completion. A timeline is also something that grows, as if it were expanding into something – not space necessarily but something space-like, something that houses it, for which the page on which the line is drawn stands proxy. The present moment is represented as the moving tip of the line and, as moment succeeds moment, the line gets longer.

Because the fundamental image is so tempting, it is difficult to resist an entire cluster of related images. For example, I cannot help thinking of the succession of days as a series of event-containers attached one to another, hung like cars on the cable of a present unreeling as a succession of "todays"; or of memory as being a glance into a sequence receding into an ever more remote distance (with remembered events acquiring their own mist of distance as they are pushed further back by their successors); and of looking into the future that also recedes in a different way. And when we are not thinking of the years passing through us, or passing us by, we think of ourselves moving – or being propelled – through the years. We and time seem to pass away together.

Let us look therefore at time as something flowing *away*.

2.2.3.1 Time passing (away)

If time were truly a dimension analogous in some important respect to the dimensions of space, it would have nothing to flow in, no direction to take, and no destination to reach. Even so, some writers seem to acknowledge this difference – that time flows and space does not – without giving up on the idea of time as "the fourth dimension". Why does the attraction of the idea of time as flowing go so deep? Is it rooted, perhaps, in the sense that time passes (and hence flows or drains) *away*?

We speak of using up space – as when we fill a suitcase – but it is not thereby spent: it can be reused. Time, it seems cannot. The events that occupy 12 December 2016 leave no time behind them when midnight strikes. The day is not there to be refilled. Of more direct existential import, as we live our lives, the time of our lives is used up and, it seems, some time – drawn from the overall span (if this is indeed finite) of the universe – is also used up. By contrast, a region of space can have an indefinite series of occupants without being used up. Space, what is more, exists in our everyday understanding, independently of being occupied.[13] That a region in space can be endlessly occupied and reoccupied (one of the bases, as we saw in Chapter 1, of the emergence of explicit time) without being "used up" is reflected in the fact that we can visit, leave, and revisit the same place. In contrast, we cannot occupy and reoccupy the same period of time. I cannot, for example, return to the time when I was 40 or pop back to last Wednesday – notwithstanding what the time travellers say (of whom more, much more, presently in §2.4). My fortieth year and last Wednesday are not merely out of reach but no longer. I, and the world I live in, have moved inexorably on. They clearly haven't moved on spatially. Nor have they moved on in time, because time has gone with them. It is this, or something like it, that may underpin the notion that time is something which passes away – and since it moves seamlessly – that it "flows".

The idea of the "flow" of time is a commonplace but it is affirmed by some major thinkers, none more eminent than "the incomparable Mr Newton": "Absolute, true and mathematical time, of itself, and from its own nature, flows equably without any relation to anything external and by another name is called duration."[14] This is not an entirely surprising position for a scientist who devoted such efforts to making quantitative observations. The measurement of time involves observing the successive positions of a marker – such as a moving shadow, sand flowing in an hour glass, or a moving finger on a clock face. We project the movements within these items into time itself which consequently seems to undergo a comparable passage, movement, or flow. Prior to formal measurement, our perception of time – of temporal depth, of this which is before and that which is after – was already inseparable from motion. As discussed in Chapter 1, our most basic experience of "what was", "what is", and "what will be" is of successive positions occupied by an object, in which both the positions and the object outlast the occupancy of the positions. Again, the passage of the *marker* of time is projected into time itself and the movement between successive positions presents the transition from past to present to future as a movement within, or of, time itself.

It gets a bit more complicated. Classical physics is often described as the search for, and the application of, laws according to which matter moves in space and time.[15] While, however, it makes sense to think of matter moving *in* space, we tend to think of matter moving *over* time. This encourages the sense that it is time that is doing the moving (unlike space which is, relatively even if not absolutely, still). More generally, we transfer our sense of the dynamism of the events, comprising the unfolding world, that "take time", to time itself.[16] The succession of time-consuming and time-ordered events is seen as a flux of time or as evidence of time as a flux, bearing events on its bosom. The idea of time as flowing has inspired much wonderful, as well as banal, poetry, using metaphors that portray it as a stream, a river, or a torrent, bearing things and events (including our own lives) towards us and sweeping them away. We see events as "tense tourists", starting off in the future, passing through the present and ending up in the past. As we shall discuss (§8.2.2.2) this is mistaken and is responsible for most of the arguments that discredit tensed time and for the errors leading to logical fatalism. It is, however, compelling, particularly when it is supported by confused notions, inspired by the calendar, of time divided into labelled portions, and of days and dates as containers for events, on the move.

2.2.3.2 Against flow: lumps of time on the move

When time becomes calendric, the marks to indicate the successive days and years are set out in space and we think of these items being literally close to, and far from, the present. A particular day may be a few marks or cells away, getting closer as the number of intervening days diminishes, arriving "here" at the present, and then drifting further away as more days intervene. We think of the Great Day and its Great Events being first "a long way off", then "here at last" and finally "receding" to become "a distant memory". It is the beginning of 12 December. Christmas Day is 13 days away. Twenty-four hours later, we say it is 12 days away. It has "come closer" and every 24 hours it will come a day closer still. Eventually, it arrives, and by 7 January it is again 13 days away. The notion that the day in question has travelled is irresistible: it has moved towards the present, passed through it, and then entered the past. We can build up our resistance by examining the nature of the journey and the nature of the traveller.

The fact that the days move towards us one day per day, and that it takes a day (no more, no less), to bring an index day one day nearer, should make us suspect that the idea of days travelling towards us is not based on empirical observation. The day's journey – if one takes it seriously – is something between a passage through time and a passage of time; partaking of both but not fully either. When 25 December has arrived, it has not got closer to 12 December, which was the reference point from which it was accurately described as being 13 days away. By definition, 12 and 25 December must remain 13 days apart. And this is true of 25 December's position with respect to any other temporal landmark – for example 1 December or an event that occurred on 12 December. So there is no temporal journey. (Another aspect of this is that the state of the world on 12 December does not get closer to that it will have on 25 December as the days "pass". 12 December remains as it was at midnight on that day.)

The other problem relates to the item undertaking the journey. Even if we allowed that (future) 25 December had a real existence we would still have to ask what it was made of. Clearly, it cannot be made of events because nothing has happened yet. What is more, it has no guaranteed contents. Our plans and expectations may be defeated. If it is made of anything, it must be made of pure time. So we have a piece of (empty) time journeying through time – an idea whose problems hardly need spelling out. But we have also to ask whether 25 December, if it exists at all as a stretch of time, exists as a whole that moves as one. We are inclined to think so because it is allocated a bounded space of its own in calendars. But of course those boundaries have no real existence. We do not have to open a door at midnight to get from 24 to 25 December. Which brings in the question of the size of the traveller – the bolus of time – if time were travelling towards the present. It is a question to which there is no sensible answer because dates are neither occurrences nor events, nor objects, that can seem to pass towards and away from us.

2.2.3.3 Against flow: fundamental arguments

The most obvious objection to the idea that time flows is one that we have aleady noted: this would be a rather odd thing for a dimension to get up to. Up–down, etc. don't move through space. How could they when they are (aspects of) space? Nor do portions of space move through space. An object a kilometre long may move closer but we cannot think of a kilometre (or a cubic kilometre) coming any nearer. Not even the strongest form of substantivalism could countenance space moving in space – that is to say in itself. This argument may be countered by asserting that, yes, time is like space in being a dimension but it is unlike space in being dynamic.

Accepting this merely makes way for another objection, almost as obvious. If time flows, it must flow at a certain speed. What speed would it flow at? The obvious answer – one second per second or one year per year – is clearly unsatisfactory. The presence of time on both the denominator and the numerator indicates that the "rate of" in question is entirely empty. Postulating a hypertime on the denominator in which time flows – so that one interval of ordinary time takes the same interval of hypertime – is both expensive and unclear. Is hypertime an absolute marker of the passage of time to make sure that ordinary time is, as it were, kept to time? Or does hypertime, too, flow and measure its rate of flow against a higher-order hyper-time? The question is unanswerable but it indicates quite plainly that the appeal to a second-order time to make sense of the flow of time creates more problems than it solves.[17]

The difficulty is linked with a kind of circularity that haunts the notion of time as something that is flowing – namely that it implies that in some respect it is itself changing or is a universe-wide sequence of changes. This does not seem possible: changes take time and so time must be presupposed in change. The circularity is concealed by fancy footwork between time and events which permits each to provide an external source for the other's dynamism.

The notion that the speed of the passage of time might be measured relative to something other than time (or hypertime) opens up the possibility of relative motion between the flow of events and the flow of time – which is unintelligible. It also raises the possibility that, if time is flowing like anything else that flows, the rate of flow of calendrical time should be able to vary. It clearly cannot: one day must take a day to pass. What is more, the rate of flow of time is not something that could be a matter of empirical *discovery*. If we found that Wednesday arrived only two days after Saturday, we would not conclude that time had speeded up but that we had got muddled over days.

The idea of passage, then, is fraught with contradictions and is close to unintelligible. But it remains irresistible, particularly when it is associated with certain images, such as a flowing river. Time is, it seems, inseparable from change (but see §10.2). The most basic and universal mode of change is movement. Hence the sense that time is a kind of Ur-movement. If so, its movement requires smoothness and continuity, must take place on a broad front, and yet have an overall direction. The image of a worldwide river – of a jointless flux – seems to pick up on all of these characteristics. It works – or does explanatory work – however, only insofar as it is taken literally. And once it is taken literally, it runs into difficulties.

There is a small difficulty of the fact that a *river* does not flow, in the sense of itself moving. It does not, for example, move out to sea; otherwise maps would always be out of date. What does move is the water in it; or the water that passes through its banks. The idea of the river is of a *form* of the passage of water; this form is called (for example) "the Mersey" and, unlike the water, it does not move – or only slowly.[18] The form, what is more, has to be maintained by something that is other than water. The idea of time as a river therefore requires something corresponding to the (relatively stable) banks between which the water flows that define the form and position of the river as shown on a map. With respect to what "banks" does time flow? There is clearly no relatively unmoving reference point with respect to which time flows. Within space, movement is established with respect to an inertial frame of reference that is relatively static. We can find nothing within time to correspond to the difference between that which moves and that with respect to which it moves.

One, perhaps insufficiently remarked, reason for being suspicious of the notion that time flows is that it seems to be more evident in certain events and processes than others. If time's flow were real, it would be universal and one might expect therefore that it should be universally and equally evident – or, being universal, not evident at all. Indeed, given that we ourselves would be entirely taken up in the passage of time – there would be nothing of or in our thoughts, bodily processes, or world outside of it – it is difficult to see how it would be evident at all. Against what it would stand out? (Compare this with the argument that, if the universe were uniformly and entirely red, it would not be explicitly red.)

Some in fact have argued that we do not directly or indirectly experience the passage of time and those who claim that we do experience it usually appeal to perception of the changing of the present moment evident most typically in our perception of motion.[19] The argument that visible change is sufficient proof that time passes confuses the properties of events with the properties of time itself – which we shall discuss presently.[20]

The notion of "the passage of time" therefore is unsustainable. So why is it so central to our time-talk? What is more, why do so many otherwise sensible and competent philosophers subscribe to it?

2.2.3.4 Against flow: the conceptual source of the tenacity of the idea

There are many reasons for the enduring attraction of the idea of the flow of time. Here are some of the most important:

A. Confusion between the properties of events occurring in time and the properties of time itself.[21]
B. The notion of "times" (instants, "nows", days, etc.) as *occurrences* and hence as quasi-events that follow one another.
C. The belief that, if time is not flowing, it must be frozen and, if time is frozen, the universe must be frozen as well.

A. Confusion between the properties of events that occur in time and the properties of time itself

Consider the opening paragraph of Oaklander's essay on "The Problem of Time and Change":

> Time has two aspects when we ordinarily talk about, think about, and experience the world ... [W]e conceive of time as something that flows or passes from the future to the present and from the present to the past. Thus, for example, the inauguration of the fiftieth president of the United States is in the relatively distant future, but with the passage of time it will become less so and eventually will become present. And then, after its spotlight in the NOW, it will recede into the more and more distant past. To speak of events as moving or flowing through time is to conceive of them as undergoing *temporal becoming*.[22]

Oaklander begins by talking about time as something flowing or passing from the future to the past, proceeds to talk about events passing from the future to the past, and ends by talking of events moving or flowing through time. First, it is time that is on the move; then it is events moving along with time; and finally (to judge by the last sentence) we have events moving through presumably static time. Dynamism seems to pass back and forth between time and events. From time flowing from future to past, we move to the idea of events moving from future to the past. This is not a case of relative motion, with time flowing round temporally static events, because if one went backwards, the other would go forwards. Somehow events and time are both on the move, with time, perhaps, providing the momentum. One gets a vague impression of events being not only tagged by times but, in virtue of being attached to those times, being dragged along with them. Event E occurred at t; t is now receding into the past; so E, too, must recede into the past.[23]

It is unclear, then, whether events get their dynamism from dynamic time or whether time gets its dynamism from the dynamism of events. The issues are further blurred by the way events are presented. To examine this confusion – evident in the passage from Oaklander – let us look at a simpler example.

(a) A car passes down a road from point P_1 at t_1 to point P_2 at t_2.

(b) There is an event E (the passage of the car between the two positions) that unfolds from its beginning (when the car is setting out from P_1) to its end (when the car is arriving at P_2).

(c) There is: *the fact that* the car passes from P_1 to P_2 which corresponds to a past event (in the bag and eternal) any time after t_2; an event that was presently occurring between t_1 and t_2; and an event that we can see retrospectively was entirely in the future before t_1 and partly in the future between t_1 and t_2.

Where is the flow to be found? The most obvious location is in the actual, literal passage or movement of the car from P_1 to P_2, in E. This, however, does not deliver dynamism to *time*. The reason for saying this is that E is too local to sustain the dynamism of something as global as time. E is just an instance. The dynamism of events is ubiquitous: there is a continuum of visible and invisible events extending throughout space and time. When one event stops another starts; where there is quiescence here, there is activity there. It seems possible, then, to argue that the dynamism of time may be made explicit in particular events but is maintained through the unceasing global totality of events. However, events will still not make time flow if the latter is seen as something in itself and separable from events.

Oaklander's example is a completed event, with its beginning, middle and end gathered up, designated by a noun phrase: "the inauguration of the fiftieth president of the United States". There is not much dynamism there: the event is frozen in completion – as if the "-ing" of process is arrested to the "-ed" of the done and dusted. The dynamism internal to the event is transferred elsewhere. Oaklander seems to find it in the passage of the complete (and hence seemingly completed) event through successive tenses. These are not, however, alterations in the event, unless one believes that the inauguration enjoys an antenatal existence when it is just like itself but has the additional inflection of being future and a posthumous one when it is past, in addition to the existence it has when it is taking place. In reality, the event, cast in the form of a noun phrase, is pickled as an eternal fact – which is why it can sail through tenses apparently unscathed, undergoing the dramas of coming into and going out of existence, and outlive the time when it is actually happening. However, as a fully baked fact, lifted out of its particular time and circumstances, it seems pretty static. Similarly, "The fact that the car went down the road" is static, silent, and unchanging. It seems (as we shall discuss in Chapter 9) to inhabit a low budget eternity.

There is, then, the world of difference between the car that passes by, the event that passes (or, strictly, unfolds), and the fact of the car's passage that remains forever unchanging after the event has happened. Even so, the uncertain location of the dynamism of time – what it is that is passing – keeps the idea in play, as it draws variously on the dynamism of events, the dynamism of their coming into being, and the seeming dynamism of their passing through tenses. In the latter case, it is unclear whether it is time that provides the dynamism directly by providing the tenses through which events are supposed to sail.

The dynamism of the experienced world is, of course, presented to us in the succession of experiences, which seems to have an intrinsic dynamism. There is a sense, therefore, in which the river of time is borrowed from the stream of consciousness, which is itself both ceaselessly changing and jointless because continuous.

B. The notion of "times" (instants, "nows", days, etc.) as occurrences and hence as quasi-events that follow one another

There are also grounds for suspecting that the dynamism of flowing time is conceived at least by some writers not as residing in events such as E, the passage of a car down a road, but in the transition from t_1 to t_2 that marked the interval in which E took place. This places becoming at the very heart of time itself. In order to make sense of this mode of becoming, we have to embrace either the idea that times such as t_1 and t_2 are in themselves *quasi-occurrences* or that the replacement of one time by another – the replacement of t_1 by t_2 (taking in all the intermediate times) – is an *event*.

There are many problems with the idea of times, or the succession of times, as occurrences and we shall return to them in §10.2. For the present we shall focus on the ones that are most relevant to the idea of passage. Let us compare E – the passage of the car from P_1 to P_2 – with the passage of time from t_1 (when the car left P_1) to t_2 (when the car reached P_2). The passage of the car takes place in something other than the car (a road) and is other than the car (because the car can be still as well as moving, and rust as well as move or keep still). The transit of the time, by contrast, clearly cannot be separated from time itself. The not-quite-separate medium of "hypertime" has already been discredited. Treating instants or stretches of time as occurrences would have other odd consequences. It would oblige us to accept, for example, that Wednesday is a macro-event additional to all the events that take place on Wednesday. When we are asked to list all things that happened on that day, we would have to include "Wednesday happened on Wednesday". Similar considerations would apply to the transition from Wednesday to Thursday or from any t_1 to any t_2. In sum, the notion of intrinsic *temporal becoming* – the becoming of time itself without anything else being involved – is highly suspect. And there is nothing else for "the passage of time" to be other than the intrinsic becoming of time. And for this becoming to be translated into passage, we need to posit that time is intrinsically divided into times in the plural, and these have their time of being, of occurrence.

We shall look critically at this in §10.3.2, where plural times are proposed to consist of naturally occurring instants.

C. The belief that, if time is not flowing, it must be frozen and, if time is frozen, the universe must be frozen as well

It is the first part of the argument we must address here: if time is not dynamic and does not flow, then it must be static and be frozen. The conclusion does not follow from the premise. It is more likely that *neither* property – dynamism or stasis – is appropriately ascribed to time. Just as we are not obliged to conclude that if time is not blue, it must be some other colour. We think we are so obliged only because the notion of time is insufficiently disentangled from that of the events that occur in, or states that endure in, time. Consider the car in the street. Here the contrast between movement and stillness is real and it is reasonable to conclude that if the car is not moving it is still.

The second part of the argument, based on the presupposition that dynamic time is necessary for a dynamic universe – in which events can take place and becoming is possible – is the obverse of what we have hitherto noted: instead of projecting the observed restlessness of the universe into a putative dynamism of time, it injects the latter into the universe to allow it to be restless. We may reject this for several reasons. It presupposes that dynamic time must precede all events: that it is time on the move that gets everything else on the move. This in turn presupposes that time could get on with flowing in a universe void of events, an assumption that is open to challenge – as we shall discuss in §10.4.2. And it also makes it difficult to see how the dynamism of time could be resisted, so that (as is the case) some parts of the world are static, others are slow moving, and yet others are spritely. If the universe were driven by the universal temporal motor, what could account for the difference between the seemingly static rock and the dynamic river when dynamic time is donated equally to the enduring one and the volatile other? The absurdity of the idea of a temporal dynamism distributed unequally through the universe is the other side of the absurdity of the idea, earlier discussed, that the intrinsic nature of time is closer to some of the elements of the material world than others – so that we talk of a "river", and not, say, a "rock" of time. We would expect the dynamism of time to be equally apparent in all the contents of the universe such that the becoming of the latter would be identical in some respect with the becoming of time itself.

At any rate, the uneven distribution of dynamism in the world does seem to justify the question that, if time truly is dynamic, how dynamic is it; and – to return to the earlier question – if it flows, how fast does it flow? To the objection that to ask this question is to take the idea of the flow of time rather literally, we may respond by asking if it is not taken literally what meaning remains to be ascribed to it; or, indeed, what the implications are of asserting that time is dynamic.

It is evident from the Oaklander passage quoted earlier that there is a deep connexion in some thinkers' minds between dynamic and tensed time: the former, it is implied, permits the latter; flowing time sweeps events from the future to the present and then to the past. Barry Dainton asserts that "the eternal-dynamic dispute maps neatly on to the tensed tenseless dispute".[24] Michael Tooley goes further, arguing that "the fundamental thing that separates tensed and tenseless accounts of the nature of time is … acceptance or rejection of a dynamic conception of the world".[25] It is this supposed connection between tenses and the passage of time that discredits the notion of tenses in the minds of some.[26] This is unfounded, as we shall discuss in Chapter 5.

Equally unfounded is the claim that, if time does not flow, it is not real. J. M. E. McTaggart (whom we shall discuss in §5.2) argues that since the temporal relationship between two events does not change (leaving aside considerations from special relativity), then there is neither change nor time. If A occurred before B, then it will always have occurred before B: this relationship seems frozen for eternity. It is, of course, a mistake to infer from the fixity of the relationship of succession that there is no succession; that because the before–after relationship is true for all time there is no such relationship, and hence no real succession, no change, no flow of events – as well as no flow of time. The argument would not have got off the ground had there not been a confusion between events and the fact that they took place. To return to our example, the event E of the car travelling down the road has an intrinsic dynamism but *the fact that* it took place is not dynamic. E took place at a particular time, had a beginning at a particular time t_1 and an end at a particular time t_2, occupied the interval t_1–t_2, and assumed its temporal place in a series of events so that it occurred after the driver got into the car and before the driver got out of the car. None of these is true of *the fact that* the car travelled down the road. Facts do not occur at particular times, do not last for definite stretches of time, and are not in temporal relations to other facts.

The notion of temporal passage or flow, therefore, does not stand up to scrutiny. However, the idea of time as a river is powerfully attractive to those who want to think about time but not too hard. As we have already noted, the stuff that flows in rivers (water) is jointless as (apparently) is time. And they drain away. Time, likewise, seems to get used up by its guests, unlike space which is not consumed by occupancy. The idea of temporal passage captures this character of time as passing *away*. We have already mentioned the contrast between spatial locations that can be revisited and reused indefinitely and temporal locations that cannot. 25 December 2015 lasts from midnight 24 December until its own midnight. After that, it is used up forever, no longer available to "house" events. This is a trivial truth of course: after 25 December, it is no longer 25 December. But it captures our sense that when a period of time is "over", there is less time remaining. This applies particularly to items that have a shelf-life, most notably and most poignantly, creatures such as ourselves that have an allotted lifespan. If this is limited, then not only have certain times passed but available time seems to be shrinking. We may not be able to say precisely how much time we have left (leaving aside the exceptional case of a man under a sentence of judicial execution with no chance of reprieve) but we do know that the older we are the shorter our remaining life expectancy. Whether this applies to the universe as a whole – and to time as a whole – is a matter for conjecture; but if its span is finite then the passage of time might seem to mean the shrinking of time, its passing away. Time is not reusable because the "re-" betrays that reuse corresponds to a different time. So it seems to drain away; hence the river (and the sands) of time. It is also crucial to the argument against time travel to be discussed in §2.4.

So much for the rather cloudy idea of the passage of time as time passing *away*. This is the only aspect of the idea of passage that seems to withstand scrutiny. It is not very much; even so "the flow of time" seems to be indispensable in our everyday conversation and in philosophical discourse. How can this be? To answer this we perhaps need to look to psychology.

2.2.3.5 Against flow: the psychological source of the tenacity of the idea

Mellor tries to make sense of our attachment to the idea of the flow of time by arguing that flow is not a property of time itself but of our beliefs about events that take place in time. He connects the notion of the passage of time with tense – with the intention of discrediting both. Adapting McTaggart's terminology, he traces dynamic ideas of time to so-called "A-beliefs" that allocate events to tenses, to the future, present and past – echoing Dainton's claim about the close connection between attachment to tensed and to dynamic time. A-beliefs are contrasted with B-beliefs that are about time as a mere series of events that are "earlier" or "later":

> We have so many A-beliefs that we must always be changing some of them, especially our now beliefs. These changes embody the psychological truth in the metaphysical falsehood that time flows, i.e. that events like Jim's race really are moving in A-time from being tomorrow, to being today, to being yesterday, and so on.[27]

It is this – the fact that we are constantly having to change our tensed beliefs, updating our beliefs as to what is "future", "now" or "past" – that generates "our undeniably real experience of time flowing" but it "gives us no reason to think that time flows in reality".[28] There is nothing unreal in this, Mellor argues: the passage of an event from future to present to past "is a real process of change – but only in me, not in e [the event itself]".[29]

As will be evident in future chapters, I think Mellor throws out the clean baby (of tensed time) with the dirty bathwater (of the notion of time as flowing). This is at least in part because he gathers up the sense of a change of tense into the individual psyche. But the transition from the belief on 12 December that Jim will race tomorrow to the knowledge on 13 December that he is racing today and on 14 December that he raced in the past is not purely intra-psychic. It is as little a matter of psychology as the passage from "Christmas is in two days' time" to "Christmas is today" to "Christmas was two days ago". These are facts that belong to the community of minds at least as much as "Christmas" and "25 December". As we shall see in Chapter 5, dismissing

A-series temporal statements (that are tensed or include implicitly tensed terms such as "yesterday" and "tomorrow") on the grounds that they are intra-psychic will have the undesirable consequence for those such as Mellor himself – who feel that B-series time ("earlier" and "later", dates such as 12 December, etc.) is "real time". It will draw attention to the psychological components of the latter and by the same token undermine *their* claim to reality.

If we are to discredit the idea of flow or passage as intrinsic properties of time, we need to clarify the phenomena (psychological or communal) that explain our propensity to speak and think of time as dynamic. What is perceived? A succession of beliefs – and my associated inclination to say "X will happen", "X is happening", and "X has happened" at different times – does not seem to get to the heart of the feeling of flow, though what that feeling really is (beyond something that our way of talking about events makes us think that we ought to feel) is unclear. As for the idea that events move from one part of time to another – from the future to the present to the past – this, though tenacious, is misleading, as we shall discuss (see especially §8.2.2.2.) The nature of this movement – real or apparent, objective or psychological – is baffling. After all, we know that, if an event occurs at t_1 it cannot (also) occur at t_2. So an event's movement in time cannot be of the kind that we would designate by "the passage from time t_1 to t_2". If there is to be any movement and the event is to remain attached to t_1, it is t_1 that must move – coming nearer, arriving (at the present) and moving away. If this is a real movement, then the question returns as to what t_1 is moving *in*. So too does the question as to whether this idea of t_1 moving is effectively making moments of time items in themselves, that exist – indeed occur – independently of any events or, indeed, of a material world, something we have touched on already.

As we discussed earlier with respect to dates, there is no net movement: t_1 will advance towards the present only as fast as the present moves towards t_1. We must not, however, conclude from this that both parties are moving but at equal speed. This is entirely wrong, but an inevitable consequence of succumbing to the notion that t_1, etc. are items in themselves that exist before and after they become present, so that they can move towards a present that is moving towards it. It should hardly be necessary to point out that t_1 cannot exist before and after the present (t_1) at which it becomes the present. It cannot outlast itself, enjoying the status of t_1-in-waiting prior to t_1 as it is heading towards t_1 and t_1-afterlife after t_1.

Is there any way of rescuing the notion of time as flux? Perhaps we could dismantle the banks and see time as flowing in all directions at once, like water spreading two-dimensionally over a flood plain or three-dimensionally like a growing balloon or the expanding space of astrophysicists. This would at least capture the "everywhereness" of time – corresponding to the (spatial) ubiquity of the events that unfold in, and measure time, and the universality of the temporal relations between events and times. And it would also deal with the suspicion we should direct at the idea of something that flows but can flow only in one direction – forward and not backward and certainly not sideways. Unfortunately, however, this interpretation would remove one aspect of time that is valued by those who find the "river of time" intuitively attractive; namely, its (seeming) one-dimensional (seeming) directionality (something which we shall deal with in due course). And it would exacerbate rather than remove the problem of what time is moving in: we now have to find two or possibly three hyper-temporal dimensions to house its expansion.

Even so, this may highlight the distinctive attraction of those dynamic accounts of time that focus on accumulation and expansion rather than movement of time or parts of it. These include the "growing block", "growing line" and "moving spotlight" images of dynamic time.

2.2.3.6 Dynamic alternatives to flow

The dynamic alternatives to flow either set aside or modify the notion of time as something in motion, but retain the idea of a mode of becoming inherent in time itself (as analogous to that of events in time). The growing block theory sees time expanding or accumulating rather than moving. The moving spotlight theory is ambiguous as to the becoming of time: whether or not it is already-existing time that becomes by coming into the present. Its becoming takes the form of "nows" (real, because present, time) picked out by a spotlight, so that movement, dynamism, is as it were outsourced to something that seems to be other than, or at least not entirely identical with, time.

The growing block (and the growing line)

The idea that time does not flow or spread but accumulates – the "growing block" theory – is particularly associated with C. D. Broad. According to Broad, temporal passage is the continued growth of the sum of existences.[30] By "existences" he does not mean material objects but states of affairs and events, that become facts and information. Future events are non-existent but present events obviously do exist and, less obviously, so do past ones since, Broad argues, nothing has happened to them by becoming past: this involves no intrinsic change. Thus "fresh slices of existence [are] added to the total history of the world".[31] Physical reality at any moment consists of a space–time block of present and past facts (but no future facts) and, as time passes, there is more past time and thus more of what has happened.

Thus we have a kind of passage without passing away: nothing is lost. What is more, there is passage without any quasi-spatial direction: "into the past" is clearly not the kind of direction that seeks or requires an arrow. And, most attractively, time that grows but does not flow does not raise difficult questions about the "speed" of passage.[32] The notion of time as an accumulation also corresponds to our sense that what has happened cannot unhappen, so that the sum total of (happened) happenings will increase. We can turn the clock back in the loose sense of reversing a change but doing so is an additional happening and time, of course, is not reclaimed.

There are, however, other problems. Firstly, that which grows with time is not time itself but "existences" that happen in time. This may seem like an added attraction: we are happy to outsource whatever it is that corresponds to our idea of the passage of time to something a bit more tangible – events that come and go and/or the fact that they have happened. However, it remains questionable whether even events can accumulate in the way Broad envisages: yesterday's events are not in some sense still present as the latest addition to the sum total of events in history. While events do not unhappen, they are not continuing to happen posthumously as it were; while they are not taken back, neither are they ongoing. And as for states of affairs, consider my car when it was new a year ago and the same car, somewhat battle-scarred, a year later. The earlier state of the object is clearly not preserved in some form.

What is it, then, that accumulates with time? We need to clarify "existences". Perhaps they are facts: facts such as "that E took place at a particular time t".[33] These facts, however, must depend on something else to bring them into being as existences. The most obvious candidate is human memory or memory articulated and preserved in records. In the absence of memory, the events corresponding to them do not have any kind of (present, continuing) existence, except implicitly in their present consequences. If the events comprising the sum total of existences are not made to exist beyond the time at which they happen, they have only a virtual existence – a point underlined by the fact that there are many ways of organizing the past corresponding to many types and token facts. (Imagine trying to answer the question: "how many facts were contained in yesterday?" – we would not even be able to address it in principle.) This is not to deny the reality of the past – something we shall discuss in Chapter 7 – but simply to point out that growing block won't grow unless there is some means of retaining what has happened beyond the time of its happening.

There is also the question of the means by which the block is brought together. It is unlikely to be self-totalling, so that, for example, the Battle of Hastings, the Battle of Waterloo, a cricket match a few days ago, and the pain I just felt in my side just now, spontaneously gather themselves into a unity. In, or in virtue of, what is the block totalled, do its parts co-exist? The same question applies to *the amount of time* that is proposed to grow with the block, the "our yesterdays" adding up to an ever-increasing "All". The existence of this total presupposes that those yesterdays have a posthumous existence. Of course they do so but only in our individual and collective memories. If that existence seems more substantive than it is, it is because they are recorded as the leaves of a diary or the contents of the boxes on calendars.[34]

This helps us to clarify an essential fault with the growing block theory: the putative growth is predicated on the notion that the universe keeps a tab on itself and that (say) the present effects of past causes retain the memory of their progenitors or that successive states of the universe in some way retain their predecessors. While the pages of history can be placed together in one book, existing simultaneously as a record, and getting fatter as the centuries pass, the successive moments of time, or events or states of affairs associated with those moments cannot. The page devoted to Wednesday 25 April and the page devoted to Thursday 26 April can lie within the covers of the same book – so that the book gets fatter as history unfolds and is written – but the two days, 25 and 26, cannot be together in this way. They cannot be successive *and* simultaneous; separated in time and, at the same time, not separated in time.[35] Yes, there is a larger past in 2000 CE than in 1000 CE but this does not mean that there is more time in the sense of a greater capacity for events; that there is more available time. Past time perishes as it is born: it is "gone time". Space, by contrast, does not perish as it comes into being; indeed, it does not come into being (outside of the cosmogeneses of astrophysics – see note 38). Events take up space without as it were consuming it but they take time; space is there to be used and reused but time is used up. Thus it shrinks as fast as it grows; and from the viewpoint of a living organism, that which is used up is not replaced *for* it.[36]

The fundamental fault with the growing block is evident in Broad's description of it, quoted earlier: "fresh slices of existence [are] added to the total history of the world". The word "history" is smuggled in, so that a succession of events elides into a growing timeline. Even if we allow that the successive states of the universe are self-totalling, so that the block will grow, it is not evident that this growing total will translate into growing quantities of elapsed time. Can we assume that "More time means more events (or facts)" implies that "More events (or facts) means more time"? There is a sleight of hand in reading time out directly from a growing quantity of states of the universe, so that time becomes itself something whose total is growing and whose latest addition is an ever-changing "now" or "the present".[37]

The attraction of the growing block image is that it seems to retain a dynamic notion of time. This, however, is illusory because any flowing is located in the collective (overwhelmingly human) consciousness or record of successive states of the world; in the *registration* of increase, not in time itself. And this is true also of the alternative metaphor of time as a *growing line.* The advancing tip of the line is the present moment and completed events can be located at different points on the line that grows behind that tip. This seems to capture "before" and "after" as well as the relationship between a "now" and its "past" and "future" but, as hardly needs spelling out, it retains the problems associated with growing block. "Time as a line" fits, of course, with its status as a fourth dimension, if we overlook the awkward fact that the other three dimensions are not usually in the business of growing.[38] It is not, however, as straightforward as it might seem. First of all, there is a qualitative difference between the tip of the line (however that is defined) where there is movement, or growth, and the rest of the line which is an inert deposit. Behind the tip, the line is a static trace of something that was once dynamic. To put this another way: the line is both the moving (present) moment and the total of previous moments; it is dynamic at the tip but remains static throughout the remainder of its length. If it were not, the line would be a mess. (The exception is when the succession for which it stands is reactivated by being scanned.)

The line analogy is flawed in another way. Think of a linear object such as a road. We may say of it that it "goes" somewhere, but of course it is motionless. The supposed linear object that is time *is*, by contrast, purely its going somewhere, its moving on to new (temporal places). If time were a road, we would have to conceive of a road that was purely road-building and not the built highway, a line that was simply the being-drawn and not that which has been drawn.[39]

If despite its many flaws, the notion of time as a line seems compelling, this may be because it captures something of our sense of what is central to time-filling, time-consuming, time-creating (the incompatibility of all these three inseparable descriptors is significant) happenings: namely change, whose paradigm is motion, reduced to distance covered, reduced in turn to a trajectory signified by a line. The application of "direction" to events other than objects in motion is, however, somewhat problematic. It is doubtful whether it can be used in a fully non-metaphorical sense outside of spatial displacement. When an object turns from red to blue, *blue* → *red* has an "orientation" only in contrast to *red* → *blue*. However, the "reversal of direction" must not be taken literally, unless we are prepared to say that the turnaround is 180°. Nevertheless, all change – economic trends as well as the flight of birds – can be (or seem to be) represented as, and reduced to, a type of motion in a kind of space broadly construed. So a change in the colour or temperature of an object can be represented as a "movement" from one location on the spectrum (set out in vector space) to another or a "movement" from one position on the temperature range to another. We should not confuse this representation with that to which it refers.

Both the growing block and the growing line images translate the passage of time into the sum total of events and *that sum total* is seen as a passage, pure becoming. It is to see time as something that comes into being rather as events, states of affairs, and objects do; as a process of continuous occurrence in its own right.

The moving spotlight

So much for "passage" or "flow" capturing time that is both passing and passing away – a dynamism that is borrowed from events – and "the growing block" where passing time in one sense does not pass away but is stored in the form of the sum total of the facts about those existences that have come into (and gone out of) being up to the present moment. There is another metaphor which is particularly attractive because it addresses our intuitions about *tensed* time: the idea of time as a moving spotlight. It also avoids the problems of storage, the self-totalling implicit in the growth of the growing block or line. Time, seen as a moving spotlight, consists of a succession of transient, perishable moments – more precisely of "nows" – or perhaps of a series of token nows that maintain, through successive instantiations, an unchanging Now. The passage of time resides in this succession in which, as Gödel put it, "*reality consists of an infinity of layers of 'now' which come into existence successively*".[40] The flow of time is a succession of present moments. The idea endeavours to capture the fact that first t_1 (with the events associated with it) and then t_2 (with the events associated with it) are present; in short that a succession of moments takes on the mantle of "now".[41] The events that take place in those moments or the objects present in them enter the spotlight of current existence.

A classic expression of the moving spotlight idea of time is again by Broad:

> We are naturally tempted to regard the history of the world as existing eternally in a certain order of events. Along this, and in a fixed direction, we imagine the character of presentness as moving, somewhat like a spot of light from a policeman's bull's-eye traversing the fronts of houses in a street. What is illuminated is the present, what has been illuminated is the past, and what has not yet been illuminated is the future.[42]

According to this image, each moment in time has its moment in the sun of "now". It can be seen, first of all, that the image is ambiguous as to what it is that comes into the sun: the moment itself or that which furnishes, or takes place in, or is permitted by, the moment.[43] We thus seem to have two independent series: the succession of instants (t_1, t_2, etc.) and the succession of states of the universe (S_1, S_2, etc.). That seems rather odd for two reasons. First of all, it seems to license the idea of moments such as t_1 assuming their rightful place as "now" – or rather a particular now – which is, of course, inseparable from t_1. In short, t_1 takes up its allotted place in itself! Secondly, it would suggest that the states of affairs are unfolding independently of time; at any rate that their existence is independent of their being "now", in the spotlight of the policeman's bullseye. This notion – effectively of states of affairs or of the universe waiting in the wings to become present, having their moment on the stage and then returning to the wings – is questionable, for the same reason as it is wrong to think of events as "time tourists", anticipating and outliving their own occurrence, as if they were able to be about to happen, be happening, and having happened all at the same time.

The alternative interpretation – namely, that the succession of times brings the succession of states into being – is equally unsatisfactory. The moving spotlight seems to have two jobs to do: making that which occurs occur and also making it exist as a present reality. This would ascribe causal powers to time itself. We shall examine this in Chapter 10. But let us here touch briefly on why this cannot be right. If instants were able to bring about states of affairs, then all states of affairs would have two kinds of causes: the causes that we usually ascribe to them (their private causes, as it were); and time itself (the common cause of all happening). And time, being the prior condition of existence of any state of affairs would, as it were, be the senior cause. What's more, if time were homogeneous, then it would presumably have the same causal effect under all circumstances, which would make it impossible to see how it could operate in a variegated world, where heterogeneous causes are associated with heterogeneous effects or where the world unfolding in time endlessly changes into something different.

Manifestly, any attempt to separate the spotlight from that which is spotlit – whether it is time shining a light on itself, or a succession of nows illuminating, or even midwifing, a succession of states of affairs – leads to contradiction. If this is less obvious than it should be, it is because we tend to ascribe to states of affairs in the absence of time properties that they can have only in the presence of time; in other words project timeliness into timeless states of affairs. In addition, we equally inadvertently ascribe to times themselves a property that properly belong to states of affairs – namely causal efficacy – in virtue of which states of affairs are brought into the present; that is to say into current actuality. Finally, the idea of a *moving* spotlight is another example of the projection into all of time the motion we see in certain events.

This metaphor – really another one of passage – is even more hapless than that of flow. For a spotlight to illuminate a succession of moments, as it were from the outside, those moments would have to be in existence already, awaiting their time in the limelight. Otherwise the spotlight, or its successive positions, would have to be identical with the moments it illuminates. If it *were* identical with them, the spotlight would be redundant; at any rate we would lose the notion of something other than the moments making the moments present. The idea of moments waiting in the wings and being picked out in succession – so t_1 is picked out and becomes present, followed by t_2, and then t_3 – is clearly rather problematic. Are we to assume that t_3 is already in place at t_1 waiting for its cue – or auto-cue, given that the cue is t_3 itself – by which time t_1 will have had its moment of glory but will still remain as an "emeritus-now"? Are we to imagine t_3 pre-existing itself, awaiting during t_1 and t_2 its moment in the spotlight at t_3 and then outliving itself from t_4 onwards as part of a departing troop of moments? The notions of times-in-waiting is even more obscure than the idea that events that have not yet occurred are "in the future" awaiting their turn in the present. This is particularly awkward because, for its moment in the spotlight to be at t_3, the latter would have already to be in existence, at least to specify the temporal point of its own emergence. And yet all of this is licensed by the imagery in Broad's account of "the moving spotlight".

We may be tempted to look outside of time for a candidate to assume the role of the spotlight making successive moments present, and (possibly) plucking events and states of affairs out of mere possibility into momentary actuality. The obvious candidate is consciousness but there are at least two reasons why this seems unsatisfactory. Firstly, it is unlikely that an *individual* consciousness – while it may make events, etc. present to itself – could define the present tense, or the sum total of what is present. At the very least, we would seem to require the sum total of all consciousnesses, perhaps all actual and possible consciousnesses. If we merge the idea of "now", with the spotlight and the spotlight with consciousness, we are left trying to make sense of successive moments of consciousness awaiting (one presumes) their turn as "now" or as "now-makers" that can realize potential events or states of the world as actualities.

Otherwise there would be a flow of time unique to each conscious being. And this points to a greater difficulty: it makes consciousness too active in determining what counts as the present, and hence making what is present be present. We – individually or collectively – do not choose the present moment, nor for the most part, what is present, though we may influence some of its contents. "Now" is, overwhelmingly, what is served up: we are recipients of happenings. Even less do we have any say over what moment in time counts as the present – when, for example, 12 noon on

25 December should count as "now". So we – individually or collectively – are not the moving spotlight. As well as giving too much power to consciousness to make the potential actual, this view would simply move the problem on. By what means would the successive moments of consciousness acquire the status of "now"? We should therefore abandon the notion of consciousness as playing on the world and bringing it into the present. But this leaves the "spotlight" entirely uncharacterized.

We have focused on the spotlight but there are also many residual ambiguities in the notion of the *spotlit*. How big, for example, is the time-slice illuminated by it? Intuitively, we feel that something like a whole day is too fat to count as the present. What moves, then, is a rather slimmer "now" illuminating a succession of moments. How slim? A minute, a specious present of a few seconds, or something closer to a mathematical instant? As we shall discuss in Chapter 6, our experience of (present) time is not bounded by the limits of any putative "instant" or indeed "specious present": there is a sense in which the present (pregnant with past and future) extends to longer stretches – days or hours. "Today" and "nowadays", after all, are terms that make sense to us. If we concede that the spotlit is a blob rather than a pinpoint, it is even more difficult to grasp the notion of "nows" each having their moment in the sun of (present) reality.

This last image reveals a further problem in the relationship between the spotlit and the spotlight. The idea of a moment having its moment in the sun threatens the return of a second order or hypertime in which first order times are allocated a time and between which they can move. And this is of course the consequence of the very idea of times, or dates, coming nearer (in time) to a particular time, that in which it is the present, irrespective of whether it is given a name such as "12 December" or simply designated by a generic term such as "a moment". It is hardly necessary to reiterate that the hypertime through which time must move – if it is to move at all – is not only unintelligible but the first step into an infinite regression – of hyper-hypertime, hyper-hyper-hypertime, etc. – in which time and hypertimes, etc. must move.

It will be evident that the moving spotlight seems to have inherited all the problems of flowing time and added some of its own. "Now" playing over a scene of co-existing states – that are somehow already in ghostly form waiting to be clothed in actuality – is difficult to make intelligible. It construes time as something that not only makes things present but also brings them into existence. It assumes, furthermore, the ontological equivalence, at some level, of the contents of the future and the past; as if the future is populated by objects- and events-in-waiting, patiently enduring until they are kissed into now-being by the arrival of the present tense and enjoy their moment in the sun. This becomes particularly clear when we mingle the notion of the spotlight with that of consciousness: there is an inescapable conflation of what is happening with consciousness of what is happening; or the emergence of what is happening into consciousness. (Whether the "happening" of what happens is due to consciousness is something we shall discuss in §10.4.4).

The idea that the present is a moving spotlight picking out successive points on a somehow pre-existent static timeline is equally unattractive. It would make of time the creation not only of itself (which it may well be as it seems unlikely to be generated by anything else) but also of everything else – summoning states of affairs, events, processes, and objects into being, or at the very least lifting them from possibility (when they were future) to actuality and subsequently banishing them to the state of has-beens. The analogy merges two things that (perhaps) should be kept separate: the movement from time t_1 to t_2 to t_3, etc.; and the succession of events that constitute the changing present of "what is going on". It could be argued that this conflation might be justified if t_1, t_2, t_3 are containers for possible events, and/or events at t_1, t_2, t_3 constitute t_1, t_2, t_3. But moments of time and actual events cannot be assimilated to one another. It seems sensible to keep 12 noon and what happens at 12 noon distinct.

It may be thought that I am taking the analogy too literally. If, however, we dismiss every objection to the moving spotlight theory as the result of excessive literal-mindedness, it is difficult to see what remains that would have any explanatory or even descriptive power. If the moving spotlight were really just another name for "becoming", as successive states of the world become successively the present state of the world, it does not take us very far. But beyond this modest interpretation of the metaphor lies irremediable muddle and worse.[44]

There is a less ambitious version of the moving spotlight theory which seems to avoid the kinds of problems we have discussed but it does so at the price of seeming, and in my view being, a truism. Brad Skow argues that "Now moves from the past to the future".[45] This can correspond to a moving now and the latter to "the passage of time (itself)" only if Now is a particular point of time – say t_n – which begins in the future and ends in the past. Then we have the absurd notion, already touched on, that t_n passes via itself from t_{n-x} to t_{n+x}, where x is any time. The defence that "Now" is a general term, encompassing all moments in time, only compounds the problem, because what we then have is an entire class of instants on the move, pre-living and outliving themselves. If "Now" is not actual instants of time but merely a relationship between an utterance and the time of the utterance then nothing is on the move.

2.2.3.7 Further reflections on dynamic time

I hope the foregoing is a persuasive case for setting aside the quasi-spatial notion of time as something that flows, that there is something called "the passage of time" which is a universal change, an ongoing process, or a succession of events. It will have been apparent that one of the many reasons that it is difficult to shake off the notion is that it is slippery, encompassing at least three kinds of putative passage: of events or successive states of the world; of calendrical time; and of time *tout court*. Or to put this slightly differently, the passing of events, the passing of the days and years, and the moment-to-moment passage of time. The middle kind is the one that gives most credence to the notion of flow. As we have already discussed, it is almost impossible to resist thinking of days, months, and years coming closer, arriving, and then receding. As items on the move, however, they are even more implausible than time itself. We are invited to imagine blocks of time, empty crates travelling from the future towards the present to be loaded with events before proceeding to the past. It is difficult to see what the days are journeying *in*, what propels them forward, if it is not a second-order river of time upon whose bosom they are borne. We could have only talked ourselves into such a notion of the flow of time through taking calendars, and their contents, seriously as items that exist independently of the notational system by which we capture future and past time.

We know of course that a morning passing is nothing like a bus passing and dinner approaching is nothing like a place getting nearer as you walk through it. In the case of ordinary motion, there is a difference between something coming towards you and you moving towards something but as The Big Day approaches, it makes no sense to allocate credit for this, least of all crediting ourselves who are looking forward to The Big Day: it and we have no choice over its getting nearer. This is all obvious but it may be difficult to escape these ideas because there is something deeper than an attachment to conceptual muddles in our propensity to ascribe dynamism to time and to think of it as something flowing or growing in itself. It is our sense of the irreversibility of what is happening in the world and our lives and with it the sense of the implacability of our progress towards things, especially those we dread – future ordeals, losses and extinction; the day of the examination, of the departure of a loved one, of the surgical operation; or, even though it has not been decided, the hour of our death. Whatever we do, whatever way we face, whatever our direction of travel, we are always getting nearer to the end of our life: time does not merely advance, it "marches" on regardless, frogmarching us along with it. Nothing, we say, can make time and hence our lives "stand still". And we think of the days – of a holiday – "slipping" or "rushing" by. Our allocation is "used up" – the number of our numbered days gets smaller – and, when we fall ill, we ask the doctor how much time we have got left. Swept into and out of being, we feel as helpless as logs on a torrent, propelled towards The Great Drop. Hence time, in the words of the hymn-maker Isaac Watts, as "an ever-rolling stream/Which bears all its sons away".[46]

There is, in addition, the fact discussed in the previous chapter, that our sense of explicit time, of time as something in itself, is closely linked with our experience of motion as revealed to us through vision. Movement and space loom large in our minds when we are conceptualizing time. This can be misleading, as illustrated by this fundamental contrast with time: when an object comes nearer to or goes further from us, either we or it are moving; whereas when a date or planned event seems to come nearer to us, or to recede from us, it seems to be time, not the date or the event that provides the movement. We don't have to do anything. If we want Christmas morning to come more quickly our best strategy is to fall soundly asleep for the first 24 days of December. Even so, this connection between explicit time and observed movement – reinforced in clocks that measure time by spatial displacement – makes it seems as though time is a kind of motion. Which is why, when an object moves from position A which it occupies at time t_1 to position B at time t_2, we sometimes think of the replacement of t_1 by t_2 as a kind of change comparable to the object's change of position or that change of position requires another real change, the "passage" of time *from* t_1 to t_2, such that time has as it were "moved *its* position".

For these reasons, it is easier to show the incoherence in the idea of the passage of time than to banish it from our thoughts and intuitions. It does seem to reflect our sense of a dynamic universe; as the logician C. I. Lewis put it "the passage of time as actual" is "given now with the jerky or whoosh quality of transience".[47] It is, as Richard Gale, says, "the flow and go of very existence, nearer to us than breathing, closer than hands and feet".[48] "It is simply that we *find* passage, that we are immediately and poignantly involved in the whoosh of process, the felt movement of one moment into the next."[49] It is as if time were a special, pure "whoosh" inside the "whoosh of event", lying at the heart of becoming, of our perception of becoming, its translation into explicit time, and its eventual translation into measured time. Of course, if time really is the marrow of all change, common to all happening, it must be different from the particular events it supports – either through permitting them, bringing them into being, or creating a kind of space of possibility into which events and processes unfold. More to the point, it cannot share some of the properties of events. If, on the other hand, times *were* sufficiently distinct from events – so that we can isolate a distinct passage of time from the passage of events – odd questions start to surface. For example, how do events keep up with the overall flow of time? If, on the other hand, events are that in virtue of which time flows, then time cannot flow independently of them.

Finally, we should remind ourselves that, if time were a dimension comparable to those of space, it would make no more sense to think of it flowing than to think of length moving longways or, perhaps, upwards or sideways – or even come to that moving in time – getting "later" or translating from the future to the past. If time were space-like in this fundamental respect, it should no more move than space does.

To the objection that I have been too literal-minded in my dealings with "the flow of time", I offer this defence. Only by taking the idea literally is it possible to see through it. My aim (to borrow a phrase from Wittgenstein) is "to teach you to pass from a piece of disguised nonsense to something that is patent nonsense".[50] And "you" here includes myself.

Similar objections may be raised to my way of dealing with two further consequences of the spatialization of time or its reduction to mere membership of the group of four dimensions – which may still be influential even when the illegitimacy and incoherence of space-like or space-based notions of time has been demonstrated. The second is the notion of time travel, which I will discuss in §2.4. The first is the "arrow of time", to which we shall now turn.[51]

2.3 IS THERE AN ARROW OF TIME?

2.3.1 The origin of the arrow

> The happy highway where I went
> And cannot come again.
>
> Housman, *A Shropshire Lad*, poem XL

[A] fundamental asymmetry in all the possible structures of the universe could provide a basis for the arrow of time.

Barbour, *The End of Time*[52]

While many, perhaps the majority, of philosophers of time would be content to abandon the notion that time "flows", "passes" or "moves", the quasi-spatial idea that time
has a "direction" is more adhesive. Although it is associated with the conception of
time as a fourth dimension on a par with the three of space, it should, however, like
flow, be incompatible with it, as we have already noted. The spatial dimensions do
not have a direction. This is not merely because space is isotropic. It's more basic
than that. Together, the three spatial dimensions do not themselves have a direction
but open up the *possibility* of direction. Clearly, the possibility of direction opened
up by space could not be extended to time. It would not make sense to say that time
was pointing from left to right or up and down or in some intermediate direction
compounded out of the spatial dimensions.

Again, as already noted, the idea of time having a direction is at odds in another
respect with its being assigned the status of a dimension: it is one way. If we were
(legitimately or otherwise) to assign a direction to spatial dimensions, they would
have to be two-way. Up–down is inseparable from down–up. The line from A to B is
also the line B to A; any path going from a lower point to a higher point is also a path
going from a higher point to a lower point (though *pace* Heraclitus, the way up and
the way down are not the same!). The bi-directionality is rooted in another difference:
spatial dimensions such as up–down are static: they have no intrinsic movement.
If they did, they'd be in some difficulty: movement can be either way (up–down or
down–up) but not, of course, both at once. By contrast, the path between earlier
time t_1 and later time t_2 can be traversed in one direction (earlier–later) but not in
the other direction (later–earlier). The path from t_1 to t_2 is inescapable while the
path from t_2 to t_1 is blocked. In the case of time, unlike space, there is no distinction
between the dimension, the (supposed) movement in it, and the direction of that
movement. Those dis-analogies between space and time again.

The idea of time's (uni-)directionality is as it were the last residue of the "flow of
time". Many physicists and philosophers of time feel that this unidirectionality is not
simply a matter of definition – that t_1 is bound to be earlier than t_2 merely because
the latter is later than it – but is connected with something fundamental about the
universe in which we live. The hunt has therefore been on for a universal property of
objects and events that will give time a direction, at least in the very restricted sense
of its moving "forward" but not "backward", the other possibilities (up and down or
side to side) not being on the table. This something will account for the difference
between the temporal dimension and the three spatial ones; namely that direction
and movement are inseparable in the case of the former but not the latter. We can
wander at will in space but not in time (as we shall discuss in §2.4 when we address
time travel). The multiplicity of the dimensions of space makes movement independent of those dimensions. While I can move in the up–down, side–side or back–front
axes, I can (as I do for the most part) move in directions intermediate between these
axes, or directions created out of different contributions from these axes.

We can approach this contrast differently by arguing that there is an intrinsic temporal order to events to which there does not correspond a spatial order. Consider three objects:

   A   C   B

There is no constraint on the order in which I visit them or visit the spatial locations they occupy. The journey A → B → C is no more or less legitimate or possible than A → C → B, or C → B → A, or C → B → C → A. There is no order of coexistent objects, as there is an order of succession of states or events. The fact that B is between A and C does not of itself oblige me to visit B before I visit C if I am setting out from A. I can take any route and if necessary deviate in order to bypass B to get to C before visiting B. Indeed, we could argue that it is the order in which we visit A, B and C that orders them: they are arranged along our chosen trajectory. Time, however, appears to have a built-in trajectory: it *is* a trajectory.[53]

It is tempting to explain this difference by saying that temporal points happen in a certain order while spatial do not happen at all and so are not ordered. This temptation ought to be resisted not only because of the doubtful status of "points" in space (see §3.4.1),[54] but also because there is something deeply suspect about the suggestion that points in time – or "times" – *occur* at a certain time and in a certain temporal order. It makes them quasi-events, as occurrents, and also threatens the return of the idea of time being located in a higher order or hypertime. Even so, there remains a clear difference between space that is intrinsically directionless because it is the womb of all directions and unidirectional time. It is awareness of this difference that motivates the all-too-familiar metaphor of "the arrow" of time, introduced by the astronomer and physicist Arthur Eddington.

An arrow seems to have two features that commend it: it has a direction; and for those wedded to the idea that time flows, it can even be in motion.[55] What is more, its direction, with or without flight, comes from its differentiation into head, shaft and tail. So far, so good: we have echoes of the mandatory direction of time – from earlier to later rather than the other way round. After this, the analogy falls apart. Unlike a literal arrow, time's arrow if it really could move, could move in only one direction. Real arrows can be pointed in any direction and even be sent back to where they have come from. Nevertheless, the arrow metaphor is ubiquitous.

Here are a couple of examples. When we represent the successive states of a system we tend to connect them by means of an arrow that points from the earlier to the later state, thus:

   S_1 at t_1 → S_2 at t_2

You might say "This is only a convention", but it is a remarkably tenacious one. It is present throughout classical chemistry:

   $2H_2 + O_2 → 2H_2O$

And the relationship between cause and effect (something to which we shall return briefly in §2.3.5 and at greater length in §11.2) is often pictured thus:

cause → effect

And, finally, it is not unusual to see successive moments of time presented in this way:

earlier → later

Notwithstanding its faults, therefore, "the arrow of time" is seemingly inescapable, perhaps because it conflates many different views on time: that it moves; that it has a direction; that it moves in a certain direction; and that events have a certain temporally irreversible direction. It is the latter, the most conservative and least vulnerable, image that I want to focus on here.

The question that seemingly justifies the search for metaphors, such as the arrow, for the directionality of time is: "what is it that makes one event E_1 earlier (or later) than another E_2?" The answer would appear to be pretty straightforward: "the fact that E_1 *was* earlier (or later) than E_2." In short, the relationship "earlier than" and "later than" is irreducible to anything else; it is mistaken to look outside of time for criteria to justify saying of an event that it is "earlier" or "later" than another and to explain why it is possible (indeed inescapable) to pass from earlier events to later ones but not the other way round. It is, however, illuminating to examine the extra-temporal bases that have been invoked to explain the directionality of time: the thermodynamic, psychological, informational and causal arrows. They do not quite address the same questions but they are closely connected aspects of a single inquiry.

2.3.2 The thermodynamic and other irreversibility-based arrows

> It is not *a priori* that the world becomes more disorganized with time. It is a matter of experience that the disorganization comes at a later rather than an earlier time.
> Wittgenstein, *Lectures on Philosophy*, para 15

> I find myself more than half-convinced by the oddly repellent hypothesis that the peculiarity of the time dimension is not…primitive but is wholly a resultant of those differences in the mere *de facto* run and order of the world's filling.   Williams, "The Myth of Passage", 112

If we are looking for a characteristic of the material world that will give time a direction, it, too, should have something that can be construed as a direction – at least to the extent of being one-way – and it should be ubiquitous. The second law of thermodynamics seems to meet both of these criteria. According to this law, a closed system will tend towards increasing entropy or disorder. This is illustrated throughout nature. Concentrations of heat, of diffusible substances, of gases, etc. will spread to fill any space made available to them and in that space there will be an evermore homogeneous distribution of the relevant variable or substance. If you bring together two liquids such as water and alcohol or a crystal and its solvent, they tend to mix until there is a macroscopically even spread of the two components. The reverse process does not happen – or very rarely happens – spontaneously. For example, we do not see a spontaneous separation of a mixture of the two into pure alcohol and pure water. The direction of the unfolding of events with time towards increasing homogeneity, or disorder is that of increasing entropy. "Later" consequently means in a state of higher entropy compared with "earlier".[56]

This connection was expressed by Eddington as follows:

> Let us draw an arrow arbitrarily. If we follow the arrow and we find more and more of the random element in the state of the world, then the arrow is pointing towards the future; if the random element decreases the arrow points towards the past. That is the only distinction known to physics. This follows at once if our fundamental contention is admitted that the introduction of randomness is the only thing which cannot be undone. I shall use the phrase "time's arrow" to express this one-way property of time which has no analogue in space.[57]

The spontaneous trend towards "thermodynamic equilibrium" is essentially a mixing up and evening out of the material contents in the world, one manifestation of which is the degradation of complex items, a loss of order or structure within closed systems. The one-way passage of events towards de-differentiation is associated in physics and engineering with loss of energy available for use (as when heat passes into the surroundings of the heated object); and in homely everyday life with upsets such as the breaking of a cup which can be brought about by a simple event such as its being dropped and cannot be as easily or entirely reversed. The irresistible passage from earlier, comparatively lower entropy states (whole cup) to later, higher entropy states (the broken cup) and the barriers to the opposite ordering of these states – for example, returning the higher entropy broken cup to its lower entropy state of wholeness – suggests that there is a natural tendency in the material world according to which earlier states of the universe as a whole are tagged by a higher level of order and later states by a lower level of order, or increased entropy.[58]

Such a net change in the universe over time will seem to be puzzling given that the laws of classical physics are time reversible. For example, the laws of motion do not dictate that the passage from whole cup to broken cup should be privileged over the passage from broken cup to whole cup. A film showing the broken cup reassembling itself would not show the laws of physics being broken. So there should be no overall trend towards increased entropy over time: there should be to-ing and fro-ing here and there without a net change. However, the apparent clash between the reversibility of Newtonian mechanics and the irreversibility of thermodynamics can be resolved. It is, as Ludwig Boltzmann pointed out, a consequence of the fact that there are many more possible disordered states than there are ordered ones. The passage from non-equilibrium to equilibrium states (as when local heat is dissipated into the world at large) is in accordance with statistical probability. This dictates that random change – as is seen at the molecular level – will overwhelmingly result in a macroscopic passage from lower to higher entropy rather than the other way round.

The notions of "order" and "disorder" here are very generously interpreted. For example, a local area of warmth will correspond to a collection of molecules whose average speed is greater than that of the speed of the molecules in the surrounding universe. Likewise, a gas will expand to occupy the space made available to it: the situation where the gas fills only half that space is thermodynamically unstable; and the only way that this can be reversed is by putting in energy from the outside. As Craig Callender has put it:

> Boltzmann's insight was to see that those macrostates we call "equilibrium" macrostates are such that they are realized by many more microstates than those we call "non-equilibrium" macrostates. And in general, higher entropy macrostates can be realized by more microstates (classical or quantum) than those with lower entropy.[59]

In the case of the universe as a whole there is no outside. Successive states of the universe will thus be increasingly disordered, eventhough there may be local decreases in disorder as when an organism (a blob of relatively low entropy) grows; or where agents make an artefact or in some other way manipulate the world to conform to their idea of order. The overall tendency will, it is argued, deliver time's arrow: a state S_2 of the universe as a whole is *after* state S_1 if S_2 is more disordered, closer to thermodynamic equilibrium, than S_1.

There are two reasons why the universal tendency of entropy to increase does not generate the requisite arrow. Firstly, the relationship of succession, of before and after, requires that the two states – or any states – should be brought into relation, so that one counts as "before" and the other as "after". Something (more precisely *someone*, as we shall discuss) has to relate them. There is nothing intrinsic in S_1 that makes it "earlier than S_2," particularly as S_2 by definition won't have arrived so long as S_1 is around – or for that moment make it "earlier than $S_{4'000'000'000}$. "Earlier than" and "later than" are inescapably relational; the successive states of the material universe, however, are what they are in themselves: they do not relate to anything other than themselves.

Indeed, the relations that would be required to derive temporal ordering from entropy states of the universe as a whole are even more complex. If "later" means "in a more disordered universe" and "earlier" means "in a less disordered universe", then the claim that event A was earlier than event B would have to be derived from a relationship to the universe as a whole and, what is more, to the determination that events A and B are located at the same time as, respectively, less disordered and more disordered states of the universe. In short, we would have to get "at the same time as" free – without reference to the relative order or disorder of the universe.

For these reasons, we can therefore set aside the claim made by Ilya Prigogine that scientists have "rediscovered" time, and hence the arrow of time, in virtue of having discovered of new modes of irreversibility at both the macroscopic and microscopic level.[60] We must resist the assumption that, if all the processes in the universe and all state transitions were reversible, then time would have no direction and there would be no basis for "earlier" and "later", whereas if these processes were reversible, there would be such a basis. The conflation of the irreversibility of physical processes and the irreversibility (or directionality) of time begs the question of how "before" and "after" originate. Consider this state transition E_1 taking place at t_1:

1 E_1: State$_1 \rightarrow$ State$_2$

This may be reversed in event E_2 taking place at t_2:

2 E_2: State$_2 \rightarrow$ State$_1$

Even if the states in question were states of the entire universe, time would not have been put into reverse. Although there is no clock outside – or, according to (one interpretation of) relativity theory, inside – the entire universe, the before–after relationship between t_1 and t_2 would have been maintained and, likewise, the before–after relationship between E_1 and E_2. What is more, revisiting State$_1$ is not the same as *being in* State$_1$ the first time. They are successive realizations, instances, or tokens of the same time states of the universe and they have the temporal order of succession. E_2 at t_2 does not make E_1 unhappen: E_2 is not the unhappening or taking away of E_1. And even if it were, there would be a prior temporal order between E_1 (happening) and E_2 (unhappening). In short, irreversibility is neither necessary, nor sufficient, for any putative direction of time; nor would universal reversibility deprive time of any putative direction dependent on the characteristics of the states of the universe.

To develop this with an additional point: there is a fatal conflation here between event-types and types of states of the universe on the one hand and on the other actual (that is to say individual, singular) events and states. The fact that the laws of the universe (in particular the laws of motion) are time reversible does not mean that the distinction between "earlier" and "later", which relates to the expression of those laws in particular circumstances, is lost.[61]

That there is a fundamental difference between states of the universe and times can be demonstrated by considering a frozen universe. The universe in State$_1$ at t_1 is still in State$_1$ at t_2. If states defined times (as in the notion that increasing entropy states give us successive times), then State$_1$ = State$_2$ would imply that $t_1 = t_2$. In other words, there would be no passage of time between the two states; or the two states, being phases of an unchanging state, would be at the same time. In short, if stasis were universalized, time would come to a halt. This seems counter-intuitive, though we shall examine it again in §10.4.2 when we discuss temporal vacua.

Henri Poincaré highlighted the problems with the thermodynamic arrow when he demonstrated that, given a long enough time, even very improbable outcomes might materialize. It was therefore possible that the trend of entropy could reverse, with the universe becoming *less* disordered in successive moments. A finite collection of particles confined to a container and moving in accordance with Newton's laws of motion that Boltzmann had relied upon would eventually return to its initial state, so called Poincaré cycling – the once and future state of the universe. This would then mean that in one part of the cycle the same two states S_1 and S_2 would have the opposite time relationship, with S_2 (more disordered), occurring before S_1 (less disordered). Even though Poincaré cycling, which envisages phases in the history of the universe when entropy is falling as well as phases in which it is increasing, may take longer than the age of the universe so far – and Boltzmann showed that this was the case even for a small system comprising only a few hundred gas particles – it seems to open up at least the *logical* possibility that the (thermodynamic) arrow of time can do a 180° turn and "point" or even "flow" backwards. One particularly baffling consequence of this would be that a particular event could be both before and after another event.[62] Let time t_1 be defined by a specific state of the universe associated with a particular level of entropy S_1 and (later) time t_2 be defined by another state of the universe S_2 with a higher level of entropy. If the events *are* causally connected, or E_1 at S_1 is an indispensable part of the conditions that permit E_2 at S_2, there is an obvious problem. Events will have to occur before the conditions which permit them or the causes that bring them about. (We shall look at this again in §§ 2.3.5. and 11.3 when we look at the apparent connection between the causal arrow and the thermodynamic arrow of increasing untidiness.[63])

The paradoxes created by the logical possibility of Poincaré cycling are the consequence of the confusion at the heart of the notion that times can be defined by the comparative levels of disorder in the universe. Times have priority over states of the universe and the transition from an earlier to a later time is only contingently characterized by the passage from a less to a more disordered state of the universe – a hugely more probable transition than from a more to a less disordered state. The fact that the latter is improbable but not impossible shows that the direction earlier–later cannot be rooted in the nature of the transitions.

There is another, widely discussed problem. If entropy tends to increase with time, the universe must have begun in a relatively ordered state. What is the explanation of the low entropy of past states of the universe? Boltzmann himself acknowledged the possibility that: "when we follow the state of the universe into the infinitely distant past, we are actually just as correct in taking it to be very probable that we would reach a state in which all temperature differences had disappeared, as we would be in following the state of the world into the distant future".[64]

Given that the universe had to start in some state, it might be argued, there is no reason why it should not start in a low entropy state. When there is no initial population of possibilities to draw upon, nothing on the denominator as it were, each initial state is equally possible, though the proportion of those with higher entropy will be greater than the proportion of those with lower entropy. What is at issue are the probabilities governing the *transition* from one state to another. The passage from State$_1$ at t_1 to State$_2$ at t_2 has to be along the steepest gradient from the less probable to the more probable, the latter being defined as "having more possible realizations". State$_2$ doesn't have in itself to be probable: it simply has to belong to a class of states that are more probable than the class of states to which State$_1$ belongs. No individual, actual state of the universe, or of a locality within it, has other than a negligible probability of coming into being, given the zillion-trillion range of possible configurations. What are at issue are second-order probability considerations: namely, that it is more probable that there should be a transition from a less probable state to a more probable one than vice versa. A state is more probable if it exemplifies a larger population of (relatively disordered) possibilities than if it is an example of a smaller population of (relatively ordered) possibilities.

This may address the mystery of the initial low entropy of the universe. In the case of the first moment of the universe, there is no preceding state and all states are equally possible, so the universe could just as well have started in a low entropy state (as it did) as opposed to a high entropy one (which it didn't). It is what follows afterwards which is governed by the transitional probabilities; and these arise only after there are initial and subsequent states and physical laws regulating the transitions from one to the other.[65]

Our critique of the thermodynamic arrow rests on the fact that we have to determine, *independently of any of their characteristics*, which of two events, or even which of two states of the universe, is "earlier" and which "later". The very idea that we *progress from* "less probable" (low entropy) states *to* "more probable" states seems to *presuppose* a temporal order not to *create* it. Time, and the direction of time, is built into the very idea of change, of an entity moving from one (prior) state to another (posterior) state, irrespective of what form the change takes. Without an independent sense of time order and the ordering of times, we could not have arrived at the second law of thermodynamics.

An adjacent point is argued with great clarity by Huw Price: "[W]e are inclined simply to help ourselves to the principle that the past explains the future, but what could possibly justify that inclination here, where the temporal asymmetry of the universe is what we are seeking to explain."[66]

And he develops this as follows: *Unless one temporal direction is already privileged, the statistical reasoning involved is as good in one direction as in another.*[67] A particular trend in the state of the universe with time (e.g. towards increasing untidiness) does not give time an externally definable directionality; on the contrary, directionality in time is required to make this trend the basis of temporal asymmetry. A trend can be seen as the basis of "forward in time" as opposed to "backward in time" only if we establish in advance the order of events or states, so that we can see that State$_2$ *follows* State$_1$. To put this another way, "No theory of the evolution of a physical system over time can produce different results for the two temporal directions, unless it treats them differently in the first place."[68] It is, in short, our asymmetry of gaze – which is neither omnitemporal nor atemporal – rather than the entropy gradient that delivers the asymmetry in time.

It should by now be evident, that the relationship earlier-to-later, cannot be defined even less created, post hoc by trends in the physical world, if only because those trends, being time trends, presuppose that "earlier" and "later" have already been established. Even so, philosophers and physicists have looked to even broader one-way or irreversible trends in the universe to account for the apparent unidirectionality of time. There is the Cosmological Arrow, to be found in the totality of the universe's irreversible processes, that gets its direction from the expansion of the universe and may turn round if, as some believe, there are alternating phases of expansion from the Big Bang and contraction towards the Big Crunch. Particle physics offers kaon decay which may be time irreversible. Quantum mechanics offers wave function collapse which is also time irreversible though this, according to some modern interpretations, may be a consequence of the putative thermodynamic arrow though the role of the observer, and the measurement problem (which we shall discuss in §3.5.3.1) make this a contested source of the arrow of time.[69]

Intuitively easiest to grasp is the arrow of radiation. It is illustrated by dropping a stone into a pool, which results in concentric waves spreading across the surface of the water. This is clearly a process that could not go into reverse; for in order for this to happen, it would be necessary, as Karl Popper pointed out, to assemble "a vast number of distant coherent generators of waves, the coordination of which, to be explicable, would have to be … originating from one centre".[70]

I won't discuss these different arrows separately. Whether or not they are, as has been argued, in some direct or indirect way a manifestation of the second law of thermodynamics, they do seem to share a family resemblance and a formal similarity, so that they will fall by the arguments we have just presented. In all cases the focus is on an irreversible, or at least difficult to reverse, transition from past to future, from a relatively tidy to a relatively untidy state, or from a single event to a multitude of consequences (something we shall touch on in §2.3.5 and discuss in more detail in §11.3). The important point for the present is that they fail to generate the requisite temporal asymmetry, the difference between the tip and the tail of the arrow, for the same reason as does the appeal to increasing entropy; namely, that we have already to identify that certain states are temporally prior to other states in order to register that there are trends which are irreversible. Without this prior determination, we have no grounds for arriving at the conclusion that the more disordered states typically succeed less disordered states; or (as we shall discuss presently) that causes typically precede effects. They may enable us to identify particular pairs of states as "earlier" and "later" in the absence of other clues – as when we are presented with series of pictures, such as of a stone dropping into a pond or an egg being broken – but they do not constitute earlier and later in themselves. There are, after all, many *reversible* local processes as when a pendulum, having swung to the left, swings back to the right, in which there is a clear temporal order, though we could not diagnose which of two positions occupied by a pendulum was before and which was after. Temporal order and diagnosis of temporal order (in the absence of direct perception of the events in question) are two different things. There is no intrinsic "beforeness" in a tidier state or "afterness" in a less tidy state of the universe or a system within it.

We should be suspicious of the appeal to irreversibility as the basis of the direction of time for two further reasons. First, irreversibility is more evident in some processes than others – for example the breaking of an egg as opposed to the swing of a pendulum – whereas, if it were a marker of the universal direction of universal time, it should be equally apparent everywhere. Secondly (and this is the more important point), there is a logical (as opposed to thermodynamic) irreversibility in the case of token events. Even if I could unscramble an egg, I could not take away the fact that the prior scrambling had taken place. Token events cannot be made to unhappen; so the counter-thermodynamic unscrambling of the egg would not reverse time. The temporal sequence would remain: egg intact (at t_1) → egg scrambled (at t_2) → egg intact (at t_3). In short, the history could not be taken away even if thermodynamic reversal were scaled up to the sum total of the universe.

2.3.3 The psychological arrow

The sense of earlier and later begins locally and extends outwards. It relates most directly to particular events experienced by a particular observer. While every event in the universe is in theory temporally related to every other event, without an observer to experience the events, and to connect them, they are neither "earlier" nor "later", "before" or "after". For example, an unobserved event on a distant planet does not have this ordering in relation to the events that I am aware of as going on around me now or indeed other unobserved events on that planet. This is why some have argued that, if there is an arrow of time, it must be built out not of the intrinsic properties of material events but out of the linkage of events through the experienced succession of our experiences of them. Without this linkage, two happenings would not as it were reach beyond their own boundaries to relate to each other. Thus the case for time's arrow being a "psychological arrow".

The question that then arises is whether the directionality of time transcends the psychological (such that the latter merely reflects something that pre-exists conscious beings) and exists in itself as an intrinsic property of the physical universe. The testimony from physics is somewhat confused. The overall trend of the natural sciences has been to liberate the observer from individual, subjective perspectives. By instrument-enhanced, quantitative, and more broadly mathematized, observation we endeavour to transcend the fallibility of the bodily-dependent and biographically-tinged limitations of our eyes and ears in order to see things as they are in themselves; we endeavour to ascend to Nagel's famous "the view from nowhere" and indeed (as Huw Price puts it) to an atemporal "view from nowhen".[71] The result is a body of knowledge – such as the history of the origin and evolution of the solar system – that belongs to no-one in particular, but only to the community of human minds. It is equally faithful to (and equally remote from) everyone's actual experience; as a result it defines key aspects of possible experience in the broadest possible terms. Do the notions of the direction of time and of "earlier" and "later" survive unchanged at this great distance from our actual conscious experience? Or does there come a point, as we shed more and more of the living breathing, parochial observer, and aspire to the condition of a universal observer forged in the community of minds as expressed in mathematical physics, when we lose the basis of the arrow?

If we believe that the arrow depends on events being located at a definite, absolute point in an absolute time frame, the answer to this question must be "No". In the local frame of reference in which we pass our lives, the temporal relationships between events is fixed: there is no question that E_1 took place before E_2 and the relationship of succession between them, which gives the experience of succession, is secure. However, viewed from the Nowhere (or more strictly the mathematical Everywhere that privileges nowhere in particular) of relativity theory, the relationship between the two events – unless they are causally connected – is intrinsically neither one of succession nor of simultaneity. There is no temporal order independent of all observers or inertial frames of reference.[72] This is a consequence of the principle owing to Mach, which Einstein embraced, though not consistently (least of all when he was affronted by the unintelligibility of quantum theory[73]), that there is no reality beyond that which can be observed, no reality-in-itself beyond actual or possible experiences. Reality is defined as the sum total of actual and possible experiences, not something separate from experience. This seems simultaneously to locate any arrow of time inside human consciousness and at the same to discredit the arrow – at least in the view of the fundamentalist physicist who believes that what (objective, quantitative) physics reveals is (and will be) the metaphysical truth, and the whole truth, about the world.

The only way to preserve the arrow in physics would be to find it not in the irreversible succession of experienced events (because that succession can be reversed from another frame of reference) but in the actual nature of the laws governing those events and linking one state of the universe with another – hence we find ourself heading back to time-irreversible processes and laws such as the second law of thermodynamics. The temporal asymmetry which distinguishes "early–late" from "late–early", and permits the former but not the latter, is then generated not from within perception (of succession or simultaneity) but from measurements of something that appears to be independent of time. While these measurements are ultimately derived from perceptions, they are not based on observations dependent on individual observers. However, it is this latter scientific virtue that disqualifies them as markers of temporal directions, as we have seen from our examination of asymmetric processes in the previous section.

Locating the arrow of time in the human psyche, therefore, raises as many questions as it answers. If we reduce the directionality of time to the *experience* of the succession of events, within our minds, our bodies, or the observed material world, we run into trouble accounting for those aspects of succession that are more objective, or less observer-dependent, than others. The psychological theory of the arrow sits ill with the fact that something outside of consciousness, or a conscious individual, is the final determinant of the succession of events. What is more, implicit in the notion that time's arrow is based on our perception of the succession of events, is the assumption that there is a succession of events to be perceived – that temporal order and direction is intrinsic to the events we perceive that gives rise to the experience of succession. There is a confounder arising out of the fact that the order in which we perceive things also to some extent depends on us (just as what I perceive depends to some extent on where I choose to look from and the direction of my gaze). But this is not sufficient to determine the order of events, though it does determine the order of my perceptions.

Consider a simple example. Suppose I am looking round at a group of smiling people, I will see the smile on the face of Mr A before I see the smile on the face of Mrs B if I pan round in one direction and the reverse if I pan round in another direction. This does not, however, determine the temporal order of the smiles. If Mr A started smiling before Mrs B, this is not altered by the fact that I perceive Mrs B's smile first. The psychologizing of time's arrow, in other words, does not accommodate the objective reality of temporal order or those features of it that cannot be relativized, as, for example that which is in a fixed inertial framework, as is the case with the everyday observer, or where the salient events are causally related; where for example Mr A's smile triggered Mrs B's. We acknowledge that the sequence of events and the sequence of our experience of events are distinct – something that is more obvious when we consider the order in which we become aware of something as a matter of general knowledge. The Big Bang (if it occurred) was the first event but it has only recently become an object of knowledge.[74]

The psychological reduction of the directionality of time – and of what makes "before" before and "after" after – is open, therefore, to a variety of objections. The most obvious relates to what the French philosopher Quentin Meillassoux has called "ancestrals" – any reality such as an event anterior to the emergence of human or any other kind of consciousness – and the present evidence of them.[75] It is obvious that the solar system came into being before there were living creatures, living creatures before sentient beings, and sentient beings before human beings. The overwhelming majority of the history of the universe with its temporally ordered events took place before any kind of psyche emerged to register them. And if our perception of the succession of events reflects their temporal order in our locality, then the psychological arrow seems to depend on a physical arrow. At any rate, the private perception of the succession of events is transcended by dates that at the very least belong to the shared history of humanity and in fact seem to transcend it. (We shall return to Meillassoux's arguments – which are directed against the idealist "correlationism" or Kantianism according to which objective reality is inseparable from subjective experience – in §10.5.)

We have reached an *impasse*. The endeavour to find the directionality of time in the asymmetry of physical processes – such as is reflected in the second law of thermodynamics – may be doomed anyway because it overlooks the necessity for a conscious observer to translate the states of the universe or of local systems within them into a *succession* that has been picked out and connected.[76] However, the radical conclusion that the directionality of time is entirely internal to our psyche – and to our sense of the past and the future – makes it difficult to see the connection between the succession of our experiences and the ordering of events that appears to be independent of anyone's experiences.

2.3.4 The arrow of information

The complementary deficiencies of physical and psychological bases for the direction of time may in part explain why the notion of time's arrow being an "arrow of information" has had such a good run for its money. "Information" in common (sloppy) usage is something that can be seen as having a recto of psychological contents and a verso of physical events.

Notwithstanding the selling point of this arrow – its combining physical processes and psychological events – the focus is often on the latter, with tensed time playing a key role. We look back at the past in knowledge of what has taken place and we look forward to the future in ignorance of what may come to pass – and it is this that provides respectively the head and tail of the arrow. To put this another way, the forward movement of time is an *accumulation of information*, reflected in a difference between what we have known and what we will know; or between a remembered past of irreversible, determinate events, and an unknown, indeterminate future.

This is expressed most clearly by the physicist Paul Davies: "The fact that we remember the past, rather than the future," he says, "is an observation not of the passage of time but of the asymmetry of time."[77] Given that (as he and many others believe) memory is a matter of "information", the difference between the determinate past and the indeterminate future is also a matter of information. We obviously have more information about the past than we do about the future. Indeed, in one sense we have *no* information about the future, except at a probabilistic level. So, as the indeterminate future becomes a determinate past, information accumulates.

Now it is of course obvious that the difference between past and future, or between "before time t" and "after time t" cannot be merely the difference between what I know and what I don't know; cannot be reduced to the difference between my knowledge and my ignorance. No "Arrovian" would wish to advance a hypothesis so vulnerable. It might have all sorts of undesirable consequences, such as for example that an event would pass from the future to the past only when I (or someone) got to know of it; and, even, that it would be returned to the future when I (and everyone else) had forgotten it. It is not about information understood as personally held knowledge, what I happened to know, but about what, for reasons that lie outside of me, I or anyone else could possibly know. What is in the past, irrespective of whether anyone knows it or not, is knowable because it has happened; whereas the future is not knowable because it has not happened.

This reminder of the ontological as opposed to merely epistemic difference, between the relatively information-poor future and the relatively information-rich past explains why information is insufficient to deliver Time's Arrow. The Arrow of Information seems to merge two processes that should not be conflated: namely states of the world getting to be known (increasing information in the narrow sense) and states of the world passing into existence – from possibility to actuality. The confusion is the result of the way (in this context as in many others) the idea of "information" is widened to include the passage from indeterminacy to determinacy in the case of *material* events in the absence as well as the presence of consciousness. Some explanation of the source of this confusion is justified.

The massive expansion of the catchment area of the word "information" is one of the most striking trends in recent philosophical and scientific discourse. I won't go into this in any detail here as I have discussed it elsewhere.[78] Suffice it to note that a term that originally designated intelligence, news, gossip, facts exchanged between people – between an informant and one who is informed – is now being used to designate any kind of transaction in the material world. The flimsy rationale for this is set out by David Chalmers, who speaks for many: "[W]herever there is causal interaction, there is information, and wherever there is information there is experience. One can find information states in a rock – when it expands and contracts, for example – or even in the different aspects of an electron."[79]

This greatly expanded notion of information has been particularly attractive to some philosophically inclined physicists. John Wheeler famously argued that IT came from BIT – that the universe is a massive information processing machine.[80] There is, of course, more to be known about a universe that has a history of 2 billion years compared with one that has a history of 4 billion years – namely 2 billion years' worth of happening. It does not, however, follow from this that more *is* known. The "more" of the first 4 billion years compared with the first 2 billion years (long before conscious life emerged) is not more information.

The vision of the History of Everything as a progressive accumulation of information makes it easy to merge the fact that the past is known, while the future isn't, with the fact that the past is determinate while the future is not; to conflate knowledge and knowability. This confusion is sometimes compounded by another that brings the thermodynamic arrow back into the frame: the identification of information with, on the one hand, entropy (something intrinsically remote from consciousness) and, on the other, memory (which, in my case at least, is inseparable from consciousness). Paul Davies again: "As physicists have realised over the past few decades, the concept of entropy is closely related to the information content of a system. For this reason, the formation of memory is a unidirectional process – new memories add information and raise the entropy of the brain. We might perceive this unidirectionality as the flow of time".[81]

Exposure to events creates memories; memory is the accumulation of information; information is increased entropy; the increased entropy of our brains not only gives us a sense of the passage of time but also underpins the reality of the directionality of time. Let us deal with each of these assumptions in turn.

The first two are easily dealt with. To reduce memory to information in the sense of factual knowledge is to traduce it. It is wider than that: it includes much that is not accessible as information (such as changes in unconscious presuppositions and the acquisition of skills); and much that, though accessible to recall, is not information in anything other than a strained sense – such as the sad recollection of a day that has passed. This would not be a problem for Davies and others. Their notion of information is, as we have seen, much wider than this. Which brings us to the second part of his argument – or association of terms: information is identified with entropy. It is worth tracing the steps that leads to this conclusion.

When you are sending me a signal, the quantity of information (according to the engineering definition) that you transmit depends on how much uncertainty you resolve. If there are only two possibilities, and the signal tells me which one, then the delivery of the signal gives me one binary digit of information. If I were sending randomly determined letters, then each letter would resolve a greater uncertainty: the probability of any given letter being sent is 1 in 26 and the arrival of a signal bearing a letter delivers 4.7 bits of information. There seems to be a correlation between the amount of uncertainty resolved and the quantity of information transmitted. A more chaotic system simply contains more information – or potential information: it is richer in uncertainty. There would be more facts to know about it. It would be less susceptible to summary or algorithmic compression.

The slither between potential and actual information – or between a system and what there is to be known about it – is a symptom of another invalid conflation: of "information" in the engineer's sense with "information" in the conventional sense. In fact, the engineer's quantification of information in terms of uncertainty reduction presupposes the prior existence of the uncertainty that has to be generated or entertained in order for an event to count as something that resolves it. Uncertainty will be very context- and, indeed, interest-dependent. If I am expecting a message consisting of 1 out of the 26 letters of the alphabet then the single-letter message that turns up will deliver 4.7 bits of information. If the options, however, are framed as "letter" versus "number", then the receipt of any letter will count as one bit of information. If I am wondering whether the transmission system is working, then the arrival of *anything at all* would count as an additional bit of information. Other information may be carried by the transmission of the letter; for example, whether you – the sender – are cooperating with me, are competent, are still there at the other end. In sum there is no measurable information, even in the engineer's sense, without an uncertainty being proposed or felt that an event will resolve and, thus resolving the uncertainty, will count as a signal. These ambiguities arise even if we set aside the significance of the semantic content of any message I receive. Suppose I am desperate to know whether you are alive or dead. The letter "A" for alive or "D" for dead will each carry one bit of information in the engineering sense. The significance of each letter, however, is boundless. Each carries a huge piece of information that is not captured in the tine of a fork.

The extension of information to encompass events in (unobserved) rocks and electrons *á la* Chalmers is the ultimate consequence of separating the notion of information not only from meaning/significance but also from any conscious being who is informed, who entertains the uncertainty that needs resolving. The profound difference between a signal that resolves uncertainty from that which the signal is *about* has been collapsed. By this means, every event can be made over into an information-bearing signal, so that the unfolding of the universe becomes a unidirectional accumulation of information.

Thus the background to the connection between the Information and the Thermodynamic arrows; between information and entropy; and the assumption that a disordered system, which has more unpredictability and requires more messages to describe, is richer in information than an ordered one. The informational richness of a signal sent by one conscious being to another into the system or region of matter (with or without any system) it describes is projected (by something akin to magic thinking) into the universe itself.

That this notion gets past many quite serious thinkers reflects the extent to which we are (far too) accustomed to talking about information being embedded in the (material) states of affairs that information is supposed to be about. Such talk collapses the gap of "aboutness" and finds information in the physical world. Overlooking "aboutness" lies at the heart of many of the wrong paths taken by the metaphysics in the physics of time. We shall look to this – to intentionality – to develop a true image of the nature of (human) time in Part III of this book.

For the present, it is sufficient to note that the removal of consciousness from information is a key step in connecting the thermodynamic trend towards higher entropy with the difference between a remembered past and a future of which we are ignorant. The present state of any evolving object would be a bidirectional glimpse into a past (which would be related to its own past) and into a future. The lowliest item in the physical universe would have the very tensed time that "believing physicists" (according to Einstein himself) hold exists only as an illusion in the human brain (including the brain of physicists) – an item that, as a material object, should not have the physical capacity to house the tensed concepts their owners believe in.

Seeking the directionality of time in "the flow" or "accumulation" of information, therefore, results in conflating the difference between (tenseless) "earlier" and "later" with the (tensed) difference between a past we can remember and a future we may anticipate; between a past of which we can have certain knowledge and a future about which we can only speculate. The putative intrinsic directionality of time is conflated with the asymmetry of the temporal gaze of a conscious individual located in time. The information arrow (to reiterate an earlier point) confuses an epistemic difference – connected with what we know or can know – with something more substantial; between a determinate past and an indeterminate future. The difference in short is not merely epistemic but also ontological or constitutive.[82] Not knowing the future is different from ignorance of the past because there is nothing to be known – though it can be guessed at with more or less shrewdness – as the future hasn't yet gone one way or another. Regarding the future, we are all (relatively) in the same boat. Even when I have a privileged position (as when I can see two cars on a collision course, though the drivers cannot see one another or when I have insider information relevant to the stock market) I still cannot be sure that there will be a collision or the shares I am considering buying will rise. The determination of the future as it enters the present is not merely a matter of becoming potential information: it is about something out there that has changed.

In summary, confusion of the directionality of tensed and tenseless time, and of epistemic limits and ontological realities, in the Information Arrow is not at all surprising, given the proliferation of meanings in the contemporary usage of the word "information". As such, the Arrow of Information is decidedly uninformative about the directionality or asymmetry of time.

2.3.5 The causal arrow and "the asymmetry of influence"

> Attempts to meddle with the past are futile
> Kutach, "The Asymmetry of Influence", 247[83]

It is necessary therefore to look elsewhere for universal characteristics of the universe and of the events that arise out of them that will determine their temporal order. For some writers this is to be found in an "asymmetry of influence" evident in the direction of causality: that which we consider past can causally influence the future but future events cannot have a causal influence on past ones; more generally, a tenselessly earlier event can influence a tenselessly later one but not vice versa. The influence of E occurring at time t will always be observed after time t and never before time t. Mellor takes this further and asserts that "Time is the causal dimension of space–time",[84] adding that the correlation between causal and temporal order "is not because time order fixes causal order. It must be the other way round."[85]

The causal arrow has several apparent attractions. Firstly, relativity theory does not relativize the temporal relationship between cause and effect. If I observe that A causes B, then it is not possible for there to be a frame of reference in which B causes A. This is because, in order to interact, A and B have to occupy contiguous locations in space–time and space–time intervals (unlike purely temporal or purely spatial relations) are invariant, irrespective of the frame of reference from which they are viewed. Their relationship is real in the sense of being observer-independent. Given that causal chains extend indefinitely, this applies to the entire nexus of causation. That is why Hastings may have a distant effect in bringing about Agincourt, or at least raising its probability of its occurring, but Agincourt could not return the compliment. Secondly, our common sense experience of what is happening can seem to be reduced to a network of causes and effects in which the former precedes the latter. We cannot imagine an effect bringing about its cause and this is not just for purely definitional reasons. It makes *physical* sense that the lightning flash should cause the thunderclap and not the other way round. Thirdly, an event could not influence its cause because then it would stop itself happening, rather like a time traveller making his own existence impossible by killing his ancestor. This is one of the reasons why we take it for granted that events depend on prior events in earlier times and not posterior events in later times. It is also a truism: E_2 cannot depend on E_1 unless E_1 has already occurred. Fourthly, without the cause already being in place as a target, the effect could not alter it. Finally, it seems to bring temporal succession into the very structure of material necessity that is built into the world – an advance on the psychological arrow.[86]

The reasons why causation does *not* deliver time's arrow go very deep and are of the greatest interest. Firstly, identifying something as a discrete cause and something else (or some things else) as its discrete effect(s) depends on *observing* that causal relationship. The events in question are not self-defining, self-circumscribing. The physical world is not in itself a linear chain of causes and effects: it is a broad unfolding of densely interwoven processes from which particular chains of causes and effects are picked out, according to our interests. You could not, for example, even in principle, state how many causal pairings there are in a room, any more than you could say how many facts there are in the room. Causes are those things that we see as salient, most obviously because – as many philosophers have pointed out – they may be handles by which we manipulate the world in accordance with our wishes or may allocate responsibility, as when we say that the cause of a crash was a driver's carelessness, although we could have identified many other causal ancestors and relevant conditions. In other words, what counts as a cause of an event, and what event shall count as the effect of another event, is relative to observers and their interests. You might concede this – and we shall discuss this more carefully in §11.2 – and still maintain that there is a non-negotiable temporal relationship between picked-out events and picked-out causes. However, the act of "picking out" cannot be ignored and it is this that takes us to the heart of the matter: the relationship between causation, consciousness, intentionality and explicit time.[87]

Secondly, the observation that effects succeed their causes may not provide an independent marker of the intrinsic directionality of time since we judge of two events E_1 and E_2 that E_1 is the cause *because* it occurs first and that E_2 is the effect because it occurs later. In other words, we assign roles on the basis of the perceived temporal order and not the other way round. That temporal order is the more fundamental and universal relationship between events becomes evident when we observe events (the overwhelming majority) that are not causally connected or do not appear to be. I see you walking along the road and shortly afterwards observe a plane pass overhead. They are obviously causally unconnected events but I have no difficulty saying of the former that it is "earlier" and of the latter that it is "later".

This puts into question Mellor's assertion, just quoted, that the correlation between causal and temporal order "is not because time order fixes causal order. It must be the other way round." Mellor tries to deal with this by arguing that those events which are causally connected establish the framework for ordering those that are not: it is as if a subset of salient causal relations creates the clock for those that are temporally related but not causally connected.

This seems rather an ad hoc rescue of a vulnerable position. Nevertheless, the reasons why causation does not deliver the direction of time are deeply interesting and discussion of them will be postponed until Part III when we have quite a few more ideas in place. Suffice it to say for the present that they touch on the relationship between time and consciousness, and the vexed and puzzling relationship between "physical" and "human" time.

2.3.6 Quivering the arrow

> The Moving Finger writes; and having writ,
> Moves on; nor all thy Piety nor Wit
> Shall lure it back to cancel half a Line,
> Nor all thy Tears wash out a Word of it.
>   *The Rubaiyat of Omar Khayyám*, LI (tr. Edward FitzGerald)

In view of the foregoing, it is not surprising that there are philosophers who reject the very idea of grounding the direction of time in some general character of the unfolding universe, or the hope of finding a universal "diagnostic sign" which would enable us to determine which of two events or states was "earlier" and which "later".[88] Even Tim Maudlin, who believes that time flows and has a direction, argues that its passage is not supervenient on some character of the universe. It is a primitive, non-reducible physical fact.[89] And Huw Price has argued as follows: "The contents of time – that is, the arrangement of physical stuff – might be temporally asymmetric, without time itself having any asymmetry. Accordingly, we need to be cautious in making inferences from observed temporal asymmetries to the anisotropy of time itself".[90] Content asymmetry does not generate time asymmetry because the former presupposes the latter – the irreversible relationship between earlier and later events.

One thing that will come through in the preceding discussion is a certain amount of confusion in the literature. It is not, first of all, entirely clear what work the arrow metaphor is supposed to do. At its very least, it is an attempt to capture the notion that time has a direction. While this seems to be less vulnerable than the more florid notion of time as "flowing", it is still problematic. Given that time is supposed to be unidirectional, it would have to *be* any direction it had. Indeed, it seems to stretch the notion of direction to extend it to something is intrinsic to a dimension. The directions we find in space are directions permitted by, not identical with, the spatial dimension. You need to have more than one dimension to create a direction, not only because dimensions are merely permissive – defining a space of possible transitions – but because only this makes it possible to have a *range* of directions.

The directionality of time is most fundamentally expressed in the fact that there are times called "earlier" and "later" such that, while it is not possible to go from the latter to the former, it is mandatory to go from the former to the latter. It seems pointless to spill any ink over a truism. You can, by definition, only reach a later time after an earlier time. If you came to an earlier time later than the earlier time, *it* would be called the later time. Or, if it were possible to revisit the earlier time, the visit would be at a later time. If someone travelled to t_1 *after* t_2, then the latter would be deemed to be earlier than t_1. Revisiting t_1 would be possible only if it "occurred" twice – presumably at different times.[91] This is doubly objectionable: it treats times as occurrents; and as token occurrents that can occur more than once.

The Arrovians, however, are after more than trying to uphold a truism. They want to understand the (physical, external) basis of the asymmetry between the past and the future; of the sense we have of passing from future into the past and of the former being open to manipulation and the latter not. This basis would, they feel, also underpin the directionality of physical, non-human and tenseless time-in-itself linking it with the direction of the increase of entropy and of causation.

My essential argument is that the idea of the arrow is, first and last, a muddled response to the erroneous notion that time is a dimension. We are used to representing dimensions by means of lines and lines have a direction and therefore time, being a dimension, must also have a direction. However, it does not follow from the fact that dimensions are *represented* by lines that they are intrinsically directional. Even if the individual lines representing the dimensions had a direction, they would extend infinitely in two opposite directions – away from and towards the origin. When we depict the three dimensions of space, we draw lines at right angles to one another representing respectively the x, y, and z axes. But none of these dimensions has an intrinsic direction: they simply have a directional relationship *in contrast with* one another. The x axis has to be at right angles to the y and the z axes.[92] The y axis likewise: it has to be at right angles to the x and z axes. It is the mutual separation by 90 degrees that defines the axes and these in turn will define the direction of something (else) that *does* have a direction – for example a movement of an object in the space defined by the axes. The axes themselves no more have a direction than "length" has a length, "height" a height and so on. In short, as noted at the outset, if we take seriously the idea of time as a dimension on all fours with the three of space, we should not countenance the idea of it as being directional in the sense either of (a) moving and moving in a certain direction or (b) being statically directed. So the temporal arrow is as incompatible with the very idea of time as a dimension that prompted it as is the idea of time flowing.[93] Nevertheless, this does not stop the habit some thinkers have of outsourcing the directionality of time to other properties of the physical world though we find, in the end, that nothing else can fix the temporal sequence of events other than their *de facto* order of occurrence.

The quest for the basis of an arrow of time is just as fruitless irrespective of whether or not we first remove the seemingly more vulnerable notion of the "flow" or "passage". At root is a spatializing tendency we need to resist. Another source is the projection of passage or flow from events that occur in time to time itself which can be challenged as follows. Consider the event E of an object O moving from position P_1 to position P_2. What moves or flows is not E but O. The event itself does not pass through space: it *is* a passage through space. And while the occurrence of events is not a kind of passing or flowing of E through space, we may speak of its "passing" from its beginning to its end. "E", however, refers to the whole, completed event – not to its beginning or end or the transit between them – and this totality does not "pass" or "flow", not even in order to pass or flow into or out of being. When an event takes place, it does not pass by us as, say, an object moving from one position to another passes by us. Its dynamism is internal to it, evident when it is ongoing, no longer when it is done and dusted.[94]

If, as we have noted, individual events do not pass in a particular direction as moving objects do (unless we falsely think of passing into and out of existence as a kind of directional passage), how little does the passage of *all* events taking place at any time amount to a kind of direction. Look at what is happening in the scene before you. Objects are moving hither and thither or remaining at rest, events are happening and coming to an end: there is nothing in this to suggest an overall direction of anything.[95]

There may be another source of the attractiveness of the metaphor of the arrow of time – one that was active in the collective imagination long before Eddington introduced it into the philosophical discussion of physical time. Arrows wound, and then kill, and the image reflects our sense of the world being out of our control and potentially dangerous; it captures the way we are skewered on to the same totality of unfolding events that gave rise to us, our helplessness before the inevitability of things, the fact that the laws of nature cannot be bucked. It expresses a profound, existential anxiety that underpins the fundamental narrative of our life: the passage from birth to death. You can wind the clock back and set it to zero, and make a fresh start; but there is something you cannot wind back – time itself – in order to recover the lost days, to take back or amend what has happened and what we have done. The notion of the unidirectionality of time, in short, is inseparable from our awareness of our mortality, of a life that has a diminishing quantity ahead and an increasing quantity behind; of birth as a one-way ticket to the grave. And a sense of our ignorance in the face of the future – contrasted with our knowledge of the past – lies at root of the "arrow of information". We may know how things turned out; never how they will turn out.

To what extent this truly explains the tenacity of the metaphor of time's arrow, I cannot be sure. What does seem to be the case is that Arrovians want to confer direction upon time and then to reduce the direction to something non-temporal. More precisely, they want to treat the fact that earlier comes before later as both a fundamental property of time and yet susceptible of further explanation. But time simply *is* a matter of earlier before later and the necessary precedence of the former over the latter. That this very obvious fact seems to require explanation is also the result of seeing time as space-like and its asymmetry as therefore puzzling. If space were understood in time-like terms we would be puzzled by its being the same in all directions, that it was possible to travel freely in it, and that distinct parts of it coexisted such that there was no order governing visiting different items in space.

According to G. J. Whitrow's persuasive judgement, the attempt to understand time in non-temporal terms will always fail:

> [A]ny theory that seeks to derive the *entire* concept of time from some more primitive considerations – for example, assumptions of a causal, probabilistic or statistical nature – is foredoomed to failure. For any theory which endeavours to account for time *completely* ought to explain why everything does not happen at once. Unless the existence of *successive* (non-simultaneous) states of phenomena is tacitly assumed it is impossible to deduce them…In the final count, time is a fundamental property of the relationship between the universe and the observer which cannot be reduced to anything else.[96]

The arrow of time is a striking manifestation of this failure to see the irreducible *sui generis* nature of time: it is rooted in the belief that if there were time-asymmetric processes and these were universal then time would be directional and its directionality explained.

Let us now examine another very prominent expression of the irresistible spatialization of the way we think about time: time travel.

2.4 THE MYTH OF TIME TRAVEL: THE IDEA OF PURE MOVEMENT IN TIME

If any part of this book counts as a grudge match, the present section qualifies most clearly. Although I shall be examining the notion of time travel as a consequence of treating time as a dimension on all fours with those of space, indeed as a reduction to absurdity of the quasi-spatial conception of time, my hostility to time machines and the like goes back to my schooldays and to the irritation I felt with the knowing smile of those of my schoolmates who had read or read about Einstein and were confident that the paradoxes of relativity gave them insights into the true nature of the universe denied to their less mathematically gifted fellows, myself among them. It is here that you will find the origin of any overkill that you might detect in the pages to come. For I attack time travel on no less than three fronts: (a) the contradictions built into the very idea of (pure) temporal journeying; (b) the difficulty of arriving at any particular destination; and (c) the necessary impotence of the time traveller. The most obvious problems arise from the contradictions that result when the traveller goes backwards in time – which I will focus on here – though difficulties attend the idea of travel into the future, because it is equally rooted in the image of time as a quasi-spatial dimension.

The link between the myth of time travel and the idea of time as a dimension comparable to space is most directly set out in the famous passage from *The Time Machine* I have already quoted:

> "Clearly", the Time Traveller proceeded, "any real body must have extension in *four* directions: it must have Length, Breadth, Thickness, and – Duration ... There are really four dimensions, three, which we call the three planes of Space, and a fourth, Time ... *There is no difference between Time and any of the three dimensions of Space except that our consciousness moves along it.*"[97]

While most fictional time travellers (and, as we shall see, there is no other kind) travel in space as well as time, landing on an alien planet at some future or past time, time travel in its purest form, is a one-dimensional displacement from year X to year Y and depends on a disconnection between space and time.

It could be argued that we are always time travelling, moving "forward" at one second per second. I can get to next Wednesday by doing precisely nothing. However, we contrast travelling in time with moving in or with time. It is always assumed that we not only *can* but *must* do the latter: if time is moving, then we must move with it; if time is not moving, then we stay still with it. While one can electively travel from one place to another, we cannot *choose* to travel from t_1 to t_2 because we cannot choose not to travel between them, even if we arrive at t_2 a corpse. We have to "go with" (to use the notion that is now, I hope, discredited) "the flow". Everything, in that sense – people, chairs, and rocks – is a time traveller (or at least a time mover). There is, however, a difference, captured by David Lewis: "[Time travel] involves a discrepancy between time and time ... The separation in time between departure and arrival does not equal the duration of the [time traveller's] journey".[98] In short, the traveller would be proceeding at more than the standard one second per second – irrespective of whether she is travelling into the past or the future. This is what would be required to get to the future before it is the present for everyone else – say to a week on Wednesday by next Wednesday. And in order to get to *last* Wednesday, she would still have to out-run time – to move backwards faster than she is moved forward. (Something to which we shall return). So the traveller has to travel in one dimension to the extent that with respect to that dimension, and that dimension only, she is out-pacing the intrinsic dynamism of the dimension in which she is travelling. It is this, as well as the deliberate nature of the exercise, that distinguishes time "travelling" from mere movement in or, less contentiously, existence in, time.

I want now to examine three insuperable barriers the putative time traveller would have to overcome:

- *travelling* – the troubled journey;
- *knowing how/when to stop* – the difficult arrival;
- *being active at, or even conscious of, the destination* – the necessary impotence and unawareness of the time traveller.

2.4.1 The troubled journey

We may travel in space in any direction. I can just as well move from A to B as I can move from B to A and B and A may have any combination of coordinates, so long as they are not separated by greater distances than I could cover travelling at less than the speed of light for the duration of my life. And whenever we move (or so common sense tells us), we are out-pacing the space around us, since – irrespective of whether one is substantivalist or relationist about space – it is a collection of (relatively still) reference points against which movement counts as movement. It is the job of surrounding space to define zero miles per hour for our locality – for the place where movement matters – even though this will not apply in another frame of reference. Thinking of time as a dimension on all fours with space, encourages us to entertain the possibility of time travel analogous to space travel, where "travel" is defined as deliberate, voluntary, targeted movement as opposed to mere motion. Importantly, the target needs to be specified in advance – otherwise this would be travelling to "nowhen" which would not count at travelling – and from this, as we shall later see, many problems arise.

A cursory inspection of movement in space, as discussed already, should be sufficient to demonstrate that this encouragement is ill-advised. First, we can reverse our movement in space *because* space does not itself have an intrinsic direction or quasi-direction comparable to that which obliges us to move from that which is earlier to that which is later and not vice versa. This may not seem to count as an objection if we argue that time really is analogous to space and that the seeming impossibility of moving backwards in time is an illusion. This only delivers us to the next objection.

If time is the very medium of change (including movement) how can we go against it (as when the putative time traveller goes into the past) or race ahead of it (as when she travels into the future)? What change could out-pace time – the time of its own occurrence? And there is a third objection. Any movement in space is a movement in all three dimensions of space: we cannot move purely along "length". When I cross a road, I cross three-dimensional space. While it may seem as if I can arrange axes, in order that my movement is in a straight line parallel to the x axis, so that values change only in that single axis, all actual movements of actual bodies (with irregular shapes, and all bodies, particularly human bodies, have irregularities), will involve moment-to-moment changes in the values against all three axes. In short, real movement (as opposed to the abstracted presentation of trajectories) will be three-dimensional. More precisely – and more importantly – it will be four-dimensional: movements take time. When I – or a pebble – move from A to B, my journey will involve changes in the values of x *and* y *and* z *and* t. And this is true of any change or event. Nevertheless, that its world-line is four-dimensional is precisely the starting point of those who see time as a dimension and are thereby encouraged to imagine that time travel is possible. Finally, whether we are travelling into the future or the past, we have to move in such a way as to go counter to the sum total of events in the rest of the universe by which time is measured.

Let us, however, stick with the notion of time travel as a pure displacement from one time to another, so that when I set off for (say) 1066, any space travel is incidental, as it were a contaminant. Is this one-dimensional movement, possible, leaving aside relativistic (as well as common-sense) considerations that make space and time inseparable? The answer must be no. What are the grounds for saying this?

Supposing I decide to visit my present neighbourhood of Bramhall, Cheshire, in 1066. The study in which I am sitting will clearly be different from what it is now: it will not yet have come into existence. Nor will my house, the road going past it, the trees in the nearby field, and so on. All that will be available for me to visit will be the putative location in space, the imaginary container, presently occupied by my study but in 1066 occupied by (say) forests. The question then arises whether this will count as "the same location" and my journey count as pure time travel. The answer is no, even if I do not narrow the definition of the location to recognisable contents, but allow anything that has the same mathematical coordinates with respect to an identical frame of reference, to count as my present location. This is because the notion of "the same coordinate values" – of a mathematically defined place unchanging over 1,000 years – will be a difficult one. The distribution of matter will be different in 1066 compared with 2014 and so space–time in this locality will have a different structure. The same place will not therefore be the same place, even if we define both places using coordinates supported by the (relatively) fixed stars. These will have changed. So to get back to the same place at a different time will require some space, as well as time, travel.

Most time travellers anyway are a little more adventurous. They want to go places as well as to times. Supposing I decide to visit a particular place in the past in order to witness an event that happened there; for example, to go to Hastings to see the actual battle that took place on 14 October 1066, in particular to observe the famous arrow enter Harold's eye.[99] Then I would have to travel a certain "distance" in time (roughly 950 years from today) and a certain distance in space (roughly 250 miles from where I am presently sitting). This would require me to combine pure (motionless) time travel with actual spatial displacement: my time machine would have to be a space–time machine. (And this is true whenever we visit some part of the past: our destination is a slice of history that occurred in a certain place.) There would therefore be two time scales to reconcile: the time scale of the "journey" from 2014 to 1066 (of which more presently) and the time scale of the journey from here to Hastings – which would depend on my speed of travel.

Leaving aside the difficulty of defining the trajectory of spatial journeys in past time – the problem of assigning a location to the start, the middle and the end – it would be impossible to reconcile the time scales. It would be necessary to retain the normal sequence of "before" and "after" for the spatial component of the journey to the Battle of Hastings – Bramhall to Hastings – while at the same time violating it (for the temporal component – 2014 to 1066). It would take a certain amount of time to get from Bramhall to Hastings and (perhaps) a certain amount of time to get from 2014 to 1066. The successive stages of the spatial journey would have to be associated with successive moments in conventional time, while I, the time traveller, would also be going from "later" to "earlier" to "earlier still" in a trajectory independent of conventional time.

Time travel (either with or without space travel) not only has to deal with civil war within time but also the separation of movement in time from movement in space in a manner that is at odds with the mandatory four-dimensionality of movement as it is understood in common sense and classical physics. The traveller has to engage in a one-dimensional movement of a four-dimensional person, reducing a journey to the equivalent of a pure line or even a pure length – essentially to the mathematical representation of one of its dimensions. That may seem tricky but it is only the beginning of the contradictions built into time travel. The most important relate to the time traveller's need to break, and then to resume, her existing causal connections with the rest of the universe. The time traveller has to shake off one set of causal relations, be liberated from causation for the duration of the journey, and then hook up with another set of causal relations when she comes to rest. She has, so long as she is travelling, to be causally insulated from the rest of the universe. In short causal connectedness requires to be picked up and put down at will.

In the traditional model, the traveller enters some sort of device. If it is a kind of time-ship (as opposed to a spaceship), in order to transport its passenger to the past it, too, will have to break off its present spatio-temporal, and hence causal relationships, and eventually resume another set when it "lands" (to use an unreconstructed spatial term). Only by this means will it coexist, be simultaneous, with its human cargo, a necessary condition to ensure delivery. Such a divorce from the causal nexus it leaves behind could not be complete because dodging the effects of events in the world it has left behind (including those by which it was manufactured) would itself have anomalous consequences. Even if there were no "causal re-fuelling" required on a journey that is continuing on inertia, the initial liberation from causal ancestors would make it impossible to exploit that inertia.

Time travel, in short, requires that a part of the universe should break ranks with the rest of the universe, without this impacting on anything else that is not there for the ride. This follows from, and is a necessary condition of, the fact that the machine is going backwards in time, while the rest of the universe is moving forward in time. The traveller is heading towards (say) 1066, while the universe, which she left on 2014, is heading towards 2015. All the usual rules of material engagement are suspended.

The only way to avoid this divorce would be for *everything else* to come along for the ride. If, however, the entire universe were wound backwards, there would be no experience or indeed reality of travelling away from the present into the past: there would be no clock – or consciousness – unaffected by the backward movement from the present able to register the journey. The machine would not make net progress to the destination.[100] Time travel, in short, requires one small part of the universe – human plus machine plus entourage and effects – to break ranks with the rest. The time machine is required to be out of joint.

The notion that one part of the universe can change without any other part being affected is untenable. Everything is directly or indirectly connected with everything else. The ragged hole left behind by the disappearing time traveller, her machine, and her baggage will send out ripples. As McTaggart once said, if anything changes, then all other things will change with it – if only the relationship of the changed item to the rest of the universe.[101] The ragged hole in the causal net of the world left behind by the time machine will have limitless consequences: "The fall of a sand-castle on the English coast changes the nature of the Great Pyramid".[102] And we have all heard of the butterfly effect, whereby a butterfly fluttering its wings in Glasgow may ultimately lead to a hurricane in Puerto Rica.[103] In other words, the time traveller whose departure depends on breaking with the causal nexus in which she is located will herself have effects on the time-slice of the universe she has left. We should therefore be sceptical of the special, unilateral suspension of causation for the time traveller, this temporary breaking free of "the surly bonds" of causal connectedness. And this is true *a fortiori* of someone who has broken the causation that lies at the heart of classical physics and yet is persuaded by those laws to believe that time travel is possible.

This is not the end of the troubles that attend the time traveller's journey. First, we may assume the journey itself takes time. In which case, the traveller is moving in two temporal directions at once: travelling voluntarily towards the past and moving involuntarily towards the future. A consequence of this is that she will be in two dates at once: the today she shares with the people she has left behind, who are also moving forward in time; and the date corresponding to the point she has arrived at on her journey. This justifies our saying that (for example) she has arrived at 14 October 1066 (her time) on 12 January 2016 (others' time). To say this may strike the reader as pre-Einsteinian but even the special theory of relativity cannot deal with the simultaneous *opposing* temporal directions of the journey. What is more, the journey must take *some* time. This is a necessary condition of arriving at a destination – for if time travel were instantaneous, it is difficult to see how the distance travelled could be regulated, so that the traveller could arrive at the chosen destination of 1066 rather than shooting past it to the putative beginning of time 13.75 billion years BP. If so, it is difficult to imagine by what clocks the duration of journeying would be measured.

2.4.2 The difficult arrival

The difficulties experienced by the time traveller in the departure hall and in transit are as nothing to those that attend her arrival. The first is something we have touched on already. If the journey takes time – which we assume it must unless we can travel in time at an infinite speed – the target will recede as it is approached. This could be a problem if time travel is slow. Supposing the traveller sets out for 1066 in 2014 and it takes her 10 years to get a decade nearer to 1066, she will be swept away from the date at the same speed as she is approaching it. To put this another way: it will take her until 2024 to get to – 2014. She is like a swimmer swimming at 2 knots relative to the water against a current of 2 knots. It is no use saying that the private time of the traveller is insulated against the public time of the world because her target is a public target – a year 1066 that (for everyone) is 937 years away from 2014 – because her arrival is personal. (We shall return to the nature of the target in due course.)

Time travel to the past, then, is a race against time and it is one that can be won only if the rate of backward movement is faster than the rate of forward movement. This requires that there should be some measure common to both the forward speed of movement of the time she has left behind and of her backward movement in time. The notion of the speed of time would make sense, as discussed in §2.2.3, only with respect to a *hypertime* – a second-order time that would compare the forward passage of time (reflected in the ageing of her body) with her passage *against* time.

If we reject the idea that we must imagine the *speed* of backward movement in time, then, as noted, we shall have to reject the idea of the time traveller having, and certainly successfully arriving at, a specific temporal destination. If she is setting off from 2014 and aiming to reach 1066, then she will need to proceed at a speed of (say) one year a day and continue for 937 days plus the 937 days by which 1066 will have receded during the journey. In other words, any destination will have to be reached by maintaining a certain speed of travel for a certain period of time: time-distance travelled is the product of the speed of time travel and the time for which travel is maintained. We cannot, it seems, escape the unattractive appeal to a hypertime to measure the speed of the backward journey through time, and possibly the time for which that speed is maintained.

The argument that it is equally meaningless to talk about the speed of time travel as it is to talk about the speed at which time of its own accord passes and that we should not think of the time traveller having to "outpace" the intrinsic movement of time, does not hold up. If we go back to David Lewis's minimalist definition of time travel – whereby the interval between the time of departure and that of arrival is longer than the duration of the journey – we see the two measures of time's passage in play: there is the time it takes to get from the beginning to the end of the journey (as measured by time in the universe the traveller has temporally broken with); and there is the time that has passed between the beginning and end of the journey (as measured by, say, the traveller's wrist watch). For time travel to take place, the traveller must pass through times faster than times pass.

Even if we could get over these little difficulties, it would be interesting to know by what means the traveller would successfully *alight* on reaching a target date. (To repeat a point made earlier, *travel* as opposed to mere movement assumes that the journey is under her control, that she has a destination in mind.) How could the machine be brought to a halt at the chosen destination? Given that the time traveller must shake off the causal bonds as she sets off, and is beyond the grasp of causation in all intermediate locations, what causal brakes could be applied? How could she rewire herself and her machine into the causal nexus?

But there is a deeper problem than this and it may have been apparent when I argued that a time traveller who took a year to travel one year backwards would not make progress towards the destination. There is an obvious riposte to this concern: by what measure would the journey have lasted a year? And by what criterion would it be 2015 by the time she had reached 2013 in her journey from 2014 to 1066? If the traveller has reached 2013, she is in 2013 and that is the end of it. Only those she has left behind are in 2015. That is the whole point of time travel: never mind what is happening in the universe she has left behind – she has left it behind, she is not inside it. Well, she is and she isn't. She has to leave it in order to travel but she needs to remain in it in order to have a definite destination that was defined, in the world from which she left , as "937 years ago". In other words, 1066 is, or seems to be, a public target but it cannot be kept in view if she enters entirely local or private time. Just as I do not arrive at Greece by thoughts that reach out to it, so I do not arrive at 1066 by means of some entirely private route that has no place in the shared world. After all, if the route is through a private dimension, the target, too, is private. But presumably the traveller is heading to 1066 in order (say) to witness the Battle of Hastings, to observe William the Conqueror on the throne, and to see people behaving in the way history books have told us that they did in that year. Without the (public, objective, shared) contents of 1066, the target year is just a number, not a temporal location. The traveller can't have as her destination something she shares with the universe she has left behind (in which it was defined in space and time) while also getting to it by means of a journey whose temporal coordinates are utterly private to her. This is connected with the important, but unanswerable question, of what time the traveller will arrive at her destination. It cannot be 1066 and it cannot (of course) not be 1066. And it is no use saying that this contradiction arises only in the context of a now contested notion of Global or Unitary time. Without the latter, 1066 and the events in it would not be envisaged as somehow being located, so they could be a destination.

This tension between public and private time – between historical and individual time – will return to haunt us, as we shall see. For the present, let's look at the traveller's destination a bit more carefully. It is obvious that it is not possible to arrive "in 1066" – that is to say in *the whole of 1066*. Time *per se* does not exist in years. It is necessary to arrive at a particular moment in 1066 – say, 12:01:59 on 14 October.

But would this then licence roaming around 1066 or even the whole of 14 October, the day of the battle? Would the traveller have to reboard the time-ship in order to proceed to the next moment? Or would she be imprisoned in an infinitely thin time-slice? It is difficult to see how our fat time words – "1066", "14 October 1066", etc. – could be built into the destination of a time-ship. We usually overlook this problem because we tend to think that when the traveller alights from the time-ship, she can then avail herself of the forward movement of the local time. In other words, she arrives at 12:01:59 on 14 October 1066 and, by dint of her staying around, the time which is in the past (1066), can pass again, for as long as she wants it to. In other words, she arrives at a moment on 14 October 1066 and (say) leaves a week later. This raises a very great problem as we shall see.

Before we examine this problem, however, let us return to another closely connected with it: movement in space. The time-ship does not have the capacity to take the traveller to a particular place: its navigation system takes note only of time. If it offers pure time transport then the best it can do is to leave her in the same place from which it set off, but 937 years earlier; however, as we have seen, the notion of "the same place" maintained across the time, in the face of a total change of material and social contents and material and social context, is dubious. The alternative to delivering the traveller to a particular place – namely, delivering her *to the entire universe* at a particular moment, a time-slice of everything, a foliation of the entire space–time manifold – is even less attractive, particularly as relativity does not allow distant simultaneity or a worldwide Now. Even if the machine could spread itself out in this way, the time traveller could not. She would have to alight *somewhere.* But could she then move, even to the extent of breathing? Pure time travel makes *space* travel suddenly seem problematical.

If these questions are usually overlooked in the literature of time travel, it may be because there is a confusion between journeying to a time as identified by a date ("1066") and journeying to an earlier state of the universe that happened to be its state at that date (e.g. in 1066). Both definitions of the destination have distinctive problems. The first assumes that dates have an existence, substance separate from, and independent of, their contents, of any state of the universe. The second is that they remain "in store" even when their time is past, so that they are available to be revisited at or from a later date; in other words, that the past states of the universe are present, or retained, or available, even when the world has moved on. This is particularly difficult in the case of a manifestly complex event such as The Battle of Hastings (and all events are in fact complex). The target would have to be completed – to be there to be visited – and yet reignited into "ongoingness" in order to be experienced or observed, never mind to be acted on. It would have to be both done and dusted (if it is to count as being in the past) and at the same time open for visitors, even if the latter do not actually interfere with it.

It is only because time travel myths are vague as to whether they are about dates or states of the universe do they seem conceivable. The confusion between times (or dates) and states of the universe at those times (or dates) has further important consequences, relevant to what the traveller is permitted to do, or even experience, when she arrives at the chosen destination. There is an assumption not only that the target date is kept in aspic but that it absolutely or intrinsically has a temporal – indeed a tensed-temporal (e.g. in the past) – relationship to the date from which the traveller sets out. Ironically, this is not even consistent with the relativity theory that, in virtue of placing time on a footing with space, was what made time travel seem conceivable in the first place. We shall return to this.

2.4.3 The necessary impotence (and unawareness) of the time traveller

So the traveller has problems in the departure lounge and in the arrival hall and in the journey in-between, en route to landing no-place-in-particular, in an infinitely thin time-slice. There are obvious limitations on what she could be permitted to do when she disembarks from the ship. This is connected to the best-known objection to time travel, one that arises out of the fact that travelling backwards in time seems to involve, or at least permit, moving against the grain of causation and going back-wards from present effects upstream to their causes.

Suppose, to take a well-known concern, she returns to the day when her parents first met. She distracts one of them. As a result, they do not catch sight of one another, their relationship never happens, and she is not born. By interfering with the past, she has removed the essential condition for her journey to the past: namely, that she should exist. The things that she must be prevented from doing will include not merely headline events such as stopping her parents meeting, but anything that disturbs the conditions which led to her being born and able to undertake the journey to the past. Since, however, every event has the capacity to deflect the subsequent course of the universe, howsoever slightly (the butterfly effect again), there appears to be no way of defining those events that should be forbidden on the grounds that they will interfere with the time traveller being born or even with the life that led up to her wanting to become a time traveller. To be entirely safe, she should be forbidden to act at all, because there cannot be bespoke, local tinkering, since its consequences cannot be contained in view of the connectedness of the world.

But even a limited visa or causation permit, forbidding all interference with the way things are at the destination, would not be enough to ward off problems. By the very fact of her arrival – eating, walking, breathing or even looking – she must alter what happens at her destination. Not only is she bound to impotence and must forego the hope of (say) righting past wrongs (a common motive for fictional time travellers) she must be forbidden to do all the ordinary things necessary for survival: standing, eating, breathing. What is more, given that awareness of one's surroundings requires interaction, energy exchanges, with it, she must not look at, even less touch, the world within which she has found herself.[104] Time travel plus mere aware-ness of her destination would not be as undisruptive as the "mental time travel" we are familiar with from the faculty of episodic memory. When I recall a state of affairs, I am no longer interacting with it. Any causal interaction was in the past; all that remains is the intentional leg of the perceptual experience – the "aboutness" that the memory is about. This is extra-causal, a tear in the causal fabric of the world, as I will discuss in Chapter 12. My memory of a token event does not touch that event.

Once the traveller has interacted with the destination, even only sufficiently to be aware of it, she cannot leave the place as she found it, so as not to interfere with the future, including her own life leading up to the moment of embarking on her journey. The causal chains set running by her lightest footfall would already be beyond her capacity to cancel: footprints and eye prints are equally inadmissible. In short, the time traveller is denied anything on her arrival that would constitute actual arriving.[105] (And we are assuming that she is not a disembodied spirit because this would make the idea of arrival – and at a particular place and particular time – meaningless.)

Even if, by some extraordinary dispensation, the ripples it causes are prevented from impinging directly on her subsequent existence, the time traveller's arrival will still have paradoxical consequences. They will have an impact on the subsequent history of the universe, and hence on the contents of the day from which she set out, since every event has a direct or indirect influence on every other event.

Supposing she sets out on 15 September 2013 and arrives at 6 June 1933. The target date will have two versions: the one whose contents were complete by midnight on 6 June 1933 and another whose contents had been altered by the time traveller. The contents of 6 June would not, it appears, be finalized until after 15 September 2013 – or later if other visitors come from later dates. The traveller's day of departure from the present, likewise, will have at least two versions: the one that was obtaining when she set out; and the one that subsequently came into being as a result of the spreading ripples created by her arrival on 6 June 1933. These would also affect all the dates between her arrival at 6 June 1933 and 15 September 2013 when she set out on her travels. It doesn't matter how trivial the difference is: *any* difference is sufficient to create two versions of the days in question. So we have the paradox of the contents of the days being altered after they had come to an end. The contents of 6 June 1933 would have been *both* completely determined by midnight on that day – one reason for her choosing that as her destination – *and* altered at some subsequent time.

How will these two versions of the days relate to one another? Do they exist side by side, simultaneously as parts of parallel universes? Seemingly not, as they will not be genuinely parallel; for they will not come into being at the same time, or not at least if time travel takes time and the effects of the time traveller's interference with each day's causal ancestors also takes time to work through. The version of 15 September 2013 that she sets out from will be in place at the beginning of her journey into the past. It will therefore *precede* the version of the day that will result from her arriving at 6 June 1933 and, as a result of that arrival, disturbing the course of subsequent events right up to and beyond 15 September 2013.

The difference between the two versions of the *destination* day is particularly profound. Before she sets out on her journey, the traveller will be present in 6 June 1933 only as a future possibility not yet born; after she has landed, she will be present in it as a fully grown up actuality. In this case, the first version of 6 June 1933 will be in place 76 years before the second version. And yet they will both lay claim to being the same day. This is, of course, contradictory: the least we might expect of a day is that it should be simultaneous with, and identical to, itself! And, as we have seen, there is simply no way of reining in the time traveller to make sure that the two versions of 6 June 1933 and 15 September 2013 and all days in-between have the same contents.

It is interesting that the arguments against time travel have focused on killing parents, or otherwise removing the conditions that made it possible for the traveller to exist. What if the traveller merely travelled back by 1 day and killed herself? The question illuminates how time travel requires not only that there should be two versions of the same stretch of time but also two versions of the traveller: the one who undertakes the journey and the one who is already there. These two versions come face to face when the traveller kills herself – or rather one version of herself: the visiting self and the visited self. If she succeeds in killing the visited self, then she will of course kill the visiting self. In short, the experiment requires the coexistence of two phases of herself and also forbids them.

An ad hoc law of nature that somehow ensured that she would be able to arrive on target and that her stay would not have any enduring effects locally, or that those local effects would be sealed off from the rest of the world on that day and subsequent days, carries little appeal. But without this ad hoc arrangement, that flies in the face of the physics upon which the very possibility of time travel depends, each visitor would generate an alternative history subsequent to the target date, and those histories would all be in conflict with one another simply in virtue of being different.

However we try to wriggle out of this, time travel to the past therefore, commits us to allowing at least two versions of the visited day and all days subsequent to it, including the day of departure. This offends our idea that the contents of 15 September 2013 should be fixed once and for all; that the account is closed at midnight; and there is not even standing room for additional events irrespective of whether the day was quiet or action-packed. (From the point of view of physics, of course, all days are equally action-packed). What is more, the two versions of the same day would be separated in time: Version 1 would be fixed before the time traveller's arrival and Version 2 after her arrival. The day would therefore be both later and earlier than itself.[106]

How did we arrive at such an absurd conclusion? As always, the first and crucial step on the road to lunacy is an assumption that is difficult to take exception to – though we must. It is the assumption that the past exists in such a way that, if we could travel backwards in time, we could visit definite parts of it. This assumption, as we have already discussed, is at least in part based on the melding of the notion of an actual day (or month, or year, or century) with its fixed contents, and a date. Let us explore this a little further.

There is an obvious distinction between a day and a date: the former is the contents of a particular stretch of time, the latter its notional container. I emphasize "notional" because there are no sharp boundaries at either end of the day, other than those we have imposed via our clocks and calendars. We pass from 23:59 to 12:01 without any discontinuity, boundary or interruption. Nothing is obliged to stop or start at the edges of a day, or an hour, or a year. The distinction between the container and the contents is important. The contents of 12 December 2013 do not exist before or after that day, or not at least in the sense that they exist *during* that day (the way in which they do exist will be discussed in Chapters 6 and 7 respectively). However, the *date* 12 December 2013 exists both before and after the 12th. We can see it on the calendar, or our diaries, and we can plan for it, with the aim of predetermining its contents. On 10 December, we can move our finger on the calendar forwards to 12 December and of course we can talk about what we are planning to do then, populating it with various appointments, for example. Likewise, we can look back on the calendar date, remembering what happened. 12 December, unlike any particular contents, is guaranteed to happen (even if the solar system comes to an end) because it is defined purely numerically as being at such and such a temporal interval from now. 12 December 2011, which lies 2 days ahead on 10 December 2011, will be guaranteed to be "now" 2 days later. And it will still exist, insofar as it ever does, on 14 December 2011. As a location in a notational system it is just as real (and unreal) on 10 and 14 December as it is on the 12th. The material existence of dates – the sense in which they are items – is realized in, and distributed through, the written and spoken tokens that signify them. The date, however, is not a day with its events; neither an event, nor time, but the skeleton of time; it has no substance or causal effect in its own right, except insofar as its tokens may prompt human actions. Unlike the events that happen on 12 December, "12 December" does not exist as a set of causes or effects in its own right.

Even if we resist confusing dates with the days that realize them we still may be deluded into imagining that they are visitable. Especially when they are set out on the calendar, they seem deceptively analogous to spatial locations that are still in place after any particular events that have occurred in them are over.

And yet, if dates are deemed to be worth visiting, it is because we imagine that we can visit the events, states of affairs, and objects that "occupied" them, so that, if we visit 14 October 1066 between 9 a.m. and 4 p.m., we might witness the Battle of Hastings, even if we cannot take part or in any way change the outcome. The permanence of dates – which do not "happen" but are merely containers or temporal labels for what happens – is transferred in our minds to their contents which can therefore be visited by a traveller from the future. This is an expression of the spatialization of time – or times – that makes it seem as if we can visit one time from another time. The time traveller wants to have it both ways. She wants to visit the Battle of Hastings by visiting the date of the Battle of Hastings – and this presupposes that the date holds the contents of the day intact and inviolable – and she wants at the same time to alter its contents even if only sufficiently to add to them through the interactions necessary to be aware of those contents.

The very idea that the time traveller could have a destination to go to, that there would be something to see when she got there, that she might be able to act in, arrive at, or even be aware of, her chosen spot in the past, is connected with the self-contradictory idea that you could revisit time t_1 from time t_2, and that revisited time t_1 would be, as it were a second token of a type t_1. But stretches and instants of time are unrepeatable tokens, not instances of a type. This confusion between tokens and types is widespread in discussion of events as well as times and is based on a failure to acknowledge that what has happened is singular, underlined by the fact that it happened at a definite time (and place). The Battle of Hastings is not "a class of Battle of Hastings". It is not therefore available to be experienced or sampled at a later time.

This crucial point is overlooked by some serious thinkers about time. Consider, for example, this claim from Maudlin: "[T]he topology of space–time … allows for a sort of time travel: an observer who always "goes forward" in time can return to an event he has already experienced".[107] Against this, we need to point out that, in virtue of a) being visited (and hence, however subtly, changed) and b) being present at a different – later – time, the event must be a different entity, however similar it might be to the index token event. All past events, of course, are token events. You cannot revisit a token event and tinker with it, even less reverse it. That which has happened cannot be made to happen differently even less unhappen; even less can its causal consequences be taken back or *a fortiori* its causal ancestors. This is not to say that states of affairs cannot be reversed: you untidy a room and I tidy it up again. But that is not interfering with the token event of the untidying but simply adding another event that restores the status quo ante. This will become clearer when we appreciate that only future events are types – or purely types – and hence are not events (something we shall discuss in §8.2.2).

There is another very important sense in which the time traveller needs to have things in two incompatible ways. She wants to take advantage of a world picture developed most completely in relativistic physics in which time is a fourth dimension. At the same time, what she is doing is not mere moving but *travelling* – from the present (the beginning of her journey) to a past destination (the end of her journey). She is conceived of as an *agent* who undertakes a journey, defined by egocentric markers such as "beginnings" and "ends" and "here" where she is and "there" where she aims to be. And it is difficult to characterize *actual* time travel without appealing to tensed time to specify where the traveller is ("now") and where she is headed ("the past" or "the future"). The destination of any journey – a date such as 14 October 1066 or an event such as The Battle of Hastings – what is more is held in the community of minds. None of these elements – necessary to make what happens *travelling* as opposed to mere motion, to be the deliberate behaviour of a conscious agent – has any place in the four-dimensional manifold of relativistic physics. Any putative time traveller would have to do without the egocentric parameters of the journey (beginning here and ending there), consciousness, intentionality, tensed time (including the "now" which marks the beginning of the journey), and all those characteristics that are necessary for agency, including travelling. Time travel has to be experienced and *done* to count as travel.

More broadly, the causally closed physical world of time as a fourth dimension is not available to be manipulated by human agents, certainly to the degree that would be necessary to "set off" for a particular destination (even if that is broadly characterized as "the past" or "the future") and arrive there, ready for action or even for observation. The space–time manifold and the worlds of individuals are mutually exclusive. The notion of individual time travel in a purely physical universe is thus self-contradictory. This would be true even if it did not require the traveller to requisition causes to activate and regulate the journey and at the same time break with them to permit the journey.

There is a more general principle here: you can't have your cake (e.g. a block theory of the universe in which all of time and all happening – past, present, and future – coexist) to hold open the possibility of time travel and eat it (the egocentric world(s) of ordinary agents who do things such as travelling and make a difference when they arrive). This veto applies *a fortiori* to the kind of time travelling that seems to be permitted by more exotic consequences of contemporary physics. Gödel suggested that making a long space journey in a rotating dust-filled universe might permit time travel.[108] As Palle Yourgrau has pointed out the primary philosophical point of Gödel's paper was deeply subversive of a realistic interpretation of the general theory:

> The deduction, from the General Theory of Relativity ... of the possibility of time travel shows that time is ideal – a mere appearance imposed on reality by a kind of "optical refraction" of the subjective lens of the mind but reflecting nothing objective in the nature of things.[109]

Ouch! Einstein, the Machian-turned-Parmenidean, might not have appreciated being exposed as a Kantian as well. The even more exotic notion of time travel through wormholes – short cuts connecting two separate points in space–time – suggested by Kip Thorne seems to offer little hope to the aspirant time traveller. The transformation of such a wormhole into a time machine would require two things. The first is scaling up nanoscopic entities, generated by mathematics, to the size where they could be usable by macroscopic time travellers. The second is finding wormholes in a world-picture defined by general theory of relativity.[110] The goal of uniting general theory (that raises the possibility of time travel) with quantum field theory that provides the necessary wormholes remains elusive. These problems are, of course, additional to the general objection, already lodged, to retaining the egocentric agent with particular goals, given that she cannot be accommodated in the world of physics. Even if contemporary physical theory allowed closed time-like curves – and it remains uncertain whether or not it does[111] – these would not be tracks along which humans or any sentient beings could satisfy a thirst for time travel. A loop in time is not a journey someone can voluntarily undertake.

One does not, however, need to dig so deep. Anyone who imagines that it is possible to travel in time has misunderstood the basics of four-dimensional physics. We could no more displace our bodies in pure time than we could propel ourselves through Minkowski space–time as if we were walking through 3-dimensional space. As Arntzenius and Maudlin have said, "The only serious proof of the possibility of time travel would be a demonstration of its actuality".[112] Until then, we have every reason to believe that time travelling is a myth with even less plausibility than witches' broomstick-travelling.

2.5 FURTHER REFLECTIONS ON TIME AS A DIMENSION

In this chapter I have looked at some of the consequences of treating time as one of a quartet of dimensions whose other three members are spatial. While, as we have noted, it may not be entirely just to accuse physicists of reducing time to space, the fact that time joins the three others as a fourth member of a quartet, and that it is in the predominantly spatial sense of vision that time becomes explicit to us, it is inevitable that the reduction of time to a dimension supports a quasi-spatial notion of it. This is reinforced by the way time is represented in clocks and graphs, where successive moments are set out in space, and seconds are seconds of an arc that can be "split" and displayed as smaller angular displacements. Of course, special relativity gives space and time a single measure, uniting them in a four-dimensional geometry (which we shall discuss in the next chapter) and allows space–time distances to be partitioned in different ways into spatial and temporal components, depending on the inertial framework from which they are being measured. A change in frame of reference may turn a space-like separation into a time-like one or simultaneity of events at different places into temporally separated events at the same place. So there are grounds, too, for seeing space as being misrepresented.

Spatialized time may be complemented by temporalized space. In everyday life, we often describe distances in temporal terms. Varlam Shalamov in his *Kolyma Tales* describes the Yahut people for whom time and distance measures are interchangeable and distances are often described as "time to be crossed".[113] "A day's walk", "an hour's drive" are common ways of describing distances. And time may be used to define the essentially spatial concept of longitude, which is defined by the discrepancy between the time as reported by the clock set in Greenwich and the local time as recorded by the position of the sun. The latter indicates how many degrees of longitude a ship is east or west of Greenwich. We think of vertical spatial slices of the earth as "time zones".

And, at the most fundamental scientific level, there are places where time seems to triumph over space. Two lengths are regarded as equal by definition if they are crossed by light in equal times and the length of an object seen as the time light takes to traverse it. More generally, physical distances are best thought of as being determined by time measurements. It is customary for physicists to think of time and distance measurements to be basically interchangeable, via the speed of light (years to light-years, seconds to light-seconds, etc.). However, time measurements are now so much more precisely determined than distance measurements that the metre is now *defined* so that there are precisely 299,792,458 of them to a light second.[114] Indeed, we can think of the finitude and constancy of the speed of light as not being about light itself but about the relationship between time and space.[115]

However, the spatialization of time has a more powerful hold on our intuitions than the temporalization of space. We have seen how this is evident in our conception of time as a river, or as flowing, or as having a direction (captured in the metaphor of the arrow) and in the myth of time travel, of voluntary movements in both directions of time comparable to voluntary movement in space. All of this is in despite of the fact that the treatment of time as a dimension comparable at a deep level to space is inconsistent. Space houses "flowings" but does not itself flow; and while movements in space have a direction, it is not itself a direction or directed but is the womb of direction, the possibility of there being directed movements. Nevertheless, spatialization has such a powerful grip on our thoughts that even this disanalogy does not loosen its hold.

Moreover, time has not been singled out uniquely for spatialization. This is a pervasive feature of the scientific representation of the world and it offers an important transition to the reduction of what there is to numbers – which we shall talk about in the next chapter. That the very idea of a dimension is rooted in that of space is betrayed in the standard definition of a dimension as "measurable or spatial extent of any kind, as length, breadth, thickness, area, volume, measurement, measure, magnitude, size".[116] The notion of a phase state – fundamental to the scientific description of the physical world – is that of a *space* in which all possible states of a system are represented, with each of these states being marked by a unique point. This can be used in many contexts, including ones remote from its thermodynamic birthplace.

The hegemony of the idea of "space" in natural (quantitative) science is beautifully captured by W. V. O. Quine:

> The mathematician generalizes, as is his wont. He begins by noting that we can specify any point in space by assigning values to three independent variables: (1) how far up; (2) how far out, and (3) how far over. Such is the tridimensionality of space. Generalizing, then, he speaks of a class of entities of any sort as *n*-dimensional if there are *n* independent variables such that each member of the class is specified by values to all *n* variables, and each assignment of values to all *n* variables specifies a distinct member of the class. Predictably the mathematician also generalizes the word "space" correspondingly, calling the class an *n*-dimensional space.[117]

Let me give one example which illustrates how far this can go: colours and the appreciation of colours. It is possible to locate colours in a three-dimensional space, whose axes correspond to long, medium and short wave reflectance, each stimulating a particular set of retinal cones. Any given colour then occupies a particular location in this space defined by the values read off from each of the axes. According to Paul Churchland, this model allows us to see how the brain "represents" individual colours or indeed *any* sensations: "sensations are simply identical with ... a set of stimulation levels (spiking frequencies) in the appropriate sensory pathways" – locations in the colour space.[118] For Churchland – whose neurophilosophical thinking still has many adherents – this can be extended to encompass all conscious experience. There is a unique coding vector – a list of numbers, a set of magnitudes, read off from axes – for every human experience. Consciousness is simply a multitude of positions in a multitude of phase spaces. The scene is set for what C. B. Martin has called "Pythagoreanism of the brain"[119] – and which we shall discuss in §3.6.

Views such as this highlight the domination of spatial imagery or, where imagery fails, of spatial discourse in the physicist's account of "what there is", encompassing even consciousness. The extended idea of space is an important step towards the exsanguination of phenomenal reality in natural science and the replacement of qualitative experience by numbers. It is interesting in this regard that, when physicists cut free from the limits of intuitive understanding and follow the maths wherever it takes them, and they multiply dimensions, the newcomers are deemed to be spatial rather than temporal. There is no question of a "volume" or "area" of time. Consider, for example, string theory which boasts 10 dimensions. Only one of these is time, the extra seven all being "spatial", albeit usually curled up and thus hidden from sight.

Far from the concept of time being a victim of imperialist conceptions of space, therefore, both parties lose out as they are stripped of their experiential character and reduced to pure quantities. The fundamental dissimilarity of space and time is not defended, and their different phenomenal reality respected, even though the former is, say, measured in cubic centimetres while the latter is measured in seconds. The difference between the units is outweighed by the similarity of units *per se:* cubic centimetres and seconds are both quantities of ratios, derived from ever more remote and hidden standards, such as the standard metre. It does not matter whether reduction to quantities is performed by clocks or rulers. The profound difference between the spatial "here versus there" and the temporal "now versus then" is lost in the journey to numbers. Attempts to revive the difference between space and time within space–time by arguing that a time-like vector is one that links two events that are causally connected while a space-like vector is one that links events that are causally disconnected are – as we have already touched on and will discuss in depth in Chapter 11 – too little, too late.

In summary, while we have in this chapter examined the potency of a spatial image of time, the reduction of space – to points, lines, and ultimately naked numbers – is of equal concern. It is to this reduction of space we shall now turn our attention.[120]

CHAPTER 3

Mathematics and the book of nature

[The universe] is written in the language of mathematics, and its characters are triangles, circles, and other geometrical figures ...
Galileo, *The Assayer* (extracted from Burtt, *The Metaphysical Foundations of Modern Science*, 85)

Let no-one ignorant of geometry enter here.
Plato (inscribed at the entrance to his Academy)

3.1 FROM PLACE TO DECIMAL PLACE 1: GEOMETRIZATION OF SPACE

This book is about time and yet much of the present chapter will be devoted to space. You are entitled to an explanation. The explanation is not to be found in the fundamental postulate of post-Einsteinian classical physics that, as Minkowski put it, "space by itself and time by itself will recede completely to become mere shadows, and only a type of union of the two will still stand independently on its own".[1] No, it reflects my belief that space and time are equally traduced by the scientistic assumption that the world seen through the eyes of quantitative science, in particular mathematical physics, is the world period. When time is thought of in quasi-spatial terms – due in part to its initially being made explicit through vision, the most spatial of the senses – this is not a triumph of space over time, but the first step towards the triumph of quantification, of number, over both space and time. Reduction to pure quantity finishes off what was started by the spatialization of time: the loss of time as it is experienced in our lives. The reduction of time to a one-dimensional space that can be mapped on to the line of real numbers was made possible by the prior quantification, more specifically geometrization, of space.[2] Time reduced to a dimension – the Fourth Dimension – is ultimately time shrivelled to a quantity, to something which can not only be measured but *is* that measurement, so that the distinction between the duration of events, of the intervals between events, and the "when" of events is lost in their reduction to mere numbers.[3]

The initial focus in this chapter on the reduction of *space* to pure quantities, to pure extension, is not, therefore, a digression. To understand the fate of time in physics, we need to understand the scientific impoverishment of space, the denigration of the image of habitat as primitive clothing concealing a geometrical reality and, more generally, of the reality of our surroundings to a mathematical volume.

Geometry is not only the most obviously visual of all the branches of mathematics; it also lies at the root of physics, whose foundation is in mechanics, the most general and most powerful description of movement and, more broadly, of change. This is captured in Galileo's vision of science as expressed in the quotation at the head of this chapter; and in coordinate geometry, where the mathematization of space is developed to the point where locations and changes of location are the mere values of algebraic variables set out in Euclidean space.

Since the early years of the last century, Euclidean (as opposed to non-Euclidean) geometry has been seen as only one of many ways of representing space in order to render it – and the most general patterns of movement of physical objects – amenable to being quantified. But that has not altered the fundamental story: namely, the stripping down of space to its geometry and hence to mathematics. This has had complex consequences, with space being at once upgraded to the status of an active player in the universe – its curvature in the vicinity of objects that have mass, being the reality of gravity – and downgraded to a set of numbers. By this means, space has finally parted company from perception, and from lived experience, and is occupied not by places but by decimal places.

Of course this is not something that worries, or even should worry, physicists. The space of mechanics and of moving material objects and force fields is not the space of the shopper, the doctor doing his rounds, or the tourist. Mechanics is not psycho-geography. Indeed, its extraordinary explanatory, predictive, and practical power has come from shedding what might be regarded as irrelevant baggage. So long as it is not claimed that the physicists' space is more fundamental than, or is the ultimate reality or truth of, lived space, then no harm is done. Unfortunately, this is precisely what is often claimed – or at least implied.

The general theory of relativity takes to the limit the representation of the most basic and ubiquitous mode of change – movement – as an alteration of the value of variables measured against coordinate axes. As Stephen Hawking and Leon Mlodinow put it: "General relativity has transformed physics into geometry".[4] How has geometry come to assume such a hold over our thinking about space, to the point where we believe that the essence of space, and of changes taking place in it, is a set of truths expressed geometrically?

3.1.1 The essence of geometry

Geometry is the meeting place of logic and space, in which the latter is populated and defined by items such as "line" whose definitions have axiomatic status, and, in arguments that reveal (apparent) necessity in extensity, logically unassailable premises are connected with conclusions and a triumphant "QED". In Euclid's *Elements* the geometrization of space is expressed in a succession of theorems (many of which had been discovered by his predecessors) that deal with the relationships between lines, angles, and volumes, and are bolted together into a comprehensive deductive and logical *system*. Euclidean space as it is typically presented has three dimensions[5] subsequently employed in classical mechanics to specify the positions, the size and the movements of objects. These dimensions are founded in locations specified by zero-dimension, or dimensionless, points.

Points mark the beginning and end, or the intersection, of one-dimensional lines. Lines may be linked to create figures that enclose two-dimensional planes; and these in turn connected up into those figures such as cubes and spheres that define, or notionally enclose, pure volumes of space. Points do not occupy space, at least in part because they are supposed to *be* space. We shall return to this crucial fact in §3.4.1. For the present, we note that the point is an entity that is somehow able to be a location in space without occupying space. This paradoxical achievement is also demanded of lines (which we shall examine in §3.4.2) and plane figures. They do not belong to the sand, the wax tablets, or the page on which they are drawn. It is their markers not the items themselves that occupy space. Only a three-dimensional *material* entity can occupy and consequently specify a particular region of space.[6]

While it is easy to accept that points, lines and planes do not occupy space, it is tempting to think that *three*-dimensional, purely geometrical, entities such as spheres or cubes do. We shall resist this temptation when we remember that geometrical cubes and spheres are not cubes or spheres *of anything*. They are as much abstractions as are planes and lines and points. They have no content: they are mere forms, pure outlines. They no more occupy space than the word "dog" occupies a kennel, even though a sentence may specify that a particular dog is in a particular kennel and the logic of discourse does not allow the same dog to occupy another, distant kennel at the same time. The space-occupying, spatially located line drawn in the sand or on the page signifies a geometrical line that occupies no space. This line stands for a generality of lines and, through this, for a pure distance or a pure direction. And the same applies to diagrams of planes and of volumes such as cubes and spheres. The purest form is the emptiest form: it is content-free. The form of forms, the emptiest of all forms is, in the end, so general that it is formless: it lacks even boundaries, shape and differentiation. It is mathematical space itself, removed from any place or even the image of place.

Thus geometrized space, the framework in which the unfolding universe, motion, change, as represented by physical science is captured.

3.1.2 Geometry comes out of the shadows

How did we come to geometrize space? To understand the reduction of space to pure extensity – interpreted for some as the quantified receptacle of quantified objects and events, a numerically defined holder of items themselves most authoritatively represented by numbers – we need to return to vision and the visual field in which space, as well as time, first becomes explicit.[7] The journey from place to decimal place begins with the gaze in which we who gaze are displaced in virtue of being located in a larger space than ourselves. But let us be more specific.

As we discussed in Chapter 1, when we look, we see that which is visible and also that which is visibly invisibly, so that that which is hidden from sight may be nevertheless *visually present* as obscured, occluded. Analogously, we see darkness as well as light. Visible darkness may be generalized, scattered or focal. The most obvious manifestations of focal darkness are the shadows cast by objects. The shadow may be attached to the base of the object but is otherwise distinct from it. And in the case of, say, the shadow cast on the ground by an elevated object – such as a leaf on a tree or a bird flying overhead – there is complete separation.

Shadows give the form or outline of objects without their content. On this count, they are a more radical advance into abstraction than reflections, which replicate aspects of appearances, such as colour, though they may transform them as when a tree is reflected in the warped mirror of the ripples on a stream. Shadows portray nothing of the objects to which they belong other than their shape, transformed to a lesser or greater degree (depending on the angle of the light), an indication of their size (relative to other objects casting shadows) and their motion, which they track. Colour, visual texture, blotches within the boundary of the object are lost, along with all non-visual properties. The shadow has only shape, size, and motion – those primary qualities that scientists, beginning with Galileo, came to regard as the only true reality.

The shadow, in summary, is a natural abstraction: it gives (one version of) the form of the object independently of its content. Shadows are naturally generated proto-diagrams that signify their parent objects; as such, they are not only abstract but generalized. The shadow of a tree trunk is on the way to being the shadow of *any* tree trunk or, more important for our present considerations, of any item of a particular (geometrical) shape.

And shadows have another characteristic that makes them *diagrammatic*: being two-dimensional, they lack depth. They are naturally occurring precursors of geometrical figures that indicate regions of space without occupying any space. (This is why, incidentally, they can move with their parent object without ever colliding with anything: shadows obstruct the passage neither of objects or other shadows.) As outlines – the external borders of objects replicated and placed outside of their boundaries – shadows contain the germ of the idea of a line or a figure separate from any object. *Disembodied extension*, replicating size and shape, prefigures pure quantity separated from material reality. The visible relationship between the shadow and the object may also lie behind the idea of the *angle*, understood as a pure relationship between directions represented in one-dimensional lines.

We may, in short, think of shadows, the self-geometrizing of objects, as the source of the extraordinary notion of entities, such as lines and angles, in or of space that nonetheless do not occupy space and are distinct from those things that occupy space, that are immaterial entities of pure magnitude and direction. Lines, angles, and planes are items that, belonging to no particular object, are of space itself; and they inspire the idea of space having properties – in which space-occupying and spatially related objects participate – that constitute its intrinsic topology. Our perception of shadows thus makes a decisive contribution to the origin of the geometries that analyse space as something in itself, leading ultimately to space as the Newtonian motionless theatre of movement and as the empty, universal container of objects that are full of themselves. The shadow is the bridge between objects and space and gives birth to the idea that objects, the space they occupy, and the space that surrounds them share something fundamental – most obviously in sharing dimensions.

Once figures – and consequently length, surface area, volume and direction – are given independent existence, it is possible to think of them as existing in certain quantities, just as objects do. There are long lengths and short ones just as there are long cucumbers and short ones; and there are big and small geometrical cubes just as there are big blocks of marble and small ones. This is an important source of those intuitions that ultimately make possible the mathematization of our perception of "How much?" and the transition from the semi-quantitative sense of "lots of (or not much) stuff" to "quantities of units [of stuff]".

The shadow – a spontaneously occurring replication of the form of an object, an abstract self-portrait as a negative – lies at the root of the separation of size and distance from individual objects and our perception of them, so that size and distance become things in themselves, refashioned as parameters, as variables that take values, as pure dimensions. The notion of length, abstracted from objects by shadows, may be reattached to material particulars when a ruler (or a proto-ruler such as a body part – a foot, a hand, a forearm) is applied to objects as well as to distances.[8] But the actual process of measurement is marginalized – the placing of the arm against the measured object – compared with the result, so that the output is an unencumbered number.

Not all objects that cast shadows have straight edges. Indeed, the overwhelming majority of natural objects have irregular borders. The focus on straight lines, however, and on the regular volumes that can be constructed out of them, is motivated by the need to generalize. Simple figures are the least eccentric, being closest to the averaged form of all actual shapes, which is why (long before it is a matter of mathematical description) they seem simple. What is more, the propensity to privilege straight lines may be reinforced by the observation of light beams which seem to be the purest expression of space, or space least contaminated with that which is other than space. What could put space more directly into italics, make it "utter itself" so to speak, than a column of light? And its seemingly straight path is closest to the averaged total of all curved paths – a mid-route between deviations to the right and deviations to the left. The apparent path of light matches the free or inertial movement of rigid bodies.

This last thought does not dislodge shadows from their central role in the origin of geometry. Shadows are everywhere while the circumstances under which discrete beams of light deliver visible, abstracted shapes are comparatively few. Even so it is reasonable to speculate that light beams, being rare compared with ubiquitous shadows, would have a special impact. Consider a couple of examples, where light is evident as something separate from the illuminated field. One is a beam of light, thickened to visibility by dust or mist. The other is the luminous object – such as a moon. In both these cases, there will be pure geometrical forms – the line in the first instance and a sphere or disc in the second. Other examples – stars and flames – would not generate clear, abstract, forms. If visible light has a role in the transformation of space into geometry, it will have been to reinforce, with striking, magical exemplars, whatever has been delivered by shadows.[9]

The visual field is not just a series of static tableaux. As we move, objects change their relationships to us. I walk towards a tree. First it is ahead of me; then it is beside me; and finally, it is behind me. More importantly, it changes its apparent relationship to other objects in my visual field. My walking sets in relative motion a coordinated ballet of objects altering their apparent relationships to one another. There is a highly complex, though entirely reliable, choreography based on the apparent speed of movement of the objects with respect to me. Nearby objects seem to move backwards relative to my forward movement. Somewhat more distant objects, whose change in angular relation to me is slower than that of nearby objects, apparently move backwards more slowly. Consequently, they seem also to move forwards relative to the nearby objects. I know that these apparent movements – the sliding panels of foreground, middle ground and background – are not real. The trees next to me are not moving backwards; nor are the trees over there moving forwards relative to the nearby trees and to my moving body. The effort of ambulation makes clear which body (mine) is the source of the relative motion. Nevertheless, as I travel, I see the coordinate transformation of the relation between things relative to a moving observer – myself. This exquisite formation dance is a representation of pure spatial relations and underlines a sense of space as something in itself. What is more, it may lie at the root of the idea of covariance, of a pattern of relations or a structure remaining unchanged in the face of change.

We may imagine the *geometry* of movement, and hence of the visual space in which it takes place, being foregrounded when the notion of length – already given a shadow-based existence independent of any material objects (even though it may be a property of an object) – evolved into the notion of distance. Distance (from or between) is length abstracted from all objects, from size, and applicable as much to the interval between objects as to individual objects. Journeys can be thought of as, or reduced to, their distances – such as "a long walk" or "a long way". They are ripe to be represented as pure spatial extensity, their essence being captured by a line separating point of origin and destination. When journeys are pruned to trajectories, stripped of the bespoke experience of any individual undertaking them, a straight line is proposed as the true path between departure and arrival, the beginning and end being designated as points bounding that line, and the distance between those points as the shortest route. The journey becomes the realization of an ideal, abstract route, a line straighter and consequently shorter than any actual journey could be. (No-one can move along a straight line: there is always some wobble.)

So "true" or "physical" or "objective" distance is something purified of any actual terrain that anyone might travel across. In reducing journeys to trajectories which can be amenable to geometrical analysis, we denude "participatory" or "hodological" space of human significance and reduce it to a nexus of lines, planes and volumes.[10]

Geometrical location is entirely without *genius loci*: it, and the space accommodating it, is ripe to be reduced to numbers whose lack of connotation reflects space as pure extensity: space as "an infinite expanse of *featureless emptiness* within which physical bodies are located and move".[11] The passage from spatial figures such as lines and squares and circles to figures defined by numbers enables space to be investigated without the contaminants of particulars – actual material objects with their aura of significance – making of space an homogeneous, boundless whole, uninflected by place or purpose or meaning. Even the most fundamental differences – between the occupation of space by objects and the space that is occupied, and between occupied and unoccupied space – are lost in the reduction of all space, occupied and unoccupied, to pure extensity.

There is neither space nor time to do justice to the extensive, literature that has grown around the contrast between lived, human and dead, geometrical space.[12] The cultural history of our attitudes to space is not, however, central to our present concern, which is to understand at the most abstract level the origin of our sense of space as "something in itself", independent of particular objects and viewpoints, at the same time a kind of nothing, purged of human meaning, and disinfected of *genius loci*; as the abstract unchanging theatre of all that happens, whose essential being is to have, or to be, a pure extensity whose properties are teased out in various geometries.

The emblematic geometer drawing lines in the sand builds on the abstraction of space from objects, and from the viewpoint of the observer of particular objects, that begins with the observation of shadows. The spaces, or aspects of them, that he draws are illustrative of the general structure of space. The figures are not "this line" but "any line" just as shadows that happen to be the shadow of a particular object could be the shadow of any class of objects of the same shape; they are exemplars of generalities, particularly evident when the shadow is untethered from the object. The process of abstraction is taken further when the lines are drawn not, say, in the sand on which we walk, but in a place apart, created out of material (paper) manufactured for that purpose and using an artefact (a pen) and in another material (ink) also manufactured solely for the purpose of inscription.[13]

The notion that space *is* geometry is underlined when we speak (by transferred epithet) of "Non-Euclidean" as opposed to "Euclidean" space, even though the latter may seem closer to lines drawn in the sand. Space, promoted from being emptiness to something that at least has a topology, a structure that geometry discovers rather than constructs or imposes, is at the same time reduced by being conflated with its own mathematical representation. This prepares the way for the idea, now dominant, that the last word on space (and indeed everything in it) is a number – or a pattern of magnitudes.[14]

3.2 FROM PLACE TO DECIMAL PLACE 2: GEOMETRY BECOMES NUMBER

> [In classical physics] the state of each object in the world can be completely specified by assigning values to all the object's quantitative properties (such as its position, its velocity, its mass, etc.).
>
> Halvorson, "The Measure of All Things", 2

I have suggested that the elements of geometry have been presented as gifts of nature, arising out of the spontaneous abstractions that are shadows. These gifts have of course to be received by a prepared mind, a consciousness with the necessary cognitive equipment. The world of chimpanzees is as rich in shadows as that of humans but they have yet to produce their Euclid.[15] The gifts include lines, plane figures, and angles, the latter derived from a universal relationship between objects and their shadows that obtains at a time of the day when the sun is in a particular apparent place in the sky. These "airy nothings" (or, indeed, "airless nothings") – lines, planes, and volumes – given a place of their own, are available to intersect with another mode of perception unique to humans; namely the ability to perceive numbers in themselves – enumeration freed of the enumerated – to which we shall come presently. Numbers are mapped on to lines. Angles are quantified as proportions of complete circles. Lines transformed into numbers multiplied by each other give rise to planes and volumes, also presented as numbers. Numbered lines will ultimately be used to map positions in space, as axes in coordinate systems, so that space and the motion that takes place in it – the fundamental mode of change – can be captured and transformed into unfolding patterns of numbers.

In its simplest form, mapping numbers on to lines (and hence on the generalized space for which they stand) requires defining the beginning of a line as zero and treating the line as being composed of equal stretches corresponding to the intervals between integers: 0 1 2 3 4 5 6 7 8 9 10. The numbers – which do not themselves occupy space, though the symbols used to mark them do – designate locations on, or the parts of, the line. They are the intermediaries between pure quantity and something that is, or looks like, a spatial location, though this appearance is, as we shall see in §3.4.1, deceptive. A limitless quantity of locations can be identified using decimal expansions: 1, 1.1, 1.2, 1.1.1, etc. The generalized interval in or of space designated by the line – already distilled to pure distances in no particular place – is thus further reduced to numbers. We may imagine this as a dialectic process: space, abstracted to representative lines, whose increasing magnitude as the eye journeys from one end to another is captured in a sequence of numbers, is enumerated; and numbers, set out on a line, are "*deline*ated". The passage from one end of the line to the other, transformed into a journey from 0 to 10, is a journey in nowhere, from and to nowhere, that is defined by a mere accumulation of quantity.

And so to the second step, central to the emergence of a modern representation, and hence transformation, of space: making lines into axes. Though some of his ideas and approaches were anticipated by Greek mathematicians, and also by Omar Khayyám (whom rumour has it was also an estimable poet), Descartes' invention of coordinate geometry was an intellectual event of the first importance and a key step in the development of modern science, the modern world, and the modern mind. For our purposes, the essential feature of Cartesian coordinate geometry is the completion of the translation, and reduction, of locations in space to points designated by numbers and intervals in space to numerical intervals. The numbers are read off from axes located arbitrarily in space, standing for "any point in space". A home point or origin of each axis is designated as zero, 0; and, given that three axes are required to specify a unique spatial location, 0, 0, 0 defines the origin of the framework within which all other points are located. The lines or axes, grow out from that point, at right angles to each other, to designate the three coordinates which embrace space – and separate those dimensions which in physical reality are inseparable because they cannot exist alone. Any location can be specified by the three values of the x (length), y (height) and z (depth) axes; for example $x = 2$, $y = 3$, $z = 4$. Any journey – whether the fall of a stone or a pilgrimage to the shrine of a saint – can be described similarly as a transition from one set of coordinate values to another. The start and end of a journey may be represented by two map references (providing the horizontal locations) and contours (providing the vertical ones).

The passage from geometry to numbers was not entirely smooth. There was an early scandal around Pythagoras' theorem. Legend has it that Hippasus, a member of the Pythagorean School who was foolish enough to think for himself, noted a problem in determining the length of the hypotenuse if the opposite and adjacent sides were both 1 unit in size.[17] The square of the hypotenuse, equal to the sum of the square of the opposite plus the square of the adjacent sides, amounted to 2; from which it would follow that the length of the hypotenuse would be the square root of 2, to which no definite number corresponds. The diagonal of any square, being incommensurable with its sides, could not be expressed either by a whole number or a fraction. The fatal (and it must be added hugely fruitful) step that caused this problem was to think of a "length" as being something in itself and yet, at the same time, also a number – something that can be multiplied by itself.

We shall return to what we might call "Hippasus' rot" in §3.4.2. For the present, we note that the problem reveals a deep ambiguity in the notion of a line and whether it is or is not equal to, or identical with, a number. If the line were both a pure length and an item in the real world, multiplying it by itself would seem as senseless as, and even more challenging than, multiplying a cat by itself. The ambivalent status of the lines that make up the sides of geometrical figures such as a triangle – are they things in the world or (as Plato and Galileo suggested) the eternal, extra-worldly essence of certain things in the world? – is highlighted by the vexed relationship between a line and "its" length when it is stated (and of course in one important sense correctly) that multiplying a line (strictly a line segment as lines are infinite) or its length by itself will form a literal square that will enclose two-dimensional space. That square is both numerical and quasi-spatial, so that the square of a *number x* is the number of units of area (say square centimetres) in an envisaged square whose sides are x (say centimetres). Such a square encompasses x^2 square centimetres.

The problematic nature of operations such as "squaring" becomes manifest as soon as it is appreciated that the power of a number can be raised indefinitely – even beyond cubing (x^3) – and so beyond the point at which the mathematics is still connected with intuitive geometry. From the purely mathematical point of view, there is no reason why the series should stop at cubing. But number and geometry – insofar as the latter connects with space, or at least the space we occupy and walk through – part company when we talk about fourth, fifth and higher powers. This is numbers doing their own thing. Nevertheless, they still seem to be taking space with them; moving it ever further, we might say, away from "my place" and "your place", living and liveable space, to decimal place.[18]

The relationship between space and the arithmetical presentation of space becomes more deeply questionable as the arithmetic develops. Consider how a line can be continued backwards from zero into the territory of negative numbers:

$$\longleftarrow \qquad\qquad\qquad \longrightarrow$$
$$-5 \ -4 \ -3 \ -2 \ -1 \ 0 \ 1 \ 2 \ 3 \ 4 \ 5$$

Though negative numbers were resisted by European mathematicians until the seventeenth century (they did not include them among the "natural" numbers), except as expressions of debts, they make excellent arithmetical sense and prove to be a mighty potent tool. They do not, however, make any kind of spatial, or indeed material, sense.[19]

We may map trajectories reduced to lines into minus territory if, for example, we subtract one trajectory from another smaller than it. In real life we cannot literally subtract real distances from others smaller than them, any more than we can travel a negative distance. Of course we can make negative progress to a goal, as when we go backwards. The identification of the destination as a number turns the wobble in the journey, as when I go back to collect something I have forgotten, into a minus journey. But in reality nipping back for something left behind is no less a positive journey – though more irritating – than the original journey from which I have had to dismount. Two steps backwards are not minus steps, to which two other steps would have to be added to get zero steps.

The problem with negative numbers is not of course confined to the algebraicised geometry of space. When I owe you money, say £10, and have none of my own I may be said to have minus £10 and this corresponds to the fact that you could give me £10 by forgiving my debt and I would still have no (net) assets. But minus £10 cannot correspond to something that exists, just as there is no such thing as "minus 10 sheep" even though, when I have zero sheep, I may still owe you ten sheep. My minus 10 sheep, however, do not amount, say, to an anti-flock that would annihilate any flock they came in contact with. They relate to a debt I incurred in the past, when I borrowed 10 sheep off you, and managed to lose them. In short, the negative number reflects a relationship between past and present. It is intimately connected with the temporal depth of human life and experience – which is not to be confused with the physicist's four-dimensional space–time. The minus 10 sheep would disappear when I died and my debts were cancelled. No negative sheep would have to be slaughtered or positive ones resurrected to bring about this miracle.[20]

The disconnection between numbers and "real" space is easily seen if we draw a line, like the one above, in which leftwards movements count as decrease and rightwards movements as increase. If we pass leftwards through zero we shall reach the domain of negative numbers but not, it scarcely needs saying, of negative space. What gives a location a negative (or come to that a positive) value is assigning the value "0" to some other point in space and arranging the integers along a direction of movement. This permits us to specify a point in space as "−1, −2, −6" (corresponding to the values it has in a given coordinate scheme); but the location itself is not negative. The contrast between positive and negative locations in coordinate space does not correspond to anything in real space, since any given point in space – say the location of my body – can be assigned positive or negative values, depending on the coordinate framework in which we enclose it. We have to lay down an "origin" specified by "0, 0, 0", and stipulate conventions governing which directions will count as positive and which will count as negative, in order to generate the appearance of negative locations. It is an *appearance*; the reality is that the negation is purely mathematical.

So the relationship between geometry and real space, insofar as it is mediated through numbers, is conceptually fraught. I could elaborate at length but I want to focus on one number because of its intrinsic importance and because it is geometry that supplies what little intuitive sense the number possesses. I am referring to the square root of −1, otherwise known as i. If it is difficult to imagine a journey of −1 miles, it is even more difficult to imagine the square root of −1 being a measure of distance or of anything to do with space. As Barry Mazur has put it, "If we think of square roots in the geometric manner ... to ask for the square root of a negative quantity is like asking 'What is the length of the side of a square whose area is *less than zero*?'"[21] which seems like listening to the sound of minus one hand clapping. When Leibniz described i as "that amphibian between being and not being", he was perhaps being rather generous.[22] After all, while we might (just) imagine a negative journey – not as something that is anti-travelled but as a travelling backwards, away from our goal – imagining a square with negative sides must be beyond us.

There is a way of imaging (if not fully imagining) this imaginary number i. Consider the numbers on the line below:

$$-5 \ -4 \ -3 \ -2 \ -1 \ 0 \ 1 \ 2 \ 3 \ 4 \ 5$$

We can envisage rotating the right hand (positive) half of the line in the plane of the page through 180°, round a hinge at zero, so that it lands on the left hand (negative) half of the line. We may think of this rotation of the line by 180° as being equivalent to multiplying the values on the right by −1, as a result of which 1 becomes −1, and

2 becomes −2, and so on. Mathematicians then argue that rotation of the line by half this amount − namely 90° − is effectively the equivalent of multiplying by the square root of −1. How do they arrive at this conclusion? As follows. If the operation of rotating the line through 90° were carried out twice, the result would be rotation through 180° − the outcome of the first operation we considered, namely rotating by −1. Rotating through 90° twice would therefore be the equivalent of multiplying by −1, that is to say, by the square root of −1 multiplied by itself. So rotating by 90° would be equivalent of multiplying by the square root of −1. Consequently, while this imaginary number − identified like other complex numbers that involve i with points on a line (or with points on a Euclidean plane) − it can be seen to make geometrical sense, which underpins its numerical sense.

Or does it? Only if you allow geometry, the mathematical account of space, finally to bid farewell to the space in which we live, move and have our being; and in which things fall, rise, and are transported from one place to another. The journey to this final divorce has many stages, as we have seen, but the most important is to identify space with abstract entities such as lines that do not occupy space (they have only one dimension). However, mathematicians allow them to retain sufficient of their space-like qualities to be able to undergo operations such as "rotation" and do so through quantities like 90° − the kind of angle we normally associate with homely relationships such as that between the wall of a house and the ground it stands on. But the idea that "rotation" can be expanded to encompass something analogous to multiplication − when numbers are set out on, or count as points in, a line − lifts this fundamental spatial transaction out of the kind of space in which we stand, walk and dance. In short, if taken literally, this extended sense traduces it.

What is not at issue is whether i corresponds to anything in the physical world; whether it is part of physical reality. That would be a tricky question to address for at least two reasons. Firstly, answering it would require us to determine the extent to which *any* number (as opposed to written down symbols) is part of physical reality − a matter that could be approached only after much clarification. (We shall attempt to do this in §3.6.) Secondly, the notion of "physical reality" has over the last century become extraordinarily complex − and the term has become very hospitable indeed. At the quantum level, items such as probability amplitudes are regarded by many as "real". And the extent to which physical reality has determinate characteristics in the absence of measurement remains, 90 or more years after Heisenberg's uncertainty principle, an unanswered − perhaps unanswerable, perhaps meaningless − question. What *is* at issue is that, once space and motion fall into the domain of mathematics, they are stripped of much that they mean to us in everyday life.

This is self-evident in the case of a purely mathematical operator such as the square root of −1 whose meaning does not connect with anything we might encounter in the realm of daily experience. More importantly for our present argument, is that this divorce from the space in which we live and move applies just as much to fairly straightforward "mathematizations" − such as the identification of spatial locations with points in a coordinate space or complex numbers with points in the Euclidean plane or in the analogy between the geometric problem of cutting an arc of a circle into n equal parts and taking the nth root of a polynomial – as it does to those that involve seemingly unintelligible concepts as the square root of a negative number.

In brief, it seems that when space becomes numbers, it loses its spatial character. This is not only because numbers can be manipulated in non-spatial ways – to generate items such as i and so on – but because they can be applied to items (such as "pain intensities" and "economic trends") to which the notion of extensity does not apply. Just how little numbers apply to space as we inhabit it, is reflected in the fact – regretted by no less an authority than the mathematical physicist and astronomer Sir James Jeans – that "time is mathematically attached to space by so 'weird' a function as the square root of minus one".[23] At any rate, the minus sign is the most prominent difference in the relativistic metric between temporal and spatial coordinates.

None of this seems to deter physicists from assuming that space (or space–time) is mathematical through and through, reflected in a tendency we have already noted to refer to space as "Euclidean" or "non-Euclidean". This may be shorthand but it reveals an essentialist attitude to the ways we choose to represent space, not quite as naïve as describing the Sahara as "six-lettered" but likewise important for importing our ways of thinking into that which we think about. Those of us who want to resist this may take comfort in the current battle between algebra and geometry for dominance in the physical description of the world. The failure to arrive at a "theory of everything" that unites quantum mechanics (whose most complete expression is in the language of matrix algebra) and general relativity (whose soul is geometric) may have more to do with this internal conflict between mathematical expressions of reality than the fundamental reality of things. Certainly, the attempt to resolve it through string theory has been mathematical through and through with little or no contact currently being made with physical reality and none in prospect. (We shall return to this in §3.6).

It is worth dwelling on the fact that the trouble with connecting numbers and space arises at quite a basic level. Consider any given number – say "1". There is an ambivalence in the very idea of it. Is it the unextended mid-point between its neighbours – 0 and 2, or 0.9 and 1.1, or 0.99 and 1.01? Or is it an extended numerical stretch occupying the entire interval between 0 and 1? In the case of real numbers mapped on to lines, it is the former. In the case of units – as in "1 inch" it is the latter. Where it is the former, "1" and other numbers correspond to extensionless points, so that (extended) lines cannot be built up out of numbers. In short, numbers can generate extensity only if they are attached to something else, to give them extensity.

So much for the problems of translating space into numbers. Our concern with the mathematization of space is primarily because it lies at the root of the mathematization of (quasi-spatial) time. This is part of a ubiquitous trend towards mathematization of the phenomenal world, or the mathematical displacement of the phenomenal world, or the reduction of quality to pure quantity, via the use of spatial metaphors. It begins with the intuition that motion (in space) is the primordial mode of change; that change is not only appropriately recorded by means of displacement on a scale of numbers set out in space, but that is what the change essentially is. The reduction of changes to movements in space that generate pure quantities, numbers, is problematical when the changes in question relate to phenomena that are irreducibly qualitative.

Let us return to an example we have already touched on: colour. It is possible, of course, to track changes in colour in terms of movements along a frequency spectrum whose values are set out in space with, for example, short-wave violet colours on the left and long-wave red colours on the right. The change from violet to red can be seen as a "red shift" from left to right. This spatialization can be taken further by regarding each discernible colour as a value of a variable that is set out on a colourless line. If other "dimensions" of colour are taken into account, for example intensity, hue and saturation, any particular colour can be located at a point in a (colourless) colour space defined by a number of axes (say 4) corresponding to each of the "dimensions" along which colours can vary. These points, thus captured in coordinate space, can be expressed by numbers corresponding to the values of these variables.

This not only divorces the idea of space from space as it is lived and perceived but also from space as originally understood by the founders of the scientific revolution who inaugurated the process of reducing time, space, and motion to numbers. So-called secondary qualities (*vide infra*) are reinserted in "space" from which they have been exiled. Consider this famous passage from Galileo in which he identifies that which belongs to the material world, to nature itself:

> I feel myself impelled by necessity, as soon as I conceive of a piece of matter or corporeal substance, of conceiving that in its own nature it is bounded and figured in such and such a figure, that in relation to others it is large or small, that it is in this or that place, in this or that time, that it is in motion or remains at rest, that it touches or does not touch another body, that it is single, few, or many; in short, by no imagination can a body be separated from such conditions; but that it must be white or red, bitter or sweet, sounding or mute, of a pleasant or unpleasant odour, I do not perceive my mind forced to acknowledge it necessarily accompanied by such conditions; so that if the senses were not the escorts, perhaps the reason or imagination of itself would never have arrived at them.[24]

This is the rationale for the critical distinction between primary qualities – shape, size, location, and motion which cannot be imagined away without imagining away matter itself – and secondary qualities – such as colour, taste, and so on.[25] The former belong to the material universe, are amenable to mathematical treatment, and alone have ultimate reality. Increasingly, whatever could not be captured mathematically was in danger of being regarded as ontologically dubious, as an illusion. As the philosopher of science E. A. Burtt says, "In the course of translating this distinction of primary and secondary into terms suited to the new mathematical interpretation of nature, *we have the first stage in the reading of man quite out of the real and primary realm*."[26] Burtt was prescient, writing this before the advent of intellectual fashions such as neuromania in which consciousness itself was reduced to abstract patterns of nerve impulses located in different kinds of spaces by a physico-mathematical gaze. Items such as "the self", "agency" and even "qualia", which, because they eluded this gaze, were accused of being non-existent – albeit by thinkers who were selves that presumably felt that they were freely deciding this on the basis of phenomenal experience.[27]

This was almost certainly not Galileo's intention. However, the spread of the idea that "the book of nature" was "written in the language of mathematics" into areas beyond the science of motion paralleled the rise of mechanical science and opened the way to the assimilation of the sciences of heat, colour, optics and electromagnetism, and the associated unification of the foundations of natural philosophy into, fewer, ever more general, abstract and quantitative, laws. There was a progressive conflation of primary qualities, that which can be measured (indeed that are fundamentally quantitative) with nature herself (or the truth about her underlying reality). Nature, as "a system of magnitudes" was in danger of losing all appearances since numbers alone have no appearances. (Or those they do have are not part of their quantitative essence. The symbol "1" may be in black but there is nothing black – or indeed blue – about "1").

The phenomenal experiences of colour, of warmth, of taste and so on are demoted to ontologically suspect add-ons that can be made respectable only by incorporation into a particular corner of the material world – namely the brain – and being identified with physical events in said brain. The mind–brain identity theory, which identifies "subjective" experiences with measurable activity in the brain, promises to bring them within the realm of quantitative science and hence rescue them from the taint of unreality. This rescue operation identifies conscious experiences with firing patterns in the brain and the latter as realizations of the values of variables in multi-dimensional spaces corresponding to, for example, the spectral frequency, the hue, saturation, etc. of colours. Thus translated, Galileo's secondary qualities can be readmitted to "the real and primary realm". And if the scientist is willing to recognize his consciousness as material events, he, too could be redeemed as an object worthy of a place in the scientific world picture.

The intellectual price of this is (as we shall discuss in the next section) to remove any kind of intelligible basis for the phenomenal appearance of the material world. The ultimate consequence of the mathematization of appearance as a set of firing patterns instantiating locations in spaces standing for variables is the disappearance (or dismissal of the reality of) of appearance.[28]

Thus the consequences of mathematizing space and extending the notion of mathematized spaces to encompass the contents of conscious experience. The latter is allowed to be real only insofar as it is traduced as the numerical values of quantitative variables. In reality, the gap between the experienced world and what post-Galilean science counts as pukka reality widens. It is expressed in the distance between what is measured and what is experienced. Space shrivels to lines from which planes and volumes may be constructed and this reduction presents it as bare quantities, mere numbers. Quasi-spatialized time follows suit, joining the other three as the fourth member of the quartet of axes of four-dimensional space–time, which describe motion, and aspirationally all events, as ultimately made up of patterns of motion on a microscopic scale. Time is the quantity (little) "t" taking its place alongside the dimension x, y and z that are length, breadth and depth. They lack any of the characteristics we associate with the space (or time) we inhabit: "x" as a number is neither long nor short, "y" is neither thick nor thin, and "z" neither high nor low, deep or shallow. Just as space is pruned to mere extensities represented by leafless lines and abstract locations that are collections of points defined by numbers, time is likewise impoverished: it is neither future nor past, neither agonizingly drawn out nor poignantly brief. Journeys are stripped to naked trajectories defined by measurements linking locations that are defined as sets of numerical values against immediate reference frameworks marked by axes. "Here" and "now" become numbers that are nowhere and nowhen. Nothing in them corresponds to experience or indeed content: they are pure, that is to say mathematical, form.

It is time, now, to examine this mathematized world of space – and time – and space–time. And for this we need to go a long way back: to elementary counting and basic measurement.

3.3 X, Y, Z, T: SPACE AND TIME STRIPPED BARE

> [Descartes'] system married algebra and geometry to give every geometrical shape a new symbolic representation with zero, the unmoving heart of the co-ordinate system, at its centre.
>
> Webb, *Nothing*, 32

The collective cognitive journey from the appreciation of items as "large" or "small" or "near" or "far" to measuring their size and distance in units involves at least two very large conceptual leaps: from seeing to counting; and from counting to measuring.

Though counting is rooted in the body, it represents a striking separation of embodied subjects from themselves.[29] The primordial digits are the fingers of our hands. They signify a multiplicity of items which, though they are quite different, "count" as the same. From the standpoint of counting, items as different as the little finger and the thumb are each "one". The forefinger also has another role in quantification, pointing in succession to the items to be counted – transferring the imposed equality of the fingers to the outside world. The entities that are picked out – sheep, or sheep and goats, people, tools – are each registered as "one". The differences between sheep, or between sheep and goats, or between one person and another, or between a hammer and a nail, are temporarily erased, as they are reduced to instances of a chosen category. The separation between that which is numbered and the act of enumeration is prefigured in the process of "picking out". The item that is picked out is not picked up: it is not touched but pointed to. In the space between the fingertip and the object that is counted arises the gap between carnal and arithmetical digits.

The reduction of parts of the body, such as the fingers of the hand, to "one such-and-such" is taken further when they are used in measurement. Measurement differs from direct counting in three connected ways:

(a) That which "counts" as 1 does not bring its own borders, as does (say) one sheep. There has to be a definition.

(b) Within the borders of a naturally delimited item the count may exceed one (one sheep may be several cubits long and one cut of meat may be 6.5 pounds).

(c) That which is counted is an *aspect* of the item, such as its height, and not the item itself – as when a horse is measured to be 15 hands (high).

To use a part of one's body to measure the size of something involves suppression of the specific character of both the object being measured and the bodily part being used – it is "any" foot being deployed merely to be an abstract aspect of itself – to make the measurement. It is difficult to appreciate just how extraordinary this is; how far it is from our basic relationship to our body – or from any relationship any other animal has to its own body.

Supposing I am measuring the height of a wall using my forearm and arrive at the figure "10 cubits". If you want to challenge that, you do not measure it using your forearm because forearms differ in size. Instead you watch me repeating the measurement. In so doing, I set aside the privileged relationship of my body to the world. In the end we all set aside this privilege and manufacture a measuring rod whose length represents that of the average, or anyone's, that is to say no-one's cubit. The standard cubit – just as much as the standard metre in its temple in Paris – assumes a distance from one's own bodily being, and, more narrowly, one's own viewpoint.

Out of the suppression of the features of both the measuring device and of the item being measured arises a number. We can put this another way: a measurement which describes (say) a wall as 6 cubits makes the magnitude of the wall a *ratio* in which the features of the wall and the features of the forearm are cancelled out as each is reduced to a pure quantity and the relationship between them to a number. The wall is a proto-numerator divided by an elbow that is a proto-denominator. Newton himself put it thus: "By *Number* we understand not so much a multitude of unities, as the abstracted ratio of any Quantity, to another Quantity of the same kind, which we take for unity".[30]

A key characteristic of scientific quantification of nature is the marginalization (and indeed progressive removal) of the phenomenal appearance of the (measuring) body and, equally, of the (measured) world. It does not matter what my counting finger or measuring arm looks or feels like. As for the item that is being measured, all characteristics other than that of pure magnitude are set aside. This is necessary in order that body part and measured item may meet in something they have in common – extensity. To say of a wall or a tree that it is two cubits high is not to say that a forearm is like half the wall or half the tree or that the wall or the tree is like two forearms. Each exemplifies an abstraction that can be applied to both of them. Let us look at this "de-phenomenalisation", or exsanguination, of the phenomenal world in a bit more detail.

Consider a table. It has a rich variety of visible, tactile and other phenomenal appearances; it has a location and spatial relations to other objects. It is something that we relate to in a wide variety of ways: we deem it as beautiful or ugly or handy or inconvenient, as superfluous or appropriately filling a room, as belonging to me or to someone else. And so on. All of these relations are viewpoint-dependent – some literally so (the angle of vision) and some metaphorically so (the interest we have in the table). We may disagree over them. Some disagreements can be resolved by resorting to measurement; others cannot. Measurement would not demonstrate that you are right to think that the table is ugly, convenient, or handy when I disagree with you on all three counts. But it can resolve some disputes. You may think it is larger than another table but of the same shape while I think it smaller and of a different shape. Its size and shape can be recorded and compared with the size and shape of the other table. But those aspects that are not amenable to measurement – ugliness or beauty – are seen as irrelevant or at least secondary to physical science. The marginalization of experience, however, goes much further than this.

Let us think how the table would be presented to the quantitative gaze. Its size is a set of dimensions – say 2 feet by 3 feet. Its shape can be captured by a set of angles (e.g. the 90° angle between its sides). This being "90° at all four corners" does not look like the phenomenal appearance of "square" though, of course, it corresponds to it. Its weight, tensile strength, density and so on are all reduced to numbers which do not capture anything of what it feels like to lift it, to sit on it, or to grip it. (This is the obverse of the fact that we can accept as valid, even meaningful, quantities, such as the speed of light, the distance across the galaxy, the population of the world, that correspond to something we could not possibly experience.) In pursuit of the objective – that is to say quantitative – truth of the dining table, we shed even basic aspects of subjective experience. When I look at the table, I look at it from a certain angle and from a certain distance and it may or may not be fully or partly visible. From the side, its top may look diamond-shaped, while from above it may look square. The measurement factors out this source of variation: the table is 2 feet by 2 feet with right angled-corners and that's the end of it. This captures its squareness, independent of any appearance, square or otherwise, it might have.

And that, of course, is the point of measurement: it seems to grasp what the table is in itself and not how it appears to you which may differ from how it appears to me. It puts an end to quarrels – or at least moves them on. For it is not entirely true that the table is *in itself* 2 feet by 2 feet. Relativity tells us that the measured size of the table will depend upon the relative velocities of the frames of reference in which it and the observer are located and there are no privileged frames of reference to which the table-in-itself is revealed. But measurement brings us closer to the quantitative aspect of the table – by stripping it of its phenomenal appearance and marginalizing the individual experiences of those who encounter it.

This is only the first step in the journey of quantification towards an evermore abstract and general presentation of what is there. We move from individual objects and events, to classes of objects and patterns of change and of stability in the world captured in mathematical relations; to the laws of the natural or material world that apply equally to ships, and shoes, and sealing wax, and cabbages and kings. Abstraction continues to the point where the eye that looks round the world is replaced by a summarizing gaze made of purely mathematical relations between variables, as in $E = mc^2$. This colourless, odourless, weightless, equation whose instantiations are seen from no angle or distance, is a gaze on a world exsanguinated of phenomenal appearance.

We may describe this, using Heidegger's term, as the "de-experience" (*Entleben*) of experience.[31] As in the case of the beginning of the explicit sense of time, the path to de-experience, is particularly associated with vision, though of course the visual field is rich in experiences. There is a literal distance between ourselves and that which we see; while "seeing may be believing" something more is required fully to experience something. Vision does not give us the weight, the resistance, of the object, its obdurate reality which requires effort to overcome. This is the other side of the positive fact that vision "rises above" that which is perceived. Any given visual field far exceeds the eye that sees it, unlike, say, a touched surface, where at any given moment, my finger can palpate a surface equal to its palpating tip and my hand grasp only a handful. In many cases the cognitive content of sight is vast compared with the quantity of sensation. It is a wider, more complex, but thinner sense. We could put this another way: vision is an *uncoupled* sense. The least immersed of the senses, it makes contact at a distance: it is a light-mediated interaction with what is there – and is half-way to the chill of knowledge (mediated by signs standing for general classes or abstractions) that is disconnected from us – as we scan around and jump from looking at this and at that. We rise above, and are at a distance from, that which we see. We also see *that* it is at a distance from us, that it is other than us. It is as seers that we are most clearly embodied subjects *offset* from a world of objects. The object of the gaze does not directly impinge on us and, in most cases, what we see does not concern us, though it may provide a background that renders what concerns us intelligible. When we look, we also (in more than one sense) *over*look.

By contrast, we are touched by what we touch, and are invaded by what we smell and taste. And that which we hear, though it may be heard as being "over there", is not given to us separately from our experience of it. Of course, we may say that we hear a bird or a car but the object is an explicit inference not revealed directly by the sound. Indeed, the sound is separate from the object – radiating out from it – while the sight of it is not. We can hear an object without knowing where it is but we cannot see an object without seeing where it is.

Sight is the most fundamental form of explicitness, of "thatness", the primordial form of the revelation of our surroundings as "thatter".[32] Because, as lookers, we are not immersed in that which we see, we are able to see *that* we see what we see from a particular viewpoint and, what is more, to see the possibility of other viewpoints – a possibility rendered visible in the visible gaze of others and underlined by gestures such as pointing that express what is visible to those other viewpoints. In short, vision which reveals its own viewpoint *as* a viewpoint, the viewpoint of one who sees himself and sees *that* he sees, opens the way to an idea of a shared or objective way of seeing.

This distancing from our own experience is taken further by measurement, which addressed equally to all viewpoints, that is to say, to no individual viewpoint and is

– or aspires to be – from no viewpoint at all. The object is reduced to its "objective" characteristics, those which it has, or seems to have, "in itself". An accurate measurement will generate the same result whoever is doing the measuring. If I say the table is 2 feet by 3 feet and you say it is 1 feet by 3 feet we cannot both be right, though we might both be wrong, assuming we are not travelling at relative speeds close to the speed of light.

The partially de-experienced object revealed to the gaze is completely de-experienced in measurement. Even though the act of measuring is necessarily an experience, the resulting measurement is not a report on an experience the way that describing what you see is. This is particularly obvious when the measurement is written down as a number. It does not matter where the measurement is recorded, the size, the colour or the font of the characters, whether they are inscribed on stone, parchment or computer screen – they are still "the same measurement". The phenomenal appearance of the actual measurement, in short, is irrelevant. This is highlighted when measurement is automated by an unconscious recording device (though the need for consciousness is not dispensed with, only postponed – as we shall discuss in §3.5.3.2 on the Twin Paradox).

That this transition from direct experience of a phenomenal reality to a "dephenomenalised" world of quantities has been of immense benefit is not in question. If anything has distanced us from the relative helplessness before nature that is the condition of all other living beings, it is our ability to measure – and hence to predict and control – our surroundings. My concern, here, however, is with the suggestion – implicit in the passage from Galileo quoted earlier – that only objective measurement captures things "in themselves", and only that which is susceptible to objective measurement (essentially primary qualities) is "real". The subjective viewpoint which corresponds to a directly experienced world is then regarded as flawed, or at least merely preliminary or cognitively inferior, and that which it reveals is seen to be of dubious ontological standing. The world of smells, colours, tastes, feels, warmth and chill, not to speak of pain and pleasure, joy and sorrow, love and hate, fades along with the experiencing subject for whom these things are important. Natural science, which advances by setting aside what is seen to be subject-centred, will offer a subjectless account of space and time: "here" and "there", "close by" or "a long way off" – not to speak of "now" and "then" – are lost. Geometry is space viewed from nowhere – or from (what amounts to the same thing) everywhere. It is what is conserved through all changes in the observer and all changes of observer; indeed, through all changes.[33] The geometrization of mechanics in the general theory of relativity is the final outcome of Einstein's quest to arrive at an account of the world in which the laws of nature were invariant irrespective of the frame of reference of the observer.

It is hardly surprising, therefore, that when time and space are reduced to measured, objective quantities, they lose their distinctive characteristics. We have already seen how it would be inevitable, when time joined the spatial dimensions as one of a gang whose numbers are now expanded to four, the problem is not just that it would become space-like (through its joining a group in which spatial dimensions outnumber it 3 to 1) but that time and space would both lose their distinctive characteristics.

They are each merely values of a variable marking locations and distances in what sooner or later would be called "space–time".

The consequences of this for time are obvious: the experience of duration, of intervals, of succession, of when, in what order and how long, are gathered up into the thin dimension t, in which all of these qualities are mere quantities of units, essentially numbers. The difference between an hour of utter grief and two hours of ecstasy is the difference between 3,600 and 7,200 seconds. The important point is that all seconds are the same.

The reduction of time to quantity of time is not entirely new. Aristotle, after all, defined time as "The number of change with respect to before and after".[34] What is new is the degree to which time as the parameter or dimension "t" has penetrated our time consciousness. Once time is made into a quantity, it can undergo the transformations that we saw space submit to, entering the domain of mathematical operations. It can be a numerator or a denominator. This is clearly demonstrated in the concept of velocity: space divided by time. Time can be squared. It can be substituted for by other variables; or other variables can be substituted for by it. For example, as we noted, the latest definition of the fundamental unit of length the metre is the length of the path travelled by light during a time interval of $1/299792458$ of a second. Time as "t" becomes a timeless number as in $v = d/t$ (velocity = distance divided by time). There are things you can do to "t", time as pure quantity, that real stretches of time such as afternoons would not permit. Anyone who tried to multiply a bargain break weekend by itself would have their work cut out.

This precision of quantification is, of course, hugely effective in enabling us to manipulate the world; and not only at the level of high science but also in everyday life. We synchronize our watches and say "See you in 2 hours' time" and those 2 hours are pure quantities, defined not by any experiences either of us may have in-between our planning to meet and our meeting.[35] The mistake is to think that quantities of time are time itself; or that time is a pure quantity; or that our ways of measuring time are the last word on time. More generally, to believe that the mathematical account of the world is the world in which we live; the true "in-itself" of what is out there. (To this we shall return in §3.6).

We have grown so use to populating our world with numbers that we hardly notice how strange this is and how it separates the actualities before us from themselves. We have been accustomed, for example (as quoted in the epigraph to this section), to Descartes' system, which "married algebra and geometry to give every geometrical shape a new symbolic representation with zero, the unmoving heart of the coordinate system, at its heart".[36] Zero at the heart of space! And yet zero has had a relatively short existence in human consciousness. It is a consequence of another relative innovation:

> [The seventh-century Indian astronomer] Brahmagupta was the first person we see treating numbers as pure abstract quantities separate from any physical or geometrical reality ... As soon as numbers became abstract entities ... a whole world of new possibilities is opened up – the world of negative numbers.[37]

The Galilean–Newtonian revolution reduced the changing world to a realm of primary qualities, of magnitudes, of numbers. And yet the world seems to elude the grasp of mathematics, even when we exclude phenomenal experience. I want to remain with space to examine this further.

3.4 SPACE: BEYOND THE REACH OF NUMBERS

To examine the failure of mathematics to grasp what we might call real or actual space, I will begin by focusing on two concepts associated with the reduction of space to pure quantity via geometrization: the point; and the line (or the idea of length).

Let us begin with points.

3.4.1 On spatial (and temporal) points

The notion of the point lies at the root of the mathematization of space via geometry and consequently at the heart of "dephenomenalized"[38] mathematical conception of the world. Mathematically, space and time are made up of dimensionless (and hence featureless) points. It is via the concept of the point that mathematics advances from being a description of the magnitudes, and patterns of magnitudes, of nature to its very fabric or substance. Indeed, as Jeremy Butterfield and Chris Isham claim, "space–time points" of zero size are not only "genuine objects", they "are the basic objects of physical theory".[39] The Minkowskian world is a four-dimensional manifold, whose elements are world-points; and space and time are forms of arrangement of world-points. In quantum field theory, the basic elements are points of zero size.[40] This has not gone uncontested – and there is clearly more to real spaces than a set of numbers – but it is a tribute to the continuing importance of the notion of "the point", which was evident in early mathematics, though it was of the spatial rather than the spatio-temporal variety.

It is there, after all, at the beginning of Euclid's *Elements*: "A *point* is that which has no part". Points are indivisible because there is nothing to divide: they are entirely without extension; they lack volume, surface area or even length. *They do not occupy any space.* This is equally true of a line (which is length without breadth or depth) and also of a plane, which has breadth and length and seems to enclose space but does not fill any because it has no depth. But the lack of real estate is most clearly true of a point, which is zero-dimensional.

This provokes the naïve inquirer (what all philosophers should be – at least knowingly) to ask a question: If a point does not occupy space, how can it be located in space?[41] How can a spatial nothing (defined entirely negatively – "having no parts", "dimensionless") designate one bit of space rather than another bit of space? And come to that, how can we claim that one point in space is such and such a distance from another point in space – a distance traced by the length of a segment of a line?

Surely something can have a location in space only if it *occupies* some of it. If it is not extended, what confers upon it a location in space, even less enables it to *be* a location in space, or *be* a bit of space? You and I are next to each other in virtue of occupying adjacent volumes of space. If an ordinary object had to provide the space it occupied, space occupancy would be a rather challenging business. Points seem to have several jobs at once: to be a location in space, to occupy a location in space, and to be *at* a location in space.

You might not see this as a real question if you conflate the mathematical (or geometrical) points we are talking about with the material means we use to represent them, such as dots and blobs of ink. Real objects such as ink marks are not dimensionless. They *do* occupy space, otherwise we couldn't see them. Being designated by such a mark is the most obvious way in which a point borrows space from something else to lay claim to a location in space. (Lines, and planes, of course, do the same thing; they, too, are squatters but points are the most bare-faced parasites.)

The space-occupying *mark* has a spatial location but it is self-evidently not a Euclidean geometrical point because it *does* have parts; it is extended. We can cut a dot in half, by cutting through the paper bearing it. So the biro mark is not itself an unextended point but an extended (visible) sign of an unextended point. This is evident from the fact that we can use a variety of methods to specify a point: alphabetical label ("point P"); an alphanumeric label ("point P_1"), or a purely mathematical label ("2, 3, 7"). And, unlike mathematical points, their markers have qualities – such as being coloured.

Every method of representing points is in a sense a misrepresentation, designating what should be a concept without any ownership of space as if it were a percept evidently located somewhere or other. This is illustrated by the fact that we often represent points by *circular* dots that are equal in all directions. This shape seems to be true to an entity that is equally null in all directions![42] Any perceptible feature of a point is a contaminant, leading one to conclude that only when a point reaches vanishing point is it truly itself. When we visualize or represent a point, we traduce it because its zero radius puts it below any visual acuity.

There is another, deeper mode of spatial parasitism that enables geometrical points to seem to inhabit locations in the world (and consequently to be located at one place – "at one point" as we loosely put it) without taking up any space: the use of mathematical coordinates both to designate and locate points. Points exist only insofar as they are coordinatized. We can specify a point in space by characterizing it with respect to three axes, corresponding to the three dimensions of space, which will uniquely define a position. So I can refer to a point as being *at* "$x = 2$, $y = 3$, and $z = 4$", where x, y and z are three axes that capture the range of values for up–down, side–side and back–front. By this means, it seems possible to designate a point in space without using anything that occupies space. Axes assign numbers to points. Numbers with their exactitude (a kind of tautological exactitude – "1" is exactly "1": it does not spill outside of itself) can specify a point in space without occupying a point in space.[43] End of problem.

Not so fast. We need to look a bit more closely at the intermediary by which the Euclidean point is plugged into real space, attached to a specific place: the coordinate system, whose three axes, taken together, establish a frame of reference, and define the position of the extensionless point by means of numbers. Does this frame of reference mark off a volume of space in which points can be situated? Surely, you might say, it is located in space – real space this time – and is consequently able to guide extensionless points to a location in real space.

Not so. Typically, the axes are located on a page, where they form the elements of a diagram. The space they enclose is not the space where the page, or I who am writing on it, is located. "$x = 2, y = 3, z = 4$" in a diagram in a book I am reading in Stockport station, is not itself a spot in Stockport station, even though the page on which it sits is in my hand at Stockport station. The geometric point is not in Stockport in the way that Stockport station is in Stockport or the way that my book is in Stockport station or in my hand. Consequently, the point on the page isn't a point in real space, the kind of space you can walk through and dance in and bodily occupy. My finger pointing to a point in that space does not belong to that space. The point is mathematical and is located in the abstract thought-space of mathematics. If the axes seem to allow the point to occupy a location in real space, it is because the coordinate framework to specify a virtual viewpoint, planting or upholding such positions, is realized in lines drawn in real space. But the space of the page is not the space of the axes. This is evident when the axes are used to illustrate something general, for example the parabolic trajectory taken by any missile.

The parasitic nature of points, borrowing their location from a coordinated space anchored to a stipulated 0, 0, 0 origin, is no less the case when the axes are invisible, as for example in the coordinate space used by General Positioning System. The reference upholding the coordinate space is based on signals sent out by satellites and harvested by the device.

For the coordinates to be the basis of a real viewpoint revealing a real corner of actual space – such as the one in which I am now sitting – they would have to be related to another coordinate framework. This would give new coordinate values to the 0, 0, 0 of the first framework. Unfortunately, this in turn would have to be located in a third framework. The looming infinite regress is self-evident, as is the fact that coordinate systems are necessary to reconcile the notion of a point (which has no extension) with that of something that can mark an actual location. The coordinate framework connects – or seems to connect – the virtual, general space of points identified by numbers with actual spaces we can live in, walk through, etc.

This then is the illusion: a numerical "address" is a virtual or fake address and does not designate a location, even less a habitation. This is true not only in the obvious sense that the number isn't where its tokens are but in a deeper sense which warrants examination. Numbers are ordered one-dimensionally, but three dimensions are required to define a point in space. There is nothing in numbers *per se* corresponding to the right angles that differentiate the three dimensions of space. This presents a problem given that, according to Reichenbach, while there is no limit to the number of dimensions a space may possess, there is "a physical law that objects capable of physical existence must have as many dimensions as the surrounding space".[44] And numbers themselves do not have an intrinsic order other than the linear one of increasing magnitude that connects cardinality with ordinality.

This failure to get physical reality out of pure magnitude lies at the heart of the difficulty of finding the directionality of time ("earlier" versus "later") in a mathematically portrayed world. But there is also a problem in space: while specifying locations requires three numbers, intervals and extensity require only one number, though the number that captures the latter is contaminated by units (inches, etc.). This dual and different use of numbers – as joint definers of a spatial location and as single definers of an interval in space – should raise the spectre of conceptual incoherence.

More directly relevant to our present concerns is the fact that what is required to bring the regress of coordinate frames of reference to an end is the point of view of a conscious being who stipulates what shall count as 0, 0, 0. This is more important than may at first be apparent. It connects with the observations we shall make on "The Erasure of the Observer" (§3.5.3), and the irruption of viewpoint as the basis of freedom in an apparently causally closed world (§11.3.1 and Chapter 12). For the present, we note that there is *no particular place* in mathematics. Coordinates no more designate actual places on their own than do points. There are (to reprise and rephrase an earlier argument) no (real) places in diagrams or mathematized reality. Geometrical space, based on points, is space without place. It has no real "at": this would be outside of mathematics. This is not, of course, an oversight. It is, however, an insuperable limitation.[45]

The parasitism of points – from which we may conclude that there is no difference between their presence and their absence, that they have no "in-themselves" – has two aspects. The first is their dependence on higher dimensions: they borrow existence from segments of lines which they delimit (which in turn borrow existence from two-dimensional surfaces, themselves parasitic on volumes). The need to have dimensions "on account" as it were results from the fact that, though dimensionless, they are supposed to be the building blocks of dimensioned spaces. Unfortunately, you can't build up a line out of points or a surface out of lines, or a volume out of surfaces.[46] As for the distance between two points, this would be a distance between two nothings. Points can generate distances only if they hitch a ride on an object or marker at either end of the interval. The second aspect of the parasitism of points is the need for material stuff that tethers geometrical entities to locations and to actuality. And the third is the *viewpoint* that allocates points to an extra-punctate framework – which we shall discuss in §3.5.3. For the present, we note that the idea of a "point" seems to encompass that which is pointed out and that which points it out: the point is required to be self-pointing, self-locating.

From this we may conclude that Euclidean (and indeed non-Euclidean) space, founded on points, is not the space of real places. This cuts deeper than the truism that a diagram is not the situation it depicts or the map is not the terrain. The concept of a mathematical point lies at the origin of the progressively widening divorce between space experienced as place, as a nexus of meanings, walkable and habitable, and space as empty extensity, as pure quantity; the fundamental rift between the space of mathematics and the space that surrounds us.

The gap is concealed because we use space-occupying signs such as biro marks to represent points or to capture them in values generated in association with a frame of reference whose necessary further supports are hidden from us. The frame of reference, except insofar as it is being used for abstract mathematical demonstrations, has to be established non-mathematically, as when I use my lived surroundings, as opposed to mere lines, to establish a frame of reference. $x = 2$, $y = 3$, and $z = 4$ does not generate a point in real space unless I have located the axes in a place defined non-mathematically, with myself or someplace I have chosen as the point of origin, at the heart of "egocentric" space. Without an audit trail leading back to egocentric space, mathematical space is not really space at all. (In making this point, I think I am at one with Ernst Mach – of whom more in §3.4.3.)

The mathematical account of what is there seems to be stand-alone and self-sufficient only because the individuals or the communities that generate and apply the axes – enabling them to get a grip on the real world and to have a concrete reference to real places – are off-stage. There is in reality no frame of reference without reference outside the activity of framing; something (more precisely some*one*) has to plant 0, 0, 0 in space otherwise empty of coordinates.

The habit of inscribing mathematics on space itself, of making the most general modes of extension a hive of mathematical symbols, may lie at the root of the long-standing controversy as to whether space is punctate or continuous. The notion that it is composed of zero-dimensional points seems to provide a happy resolution: punctate space is continuous because the points in question are infinitely small and without boundaries: we don't have to get from one point to another because there is neither space within nor space between points. Between any two points, there will always be another point because, points being infinitely slim in all directions, can always squeeze into any imaginable gap between points. Unfortunately, this imposes on points two conflicting duties: to mark locations in space with infinite precision, for which purpose they have to be unextended; and to occupy or to be the distance between these (separate) locations, in which case they have to add up to extension. With such directly contradictory demands placed on them, it is surprising that points don't suffer a nervous breakdown. Instead, they have left that to mathematicians.[47]

The general message, applicable equally to space, time, and space–time, is that we should be aware of the extent to which the scientific account of these fundamental features of the world is driven by what works mathematically. This is expressed lucidly by W. H. Newton-Smith in relation to points in time:

> [O]ur belief in the continuity of time does not relate to any argument relating to infinite divisibility, it arises from our projecting on to the world the richness that is present in the mathematical system [of real numbers as opposed to mere integers] which we have found to date to be essential to the construction of viable physical theories.[48]

The notion of continuous time, whose "points" are entirely extensionless, maps on to physical theories which rely on the real number system which allows limitless interpolation of numbers between neighbouring numbers. If the best theory relied on integers, then time would be mapped as consisting of discrete, finite intervals.

A. N. Prior's assertion that "instants" or discrete points of time are "artificial" is blunter.[49] This seems just, given that "instants" and "moments" presuppose temporal location without duration. We shall return to this in §10.3.2. At any rate, the problem with points in space is replicated with points in time. There is a contradictory endeavour to alight "at" an instant without a "during an instant"; to get a location in, without occupancy of, time.

We could attack the notion of spatial points by means of the kind of logical argument beloved of scholastics. Spatial points are, by definition, smaller than any existing thing. Nothing that really exists can be smaller than all existing things. Therefore, points do not exist. (This supports the argument that we have already made: the existence of points is borrowed, parasitical.) Arriving at such a conclusion spares us having to address rather difficult questions. There is another scholastic anxiety (that will become evident when we address Zeno). If space were composed of unextended points, stretches of space would not be possible and, if they were possible, it would be difficult to see how there could be any difference between different stretches of space, since all stretches would be built on the same (unachievable) infinity of points. Moreover, in order to comprise lines, points would have to be aligned. This would demand of them not only location but, as it were, an orientation, and the capacity to pool their distinct nothings to something more than themselves. If, additionally, spatial points were real (even physical) entities, we would be entitled to ask the question: "Do adjacent points exist simultaneously?"; after all, it would be possible for points to be side by side only if they were coexistent. However, we might equally ask whether they come into and go out of being and whether they have a duration.[50]

That these questions are manifestly absurd underlines how points are essentially mathematical, so that the question of simultaneity of existence, of occurrence and of duration, does not arise – just as it does not arise with numbers. "2" does not exist simultaneously with (or, contrariwise, as a temporal successor to) "3" and this is equally true of points "$x = 2, y = 3, z = 6$" and "$x = 2, y = 3, z = 7$" or "$x = 28, y = 19, z = 4$" which do not come into being or last a certain period of time. (Indeed, they are for those of a Platonist persuasion eternal.) The absurdity of the questions is not mitigated if we substitute the more respectable space–time points for spatial points and instants of time. They still have somehow to coexist (both simultaneously and successively and side-by-side) in order to constitute the spatio-temporal manifold and yet the notions of space–time points occupying a particular location in space and coming into, and going out of, being at a particular point in time are unintelligible.

Once we accept that (spatial and temporal) points are purely mathematical entities – so that for example the points in Euclidean space corresponding to complex numbers, are not in real (walkable) space – we can set aside other challenges, such as trying to explain the mystery of how extended spatial intervals could be constituted out of extensionless points or how the decomposition of extended spatial intervals could generate non-extended points after a finite series of operations. The non-extendedness of the point then merely corresponds to the fact that a *number* has no extension. Numbers are exactly themselves. This is true, irrespective of whether it is an integer such as "1" or a figure such as "1.233333".[51]

There is a problem not only with points but also with lines – and with those one-dimensional, extended entities that are supposed to exist in the material or lived world: lengths. These will be our next port of call. For the present, we note that the notion of the spatial point is a key instrument in the purification of places in the world to spaces that are pure magnitudes and in the reduction of space to an array of numbers.[52]

3.4.2 On lines and lengths

> Line itself does *not* exist in the observable world.
>   Petherbridge, *The Primacy of Drawing*, 90

Intuitively, by a "line" I mean an open line in space that does not self-intersect and does not close back on itself as a circle does. We conceive of geometrical spaces primarily by means of such lines.[53]

The dimensions of a space (or object) correspond to the minimal number of coordinates needed to specify each point within it. A line has a single dimension because only one coordinate is needed to specify a point on it. Although they are an advance on zero-dimensional points, lines (strictly line segments) are no less elusive than points. Their relationship of priority to points is contested: either points are the progeny of lines, being the intersections of lines (or the mode of contact between a tangent and a curve); or lines are generated by sets of aligned points or the shortest distances between locations defined by two points.[54] In either case, it is evident that lines, too, are mathematical constructions. Even so, they do seem to have more of a toehold on reality than points.[55] Real objects, we are told, have lengths, breadths and depths. Lengths (and breadths and depths) are segments of lines that seem to belong to tangible objects. All, however, is not as it appears.

Like points, lines ultimately correspond to a number, though when it is a question of (the) length (of an object), the number is attached to a unit. Asked what the length of an object is, we shall respond with a number of units: it is 6 (inches) or ½ (a foot). It may seem as if the numbers not only touch the object in question, as when a ruler is applied to it, but are actually inherent in it as a property: that the object has, even instantiates, a length – and that that length is a number.

On closer inspection, lengths prove more elusive. The relationship between mathematical lines and material lengths is somewhat complex: the straight and the curved lines that figure in the theorems that describe Euclidean space are pure straightness or curvedness while no measured length in the real world is purely straight or curved. Although the edge of a material object may be represented by a line, the edge is not itself a line. The edge may be defined with increasing precision and fidelity to its idiosyncrasies, its wiggles, but it will never conform exactly to a line. To bring this into focus, let us look at a famous paper: "How long is the coast of Britain?" by Benoit Mandelbrot.[56]

Mandelbrot noted that the measured length of a coastline depends on the scale of measurement. If you measure the length using a yardstick, you would get a shorter result than if you measured it with a one foot ruler. This is because the coast has irregularities and the larger the measuring device and the unit of measurement, the more the edge is ironed out. A yet more precise measure, using a micrometer, would give a higher value still, because it would follow an even wrigglier route, being more faithful to the ins and outs of pebbles, their rough surfaces, and the ups and downs between grains of sand. The measured length would increase to infinity as the measurement scale approaches zero. This observation can be generalized to any real material object – such as the length of a table or the circumference of a cricket ball. If the ultimate goal of precision were a mathematical point-by-point correspondence between the measured item and the measuring device, then all lengths would be infinite.[57]

This throws the very notion of the length of a material (that is to say an actual) object into question. No actual object can have a boundary that conforms exactly to a line: it cannot be smooth enough to be contained within a single dimension. Most objects are obviously irregular at a level visible to the naked eye. This is overlooked when we are concerned only with the good-enough measurement appropriate to our practical needs; then we think of the measured length as an intrinsic property of the object being measured. We say (for example) "The table is 2 metres long". Even when we qualify this, by saying "This table is roughly 2 metres long", there is still an ambiguity. The table itself does not have a "rough" length as an intrinsic property. The roughness is relational: it lies in the relationship between the measuring tool and that which is being measured. If an object has an intrinsic length, it must be "exact". Rather, it is beyond exact: it must be precisely the length it has. The measured length, understood as a measured line, is not a property inherent in it: it is a relationship. When we measure the length of a rectangular table, we are determining the (shortest) distance between the two points that *we choose* to mark its beginning and end. This line may pass through or over material locations on the rough surface of the table. And the measurement ignores the fact that what we may legitimately choose as the boundary of the table may be ill-defined, given that (for example) when the table is illuminated there is a penumbra of electrons ejected by the light in the immediate vicinity between the table surface and the surrounding space. The fact that the wiggles the "plumb" line skips over or under are minute does not close the conceptual gap between lines and the lengths of actual objects.

In making a measurement, we apply one real, rough-edged object (with visible or microscopic bumps) – say a ruler – to another – say a table. In order for the length we ascribe to it to be intrinsic to the table, it and the ruler that measures it, would have to conform to a geometrical ideal – or at least to have precisely matching outlines. No actual objects can conform to each other in this way. This is highlighted when we purport to represent a length in a material sign, such as a pencil line on a sheet of paper. Pencil lines have width, depth and microscopic local wobbles. Though these may cancel out (or not accumulate to a net deviation), and they are straight in their signifying intention, they are not in fact straight. If we usually overlook this it is because the measurement we extract from the application of the ruler to an object is a ratio of two virtual lines extracted from two things (the ruler and the object) whose roughness cancels out so that the edge of each counts as a straight line. We could put this another way by saying that the gap between measurement and reality is suppressed by the fact that the roughness of the edge of the ruler cancels out the roughness of the edge of the object; there is, as it were, roughness on the numerator and the denominator.

The critique of the notion of spatial lengths – understood as lines corresponding to a geometric dimension as real items – needs to go deeper. We should note, for example, that the figures on the numerator and the denominator are not part either of the object or of the measuring device. Only in the context of measurement does the table have a length of "two feet" and the standard ruler have a length of (say) one foot. To emphasize this point, we may remind ourselves that the line whose length is measured connects two points that mark its beginning and its end; and points, as we have seen, exist only mathematically. In sum, the arithmetical-geometric length of the object does not correspond to a perceptible edge that bounds it. In short (to go back to the original example), a coast does not have a length, though a coast*line* does. But a coast does not have a determinate coastline. Coastlines are not located between the land and the sea but on sheets of paper.

These observations apply with just as much force if we replace Euclidean with any of the non-Euclidean geometries that are on offer. The shortest path between two points may be a straight line (Euclidean) or a curved one (non-Euclidean) but no actual trajectory or edge of a material object will conform precisely to a straight or curved line. Nothing that occupies space and is subject to wobble – in other words any material object – can stick to a mathematically describable line.

Length as a traceable line identical with a border of an object exists therefore only as an asymptotic, mathematical ideal. Any measured length will be the result of a choice depending on the precision with which the border of the object is adhered to. Such precision can be extended indefinitely but will never reach the ideal exactitude portrayed in the geometrical conception of a line. Even if the level of precision has been settled on, we shall still have to make decisions that, from the point of view of the object, are arbitrary. Should the line standing for the length of the object pass to the left or to the right of a particular grain? Which aspect of the grain – its inner or outer border – counts as the border of the object?

This indeterminacy is compounded because measurement goes beyond simply tracing the boundary and quantifying it: it is also unitized. There is no unit of measure so small that it will be faithful even to the observed lengths of object: just as the traced border is an approximation to the imagined "real" border of the object, so the, necessarily unitized, measurement is only an approximation to the traced border. Borders will not correspond to whole numbers of units, or of tenths of units, or of hundredths of units. No units – notwithstanding that they are defined mathematically to an absolute precision ("1" remains more than 0.999 … and less than 1.000..,1 however many nines and zeroes there are before the run is broken) – will map on to the rough edges of the world.

The fact that mathematical exactitude can be approached but never reached should not prompt the conclusion that something such as length really does exist as an intrinsic property of material objects, beyond measurement. Length does not belong to the object in the sense that it is "out there" waiting to be picked up and discovered. Nor should we conclude that what is at issue is merely a question of measurements based on the notion of lines representing length, depth, thickness failing "to capture the essence of irregular shapes".[58] We should draw a more radical conclusion; namely, that "length" (in part) and the line that describes it (wholly) are mathematical constructions that connect with the material world but are not inherent in it. *All* real shapes are irregular, in the literal sense of not conforming to any (ideal) rule(r). While Lee Smolin is correct to say that "a straight line is an idea"[59] – and hence not an item in the world – we need to be more radical in our thinking and acknowledge that *all* lines (straight, curved or wobbly) are ideas and that length, if envisaged as the defining property of a line, is an idea within an idea. The notion of (say) the true length as the shortest distance between its limiting points imports too much geometry into the space we actually inhabit (in our case) and occupy (in the case of our living bodies and other objects).

We should therefore look critically at the elements with which Euclid populates his *Elements* and subsequent geometers construct their notions of space. While Euclid (like his non-Euclidean successors) is concerned with the direct measurement of the magnitudes of real objects (and, later, real trajectories), or rather with their indirect measurement on the basis of calculations that use observations and general principles, geometries are nevertheless of an absolutely general and hence ideal nature. The lines, planes and volumes that they deal with are idealizations: no triangular object has three absolutely straight line borders meeting at angles that total precisely 180°.

The space of geometrical theorems, propositions, and definitions, is therefore devoid of material objects. It is empty space; and yet it has – or is supposed to have – a definite structure. The very fact that items such as length, right angles, straightness or curvature, can exist in the absence of any object confirms the correctness of our more radical conclusion – that objects do not intrinsically have length, area or volume, etc., as constitutive characteristics. Realizing this should stop us from falling into the trap of thinking that the length of an object is something out there that we approach by successive approximations.[60] Length, breadth, area, volume, curvature are crystallizations of lines into empty space which objects may be seen (roughly) to instantiate when they enter space. This is not to deny, of course, that one object is longer than another, or that a third object is more curved than the other two; only that what is being compared are not entities that somehow manage to combine being mathematical ideals with being pieces of material reality. Appreciating this is essential to grasping the relationship between mathematics and reality, which we shall examine in §3.6.

This is an appropriate juncture to return to Hippasus' rot, because the disease is more widespread than is generally appreciated. Hippasus, it will be recalled, pointed out that if a triangle had sides each of 1 unit, then it would follow from Pythagoras' theorem that the hypotenuse would be the square root of two. This is an irrational number – recently calculated to 200 billion decimal places with no end in sight. This problem does not apply solely to a subset of right-angled triangles that happen to have vertical and horizontal sides of a particular size. Any straight line – whatever its length – is capable of being joined by another of equal size at right angles to it. Each of these could be regarded as a single unit, being equivalent to one of themselves – if you like we could call the line "One Raymond" in length – and thus capable of being joined at their tips by a hypotenuse. The length of the latter would then also be an irrational number of Raymonds. In other words, Hippasus' rot is not just a little local difficulty. It potentially spreads through the entire world of geometry – hence the (legendary) alarm and outrage of the Pythagorean faithful. Any real line could be seen as an hypotenuse slung between two equal right-angled lines which could be described as consisting of 1 unit and thus as having an irrational number for a length.

Hippasus' rot highlights the gap between lines – any lines – and the physical world, and the even greater gap between them and the world we live in. So long as lines are purely mathematical entities, quantities void of qualities, they cannot be items in the real world and should not be confused with, for example, edges of objects or distances between locations, or journeys. Real objects have measured lengths but those lengths, like the lines corresponding to them, do not exist as independent entities in the world; indeed, they are ratios, between a standard length and the length of the measuring rod. Ratios, like denominators, do not populate real space. The legend that Hippasus was exiled or murdered for leaking his discovery may be ill-founded but the punishment would have been proportional to the significance of his action because it undermined the claim that the stuff of the world was numbers.

3.4.3 Concluding thoughts

To think of space as "Euclidean" or "non-Euclidean" and the objects we live among as intrinsically having geometrical properties such as length or area or volume is to mistake the mathematical shadows of things for their substance. To say this is to adopt a more radical position than that which merely denies that mathematics is the final, privileged or sole truth about the world. I am claiming that mathematics does not reach the intrinsic nature of things, something that will be explored further in §3.6. Points and their self-specified positions, lines and their lengths, etc. do not correspond to anything real.

Of course, there is more to the quantities that feed into the mathematical world picture than numbers: 6 inches or 5 grams for example are numbers *of* units of length and of weight respectively. Even at the most basic level, therefore, the mathematical picture of the world is composed of impure quantities: it is quantities *of stuff* and stuff is more than quantities. However, as the mathematization of nature proceeds, the picture that is generated moves further from natural items to units and thence to laws governing the relationships between unitized entities.[61]

Mathematization advances from counting naturally occurring items (5 sheep) to counting units of abstracted items (500 kilograms of meat); from describing individual movements in unitized terms (5 metres per second) to capturing the relationship between, say, abstracted forces, the masses of objects, and resultant acceleration ($F = ma$); and, finally, to bringing together these mathematically described principles or patterns of movement into laws that encompass heterogeneous kinds of entity, such as electromagnetic energy and mass, resulting in purely mathematized accounts of the world, for example, $E = mc^2$ where even the most fundamentally different items (energy in the broadest sense and mass in the broadest sense) sink their differences and become translatable one into the other. So while basic parameters in physics such as weight and density are quantifiable – and indeed expressed in quantities – they are not purely mathematical concepts; but as they become subsumed into higher order variables connected in evermore general laws, they lose the last toehold in qualitative content and are increasingly dissolved into the space of mathematics. We leave the space (and time) we know and enter a different kind of space and time defined mathematically.

And this de-differentiation is evident even at the most elementary level. We might think that there could be no more basic spatial difference than between an angle and a line; and yet the mathematics of i invites us to treat rotation through 90° as an *arithmetical* operation involving imaginary numbers. The reduction of space to numbers – notwithstanding that contemporary physics also makes it an active player in the universe – empties it of specific properties: even of the fact that it is extended; that it has three dimensions; and that it is different from time. The geometrization of space and the subsequent algebraic reduction of geometry reduces it to numbers.

To generalize from the example of space: measurement does not generate an undistorted mirror made of that which it measures. The progression from experience based on perception to measurement is an abstraction from the object that is being measured; and the generalization of measurements is a withdrawal from any actual situations in which we might find ourselves. While, for reasons we shall discuss in §3.6, this may enable us to act more effectively in the real world, we must not conclude from this that the "de-phenomenalised" entities that populate the mathematical world are the real deal. That measurement does *not* get the measure of all things is true even of something as seemingly featureless as the background space in which we live, move and have our being. Which brings us to an interesting irony in the history of ideas.

Ernst Mach, whose philosophy of science initially inspired Einstein's journey to the geometrization of space and time and, indeed, of the material world, emphasized that space was not reducible to the space of the physicist. Physiological space – bounded, finite, and non-uniform and constructed by our cognitive structures – was more fundamental than the pure extendedness, infinite, unbounded and homogeneous, of physics.[62] This hierarchical ordering was in part connected with Mach's belief that science was and should be rooted in our experiences.[63] Any entities proposed in science should be directly or indirectly supported by our experiences. In short, the idea of reality without the possibility of experience was without meaning. Unfortunately, this part of the Machian inheritance influenced philosophy perhaps even more than it did physics though the philosophical movement most influenced by it – logical positivism – was totally in thrall to physics.

3.5 SOME CONSEQUENCES OF MATHEMATICAL LITERALISM

It would be foolish to deny the descriptive, explanatory, predictive and operational effectiveness of the mathematical account of the material world or dismiss the deep, and extraordinarily wide, truth of its ways of making sense of things, which must somehow account for this effectiveness – its enhancement of our capacity to make predictions and, through this, to manipulate the world. At every moment in our lives, we are guided, protected, served, illuminated, entertained, and borne up by the ideas, methods, techniques, and technologies based on mathematical physics and the other natural sciences that are so indebted to it. In science, predictions based on quantitative data and a long series of calculations are again and again fulfilled in reality. It is a mistake, however, to conclude from this that numbers, or the numerically reduced versions of the material world, and of space and time, are the whole, final truth about the reality in which we pass our lives, or mark the path to such truth. This is, to use a metaphor which may seem more than a little appropriate in view of the earlier discussion, to mistake the shadow for the substance.

The most spectacular expression of mathematical literalism is the present front-running account of the origin of the universe, explaining how it was able to arise from Nothing without the assistance of God.[64] There are fundamental problems with this account of the Creation – and we shall discuss them in §10.3.4. Here, however, I want to focus on more humble examples of problems arising out of confusing mathematical models of certain very general patterns of physical events with the world itself. This will take us to the time and place– Ancient Greece – where our present troubles began.

3.5.1 Zeno's paradoxes of motion: confusing mathematical and walkable space

> Diogenes the Cynic, unable to answer [Zeno's arguments against the reality of motion], got up and walked away, deeming a proof by action more potent than any logical confutation.
>
> Aristotle, relayed by Simplicius[65]

Zeno put forward his paradoxes of motion in order to support his teacher Parmenides' claim that motion (and indeed all change) is logically impossible and hence illusory. As an illustration of the consequences of mathematical literalism, it would be difficult to improve on the Dichotomy Paradox.

I am running for a bus. The kind-hearted driver has signalled that he will wait until I arrive. According to Zeno, his kindness will be ill-rewarded. In order to complete the distance between myself and the bus, I have first to cover half the distance; in order to cover half the distance, I have to cover half of half, or a quarter, of the distance; in order to cover this … Well, everyone can see where things are going: ad infinitum. Since the process of halving (or dichotomizing) can continue forever, it would appear that I would have to complete an infinite number of tasks in order to close the gap between myself and the bus. Given that it seems impossible to complete an infinite number of tasks in a life of finite duration, I will never reach the bus.

Something has obviously gone wrong. After all, I usually catch buses that wait for me. Zeno's argument, however, would not even allow me to start chasing the bus. To complete the first step on the way to the bus, I would have to complete half a step, and a quarter of a step, and an eighth of a step and so on. It's worse than that: not only I am stuck *at* the starting point; I couldn't get *to* the starting block in the first place unless I was there already. This would still be impossible even if I were born in the very place where I started chasing for the bus, since my mother would somehow have had to get to that spot in order to give birth to me, unless she, too, came into being at that point; and the same would apply to her parents; and so on. A journey *to* a starting point, necessary for the journey to start somewhere, therefore, is seemingly as paradoxical as the journey *from* the starting point. And the driver, by the way is in the same boat. He could not get to the bus stop to await me with thinning patience. In short, not only would the journey be impossible to complete: it could not be set up as a task to be completed. If no-one can get from A to B, nobody can get *to* A or B either. (And in the case of the race between Achilles and the Tortoise, they could not meet to compete against one another.)

All of which is compatible with the Parmenidean world picture, according to which there are no happenings in a universe. Happenings would include token events such as Zeno's putting forward his argument, getting from its beginning to its end. Zeno, it appears, has proved that he cannot execute proofs. This pragmatic self-refutation extends to the speech acts of which the argument is composed. Finishing a sentence, even speaking a single word, can be divided into an infinite numbers of steps.

A common ploy for dealing with the paradox is to suggest that Zeno made a *mathematical* error. He fails to notice that, as the distances to be covered are divided into smaller portions, the time taken to cover them also falls proportionately. As a consequence, although the number of portions of time into which my race for the bus can be divided is infinite, they belong to converging series that adds up to a finite quantity. Let us suppose that I intend that my dash for the bus will take 10 seconds, then half the journey will take 5 seconds, a quarter of the journey takes 2.5 seconds, an eighth takes 1.25 seconds, and so on. As this series extends, it gradually converges on 10 seconds, even though the number of steps is infinite.

This mathematical solution does not deliver what is required. As Peter Cave says, "To converge is not to reach".[66] We could put this differently: not only does mathematical convergence not result in arrival; it does not count as journeying at all. Mathematical convergence to a mathematical limit is not spatial convergence on a particular location in space, such as that occupied by my bus. Zeno got us into difficulties by making real movement a matter of mathematics so that walking a particular distance seems like the *mathematical* problem of completing an infinite, though convergent series. We can escape from Zeno by refusing to think of locomotion as an act that involves, or even consists of, passing through mathematical stages.

We should be alerted to the invalidity of mathematizing my dash for the bus by the fact that Zeno's take on travelling would yield the same (infinite) number of mathematical steps irrespective of whether the journey were 10 yards, 100 yards or a million light years. Zeno's argument collapses the distinction between large and small distances – and hence loses the very idea of "distance": the gaps between my index finger and my thumb on the one hand and that between my index finger and a distant star on the other both have an infinite number of divisible components, of non-extended points. Not only could I not get closer to the bus if it involved accomplishing an infinite number of steps, the notion of "getting closer to the bus" would have no meaning because all distances would have the same number of mathematical components: every location would be an infinite number of steps from every other location. Spatial division infinitely continued leads to individual spatial points and there is the same number of points in the line signifying any distance between two points – namely an infinite number.

In short, mathematics loses its grasp on real extension and, given our earlier observation in §3.4.1 that points are not located in space, it has also lost its grip on location. One could even say that the mathematization of distance in this way has emptied it of actual spatial content, of space that can be inhabited, traversed, or lived in. The root cause of our problems is the failure to appreciate that when I walk, I walk through *lived* not mathematical space, *taking steps not fractions* such as ½, ¼, etc.

Zeno's dichotomy paradox applies to *times* as well as to distances. To hold your breath for a second you would have to hold it for a half-second, quarter of a second, an eighth of a second, etc. It might be argued that *seconds* – unlike distances crossed – do not have to be *accomplished*: they happen of their own accord and a second will come to an end in a second. The mathematics of the *action* of holding one's breath, however, is like that of journeying: it can be dichotomized without end. And the mathematics applies to events other than actions. It would apply just as much to mere happenings such as the fall of stones. Or to other changes, such as the alteration of the colour of an object from red to green. The trajectory, presented as a quasi-mathematical, quasi-spatial distance to be crossed, would be composed of an infinite number of intermediate places or states, discovered through the perfectly legitimate mathematical operation of division. Zeno would be happy with this, of course, because his paradoxes were intended to demonstrate the illusoriness not only of all motion, but of all change.

It will be evident by now that it is a mistake to look to more, or more advanced, or better, mathematics to solve a problem that has arisen as a result of mathematization of the material or lived world. Zeno's fundamental error is not due to bad or primitive mathematics but to a false belief that the space through which we chase buses, or the world in which stones fall, is a mathematical entity so that the mathematical description of motion, or indeed of anything else, trumps the experienced or lived reality of it; that the failure to match a mathematical description of a piece of the world as we usually conceive it proves that we conceive it, indeed *experience* it, incorrectly.

The error of conflating a mathematical series with real space is highlighted by considering the difference between mathematical steps and walking steps. Taking an infinite number of footsteps would be difficult enough but would be even more difficult taking each of these steps separately. The nimble-footedness required to keep within the bounds of one step at a time would be beyond my capability long before I got to divide the journey into an infinite number of discrete steps. I could not run (literally) into the mathematical difficulty Zeno envisages because I cannot help walking in strides rather than in indivisible fractions. As Cave puts it, "Divisibility differs from constitution and composition,"[67] Zeno is guilty of "mistakenly transforming abstract fractions generated endlessly by mathematical rules into physical divisions that must be traversed when physically traversing".[68] This is why attempts to resolve the paradoxes mathematically are misguided. Mathematics is the problem not the solution.

The inescapable end-point of mathematical division is the spatial, or spatio-temporal, point, of which there would be an infinite number. Even if I were able to visit each of these points, I would not make any progress. Passing through a point is no passage at all since, by definition, there is no interval between the entrance to and the exit from it. Since the points are not extended, ticking off an infinity of them would not add up to a finite distance crossed: an infinity of extensionless points does not add up to any extension at all, particularly since no gap is permitted between points. If an actual infinity of points did add up to a distance, that distance would be as likely to be 10^{43} centimetres as 10^{-43} centimetres. The fact that they do not add up to any particular distance, reveals that they do not add up to any distance whatsoever.[69]

But there is another way of expressing this argument that bears more directly on the relationship between mathematical space and the inhabited space of our lives and actions. The infinite series that converges to "1" does not converge to "1 *actual journey*" (or any number of whole journeys). The "1" which is the end-point of convergence is "1-anything". We have to import something from without in order to make "1" into a completed journey; into, say, "1 bus chase". We could add, for example, a unit of actual distance, such as "yards of pavement". Then the steps would no longer be purely mathematical steps but real steps or stages. My dash to the bus would be divided into 50 yards of pavement + 25 yards of pavement + 12.5 yards of pavement, etc. until we get down to tenths and millionths of yards of pavements at which stage issues of nimble-footedness would come in.

It is incorrect to think of processes, especially voluntary actions, taking place over intervals and in steps shorter than their intrinsic divisibility. And we can then see that the problem of the impossibly many steps of Zeno's paradox presupposes that they can actually be taken (separately and successively) despite being impossibly small. As Cave says of another paradox – Achilles and the tortoise – "In some races, the smallest distance … Achilles could run in his hobnailed boots may be one yard …". The mathematical impossibility of an infinite number of infinitely small steps is headed off by their physical impossibility. The mathematics of converging series could not capture the difference between walkable and unwalkable fractions of a journey. There is nothing in the maths to reflect the cut-off between steps that are large enough to be taken separately and those that are too small to be taken separately. Nor, indeed, does the maths identify those that are too *big* to be taken as a single action; for example, the first mile of a ten-mile race.

In short, to fall foul of Zeno's paradox in real life would require impossible things of us. Covering a journey one millionth of a yard at a time would need fancy footwork well beyond the limits of our ambulatory acuity.[70] And it is no good Zeno arguing that one footstep is made up of an infinite number of fractions of a footstep because beyond a certain number of divisions, it is impossible to perform the dividends separately. Peter Cave again: "What is and what is not possible with regard to abstract mathematical series do not carry over to what is and what is not possible in the world of wood, runs and restings".[71] So we could not get into the mess Zeno envisages: "That an infinite series can be summed does not mean that it can be walked through."[72] Or that it needs to be walked through for a task to be completed. The mathematics is a latecomer, applicable only to walking *after the fact*.

What Zeno reveals is not that mathematics proves the impossibility of the movements that we perform through a finite space in a finite time but that mathematics does not capture such movements. More broadly, the mathematical description of space is not the story of lived space and our journeys through it. We cannot walk in mathematical space (or space–time). Nor can we hurry or dawdle. Which is no restriction, because our walking and other activity – and indeed other changes in the world – do not take place in mathematical space. In the actual world, we walk in strides not in mathematical fractions which, of themselves, are not fractions of anything. The walker is a living being, not a mathematical point making a mathematical journey along a one-dimensional line from one mathematical point to another. Mathematics crash diets my position at any given moment during any journey to an unextended point at the notional centre of the place I occupy; in fact, however, I am extended. I am inescapably located at more than one mathematical place at once. Indeed I am at an infinite number of mathematical point locations. Neither I, nor Achilles, nor a falling pebble is a single mathematical point on the move. The very fact that we exist means that we are not zero-dimensional points moving along one-dimensional lines, though the mathematics that distils the journey (as a line) from our journeys may persuade us that we have to think thus.

The other side of this truth is that numbers – like mathematical points as we discussed in §3.4.1 – do not of themselves specify real locations or real distances. They seem to do so only by borrowing locations from outside of the mathematical scheme of things, by means of axes that have an implied frame of reference, that is an implied viewpoint, installed by individuals with definite viewpoints. (Something we shall return to in §3.5.3). Without such an extra-mathematical implicit reference to a world in which mathematicians walk, pebbles fall, and colours fade, the numbers do not count as locations or distances. And changes of locations would not count as movements. Under such circumstances, no object would have a definite location and the difference between movement in space and keeping still would be lost. This is what, of course, happens when we mathematize the entire world: the result is the unchanging space–time continuum – a conceptual totality of all that has taken place somehow added up, though observed from no viewpoint.

It will seem obvious that that cognitive parvenu mathematics – appearing on the scene billions of years after animate and inanimate objects were set in motion

– cannot retrospectively prove that the restless universe is in fact frozen. Instead, we must conclude, more plausibly, that Zeno's paradoxes merely demonstrate the limitations of mathematics; or, rather, reveal what elude mathematics, namely actual events. Every change seen through the mathematical lens Zeno applied to motion is the same as every other change – consisting of halves plus quarters plus eighths, etc., or thirds plus ninths plus twenty-sevenths. They all share the same mathematical structure and the same impossibility, if only because there is no change within mathematics. My running for a bus, Achilles chasing after a tortoise, Zeno explaining his paradoxes, the sun setting and shadows lengthening, or a stone falling towards the earth, are equally caught up in the Parmenidean paralysis. If we were to accept the consequences of the paradox, the very conditions under which the paradox can arise, and be stated, would also be ruled out. Zeno has talked himself out of existence: neither he nor his paradoxes (nor his interlocutors) could have *come into* being.

This applies to another of his paradoxes: Achilles and the tortoise – which may be seen as analogous to my trying to catch a bus, with a slightly less kindly driver, so that it is very slowly drawing away from the stop. Achilles challenges a tortoise to a race but decides to give him a head start of 100 yards. Off they go and Achilles, leaving position A_1, attempts to reduce the distance between A_1 and the tortoise's starting position T_1. Every reduction in the distance appears to require him to traverse an infinite number of fractions of that distance. However, the tortoise, too, is susceptible to the same mathematical paralysis; this therefore factors out and it's game on again. After all, while they both have to traverse the same number of mathematical distances, whatever distance Achilles has to cross, the tortoise will cross it more slowly. It is this difference that the race in real, as opposed to mathematical, space will pick up.

There is, however, a twist in the tale: by the time Achilles has reached T_1, the Tortoise will have moved to T_2. Achilles has more work to do. Unfortunately, while Achilles is running from T_1 to T_2, the tortoise will be busy moving to T_3. The creature will, it seems, remain permanently just out of reach: its position will be an asymptote towards which Achilles approximates ever more closely but never reaches. Again, this would apply only if "catching up with the tortoise" were a mathematical rather than a physical operation. In the world of space reduced to numbers, "faster than" and "slower than" lose their difference. In the real world of runners and riders, however, as Achilles gets closer to the tortoise, he will have increasing difficulty avoiding treading, or leaping over, the beast. There will come a time at which he cannot take a step small enough to avoid overshooting the target.

The confusion between mathematical steps and ambulatory ones, between footsteps and fractions, or between the idea of movement in mathematical space and actual movement – central to the paradox – is an instance of the more widespread confusion between mathematical and physical space, at least in part rooted in the belief we have already touched on that mathematics reveals the ultimate truth about physical reality or, even, that mathematical objects are the fundamental stuff of the world or, at least, its primordial materials – something we shall discuss in §3.6. There is also the wider assumption that, if mathematics (or quantitative science) cannot accommodate something – for example movement – then we should doubt its reality. There are other casualties of this kind of thinking; for example, free will, the self, and consciousness itself – all of which are difficult to discover using the objective, quantitative methods of neuroscience. We shall return to this in Chapter 12.

There may be something else at work behind the scenes here: a civil war within mathematics. Look again at the idea that completing the first half of the journey is step distinct from the second half of the journey; the first half of the first half from the second half of the first half; and so on. Space, the mathematical representation of movements through space, and real live locomotion, are conceived as *discontinuous*. The paradoxes arise not just because this is an unrealistic – or incomplete – representation of space but also because it is at odds with another (mathematical) representation of space.

When space, trajectories, and real live movements are mathematised, they can be represented arithmetically or geometrically. The geometrical representation of movement generates a line that is manifestly continuous. Even if the line were considered as being composed of discrete points, they would be fused in the manifest image of the line. By contrast, the arithmetical representation of movement by anything that falls short of the sum total of real numbers would be discontinuous, saltatory. The moving item passes from one position to another and the positions are interruptions to space: they are locations *in* it. There is a gap between one number and the next, just as there is a gap between 1 and 2, or between ½ and ¼, or between 0.5 and 0.5000001. This is true, irrespective of whether the numbers are "whole" numbers, or whether they are fractions or even decimals. This follows from the fact that between any two neighbouring numbers, there is always room for the interpolation of another number. There is a numerical space which can accommodate a potential infinity of numbers. Consequently, space conceived typically through integers, is discontinuous. This points to an alternative understanding of the aetiology of Zeno's motion paradoxes. While the consternation they cause is the result of confusing the mathematical representation of the world with the world itself, the particular form they take may result from a fundamental incompatibility between geometric and arithmetic modes of mathematical representation.

In summary, to accept that Achilles has a problem, we have first to imagine his journey as a line. More generally, we must assume that real journeys are equivalent to movement along a trajectory which can be represented by a line, to pure quantities which are not quantities "of"; in short, to reduce real movements to that which can be extracted from them mathematically as a line. This line has no properties other than extension. Its location, and the actual experience of any journey – effort, sweating, stumbling, sense of purpose – are irrelevant. (That is why the paradox applies equally to Achilles or a falling pebble.) The second step is to rethink that line arithmetically as something that can be halved not merely in principle but is in fact. It is broken up into distinct aliquots: halves that can be halved and halved and halved; thirds that can be trisected and trisected and trisected; and so on, right down to notionally indivisible points. There is a tension between these two views of the journey represented by a line: (geometrical) that sees it as continuous (and it is portrayed as such); and the other (arithmetical) that sees it as composed of distinct, and hence as discrete, components.

This conflict between a discrete number system and continuous geometry, with the latter seeming to be closer to the perceived and lived reality of the world, has been characterized by Tobias Dantzig as "staccato" versus "legato": "The harmony of the universe knows only one musical form – the legato; while the symphony of numbers knows only its opposite. All attempts to reconcile this discrepancy are based on the hope that an accelerated staccato may appear to our senses as legato".[73]

A related point is made by Unger and Smolin:

> The dominant, modern program of discrete mathematics is inadequate to the task of representing the vulgar (non-mathematical) idea of the continuum as uninterrupted non-discrete flow. The sequence of real numbers remains a series of steps: the steps fail to melt into a flow by virtue of being uncountably infinite.[74]

The most profound advance in the endeavour to get continuity – and continuous change – and hence change (given that, at the macroscopic level, all change is continuous) – out of arithmetized/algebraic reality is the calculus. But it still seems like a mathematical fiddle. The incurable approximateness of any endeavour to recover continuities (such as continuous movements) from a mode of representation that is intrinsically discontinuous demonstrates that, while there is a mathematics of motion, motion is not itself mathematical. It is possible, therefore, that the particular form of Zeno's paradoxes may result from not only the projection of mathematics into the extended material world but also of a domestic dispute within mathematics that treats an abstracted representation of movement in two rival ways – as a continuous line, and as a (granular) series of numbers – and cannot reconcile them. They are incommensurate.[75]

Zeno has another paradox up his sleeve: the paradox of the flying arrow that is extended (as I am), occupies space (as I do), but still cannot move. At any given point in time, or instant, Zeno tells us, the arrow occupies a space identical with itself. It cannot, that is to say, exceed its own boundaries, cannot "put out" beyond itself: it is where it is. But, Zeno argues, all of time consists of instants; so the arrow must remain confined within the boundary it has at an instant. It cannot therefore fly. Since arrows *do* fly and St Sebastian did not merely die of fright, something must have gone wrong.

At the most obvious level, there is the problem of judging the velocity of an arrow at an instant. The notion of "instantaneous velocity" is perfectly respectable but it is not one that can be arrived at by dividing how far the arrow moves in an instant, which is no time at all, by the time in question. It is obvious that an arrow cannot move any distance at all in *no* time. If any distance were travelled in zero time, the traveller would have an infinite velocity and this would apply to all moving arrows, whatever their apparent speed. Velocity must be measured – and has meaning – only over an interval of time greater than an instant. Indeed, if an arrow maintained a given velocity only over an instant, which is to say over no time, one would say that it had not achieved that velocity at all. All that one can have at an instant is a position.

The very notion of the arrow-at-an-instant is the product of a freezing glance and it is this that arrests the arrow in the position occupied by itself. The flying arrow paradox merely asserts that an object cannot occupy two positions at a given instant in time; or that it cannot get from one position to another in no time at all. It seems like a paradox only because we are invited to see movement and time from two incompatible viewpoints at once: position *at* an *instant* of time and movement *over* a *period* of time (however small).

When mathematicians talk about instantaneous velocity, they are not really talking about movement in no time. In the case of uniform motion in a straight line, instantaneous velocity is derived from the measured total distance travelled over a measured period of time. In the case of variable velocity (as in uniformly or non-uniformly accelerated motion), "instantaneous velocity" is an idea – an unreachable goal – of ever more precise tracking of velocity over smaller and smaller intervals of time to a level at which inaccuracies are unimportant. This does not involve self-contradictory notion that combines being *at* an instantaneous position with *passing through* that position at a certain speed.[76] Instantaneous velocity must not be taken literally as a measure of the velocity *at* an instant. An instant, after all, is not "a very small period of time" belonging to the same series as "hour", "second", "millisecond", "nanosecond", etc.

The flying arrow seems to be at rest only if we consider it over a period of time – zero – too short for any movement to take place. Its stillness over zero time does not translate into stillness over any period of time greater than zero. Its Zenonian stasis is therefore the consequence of merging the notion of "*at* a time" (when the arrow occupies a position) and "*over* time" (when it occupies a succession of positions). We could express this distinction by noting that the flying arrow does not *maintain* stillness, it does not *keep* still. Not moving in an instant, over no time at all, does not count as *staying* still. Both instantaneous velocity and instantaneous stillness (zero velocity) are contradictions in terms.

The flying arrow flies, given time; and it is given time because its time does not have to be put together out of instants. If we fail to grasp this, it is because our conception of an instant – a mathematical artefact – hovers in an intermediate realm between "no time at all" and "a very tiny stretch of time". If we are inclined to think of an instant as a vanishingly small stretch of time that has not completely vanished it is because we are able to allocate it a location and, as with spatial points, we imagine since it has a location, it must somehow *occupy* one place rather than another: it has a toehold, even though it has no toes or indeed anything else. Like spatial points, temporal instants (moments, points) exist only as numbers in a coordinate scheme.

Although this was not his intention, Zeno has done us the service of demonstrating that the notion of a point in time is a purely mathematical construct and that mathematical items, unlike arrows, do not move or host movement. More generally, he has reminded us – if we needed reminding – that mathematical space and time are not the space and time in which you and I and Achilles and arrows and pebbles move and have their being. Mathematical space is constructed of spatial and temporal points given quasi-existence by being made manifest as numbers that have no intrinsic extension, even less mobility.

The fact that, according to Zeno, a change such as standing up from sitting down is no less impossible than lifting one's self up by the hair on one's bald head at a speed greater than that of light, should demonstrate that Zeno has nothing to say about the real world. He might have been happy with this, arguing that what we take as the real world is an illusion. His aim was not to flag up a little local difficulty but to bring the entire universe to a grinding halt. Since Zeno gives logic (or his version of it) the last word, if things cannot move in theory, they cannot move in practice. The wrong counter-argument is to say that if we can walk in practice, there must be something amiss with the theory. The better counter-argument is to say that theory is not the last word because, if it were, there would be no word (and hence no theory) since formulation and communication of the theory, too, requires movement. Zeno, after all, had to open and close his mouth.

The broader conclusion we may draw from Zeno's paradoxes is that we should not confuse the mathematics of change with change period because then change will prove impossible. Walking is not a mathematical event any more than breathing is an intake of the symbols O_2. Getting from the beginning to the end of a race-track is no more like counting than it is like a proof. The apparent problem of demonstrating motion mathematically does not mean that motion is impossible but that the mathematics of motion is not identical with, or constitutive of, motion. The sin of confusing movement with its mathematical representation is compounded when the motions in question are *actions* (such as running for a bus).[77]

There are *no* mathematical events. Mathematical entities are eternal inhabitants of a frozen world. We shall return to some of these themes in §3.6.

3.5.2 The ideas of curved space and dilated time

> Shut up and calculate.
> Richard Feynman (according to David Mermin)[78]

I can remember when I first came across the notion of "curved space" and the protests it awoke in me. I kept my feelings largely to myself, partly because I was only too aware that the history of science had shown that our everyday intuitions and common sense are poor guides to the nature of the material world,[79] and partly because I did not know how to formulate my objection to the concept in a way that did justice to its richness and profundity, and that took into account its immense predictive and even explanatory power. The feeling of protest has not diminished but now I can see that it is possible to object to the idea of curved space in a manner that does not merely betray a stubborn attachment to unreformed pre-scientific common sense or to the daft idea that Einstein got his physics wrong and the even dafter idea that I am the one to correct him.

At the heart of the matter, I believe, is something identified in our discussion of Zeno's paradox of motion; namely a mathematical literalism that confuses the way we represent things mathematically with the way things are in themselves. It is a prime example of what Alfred North Whitehead called "the muddle of *importing the mere procedure of thought into the facts of nature*".[80] The homely analogies used to make the idea of curved space intelligible exemplify a mistaken tendency to try to rediscover the phenomenal world in the mathematical models of physics.

Let me begin with the stubbornly naïve grounds for protest. It seems absurd to assign a topology – "straight" or "curved" – to something that common sense defines as emptiness. Or it does so as long as we retain the ordinary sense of "straight" and "curved". A curve is something we discern in a boundary, separating (for example) an inside (of an object or a figure) from an outside; separating matter from empty space or one part of space from another. It is a border "between". And trajectories across space may be straight – as when an item takes the apparently shortest route between two locations – or curved, as when a less direct route is taken. And objects can have a curved surface, as does a football or a flat, straight-edged surface, as does a kitchen table. These distinctions are applicable to items located or inscribed *within* space. But what are we to make of the notion of space itself being curved?

The reason for describing space (or space–time) as curved – with non-Euclidean consequences such as that the shortest distance between two points may have non-zero curvature, the sum of the angles of a triangle may be greater or less than 180°, and parallel lines may meet before infinity – is to make sense of accelerated motion, whether under the influence of gravitational forces or in response to impact. We will come shortly to the rationale of this but first I want to examine the way the popularizers of general relativity try to appease affronted common sense by simple analogies. These analogies are deeply flawed because they treat the curvature of space as if it were extrinsic rather than intrinsic – a contrast we shall come to in due course.

The standard ploy is to translate curved space into a curved surface, such as that of a large sphere on which longitudes and latitudes have been marked. The shortest distance between two points on such a sphere, they claim, will not be a straight line but a curve, as when I move my finger over a football. What is more, the angles of a triangle drawn on its surface will not add up to the Euclidean 180° but will vary depending on the curvature of a ball, which will in turn vary as the ball is inflated, and the location of the triangle – whether it is near the equator or near the poles.

Why is this a mistake? For two reasons. Firstly, it invites the literal-minded, even bone-headed, response that the shortest distance between two points on a sphere such as a football will still be a straight line, though – because this involves piercing the leather at two points – it won't be the shortest *convenient* distance which latter will follow the curved surface of the ball. A rigid or impenetrable sphere mandates a curved journey over its surface but there is nothing *physically impossible* about taking a diametrical path from surface to surface.[81] And it is *physical* possibilities we are talking about, not convenient or sensible ones. (After all, there cannot be any barrier to passage through empty space.) Secondly, the triangles drawn on the surface of the football are not "non-Euclidean" because they are not triangles in the original and subsequently canonical Euclidean sense of items consisting of three straight lines. Indeed, we could regard the example as showing the difference between a curved and a non-curved *surface* and the constraints on movements that may result from curvature. This is not the same as showing the nature of the *space* in which the ball is located: it does not clarify what is meant by the curvature of space itself. Indeed, the very fact that the illustration appeals to an explicitly spherical object with a curved surface as opposed to a square object with flat surfaces, demonstrates this. In short, the analogy universalizes all objects in (non-zero gravity) space as being effectively curved which raises the question of how the difference between straight and curved surfaces, not to speak of straight and curved trajectories, arises. The constraints exerted by a curved object can be overcome and straight paths can be adhered to; but this is not true of the constraint captured in the notion of the curvature of empty space. Yes, while the earth may have a curved surface, it is not curved "through and through", as curved space (which lacks surfaces) is supposed to be. Within the earth's two-dimensional curved surface is its three-dimensional substance, which being neither straight nor curved, permits straight or curved paths through it. Unless, of course, you are a two-dimensional creature of zero thickness, which I presume is not the condition of anyone reading this.

Physicists will smile at taking the analogies too literally. But if they are not taken literally, they do not help to mediate between maths, our intuitions, and perceived reality. And the analogies do indeed lack explanatory power. Worse, they are seriously misleading. Though it is not uniform, the supposed curvature of space *is* – unlike the curvature of a sphere – continuously distributed. Its curvature is that of a *field*, being proportional to the intensity of the gravitational forces distributed through it, curved at every point and in every part. Contrast this with a curved object, such as football. The material inside it – air – is not curved, as if it were fitted within it like an infinite number of Russian dolls; only the surface is. Or imagine something solid such as a marble sphere: while the surface, the boundary is curved, the stone within it is not curved. Its curvature is that of surfaces, in this case a two-dimensional surface. That is why it is possible to carve out a straight-edged cube from within it.

In short, it does not make other than mathematical sense to think of anything as being curved (or indeed straight) all the way through, *through and through curved*: only boundaries, edges, surfaces and motions are curved (or straight). After all, circles are permitted to have straight diameters and limitless families of chords and tangents that touch their curvature at, respectively, two places or one. The idea of space itself, or space–time, as curved raises the question of what it is it curves into, or with respect to what it is curved. A curved trajectory or curved surface curves away from and towards locations or objects other than it. We cannot think of space, or portions of it, curving away or towards in this way.

I could go on but the point, I think, is made: the seemingly unintelligible, indeed outrageous, notion of the curvature of space itself is not rendered more intelligible or less outrageous by images of trajectories on the surfaces of curved objects. Such images are fudges. Indeed, to impute the primary quality of an object (shape) to space itself is to break down the difference between space and the items that may occupy it. This, however, is precisely what general relativity does, and not by accident, either. The objection to the analogy of a football carries weight only because, in the endeavour to make the notion of "curved space" more intuition-friendly, it conceals how radical is the theory behind it and how remote it is from actual or imaginable phenomenal experience.

We can summarize the way in which these images are at fault very briefly. The images used in popularizations of relativity illustrate intrinsic curvature of space with examples of objects that have extrinsic curvature. The intrinsic curvature of space does not relate to a background and it is not altered by (for example) bending a surface without stretching it. There is no such background. It is the curvature of a surface determined as if from a perspective confined entirely to the surface. Curvature is characterized for each point on the surface (or for the infinitesimally small neighbourhood surrounding each point on the space–time manifold) without requiring a larger Euclidean "outside" space in which to locate the surface. In the absence of the contrast between space and the items occupying it, "straight" and "curved" no longer have the meanings we normally assign to them. They are being asked to breathe in a vacuum.

We should accept, therefore, that there is no way of making common, phenomenal, or anything other than mathematical, sense of curved space. The divorce between the common sense that guides us in every moment of our lives and general relativity is complete. What then is the rationale for the claim that the notion of curved space captures a fundamental aspect of physical reality? After all, interpreting the laws of motion in terms of the topology of space seems a rather brave choice. It comes from projecting the way things are mathematically represented into those things themselves.

Volumes of space can be represented through three axes enclosing them; a position in space by means of values derived from those axes; and a movement in space by means of a line joining two positions. Locations on these axes represent pure quantities. If a fourth axis is used to represent time as another pure quantity, any change can be represented in the form of a line. The relationship between the location of an object and the passage of time – velocity when the transition is in a sustained direction – can also be represented by means of such a line. If velocity is constant in the absence of other forces, the line is straight in space and in space–time. If velocity is accelerated, the line is straight in space but curved in space–time as, in successive intervals of time, more space is traversed per interval. It is the latter that is the key step towards the notion that space–time in itself is curved in a gravitational field: the graphical representation of accelerated motion in space–time is a curve. Two other steps, however, are required.

The first is to assume that positions in space or time and the transition between them, the state of being at rest or in motion, are not absolutes, calibrated against space-in-itself or time-in-itself. Spatial distances and time intervals are observer-dependent, though space–time intervals are invariant. That much comes from the special theory of relativity. It delivers something we shall address presently – the notion of time dilation. The second step is to relativize the difference between the state of rest and that of uniform motion in a straight line. This brings us to what Einstein described as "the happiest thought" he ever had: that inertial and gravitational forces are the same such that entering a gravitational field is the equivalent of being accelerated in response to an inertial force.

Imagine that you are in a lift in outer space and you have no reference points against which to calibrate your motion. You feel a pressure under your feet. You do not know whether this is due to the acceleration of the lift which your body, like any other body, will resist due to its inertial mass or whether it is due to an increase in the gravitational field, so that your body feels heavier. Einstein understood that this was not a temporary ignorance – which could therefore be corrected – because there are no absolute reference points (in, say, a background space) against which you could decide whether what you are feeling is acceleration (and inertial forces) or entry into a gravitational field. Gravitational mass (or weight) and inertial mass (or resistance to change in velocity, including those of your body in the lift) are not merely equivalent – and quantitatively identical as the Hungarian scientist Loránd Eötvös dedicated his life to demonstrating – but are two aspects or manifestations of the same thing. To enter a gravitational field is to enter a place where uniform movement against the field is the equivalent of acceleration or deceleration (and requires the same amount of work). In this field, then, the trajectory of uniform motion in a straight line is effectively curved in space–time, like straight line acceleration. Or rather (and this is the crucial step for our argument) their *representation* would be curved, reflecting the fact that circular motion is effectively continuously accelerated motion. The stronger the gravitational field, the greater the resistance to movement away from the source and consequently the more tightly curved the representations of the movement.

We can see now why physicists find it useful to think of space in a non-zero gravitational field as curved and Euclidean geometry as a reflection only of the topology of space infinitely remote from any masses associated with gravitational fields. The lines that represent the trajectories of objects are curved because that is how acceleration and deceleration are represented in space–time graphs. To enter a gravitational field is to enter a place where motion is accelerated or decelerated, in the absence of any inertial input. Straight line motion is bent without the application of an inertial force.

This has mathematical consequences. For example, the constraints introduced by a gravitational field may mean that the shortest spatio-temporal distance between two points may be a curve rather than a straight line; indeed, since no part of space is uncontaminated with gravitational forces, it will always be more or less curved. For this reason, the appropriate geometry of space is not Euclidean (where the shortest distance between two points is a straight line and the sum total of the angles of a triangle is no more and no less than 180°) but non-Euclidean where these two fundamentals do not apply.

By using a geometry that is not committed to the Euclidean constraints in determining the distance between two points (a so-called metric), it is possible to arrive at a description of the physical universe that over-rides all the variations seen by individual observers located in different inertial frames and arrive at an invariant that does not, however, break with the special theory of relativity and presuppose the existence of absolute time or absolute space. It will describe the principles of universal covariance that will ensure that the laws of physics will be the same for all observers. Relativity theory, in short, will recover absolutes at a different level – in a higher order, more abstract place – from that which it undermined. At this absolute level, straight-line – or shortest distance – motion in a non-zero gravitational field will be represented as a curve.

And all of this, to emphasize, works fine: non-Euclidean geometry underpinned by tensor calculus delivers what is required to give the most powerful imaginable description of motion. As Barry Dainton expresses it:

> Using the tensor apparatus to represent the properties of space has a useful feature: the quantities thus represented (if not the actual numbers employed) are independent of the system of coordinates used to refer to points in space. Coordinate independence (or "covariance") is a criterion of a quantity being physically real as opposed to an artefact of a particular mode of representation. The mass of a truck does not depend on whether it is measured in pounds or kilograms, and just as pounds and kilograms are interconvertible, so, too, are the tensor representations of geometrical quantities based on different systems of spatial coordinates. It was this property that led Einstein to seek out the tensor apparatus when formulating the general theory of relativity.[82]

The contestable step is to impute to space itself the properties that are revealed by motions in space (everything from lumps of rock to beams of light) *as they are represented* in a certain way. This is the end-result of reducing motions (indeed all changes, all events) to lines defined by axes corresponding to the four dimensions of space–time. Presenting both movements in space–time and the space–time within which they take place as lines is perhaps the key step to fusing space itself with the representation of movements and presenting both as curved. The fact that movement in a gravitational field is curved (that is to say accelerated or decelerated) in the absence of inertial forces acting on the object then suggests that it must be the curvature in the very fabric of space or space–time that makes it take this curved path. The movement is portrayed as a curve but, to repeat, it is a curve (or a straight line) *only with respect to a mode of representation* – one that reduces it to a succession of mathematical locations defined according to axes that make locations purely numerical.

All attempts to connect, or reconnect, the counter-intuitive and conceptually opaque notion that space itself can be curved with common sense are therefore fudges. We should accept that there is no rapprochement between the world as we live it and the world as it is revealed by physics. It does not follow from this that the truths of everyday life are inferior or, on the contrary, that physics is "wrong". To argue the latter would be to combine arrogance with something bordering on lunacy. Relativity theory makes a generalized account of the science of motion expressible with the maximum of economy. It preserves the fundamental notion of light travelling by the shortest route (almost as good as "the rectilinear propagation of light" that we all learned in basic physics), and by breaking down the difference between the gravitational field and space itself it avoids having to think of gravity as an attractive force being transmitted through space instantaneously, which would break the well-founded veto on velocities greater than that of light. Space is bent in order that the honour of light as the fastest and straightest phenomenon in the universe may be saved. Given that the general theory of relativity is the best, most compact way of describing quantified physical reality, it is not surprising that it is such a potent way of predicting quantified physical reality.

The point that I am making is that, while the truths of physics are used in the technology that directly or indirectly impinges on every moment of our lives, they are not the last word, the ultimate truth. The mathematical truths of physics – for which it is convenient and indeed powerful to think of space as curved – are only one kind of truth. To speak of space as straight or curved is to use a shorthand that collapses the difference between space, movements of objects in space, and the graphical, mathematical representation of the laws governing, or the constraints on, spatial movements. It does not follow from the usefulness of thinking in this way that our usual distinction between objects in space and the space that houses objects is an illusion.

The confounding of the image of space with a particular way of representing movement – and the velocity of movement – was several thousand years in the preparation. From the discovery of geometry to the geometrization of space there was a long period in which Euclidean geometry proved useful to make spatial predictions – as in determining the height of objects that could not be measured directly, in calculating how to maximize the space enclosed using limited materials, in predicting the path of projectiles – and so on. This, along with advances in mathematics, eventually paved the way for the "discovery" that all but zero gravity space was not Euclidean but non-Euclidean. In fact, space is no more straight than it is curved; nor is it either Euclidean or non-Euclidean, though Euclidean geometry has more limited uses for understanding trajectories than was appreciated before Einstein generalized mechanics to take account of the events that took place at velocities closer to the speed of light than we ordinarily encounter in daily life – particularly at the subatomic level. Thinking of space as Euclidean or non-Euclidean is just one example of the wider tendency to confuse the way we represent what is there with the intrinsic properties of what is there.

It is an inescapable consequence of reducing space to numbers – as merely a partner in a metric between intervals that are defined mathematically in terms of four parameters – and disinfecting it of place. The differences between extensity of objects, of the intervals between objects and (in the case of the gravitational field) the nature of the interaction between objects and between objects and forces, are lost as they are all gathered up into a mechanics of a higher generality. Matter takes on the properties of space and space the properties of matter. Empty space, sharing with objects the same dimensions reducible to numbers, can then be thought of as if it, too, had shape. Its (shaping) shape can make it an active player in the physical universe. And its dimensions, purely mathematical, can be multiplied – as in some versions of string theory, where the notion of "curved" space is elaborated to encompass up to seven extra dimensions that are themselves tightly curled up, so that they are detectable only by the modelling strategies of a theorist.

The attempt to make everyday sense of the seemingly unintelligible conclusion that space in a non-zero gravitational field is curved by appealing to metaphors involving footballs and the surface of the earth reflects a wish to run with the mathematical hounds while hunting with the hares of phenomenal experience; to try to make a direct connection between the world of sensory appearance and the realm of mathematical description. Unsurprisingly, it fails: we cannot follow the mathematics to the end and at the same time save the appearances. Mathematics cannot get a grip on phenomenal reality and it cannot include the latter in its territory. The conclusion that one – mathematized reality – is right and the other – our lived reality – is simply wrong has been gathering adherents as physical sciences dazzles us with its increasing predictive, explanatory, and practical power. We shall examine this question of the relationship between mathematics and reality in §3.6. Let us for the present briefly look at what relativity does to time.

Time, as we have discussed, has been denatured by being reduced to a dimension, then to a measurement, and finally to one of a quartet of partners in a line that represents a succession of measurements. The thought processes that lead to space being bent or straightened out are those that permit time to be dilated or contracted. They include the performance of mathematical operations on time reduced to a parameter t. As t – rather than as, say, tea-time – time can be squared, square rooted, placed under another variable as a denominator, and placed on top of another variable as a numerator and so on. Purified to a number, time is ripe to be incorporated along with space into a geometry of the physical universe. Against the background of mathematical operations that create entities such as t^2, "time dilation" hardly seems an eccentric or even bold notion.

There are many situations in which physicists see time as dilated. I want to focus on one of the most well-known examples. "Time dilation" may be observed when a clock A enters a more intense gravitational field compared with clock B. Under such circumstances, "the flow of time" is seen to be more sluggish, as if gravity introduced a kind of viscosity into time. This dilatation of time, due to the increased curvature of the path of light signals is not merely an impression that can be corrected by a measurement from some universal clock, independent of any frame of reference, of what is "really going on". Access to the nearest we get to "what is really going on" has to be mediated through signals that travel at the maximum possible speed – that of light. And (in accordance with Mach's verificationist principle of the unreality of unobservables) there could not be anything corresponding to what is "really going on" that is in principle unobservable.

But the notion of *time itself* slowing or speeding up is mired in the idea, that we discussed in §2.2.3, of time passing at a certain rate – or different rates in different circumstances – and this would require us to refer to a hypertime against which its speed could be measured. What is affected by relative movement (or a gravitational field) is not time itself but precisely what is described: measurement on a clock and noted by an observer of the clock. Time dilatation is a quarrel between clocks, not a local ballooning of time itself. To translate this into literal dilatation – in which (say) seconds become more capacious, able to accommodate more events, as if the latter had a fixed (absolute) duration – is to confuse measurements of time with time itself. As Plotinus said, "to measure something is not to grasp that something".[83] Admittedly it appears that we do grasp things more firmly through measurement, however, because we seem to get our (individual, unreliable) selves out of the way. Measurement, which is objective, in the sense of being repeatable within and between people, and giving rise to predictions that any observer would confirm, would appear to be "on the side of the object", "out there in reality".

This is our cue to discuss the presence – or, rather, the absence – of the observer in contemporary physical understanding of space and time. *Pace* David Mermin (or Richard Feynman), this will give us grounds for *not* shutting up, even those of us who cannot calculate, since the essence of time lies beyond the reach of calculation, not the least because it is bound up with the one who (observes, measures) and calculates. We should not, however, stop at John von Neumann's dismissal of the attempt to make sense of mathematical physics – "In mathematics you don't understand things. You just get used to them."[84] For we have got a little *too* used to what mathematics serves up and to the habit of reciting, hosting, accepting thoughts that we can neither truly imagine or understand. We nod things through that we ought – for the sake of the observer, our living selves – to challenge.

3.5.3 The erasure of the observer

> The great advances in the physical and biological sciences were made possible by excluding the mind from the physical world. This has permitted a quantitative understanding of that world, expressed in timeless, mathematically formulated physical laws.[85]
>
> Thomas Nagel, *Mind and Cosmos*, 81

3.5.3.1 The observer and the observation post as a set of numbers

> [W]e have no satisfactory physical theory at all – only ill-defined primitives such as "measurement", "observer" and even "consciousness".
>
> David Wallace (quoted in Halvorson,
> "The Meaning of All Things", 139)

At first sight, it might seem that the observer, the conscious subject, is enthroned at the centre of contemporary physics. Relativity theory is founded on the fact that observations and measurements and the order of events are viewpoint-dependent, and that there are no privileged viewpoints. It was in part inspired by Einstein's conviction, based on Ernst Mach's philosophy of science, that there is no reality other than that which can be observed, no reality-in-itself beyond actual or possible experiences and that, consequently "the task of science is not to set up theories of the world but merely establish empirical connections between directly observable phenomena".[86] And to bring science home to the experience of the scientist, Mach argues that "the material world is a complex of sensations".[87] The leading interpretation of quantum mechanics asserts that, at a fundamental level, variables such as momentum, position, spin, wave or particle form are indeterminate until a measurement has been made. Whether an entity is a wave or a particle depends on what kinds of measurements are made on it. In short, the observer seems to be an indispensable part of the universe as revealed to physics, to be present in the characterization of motion and location and relative position at the macroscopic level, and to permeate the very interstices of the subatomic world. This has prompted respected physicists and popularizers of physics to talk of "the ghost in the atom".[88] In the first flush of excitement after the development of quantum mechanics, Sir James Jeans asserted that "the universe is more like a great thought than a great machine".[89] The apparent reinstatement of the observer is captured in the speech ascribed to Niels Bohr in Michael Frayn's *Copenhagen*:

> You see what we did in those three years, Heisenberg? Not to exaggerate we turned the world inside out! ...We put man back at the centre of the universe ... Throughout history we keep finding ourselves displaced. We keep exiling ourselves to the periphery of things ... Until we come to the beginning of the twentieth century, and we're suddenly forced to rise from our knees again.[90]

And Hawking and Mlodinow assert that "there is no way to remove the observer – us – from the perception of the world".[91] Most strikingly, John Wheeler famously asserted that "No phenomenon is a real phenomenon until it is an observed phenomenon"[92] and even claimed that "the observer plays a key role in bringing the universe into being".[93] And of particular relevance to our present investigation, the quantum physicist and champion of Henri Bergson, Satosi Watanabe reported that "modern physics has found the lost link between psychic time and physical time".[94]

All, however, is not as it seems: what is given with one hand is taken away with the other. For a start, "the observer" who measures what is happening in physical systems to many decimal places of accuracy is quite unlike Raymond Tallis who is currently casting casual and unreliable glances at the world around him. The scientific observer is not really an individual with all his foibles and fallibility, a local reporter at the centre of a small locality. More importantly, physical science – especially since the Galilean revolution – is characterized by the progressive *erasure* of the observer; and twentieth-century physics, rather than bucking this trend, has continued it. The last century has enthroned the observer in the universe as represented by mathematical physics only by assimilating the observer more completely into that world; ultimately by mathematizing the observer. The "ghost in the atom" looks suspiciously like a set of mathematical points rather than a nebulous haze of generic humanity. Mankind, far from being reinstated in the centre of the universe is mummified, on the basis of observations that are the values of a set of variables, into a swarm of numbers.

At a very basic level, the mathematician, or physicist has no specific character-istics. And this is true of any observer, or measurer, including Einstein's and Bohr's observers. All the characteristics that enable a flesh-and-blood human being to be an observer are irrelevant from the point of view of physics. It hardly needs saying that the "observer" in physics is not a person, even less a living one, man or woman, young or old, happy or unhappy, rich or poor. But he or she is less than an "it", lacking even a phenomenal appearance – never mind history, preoccupations, duties, character, and purpose. As Erwin Schrödinger put it: "a moderately satisfying picture of the world has only been reached at the high price of taking ourselves out of the picture, stepping back into the role of the non-concerned observer", adding that "while the stuff from which our world picture is built is yielded exclusively from the sense organs as organs of the mind ... yet the conscious mind itself remains a stranger within that construct, it has no living space in it".[95] Objective science advances by excluding what Schrödinger calls "the subject of Cognizance from the domain of nature".[96]

This we might expect: such characteristics are irrelevant to the business of phys-ics. And science has advanced as a result of the work of a community of scientists whose individual members as it were get themselves out of the way. Even where an equation is named after the individual who first described it, that individual is a mere tag, lacking any characteristics. There is nothing Austrian or bespectacled about Schrödinger's wave equation. Observer independence is a mark of objectivity and generalisability. But the ontological crash diet physics inflicts on the observer goes far beyond this. In the last analysis, the observer in physics is merely a location in a mathematically defined frame of reference mathematically related to other math-ematically defined frames of reference. Far from being enthroned she is erased. To jump ahead a little, the mathematical, physical account of the universe which aspires not only to Nagel's "view from nowhere",[97] or indeed from "nowhen" (to borrow Huw Price's coinage), is necessarily a view from *no-one*. The ballet of coordinates that terminates in, say, the field equations of the general theory of relativity, is a dance of mathematical variables realized in a structure of space–time points. Ultimately, the observer does not occupy a location in space–time but *is* an imagined set of points in space–time. The gaze of the physicist is assigned to the unwatering, unblinking, insentient glass eye of mathematical relationships. This is the gaze that reveals laws of nature that Einstein insisted "would remain the same even if no-one perceived them".[98]

There are several paths to this extraordinary outcome. A crucial step is the confla-tion of the observer with a recording device whose records may or may not ultimately enter someone's consciousness. To this we shall return presently. But let us first glance at the nature of measurement.

As we have already seen, measurement looks past the phenomenal characteristics of the object; and objective measurement (quite properly) marginalizes the view-point of the observer. In getting at the object in itself, measurers get themselves out of the way. What the object looks like to them and where it is in relation to them, its secondary qualities, and, of course, the tertiary qualities relating to its value, are all set aside. This draining out of the experiences of the observer and the paring down of the experienced world progresses as (physical) science advances and measurement is assimilated to the activity of looking for very general patterns in the states and evolution of the material world. Measurements become data, data are aggregated in the form of graphs or tables, and aggregated data – animated by the intuitions and conjectures of the science community – give birth to equations that in some case express laws. The relationship between the datum and the living individual who obtained it eventually becomes so remote that it is possible to imagine that the conscious subject is an optional extra.

Any residual presence of "I" or "we" must be exorcised because it is a warning that the observer has got in the way of the observed and distorted the mathematical image of it. As data acquired by any number of observers, and confirmed by any number of other observers, add up, and laws are conjectured, and checked against further data and other laws, the world is increasingly emptied of subjects and of the phenomenal appearance of objects. The laws describe mathematical relationships between abstracted properties. Higher levels of classification minimize specific contents. That which applies with increasing generality must apply less and less to what is particular in actualities: the Theory of Absolutely Everything ascends to a Theory of Nothing in Particular about a universe that is inhabited by No-One in Particular or No-One at All.

This is not a recent trend. The early nineteenth-century scientist Mary Somerville noted how "The progress of modern science, especially within the last five years, has been remarkable for a tendency to simplify the laws of nature, and to unite detached branches by general principles".[99] She was writing in 1834! We are left ultimately with laws that relate variables at higher and higher levels at the end of a journey that starts off with (say) $V/i = r$ (voltage divided by current = resistance), proceeds to the great unifying laws of the physical world, such as the Maxwell equations which connect what happens in electrical circuits with optics and electromagnetism; and thence to the all-encompassing statement of the relationship between mass and energy, $E = mc^2$. Thus does science advance towards a single blank stare at a world seen by no-one from nowhere; that encompasses everything in general by looking past everything in particular.

So much for the "observed" world as related to the sum total of all possible observers. What, however, of the observer? His/her marginalization, even obliteration, was well advanced in classical physical science by the end of the nineteenth century and, notwithstanding "ghosts in the atom" and Mach's verificationist influence, with the insistence that theories be tested against the tribunal of experience, neither relativity theory nor quantum mechanics really has brought him/her back. This act of erasure, however, is in part concealed by the conflation of the observer with other items – notably measuring or recording instruments and inertial reference frames.[100]

First measuring apparatus. Consider these quotes:

> It is true that for the sake of convenience authors of works on this issue [relativity] have often introduced "observers" who are assumed to perceive the phenomena. But these observers can just as well be replaced by

recording instruments, and whether or not they are living and conscious is irrelevant.[101]

At a given instant E on the world-line of an observer A (*who need not be regarded as anything other than a recording instrument*), all the events from which A can have received signals lie within the backwards-directed light cone with its vertex at E.[102]

Whitrow's idea of "a recording instrument" folds the observer ("recording") and her agency ("instrument") into an insentient material object. Bertrand Russell, in his explanation of relativity, dismissed the natural idea that the observer might be "a human being, or at least a mind" and asserted that it was "just as likely to be a photographic plate or a clock".[103]

This conflation is particularly striking in discussions of the so-called Twin Paradox which we shall examine in the next section. Alain Sokal and Jean Bricmont, in the course of chastening postmodern critics of science, point out with barely concealed patience that "Paul [one of the twins] could be, for example, a photodetector coupled to a computer, and after the experiment everyone could consult the computer's memory to see which beam of light came in first."[104] The observer is brushed to one side as an "everyone" who after the experiment consults the computer's "memory". We shall leave aside the standard transferred epithet of "memory" – access to tensed time – being applied to computers (material objects) for the present and note while the conscious observer is still involved, consciousness is (a) delayed and (b) distributed between those many people who have created the detector or detecting system and have consumed the result. It is possible to postpone a (conscious) reading of a recording or automatic inscription device but not do without it altogether. The state of, or an event in, a recording device is not a record or measurement, even less an observation, unless the record is *read*. At some stage there has to be direct witness.

All of which is sufficiently obvious, one would think, not to require spelling out. The reason it does require spelling out is that descriptions of recording devices tend to be anthropomorphic. This is particularly true of the way computers are spoken of: they "calculate", "remember", "decide" and so on.[105]

The upgrading of "detectors" to stand-alone, or stand-ins for, observers in relativity theory reflects the fact that the "observer" is in reality the occupant of a virtual viewpoint, an imagined point of registration of events, or of arrival of signals (that can be signalling to no-one). That the characteristics necessary to constitute a real observer (a physicist, for example) are absent is illustrated by the fact that the entire measurement situation can be captured in a diagram unhaunted by any consciousness. The location of the "observer" is not a "here" to which there corresponds surroundings that counts as "there": it is "deindexicalised" and consequently not the location of an observer at all.

The distance between conscious awareness and measurements on instruments is captured in this aside by Jim Al-Khalili in his account of the paradoxes of special relativity. He considers what the observer travelling next to a light beam might see and then signals "a note of caution" in using the word "see": "I am using the term 'see' here just to mean 'measure' in some way – for example, in the case of a pulse of light, by recording the precise time it triggers devices along its path."[106]

Because the record can be looked at by anyone at any time – underlining the disconnection between the measurement and the consciousness of the observer – it seems as if it stands on its own as a record, as an observation, and the recording device becomes a proxy for an observer; as if an unwatched watch is still a watch and readings that are never, and never will be, read are still "readings". And it is standard to think of the natural world as being populated by clocks – periodic processes that count as clocks irrespective of whether they are explicitly used as such by a conscious physicist making observations. Such a clock could make measurements on its own, declaring to an unconscious world what time it is or how much time has passed. This example of knowledge in the absence of a conscious knower is, of course, epistemological nonsense but it is a logical consequence of adopting a world picture in which conscious human observers and clocks (and other automatic recording devices) are treated as equivalent.

The vice of ascribing clock-hood to physical processes that have certain properties such as periodicity is not unique to special relativity and its popularizations. Indeed, the entire universe has been described as a giant clock, its unfolding as the intermeshing of a vast numbers of clocks large and small. We talk about rocks and fossils being "clocks". The fact is that any event – or train of periodic (and assumed to be isochronous) events – can be or not be a clock depending on whether it is used to time the "when", "how long" or "in what order" of other events. It is a matter of the use to which physical events are put that determines whether they count as clocks. The rotation of the earth round its own axis and round the sun did not of course become a calendar until it was used as such by conscious beings. No processes generate data – irrespective of whether they are constructed apparatuses or naturally occurring like fossils – without being interpreted by a conscious subject.

Conscious observers are not simply part of the nexus of interacting events in the way a piece of apparatus is. They have to stand outside of that nexus in order to turn the states of certain parts of it into measurements. Observations are contrived events made by people for certain explicit purposes. The universe is not self-observing; the physical world is not one giant physicist.[107] Pointer positions or numbers on the clock do not of themselves count as observations made or time told. The pointer position is as uninformative as the accidental shadow cast by the apparatus on the surface on which it is standing and, in the absence of a trained observer who needs its information, 1 says as little to the world at large as it does to the insect crawling over its face or to the walls of the laboratory. A measurement is not merely an effect of a physical event on a physical body; it is the result of an action carried out in pursuit of a particular end. This clearly could not be said of a physical instrument, which is indeed the passive recipient of physical events as causes with what may become readings (if they are read) being mere effects.

The confounding of the clock with the clock-watcher or, more generally, that which is measured with the measurement and/or the observer who makes the measurement is an understandable extrapolation of the fact that measurements are only contingently made by particular individuals: they are not personal to them. An accurate measurement has nothing to do with any "who" and the laws of nature are the result of a journey out of viewpoints. The general theory of relativity may have been constructed by Einstein but insofar as it is true it is not Einstein's individual take on the world.

That even orthodox exponents of relativity theory are aware of the difference between a true observer and an insentient recording device is indirectly acknowledged through the difficulty reported in accommodating recording devices in their account of the physical world. Consider the device most relevant to our present concerns – the clock. Tim Maudlin describes such a clock:

> A light clock is a ray of light that is reflected back and forth between two mirrors. We assume that there is a mechanism ... that can register when the light ray reaches one of the mirrors and "ticks" when this occurs. We also assume that some mechanism keeps count of the ticks. In this way, the device assigns integers to particular events along its world-line.[108]

One could be forgiven for getting the impression that the rays bouncing back and forth between the parts of a mechanism would tell the time without anyone observing them; indeed, without anyone to tell the time to. But of course, notwithstanding the liberal use of anthropomorphisms "register", "keep count", "assign", they do not. It makes the status of devices such as clocks (and measuring rods) rather awkward to characterize. Einstein himself was acutely aware of this:

> One is struck [by the fact] that the theory [relativity] ... introduces two kinds of physical things, i.e. (1) measuring rods and clocks, (2) and all other things, e.g., the electromagnetic field, the material point, etc. This, in a certain sense, is inconsistent ...; strictly speaking, measuring rods and clocks would have to be represented as solutions of the basic equations (objects consisting of moving atomic configurations), not, as it were, theoretically self-sufficient entities.[109]

The problem is serious:

> Nature does not have to settle whether a given mechanism counts as a "clock" in order to determine how it should behave. A term like "clock" unlike "light ray" or massive particle cannot appear in the statement of any fundamental law.[110]

Clocks and measuring rods have no place in the universe described by the physics of motion, time, and space because they do not *count* as clocks or as measuring rods without conscious beings who use and consult them and such beings have no place in that universe from which the observer has been erased. What makes a measurement the privileged set of events it is won't be found in the physical properties, but in the explicit purpose, of those events. If people are conflated with recording devices, the latter have to make and receive measurements of their own accord. While clocks are "in" time, they are also – when they are used – devices that stand outside of time, telling us what time we are "at" – of which more in §4.5 *et passim*.

There are worse fates for "observers" than being turned into an insentient unwatched clock or a measuring rod that there is no-one to use to measure anything. They could become the unacknowledged authors of a frame of reference. In special relativity an observer is a frame of reference from which measurements are being made. While for Einstein – at least in his early expositions of special relativity – the typical observer was a passenger on a moving train, an individual on a (relatively) still embankment, or a daring traveller on a light beam, more recent popularizations of the theory seem to turn the observer into unhaunted frames of reference. According to philosopher Bradley Dowden's article on time for the *Internet Encyclopedia of Philosophy*, while "[the] observer's frame of reference is a perspective or coordinate framework from which measurements are made ... [t]he observer need not have a mind".[111] Indeed, if as is standardly assumed, the frame of reference (of, for example, a clock) is merely a set of Lorentz coordinates in which the clock's speed is zero, from which the motion of objects is measured, then the observer vanishes, notwithstanding the slipping in of the word "perspective" that is haunted by a smidgeon of consciousness. It becomes a courtesy title, or a conceptual relic, as Steve Savitt seems to imply, when he dismisses the very notion of the observer (in a bracketed aside) as "(the usual anthropomorphized way to refer to admissible coordinate systems)".[112] The distinction between the observer and the coordinate system seems to have gone the way of that between observer and apparatus. As a popular source puts it: "Today it is common to find the term "observer" used to imply an observer's associated coordinate system (usually assumed to be a coordinate lattice constructed from an orthogonal right-handed set of space-like vectors)."[113]

This raises fundamental questions. Just as it seems difficult to imagine a measurement without a conscious measurer (or a clock without a clock-maker telling the time or without a clock-watcher using a natural process to time events) it seems equally difficult to conceive of a frame of reference arising spontaneously without the direct or indirect sponsorship of an observer. Space itself does not spontaneously crystallize into coordinates, linked to origins, becoming self-populated by a blizzard of zeroes appearing in fused triplets (or quartets in the case of space–time) – any more than space–time gives unassisted birth at each of its points to light cones linking past and future. If it did, chaos would result. They would conflict with one another, giving an infinite range of different values for each space–time point without the local privileging provided by the "here" and "now" of the observer to settle which frame of reference should prevail.

Fortunately, this mess is avoided because frames of reference are not naturally occurring phenomena in the material world.[114] Every frame of reference presupposes an implicit conscious observer or viewpoint notwithstanding that the fully developed theory tidies him or her away. While the idea of a "frame of reference" is still allowed to retain the connotation of a viewpoint bounded by the horizon of a conscious field, to make sense of the idea of measurement (or to make a series of events into a measurement), consciousness is banished from the completed theory, which cannot accommodate it.

The issue is of central importance to the metaphysics, though not the physics, of time because the notion of a frame of reference goes to the heart of relativity theory. As Maudlin has pointed out: "Light in itself has no speed since there is no absolute time or absolute space in Relativity" (and so no absolute spatial distance to put on the numerator or absolute temporal interval to place on the denominator); but *relative to a coordinate system* we can assign light a *coordinate* speed".[115] It is perhaps to lay the irony on a bit too thick to say that it is good to know that not only has light not got a speed (it is folded into the structure of space) but that the speed it does not have is (a) constant and (b) 186,000 miles per second. The latter is remarkably precise for something that does not have an intrinsic existence, though it is the ultimate reference for all other measurements to the point where its authority has to be accepted at the cost of any number of counter-intuitive conclusions, some of which we have already discussed.[116]

Without a viewpoint, distinct from the material that is viewed, there is nothing ultimately – however indirectly – to which to tether the axes of coordinate space. Indeed, a particular point in space, and a particular trajectory have an indefinite number of potential coordinates and consequently numerical values corresponding to imaginary observers. I am at this moment located in an infinite number of potential coordinate spaces. None of these is actual in the absence of an imaginary or real observer. The assimilation of the observer into what is essentially a mathematical configuration does not seem to allow for any actual experiences. Mach's principle that only that which is experienced or in principle experiencable is real, which as we noted provided part of the justification of special relativity, seems therefore to have ended by extruding that in virtue of which there is experience at all: the observer. Frames of reference without any basis for reference are essentially aspects of a mathematical lattice, a pure structure of space–time points from which experience, defined in part by frames of reference, does not seem likely to arise.[117]

It is because all of this is so obvious that it is overlooked. Indeed, to draw attention to it seems like missing the point: objective science, above all physics, *begins* by leaving the *individual* (real, sentient, situated) observer behind. As Eddington expressed it, relativity theory (that, in the form of general relativity, used tensors) "symbolized absolute knowledge; but this is because it stands for the subjective knowledge of all possible subjects at once".[118]

The problem of merging all possible viewpoints is that we end up with no viewpoint at all; and with fake observers that are in fact insentient devices, that lack the capacity to observe, located in mysteriously self-stipulating frames of reference. If the physics that reduces the observer to part of the material world were the sum of truth about things, there would be no observations, no measurements, and hence no physics or physicists. Their possibility depends on allowing there to be privileged frames of reference – the "nows" *at which* observations (including observations of clocks) are made.

This is clearly relevant to the question of the distance between physical time and lived time, between the little t of physics and the time of our conscious lives. As we shall examine in Part II, the latter cannot be reduced to the former; but of more immediate relevance is the fact that clock-time straddles both. There is no clock-time without observers. The observer is inescapably psychological and cannot be excluded from the physics of time if the latter is at least in part rooted in observation.

That this is less obvious than it should be is in part because the observer in the case of a scientific investigation is not one person but an entire community of minds extending over time, geography, cultures and societies and the possibility of an observation may be set up by one person and actually made by another.[119] The loss of the observer seems to undermine even the thin, purely relational time that special relativity put in the place of substantive, absolute Newtonian time, because that in virtue of which relata are related – consciousness – has evaporated into space–time points mathematically defined.

We have therefore to disabuse ourselves of the myth that physics after Planck and Einstein brought observers to the centre of its investigations, incorporated them into its world picture, and then transcended them in creating a world picture that captured the true nature of time, such that it was in a position to pronounce on which aspects of time (tense, for example) are real and even whether time itself it real. The observer in contemporary physics is a virtual or quasi-observer generated in order to frame thought experiments or to imagine possible outcomes of interventions. It is a meta-observer – an abstract category of all possible observers relevant to a particular class of observations. Ultimately, however, it becomes a contradiction: something that reveals the spatio-time manifold, the total of all happenings in the history of the universe, from an impermissible outside. The implicit meta-observer (required to generate, but hidden in, equations like the field equations of the general theory of relativity) is a mathematical view on a mathematical field; a gaze transformed into a set of equations that has no viewpoint.

The elimination of a real as opposed to a mathematically defined observer yields an image of reality as a tenseless space–time continuum in which the entire history of everything is taken together. This is clearly problematic – but not for the reason that people sometimes think. The commonest objection to the metaphysics of general relativity is that the space–time manifold is a still, frozen unchanging block that fails to reflect our fluid, changing world. However, as several philosophers, notably J. J. C. Smart, have pointed out, the sum of everything – changing and non-changing – must itself be unchanging.[120] This, however, is a matter of definition, a logical not an empirical truth: nothing can be added to a total, neither additional objects nor additional events. Being Australian, Smart illustrated this with an example from cricket. If, in talking about a cricket ball, we are referring to the entire history of the object in question, then nothing (further) can happen to that item. And this applies equally to the universe: the total of its objects and changes cannot change.[121]

Given, what is more, that there could be no second-order space–time change-space in which the continuum could be seen as changing, any view on the manifold, seeming to contain everything changing and unchanging, would contain it all at once in a kind of simultaneity. It would make of all happening a *frozen array*, in which the happening and having happened and not yet happened, are indistinguishable. Actual happening requires a privileged "now" – supplied by a real, sentient, observer, who is distinct from that which is observed, being neither a piece of apparatus or a coordinate frame – which relativity forbids.

What Einstein – and more generally physics – offers us as ultimate reality is the sum total of things viewed from no viewpoint, an item that is even more thoroughly self-cancelling than Nagel's "view from nowhere". We arrived at the idea of this actually unsustainable viewpoint through taking too seriously the mathematics which offers or generates *virtual* viewpoints that seem like places inhabited by someone. You can do maths on uninhabitable viewpoints – and to great effect as Einstein did when, as a teenager, he envisaged himself travelling on a light beam and tried to imagine what he would see. The very fact that the Einsteinian quasi-observer can occupy places that could not be occupied by a conscious being is no accident: numbers do not require board and lodging. But we must not be misled into thinking of these places as viewpoints as ordinarily construed. The maths of coordinates can pass unscarred even through the cognitive vacuum labelled as "the square root of –1". No flesh-and-blood observer would be as robust. "Observer" is a merely honorary title, the location of a quasi-consciousness that is not conscious at all.

Where the conscious observer is permitted a place in the scheme of things, it is often as the source of profound illusions. One can understand, while deploring, Hermann Weyl's characteristic attempt to marginalize observers, by denying them a place in fundamental reality, even at the cost of denying the reality of happening: "The objective world simply is, it does not happen. Only to the gaze of my consciousness, crawling upward along the lifeline of my body, does a section of this world come to life as a fleeting image in space which continually changes in time."[122]

"Only to the gaze of my consciousness" implies "not in reality" – although that consciousness must itself have some kind of reality; and so, also, must whatever it is that allows it to "crawl upward" along the "lifeline of its body" and thereby introduce becoming into a world of being. There is no way this awkward character could be assimilated into the material world or replaced by unconscious recording devices Even less could it be present in the unobserved physical world. Even so, the usually reliable Smolin asserts that "photons, since they travel at the speed of light, don't experience time at all" as if they would experience time if they moved more slowly.[123]

The distaste for the idea that anything actually happens – as evinced in the passage from Weyl – is reflected in resistance to the notion that events happen at a definite time. We naturally think that the time that events take place is the time they are observed to take place when we are at, or near to, where they are taking place. This is rooted in the common-sense notion that the gap between an event occurring and its being observed will be smallest if the observer is close to the event rather than being three billion miles away from it. The close-up observer will be best placed, so common sense tells us, to say when the event "really" or "actually" took place and his sense that it is taking place "now" will be privileged. The response of the physicist is of course: check your privilege. We should avoid, they say, thinking that it can translate this "now" into a universal "now" and that the authority of the on-the-spot observer will still survive in the world of objective time measurements, according to a universally agreed system, a cosmic time. The observer's authority is only a local authority.[124]

Even so, there is an irreducible aspect of the authority of a conscious observer which can never be transcended. After all, the observer at a distant point from the event still must relate his observation of a distant event to a nearby one (e.g. the fingers assuming a certain position on a nearby clock). In short, the "now" rooted in what is happening in the vicinity of the observer cannot be transcended by a nowless universe of mathematically defined space–time locations – as Einstein was uncomfortably aware. "Now" is an essential basis of observation. Smolin again: "There are aspects of the real universe that will never be representable in mathematics. One of them is that in the real world it *is always at some particular moment*."[125]

The mathematized (as opposed to the flesh-and-blood) observer does not live, observe, experience, or in any sense *occur*. The scientifically unacceptable tendency of real observers to imagine a real, frame-of-reference independent difference between what has already and what has not yet happened (not to speak of motion and stillness, near and far), makes them impossible to accommodate in the universe of mathematical physics on their own terms. Observers are allowed into the physicists' world picture only insofar as they are material objects, describable as are other material objects in terms of space–time points.

J. R. Lucas addresses this issue from another direction, by emphasizing the distinction between events really happening and their being observed, with respect to the collapse of the wave-packet in quantum mechanics, "when many possible eigenvectors, with their associated eigenvalues, give way to a single eigenvector with one definite eigenvalue":

> [T]here is a definite moment of truth when possibilities become definitely true or definitely false. There is a fact of the matter, quite independent of whether we know it or not, and of how and when we know it. Knowledge may be unable to travel faster than the speed of light, but reality does not have to travel at all. Galaxies may be thousands of light-years away, and we shall be able to assign a date to a particular collapse only thousands of years after the event, and our assignment may depend on an idiosyncratic choice of frame of reference, but nonetheless there will have been a definite moment at which the event occurred independent of any frame of reference.[126]

In short, he rejects Mach's identification of reality with experience which, whether or not Mach wanted this, has had the perverse consequence of experience being marginalized in a portrait of the world as mathematized material reality. Just as observations cannot be reduced to the recordings on measuring devices in the absence of consciousness (and observers are not measuring devices wired into physical systems) so, Lucas emphasizes, the obverse is true: the occurrence of physical events in physical systems cannot be dissolved without remainder into observations.

We can illustrate this with the more homely example of a continuous process whose components have a necessarily fixed order, though it would be wrong to think of this as being due to a causal relationship. Consider a thrown ball flying through the air. The ball necessarily passes through a succession of positions that respect the continuity of space, indeed of space–time. The ball in parabolic flight occupies in succession all the locations between my hand and the ground on which it makes landfall – passing through P_1, P_2, P_3, etc. Different observers may observe the ball occupying different positions in a different order. There is, however, a definite order in which the ball did – and must – occupy the series of positions. In short, if there is a definite event (i.e. an event definitely happens) then it must have its elements connected in a definite order. If there is no definite event, then there is no event period and we are back with Weyl's world in which nothing happens.

The observer is even more problematic if one thinks of the universe as a set of space–time points. The distinctions between a) the observed (material world), b) the observer making the observation, and c) the observation being made seem to collapse. What, for example, are the distinctive characteristics of those events that are observations (or measurements?) How does the space–time point x, y, z, t come to be known as "x, y, z, t"? And, to refer to an earlier question, by what means do frames of reference arise or, more precisely, the observer who makes the material world into a set of frames of reference? Behind this is the deepest puzzle – and indeed contradiction – of the physical world picture: the emergence of *localities* with local times and spaces, the *sense* of absolute space and near and distant simultaneities, and those quasi-occult forces called "causes".[127] For the present, we note that the world picture of the physicist does not have a place for the physicist or, indeed, allow for world pictures or the observations upon which they are built.

If the observer presents problems to relativity theory, they are as nothing to those they pose to anyone trying to make sense of quantum mechanics, even though it is supposed to be even more observer-friendly. The status of the observer – is it a flesh-and-blood conscious human being, material recording device, or a mathematically defined frame of reference encompassing one or the other? – is even more ambiguous and vexing.

This is highlighted by the so-called "measurement problem" that some think threatens to bring the theoretical framework of quantum mechanics into disrepute. As Hans Halvorson says: "The measurement problem supposedly shows that an observer (like you or me) could not ascertain facts about the physical world by making observations, and so (among many other things) could not actually test quantum mechanics".[128] How is this claim justified? The measurement problem is a consequence of perhaps the most familiar, as well as notorious, features of quantum theory: its discovery that the properties of subatomic entities – as wave or particle, as having spin-x or spin-y states – are superposable. All quantum states are superpositions of more than one state. This, the so-called quantum indeterminacy, is maintained until observation causes "collapse of the wave function", when the composite state of the entity as, say, wave-and-particle resolves into one or the other. It might be thought that this should not be relevant to the status of the observer since the latter is not a subatomic entity.

Unfortunately, superposition is not confined to subatomic entities and it comes back to haunt the science itself because superpositions "percolate upwards" such that anything composed out of subatomic particles also has superposed states. This applies not only to rocks and trees but also to the bodies and – crucially – the brains of human beings and of their subset experimental physicists who make the observations upon which quantum mechanics is founded. While it is true that superposition becomes harder to maintain as we move towards the macroscopic world, there is no principled way of defining the upper limit of superposition.[129] It can be formally demonstrated that, if we adhere to Schrödinger linear dynamics, we end up with a situation in which, it would seem, there must be superpositions of macroscopically distinct states of the apparatus, and of any macro-system. This will include the brain of the observer.

There is worse to come: the phenomenon of "entanglement", such that two objects are so entwined with each other that they do not have *any* individual characteristics. When one is determined to have spin in one direction, the other spins in the opposite direction. This also percolates upwards towards macroscopic physical objects, including the measurement apparatus, which encompasses the laboratory, and the equipment. For most physicists, the macro-system underpinning the measurement process is the brain of the physicist, whose states supposedly reflect the processes of observation or measurement. Superposition, entanglement, and upward percolation, means that state of the brain of the observer remains indeterminate unless observed by the brain of an observer itself observed by the brain of an observer – ad infinitum.

In short, quantum mechanics predicts that physicists whose brains confirm quantum mechanics on the basis of observations will not have definite states corresponding to definite measurements. Hence Halvorson's conclusion quoted earlier: that the measurement problem seems to imply that "quantum mechanics entails a fact ... that would utterly destroy our ability to test the predictions of quantum mechanics"[130] – or indeed to arrive at any theory that would be exposed to testing against predictions.

It has provoked some desperate responses. David Wallace, a leading philosopher of physics argues that "the measurement problem threatens to make quantum mechanics incoherent" and to a cry of despair: "we have no satisfactory physical theory at all – only an ill-defined heuristic which makes unacceptable reference to primitives such as 'measurement', 'observer' and even 'consciousness'".[131] And it has prompted the development of alternative interpretations of quantum theory to the Copenhagen approach which is particularly associated with embracing uncertainty and indeterminacy. This approach is espoused by the overwhelming majority of physicists – at least those who adopt any position (most just "shut up and calculate"). These alternatives are deeply unattractive. Wallace's own preferred "many worlds" hypothesis, is a very expensive way of saving the (mathematical) appearances. It postulates that when a physicist makes a measurement, the universe splits into several branches, and the physicist splits into several copies of his or herself. The instantaneous creation of an entire universe – with very distant regions – would seem to be at odds with special relativity and the constraint on the speed of the transmission of influences. As if that is not bad enough, "many worlds" is not susceptible to empirical testing – something of a disability for a scientific hypothesis. It cannot be either confirmed or falsified because the Other Universes are causally disconnected from our own. Indeed, this is a necessary feature of an hypothesis that tries to deal with superposed incompatible states by allocating them to different sealed off universes that are not competing with one another to occupy unique logical spaces. An entity can be both A and not-A if it is allocated separate billets, separate worlds, for its A and not-A states.[132]

Other ways of eluding the self-destruction of quantum theory – such as the "hidden variable" theory of David Bohm and the dynamical reduction theory of Ghirardi and others (both discussed by Halvorson) – have commanded little general acceptance and have unresolved problems. They look very much like ad hoc responses to brush aside an awkward discovery. The problem is at root connected with the one we identified in the case of relativity: collapsing the distance between the observer and the observed world. The mistake in both instances is to entangle the physicist (and other conscious human beings) with the physical world.

And this is Halvorson's conclusion. He argues, on the basis of the measurement problem, that the minds of physicists, or indeed any conscious observer, whether they are vaguely gawping or precisely measuring, must be distinct from the system they are observing and, in the case of the physicist, from the devices they use to observe it. In other words, there must be something that is quarantined against the encroachment of the measurement problem. For Halvorson (and for some other writers such as Henry Stapp) this means dualism, with mental states being logically independent of physical states. The former, unlike the latter, are not susceptible to the fatal superposition that threatens to engulf quantum mechanics. As we know from direct experience, Halvorson points out, we experience things in definite states. (This, of course, is one of the thrilling mysteries of ordinary consciousness: how the dynamic experience of a dynamic world gives us an impression of a stable reality. An adjacent mystery is how in the conscious moment we can unite items that are, however, discrete parts of a conscious field; a disentangled unity that permits us to be aware separately of elements that we are also aware belong together.)

The measurement problem in quantum mechanics is a particularly acute manifestation of the observer problem, of finding a place for a distinction between the physical world and the measurements or observations that underpin the physicist's picture of it. The very fact that Halvorson has to remind us of basic facts about ordinary perception – and is in a minority in doing so – highlights how widespread is the tendency to confuse or conflate observers and the physical recording devices they use.

This tendency is illustrated by a recent interpretation of quantum uncertainty, espoused by, among others David Mermin, that is regarded as revolutionary. It is called quantum Bayesianism, or QBism. According to QBism, quantum uncertainty reflects our subjective sense of probability and hence uncertainty:

> Quantum states, wave functions and all the other probabilistic apparatus
> of quantum mechanics do not represent objective truths about stuff in the

real world. Instead, they are subjective tools that we use to organize our uncertainty about measurements before we make them. In other words, quantum weirdness is all in the mind.[133]

This has not been received with universal enthusiasm. According to some physicists, QBism is at odds with the idea that nature can be described from the perspective of the detached observer – presumably because the observer has to be attached to observe.

The assumption of attachment, seen in terms of physical causation of observations by the observed events, is a symptom of the domination of physicalism. Placing physical events such as the responses of recording devices on all fours with observations by regarding the latter also as physical events – in the brains of physicists – is consistent with the reduction of mind to material events in the material world, more specifically neural activity.[134] Even those who do not buy dualism must acknowledge that the observer cannot be on all fours with, even less assimilated to, the observed physical world. As we shall discuss in §12.2, perception, and the observations built on them, have an intentional relationship to their objects which cannot be assimilated to causal or other material connections. There is nothing in the relations between material events that makes one be *about* another, even less making one be a *measurement of* another.

Observation begins with the sentience of a complex organism for which some items are salient and others are not, some are near and others are not, and so on. Sentience in humans evolves to observations of objects by subjects – explicitly public objects by individual subjects – and shared or communal or communicated observations form the basis of measurements and the idea of objective reality. Sentience, with its localities, its inseparability from "here" and "now", has no place in physics at its most developed. It happens that it cannot be plausibly seen as simply one among other *effects* of the material environment on the material organism, analogous to, for example, the effect of radiation on a Geiger counter recording the number of particles impacting on it. At the heart of perception is intentionality which seemingly reaches causally upstream from (say) the experience of the effects of the object to the object that caused it. If the causal theory of perception were the whole story, it would have to explain how an effect could perceive its own cause or causes.

This is even more evidently true of those extremely complex prepared perceptions we call observations and more clearly yet in the case of measurements. Unlike the events seen on measuring devices, measurements are not mere material effects. And the result of a measurement is not just an effect of an apparatus, even less of the physical events that it measures, on the scientist in the way that a blink is an effect of the light on his eyes. A measurement is the intended product of an action. There is a huge gulf – many intermediate steps, concepts (largely presupposed) between what happens in a measuring device (which can continue to happen in the absence of any measurement being made) and a measurement; between the material set up that allows for a measurement and the act of measurement or observation; or *a fortiori* between a measurement device and an observer. Measurement, unlike the continuous sense experience of everyday life is intermittent, mediated, and dephe-nomenalized such that the indispensable "observer" is almost completely effaced.

The journey from sensations to the values of x, y, z and t is a long one and cannot be wrapped up in the mechanical frame of reference that underpins x, y, z and t. And a set of numbers could not trace that journey. Nor could it capture the sensations that form the starting place of that journey. "The observer" is clearly irreducible to manifestations of the observed physical world without being first reduced to numbers in a world of numbers. And if reduced in this way, it (he, she) entirely loses its (his, her) status as an observer.[135]

3.5.3.2 The twin paradox

> If we placed a living organism in a box ... one could arrange that the organism, after an arbitrarily lengthy flight, could be returned to the original spot in a scarcely altered condition while corresponding organisms which had remained in their original positions had long since given way to new generations. In the moving organism, the lengthy time of the journey was a mere instant, provided the motion took place with approximately the speed of light.
> Einstein (quoted in Whitrow, *The Natural Philosophy of Time*, 93)

The conflation of the observer of the physical world with the physical world itself is evident in one of the most famous consequences of the special theory of relativity: the twin paradox.[136] As we shall see, its most troubling consequences arise from the assumption that the twins are essentially material objects – organisms fundamentally akin to other physical objects, such as the rocket in which one of them ascends or the earth on which the other stays put or the clocks that enable them to track the time – rather than subjects. The twins as conscious beings are conflated with the biological material of which they are made, with physical devices such as the rocket, and with the clocks used to make measurements. Most importantly, time (including time as consciously experienced) is conflated with readings on clocks.[137]

This is rarely asserted explicitly but it slips between the cracks of popular expositions of relativity theory. Consider this passage from physicist Brian Greene: "Whenever we discuss speed or velocity...we must specify precisely *who or what* is doing the measuring."[138] The slither between "who" and "what" says it all. The observer seems to merge with the instrument that permits her to make observations. More specific to the twin paradox is the confusion of observers with material objects such as spaceships in this passage by philosopher Steven Savitt: "Given an 'observer' or (in the example most used nowadays), a spaceship far from any planet or stars, its path in space–time is a straight line."[139] The conflation of observers (albeit in scare quotes) with material objects located in space is taken to its limit in a discussion of time travel by Chris Smeenk and Christian Wutrich. Time travel, they say can be "understood as the existence of closed world lines that can be traced out by physical objects".[140] Note that it is *physical objects* to which travelling is ascribed though, as was pointed out in the previous chapter, travelling implies purpose, voluntary movement towards a goal, rather than mere motion. They then, however, slip back from objects to something like people. Time travelling is described as the possible trajectory of an *observer* "looping back on itself in time, to form … a closed timelike curve (CTC). In these universes travel is possible, in the sense that an observer travelling such a curve would return to exactly the same point in space–time at the 'end' of all her exploring".[141]

We have drifted from physical objects to an observer that is sufficiently human to be ascribed a sex. Such zigzagging between naturally occurring material objects, artefacts such as spaceships, and observers who see the objects and use the artefacts creates the necessarily blurred framework for thinking about the twin paradox in the conventional way. It enables a translation of measured time into time itself. The slowing of clocks and other material processes is interpreted as a slowing of time.

At the heart of the paradox is the prediction from special relativity that clocks (and other processes that may also be regarded as markers of time) are slowed when they are accelerated. What is the basis for this expectation?

Electromagnetic theory gives a fixed value for the speed of light (c).[142] All observations have confirmed that measured speed is constant, irrespective of the relative frame of reference of the light source and the observer. Consider a light source 300,000 km away. The signals will take one second to reach the observer, given that the speed of light (c) is (approximately) 300,000 km per second. Supposing the observer moves towards the source of light at 240,000 km per second, or 5/6 c. Two things might be expected, by the *pre*-Einsteinian principle of relativity of motion: firstly, that the light will take a shorter time to get to the observer, since the distance to be covered is reduced; and this is in fact the case. Secondly, it may be anticipated that the measured speed of light will increase: light from the source will move faster towards the observer. This proves not to be the case: the observed speed of light is a constant, as demanded by the Maxwell equations describing the properties of electromagnetic waves, and will not be altered by the relative motion of the source and observer. A pulse of light will come towards me at the same velocity irrespective of whether I stay still and wait for it to arrive or go out to meet it, even though in the latter case, the relative velocity of the light signal coming towards me should be increased.

This seems to undermine the basic, common sense every day principle of the relativity of motion whereby, for example, when I walk at 3 mph along the aisle of a train going 60 mph in the direction of travel, my speed relative to the embankment is 63 mph. The speed of movement of the source relative to the observer is affected by an intrinsic variation in time itself: increasing speed dilates (or slows) time or, more precisely, the relative speed of the passage of time depends on the relative speed of the frames of references of the observers recording its passage. Clocks are slowed. In the case of clocks travelling at 240,000 km per second, they will go at 60 per cent of their normal rate, or 36 minutes to the hour kept by a clock at zero velocity.[143] The slowing of clocks – "natural" ones such as muons and artificial ones such as caesium clocks – when they are accelerated to high speeds has been verified in many circumstances.[144]

Clocks – and any process we might use as a clock – are slowed but should we conclude from this that time itself is stretched? If we identify time with the behaviour of clocks, we are indeed obliged to draw this conclusion; if, that is to say, we conflate the means by which we measure time with time itself; or – and this is to our present point – with measurement and the means of measurement on the one hand with the observer on the other. To do so is to erase, or at least to conflate him or her with the physical observation that is made. Exploring this brings us to the twin paradox.

Consider identical twins. Twin 1, whom we shall call "Stay-at-Home", remains on earth. Twin 2, whom we shall call "Space-Traveller", takes a return journey into space at a speed 5/6 that of light. Let us suppose 20 years pass according to the earthbound twin's clock. According to Space-Traveller's clock, during this time, 12 years will have passed. When Space-Traveller returns, she will be 12 years older while Stay-at-Home will be 20 years older. The twins have thus managed to achieve different ages. What is more, for Space-Traveller, the interval between when she said farewell to Stay-at-Home and when they were reunited will be 8 years less than it will be for the latter. There is no inconsistency in this, as Paul Davies says: "You just have to accept that different observers experience different intervals of time between the same two events. There is no fixed time difference between the events, no "actual" duration, only *relative* time differences."[145] The key words are "observers" and "experience" which are not identical with (physical) clocks or with what is displayed on them. An observer is not reducible to a clock or to any source of equally spaced periodic events that can be regarded as a (potential) clock. Conversely, clocks – grandfather in the hall or caesium in the lab – are not, intrinsically, observers. These general caveats are relevant to our critical examination of the twin paradox.

The crucial point is that the paradox has a larger cast of characters than is usually appreciated. They tend to be merged. There are events: ordinary uncommunicative events (such as the rocket and Space-Traveller leaving earth or landing on a distant star); flashes of light that become *signals* in the minds of conscious beings such as the twins; clocks that are used to *record* the time intervals between what count as signals. And there are objects such as the spaceship, clocks, and the two twins. They are all treated as if they belonged to the same physical system, not merely subject to the same laws but capable of being captured in, fully accounted for, by the science of mechanics. The Paradox arises not out of the physics but out of this crucial but overlooked assumption which in turn derives from the conflation of the twins with material bodies (or their material circumstances), and clocks with those who use them to make measurements. The conflation is part and parcel of the erasure of the observer that we examined in the previous section. If, however, we do not accept that the twins are identical with their material bodies in precisely the same way as a spaceship is identical with the matter[146] in it and that the states of material clocks are not intrinsically (in the absence of a conscious observer) reports on time, then the Twin Paradox becomes less alarming and, what is more, reveals less than it is supposed about the nature of time. The key point is that the twins (and/or the community of minds to which they belong) transform flashes of light into light *signals* and states of a material object into times *recorded* on a *clock*. Outside of the consciousness, light flashes do not count as signals and states of objects do not count as "times told on a clock".

No-one should doubt that the clocks that accompany the twins will be found on inspection to have recorded different intervals of time between the departure and return of Space-Traveller; and the material of the twins' bodies – also a kind of clock, recording (for an observer) the passage of time – will also have aged differently. As Brian Greene has put it: "After all, if time elapses more slowly for an individual in motion than for an individual at rest, then this disparity should not apply just to time as measured by watches but also to time as measured by heartbeats and the decay of body parts".[147]

But there is no simple relationship between the age of either twin and the physical age of their material body, unless we assume that the twins are their bodies (as opposed to being embodied). If we accept that they are not just their bodies in the way that, say, the rest of the cast of characters such as clocks and the spaceship is identical with its material, then the interpretation of the thought experiment gets more complex and less disturbing. For a start, it is not entirely clear that the conscious experience, the quantity of lived life, of the two twins will obligingly mend itself to the measurements recorded on their respective clocks. There is a fundamental difference between, say, Space-Traveller being 40 years old and her spaceship being 40 years old. The spaceship is not 40 in the way that Space-Traveller is 40. The twin paradox, which overlooks this, results from stitching consciousness into the material world so that time as measured by the physicist is time as it is in itself. This is inadvertently hinted at in Greene's discussion of muons:

> If a stationary muon can read 100 books in its short lifetime, its fast-moving cousin will also be able to read the same 100 books, because though it appears to live longer than the stationary muon, its rate of reading – as well as everything else in its life – has slowed down as well. From the laboratory perspective, it's as if the moving muon will live longer than a stationary one, but the "amount of life" the muon will experience is precisely the same.[148]

Naturally, a muon no more experiences anything than it has a life or reads books. Greene is not, of course, serious about the idea of the book-reading muon. But the fact that he reaches for this analogy is telling. It closes the gap between conscious observers and purely physical entities. There is no "what it is like to be a muon" or indeed to be any of the other naturally occurring "clocks" – strictly, merely potential clocks – in the material world. With the twins, however, it is quite different.

This much we must concede: the accelerated ageing of Stay-at-Home's body compared with that of her space travelling sibling is no different from the time-dependent physical changes in, say, the metal of the rocket sent out into the space: arthritis and rust belong to the same ontological realm. The disturbing consequences of the thought experiment have their origin in the assumption that the fate of the body is identical with the experience of the person; that matter and consciousness are fused. The "older" twin, who remained at home however, may not be really older, given that being old *in the sense that is salient for humans* is not solely a property of the body but of how we experience our body and the experiences we have through our body.[149] Yes, Stay-at-Home's bodily parts will be more decayed but she will not have had more experiences – whatever that means. The lapse of time on a clock is not directly translatable into a quantity of experience or even a sense of lapse of time.

The essence of the present critique of the metaphysical significance that is ascribed to the twin paradox is this. The paradox assumes that time itself is entirely captured by the documentation of its passage on clocks (including the informal or potential clocks of changes in other material objects) and that the subjective experience of time (which is *not* shared by the clocks, the rockets or the greater parts of the twins' bodies – legs, spleen, arteries, etc.) is irrelevant. It sees the twins, their bodies (alive or dead – because a dead body can be a "clock" for an external observer such as a forensic pathologist, registering the passage of time from the moment of death), and the spaceship as simply parts of the same mechanical system. While the twins' "ageing" is of course linked to physical – more precisely biological – states, that is not the whole story. Getting older is not precisely analogous to rusting (say, of a spaceship), wearing away (say, of a clock) or rotting (say, of the twins' bodies). Being old and having had so many years of life is a qualitative state as well as the outcome of quantitative processes. The latter lie within the scope of physics, the former most certainly does not. Physics can give us no clue to the difference in the psychological states of the two twins. Two identical pebbles subjected to the different treatment meted out to the two twins would also change at different rates. The Stay-at-Home pebble would not undergo anything corresponding to "accelerated ageing". The latter requires something more; for example, a faster accumulation of experience and a more rapid extension of an interior narrative.

If we are entirely sincere positivists and accept the Machian principle, underpinning the special theory of relativity, that only that which is observed – or at least observable in principle – is real, we cannot exclude the conscious observer from our picture of the physical world – though we have to acknowledge that the observing subject is not accessible to objective observation. So we have to take account of the twins as observers – and not merely as material objects analogous to spacecraft and other such objects that figure in mechanical science – when we are trying to make sense of what is happening in the thought experiment. We could put this more bluntly by saying that "Einsteinian time" is not "time period". It does not even tell the whole story of measured time because it overlooks the consciousness of the observer necessary to turn a certain sub-class of events into clocks that transform time into minutes and accounts that can be compared, which is why "time dilation" applies as much to muons as to human bodies, though muons are unaware of it.

It is the ineliminable observer that makes the outcome of the thought experiment so paradoxical. If it were a question of two pebbles, one of which was earth-bound and the other had a return journey to a distant star at near the speed of light, their different rates of change would not be a cause for concern. We accept that items change at different rates in different circumstances.

If this is overlooked, it may be because not enough attention is paid in the thought experiment to the special (from the point of physics) nature of the interaction between the twins. This is particularly apparent at the start and finish of Space-Traveller's journey. It is because the twins compare notes, and begin and end side-by-side in the same "now", where one is now older than the other, that the result seems so disturbing. The translation of the sequences of events affecting the two bodies of the twins into one ageing faster than the other, and one experiencing the passage of more time than the other, is not a conflict within the material world but between two observers who are used to having identical local or proper times. (And this is just as true if we leave the comparison to a third party.) The relevance of this to limiting the significance of the paradox of the twins is captured in this passage from Savitt, from which we have already quoted:

> If each inertial frame has its own sets of simultaneous events, and the principle of relativity states that no physical experiment or system (and we human beings are physical systems too) can distinguish one such frame or another as (say) genuinely at rest, then we are able to discern no particular set of simultaneous events as constituting the now or the present.[150]

It is because we human beings are not (just) physical systems that those comparisons that give rise to the apparently disconcerting consequence of relativity are possible.

And there is, of course, a "now" of the present when the two twins compare bodies and wrinkle counts and this difference in the speed of the dermatological clocks correlates with the different rates of literal clocks. It is of the most profound significance that there is no local time – just as there is no "now" or "at the same time" – in the absence of observers. (Indeed, as we shall discuss in Chapter 11, there are no localities prior to the irruption of conscious subjects who alone are able to be observers.) The differences between the twins' lapses of time are not intrinsic to unobserved time itself but to the measurement of time by observers – who are not merely material objects, as their bodies (dead or alive) are. This measurement, the result of which is dependent on the relative frames of reference of the measurer and that which is measured, does not grow out of the system that is being measured but is something that is discovered by the application of measurements from without.

The paradox arising out of the thought experiment is not due to a quarrel between clocks or between spaceships and bodies acting as proxy clocks that seem to have passed different periods of time in what appears to be the same time. No; it is in the quarrel between clocks and the interval between two "nows" that transcend clocks: the "now" when the twins parted company and the "now" when they were reunited. The paradox, or at least its power to shock, resides in the incorrect assumption that the two nows belong to the same time-as-a-dimension that the spaceship and the bodies of the twins belong to. Then we would have a single line whose ends were separated by both 12 years and 20 years. The ends, however, do not belong to the same line.

Our astonishment therefore should be targeted on the "nows" – the simultaneities that define those intervals – before and after the journey into space, that generate the paradox. Given that an observer is necessary to privilege a part of the material world, along with its velocity, as a frame of reference and to privilege a moment of time as now, a location in space as here, and a position in space–time as here-and-now, it does not make sense, in the absence of such frames of reference, even to say that Space-Traveller left the earth before she returned to it. The twin as observer cannot be assimilated into, even less trumped, by the twin (or the twin's body) as an object of observation. There is a "what it is like to be" either of the twins that includes having certain experiences of the world around them that is not identical with the twins' bodies as material objects captured without remainder by the relativity theory. It is only because twins are both observers and self-observing entities that measurement is possible. As such, they have local time – their own account of time; and it is only from the viewpoint of local time that timing – with the paradoxes that follow – is possible. To put it bluntly: without the kind of time that relativity is supposed to have discredited, the paradox could not arise.

This is most evident in the putative encounter between the twins – when Space-Traveller is astonished to discover how old Stay-at-Home is and Stay-at-Home is scandalized by Space-Traveller's youth or when a third party is surprised at the discrepancy between their ages. These are possible only if we imagine a now in which the relevant observations – of one twin by the other or of both twins by a third party – takes place. That now lies at the heart of any observation or indeed any measurement, including those measurements that eventually lead to the science of mechanics and relativity. The paradox seems paradoxical only if we conflate the time implicit in physical processes (such as the ageing of the twin's bodies or the rusting of the spaceship) with the time made explicit through measurement, expect them to agree with one another, and are consequently surprised at the tension between them. The paradox in short arises from something that is overlooked in relativity theory; namely that physical processes are not, in themselves, clocks. To repeat Einstein:

> One is struck by the fact that the theory [relativity] ... introduces two kinds of physical things, i.e. (1) measuring rods and clocks, (2) and all other things, e.g., the electromagnetic field, the material point, etc. This, in a certain sense, is inconsistent ...; strictly speaking, measuring rods and clocks would have to be represented as solutions of the basic equations (objects consisting of moving atomic configurations), not, as it were, theoretically self-sufficient entities.[151]

Clocks fit in awkwardly into the material world.

The power of the twin paradox to cause dismay is a testament to the extent that we imagine that physics has the last word on the nature of time. In challenging this we need to embrace Plotinus' argument (against Aristotle) that to reduce time to a number, a quantity (of change) is not to grasp its essence.[152] To think of time as something that is grasped by measuring it – so that we can conclude from measurements that it is dilated or contracted under certain conditions – is to overlook something absolutely crucial: that the measurement of time relies on an observer who eludes measurement and whose existence – necessary to establish a frame of reference and the simultaneities that make measurement possible – is excluded from the physics of time, being a prior condition of it. Relativity, it seems, takes only one *relatum* in the relationship between the observer and the observed seriously – namely the observed – and the observer when not ignored entirely is regarded simply as another observable.[153] Overlooking this is the result of conflating lived experience with observations, observations with measurements, measurements with effects on material objects that have been designated as clocks, and states of material objects with clock readings. The fundamental nature of this error is captured again by Plotinus: "To make number essential to Time is like saying that magnitude has not its full quantity unless we can estimate that quantity".[154] Or indeed like saying that its nature is its (measured) quantity. The intrinsic absurdity of this position is made explicit in the assertion by Hermann Bondi that "time must never be thought of as pre-existing in any sense. It is a manufactured quantity".[155]

This is a predictable consequence of the implicit assumptions behind the paradox: (a) the physics of time captures the essence of time; (b) the essence of time is its quantity; and (c) its quantity is as recorded in any physical processes that count as clocks not as (say) experienced by conscious beings.

Indeed, if there were only clock-time and *any* material process counted as a clock, then there would be no clocks and no clock-time. There is a need for a time – "now" – in which we *consult* clocks. Lived time is not only contrasted with clock-time but that in virtue of which there is clock-time; in virtue of which sites of recurrent, isochronous events become clocks and events take place *at* a particular designated time.

The somewhat knotty relationship between time and consciousness, or between time as a dimension and the conscious subject, is highlighted by the famous passage from H. G. Wells we have already cited in Chapter 2 when we discussed time travel:

> "Clearly", the Time Traveller proceeded, "any real body must have extension in four directions: it must have Length, Breadth, Thickness, and – Duration … There are really four dimensions, three, which we call the three planes of Space, and a fourth, Time … There is no difference between Time and any of the three dimensions of Space except that our consciousness moves along it".[156]

The suggestion that the passage of consciousness "along" time – in virtue of which time is distinguished from the other three dimensions – is to be treated as a mere detail tells us a lot about the consequences of reducing space and time to dimensions. It shows how it inevitably leads to the marginalization of consciousness. Far from installing consciousness at the heart of the physical world, four-dimensional physics and relativity diminish it – as the mere difference between time and space. The spirit of "mere" is equally apparent in the passage also worth quoting again from Hermann Weyl:

The objective world simply is, it does not happen. Only to the gaze of my consciousness, crawling upward along the lifeline of my body, does a section of this world come to life as a fleeting image in space which continually changes in time.[157]

The gaze of consciousness thus regarded is not as something that transcends the objective world (which it does) but merely as something that gets it wrong; or rather that curdles our vision of it, a vision that is clarified in mathematical physics, which shows that nothing actually happens.

3.5.3.3 The erasure of the observer: some conclusions

The *logico-physical philosophy of time* ... assumes that time is best understood through a careful analysis of temporal concepts, informed by the best physics and mathematics. But it is not part of this view that every aspect of time is comprehensible without reference to the subjective viewpoints of agents.

Currie, "Can There be a Literary Philosophy of Time?", 44

It will be evident from the foregoing that the observer in contemporary physics, far from being enthroned at its centre, is suppressed. In relativity, he/she is conflated with (insentient) material objects, often recording apparatuses, or inertial frames of reference from which observations are made. In the latter case, he/she is half way to being reduced to a set of coordinates that confer values on space–time points or regions and on the events that they constitute or which take place in them.[158] The conflation of the observer and the observed physical world is the product of a two-way process: physical systems (clocks and rocks) are spoken of as observers; and observers, human beings, are treated as physical systems. In quantum mechanics, superposition threatens to engulf the observer (identified with his/her brain) in the indeterminacy of the elements in the quantum field, such that definite observations, measurements, would be impossible. The measurement problem in quantum theory makes explicit that what relativity theory seems to allow or even require, namely the merging of the observer with the observed world, cannot be permitted if physics itself is to be possible. The observer needs to be offset or cordoned off from the material world revealed by observations and interpreted by physicists. It has to transcend what is revealed by physics.

Observations in the usual sense are from a locality, and it is this that is characterized as an inertial frame of reference. Without the latter, there are no observations. No group of objects or mere point, or set of points, in space–time would of themselves amount to a frame of reference and, although points may be defined mathematically, their actual values will be borrowed from the coordinates that are placed around them by the observer as we discussed in §3.4.1. They require, that is to say, an at least implicit viewpoint to create the axes that give the points within it definite values. An account of space, time, gravity, and motion described by laws of physics that are invariant under say a Lorentz transformation, irrespective of the status of the viewpoint (location, velocity, acceleration) of the observer, does without actual viewpoints and actual observers, and hence leaves out those conditions in which observations are possible.

A view of the universe as an immobile spatio-temporal continuum – one interpretation of reality according to general theory of relativity – is the inevitable consequence of an approach that squeezes out the observer. This universe is unchanging not only because it is the sum total of all that there is, will be, and has been, but also because it has no points of view built into it. The field equations of general relativity do not house actual events because an event viewed from nowhere – neither near or far, large or small, before or after, drained of phenomenal qualities – would not amount to an event. There is no coming into being (or going out of being) in the manifold. While it is possible to introduce individual viewpoints by hand – and so get things particularized and moving – they would not belong to the ultimate (mathematical) reality. They have no part in the universe of physics and, indeed, should be excluded from it.

A defence of the marginalization and eventual liquidation of the conscious observer might go as follows. While science begins with individual experiences – those associated with inquiry-driven measurements – scientific accounts gather up those experiences into a theory which describes in the most economical way the sum total of the empirically actual and possible. This necessarily transcends individual experience, and is liberated from any individual viewpoint, indeed any viewpoint in the everyday sense. Mathematical physics is simply the most advanced development of the de-experiencing process (see §3.3) that began with the visual sense, a sense that could see *that* it was seeing and hence could critique its own viewpoint with intuitions of rival viewpoints. It was embarked on a process of squeezing out itself: overlooking its own viewpoint, itself *as* a viewpoint. At its terminus is a view of the world that gathers all actuality and possibility under a single de-focused gaze. It approximates to what Lucretius spoke of when he spoke of "the sum total of all sums total that is eternity".[159]

That is true up to a point. But it debars physical science from making metaphysical claims. Mach perhaps confused a way of demarcating testable and useful scientific theories, and separating them from useless speculation, with a judgement as to what is ultimately real. The confusion may have been encouraged by something else that Mach (and many of those influenced by his world picture) believed. It has been aptly summarized by Leszek Kolakowski:

> [T]here is no difference between ordinary experience accessible to any being endowed with a nervous system and scientifically organized experiment. There is no break in continuity between science and spontaneous modes of everyday experience, nor even between science and modes of behaviour characteristic of the entire animal world.[160]

Closing the gap between scientific observation and the kinds of experiences available to all sentient creatures makes it easier to assimilate the observer to the observed. Indeed, where the discipline of physics grows out of the irritation of nerve endings, (that is to say physico-chemical activity in the nervous system) it is close to being itself something entirely physical.

This is not the place to discuss the "naturalization of knowledge".[161] It is sufficient to remark that, if we are able to close the (huge) gap between immediate sense experience and the massive cognitive structure of science, embracing both in a biologically based scientism, it is easy to understand why the ordinary observer, the bystander who watches trains moving out of stations and stations relieving themselves of trains, should be fused with that which he or she observes.

We are entitled then to look physics in the eye and say "You don't tell the whole story". The full story would have to allow the reality of the observer separate from that which is observed. And it would also have to account for the origin of the world of everyday experience which lies beyond the reach of physics. In the Einsteinian manifold there is no "here" or "there" and there are no journeys from "here" to "there". If locations are mathematized, movement is not movement as we know it: the movement of things around us and the movements we make ourselves.

But these things are essential to our lives, to the lives of observers, and, in particular, to our nature as temporal beings. And, given that physicists are temporal creatures like other humans, they are essential to physics itself. If, as Einstein said, "there are no preferred observers in the universe", we might ask whether if that were entirely true there would be any observers at all, given that all observers prefer themselves in the sense of being at the centre of their experienced world.

Consider the development of this idea in one of the cornerstones of contemporary astrophysics: the cosmological principle. This states that there is no centre to the universe, that matter is distributed similarly in all directions (isotropic) and same everywhere (homogeneous) when it is considered on the largest scale. All observers everywhere in space and in all times, would have the same large-scale view of the universe. In short, it assumes that the universe seen aright would be like the Parmenidean One: unchanging and undifferentiated. But what sort of view would that be? It would be unlike the world revealed to living, flesh and blood observers like you and me, who are situated at the centre of a universe differentiated according to place, time, qualities and quantities, and meaning and significance. To be a real observer – an observer who makes observations, who experiences and measures – is to have a take on the universe that is different from that of another observer; to have a world arranged in accordance with the self-preference that is built into the very possibility of experience.

We need to ask ourselves what remains of the notion of "the observer" once we extend it beyond the individual person, or a group of persons checking each other's experiences, to a so-called "fundamental observer" who (or more precisely "which") represents the viewpoint of entire galaxies that are associated with the bulk distribution of matter through the universe, whose "now" is a preferred foliation (that is the good news) but it is based on a universe-wide clock rooted in major mass centres (that is the bad news). The times kept by fundamental observers fit together to form one common universal time:

> [A]ccording to these observers, there are successive states of the universe as a whole which define a cosmic time. In terms of this, all events have a unique time order. The anomalies and discrepancies of time-ordering that arise in connection with the special theory of relativity are due not to the nature of events themselves but to the introduction of observers moving through the universe relative to the fundamental observers in their neighbourhood.[162]

These "discrepancies" will include the twin paradox, dealing with paired observers who are localised in the universe and moving in different ways with respect to these fundamental observers. So we recover cosmic time from the point of view of fundamental observers for whom there will be a common linear time order. But are these really "observers"? They are mathematically derived ideals composed not of flesh and blood but of clusters of mathematical terms to which are given general values. The "viewpoint of entire galaxies" is not a viewpoint.

In other words, if the world according to our most advanced physical theories were the whole story, there would be no basis for the emergence of that in virtue of which the universe comes to have ideas – true or false, complete or incomplete – about its own nature. If the whole story of the world were the world according to physics, there would be no physicists, no "according to", and no conception of a world. The Machian naturalization of knowledge, seeing it as the product of events in neural tissue, as part of a continuum of consciousness that begins with sensations and ascends towards the Theory of Everything, not only makes the key characteristics of knowledge – generality, reliance on notions such as "the universe", and its being *about* and true *of* the material world – utterly incomprehensible. It would make the very terms in which we understand the material world, and on which we arrive at a purely mathematical understanding of the world, impossible.

3.5.4 Time and the physicists

> Denial of the reality of time ... widens the gulf between science and consciousness to such an extent that it renders all our experience questionable, including the perceptual experience in which we must translate, and on the basis of which we must make, our scientific discoveries.
>
> Unger & Smolin, *The Singular Universe and the Reality of Time*, 521

> Why promote space-time from a 4D diagram, which is a useful conceptual device, to a real essence? By identifying my abstract system with an objective reality, I fool myself into regarding it as the arena in which I live my life.   Mermin, "QBism as CBism"

The thesis of this and the preceding chapter has been that physics, the discipline that above all others mathematizes our understanding of the world, has impoverished time (and space) – allowed it to waste away to a mere variable (little) "t" that is remote from the complex temporality of our rich human experience. There is, however, no consensus among physicists about the nature of time, or even whether or not it is real. I have discussed the views of various physicists in passing but in this section I would like to highlight this variety of views that physicists are committed to, implicitly if not explicitly. Conflict is evident even among those who argue that physics can do without time. Do they mean that physical theories will be more effective if they leave time out or that time is not itself a feature of the fundamental reality of the universe? And if it is a question of the truth about the universe rather than more effective or even more convenient theories, does the absence of time in physics mean the absence of tensed time, of the preferred direction or arrow of time we discussed in Chapter 2, or of something more fundamental, namely objective time intervals and the time ordering of events? Whatever the answer to these questions, it is worth noting at the outset that those physicists who strip time down to a mere parameter that is vulnerable to being dispensed with are more faithful to the *weltanschauung* of (mathematical) physics than others who try to retain a richer view of time.

At one extreme is the view, expressed by Carlo Rovelli, a leading figure in the endeavour to unite quantum mechanics and relativity theory.[163] According to Rovelli, time is a notion that makes sense only for describing a limited region of reality. It will disappear when quantum mechanics and general relativity are united to encompass all aspects of the entire universe: "mechanics will become a theory of the relations between variables, rather than the theory of the evolution of variables in time".[164] His argument is in part based on the apparent circularity in the measurement of time. When we measure time, he argues, we are just comparing clocks in what is a closed circle of mutual validation: we check clock A against clock B and clock B against clock C and clock C against clock A. Think of the most famous example: the moment when Galileo realized that the swings of a pendulum were regular and could be used as the basis of clocks. Galileo used his pulse to demonstrate that the swings of the chandelier in church were really regular or isochronous; he then used the chandelier to time his pulse and that is how things have always been.

Rovelli, however, seems to overlook that this apparently closed circle – which suggests that we have no way of checking which clocks are measuring time more accurately – is broken in two ways. First there is the increasing consistency of clocks: atomic clocks are more in synch than pendulum-based clocks. Secondly, and more compellingly, is the discovery of laws – laws of motion for example – which enable periodicities to be predicted independently of direct measurements. There is a network of laws that have a precision that go beyond actual measurements (something which I will discuss in §3.6) – which is why we can be sure, or it makes sense to be sure, that a caesium clock is more accurate than a clepsydra. (We shall examine this in §4.4.)

Halvorson has argued that "quantum theory rules out the possibility of any quantity that one might call 'the time interval between two events'" because of the formalism employed in the theory – in which quantities are represented by operators – such that time is not a *quantity* at all.[165] This is already expressed in the canonical quantization of general relativity that results in the Wheeler–DeWitt equation which does without a time variable and seemingly corresponds to a universe frozen in time – or frozen out of time.[166] The assumption is that if something does not figure in the most comprehensive and predictively powerful equations, then it is not real.

Somewhat at an angle to this, a recent paper[167] has reported an apparent experimental proof of an idea first put forward a couple of decades earlier that time is emergent from subsystems within an overall timeless universe, using observation of the quantum entanglement of photons. The authors compared the change in entangled particles with an external clock deemed to be entirely outside the universe. (Don't ask). They appeared to be entirely unchanging. In the case of an internal observer, however, there was evidence of change independent of universe entanglement and, regarding the photons as a "clock" (again no comment), this indicated a flow of time. The experiment seems to show more than that the totality of the universe (viewed from a presumably virtual outside) does not change (a truism) but also that there is genuine change within subsystems of the universe. Needless to say, the assumption of the two viewpoints, one of them local, and treating elementary particles as clocks, is problematic in view of the discussion in the previous section (§3.5.3.3), but one should perhaps be grateful for small mercies.

And larger mercies may be on offer. According to Karel Kuchar, while "relativity does not care much about privileged time … quantum mechanics is hooked on it. When it is not given, it demands an adequate substitute".[168] The reasons for this are buried in the equations beyond the reach of all but the cognoscenti, but there are seductive intuitions that support the notion that there is something in quantum mechanics corresponding to the asymmetry of information that is experienced by humans who can see (or at least recall) the past but cannot see the future.

This is most obviously rooted in a more fundamental temporal asymmetry – namely that the past is determinate and the future indeterminate. The wave function collapse that occurs after interaction with an observer reduces a superposition of several possible states of a wave function to a single definite state: many possible eigenvectors with their associated eigenvalues resolve to a single eigenvector with a single eigenvalue. This is consistent with a more general, current notion, of time as the passage from an open future through the actuality of the present to the unalterable fixity of the past. The "now" that is the filter is clearly linked to the observer. This is endorsed by Lucas, who argues that "quantum mechanics" – at least on a realist construal – "is rather kind to time. In quantum mechanics time is mostly an independent variable, not under pressure to be anything else":

> There is a world-wide tide of actualization – collapse into eigen-ness constituting a preferred foliation … of co-presentness sweeping through the universe: a tide which determines an absolute present. In this, quantum mechanics goes beyond anything that thermodynamics and cosmology suggest, which, although witnessing to there being a definite directedness in

time, do not pick out any particular time as pre-eminently real – the moment of truth when possibilities become actual or else fade away. Quantum mechanics ... now appears to be irremediably probabilistic, and not only insists on the arrow being kept in time, but distinguishes a present as the boundary between an alterable future and an unalterable past.[169]

The idea of quantum mechanics as the friend of time, even of tensed time, is not without its problems, not the least being the difficulties (already discussed in §3.5.3.1) with observation and measurement in quantum mechanics.[170] The observer as the bestower of determinacy has somehow to get his/her determinacy from elsewhere. However, the transition from amorphous waves that have no location – only probability functions – to definite particles does seem to resonate with basic ideas about both quantum mechanics and tensed time. Penrose and Percival suggested half a century ago that the increasing amplitude of fluctuations in a quantum vacuum (the apotheosis of zero) – which increases the probability of a universe coming into being – gave a direction to time.[171] Leaving aside the circularity that this quantum arrow shares with other arrows of time – "increasing amplitude" means "increasing amplitude *with time*" – this does at least show that quantum mechanics and time are not necessarily mutually exclusive; or not at least in the eyes of all the adepts of the Black Art. But the argument is more than a little entangled. This is evident from the excellent discussion by Hilgevoord and Atkinson.[172] A few passages capture the uncertainty:

The [Schrödinger] wave equation evolves in time and gives probability amplitudes and transition rates for physical entities with respect to external time; the total probability is conserved in time.[173]

It is obvious that [the theory of quantum gravity] will have drastic consequences for the concept of time.[174]

Whereas quantum mechanics still contains the absolute time t, no such time is available in canonical quantum gravity. One should thus expect that the equations of quantum gravity are fundamentally timeless.[175]

Upon quantization, spacetime disappears in the same way as a particle trajectory has disappeared in quantum mechanics; only space remains.[176]

There is much dispute over whether relativity theory eliminates time from the world. Special relativity disallows "substantive time" as an independent background to events but (as we shall discuss in §10.3.3) the situation with general relativity is more ambiguous. It is not clear, at any rate, whether our everyday experience really is predicated on the notion of a substantive time-in-itself. The reduction of time to the fourth dimension, however, has more serious consequences, which we have already discussed. Consider again Minkowski:

The views of space and time which I want to present to you arose from the domain of experimental physics, and therein lies their strength. Their tendency is radical. From now onwards space by itself and time by itself will recede completely to become mere shadows, and only a type of union of the two will still stand independently on its own.[177]

As we have already noted, this does not necessarily mean that time has become space but that, while intervals and locations can be either time-like or space-like, they are intrinsically neither the one nor the other: they are space–time intervals and locations. Space, however, is the dominant conceptual partner, if only because it is easier to represent on the page, and easier, for the reasons set out in Chapter 1 literally to "envisage". What's more, it brings three as opposed to just one dimension to the party. The notion of space–time therefore seems more space-like than time-like.

Even those physicists who do not conclude that time is essentially space-like, may be inclined to agree with Einstein's famous assertion that "for us believing physicists, the distinction between past, present and future is only a stubborn illusion".[178] The attack on tensed time from physics will be discussed in §5.1 but it is sufficient here to note the outline argument. Measured time relations between events will depend on the viewpoint (more accurately, the inertial frame of reference) of the observer. Consider two events, A and B. Two different observers moving in different ways may judge of A and B, that they are simultaneous (in each other's "present"), or that A is before B (so that A is "past" when B occurs) or that B is before A (so that A is in the "future" when B occurs). There is no referee, occupying a privileged view point, who can adjudicate between these three judgements. To put this in relativistic terms, there is no privileged foliation of the manifold – a hyperplane of simultaneity – to determine what counts as present, as past, or as future.

General relativity has negative implications for time as the possibility of change. Indeed, Einstein happily accepted the title of "the Parmenidean" from Karl Popper: "I called him 'Parmenides' since he believed in a four-dimensional block universe, unchanging like the three-dimensional block universe of Parmenides".[179] Thus Einstein as (an unlikely) Block-head. General relativity (for some) "regards reality as a single entity of which time is an ingredient rather than as a changeable entity set *in* time".[180] Consequently, all times (and their associated events) timelessly coexist. The force of the "co" in "coexist" is of course deeply problematic. And the coexistence of some events would be impossible to conceive: the shops are always open and always closed and, what is more, there are neither times when they open nor times when they close.

This is explored in considerable detail by John Earman who investigates whether McTaggart's argument for the unreality of time, based upon the unreality of change, is upheld by the general theory. He concludes that there is a real problem about change "which seems to imply that there is no temporal change in any genuine physical magnitude, i.e. there is no … property change".[181]

There is a consolation prize of sorts: "a D-series of time-ordered coincidence events" that emerge from the deep structure of the general theory, which are objects of predication that come and go and so accommodate property changes.[182] Earman, however, doubts whether they are real and whether they can be invoked to melt the frozen dynamics of the block universe. The default position is that "genuine changes in physical magnitude" – the basis of any qualitative change – "are not to be found in the world itself but only in a representation", which Earman accepts that many will view as "patently absurd".[183]

Quite compelling appearances, such as are evident in your reading this sentence, irresistibly suggest that change is part of the real world. However, the freezing out of time and the freezing of the universe are connected: they are both (unsurprising) results of the mathematization of reality, which has as one of its basic tenets the notion of conservation – the preservation of identity and even constancy beneath the surface appearance of change such that the laws of change can be represented as the underlying invariance of the world beneath surface alterations. This has, of course, been a key idea of western thought since Parmenides expressed the notion that which is (really) real does not change and stability is the mark of that which is real.[184]

This conviction has protean expressions at many levels in science. Chemical equations describe changes while at the same time asserting that, at the level of the fundamental constituents, namely atoms, everything is preserved. This was generalized to the law of the conservation of matter, later further generalized – in order to accommodate the transformation of matter into energy – to the law of the conservation of mass-energy, which says that the quantity of the fundamental stuff of the material world remains unchanged beneath the visible transformations. When, as has increasingly happened in science, mass-energy is defined not in terms of perceptible phenomena such as warmth or brightness or heaviness, but as mathematical abstractions corresponding to a measure of pure magnitude, the laws of conservation, of that which is unchanged, become rock solid. What is more, the mathematical equation, by putting the beginning and end of a process in the same place, in a sense cancels change.

This is only the starting point for contemporary mathematical physical science. The theory of relativity was driven by the deep intuition that has guided much science – that reality is to be found not in individual events experienced by individual people but in the *pattern* of happenings as they would be experienced by all and everyone; a pattern whose best descriptions are unchanging laws that are invariant across all possible observers over all times. In the case of quantum mechanics, where the notion of entities with persisting existence and definite locations is somewhat under siege, symmetry has emerged as the key notion: an essentially spatially (or spatially conceived) pattern – that is conserved. If symmetries are ultimate realities and symmetries are conserved, then nothing really changes. In both science and mathematics, a symmetry is change without change, or apparent change where, fundamentally, there has been no change. That quantum mechanics, and its more ambitious descendants (such as quantum gravity and string theory), lose time so completely is perhaps simply a reflection of the fact that these are the most highly and indeed purely mathematized accounts of the universe. Quantum field theory, for example, quantizes classical field theory by going through the equations and replacing physical values with "operators", with operations such as "differentiation" and "square root", which generate not physical values but ranges of probabilities.

Not all physicists are happy with the loss of time in physics. Unhappiest of all is Lee Smolin and no discussion of the "chronicidal" tendencies of physics would be complete without reference to his writings. In recent books, he argues that the current troubles of physics – in particular the problem of reconciling relativity theory and quantum mechanics – will not be overcome so long as physicists hold to the view that time is unreal.[185] Against this, he asserts that, not only is time real but that nothing we know or experience gets closer to the heart of nature than the reality of time. Time is absolutely fundamental.

Most interestingly, from the point of view of the present inquiry, he shares the view advanced in this book that the elimination of time has its origin less in any particular theory than in the habit of physicists taking the mathematical objects they deal with as if they were not merely real (so that they are independent of our intellect, discovered rather than constructed) but (as we shall discuss in the next section) actually constitutive of reality itself: "Curves and other mathematical objects do not live in time" – though of course their tokens, and the experience of their tokens, do – is one of his many statements to this effect.[186] This goes all the way back to at least the first scientific revolution in which motion is portrayed as a curve on a graph, so that time is represented as if it were another dimension of space:

> Motion is frozen, and the whole history of constant motion and change is presented to us as something static and unchanging … We have to find a way to unfreeze time – to represent time without turning it into space. I have no idea how to do it. I can't conceive of a mathematics that doesn't represent a world as if it were frozen in eternity.[187]

The reason why physics would inevitably mislay time, therefore, goes further back than recent developments: it resides in the mathematization of the world that makes temporal locations into numbers and the intervals between temporal locations into the numerical difference between numbers. If quantum mechanics has a particularly acute problem with time, it is perhaps because it is the most mathematically developed account of the world. And as it reaches out to be united with the general theory of relativity and string theory emerges, nothing of non-mathematical substance – practical consequences, empirical tests – remains.

It is evident, if we are to rescue time, we need to give up taking literally equations and laws and the mathematical objects out of which they are composed, and desist from drawing metaphysical conclusions from physics. Smolin's view is at one with the view that Bergson developed throughout his philosophy: that, since the sciences are so organized as to ignore time as we experience it, it is hardly surprising that they lose time.[188] Smolin is clearly of the party (a minority, he believes, among physicists) for whom the inability to find time is (as George Musser has described it) "a hole at the heart of physics".[189] They regret that "as researchers try to formulate more fundamental laws, the little t evaporates altogether". But only if we assume that physics, reduced to the relationship between pure quantities – in short the mathematical account of the world – is the definitive, or at least most authoritative statement on what the world consists of, should the absence of time in its version of fundamental reality, prompt us to discard, or at least to feel that we must revise radically, our conception of time.

Before we proceed to defend time as it is understood outside of physics, let us address head on the question of the extent to which reality is truly represented in mathematics or, indeed, whether mathematics, in some sense difficult to specify, is constitutive of the world. The notion that (timeless) mathematics reveals, or constitutes reality, is the other side of the idea that what is really real is timeless.

3.6 MATHEMATICS AND REALITY: THE WORLD AS A SYSTEM OF MAGNITUDES

> Numbers and other mathematical objects are wanted in physics anyway, so one may as well enjoy their convenience as coordinates for physical objects; and then, having come thus far, one can economize a little by dispensing with physical objects ... As physicalists we have welcomed bodies with open arms ... On the other hand the mathematical objects attained the ontological scene only begrudgingly for services rendered ... It is ironical then that we at length find ourselves constrained to this anti-physical sort of reductionism from the side of physics itself ... Physical objects, next, evaporated into space-time regions; but this was the outcome of physics itself. Finally, the regions went over into pure sets; still, the set theory itself was there for no other reasons than the need for mathematics as an adjunct to physical theory.   Quine, "Whither Physical Objects?"[190]

The tendency to read our notational systems into the world which they are used to describe – what, as we've seen, Whitehead called "the muddle of *importing the mere procedures of thought into the facts of nature*"[191] – has a long history; indeed it goes all the way back to the earliest days of science and philosophy.[192] It is there in the notion traditionally ascribed to Pythagoras that "All is number" so that the very fabric of the world is made of numbers; or that, as Aristotle put it, "the principles of mathematics were the principles of all things"[193] – a view echoed in Galileo's less radical assertion we have discussed that "the book of nature is written in the language of mathematics". When contemporary physicists and philosophers describe space as "non-Euclidean" rather than "Euclidean" a well-founded preference for one set of mathematical tools over another turns into a claim about the most general nature of the physical world. Inverted commas round the description of space as "curved" and time as "dilated" are somewhat thin on the ground. And paradoxes arising out of the mathematics of motion in space are, 2,500 years after Zeno still taken seriously as having metaphysical significance.

What is more, there are physicists for whom mathematical realism is an article of faith, some of them pre-eminent in their field. Bryce DeWitt, one of the fathers of the Wheeler–DeWitt equation, is among them:

> The real world is faithfully represented by the following collection of mathematical objects. The use of this word ["faithfully"] implies a return to naïve realism and the old-fashioned idea that there can be a direct correspondence between formalism and reality. The symbols of quantum mechanics represent reality just as much as do those of classical mechanics.[194]

The "just as much" would be reassuring if it did not mean "a lot" rather than "not at all". Otherwise, it is simply an assertion that quantum mechanics is a mirror of reality.

The fact that the endeavour to save (the reality of) the (mathematical) appearances leads to such a desperate measure as the many worlds interpretation of quantum mechanics (discussed in §3.5.3.1) indicates the power mathematical realism has over some very eminent minds. Adrian Kent points out that DeWitt need not be at all defensive, given that "mathematical realism has been more or less continuously advocated by distinguished physicists throughout [the twentieth] century".[195] Possibly; but the situation in which interpretations are developed to save the mathematical appearances is something of a decline from the time when, for example, Copernicus developed a different mathematics of the solar system to save actual appearances.

However, he might take comfort from James Ladyman – whose views we shall discuss presently – who has argued that metaphysics should be rooted in physics, since the fundamental description of reality is one in which the world is described by reference to mathematical models:

> What makes the structure [of the world] physical not mathematical? That is a question we refuse to answer. In our view, there is nothing more to be said about this that doesn't amount to empty words ... The "world-structure" just is and exists independently of us and we represent it mathematico-physically via our theories.[196]

How different this is from the view of Russell – a great mathematician as well as a philosopher – who remarked that "Physics is mathematical not because we know so much about the world but because we know so little; it is only its mathematical properties that we can discover."[197] This acknowledges that mathematical descriptions are profoundly simplifying; and the more general they are, the more they endeavour to encompass the totality of things, the more the world they purport to portray is emptied. Fundamental theories in physics reveal only the structure or the form of an otherwise unobservable (or unobserved) world and not its actual nature.

My target in this section is not of course mathematics itself or even the use of entities such as i and other exotic creatures in the mathematical menagerie to help us to explore the world and to predict and manipulate what happens in it and in that part of it where its happenings are things that happen to us. The most abstract mathematical physics, for example quantum mechanics, "works" in several non-trivial senses: it delivers practical benefits through the technology based on it (including the computer on which I am typing this sentence); it is internally coherent; it coheres with other theories of extraordinary theoretical robustness, scope and practical value – notwithstanding some profound conflicts as with the general theory of relativity; and it makes astoundingly precise predictions that can be tested.

Rather, it is "mathematical literalism" that it is to be challenged. It has many possible forms.

(a) At its most modest, it is the belief that mathematics is a mirror image of the world or that it is the most faithful portrait of – or will provide the last word on – its underlying reality.

(b) Less modest is the belief that when the mathematical account of the physical world is complete, we shall have the whole truth of the world – a theory of everything.

(c) At its least modest, mathematical literalism is the claim that mathematical objects are constitutive of the world: "All (seen correctly) is number".

This last claim requires further clarification: we still must specify what kind of items we are talking about; whether we include imaginary and complex numbers or hold, along with Kroneker, that only the integers are naturally occurring and that the rest are man-made; and whether we are thinking of patterns of numbers, relations between patterns of numbers, equations, matrices, geometrical forms and entities such as points and so on. En route to industrial strength Pythagoreanism is a relatively cautious mathematical realism which holds that numbers are real entities, existing in themselves, being more than mere elements in a notational system upon which they depend for their existence.

As physics moves towards a unified account of the natural world, it becomes more purely mathematical. The world is seen as a set of mathematical patterns, preserved across change, of highly generalized events. The items that are postulated in order to grasp the world become increasingly exotic and consequently remote not only from our immediate experience of the world but from anything of which we can make intuitive sense.[198] They are not, and could not be, suggested by the actual world we look at, walk around, bump into, and grapple with. Characters such as the (unimaginable and unthinkable) square root of −1 move to centre stage. Meanwhile the contents of our direct experience vanish. Secondary qualities such as warmth, colour, loudness, all disappear, though for a while they may be represented by quantitative proxies such as degrees of temperature, wavelengths of electromagnetic radiation, and frequency spectrograms, before the laws applicable to their particular domains are subsumed into higher order laws with even greater generality.

En route strange things are done to the furniture of the world: we have mentioned the way time is multiplied by itself and subjected to indignities no pre-scientific entity such as an afternoon would submit to. But there are others that are more striking still. Consider the extraction of the speed from light and setting it on a course – remote from dazzle and brightness – where it can be multiplied by itself (as in $E = mc^2$) or placed under a denominator.[199]

Notwithstanding the admitted unintelligibility of the most powerful and comprehensive scientific theories – those rooted in quantum mechanics – the progressive mathematization of the world seems to many to constitute progress towards ever more complete understanding. Unification of the laws of nature creates the feeling that we are arriving at a view of the world that is not merely synoptic but explanatory – offering "how" and even "why".

This free pass from "how" to "why" has been highlighted by Richard Hamming:

> Not that science explains "why" things are as they are – gravity does not explain why things fall – but science gives so many details of "how" that we have the feeling we understand "why". Let us be clear about this point; it is by the sea of interrelated details that science seems to say "why" the universe as it is.[200]

The transition from a set of phenomena seen as exemplifying certain general principles or trends to seeing them as a subset of an even greater set expressing even more general laws and principles certainly adds to the predictive and manipulative power of science but does not fully answer to our feeling as to what would count as an explanation. At the very least, this is because very general laws have little grasp on the singular actualities that make up the flow of experienced reality. The notion of "causal laws" – that tries to unite the local "oomph" of causes making things happen with the general guidance of laws shaping the happening – is an awkward marriage, as we shall discuss in §11.2.

The most radical version of mathematical literalism – the view that the world is made out of mathematics, that its very substance is numbers – has a long history. Consider this passage from Alexander Polyhistor, the first-century BCE Greek scholar:

> The first principle of all things is One. From the One came an indefinite Two, as matter for the One, which is cause. From the One and the Indefinite Two came numbers; and from numbers, points; from points, lines; from lines, plane figures; from plane figures solid figures; from solid figures, sensible bodies.[201]

The material world, it seems, is a relative parvenu compared with mathematical entities. Three is more fundamental than, say, three sheep. The universe is contaminated mathematics.

This seemingly eccentric view has gradually regained respectability as pure mathematics has assumed a central place in rational mechanics and, more broadly, physical science has become progressively mathematized. Mathematics has been promoted from an instrument to assist scientific progress towards truth about the world to that of which the world is true. Numbers as powerful tools are promoted to numbers as objects in themselves and, finally, acquire the status of being the very fabric of the universe.

One of the most spectacular contemporary expressions of this is the world picture proposed by the theoretical physicist Max Tegmark. According to his "mathematical universe hypothesis" (MUH), natural realities are mathematical structures – a set of abstract entities with relations between them.[202] This is to be understood literally. For example:

> [L]ight is simply a wave rippling through the electromagnetic field, so if our physical world is a mathematical structure, then all the light in our Universe (which feels quite physical) corresponds to six numbers at each point in space-time (which feels quite mathematical).[203]

> Light boils down to numbers at space-time points that are also defined by numbers.[204]

The world according to Tegmark is a nexus of pure magnitudes that are not the magnitude of anything (else) or, yet more abstractly, a structure abstracted from patterns of magnitudes. Even more boldly, he proposes not only that all reality is mathematical but also that anything which is mathematical is real. What he calls his "mathematical monism" denies that anything exists other than mathematical objects: "our physical world is not only described by mathematics but ... is mathematics".[205] Even conscious experience is composed of mathematical substructures that are mysteriously but conveniently "self-aware".[206] This may be nonsense but at least it deals with Putnam's critique of Platonism, namely "that it seems flatteringly incompatible with the fact that we think with our brains, not with immaterial souls".[207] Our brains, it appears, are made of Platonic mathematical objects. (Though this only moves the problem on to that of understanding how we can access eternal mathematical objects via token thoughts targeted by non-eternal tokens in a voice or on a page.) Maintaining that all reality is number requires what Martin has called "Pythagoreanism of the brain".[208] Qualitative experiences are translated into quantities of neural discharges whose nature is defined by their location in phase spaces – as we discussed in §2.5.

Tegmark's universe is frozen: "the only intrinsic properties of a mathematical structure are its relations, timeless and unchanging",[209] so that time is an illusion, as is change. (Why therefore he believes he might change our views as a result of our reading his book remains a mystery, unless he also believes that the changes in our views – and his part in changing them – are not ultimately real.)

We note in passing that physics that began as the most hard-headed of the sciences should have, in its theoretical upper reaches, as a result of commitment to ever wider generality, seen the world evaporate to abstractions. This is an irony observed by Quine in the passage quoted as an epigraph to this section.

Reducing the universe to a pattern of numbers is an unsurprising consequence of exsanguinating qualities and dissolving *thisness* and *whatness* into *how-muchness*. The destination – a Pythagoreanism of numbers in space–time with space–time itself, along with its contents, collapsing into numbers – could have been seen in advance. The Quinean irony is matched only by this one: that its theory of everything should, in virtue of being increasingly a theory of nothing-in-particular, start to look like a theory of nothing-at-all.[210]

Tegmark's MUH abolishes the distinction between mathematics and physics, between mathematical and physical objects (reducing the latter to the former). Even those who are convinced that qualities ultimately boil down to quantities – and are happy to ignore Feynman's problem of finding "frogs, musical composers, and moral-ity" (*vide infra*) – are aware of difficulties of squaring different ways of reducing the world to numbers with the reality of irreducible qualities in experience and appar-ently in the experienced world. Some philosophers deal with this by replacing the idea of numbers or quantities with that of mathematical *structure* and by extending structure to encompass symmetries or, indeed, what remains unchanged beneath apparent change – change in the world or change in scientific theories. This is the view known as structural realism. It is worth examining in some detail because the varieties of structural realism inadvertently do us the service of helping to pinpoint what is amiss with various modes of mathematical realism, even those that are less radical than Tegmark's reduction of the world to mathematical entities.

There are two main influences behind structural realism. The first is from quantum mechanics and the second from reflection on the history of science. The connection between structural realism and quantum mechanics is accessibly summarized by Meinard Kuhlmann.[211] He begins by examining the two concepts central to quan-tum physics: that of a "particle" and that of a "field". Both of these kinds of item are in conceptual trouble. The particles of quantum field theory are (a) not entities with specific locations that change in time as they move; (b) they are not necessary for things to happen; (c) their very existence depends on the nature of the observer; and (d) they do not have definite, monadic or intrinsic properties independent of other particles (they are entangled). As for the fields in quantum field theory, they are not like classical fields, in which a physical quantity is assigned to each space–time point within them. Quantizing physical field theory replaces physical values with operators or mathematical operations such as differentiation or taking a square root – a conse-quence of the fact that quantum mechanics does not deal in determinate values but in probabilities which have to be combined with other operators to assume a definite range. Neither particles nor fields, Kuhlmann concludes, provides ontologically sat-isfactory accounts of the physical world and how it works.

We therefore need to look elsewhere than thing-like particles or soup-like fields for the elements of fundamental reality; namely to the *relations between* elements – and hence to structures.

The more modest claim is that, irrespective of what reality consists of, this is all we shall know of it. This is so-called *epistemic* structural realism – which is not far from Russell's observation about our picture of the physical world quoted earlier: that it is mathematical not because we know so much but because we know so little. The more radical claim that we are restricted to knowing only structures because *that is all there is* licenses the more radical form of realism, labelled *ontic* structural realism. What we observe are not things in themselves or changes in themselves but symmetry transformations in which fundamental structures are preserved. There are no consequences of symmetry transformations at a fundamental level. Or, to put this another way, that which is truly real is that which is unchanged. If a symmetry is defined as a transformation that leaves all relevant structures intact, and if structure is the essence of reality, symmetry-preserving transformations are only apparent, not real, changes.

The other motivation behind various forms of structural realism[212] – particularly epistemic structural realism – has come from the history of science and the need to reconcile two facts: (a) that science regularly undergoes revolutions in which its fundamental theories change; but that (b) it is nevertheless our best approximation to the truth about the natural world. The former points to, and the latter seems to undermine, realism about successful scientific theories: they simply "work". Epistemic structural realism argues that something fundamental is conserved even as science discards one theory in favour of another – namely the structural or mathematical content of theories; more precisely a set of mathematical relationships describing the structure of reality. Scientific theories give information only about the structure of an otherwise unobservable world and not about its constitution or intrinsic nature. It rejects the reduction of theoretical terms such as "atom", "electron" or "black hole" either to disguised ways of referring to directly observable phenomena or simply to terms of the art that have no genuine referents in the real world.

One might respond to this by pointing out that more than structure is conserved as science progresses. Some empirical content of even quite ancient science still retains its standing as true. Archimedes' observations on levers and on the method of measuring density have not been falsified; and many laws relating all sorts of phenomena survive successive scientific revolutions, though they may be found to have a narrower application than had been thought. Not all science, what is more, is fundamental – and this includes much of the science necessary to pursue fundamental science. The Large Hadron Collider was built using the science of many epochs. The cumulative body of facts, methods, expertise, and techniques *is* relevant if we are looking to science for metaphysical guidance. As too is the global presence of the unreformed manifest image of the world in the working as well as the recreational lives of scientists. Let us, however, accept paradigm shifts as part of the rationale for structural realism.

Ladyman and his co-authors in *Every Thing Must Go* go beyond epistemic structural realism, embracing ontic structural realism, as an inescapable consequence of accepting the authority of quantum mechanics.[213] "Things" in the everyday sense are ontologically dubious: at best second order; at worst, phantoms. More radically, things that are identical with themselves, self-subsistent, and localised, also must go. Quantum particles and space–time points (placed in the same basket in a way that might already raise suspicions) may be the values of first-order variables but do not obey the law of identity: "for all x, x is identical to x". Relations, or more precisely, relational structures are more fundamental than objects; indeed, in the last analysis the former have primary existence and the latter are not really real. The idea of an unobservable realm that underpins structures is anti-scientific and hence has no place in a metaphysics or ontology that wears the charge of "scientism" as a badge of honour (*vide infra*). Reality *is* simply a structure described by a set of mathematical relationships whose surface appearance is what we call "the laws of nature". Structure and relations have ontological priority over things or objects, even elementary particles.[214]

This is clearly counter-intuitive. Surely, we protest (as have many philosophers quoted by Ladyman[215]), relations *presuppose* relata: distinct, independent, existences that are brought into relation. "Relations between" presuppose the "be(ings)" to uphold the "tween". The claim that it is "relations all the way down" because the relata turn out to be ensemble of relata is a desperate ad hoc claim that simply moves the bump in the carpet. Likewise, structures must, we feel, be structures *of* – of objects or ensembles that are not structures: they must supervene on, or be assembled out of, relata that are items in themselves that have intrinsic properties. If structures are all that is really there, then there is nothing for there to realize the structure.[216] Arguing that reality is the structure of reality, described in a certain way, seems to be a spectacular example of putting the cart before the horse. Or the outline of the horse before the horse. What is more, a world of structures seems frozen because, if anything is to happen, it must happen in or to individual objects; otherwise we have only the unchanging whole of wholes.[217]

All of this may seem to invite impatient dismissal. But it is important because in many respects it brings to a climax certain trends in thought about the relationship between mathematics and reality. Even so, we must acknowledge that giving onto-logical priority to relations over self-subsistent relata is even more weird than appears at first sight. When we consider the macroscopic world of objects and events, their being in relation to one another depends upon their being picked out together. That which picks them out is a consciousness motivated by salience-defining concerns. It is this that confers the epithet "in the next room" on my biro, which could equally have been described as "on the table", "ten thousand miles from New York", and so on; or the epithet "earlier than your smile" on a note that is being played, which could equally correctly have been characterized as "before 'a later note'", "one thousand years after the Battle of Hastings", or "13.8 billion years after the Big Bang". In short, relations not only require the prior existence of relata; they also require a conscious being supporting the act of synthesis that binds them together; that makes what is merely a potential relation into an actual one.

The only exception to this is consciousness itself, which is essentially, constitu-tively relational. Consider ordinary perception: it is in essence an intentional rela-tionship that brings together subject and object but is not located in either subject or object. Intentional awareness *is* relational all the way down – something that we shall discuss in Chapter 11. It is therefore another Quinean irony that apparently hard-nosed ontic structural realism, wearing "scientism" as "a badge of honour", should import the properties of consciousness into the heart of a physics most remote from it – though it may not acknowledge this. However, it is perhaps not surprising that, when the conscious subject is finally erased from the picture of the world, objects and their localities, more precisely necessarily local objects, disappear as well.

The advocates of ontic structural realism seem to be voluntarily enmeshed in the difficulties associated with the quantum measurement problem that we discussed in §3.5.3.1. They accept that, at the fundamental level, physics has shown that reality is not composed of discrete, independent, localised objects. The phenomena of quantum entanglement are interpreted as demonstrating that the entangled entities have no intrinsic properties, and that they do not have independent identities. Ontic structural realism seems to assume that what is true at the fundamental level is true at the macroscopic level; effectively that the superposition that opens up the way to entanglement has no upper limit, so that discrete, localised material objects are illusory. Given that this leads to the measurement problem, one of the consequences of taking mathematical physics literally in the way that Ladyman does would be that James Ladyman's own quantum-mechanics-based thoughts – and indeed the apparently self-identical James Ladyman and his apparently self-identical volume *Every Thing Must Go* not to speak of the equipment, buildings, and personnel necessary for research into quantum mechanics – would also be phantoms. If reality is what is measured and/or what can be measured and/or the results of measurement, it is hardly surprising that (given that the universe does not measure itself) reality seems to have been brought into determinate existence by measurement. And it is equally unsurprising that that in virtue of which there is measurement, which must precede actual measurements, namely the measurer, the physicist, must be a source of embarrassment, an awkward customer that, as the measurement problem indicates, does not survive the extension of quantum phenomena beyond the subatomic world.

Ladyman's suggestion that everyday material objects, such as tables and chairs and cats and dogs, may be constructs, "pragmatic devices used by agents to orient themselves in regions of space–time, and to construct approximate representations of the world"[218] seems implausible for several reasons. It does not explain (a) why such devices would be any use if objects were not fundamentally real, (b) why, if space–time were not really mapped out in the distribution of objects, proposing them should help to "orientate" us, and (c) what the status of "agents" in this context would be if they were not really macroscopic objects like you and me interacting with macroscopic objects such as tables, chairs, and each other. The least one would expect of an agent or an observer is that he/she should be a localised object occupying macroscopic space. While contemporary physics may oblige us to set aside the notion of solidity as a plenum, it should not require us to deny solidity *per se*, even less localised solid objects. They are, after all, the most fundamental furniture of the world we negotiate and use in everyday life.[219]

It may seem odd that a philosopher should be willing to give up on everyday experience so radically – so that, for example, the apparent locality of apparently solid objects such as his own body or the chairs it sits on is something between an illusion (if you espouse smallism) and an emergent property – in order to align his metaphysics with contemporary physics. The appeal to Occam's razor – in the latest form of not allowing the existence of entities that are not accommodated by, or indeed required by, advanced science – seems to have resulted in self-abolition. It illustrates how over-enthusiastic deployment of the Occamist shaving tackle may result in cutting your own throat. There is (to change metaphor) a kind of Escher circle. The laptop in your room is evidence for the effectiveness of quantum theory. The effectiveness of quantum theory is evidence of its truth to reality. Its reality does not include self-identical objects. Thus neither your laptop nor the room in which it sits really exists. QED.[220]

This is, however, consistent with Ladyman's scientism and setting out the role of the metaphysician as something between a standard bearer and a bag carrier for physics:

> Any new metaphysical claim that is to be taken seriously ... should be moti-vated by, and only by, the service it would perform, if true, in showing how two or more specific scientific hypotheses, at least one of which is drawn from fundamental physics, jointly explain more than the sum of what is explained by the two hypotheses taken separately.[221]

More generally, Ladyman *et al.* see the role of metaphysics as "critically elucidating consilience networks across the sciences".[222] It is evident that that consilience will be arrived at on terms dominated by fundamental physics and the agenda will be essentially reductive.

Given that "the badge of honour" – scientism – looks more like a cross, it is inter-esting to consider why it is worn with pride. After all, it does not follow – from the fact that all that is preserved as we progress to ever more successful scientific theo-ries is a mathematical structure – that the universe they are about is a mathematical structure. The most obvious reason for rejecting this view is that it collapses the dis-tance between theories and their intentional objects, it squeezes out the "aboutness" of theories – enshrined in the distance between the community of physicists' minds and the universe. The belief that nature speaks the language of mathematics assumes (a) that it speaks (for) itself, and (b) that it *is* that which it speaks.

Since this criticism is obvious, there must be some other explanation for the attrac-tion of ontic structural realism – and the reason why it justifies close examination. It arises from a more general (apparent) case for the mathematization of the universe – which inevitably leads to the ontological privileging of structures and relations over self-subsistent objects. The case is rooted in what has been called the "unreasonable effectiveness" of mathematically based physics in extending our ability to control (and hence presumably understand) the material world. Armchair metaphysicians have nothing to show for their millions of words over several millennia that can compare with the fruits of the science of the last few centuries. Metaphysics, it is concluded, must therefore follow science along a journey that sheds phenomenal appearances, locations, macroscopic objects, events that take place at a particular time, items such as discrete atoms, for universal patterns that, being universal do not change. This is probably the commonest rationale for deciding that (to use a distinction from the philosopher Susan Stebbing) "the world of physics" is "the phys-ical world".[223] Indeed, not only the physical world – the material universe of matter, energy and the rest – but the world period.

At the heart of physics is mathematics and the more powerful and fundamental the physics, the closer it is to pure mathematics. Mathematics does not deal with things but captures the relations between or within things – objects, events, processes, forces, fields, and so on. The reality that is mathematical is relational, and the relations are organized into ensembles, into patterns of the most general nature, structures whose paradigm expression would be the matrices corresponding to quantum fields. The uncritical pursuit of physics into places where even most physicists would agree intelligibility itself gives out is therefore justified by this aim: to see the universe as an array of relations which are indistinguishable from an ensemble of mathematical (reification noted) "objects".

The privileging of relationship over any items being related and of structure over event – which makes the idea of the universe unfolding in time through causally connected states or events deeply problematic – has many other sources.

Patterns of relationships are more user-friendly to the intellect than conventional material objects in virtue of being more soluble in mathematics. Matter, in the form of the cloddish reality we know in everyday life, is not soluble in this way, though its general patterns or relationships of motion, are. Structures by being frozen seem more user friendly to the intelligence.[224]

Tegmark's mathematical literalism and Ladyman's ontic structural realism are hardly conventional views among either physicists or metaphysicians. However, many physicists are mathematical realists to the extent that they believe that the mathematical portrait of reality is the most accurate, penetrating, and truthful account of what there is: what kinds of things there are and how they unfold or do not unfold in time. And it is easy to see why. The potency and overall beneficence of technologies based on mathematical physics have greatly extended the life expectancy, health expectancy, comfort expectancy and fun expectancy, enjoyed by many of us. Mathematical physics *works*, when it comes to operating on and with the material world to realize our goals. How could this be so unless there were something essentially mathematical about nature? As Hilary Putnam has put it, "scientific realism is the only philosophy of science that does not make the success of science a miracle".[225] And the success is that of mathematically based science.

This is the issue that lies at the heart of Eugene Wigner's justly famous paper on "The Unreasonable Effectiveness of Mathematics in the Natural Sciences". The question addressed by Wigner is particularly pertinent given the widening gap between the world as experienced through our senses and the world as portrayed in mathematical physics.

The most obvious link between mathematics and material reality – and the key to the mastery of the former over the latter – is measurement. This reduces what is physically out there to numbers of units. But we can usefully examine the divergence between what we experience directly and what is captured mathematically first by examining something even more basic; what must be the least contentious act of mathematization: counting items and (almost as basic) adding them up. This is counting without the mediation of artificial units: the counting of self-defining or naturally occurring units. Let us return to an earlier example.

Consider a farmer counting his sheep. There are three over there and three over here and this makes six in all. The sheep are aggregated together as "2 lots of 3" or "1 lot of 6". This mode of aggregation – a conceptual aggregation – is profoundly different from the primordial active aggregation of herding or penning. The latter locates the sheep in the same space; it is spatial relocation. The former has nothing to do with space. When my sheep are brought together mathematically and I discover that I have 6 altogether, they are *not* "all together". Indeed, my sheep would (numerically) amount to or be "6 altogether" even if they had strayed in different directions or disappeared who knows where. The aggregation by counting – what we might call one-by-one aggregation[226] – is more complex than might appear at first sight.

I glance at, or point to, each of the sheep in turn and recite the next number in the series. The sheep are abstracted from space and all spatial relations to each other. My counting finger lifts each sheep out of its environment, out of any biography, out of its relation to other sheep. And although we say "1" when we point to Dolly, "2" when we point to Nelly and "3" when we point to Mary, from the point of view of enumeration, they are anonymous. I can count sheep without knowing their names. Each – young or old, well or ill, fat or thin, over there or over here – is just one sheep; we could change the numbers attached to particular named sheep if we counted them in a different order.

They thus lose their identity as individual sheep. But that is not all: they are half way to losing their "sheepness" being reduced merely to (any) "one" of the category they are considered as belonging to. They are half way to being units – natural units, as it were. To join the numerical group is to be lost in aggregation, like snowflakes being absorbed into a drift. This process is taken further when we start trading sheep and see them in terms of exchange value; the abstraction advances. A sheep is transformed from a presence, located at a particular point in space, to a unit of exchange to which the notion of spatial location, or individual identity, or even categorical identity, does not apply.[227]

Both space and time are lost.

So the divorce between mathematized reality and experienced reality begins at a very basic level – before mathematical operations such as multiplication and division, before the invention of zeroes and negatives, before imaginary numbers. And that distance is further widened to a significant degree when we "do sums" with sheep – adding and subtracting them. When we do those sums on our fingers, enumerating fingers that correspond to marking off sheep, we take a further step away from the bleating, grazing, defaecating reality. The gap between enumeration and the enumerated widens when the relevant numbers are spoken in the absence of the numbered (as when I report that "I have 6 sheep"), or when the numbers are written down, and definitively assigned to a different kind of space (pages, for example) from any which sheep could occupy.

The reduction of items to numbers is taken further when naturally occurring entities counting as a general "one" are replaced by units. An early example would be the reduction of the items themselves to numbers by referring to them as so many "head" of sheep. Each sheep is equivalent to every other sheep because each has one head and counts as one head and hence as one. Their individuality is lost as they become reduced to pure quantity, which will prepare them to be marketized as so much exchange value or a quantity of quantities when they are described, say, in terms of their weight or length. Unitization can ascribe similar quantities to entirely different items. A human being, a tree, and a rock can all be five feet tall.

In summary, when we start exploring the mystery of the effectiveness of mathematics – with its arcane operations, and its long chains of reasoning involving items such as "the square root of minus 1" that do not have an obvious connexion to the world of our sense experience – we have to recall that this mystery begins with these seemingly straightforward, homely, everyday, activities around counting. Addition, subtraction, and multiplication and other elementary operations lift quantities out of the world and, reducing them to numbers, enable them to be operated on in a different kind of space – in the virtual spaces of thoughts and pages. The effectiveness of mathematics, however, becomes more obviously mysterious, even "unreasonable", in relation to its role in the advance of ever more powerful natural sciences, where it is more than a mere tool for aggregating and connecting naturally self-delimited countables and permitting the legitimate generalization of quantitative observations.

It has, as Eugene Wegener has pointed out, played "a more sovereign role in physics", in guiding our attempts to arrive at the most general account of the physical world. "The mathematical formulation of the physicist's often crude experience leads in an uncanny number of cases to an amazingly accurate description of a large class of phenomena"[228] – suggesting that mathematical language touches on a deeper truth than is accessible by our senses. A similar thought is expressed by Hamming: "constantly what we predict from the manipulation of symbols is realized in the real world".[229] And he also notes both "the enormous usefulness of the same pieces of mathematics in widely different situations" and the internal coherence of the various fields of mathematics such that the simplest algebraic equations can be mapped on to the simplest geometrical entities, as if they were different expressions of a deeper mathematical reality.[230]

One of the most familiar examples of the unreasonable effectiveness of mathematics in the physical world is also one of the most striking: Newton's law of gravitation. The numerical coincidence noted by Newton between the speed of falling bodies on earth, the parabolic pathways taken by thrown rocks and the elliptical orbit of planets, led to a law with a universal application: "The law of gravity which Newton reluctantly established and which he could verify to an accuracy of about 4% has proved to be accurate to less than a ten thousandth of a per cent."[231] This illustrates Hamming's more general point:

> [S]cience is composed of laws which were originally based on a small, carefully selected set of observations, often not measured very accurately; but the laws have later been found to apply over much wider ranges of observation and much more accurately than the original data justified. Not always … *but often enough to require explanation.*[232]

An even more spectacular example, invoked by Wigner, was the importation of matrix algebra into quantum mechanics which has proved extraordinarily powerful in understanding and predicting what is going on at the subatomic level.[233] Matrix algebra was originally invoked in response to the observation that some rules of computation given by Heisenberg were formally identical with the rules of computation with matrices established in the nineteenth century. Application of rules of matrix mechanics to situations in which Heisenberg's rules did not apply – indeed were meaningless – made predictions that agreed with experimental data to within one part in 10,000,000.

So our mystery has at least two distinct aspects. The first is that mathematics, beginning with elementary operations such as counting, abstracts from the properties of the world we see around us. Sheep, lifted from space, are aggregated into numbers that are entirely without ovine or indeed any material or even spatial properties. (There is no more effort in referring to 100 sheep than in referring to one sheep.) Addition, subtraction, measurement and exchange, further empty the described world of the characteristics we experience as we walk around, bump into, and live in, it. The second is that mathematics, deploying unimaginable, unthinkable entities such as the square root of −1 and operations such as multiplying by the square root of −1, can generate an account of what is out there that has hugely amplified our ability to predict and manipulate the material world. It is this that has prompted the belief that the maths that takes us away from the world of appearance and experience brings us closer to its hidden (mathematical, timeless) reality.

We might be tempted to respond to the "unreasonable" effectiveness of mathematics by arguing (in accordance with Russell's observation noted earlier) that it is precisely because it does *not* capture the (experienced) physical world, only those aspects which are amenable to mathematical reduction, that it is so powerful. While there may be a measure of truth in this, it cannot be the whole story, for two reasons: firstly, mathematics opens new worlds that did not seem to be required to be explained in the first place (most notably the subatomic world); and secondly, mathematical physics has an ability to manipulate the physical reality into which we are pitched, and which we experience as the primordial theatre of our lives, through the science-based technology it has had a central role in shaping. The effectiveness of mathematics goes beyond a mere "put up job" where a mathematized universe matches a universalized mathematics.

Even so, while we acknowledge the unreasonable effectiveness of mathematics, we must also recognize, along with Russell, how much of the world lies outside of the grasp of mathematical description and prediction. It is obvious that it does not capture many aspects of our lived experience; for example the humiliation and pain of a man falling down the stairs though he does so in conformity with the fundamental laws of motion. More significantly, we have already noted the absence of secondary qualities – in other words *all* qualities – in mathematics. But Wigner brings the criticism nearer home by pointing out all the *physical* things that are left out from the laws of physics: "the laws of nature are all conditional statements and they relate only to a very small part of our knowledge of the [physical] world":

Thus classical mechanics, which is the best known prototype of a physical theory, gives the second derivatives of the positional coordinates of all bodies, on the basis of the knowledge of the positions etc. of these bodies. It gives no information on the existence, the present positions, or velocities of these bodies.[234]

Elsewhere, he summarizes these aspects of the physical world that lie outside the laws as "initial conditions". They include, in addition, the fact that there is something rather than nothing, that there are certain constants, that there is one set of laws and not another set, and so on.[235] Supplementing the number of laws or discovering laws of greater generality would not dispense with the need to have initial conditions – which is why the attempts by physics to trespass on the territory of theologians and produce their own creation story have proved so unconvincing. You cannot simultaneously generate the laws of nature *and* the substrate upon which they operate; or create the latter out of the former; or have the latter ready-in-waiting independently of the former (See §10.3.4).

What is more, the mathematical account of the world not only excludes its experienced, phenomenal qualities but also the *singularity* of actual events that really take place, at a particular location in space and time, leaving only general possibilities defined by covariance of patterns of quantities. This singularity is the correlate of real (as opposed to a mathematical) observer – an observer who of necessity privileges certain events and who, despite the generality of the conditions that makes her possible, has an irreducible individuality. Someone is always "one".[236]

The absence of singularity (leaving aside the contested singularity at the start of the universe) in the laws of physics, indeed the absence of actuality, uncovers what mathematics reveals of reality: its most general form, pattern, or structure but not the content or stuff of reality itself – as illustrated by Ladyman's ontic structural realism. Our quantification-based equations can successfully predict certain quantitative aspects of events but not encompass all aspects even of those events they predict. They do not take us down to actuality – actualities which are necessarily experienced in localities. It has spectacular successes, as in for example, the vindication of relativity theory in the precise guidance that we get from GPS systems which depend for their accuracy on corrections that relativity predicts. But what they deliver is a purely mathematical definition of space, remote from place and actuality. The latter is put in by the user. That quantum mechanics, the most highly mathematized branch of science, should have trouble not only with observers (as discussed) and with locality (and with local causes – of which more in Chapter 11) but also with its intellectual peer, the general theory of relativity, should not come as any surprise.

So we can accept and be grateful for the "unreasonable" effectiveness of mathematics without at the same time feeling obliged to believe that the universe is in some sense intrinsically mathematical or that mathematics is the last word on, or the most faithful portrait, of the world.[237] Mathematics is a lens turning our shared experience into an image of a world that vastly outsizes both ourselves and the parishes in which we each live. We investigate the world mathematically in order to overcome the fact that individually and even collectively (at the level of the community and the species) we approach it from a particular place or angle. It is our way of getting outside of our perspective or location, though it is only from a particular perspective or location that actual experience is possible. Mathematics is thus a bridge between what we are and what is "out there", without being constitutive either of what we are or of the physical world. To conclude from the fact that, if mathematics greatly extends our gaze into the world it must be constitutive of that world, would be in some respects analogous to citing the success of astronomy as evidence that the stars are made of telescopes.

And it is, of course, obvious (to return to Wigner) that for most of its history, even physics – the most mathematized account of the natural world – still has a non-mathematical element. Its laws do not have the mathematical purity of axioms or proofs. Consider, for example, a law of motion $f = ma$. Though it expresses the mathematical relations between parameters, those parameters themselves are not mathematical objects. In short, $f = ma$ is not like $1 + 1 = 2$ or $a = bc$ where b is 0.5 of a and $c = 2$. The notion of "force" is not like that of a parabolic line or a right angle. The differences between the components – between f and m and a – is not the same as the differences between two mathematical entities. To spell this out a little more: the relationship between the variable and its value in the law $f = ma$ is not the same as the relationship between variable and value in, for example, $A/B \times B = A$. "A" and "B" are "any (unencumbered) numbers" whereas f (say) is a force translated into units by measurement. The difference between the two equations is also revealed in the fact that one is necessary, true in all possible worlds, and the other contingent. That $A/B \times B = A$ is true, given that it could not be otherwise, could hardly count as a discovery. A full mathematization of the world would make not only values but also the variables they instantiate into mathematical entities. Indeed, the distinction between values and variables would be lost.

In short, although the laws of physics are cast in mathematical terms, they are not entirely mathematical and – *a fortiori* – neither is the nature they help us to predict. If it were, it would not have any qualitative or distinct properties.

We can see such (distinctive) qualities being lost when mathematical equivalences are taken to mean identity. The loss is evident even at a fundamental level. For example, treating gravitational and inertial mass as identical to each other and identical with topology of space–time means that all three lose what little distinctive qualities remain to them once they have been quantified. And the only field of physics in which the world is rendered almost entirely in mathematical terms is quantum mechanics which, of course, is unintelligible and incompatible with the moment-to-moment deliverances of daily experience. It is scarcely surprising that it not only runs into internal difficulties, with the constant threat of infinities, but also, for reasons we have already discussed, that it has a problematic relationship to the macroscopic world of classical physics and of our lives.

Unger and Smolin argue that the "unreasonable" power of mathematics in the natural sciences that Wigner spoke of is entirely reasonable because it picks its substrates with care, leaving out mathematically intractable phenomenal qualities, time, and of course everything connected with value and significance. It confines itself to those aspects of reality which it is particularly suited to capture, reflect, or express: "mathematics is an understanding of nature emptying the world of all particularity and temporality: that is a view of the world without either individual phenomena or time".[238] According to the ancient Greeks, the aim of science was "to save the phenomena". Now science sometimes seems to be saving itself by evading phenomena; and some theories at the cutting edge, most notoriously string theory, seem to be developed mainly to save the ("de-phenomenalized") mathematics.

The realism of mathematics, then, is "selective". As pioneer of quantum mechanics and computers John von Neumann put it:

> [A] mathematical formulation that is chosen to represent the underlying problem may represent it only with certain idealizations, simplifications, neglections [sic]. This ... is closely related to the methodological observation that a mathematical formulation necessarily represents only a (more or less) explicit theory of some phases (or aspect) of reality not reality itself.[239]

As we have emphasized throughout, the effectiveness of mathematics in natural science is reasonable because it is limited; most importantly it is confined to a model of the universe based entirely on quantities. The kinds of things that it gets staggeringly right are precisely the things that you would expect it to get right. It might predict with amazing accuracy the quantity, location and wavelength of such and such nanometres of light but not the experience of red. Likewise, a GPS device can guide us from one mathematical point in space to another to a degree of precision that would not have been possible had not general relativity been valid; but it says nothing about either place or the places between them.

We exaggerate the power of mathematics, Unger and Smolin argue, because we overlook this selectivity of its realism:

> The less we grasp the non-mathematical reasons for the application of mathematics (and ... we understand them only very incompletely), the more enigmatic and disconcerting the application of mathematics will appear to be. We will be tempted to bow down to mathematics as the custodian of nature's secrets.[240]

Quantitative science at its most fundamental presents nature as denatured. As Unger and Smolin note acidly: "The self-denying ordinance that is the source of its power provides no license to impose that ordinance on the whole of experience. Scientism is not science".[241] Nor is it warranted by science.

For Unger and Smolin, as it is for the author of this book, the most important missing ingredient in the mathematical portrait of the world, its *selective realism*, is time (and possibly change). This is precisely because mathematics is structural. However, as Unger and Smolin say, "history" – the unfolding of the universe in time – "trumps structure".[242] Ontic structural realism is a direct consequence of not appreciating that the realism of mathematics is selective.

Because ordinary experience of the coherence of the world in space and time, the experience of solid objects, and the colour yellow lie beyond mathematics they should not be dismissed as illusions (after all they won't go away if we take the right kind of medication and they are not confined to individuals), nor as merely epiphenomenal, nor as relics of primitive science, or folk physics comparable to discredited Aristotelian ideas of what we have subsequently come to know as inertial and gravitational forces. At each step, mathematical science gets more nimble as it sheds baggage; but the baggage it sheds is the world we live in, that which underpins the "there" of what is there.

That which lies beyond mathematics is not unreal but evidence of the (self-imposed) limitations of mathematics, which strives towards quasi-axiomatic certainties. Mathematics takes different forms but it encompasses axiomatic systems and tools which are useful insofar as they make contact with reality; but they do not add up to a portrait of reality itself; and even less are they the ultimate reality. As Einstein himself expressed it: "As far as the laws of mathematics refer to reality they are not certain, and as far as they are certain they do not refer to reality".[243] The world is not a nexus of mathematical necessities.[244]

It would be absurd and deeply ungrateful not to acknowledge the huge contribution mathematics has made to our understanding of the world and our ability to control it; but gratitude does not oblige us to adopt a Pythagorean notion that the world is fundamentally composed of mathematical objects such that the whole, fundamental truth about it is captured in the mathematical models developed in advanced physics; that the universe is isomorphic to a mathematical construction; that it is *super*-maths that is revealed piecemeal through actual mathematics.[245]

And the effectiveness of mathematics deployed in a theory is not always dependent on or proof of, the theory being true of the world. This is a manifestation of the thesis (ascribed initially to the French philosopher of science Pierre Duhem and then to Quine) of the underdetermination of scientific theory by evidence. It is beautifully expressed by John Stuart Mill:

> Most thinkers of any degree of sobriety allow that an hypothesis ... is not to be received as probably true because it accounts for all the known phenomena, since this is a condition sometimes fulfilled tolerably well by two conflicting hypotheses ... while there are probably a thousand more which are equally possible, but which, for the want of anything analogous in our experience, our minds are unfitted to conceive.[246]

Larry Landau has been one of many philosophers of science who have pointed to the double dissociation between the truth and success – even "unreasonable effectiveness" of theories. Among the most striking examples he cites are the chemical and physical theories of the late nineteenth century which explicitly held to the discredited central dogma that matter was neither created nor destroyed. Landau notes that not only may theories that are subsequently considered to be false be useful but also that theories subsequently considered to be true may prove to be useless for quite some period of time:

The chemical atomic theory in the 18th century was so remarkably unsuccessful that most chemists abandoned it in favor of a more phenomenological, elective affinity chemistry. The Proutian theory that the atoms of heavy elements are composed of hydrogen atoms had, through most of the 19th century, a strikingly unsuccessful career, confronted by a long string of apparent refutations. The Wegenerian theory that the continents are carried by large subterranean objects moving laterally across the earth's surface was, for some thirty years in the recent history of geology, a strikingly unsuccessful theory.[247]

Lawrence Sklar has discussed an instance of underdetermination closer to our present preoccupations:

> [G]iven the plausibility of the allegation that our geometric theories of the world [e.g. general relativity] outrun in their content the possibility of unique specification by all possible empirical data, how can we possibly avoid the skeptic's assertion that we ought not to claim to have genuine knowledge of the geometry of the world? Further, doesn't the sceptical threat present in the geometrical case generalize to a threat of skepticism against alleged theoretical knowledge in general?[248]

Ouch! The "selective realism" of mathematics implies that the truths of mathematically derived and expressed theories do not capture either the whole or the fundamental truth of nature, of our condition, or of our place in nature. That is why mathematical models can have tremendous predictive power and dovetail beautifully with other models and still be only provisionally or partially true. Think, for example, how powerful the most powerful of all scientific theories – quantum mechanics – was even before it learned how to renormalize infinities and how powerful it remains, although those infinities have the habit of returning when attempts are made to unite it with the second most powerful theory – the general theory of relativity. There is no clear point at which we can say a model is a mirror image of reality.

In making this point, we find a perhaps surprising ally in Stephen Hawking (he who once spoke of seeking to read the mind of God):

> In our view, there is no picture- or theory-independent concept of reality. Instead, we adopt a view that we call model-dependent realism: the idea that a physical theory or world picture is a model (generally of mathematical nature) and a set of rules that connect the elements of the model to observations. According to model-dependent realism, it is pointless to ask whether a model is real, only whether it agrees with observation. If two models agree with observation, neither one can be considered more real than the other.[249]

Even more surprisingly, he adds:

> Although it is not uncommon for people to say that Copernicus proved Ptolemy wrong, this is not true ... Notwithstanding its role in philosophical

disputes over the nature of our universe, the real advantage of the Copernican system is that the equations of motion are much simpler in the frame of reference in which the sun is at rest.[250]

This is close to Poincaré's view that the laws of mechanics are conventional, being selected on the grounds of simplicity, for simplicity – mind-portability – may be a proxy for objective, fundamental truth.

Smolin quotes Hermann Weyl, in whom the Pythagorean dream of a complete mathematical account of universe that is in essence mathematical shone particularly brightly: "I am bold enough to believe that the whole of physical phenomena may be derived from one single universal world-law of the greatest mathematical simplicity".[251] We need our physicists to be that bold; but we, too, need to be resolute in resisting this dream of simplification and the rhetoric of "theories of everything" and a "mathematical universe". Given the manifest complexity of the world and of the most trivial item in it, "a law of the greatest mathematical simplicity" would seem to look though, or past, rather than at the world. What is more, the notion of "physical phenomena" has an important ambiguity, given that the advance of physics is characterized by increasing distance from the world of phenomena.

In this regard we have another surprising ally in one of the greatest physicists of the last century, Richard Feynman:

> The next great awakening of human intellect may well produce a method of understanding the qualitative content of equations ... Today we cannot see whether Schrödinger's equation contains frogs, musical composers, or morality – or whether it does not.[252]

It seems unlikely that we shall rediscover qualities – and judging by the items listed they would seem to be secondary and even tertiary qualities – in more or better (necessarily quantitative) equations. Feynman still seems to believe that everything can be completely known through (presumably mathematical) equations. At least, however, he understood the limitations of physics, if not perhaps how profound those limitations are. Its mathematical portraits can neither accommodate the embodied subject that constitutes the observer nor can it do without him or her. It cannot dispense with time but seems unable to resist freezing time and denying change.

The contradictions at the heart of a mathematical physics that claims to be on the way to a theory of everything (including the physicist) could have been anticipated from the Galilean revolution which pushed to the margins the sentient beings that made physics possible. But they go beyond the impossibility of finding physicists, and observers, in physics. They have wider metaphysical ramifications for thinkers, impressed by the successes of a natural science based on the elimination of the qualities, the perspectives, meanings, the first-person reality, of human consciousness, who subscribe to physicalism. We cannot reconstruct the mind using only materials that have been developed by putting mind to one side. The most promising quantitative scientific approach to the reconstruction of mind – neuroscience – which has also progressed through setting aside qualia (and qualities), the self, and the first-person perspective fails dismally, which is hardly surprising. We would not expect a science free of them to be able to give an account of qualia, qualities, etc. The fact that it cannot do so is not proof that those ubiquitous and inescapable aspects of reality are in fact unreal but that the science is inadequate to them – and not by accident either.

This difficulty is well described by Edward Feser:

> Those who suppose that the scientific picture of matter is an exhaustive picture are stuck with a dualism of, on the one hand, a material world entirely free of irreducibly qualitative, semantic and teleological features, and on the other hand a mental realm defined by its possession of irreducibly qualitative, semantic, and teleological features.[253]

It is not possible for the mathematical physicist to lift up the ladder behind him once he has ascended into the Platonic heaven of a nexus of mathematical constructs because he himself, his community of fellow scientists, the life he lives, and the world in which his discoveries are actually used and prove their worth, necessarily remain in place and inescapably real. David Hilbert was not merely a set of points in Hilbert space. A Hilbert space could not have come unaided to knowledge of itself.

It is a mistake, perhaps, to set up a straight competition between realities, asserting for example, against the scientific views we have discussed, the phenomenological view that the ultimate features of reality are those which are revealed to us in our pre-analytic experience. To do so would fail to make sense of the fact that science has greatly enhanced our ability to act on our individual and collective wishes and needs; and would also presuppose that we could assume a viewpoint, transcending both ordinary experience and fundamental physics, that could adjudicate between the competing claims to reality of the scientific and everyday image of the world.

When we address the question as to whether or not mathematical physics reveals the fundamental reality of the world, and even shows our everyday experience to be sham, mistaken, or seriously incomplete in some way, we need to pause over the notion of "reality". "Real" is a floating qualifier. As J. L. Austin pointed out many years ago the notion of "real" arises in response to the suspicion that something is *un*real.[254] Of the contrasting couple, it is "unreal", not "real", that, as he put it, "wears the trousers". So, in addition to the question "What makes the mathematical view of the world more true to reality?", we would need to ask "What is unreal about the deliverances of our everyday experiences?" In what sense are we using the word "unreal"?

It is obvious that hallucinations and dreams are unreal; the illusion of their reality will be corrected by their transience and by the disappointments and frustrations we have if we proceeded as if they were real. In short, hallucinations and dreams and the like are experiences that are corrected by the vast bulk of the experiences at the same level that are inconsistent with them and by the manifest failure of actions based on the trust that they are real. In other words, the corrections take place within everyday life. Admittedly, there are illusions that require something more than additional experience to correct them; for example, the illusion that the sun moves across the sky during the day, or sinks below the horizon in the evening. This requires measurement, theoretical calculation, and mathematical modelling. But you can live an entirely geocentric existence and still function perfectly well in daily life. What about a more radical global claim, for example, that *all* experience is somehow mistaken, so that our experience of colours has nothing to do with the reality of light? Or the claim that objects are not solid, or made up of components that have a definite location, but that they are largely empty space and that which fills the empty space consists only of probability waves? This is of a different order from something that requires mere focal correction. It is, for example, more than a little stubborn. It is impossible to see, or to treat, a chair as it is seen through the eyes of fundamental physics. There is nothing unreal or merely mistaken about the object of immediate experience.

That is why it is a misuse of the notion of reality to argue that the world of daily life is a four-dimensional life-long illusion. It is more accurate to argue that the scientific image of the world captures one aspect of reality and that the manifest image captures another. Neither is superior. If it was a question of ranking them, the manifest image of daily life is closer to reality. Unlike the scientific image, it is not generated at the end of a long chain of observations, measurements, and theorizing; nor does our folk ontology (unlike fundamental science) change every few decades. The underdetermination already discussed of physical theories by the empirical data on which they are founded is even more evident in the relationship between physics and metaphysics. What is more, there is a kind of completeness, what we might call an existential completeness, in our ordinary transactions with objects – as when I pick up a ball and throw it – which is absent from the theorizing that is endlessly open to modification, extension and rejection. The everyday image is *lived* – every hour of every day. Grounds for discarding our traditional ontology on the basis of advances in physics seem very shaky indeed.

Against this, it may be argued that the scientific image is closer to the truth of the universe at large because it hugely extends our power to act, to shape the material world, to communicate and, through this, to shape the social world. The power of, say, quantum mechanics is staggering not only in terms of the reach and precision of its predictions – which both test the theories and guide us through the world – but also in the technologies (the majority of the most significant of the latter half of the twentieth century and the twenty-first century) it makes possible. But should we conclude from this that the existential truths of the manifest image are *inferior, wrong, ideas we have grown out of*, etc.? The assistance from the technologies is still focal and the confirmations of its truths are discontinuous and in this respect are unlike the global continuity of the everyday lived world in which we use those technologies. After all, we do not leave that world behind as we enter the electronic era. We listen to a solid radio as we park our solid bodies on solid chairs. And physicists make their way to laboratories and work in them as if they were in the same reality as they inhabit when they are off duty. In short, the scientific image of the world supplements the manifest image but it does not supersede it. To return to our earlier example: the laptop in the room, which functions on the basis of quantum mechanics, does not prove that there isn't a laptop in the room.

The assumption that mathematical physics has burned off what is merely a veil of misleading (qualitative) appearances is therefore ill-founded. This book, which is dedicated to rescuing time from its reduction to a quantity, will not *pace Feynman* look to *more (or better) equations* as a means to this rescue. For the present, however, let us look most directly at the quantification of time; at how time got clocked.

Addendum 1
Some sideways glances at Henri Bergson

There are obvious points of convergence between the views set out in the present chapter and earlier, and those of Henri Bergson. While I have flagged some of them up in passing, a "compare" and "contrast" might be of interest to some readers.

Our most significant points of agreement are:

(a) Natural science cannot capture qualities – indeed sets them aside on principle – and reduces the world to "a system of magnitudes". I share his view that there is "no point of contact" between the non-extended (qualities) and the extended (quantities). "One can interpret the one in terms of the other; but sooner or later, in the beginning or the end, the conventional character of the assimilation must be recognized."[255]

(b) Physics traduces time by spatializing it, so that temporal intervals are reduced to quasi-spatial magnitudes and duration is temporal extensity (analogous to spatial extensity):

> [W]e set our states of consciousness side by side in such a way as to perceive them simultaneously, no longer in one another, but alongside one another; in a word, we project time into space, we express duration in terms of extensity, and succession takes the form of a continuous line or chain, the parts of which touch without penetrating one another.[256]

We have to acknowledge that implicit (heterogeneous and continuous) time is not replaced by explicit mathematized time. These are some of the reasons that while an interval represented by "t" can (seemingly) be multiplied by itself, an afternoon or a week's holiday most certainly cannot

(c) Einstein had developed a brilliant theory of time but he had lost key aspects of our experience and intuitive understanding of time. Einstein was not justified in presenting his physical account of time as a metaphysical one and arguing that what lay outside of physics was merely "psychological time". Einstein's theory is "metaphysics grafted upon science, it is not science".[257]

(d) There is a widespread tendency, most pronounced in natural science, to confuse symbolic representations of the world – either in language or by the tools or units of measurement – with the reality in which we walk, work, and live.[258]

(e) Another point of contact with Bergson – more relevant to the later parts of this book – concerns our understanding of the nature of consciousness and, in particular memory. They are inexplicable in material terms and this is central to my defence of tensed time in Part II and the exploration of its significance – notably for human freedom – in Part III.

(f) Finally, I would defend Bergson against Bertrand Russell's charge that he was a visualizer and that he mistook this personal idiosyncrasy for a key to the nature of the intellect. This is a charge that, I suspect, Russell would lay against me.

Our points of disagreement are almost as important.

(a) While time is misrepresented by being spatialized, I feel that space is also shabbily treated when it, too, is reduced to a cluster of dimensions and rendered as a pure quantity, as mere extensity. Time as "homogeneous duration" is no more profoundly misrepresented than space when it is seen as "homogeneous extensity".

Admittedly, Bergson does sometimes appreciate that space, too, needs defending against quantitative science. When he asserts Kant-like that "homogeneous space" (space suitable to be reduced to number) is "a form of our sensibility" he does not get to the heart of the problem, though he acknowledges that "homogeneous space" has its source in our cognitive activities. But we should not think of that source as being as deep as Kantian forms of sensible intuition but as something more recent: it is a child of the science which reduces place to decimal place, otherwise there would not be alternative ways of seeing space. Admittedly, space is primordially shared – and to this extent neutral and continuous – but this shared space is not geometrical or coordinate space. Joint attention and shared activities make for common space, but nothing could be more heterogeneous than a space fashioned out of the meetings between humans engaged in their shared lives. Bergson recognized this when he acknowledged the difference between homogeneous mathematical space and heterogeneous lived space.[259] And, as Barry Dainton has reminded me, later Bergson was less disposed to view space as "mere extensity" and linked it more closely with consciousness and *durée*.

(b) Nor do I accept Bergson's way of conceiving number as spread out in a line. If numbers were intrinsically spatial in this way, reducing space to numbers (as is the practice in physics) would seem to have some justification.

(c) We both of us connect time and free will – though we do so in different ways – but his idea of evolution as "creative" and his notion of the *élan vital* that lies at the heart of life are not, I believe, helpful for understanding life, even less human life. It spreads the characteristics of conscious life – even of agency – too widely through the universe.

(d) Finally, for reasons that will be evident from the critique of ontic structural realism, I do not accept Bergson's denial of the reality of discrete objects.

Addendum 2
A note on intelligibility and reality

In §3.6, we investigated the belief that mathematics provides the most accurate and comprehensive account of the real nature of the universe. In its most extreme form, this view merges with the claim that the universe is an abstract mathematical structure and such objects as it has are mathematical entities. These claims are so extraordinary and, as we have seen, so obviously incorrect that they require explanation. We need to examine the criterion of "reality" that makes mathematically satisfying but intuitively opaque, indeed outrageous, theories seem to be the royal road to finding reality and (increasingly mathematical) physics as the best guide to metaphysics and ontology.

While it may seem new, the mathematical universe hypothesis and such-like are rooted in an idea that has had a long history; namely that the touchstone of reality is stability: real entities are eternal and unchanging. In the Western philosophical tradition, it goes back to at least Parmenides though Plato was the key to its wide acceptance.[260] Mathematics, which does not, and indeed cannot, admit time and change, would seem, therefore, to be the form of intelligibility closest to that which is real. Mathematical entities are the paradigm of beings that are unchanging and, indeed, eternal. Therefore, mathematics is either closest to, or identical with, reality. QED.

An important tributary to this mode of thought is the faith that "the real is rational", so that the more purely rational thought is, the more it will approximate to reality. Mathematics, which at its purest deals in logical necessities – tautologies according to early Wittgenstein – is a supreme expression of rational thought. Another reason, then, for expecting that the truest portrait of what is really there will be mathematical and, even, that what is there should itself be mathematical.

This secular basis for mathematizing accounts of the true nature of things has the advantage of resonating with religious doctrines according to which the Creator is Himself unchanging and eternal, the Most Real, entirely rational, at least in part discoverable by reason and largely hidden from the world of everyday experience. There is an important point of intersection between secular and religious validations of the assumptions that the Real is eternal, unchanging, and accessible to pure reason in the *logos* – an immensely complex notion that captures or reflects the extraordinary fact that the world is somehow intelligible to us. From the *logos* of the admittedly change-intoxicated Heraclitus that was the intelligence of the philosopher reflecting the intelligibility of the world to the *logos* that is the word of God that began all things, there has descended a braided stream of ideas about a world unfolding according to the Principle of Sufficient Reason.

The strength of this faith in hidden, unchanging gods, and hidden, unchanging fundamental mathematical physical laws, is such as to make acceptable the progression of science to accounts of reality that are entirely at odds with the flux of experience and our intuitions about what is there, what kinds of things there are, that hold sway in daily life. The superior validity of a mathematized reality can be defended at whatever cost to our intuitions. This has been expressed with exceptional clarity by

Ernan McMullin: "Imaginability must not be made the test for ontology. The realist claim is that the scientist is discovering the structures of the world; it is not required in addition that these structures be imaginable in the categories of the macroworld".[261]

So how does stability justify its status as the mark of reality, to the point where ideas such that the world is made of unchanging mathematical entities or structures are taken seriously? Leaving aside an internalist history of ideas, we might look for the roots of this belief in everyday intuitions, later to be discarded, of what is real. It begins, perhaps, with the notion that only that which can be checked or validated is real. A paradigm case of something that is *un*real such as a visual hallucination fails on several counts. It can be seen but only temporarily. If it persists, what is promised by sight is not delivered to touch or the other senses. It cannot be walked around: there is not a constant presence from different perspectives. Nor can it be shared by others. I cannot see it from the back or touch it, you cannot either see or touch it. The hallucination, in short, exists only in relation to the perspective of the single sense of a single individual.

There are several respects, then, in which a hallucination is contrasted with a "real" object that can be seen from a multitude of perspectives of a multitude of people. We can gather these under the general characteristic of stability. A real object is stable, not only in the sense that it does not vanish in the blink of an eye or when a light is switched on – indeed it persists through intermissions in the experience of it – but also because it has a core that is conserved across a multiplicity of senses and an indefinite number of individual people. It is "there" to be visited and revisited, to be explored and re-explored by any number of people. The stability of "real" physical objects is the most elementary form of reality and, indeed, gives rise to the notion of "objective reality".

At the heart of this basic judgement as to what is real is the notion of something that is *invariant* in the face of change in the sense of being independent of necessarily perspectival experience. A real object is something I can touch as well as see, walk round the back of it as well as see it in front of me, and you or anyone can see it as well as I can. This constancy – that which is shared by vision and touch, front view and back view, your view and my view – is clearly not a particular sense experience. The intrinsic reality of the object-in-itself transcends the fluctuations of, or the succession of, the experiences *of* it. The independence of perspective as a criterion of reality, reaches all the way to the theories of the utmost generality. The passage from Dainton which we quoted earlier captures one aspect of this:

> Using the tensor apparatus to represent the properties of space has a useful feature: the quantities thus represented … are independent of the system of coordinates used to refer to points in space. Coordinate independence (or "covariance") is a criterion of *a quantity being physically real as opposed to an artefact of a particular mode of representation*.[262]

Things from the sum total of possible viewpoints – the same as no viewpoint – remain unchanged.

But we are getting ahead of ourselves. The point is that there is a gap between the fluctuations of our sense experiences of objects and the relative stability of the object and it is the latter that wins the certificate of reality. Immediate sense experience – notwithstanding that it is the final tribunal of what counts as real in everyday life – is tainted with the stigma of cognitive inferiority. The very notion of confirmation, or validation, presupposes a question mark placed over the flux of immediate experience and privileges that which remains unchanged, if only long enough to be visited and revisited indefinitely and from different viewpoints to confirm what has been observed.

The object's stability – the conservation across senses, angles of view, across people, and over time – is inseparable from the intuition of its reality.[263] The gap between fluctuating sense experiences and (relatively) unchanging reality is greatly widened as measurement assumes an ever more dominant role in defining what is there. A measurement may be based on observation but it is an observation that is alienated from its nature as a sense experience and from the person making the measurement. Firstly, a measurement is a discrete act that is not dissolved in the sensory field. It is a kind of interruption in the informal flow of sensation, a particularly authoritative mode of scrutinizing what is out there to determine its nature. Secondly, it is an attempt to overcome viewpoint that is inseparable from sense experience. The table looks small when it is a long way away and looks larger when it is nearer. But in the arithmetical gaze of measurement it is neither large nor small: it is 2 feet wide by 2 feet long. The fluctuating phenomenal appearance is dismissed in favour of something that can be validated or confirmed. You and I may agree to disagree over whether the table looks large or small but we cannot agree to disagree over whether it is or is not 2 feet by 2 feet. Thirdly, the outcome of measurement – 2 feet by 2 feet – has little to do with the phenomenal appearance of the table. After all "2 feet by 2 feet" can apply to any item that happens to be of that size and shape: it is as applicable to a table as to a paving stone. Finally, the phenomenal appearance of actual output of measurement, the record, is irrelevant. It can take the form of spoken words or written inscriptions and the exact form of the latter – size and colour of the characters, for example – is irrelevant.

Measurements are deemed to take us closer to the "objective reality" – confirmable reality, intrinsic reality, reality period of the object. The distance between what counts as real and what is experienced grows ever wider as science measures more and more things (with an accuracy that lies beyond sense experience) and increasingly indirectly, involving the mediation of intermediate concepts and evermore complex instrumentation. The important point is that the stability of the report – its repeatability – is connected with the stability and reality of that which is reported.

The other trajectory of science is to ever greater generality. Beneath local differences, general identity is found: A and B are really both examples of, or expressions of, C. Ultimately the view from nowhere and nowhen, of something that is invariant, becomes the window on to evermore solid truth. What is really out there, which is beyond the limits of our gaze, is captured in the quantitative natural sciences. And so its general laws which ultimately present dephenomenalized reality as stable, timeless structures, are conflated with reality *per se* and that which is visible through its mathematical methodology becomes confounded with ontology.

The Mathematical Universe Hypothesis according to which the world is a crystal of mathematical structures derived ultimately from quantities is only an extreme expression or logical conclusion of these trends that began with the passage from the fluctuating experience of the material world to the hidden stability of the reality beyond sense experience. Even so, the position is so counter-intuitive – indeed at odds with the stubbornly unchanged deliverances of our everyday experience – that other allies are needed. And they are found in certain traditions – rejected by science – that have penetrated human thought. There is the unchanging, invisible (indeed beyond sense experience) God; and there is the influence within metaphysical thought of Platonism, where intelligibility and reality are united in an image of unchanging entities generated by thought and hidden from the senses.

This brings us closer to another link between the criterion of intelligibility, stasis, and the decision as to what counts as real. In making things *intelligible*, we as it were freeze them, or look for something unchanging within them. We see this link most clearly in Plato. When we make sense of objects they are allocated to categories. In our everyday experience I *recognize* this object as a "table". Our discourse about objects we all recognize is mediated through general terms. For Plato, a table – open to the flux of experience – is intelligible to our eternal minds in virtue of being the individual token of a universal, unchanging type – a Form or an Idea. The intelligibility of the table is not rooted in its homely use and our equally homely needs but in its participating in a general, eternal Form. Intelligibility is inseparable from stasis because generality is rooted in something that transcends the flux of the world experienced through our senses. A special reality attaches to that which can be grasped only by thought, which has itself to hold still, to be stable. That which can be grasped by thought – which of course transcends the fluctuations and idiosyncrasy of ordinary experience which is ultimately incommunicable and lacking in common existence – is real.

To some extent, Plato was building on the fact that words arrest by reification – "A table is a table is a table" – and changes of a token table during its lifetime as a table are erased by this tautology. (Indeed, change becomes problematic, so long as identity is maintained.) The word super-reifies the *res*! Nouns, in short confer a higher order thinghood, which is a mark of reality. The word "smoke" arrests smoke, turning its wriggling, self-mangling columns to stone. Even the concept of "change" itself becomes real through reification, though being arrested in thought or on the page.

What Plato, perhaps was dimly aware of (though he did not himself write) was that token objects are instances of classes that do not occur at a particular time or place. This is most obviously true of token thoughts. And there is a third order freezing when thoughts are inscribed in space. By this means, the intelligible, held steadily in the external mind of the printed page, is stabilized further. The (generally) intelligible is always distant from that which is currently happening; or rather the happening and the intelligibility are distinct.

The arrow of increasing intelligibility points in the direction of increasing generality and this is destined to be ever more reductive, finding the highest common factor in disparate things whose common reality is arrived at by setting aside their individual features. This is reflected in the following passage from Steven Weinberg:

> The explanatory arrow points downwards from societies to people, to organs, to cells, to biochemistry, to chemistry, and ultimately to physics. Societies are explained by people, people by organs, organs by cells, cells by biochemistry, biochemistry by chemistry, and chemistry by physics.[264]

The passage from infinite variety – for example, societies and what is in them, or people and what they think, do, and feel – to highly restricted variety – such as the Schrödinger wave equation – makes the world more mind-portable and this is empowering to the intellect. It offsets the losses associated with the passage from everyday experience that makes immediate, intuitive but local sense, to the denizens of the subatomic world where all that remains is a mathematical model that seems like the pure outline of intelligibility but is actually unintelligible and unimaginable. It justifies the implicit assumption in the arrow of explanation that if A explains B, then A is more real than B or A is what B really is. The world as a unified uncollapsed wave function is the *terminus ad quem* of the journey along the vector of explanation as Weinberg has set it out so clearly. The trade-off is clear: intuitively meaningful manifest images, transient, mind-elusive, and contingent, for frozen necessities, that are graspable in the sense at least of being mind-portable.[265]

Thus the reduction of the world to simple equations of huge generality, that are essentially static, and to a frozen mathematical crystal is the final stage of the ascent from the fluctuations of the real world to something seems necessary rather than contingent and capturable by the basilisk gaze of the pure intellect.[266] The latter accommodates change poorly because it is offensive to reason: if "the real is rational" it will be unchanging. The rational, anyway, cannot change because it would have to pass from rationality to irrationality or arrive at rationality via irrationality.

It might be argued that there is a profound discontinuity between physical and mathematical explanation; that intelligibility does not develop along a single trajectory. There is important truth in that. Physical explanations (in which laws do not entirely free themselves from localities and locally acting causes) continue the path opened up by the passage from sense experiences to objects that are real in virtue of stability across observers, viewpoints, and time. Mathematical explanations continue the trajectory opened up by the passage from observation to numbers. However, both are needed: for physical theories to have quantitative generality; and for mathematical theories to have application to the material world. The final triumph of mathematics not only in physics but over physics – such that "every thing must go" – is the result of a misunderstanding that Kant noted:

> The light dove, cleaving the air in her free flight, and feeling its resistance, might imagine that its flight would be still easier in empty space. It was thus

that Plato left the world of the senses as setting too narrow limits to the understanding, and ventured out beyond it on the wings of ideas, in the empty space of pure understanding.[267]

A purely mathematical world would be a world of pure mathematics. Ultimately a world picture dissolved in mathematics would be a nexus of propositions that guaranteed each other's necessity, hinged on an ur-proposition, an axiom, that was self-evident. Unfortunately the world is stubbornly contingent because it persists in existing through particulars and these cannot have a built-in logical necessity. It cannot come into being through sheer force of self-evidence. The reality "out there" that has to be "there" and "out" cannot be liberated from its starting place in the rag-and-bone shop of items encountered in particular locations at particular times. The pursuit of intelligibility-without-remainder requires the removal of all that makes for actual life, indeed for actual existence. The basilisk stare that looks through all change to unchanging reality blinds itself.

In the end, therefore, physics can never become mathematics and pure transparent explanation. The empty stasis of mathematics cannot substitute for the experienced world, and the latter cannot boil down to the former, though, as we have seen, some find the temptation to think this way irresistible.

CHAPTER 4

Clocking time

4.1 THE MYSTERIOUS VERB "TO TIME"

In our commitment to rescuing time from physics, and from reduction to the mere value of a variable, a quantifiable dimension, we have rather taken for granted something deeply mysterious. While all beings (pebbles, trees, monkeys) are, in some sense that we have yet to determine, in time, only one kind of being turns time into an activity. We humans are alone in *timing* being and beings, in timing what happens – including (or especially) what happens to us and, indeed the span of our lives – and in being on time. We portion time into days and we number days and parts of them; and, apparently uniquely among sentient creatures know that our days are numbered.

Our passage from experienced time to timed time – which builds on the explicitness of time afforded by vision – depends on our utilizing as clocks a subset of the processes in the material world of which we are a part. It is not enough that there are putatively isochronous periodic events, such as the swinging of pendula, the succession of night and day, and the apparent rotation of the stars. We have to see that they might be used to determine the duration and temporal location of other events and processes. And this presupposes a distinction between, and the relations between, events that fill (an interval of) time, events that constitute time ("at" – *vide infra* – "how long", "in what order"), and events that are used to measure, or determine a location in, the time. The subclass of events that are generated or domesticated in order to mark time with their periodicity is stranger than we customarily acknowledge. They are in time and, courtesy of us rise above time so that they can be about time.

We should not therefore allow our objection to the reduction of time to a dimension and then to pure quantity to blind us to this astonishing fact. Or cause us to overlook the extraordinary truth that, notwithstanding the gap between lived and measured time, between human time and time shrivelled to "little t", measurement has enabled us to extend, protect, enrich and enhance our lives; to have the time of our lives. "Measurement began our might", as Yeats said: it extended our powers beyond anything that could be imagined by our pre-numerate ancestors.[1] So a certain amount of astonishment and a good deal of gratitude is in order before we move on from this critique of what science has done to our conception of time and we proceed to look at the human time it has traduced. This chapter, in other words, is something of a corrective to the negative stance of its predecessors.

Measurement-based science has not only enabled us to see more of how the material world "works" – at least insofar as to enable us to work on it more effectively – but it also greatly extends our temporal gaze. In recent centuries, we have come to situate ourselves in a "deep time" revealed by archaeologists, evolutionary biologists, geologists and astrophysicists. We locate our lives in a time span that exceeds the duration of our individual lives by billions of years. The measures that have made us collectively mighty have created a mirror in which we are individually, existentially small. As the terminally pessimistic philosopher E. M. Cioran put it, "human life loses its value when seen from afar, either from the standpoint of distant space or distant time"[2]

Thus the consequences of being creatures for whom time is explicit and by whom, eventually, events, including that of their own lives, are timed. The strangeness of the activity of timing is reflected at least in English by the fact that there is no analogous verb for space. We do not talk of "spacing" in the way that we speak of "timing". We speak of measuring lengths and volumes of objects and of distances between them. The sense, implicit in the verb to time, of accessing time directly is, of course, confusing and leads to the endlessly debated notion that (for example) clocks measure "the passage of time" – something we shall examine in §4.4.

There is another aspect of timing – also easily overlooked. It is that we tell "the time" *at* a time. This seemingly trivial point is in fact of the greatest importance. Suffice for the present to acknowledge that I note that it is 4:30 *at* 4:30: "I looked at the clock *at* 4:30 and saw that it was 4:30". This underlines the extent to which as timers, we both stand outside of time and are immersed in it. To know (correctly) that is 4:30 is to be at 4:30 and to be looking on 4:30 as if from a temporal outside.[3] There is a time (a) at which I note the time and (b) the time that is noted. (a) and (b) are not identical even though (if the clock is accurate and I have read it right) they are "the same time". This becomes evident when we look at a clock that we do not trust: "I looked at the kitchen clock at 4:30 (at least according to my trusted watch) and I saw that it said 4:35 and realized that the clock was 5 minutes fast". The complexity inherent in the assertion "It is 4:30" will be examined in §4.5 and I will return to it in §6.1 when I discuss the idea of "now" and the links between "it is 4:30", "It is now", "Now is 4:30" and so on. (We don't of course need a clock to tell us that it is "now" any more than we need a calendar to inform us that it is "today".)

The complexity of these relationships becomes even more apparent when we perform the most basic actions associated with the verb "to time": noting the temporal duration of events and their temporal relations to each other. When I time how long it takes for something to fall to the bottom of a cliff, or to melt, or to traverse an interval of space, I can arrive at a conclusion of this sort: "The process took 10 seconds and I measured it at 4:30"; or (more precisely) "The process took 10 seconds and I measured it between 4:30:20 and 4:30:30." Under these circumstances, the timing of the process takes as long as the process itself and both the process and the timing are located in the same stretch of time. There is a "how long?" of the process and an identical "how long?" of the timing of the process; and there is a "when?" (or "where temporally at?") of the process that is timed and of the process of timing.

The complexity of the temporal "at" is captured in the simplest account of the time of an event. This passage (already quoted) from Einstein's 1905 paper on relativity is deceptively simple: "When I say, for example, 'The train arrives here at 7' that means that the passage of the little hand of my watch at the place marked 7 and the arrival of the train are simultaneous events."[4]

The importance of these relationships is that they highlight the otherwise over-looked conscious subject at the heart of the objective observations upon which the reduction of time to pure quantities disinfected of the ghost of the human is founded. It reflects a paradox: in subjecting time to timing, we seem to have succeeded in some respect to have stepped even further out of time – while of course, remaining within it, and yet seeming to exclude ourselves from it. This is the most profound mystery of clocking time.

4.2 LIGHT AND DARK; DAYTIME AND NIGHT-TIME: SHADOW CLOCKS AND BEYOND

If, as argued in Chapter 1, our explicit sense of time began with vision, it seems evident that our sense of time as a measurable quantity began with things we can see. There are certain recurrent visible events that can be relied upon to happen at regular intervals and to continue doing so seemingly forever. What is more, they are global and visible to all. I am referring, of course, to the cyclical passage from day to night and from night to day. This, the most universal common sensory truth of our lives, more widely shared even than the weather, is the ultimate source of the gap between the immediately presented temporal depth of the visual field and our widening sense of temporal extensity. Dawn, noon, and sunset, are at once locations of the sun, places in the sky, and times, and they are universally evident: time spatialized (as distinct times), made explicit, and made public. It is natural or world-time.

The cycle of day and night has been imposed on humans throughout their history. We are collectively and inescapably aware of it and it plays a key role in the organization of our lives: until comparatively recently in human history, works and days have gone together.[5] It is hardly surprising therefore that dawn, when the light returns, is the archetypal beginning and even supplies an image of the primordial beginning, when the universe itself began. The creation story in Genesis opens with the command that there shall be light (though palpable darkness also requires creation[6]); and it was this command that transformed the void into the world, and chaos into cosmos. Conversely, our passage out of explicit time, when we die, is envisaged as a descent into darkness (though in reality the darkness, too, goes out).

The alternation between day and night has had, for most of human history, a constancy, a reliability, that is "good enough" to orchestrate those of our activities that need coordinating. The apportionment of time between day and night will of course vary from season to season but we can still arrange to meet at dawn or when the light fails. There are more local consequences or expressions of this universal cycle of revelation and concealment of what is around us. Illuminated objects cast shadows, the visible darkness that, as we have discussed, re-presents them as their abstract forms. These lengthen towards evening before they converge in the universal shadow that is the night. The natural universal time marker of the succession of days can be supplemented by more local items: the early clocks whose dial was the earth itself and whose index was a shadow cast upon the face of the earth.

The most portable of the shadow-clocks that might mark time is inescapable: the one that is cast by our own body. We discussed the "peasant's clock" in §2.1, and how it might enable us to coordinate our shared lives even when we are not in sight of each other with respect to times that are beyond the past and future revealed in the visual field. We can arrange to meet when, for example, our shadows are as long as our bodies or multiples of the length of our feet. Our shadows, synchronized in their waxing and waning by the sun beneath which we all live, orchestrate the ballet of our shared lives. By these means our hours can be co-ordered and our paths intersect when it is appropriate: we can make and honour appointments.

The peasant's clock may seem primitive but the passage from visible object to visible silhouette, and from visible silhouette to abstracted length is not only cognitively complex. It is also a decisive step in the transformation of our sense of time from that which is directly yielded by visual experience to time as a dimension, ultimately as a quantity, as a number. It lies at the origin of more sophisticated uses of the variation in the length and angle of shadows that will correspond not merely to day versus night but to "the time of the day". "The time of the day" expresses something else: time placed outside of our individual selves, the time of the physical world that is experienced in common. This time will not be specifically my time (corresponding to anything I am doing or feeling – fresh or tired, for example) or your time but anyone's or everyone's time. The peasant's clock connects time with a generalized human body (its time is common to *any*body and, indeed any material body), and opens the way to the use of angles and lengths of shadows attached to *any* objects to mark time. We are en route to a universal, global time that is common to all people and objects in all places.

While the peasant's clock has its virtues, not the least being universal availability, portability and the ease with which such clocks may be synchronized, ensuring that appointments might be fulfilled between people who cannot keep each other in view, it gives only rough locations in time – morning, noon, afternoon, evening. What is more, it does not directly record intervals of time: it may give the "position" but not the "quantity". Hence the development of artefacts that have the specific purpose of exhibiting the time of day and measuring how much time has passed, as when, for example judging time allowed for rituals or for a public address. Foremost among them are items that cast sharp, large shadows on a special piece of ground; namely, the dial at their base. A striking early example is the obelisk which not only liberates timekeeping from the body but sets it in a public space and, what is more, also measures quantities of time, swept out by its moving shadow.

The principle of the obelisk was realized in the sundial around 1,500 BCE. The sundial tracks the apparent movement of the sun round the earth by casting the shadow of its style or gnomon – aligned with the axis of the earth's rotation – on to a surface etched with lines marking hours and parts thereof. It reports local solar time (good enough for ancestors who had not yet joined the jet set), bringing the majestic passage of the sun – broadcast through the radiance it sends even-handedly into the gigantic darkness around it – down to a particular part of the earth. Its working parts – the sun and the earth – are separated by 93,000,000 miles. The sundial's day-hand depends on the earth's rotation round its own axis every 23 hours and 56 minutes. And its year-hand is based upon the earth's multi-billion-mile orbit. Thus do we use the sun's epic journeying to orchestrate our little movements and domestic activities.[7] (To vary a saying of Douglas Adams: "Time is mysterious; tea-time doubly so.") The Copernican revolution and the uncovering of deep space occupied by billions of planets and of deep time reaching back billions of years has not diminished our concern for the minutiae of our own lives.

It is thrilling to contemplate the story of timekeeping, even at this early stage in its history, the soundless ticking of the obelisk and sundial capturing the twin rotations of our planet – on its own axis and around the sun – that usher in our days and years and brush them away. The movement of the shadows prefigures the geometrization of time, with the passage of hours and the o'clock of the day corresponding to degrees of arc and the dial of the sundial as the forerunner of the clock-face.

The heavens also provided a source of timekeeping through its night-lights – the stars – which were available throughout what came to be the (roughly) 24-hour cycle. Sidereal clocks depend on observing the earth's motion with respect to the fixed stars rather than the sun; more specifically the observation of the same star passing the same place. The underlying principle and the consequent influence on life was, however, the same: the astronomical events requisitioned by shadow-clocks open the path to orchestration of the great cooperative enterprise of civilization that encompasses the synchrony of public events and the intersections of private assignations have certain essential features: (a) they are recurrent; (b) they have a fixed frequency; and (c) they return to their beginning state at each repetition – fro-ing reverses to-ing.

There is a wide cognitive gap between the informal observation of times of the day as signified in the changing length and angle of shadows and the use of a sundial or obelisk to quantify the passage of shadows as the passage of time recorded in a particular locality. Almost as wide is the gap between chronometers that exploit naturally occurring events and those that generate the recurrent events they use to measure time intervals. In the case of the water clock (or clepsydra or "water thief"), each drop counts as one; but there isn't the same kind of literal cyclicity as is seen in an astronomical timepiece. The water clock (like oil lamp clocks with marked reservoirs) has the advantage of not being dependent on the light. It can watch over the hours of darkness as well as over those of sunlight and it runs as well in cloudy weather as in sunny.

The clepsydra exemplifies a principle present throughout the history of clocks: the expression of time as space and of space as pure quantity. The volume of accumulated water is translated to the height of a column; time is consequently measured by the ascent up the side of the container marked to indicate equal intervals. This is an early version of digital-to-analogue and analogue-back-to-digital conversion. The discrete drops (each counting as one – digital) add up to the volume in the receptacle (analogue) and the volume advances up the numbered sides of the receptacle (digital).

There are obvious problems with a clepsydra, the most important being that successive drops may not be precisely equal in size and the intervals between them may vary depending on (for example) how full the input column is, determining the pressure of the water, though more sophisticated varieties had built-in pressure regulation and ultimately water-driven escapements. Comparable problems of poor control over the rate of events are evident in candles marked in increments, oil lamps with marked reservoirs, hourglasses, and so on. Social organization and subsequently empirical science created a need for clocks in which the frequency of the events captured in, or generated by, them was more closely controlled.

Hence the development of mechanical clocks generating "quality controlled" repeated occurrences rather than relying on naturally occurring ones. This was a crucial step in the history of timekeeping which "is the story of the search for ever more consistent actions or processes to regulate the rate of a clock".[8] Unfolding processes – moving shadows, filling receptacles, burning candles – were superseded by repetitive ones marking equal increments of time. The processes by which they were generated was separated from the means of keeping tracks of these increments, totting them up, and displaying the result – another huge conceptual leap.[9]

Mechanical clocks came into widespread use in thirteenth-century Europe. They employed weights, springs and an escapement mechanism to break up the smooth unfolding of the spring into discrete, equal units, thus counting stretches of time of fixed and equal length. ("Stretches", "length" – the spatialization of our conception of time is inescapable!) At first they had no face or hands but struck a bell every hour. ("Clock" comes from *clocca*, meaning bell.) More sophisticated mechanical clocks were introduced in the early fifteenth century. In a common design, an uncoiling spring moved hands over a face, so that time was presented both visuospatially in analogue form (the displacement of the fingers over the face) and in digital form (the numbered positions on the face).

The next key step involves Galileo and the pendulum but I want to pause at this point to consider how far we have already travelled in transforming our sense of time.

The first thing to note is that clocked time is in equipoise between the sense of time as continuous and the sense of time as discrete – which may be the source of the intuitions that have fuelled the discussion as to whether time is or is not granular, is or is not made of distinct instants – which we shall discuss elsewhere, especially in §10.3.2.[10] The input into the process of measurement in the case of the mechanical clock is the discrete, bounded event: the tick or the tick-tock. The output is a piece of space traversed – space that is continuous. That continuous space, however, is again broken up into discrete, numbered components. On a clock face, distinct locations are placed on a continuous circular track and the sweeping hand (in later clocks at any rate) moves, or appears to move, continuously in order to tick off discrete units of time.

The second point is that events are generated (as in successive tick-tocks) for no other purpose than the measurement of time. They are meaningless in themselves, as will impress itself on anyone sitting in a quiet room with only a clock for company. This is true even in the case of a device such as a water clock, where the drops are disconnected from any function they may have in quenching thirst or washing our face. (Drinking the water from the clepsydra would be something of a *faux pas* – though magic thinking may lead to the hope that it could bring eternal life.) The intrinsic meaninglessness of the clock's activity is underlined by timepieces such as those I remember from my childhood in which successive ticks were associated with representations of activities like a hen bending up and down, pecking on the ground. The meaninglessness of the events is linked with something else: that they are used, or are generated, simply to *be* temporal units. However different they prove on close inspection, they are by fiat as it were, identical, equal in the eyes of the timekeeper: whatever the shape and size of successive drops each drop is just a drop; likewise, each tick is just a tick.[11]

This uprooting of events from anything other than their meaning as ticks or their equivalent, is in part responsible for the impression that a clock is a device for directly measuring the passage of time; that ticks scarcely qualifying as events are themselves pieces of time. It is not for nothing that we are tempted to use transferred epithets such as "the sands of time": the timer seems to gather and measure purified time inside its workings. Whether (or in what sense) clocks really do measure time is something we shall examine in §4.4.

One of the key drivers of the search for ever more accurate timekeeping was the post-medieval globalization of trade. With this came the necessity to determine your position chronometrically when you had sailed beyond all familiar landmarks. Another was the increasingly complex micro-management of society, as the role of the sovereign and the authorities expanded, with the associated requirement for power to be asserted through ever closer temporal coordination of behaviour. The need to know what the (agreed) time was became ever more pressing as the appointments (in the widest sense) that citizens made with each other were more distant in time and agreed between individuals who were ever more separated. An extraordinary pre-wireless expression of this was the telegraphing of time throughout the UK, with the result being received and broadcast so that individuals could set their watches. But this is a topic for another book; it is enough for us to note that these social drivers did exist and they were reinforced by the needs of the emerging science of mechanics, where timing events was central.

4.3 THE PULSE AND THE PENDULUM

It is time to visit an iconic moment in the history of our relationship to time: the famous episode where a bored teenage Galileo – when he was in church observing this material world instead of thinking about the next, immaterial one – observed that the swinging of the chandelier seemed to be isochronous. Each swing took the same time: the period of the pendulum was independent of the amplitude of the arc of its swing.

This is interesting for many reasons but two are salient. The first is that Galileo is said to have checked the isochronicity of the pendulum against his own pulse.[12] The second is that he inspired others to use the pendulum to time events – although the idea of a pendulum clock was not fully developed by Galileo until decades later when he was near the end of his life; and it was not fully realized in practice until after his death. The most pertinent early use of the pendulum was in the "pulsilogium" designed by his friend the physician Santorio Santorio to measure the pulse of his patients. This employment of an harmonic oscillator in which the duration of some kind of to-ing and fro-ing is absolutely regular – the heart of every subsequent clock – to time a pulse was a transformation of our sense of the relationship between our-selves and time; between time "in here" in our bodies and time "out there" in the world.

Galileo's use of his pulse to check the constancy of the frequency of the pendulum – instrumentalising his own heart rate and externalizing the time felt in his own body to the world – was therefore a leap of thought of almost metaphysical profundity. The projection of time into the outside world from one's body – which, because it externalizes the body's own time, goes beyond the process by which time is made explicit through vision that we discussed in Chapter 1 – is a huge step towards a divorce between experienced and measured (which takes on the status of "real") time. The second step – his physician friend's use of the pendulum to check the speed of the pulse – was a further externalization: the pulse becomes a parameter which is measured by an individual who is experiencing it indirectly. What is more, that individual's judgement is mediated by an external, material event.

The pendulum is the paradigm case of a harmonic oscillator which, displaced from an equilibrium state, returns to it, overshoots, and heads back towards equilibrium, indefinitely. Crucially, each swing of a pendulum of a particular length takes the same time irrespective of the amplitude of the swing or the weight of the bob, or whether the pendulum has just been set moving or is approaching stasis. This proved an advance on the coiled spring devices used in earlier mechanical clocks and Huygens perfected the pendulum-based clock in 1656. Much effort was invested in ensuring that the length, and hence the period, of the pendulum did not change in different physical conditions, most notably with alterations in temperature, such as when a ship sailed from temperate to tropical zones, a problem that was finally solved by John Harrison in 1761.

With the fundamental principle of a clock driven by an harmonic oscillator estab-lished, the hunt was on for repetitive activities that occurred at more precisely equal intervals. The pendulum was still checked against astronomical time.[13] It was not, however, dethroned until the twentieth century, when the vibration of crystals, at a known frequency, in an electromagnetic field – the so-called piezo-electric effect – became the harmonic oscillator of choice. In the second half of the twentieth century, the focus shifted to the frequency of transition of an atom from one energy level to another. The atom of choice was caesium, which executed 9,192,631,770 cycles in one second. This finally replaced the traditional time divisions ultimately defined in terms of the earth's motion. The caesium atomic clock of 2002 was said to be accurate to 30 billionths of a second per year, its frequency being some million times more stable than the rotation of the earth.

Such precise measurements of time raise two questions. First, in what sense does the clock measure time as *something in itself* – both beyond our experiences, and separate from perceived events? And secondly, how is it that we can arrive at ever more accurate measures of time, if time is *not* something in itself, existing in or flowing though the devices we use to measure it? These two questions are inseparable and they merge in one more fundamental: If time is being measured with ever greater accuracy, an accuracy that lies beyond our immediate or personal consciousness, is the clock measuring time itself, out there, independent of us? What, in short, is a clock doing?

4.4 WHAT DO CLOCKS (REALLY) DO?

> Time should be so defined that the equations of mechanics should be
> as simple as possible.   Poincaré, "The Measure of Time", 227

What do clocks do? The answer is surely simple: they tell the time; and if they are any good, they tell the right time. But behind that simple answer are complex, and perhaps not entirely resolved, arguments. So we ask again: what do clocks (really) do?

A clock is a device that records and sums naturally occurring or artificially generated, standardized, events – dripping of water drops, swings of a pendulum, vibrations in piezo-electric crystals – occurring at what are assumed to be equal periods. By this means, it times other events – their duration, their frequency, and their temporal location relative to other events. The events in the clock that enable it to time other events are assumed to be temporally equal within and across clocks. They are registered and gathered up, and their growing sum displayed, typically as a distance moved on a dial or (more recently) as an increasing number. The events, as we have said, are meaningless in themselves: any meaning that may be ascribed to them is as irrelevant as the colour of a numerical symbol. They are stripped of everything other than the temporal intervals between them. This is one of the reasons why we are inclined to think of a clock as a place where pure time is made explicit such that definite quantities of it can be laid, like a ruler, alongside events whose duration, frequency or other temporal characteristics are to be measured. Notwithstanding the arguments in §2.2.3, there is an irresistible temptation to think of a clock as measuring "the passage of time", as somehow standing to one side of the flow of time – on the banks of the river, as it were – allowing we who consult it to do likewise, so that we can "time" what happens, as if from without, notwithstanding that we and the clock and the act of recording time are immersed in time.

There is another reason why we might be tempted to think of a clock in this way, so that its role in helping us to time events suggests that it is a site where pure time passes through like a stream making a mill paddle revolve, and its quantity gets measured. It is this: we think of the history of timekeeping as being one of progressively increasing accuracy. Does this not suggest that we are closing in on time itself? By what criteria do we justify the claim that one clock is more accurate than another?

The question has a particular force because we cannot directly compare intervals of time to find out whether one is longer or shorter than another and then use this to calibrate our clocks. All time measurements have to be mediated by clocks. This is quite different from the situation with spatial measures. I can place two objects directly side by side to see if they are the same size prior to making mediated comparisons of size by placing each of them separately next to a ruler. While we might relatively easily judge of two simultaneous or overlapping events whether one is of longer duration than the other, we cannot re-run singular events to check our judgement. We are even more disadvantaged when it comes to non-overlapping events: we cannot align them except in our memory and this is vulnerable to many sources of error, not the least being that the more recent event may "loom larger" than the more distant one.[14]

The trust we place in clocks is therefore more vulnerable than that which we place in rulers. The particular point of the question "What do clocks (really) do?" is illustrated by the example we have already discussed, of Galileo and his friend Santorio.[15] Galileo checked the regularity of the pendulum – the isochrony of the swings – with his pulse and Santorio timed his patient's pulse with the swing of a pendulum. One measured the pendulum against a pulse and the other measured the pulse against the pendulum. They could of course be further checked against sundials and other recorders of astronomical time but this would presuppose trust in the accuracy of the astronomical clock provided by the sun, which, as we have seen, is justified only up to a point.[16] We seem to be in the grip of a measurement circle and it is difficult to see how we could break out of it. As Rovelli puts it: "How do we know that a clock measures time, if we can only check it against another clock?"[17] He concludes that the variable t measured by the clock is merely "a convenient assumption" and he argues that we should drop it.

Even if we do not take that radical step, we still need to face up to a genuine challenge to the Whiggish idea that the history of timekeeping is one in which we are measuring time with increasing accuracy. We can check that one clock G is a gold standard and another clock B a mere bronze standard only if we already have a platinum standard clock P by which to judge the relative performance of G and B but that is precisely what we seek. By what criterion could we determine that G is more accurate than B – or that P has the authority to adjudicate between two clocks that disagree?

In order to see how we might break out of this circle, and that the journey from Galileo's chandelier-clock checked against his pulse to a caesium clock supposedly accurate to 30 billionths of a second per year, represents real advance, we need to acknowledge that progress in timing cannot be separated from the progress of physics as a whole and, in particular, its development of a network of theories that, while they take their rise from observations, predict other observations with a precision that goes beyond anything that could be directly measured.

It is useful to recall at this point Wigner's remark quoted in the previous chapter that "The law of gravity which Newton reluctantly established and which he could verify to an accuracy of about 4% has proved to be accurate to less than a ten-thousandth of a per cent."[18] The *theory* specifies what is really happening with a precision greater than any of the observations on which it is based.[19] So the theory of the pendulum, based on investigating pendulums of different length, gives a precise estimate of the period of any given pendulum (for small swings). This will not be observed with real pendulums where there are confounding factors such as air resistance, friction at the point of attachment, and the mass and wobbliness of the string. The *theoretical* (ideal) pendulum would show a relationship that would be predicted, to an observationally unattainable degree of precision, by Newton's Laws of motion and gravitation.

This relationship gets more securely grounded as it is incorporated into an increasingly extensive meshwork of theories – encompassing the laws of motion and the theory of gravity. We get an evermore accurate handle on what observations *should be* in advance of making them; and so we can anticipate how a clock, superior to any that we have so far, would behave. It is this intermeshing of laws that enables us to adjudicate between clocks and say that clock G is more accurate than clock B and clock P is more accurate than either G or B so that it can tell us that G is more accurate than B. The higher level law – and the law of consistency of laws – enables us to choose between time measures and hence to select the time measure that will predict the widest ranges of observations (and consequently experiences) with the greatest accuracy.

To some extent, this will involve changing the nature of what it is that is measured. Lawrence Sklar illustrates this in the case of temperature. We begin with subjective awareness of hot and cold and then find an objective correlative of these experiences in devices that exploit the fact that many substances have linear coefficients of volume that change with temperature. The discovery of the laws of thermodynamics changes our understanding of temperature. "At this stage the concept of temperature is principally tied no longer to subjective experience or the results of thermometric measurements, but to its role in fundamental thermodynamics and statistical mechanics".[20] Sklar connects this principle with the idea of objectively accurate measures of time. "The temporal metric", he says "has received its deep objective clarification by the embedding of the notion of equal temporal interval" into the fundamental laws of mechanics.[21] There is a profound connection between our measures of time and the laws of motion, which, as we have seen, have been verified to be accurate to a degree that exceeds many thousand-fold the accuracy of the data upon which

Newton first proposed them. More generally "the metric of time has entered into many laws of foundational physics"[22]. A similar point has been made by Newton-Smith: "the selection of preferred clock systems ... is intimately bound up with the choice of physical theories".[23] He quotes Reichenbach's assertion that "the extension of being isochronic is to be fixed by reference to our best physical theories".[24]

The latter, of course, derive their authority not only from their consistency with existing theories, or their capacity to generate new ones, but from the power of those theories to predict what we experience, observe, or measure, to extend our ability to create technologies that will help us to get things done, and to anticipate the physical outcomes of our actions. In short, assessing the accuracy of time measurement goes beyond consistency with other time measurements – with clocks endorsing clocks – but involves laws that encompass both temporal and non-temporal parameters. There is an authentication trail that leads from personal experience, to collective experience, to scientific measurement that reaches beyond actual experience to the structural and quantitative aspects of possible experience, and back to experience. This is most obviously illustrated by technologies such as GPS that enables our cell-phone-coordinated lives to dovetail over the entirety of inhabited space. "More accurate timing" means predicting a greater range of measured events more accurately, consistent with laws that have ever greater scope. This is clearly not merely a matter of convention – or not, at least, in the conventional sense.

The development of theories or laws, on the basis of approximate observations supported by relatively primitive instruments which are then confirmed by what are regarded as more accurate observations and then stitched into the meshwork of interlinked observations tethered to evermore fundamental theories, enables science to move from a seemingly unbreakable circle of validation of instruments to the open beyond. In other words, we can escape from the apparent closed circle whereby we demonstrate that clock G is more accurate than clock B by referring to clock P whose claim to being a better measure of time would require us to have reference to another clock ad infinitum. Outside of the circle we have laws predicting the time that events should take and we can use those to test clocks that time those events. For example, the frequency of the caesium atom's oscillations could be calculated, on the basis of quantum theory, in advance of any timing.

The harmonic oscillators that were developed in the last century rendered swinging pendulums obsolete in physics and to a great extent in the technology we use in everyday life. Consider again the caesium clock, which uses the frequency of electromagnetic microwaves. One second is equal to 9,192,631,770 periods of radiation between the two hyperfine levels of the caesium atom. That this is constant and repeatable, and introduces minimal sources of error in measurement and prediction, could be arrived at theoretically but there is also another check, ensuring that the waves are of an entirely identical temporal size: namely, that they are *superimposable*, something that can be tested for by the presence or absence of interference patterns. These are precise measures of self-consistency and consistency with clocks of the same kind or self-congruence over different stretches of activity. So checking caesium clocks against each other and seeing whether or not over a significant period of time they do not get out of synch is not like buying two copies of the same newspaper to check the veracity of the stories they contain. If they remained in synch, this would not be simply because they were prone to the same kind of error.

The most advanced, that is to say reliable, clocks are checked not only against experience, against other clocks of the same kind, and against clocks of other kinds, but also (and most importantly) against the clockwork of the entire universe insofar as it is revealed by theory, so that we can ascertain that they are closer than their rivals to the beating heart of the totality of things. The closed circle of the pulse and the pendulum has been opened up to embrace the entire universe.[25]

This is one reason why we are tempted to see the clock as metaphysically privileged, as directly measuring the passage of time, and giving us the fundamental reality of time. It does not justify our doing so because the physics, for all that it is the most wide-ranging quantitative general account of the material world, empties time of many of its essential features and, in fundamental theories, may lose it altogether. However, our inclination to grant metaphysical standing to the physics of time – to believe that clocks measure time directly, time in-itself – has a homelier origin. The clock is not merely a source of events that are then compared in some respect with other events: it rises above specific events to be available to be related to an indefinite range of events in whatever vicinity it finds itself. This is clear even in the case of the humble kitchen clock, where its ticks and tocks and finger positions say something about everything else that is happening in the kitchen, whether it is the egg being boiled, the lateness for an appointment, the cooling of hot coffee, the boredom that overcomes us because nothing is happening, the speed of the traffic outside, and the realization that it is time to feed the dog.

Some have argued for a different understanding of a privileged relationship between clocks and time; namely that they in some sense *generate* time; that the seconds they dole out are not merely chopped up pieces of the time that is passing through them or around them but something they as it were create. The astrophysicist Hermann Bondi suggested this. "Time" he said, "must never be thought of as pre-existing in any sense; it is a *manufactured* quantity".[26] To which we would want immediately to respond: manufactured by whom? And, more tellingly, manufactured when? How long did it take? And, finally, the question that may make sense of what seems to be a senseless assertion: manufactured by what means?

If there is a sense in which clocks seem to manufacture time, it is by, as it were, giving it a visible surface; by apparently extracting it and placing it before us. Self-evidently, they represent a decisive step in the process by which time, made explicit through vision, looks increasingly like something that has an existence in itself. The clock on the wall that marks the passing of the morning seems to reveal something that is outside of the morning: above it, in one sense, even though in another, it is inseparable from it. The clock is the site of a succession of events – ticks and tocks and hand movements – that belong to the matitudinal hours as much as the conversations in the room and the to-ings and fro-ings that fill the morning. The ticks and tocks, and the event of consulting the clock, are no more above the temporal fray than the events that are allocated times by it. After all, timepieces have many components that do not relate directly to the measurement of time (such as the outer case and the film of oil between the moving parts) and there are many events in the clock that are also unrelated to recording time – for example, the fading of the numbers on the face, the wear and tear of the escapement mechanism, the sounds produced by the ticking. This subjection of time-measurers to the processes that also affect that which they time can often be quite poignant – for example, the moss and rust on the sundial advancing as soundlessly as the ticking of the gnomon; or the effacement of the name of the original owner on the pocket watch handed down the generations. Every aspect of the clock, and the events in it, are just like those events it clocks, temporally wired into the general flow of events.

The fact that the clock is not above the temporal fray undermines the notion that it "measures the passage of time" because the latter would suggest it was outside time, just as we measure the flow of a river from a point on the bank which is at once outside of the river and stable with respect to it. But are we making rather a meal of this issue? Consider measuring the length of an object or the width of a gap between two objects: we are making spatial measurements but we do not conclude that we are doing this from outside of space.[27] Indeed, our measuring devices have to get alongside that which is measured in order to measure them. A ruler that was outside of space would be of no use to us. However, there is an interesting difference. We measure sizes of objects, distances between objects, but not pure space: what we quantify is space occupancy, even if in those cases in which what occupies the measured space is a gap between things that occupy space.

There is, however, another consideration that takes us in the opposite direction: the nature of measurement itself. Let us remain for a moment with space. When I measure the length of an object, I place another object, a ruler, against it. This is the means by which I literally apply units to the object in order to unitize it; to make it into a number of standard items (e.g. 6 "centimetres"). By turning the object into a number of units, I do two things – one obvious and one less obvious. The first is to strip it of its singularity: when I say of something "It is 6 centimetres", I am essentially asserting its identity in the pertinent respect with all items of equal length and suppressing its particularity. Under the rule of the ruler, goats, arms, mountains, masterpieces and kings, are treated equally. They are all the bearer of their sizes and the latter are reduced to multiples of a standard size. Secondly, I am removing it from its particular location: "The object is 6 centimetres" is true irrespective of where it is and I am (leaving aside relativistic considerations which are irrelevant to ordinary experience). The application of the ruler to the measured object generates a truth about the two objects in space that is not itself in space. Measurement as it were lifts the item out of space: "6 centimetres" is not a spatial relation in the way that "over there", "next to" are spatial relations. What we get is pure spatial extensity but "de-located". Better, we get pure space; space separated from place; space reduced to extensity, to naked magnitude.

And we feel that something is comparable with clocks. This is why we seem to be perhaps measuring pure time or (since time is traditionally said to "pass") measuring the passage of time. There is, however, an important difference between spatial and temporal measurements. When I measure the length of a table, I place a spatially extended material object against the spatially extended material table to determine the latter's length. I cannot do this directly in the case of time. Standardized events (in the clock) are counted against the event or interval that is being timed. In that sense, duration is being measured against duration but the visible "side-by-sideness" of a ruler placed against a table is missing. In order that the ruler can measure the table, the one has to be applied to the other and this is only tenuously analogous to what happens when an event is timed.

There *is* a sense in which a clock has to be next to an event in order to time it. In the ordinary case, we look at the clock face and at the event (for example you running 100 yards) and compare the positions of the fingers at the start and end of the event. The distance moved by the fingers measures the duration of the event. So we have to bring the clock and the event into the same visual or sensory field (directly or via mediation) in order that the one can be used by us to time the other. But what about using a clock to tell what time it is? Here, no location is necessary, so long as the event we are interested in and the clock are not separated by time zones. This highlights a difference between the duration of events (and time intervals) and location in time.

Have we demystified clocks? Perhaps. When we look at the events in a busy room, it remains difficult to shake off the idea that there is one set of events that seems to be temporally privileged compared with all the others, notwithstanding what has just been said. These are events that not only occur in time but are used by us to time the duration of other events (the food cooking, the lateness of our guests) and to locate what is happening in time – to say that (for example) everything that is happening now is happening at 4 o'clock. The clock is a general comparator. It is this that makes it seem as if the comparison with respect to time is a manifestation of time itself and that time is a pure quantity. And this is how the translation of time into space – which happens in some sense when any steady movement persists over time – and thence into numbers in a clock seems to reveal time as it were *in itself.* Or, at the very least, the events in the clock measure time while everything else in the kitchen is measured against time.

Let us return to basics. A clock has three essential elements: periodic, isochronous, rhythmic events (borrowed from nature or generated purposefully); a means of displaying the accumulation of those events; and an observer who reads what is on the display. By focusing on one or other of these elements at the expense of the remaining ones we arrive at a false notion of what clocks do and how they do it. If we look at the events on the dial, we see the finger moving, or successive numbers coming and going, and feel that what is happening is "the passage of time". If we look at the interior, we see a paddle being driven, and time passing through it. If we focus on this and the observer, we may falsely conclude, with Hermann Bondi, that time does not pre-exist our measurements of it; that rather it is a *manufactured* quantity.

It is more accurate to say that clocks present the temporal element of events separate from any other aspect; that what the clock offers is not a manufactured product but a distillate. When I say of a conversation that "it began at 4 p.m., it lasted 15 minutes, and it occurred an hour before the fight broke out", I have removed from it everything except its temporal characteristics. Of course, I can subsequently fill them in but for the present, what is given us by the clock is pure time, winnowed of every other aspect of the conversation that is timed. We have it seems *extracted* time from events in order to quantify it; and since we have done so by recording the succession or passage of events, we seem to be measuring the succession of stretches of time, the passage of time. The question we need to ask ourselves is the extent to which the idea that we *extract* time from events justifies our thinking that we have *manufactured* it or the opposite view that we are directly measuring something that exists in itself. Neither of these views is fully justified but they owe their origin to the feeling that the act of "timing" either reveals or confers the essence of time, an essence that is concretely represented in the axes that capture "world-line" graphs.

It is certainly the case that the habit of separating out time as something in itself, as an independent constituent of things, was irreversibly entrenched in scientific thought with the Galilean–Newtonian revolution. The construction and dissemination of reliable clocks – resulting in an increasingly high level of agreement between observers – reinforced the sense that it had an independent reality captured in its mode of representation – in measurements. The psychologist E. L. Thorndike once famously asserted that "whatever exists at all, exists in some amount".[28] This is, to put it mildly, contentious; but it does suggest an obverse: "Whatever exists in some measured amount, may seem to exist in itself" – and to exist in a way that is captured by this amount. It is what we may call "the quantitative theory of time" – the main target of this book. This prompts another thought: that the extraction of "the flow of time" from "the succession of events" by means of counted periodic events is the *same* as manufacturing it. Does bringing the explicitness of time that begins with vision to a higher level in the shared explicitness of public time and ultimately objective scientific time – time that reaches beyond any human subject – amount to creating it? This is a question to which we shall return in the final part of this book: it reaches to the heart of our preoccupations.

While we want to resist the notion that a clock measures the passage of time but rather compares events in the clock (the timer) with certain salient events outside the clock (the timed), we cannot completely eliminate the use of the word "time" in our description of a clock. Firstly, the comparison of the events in the timer with the events that are being timed is *with respect to their temporal duration*: a clock says nothing about the size or colour or meaning of events. Secondly, the events in the clock are chosen because they are identical in one temporal respect, namely that the time interval between them is precisely the same. That is why each can count as "one" and, counting as one, their succession is ripe to be translated into "counting time". The meaninglessness of the events generated by the clock is another way in which the timer is differentiated from the (meaningful) timed. They are summed and displayed and it is this that reduces clock time to a pure quantity. "A second" does not correspond to the perception of the sequence of events because what is perceived is a number and we look past the phenomenal appearance of the number in order to make sense of it. The clock, as it were, separates time from the *experience* of change, of duration.

One final thought. There is a popular image of the universe, which unfolds according to certain laws that have time as a variable, as a great clock: it goes according to time. This act of retrospectively reading our technology into the totality of things is not customarily regarded as a joke. Indeed, Paul Davies has taken it seriously even at the subatomic level when he argues that "some particles, such as muons, have a built in clock because they decay with a definite half-life".[29]

But it is a gross anthropomorphisation to speak of the physical world in this way. There are many billions of periodic, rhythmic processes going on constantly but they are not clocks until they are used as such. The variety of items we use to measure time – our own shadows, the dripping of water, the movement of a pendulum, radioactive decay, subatomic resonance – is itself testimony to the fact that nothing is a clock until it is used by us for that purpose. Flowers come into bloom at different times but their succession amounts to a flower clock only in a public park. It is "the beholder's share" that we should look for when we seek what is special about the events in a clock.[30] Clocks in themselves no more "tell the time" than do shadows – or than they attend to their own ticking. We slip into talking in this way because I can find out what time it is equally by looking at a clock myself or by asking you to do so on my behalf and report what time it is. The clock seems to be doing what you are doing when you answer my question as to what time it is. We consult people and we consult clocks. However, the clock – muon or grandfather – tells nothing in the absence of one who consults it. This is a topic to which we shall return in §4.7.[31]

4.5 TELLING THE TIME: "AT" – FROM CLOCK TO O'CLOCK

An important word at the heart of timing is not, at first sight, very impressive. It has, after all, only two letters. The word is "at" and it lies at the heart of the transformation of time into timing. It is ubiquitous in all our timing-talk. We tell the time at such and such a time and if the time is told correctly, the time is what is told at the time we tell it. We time the duration of events by noting the time at which they begin, and at which they end, and our timing takes place at (that is to say during) the time (or apparent time) of the events. I could go on but I will spare the reader more apparent truisms, as I hope the point is sufficiently made that they are more than truisms.

"At" most immediately relates to location in, rather than quantity of, time. The primordial "at" is the "now" at which the (correct) time is noted, recorded, detected, reported (and "at" which events take place). Where the dominant ways of thinking about time are rooted in physical science, the basic "at" is thought of as a space–time point, defined by a number in relation to a set of coordinate axes. "Now" by contrast leads a precarious existence, as Einstein noted in a famous conversation with Rudolf Carnap that we shall discuss in Chapter 6:

> Once Einstein said that the problem of Now worried him. He explained that the experience of the Now means something special for man, something

essentially different from the past and the future but that this difference does not and cannot occur within physics. That this experience cannot be grasped by science seemed to him a matter for painful but inevitable resignation.[32]

The implication is if we lose "now" – so be it. Thus Einstein. But if "now" is the ground floor of "at", then without "now", there is no timing. The insentient space–time points of the physical world do not after all mysteriously locate themselves with respect to coordinate axes, and thus acquire (numerical) values. As we noted in §3.5.3.1, coordinate axes do not arise spontaneously: space does not spontaneously crystallize into coordinates, linked to origins, become self-populated by a blizzard of 0s appearing in triplets (or quartets in the case of space–time).

The now *at* which timing takes place is invisible because it is taken for granted. That it is 6 a.m. at which I note that the time is 6 a.m. is lost in the assertion that "It is 6 a.m." It is a necessary condition for the truth of the assertion which, given that our usual intention is not to mislead, and our usual assumption is that the clock is accurate, hardly needs to be spelled out. But not spelled out, it disappears from view.

The elision of "at" whose primordial form is an implicit "now" has serious consequences, and has much to do with the erasure of the observer, discussed in §3.5.3.1. Another consequence may be the disappearance of time itself. If time is a pure quantity, or the value of a variable identified by one of four numbers characterizing a space–time point, then in the absence of those values being determinate, there is no specific time. However, variables can be assigned or determinate only from the viewpoint of an observer, that imports a now (and a here) defining a frame of reference. The "now" and "here" are the dimensions of the "at" from which the parameter is assigned values. Take away "at" and there are no values; take away the values and nothing remains in a physical universe that has already been reduced to a system of magnitudes.

If this does not look like the truism it is, this is because we are so used to extruding the observer from the coordinate systems into which time is assimilated, somehow imagining that the system will be provided free. We imagine that there is an "at" built into the space–time manifold, that justifies assigning values to locations within it; that the "at" upon which observations were made can subsequently be left behind, a ladder that to be drawn up and forgotten when you are safely in the Platonic heaven of the four-dimensional continuum. But this is an illusion because without "at" there is no basis for those measurements upon which relativity ultimately depends. More specifically, there would be no basis for discriminating between the correctness of saying that "It is 6 o'clock" at 6 o'clock and the incorrectness of saying "It is 6 o'clock" at 7 o'clock. Without this "at", there is no answer to the question of what time it is. There is no such thing – which is precisely what physicists would say. To imagine that there could be an absolute – or definite – time assigned to a point in the manifold, or to an event at that point, would be an elementary mistake.

The absence of "at" also removes the possibility of assigning a definite size to the temporal interval between events. After all, my judgement that event E lasted one hour must be based on my observing the clock reading 6 p.m. when it began and 7 p.m. when it ended and that I was making the two observations, at respectively 6 p.m. and 7 p.m. And, by the same token, the removal of "at" – which eternizes the moment – would take away the possibility of assigning a temporal order to events. And while (of course) there is no universal "at", without "at" there is no basis for measurement and hence for physical science.

The "at-less" world of relativity would – as we have already demonstrated in §3.5.3 – be one in which the kind of observations that Einstein refers to in the passage already quoted would not be possible: "When I say, for example, 'The train arrives here at 7' that means that 'the passage of the little hand of my watch at the place marked 7 and the arrival of the train are simultaneous events'. His later collaborator Leopold Infield wrote that this was "the simplest sentence I have ever encountered in a scientific paper".[33] It will be evident by now that it is not at all simple. Timing takes place at a time and takes the time defined by such places.

The fact that the "at" which lies at the heart of timing (most pertinently the timing upon which relativity theory in particular and physics in general is based), has no place in the physical world is the most fundamental refutation of the claim of physics to have the final say on time. Time without timing – without time being made explicit *at* times – is a world without physics (and much more besides – most obviously "now"); indeed, not the world as we know it; and it could not accommodate such a world. This highlights how the seeming unexceptionable assertion that there are no absolutes of temporal location, absolute magnitudes of temporal interval, or temporal orders of events, can lead ultimately to the conclusion there are no times, time intervals, or time orders, if we regard physics as the whole story of time and timers (young and old) as being entirely assimilated into the material world portrayed in fundamental physics.

One final at-related point. In our discussion of the erasure of the observer in §3.5.3 we noted that a measurement was not merely to be equated with the effect of a physical event on a physical instrument. Measurements are actions and the products of actions made by and for conscious observers. When I look at my watch to time an event, the resulting measurement is not merely an effect of the interaction between the device and my body, although this is necessary. There is a profound difference between how a change in the position of the fingers on the face gives rise to a measurement and the way that change in position causes an alteration of the position of the shadows cast on the face. In the case of using the watch to time something, the distance between the events in the watch, the events in the watch-user, the events being measured, and the measurement, is not reducible to differences in spatiotemporal intervals. (We shall return to this issue in Chapter 12.)[34] Bergson's position that Einstein created an excellent theory of clock-time but missed out on lived time is too generous. Clocking time – and the temporal "at" ascribed to events – lies beyond physics.

Clocked time is inseparable from the shared consciousness of living human beings. A clock straddles physics and humanity. It is easy even for sophisticated philosophers to forget this. Tim Maudlin, for example, states that:

An ideal clock is some observable physical device by means of which num-bers can be assigned to events on the device's world-line, such that the ratios of differences in the numbers are proportional to the ratios of interval lengths of segments of the world-line that have those events as world-lines.[35]

It is not sufficient that the device should be "observable": it should be observed. Clocks tell the time only when they are asked; when they are constructed and used to do so. Only then do the numbers count as numbers and the numbers mark intervals of time.[36]

To vary Douglas Adams once more: "Time is mysterious; clock-time doubly so."

4.6 ORCHESTRATING OUR LIVES

And strangers were as brothers to his clocks
                                   Auden, "In Time of War", sonnet VIII

Mechanical clocks have ruined our lives. In medieval Europe the first mechanical clocks appeared around 1270 but it was several centuries before they were widely available and longer still before they began to dominate our lives. The explosion in clock and watch ownership – the so-called hor-ological revolution – changed for ever our perception of time. The remorse-less ticking of those treasured timepieces transformed the way we worked, ushering a new era of rigorous time-discipline and synchronized, soulless routines, almost obliterating the seasonal rhythms of a more humane, pre-industrial age. Humanity laboured under the tyranny of clocked time.[37]

The consequences of timing are immeasurable. Our society and our individual lives within and offset from it are transformed into a multitude of intermeshing ensembles harmonized by timepieces. Inside evermore tightly drawn temporal meshes, the clock rules our every moment: we watch time and time watches us; and the portability of the watch compared with, say, the obelisk, makes the watching and the watched more intimately locked together. The living rhythms spelt out in our breathing, our walking and our beating hearts are overlain by something profoundly different, symbolized by the way the watch we consult with fast-beating heart is placed on top of our heart or grips our wrist. We dance or jump or run or stumble to the stipulated rhythms of the shared day, of the common world. We eat and sleep not according to our bodily appetites and needs but according to the calendar and the clock.

It is not clear how recent is the tyranny of clocked time. Paul Glennie and Nigel Thrift argue, against E. P. Thompson, that it antedates the industrial revolution and the discipline imposed on those who labour in increasingly Taylorized factories.[38] The clock permeated the houses of the clockless, in the sounds of the bells summoning them to mass, announcing that the market is open, or declaring the curfew ("tolling the knell of the parting day"). What no-one disputes is that the clock has penetrated ever more ubiquitously into the capillaries of our daily lives, private, public, and professional. Increasingly, time is money and the sweat of our metaphorical brow becomes a metaphorical clepsydra.

This is not all bad, of course: our lives have been vastly enriched, and we are collectively and individually empowered, by coordination: dancing to the music of clock-time, we can work together more effectively to meet and anticipate our basic needs, to generate evermore complex ways of exploiting nature, and to erect defences against a universe that has no particular care for us. Our powers converge in actions on a scale that far exceeds what we have achieved through the accidents of co-presence in space. And we must not underestimate the extraordinary nature of this achievement.

To take a salient example: the operating theatre. There is the surface orchestration of the lives of all the experts – surgeons, nurses, technicians, anaesthetists, cleaners, and engineers – necessary to make the procedure happen and happen safely. But beneath this, there is an almost bottomless subsoil of temporally coordinated life. Think of a vital but often forgotten member of the cast: the engineer responsible for making sure the complex machinery in the theatre works, and works to time. He himself must arrive on time and his journey will have depended on a multitude of conductors, ranging from the alarm clock he set to wake him up to the traffic lights whose efficient working (regulated from some central place) made sure that he was not held up forever in jammed traffic. His assumption of his present post as a medical engineer will have been the end stage of a long journey that has depended upon meeting with others at preset times. His skills and training, for example, will have involved a multitude of people whose tabled time will have meshed with his, so that he was able to benefit from the wisdom and technical expertise of his teachers. The equipment on which he learned his skills – either directly or as illustrations of general principles – had to be manufactured, delivered, maintained and demonstrated by an endless army of individuals turning up on time and timing their activities to fit in with those of others. The equipment itself will have a multitude of components based on clocks – visible and hidden – created by other clock-watchers and on physical principles whose discovery and application and commercialization involved yet more armies of clock-drilled people. At every point in his life, our engineer will have been borne up by myriads of clock-conducted fellows.

This is a beneficent example. There are other less heart-warming instances of the consequences of orchestration. The gigantic torture machine that is North Korea is an extreme instance of how the imposed brotherhood of clocks can subordinate individual life entirely to a collective existence, a Big Brotherhood, where each is reduced to an atom in an engine of power servicing the needs of a small elite. The scale of the catastrophic wars of the recent centuries would not have been possible without clocks to bring men and *materiel* together on a giant scale, permitting destruction to be both precise and ubiquitous. The synchrony and orchestration that enhances our ability to realize our collective power and knowledge and to enhance that collective power with our ever-increasing collective knowledge, unifying ever greater numbers of us by means of ever closer and denser connections, make it possible to hurt each other with appallingly enhanced efficiency. As time gets further from subjective experience and, led by the eye, opening our way to an explicitly shared world, goes further from our beating hearts, heartlessness may install itself in the heart of our world. If we strangers are made as brothers by clocks it may be at the price of becoming self-estranged. Our evermore precise timekeeping may be a mode of time losing. By facilitating the passage from bodily experience to disembodied information, from the personally endured to the impersonally mapped, clocked time may have liberated us into an ontologically lighter world of facts and possibilities, of abstractions, but this may also leave us feeling a little emptied.

There are lesser woes that may follow from this than the kind of global horror humanity may self-inflict through totalitarian politics and total war. The kitchen clock, my watch, the peeps from the radio, preside over my hurry, your hurry, the hurry of widening rings of friends and strangers who are the soft inflectors of the infinite hard clockwork of the universe endlessly extending possibility. Hence the paradox that our orchestrated lives may be emptied even as they are enriched. The ever-greater efficiency of an evermore intimately clocked world adds to our opportunities but this may drive a positive feedback in which we demand more of the world and the world demands more of us. Uniquely human hurries are directed towards appointments and by obligations instead of away from predators and other natural threats or towards food and drink and immediate objects of appetite. We run not because we are being chased but because we have looked at the clock and seen that we have only 20 minutes to get to that all-important meeting. The occasion of our rush is not a physical stimulus or a biological threat or promise but an abstracted interval of time – 20 minutes – a temporal relationship between a point in a notational system and "now" whose location has been identified by the clock.

As we seem to get a grip on time, via those numbers, time tightens its grip on us. Like Gulliver in Lilliput, we are held down by a multitude of threads, even though our hastes become more manic and our passage from one thing to the next is a more fluent slide. We supplement the treadmill of work with a treadmill of pleasures. Hurry may seem to be a constant condition, even if the hurry is to catch a plane to go on holiday, to get to a concert on time, to meet an engagement whose sole purpose is for a relaxed get-together. Lateness has more complex consequences and the virtue of punctuality makes us endlessly anxious. We are forever on the edge of being late and any dereliction in this respect causes us anguish: we are mortified and the others are impatient. The quickening of pace is evident in every aspect of our lives and, for those of a religious persuasion, extends beyond our lives. The church bell nags us not to be late for the service.[39]

The tyranny of the clock asserts a pre-emptive sway over an ever-extending future. The calendar on the wall says what is going to happen or ought to happen in the future. Our days are spoken for days, weeks, months, years ahead. A phone call on the morning of 12 November 2010 commits the afternoon of 14 July 2012. The future we may not even live to see is populated with constraining possibilities, with private, shared, and public intentions, with mutual obligations.

New forms of communication permit an instantaneity of response and consequently seem to demand this. Others expect immediate or continuous availability and we in turn expect this of them. We are electronically skewered by emails, texts, phone calls. Our lives are coordinated, shaped, even filled, not by the stars but by satellites that orbit round the nearer heavens. As we "communicate" more electronically, we seem to communicate less. We are attenuated – or "e-ttenuated" – a paradox that symptomatizes what is happening more generally: that, as we travel faster and our journeys are increasingly effortless, so we seem to travel lighter, indeed to *become* lighter. The inability fully to experience our experiences, except when those experiences are unpleasant (hunger, cold, pain, terror, grief), particularly when we seek experiences for their own sake, becomes ever more evident. We look to boredom to restore to time its weight, so that it hangs heavily.

Enough of complaint. Let us return to the miracle of clocked time and the ability that it affords us to locate ourselves in a temporal ocean much deeper than the rock pools of our little lives.

4.7 TOWARDS DEEP TIME

> [The clock] disassociated time from human events and helped to create the belief in the independent world of science.
> Lewis Mumford, *Technics and Civilization*
> (quoted in Carr, "Is Google Making Us Stupid?")

Clocks affect our sense of time in many different ways. The most profound effect is to undermine our confidence in our immediate sense of the duration of events. Clocks have the last word; in any quarrel with the clock, the clock always wins. When we are surprised at how quickly or how slowly time has passed we question our own judgement not the accuracy of the timepieces that tell us that our judgement is faulty. There is the old joke about attending a Wagner opera. You enter a darkened auditorium at 5 o'clock. The curtain rises. Two hours later, you look at your watch and see that it is 5:15. We blame Wagner – or our philistinism – for the disconnection between experienced and real time rather than our wristwatch.[40]

Almost as fundamental a consequence of out-sourcing our temporal sense to clocks is the great extension of the temporal depth of our present situation. In Chapter 1 we examined the origin of explicit time and temporal depth in the visual sense. I can literally see the no-longer and the not-yet in the positions no-longer-occupied and not-yet-occupied by a moving object. The positions outlive the object's occupancy of them, being present both after and before the object passed through them. Consider now what happens to our sense of temporal depth as a result of engaging with clocks. We do not have to mobilize anything particularly technologically advanced: an obelisk will make the point.

I see that the shadow indicates that it is noon. Either side, there are markers indicating where the shadow was at dawn and where it will be in the evening. A single glance will consequently take in the entirety of a day. The temporal depth of my visual field is greatly extended beyond that which I can or could see to positions that could not even in principle be seen. This is of course simply a beginning. On a more humble level, the hour-glass brings the future (the sand in the upper storey) the present (the sand passing through the middle) and the past (the sand in the lower storey) into the compass of a single glance. In the case of a mechanical clock, the expansion of the past and of the future is even more obvious. Four o'clock in the afternoon – the present time – is located in a circular array which encompasses the entire cycle of night and day. It visibly sits between 2 o'clock and 6 o'clock.

The extension of the visual presence of the past – the position which the hour hand pointed to – and the future – the position which the hour hand will point to – does not, of course, stop there. The cycling of the hands continues indefinitely. Seeing them moving, and observing that they return to the same places again and again, underlines the idea of the entire dial as a set of positions which outlast the present cycle. The clock face is a visible symbol of an indefinite number of days, each of which is in some sense equal. Today is not privileged: 4 o'clock on the clock today looks the same as 4 o'clock yesterday and tomorrow and the day before and the day after. Looking at the clock face, we can see places which have been visited any number of days in the past and will be visited any number of days in the future.[41]

However, this is not the entire story of the origin of a time deeper than vision allows. The earliest time pieces – obelisks and so on – captured the notion of time as having smaller and larger cycles. There was journeying and return: each day is a new beginning after the previous day's ending. At the most public level, there is the recurrent passage of the sun across the sky that set clocks. There are other cycles that extend our temporal sense beyond clocks to calendars: the waxing and waning of the moon; and the cycle of the seasons with the predictable fluctuation of weather from hot to cold and back again and of the duration of daylight, of flooding (the Egyptian year was divided into three – two seasons separated by the inundation when the Nile overflowed its banks) and, more directly, of the length of the day. The earliest, Sumerian calendar, began with the sighting of the new moon. The past and future sizes of the moon, preserved in collective, collaborative, memory, was an increasingly capacious placeholder for time going beyond now, beyond the visible past and future, to a future which could add up for ever (though the possibility of greater cycles that would take us back to the beginning was not ruled out) leaving behind it an ever deeper past.

It was this visibility of invisible time that primed us to see other modes of the invisible past in the visible present. All objects are potentially fossils, signifying not only their own past (evident in their present state) but also the past objects with which they were co-present: a past world. This is particularly clear in the case of arte-facts – the battered suitcase covered with travel labels, the cracked mug, the peeling wallpaper, the table in the style of an earlier period, or (to go a little further back) a blood-stained or chipped hand axe – where there is an audit trail maintained by witnesses from then to now. But the revelation of the past in the state of present objects far antedates that: the rotting log, the mossy stone, speak as eloquently of past times.

That these items wear their ancientness on their sleeve, and so confer added temporal depth to the visual field in which they take up residence, is not self-evident: the immediacy of our appreciation of their oldness (or comparative or brand newness) is deceptive. It depends upon the fundamental extension of the visible invisibility of the past and this is made explicit by the clock that harbours futures and pasts.[42] Once this is in place, the past is open to be extended without limit: we are set on a course that leads, via history, archaeology, and geology, to a sense of ourselves being located in an almost bottomless ocean of time. When the bottom is located, it may as well not be there; for it is (so we are to believe) just under 14 billion years from the present day in which I am writing. The visibility of invisible has led us to knowledge of the unimaginable. Though we are made mighty by measurement, measurement reveals us as minute, transient occupants of a handful of days in a universe that has so far outspanned our lives – by perhaps a hundred-million-fold.[43]

The notion gradually forms that the entire history of the universe has quasi-horological time starting with the Big Bang. This sits uneasily with the treatment of time in relativity but Unger and Smolin have suggested that "The clock of cosmic time is the universe itself"[44] The discussion in the previous section makes clear why the totality of events cannot be a clock, given that a clock is a local register of "at". Merging the clock face, the mechanism, and the clock-watcher will result in no time being told.

We have left unfinished a good deal of business regarding the relationship between subjective time (time as our perception of the succession and duration of events) and objective time (time as clocked and as structured in the history of mankind in particular and the universe in general). We shall return to this in §10.5.

4.8 FURTHER REFLECTIONS

Our exploration of clock-time has left many trailing threads. I have criticized the notion that clocks measure the passage of time but have not really addressed what it is that they do. To say that they compare events with each other, rather than placing events against quantified time, does not help because we have still left incompletely defined the respects in which they compare events; namely, the time at which they take place, their temporal order, their duration (in time), and the time intervals between them. The kitchen clock does not compare my eating my porridge with your eating your porridge. It compares these events, and everything else that happens in the kitchen, or relevant events outside the kitchen, with respect to time.

The clocks that we use to time events neither grasp those events nor take hold of time itself. The latter thought, again echoing Plotinus' assertion that "to measure time is not to grasp it", is not perhaps all that revolutionary, though it touches on something central to this book: that, to measure *anything* is not to grasp it.[45] Measurement does not reach beyond measurement; it delivers the numerical form of things not their actual constitution. This is the truth behind Russell's profound observation, already discussed, that "Physics is mathematical not because we know so much about the world, but because we know so little; it is only its mathematical properties that we can discover."[46] This is perhaps more evident in the case of timing than in the case of, say, "spacing" or even measuring temperature. The clock does not take hold of time and apply its own kind of ruler ("How much time?") or grid ("What time is it?") to it.

Which may be why we feel that what we call "timekeeping" is somehow "time-losing", something that is reflected in our anguished sense, referred to in the previous section, that in the clock-orchestrated busyness of our lives, time is dissipated. We wake up to find that a week has vanished, the looked forward to occasion has come and gone, our children have grown up, and we are old. If time regains its substance it is under unpropitious circumstances, as when we are up all night with a scream-ing infant and the clock refuses to advance towards dawn or we know that we have another four hours to go before the dinner party ends and we can flee our own and others' empty chatter or, somewhat more seriously, we have another year to go before our course of chemotherapy is complete and we can look forward to feeling less wretched at last. Otherwise, the reduction of time to numbers seems to empty it, locating us in a temporal place that is neither here nor there.

We sometimes resent the authority objective time has over us; that the clock, and not ourselves, says what time it is, whether it is early or late, and how long or how short our experiences are. An hour on the clock must be the real thing – it's the hour we are all agreed on and which mirrors the unfolding of natural processes (the time the sun takes to move from one part to another of the sky, the time it takes for the potatoes to cook); it's the hour of our living bodies that are the condition of our existence. And yet the hour seems either too fast or too slow. Most frustratingly of all, we don't know what it would feel like if the passing of an hour felt just as fast or slow as it should. What would be the undistorted, undistracted experience of a minute be *like* – something to which we shall return in §10.5.

The same problem does not arise in relation to space – or not so obviously. An inch looks like an inch and a foot like a foot – even though our estimates may vary. This may be because of a fundamental difference that was implicit in our discussion in Chapter 1 and has pervaded all that has followed from that; namely that space is already outside of us, public and shared; whereas time begins inside us, our imme-diate experience of the succession of the events in our body – breathing, heart-beat, walking, before it is made explicit as something that has depth. Time has to be "brought out" by the magical power of one of our senses – vision.[47] Space on the other hand, is, of itself, out there, as the most basic form of our "surroundedness", as finite, bounded beings. I can see the spatial edges of my body (though not the limits of the space it will occupy over the course of my life) but I cannot see its temporal boundedness, the birth and death that limit it.

At any rate, this is why a clock has to do more to make time visible than a ruler has to do to make space visible. In the case of space, measurement and visibility are clearly distinct; in the case of time they are tangled together in a way that has generated many of the problems that have prompted this book. To put this another way, the measurement of space does not involve such a fundamental act of "making explicit" as does the measurement of time. It is this that gives credibility to dubious claims, such as those of Hermann Bondi, that we, or our clocks, generate time. To what extent it is true that making time explicit actually brings it into being – that measuring time is not merely gasping it but somehow making it *be* – is something that we shall return to in Chapter 10.

At any rate, we feel that there is something at the heart of time that lies behind and beyond and beneath what can be captured in numbers of seconds, hours, days, or centuries. That something is, at least in part, inside ourselves; something more primordial than the visible time outside of our bodies: the sense of sequence and succession manifest in the explicitly cyclical activity of breathing and the beating of our hearts which does not immediately present itself to us as cyclical. (The successive systole and diastole of the cardiac cycle, and the circulation of the blood, were late discoveries.) But there is perhaps something more yet: whatever it is that is at the heart of the flux of events we see around us, the whoosh inside the whoosh of events that makes whooshing possible. This is our intuition of time as something in itself that goes beyond not only the numbered units (say) but also beyond my sense of how long things are lasting, how far apart they are, and my perception of the sequence of events. (And of course, time *does* go beyond that: no unmediated perception would tell me what time it is, what time of the day, of the year, of the century).

Beyond the "whoosh" there is coordination of events and processes, the sense of the world as a law-driven machine, whose fundamental variables are space and time, the primordial modes of separation and connectedness. The German philosopher and disciple of Wittgenstein, Friedrich Waismann discusses this in relation to the unification of the laws of nature:

> The fact that only one system exists in which all correlated sequences are linked now assumes a profound significance. It is no less significant that the time scale, based on this system, is in keeping with our natural estimation of the lapse of time (for short intervals, anyway) and, further, that it leads to the formulation of simple laws of nature. That this is so does not follow from the mere idea of a time scale; it is conceivable that the time scale of the clock should not lead to simple and transparent laws, and that it should have to undergo some transformations before it could serve the purpose of rendering "the equations of mechanics as simple as possible" to use Poincaré's words.[48]

And J. R. Lucas puts an interesting gloss on this thought:

> Isochronous intervals are determined by periodic processes such as the rotation of the earth, its orbiting round the sun, the vibration of a caesium atom. It is a contingent fact that these processes all keep in step; it could be that there are two families of processes each in internal harmony, but out of step with each other, the infinite past of the one constituting only a finite past as measured by the other, with accompanying difficulties in deciding

which, if either, was the more fundamental. But, so far as we know, all natural processes keep in step: there is "a natural rhythm to the universe ..."[49]

A good point to conclude our meditation on the tangled mysteries of clocked time and the activity of "timing". While every event in the universe is (potentially) timed by the sum total of all the other events in the universe, the differentiation into timer and timed (not to speak of the index event that is timed) is a legitimate source of wonder.

Epilogue
Finding lost time: physics and philosophy

We no longer need feel obliged to construe time in a non-temporal way in order to be truly scientific or philosophically respectable.

Lucas, "A Century of Time", 11

Sometimes I feel physics has been corrupted into a kind of bad mystery religion in which its priests … step out among the laity amidst mind-clogging clouds of incense (the aura of physics) to make claims about the nature of reality on the basis of technical rituals they perform behind an iconostasis (mathematics).

William Simpson, personal communication

For wanting to prevent conflict between science and philosophy we have sacrificed philosophy without any appreciable gain to science.

Bergson, *Creative Evolution*, 197

In this, the first part of our endeavour to rescue time from the jaws of physics, we have challenged the reduction of time to a pure quantity, to little t. Thus reduced, it was always in danger of disappearing altogether. The journey to extinction has taken the particular path it has because of the conditions under which time first became fully explicit; namely through the most spatial of the senses, vision. Explicit time, even before the rise of natural science, was liable to being spatialized.

Spatialization need not have resulted in the extreme impoverishment – even elimination – of time evident in contemporary physics, however, had it not been for the fact that from the start of the great scientific revolution that unfolded during the sixteenth and seventeenth centuries, when the science of motion was enthroned at the heart of physical science and physical science was emerging as the definitive portrait of the reality underlying the appearances of the natural world, had also denuded space to a pure quantity. The reduction of time to little t was a consequence not only of its being treated like space but of the geometrization of space and its reduction to bare extensity, naked quantity.

It is therefore too simplistic to blame only the most recent developments for the current diminished and even precarious existence of time in natural science. Special relativity, however, did formalize the reduction of time to a dimension on all fours with the three dimensions of space. Given that spatial dimensions outnumber those of time and are easier to envisage, when time joined space as the fourth dimension, *it* was always going to be thought of as analogous to *them*, rather than the other way round. The joint assault on space and time was completed by their forced marriage in a manifold of space–time points.

Time placed on all fours with spatial dimensions was effectively frozen or even annulled. This was reinforced by the graphical and geometrical representation of motion, and hence of all change. Consider, for example, a missile fired from a gun.

The resultant path can be represented by a graph with three axes: the vertical axis defines the height of the missile above the ground; the horizontal axis corresponds to the distance from the gun; and a third axis represents the time that has passed. This path is evident all-at-once: its beginning and its end are seemingly co-present; a glance can take in the gun from which the missile sets out, the landing place on the ground, and the journey between them. Thus time, reduced to t, alongside axes x and y, is not only a pure quantity, but it also frozen like space. Spatialization, mathematization in the form of geometrical representation, and freezing are closely connected, serving a vision of the world as a crystalline system of magnitudes.

What is lost when time is reduced to little t, to the value of a variable represented by an axis, is the lived experience from which physics takes its rise and to which it is ultimately answerable. Little t is time isolated from anything that matters, anything that is done or felt, and even anything that happens. Those aspects of time that are associated with the moment-to-moment, always open, always incomplete, realm of significance irreducible to quantifiable dimensions, where we locate our regret, satisfaction (at or with the past), immediacy and here, now and presence (in the present), and goals, plans, hope, fear, and anticipation (for the future) – they are all lost. Most fundamentally, time as the condition of the possibility of experience, and indeed of experiencers such as ourselves, is eliminated.

Traditional intuition-driven philosophical investigation has often proved a poor guide to the fundamental nature of reality, as the Galilean demolition of Aristotelian physics illustrated so dramatically. It is, however, bad science as well as bad philosophy to conclude, from a limited number of clashes between (say) physics and philosophically based metaphysics from which the latter appears to have come off worst, that the latter is and always will be at fault. Equally baseless is the assumption that an inquiry that does not involve or depend on equations cannot be fundamental or that what physics, or other natural sciences, cannot accommodate, find, or deal with, must be unreal. John Norton has argued against "the vanity that our physical theories of time have captured all the important facts of time".[1] More generally, it is reasonable to question whether "we can infer that something – like a privileged reference frame – does *not* exist from the fact that it is *not* mentioned in a successful scientific theory".[2]

Of Time and Lamentation has been and will be an unashamedly philosophical inquiry that does not take its orders from science. Of course, the natural sciences have much to tell us about the world we inhabit. In the case of biology, they may cast some light on our own nature, though it will have more to say about ourselves as organisms and less to say about ourselves as persons than the arts, humanities, and the so-called human sciences. While Tim Maudlin's suggestion that "metaphysics, in so far as it is concerned with the natural world, can do no better than reflect on physics"[3] is far from the dismissive tone of those such as Weinberg and Hawking who inform us that "philosophy is dead", it does not row back far enough. After all, the proviso, "insofar as it concerned with the natural world" touches on what, traditionally, has been the central preoccupation and subject matter of metaphysics. More worryingly, the advice "to reflect on physics" suggests that philosophy should still approach the natural world through the lens of mathematical natural science; almost that the best way to do metaphysics is to ring up the physics department every two weeks to ask for a progress report. Waiting in the ante-room of science for metaphysical truths to emerge to pass on to fellow philosophers, does not allow that metaphysics independent of physics may conceivably have a role in assisting physics, at the very least to make sense of itself, irrespective of whether or not it can help the current difficulties of reconciling general relativity with quantum mechanics, dealing with the inescapable paradoxes of the latter, or help physics out of the apparent cul-de-sac of string theory.

While it would be foolish of philosophical metaphysicians to ignore physics, it would be at least as foolish to ignore the deliverances of daily experience. Metaphysics should bring both to inquiries into "what is there", and more specifically the nature of space, time, substance, and causation and the place of mind in the cosmos. Physics should not be regarded as the chief or even a privileged witness. We should begin and end with the existentially inescapable realities in which we enact our lives and from those intuitions which, although they are theoretically overturned by physics, are unshakable in the world in which physicists, like the rest of us, live their lives and in which physics is therefore possible. This is a world in which there are not only J. L. Austin's "medium-sized dry goods", but also actions, and causes – to name just a few features that physics at the most fundamental level seems unable to accommodate. There is still an important place for a philosophical investigation that does not take its instruction from science. Such an investigation would include what Wittgenstein characterized as "assembling reminders for a purpose",[4] which will occupy the second part of *Of Time and Lamentation*.

It is inevitable at this juncture to refer to Wilfrid Sellars's contrast between the "scientific" and "manifest" images of the world, and to define the role of the philosopher as being to mediate between the former and the latter. "The aim of philosophy, abstractly formulated" he begins:

> is to understand how things in the broadest possible sense of the term hang together in the broadest possible sense of the term. Under "things in the broadest possible sense" I include such radically different items as not only "cabbages and kings", but numbers and duties, possibilities and finger snaps, aesthetic experience and death.[5]

Sellars defines "the manifest image" as "the framework in which man came to be aware of himself as man-in-the-world", in which he encountered himself and through this became man. It is the image of the world of everyday experience, common sense, ordinary getting-about consciousness. It will, of course, be influenced by disciplined inquiry as well as the direct observation of correlations between events, of how the world hangs together. It is not merely the folk world picture of pre-scientific man. There is, however, an important contrast with the scientific image, not only because its primary objects are persons. The scientific image "involves the postulation of imperceptible entities, and principles pertaining to them, to explain the behaviour of perceptible things".[6] They would include invisible items such as atoms and their component parts, fields, and forces, and the mathematics that describes them.

Sellars's concern is "in what sense, and to what extent, does the manifest image of man-in-the-world survive the attempt to unite this image in one field of intellectual vision with man as conceived in terms of the postulates of scientific theory?"[7] There is, of course, a dialectical interplay between the images which are anyway idealizations, particularly in the case of the scientific image which is a work in progress, explicitly incomplete. Even so, there is "a clash of images". To which should primacy be awarded? Sellars explores the possibility that the manifest image could be superseded by a scientific image that incorporates it. Ultimately, the image of man as "a complex physical system" would prevail. His discussion is commendably honest because he acknowledges that sensations, free will, and the irreducibility of "we" (among other things) do not seem to fit into the scientific image. Even so, he imagines the possibility in future of "transcending the dualism of the manifest and scientific image of man" with the former being eaten up by the latter. This seems to be an unwarranted regression from the "stereoscopic" or "binocular" view of the world that he refers to at the outset of his discussion, in favour of Blake's "Single vision and Newton's Sleep".[8] Sellars, what is more, dismisses the claim that "the scientific image cannot replace the manifest without rejecting its own foundations".[9] This is fundamental: the erasure of the observer is necessary for the claim to completeness on the part of physics and yet impossible if there is to be such a thing as physics. More specifically, if the world were entirely the entangled reality described by quantum mechanics, quantum mechanics would be impossible. And if the universe were only the spatio-temporal manifold of general relativity, then there would be no circumstances in which the general theory of relativity could be formulated.

In many ways, Sellars's brilliant essay is unintentionally the most powerful imaginable critique of the notion that the agenda of philosophy – in its endeavour to see how things in the broadest possible sense hang together in the broadest possible sense – should be driven by science or by philosophers lapping up the latest intelligence from science. It is, incidentally, equally misguided to think that the agenda of philosophy should be defined by those things that do not interest science, such as ethics, politics, aesthetics or (analogous to the God of the Gaps) those things that science cannot yet deal with or has not yet got round to, but will do one day. In short that philosophy will deal either with secondary unsexy subjects or is an interim or second-best approach to things of the first importance – a philosophy of the stop-gaps. It should be more ambitious than this. Science is methodologically non-anthropocentric; the arts and the humanities are naturally centred on humanity. The role of philosophy could be to mediate between the two, so that we might transcend the profound divisions within our cognitive life.

We need, however, to challenge even the seemingly even-handed position that the two images of the world – and of humans as persons and as complexes of physical particulars – are equivalent in cognitive scope and existential import. This exaggerates the presence of the scientific world picture, in particular that of physics, in everyday living. Of course, our days are packed wall-to-wall with the artefacts, technologies, and procedures that are made possible by natural science. But the notion of a world populated by real, solid localised objects is not thereby displaced or marginalized or even seriously challenged by the quantum vision of a universe consisting of mathematical structures that are not realized in localised self-subsistent entities or may amount to a single, undivided, wave function. This is not simply because of cognitive inertia, or lack of imagination, or evolutionary constraints on consciousness,[10] that prevent us from looking past the manifest surface to the underlying reality. As we have seen, accepting, for example quantum mechanics as the truth, the whole truth, and the ultimate truth of the universe would make it impossible to see how such truths were arrived at. (I am referring, of course, to the measurement problem discussed in §3.5.3.1.) We should accept that the scientific image remains the junior member of the "scientific-manifest" pair. The manifest image has temporal priority and retains existential and logical priority. So the investigation of the manifest image should form the larger part of the task of metaphysics.

This said, what does philosophy bring to this task? There is conceptual investigation, which P. F. Strawson saw as central: "[O]ur essential, if not our only, business is to get a clear view of our concepts and their place in our lives."[11] and "[T]o establish the connections between the major structural features or elements of our conceptual scheme".[12] This is exemplified in Strawson's own "descriptive metaphysics". It is, however, the kind of metaphysics that is rejected by philosophers such as Ladyman in virtue of its appeal to intuitions.[13] And yet – given the uncritical way concepts such as "instants" or "time-points", and notions such as "the passage of time" are active within the time-talk that is part of the starter-pack of physics – examining and challenging intuitions, the taken-for-granted, the prior invisible framing of scientific inquiry and understanding, is essential. The endeavour to raise the level of clarity and explicitness in metaphysical discussion – if that were all that it achieved – would be sufficient in itself to justify philosophical metaphysics.

The concern expressed by Ladyman and others is that traditional metaphysics, located in the armchair, is neither informed by, nor does it generate empirical information. Newton-Smith (who seems to confuse analytical philosophy with an *a priori* approach to metaphysics) argues at the outset of his classic *Structure of Time* that "Contrary to a long and venerable philosophical tradition, the investigation of the structure of time is an empirical matter and as such cannot be conducted in an entirely *a priori* manner".[14] It is not, however, factually true that this is how philosophers have approached the metaphysics of time. Philosophers, too, look around them and reflect on what they see. It is a special kind of looking round, motivated by the suspicion, articulated by Wittgenstein: "The aspects of things that are most important for us are hidden because of their simplicity and familiarity. (One is unable to notice something – because it is always before one's eyes.)"[15]

Which takes us to what else, other than conceptual analysis, philosophy will bring to the table: phenomenological investigation. This – the phenomenology of lived time – will be the theme of the next part of this inquiry during which I hope that it will become evident that time, beyond the essentially timeless, quantitative parameter of the physicist, notably tensed time, is not a chimera; or merely "psychological", a second order, manifestation of temporality that physicists can toss to philosophers. We shall focus on tensed time, on the triptych of the present flanked by the past and the future. If this results in turning the tables on the relationship between the physical time and lived time, well and good. At the very least, it will put physics back in its proper place since, as Ian Dunbar expressed it:

> No discoveries in physics can falsify what we directly experience (although they can falsify rash deductions we might make from direct experience). Physics depends ultimately for all of its results on this experience – if it were shown to be systematically illusory, then the grounds for believing in physics would be lost.[16]

Or as Mermin has put it: "quantum mechanics has brought home to us the necessity of separating ... irreducibly real experience from the remarkably beautiful, and highly abstract superstructure we have found to tie it together".[17]

Having, I hope, done justice in the second part of the inquiry to the richness of lived time, I will, in the third and final part of this inquiry, address the question of what remains of time in itself, when we not only rescue it from physics but also strip it of the dubious metaphors that clothe our everyday, common sense understanding of this most elusive, and inescapable, most obvious, and yet most mysterious, aspect of our condition. What remains will be essential to our very nature as human beings – as beings "whose being is an issue for itself"[18] – and as conscious agents who have a margin of freedom actively to live their lives. The condition of such creatures is far from the desert of quantities and mathematical structures to which quantitative science would reduce the chiaroscuro of light and shade, of plenitude and emptiness, of meaning and meaninglessness that is the world in which we pass our lives.

PART II
Human time

CHAPTER 5

In defence of tense

He has departed from this strange world a little ahead of me. That means nothing. People like us, who believe in physics, know that the distinction between past, present and future is only a stubbornly persistent illusion.

Albert Einstein, letter to Michele Besso's family
(quoted in Isaacson, *Einstein*, 540)

[We feel] the view from Nowhen is the view that scientists do and philosophers should adopt. The urge is powerful but misguided.

Lucas, "A Century of Time", 3

[P]hysics – and science itself – will always be against tenses because scientific methodology is always against superfluous pomp.

Callender, "Finding 'Real' Time in Quantum Mechanics", 221

5.1 THE ATTACK ON TENSE: THE PHYSICISTS

While only a minority of physicists would like to do away with time completely, many, perhaps the majority, are content to dispense with tensed time. The shortest of the numerous arguments for maintaining that "the distinction between past, present and future is only a stubbornly persistent illusion" derives from special relativity and goes like this. The observed time relations between events will depend on the viewpoint (more accurately, the inertial frame of reference) of the observer. One observer will see that A is past with respect to B, another will see them in reverse order with A future with respect to B, and a third may judge them as being simultaneous with A and B co-present. All three are equally valid. There is no referee, occupying a privileged viewpoint, who can adjudicate because, to the democratic eye of physical science all observers are equal. To put this in relativistic terms, there is no privileged foliation of the manifold – a slicing of space–time into spaces at different times – no "now" acting as a universal reference point, underwriting the present.

In the absence of a privileged viewpoint, there is nothing corresponding to the "real" temporal location of an event in relation to another event. "At a given time" is not a relativistic invariant notion. Anyone setting himself up as a referee is in the same boat as the others: he is just another individual at another viewpoint and not privy to locations in an absolute time in which events "really" take place and their "real" temporal order determined. If we think of "now" as a set of events, we can see that events that are located as taking place before "now" are not intrinsically past since another observer may observe them as taking place after "now" – that is being in the future with respect to those events we have used to define "now". What is more, "now" – understood as being made up of an indefinite number of events occurring at the same time – lacks physical reality. The very idea of distant simultaneity is discredited and, so too is that of a set of distant events adding up to the present moment or, indeed, a moment, as Steven Savitt points out:

> If each inertial frame has its own sets of simultaneous events, and the principle of relativity states that no physical experiment or system (and we human beings are physical systems too) can distinguish one such frame or another as (say) genuinely at rest, then we are able to discern no particular set of simultaneous events as constituting the now or the present.[1]

Savitt continues:

> The special theory of relativity tells us that there is an infinity of planes of simultaneity passing through any given space-time point and that no physical test can distinguish one from among the lot. What was metaphysically distinguished is now physically indistinguishable. Assuming that we humans are complex physical systems, then we have no way to distinguish the present from amongst the multitude of presents.[2]

We have challenged the idea that "humans are [just] complex physical systems" in §3.5.3, but let this pass for the present: our aim is to examine certain received ideas in physics, where, as Rovelli expresses it, "the notion of the present, of the 'now' is completely absent from the description of the world in physical terms".[3] For Einstein, as the quotation at the head of this chapter illustrates, this is to be taken literally and it has major implications for our understanding of our lives. Our birth and death are mere time slices of our bodies which, even if we are unable to recall or anticipate them, had always been there.[4]

The discussion in Chapter 3 should remove any surprise at this result. It is an ultimate, and inevitable, consequence of mathematizing the world, in which events and viewpoints are defined mathematically, as numbers in a mathematically defined, inertial framework. There is nothing "now-like" about 0, or "past-like" about −1 or "future-like" about +1. Lee Smolin expresses it thus:

The real universe has properties that are not represented by any fact about a mathematical object. One of them is that there is always a present moment. Mathematical objects, being timeless, don't have present moments, futures or pasts.[5]

So what remains? According to the "block-universe" account, it is the space–time continuum in which the entire history of the cosmos is taken together. For some, this means that not only is tensed time abolished but time is also wiped out. Smolin again:

Relativity strongly suggests that the whole history of the world is a timeless unity; present, past and future have no meaning apart from human subjectivity. Time is just another dimension of space, and the sense we have of experiencing moments is an illusion behind which there is a timeless reality.[6]

The reader may have observed a certain amount of overkill. Physics that doesn't like tense may also have trouble with time itself. Indeed, the tenseless B-series – which allocates events to an order of "before-and-after" – is discredited at the same time as the tensed A-series which says that at any given time there are spatially separated events that are present and others that are past or future. Space–time intervals are invariant; but the apportionment of this interval between space and time is not. By the same token that distant simultaneity – a zero-time interval between events – is demonstrated to be entirely frame-relative, so a definite positive time interval between events is also observer dependent and not intrinsic to the related events.

As we may anticipate from the discussion in Part I, there are even more drastic consequences. If there is no physical reality corresponding to the difference between the past, which we think of as done and dusted, and the indeterminate future which is open, there is no basis for an unfolding world.[7] As Hermann Weyl argued, the four-dimensional space–time of physics is not merely void of tensed and tenseless time but of *becoming*: "the objective world simply is, it does not happen".[8]

This may seem an over-interpretation of what relativity requires us to accept about physical reality. If, however, there is no difference between past, present, and future, then what has occurred, what is occurring now, and what will occur must in some sense co-exist. In the absence of the difference between events that have happened, events that are ongoing, and events that have not yet happened and (indeed) may or may not happen, there doesn't seem to be much chance of anything happening at all. Alternatively, happening would be riddled with contradiction: event E would have to be about to occur, in the process of occurring, and having occurred – all at once. No wonder Weyl suggests that any becoming or happening is merely the appearance of happening as a result of a conscious observer coming upon parts of the block universe and lighting them up. This is a universe in which the ontologically dodgy Prince or Princess Charming of consciousness wakens the Sleeping Beauty of slumbering reality, his or her moving gaze giving the impression of change in an intrinsically eventless physical world, where nothing really happens because everything has happened already *and* hasn't happened yet.

It is of course deeply puzzling that consciousness should be the sole source of (apparent) change for at least two reasons. First, it would have itself to change and thus enjoy the unique privilege of being free of the spell that freezes the physical world. And secondly if, as some believe (not the present writer, I hasten to add) consciousness itself is identical with brain activity, and hence with physical events in the physical world, it too should be frozen along with the rest. (We shall return to this denial of change in §10.4.4.).

The attack on tensed time, therefore, could be repulsed by pointing out that it mobilizes weapons that result in the death of B-series (before-and-after) time, of events occurring at a definite time, and ultimately of events occurring at all – of becoming. This may be why not all physicists feel comfortable with the attack on tensed time – as noted in §3.5.4. Some have looked to quantum mechanics or even a future quantum gravity to rediscover tensed time but the prospects in this area seem discouraging or at the very least utterly confusing to all parties.[9] At any rate, there is something amiss in a picture of the world that not only denies the basis for our different attitude to tomorrow's dental appointment and yesterday's dental appointment, or to a future betrothal and a subsequent widowhood, but also denies the difference between a future about which we are ignorant and a past of which we have reliable knowledge, or, most fundamentally, a future that is at least apparently indeterminate, that has not happened and cannot exert any influence on present events except through being proposed as possibilities, and a past that is seemingly fixed and determinate, that has happened and has influenced subsequent events. If we take certain theories in physics to be the last word on the metaphysics of time, we lose, it seems, not only existential, tensed human time, but also temporal succession and ultimately happening itself. This, however, is the inevitable consequence of reducing time – tensed or tenseless – to a pure quantity, to a variable, a mathematical object. In mathematics – the pure form of possible events – nothing can happen.

Our present concern, however, is specifically with tensed time and the tenses that are the subject of this section of the book. If tensed time can be made safe, then perhaps time period can look after itself. Prominent among physicists who wish to argue that it is, after all, possible to explain the origin of tensed time in a four-dimensional world with a classical space–time geometry, is James Hartle. He has argued that, although in truly objective terms, there is no past, present or future, or indeed an order of events, we are creatures who live in a world in which we are limited to interactions that occur many millions of times slower than the speed of light.[10] As "information gathering and utilizing systems" (IGUSs), we have a sense of "now" that taps into the local physics in which all events *appear* to be simultaneous with a present moment. In such a world, the differences between space–time frames are small enough (compared with say the scale at which the finite speed of light makes a difference) to be unimportant. Consequently, we are in a coherent world where something such as a widespread "now" can be shared. At the very least, "now" encompasses say an organism and its prey, so that the former can catch the latter. In short, the sense of now, and our ability to respond to it, is essential for survival. To put this another way, there is a present composed of things that are present in the sense that the organism has *to take account of* them. They have an immediate salience.

This deflationary defence of tense begs many questions. Most damagingly, it presupposes precisely that which it has to find, namely that there is an objective, definite time interval and time order within the organism between perception and action, and a real near-simultaneity between the organism being in a certain vicinity and the predator or prey also being in that vicinity. They are assumed to be temporally as well as spatially side by side to an extent that extends beyond the range of current causal interactions which relativity allows to define an invariant spatio-temporal interval of zero. It would be interesting to test the argument further by asking how it is that there have emerged conscious creatures that do have a sense of "now" in a physical world that cannot accommodate "now", given that (for writers like Hartle) the biological boils down to the physical. Given that the apportionment of space–time intervals between events is frame of reference dependent, how does ("real, frame-independent") physical proximity and simultaneity crucial to life, arise?[11]

This opens on to large questions about the relationship between sentience, perception and knowledge on the one hand and, on the other, the world as it is revealed to physics; between the generalizing, synoptic glance of physical science and the localities which sentient creatures inhabit – and in an important sense generate – by planting centres in a universe that is intrinsically acentric and that (as we discussed in §3.5.3) cannot even accommodate the observer necessary to populate spaces with frames of reference. This is something we shall return to in §11.1.

It is significant, however, that Hartle establishes his argument on the basis of *robotic* IGUSs, to which he ascribes an "external environment", a present tense which consists of the present content of its register (or the most recently acquired image of its external environment), a past consisting of earlier contents of the register, and a future which (it seems) is its future state. In short, he ascribes to a robot (which has the virtue from the point of view of his argument of being a purely physical system) properties or capacities it could not possibly have; namely that of not being identical with its present state, of being aware of what is around it. This awareness is wrapped up in the weasel word "information" that elides the distance between that which is, and that which is not, conscious or between the changing physical state of an entity and the acquisition of knowledge (see §2.3.4) and making decisions.[12] At any rate, the causal interaction between a robot and "its" "environment" would no more require to be mediated by a "now" – so that the robot's responses were timely – than would the interaction between one billiard ball and another. Timeliness is swallowed up into the causal relation.

For the present it is enough to note that there are at least some physicists, even among those who would like to believe that they are on the road to the theory of everything, who are uneasy about losing tense. No-one was unhappier about this than Einstein himself. He was aware that there was another side to the embarrassment physics presents to "now"; namely, the embarrassment "now" presents to physics. He said as much in the famous discussion with the philosopher Rudolf Carnap already alluded to:

> Once Einstein said that the problem of Now worried him. He explained that the experience of the Now means something special for man, something essentially different from the past and the future but that this difference does not and cannot occur within physics. That this experience cannot be grasped by science seemed to him a matter for painful but inevitable resignation. I remarked that all that occurs objectively can be described in science; on the one hand the temporal sequence of events is described in physics; and on the other hand, the peculiarity of man's experience with respect to time, including his different attitude to past, present and future, can be described (in principle) in psychology. But Einstein thought that these descriptions cannot possibly satisfy our human needs; that there is something essential about the Now which lies just outside the realm of science.[13]

The very notion of an unnegotiable "now" undermines the radical democracy of physics which gives no viewpoint priority over any other; which (more accurately) offers a no-view from nowhere; or (what amounts to the same thing) an imaginary and impossible viewpoint that the totality of the material world would have on itself. Such a viewpoint can only be mathematical, as we have already discussed. In short, it is not a viewpoint at all; or it is a curiously eyeless one, which does not have its own field, its own near and far; an abstract placeholder in an egoless space that is the opposite of the egocentric space of our daily lives, of the world as we live it.[14] Even if we accept this viewless viewpoint, and concede that individual experience, even the experience of someone who is "on the spot", which ascribes time relationships to events, is not the last word, it remains a necessary first word. But there is an important sense in which it is also the last one; for it is that in which physics is conceived, understood and used.

As we discussed in Chapter 2, most physicists do accept a non-negotiable time relationship in causally connected events – such that the cause *must* always have *really* occurred before the [its] effect. As Dean Zimmerman has put it: "For any events e_1 and e_2, e_2 is causally dependent upon e_1 only if, when e_2 was happening, e_1 had already happened."[15] But this is not entirely without problems, not the least because of the confusions around the notion of "cause". The designation of events as causes and as effects depends in different ways on viewpoint and this is not rescued (as we shall return to in §11.2) by appealing to a temporal arrow of causation.

Shrinking the conscious subject to an observation point in turn reduced to a group of values assigned to mathematical variables and discarding memory and anticipation keyed to a "now" (in turn rooted in "me", "here"), empties time of something central to it and most certainly of what matters to us. It is not self-evident that psychological reality is less real for not being found in, reducible to, physical reality; or for being beyond the reach of physical science. The discovery that there are certain important aspects of reality (and they range from so-called secondary qualities, through tensed time, to selfhood and agency) that cannot be captured by, or accommodated within, physical science can be turned on its head: it demonstrates not that they are, after all, unreal but that physical science offers an incomplete account of reality. A world picture that relegates pains, colours, and the temporal order of my birth and death to the ontological second division and yet allows fluctuations in a quantum vacuum the power to give birth to the totality of things (see §10.3.4) requires a better defence than physicists can mount.

The rediscovery of something like a Newtonian absolute "now", agreed throughout the universe, in the cosmic frame of reference at rest with respect to background cosmic radiation, supplies something of what is needed.[16] It is this that dates the beginning of the universe to 13.7 billion years before the present. If we are agreed on this date, two consequences follow. The first is that 13.7 billion years' worth of events are past to *all* current, that is to say living, observers. The age of the universe is not observer-dependent. The past therefore *does* have a place in the objective physical order of things. Secondly, so do the present (for the Big Bang is not a contemporary event for any of us) and the future (for the Big Bang is not in the future for any of us). In other words, the pastness and non-presentness of the Big Bang are objectively real. Because this pastness is – and must be – true for all observers, these aspects of tense cannot be eliminated in favour of a B-series relationship of "before" and "after". So we have an aspect of tensed time that is unchanging and ownerless, which nevertheless gives a physical respectability to the existential absolute now, maintained not by observers reduced to mathematical points but by breathing living individuals who look forward in hope and look back in anger. Everyday "I-time" and "we-time" with their profound distinction between past and future are not, therefore, ready to be consigned to the ashcan of human thought.

Even if the appeal to a cosmic frame of reference is rejected, it remains the case that physics would not be possible without tensed time and the kinds of creatures for whom things are near or far, occur earlier or later, occur now and can be seen as being once in the future and are now in the past, and so on. If the world as reflected in physics were the world period, the sum total of reality, physics would not be possible. The hundreds of thousands of plans that converged in the building and running of CERN are steeped in tensed time. Physics does without "tomorrow" and "yesterday" but physicists cannot do without them in any part of their lives, including that in which they do physics.

This might provoke the counter-argument that physicists doing physics is only a minute and very recent feature of the physical world. Such an argument, however, assumes that physics can somehow transcend its own conditions to reveal a world without physicists. Against this, it might be pointed out that the conditions of the possibility of physics must be part of the physical world if physics is supposed to give, or aspires to give, a complete account of reality. To confine what can be said about time to what is true of time in the world of physics is to extrude us from the nature of time and hence from our picture of nature itself, though in our absence – or the absence of any sentient creatures – there is no picture of nature nor even the possibility of it. If the world picture of physics encompassed all that was real, the world could not be depicted.

A tenseless world in which all observers are reduced to mathematically reconciled values of all possible variables, is a world without observers; and, indeed, a world reduced to the relationships between patterns of quantities, lacking the real items necessary to give values to variables. That this is often overlooked is due to the fact that the result of measurement – which takes place in a here-and-now and is performed by someone – is typically a number that bears no trace of the here-and-now or the measurer. The measurement, the datum is timeless, tenseless, placeless, and personless. The realm where simultaneity – between events and their being observed, and between the components of an observation (the device and the object of study) – reigns can never be left behind. It is simply forgotten. "Time", Bernard d'Espagnat observed, "is at the heart of all that is important to human beings".[17] To reduce time to tenseless physical time is to lose what lies at the heart of that heart: to lose the human being – and, in a crucial sense, to lose time.

Taking tenseless physics as the last word on time may have strange consequences. Consider Paul Davies' touching suggestion (quoted in the Preface) that this might wipe away all our tears:

> And what if science were able to explain away the flow of time? Perhaps we would no longer fret about the future or grieve for the past. Worries about death might become as irrelevant as worries about birth. Expectation and nostalgia might cease to be part of the human vocabulary. Above all, the sense of urgency that attaches to so much of human activity might evaporate.[18]

Given that the physical theories most hostile to tense – special relativity[19] and many variants of quantum mechanics (but see §3.6) – are seriously incompatible with one another and that any theory that reconciles them will without doubt require major revisions to our fundamental concepts, we should rein in our faith in what physics has to say about tense. Don't throw away the handkerchiefs just yet.

5.2 THE ATTACK ON TENSE: THE PHILOSOPHERS

5.2.1 Tense as all talk

We are used to physicists erasing tensed time and we may ascribe this to the habit of cultivating a rather narrow viewpoint, more at home with material objects than with people, with equations than lived experience. When philosophers join them, however, things are getting serious.

This is not, of course, a recent trend. There is a long tradition – from Parmenides[20] to McTaggart[21] – of philosophers denying the reality not merely of tense but of time altogether. This has been an unpopular view among philosophers since G. E. Moore[22] and others in the analytical tradition, as well as many continental philosophers, argued that the reality of time was existentially undeniable.[23] As Moore remarked, anyone who claimed to believe that time was unreal while at the same time agreeing that he had eaten his breakfast before his lunch could not be taken seriously.[24]

More recently, however, philosophers have trained their guns specifically on tensed time. Indeed, most philosophers in the analytical tradition affirm the reality of time, but regard time as tenseless, with tense having the diminished ontological standing of something analogous to a secondary quality that exists in our minds but not out there in the real world. Prominent among these is D. H. Mellor.[25]

Mellor, like most philosophers of time in the analytical tradition, tense-deniers and tense-affirmers alike, begins with McTaggart's distinction between "A-series" and "B-series" time. The "A-series" is "that series of [temporal] positions which runs from the far past through the near past, to the present, and then from the present through the near future to the far future, or conversely". The "B-series" is "the series of positions which runs from earlier to later, or conversely".[26] The A-series is also associated with terms such as "yesterday", "today" and "tomorrow", as well as "soon" or "recent" that are pegged to the present as a reference point.

Mellor's key argument for the tenselessness of time is that we can replace A-series statements by B-series statements without loss of content: tensed statements can be translated to untensed ones that have the same truth-makers.[27] The metaphysics of the relationship between tensed and tenseless time is thereby reduced to the semantics of tensed and tenseless discourse, with the latter having priority: tense is not an objective feature of reality. A-series assertions about events being past, present or future, can be rephrased, without loss of meaning or change of reference, or alteration of truth value, as assertions to the effect that one event is earlier than, the same time as, or later than, the present. As for the present, this is simply the time t when the statement is being made. When we say that "Event A happened in the past" what we mean is that "Event A happened before Event B" where Event B is the (present) utterance, the very speech act, which states that "Event A happened in the past". To put this another way, what makes a true tensed utterance U such as "Event E is future" true is a tenseless (before-and-after) relationship between U and E.

There is therefore nothing mysterious about, say, "The Past": it is simply "earlier-than-now"; and "now" isn't located in an irreducible tense, namely "the Present". It is simply the *time of the relevant utterance* – let us say 4:15 p.m. on 12 December 2012, which, clearly, is intrinsically neither past, present nor future. Any event E that took place before my utterance U at 4:15 p.m. on 12 December 2012 would be "in the past" and anything after would be "in the future". Other utterances, spoken at different times (say 4.15 p.m. 13 December 2012) would assign other tenses to Event E. So the A-series present-past relation can be reduced to B-series "after-before" relations and the A-series present-future relations to B-series "before-after" relations. Another way of putting the argument is to say that (for example), in the utterance U "E is happening now", "now" is self-reflexive token whose referent is the time at which it is uttered. It enables utterance U to be token-reflexive referring (implicitly) to the time at which it is uttered.

Other statements that contain tensed terms can likewise be reduced. Consider Mellor's example, "Jim will race tomorrow". This is true if and only if it is uttered on Day 1 (e.g. 12 June) and Jim races on Day 2 (13 June). The future-tensed statement boils down to "This assertion tokenized in an utterance U uttered one day before the event E it asserts as taking place." Thus tense is translated into an interval of "before-after" and consequently eliminated. Likewise, "Jim raced yesterday" is true if and only if Jim races on 13 June and the statement U is made on 14 June. The dates 12, 13 and 14 June are not intrinsically past, present or future. Which they are depends on the date of any statement that involves or implicitly refers to them.

Mellor's wish to dispense with tense as a feature of time itself, or of the world, arises in part because he wants to avoid the arguments that McTaggart deployed in denying the reality of time by discrediting tensed time. For Mellor time *is* real but it is tenseless. Events in themselves, McTaggart says, cannot be past, or present or future – or more precisely future, present and also past – because this would involve a contradiction and no real entity such as an event can have contradictory properties. If being future, being present, and being past *are* non-relational, that is to say intrinsic, properties, then no single event can be future, present, and past. If I predict that a certain horse will win a race, and it does win a race, and I believe in the reality of tenses, I have to envisage an event E which was in the future and yet was identical with an event that subsequently became present and eventually entered the past. This event, therefore, would be different from itself in respect of having different tenses.

We cannot wriggle out of the difficulty of an event having contradictory properties, Mellor says, by arguing that it is not the same event that is future, present, and past; that, for example, the event of the horse winning the race ("The horse wins the race") is not the same as the event that I predicted ("The horse will win the race"). If the "two" events were different, the bookie would not be obliged to pay up on the grounds that I placed my bet on a future event but it was a present, not a future, event that happened!

In fact, denying that "the horse will win the race" and "the horse has won the race" are "the same event" is actually key to dealing with McTaggart's problem. In §8.2.2, I shall criticize the notion (seemingly crucial to Mellor's argument) that utterances which refer to events as future, present, and past respectively have identical referents. The notion of events as "tense tourists", that they pass through the future to the present and end up in the past, as if coming into existence and being completed were changes in location or property of the same events. The emphasis of my present critique of Mellor (and of much of the philosophical opposition to tensed time), however, will have a different focus. It has two key elements.

Firstly, it is not possible to reduce tensed statements to tenseless ones without bypassing the fact that such statements are made by conscious speakers and these will provide implicit tense in all utterances, irrespective of whether said utterances are explicitly tensed or not. The conditions necessary for an utterance to be uttered will not enter into its truth conditions *though they are essential for there being truth conditions.* Fully to grasp what is done when we assert something, we need to go beyond truth conditions to explicitness conditions. Before statements such as "today is Wednesday" or "He has just left" or "he will come shortly" can have definite truth conditions, they need explicitness conditions and these are, as it were, off-stage (and indeed off-page in the case of written statements). But they are essential: they are the condition of assertions having truth conditions. Tensed statements have an implicit, lived, existential "now". The knowledge that E took place at time t does not locate it in the past unless we know that it is presently – that our standpoint is – any time after t. That is why knowing that the meeting begins at midday is not the same as knowing at midday that the meeting is beginning: we would still have to consult the clock to check that 12 midday is now and now is 12 midday.[28]

Secondly, the reduction of tense to a ("mere") relation (between events U and E) would not effectively eliminate it or impugn it as unreal. If it did, then tenseless time – the B-series of "before" and "after" – would be eliminated by the same argument. There is no intrinsic ordering of events unless events are picked out to be ordered. There is, for example, nothing intrinsic about Event U being early or earlier and Event E being late(r). If these were constitutive or monadic properties of E and U, then B-series events would be both earlier and later (before one event and after another) and these properties would be at once incompatible and even more inescapable than being past and/or future because they would be "earlier" and "later" at the same time. An event on Wednesday would be both intrinsically "earlier than" (e.g. an event on Thursday) and "later than" (e.g. an event on Tuesday).

Let us look again at Mellor's way of disposing of tense. "Event A happened in the past" he claims boils down to "Event E happened before Event U, where Event U is the event of asserting that Event E has already happened and is therefore in the past". "In the past" means "before now" and "now" can be reduced to "the time of Event U". But to say this overlooks that Event U counts as "now" only because of the speaker's conscious awareness of being in a present which divides time into past and future. It is the *speaker* not the (objective, observed, material) event of the emitted sentence that establishes the now; and while now has only dubious reality in the eyes of physics (despite Hartle's attempt to embrace it), it is nonetheless real. That I am speaking "now" is both a truism and a profound truth – an existential presupposition that is too deep to count as a mere truth-maker of whatever it is I am saying. It marks an undeniable boundary between actual events that are recollected and possible events that are anticipated. This boundary, what is more, enjoys the objective reality of being shared with others. We share a "now" with other people, and that shared now is underpinned by events, processes, and objects out there. It is far from being subjective in the way that, for example, my view of a room is subjective. Tensed time is time seen from within by creatures who are aware of being in time and at a point in time. Such awareness is not egocentric: it is mandatorily shared. A soldier at the Battle of Waterloo is aware that his actions and what he observes are part of a wider sequence of events and may well be aware that the Battle of Hastings was in the past. The awareness is of course confined to conscious beings. No bullet or material object at this Battle shares this awareness. They may be the substrate, the content, of now but they do not situate themselves in a now, in the sense of being explicitly related to a sphere of co-occurring events and coexistent objects.

The essential point is that it is a conscious individual, not a physical Event U (the speaker's utterance, which could be captured on tape as a purely material event) tagging a time, which lays down the "now" with respect to which events are past, future, or present. If, however, we overlook the speaker and restrict our attention to the objective relation between Event E (the referent of an utterance) and Event U (the utterance), and deny the importance of the *person* – or more importantly the interlocutors – who manufactured Event U, and for whom it was "at now", and who conferred meaning upon it, we will indeed fail to find tensed time – and thus arrive at the erroneous conclusion that tenses are unreal.

The correct conclusion is that physical events are not enough to establish tensed time. The deficiency lies within the material objects and events. But, as already noted, they are equally insufficient to generate the *tenseless* series of "before and after", the very B-series time which so many detensers are eager to defend. Everyone agrees that some times are before other times. But no time is *in itself* "before" or "after" any more than a time is in itself "past", "present" or "future". 12 noon 22 December 2012 is before all times after itself and after at all times before itself. If this were a constitutive feature of times, McTaggart's argument would be just as applicable to tenseless as to tenseless times: 12 noon would have a McTaggartian nervous breakdown trying to be both before all the times in the afternoon and after all the times in the morning. Since McTaggart was committed to demonstrating the unreality (because of the self-contradictory nature) of time itself, this would not worry him. Mellor, on the other hand, who wishes to uphold the reality of tenseless time, should be concerned that his arguments against tense, if valid, are equally fatal to the B-series. "Before" and "after" are just as description-dependent (and hence utterance-, viewpoint-, and ultimately consciousness-dependent) as "past", "present" and "future", though they are dependent in different ways.

If we excluded the conscious individual (for example the speaker) from our understanding of time, we would of course lose all those indexical terms whose reference depends on the situation of the speaker. "Today", "tomorrow", "yesterday", "next week", "last month", "a few years hence", "a long time ago" would all vanish along with "now". So, too, of course, would semi-quantitative terms such as "soon" and "recently" which seem to lie on the border between lived and measured time.[29] Tense has a first-level objectivity. That an event is ongoing, that is to say present, or past (completed), is not subjective, even though the judgement may not be shared between individuals separated by large distances. Without this distinction, organized time sense, at least as it is lived, would effectively disappear. To illustrate this, let's take a preliminary glance at "now". (It will have its place in the spotlight in §6.1).

Does "now" really reduce to a kind of tautology, for example, "12:30 p.m. 12 December 2012 is when it is 12:30 12 December 2012"? To put this another way, does that re-description really eliminate the aspects of "now" that detensers want to jettison? The analysis of now as "time t when it is time t" is a generic description and does not capture an actual now. It does not say which now is *now*. Just as saying that "today is day x when it is day x" does not tell us what day it is, what day it is today – how or in virtue of what a day qualifies as "today". The rules for using the terms, "now", "today", etc. do not deliver an actual "now", "today", etc. because the latter correspond to something singular. "Now" can acquire singularity only through the lived moment of a person whose temporality it makes explicit – that is in turn made explicit through an utterance at a particular time. To put this another way: there is more to "now" than an identity relation between tagged times and themselves; there is more than an empty tautology. An extra relation is required.

It is perhaps easier to see this in the case of future-oriented terms such as "tomorrow". If today is Day 1, then tomorrow will be Day 2. But that will tell us nothing more than merely the rules for using words unless we are already able to say what "today" refers to. We have to unpack the assertion further as, for example, "If (a) today is 12 December 2012 then tomorrow will be 13 December 2012 and (b) today *is* 12 December 2012, therefore tomorrow will be 13 December 2012". Tenseless assertions merely relate one event or date to another and remove the relation of the events or dates to "today" or "tomorrow" which are connected with the conscious subject. If I say of the assertion "Event E happened yesterday" this is the same as saying "Event E happened on 13 December" only if it has *already* been established that I, the speaker, am speaking on 14 December. And I can *mean* by my statement that the event happened on 13 December only if I know – or believe – that today is 14 December. This is an additional piece of knowledge incorporated into my utterance necessary to translate the tensed to the tenseless assertion. The two are therefore not equivalent. The statement that "Event E took place on 12 December" does not amount to the statement that "Event E took place yesterday" unless I and my interlocutor know that today is 13 December. I know of necessity that I am talking "today" but not of necessity that "today is 13 December". What I cannot be mistaken over is the existential reality that "It is today" – lost in the translation from tensed to tenseless statements. These are the existential truth conditions that underpin the truth-makers of tensed statements.

Consider the translation of (a) "It is raining now" into (b) "This utterance is taking place at the same time as a period during which it is raining". The two statements have the same truth conditions, the same truth-makers. But do they have the same meaning? Only by virtue of retaining in (b) the (easily overlooked) indexical "this" in "this utterance". The meaning of a demonstrative such as "this" cannot be separated from a conscious human subject. The token-reflexive form "this utterance" may seem to make the relationship an internal one of language but personal-space reality seeps in from the sides: "this utterance" unpacks as "this one I am uttering now" which has three indexicals, including an unreduced and irreducible reference to the present tense – the present moment of "now". That is why I cannot infer from "It is raining on 12 July" that it is raining *now* unless I am additionally informed – either directly or indirectly through indexicals such as "this sentence being uttered" – that "Now is 12 July". And if it is conceded that seemingly tenseless sentences require the anchor of a reference to the present tense to give them complete meaning, then tense returns; indeed, all three tenses, because if the present is an irreducible reality, we have the basis for the distinction between past and future in the border between them.

"Now" refers to the time at which an utterance is made but not to what is on the clock. "Now" uttered at 2 p.m. does not of itself refer to 2 p.m., otherwise clocks (and calendars) would be redundant. This exposes the frequent ploy of the detensers who try to reduce sentences such as "E is happening now" to a relationship between an event and a date. Dates, incidentally, are not legitimate partners in a B-series relationship because they are not events but human artefacts belonging to notational systems constructed to house events. "Now" underlines that there is a fundamental aspect of time that cannot be captured by clocks, even less by physical systems that may be used as clocks.

There is another irreducible difference between A-series and B-series relationships. To say that E is past, is not merely to say that it is earlier than a given event, for example D, but that it is earlier than *everything* that is presently occurring or will occur in future. By contrast, to say that E is (B-series) "earlier" requires specifying a relation to a particular event or set of events. "Earlier than D" is not the same as "Earlier than Now" most obviously because "now" is not a particular event or even a definite set of events. It is the sum total of events that count as being simultaneous with the token utterance "Now". The token utterance U is one small part of "Now". That is why "Now" is the implicit context of U, not U inside itself.

My argument essentially is that tensed time is not a property of, or intrinsic to, stand-alone spoken statements, any more than it is a property of statements on a page (a timeless zone, where assertions are cited rather than genuinely made or await being realized in a reader to whom they are addressed) uprooted from any speaker. It is the conscious speaker and the fact that he or she is speaking at a particular (present) time that establishes the (present) tense of the utterance. That is why tense is connected with fundamental attitudes such as regret (for the past) and anticipation (of the future). The attempt to reduce the basis of tense to language, specifically to truth-makers of assertions, will necessarily fail because we cannot remove the speaker (and her listener(s)) without missing the existential point of tenses. When we translate the tense of an assertion such as "Jim will race tomorrow" into a relationship between the utterance U "Jim will race tomorrow" and Jim's racing the day after U, we have not eliminated tense, we have buried it by treating Event U as a stand-alone occurrence that does not rely for its meaning on the existential situation of a speaker who has asserted it. That which Mellor and many other detensers cite as evidence for the unreality of tensed time is precisely what makes it an irreducible and indispensable aspect of time.

Given that this should seem obvious, it may be a source of wonder that it is overlooked. The explanation lies in the pervasive deindexicalisation of our discourse. Everything we say is said at the time it is being said, is implicitly said now. It is a commonplace that the removal or suppression of indexicals – and the passage towards fully deindexicalised discourse – is closely associated with the rise of science and the advance to the scientific "view from nowhere". But deindexicalisation begins a long way before that: it is implicit in the timeless (and hence tenseless) intelligibility of discourse and is made explicit in discourse about discourse. "Now" refers to the time at which I say "Now". However, the word "now" is a type that has any number of tokens. When I say "now", I mean the now of my utterance of now. But the verbal type "now" itself has no particular now to which it is attached, as is made obvious in this paragraph in which I am talking about it. As a type that is *mentioned*, as opposed to a token that is *used*, it does not of itself refer to the time of its utterance. It refers to no time. Written "now", arrested on the page, for example, does not count as a constant iteration, or tracking, of the present moment. Conversely, events that are happening "now" do not broadcast that fact; and this is equally true of all conscious actions, *including utterances*, in which "now" is implicit. So the "now" that is established through Event U as uttered by the person who is speaking it does not have to say that it is happening now: it does not have to wear its "nowness" on its sleeve. This is its ineliminable tensed nature – so that it cannot be translated without loss into a time *t* when a token of "now" is uttered, though it can appear to be so reducible.

What the glamour of science (largely but not fully earned) does is to make deindexicalised discourse seem like the last word on what is real; or, indeed, deindexicalised words the last word on what is real. Consequently, indexical statements seem somehow to carry a *lesser* freight of truth or reality than ones that are not cluttered with indexicals; that to say that "E happened yesterday" is to say less than "E happened on 12 December 2012". If this were true, then to say "12 December 2012 is today" would have no truth content. If we are inclined to think this, it is because the truth value of indexical statements is not eternal and will in many cases depend on who is saying them or the circumstances of the person who is saying them. This is obvious in the case of space. "Cambridge is here" is true only if the speaker is in Cambridge whereas "Cambridge is 50 miles from London" is not so dependent. The first statement seems less objective and so seems to fall short as a *fact*. But conveying an objective, (relatively) invariant fact is not the only source of content in an utterance. "I am in pain" is even more subjective and subject-dependent but it hardly lacks an irreducibly real content that could not be entirely captured by "C-fibres are firing in the brain of a body whose centre is located at coordinates x, y, z, t". The prejudice against tense is a prejudice against subjective experience and against subjects who, having such experiences, look back to the past and forward to the future because they live in the present.

But it goes beyond a prejudice against subjective experience, since the indexicality of tensed statements – such that their truth-makers are sensitive to the time and place of the speaker – is not specific to a particular individual in a particular state: it is not like an-appearance-to-me. The indexicality is not anchored to a consciousness. It is public and collective: "now" would not have any meaning if (unlike, for example, the *experience* of red), it could not be shared. Indeed, the sharing may be very wide, as in the case of the millions listening to a radio programme. There is, what is more, nothing in tense that warrants its being classified along with the delusions, illusions, and hallucinations that bedevil phenomenal consciousness. You and I could not disagree whether it is now because we would have to have a shared now to express our disagreement. In this sense, tense reaches a first-level objectivity.

While tensed time does not appear to have a reality that physics can capture or do anything with, this does not mean that it is not objectively real. Its objective reality is dramatically demonstrated by its key role in our individual and collective freedom that depend on tensed time. The very fact that tensed time is not part of the physical world is a necessary condition for our existence as beings able to operate on the physical world from the virtual outside of the human world, for our being *homo ex machina*. We shall examine this in detail in Chapter 12.

In summary, tensed and tenseless statements cannot be translated into one another without loss of content. If the implicit indexicals in tensed utterances were eliminated, the cognitive significance and explanatory power of such utterances would be altered, indeed diminished. The content that is lost is that which is folded into the utterance, the implicit token-reflexivity of ordinary speech involving tensed terms. This is only partially visible when terms such as "now" and "tomorrow" or even "soon" are deployed and it is all but hidden in most tensed utterances such as "I will do this" or "I have done this". The token-reflexivity in turn depends on the shared awareness of the shared circumstances of the speaker and the recipient. Such awareness is existential and not intra-linguistic.

So much for the argument that tense is all talk.

5.2.2 What tense is not

The case against tensed time is rendered more persuasive by false assumptions about the nature of tense. The most important of these are that being tensed is an (intrinsic or constitutive) property (of events or states of the world) or that tenses are realms defining locations. Let us examine these assumptions in turn.

5.2.2.1 Tenses as properties of events or states of affairs

> Tenses are no more properties of events than the times at which they happen.
> Dainton, *Time and Space*, 69

Let us focus on events. Are the defenders of tensed time necessarily committed to the notion that future events have the property (common to all of them) of "futurity"; that present events are all characterized by "presentness"; and events that are past are all tinged with a metaphysical sepia of "pastness"? Do those who believe in the objective reality of tensed time hold that "being future", "being present", and "being past" are predicates corresponding to phenomenal properties? This seems hardly likely. What could it possibly mean to ascribe a common property – "futurity" (to all that has not yet happened and may not happen), "presentness" to all that is happening, and "pastness" to all that has happened. These are too general to count as properties or predicates. To think that all that is present shares the property of "happening" is clearly absurd. What phenomenal properties or other characteristics do The Battle of Hastings, the spilling of a drink in 1645, and a sneeze I have just sneezed, share though they have in common the fact that they are past? It is not as if there were something corresponding to "-ing" shared by all present, ongoing events, and something designated by "-ed" shared by all that has happened. To ascribe a common property of "futurity" to all that has not yet happened is even more dubious given that the future is populated with events that may not happen at all. What could events and non-events have in common? What properties could a non-event call its own? What could the properties be attached to?

The idea of tenses as the *successive* predicates or properties of individual events as they pass from "about to happen", to "happening" and on to "happened" is equally absurd. It not only incorporates the problematic idea that all events indexed to a particular tense have a definite property in common, it also assumes that events visit each of the tenses in turn, with everything unchanged apart from their tenses. We shall tease out the fallacies in this idea in §8.2.2. Suffice it to say, the idea of an Event E remaining essentially unchanged when it passes from not-yet-being (non-existence), to coming-in-being (occurring at present) to no-longer being (past), is clearly nonsense.[30]

Defenders of tensed time such as myself must not be thought of as being inescapably committed to thinking that "pastness", etc. are real properties of events and that every event passes through a succession of tensed states – being future, then present, and then past. After all, as we have noted, believers in B-series time, are not committed to thinking of events as being in themselves, or constitutively, "before" or "after". If they were, they would be in trouble, because any given event would have to have the properties of "beforeness" or "afterness" at the same time. Such a contradiction would discredit the B-series by the same token that McTaggart believed he had discredited the A-series. Event E_2 would be both after Event E_1 and before Event E_3. And if the series of events ran into gazillions as it does, then each event would be the simultaneous site of a gazillion times gazillion states of "beforeness" and "afterness". The Battle of Hastings would be the meeting place not of two armies but of two aspects of the history of the world – the sum total of the events that preceded it (that colour it with "afterness") and the sum total of the events that succeeded it (that colour with "beforeness").

We defenders of tense no more believe, or are obliged to believe, that events are *intrinsically* "past", "present" or "future" than they are *intrinsically* "earlier" or "later" or than we believe that objects are *intrinsically* "here" or "over there", "close to" or "far away". It does not follow from this that tense is an empty concept that should have no place in an account of time. We can agree that "no event is in itself either past, present or future" without having to accept that reference to past, present or future, refers to nothing that has any reality. And while it is true "Nothing is in reality now or then"[31] it is equally true that no object or event is in reality (that is to say, in itself) "before" or "after". If tense were a property of events, it would necessarily be the present tense. But the present cannot exist alone, any more than left can exist without right or up without down. If past and future have no reality, in virtue of failing to be properties of events, then the present, too, would lack defined meaning – an argument we shall deploy against presentism in §6.2.3.

If we reject the idea that being tensed is a property of events or states of affairs, we lose one of the most powerful motives for being a detenser – which is to avoid McTaggart's attack on the reality of time. If tenses are not properties, then the possibility that events might have the contradictory properties of being (say) both "present" and "past" cannot arise. The mistake is to assume that, if tensed time is real, we must be ascribing properties to events when we say that they are, for example, "present" or "future". We cannot, of course, ascribe a property to something that has not happened. As for past events, it is absurd to think that they acquire a thickening patina of pastness as the interval between the present and the time they happened grows longer.

5.2.2.2 Tenses as locations

Nor need the defenders of tensed time think that they have to be committed to the idea that the tenses are places or domains that events inhabit in succession. This defender doesn't anyway. *Pace* L. P. Hartley (or his famous metaphor not to be taken literally as a philosophical claim) the past is not a foreign country (nor is the future), not least because the present isn't a "country". Of course, we do talk about an event having taken place in the past (though it wasn't past when it took place) or being about to take place in the future (although it won't be the future when or if it does take place). This also feeds into the impression that there is a kind of homogeneity – a common temporal hue or tinge – about "past" and "future" – an impression that is dispelled when we think about the third panel in the "triptych", namely the present. Although we modify the supposedly homogeneous past somewhat with stratifying talk about the "recent" or the "distant" past these seem rather informal distinctions compared with the profound difference between any past and any future. The suggestion that all events taking place at a given time have something in common – other than the bare fact, unadorned with predicates, that they took place at the same time – and that how much they have in common attenuates as the slice of time under consideration is fatter is clearly an empirical assertion that has nothing going for it.

The numbering of, say, the past as a succession of dates underlines its apparent qualitative homogeneity by making purely quantitative distinctions within it. It is easy to see why we might be more inclined to speak and think in this way when we format past and future time with clocks, calendars, diaries and timetables. Indeed, the very events that are past, or the possibilities that are in the future, seem themselves to be ontologically more robust – notwithstanding their current non-existence – by being associated with a labelled niche in a temporal array of dates set out in space, as on a calendar. When, on 12 November 2012, we write "birthday party" in the box marked 12 December 2012, we give the future event – which is a mere possibility that has only putative and general features and may not occur – an apparent solidity which in the days after the party seems to have been real. The continuing presence of the birthday party inscribed in that box after 12 December, the birthday and the party are over makes it and the box also seem more solid, and the future of which the box is a part more domain-like. The box is like a holder and it seems to give literal force to the question of what "the future holds" or "holds in store". And this beguiles us into imagining days, and their contents, "coming closer", "passing through" the present, and "receding" further into the past, as if through a succession of homogeneous media corresponding to the three tenses.

The image of tenses as domains is an expression of our tendency to spatialize time, so that different times can co-exist in a kind of side-by-side. It begins with the notion of "looking ahead" to the future and "looking back" at the past. Our ways of thinking about the future reinforce this spatial sense. The idea of (past and future) days as free-standing holders for events, stacked up one behind the other, is reflected in what is for me the most enduring image of *The Time Machine*, when Wells describes what happens as the machine gathers speed. The passage through time is represented as the passage through days and the latter are reduced to stretches of light: day*light* stands for day*time*. Day and night succeed one another with increasing rapidity, and the frequency of alternation reaches the point where the impression the Time Traveller has is of a grey blur, like the pages of a book being riffled. The journey through time is translated into a passage through or, more precisely, a passage alongside, days hyphenated by nights. This reinforces the sense of the journey as quasi-spatial.

5.2.2.3 Faux amis *of tensed time*

We have rejected a couple of characteristics ascribed to tensed time that have bolstered the arguments of some detensers. However, tense also has its *faux amis*, assumptions that provide a spurious support for the objective reality of tensed time. The most compelling to some is that time has to be tensed if anything is going to happen – if becoming is to be possible. This is reflected in Oaklander's claim – against the denial that pastness and futurity are properties of events: "If temporal becoming is not to be understood as a species of qualitative change, then how is it to be understood?"[32] We have already rejected this notion that happening – temporal becoming – is a qualitative change in the thing that happens because having (already) come into being is a necessary precondition of having qualities. Existence, as has often been said, is not a predicate; rather predication is predicated on existence. To look at change at the level of existence – Item X passes into and out of Being – is to go beneath the level of qualities.

What makes this less obvious than it should be is the notion – first criticized by Parmenides[33] – that that which comes into being must have had its own private pre-being out of which it came. That, for example, $E_{present}$ came out of E_{future} which does not yet exist but has a specific billet "in the wings" where it is waiting. This brings us back to the notion of events as tense tourists, visiting the future, the present, and the past in turn in virtue of having as their successive states E_{future}, $E_{present}$, and E_{past} all of which somehow manage to have the specificity and singularity of E_{past} the completed event. (See §8.2.3). If tenses were states of events, they would have somehow to be earlier than, later than, and at the same time as themselves.

This is the route by which some philosophers arrive at the conclusion that tense is a necessary condition of anything happening. It is a view encapsulated by Steve

Savitt (who rejects it) that becoming depends on events "changing their properties of pastness, presentness or nowness, and futurity".[34]

To see how absurd it is to think of tenses as specific properties of events, let us take a particular example. Consider the Battle of Hastings in 1065 (when it was in the future), in 1066 (when it was happening) and in 1067 (when it was done and dusted). It is obvious that we are not talking about a single item that has three successive properties. In 1065, when it might not have happened at all, it had no properties. In 1066, it had characteristics that evolved during the period of the Battle. In 1067, it had definite, unchanging properties. The passage from no properties, to emerging properties, to definitive, unchanging properties, is clearly not the replacement of one property by another.

While we may set aside *events* as having "pastness", "presentness", "futurity" as one of their constitutive or monadic properties or being located in one or other domain, the argument becomes interestingly complex when we think of instants or of "stretches" of time such as dates. Consider stretches. We are inclined to say on 12 November 2012 that 12 December 2012 is in the future, on 12 December 2012 that it is in the present, and on 12 January 2013 that it is in the past. It seems inescapable to think of the date as having three states. Does this not generate the McTaggart contradiction? How can a day be at once future, present and past? In this case, the problem does not arise because the pastness, presence or futurity of a day is explicitly defined by the viewpoint from which it is observed: it cannot be both at once. The question of its identity does not arise as it does in the case of a token event: 12 December has no identity other than its relationship to other days. It is a location in a temporally ordered sequence of dates. It can be present only on 12 December and past after 12 December and future before 12 December. It cannot be both future and present or present and past at the same time. Its "arrival" and "departure" are not like an event coming into and going out of being. 12 December is not something – an event or such-like – waiting to become today on 12 December. As we discussed in §2.2.3.2, dates are even less able to precede or outlast themselves than events.

What's more, there is nothing in the specification of 12 December that prescribes that certain token events will take place in it. We may be deceived into thinking this when days have names as well as numbers: Sunday, Christmas Day. Even then there is no fixed – guaranteed or definite event – content. Sunday may be declared a work day and Christmas – or the events planned for it – may be cancelled or not come about. A nuclear catastrophe may prevent Christmas having any of the expected content, or any human content at all, but it cannot prevent 25 December from arriving, block the numerical series of days. Dates are slices of time that tag the temporal location of events and are not events themselves; so they cannot be altered materially by change of tense as they have no material to change. There is no contradiction in 25 December being first future, then present, and then past because up to and including 24 December, it has no events, it does not have its full freight of contents until midnight on 25 December and has no present contents from 26 December onwards.

Another spurious support for the objective reality of tensed time is the claim that tense is necessary for time to pass. We have already examined the fatal flaws in the notion of temporal passage but let us examine the idea that the quarrel between tensers and detensers maps on to that between those for whom time is dynamic and those for whom time is static.[35] The alleged connection between tense and a dynamic conception of time has many aspects, but one of the common assumptions is that tense implies, or permits the advance of "now" into a (or *the*) future and away from a (or *the*) past; or the movement of a (or *the*) future towards "now", and thence into the a or the past. For example, "today" is successively 12, 13 and 14 December, and 13 December is successively future (on 12 December), present (on 13 December) and past (on 14 December).

The plot (or the confusion) thickens when the supposed movement of "times" such as "now" and "today" through tenses is conflated with the supposed movement of events through tenses. Oaklander (who is in fact a detenser) perpetrates this conflation when he portrays (as quoted earlier) the ordinary way we think about tensed time thus:

> [W]e conceive of time as something that flows or passes from the future to the present and from the present to the past. Thus, for example, the inauguration of the fiftieth president of the United States is in the relatively distant future, but with the passage of time it will become less and less so and eventually will become present. And then, after its spotlight in the NOW, it will recede into the more and more distant past.[36]

Two kinds of things appear to be on the march: time itself; and events occurring in time. Let us designate the time when the fiftieth president is inaugurated as tp and the event of the inauguration Ep. Both undertake the journey from the distant future through the near future, into the present, and thence to the near and distant past. It is assumed that the motor is time itself; that it is tp's momentum that propels Ep rather than vice versa if only because tp contains a vast number of events (even if one restricts the scope of simultaneity) and Ep could not assume responsibility for herding all of the co-occurrent happenings, the whole set of events or part-events taking place, at tp and driving them to the present and on to the past.

This gives time itself a heavy burden of responsibility. The passage of E_p from the future to the present, would amount to E_p's coming into existence. We shall discuss the dubious notion of time as causing events to come into being in Chapter 10 but for the present, we note only the regrettable tendency to conflate passage of times and passage of events when tense is seen to be a necessary condition of time being fluid enough to pass.

Oaklander's assertion that "we conceive of time as something that flows or passes from the future to the present and from the present to the past" would certainly discredit supporters of tensed time, such as myself, if this were what such support would commit us to. Neither time itself, nor individual times, could change tense. How could a moment in time t_1 start off in the future, move to the present, and end up in the past, while remaining the same element of time? To suggest that t_1 is future at t_{1-n}, present at t_1, and past at t_{1+n} would be either to locate times in hypertimes or to suggest that times have a multitude of different locations in the very series of which they are a part – both of which are impossible. Tensed time would clearly be discredited if it were associated with such naïve ideas about "the passage of time".

Tense, in short, hardly becomes more respectable for seeming to be the necessary basis for ensuring that time flows.

5.2.3 The world as tenseless facts?

The most telling point against those who would wish to discard tensed time while maintaining that time itself is real is one we have touched on already: arguments that discredit tensed time on the grounds that terms such as "past" and "future" are "mere" (external) relations seem to pose an equally serious threat to the "before" and "after" tenseless time of events and, indeed, to the before and after of times themselves. Even if one accepts that tensed time is ("merely") relational, this does not make it unreal or ontologically second-rate; or hovering in some nowhere land between relata. The fact that I am taller than you is not one of my properties – rather it is a relationship between one of my properties and one of your properties – but this does not make "taller than" an unreal feature of the world even though it is not to be found in the two objects being compared or indeed anywhere else. The distinction made by Russell that "past, present and future arise from the time relations of subject and object, while earlier and later arise from the time relations of object and object"[37] needs to be supplemented by the observation "the time relations of object and object" just as much as the relations of future, etc. that also need to be brought out by a conscious subject.

It may be that Mellor is aware of this threat to tenseless time (whose reality he upholds) and why he tries another strategy to disinfect our descriptions of events of what seems like an inescapable indexicality that would link them to tense. He espouses an argument, to which the philosopher of time Michael Tooley also subscribes, that "reality consists of tenseless facts".[38] Irrespective of whether *language* is indispensably tensed, the argument goes, that of which it speaks – facts – are tenseless. Even the facts that make tensed statements true are tenseless.

There are two counter-arguments to this view. Firstly, the arguments that underpin it inadvertently dispense with tenseless time as well as tense. Secondly, the claim that the world consists of "facts" is open to challenge.

To take the first point. Facts are not only tenseless but, like "propositions, numbers, and universals" (to cite Tooley's other examples), are also timeless. There is an obvious sense in which, for example, numbers do not come into being in time, do not last for a period of time, and do not perish. They have no intrinsic temporal order, or duration, any more than they occupy a location in space or have a spatial order. Of course, numbers may engage with time in a variety of ways. The most obvious is counting, when objects are enumerated or when numbers themselves are recited. But there is no intrinsic temporal order in numbers, as opposed to their tokens when they are used on a particular occasion. Two comes before 3 and after 1 in ascending order of magnitude but this has no relevance to temporal before and after: 321 is as acceptable as 123.

And it is scarcely less obvious in the case of propositions — which have the form "That x is the case" — that they, too, are not only tenseless but also timeless (and spaceless). Propositions may engage with time when they are expressed in a token utterance but it is the latter rather than the proposition that is in time. When I first say, "I am hungry" and then say "Russia is a cruel place", this does not assert or establish a temporal relationship between my being hungry and Russia being cruel.

Let us now focus on facts. It is easy to see how they may be construed as tenseless — and I believe that if they are viewed correctly, they are tenseless. However, by the same token they are also timeless (and spaceless). The facts that encapsulate, or are of, timed events do not share the time of those events. While the Battle of Hastings took place in 1066, *the fact that* the Battle of Hastings took place in 1066 does not take place in 1066 or at any other time. Facts are not *occurrences*, a special kind of second order events, which have a temporal location: the fact that E happened is not an additional happening. Nor do facts have a duration, any more than they have a spatial extensity. *The fact that* the battle in 1066 took place at Hastings does not itself take place in Hastings. We could just as well (or as ill) say that the fact takes place in the classrooms where its date is taught or that it had an intermittent existence corresponding to those times when it was iterated, or recalled.

The contrast with events could not be more clear cut. Events are "occurrings" and are so only so long as they are incomplete, ongoing rather than "ongone". Facts are not ongoing. The fact that the Battle of Hastings took place in 1066 is not an unfolding reality. It is separate from the latter in two ways: it concerns reality that was once unfolding (ongoing instead of ongone) and it is *about*, not identical with, that (ongone) reality.

This difference is also illustrated by the contrast between the supposed causal efficacy of events and the actual causal impotence of facts (as opposed to the event of their being asserted or recalled). The Battle of Hastings had consequences that are still unfolding. The fact that there was a Battle of Hastings, however, does not bring about effects of its own, separate from the Battle, though the *event* of my asserting that fact may have effects, such as changing your mind or provoking your disagreement.[39]

To think of the world as being composed of facts is a way of folding tense (and, as it turns out, tenseless time as well) into our description of it. By then conflating the description with that which is described and hiding the presence of time in the latter, it is possible to make the world seem to be tenseless — or indeed timeless. This last point is illustrated by McTaggart's argument against tenseless time. If Event A occurs before Event B, he says, there is a before-after relationship between them that is eternal. A is forever before B: the relationship between them does not change. On this basis, McTaggart argues that the relationship between A and B is more like the spatial relationship between the cold and the hot end of a poker.[40] The argument fails of course: an unchanging temporal relationship is still a temporal relationship; and the fact that it does not change with time shows only that there is no hypertime in which it might change. What is unchanging is the fact that A is before B but it does not mean that there was no change such that B succeeded A.

Which brings us to the second counter-argument: does the world really consist of facts – tenseless or otherwise? That it does is expressed in the opening of Wittgenstein's *Tractatus Logico-Philosophicus*: "The world is all that is the case. ... The world is the totality of facts, not of things."[41] While it is not entirely clear what Wittgenstein meant, it seems to me to have licensed the belief that facts are items on the ground, "out there", and as real as, or even identical with, events. Against this, I would argue that facts are not items on the ground or in the air – like trees and breezes and forces; they are not material entities in a material world. They belong to the discursive space of the community of minds. They are the product of a consciousness, or rather the joint product of an indefinite assembly of consciousnesses, articulating states of affairs in the language of the collective.[42] Unlike events, they do not *take place*. What is more, facts do not interact with each physically; rather such interactions as they have are logical. They are items of knowledge that, as Sellars might say, belong to the Space of Reasons rather than the Space of Nature.[43] Their form is "*that* such-and-such is/was the case" or "*that* such-and-such is/was believed/ hoped/ denied to be the case". The "that" – which is almost invariably overlooked[44] – distinguishes facts from the kinds of items such as events and processes that take place at, and last, a certain time (and occur in a certain place) or objects, that have a certain duration and location (and size).[45] It is through being timeless that they are tenseless and they are the route by which tensed statements can seemingly be reduced to tenseless assertions.

Supposing I state this fact F: "It is true that Event E was the case." F will be true (that is, count as a fact) if Event E takes place before Event U, namely the (speech) act or utterance stating of fact F. Whereas there is tense inside the statement, F itself is tenseless. What is not tenseless, however, is Event U which is present and provides the point of reference that makes F a fact as opposed to a falsehood.

In other words, the elevation of an event to a fact, the use of "that" – so "E happened" becomes "*That* E happened" – detenses the implicitly tensed nature of the assertion. While "E is happening" refers to a present tense event, "That E is happening (at such and such a time)" is a tenseless fact. Replacing events, processes, and objects by facts is thus the quickest way to eliminate tense from the real world. But in practice, it would also remove tenseless time along with tense, my first counter-argument to the notion of the world as being made up of tenseless facts – to which I now return.

Let us illustrate this with a homely example: the cat may have entered this room 5 minutes ago but *the fact that* he entered the room is not something that took place 5 minutes ago. *The fact that* event A took place at 6 p.m. did not take place at 6 p.m. nor at any other time. Ditto the fact that Event B took place at 6:30 p.m. Suppose the cat entered the room at 6 p.m. (Event A) and left the room at 6:30 p.m. (Event B) then it would be true that Event A took place before Event B and that Event A was past when Event B took place. Consider now the fact that the cat entered the room at 6 p.m. (Fact A) and the cat left the room at 6:30 p.m. (Fact B). It would not make sense to say that Fact A was either before Fact B or that Fact A was past with respect to Fact B.

The realm of facts is not one of temporal succession; indeed, it is a frozen world of items that do not stand in temporal relations to one another. It is the "that" which freezes. That is why we can give the facts in any order without creating a mangled portrait of what is there. We can say that the cat left the room at 6:30 p.m. before reporting that it came into the room at 6 p.m. The facts are not part of the unfolding material world; rather they are items that straddle intra-linguistic and extra-linguistic realms. A (true) fact has two inseparable faces, like the recto and verso of a sheet of paper: the first face is an assertion of something and the second the something that is asserted. Facts are neither an item which inhabits a page (so we do not tear up the facts when we tear up a sheet of paper); nor are they something that has a stand-alone existence in the place where the events corresponding to them took place. This is the sense in which facts are *facta* – "things which are made" – though they are not, of course made *up*. Of two would-be facts, "The Battle of Hastings took place in 1066" and "The Battle of Hastings took place in 1067", both are made but the latter is in addition made up, or requires a made-up entity called "the 1067 Battle of Hastings".[46] Facts are made insofar as they are scissored out of what-is by (typically declarative) assertions. They do not correspond to a reality external to them but are a reality inseparable from that which cut it out. The fact that the cat entered the room at 6 p.m. is lifted out of the unfolding of events in the room and the wider universe of which it is a part.

The failure to maintain the distinction between an event that takes place at, and takes, a certain time and the tenseless fact of an event's occurring which does not take place, even less at a particular time, is what gives credibility to the key argument of the detenser. But, as will now be evident, detensers such as Tooley and Mellor should have been warned off this approach by McTaggart's classic paper, which shows how this leads to the conclusion that time itself (not just tensed time) and indeed change are illusory. Effectively, McTaggart argues that, since "The fact that Event A occurred at time t", if it was ever a fact, will be timelessly so, the world is timeless. If, however, we remember the essential distinction between "Event A occurs at time t" and "Fact A – the fact that Event A occurs at time t" we are not pushed to the conclusion that the world is timeless – or tenseless. When we gather up (say) the cat's entry into the room at 6 p.m. into "The fact that the cat entered the room at 6 p.m." time, as well as tense, is buried and we have the timeless fact that the event happened at a particular time. So timeless facts lift us out of the flux of events: they have a modest, local eternity.[47]

Once there is a fact F, it is a fact F forever. Particular facts, as McTaggart pointed out, do not change; nor (unlike events) are they change. Change is real because new events can take place licensing new factual statements, generating new changeless facts. An object that was once green may become red and then brown. This is a change. *The fact that* it changed from green to red to brown is not itself subject to change. The fact of the change which encompasses both ends of the change, is not itself a change (though the token assertion of it is a change, an uttered, that is to say in an unfolding, sentence). If it were a change, then every real change (an object going from green to red to brown) would spawn an infinite number of changes; namely, all the quasi-occurrences of *the fact that* the object changed colour which "occur" when the fact of the change is stated.

Consider an apple passing through a succession of states, S_1–S_3, as it first ripens and then rots:

$$S_1 \text{ Apple}_{green} \quad \rightarrow \quad S_2 \text{ Apple}_{red} \quad \rightarrow \quad S_3 \text{ Apple}_{brown}$$
$$t_1 \qquad\qquad\qquad t_2 \qquad\qquad\qquad t_3$$

The fact that the apple ripened and then rotted – portrayed in the diagram – does not take place at a particular time – t_1, t_2 or t_3, nor over the interval t_1–t_3. The process is gathered up into something complete, in which the beginning and the end are co-present.

This is what motivates McTaggart's half-truth that, "If event N is earlier than event O, it always will be, and always has been". It is certainly the case that the temporal relation once established is subsequently always the case – it is an unchanging fact. It does not follow, however, that it always has been the case. In fact, it won't be the case until both events have occurred and the relationship between them picked out. At any rate, the "earlier than x" relation cannot come into being until x has occurred and in a temporal relation to other events.

While facts, as we have already noted, are not made up, they are *facta* – that is to say they are made. They are fashioned out of language. And language, insofar as it is intelligible, is tenseless, indeed timeless, though it has tenses and refers to times, and the speech acts that employ it occur at, and take, time. This is the sense in which discourse freezes that of which it speaks – something that philosophers have been aware of in different ways since Plato. It is most dramatically illustrated in the case of the word "change": by encompassing the beginning and end of change, and all change, it conceptually arrests change, it brings it to a halt on the page and in some sense in our minds.

Behind McTaggart's argument is another fallacy. It is the idea that, if time itself does not change, it is not real. It is this that underpins his obvious error that if temporal relations between events do not, indeed cannot, change (they are done and dusted), so temporal relations are unreal. On the contrary, if the apparent temporal interval between token events E_1 and E_2 *were* always changing, then we would have grounds for doubting its reality.

Mellor's key argument against tense, trades, perhaps unwittingly, on the ambiguity of statements that are at once transient (token) events (as instanced by my saying at t_1 "Jim will run a race tomorrow") and bearers of general, that is to say, tenseless and indeed timeless meanings. These two faces of words can be used to illustrate a connected point. The word "now" has a general face that gives it meaning (the time of any utterance in which it is properly used); and the singular face corresponding to its use at a time to refer to that time. That is how "now" can be both always, ever-present – as it is not committed to any given present moment – and genuinely "of this moment" as I use it to make a particular statement. The verbal type "now" has a splinter of eternity in its heart, though it is a lopsided eternity that has a beginning but not an end.

The tenseless core of the most explicitly tensed statement is the basis of its (necessarily general) intelligibility. Indeed, if statements did not have a meaning that lay outside of tense, they could not assert tense – from the outside. When I say that "Event A has happened already", the *meaning* of my assertion is not in the past, though the token sentence in which I assert it is past as soon as it is complete. The "pastness" of the assertion is carried by the meaning but the meaning, in order to do this – to mean what it should mean now or at any time – has itself to be tenseless and, indeed, timeless. (That is why, of course, it can be explicitly lifted out of any time and still retain its meaning, as when it is cited, as I have done just now.)

This is where we should seek the explanation and resolution of the so-called paradoxes of tensed time. Tensed statements are indexed to a point of view – an individual consciousness located at a particular point in time (and of course in space – utterances are uttered "here" as well as "now") – and yet the assertions seem viewpoint- free. "There was a cat in the room" has a timeless sense and a tensed reference. When I *mention* this sentence (as by way of illustration) it is timeless – which is why you know what it means; but my use of it is timed and its actual connection to "now" upholds the tense. The necessary omnitemporality of the meaning of words (and indeed their "omnilocality") enables sentences to be used in different circumstances to convey portable, general sense. They straddle the here-and-now of experience and the realm of factual reality.

5.2.4 Further observations on tense

Upholding the profound distinction between on the one hand facts – articulated reality – and on the other events or states of affairs enables us to look critically at the key step in Mellor's reduction of tensed to tenseless time. He argues that "Event A took place in the past" and "Event A took place before this utterance", have the same truth-makers and so have the same meaning and reference. I would argue that, while for any true proposition there is something that makes it true, the something in question is not merely or just a truth-maker even when it has been elevated from an innocent material event to a truth-maker by a conscious speaker asserting it: it takes two to truth-make.[48] That is the first point. The second is this: whatever occurrence it is that makes a statement true, it always exceeds – and always has to exceed – that which is required to make it true. To take a simple example: "The cat came into the room 5 minutes ago" may have the same truth-maker as "The cat came into the room 5 minutes before this utterance" but the cat's entry into the room necessarily has more characteristics than are needed to make either statement true. For example, the entry will be from a certain angle, will involve a certain trajectory, etc., will result in the cat assuming a certain position, and so on. The content of a statement is not identical with any actual event or state of affairs that makes it true. This may seem a pedantic point but it will prove central to the argument against logical fatalism when we consider future contingents such as "tomorrow's sea battle" in Chapter 8 and the general notion of events as tense tourists visiting in turn the future, the present, and the past.

The pertinent point for our present concerns is this: two statements may have the same truth-makers but have different contents. This is the other side of the fact that any real event will have numerous features in addition to those that make an assertion true and those additional features will vary from event to event. So just because "Event A is in the past" can be reduced or recast to "Event A is before this utterance Event U" this will necessarily involve the loss of something – in this case the speaker underwriting the present that locates events before the utterance in the past. This loss will not be noted if we overlook the difference between events on the one hand and events that have become facts or truth-makers as a result of being asserted by conscious human beings on the other.

The attempt to replace events by facts understood as truth-makers goes to the heart of the flaw in Mellor's way of abolishing tenses as a fundamental aspect of reality; namely that it sees the question of tensed and tenseless time – and whether the latter is reducible to the former – as something to be resolved *within* language without any consideration as to the nature of language itself. In particular, it overlooks the fact that events and states of affairs count as truth-makers only to a consciousness anticipating what will be the case, seeing what is the case, or recollecting what was the case. Only when events are registered and related to assertions do they become truth- or false-makers. What's more, we need truth *bearers* – people like you and me – for what is out there to be truth-maker or a false-maker. A tape recording of the sentence "It is raining now" playing endlessly would not make rain, when it occurs, into a truth-maker.

Mellor addresses the issue of tense from within the relationship between utterances and what is the case without fully acknowledging that utterances have to be consciously meant and intended and that what they assert becomes a truth-maker only for a consciousness seeking something to specify some general requirements. And this applies equally to B-series statements as to A-series statements. Yes, what makes "E is past" true at time t is the fact E is earlier than t. But it is not the whole story: t does not become a reference point of its own accord: it is *someone's* reference point. To make a more general point: language is the curator of the past (and *a fortiori* of the future) but this does not mean that tensed time is intra-linguistic. This is particularly clear when we think of "the present". Statements of the kind "E is present" have their roots in the notion that something is, or could be, present in the sense of being *present to* (someone). Event A is not present simply in virtue of being simultaneous with other events, such as an utterance U. No number of simultaneous events would constitute "the present" – because, in the absence of a unifying consciousness, they would not add up to a group of co-occurrent happenings. What's more E does not pick itself out; "E is past" is indeed a *relation* as Mellor asserts; and it is a relation between *someone* and an event. Just as is "now". The fact that "now" is 12 noon isn't delivered by 12 noon itself, notwithstanding that at 12 noon it is now 12 noon. Nor does the assertion "It is now 12 noon" made at 12 noon tag "now" as 12 noon without it being assumed that I am telling the time at 12 noon, that the "now" I am looking at the clock is 12 noon. Likewise, there is a difference between "Tuesday 8 May 2012" which is when I happen to be writing this and "today" because Tuesday

8 May 2012 can be, indeed must be, tomorrow, today and yesterday, whereas "today" cannot.

It will be evident that the inseparability of tensed time from consciousness is not an argument against the *reality* of tensed time if only because, as we have seen, B-series tenseless time would fall by the same argument. There are many aspects of time that a tenseless account does not capture – nor indeed would wish to. There are relatively minor deficiencies, for example the difference between on the one hand the temporal distance between two events and on the other the relationship between an event and "the present" which latter cannot be reduced to a particular event, such as an utterance marking that present. The Battle of Hastings is continually receding from the present at one year per year; it becomes more and more "ago" and the gap between "now" and "then" widens. By contrast the gap between Hastings and Agincourt is constant. *Pace* McTaggart, that this interval is unchanging does not imply that it is not temporal, that it is like the interval (to use McTaggart's example) between the hot and cold end of a poker. The price of denying the reality of the difference between a future that is anticipated and a past that is recalled is to lose temporal relations altogether.

Mellor, like Hartle (see §5.1) believes that we can explain the illusion of tensed time on the grounds of its evolutionary value. We impose unreal tenses on tenseless real time so that we act at the right time. This seems implausible. The intuition that 12:30 on 12 December 2012 is "now" will help us to act in a timely fashion, however, only if 12:30 on 12 December 2012 truly is "now". The tautology that "12:30 on 12 December 2012 is on/at 12:30 12 December 2012" would not be of much use to a beast needing to feed, fight, flee, and copulate in order to survive. What is needed is not an illusion of tense but a compelling sense of reality, which is hardly something animals need to be taught.

Some philosophers, notably A. N. Prior, have taken a position opposite to that of Mellor, arguing that tensed time is more fundamental than tenseless time: "Past and future are in fact not to be defined in terms of earlier and later, but the other way round. 'X is earlier than Y' means 'At some time X was past and Y was present' and 'X is later than Y' means the opposite of that."[49] One could be forgiven for thinking that Prior was not entirely the saviour that tenses need, given his commitment to seeing tenses as "logical operators" but that would be unfair. He did not make the error of confusing the logic of temporal statements with the structure of temporal reality.

Keeping these two things – language and the structure of time – separate is a key feature of what has been called "the new tenseless theory of time" which also subscribes to Mellor's view of the practical need for tensed time: "According to the new tenseless theory of time, tensed discourse is indeed necessary for timely action, but tensed facts are not, since the truth conditions of tensed sentences can be expressed in a tenseless metalanguage that describes unchanging temporal between and among events".[50] Oaklander's separation of the logical and ontological functions of language enables him to argue that even if tensed utterances prove not to be translatable into tenseless ones, this has no ontological implication. This, however, is more a statement of faith than a fully worked out argument.

We must not throw the baby out with the bathwater. In asserting the (at least equal) *status* of tensed and tenseless time, we should not deny the profound differences between them. There is much to be said about "present", "past" and "future" that would be lost if we assimilated tensed time to "physical time" and argued that it qualified as a legitimate aspect of the world seen through the lens of physics. And it is worth finally, reiterating that, in restoring tensed time to its rightful place, is not to subscribe to certain untenable views about tenses. Subscribing to real tense does *not* require that one should believe that: (a) the past, present, and future are quasi-realms; (b) that being "past", "present" or "future" are properties of events or other items in the world; (c) that – arising out of (a) and (b) – there is an homogeneity about the events in each of these "realms";[51] and (d) that events pass through time by doing a grand tour of future, present, and past or that time itself passes in this way, with moments and dates journeying from the remote future, through the present, to the past.

5.3 TENSE REGAINED: TIME AND THE CONSCIOUS SUBJECT

The philosophical critique of tensed time depends upon the same assumptions that make physics unable or unwilling to accommodate this aspect of time: the marginalization of the conscious subject.[52] As we discussed in Chapter 3 (see especially §3.5.3), in relativistic physics, while subject as observer is installed at the heart of the system of understanding, he/she is at the same time eliminated by being reduced to a point location in turn defined with respect to a set of coordinates or a frame of reference. In the philosophical discrediting of tense, the subject is pushed off stage by the utterance which "takes place" (rather than is performed) at a certain tenseless time: the utterer's presence and intention (which elevates the material states of affairs to which it corresponds into truth-makers) are suppressed.

The underlying presupposition is that that which is real for conscious human beings is "merely" or "only" *real for them* and not really real. This is to tar all of human consciousness with the brush of those mind-dependent unrealities such as hallucinations and things we get wrong; and to assume that in progressing towards a physics-based account of the world, we have woken out of subjectivity as out of a dream. Tensed time is to be set aside as something belonging to our cognitive childhood comparable to the belief that objects fall to the ground because they want to or that the sun goes round the earth which is the centre of the universe.

In fact, to deny tensed time, is to deny the fundamental reality of the "that I am", the existential intuition[53] that is the ground upon which we stand. Detensers therefore demand that we should wake up out of ourselves, and out of the "now" and the "soon" and the "recent" that is the very fibre of our being. More broadly, the continuing inescapable presence of subjectivity in the world we live, love, work, breathe, and die – our unshakable existential commitment to this world – confirms, however, that it is at least as real as the world revealed by science and not merely an epistemically primitive state from which science should liberate us. So the fact that tensed time is inseparable from human consciousness – and "the world as tenseless time" is a world without consciousness – does not discredit either it or the notion of a "now" that separates a past that is recollected from a future that is anticipated. While "now" seems to elude physics, it is ubiquitous in the lives of physicists doing experiments. It is not (surely!) suggested that physicists are somehow outside of the real universe when they are doing physics. If the physicalist world picture does not allow for the existence of physicists who are making that world picture, there is something amiss with this picture.

Some philosophers seem entirely unfazed by this criticism of metaphysical scientism. The practical and theoretical success of physics seems to proclaim its metaphysical authority. "[N]o cognizance is taken of nowness (in the sense associated with becoming) in extant theories of physics", Adolf Grünbaum noted, and then added: "If nowness were a fundamental property of physical events themselves, it would be very strange indeed that it could go unrecognized in all extant physical theories *without detriment to their explanatory success.*"[54] From this, however, we may legitimately conclude only that tense has no place in the physical world – or to reiterate Susan Stebbing's crucial distinction – the world as revealed by and to physics. The incorrect conclusion that it has no reality period would lead directly to self-contradiction. As Grünbaum points out in the same article, there is no place either for *becoming* in the four-dimensional space–time continuum. If, as he feels, it is a coinage of our minds then it is difficult to see how our minds do the necessary coining given that (as he also believes) the mind is identical with physical activity in a physical brain. Coining, after all, is a mode of becoming.

One of the most compelling expressions of a seemingly irreducible component of tensed time is that we have different attitudes towards past and future events. As Dainton points out, although I suffered horribly at the dentist last week, I wouldn't now be willing to pay £10 to make it so that I had never had that experience, whereas I would be willing to pay £100 to prevent my suffering next week, especially if this were the only sure-fire way to prevent it.[55]

Some may not be persuaded even by this. The different attitudes to "past" and "future" events, they maintain, does not point to something about the nature of time, "only" about our own nature and, given this, however constant and ubiquitous a feature, it is not really real, but ontologically second-rate. Another tack is needed.

One strategy is to highlight how the irreducible objective reality of the future and the past is reinforced by the fact that, while they are accessed privately and are tailored to our personal interests, they are also ubiquitous in our collective experience and the coordinated conduct of our lives. Future and past times and events are shared realities that can be looked back on, or forward to, collectively. You and I cannot disagree over whether Event E happened yesterday or will happen tomorrow, or, indeed, whether E is ongoing (present) or complete (past) without one of us being wrong. What is yesterday to me is yesterday to you. This first level objectivity connects with the kind of objectivity that is respected in natural science. The tense-free order of the physical universe – as revealed by geologists and physicists and astronomers – builds on the calendrical time that grows out of our shared human enterprises regulated by a sense of time that is rooted in the regularities of the natural world such as the movement of the sun. So talk of "tomorrow" and "yesterday" may be empty from the standpoint of a subjectless physical world but this does not mean either that it is empty period or that it is entirely disconnected from that world.

As we shall discuss in Part III, tensed time is crucial to the relationship between intentionality, consciousness, time, agency, and the nature of the intelligible world. We need tense not merely to act in a timely fashion but to act at all. I mention this to underline that the defence of tense in this chapter is motivated by the belief that it is not only an important aspect of time but that it is indispensable. If tensed time seems to be more contaminated with consciousness and compromised by a human viewpoint than tenseless time, it is because we overlook the necessity of the observer to make time explicit, irrespective of whether it is tensed or tenseless, A-series or B-series. That time should somehow shake itself free of human consciousness when we measure it − so that "Event E_1 is 10 seconds before Event E_2" is considered to have a fundamental reality lacking in "Event E is past" − is an illusion. This may be concealed when we translate "E_1 is before E_2" into "The interval between E_1 and E_2 is 10 seconds" which seems to be a feature of consciousness-free universe. Conscious experience, however, is a necessary prerequisite of measurement. What is more, the measurement − "3 seconds" or whatever − leaves something real out of time, particularly if we forget that measurements have to be made by conscious subjects. The denial of tensed time is part of a wider denial of the role of perception in making time explicit (discussed in Chapter 1) and indeed what the French philosopher Maurice Merleau-Ponty called "the primacy of perception".[56]

This brings us back to a key point from Part I: that time is not "just" or "fundamentally" clock-time. Clock-times − underpinning the great systems of thought in physics that deal with time − have to be experienced "now" in order to count as records of what is "out there" or of the "patterns of events". But there is a less obvious point, discussed in §4.5, concerning the "at" of time. Clocks tell the time only when they are asked. They pronounce that it is 12 noon only when they are consulted; and 12 noon is "the time" if they are being consulted *at* 12 noon. Events and states are not intrinsically clock readings. Without an informed, trained, consumer, we just have an event that has as little significance as a shadow cast by a rock, though the latter also has the capacity to be used as a sundial.

The construction of our complex sense of "before" and "after" − indeed of a universe in which events are ordered in this way − requires some sort of matrix to house them. This is provided by a structured sense of the past and the future, tethered to the present: "shortly", "in a while", "tomorrow", "yesterday", "such-and-such ago". These tensed terms open up our sense of time to enable us to assign events the temporal order that is, eventually, extended via quantification to a notional all-encompassing sense of order, gathered up in the conception of the universe or the physical world as the sum total of everything. The temptation to think of tensed relations ("in a while", etc.) as being subsumed in and superseded by tenseless numbered temporal locations can be resisted when we realize that the relations "before" and "after" are between events that are picked out by a conscious human being for whom they have salience. They are, as already noted, as consciousness-dependent as tensed relations. It is the reduction of tenseless relations to numbers that conceals this and hides the fact that these relations are not properties of the material world. We cannot remove "just now", "ago", "in a while", "tomorrow", "yesterday" from our mode of being in the world any more than we can remove the foundations from a house once it has reached a certain height.

Episodic memory, in which earlier events are present not merely as implicit in their current consequences but as items explicitly located in the past, and what we might call episodic anticipation, in which we await events that are explicitly in the not-yet, are irreducibly tensed. When this is acknowledged, then Mellor's claim that "The A-scale is the only way we have of locating events in time; a compelling way, indeed, which we could not do without, but not the way things are in reality"[57] prompts us to question what he could possibly mean by "reality" here – unless he means the world in the absence of consciousness. If this is what he intends, then, as we have seen, he might be hard put to defend tenseless locations of events. What would "12 December 2012" mean before humans appeared on the scene? Or "a year before such-and-such an event"? If we are inclined to think of it as independent of humans, it may be because we have developed this timescale into something that is so thoroughly collectivized, that its origins are as it were laundered of their association with human consciousness. What does "the way things are in reality" mean if that excludes how they appear to us, particularly if appearing to us is the *sine qua non* of our accessing reality at all? Physics cannot shake off its origin in "the observer": it is not merely the taking off point but also the destination. The dream of shedding the human viewpoint to reveal reality in itself would be rather like the dream of "the light dove" who in Kant's analogy, sensing the resistance of the air, feels that it would fly better in a vacuum.[58] The observer remains stubbornly at the heart of physics, though his/her reduction to a cluster of mathematically defined points hides this.

I have endeavoured to make a case for the reality of tensed time, as a prelude to investigating the complex richness of time's three tenses. I have also argued that the inseparability of tensed time from (human) consciousness does not damn it as having inferior reality. After all, the existence of the B-series, which depends on events being picked out in order to be placed in a relationship of "before" and "after", is also in this respect consciousness dependent. We may think of the B-series as one in which the reference point is outsourced to one of two events, acting as a proxy for the me-here that provides one of the relata in the case of A-series time. Or there is a viewpoint which is spread evenly between the two relata. And this points to a wide truth, captured in Merleau-Ponty's assertion that "Time presupposes a view of time."[59] A world without viewpoint – the four-dimensional continuum considered as a totality – is a world not only without tensed time but also time period and indeed change or becoming.

Defending tense by arguing that tensed and tenseless time are both tarred with the same brush brings us up against a real tension in understanding the relationship between time and consciousness. Invoking consciousness as central to time, we may seem to be in danger of denying the objective reality of the temporal order of the world, in particular the universe before conscious beings arose, something we shall discuss in §10.5.[60] On the other hand, time cannot be slimmed down to a physical dimension independent of consciousness, if only because its apparent directionality – which as we have seen is at odds with the idea of it as the fourth member of the spatio-temporal quartet – has to be found within consciousness. Stand-alone, pure physical time would lack the asymmetry that marks time as we experience it and as it matters to us. To anticipate our discussion in Part III, in order to get directionality into time, we need to have a reference point; or, indeed, two reference points – a beginning and an end. The master beginning, the beginning of all beginnings, and the master ending, the ending of all endings, are birth and death. Within these beginnings and endings are the stories – of growth, progress, of passage from a start to a conclusion – that characterize our lives. This directionality is not to be found when the observer is crash-dieted to a collection of numbers defining temporal locations and intervals. "73" is no more grizzled than is "12".

So the temporal order of the universe is more deeply intertwined with the living, conscious individual suspended between life and death, passing from the beginning to the end, from many subordinate beginnings and subordinate ends, than physics can allow or accommodate. Time, in short, is at one very important level narrative or narratable time. This is the time that is divided into the past – the journey so far completed from birth – and the future – the yet to be completed journey to death. It is the time of memory, regret, backward looks in satisfaction, of a sense of accumulation, of growth; and of anticipation and hope and fear and anxiety and excitement. It is the time of hurry, of waiting, of relaxation, of impatience. This is the kind of time that real, as opposed to virtual, observers are immersed in. The person who sees what time it is on the clock does so at a particular clock-time that has a place in her life. Looking at the clock has a place in her history, has a purpose, has a meaning that relates to her intentions and feelings. This is time as forward-looking "care" (to use Heidegger's term) rooted in past experience.[61]

One of the reasons for resistance to accepting that the human experience of time highlighted in tense is part of its fundamental reality is that our perception of the quantity of time that has elapsed is highly variable, correlating poorly with the interval recorded on clocks. Our judgement of the quantity of time that has elapsed will depend upon how interesting and dense our experiences, and how they affect us or fail to affect us emotionally. It will also be influenced by the frequency with which we *reflect on* how much time has passed and, in particular, how often we consult the clock.[62] These apparent deficiencies in our judgement of the quantity of time that has elapsed during an activity would prove that lived time is not time itself but "merely subjective" time only if clock-time were the whole or fundamental truth of time; if time were simply its own quantity, such that accurate and repeatable measurements captured its essence, and we have seen that this is not true. Even so, it is an adhesive intuition and lies behind our thinking when we tell ourselves that we are going to "make the most" of the time we have – being together, or on holiday, or free.

I hope that this chapter has provided sufficient reason for accepting that tensed time is (at least) as real as "before" and "after" time; that, as Prior has noted, the temporal modalities past, present and future are basic ontological categories of fundamental importance for our understanding of time and the world.[63] And that in our individual development and human history tenseless facts *supervene* on tensed experiences and realities and that "earlier/later" and "before/after" are no more basic or primitive than "past/present/future". The orientation that provides the hinge between past and future – namely the present – seems existentially fundamental.[64]

If tenses really were mere illusions, they would be illusions that we could wake out of though only at the price of lapsing into animal sentience that lacks even a present tense, a state described by Nietzsche:

> Consider the herds that are feeding yonder: they know not the meaning of yesterday or today; they graze and ruminate, move or rest, from morning to night, from day to day, taken up with their little loves and hates, at the mercy of the moment ... The beast lives unhistorically; for it "goes into" the present, like a number, without leaving any curious remainder.[65]

Tensed time is, in short, central to our humanity, our being fully fledged centres of worlds. Indeed, this connection is in no sense accidental or superficial. Lucas has argued that "It is part of the concept of time that it is connected to us, whereas it is not absolutely necessary ... that space should be connected to us. The essential egocentricity of time is reflected in the ineliminability of tenses."[66] Taking tense seriously (and doing it justice) therefore involves more than conceding that tensed discourse cannot be reduced to tenseless discourses and that the language of tenses is primitive and irreducible.[67]

The importance of tensed time is inseparable from the fact that it does *not* have a place in the physical world; that is to say, the world according to physics. Indeed (as we shall discuss in Chapter 12) it is because tenses are *ex machina* that they are so central to our capacity to be agents. Tensed time as virtual time is the key to our being able to act upon the world as if from without. The connection between tensed time and action is acknowledged even by those who would question its reality, such as Mellor. As Lucas has expressed it:

> Mellor holds that tense is...projected by us on to an untensed system of dates so that we can act in a timely fashion when the situation calls for it. Tenses are like secondary qualities. We paint them on the world, but are led to do so by reason of our being entropy-increasing organisms agents that need to know when the time is ripe for action.[68]

Much about this is wrong but it is at least an acknowledgement of the relationship between agency – the possibility of free action – and tensed time. Tensed time is the most elaborated form of explicit time and is thus most intimately associated with our freedom. It is because the time we are at is not an instant of mathematical or physical time that we are able to be outside of the moment we are in. The reality of agency and hence of the tensed time on which it depends is attested by the fact that we have so deflected the course of the planet we live on as to justify the present era being called the Anthropocene.

It is time now to move on from a general defence and characterization of tensed time to examine the phenomenology of the three tenses. We shall begin with the present (Chapter 6) that most immediately engages us; move on to the past that we look back on (Chapter 7); continue into the future that is anticipated (Chapter 8); before briefly alighting on eternity (Chapter 9), an "after-time" that is simultaneously so attractive and repulsive to time-torn creatures such as ourselves.

By looking closely at tensed time, we shall at the very least, encounter the time of impatience, endurance, waiting, and hope, and go some way towards recovering what has been lost in the long journey from our pulse to the segmented, unitized, time of our clocks, and thence to the realm of numbers. We shall rediscover the time of flesh and blood individuals living their lives.

CHAPTER 6

Living time: now

6.1 NOW

6.1.1 Defining now

> "What day is it?" asked Winnie the Pooh. "It's today" squeaked Piglet.
> "My favourite day" said Pooh.
>
> A. A. Milne, *Winnie the Pooh*

Anyone inclined to think that the present is the least mysterious of the tenses, that it is more straightforward or even more basic than past or future, will change their mind once they look hard enough.[1] The trouble begins with the most elementary face of the present: "now", which, as we noted in the previous chapter, Einstein observed (with some regret) lay as far beyond the reach of science as other aspects of tensed time. No foliation of space–time is geometrically special, and certainly not in the way that the present moment is special. The fact that "now" eludes the grasp of physics may seem scarcely surprising. It is an indexical anchored in "I" or "we" and first-person being and hence is absent in no-person physical science, notwithstanding that the mathematized account of the world aspires to describe the framework of all possible experiences. Even so, it seems to have a reality that goes beyond the apparently equally indexical "here", as we shall discuss in §6.1.3.

Poincaré pointed out that in mechanics something is missing in its grasp of simultaneity: it reduces the *qualitative* problem of simultaneity to the quantitative problem of time measurement.[2] Some might argue, however, that "now" eludes physical science not because the latter has an impoverished sense of simultaneity but because "now" entirely lacks content and Einstein should consequently not have fretted. Certainly "I am now" and (of the time) "It is now" smack of empty logical necessity because "now" is defined by the time at which the assertion using the token "now" is uttered. It is, however, substantive in a way that Mellor inadvertently highlighted when he attempted to reduce now (and tensed time) to the relations between utterances and that of which they speak.

Why no-one would bother saying either "It is now" or "I am now" may seem obvious but the reasons are worth spelling out because they are different in the two cases. "It is now" unpacks the fact that in its use in particular utterances, "now" refers to the (present) moment in which the utterance is being made: the utterance, that is to say, is devoted to making explicit one aspect of itself. "Now" cannot be shaken off: we cannot say "It is then" because this would amount to "It is (now) not now". "Now" also adheres to me, like a shadow, in "I am now" for the same reason: namely that the utterance, by being in the present tense, refers to the same moment as that in which it is uttered – the present moment, specified in the word "now". But – and this is the point – in this latter case things are more complex. The "now" of the "I" is a lived now, an endured, enjoyed, even enacted, now; and this now, partaking of first-person singular and plural being, has temporal depth. The now I am "at" at any given moment, goes beyond the bare tautology of an identity between the time of an utterance U and the time referred to in the utterance U. Lived now is fatter than the punctate now of the mathematical imagination or the world of physics; than the "now" of t_1 at t_1. We shall return to this in the next section but before doing so, let us look at another way of capturing now.

Supposing I say "It is now 12 o'clock on 12 December 2012". This will be true when, and only when, it is uttered at 12 o'clock on that date and false at every other time. We can both "eternize" and "tautologize" this kind of statement as follows. We eternize it by saying "It was true that I uttered 'It is now 12 o'clock on 12 December 2012'": this *factual* truth is true for all time. It is tenseless which is why (as we discussed in Chapter 5) Mellor, aiming to drive tensed time out of the real world, chose to make facts the basic stuff of reality. By contrast, "It is now 12 o'clock on 12 December 2012" is not an (enduring) fact. At 12:15 the statement is false. We tautologize it by saying "Any statement of the form 'It is (now) t_1' is true if/when and only if/when it is uttered at t_1". This rephrasing seems to make the "now" redundant: the present tense of the verb in "It is t" implies "It is (now) t".

What is the connection between rendering "now" statements eternal and rendering them logically necessary (and hence true in all possible worlds)? It is the ascent from particular utterances made by a particular person at a particular time to the general relationship between utterances and the times to which they refer, where this is assumed to be the time of the actual utterance. It is a way of taking out the indexical essence of now statements and rendering them amenable to logical handling – but not, of course, to scientific treatment.

Another way of doing this is to discard now once it has been given an objective value. "It is now 12 o'clock on 12 December 2012" can be stripped of its explicit now. "It is 12 o'clock on 12 December 2012". We seem to leave "now" behind and ascend to a nexus of times that belong not to one person, but to all persons, recording devices, and (notwithstanding Einstein's well-founded regret), apparently, to the material world itself, whose times are inscribed by the sun and more distant stars. But this is an illusion: "now" remains stubbornly irreducible. Indeed, you can't translate it into objective temporal relations such as "at the same time as" because simultaneity is observer-dependent. Simultaneity is in the sensorium of a beholder or her proxy an inertial frame of reference. The fact that event E_1 at one place seemed to occur at the same time as another event E_2, or as an indefinite number of events E_2 to E_n, does not make the time of the occurrence of any of the events count as "now", or add up to a global now.

So, while it is tempting to think of "now" as an arena of all the material events that are simultaneous with an index event, one event at least has to be perceived by a subject as occurring "now" in order to extract "now" from simultaneity. "Now" in short, is an interloper, in the nexus of material events that, according to special relativity, adds up to a space–time continuum. John Locke's assertion that "this present moment is common to all things that are now in being"[3] incorrectly assumes that there is a present common to everything that exists, a universal "now" such as had been envisaged by Locke's touchy friend Mr Newton. This is an image of "now" as it were expanded widthways from a centre to encompass the totality of what exists. The index event, however, acquires its status as the centre only from the "I-now" or "I-implicitly-now" registering it. (The – albeit limited – inter-subjective agreement as to what is now – so that "I-now" is "we-now" – may conceal the indexicality of now.)

It is difficult to formulate a satisfactory account of a physical now. The standard description of it as "a global hypersurface of simultaneous events" tries to run with the Newtonian hares (a universe of simultaneous events) and the Einsteinian hounds (the connection is through four, not three dimensions) and fails dismally. It invites us to imagine a universe of simultaneous events that are spread through space which the Einsteinian veto on distant simultaneity denies as possible.[4] If they are simultaneous, they must be observed as such and if they are spread through space, they cannot be perceived as occurring simultaneously – and hence are not simultaneous. (The simultaneity can be understood as a virtual, mathematical simultaneity in which all separations are space-like.) As events are further and further from me, the news of them will be increasingly delayed, and this increasing lateness will mean according to relativity that they *are* later. The receding spatial zones are receding time zones and the recession begins from the observer who is the bearer of now; and around "now" is the not-yet and no-longer. While the recession hardly matters practically for the difference between my mouth uttering "The tree is shaking in the breeze" and the tree over there shaking in the breeze, the metaphysical point is as valid for the gap between me and the tree as between me and a distant star.

The "hypersurface" fudge is one that we live out in our everyday life. The intuition of global simultaneity – or a simultaneity without spatial boundaries – is central to our intuition of a coherent world. "Now" must be the same for more than one person otherwise there would be no authority in the assertion that "It is now 12 o'clock". Part of the authority comes from the synchronization of our watches: we say that, within certain agreed objective time (i.e. space) zone, it is the same time for all of us. When we synchronize our watches, we do not simply agree as a community to choose certain arbitrary time labelling and scales. They fit into broader "clockwork" of the physical world. Even so, when we both agree that "it is 12 o'clock" we are stretching the "now" to encompass a (tight) cluster of "nows" corresponding to the slightly varying viewpoints of an indefinitely large group of individuals. In France they ask "what time do you have?" and in England "what time do you make it?". There is a half-truth on both sides of the English Channel: we make the time that we collectively have, where the boundaries of the collective are agreed in advance. Our personal "now" is over-ridden in favour of harmonization – unlike our personal here (of which more presently) – so that "now" seems to be spread all over the area marked out by a time zone. We bury our (insignificant) differences.

Indeed, incorrigible Newtonians as we are in practical life, we have a sense of "now" that spans the universe, of a present moment from one end of being to another (as is picked up in John Locke's definition above). When I ring you in Australia, I note that your clock is 12 hours adrift from mine; we are running to a different time. But I don't question our sharing a "now"; indeed, it is the necessary condition of our talking to one another. I ask what time is it *now* where you are and compare it with the time it is *now* where I am. So the gap between our subjective experience and "now" that is inserted by referring our now to a time on the clock is only apparently closed. Indeed, it is still there, though hidden, when I consult the clock to find out the time now: I consult the clock now as well. It is because I consult the clock now that the clock tells me the time now.

The inescapable "nowness" does not imply that we can read time off from now. There is nothing distinctively "12 o'clock 12 December 2012" about any now, otherwise we would not need clocks and calendars to tell us what time it is. "It is now" requires no evidence but "It is now 12 o'clock" is a piece of knowledge that does require evidence. The evidence is not present to us as experience: "It is (now) 2011" is not experienced in the way that I experience "It is warm" or "My arm feels warm". While we may see straight away that it is morning in a familiar place, we could still be deceived; and more exact "now" (that it is 10:10 a.m. in the morning) or less exact "now" (that it is 2012) will require objective evidence. You cannot, in each case, tell by looking. (The obverse of this is that there is nothing "now" or "now-like" about any moment in time – otherwise that moment would remain forever now.)

The fact that none of this would make any sense in physical systems does not expose our lives as being based on illusions but demonstrates that we are not (just) physical systems. It underlines, also, how complex the notion of "the present" is. It encompasses: (a) a privileged foliation in the manifold defined by a grouping of events; (b) a moment in time on a putative universal clock; (c) the time in which experiences are had, transcending the time of the objects of our experience; and (d) the time that matters above all other times.

The explicit sense of now – that opens up the question, "What time is it now?" and makes the question "When is now?" not empty, requiring more than the answer "Now is now" – separates the present moment from itself. It situates that which is present before us in a present *tense* and makes it part of a present moment that, as soon as it is fully present, is past. It opens the present to other times. The present, in short, is not a mere dot, or a widthless boundary between no-longer-existence and not-yet-existence, because it would be uninhabitable. Now has depth. It is fat and can get fatter.

6.1.2 Fattening now

> [The present] is a point of time so small that it cannot be divided into even the most minute particles of moments ... Such a time must fly so rapidly that it has no duration and no extension.
>
> Augustine, *Confessions*, 269

One of the most familiar ways of envisaging "now" is as a point – a point in time, of course. That this point can expand widthways, as it were into the three dimensions of space, a foliation of the manifold, tempts one to see it as a line moving broadside, at right angles to a timeline, or the edge of a growing block behind which is the sum total of the past. The basic, inescapable, expansion of now, therefore, is into the space which holds together all those things that are deemed to be simultaneous with each other, to be occurring at a given moment, one so recent that it is not yet in the past. This expansion is constrained by relativistic limits on distant simultaneity, restricting the scope of now to a parish defined by a viewpoint (usually sloppily conflated as we saw in §3.5.3 with an objective inertial frame). Strictly, simultaneity is absolute and invariant only where paired events are not separated in space: "now" lives on borrowed space. I want here to focus not on this widthways expansion into space but on temporal depth; on expansion within time itself; on the presence within now of before and after. (Though we shall find, quite other than for Minkowskian reasons, that the spatial extensity of now is not easily extricated from its inner temporal depth.)

The key to investigating the depth (or width) of now is to appreciate that the present moment is a psychological, indeed existential, entity, not a mathematical one. It is not a dimensionless point, the tip of a one-dimensional quasi-spatial line, a knife edge separating past from future. If there is no physical "now" (as Einstein mourned), there is certainly no mathematical now, any more than there is a mathematical "then". To think of "now" as a point is to confuse psychology and human existence on the one hand with mathematics on the other. Contrary to the usual way of thinking of things, it is the mathematical punctate now that is "the specious present" rather than the now of experience.

This point was made with his usual force and clarity by William James. The present is not a knife edge "but the short duration in which we are immeasurably and incessantly present". The *strict* (durationless) present is "an altogether ideal abstraction, not only never realized in sense, but probably never even conceived of by those unaccustomed to philosophic meditation".[5] In short, in our endeavour to find something habitable in the present, we should not have started out from an ideally pure present narrowed down to a (mathematical) instant. A putative instantaneous now would be an unhappy mixture of the nowless (and indeed tenseless and possibly timeless) mathematical temporal point and the lived present. An instant borrows its claim to be "of time" from the system of coordinates to which it notionally belongs.[6] The idea of the present as an instant, in summary, would change "there is no time like the present" to "there is no time in the present".

That this is not always understood by even the brightest intelligences is illustrated by Gödel's confused construction of actual time: "The existence of an objective lapse of time means (or at least is equivalent to) the fact that reality consists of an infinity of layers of "now" which come into existence successively."[7] An "*infinity* of layers of "now"" would indeed be required to make actual intervals of time out of a present conceived as a succession of extensionless instants irrespective of whether the interval in question were the gap between tick and tock or the time span of the universe – a clear demonstration that this account of time is flawed. There are no actual (as opposed to potential) infinities in nature. They would, however, have to be actual if actual intervals of time were to be constructed from components that were effectively zero in duration. It is also difficult to see how zero intervals could qualify as intervals specifically of *time* – or indeed of anything. And what is more, it is difficult to see how they could accommodate a present where "happening" intervenes between the-not-yet-happened and the already happened.

Notwithstanding the problems that inevitably arise if we start from mathematical instants as the basic element of time (tensed or otherwise) and the idea of "now" as unextended, it is not easy to shake off the notion of time being doled out instant by instant. The adhesiveness of this notion is reflected in the tendency to speak of a liveable now that could house ordinary consciousness as "the specious present" – as if the real present were instantaneous and anything thicker than that must be in some sense illusory.

"The specious present" denotes the slice of time that counts as present, or the temporal depth of a unified experienced whole which spreads beyond the instant. The term was coined by the nineteenth-century psychologist E. R. Clay but given wider currency by William James. The psychological and philosophical literature on this topic is prodigious.[8] The phrase captures the fact that our present moment has depth in virtue of making co-present events, or stages of events, or processes or phases of processes, that when observed objectively are seen in fact to be separated in time. In short, it is the experience of simultaneity stretched beyond the simultaneity that would be permitted from the viewpoint we occupy. This has been well expressed by Jenann Ismael: "The Doctrine of the Specious Present says that if we consider a particular temporal cross-section of experience at a point t in time (call it a t-section), the content carried by the t-section has temporal breadth. It spans a finite interval of time centred on t."[9]

The "specious present" proves on close inspection to be rather complex. Studies have differentiated three modes of the immediate present.[10] There is "the functional moment" which designates a timescale at which we can differentiate one event from another. For hearing, this is 2 milliseconds and for vision tens of milliseconds. And two events must be at least 50 milliseconds apart before you can tell reliably which came first. The next level is "the experienced moment" – 2–3 seconds wide – which is the interval within which we can integrate jumbled stimuli into a comprehensible whole. This is the "subjective present" which allows us consciously to perceive sequences of events. How this happens is not known but it has been described as a "psychological illusion based on the past and a prediction of the near future" – a strange illusion, it must be said that must generally reveal objective truth. The top "now" of the hierarchy is the "mental present" constructed out of present moments. This "mental present" operates over a time span of the order of 30 seconds and gives a sense of continuity. It underpins the feeling that it is I who am experiencing the events. It is the "now" of the "I" of the narrative self.

Such a temporal breadth (or depth) of experience is necessary if we are to experience events at all. No event or experience of an event has a mere point duration. We could not hear a melody, if we did not hold all the notes together as a sequence. And we could not see a motion such as a car coming down the road if we did not take its successive positions in some sense together. (The latter is the basis for our perception of time as something in itself, for making time explicit, as we discussed in Chapter 1.) If "now" were not fat, we might be able to eat a whole meal (though not, perhaps, formulate the intention to do so) but we could not experience, even less enjoy, it as a meal. We would not even be able to enjoy or experience an entire mouthful. A mathematical instant would not be wide enough to accommodate the experience of even a single note, never mind a melody, if it lasted (as it must) more than a mathematical instant. Or any movement. Or any change.[11]

Individual extended experiences must be located in a wider temporal field. If consciousness were constituted out of instantaneous experiences of instantaneous events, or of instant-slices of events, it would be disconnected, worldless, meaningless, and in a real sense empty – empty of objects and of events as much as of "I". Experience must be of things that take time (events) or endure through time (objects) and must itself take time. For the "happen*ed*" to be experienced as having happened, phases of its "happen*ing*" must be held together. "-ing" signals the fact that the present is irreducibly ongoing, a participial. Walk*ing* cannot be translated into a succession of positions disconnected from one another. Nor could we see an object as a whole, as having more than one property, and being in a certain external relation to us, and as stable, without bringing together a succession of experiences generated as we roam over it. The enduring object that is now before us is revealed to us through what we might call "a running succession" of experiences. Our sense of items being real is inseparable from our bringing them to a halt in enduring stasis in our presence.[12]

Ordinary experience therefore requires that we need to hold together non-infinitesimal intervals of time. A succession of temporally depthless perceptions would not deliver the perception of succession. Even at the most basic level, perceived "now" is explicitly open to not-yet and no-longer. This must not be misunderstood. When I hear a succession of notes as a melody, as a *succession* of notes, they are not fused, losing their individual identity in the higher identity of the succession. Nor do "earlier" and "later" translate into characteristics we might see in present sensations, so that, for example, earlier notes, incorporated into the succession, would be experienced as being quieter than later ones. This is, however, how we would be obliged to see things if we accepted the notion that memories are like "pale copies" of present percepts. In reality, a memory of a yellow of a certain hue is not like an experience of a paler yellow; a memory of a note is not a quieter version of the experience of the note, with remembering prompting us to turn up the hearing aid. Memories of toothache may be painful but not in the way toothache is.

If the present were a succession of unextended moments, it would not be able to accommodate any ideas – including ideas such as "now", "the present", and "today" – which require a temporal spread to be entertained. A present of instants could not even house the idea of an instant. Even to experience a world as present, therefore, we need a present moment that is thicker than a notional mathematical point, unless there could be a direct experience of succession somehow compressed into a durationless conscious experience.

The present, as already noted, is impregnated with the past. It is important not to exaggerate the extent of this. The psychologist Donald Hebb suggested that "what we experience is really the memory of immediate past experience and depends on short-term memory."[13] This risks denying the present its own territory as thoroughly as does the mathematical reduction of "now" to an instant. Edmund Husserl's emphasis on the presence of the past in the present – in the form of "retentions" – is qualified: the core of the present remains "the primal impression" and, what is more, it is as impregnated with the future in the form of "protentions" as it is with the past ("retentions").[14] (We shall discuss this in more detail in §10.4.3).

This does not alter the fact that the past is key to the present if only because it is in virtue of past experience that what presently surrounds us, the situation we are in, is intelligible, so we have an idea of what is before us, where we are, and indeed who we and others are. As for the immediate presence of the future, at the most basic level, perceived objects are experienced as items that have hidden possibilities that could be disclosed. In the opening chapter, we talked about the visible invisibilities of the material world. These include the properties that are implied but not directly given to vision (such as appearance of the back or inside, weight, texture, pliability, etc., of the object). There is also that which is hidden behind that which is visible, what lies beyond the bend in a track, what exists over the horizon. An aspect of this is captured in the psychologist J. J. Gibson's designation of objects as "affordances": they are possibilities of things that might happen, including things we might bring about. The world around us is a nexus of significances.

Our needs, expectations, hopes and so on open up the sense of "what" and "where" and "who" and "how" to a future of possibilities, opportunities, threats, obligations. This is replicated at many levels; so, for example, each moment of my walk to the shops informs me where I am and where I will be next and what I must take account of in completing my journey, a journey that itself is impregnated with a future – the future needs that I anticipate in shopping, and so on. If the present were depthless, consisting of a succession of durationless points, it would be a senseless flurry of sensations.

This depth is further enhanced by the explicit sense of the past that goes beyond the kind of basic memory necessary to make the world intelligible (and even further beyond the "habit memory" enshrined in such items as expectations and skills) and beyond a future implicit in having particular goals. We may at any moment be visited by episodic memories of singular events we have experienced and their circumstances or by anticipations of specific events we are expecting or intend to bring about. These out-of-time psychological moments, are distinct flecks of the no-longer and the not-yet, supplementing the out-of-present implicit in the immediate recognition of a face, or the sight of a bus that makes me hurry.

One further point: without the present being extended beyond a temporal instant, it would not be possible to experience a spatially extended world. The present would shrivel to a spatial point as well as a temporal one because experiencing an array of objects, events, and bodily experiences, that are both distinct (so that we are aware of them as separate) and together (so they belong to the conscious field) requires items that occur at, and/or are being registered at, different times to be brought together. There is a temporal smearing in something as elementary as seeing an object moving; and in registering change, when the experience of the ongoing combines that of the "ongone" with the "oncoming". What is more, we experience many "ongoings" at once in different stages of their development, with different proportions of about-to-happen and just-happened: there are embryos next to elders.

Temporal "smearing" – such that events or event stages at t_1 and t_3 are in some sense present in t_2, when t_2 is "the now" – could not result from the joining up of instantaneous dots of mathematical or physical time or out of the broadside movement through space of a confining temporal line dividing past and future. It is inextricably bound up with the connectedness of consciousness of items that are also perceived as separate, such that (for example) the experience of a patch of brown signifies something that goes beyond itself: it is inseparable from the experience of an object, say a table, which has other properties, such as being square, being over there, having a slick of light on its polished surface, and so on. The table in turn is experienced as part of an array of objects that amounts to a lay-out of a kitchen. The kitchen is in a house but also situated in our lives as part of our *umwelt*, of an open network of implicit and explicit meanings that imply or arise from each other. The meaningful presence of these components is no more stand-alone than are the meanings of individual statements in a speech, individual words in a statement, or individual sounds in a word. In short, the items of our experience are interpenetrated in a way that is more intimate than any physical spatial or temporal relation.

Importantly, while the items in a sensory field, a moment of consciousness, or a lived world interpenetrate, they are also distinguishable as discrete elements: they are one-and-many. It is this that provides the background for a fat now in which, say, a musical note is experienced as part of a melody and successive notes are co-present, as if they were simultaneous, though they are not perceived as simultaneous. Husserl's conception of the present moment as consisting of a "primal impression" flanked by retentions (present representations of immediately preceding experiences as past) and protentions that reach into the immediate future, towards future events about to happen or states about to be achieved (the next note, the anticipated phase in the trajectory of a flying object) is in a sense too narrow, too linear, an account of temporal depth.[15] The temporal depth of now is part of a wider depth of experience:

"The perceptual 'something'", Merleau-Ponty wrote, "is always in the middle of some-thing else, it always forms part of a 'field'".[16] The field is a multidimensional network or world of significance. The mystery of the depth of the present and of the sense of succession – which would seem to require the co-presence of at least two items in a sequence of items that are separated in time, the presence of that which is past and even of that which is future – is simply one aspect of the general mystery of consciousness in which many things are brought together and yet are also kept apart.

The stitching together of experiences into wholes or fields – so that, for example, the isolated, atomic sensation, like an instant of time, is a purely intellectual construct rather than a primordial reality – is on the basis of meaning, sense, or significance.[17] These latter are not occurrences nor are they items that have a certain time span: they are timeless. Significance is not a discrete characteristic attached to a particular item (object or event) in a conscious field and co-terminous with the physical time of its being present. Meaning is the splinter of timelessness at the heart of all experience, lifting it above the moments of its occurrence and enabling it to be connected with – and so make present – past and future experiences. The fact that the sense or sig-nificance of our experiences – transferred to those items (events, objects) that they are experiences of – does not have a definite duration or temporal location opens up the present to that which is not present in the sense of being currently before us.

That timeless, general meaning, is outside of the present understood as a physical time t is an easily overlooked truth. It has, however, haunted Western philosophy. It may, for example, be behind the Platonic connection between generality (of univer-sals) and eternity. Leaving that aside, it is here or hereabouts that we find the possi-bility of a virtual world of intelligibility that makes freedom and action possible – as we shall discuss in Chapter 12. Sense or meaning, which is not located at a physical, mathematical time t, is amenable to expansion through signs whose significance is, of course, general and clearly not tethered to a specific time (or place). And even though signs may be used to refer to particulars, they do so from outside the time and place of those particulars.

This is why it is misguided (and unnecessary) to assume, when we are trying to understand how on earth present experience could reach beyond the present, that we have to begin, as the nineteenth-century philosopher R. H. Lotze believed, with "persisting sensations or memory images that are simultaneous in present con-sciousness"[18] if the sensations and images in question are thought of as discrete. It may be equally misguided to try to solve the problem of the openness of the present to something beyond the present moment by postulating, as Dainton does, a linear thread of acts of awareness whose overlap spans successive phenomenal contents, such as the successive notes of a melody.[19] The spatio-temporal spread of "now" is not captured by localised break-outs from a putative momentary or moment of sensory experience. My sense that the melody is more than its present is part of a wider sense that the world and I are rooted in a past and heading towards a future.

The fundamental mistakes are to imagine that consciousness is made up of atomic contents and that time is made up of instants. The latter confuses the mathematical representation of time with its true nature. There is no mathematical present, any more than there is a mathematical now. We could highlight this in another way: to be now is to be *at* now or *at* t_1 which at a certain moment is "now". This meta-time is unique to human consciousness, transcending the material world by being *about* or *of* that world. Mathematical t_1 does not have "*at* t_1" within it. This may be what Husserl was referring to when he introduced the concept of "absolute constituting consciousness" and argued that the temporality of experiences was not itself temporal: "The consciousness of now is not itself now".[20] We could unpack this further: "Now and our consciousness of it do not converge on, even less are identical with, the physical t_1 that it is now".

The present is a present world that is had in common with others, the subject of a widely joined attention: groups of people (aggregated in many different ways) engaging with, co-existing in, and co-living, parts of a notional total world or universe. This joint attention is underlined and elaborated in communication, where our consciousness of now is made explicit as something shared, something we have together, something that is open to us, and encloses us, defining immediate and longer-term possibilities. The successful communication between individuals cancels any delay in our experiences: the speaker and the receiver are one in the transmitted meaning and we truly co-exist. When I understand what you are presently saying to me, your meaning it and my understanding it (irrespective of minute objective delays) belong to the same moment.

Communication expands "now" in two directions. The first and most literal is the expansion that comes from its making me aware of things that others are aware of and that I am not. This presence of the hidden-from-me, which began with vision, is extended by pointing, where you disclose to me something that is available to you through your positional advantage. There is something "now" existing that lies outside of my current experience. There are, of course, many kinds of pointers that join attention and share awareness beyond the primordial indicator of the forefinger. Within the semiosphere that is the human world, it is language in the narrow sense that most obviously drives the expansion of now.[21] Verbal communication inflates now beyond anyone's personal experience, beyond the sum total of their evolving perceptual field, beyond what is experienced by a particular third party, to what is or has been experienced by a generic "someone", and eventually to what *might be* experienced by someone, though it is not actually present to anyone. We have, that is, a shared sense of a boundless public "now" of events that somehow hold together in time, even though they are not synthesized in a moment of individual consciousness. The sphere of "now", of the present world, of the present, eventually extends to encompass events that are envisaged as co-occurrent though not co-experienced, which are awarded an honorary "now-hood" through belonging to the same world, or overlapping worlds, as those things that are presently being experienced by you and me. There is a foliation of space–time that commands community-wide agreement. It is an existentially privileged foliation that goes beyond the individual: that in virtue of which we live in shared worlds.

It is this expansion of "now" that licenses the false idea of a boundless now as a property of the material world, of a global foliation, which relativity exposed. As

Callender puts it, "part of the shock of relativity is its conflict with the idea of a special common now".[22] Or perhaps, we should say, *apparent* conflict – because neither the specialness nor the (limited) commonness of "now" is put in question. It is necessary to point this out because exaggeration of the significance of relativity theory in turn has led to the opposite error of thinking that "now" must therefore be unreal. And the apparent challenge of relativity theory is not as novel as may seem. Science, after all, was rooted in de-privileging human experience and human existence long before relativity made this particularly explicit. The heliocentric theory set aside an important judgement between that which is at rest and that which is in motion.

This is underlined by Mermin who also makes a fundamental point about the distant relationship between the world-picture of physics and the physical and human world:

> The events I experience are complex extended entities and the clocks I use to assign times to my experiences are extended macroscopic devices. To represent my actual experiences as a collection of mathematical points in a continuous space-time is a brilliant strategic simplification, but we ought not to confuse a cartoon that concisely attempts to represent our experience, with the experience itself.[23]

Or, indeed, with the experienced world.

On the other hand, the (misleading) idea of a "now" intrinsic to the material world has also played into the hands of physics in another way: by giving credence to the idea of the present as being independent of presence. This severs it from its roots in consciousness, thereby rendering it vulnerable to being emptied of meaning and content, en route to ultimate reduction to a non-privileged point or succession of points defined by numbers. What relativity theory really tells is not that "now" and the present are unreal but that any idea of the present divorced from presence is vulnerable to elimination. If we resist separating the present from presence, we won't go down a route which ends up with our trying to build up lived time out of durationless points and falsely imagining that living (in the present) consists of occupying a succession of temporal instants.

Mellor has highlighted one aspect of the fattening of (collective) "now" by means of language, dramatically widening the present that mathematization would make vanishingly slim. As we reach deeper into the no-longer and not-yet, so the units of time that we use to identify locations in the past and future become larger. Our time-thinking becomes more coarse-grained. And this plays back into our thinking about the present. Now swells to "nowadays" and the present grows fat on hours, days, years and centuries. As Mellor says, "we should call any A-time 'present' however long it is if, and only if, it includes the present moment".[24] The verbal now is "this hour", "today", "this week", "this year", "the present age". At any rate, we have (whole) todays, just as we have yesterdays and tomorrows in common. "Yesterday", for example, is not analogous to "over there" which is dependent on the location of an individual body – that of the speaker.

By this route, the present expands yet further and goes beyond that which is experienced as present. There is an increasing disconnection between a now that is referred to and a now that is as it were directly mentally colonized or inhabited. We expand our reference from the full "thisness" or indexicality of experienced "now" to the purely titular "thisness" of (for example) "this week", "this day" or even "this hour". By this calendrical route, we journey beyond our direct temporalized awareness towards an objective time and ultimately the mathematized time that is fully developed in natural science. While our experienced "now" has a depth that is far more than a notional instant or even the "specious present", it falls short of many "nows" indicated by stretches of time that are too thick to be penetrated by our consciousness – the now of (for example) "nowadays".

Experienced time, it seems, lies between the mathematical limit indicated by the idea of a temporal point, moment or instant, and those large slices of time gathered up in terms like days, weeks, years and so on. It is here that we find the mismatch between subjective and objective time; between experienced and measured or recorded time (see §10.5). And it is in this mismatch that we experience time as elusive (as we shall discuss in §6.2.2). An experienced hour fails to be 60 times as long as an experienced minute and an experienced day fails to be 24 times as long as an experienced hour. As for a week, or a year, or a decade ... Indeed, experience of continuing "now" fails to swell proportionately to those units by which the clock divides time or the calendar marks it. Part of the problem is that a day is not only too stretched out to be gathered up; it also belongs to the collective. Housed in the community of minds, it cannot be fully accessed in the experience of individual minds.

The fattening of "now", that is, does not mean that we can experience, even less occupy, whole stretches of time at time t. There is a residual sense in which, objectively, "now" is only modestly extended. If this were not the case and (say) "now" *were* really an entire hour or a day wide, and this corresponded to objective time, we would be able to see that which had not yet happened and would continue to experience as contemporary that which has ceased happening. The very fact that that which fattens "now" – except for its immediate surrounds – are not experiences but memories and anticipations, and their proxies in our discourse, reaches to the heart of the human present tense. A fat present is no more an objective or extended time interval than it is an instant. A series of frozen stretches of time such as days would be as little able to constitute a present tense than could a series of mathematical points. And (to anticipate the arguments of Chapter 12) the present is the arena of our freedom precisely because it is offset from the physical world – which latter at any moment is identical with itself.

The failure to appreciate this is relevant to the erasure of the observer in physical theory that we discussed in §3.5.3. The quasi-observer in physical theory is located at a space–time point, or a set of space–time points, like any physical object. That is how he/she (really "it") is ripe to be reduced to a datum on a clock. The "observer", wobbles confusedly between being a physical location (defined by coordinates), an inertial frame of reference, a recording device such as a clock, a reading from the device, and a conscious individual who reads and makes sense and use of the reading, and relates it to other readings. But the "now" that is missing – missing because a true observer is absent in relativity – is not merely an inadmissible privileged foliation, an infinitely thin temporal cut through the three-dimensions of the manifold. "Now" is the (irreducibly) fattened now that human beings occupy. In the absence of such "nows" there are no observers; indeed, no translation of the state of a particular object into a state of a recording device and this into a reading on a clock taking place *at* a particular time, related not only to the temporal coordinates of local reality but also to the life of the individual making use of the readings to serve a particular goal that, in turn, belongs to the nested goals of a lived life. And, equally, in the absence of such a (real) observer, there is no "now".

The passage from Gödel cited earlier that "reality consists of an infinity of layers of 'now' which come into existence successively" raises at least two further issues that we have not addressed in this section. The first is the difficult notion of the passage of time as being, or being the result of, a succession of "nows" – which is associated with the dubious notion that "nows" are transient in the way that events are. The second is the even more questionable notion that "nows" can themselves be in a temporal relation to one another (as opposed, for example, being a locus where temporal relations are established). And the third is most difficult of all. Gödel claims that reality consists of piled up "nows" which suggests that they are not merely elements of time but *times* – presumably with their full freight of events. These issues are not directly relevant to our present concern with the present, and with tensed time. Some we have discussed already (see, for example Chapter 2 for the idea of "passage") and some we shall return to in Chapter 10 when we try to get a perspicuous view of time itself.

6.1.2.1 Further notes on "at time t"

In §4.5, we discussed the implicit "at" in telling the time. I want to extend that discussion to connect it with the notion of "now" which has "at" built into it.

"At time t" is not the same as t. There is no "*at* time t" in the physical world – in time t physically construed. "At" requires that time is made explicit to and for someone. "At t_2" is the experienced moment opened beyond itself to refer back to past t_1 and forward to the future t_3. This being unconfined to a point in time is a characteristic not only of tensed time but is also implicit within the B-series, earlier-and-later time. Unless being "at t_2" in some sense spilled out of t_2, t_2 would not be connected with t_1, as its explicit predecessor, or t_3 as a successor separated from t_1 by the interval $t_3 - t_1$. The relationship between successive moments is a reaching across, and an affirmation of, the separateness and togetherness of the relata and is not inherent in either of them.

In short, being *at* (the moment) is not precisely being "in" in the sense of being confined to, identical with it. Event E is at time t_1 according to an observer but time t_1 is not *at* time t_1. To take a spatial analogy: the earth is within in the solar system as per our way of organizing things but it is not in or at itself. This is not just a matter of avoiding a tautology. To say that spatial point 2, 3, 4 is at 2, 3, 4 is unacceptable not because it is, as it appears, a tautology. It is because it suggests incorrectly that those points have a location that is built into the numbers rather than being localised by other things to which they are related.

"*At* t_1," emerges when an I (ego) is connected with explicit time. It is this that gives the instant t_1 (which is constitutionally featureless) a place, a relation, a name. (An I is joined with other Is to make the collaborative venture of clock and calendar time.) The I at any given time t_1 is not the same as the instant of the material world which can be mathematically characterized without remainder.

That is why there is no direct conflict between the logic of times and the psychology of "at" (a) time. Logic demands only that any $t_1 = t_1$ and that t_1 should be confined to t_1. However, t_1 confined to t_1 does not deliver *at* t_1 of itself. Consequently (tauto-) logic as a constraint does not get traction on psychology. Logic dictates that the present should be inescapable; psychology opens the present moment beyond its mathematically defined confines.

This is reflected in the sense that we live, not in a succession of instants that do not amount even to a succession, but in a world of change, of which we are an inseparable part. Consequently, we are not confined to where we are either spatially or temporally as objectively defined: we are always en route. Action, feelings, and emotions are always off and away; "ongoingness" is all-pervasive. The logic that would seem to dictate that the present is inescapable and temporally unextended does not take account of the fact that we are never entirely *in* a moment and our timetabled lives take us further from this. At best, the spatial-temporal moment provides us with an implicit centre of our unfolding world.

If we were entirely in, as opposed to *at* times, the moments of our lives would be void of meaning. The logical now, whose purest expression is the mathematical instant, cannot accommodate meaning, and could not be inhabited, even less lived. We can no more confine ourselves to the moment than Achilles in Zeno's paradox can move from unextended spatial point to spatial point. We can no more help overflowing temporally than we can help overflowing spatially. "At" overflows the moment.

It is through "at" that the moment is explicitly shared. "At 4:30 p.m." belongs to a community of minds that can stand even further outside of time than any notionally monadic individual. This sharing, and standing-outside-of-time, has in recent centuries become more explicit as we have become conscious of crossing time zones. You are in Australia and I am in the UK. We speak on the phone and I ask you "What time is it where you are?" I am standing outside of your time frame and, since your different time frame makes me aware of my own temporal location, makes my "at" even more explicit.

The logical now on the one hand and the psychological or existential now on the other are incommensurate. The failure to acknowledge this is the common root of both the apparent elusiveness of the present and the presentist sentiment that says that only what is absolutely "t_1-now" is absolutely real.

We have already seen how the fattening of "now" is in part connected with the intrinsic fatness of here, as evinced in the broad field of the conscious moment. It is time to look more directly at here and, more specifically, at the various ways in which "here" is different from its inseparable partner, its fellow indexical.

6.1.3 Here and now

In §5.1, we discussed the conversation between Carnap and Einstein in which the latter regretted the fact that "now" lay beyond the reach of physical science. Several thinkers agree with Carnap's refusal to share Einstein's regret. Consider this from Steven Savitt: "Physics is not felt to be incomplete because it fails to treat hereness. Why should its indifference to nowness be of any greater concern?"[25] The implicit assumption is that "here" and "now" are comparable at the relevant level. They are, of course, closely allied – indeed inseparable: any creature capable of being "now", that is to say experiencing the present, is also "here". "Here" is where I (or anyone) am (is) now. These indexical dimensions of ordinary experience, though they stand at the beginning of a long cognitive journey which ends with space and time losing their separate identity, are clearly distinct. They are not conjoined in the way that, per modern physics, space and time are conjoined as inseparable aspects of a space–time that subsumes them both so that the same space–time intervals can be measured as space-like or time-like separations. There is no translation of "here" into "now" or vice versa.

This notwithstanding, philosophers who want to demystify and eventually abolish tense, claim that "here" and "now" are comparable at every level and, given the unreality of spatial tenses, argue that temporal tenses are also unreal. The feeling that there is a special A-series fact associated with the assertion that "12 noon 12 December 2012 is 'now'" in addition to the B-fact that "It is 12 noon 12 December 2012" is, they argue, ill-founded because we don't feel that there is a special fact (a spatial A-fact) that supplements "I am in Cambridge" or "This is Cambridge" with "Cambridge is here". We do not conclude, from the fact that "Cambridge is here" is true only when the speaker who is uttering it is in Cambridge, that there is something special or irreducible about "here". Nor do we conclude from the contrast of "here" with "not here" or with "there" that there are (tensed) spatial facts additional to "tenseless" spatial relations such as "Cambridge is 50 miles from London", any more than we conclude, from the fact that Manchester is north of Cambridge, that "being north" or "northness" is a property of Manchester. If it were, Manchester would have to house an indefinite number of other properties, some such as being South (of e.g. Glasgow), which would be at odds with properties such as being North. In short Manchester, or any other place, would be the site of the kinds of contradictions McTaggart thought he had identified in A-series temporal facts. Cambridge's being here is no more a property of that town, or a fact about it, than its being "50 miles away" from London or "100 miles away" from Birmingham.

On this basis, it could be argued that "now" and "here" both disappear in grown-up discourse. What's more, loss of such indexicals does not await the advent of sophisticated science generating more truthful pictures of the world. They are both threatened by the transition from experience, which is indexed to the body of the experiencer, to knowledge which is not. Perceptions are local while facts are delocalised. There is a "now" of experience but not of knowledge (though knowledge may retain a grip on "now" when we establish that "it is now 12 o'clock"). It is not science, then, but the broader cognitive development from perception to factual knowledge that marginalizes "now" (and of course "here").

In view of this, and other considerations, and in the interest of keeping time separate from space, it is worth examining the ways in which "now" is profoundly different from "here" so that, for example, we cannot conclude from the tenselessness of space that "real" time, too, is tenseless.

The first and most important is that we *choose* the here we occupy but not the "now" we are "at". (Though I can choose by knocking myself out to miss out on having any now at all.) I can make "here" be Cambridge or London simply by travelling to those places. Indeed, this is something we are doing all the time. Our now, by contrast, is not something we have any control over. It might be argued that, by choosing our location, we also choose the frame of reference which will determine what events count as being present or falling within the curtilage of "now", defining its contents. But we do not do that deliberately, except insofar as we act on what is in our literal vicinity, and create events that will contribute to the "now". This will be only a small proportion of the events that belong to "now".

The difference is reflected in the difference between travelling and mere movement, which is evident in the case of space and not in time. There is a difference between walking towards something and something moving towards you. There is no comparable difference in the case of time, as we discussed when we rejected the notion of time travel. Space travelling is something we do all the time, whereas time travelling is impossible. That is why, of course, our "now" is inescapably shared with some others, whereas our "here" (with some qualifications) is our own. We usually say "*It is* now 12 noon on 12 December 2012" but "*I am* in such and such a place". You and I must occupy the same now but we cannot occupy (precisely) the same here: we cannot stand in entirely the same place. The "now" is had in common and it is compulsory, unchosen; the here is private and (under most circumstances) freely chosen.

There are, of course, ways of construing "here" which will permit it to be something that is shared. A sufficiently blobby "here" can accommodate more than one person. You and I can both sign a postcard to a third party saying that we are "here in Cambridge" and that are wishing that "you" (too) "were here". But within any given here, there will be a "here" (where I am) and a "there" (where you are). To a third party at some relatively distant place (many body lengths away) we are in the same "here" contrasted with a bigger there. But to each other, I am here and you are there. We do not have to go down to a notional spatial point to find a mutual exclusion that cannot be overcome. Indeed, "here" is intrinsically spread out and does not require "fattening" as "now" does. This is because the spatial sense is constitutionally extended. No-one is inclined to think of "here" as in reality an infinitesimal point corresponding to, for example, the location of the centre of gravity of my body or my existential or egocentric perceptual centre – say somewhere behind my eyes.

The criteria are not that strict: here can be scaled up or down. "Here" can be right next to me, this room, this house, this street, this town, this country, this continent, or this planet. All it requires is the relevant contrasting "there": just over there, or in that room, that house, that street, that town, that country, that continent, or that planet. We may be "here" in Europe when you are "there" in USA. We can speak of the human race being "here" on earth. And the boundaries between here and there are soft and flexible. I can say, "Come and stand here next to me". "Here" is not merely indexed to a mind or a sensorium but may be indexed to a group and its scale is relative to the interests of the person or group of persons using it.

But when the chips are down, I will say that I am here and you are there and you will affirm with equal vigour and validity that, on the contrary, I am there and you are here. To put this another way: my "heremost" location and your "heremost" location are necessarily different. You and I may be able to occupy what, according to a third party, is the same "here" but the *centre* of that here – the heremost – will be different for the two of us.

This is connected with the sense that "here" is explicitly private to, or centred on, me whereas "now" manifestly is not. Now is shared or communal. The difference is reflected in the different relationship here and now have to objective (geographical or mathematical) locations. I may recognize where I am now (a pub in Didsbury as it happens) but this does not necessarily locate me in the larger scheme of things. I may be quite unaware that I am 5 miles from the centre of Manchester or 200 miles from London. By contrast, if I know that it is 5 p.m., I know definitely that it is 2 hours from 7 p.m., 2 days from 7 p.m. on the day after tomorrow, and so on. These are trivial additional facts (though as in the case of the answer to the question addressed to an oncologist "How long have I got?", this may not be trivial in practice) but there are no comparable ones in relation to "here". I require additional empirical knowledge to conclude from the fact that I am in a pub in Didsbury that I am 5 miles from the centre of Manchester. The translation of "here" into "the Gateway pub in Didsbury" requires a different kind of knowledge than is required for the translation of "now" into "5 p.m. 9 September 2013". I can see that I am in the Gateway pub if it is my regular haunt but I cannot see that it is "5 p.m. 9 September 2013". I may infer the time of day from the appearance of the sunlight but not the day, month, and year without the help of a clock and an up-to-date calendar. In the case of "here", I get the first step free – "Here is the Gateway tavern" – but subsequent steps that locate "here" geographically or mathematically are not available just on the basis of looking around. In the case of "now", I cannot get the first step free just by looking round, but once this step is taken, then the location in the clock or calendrical grid of time is given. This illuminates the difference between the personal and informal "here" on the one hand and, on the other, the "now" which, though indexical, is not private to me. To iterate: We say "*I am* here" but "*It is* now". A particular "now", having been translated into a particular clock-time is assimilated into the objective system of time, without remainder. "Heres" are not dissolved entirely into objective space because there are many overlapping, private heres – endless incongruities and duplications – that do not correspond to a particular patch of space. To look at the clock, to find out what "now" is, is to link one's present moment with a temporal order that extends from the beginning to the end of the universe.

We really do "tell the time". We do not "tell the space" in the same way. This contrast between "now" which is linked by a clock to the whole of time and "here" which is not connected by a recognition of where I am to the whole of space (except as the negative of the negative "not-here") is the other side of the fact that "here" is to some degree a private, often elective space centred on a point unique to each person at each time while "now" is (manifestly at least) had in common and assigned to us without our say-so.

The fact that "now" is common, public through and through – such that any member of a group experiencing, or having access to, the same token events will share the same now – while "here" has a private core, underlines how the perspective that goes into making "now" (and "the past" and the "the future") is not evidence of their unreality, even though relativity would allow reality only to a point-like "here-now" of Minkowski space–time. "Here" by contrast really is a matter purely of (ultimately) individual perspective. That is why the failure of physical science to capture "now", and tense in general, is a serious deficiency in the way that its failure to capture egocentric terms such as "here" and "there" and the contrast between them is not.

Another difference between "here" and "now" relates to their borders. First, now does not have a border. Everything that we are directly aware of happening – though not events accessed through the mediation of reports – is happening now. By contrast, not everything is happening here: some things are happening over there and other things we are aware of happening are just beyond our sensory field. The privileged status of "now" is validated by "now" being had in common, while "here" does not designate a privileged patch in space. We can watch objects moving out of here to over there and, although there maybe no visible boundary between here and there (and here-there and elsewhere) the contrast exists. Although here has a present border, it has only one such border – a border shared with the "there" that encloses it. "Now" has no explicit border (everything that is happening is happening now) but two contrasts: with (a) the no-longer and (b) the not-yet. It is tempting to think of "here" as facing in many different directions: we can travel north, south, up, down, etc. into "there". But these are all part of a homogeneous "not-here", an outside to its inside. At any rate, there is nothing in space corresponding to the difference between the border with the past and the border with the future. This would become apparent if space were one-dimensional – "Lineland" – and its inhabitants divided the world into backwards and forwards.

Given these profound disanalogies between "here" and "now" – derived from the disanalogies between space and time discussed in §2.2 – we should reject the argument that, because there are no spatial tenses, or additional A-facts involving "here", there are no real tenses in time or additional A-facts involving "now".

There is, however, something more interesting about the pairing of this odd couple; namely the way "now" is supported, as we discussed in the previous section, by the spread of "here" in keeping open the intervals that exceed the mathematical instant or in making sure that the present is not merely a succession of non-extended moments. In the spatio-temporally spread here-now, events and processes at differ-ent stages of their unfolding co-exist: beginnings and middles, and endings are side by side. As is true with any sensory field, there is an explicit multiplicity gathered up as part of the moment of consciousness. Those happenings that are side by side are at once together and separated, one and many. Thus a temporal depth can be experi-enced in the notionally depthless "moments" of consciousness. This depth is further deepened by the fact that the "heremost" centre of here – the subject aware of herself as bodily present, as remembering, and as thinking – is incorporated into the unified multiplicity that is the field of the conscious moment. "Here", in short, underwrites in many ways the depth of the present moment. Spatial and temporal smearing – so scandalous in quantum mechanics – are the very stuff of "ordinary" consciousness.

The constrast between here and now, which highlights the specific irreducibility of now, is a powerful argument for the reality of tensed time against the detensers. While it is possible to manipulate our sense of what is happening "now" and which events are and are not simultaneous (as discussed by Callender[26]), so that our "now" is to some extent mind-dependent, this does not make it a mere coinage of our psy-chology. There is still a real difference between something happening (as experienced directly or via a signal) and something that has already happened. This is shared in all our modes of being-together (most obviously attending to each other or sharing attention to something out there). The idea that "the common now" is an illusion to which nothing truly corresponds, made necessary by the need to act in a timely fash-ion, to ensure survival, is self-contradictory, as we have already discussed. The very notion of the "timely" is inseparable from that of "now". The need to act in a timely fashion is the need to act now – a now shared by a leaping tiger, a low-hanging fruit, and the person who must respond to the threats and opportunities they represent.

6.2 THE PRESENT

6.2.1 What is present in the present?

While the notion of a sharp or even clear distinction between the temporal container and its contents should be looked upon with suspicion, we have to acknowledge that "now" and "the present" appear to be conceptually hybrid, combining a particular time (for example 12 noon on 12 December 2012 or "today") with all that is happen-ing or is present at that time. I want therefore to switch the focus from the present, as a portion of time, to what it is that is present in the present; what it is that is before or around us. Examining what is present in the present will help us to understand the seemingly enigmatic nature of the present as something that is neither a mathemat-ical instant nor a physical interval of time.

The contents of the present most naturally fall into things that are happening and things that simply are; between, on the one hand, events and processes that are unfolding and, on the other, (material, concrete) background objects whose unfolding is not evident so that they seem like something *in which* events or processes can take place or *to which* events can happen. Somewhere between events and processes are *states of affairs* which can be characterized as arrays (ensembles, clusters, groups) of objects caught up in, or the substrate of, events and processes. For some philosophers, such as J. J. C. Smart, states of affairs are the primary givens, the basic stuff of the world around us. This is an attractive choice because it seems somewhat artificial to separate events and processes from that in which they are happening or to lift out one set of events and processes from the others that constitute a field of activity. It makes sense, for example, to think of the river-flowing-between-its-banks or the traffic-filing-up-the-road, plus the context of those processes (consisting of other processes taking place in other objects), as inseparably together in what is immediately before us. Even objects that are doing nothing are still parts of states of affairs – for example, "being over there", "in the light", "casting a shadow", and so on. And "the state of affairs" seems to combine, unite, even fuse, the stasis of objects (which seem too inert) in the term "state" with the dynamism of events (which seem too lightweight and slippery to count as real stuff) in the term "affairs".

However, the idea of that which is present as a state of affairs, hints at a sense of the presence of the present as a state of being surrounded by items that are temporally confined to a present instant and this is close to a static notion of time and of the world. We tend to focus on the "states" (which are as it were what-is, viewed under the aspect of constancy, as if they have come to a halt) rather than "affairs" which are ongoing. The idea of the universe as a series of states of affairs suggests something close to the idea, challenged by Bergson, of a cinematic world where smoothness and continuity is an illusion created by the rapid transition from one discrete state to another. This seems to zap the buzz of change and freeze the universe into successive frames.

For this, and other reasons, it seems more true to experienced reality to subject happenings and that to, or in which, they happen to separate scrutiny; to set apart our inspections of events and processes on the one hand from our inquiry into objects on the other. This is what I shall do here.

6.2.1.1 Events and processes

The present is abuzz with events and processes. The distinction between events and processes is not intrinsic to either but to the temporal viewpoint from which happenings are examined. They are both changes, both kinds of "becomings". An event is a change that is conceived or imagined as a completed whole, as having happened: it is seen from without in a glance that encompasses its beginning, middle and end. A process is a change seen as if, or while, it is happening: it is envisaged from within its course. Processes are ongoing; events are "on-gone", done and dusted.[27] The passage of the car from A to B can be captured as a process that is happening or as an event that has happened, as a travelling or as a journey from A to B viewed from outside. The flight of the bumble bee is a (completed) event; the bumble bee flying is an (ongoing) process. The Norman Conquest was a process as it was unfolding. Subsequently it was an event – or an occurrent – that historians look back on.[28]

The difference between events and processes is reflected in the grammar of the difference between "-ing" and "-ed". Of course, the inside view corresponding to a process-description is artificial; at the very least, it has a temporal squint. If I say "The car is presently moving from A to B", I have encompassed both ends of the change (original location at A and anticipated location at B) in my description of the process and am not therefore truly looking at it from within. *Any* description of a change, typically a noun phrase, spans its entirety; and treating it as a process can consequently be as valedictory as treating it as an event.[29]

Something deeper is reflected here: namely how the description of any change freezes it, though there is a tension between the static noun phrase that says what the change is and the dynamism of the verb that says the change is happening. It relates to the fact that the present, the *nowness* of what is happening now, is descriptively as well as in other ways elusive – something to which we shall return in §6.2.2. We can speak only of the done and dusted, though we may speak of it as (in the process of) being done and as not yet dusted. Processes, just as much as events, are lifted out of the flow of the world, separated from a material substrate, by being cut out with perceptual or, more often, verbal scissors, in accordance with our interests and our judgement of saliency.[30] Even where present participles are deployed, the dynamic reality of the world is only partially restored by the succession of sentences linked by "and" and "and then".

The focus on events and processes reflects our feeling that the present is "what is (now) going on". What is now going on is fully grasped only when it has happened and is no longer ongoing but is "on-gone". This accounts for the tension between the idea of the present as an immediate (depthless) now and the experience of the present as something, which – if only for the fact that it is intelligible – has depth; that it reaches beyond a notional immediate moment to an indefinite past and future. That to say what *is happening* is actually to mark what has happened, makes identification of events and processes "valedictory". Events have come (fully) into being only when they have occurred, when they are complete, when they have been complete*d* (note the slither, with the "d" drawing a line round the event). In order to be, an event has to have ceased happening; it has to *have been*: its being is in something that has ceased be-ing – something that will be relevant when we consider the status of "future" events in §8.2.2.2. In its wholeness – or conceived as a whole – it is envisaged from a standpoint in which it is finished. Event E which lasts from t_1 to t_2 is not Event E until t_2 when it is over. The being of an event is separate from its occurr*ing* but not from its occurr*ence*, viewed tenselessly.

The fact that every completed event is past is evident when it is picked out: named, it is tucked up in the archive. In this sense, "the letter killeth" though it also curates the posthumous existence of the event in the aspic of a description. Once an event has come into being, we cannot as it were pedal backwards and reinsert the dynamism of a change that is now complete and has ceased. The completed, named event may even seem like a pseudo-object because it has the stasis that is the defining characteristic of an object. Its unchanging posthumous life continues unbroken which makes it seem like a continuant.

This is why events seem both indubitably real and ontologically questionable, having a dependent or even parasitic existence.[31] A perfectly respectable event such as "the rising of the sun" seems as ghostly as the Cheshire cat's smile when it is separated from its material substrate and pickled as the referent of a noun phrase. It can seem less real than an ongoing process, which at least is present, but paradoxically more solid than the latter which seems elusive because (still) unfolding – like smoke. The being of an event is distinct from its occurring (where it is always on-the-way-to-being); and yet it does not have an existence additional to its becoming, so that it would be as spatially and temporally distinct from the latter as another event would be.

The occurrence of an event – its passing from not-yet to no-longer, from start to completion – should not be thought of as a second-order or "meta-event". Likewise, we should not regard a change as itself changing. As a car moves down the road, there is not a second-order change – namely the unfolding, or the completion of, its movement down the road. Second-order changes – changes in changes – are permitted only when we reduce change to pure quantities. This permits the idea of "rate of change" to emerge. In the notion of acceleration, for example, we see a second-order change in first-order change (measured by velocity). This is not, however, movement on the move.

A key element in ascribing depth to the present is the fact that "now" is spatially spread and perceptually multimodal (hearing plus vision, etc.) so that at any given time there are multitudes of events (and processes) that are "ongoings", in different stages of development, connected and disconnected, hooked up or merely co-occurring. For this reason, the overall scene has the sense of being temporally extended. We may think of now as a loosely co-occurring set of relationships between an event (or a group of salient events) and a background of other less salient events. This relationship is replicated in a single event viewed from within as an ongoing process, with the present stage of the event being viewed against the background of its remembered beginning and its anticipated end. Here we encounter the temporal squint again, in which the whole is viewed from a part that is also viewed as part of the whole. This is the most basic level at which the present is experienced as present, past and future.

While events may acquire the status of pseudo-objects, they can do so only at the cost of being past. There is, however, another aspect of the present which makes it less smoke-like: the presence of that which is relatively unchanging; the substrate of change, undissolved in the flux of events. I am referring to "objects" or "material objects".

6.2.1.2 Objects

The relationship between the present and (stable) objects seems at first straightforward. The present is manifest in that which is present and that which is most robustly present before us are the kinds of things we can bark our shins against and which do not, like events, evanesce or, worse, achieve full being only at the point at which they enter the past. Events cease to be (or, at least, cease "be-ing") as soon as they are fully built – that is to say complete – the opposite of objects which begin once they are built. And, unlike even the most compelling hallucination, objects are publicly available, able to be accessed through a multitude of senses and from many different angles, by all and everyone. The presence of objects, therefore, seems to be the very presence of the present. Since they are by definition persisting, material objects are the explicit manifestation of duration; and of time as a seamless continuum. They are the ongoing background to goings on; the unchanging substrate of change.

"Change", as Mellor says, "needs identity as well as difference".[32] And this makes the relationship between objects and events on the one hand and events and processes on the other seem like one of codependency. Indeed, Davidson argued for a "symmetry of conceptual dependence" between objects and events: events happen in or to objects and objects are necessary to individuate events.[33] Objects don't have to be absolutely unchanging, of course; they simply have to be *relatively* unchanging, so that sufficient of them survives from the beginning to the end of the period during which change is observed. It is enough that changes within objects are more sluggish or less prominent than in the events around them.

The boundary between occurrent events or processes on the one hand and continuant objects on the other is not intrinsic to the material world. Indeed, we may think of an object as an inspissated, localised process whose unfolding might be revealed by time lapse photography. A glacier for example may be seen either as a process or as an object, depending on the patience of the observer. And an object may be given over entirely to a process, as when a block of ice melts.

Changes may affect an object's external relations (as when it moves from one place to another) or its actual properties (as when it is painted a different colour, or gets damaged). By definition, objects will survive all changes in external relations but it is a matter of decision as to how profound internal changes have to be before the object ceases to count as the same object. Whether O is still to all intents and purposes O after it has been changed will depend on what intents and purposes are relevant to assigning its identity to it.

Even so, there is a solid residue in the distinction between objects and events. It is highlighted by a quasi-logical point. It is possible for me to encounter the same object – say a table – at two different times. If, however, I heard two type-identical explosions, one at 12 noon and the other at 12:05, they would be different events, not two encounters with the same event. An event has a beginning and an end and once it has ended, it is not available for a further meeting. (We noted this in our critique of time travel §2.4.3) What is more, an object can out-last major changes. I look at a chair at 12 noon. You then smash it. I return at 12:15 and ask "Where is the chair?" and you point to a heap of wood on the floor. The chair, in short, may have an emeritus state that is not permitted to an event.

Things are not, however, entirely straightforward. According to those who subscribe to "endurantism", an object is wholly present at each moment of its existence, enduring in its entirety through time. But what does this mean? Clearly an object cannot have its whole history present at any one time. At time t_1, the subsequent history of O – what states it will be in after t_1 – is not yet determined. That is why some philosophers – those who subscribe to perdurantism – have argued that what is present before us at any given time is only a time-slice of the object O: what we see at time t_1 is O-at-time-t_1. Objects persist through time by having different temporal parts at different times.

Russell was an early advocate of the time-slice perdurantist view:

> Each of these [items such as tables and chairs] is to be regarded, not as one single persistent entity, but a series of entities succeeding each other in time, for a very brief period, though probably not for a mere mathematical instant. A body which fills a cubic foot will be admitted to consist of many smaller bodies, each occupying only a very tiny volume; similarly, a thing which persists for an hour is to be regarded as composed of many things of less duration. A true theory of matter requires a division of things into time-corpuscles as well as into space-corpuscles.[34]

This raises many difficulties. If the components are (notionally) sliced, in virtue of what are they also connected with each other? How do the slices join up to make a history? By what criterion do they count as having been cut from the same loaf? We could not speak of O-at-t_1, O-at-t_2, etc. without presupposing the notion of a persisting O which is available to be present at t_1, t_2, etc. And what is the limit to the slicing process? Why does it stop before the mathematical instant – as Russell requires – or the quantum limit?

Perdurantism has consequently been strongly opposed. Mellor, for example, asserts that "Things, unlike events, *are* wholly present at every moment within their B-times … No-one would say that only part of Sir Edmund Hilary and Tensing climbed only a part of Everest in 1953."[35]

The problematic status of objects is compounded by what Mellor means by "wholly present", which is that objects do not have temporal parts – in contrast with events, which do. An event such as a meal has a beginning (first course), a middle (*entrée*) and an end (dessert); whereas a cricket ball does not. It is because they are *not* merely temporal parts that objects can change. If they were a succession of time-slices, they would not be able to change because there would be no enduring thing to be the seat of change, a place where change could get a foothold. We could, however, construe the stability of objects as merely definitional: an object is an item that is considered as corresponding to an unchanging label over a period of time, though this unchanging label permits change within certain ill-defined bounds. And an event, when viewed as a whole, will be seen to be finished and hence unchangeable. The meal encompasses its beginning and middle and end and thereby becomes an item that is the sum of its phases. Even so, there remains a problem with considering objects as not having temporal parts and as being "wholly present" at any given moment which seems to justify our seeing objects as being presented to us as time-slices.

We may summarize the problems as follows: "wholly present" endurantism does not seem to allow for change against the background of stability; and the time-slice perdurantism does not seem to allow for the necessary stability against which, or within which, change can take place. We can evade, or perhaps more charitably, dissolve these problems by arguing that each theory simple captures different aspects of a material world in which change and stability are both real and, like events and objects, are codependent.

Objects have histories and phases that may be as distinct as those of an event such as a meal. Consider a tree. It starts out as a sapling, grows to full height, ages and eventually falls and rots on the ground. It might be argued that the example is invalid because each phase corresponds, not to a different period in the history of one object, but to a different object: sapling, adult tree, tree corpse. The terms underpin an objective periodization that goes beyond time-slices. The fact that there is no sharp point at which the sapling becomes the adult and the adult becomes a dead tree does not, however, alter the fact that it is possible without stretching things to see the tree as a succession of objects, corresponding to a succession of labels. We could, however, argue just as plausibly that what we call a tree is actually a *process* that has several temporal stages beginning with the sapling and ending with the rotting log. This, however, is a rather expensive let-out because all objects could be seen to be processes in this way. We could lose the distinction between processes or events on the one hand and objects on the other that is necessary for change to be evident. The world would deliquesce into a Heraclitean flow in which even pebbles would be part of the bonfire of change, though on a low flame.

We could approach our example in a different way. Suppose we confine ourselves to the adult tree, defined by whatever criteria we choose. It will have a history, being the site of a sequence of events every year. We cannot plausibly argue that the tree-in-winter, the tree-in-spring, the tree-in-summer and the tree-in-autumn are different objects: they are the same object passing through different phases in its history. Clearly, the leaved and leafless tree are not both wholly present all the time. So it makes sense to think of them as time-slices of the same (adult) object.

Let us regroup and look a bit closer at the notion of the history of an object. All objects have a beginning, a middle and an end: the glass just blown by the glassmaker; the glass in use; the glass falling to the ground en route to being smashed. So we can see that they do indeed have temporal stages – notwithstanding that they are not intrinsic to the glass. While the dessert is intrinsically the last phase of the meal, there is nothing in the intrinsic properties of the glass corresponding to being its last day. Do we see or in some other way encounter all of these temporal stages at a particular time so that they are present? Manifestly not. We can *imagine* how the object was (the suit when it was brand new, the person when he was young) or how it will be (the suit when it will be worn beyond repair, the person when he will be old). But this is not the same as it being present (before us) as it was or will be; indeed, we may be entirely mistaken at any given time as to how the object was or will be. So when Mellor asserts that an object is "wholly present" he cannot mean that its entire history is present at any time when it is being experienced. This would require extraordinary powers of hindsight and foresight. Nor could that history be present in the sense of being directly perceived, or at least perceptible, because the various phases of the object would be in conflict. The tree-in-winter and the tree-in-summer could not be co-present since nothing can be simultaneously leafless and leaved. And the same would apply even more obviously to the sapling, full-grown tree and the rotting log.

This point becomes clearer if we do not think of an object as having a history only if it has distinct phases which could reasonably be given different names. Consider O undergoing slow, small-scale, continuous change – the condition of most of the objects around us, indeed of *all* objects other than those undergoing fast, large-scale and sudden change. What do we see when we look at O at any given time t_1? It is obvious that we do not see O-at-time-t_2 at t_1. Or O-at-time-t_1-to-t_n (where t_1 is when O came into being and t_n when it perished) at any time t_1, t_2, t_3, etc. I cannot see the past of the object or the future of the object; or, to discuss this tenselessly, the object before or after the time I am looking at it. So the whole that is present is not the four-dimensional object, the spatio-temporal sum that is the object with its history.

Clearly, then, an object's being "wholly present" at any given time cannot require the presence of its entire history at every moment of its history. Even so, we should acknowledge that objects, in virtue of presenting themselves *as objects*, are imbued with a certain (implicit) temporal depth. This chair before me is present as something enduring: as something that has not just come into existence as I experience it now; nor as something that will cease to exist in the next instant. Sitting on it reassures me of its solidity and hence of its durability and indeed of its *reality*: I can therefore see it as an item that extends beyond the present moment, though I cannot see its future and past moments. And some objects as it were carry their past and future on their sleeve, in particular the past. The mossy stone, the battered suitcase, and the face with its cheek that is "the map of days outworn" tell of their past. The sapling and the baby's face speak of a future, though this is not the same as revealing the singular past that the actual objects have undergone or the singular future they may have. Crucially, an encounter with an enduring, stable object is the revelation of the presence in the present of something that transcends the present.

6.2.1.3 Challenging the boundary

The problem that has spawned rival schools of perdurantists and endurantists may be entirely unnecessary. When I see an object, I see a bounded, occupied area of space from the standpoint of its stability. When I see a process, I see a bounded, occupied area of space from the standpoint of change. I do not have to see the entirety of the history of an object for it to be present to me as a whole, only sufficient of it to be sure that it will have, and has had, a stable history. We may go further and break down the difference between events (that are changes that do have temporal stages) and objects (that are unchanging and do not, according to some, have temporal stages), by nibbling at the distinction between objects that (enduringly) are and events that (transiently) happen. Some of the fuzzy borderland between the two is occupied by the idea of a process. We could think of an object as a localised process unfolding at an imperceptible speed and an event as a process that we see as a whole because it is so rapid that it is completed when we take it in and we have no time to be inside of it.

There is no definite rate of change at which we are obliged to say that an item is no longer an event but a process and no longer a process but an object. A typical inhabitant of the borderland between object and process would be a glacier. Another would be a flickering flame which is captured in a noun-phrase denoting an object and yet is clearly a process: it is the same from one point of view and not the same from another. A third example would be a melting snowflake. Here, the boundary between object and process is particularly deeply compromised: the object does not survive the process — so it looks like a process without an object to define its substrate. On the other hand, the process has the same boundaries as the object and occupies all of it — so the process looks like the history of the object, artificially separated from it.

These examples illustrate that there is no unchallengeable rule for allocating items to the categories of objects or events. Where you draw the line depends on whether your inclinations are Parmenidean — where the emphasis is on stasis — or Heraclitean — where the emphasis is on *dynamis*. Any given item can be made to look event-like ("the snow is falling" is something that befalls the snow) or almost object-like ("the fall of the snow" seems as firm as snow — in some sense firmer as the falling, unlike the snow, does not melt) according to the choice of description. At any rate, the difference between an object that is "wholly present" at any given moment or an event that exists in a series of mutually exclusive temporal stages is not based on a hard and fast distinction rooted in the items themselves. If objects are stable and wholly present and events are transient and present only in parts this is a matter of viewpoint and *definition*.

We can see this when we think of people and their lives. A human body is an object, though it is always evolving. But a person is, in some sense, a process with temporal stages: childhood, boyhood, youth, etc. This bears directly on Mellor's example. While it might seem odd to say that Hilary climbed only a time-slice of Everest (though it is not entirely odd — we could imagine Everest being changed out of all recognition over centuries and say that "This is not the Everest that Hilary climbed"), it doesn't seem in the slightest bit odd to say that the mountain was climbed by Hilary in a particular stage of his life. For example, the mountain was not climbed by baby Hilary, nor was it climbed by the septuagenarian Hilary. Admittedly, the septuagenarian Hilary could still take credit for the climb achieved by his younger self and bask in continuing well-earned glory but baby Hilary could not. So "wholly present" seems to over-state what is the case. Let us suppose that Hilary lost his leg at the age of 40, we could not consistently say that Hilary's body is wholly present at 39 and at 41 because that which is present at the two times differs by a leg. And this is true, even if Hilary does not undergo major alterations or even more subtle ones such as those that are undergone by all individuals as they grow older, acquiring or losing memories, skills and responsibilities.

There is, however, a non-trivial difference between items considered as objects and items considered as events regarding their temporal phases. Consider on the one hand a suitcase considered as an object and on the other a meal considered as an event. I could not tease apart (except verbally) the temporal stages of the suitcase in the way that I can separate the temporal stages of the meal. Whatever happens to the suitcase, the stages all adhere together. The stages of the meal, however, can be separated in time and in space: the soup course can be had on one day in one room and the dessert on another day in another room. This illustrates something essential to items considered as events: that they are inseparable from their history because they *are* their history. An object, however, is a bearer of its history in two respects: it is changed by its history; and its history can be correctly ascribed to it by someone who has observed it. This is true, even though it will be a matter of definition as to when that history begins and when it ends such that it is transferred to another object or none. The object that is present at t_1 is the bearer of all the things that have or can happen to it, including that essential part of its history which is the range of uses to which it has been put, but it does not mean, even less does it require, that all this should be present at one time in its history.

So the bearer of the history (the object) is to be distinguished from the actual history; just as the moment at which I see the object is to be distinguished from the series of moments that is its existence. As a bearer of its history, O is *at* t_1, *at* t_2 and so on. Its continuation over time is not to be confused with the succession of *events* that is its history, or indeed with any succession of *events*, or even with its history described as a succession of states. To say this is not merely to iterate that we see before us as an *object* is the (relatively) unchanging location or bearer of changes (and of stability, though stability actual conceals dynamic equilibrium at a level below that of direct observation). It is to underline that, when an object such as a plate is repeatedly dirtied and cleaned, the history is not part of it precisely insofar as the plate is considered *as* something that is dirtied and cleaned. The history is something that happens to it, not the it to which the history happens. To be able to see this lies at the heart of our sense of that which is there before us.

Notwithstanding the continuous, gradual, but usually imperceptible changes in any object, there is a presumption of practical stasis. When I look at a chair across the table, I look at something that transcends the present, indeed, it transcends my present experience of it. I intuit in it properties that are not currently revealed to me, properties I could uncover in many different ways – by looking round the back of it, grasping it, testing its weight, its tensile strength and so on. This intuition of future possible experiences is intimately connected with my intuition that the object continues to exist independently of my awareness of it (so that I can lose it and look for it). Its "in-itself" existence also corresponds to its transcendence of the *moment* or *moments* of my or anyone's experience of it. I see the present of the object but what I see is not merely its present presence. Any object is steeped in absence, in that which is evidently undisclosed in it; for example, its visibly invisible interior or back. And its past and future, likewise invisible, is no more mysterious or ontologically dubious.

To say this is not to subscribe to the clearly false idea that at any given moment what is wholly present is the sum total of the actual history of the chair to date. This is clearly impossible because the chair might, for example, be in different positions. What is wholly present is the possibility of the chair having the kind of history available to, or suffered by, any chair. An object, in short, is present at any moment as a stable item capable of changes that leave something unchanged. It is this intuition that enables our sense of that which is present to exceed that which is presented. There is, as already noted, a spatial analogy. When I see an object from a particular angle I do not have to see the object from all angles to see that it is more than the object-at-the-angle from which I am seeing it. Likewise, when I see the object in a certain light. The object of my vision at dusk is not merely "barely-discerned-object" but an object (barely discerned). This is the transcendence built into perception which, notwithstanding it is transient, sees stable, enduring objects.

When we think of the furniture of the present, then, irrespective of whether it is events or processes on the one hand or objects on the other, we have a sense of temporal depth. The event/process as ongoing and the object as enduring work together to underwrite the fatness of "now". We need both.

6.2.2 The elusive present

> This hour is mine: if for the next I care,
> I grow too wide,
> And encroach upon death's side.
> George Herbert, "The Discharge", from *The Temple* (1633)

Even without the assistance of confused ideas about the nature of the present, such as the belief that the existential now has somehow to be accommodated in mathematical instants, the present can seem to be no time at all, a mere line between a past that is no longer and a future that is not yet, the virtual hinge between tick and tock. As a mode of persistence, the present seems to some an outrage to logic and common sense.[36] In this section, however, I want to look beyond the crash-dieting of the present that results from confusing experienced with mathematical time and the connected idea that lived now has somehow to flower within the constraints of an infinitely small interval between future and past, to a different kind of problem inherent in the present. Even if we acknowledge that lived moments are necessarily connected with other moments and hence not confined to themselves – indeed, embedded in a temporal landscape which lies beyond anything that could be captured in mathematical points – we are still struck by the elusiveness of the present. It bears upon us in different ways.

There is the direct experience of elusiveness in our apparent inability to *grasp* the now, to realize the promise of the French word *maintenant* and make it something that we can hold (*tenir*) in our hand (*main*). We cannot stand still in one experience because the world in which our experiences are located is hurrying on. Worse than this, even if we are not obliged to move on to the next thing, we cannot keep still because of the intrinsic dynamism of our experiences, captured in the metaphor of "the stream of consciousness". This is evident even when we are actively seeking and controlling experience. We look forward to a meal; and when it arrives, we look forward to the next course; and within each course we look forward to the next forkful; and within each forkful we look forward to each chew. Every pleasure, pastime, and project seems to inhere in being self-propelled to its completion and the satisfaction (and hence extinction) of the appetite or desire or goal that drew us towards it. This is even more likely to be the case if the event in question is framed by a larger narrative or interrupted by other events and other narratives in the hurly burly of ordinary experience. This is of course closely connected with our temporal location never being entirely identical with an objective instant: our being *at* t_1 means that we cannot fully be inside t_1.

The psychological elusiveness of the present could not be abolished without arresting experience, creating a present continuous such that that "-ing" did not become or even progress towards "-ed" and move on from one "-ed" to the next. It is difficult to imagine what lived state would correspond to this. A prolonged but non-extended, non-evolving experience which we are entirely inside would lack meaning which, as its participial form ("mean-*ing*") indicates, is intrinsically unfolding. Equally forlorn is the hope that we might seize the present by focusing on our own awareness, our sensations, if only because such items of consciousness are, when fully formed, already past. There is, however, an important truth in Bergson's assertion that "all sensation is already memory". When we focus on a fully formed experience – particularly to the point of knowing *what* it was – it should already have been had. Our grasping *mains* can serve only to wave goodbye to the moment which has always already passed as soon as we turn our attention to it.

The advocates of mindfulness encourage us to seize the present by focusing on what is presently around us, but the intrinsic dynamism of world seems also to be one in which states of affairs come into being and go out of being and do not remain in being. For an event to be fully present, all of it would have to be present at a (present) moment. It would need to be at once *ongoing* (justifying its status as an *event*) and *on-gone*, so that it is completed, in which case it would be no longer. This is not possible. Any attempt therefore to identify the present with events makes it something which is in a continuous state of evaporation. Unlike objects which begin when they are fully built, events cease to be as soon as they are completed. No wonder, as the poet Rainer Maria Rilke put it, we always

> retain the attitude
> of someone who's departing ...
> we live our lives, for ever taking leave.[37]

We therefore turn to things that are not transient: to stable objects. But it is no use my staring at the chair opposite me as an unchanging something to make present time come to a halt in pure duration. That duration, after all, is itself measured out, and hence registered, in the hectic change around it, like a river round a rock. What is more, by focusing on the stillness of the object, I lose the unfolding world that makes sense of those things in the present that are unchanging – or would, if I were successful in disciplining my attention. Such extreme mindfulness becomes a form of oblivion, a worldlessness. More usually, I, the observer, am in a continuous state of change, focusing on a succession of objects, attaching, losing and reattaching my attention to them, reminding myself why I am doing so, and losing my grip in continuous commentary about what I am doing, or trying to do, or failing to do. The intrinsic dynamism of experience does not abate when we try to withdraw from the flow: it is there in our thoughts, which refuse to stay still; which are always in a state of "thinking" not somehow arrested in completed "thought". Nothing abides any kind of completion: it is simply displaced. The sentences that (so we are told) express a complete thought seem such only when they are written down. And they remain complete only so as long as they are not read – when their dynamism, transience, and elusiveness is reactivated.

Even so, the dynamism of perception may prompt us to turn to words for rescue – to language whose sounds may fade very quickly but whose meanings are stable (hence Plato's search for eternity in the intelligible, that is to say, articulated world). But this, too, is unhelpful. Stasis is a property of verbal types and their general meaning but not of their spoken, written, or thought tokens. By the time I have said "now", the now when I said it and to which it referred, has gone or become "then". As soon as I say "it is", "it was". By the time I have said "lightning flashes", the thunder is already preparing its grumpy epitaph. The fundamental incommensurateness between the stable meanings carried by word types and the flickering phenomenal reality of moment-to-moment consciousness is a particularly clear illustration of the varnished vanishment of present time, eluding prehensile words, like a mouse's-tail-down-a-hole, a snake of water through a crack, or an edge of smoke. Clock-watching makes things worse, emphasizing the elusiveness of "now", since the clock, until it runs down, is in permanent motion. What is more, the endlessly changing borrowed now of the clock is shorn of all that makes time living; of everything to which the clock assigns a time.

When we try to grasp the instant, then, we are always too late. But if we turn our attention to larger stretches of the present – to segments of time that include the present moment – we encounter the same problem: any stretch of time that has its full cargo of content must be already past. We can prehend only a past present. Who anyway can grasp hold of a month, a week, or even a day? What should one bring to mind and how much of it? How can we rescue yesterday from oblivion and make it again present but on our, not its, terms? What is the chance of recalling the dissipated smoke of the day that has gone? None.

We are defeated by an uncashable richness. A stretch of time seems ungraspable against the (imaginary) benchmark of an exhaustive description. As Milan Kundera said:

> In the course of a single second, our senses of sight, of hearing, of smell, register (knowingly or not) a swarm of events, and a parade of sensations

and ideas passes through our heads. Each instant represents a little universe, irrevocably forgotten in the next instant.[38]

Our ability to live fully in the present seems eaten away from within by the fact that the present, or what is present, is, as we have discussed, not just present in the sense of being objectively attached to the present moment. The sense we make of the present – the timeless meanings that open the present beyond the notional moment of its being experienced – is rooted in the past and in the future we construct on the basis of the past. This is most frustratingly expressed in the difficulty of experiencing our experiences when we seek out experiences for their own sake – in the Kingdom of Ends. I have discussed this at some length elsewhere,[39] so I shall treat it only briefly here.

One of the striking aspects of life beyond the struggle for survival, beyond duties and obligations, in the Kingdom of (Ultimate) Ends, is that the experiences we have there are strongly anticipated in the form of images and ideas. The timeless heart of experiences is made more explicit in prospect. But no actual experiences could match these anticipated ones. Expected and planned experiences present themselves to us in the form of, as it were, pure ideas whereas actual experiences, even where they correspond to the prescription, are freighted with aspects that are not pre-envisaged.

Consider our most sustained residence in the Kingdom of Ends, the annual holiday. The actual game of cricket on the beach, or the walk by the sea, is contaminated with, indeed boils down to, details that lack the clear outline, the *form*, *of* what is anticipated. In the Kingdom of Ends, therefore, we feel that we do not fully experience our experiences: we are not "here"; and, most relevant to our present discussion, we are not "now". The present moment is hollowed out by this lack of an existential fulfilment realising a coincidence between the anticipatory *idea* of the events we engage in and the actual *experience* of them. We find that we can journey but not arrive, passing through the holiday in pursuit of something that will instantiate an ideal of holidaymaking.

This "problem" highlights the general condition of our conscious existence – though it is one which hardly bothers us under normal circumstances when we are not seeking experience for its own sake. The elusiveness of the present has much to do with the fact that events take time and, consequently, cannot be wholly present at any given time, irrespective of whether "any given time" is interpreted as a moment or "a specious present". If an event takes 10 seconds, it will not be wholly present after the first second, or the second, or … It will be present only after 10 seconds, by which time it will have passed.

And this is one of the reasons why we have, indeed need, art. It brings us events that have a *form*; and form ties the beginning and the end of an experience together, reinforcing and enhancing their co-presence in our mind. Events, occasions, stories, histories, can exist as a present whole. A work of art is not so much "a machine for the suppression of time" (except insofar as it speaks across the years) but a machine for the suppression of transience. This is differently realized in music, in literature, and in visual art, but the common fundamental principle is discussed in §12.4.

There are many who would wish for such problems and for whom the present is all too present. To those in pain, fearful, oppressed, hungry, bereaved, rejected, "now" might seem to be an inescapable prison rather than all-too-elusive. Indeed, the kinds of unpleasant experiences, states, and conditions that have no outside, where you are not merely arrived but pinned down – even to something as ordinary as a baby that won't stop crying – may seem to make the present *insufficiently* elusive. But such suffering would be rather too high a price to pay for the reward of a present that is entirely replete. Even impatiently waiting for something to happen – counting the days, or watching the clock, and feeling the hours, minutes or even seconds separately – does not insert us fully into time. Rather we make little excursions away from "now" and little returns to it. In the case of severe pain and distress, the excursions are very small indeed: we are nailed to something close to a present moment but only at the cost of becoming constricted – to experiences that iterate themselves incessantly and close down the present to a nag of now-now-now. Outside of such undesirable circumstances, it is difficult to develop an idea of what it would be like truly to experience the present, to fill the moment with consciousness of all the present contains, or to be filled by the moment. Or to experience not only "now" but "this week", "this year" in a manner that reached into all their interstices, and illuminated all the has-being and will-being that they contain.

The elusiveness of now, and the elusiveness of experience, relates to the elusiveness of one's self, partly revealed in the gap between moment-by-moment experience and what is revealed to a backward glance over past time, that makes us feel that we have not so much lived our lives as have been the site of lives passing through us. Ironically, this applies in my own case as much to the process of writing this book – years spent circling round time – as to other aspects of my life. Thinking about time seems less thinking about time than arguing with one's self and others about problems that have crystallized out of the mystery of time during the history of that 2,500-year-long conversation called Western philosophy. As I grapple with the problems I do not seem to be grasping time itself. And the years since I started writing have, like the writing itself, melted away.

Thus does *maintenant* slip through our *mains*.

6.2.3 The inescapable present: presentism

The seeming elusiveness of the present appears to be the opposite of what is maintained in the philosophical doctrine of "presentism". Presentism is the view that we cannot escape the present because only the present exists, and the past and future do not. Whatever exists is present; there are no past and future entities. It must be one of the least harmful isms in the world (no-one has been killed in its name), but it warrants refutation, not only because many sensible and serious philosophers subscribe to it[40] – it has, as Craig Bourne wittily said, a (bright) future[41] – but also because, once stated, it appears obviously and ineluctably true. Who is going to deny that only the present is real? That that which exists, necessarily exists in the present or presently exists? It sounds like the unassailable claim that only that which exists exists. Eternalists who believe that past, present and future are all (now) real – such that "all moments of time and their contents enjoy the same ontological status" – seem to be flying in the face of logic and common sense and have only relativity theory on their side.[42] And even so-called "possibilists", for whom the past but not the future is real, have a difficult time defining the mode of existence of past things that, after all, seem to qualify as past by not longer existing. (We shall address this in the next chapter.)

What is certainly true is that the present is the only time in which we, and anything, can *be* or *do*. We have no choice but to be "now" – which is another way of approaching the fact that we cannot choose our temporal location in the way that we can choose our spatial location. After all, we cannot enter the past or the future. Even if time travel were possible, we the travellers would still be stuck in some kind of present: the present in which we are visiting (say) 1066. It might not be anyone else's present but it would be our private one. We are "confined" to the present, though it is not a confinement that we usually chafe over. The present is the most open of open prisons.

If we were asked the question "Is there more to the world than the present moment or the contents of the same?" we may seem obliged to answer: "Of course not". Isn't the world identical with its present moment? It is what it is. This certainly seems to be the case if we think of the world as being made up of material objects and events and processes that take place in them – what we have hitherto characterized as the contents of the present. A material object such as an apple *is* its present state, irrespective of whether we do or do not feel that objects are "wholly present" in our encounters with them. An apple *is* what it is. This will seem irresistible if we unpack the first "is" as "is now". "An apple is now its present state" is a truism on which it seems hardly worth expending exhaled breath, spilt ink or transmitted electrons. This is even more obvious if we translate "now" into "at present" so that the proposition becomes: "An apple is at present identical with its present state", irrespective of whether that present state is stable or changing. As with an apple, so it is with the entire (material) universe. The sum of what is – the world – cannot exceed what it is. To put it another way: what exists is what presently exists and what presently exists is what exists in the present, that is to say, *now*. Those who would deny this and grant reality to the past and future should, presentists would say, try acting in the past or the future (as opposed to acting now in order to influence a future chain of events that is rooted in the present), or attempt (literally) pointing to, or travelling towards, something located in yesterday or tomorrow. They would be frustrated.

In making presentism unassailable, we may seem to have reduced it to truisms: that the world is what exists and what exists is what exists at any (present) moment; that the sum of what is at any given time is the sum of what is at that time; that what exists is what presently exists and what presently exists exists in the present; that the present is the sum total of that which is present, that which currently *is* (i.e. in the present tense). That presentism looks platitudinous, however, does not worry presentists who want only to deny reality, existence, or whatever, to past or future entities and to affirm the reality of (one) tense. Their claims have metaphysical content. And this is where we need to focus our attention.

The first question we might raise is whether the present could remain a *tense* in the absence of future and past to contrast it with. Would presentism not make "the present" something like a sheet of paper with only one surface, or a triangle with only one side? In other words, isn't presentism a tenseless view of time, disguised as a one-tense approach to time? The basic premise of presentism that what exists is what exists only at the present moment would not make sense because "the present moment" would not seem to have any meaning, or place any restriction on possible existence, in the absence of other tenses to contrast it with.

Escaping this difficulty by translating "present" into "present to" – making presence a necessary condition of existence – would be too restrictive. There are many things that are considered presently to exist in the absence of being present to – in the sense of being detected by a conscious organism. And all items in the sensory field of conscious organisms have aspects that are not sensed. This leaves an important unsatisfied demand: namely to find the basis for the privileging of a particular time when contemporary physics, denying the reality of distant simultaneity, withholds that privilege from any objective account of reality. The scope allocated to "now" or "the present" is, we are told, granted to it thanks only to the approximations of our unaided, untutored perceptions. In other words, presence in the sense of presence-to an individual consciousness or a collective of consciousnesses is necessary to give "the present", "now" any territory of its own. As Einstein said: "The four-dimensional continuum is no longer resolvable objectively into sections, all of which contain simultaneous events; "now" loses for the spatially extended world its objective meaning."[43] Given that absolute simultaneity does not exist, there is no way of slicing space–time into different spaces at different times – a foliation that applies to all of space–time – even less to identifying a privileged slicing corresponding to a "real" present.

Philosophers, however, are far from unanimous in believing that presentism is incompatible with supposedly a tenseless world picture of special relativity.[44] However, presentism has many other troubles. Foremost among these relates to the question of the truth of statements about the past.[45] Presentism, it seems, cannot accommodate the distinction between that which has existed (and is no longer) and that which will exist (but is not yet); but also between that which has once existed and that which has never existed.

It would be very odd to deny this distinction. The (present) non-existence of the Battle of Hastings in 1066 which once took place is quite different from the (present) non-existence of the Battle of Hastings in 1067 which never took place and now never can do. And this applies equally to the material world and the non-human biosphere. There is a difference between the Cambrian explosion of life-forms which took place 500 million years ago, prior to the emergence of sentient creatures, and an entirely imaginary Cambrian explosion taking place 1 billion years ago. The point is particularly clear in the case of singular propositions such as "Socrates died by taking hemlock" – which is true – and "Socrates died at the hands of a gunman"

– which is not. The former has a claim to correspond to a reality that the latter does not. The difference applies even to continuing states of affairs that are present now. The non-existence of the state of affairs of my being on the earth yesterday (I *was* on earth, by the way) is of a less radical order than the non-existence of my being on Venus yesterday. Of the assertions "I was on earth yesterday" and "I was on Venus yesterday" the former is true and the latter is false.

This brings us to the key difficulty for presentism – the so-called grounding problem: that of finding something in the present that will ground truths about, and justify the distinction between, true and false statements about the past.[46] This has been lucidly expressed by presentist Craig Bourne:

> What the problem shows is that there must be something that transcends the present in order for past-tense propositions that are true at the present time to link with present-tense propositions that were true at past times, and future-tense propositions that are true at the present time to link with present-tense propositions that will be true at future times.[47]

If the referents of true and false assertions about the past are equally unreal, it is difficult to see how we could maintain the difference between the truth values of the assertions. (We shall set aside future propositions for reasons that will become evident in §8.2.2.2). Indeed, it would make no difference whether E had or had not really occurred. How could we even make sense of past-referring propositions? As David Lewis observes, presentists would be unable to make sense of an assertion as simple as "England has had two kings named Charles".[48]

It could even be argued that a past event is *more* real than a present one, in as much as a truly present event is ongoing and hence incomplete. So long as E is happen*ing*, it has not yet happen*ed*. Indeed, if events existed, or were real, only when they were occurring, they would never exist; there would be no territory between "on the way" and "passed away". Lunch could not take place because, by the time it was complete, it would have ceased to be happening, and consequently be non-existent.

If the contents of the past are unreal, non-existent, it is also difficult to see how we would be concerned to assign events and the antiquity of objects to one part of the past rather than another. If the Battle of Hastings is (now) unreal, why fret over whether it took place in 1066 not 1067? If what happened on 12 December 2012 had no existence on 13 December 2012, then it would make no sense to argue whether or not such-and-such an event took place on 12 December or 11 December. More generally, dates would not have any meaning if there were only the present: 12 December would be meaningless without all its yesterdays, beginning with 11 December. More generally still, there would be no basis for assigning past events a temporal order.

There is also an argument relating to the real difference between tenses. How does presentism account for the asymmetry between past and future if they are (equally) unreal?[49] There should be only one way of being non-existent but the present past is a domain of actualities that have, by definition, been realized, while the present future is a domain of possibilities that may not be realized. The claim that "was" and "will be" boil down to "is" also raises the question of why verbs are tensed at all; why we bother with the distinction between "is", "was", and "will be".

Some presentists may not be sorry to lose the present *tense* as well as the other two. But they are still obliged to define what they mean by the present, or the present moment. And here they have difficulty. For the contents of "the present moment" – the sum total of that which is granted to exist – cannot be confined to what is present to someone or other but has to encompass all that *could be* present to the sum total of possible or conceivable observers at a particular time. But there is no such thing as "a particular time" defined independently of any particular observer or class of observers. We are back with the problem of needing a universal "now" to admit everything in the universe into a present moment; an imaginary observer with access to the totality of all that is at a given time.

Presentists perhaps have a stronger case when they look critically at alternative conceptions of time (such as eternalism) that ascribe reality to past and future events or other items. They don't deny their existence but confine their existence to that part of those events that exists *now*, in the present moment, when they are no longer past or future. The only existence allowed to past and future items is their *presence in the present*. The future is defined by, and indeed inheres in, our *present* anticipations, extrapolations, and expectations and so on. (We shall investigate this in Chapter 8). And the past is defined by its present effects.

There are many problems with this. To take one of the most obvious, consider a past event such as the Battle of Hastings. If it exists in the present only in terms of its present effects, what it is must change as the present changes. So the Battle of Hastings will be something different the day after the battle (for example, drying blood on the field), a few years after the battle (for example, the legal system established by a certain Norman king) and many centuries after the battle (for example Raymond Tallis scoring a mark in his history examination for remembering its date). So its existence as a past event would be endlessly changing. What is more, if the Battle were to be identified with its effects, and not with something that is the *source* of those effects, given that effects are hard to trace – they are endless and boundless and muddled up with the endless and boundless effects of other events – it would entirely lose its identity. The past would be such a total jumble, there would be no sense corresponding to the enterprise of finding out "what really happened". If the past event is dissipated without remainder into its present effects, why would we ascribe the event (a) to the past and (b) to a particular causal ancestor? When we speak of something as being the consequence of something that has happened in the past we retain that something, and the past to which it belonged, as an entity distinct from what is happening now. To see the Battle of Hastings as having an existence only in its present effects, is to remove the grounds for our using the terms "effects" and "its". There would be nothing to which to attach the effects.

This, as we shall discuss in the next chapter, is the problem behind theories of memory that also reduce the past to present effects in the brain, namely altered neural excitability. Present (material) effects of past events are not enough to sustain even the illusion of individual past events, never mind a past to which they are assigned. The reasons for this are worth spelling out because they take us deep into the notion of tensed time.

Let us first return to the grounding argument as it is expressed by Mozersky:

> There exist determinately true and false propositions about the past.
> Truth supervenes on what exists.
> What exists in the present underdetermines what is true in the past.
> All and only that which is present exists.
> Therefore, there are no determinately true or false propositions about the past.[50]

The key to the grounding argument is the third step: "What exists in the present underdetermines what is true in the past". This pre-empts the claim that the past exists (only) as its present consequences; or that we can translate the past into the existing present effects of no-longer-existent prior causes. Presentism thus has no means of differentiating between true and false statements about past singulars; or between "Event E never happened" and "Event E happened in the past". If past events exist only in their presence in the present – albeit in memories, testimonies and documents – there would seem to be no ultimate basis for the truth or falsity of records, accounts of things that did and things that did not "really" happen. This is an ontological, not merely an epistemic, worry.

Behind this is the argument that truth values can be assigned to statements about the past only because there is an ineradicable difference between something that (really) has happened – though it is no longer happening – and something that has never happened. Once event E has happened or occurred, it has always happened. It can never unhappen or "un-occur". It is not necessary for it to continue occurring in order to continue as having occurred. This can then be translated into "If E happened at time t_1, it will have an identity as a singular occurrent event at all times after t_1". It remains true, irrespective of whether there are evident (present, causal) consequences of E, or if steps have been taken to reverse any of its consequences. Under the latter circumstances, we say "It is *as if* E had never happened". We don't say "E never happened" or "E has unhappened". That is why, for E to continue to exist after it has happened (that is to say, as something "ongone" and no longer ongoing), it is not necessary for it to continue in being as ongoing or for the same token event E to recur – a logical impossibility. The past does not require replication in the present to exist, though its specific presence in the present will depend on (implicit) consequences or (explicit) awareness of it.

If there were no difference between something (a token past event) that happened and is no longer happening and something that never happened but was merely conjectured to have happened, then the way things are disposed at present would be inexplicable. We would have reached the present state by all and any route, with no influence from the past. To say that the reality of past events lies in *more* than their influence in shaping the present, is to make them causes of the present; that is to say independent of their effects in the present. If they are not independent, they are not causes, and what is happening in the present is not an effect. There would, in fact, be no definite – or any – path to the present.[51]

At the heart of the argument is a paradox which may lead presentists and anti-presentists to take it in turns shooting themselves in the foot. If presentists find the necessary grounding in the present of true statements about the past, they may be seen as conceding the real existence of the latter. If anti-presentists insist that the reality of the past should be represented in the present – that the current truth of past statements require that their truth-makers should be present – then they are dangerously close to gathering up the past into the present, and doing the presentist's work for them.

A more intimate assault on presentism comes from examining the nature of the present: it is shot through with the past and (to a lesser extent) the future based on the past. Let us return briefly to the topic, addressed in §6.2.1, as to "What is present in the present?" – to objects and events.

First, objects. Our fundamental intuition is that the world is furnished with stable entities – that are, were, and will be. It is not possible to make sense of an object without thinking of it as something that has had past states. In what sense do those past states still exist – in what is now the present? These past states exist in the present in the very fact that an object is not, at any given time, a mere time-slice of its own history. It is "wholly present" at any present moment, though only in the limited sense we teased out: an enduring object could not have all of its duration in the present. Nor could it be construed as a succession of infinitesimally thin time-slices in a succession of mathematical instants because, even in the case of an object that is changing, we think that there is something of it that is carried over from moment to moment. The very concept of an object is of an existent that is not a child of an instant that is annihilated as the instant in question becomes past. And what of events? Any event that takes time will, at any given instant, so long as it is happening, be between a phase that has happened and a phase that will (or might) happen. Let us focus on the former because it is guaranteed. Without that earlier phase, the event would not be the event that it is – say the movement of an object from one place to another.

Presentism would not seem to be able to accommodate either stability (of objects) or change (events). The world of the presentist is a frozen, temporally depthless one. It would have no place for becoming or for enduring being. It might be objected that this conclusion could be arrived at only by making the questionable assumption that presentists have a shrunken idea of the present as an unextended temporal instant. The response to this objection is that presentism, if taken seriously, would indeed reduce time in this way. If past times and future times are unreal, then there is no possibility of fattening the present in the way we discussed in §6.1.2.

And there are yet more worrying consequences. Presentism is not only effectively tenseless (the one-sided triangle argument made above) but timeless. How could a pure present tense accommodate "before" and "after"? Consider two events A, that takes place at t_1, and B that takes place at t_2. We want to say that A is in the relation "earlier than B" and that B is in the relation "later than A". But if we argue that there is nothing corresponding to A at t_2 by the time that B at t_1 occurs each of these relations has only one *relatum*, quite a serious deficiency.[52] It might be argued that "A is earlier than B" is a relationship that is established only after *both* A and B have occurred. But that would hardly help the presentist; because the relationship would be between *two* non-existent relata – both in the past – rather than a present existent and another in the past and therefore non-existent.

It is not possible, then, to uphold the idea of a single tense in the absence of the other two. A fully developed sense of the present is interfused with that of the past. And this goes further, as already noted, than the present having been shaped by what happened in the past. It is more than a matter of the implicit but necessary presence of the past in configuration of the present, as an effect of past events. The present location of the chair in this room is an effect of its having been carried thither half an hour ago; but that act is not entirely swallowed up in the present location of the chair. It is possible to focus separately on the chair and on the previous act that brought it into the room – and indeed argue over who brought the chair in.

Which brings us back to memory. We can have a specific or "episodic" memory of something happening. Those memories are not reducible to the present state of a physical item in the room – namely my brain. The episodic memory of bringing the chair into the room has a double intentionality – it is intentionally directed at the experience of the event of the chair being brought into the room and the experience in turn is or was intentionally directed at that event. This intentionality reaches beyond the current state of affairs in the room (and the universe) into a past state that is granted a distinct reality. The reduction of the presence of the past to the effects of the latter in the former (one unsatisfactory form of presentism) collapses a relationship based on double intentionality into a causal relationship. What is more, we may have episodic memories of events that have little in the way of present causal consequences. I may remember a dog barking yesterday but it is highly unlikely that the ripples from that event are shaking any reeds in the present universe outside of my memory. And those consequences that are mediated purely by material processes are clearly different in kind from those that are mediated by my episodic memory – something that is most clearly evident when I "rack my brains" to recall the memory.

We may explore the reality of the past from a different angle by comparing the existence in the present of a past item such as Socrates and, say, of a non-existent past item such as a unicorn. In both cases, their presence in the present is mediated by their effects. In the first case, however, their effects owe their origin to a real being who once walked the face of the earth, as well as having been written about, depicted and so on. In the second case, there are only the symbolic representations and the audit trail does not lead back to a real entity. What they have in common, in virtue of which they both populate the past, is that they are linked to the present not only by a causal chain but by double intentionality. In the case of unicorns, that intentionality is kept open by the intentionality of referring expressions rather than any experience underpinning a collective memory. The difference between an historical entity and a mythological one is that the audit trail in the case of the latter ends in discourse rather than material events corresponding to that which is spoken of; in actual footprints rather than imaginary hoof-prints.

The presence of the past, as an integral and irreducible something-in-itself, is a marker of the distance between material reality and tensed time, though this does not reduce the latter to a mere illusion. Consider a stone dropped into a pond at time t_1 causing ripples that shake the reeds at t_2. In the absence of an observer with episodic memory, the events at t_2 do not hark back to their cause at t_1. The latter does not enjoy a posthumous existence through being identified as a causal ancestor of its causal descendants. More broadly, in the tensed time of conscious human beings, present events are not confined to themselves: they refer to an explicit past. To put this another way: when we look at what is about us, we see not only *that* it is but also *what* it is and this draws on a sense of how it came to be what or where it is, and what it may become in the future. This goes beyond the fact that, in order to recognize what is around me, to make sense of it, past experiences have to be present; and in order to make agentive sense of what is around me, I have to imagine its future.

We discussed this earlier in §6.1.2 when we talked about fattening "now". But I want to go a little deeper, trespassing a bit on the territory of the next chapter. When I look at a mossy stone, or a rotting log, I do not see it as merely something present: I see it as something that has been past, that has undergone events in the past. Its past is present; and the world it belonged to is implicitly present around it. We see beyond what we see to the past of the item we see. This would not be possible if experience were merely the *effects* of the interactions with objects as they are now. The intentionality of human experience is the key to our distance from the material world of physical space–time and to our freedom to operate within it, as if from outside of it.

For presentists, there is no time like the present because there is no time other than the present. There is a less radical form of presentism – what we might call "value-presentism". This is explored by J. J. Valberg who detects a conflict between the idea that (a) "now is the time that matters" and (b) that this is always the case.[53] Now is clearly the time that matters in one sense because, by definition, this is when we have our experiences, including the memories and thoughts that make the past and future real presences. This is why, as has often been pointed out even the most "trivial" present is more important to us, in one sense, than the most dramatic past. The paradox that concerns Valberg is that "now is the time that matters" is a general principle, so it must mean that "now is the time that matters *always*". "Now" and "always" seem to be at odds. The root of this difficulty is a conflation between "now" as a term with a general meaning (roughly "when I am speaking") and "now" as a token used on a particular occasion. A given token "now" is incompatible with "always" but the sum total of "nows" could be seen as a definition of always.

In conclusion, it seems that presentism does not have much going for it and its future looks pretty bleak. The past resists reduction to a mode of the present: it is necessarily more than its presence in the present. The great mystery of the past – the real presence of past events, of something that is not present – remains. That the past seems to have no place in the material world underlines its importance for our overall inquiry and the conviction that motivates it; namely that the material world, or "what is there" according to physical science, is not the whole story of time.

6.2.4 The connection between the elusiveness and the inescapability of the present

While inescapability and elusiveness do not apply to the same aspects of the present, so we do not have a direct contradiction, they are nonetheless connected in complex ways. The inescapable present is both psychological (it lies at the heart of experience) and metaphysical (the present is inseparable from actual or potential presences). The elusive present is also both psychological (consciousness is itself changing and is in and of change so it becomes a kind of chase after itself) and metaphysical (as reflected in the naïve view of the present as an unextended interval between the future and the past). The inescapability and systematic elusiveness of the present capture two complementary aspects of our confused understanding of the relationship between time, experience and change manifest in the incorrect assumption that what is real is real only in (elusive) instant-by-instant slices to which we are (inescapably) confined, such that the instant of experience is the experience of the instant.

The idea that instants are the sole temporal realities originates in the observation of an apparent contradiction inherent in the idea of a *stretch* of time because any interval greater than infinitesimal will have a part that is not yet and a part that is no longer. If "now" is to have a more than infinitesimal width, it is suggested, it must be outside (before and after) itself. If there is at any time t a stretch t_1–t_3, then t_2 will be at once ahead of and behind itself if it is to accommodate that stretch.

The argument – or intuition – overlooks something very important: t_2 is "*at*" t_2. "At-a-time" is not inside the time in question: to be "at" t_2 is not the same as to be inside, or confined to, t_2. Being (explicitly) "at" (and at *is* explicit) noon is not to be confined to noon. Noon is connected with, located in, something bigger than any instant denoted by a putative "noon-as-a-mathematical-instant". The relationship of being "at" a time permits the indefinite expansion of the time in which one is located; in short makes it possible not to be at the time one is at when one consults or notes the time. To be "at" midday is to be unconfined by the instant as much as if one was "at" today. Without "at" there could be no notion of the time one is *in* because being in a time means (implicitly and explicitly) being part of a larger interval of time or of a time schema. A moment of time which we call t_2, and hence locating it with respect to t_1, t_3, etc., is not identical with t_2, precisely in virtue of its being designated "t_2". It is part of a series. In this sense, it is designated as outside of itself.

Physical time is not composed of *times* that (implicitly or explicitly) exist *at* times – or not at least without the assistance of time-watching conscious creatures such as ourselves. We are deceived into thinking that they can do without ourselves because we name or designate moments by something other than them – by their place in a series or a coordinate scheme or in a calendar. They have an "at" borrowed from outside; or they enter the physical series without shedding the "at" that does not belong to the physical series. Because the "at" is not intrinsic to physical times themselves, "at" times are not confined to mathematical instants: consequently, days are as valid as pieces of time as moments; and Wednesdays belongs to weeks. Indeed, while (say) weekdays are artefacts resulting from divisions imposed by a notational system, they have a foot in (observed) physical reality – corresponding, for example, to the duration of the sun's journey across the sky – they are also realities that belong to the community of minds, our shared social consciousness. In contrast, instants – which are essentially mathematical – have by definition nothing to correspond to, nothing to instantiate them.

But even mathematical time, in order to be connected up with other mathematical time, has to be outside of itself. The hidden, guilty secret of mathematical time is that it would not be possible if it were not supported by something more than mathematical time in order to become part of a time schema. If there were only instants – and *a fortiori* if there were only present instants – not only days but also dates, indeed labelled times, would have no meaning. 12 December 2015 makes sense only to a consciousness that envisages 11 December 2015 and 20 October 1922. The mistaken idea that dates could be unpacked from, or constructed out of, instants is rather like the idea that language could begin with one word (and possibly one speaker).

So much for the links between the metaphysically elusive and inescapable present, and the psychologically elusive and inescapable present. At the heart of both contradictions is the mistake of seeing the instant as basic to our understanding of human time, and indeed time itself. It is based on a confusion between mathematical constructs and the temporal stuff of the natural world and the time of natural world with time *per se* and hence human time (see also §10.3.2). The fact that we do not live entirely in a notional instant in which we are, awakens a sense of the elusiveness of the present and, indeed, of our lives, and our selves. We seem always to be chasing ourselves in, or to be reining ourselves back to, the present.

6.3 PRESENCE

6.3.1 Making present: experience, causation and intentionality

We have explored two seemingly conflicting intuitions: that the present is systematically elusive; and that it cannot be eluded. They are not precise contraries. The former is that the present moment is ungraspable; the other is that we cannot break out of the present. That something is ungraspable may be compatible with our being unable to escape its grasp, particularly if neither "grasping" and "being grasped" and that which is grasping or being grasped are not defined. It is time therefore to look a little more closely at the item in question: presence of – and in – the present. We have made some attempt to define the present in §6.2 and have noted its troubled relationship to that of presence. This left a few loose ends. They will turn out to be attached to some very large issues, as we shall discuss in Part III, but for the sake of the completeness of our treatment of this tense, some preliminary tidying up is in order.

While presence and the present, being present and being in the present, are obviously connected, they are not identical. For A to be present to B, it is obvious that there must be an overlap between the time period in which A exists and that in which B exists. They must share some of their present moments. That is not, however, enough. Two pebbles side by side occupying the same present may be co-present (in, say, someone's gaze) but are not present to one another. More is needed and that more may variously be designated awareness, sentience, or consciousness: A must *experience* B and/or vice versa.

Let A be a human being and B a material object. We are tempted to say that, in addition to A and B being temporally side by side, they have to interact. Something – energy or whatever – has to pass from B to A in order for A to be aware of B. This is still not sufficient to ensure that the one item is aware of the other; otherwise awareness would be reciprocated. My picking up a pebble would result not only in my feeling the pebble as heavy and resistant and cool but also in the pebble feeling squeezed by my warm, grasping hand, which is clearly not the case. So while there is a two-way causal interaction between my hand and the pebble, there is only a one-way direction of awareness. Whatever is happening in me has a property that is absent from what is happening in the pebble: "intentionality" to which I shall return presently. So, for the A to be present to B, it is necessary that: (a) A and B should overlap time-wise; (b) they should interact; and (c) events in one of A or B should have intentionality.

The relevant kind of interaction defines what we mean by "being in the vicinity" which links being in the present with being present. The link is not easy to define in a non-circular way but the circularity is instructive. At the most elementary level, that which is in the present, which exists or is happening now, is that of which I am aware as surrounding me plus the unperceived "infill" that occupies the gaps between those patches of my surroundings of which I am currently aware. The latter will include hidden parts of incompletely visible objects (including those, such as the legs of the chair I am sitting on, that are relevant to my confident expectations of the world that I am operating in), the invisible entities that must surround my surroundings, and that which is reported as going on in the world at large. There is no simple recipe for constructing the experiential "here": for example, I may be unaware of the paper clip on my desk but aware of the sun in the sky.

We enlarge the here that is now, and hence present, in many ways, most obviously by instruments that extend the reach of our senses and by information about "what is going on now" – present events that are present in the words (or images, e.g., tel-evisual images) that convey them. This enlargement of "here", as we have discussed, deepens the "now": the extension of that which is present objectively enlarges "the present".

That which I experience as going on around me is presented as being "now". As a matter of objective fact there is always a delay between my experience and the events that I experience. That delay is minute in the case of most of the things that I see with a naked eye but may be significant in the case of astronomical events or events revealed to me by means of, for example, telescopes. The "background radiation" that is detected by radio telescopes now may be billions of years old. However, the size of the gap is philosophically irrelevant: the principle is that it is there, even when I am gripping a stone and feeling its pressure resisting my hand – on account of the time it takes for energy to be transferred and for the transferred energy to become a perception of its source. This is collapsed into the "now". Part of any "here" is always to some degree "over there" – and this is manifestly true of visual "here" where most of the field is beyond the core "here" – whereas "now" is not eaten into by "then". The difference is examined most fruitfully through the notion of intentionality and the contrast between intentionality and causation.

Consider my perception of a glass on the table next to me.[54] According to the standard physicalist story, there is a causal chain linking events in the glass with events in me – nerve impulses located in the visual cortex. This can be represented by an arrow connecting the glass and me, with its head buried in my visual cortex, associated with neural activity, and the tail being light bouncing off the glass. An objective record of the events in the glass and the events in my brain associated with my awareness of the glass would show a time interval between them. It is small but irreducible. So the events in the glass and the events in the brain are separated in space and time. The spatial separation is explicit but the temporal delay is lost. My awareness of the glass is of something "over there" not in me but "now". The explicit spatial separation justifies representing the awareness of the glass also by an arrow – an arrow of intentionality pointing in the direction opposite to the inward causal arrow.[55] It indicates the fact that there are events in me that are *about* the glass; or are a revelation of it; or confer upon the glass an appearance – an "appearance to me". It is important to appreciate that the arrow – representing the gaze looking out courtesy of the light getting in – is not meant to indicate a second causal chain pointing in a direction opposite to that of light passing into the brain – a reverse or backwardly-facing or counter-causal chain. No; it stands for something that is not part of the causally connected chain of events that link what is happening in the glass with events in my visual cortex and ultimately with movements such as reaching for the glass. Intentionality is not part of the material world; indeed, it tears the causally closed fabric of physical reality.[56]

This arrow most obviously captures the fact that my awareness of the glass is of something – a material object – that is not only categorically different from me-as-self but a specific item at a location that is distant from me. But it also stands for the collapsing of the time interval between the events in the glass and the neural events that are supposedly associated with my experience of the glass. In fact, there are multiple collapses because my awareness of a stable object is constructed out of many experiences, synthesized over time, gathering evidence of its stability and its constancy. This process is further extended in the moment-to-moment compression of successive experiences (as when, for example, I glance round) that adds up to the presence of a "here" that is present, that is now.

The collapse of temporal intervals necessary to create an experience of coexistent objects in the construction of a here-now is all the more remarkable because it has to be focused, or discriminating: temporal depths, intervals, delays, successions have still to be experienced in the sphere of simultaneity that is here-now. Intentionality, that keeps items spatially apart from the perceiving subject and binds objects and events into a coherent present moment, has also to keep them temporally distinct. (We saw in Chapter 1 how the visual sense generates the first shallows of our explicit sense of time.)

We shall return to perception – and knowledge – in the final two chapters where an examination of causality and of intentionality will take us to the heart of human time and its connection with agency. For now, we note that the presence of that which is present "in" the present moment eludes the physics which deals with material events. The space–time manifold of physics does not allow the privileged foliation of a universal "now" and a universal, global present. But neither does it allow even local now because there is no genuine viewpoint of a conscious observer experiencing what is "there" – that is to say, here, now, and just over the horizon of here and now, within and beyond a "ken". Its account of the world has no place for intentionality – or indeed for the conscious subject, the observer. There is consequently no "at" any time; no reference point to distinguish that which is occurring now, as opposed to that which is occurring at some other time, or even more fundamentally for that which is revealed from that which is concealed; in short, for presence dappled with absence within and around it. There is no basis, what is more, for something being registered as happening, as becoming present, and being present in the present which it makes.

Before we leave the present, let us plunge into it.

6.3.2 The lived now: in the thick of the present

"Now" is the basis of presence and it is the name we give to the point at which the possible becomes actual. A key step in rescuing "now" and the present from being reduced to a dot poised between some-time and no-time-at-all is to remind ourselves of the extent to which at any putative moment of consciousness is outside of that moment. Husserlian and comparable modes of overlap between moments – in which for example, a "primal impression" at time t_2 is flanked by retentions of past experience had in t_1 and protentions towards the future experiences anticipated to be had in t_3 – do not capture the fullness of the present. They are insufficiently liberated from a linear notion in which time is conceived as a succession of discrete, punctate nows.

Let us therefore look more closely at the reality of our present moments which are not simply a single or linear unfolding. How much unfolding is, or how many unfoldings are, evident in the stream of awareness depends on the spatial scope of "now", the boundaries of a viewpoint, that defines what is co-detected as being connected or separated at a particular moment, the grain of the recollection that specifies the width of what is being attended to, and the richness of our description of it. Within the field of such a viewpoint, many sequences of events will be unfolding at once: the "now" is a point of convergence and divergence of happenings; and successive nows may add up to a stretch of coexistent, co-unfolding, criss-crossing narratives.

Consider that woman over there walking along the road. Judging by the bags she is carrying, she is returning from the shops. She is also smoking a cigarette and holding a child by the hand. She has a mobile phone in her hand and ear-phones plugged into her ears. Numerous unfolding stories are linking her "nows". There is her return to the car, marked out in repetitive steps, each of which makes sense only as part of her journey, though a stumble may inflate a particular step into a story of its own. There are the different stories wrapped in her different purchases – food, drink, cleaning materials and so on – connected with a variety of needs and activities. Soap, soap powder, washing up liquid, polish, pan scourers, all point to future actions, links in a nexus of primary, secondary, or higher order needs. The expedition of which her present walking is one of many threads woven into "today" or "this morning". As for the latter, they are soft-edged stretches of time to which artificially sharp boundaries may be applied by clocks, promises, and appointments.

As she walks, there is a story of the increasingly wearying impact of the heavy shopping bags on her free arms and shoulder, counterpointed by recurrent sense of the handbag on her shoulder tending to slip off and requiring repeated correction. Other threads are twisted into the rope of narratives being paid out: a background of physiological clocks (the beating of her heart and the repetition of her breathing); her mounting irritation with the child skipping beside her and nagging her with increasing impatience for an ice cream; the effect of successive drags on her cigarette – the nicotine rush and its fading – and the progress of the glowing end of the cigarette from tip to filter tip. This latter is itself part of a story of a gradual emptying of a pack of twenty cigarettes and a bigger story of her failing attempts to give up her habit – for the sake of another story – a child growing in her womb.

That, of course, is just for starters. We can imagine a multitude of nested narratives told from her point of view. In addition, her walking will intersect with a multitude of others' "nows" – as when she steps to one side to avoid someone coming the other way, or negotiates the cars as she crosses the road, or falls out with the person she is speaking to on the phone. Each of these others will have their own trajectories, bearing her towards intermediate or subordinate goals which she may or may not take account of. The stories may be lost, wiped, forgotten, or remain merely inchoate as they are mingled within and across people: notes, motifs, and melodies that are in danger of adding up to noise.

The stories in which she is an actor, or more or less caught up, have different time scales, from the microscopic to the macroscopic. She moves effortlessly between the Twitter-brief annotation of getting safely across the road, the paragraph-length action of making a phone call or listening to the end of a tune on her i-Player, the chapter-sized completions of the shopping expedition or clearing some space for her evening at the Bingo, and novel-sized stories such as trying to please, or make peace with, her difficult husband, and the great *roman-fleuve* of her evolving relationship with the child-becoming-adult she is bringing up.

Like this woman, we are always beyond the present even when we are most fully immersed in it. This is one of the reasons why it seems to elude us, why we cannot be where we are temporally; why, at t_1, we cannot *be* at t_1. No-one, looking up and seeing that it is 12 noon, is confined to 12 noon: 12 noon on the clock is more constrained than any habitable, or inhabited, middle-of-the-day. The future is present in the microscopic and macroscopic goals that make being here and now a permanent state of en route to there and then, to states compared with which the present is incomplete, hollowed out by lack. And the past is present ubiquitously in the sense we make of those goals – at a multitude of levels from the immediate recognition of that which surrounds us, making it so familiar that its familiarity is beneath remark, to the explicit recollections and reminders that keep us, or put us back, "on track". The profound pervasive presence of the not-yet and no-longer in our very directed-ness, in our orientation in and of the present, there is the elective, episodic past of reminiscence and future of anticipation.

These are the most obvious ways in which, as creatures in time, we are time-torn. The lived now is spread out, just as the lived here is spread out and we are not entirely at home in them and even less at one with them. The presence of the past and future extends beyond events to processes and objects. Objects of perception are "affordances": they permit certain actions that are relevant to their apparent significance, a source of beneficence or a threat or of having some kind of function – or dysfunction when they are simply "in the way". The drawer handle is a standing invitation to open or close the drawer. This possible action is a shaping of a future. And the temporal depth of the present is extended by objects that wear their antiquity or future on their sleeve – they are old or new, expressing a balance of not-yet and no-longer. Anything that is explicitly "brand new" – a baby, a seed, a suit bought from the tailor – is pregnant with its future, to be characterized by progressive transformation or continuation. A rotting log, a wrinkled face ("Thus is his cheek the map of days outworn"[57]) or anything that is battered and scuffed and worn carries the stigmata of its past. This past, which may not be not directly visible, or indeed perceptible, but must be inferred on the basis of knowledge, pervades the present, hollowing it out with past actuality and opening it up to future possibility.

The lived now and the larger now – "today", "this week", "my life at present" – bear no relationship to those one-dimensional lines that represent successive instants, or time intervals, in physics. None of the many stories, the systole and diastole of meanings, can be captured in a trajectory marked by numbers. Only when we rescue time from its reduced state as a parameter, a physical dimension, from being merely the successive values of a variable referenced to an axis in a coordinate system, and return it to our lives – to the place of terror, of hope, of ordinary forgetful or mindful busyness, of boredom, of anticipation, joy, of ordinary days – can it be seen for what it is. Even when time appears in our lives in the guise of a number – "10 minutes", "4 o'clock precisely" – those numbers have little to do with the figures that line up on the fourth of the axes of space–time. They are closer to tea-time than to the punctate 4-dimensional manifold.

It may seem that when, with almost comical chutzpah, we use the movement of the earth round the sun to determine when we shall have our tea, we not only subordinate ourselves to a now, a time, that is greater than our lives, but that we also subordinate ourselves to that which is greater than our lives, and so reduce our moments, ourselves, our worlds and our lives to mere loci in a universal space–time grid. However, this submission makes sense only because of things that make it matter what the time is, and prompt us to consult the clock, and to act on what we find. While we have displaced time outside of our bodies and even our preoccupations as we repair to the heavens to locate ourselves in daily time tables, it returns to us in the time of our lives, against which the time tables of history and the time tables of nature, are mere background.

Any given moment is part of a bigger moment called "today" and today is the successor to a countless sequence of yesterdays, a dark and backward abysm of the no longer, and a predecessor to an indeterminate succession of tomorrows. It is this knowledge that enables us to be aware that, though the moon and the lamp-post are side by side in the present moment, one is a few, and the other 4.53 billion, years old. Or to read, as did the poet Bernard Spencer, in the appearance of an olive tree "one grey look that surveyed/the builder imagining the city, the historian with his spade".[58] It is fitting that the transition from perceived to calendrical time, from the temporal depth immediately present in what is around us to an ever-extended succession of hours, days, weeks and years, from my sense of the past to the shared past of history, from my private anticipations to the collective organization that is the planned future of a group, or a nation, should have first been mediated by clocks that recorded the movement of shadows cast by objects in the light.[59]

The present tense has proved to be more complex than we might have expected of what seems prima facie to be the least puzzling of the tenses. Even when we set aside the idea of "now" as a physical moment shared by the entire universe, or as a privileged instant where the possible becomes actual, we are still left with the irreducible mystery and undeniable reality of presence. The "it-is-ness" of what-is and "what-is-now" is no less elusive than the "it-was-ness" of what was or the "it-will-be-ness" of what will be; and was and will-be are no more escapable than what-is.

It is time to look at those other two tenses and, since this is the order of their occurrence, let us begin with the past.

CHAPTER 7

The past: locating the snows of yesteryear

Where is yesterday, mummy?
          Overheard on a train (note the past tense in "overheard")

7.1 THE PRESENCE OF THE PAST

We have touched already on the presence of the past and reaffirmed its reality against presentism. We have, however, scarcely touched on "the past" in itself. The imperialism of the present is evident even in our endeavour to curtail it. By looking at the past through the lens of the present, we have done insufficient justice to its complexity and non-homogeneity. The present chapter will endeavour to rectify this.

7.1.1 Preliminary, unsystematic observations

Mais ou sont les neiges d'antan?
          François Villon, *Ballades des dames du temps jadis*

That single, poignant line has been transmitted through all the layers of the past that separate us from its author who lived in Paris over half a millennium ago. Villon's voice was silenced when he died at the age of 30. Few of us can recall anything else of the Ballade whose refrain it forms, or of the Grand Testament he left behind which contains the Ballade, or of the man who wrote it. And yet it can still move us: the poetic dart still has the power to pierce. Thinking back along its trajectory to this moment highlights the many layers of one (Eurocentric) version of the past: yesterday's sudden rain shower; last week's ward round; a holiday a few months ago; a walk 30 years past when a now grown up child was two weeks old; the Fifties of the last century, when the Second World War was still a recent, hideous memory;

Einstein's *annus mirabilis* of 1905, marked by those famous papers that transformed our understanding of the physical world; the birth of a certain kind of fiction with the publication of *Madame Bovary* in 1857; Napoleon's self-coronation as Emperor in 1804; Captain Cook's arrival in Australia in 1756; the ending of the English Civil War in 1645; 1609 and Galileo's discovery of the moons of Jupiter; the moment in 1543 when Copernicus' heliocentric thesis was offered to the world; and so back to 1463 and the silencing of the voice that uttered those lines.

Many other events will have taken place on the day he wrote those lines: gusts of wind, avalanches, births, marriages and deaths, caresses and stabbings, bush fires and germinations. Off-stage, a lion will have sunk its teeth into the haunch of an impala. Like most of the events of that year, of that century, and of the intervening centuries, they have been extinguished by amnesia, ably assisted by death. Their ripples have been damped by a thick plush of inattention, by effects – their own and those of other events – wiping out their causal ancestry, the lack of boosters to refresh their relay through the years. And the very texture, or colour, or taste of the collective awareness in which they were experienced – the worlds to which they belonged – have faded, diluted by the changes that have ultimately given birth to the world that surrounds the present moment, with the light shining on the screen where this sentence is advancing towards its full stop.

Villon's anguished cry spreads through the distant, middle, and near past. Where, indeed, are the snows, and the rains, and the sunny hours, and the storms and calms, the pains and pleasures, the anguish, terrors, joys and anticipations, of yesteryear, yesterday, yesterhour? Where are those natives of the past such that we can remember (some of) them and yet also know that they are gone forever? Our human past seems to accumulate and yet that accumulation is cancelled by loss. The flawed dynamic metaphor is irresistible: I "move forward" in time and leave things – past events, feelings, preoccupations, joys, sorrows, and relationships – "behind" in an inaccessible nowhere. The notion of time as a growing block – still irresistible, even after it has been shown to be incoherent (see §2.2.3.6) – carries with it the idea of the past as something accruing behind the present moment, though that which accrues is somehow "not quite". It is there and not there; no longer there and still there; somewhere yet and nowhere anymore; gone but, in some cases, not forgotten and, because not forgotten, not gone. It is the way of history to lengthen: the datelines grow, the stories get longer. As I "grow" older, I seem to build up into an enlarging heap of days that exist in some sense. And there is a corresponding feeling of diminution: of more that has been spent and less to spend. Yesterday – my yesterday, your yesterday, the collective yesterday – is here today and gone tomorrow. Today is the tomorrow yesterday anticipated.

While we mourn what we cannot help calling "the passage" of the days, we are as puzzled by their continuing presence, as emeritus days, as by their absence. The presence of the past is one of the most venerable philosophical mysteries; for it is present, when remembered, under the aspect of being absent. And we feel this when we look back on our lives. Past days are real and present in the sense of being ours: we acted in them, we are responsible for them, they accuse us, and embarrass us, and give us cause for quiet or noisy satisfaction. And yet they are lost, beyond recall or amendment. The total of such days accrues by stealth. I seem to have reached the end of my sixties in a fit of absent-mindedness, letting my twenties, thirties, forties and fifties slip through carelessness, with the pace not altered in the slightest degree by ten years of thinking about time. Inattentiveness is abetted by amnesia. We forget the unimportant in order that we should remember the important. And then we realize that the order of importance is not immutable. We find we have let go most readily that which we most mourn.

7.1.2 Slightly more systematic observations

In what ways is the past present? We have touched on this already in §6.2.3, where we defended the reality of the past against presentism. We noted the danger to be avoided of affirming the reality of the past by arguing that it is its presence in the present, and that that presence is its present causal consequences. Of course, every present state of the world is a result of previous states of the world: the world is ongoing, with each state of affairs growing out of its predecessor. On a small scale, the cup presently on my table is a consequence of my earlier bringing it in to the room; of my purchasing it, of its being manufactured; and so on. On a slightly larger time scale, the haggard look on your face is a present expression of a life of harrowing experiences. On a larger scale still, the present submersion of Pompeii under lava is the presence of the volcanic eruption that took place 2,000 or so years ago.

In defending the reality of the past in this way, we seem to lose it by wrapping it up in the present. In speaking of "the reality of the past" we drift to thinking of "the presence of the past" and thence to the past as it is (presently) present. But of course the past isn't just the present; and it is more than that part of it which is (still) present. Yesterday is more than that which is present of it today: it had an independent existence before today came into being. What survives of yesterday in today is not entirely a part of today in the way that what is going on today is part of this day. The passage of the car past the window now is different from the passage of the same car past the window 24 hours ago. And the car going past the window yesterday cannot be reduced to the traces of its passage, such as the tyre marks it left on the road, which I can see now. Two otherwise identical ticks of a clock – the last tick and the present one – are also fundamentally different.

Yes, past events have a reality that does not subsist in their being part of what is presently in the world, or going on in the world, or can be encountered in the world, now. If not being part of the world now disqualified them from being counted as real, then it would also disqualify the greater part of most ongoing events, where at any given time, there is only a thin band of ongoingness between the part that has not yet happened and the part that has ceased happening. In short, denying the reality of past events because they are not currently happening would push us towards an idea of time and becoming where the former is an instant housing an infinitesimal slice of the latter.

What is more, past events (or, come to that, objects that have perished), are absent in a way that is different from the way future events are absent. Past events have a personal, specific absence. "No-longer-being" is fundamentally different from "not-yet-being", given that the latter may be "never-being" that, of course, has no intrinsic characteristics. The sea battle that has taken place is definite whereas the battle that is expected to take place is indeterminate. And, as we discussed in §6.2.3, the absence of that which is "no longer" is different from the absence of things that never existed or took place. Socrates is absent and does not currently exist and yet he has a reality that Bocrates, a fifth-century BCE philosopher I have just invented, lacks. Events and objects in the past are not only the proper referents of statements about singulars, but the statements we make about those singulars have truth values. And there are truth values attached to the statement that those singulars existed at a certain time and interacted with other persons, or events or objects that overlapped with their period of existence or, indeed, with persons, such as myself, who are now recalling their existence. The truth of the statements supervenes on what exists – specifically the being of that which they assert. Such truths are not merely *effects* of past events; indeed, they count as effects because they have causal ancestor in a real past event. While present events in, and the present state of, the world are outcomes of past events in prior states of the world, the past is not entirely absorbed into outcomes- otherwise they would not count as *outcomes* (of past events).

The apparent ontological precariousness of the past in the eyes of certain philos- ophers is in part due to the prejudice against anything that seems to involve con- sciousness. The presence of the past – in "its own right" – requires connections to be explicitly made between the present and those prior events of which it is at least in part an outcome. For outside of conscious human beings, past events *are* entirely subsumed in, or lost to, their present consequences and the latter do not have the status of outcomes of their causal ancestors.

It is sometimes difficult to stop the past being swallowed up into the present; from being merely implicit. The fact that I recognize you, that I make sense of this or that, is a reflection of past experiences, even though those experiences are not otherwise present. Likewise, some of my attitudes (hostility or warmth towards cer- tain things) betray past experiences; and my skills (understanding language, reading, riding a bicycle) also speak of past experiences, events, endeavours, and the worlds to which they belong. These things may signify the past only to an observer (most often myself) who looks, beyond the sense I presently make of the world or the skills I have, to the experiences I must have had or the effort I have put in to learn skills or, indeed, to the trouble I took to ensure that I had the experiences that made it possible for me, say, to read French or ride a bicycle. The past in which I wobbled on stabilizers does not have to be present – and indeed for the most part is not present – when I ride safely down the road on a racing cycle.

This is well-trodden territory. The reader will probably appreciate that I am skirt- ing round the edge of the philosophy and psychology of memory, out of which have come many important and useful distinctions explored in a gigantic literature. One of the broadest is between habit memory and occurrent memory.[1] Habit memory is instantiated in attitudes, skills, dispositions that come out of experience and what is often rather too broadly called "learning". The very notion of habit memory is so baggy that it can encompass changes not only in the behaviour of people like you and me but also in organisms conditioned by events to react differently to stimuli and even the tendency of parts of the material world (such as elastic) to show different properties as a result of (unexperienced) events happening to them.

More relevant to our discussion of the past is "episodic memory" – recall of a particular event and of the actual circumstances in which it was experienced – and, a particular subdivision of episodic memory, called "autobiographical memory" – in which we recall events as belonging to our own past).[2] This is profoundly different from the kind of memory, which may be extended to material objects, in which prior events shape or prompt present events. A cup will be changed by being dropped. The chip on the rim is an effect of the past – the moment of the past in which it fell to the floor. In the absence of a human observer who traces states back to prior events – or infers causes from how things are now and sees their present states as the result of the impact of events on earlier states – the present state of the cup *is* what it is: the cup has no past. It is we who attach its past to the cup; and we do so rather selectively. I trace the chip on the rim to the event that caused it because the chip is salient and this makes its cause salient. If the criterion of salience did not apply, then the entire past of the cup would be present – its process of manufacture, its various postnatal states, the positions it had occupied, the times it had been used, and so on. The habit memory by which I am able to ride a bike functions irrespective of whether I can remember my early wobbling endeavours. Nonetheless, my cycling has temporal depth if I remember the days when I achieved my present fluency. I may separately recall (for example) my teacher telling me not to look at the wheel but to look straight ahead at the road. This may open up an entire forgotten world – the way the teacher looked, my feelings about being at school, the roads I first cycled down, the people I cycled with, and so on.

The point is that the presence of the past cannot be reduced to the latter's effects, typically material effects, in the present, even where the effects are evident in nervous tissue.[3] To identify the explicit presence of the past with episodic memory is, however, only the beginning, not the end, of our exploration. There are three lines we need to pursue: the nature of memory itself; the increasing depth of the past, to the point where it is captured as a nexus of facts – and where (for example) personal memory gives way to collective memory and collective memory gives place to history or historiography; and (*da capo*) the nature of past events and of the truth of true statements about them.

7.2 OUT OF SIGHT INTO MIND: GETTING THE PAST INTO FOCUS

7.2.1 Episodic memory

The most direct evidence of the reality of the past seems to be provided by episodic memory – memory for specific events and the times and places when and where they took place. This is "memory from the inside", memory of the experience that gave rise to the memory. It is contrasted with semantic memory – for facts such as "The Battle of Hastings took place on 1066" – that I do not recall from the inside, from an experience corresponding to it. If there are true episodic memories then what happened in the past is real. The relationship between the memory and that which is remembered is complex and the standing of the former as the warrant of the latter is not entirely beyond challenge.

I am remembering sitting out in the garden in the sun yesterday. The memory is some degree constructed. The very fact that I have captured it in a noun phrase "sitting out in the sun yesterday" means that it has been highly processed. I have slightly or profoundly doctored glimpses that serve the purpose of tapping into an episode that may have lasted an hour or more. What is more, I can see the experience as if from without as well as from within. So while I can summon up the world as it was around me as I sat in the garden, I can also recall myself sitting on the bench next to our little summer house, by observing myself from a position near to the steps a few yards from where I was sitting. However, the very possibility of the authenticity of this outside-of-myself memory is rooted in there being something beyond the general phrase "sitting out in the sunshine yesterday" and the feeling that what I am looking at from the outside was once actually experienced from within. I can, for example, summon up the feeling of being over-heated and the blurred vision I had when I looked up from the book I was reading.

A note of caution. The catastrophic consequence of the False Memory Syndrome that assumed epidemic proportions in the USA in the 1990s has taught us that precision of detail – and the ability to unpack more and more details from episodic memories – is no guarantee of the truth of the memory or the reality of the experience that is remembered. Indeed, when (at a more trivial level) I have a sharp image of my wallet being left behind in a particular place, it is a fairly good predictor that I left it somewhere else. Even so, such images are necessary to convey the feeling that I truly was there, at the place where I locate my memories. And, of course, there could be no false memories if there were no true ones.

An episodic memory, however precise and accurate, is not the same as having experience in the first place, for a variety of reasons. Remembering something often brings together experiences that could not be had at the same time. While I experience sitting in the sunshine *moment by moment* and the moments have a certain order, I retrieve it *synoptically*, putting the synopsis together out of butterflying visits to the garden of the past moment, recalling items in an arbitrary order. I remember that I was dipping into a couple of books. One book did not make much sense to me and I proceeded to another. I can, however, visit the two books in my memory of reading in any order; likewise, the moments of reading (how the differently formatted pages looked in the sunlight) and of what I got out of the book. Such auto-cueing is evident in the impressive manner I can visit the past in a targeted way, as in response to a request to share a memory. This voluntary component also underlines the distance between the past made present in episodic memory and the past as evident as its material effects in the present. We cannot imagine a cup racking its porcelain to recall the fall that led to the chip it now carries on its rim. The voluntary nature of memory is evident in another respect. Whereas I can position myself to have certain experiences, the shots are called by something that lies beyond those experiences – so long as they are not hallucinatory. My relative passivity before experiences compared with active memory, which may be the product of racked brains – of auto-cueing[4] – is connected with another difference: memories may be linked with a world but, unlike experiences, are not part of a continuum of surroundings; nor is their sequence subordinated to the laws and causal connectedness revealed by natural science, to the habits of the material world. Hence the magic of memory.

To remember a past experience (as a marker of a past state of the world) is to be aware that I *was* (earlier) aware of something. More specifically, it is to have an experience that is about another experience. The memory M is about experience E and experience E is about that which I experienced. M, therefore, has a double intentionality: a second order aboutness. When I recall sitting in the garden, I am having an experience that is about the experience of sitting in the garden which is itself about the garden in which I was sitting. My recollection of the garden steps in the sunlight is a recollection of a glimpse of the steps in the sunlight. This double intentionality is an important breach in the continuity of the material world.

It becomes more apparent if we espouse the orthodox but misconceived idea that a memory is a material trace left in the brain by a past experience, such that the present traces of past brain activity arising out of past experience are the presence of the past. Unfortunately for this explanation – or non-explanation as we shall discuss in the Addendum – there is nothing fundamentally different between those traces that are left in the parts of the brain that are supposed to be associated with conscious memories of a past that is explicitly present and those parts of the brain in which the past is present merely as, say, modification of behaviour, conditioned reflexes, motor programmes, in which there is no awareness of the past. The alterations in both cases are present as neural effects – more specifically, changed reactivity of nervous tissue. But there is a profound (and in terms of the neural theory inexplicable) difference between them. In the case of occurrent memory, the effects have to underpin double intentionality while in the case of habit memory, nothing comparable is required. The double intentionality of occurrent memory, permitting the presence of the past, is not something that fits into the physicalism to which the neural theory of memory belongs. In virtue of its double intentionality, memory "points" – even more decisively than perception – in a direction opposite to, or at least orthogonal to, the direction of causation. A present memory has an intentional object that is causally upstream to the past experience it is a memory of; and that experience is directed causally upstream to the event it was an experience of. If memories truly were just neural activity, they would have to be about their causal ancestors, being both the effects of those causes and as it were reaching back to them.

Memory has often been described as "mental time travel". One of the reasons for denying the possibility of literal time travel that we discussed in §2.4 is that it would require breaking and then reforming connections with the causal network. Mental time travel, however, operates at a distance from the causally closed world, a distance opened up by double intentionality. Hence our extraordinary capacity to dart from "place" to "place" in the past and, indeed, to visit specific locations at will.

We may conclude from this that neural accounts, or more generally materialistic, accounts of occurrent memory are entirely inadequate. The fundamental reason for this is that no material object such as a brain can retain its own past as something present in order to make present a previous state of something other than itself, a past event or state of the world that has been experienced. In the material world, everything is what it is, and not what it has been – never mind what it will be. Matter does not dwell on itself; on its previous states. It is subject to the law that "It is what it is and nothing more". This is another aspect of the absence of tensed time in the physical world according to contemporary physics.

One final point. We can envisage expanding circles of effects arising from a material event, like ripples from a splash. When an effect of an event encounters a consciousness (strictly the other way round) different kinds of ripples are set in motion: reverberations in a mind. This awareness of an event has consequences that are in a different space from that in which the unfolding of the effects of the event before I encountered one of them is located. These consequences are influenced by whether I judge the event or one of its effects to be important or unimportant, and consequently reflect on it or not, deliberately recall it, share intelligence of it with you, and perhaps take steps to bring it about again or to ensure that it does not recur. These consequences are quite different from those that are mediated by the laws of physical nature – something that is observed at many different levels. The physical impact of a crash between two cars is not part of the same unfolding process as the legal consequences – insurance claims, punishment (years in gaol), etc. – that may result.

7.2.2 Ever deeper past: from perception to knowledge

When in Chapter 1 we first examined the origin of our explicit sense of time, we assigned a key role to vision. There does however seem to be a gap between the immediate perception of temporal depth made available in the visual field and the temporal depth that comes from memory: yesterday is not visible nor even potentially so. Its contents do not lie as it were round a bend in the road. There is a profound discontinuity between the past as instantiated in a previous position of an object moving in front of me and the past tasted in episodic memory for which something that happened ten years ago though it may be no less accessible to recollection than something that happened yesterday. (This maps to some extent on to the difference, explored in §10.4.3, between seeing a change – for example a child sitting up – and seeing a change has taken place – for example that a child has grown up.)

The difference is obvious when we are thinking of token events which are complete: my sitting in the sunlight in the garden yesterday is not available to anyone else in the way that my sitting in the garden now is available to be observed by someone else. And no journey, even less a glance, could connect me with the appearance of my house as it was yesterday or yesterday's slam of the door, or sojourn in the sunlight in the garden, however vividly I may remember it.

This highlights ways in which the presence of that which is present and the presence of the past are different. Wherever we are positioned, we cannot see or otherwise observe the past. It does not belong to the same space as the things and processes and events, revealed and concealed, that are currently extant or happening. Its present "space" is only a metaphorical space of memory and its time is the time of recall, even though it was once located in the space that is currently occupied by the things that are around us and they still have an indubitable temporal relationship to present events and to other past events. How do we get beyond visual space – and visibility and visible invisibility – to a past that is invisibly invisible? How are we to think about the two distinct components of the double intentionality of an episodic memory – the one that reaches through time (back to the experience) and the other reaches through something like visual space (the experience)?

One path lies via items that have their invisible past written on their visible appearance. I am talking of, for example, things that *look* old: a rotting log, a wrinkled face, a battered suitcase. These are standing testimonies to a past that is gone but not forgotten and, because not forgotten, not entirely gone. Look at that suitcase, covered with scuff marks, with the remains of stickers recording holidays on which it has been used, and even a tag attached to the handle when it was last checked in at an airport. Thus different kinds of markers of the past in an object that has survived to the present. The most basic is its general state of dilapidation; the most sophisticated is the tag on the handle, with a time and date written on it. (The tag, also, may have become a little battered so it has two modes of pastness.) However, what they have in common is that they are *signs* and as such require interpretation. Without interpretation, they are merely aspects of the present appearance of a present object. We require knowledge to see that the rotten log covered with ivy is old; to make its rottenness and ivyed state a marker of processes that have taken time, time the object has endured with some of itself intact. Visible items wear their antiquity on their sleeve only to the informed eye. The presence of the past, then, is an inference: we infer the past of objects that incorporate their antiquity in their phenomenal appearance, even though we take in their ages as an inseparable part of experiencing them. Other experiences than that of the individual rotting log before me will lead me to conclude that it is old: to it I bring my prior experience of logs and their appearances. I have built up a knowledge of the typical appearance of logs at different times after being cut from a living tree. Only on this basis can I translate the damp flakiness and ivy-mantled bark into ancientness. There are objects that have what we might call "a private ivy", that wear moss on their sleeve only for ourselves – as when we revisit a town that we knew when young. Under such circumstances, the past becomes a place we can seem to visit, though what we visit is not the past but the place where it happened.

And personal associations between past and places can be very complex. When I stand on Pentire Head, I can see much of the Cornwall we have visited and revisited over thirty or more years. Panning round from left to right, I see: St Endellion church which I associate with the end of a long journey pushing our older child in his buggy to get him to sleep one afternoon in 1982; New Polzeath where we have just parked our car; the Polzeath beach which we have scribbled on incessantly over several decades; the little beach by the Camel where an ice cream was dropped by our younger son to much grief; Stepper Point the scene of last week's walk and a walk a year before that. This does not justify saying that "Time is set out in space" only that, because a location may outlive certain events that took place in it, the past may be preserved as "over here" and "over there". The times are seemingly conserved in the unchanging places where transient events took place. When we revisit them, of course, our visit is composed of other events, so the past eludes us.

Visibly aged objects are the bridge between a past that is directly observed to one that is inferred: between a past of the senses to a past of facts. The ways in which I infer antiquity from perceptual appearances may be quite complex. I can see the past event of your sleeping in the bed by recalling you lying there; or by seeing the imprint you have left on the sheets; or by inferring from your damp footprint on the floor that you have been staying the night and have had a shower. There remains still a link of intentionality between present and past: some particular item in the present is a standing sign of a particular item in the past. The present state of affairs is *about* a past state of affairs. This is a *trace*, outside of the mind, in virtue of which an explicit past is present in the present, although such natural (unintended) signs require a knowledgeable (remembering) human consciousness to make them act as proxy for direct episodic memories.

We may assume that this kind of mnestic marker goes a long way back. The lion's footprint indicating the passage of the lion is an early manifestation; but we must not date it too far back. The lion's footprint may also signal the passage – and hence the vicinity – of a lion to any number of non-human creatures. But the past it evokes for animals is not tethered in the first instance to an explicit episode: it retains the generality of a stimulus. In the case of humans, that generality is in principle at least tethered to the expectation of a singular entity, given that the past is in the first instance recalled episodically and episodic memory is anchored to a sense of self. The episodic past is "my" past and so its episodes are set in personal space. The absence of personhood in animals means that this is not possible.

Visible proxies presenting the past are visible to anyone, though not all may interpret them. They are the first step to a public memory: an explicit past not confined to private episodic memories but contributing to the beginnings of a full-blown collective past, albeit not one that is occupied equally or entirely by all of us. The natural signs of the past – footprints, impressed sheets, rotting logs – with their publicly available aboutness-of-the-past, may be seen as an important transition to a shared past ultimately gathered up in the concept of (local, national, global) history.

7.2.3 The past: reality and truth

Past events, past objects and past lives exist insofar as they live in present memories that ultimately have no home than the consciousness of individuals. Overwhelmingly, however, memories are mediated through signs that speak to communities of minds sharing a common language. These collective, or collectively available, memories take the form of facts, expressed in assertions, sought after in inquiries, and exposed to the truth tests – either "the tribunal of experience" or the authority of persons or documents. Facts are not indexed to persons: they belong to no-one in particular.[5] These memories – called by psychologists "semantic memories" – constitute the bodies of knowledge that we draw on to guide our lives. They are the substance of history – the history of relationships, of the interactions between groups of people, of communities, of nations, of arts, sciences, and technologies and so on.

The characteristic form of extended memory is the story. Stories begin small scale and personal, indexical, and are spoken rather than written – "Yesterday I saw a lion" – and may form the foundation of the narratives that discursive communities pass on from generation to generation. More recently history is stored outside of humans in various modes of documentation – pictorial and written. With the passage of memory into history we know more about the past than we can ourselves confirm or warrant. History grows beyond the possible scope – distance in time, range in space, cultural reach – of anyone's memory. It becomes transhuman.

The documentary storehouse is a place of virtual memory. It is there waiting to be heard or read and hence to be remembered. The relationship between semantic (impersonal) and episodic (personal) memory is complex. I have to remember facts and recall them. My learning them is itself an experience that I may remember and my recalling them is another episode of memory. But in the end, history, huge beyond the reach of anyone's remembering, is an autonomous realm, untethered to individuals. When we remember that the Battle of Hastings took place in 1066, we remember neither the Battle of Hastings nor 1066. We cannot recall the smell of the horses, the shouts, the pain, the horror, the texture of the soil, the disposition of individuals at a particular moment – any of those things that would be remembered by someone who was there. We remember only the fact that the battle occurred.

This is poignantly expressed by Poincaré:

> [The past] must, so to speak, have crystallized around a centre of associa-
> tions of idea which will be a sort of label. It is only when they have thus lost
> all life that we can classify our memories in time as a botanist arranges dried
> flowers in his herbarium.[6]

Our organized past is in the keeping of categories and is curated by the collective. In contrast to the swirling, eddying, turbulence of flashbacks, and associations, and prompt-driven recollections of private memory – most brilliantly captured in James Joyce's *Ulysses* (often imitated and never matched) – our public memory is structured, mapped on to calendars, allocating events their places in hours, days, years, and centuries.

When memories move "fact-wards" and away from recall of phenomenal appearance, when they become something that can be shared as opposed to something personal with an incommunicable core, when they move from episodic recall (however reconstructed) to the account of "what happened" or, more grandly, to historiography, they enter a different kind of space from the experiences on which they are based. My sitting in the garden was an experience connected by temporal and spatial continuity with my subsequently going into the house. There is a continuity, a fluidity, an interconnectedness. My episodic memory still locates my sitting-in-the-garden in its proper place but lifts it out of the surrounding space. "Sitting-in-the-garden-yesterday" is not situated in vicinity of the garden. When I recall sitting in the garden, I am not obliged subsequently to recall my going into the house: the most literal memory does not copy the spatio-temporal order and connectedness of events as they happened. This is connected with another aspect of semantic memory: there no line – or straight or wriggly, even less a line of sight – joining the present moment with the Battle of Hastings or even my cracking a joke yesterday and remembering doing so today. We are beyond the space demarcated by our senses.

And it is this that makes it more mysterious that episodic memories turned into facts, shards of the past, are connectable with, if not directly linked to, the events that surround(ed) them. Without this connectability check – the audit trail – it would not be possible to test the truth of memories and the plausibility of the accounts of the past. Supposing I am asked to give an account of my movements yesterday afternoon because there was a fracas in a pub. I say that I was in the garden reading. It must follow from this that I cannot have been in the pub where the event of interest occurred. I cannot, say, claim to have been a witness to the fisticuffs and to be an authoritative source of information about it. In short, semantic memories, even when they are quite humble, belong to a network and consequently can be tested for consistency – and reliability and truth. This is the least we demand of both the little stories of our individual lives and the big stories of our shared lives; of tales, chronicles and histories.

Living in a world of facts – a world in which the past is present as a nexus of particulars that can be asserted – is unique to human beings.[7] It may well be quite recent. Explicit factual awareness clearly requires language; and it is possible that a fully developed sense of being related to a shared and testable past may require writing, a parvenu less than 10,000 years old. Even more recent is the allocation of times and dates to events-turned-into-facts. The audit trail linking Fact A with Fact B and testing assertions against knowledge from other sources is made more robust when we have times and dates. If I was sitting in my garden at 2 p.m. on 28 July, I could not have been in the street at 2 p.m. on 28 July. Nor could I have been in New York at 4 p.m. on 28 July. The spatio-temporal continuum in which an event is located has been replaced by a lattice of numbers identifying dates and times (as well as places) extending boundlessly. This realm of facts contains items that do not translate directly into experience, such as "1066" and "The Battle of Hastings".

My experience of sitting in the garden last Monday afternoon is transformed into an event that is mapped in a way that I did not experience at the time. And this is true equally of historical events. We can establish that William and Harold could not have faced each other in October 1065 because they were in different countries according to the other facts that we have. And William could not at the time see the battle as the start of a 19-year reign or of a Norman dynasty that had such an influence on the history of England and of the man writing this sentence.

The factual past is ever-extending. The discovery of deep time towards the end of the eighteenth century, and its subsequent extension through biological and physical science has given us a backward glance of billions of years.

7.3 WHERE, THEN, ARE THOSE SNOWS? MEMORY AND HISTORY

Let us look at something a bit nearer to hand than the ladies of negotiable affections mourned by François Villon.

The other day I was writing in one of the handful of pubs where I have written most of this book and I looked up to see a woman with curly hair leaning forward to say something seemingly rather confidential to the man sitting opposite her. I have a precise memory of that event, or image of that moment, and I can unpack quite a few details from the things that surrounded it.[8] I can, for example, see where the woman was sitting in relation to myself, the light she was in, the bar that she was looking towards, and so on. Now it is clear that, while the bar, and the table, and I hope the woman, almost certainly still exist, the event of the woman leaning forward does not. It is over. So where is this snowflake from yesteryear – which, as I summon it to my consciousness again and again, seems to acquire the magic of an hallucination? In what sense does it continue to *be* even after it has completed its one and only occurrence?

Here are two candidate answers. The first is that the remembered event is still located in time – "So many days ago" or "12 noon 25 September 2010" – but is no longer located in space. If I could go back to that time I could find it at the place where it happened but if I went to that place without going back in time, I would not find it happening. An event that occupies time but not space may seem very odd – never mind that it is forbidden by contemporary physics. But the oddness is more deep-rooted: it lies in the separation of an event not only from the things that surrounded it but also from any objects in which it took place. Separating the-woman-leaning-forward from the objects, including the woman's own body, not to speak of the space in which she leant, that made it possible, is clearly a dubious business. Presenting the event as a quasi-thing, as one does when referring to it by means of a noun phrase as "the-woman-leaning-forward", makes the beginning and end of the time slice co-exist. But there is a more disturbing puzzle. In what sense does this item – rather like the smile peeled off from the Cheshire Cat (cf. §6.2.1.1) – exist? Or (to return to our initial question) where does it exist if it is not located in the place where it happened? Where are the snows of the other day?

The banal, common-sense response is to locate it in my memory. However, it raises two other questions. The first is that the memory locates that which it remembers in a world to which it belongs, a world which does not have evident boundaries and which is thought to be continuous with the world of the individual remembering the event. It presupposes a continuing trajectory connecting what appears to me as a free-floating piece of past reality with the present, even though I could not trace it.

The complexity of this is often overlooked, perhaps because in philosophy there has been a conflation of issues concerning the reality of the past and issues concerning the truth of memories. This confusion is encouraged by the focus within the philosophical treatment of the past on the grounding problem which we discussed in §6.2.3 when we put forward the case against presentism. Let us revisit that briefly.

Someone who argued that the snows of yesteryear are not to be found anywhere because they are no longer and so do not exist may be challenged as follows: If they do not exist, what is the basis for the distinction between true memories and false ones, between true and false testimony? If a true memory is as ontologically challenged as a false one, lacking its ultimate referent – the remembered event which has passed away – then perhaps there are no such things as true memories. A true memory must have something external corresponding to it – a truth-maker – that a false memory lacks. If the past does not now exist then how can there be true statements about the past?

We can separate the question of the reality of the past from that of the criteria by which memories may be authenticated. Consider the woman leaning forward. I could authenticate my memory by seeking the testimony of others who could have co-witnessed what happened. Their corroboration would reassure me that the event really took place. Alternately, if I knew the lady personally, I could ask her whether she was in that pub on that day and if the answer was yes, I might conclude that I am unlikely to have made up the specific details of her being in the pub. There could be documentary evidence such as photographs or other unique and lasting imprints of her action that would indirectly corroborate my memory of it. These ways of discriminating between true and false memories, however, do not really reach down to the question as to where, if anywhere, past events now are.

The conventional way of distinguishing between true and false memories – or memories and quasi-memories – is to appeal to something that is not usually available; namely evidence of a putative causal connection between the memory and that which is remembered. A true memory, so the story goes, is based on an experience that was in some way causally connected with that which the memory remembers. A false memory does not have such a causal relationship and has been implanted by (for example) a suggestion originating from an unreliable source or false information which has been translated into the impression of direct experience of that which the informant claimed to have happened. As we have seen, however, there are fatal objections to the idea that (an episodic) memory is a (material) effect of that which is remembered.

What is more, if we accept that the past is real, then we cannot confine the scope of its reality to that which is highlighted by the accident of its being remembered. A woman-leaning-across-a-table would be no less real for being forgotten. Moreover, the sensed reality of the remembered event is dependent upon its being implicitly located in circumstances, themselves part of a world extending indefinitely in space, time, and significance, that are not remembered. That which is revealed to the flare of recollection is implicitly embedded in an unilluminated world. Stand-alone – random, capricious, patchy, episodic – memory would not be sufficient to underpin the reality of the past.[9] The snows of yesteryear would not be adequately curated by the caprice of memory: the latter does not seem to have the capacity to confer real existence. Villon's question remains unanswered, perhaps because it raises unanswerable questions about the place of intentional objects in a world in which the paradigm of reality is the material object and the material processes with which it engages: ladies who lean forward and the tables they lean over, not the fact that they have acted in this way.

Even so, memory is essential to confer presence on a past that would otherwise be an unacknowledged source of the precursors of the present state of things. Without memory, the past would be cashed without remainder into its present consequences. One of the reasons for not reducing the reality of the past to its traces in the present would be that this would dissolve the very "it" whose "traces" are in the present. It would remove the in-itself of the past event. To say this is to be realist about the past and its contents. In a much-cited paper, in which he weighs the competing claims of realist and anti-realist interpretation of statements about the past, Michael Dummett examines the link between truth values of statements about the present and truth values of statements about the past as part of the non-decisive case for realism.[10] If it is true that I visited Liverpool on 20 December 2012 and it is now 20 December 2013, then it must now be true that I visited Liverpool a year ago. In other words, the truth of a statement about the past is not simply located in statements about the part of the present where the past is posited to have left its traces. If it is 20 December 2013 and I really did visit Liverpool on 20 December 2012, then it is true that something happened a year ago – namely that I visited Liverpool.

Unfortunately, although it supports the view advanced in this chapter about the reality of the past, I think the argument confuses the truth value "true" with reality itself. The present truth of "I visited Liverpool a year ago" does not, after all, deliver the present reality of my past visit to Liverpool. That the statement is true seems to deliver a truth-maker located in the past. This is both more and less than we need. It is more than we need. The snows of yesterday do not have to freeze our present hands; they simply have to have truly (actually) fallen – though we should not conflate truth and actuality. And it is less than we need, if we feel that the snows of yesteryear need somehow to be still on the ground for the past to be real; because, as we shall discuss in the next chapter, truth-makers of propositions can fall short of being actual existent events or any material reality.

We cannot find the reality of the past in the episodic memories of individuals. Is it to be found in the collective sense of the past? The latter has very deep roots. It begins with joint attention to what *is* there which may underpin joint acknowledgement as to what *was* there; with jointly seeing what is before us and joint acknowledgement of what was, but is no longer, before us. Yesteryear's snows, if they are yester enough, and have the necessary salience, will be gathered into lore or on to pages. The snows of yesteryear (like yesteryear and snows) are words and the shared human spaces proposed, held open, and populated by words.

So the snows of yesterday are still falling – in a space of facts created out of joint recollection preserved out of joint attention, in the community of our minds. This is more remarkable than we perhaps fully appreciate. If history were merely the sum total of individual memories, it would be a chaos, close to delirium. This may be the truth of the sum total of individual recollections of the past (consider "the medieval period" as it is being thought of now by all the people in the world who are thinking of it) but that truth is ordered into an agreed chronicle of demographic, social, technological, cultural, political and other events. And while that chronicle in turn may be subject to the vagaries of the listeners' and readers' attention, recall, forgetfulness, prejudice, etc., it stands there as a relatively resistant lattice in which ordered stories are located. Equally remarkable is the way that we can look through a multitude of intervening yesterdays – through hours, through days, through decades – to a targeted past, as if they were glass. This transparency is the product of the tagging slices of the past with words and numbers; words and numbers which do not participate in the "mists" that make up accumulated time.

7.4 A LAST BACKWARD LOOK AT MEMORY AND THE PAST

It is well to consider the strangeness of what we have just been up to: reminding ourselves, or trying to, what memory is, to recall recollection, and to see more clearly the nature of the past that it remembers. When I remember something, I am explicitly aware that is not present, irrespective of whether what is remembered is yesterday in the sunlight which I did experience first-hand or the Battle of Hastings which I have only in report. The past is both present and absent and somehow these two states are not at odds: intentionality permits a present event (an episodic memory) to be about a past event (that which is remembered.) The past, however, cannot be dependent for its reality on memory.

It is worth dwelling on this a little more. Consider an event no-one experienced – one, say, that took place in a part of the universe that lay beyond the reach of even the most powerful detectors. This event would still be ontologically superior to an event that was imagined but never actually took place. So experience and memory are not themselves sufficient to determine whether a past event qualifies as real. But without experience and memory it can not have the afterlife, as an *emeritus* event, that remembered happenings have. In other words, for an event to be (located) in the past, it must be remembered while for a past event to be real, it has to have occurred before the present.

A word of caution is in order here, regarding the status of the distant, pre-human past, and the problem raised by Meillassoux[11] to which we have already referred. Meillassoux points out that robust empirical science generates statements which, a few creationists apart, humans believe to be true about events that took place before consciousness or even before life; for example, that the earth is 4,000,000,000 years old. These statements refer to what he calls "ancestrals" – realities prior to the emergence of the human species. Their truth clearly cannot be something that is dependent on human consciousness or even, though less contentiously, of an internal correlation between our collective awareness of the world and that which is allowed to be real. The moment when the earth came into being, and much that followed in the 4,000,000,000 years beyond that, was not, and could not, be witnessed by anyone and so cannot be a matter of experience or memory. However, not only are they past but they belong to "*the* past" that stretches continuously at least from the Big Bang to this moment. In this past, we co-locate all the things we remember, all of human history, all of pre-human history, and all of pre-living history. There appears to be a break in this between things that were witnessed (or at least in principle could have been witnessed) and could in theory be remembered and things that could not have been witnessed and are presented only as facts that can be remembered. But the break is not reflected in the continuous line that we imagine to connect "a day ago", "a century ago", "a millennium ago", "a billion years ago" and "13.75 billion years ago". The "ageing" of "ago" seems to be a continuous recession. We shall return to the problem of ancestrals in §10.5. For the present, I shall focus on a related difficulty: the apparent continuity between events that are located in the past on account of having been experienced and remembered and those events that are located in the past despite not being remembered or even (in the case of pre-human times) having the possibility of being remembered.

The continuity is sustained by an overlap between past events that are known as facts but might have been remembered and past events that are known as facts and could never have been experienced and hence could not have been remembered. We do not have to go as far back as ancestrals to encounter the divide between parts of the past that are known merely as (scientific) facts and events that are experienced and then remembered. We simply have to look to items that are matters of knowledge, acquired as facts, and items that are experienced and are remembered in our everyday life. There are many things I know about the recent past (including my own past) that I do not remember. That is to say, there are parts of my past, and "the" past(s), that are not in the keeping of human consciousness in the sense of being rooted in experiences revived as episodic memories. In short, we have knowledge that exceeds our experiences. It is tempting to argue that while our past can be composed of facts that do not correspond to any experiences that *I* have had (apart from the experience of learning them), *somebody* had to experience them in order for them to figure in the past that I or anyone is aware of.

To say this is to mistake the nature of knowledge. Knowledge has a toe-hold in experience but it is extrapolated beyond anyone's possible experience. No-one could have experiences that correspond to most of the facts we ordinarily know; and knowledge is not just added up or collectivized experience. It is not just a matter of our succumbing to the temptation of what I have called "data-lean" generalizations (such as, for example, "the medieval period was dominated by a religious world-picture"). Rather it is because of the kind of things – abstractions, generalizations, numbers – of which facts are made. Of course, our disciplines, most notably and powerfully those of science, are crucially ultimately subject to what Quine called "the tribunal of experience" which facts and theories face "corporately".[12] The tribunal (as in the pursuit of the Higgs boson) is no mere accidental colloquy of judges but a highly organized exercise, building on pyramids of theory, information and technology. What is more, the facts are parts of networks or systems of facts which live within exquisitely interlocking theoretical frameworks.

These are far from human consciousness understood as immediate experiences plus the past understood as remembered experiences. The gap that opens between experiences and facts is present in every visual field that senses that which we cannot presently sense and may never do so. The first footprint in the path to ancestrals, in short, was laid down in everyday cognition that goes beyond experience. So the sharp break between the seen and the factual past, between the past we experience directly and the past that is opened up by science, that reaches not only beyond actual but possible experience (as in events that are postulated to occur before the emergence or any consciousness) is apparent rather than real.

We have spent much time defending the past against the charge that it is unreal. In the previous chapter, it was the present that seemed in need of defence. Even when it was not reduced to a mathematical instant, or a razor edge between past and future, it seemed to acquire territory of its own only by plunder. Most strikingly, "now" was fattened on nourishment from the past. The charge that the present has a parasitic existence seems to have a lot going for it and can be based on the nature of perception, on the temporal structure of events, and on certain truths about the relationship between perception and objective reality. Examining this is not a digression as will become apparent.

First, perception. Bergson, as we have noted, argued that the sharp distinction between experience and memory is illusory: "Your perception, however instantaneous, consists in an incalculable multitude of remembered elements, and, in fact, all perception is already memory".[13]

"All perception is already memory" seems to transfer experience of the present to recollection of the past. Even if this seems exaggerated, it is true that there is a hint of valediction in experiences, they report not what is happening but what has just happened. There is an important truth in this: an event is whole only when it is complete; and experience (of the event) has to build up to exceed a threshold and to be made sense of in order to count as, or to be experienced, that is to say recognized, as an event of the kind that it instantiates. It takes time, in short, for what is happening to dawn on us, by which time it has already in whole or in part "entered the past".

Some of these points were dealt with in the previous chapter. The most obvious response is that the present is not a linear sequence of discrete happenings, it is *teeming* – with events that are about-to-happen, are happening, and have happened in different quantities all side by side. The ongoing and the ongone are contemporaneous in the dense tangle of processes and stories, threads of becoming, that makes up the "now" passing into "then" and remaining "now". And the suggestion that experience lags behind objective reality – we always hear a sound or see a light after it has left the event it reveals to us – presupposes that there is a "now" when experienced events occur (though this has no place on a cosmic clock) and a "now" when the events are experienced. To allocate the former to a "real" but unobserved present and the latter to an observed but false present would hardly be in the spirit of the verificationist philosophy of science behind relativity. It would seem, moreover, as if we have an embarrassment of competing presents rather than an absence of such.

Our defence of the past does not therefore threaten the present. And this highlights an important point. Although the tenses are allocated separate chapters in this book, they do not exist independently of one another, any more than left and right could stand alone. The mutual invasion of past, present, and future – evident in this work in the way a defence of the reality of the past gate-crashed our previous chapter intended to be devoted to the present – is central to their reality. They exist not side-by-side – like notional instants or blocks of tenseless, physical time – but interpenetrate. This is reflected in the fact that where I am now (in the widest and deepest sense) and where I have come from and am headed to are inextricably connected even though they are clearly distinct. That is why the reduction of the past to that which I explicitly remember – as opposed to the source of the intelligibility that also suffuses the present (how cognition is rooted in *re*cognition) – and the future to mere episodic anticipation – as oppose to my forward-directedness – is fundamentally to misconceive my relationship to tensed time.[14]

7.5 CODA

We talk about "the past" and thereby homogenize it, concealing its irreducible variety. This may be because at the metaphysical level, the similar issues face us when we talk about the recent past (for example your reading the beginning of this sentence) or the remote past (for example the laying down of the foundation stone of the temple at Palmyra). Our philosophical discourse about the past tends to clump together: the visible past of the earlier phase in the trajectory of a still-falling stone; that in virtue of which we recognize or just make sense of something that is present before us; the private past of episodic and autobiographical memory; the past that is evident in the antiquity of rotting logs, wrinkled faces, and ruins – the "ye" dimensions; and the shared pasts of history, mythology, and astronomy.

There are many individual pasts individually recalled. There are both egocentric and shared pasts belonging to collectives of different scope. The calendar is a vehicle for a non-egocentric past; or for a past in which egocentricity has been laundered. And thank heavens (at times) for this, as recollection of a personal past can bring an unbearable sense of loss. Yesteryear always seems privileged: their snows without the slush and the cold feet. At the least, we had more time then, more "ahead". The inner time traveller assumes the viewpoint of a past self who did not know what the present self knows. This is fertile territory for regret, particularly when memory alights on past hopes that have not been realized. Events are not tense tourists (as we shall discuss in the next chapter); but we humans most certainly are, nimbly darting between the remembered past, the experienced present, and the anticipated future.

An appropriate juncture, then, to turn to the third tense.[15]

Addendum A note on memory

The connection between the past and memory is profound, complex, and deeply puzzling. In this brief note, I want only to pick up a few trailing threads arising out of the observation that memory has a double intentionality. A memory about something (an experience) that was itself about something. In the case of factual memory, we might even ascribe to it a triple intentionality. I am told the date of the Battle of Hastings. Receiving this information corresponds to an experience of or about you making a statement – first-order intentionality. The statement is about the Battle of Hastings – second order intentionality. My remembering that the Battle of Hastings took place in 1066 – perhaps in response to an examination question – is the memory of what I was told – third order intentionality. We might tease out my remembering into: (a) recalling the token utterance emitted by you (along with, perhaps, and the circumstances of your uttering it) – an episodic memory; and (b) recalling the fact communicated by the utterance – a semantic memory.

This layered intentionality cannot be accommodated in the material, more particularly the neural, theory of conscious memory. As we noted, the direction of causation – leading from the remembered event to the brain that encountered them – is not that of the aboutness of experience if the latter is identified with neural activity.

This is of concern because the causal relationship between that which was remembered and the act or moment of remembering is often regarded as the guarantor of the validity of the memory. I truly remember experience E if E is causally connected with the memory M. The usual way the causal path is characterized is that the relevant effect of E is to leave a *trace* M in the brain of the rememberer. The idea of memories as traces – central to cognitive science since Plato suggested that they were like wax impressions – is incoherent. It is demolished in a brilliant paper by Stephen Braude.[16] I will focus only on those of his arguments, that are relevant to our larger concern with tensed time.

If memories were traces, he asks, how would they deliver what is required of them? As Braude puts it, "memory traces are never strictly identical either with the things that produce them or the things that activate them".[17] In that case, how would we recognize the brain traces – or how would the brain traces recognize themselves – as being about (say) a smile on Mr Jones's face a couple of years ago? Is it because they are *like* Mr Jones's smiling face? Hardly: neural activity does not look like Mr Jones's smiling face, even less one that bears the appearance of being "two years ago". Wolfgang Kohler suggested that there must be an isomorphism – an inherent structural similarity – between the smiling face and the memory of it, between the memory and the remembered. The trouble is, the form would not have the singularity of the smiling face – and the unique context in which it is located. Even if it did, there is a more profound problem. It would be necessary already to remember Mr Jones's smiling face for the rememberer to recognize the neural activity for what it is: a representation of the smiling face. To recognize the trace for what it is, we would, as Braude summarizes it, "need to remember in order to remember".[18]

There is a more general point: representation is not something that material objects or events can do on their own: "representation can't be an intrinsic relation between the thing represented and the thing that represents it".[19] This is true for many reasons, including one that Braude highlights: the similarity or otherwise of two items that share a structure depends on the respect in which they are compared. A red square may represent a brown square if geometrical shape is the salient property but not if colour is. When it comes to memories of faces, picnics in the country, or historical facts, it is impossible to specify the relevant dimension of isomorphism: there is "no context-independent parsing into basic elements" that will represent one thing rather than another.[20] This is an expression of a more general truth: *there are no purely structural or "context-independent forms of representation"*.[21] Work would have to be done on the trace to make it stand for the object or event that caused it and which it is now preserving. We are back to the fundamental problem: to recognize trace M as a memory of event E, we have to remember E in order to see that M is a memory of it.[22]

There are even more problems with the idea of the "memory trace" of a *fact*. "Isomorphous" representation seems strained, to say the least. What would the neural picture of the fact that the Battle of Hastings was a disaster for Harold or that it took place in 1066 look like? And there are additional difficulties when we consider the triggering of the memories. All sorts of stray experiences may prompt me to think of Mr Jones's smiling face (or, come to that, the Battle of Hastings). The appeal to "associations" – or "associations of ideas" – as triggers is the recipe for chaos and makes the identification of the trace as a trace of Mr Jones's smiling face seem even more challenging. Pretty well anything may be associated with pretty well anything else. A mind driven hither and thither by associations would be in a state of delirium.

The underlying neurology is also conceptually confused. Is the trace a continuing reverberation of the circuits activated when I encountered Mr Jones's smiling face – so that we have as it were a standing wave corresponding to that experience? If it were, it would have to maintain itself and, somehow, keep intact the causal connection with the original experience which it remembers, and also keep in touch with that experience. If it was not self-maintaining in this way, there would have to be a causal connection that leaps over a temporal gap. The sustained "reverberation" idea requires us to imagine the sum of our remembered past endlessly reactivated. This would keep an awful lot of circuits rather busy – too busy one might think to register new experiences. There is also the problem of the coherence of the activity corresponding to the memory: how does it keep itself together so that it retains its unity and its identity as Mr Jones's smile on a particular occasion? The alternative – long-term changes in the firing thresholds of circuits, due to lasting changes in synapses "encoding" past experience, would make the second problem even more difficult: a pattern of heightened excitability would be difficult to maintain unchanged and it would be interesting to see how it was able to assert its unity or coherence. And we have the difficulty already alluded to of seeing how the spontaneous propensity to fire could be controlled, such that day-to-consciousness was not simply a seething mass of detritus from the past. And how, finally, could memories be summoned to order? How we could deliberately recall this or that (particularly facts that have no face to them), even less to "rack our brains" to recall something – the "auto-cueing" in which we engage so frequently?

It is easy to see the attraction of translating memories into traces in the brain: it brings memory into the fold of the materialist world picture: memories become material effects of material causes and remembering a reactivation of those causes by triggers that operate through those effects. Causal talk, however, highlights another fundamental flaw of this idea, associated with a problem we have already identified: that the effects have somehow to be maintained. The effect has to go on and on and on, so that the trace of Mr Jones's smile remains in my brain years after I encountered it. In the normal course of events effects in turn become causes and efface themselves in their own effects. This is particularly the case with singular causes and singular effects – directly relevant to the case of putative memory traces of billions of singular experiences which most typically give rise to responses expressed in behaviour or physiological changes that would seem to empty their continuing presence into their causal efficacy. The appeal to enduring structural changes as traces – for example long-term changes in synaptic excitability and transmission – would simply make this worse.[23]

The other fundamental problem brings us back to the outset of our discussion. Cerebral traces have somehow to make contact with, in the sense of being *about*, their causal ancestors, having somehow extricated themselves from neural melee of the open fields of moment-to-moment consciousness in which experiences from within and from outside the body, thoughts and emotions, resolves and intentions, occur alongside, and interact with, memories.

The memory trace as a miraculously sustained material effect of a material experience doesn't seem likely to deliver this. This is not to say that the brain is not a necessary condition of memory, that it *mediates* the capacity to remember, as Braude puts it. Of course, it is and of course it does. There can be very striking correlations between localised brain damage and loss of distinct aspects of memory. But there must be more to it than this. The presence of the past requires something that neither physics nor physical objects such as the brain can accommodate.

CHAPTER 8
Concerning tomorrow (today)

8.1 INTRODUCING THE FUTURE: ALL OUR TOMORROWS

All three tenses seem vulnerable to attack. The past is ontologically weakened by the fact that (by definition) nothing is presently happening in it, its states of affairs are no longer existent, and its material contents owe their survival to being in the present. The present seems to borrow its breadth (or depth) from the other tenses: it lives on borrowed time. And the future – as we shall see – has nothing determinate in it. To say this, however, far from undermining any of the tenses, is to acknowledge that they do not stand alone. There is no present without a past to inform it and a future to give it direction; and there is no future without a past-informed present to anticipate it. The future, therefore, requires no special defence.

8.1.1 The unknown future

When I began this book in earnest, I estimated that I had an actuarial average of about 7,000 or 8,000 tomorrows compared with my 22,000 yesterdays. Quite a few todays later, the number of the former is significantly less and of the latter rather more. I have of course a clearer idea of the number of my yesterdays than tomorrows and can calculate their number precisely because there is a precise number to calculate. This highlights a more general point, in addition to the mathematical one that I am over three quarters through the time for which Raymond Tallis is a walking, talking, thinking enterprise; namely, that the uncertainty in "over three quarters" comes from my tomorrows rather than my yesterdays: I know what is on the numerator but not what is on the denominator. While I can be certain that I have just under 3,500 fewer tomorrows than lay before me when I began this book a decade or so ago, I do not know which tomorrow will be the tomorrow after there will be no more tomorrows. Even if I had a suicide pact with myself, I couldn't guarantee that I would honour it or that I would make it to the appointed day. "Call no life spanned until it is complete" we might say. And the uncertainty applies with even more force to the contents of those tomorrows: what will happen, to me or the world, in my remaining time.

Our forward-looking gaze meets a blank wall, decorated with the contents of our imagination. There are circumstances in which we think we can see what is about to happen, as when we observe from a vantage two cars on a collision course. Even then, while anticipation may prove correct, it is not guaranteed confirmation. One car may swerve at the last minute. However, we must be correct often enough to make it worthwhile forming expectations or indeed for us to bother to act in order to shape the future. If I cannot have any confidence that the low hanging fruit will not move out of reach before I try to grasp them, then there would be little point in my stretching out my hand. And I would not attempt to meet you at an agreed venue if I thought that there was not a very high probability of your being in that place at the agreed time. While our active present is shaped by networks of short-run expectations whose nearest precincts are attached to the visible world around us, the future that makes sense of our lives – that confers intelligibility upon and motivates our actions – is overwhelmingly invisible.

The opacity frustrating our attempts to "look forward" in time has two distinct sources: first, that future states of affairs are as yet indeterminate; and secondly that even things that are determinate may be as yet unrevealed. Here's an example. Last week I had a blood test and have been told to ring up for the result. As I dial the number, I do not know what the future may bring – good news or bad. However, there are other people who are already able to know whether the news is good or bad because this bit of the future is already determined. The laboratory has already filed its report. By contrast, before I attended for the blood test, nobody knew whether the test was positive or not. And in the case of a quantitative test (such as a blood sugar) the relevant parameter, given that it is fluctuating all the time, would not have arrived at the measured value until the moment the test was taken. So my own uncertainty when I ring up for the result of the test is ignorance of something that is determinate, to the extent that it can already be known to others. It is an epistemic, not an ontic uncertainty. We justifiably distinguish between that which is indeterminate and (necessarily) unknown, that which is determinate but happens to be unknown, and that which is determinate and known.

Keeping in mind the distinction between epistemic uncertainty and ontic indeterminacy should prevent us from falling into the common mistake of seeing "the passage of the future into the past" as merely an accumulation of information.[1] However the distinction between what I don't know and what I could not know because "it" has not happened is more complicated than might appear at first sight. Firstly, knowing that something has taken place is not a simple yes/no issue. I may know that a car crash has taken place but not the details. Indeed, my knowledge will always lack some details. I could learn more and more just as the description of an event could be extended indefinitely. It is an interesting question as to whether there is a blood test value when the test has not been carried out properly or at all. In what sense does my blood sugar level – as opposed to the sugar in my blood – exist when no-one has measured it?

   Moreover, in the case of something that has "not yet" happened, and consequently may not happen at all, the nature of the "something" – particularly when it is entertained as one of a range of possibilities – is unclear. There is no comparability between an event that might happen and one that has happened. This is not a merely pedantic point because it lies at the root of the 2,500-year-old arguments about future contingents that should have crashed on take-off as Aristotle perhaps intended they should. Behind this is the observation that future contingents are incorrigibly indefinite – no description can specify them to the level of definiteness of an actual event.

   We shall return to this in §8.2. For the present, we note that, even where things go to plan, that plan is inescapably less detailed than anything that goes according to it. Consider a party which we have arranged. It begins and ends at the appointed time and takes place at the address we have chosen. All the guests we have invited turn up and there are no gate-crashers. Even so, we would be very foolish to predict what happens at the party except in the broadest terms.

   Thus, our ignorance of the future.

8.1.2 The furniture of the future

> When I pronounce the word Future the first syllable already belongs
> to the past.[2]   Szymborska, "The Three Oddest Words"

> The future must already "be present in its causes" [as the Schoolmen
> said] if I am able to predict that *something* is *going* to happen.
>   Lucas, *The Future*, 66

The future is not of course, entirely blank. While it cannot be known with certainty – foreknown would be foreclosed and indeed foreordained – we have some degree of foresight. If this were not the case, we would simply pinball through the world in a permanent present tense, possibly haunted by a past that offers no guidance to us. In practice, we swim through a sea of expectations – though we are often most acutely aware of these when they are confounded or where we share them with others. To return to a basic example – that of looking at an object in motion which we discussed in Chapter 1. We can see not only where it is and where it has been but also the position where we anticipated it will be.

   However, our knowledge is not equally secure on both sides of the present: I can be sure that the ball occupied position A one second ago but not that it will occupy position B in a second's time, even though this seems overwhelmingly likely. For the ball may be intercepted and the anticipated future not materialize. The visibility of past and future are not therefore comparable because what we recall cannot unhappen whereas what we anticipate may fail to happen. Remembering the past correctly depends on the quality of our memory whereas anticipating the future correctly depends on more than the quality of our information and the shrewdness with which we use it: the best-grounded expectations may be legitimately defeated by what no-one could be expected to anticipate. If our expectations were indefeasible they would not count as expectations at all but something rather like perceptions.

There are two sources of the future active in the present: the continuation of ongoing changes, along with the processes and events that comprise them, and the material substrate in which changes take place; and our individual or collective expectations of these ongoing changes. The respective contributions of, and the relationship between, the two in the making of "the presence of tomorrow today" is complex and, though it is not possible to separate them entirely, it helps to deal with them separately, not the least because we try to *shape* the future, on the basis of expectations of what could happen, as well as taking happening as it comes. Indeed, our lives may be characterized by the extent to which we endeavour to shape the future – our individual and shared future – and to control the extent to which it merely happens and happens to us.

Our challenge is to find out what of the future is already present before it "arrives". When we think about the presence of tomorrow today, it helps to think of today as being "the initial conditions" that, in conjunction with the laws according to which the world unfolds (or can be made to unfold), will deliver subsequent conditions. We may put this another way by identifying those parts of the furniture or contents of the future that are already in place: that which is present today which will still be there tomorrow; those things that straddle the imagined line between today and tomorrow that we cannot cross.

Before doing so, we need to set aside the notion that, while its metaphysical problems apply as much to ten seconds hence as to next year or a millennium hence, the future is heterogeneous. The time of the physicist is homogeneous: any moment or time interval t_1 is the same as any moment or time interval t_2. But tensed time, and more broadly lived time, has a heterogeneity in addition to that manifest in the three tenses. So we have to distinguish what we might call the immediate-future from the near-future, and the near-future from the middle-future and the distant-future, with the first two being usually (though not always) more salient than the third. These are no sharp boundaries and, indeed, the scope of these quasi-territories will depend upon what kinds of perspectives we are adopting – that of everyday practical life, of the historian, or of the astrophysicist.

In a much discussed paper, Quentin Smith introduced the idea of "degrees of existence" which varied according to the distance of events from present.[3] Past and future do exist (today) but to *a lesser degree* than the present. Today's dental appointment (that I am now undergoing) has a stronger degree of existence than a similar appointment a year ago or in a year's time. Unless the contrast is meant as a straightforward comparison of the psychological properties of an experience of a present event and a fading memory or an anticipation of a remote future event, it raises some tricky questions. How do we make sense of "partial" versus "full" or "maximal" existence? There can, of course, be things that seem to be real and prove not to be. An hallucination is real as an appearance but there is nothing corresponding to that which it seems to reveal. On this basis, we may argue that the false referential object of the hallucination (say a tree) has a "lesser degree of existence" than a real tree. Otherwise, we encounter the kinds of problems that Parmenides advanced: namely that things either are or they are not and there are no intermediate degrees of being: what-is is and what-is-not is not. A more generous ontology that embraces smoke as well as trees, holes as well as holy objects, and sakes as well as holes, will only compound our problems. Not only do we not know what to make of, for example, sakes but also we would not know where to locate future events on the imaginary line connecting pukka objects such as trees with ontologically dubious characters such as "sakes".[4] Degree presentism, in short, seems to add only confusion to our understanding of the contents of the future (and the past).

With these caveats in mind, let us consider what elements, of the things that are surrounding me today, already constitute the furniture of tomorrow.

8.1.2.1 The world's share

The most obvious candidates for the furniture of the future are material objects and the future tense implicit in their continuation. The mountain on which I plan to have a walk tomorrow will have to be in place for my plan to make any kind of sense. Though my walk is by no means certain, the possibility of the mountain disappearing is not a major source of uncertainty that the walk will take place. The uncertainties will come from events such as the fluctuation of my appetite for exercise or an unexpected rival attraction or competing commitments or bad weather. Objects (as we discussed in §6.2.1.2) are, by definition, stable compared with processes and events. Indeed, their stability is deeply connected with the ground-floor assumption that they transcend – are beyond, outlast – my experience of them. What I perceive of the object at time t_1 therefore, is not something that is confined to the t_1 of my perception. This is implicit in the sense that the object exists for, but not merely in, me; that it is for me but not just for me. In short, in my sense of the public nature, the objectivity, of the object.

I can say with some confidence that the objects that surround me in my study today – printer, desk, carpet, lamp, bookshelves, window, door, etc. – will surround me, if I sit at my table (as I expect) tomorrow. If I pop out of my study, I can reasonably expect that some or all of these items will be there when I return. I cannot, of course, be 100 per cent confident, though from one moment to the next my confidence is so high that it is not experienced as confidence. It is not (merely) an expectation, or an estimation of a "high probability" that this chair I am sitting on will continue to be present to support me or that the garden will remain outside of my window: I assume, rather than rely on or hope for, their continuation. Even so, my house could be demolished by an explosion between now and my return to my study.

I can increase the odds of being right by shortening the time interval over which my expectations stretch. If I confine the future to the next 5 seconds, then my confidence will converge on justified certainty. I can lengthen the odds by extending the reach of the future to a year's time, a century's time, a 1,000 years' time; and so on.

At some point, I can start to become confident that the furniture that surrounds me now will *not* furnish a future tomorrow.

The point is that there is no definite future distance at which my expectations of the continuation of objects and (in the case of fixtures) the stability of their arrangements should *justifiably* change from certainty to a mere entertainment of possibility or a pious hope. We have, as it were, a gradually thinning of the density of the future seen from today, as our imagination stretches from the near, to the middle, to the distant future, from the short to the long run. (This is not to be confused with a "degree presentism" of specific contents.) The strength of induction weakens, the arrow of projection of ongoing processes from the present loses its momentum and hence predictive power. While my study today will almost certainly have much of its furniture in place tomorrow, this will be less certain in a year's time and most definitely not true in 1,000 years' time. Some kinds of furniture will be present over a longer future than others: movables such as a cup will be less reliably in the same place than others such as built-in cupboards, the walls, and the ground on which the house stands. And fragile items, by definition, will be less likely to be in *any* place in a relatively distant future, than others. This, however, is a matter of likelihood rather than certainty; after all, cups may outlast cities, and be excavated intact from the sites where nothing else remains of the houses and streets. Even so, we may be more confident of the location of a wall in a week's time than of a chair, a cup, or a person.

There is a theoretical point at which probabilities about the survival of stuff into the future become certainties: namely, when we reach the physical limits to rates of macroscopic changes in the objects (governed by the finitude of the speed of light and of the rate of other processes.) For example, the unforeseen explosion, that demolishes the objects that surround me in my study, will take a minimal period of time to bring its destructive work to completion. I can be confident therefore that this study I expect will furnish that portion of the future that is defined by the term "one second from now" will indeed do that. Metaphysically, however, there is no difference between "one second into the future" and "one year into the future" and between the latter and "one million years into the future". They all belong to the same tense, to the "not-yet". This is reflected in the already noted lack of sharp difference between, say, "the immediate" and the "near" futures. There is a gradient along which justified certainties weaken to objective probabilities and objective probabilities weaken to ever more tenuous possibilities; and these gradients match the attenuating density of the future today.

When we are talking about the most resilient of today's contents – material objects – there is still an element of mere probability regarding their future existence. It is difficult to give clear meaning to, as it were, "probability-adjusted reality" because things either exist or they do not, as we highlighted in our Parmenidean resistance to Quentin Smith's "degree presentism". They do not "probably" exist or "possibly" exist, notwithstanding that probabilities may seem to be objective and to be measured with justifiable confidence.

Probabilities, however, come into play when we look at the interaction between the stability of the objects in the world and the forces that keep them stable or destabilize them. It is on the basis of these forces – derived from repeated observations that generate those laws on the basis of which we predict stability or change – that we judge whether objects are or are not likely to be present at some specified future date, and whether processes that we see ongoing in the present will continue to a particular future. Whether, in short, they will be part of the furniture of tomorrow. Those probabilities are not constitutive of the objects because they require to be co-produced by an interested subject thinking about the future. More generally, the material world (above the quantum level at least) does not have probabilities (or possibilities) as part of its make-up. Things are and that's the end of it.

What's more, while the probabilities we assign to the way the world (states, objects, processes) will unfold may be startlingly accurate, they will never reach 100 per cent certainty. One of the most important reasons why the Laplacean dream of precise prediction of a future specified with an unlimited degree of exactitude is only a dream (or a nightmare) is that laws of nature can be revealed only by removing many specifics of real situations as "noise".[5] But no situations are in themselves constituted of either signals or noise: the difference between signal and noise is interest-dependent. We may remove the influence of air friction when establishing the laws of falling bodies because in the case of the kind of bodies we are interested in (missiles rather than feathers, say) this source of resistance is relatively unimportant. Of course, it is possible to restore that component and arrive at more complex laws that take account of air friction but many other things will have been left out in order that the laws should have general applicability to situations which are generalized by having the same things left out. So even the most well-founded estimates of probability will not reach all the way down to the singulars of the future; of, say, a future world-moment.

In addition to quasi-stable objects, ongoing *processes* will also furnish the future: we can envisage future time-slices of the entirety of what is going on at present. And not all processes are time limited or obviously transient; though when they are not, they may look a bit like objects – as in the case of streams and waterfalls discussed in §6.2.1.2. Even so, such processes may be even less reliable as guides to the contents of the remote future than the most resilient objects such as mountains. Events, almost by definition, do not live on – they are complete; and if they are not complete we think of them as processes. (As already noted, a process is an event viewed from within the time interval it occupies.) While our anticipations populate the future with events, the latter have no obligation to occur and even if they do, there will be a mismatch between any given prediction and the occurrent event, even where the latter fulfils the prediction. The former will at some level be general – that is how prediction works – and the latter will be singular.

This point is of fundamental significance as we shall see in due course. For the present, we note only that there is an interaction between objects as the furniture of the future and future events. Objects, as the substrate of events, are a constraint on, and enablers of, future events. The latter will themselves erode objects (or states of affairs) and thus in their turn influence possible events further into the future. But events do not occupy the future. Indeed, we can say of the future, that we have seen it but it does no work. Or the work it seems to do does not reside in the material world. It is conscious agents that make it something that works to influence the present.

In summary, the future can be both indeterminate and yet real at present because its furniture and certain consistent patterns of change that will deliver it are already in place. What is yet to be determined are actual events, processes, changes; but they already have a potential home in the material objects that endure into the future. One can be realistic about the future without being realistic about future events to the point of imagining that they are somehow "in waiting".

As we move from objects to processes and then to events, it is evident that we are switching from "the world's share" to "the anticipator's" share of the furniture of the future – though not all philosophers would agree to this as we shall see in §8.2.2.2.

8.1.2.2 The anticipator's share

There is an important difference between the present and future state of an enduring object that provides the furniture of the future today. This-cup-today exists whether it is thought about or not; whereas tomorrow's cup exists (today) only if someone imagines it or implicitly presupposes and relies upon its future continuation – as when I buy a present to give you tomorrow. That is why the contents of tomorrow, unlike those of today, are patchy and pick-and-mix and they are picked out and mixed by propositional attitudes – beliefs, expectations, hopes, fears, plans, planning assumptions, and so on. Nevertheless, the future is continuously implicitly present: carrying on regardless today, without a thought for the morrow, stands on assumptions about tomorrow that largely go without saying because they seem too obvious and banal to be spelt out.

The future is furnished, then, as the result of an interplay between what exists of its own accord and as it were projects itself into the future (ordinary, stable objects, ongoing processes) and the projections we make on the basis of what we know about the present and about the general way the world unfolds or remains unchanged. There is the world's share and the anticipator's share.

In the absence of our expectations and anticipations and plans, the future lacks specificity. This does not mean that the future that has such a grip on us – being future-oriented is the most ubiquitous shaping force in our life, and accounts for much of the difference between enduring our lives as organisms and leading our lives as people – is a collective illusion. Our expectations are for the great part rooted in experience – personal and shared, casual and scientific – and are subject to the test of experience which, time and again, will have for the most part proved them to have been justified. The anticipated future in which my study is still in place, or a waterfall continues falling, is not ontologically dubious like ghosts revealed through precognition. The very fact that expectations of the future can be judged as realistic or unrealistic, shrewd or daft, implies that it makes sense to talk of a future reality or the reality of the future.

Crucially, our expectations are to a greater or lesser degree open-textured, so what will satisfy them will be specified only to a certain level. Consider a planned holiday – that goes according to plan. I form only very broad expectations of what I will experience; indeed, my motto as holidaymaker is *placet experiri.* The promises in the brochure are merely a permissive general framework for a singular holiday most of whose contents are outside of the brochure. And even the most closely prescribed anticipations have a large "tolerance" built into them. It could not be otherwise. Our expectations are of *classes* of events and states of affairs: they correspond to broad, general expectations. After all, the exact specification of an actual (singular) event – with all its actual features – would be infinitely long and the burden of making it happen would be beyond us and the probability of its happening close to zero, the odds lengthening as the bet spreads less and converges on precise actualities. This is something to which we shall return in §8.2.2.2.

Anticipations are based upon estimates of probabilities. But we are not so rational that the strength of our expectations correlates precisely with objective likelihood, and is soundly based upon previous experience accurately recalled and appropriately analysed, of frequencies of occurrence and the similarity of past and future conditions. And we must not confuse the roughness of our estimate of probabilities with the degree of openness of the future, the epistemic with the constitutive. The future appears open not just because we can get it wrong and it has an irreducibly unpredictable element but because it is not yet fixed.

The unexpected has didactic powers, enabling us to modify our behaviour and our plans. Correction can be close at hand and highly specific, or remote and very general. So I can reach for a bannister that turns out to be a shadow and fall down the stairs, illustrating by its defeat how much expectation is built into ordinary perception; how what we see are affordances that afford us certain local anticipated futures. At the other extreme, I can plan a career in medicine, with a general image of doing good, having grateful patients and living a worthwhile life, and subsequently enacting out this career plan in a billion details none of which, for better or worse, I had envisaged.

Among the furnishings of the future, anticipated events seem to be more completely generated by expectations than are the future phases of objects or of ongoing processes, even though those latter features are also based on expectations. And yet events are more truly part of the fabric of any time when the future becomes present. The future we imagine, that is, is not of objects but of happenings, for which objects form only the substrate. If I plan to walk to the doctor's surgery tomorrow to get the result of a test, my plan rides on all sorts of presuppositions about the material world interposed between myself and the surgery, the most obvious of which are the roads that form the route, as well at the compatibility of different activities (such as keeping another important appointment which I assume will take place). But this leaves much room for variation. Even if my intention is fulfilled without any digressions, interruptions, frustrations and so on, its actual contents will exceed the bounds of what is envisaged in the plan. Not only would it be unnecessary to rehearse every detail of the journey to the surgery, it would be impossible to do so because they cannot be foreseen: the people I pass en route, the traffic that rushes by, the weather and the lighting, the particular bodily sensations I experience as I turn into the car park, the precise placing of my steps, the pressure from the door as I push my way into the surgery, the person who deals with me and the exact form of the conversation, and so on ad infinitum. The difference between the presence of a bit of the future today when it is being planned and looked forward to and its presence when it comes to pass is consequently profound. We may characterize it as the difference between on the one hand a necessarily determinate, unfolding, singular actuality (the future when it has come to pass and ceased to be future) and a generality.

Much of our life is devoted to what we might call "future husbandry": we work individually and collectively to make our world a place that takes a path closer to that proposed in our hopes and further from that anticipated in our fears. Our manipulation of future states of (parts of) the world can take many forms and the relationship between what we do know and what we hope will happen in the future may be very complex indeed. The general idea that we do A in order that B shall occur has to be supplemented by the notion that we may refrain from doing A or prevent another from doing A in order that B shall not occur. And individually or collectively doing or refraining from doing A in order that B shall or shall not occur to ourselves individually or collectively is open to almost infinite elaboration.[6]

We could summarize the aims of "future husbandry" as being to mitigate the play of chance in our lives where accidents are for the most part undesirable (though we speak of "happy accidents") and diminish the vulnerability that comes from ignorance of what might happen in the absence of our interventions or as a consequence of our interventions. To do this to maximum effect, so that we translate our collective powers into manipulation of the future, we need to coordinate our activities. And this we do to an extraordinary degree as we discussed in §4.6.

This brings us to something that is not so much the furniture of the future as the shared or collective places in which, in our imagination, the furniture is housed: the times and dates that form the coordinates of the multiple networks of co-cooperative activities that constitute the society in which we live.

8.1.3 The containers of the future

We who plan for the future and anticipate and endeavour to shape its contents in order to lead rather than merely to suffer our lives need to divide it up. This makes intuitive sense: all contents – remembered, ongoing, or anticipated – require containers. There are many ways of slicing the future and housing the slices. The most obvious containers are "days" which reflect the universal periodicities observed in the earth on which we live. Future alternations of light and darkness and cycling of the seasons are tagged by records extrapolated from the past. In the relatively recent history of humankind, those tagged periods have been given names, and those names, by being written down are set out in space. Our human future is assigned to public calendars and private diaries: dates (named and numbered days, months, and years) are the scaffolding of a shared life. Appointments, promises, deliveries, honouring of debts, durations of entitlements, goals and targets, all have their due dates.

The containers seem to acquire a substance of their own. Although, they are empty temporal places, mere loci of possibility, they become quasi-items. In a typical calendar – the "year-to-view" or "year-at-a-glance" – each day is presented as a box, housing possible future events written into them which, it is intended or expected, will happen or be made to happen. The days as they "arrive" may be crossed out or, in the case of some calendars, torn off and assigned to the no-longer. The calendar is a strikingly literal expression of the transformation of time into space (each day a cell) and space into numbers (each cell is ranked in numerical order and, whatever happens in them, the number indicates that all days are born equal).[7] We do not take the metaphor of days as containers entirely literally, or not at least in English. We say that we shall meet someone *on* Wednesday not *in* or even *at* Wednesday.[8]

Dividing the future into an array of cells visited successively by, or in succession visiting (a telling ambiguity[9]), the present reinforces a dynamic image of time (already criticized, especially in §2.3.2.2), with the present being thought of as a moving spotlight playing over a succession of days that co-exist in the darkness, awaiting their time on the stage, or conversely of days moving into a static spotlight, where for 24 hours they are "today".

Less contentiously, diaries and calendars underline the extent to which the not-yet is a joint product: that we share in, and co-produce, a pooled future (even though within this we forge our own individual lives, and fit the future to our private biography and our unique trajectory). The calendar announces, first of all, that, whatever our differences, we are all inhabiting the same day. Secondly, it enables us to interact in more complex and sustained ways as we discussed in §4.4, so that the different things we do to shape the future, to bring things about rather than merely wait for them to happen and suffer them when they do, can dovetail. We converge in appointments; indeed, much of our life runs to appointment. We can form teams that are drawn from many different quarters of the world, way beyond those spatial aggregations that mark the "teamwork" of non-human animals. We have official days of celebration. These planned events are marked on the calendar as future inhabitants of the cells of time.

Our anticipations of natural events – day and night, long days and long nights, short days and short nights, the waxing and waning of heat and light, the cycles of seed-time and harvest – also become more precise, so that we can together take account of them and realize a collective strength in fine-tuned, precision-engineered, large-scale and long-term cooperation. The calendar signals the day we have arrived at and the "distance" separating us from the day we are preparing for, planning, and fearing. Our diaries, which also mark the things we plan, may also be a record of how what we planned turned out – how it was experienced – and how, in some cases, it did not.

Dates are and are not human constructs. They are ultimately founded on the giant periodicities served up by the solar system of which our planet is a part, upon global givens of the natural world that we exploit or suffer in common.[10] But their numbering, naming, and grouping into weeks and months, and the identification of some of them as special and to be allocated for festivals, are conventional. They are social facts, belonging not to my individual consciousness but to the community of (like or like-ish) minds. The natural roots of diurnal divisions, however, gives them the status of something that is more than stretches of time, though less than events in their own right. They are containers that have a whiff of content, as if they were analogous to a box which shares with its contents the property of being a material item. It is easy therefore to be seduced into imagining the successive days like cable cars hung from the wire of time, each delivering a day's worth of events; as being made of more than time, and yet being that into which time is partitioned.

This ambiguity between days as abstract containers and as items in themselves is particularly evident when we think of them as *dates*. We shall discuss dates (and times) as tense tourists in §8.2.2.3. Of course, we may dread or impatiently look forward to future dates. But what we dread or joyfully anticipate is not the date itself but an event (a surgical operation or the receipt of a present) that is "penciled in" to take place then.

8.1.4 The reality of the future

> I have come to discover, in philosophical discourse with those who
> are not professional philosophers, that it is very common for people
> to doubt the reality of the future, and it is very hard to convince them
> that the future is real.   Smart, "The Reality of the Future", 141

The future (like the past and the present) has a precarious existence. It has to be other than itself: its contents have to be present in order to be at all and, at the same time, not-present in order to be future; to be present in order to be (of) the future but not in the way that the contents of the present are present. "Tomorrow" is a kind of "impending" tray. Its furniture, as we have discussed, is to some degree present in the present: its objects, ongoing processes, and the laws governing the unfolding of events are to a greater or lesser extent in place. Even so, the future is present only through its representation, its proxies: the anticipated future state of objects or events presented as expectations formulated at a general level. For example, for an object to be invested with a future, O at time t+1 has to be present in some fashion at time t. And for an event to be in the future, E occurring at time t+1 has to have some kind of being at time t. While we acknowledge the difference between the envisaged presence of "'O at t+1' at t" and "'O at t' at t", and so are not too readily confused about the ontological status of the future time-slices of objects, we are more prone to be misled in the case of events. We are liable to think that E which occurs at t, already has a kind of existence as a future E at t-1. There is the idea of events "in the wings" as they lie in the future, waiting to strut their moments on the stage of the present, after which they repair to another lot of wings as they take residence in the past. This notion of events as tense tourists is mistaken, but profoundly and illuminatingly so, and it will be addressed in §§8.2.2.2 and 8.2.2.3.

In defending the reality of the future, I have focused on the present existence of its furniture – objects, etc. that are here today and will (almost certainly) not be gone tomorrow – and on the expectations, anticipations, and estimates of probability that discern the future in present furniture. Some would go further than I do in ascribing reality to the future, grounding it in (a) the present reality of future *events*; and (b) the objective reality of probabilities. A brief look at these is in order.

Smart has argued that future events are real along these lines.[11] Imagine a twenty-first century soldier cold, miserable, and suffering from dysentery and being told that some twentieth-century philosophers and others had held that the future (including his suffering) was unreal. He might, Smart suggests, "have some choice things to say". And he would not be mollified by being told that his suffering was real in the twenty-first century but not real in the twentieth century. While Smart argues, correctly, that "reality is not a property which anything can acquire", I believe, he draws the wrong conclusion from this. Yes, event E cannot have two states – real and unreal; but we should not conclude from this that E is real from the beginning of time. Instead, we should conclude that it is mistaken to think that "E" has the same referent when we are talking about a future event and about a present event; or, more precisely, an event that hasn't (yet) happened and an event that has happened. Thinking that "E" can have the same referent in both circumstances, misleads us into imagining that the same entity can begin in the future, become present, and end up in the past. In short, that events can be tense tourists. My position is that the furniture of the future (of tomorrow today) does not include events.

The future that is dormant in the present – in the form of the stable furniture (objects, ongoing processes, laws) that will outlast today and still be there tomorrow – needs to be activated by anticipations (implicit or explicit). These anticipations must be shaped by a sense of probability. For some, the dependence on anticipations may suggest that the future is still not really real unless those anticipations are rooted in the real world; specifically, in a sense of probability that matches emergent reality. This presupposes a particular view of the nature of probability – "the very guide of life" as Bishop Butler called it. A brief treatment of this very large topic is therefore called for.

According to Alan Hájek, there are three main concepts of probability: a quasi-logical concept which is a measure of the objective evidential support for a prediction; a measure of an agent's degree of (justified) confidence in a prediction; and an objective concept that applies to systems in the world.[12] They are not clearly separated and there is dispute as to whether there is a fundamental notion from which the others are derived. Where there are outcomes that are equally possible, then probabilities of a particular outcome are inversely proportional to the number of possibilities. In the case of coin tossing, the probability of either of the two outcomes is 0.5, assuming an unbent coin. There is subjective probability hosted by a rational agent which translates into degree of belief in a particular outcome that forms the basis of action – formalized in certain settings in the amount of your wealth you might be willing to bet on that outcome. The interpretations of probability that seem to locate it most clearly outside of the subject – leaving aside the subject's role in defining the field of interest and the range of outcomes – are frequency interpretations. The probability of an outcome within a range of outcomes is identified with its frequency or proportion of actual occurrences. There are *propensity* interpretations which, like frequency interpretations, locate probability in the world rather than in subjective awareness or interpretation. A propensity is a disposition of "a given type of physical situation to yield an outcome of a certain kind, or to yield a long run relative frequency of such an outcome".[13]

How does this relate to the question of the reality of the future? Where we see probability as rooted in the physical world – in the frequentist and propensity accounts – it seems as if it is a measure of the extent to which the future is constrained by the present, not only in virtue of the stable fixtures and fittings that straddle both present and future. It is also constrained by persistent habits of behaviour of the world, by a principle of precedence ("as things have been so shall they be"), by a uniformity of unfolding. Expectations shaped by objective probabilities seem more likely to be in touch with a real future; that is to say a future that is not only expected but actually turns out in virtue of being mandated. However, probabilities (like possibilities) are not generated by the material world acting on its own. Without prior expectation to define the field of interest, and hence the range of possibilities to be considered, the future that turns out is not an outcome that was correctly or incorrectly anticipated in the present. The future exists in the present only insofar as it is hoped for, feared, taken account of, or merely assumed. In this respect, however, it is no more to be dismissed as "merely subjective" than are the probabilities that are the essential stuff of objective, natural science.

The important point is that we can accept the reality of the future without siding with the notion that future *events* somehow pre-exist themselves by existing in the present or accepting that the probabilities that guide the anticipations that activate the furniture of the future present today are entirely part of the material world. The most potent evidence for the reality of the future is that it is the realm in virtue of which we endeavour – with a good deal of success – to shape our lives. Notwithstanding the "asymmetry of influence" and the temporal directionality of causation (see §2.3.5), a well-founded idea of the future – of what might happen and how it might be promoted, prevented, or deflected – can influence its past. What I think about tomorrow shapes my behaviour in tomorrow's yesterday (today): Wednesday's ideas about Thursday may influence what I do on Wednesday. For something that (according to some) is unreal, it is a mighty potent force.

There are, however, some writers who argue that the future is not open to suggestion; that we can no more meddle with the future than we can with the past.

8.2 THE CONTESTED OPENNESS OF THE FUTURE

Certainly, much fatalistic reasoning is rather uninteresting since it can swiftly be dismissed as trivial or obviously fallacious. Yet there is real interest in uncovering those genuinely perplexing aspects of time that, in the wrong heads, give rise to the fatalistic confusion. For it arises from the core question of how our world is composed and how we, as free agents, fit in. Central to our experience as agents is the idea that the past is "fixed" while the future is open – in some sense possible. It is the interrelation between these temporal and modal notions that gives rise to fatalist thinking.[14]

8.2.1 The indeterminate future

The idea that the future is open is expressed in two related ways: that it is indeterminate (not yet defined) and still determinable (capable of alteration by us). By contrast, the past is determinate (definite) and determined (incapable of alteration by us). Now while these two characteristics are connected, they have a different scope: all of the future is (as yet) indeterminate, while only some of it lies within the range of things we can change or believe we can. What we can manipulate depends on who "we" are – where we are positioned and our capacities and characteristics, including most importantly when and for how long we are alive and conscious and thus capable of agency.[15] The indeterminacy of the future, therefore, is not what accounts for our freedom; otherwise the scope of our freedom would be co-terminous with the entirety of the future. Indeterminacy is a necessary but not a sufficient condition of future events and states of affairs being to some degree biddable.

What is more, there is indeterminacy even within the scope of a planned action that we successfully execute in the ways in which a plan can go according to plan. If this were not the case, planned action would seem to be impossible; for if what counted as "Going to the doctor's surgery" were specified down to the last movement, the circumstances in which we bring it about would have to be precisely anticipated or controlled to an impossible degree. In other words, the open future exploited when we exercise our free will has to include a tolerance built into the specification of actions: both parties – agent and action – have to give a bit. All fits between plans and their realization must be loose fit – a good-enough fit to deliver the outcome (also specified in general terms) that we want. Actual events, by contrast, are congruent with themselves to the nth degree: they are what they are. The fact that future events are indeterminate – irrespective of whether they are planned or merely foreseen – because they are possibilities means that they are necessarily general. This, as we shall see, will be important when we come to think about future contingents and logical fatalism. If we overlook this, it is because we tend to retro-fit actual events to the expectation that proposed them as possibilities.

It is a mistake to think of determination – the descent from general possibility to singular actuality – as a material process out there in the world. The transition requires an indeterminate something first to be *proposed* by a forward-looking glance against which unfolding events are measured; and it requires a *viewpoint* to divide the unfolding of events into those that are past and those that are future. They require a "now" from which there are backward and forward glances. But the material universe at any given time is neither determinate or indeterminate. It simply "is";

and to suggest that the universe is "more determinate" at t_2 than at t_1 is clearly absurd. Nothing that is can be indeterminate or, come to that, be determinate in the sense of having this as one of its characteristics. Determinateness is no more a predicate, a monadic property, than indeterminateness.

This notwithstanding, the characterization of the difference between past and future as the difference between that which is already fixed and that which is indeterminate, is in some respects a truism. That which has happened has happened and cannot unhappen and that which has not yet happened still might not happen,[16] so that it can be in the "state" of not having happened without an impossible unhappening being required to allow or effect this. This is all that the necessity of the past amounts to: not, in other words, that it was *bound* to happen but that, having happened, it can't unhappen. While we can reverse something that has happened – for example put something back on the table that has fallen off – this does not cancel the happening. *The fact that* the vase fell off the table at t_1 isn't reversed at t_2: putting the vase back on the table may make it as if it had not fallen but does not make it that it had not fallen. Restoring the status quo at t_2 does not cancel the fact that the status quo was disturbed at t_1. By contrast, things that don't happen in the future do not require anti-happenings to cancel or forestall them, any more than things that haven't happened in the past require to continue to be made not to have happened to maintain their not having happened.

Truism or not, some thinkers have tried to draw profound conclusions from this difference between future and past. Some of these conclusions rely on confusing or conflating three ways in which the indeterminacy of the future can be construed. The first is based upon the uncontroversial (but as we shall see important and often overlooked) truth that something that has not yet happened has no determinate characteristics – and has only the honorary specification of "*something* that has not happened yet". The second draws on the idea that the world unfolds not according to iron laws that operate through causal connections but on the basis of truly random events that correspond to mere probabilities. We have already touched on the variant of this, owing to quantum theory, that, at least at the subatomic level, nothing is determinate in the absence of observation. This remains controversial. The third, which is not merely controversial but probably wrong, is that the indeterminacy of the future in a probabilistic materialistic universe, is a necessary (which it is) and a sufficient (which it isn't) condition of its amenability to being shaped by deliberate action. On the contrary, the translation of indeterminacy into something that permits free action requires (as we shall discuss in Chapter 12) something else of which tensed time is a surface manifestation: intentionality.

One of the most obvious expressions of the distinction between the past (of the world we have known) and future (of the world that we guess at) is captured in the contrast between memory (which may be accurate) and anticipation (which can only be guesswork). This should not, however, justify the reduction of the contrast between past and future to "information asymmetry", to the fact that we may know the former and cannot know the latter. (This view was critiqued in §2.3.4, where the asymmetry was seen by some writers to underpin one version of the "arrow of time".)

After all, there are parts of the past that we do not know and which could never be known – for example events without traceable present effects occurring prior to the existence of sentient beings. No; it is to be located in the difference between that which is or could be known, whether or not it is known in fact (the past), and that which cannot be known because there is nothing yet to be known though it can be intelligently guessed at (the future). The difference between a determinate past and an indeterminate future is not merely epistemic but ontological. The "determination" of the future as it "enters the present" is not simply a matter of something becoming potential information: it is about something out there that has changed, irrespective of any change in knowledge.

We have so far linked the idea that the future (in contrast with the past) is indeterminate, irrespective of what relativistic physics tells us, because it hasn't happened yet, with the idea that we can influence it. We shall now examine the two kinds of (invalid) reasons for arguing that the open, controllable future is an illusion and that our feeling that it is open, that the die is not cast, is the result of ignorance of what governs the unfolding of the world. The first reason arises from what has been called "logical fatalism" and the second, closer to physics, from the notion that the universe (of which we are a part) is causally or in some other way closed. We shall address each of these in turn.

8.2.2 The pre-determined future: logical fatalism

The temptation to give additional lustre to any discussion of logical fatalism by citing Aristotle is overwhelming. The present instance is not, however, mere name-dropping because it is his argument about "future contingents" that take us beyond the philosophy of time as narrowly construed to broader questions about the relationship between language and the world, between that which is asserted and that which is the case, and hence to the nature of truth. Aristotle was sure that his argument was fallacious but he could not put his finger on the problem.[17]

A future contingent is a predicted event, action or state of affairs that should be neither impossible nor inevitable. The key passages in Aristotle are as follows: "A sea-fight must either take place tomorrow or not, but it is not necessary that it should take place tomorrow, neither it is necessary that it should not take place, yet it is necessary that it either should or should not take place tomorrow."[18] By the law of the excluded middle, one of the two propositions – "there will be a sea battle tomorrow" and "there won't be a sea battle tomorrow" – must be true. And, what is more, it must be true in advance: "That which was truly predicted at the moment in the past will of necessity take place in the fullness of time".[19]

We seem therefore to be obliged to concede that seemingly contingent future events are inevitable. The distinction between what *might* happen tomorrow and what *must* happen tomorrow is lost. If the statement "There will be a sea battle tomorrow" is true today, then nothing that happens between now and tomorrow can head off the sea battle. The future is stitched up. All that actually happens has been waiting to happen; or the future is an army of events marching towards the present in which they occur.

The commander of the Athenian navy has not yet decided to join battle tomorrow. He believes that his options are open. Some observers think that he will engage the enemy and others think he will not. Since this covers all possibilities, it is argued, one prediction must be true and the other false. What is more, they are already true and false respectively. Let us suppose that the sea battle does indeed take place on 21 December 300 BCE. This means, so it appears, that the assertion "There will be a sea battle on 21 December" was (already) true on 20 December or any time, in however remote past, that the assertion to this effect had been made and "There will not be a sea battle on 21 December" was already false on 20 December.

The argument can be tightened up by reformulation as follows: It is necessarily true that either a sea battle takes place on 21 December (p) or a sea battle does not take place on 21 December (not-p).

> If not-p is false, then necessarily p is true.
> If p is false, then necessarily not-p is true.
> So, either p or not-p is necessarily true.

If p turns out to be true, it was always going to be true, because it was necessarily true (just as not-p was necessarily false). Thus the argument leading to "logical fatalism": by the principle of bivalence, one of a pair of contradictory statements must be true.

Something has obviously gone wrong. It is clearly not possible that a subsequently discovered truth of a proposition p should retrospectively give p (or the assertion of p) the power to oblige the event E to which it refers to happen. At the very least, this would then mean that E had two causes: the usual material causes; and a kind of logical pressure. We could characterize what has gone wrong in different ways. We might say: "It is not possible for either p or not-p to be true (yet) because the conditions that would make either of them possible are not yet in place." Or: "Being true is not an intrinsic property of a proposition, otherwise it could not be untrue. We are, after all, talking about future *contingents.*" We could connect these two responses by arguing that being true is a property of a *relationship* between a proposition and a state of affairs which latter we may, for the present purposes, call "a truth-maker". (We shall return to this in §8.2.2.4.) We could frame this objection in another way. "Either p or not-p" means only that precisely the same location in the space of possibility cannot be occupied (at the same time) by two contradictory actualities. It does not follow from this that either of the two actualities will necessarily occur; only that one, and only one, of them must. The necessity of the truth that "either p or not-p" does not spread beyond the node "either/or" to the "either" to the "or"; from the fork to one or other of its tines. Indeed, the fact that the necessity lies with the *node* should make it clear that neither of the branches – p or not-p – is necessitated.

So logical fatalism is mistaken.

But there is more work to be done; which is why Aristotle's argument – whose conclusions he did not himself accept – still exercises philosophers over 2,300 years

later. Some, most notably Jan Łukasiewicz, have been driven to take desperate measures and argue that the problem lies with the "bivalent" logic according to which
statements are either true or false.[20] Statements about future contingents are neither
true nor false, Łukasiewicz asserts, but "indeterminate"; and "indeterminate" counts
as a third possible truth value. Replacing the true vs false dichotomy by a trichot-
omy seems like a fudge and it is. It is an ad hoc remedy. It is like making "awaiting a
truth value" as "a truth value". Or BA (Failed) as a university degree. What is more,
it bypasses something that Aristotle's argument could tell us about the nature of the
future, and about tensed time, and what tensed statements reveal to us about the
relationships between our assertions and what is the case, between propositions and
the reality which they propose. Centrally, it is transferring indeterminacy from the
status of something that hasn't occurred – which is at best a general possibility – to
the relationship between a singular proposition and its supposed referent. Rejecting
bivalent logic in short is to locate the problem in the wrong place. It is the image of
a bivalent *world* – composed of a multitude of p and not-p alternatives – that we
need to question.

A more illuminating approach would be to investigate why propositions proposing
future contingents do not have truth values at the time when they are proposed – not
even the obscure truth value "indeterminate" – or, more seriously how we seem to
have got ourselves into the position of (almost) imagining that those truth values of
propositions *mandate* material events, such as a sea battle that actually takes place.
What is it that prompts us to feel that an assertion such as "A sea battle will take place
on 21 December", which turns out to be true, was already true on 20 December such
that as soon as it was asserted the bit of the future it referred to was fixed, even if
the assertion did not do the fixing? To answer this question, we need to examine the
difference between on the one hand future "events" proposed by propositions and
on the other real happenings, material events. There are many ways of capturing this
difference, which is the distance between events reduced to branches of dichotomies
and actual events on the ground; between general possibilities defined by opposition
and singular events that happen.

8.2.2.1 The referents of propositions

The notion that future events are already in-waiting gains some credence from the
fact that the events in question are represented by proxies; namely the referents of
propositions.

Consider three propositions:

(a) p_{future} – "There will be a sea battle tomorrow, 21 December" – uttered on 20
December.

(b) $p_{present}$ – "There is a sea battle going on today, 21 December" – uttered on 21
December.

(c) P_{past} – "There was a sea battle yesterday, 21 December" – uttered on 22 December.

For the logic to take us to a fatalistic conclusion, the three propositions should have an identical core referent, and consequently have the same truth conditions, so that if $P_{present}$ and P_{past} are true when they are uttered, P_{future} will also be true when it is uttered. In consequence, the truth of $P_{present}$ and P_{past} will have been foreordained by the time P_{future} was spoken. The first question we need to ask, therefore, is whether P_{future}, $P_{present}$ and P_{past} really are identical or have an identical core meaning. In answering this, let us set aside one surface difference – between "tomorrow", "today" and "yesterday" because they are indexicals which all have the same referent on the occasion in which they are used, namely 21 December. There is, however, another question that cannot be dealt with so easily: Is "a sea battle" the same in each of the three propositions? Does "sea battle" have the same referent?

It does not. In P_{future}, the referent is a generic sea battle without any individual features.[21] It is not *an* event at all. In $P_{present}$ the referent is an ongoing sea battle whose features are slowly being filled in, as the battle unfolds. It is an event-in-making. In P_{past}, the referent is a singular sea battle all of whose features are specified: it is a fully-fledged event so that we can justifiably talk about "*the* sea battle that [actually] took place on 21 December". In P_{future}, the proposition's subject "a sea battle" has a (descriptive) sense but no (actual) referent at the time the proposition is uttered, so long as the proposition is uttered before the battle takes place. That this is the case is not as obvious as it should be because the use of a phrase such as "tomorrow's sea battle" may give the illusion of a singular referent – an illusion that is particularly strong in retrospect after the battle has occurred. The future possible battle is, as it were, retro-fitted to the battle that has occurred. To put this another way, the definiteness of the event is back-dated to the time, before it happened, when it was entertained as a possibility. In P_{past}, the subject has a fully specified or saturated referent. And, finally, in $P_{present}$ the subject is in transition from one to the other, getting closer to a referent as the proposition is uttered later and later during the ongoing battle. Half way through the battle, the first half will confer a definite referent on the proposition but the second half will not correspond to a referent.

We could go further. The apparent referent of P_{future} is not an event but a general possibility which could be realized in numerous ways. It is only after the event has taken place (if it does take place) that we shall know what exactly we were referring to when we said (of the battle) that "it" would take place.

Admittedly, the sea battle anticipated in any statement about it before 21 December has some characteristics that we may specify: it is between (say) the Athenians and the Spartans and will involve ships on the sea. Beyond that, we are obliged to assume that it has (literally) countless features, all of them undetermined: exactly when it starts and ends; who does what and when; which ships are where and the participation of each of those who are involved; the outcome for individual participants (death, glory, and all stations in-between); and so on ad infinitum. In short, the (or rather *a*) future sea battle is a *class* of sea battles with a limitless number of members, while any actual sea battle is a singular in which everything – right down to details such as how loud a collision sounded to someone on the shore, the length of a rip in a sail, or the curses emitted by a particular sailor as he drowned – is determinate.

There is a fundamental difference, therefore, between statements such as p_{future} about future contingents (which are about general possibilities), those such as p_{past} about events that have taken place (which are singular events), and those such as $p_{present}$ that are about events currently taking place (which are in the process of evolving from general possibilities to singular instances). The (apparent) referents of future-oriented statements are therefore fundamentally different from the (actual) referents of present- and past-oriented statements. They would not, therefore, be expected to have the same truth-makers, truth conditions or, consequently, necessarily the same truth values. That which makes a statement about the future true would be any one of a whole class of states of affairs; while that which makes a statement about the present or past true, even though the statement uses a general term such as "sea battle", will of necessity be a particular that remains determinate at every level of inspection. We may not know the answer to the question as to what the last words of an individual drowning sailor were but we do know that there is an answer once the battle has taken place. "There will be a sea battle tomorrow" has what we might call "descriptive or narrative sufficiency" (so that there will be criteria for determining whether it has turned out to be true) but that is not the same as "existential" sufficiency (that which is sufficient for it to exist) – as is evident from the fact that it does not specify an actual event.

It is because we lose sight of this difference that we are deluded into thinking that we can get from the logic of propositions to empirical actualities; that we can carry out the miracle not only of deriving an empirical conclusion from a logical argument but (even, perhaps) of seemingly mandating the occurrence of an existent or actuality on the basis of a general rule of logic ("not 'p' and 'not-p'").

A logical fatalist might counterargue as follows. Proposition p_{future} – "There will be a sea battle tomorrow 21 December" uttered on 20 December – is indeed only one of a very large number of propositions that would be required to specify an actual sea battle. We can, however, multiply propositions indefinitely to get ever closer to the specification of an actual sea battle. Unfortunately, (or fortunately) this does not make things any better: any actual sea battle will always have (and need to have) more details than can be specified. No finite conjunction of (true) propositions could specify an actual sea battle. The senses of words are incurably coarse-grained (that's how they work, how they have a general meaning not monopolized by singular referents); but actual events – the referents of those words to which something definite correspond – are limitlessly fine-grained;[22] singular actuality is an unreachable asymptote of increasingly fine-grained description. And it is no use responding (in a manner analogous to Aristotle's own response to Zeno's paradoxes of motion) that the infinite number of propositions necessary to specify an actual sea battle exists *potentially* though they happen not to have been proposed. There is something self-contradictory in the idea of an infinite number of propositions that are not, and cannot in their totality be, proposed. What, after all, is an unproposed proposition? It sounds like dehydrated water.

In sum, a real battle, unlike any proposed battle is limitlessly detailed. A singular, that is to say actual, event cannot be specified. And any apparent specification of an event will fall short of it: a finite conjunction of propositions will leave something to be finished off and this something will be an extra-propositional reality.

Of course, most of those details don't matter because they could be altered without anything of importance changing – as in the case of my visit to the doctor discussed in the previous section; but this doesn't mean to say that actual happenings can happen without them. You could not have a battle – or indeed any event – consisting simply of salient details; even less one consisting of a single big detail – namely whether it did or did not happen. Reality – events that actually happen – is a seamless fabric of details salient and non-salient. Reality – that which actually occurs or which exists – lies beyond the specifying power of propositions.

We could put this another way by saying that: propositions about the future have sense but only apparent reference; propositions about the past have both sense and reference; and propositions about ongoing present events have a sense that is gradually being filled out with a referent. The necessary incompleteness of the reference of a proposition about the future is the mark of the latter's openness.

Even if this seems to go too far, we can see that it is a mistake to think that propositions p_{future}, $p_{present}$ and p_{past} have *the same referents*, so that if p_{past} is true, then p_{future} must also be true. The three propositions are not simple inflections of a tenseless core which could be specified as: "[there] is the sea battle that happened". Consequently, they do not have the same truth-makers. What would make p_{future} true would be any one of a broad class of possibilities; but those possibilities will have to be realized in order for p_{future} to be true. The difference between p_{future} and p_{past} is the gap between general possibility and specific actuality. On one side of the gap is logic (which sketches out possibilities in the broadest possible way – "either p or not-p") and on the other side material events and that which comes into being.

This gap cannot be closed until the proposed future has materialized; it cannot be closed from the standpoint on which it is proposed as a future possible occurrence. This otherwise obvious truth, that a future contingent proposition can only have a retrospective, not a prospective, truth value – is obscured by the grammar: the noun phrase "tomorrow's sea battle" has a solidity that feels like that of "today's sea battle" and "yesterday's sea battle". Propositions containing it seem to have a definite, hard-edged reference and consequently to be susceptible of bearing a truth value. Which is why the battle can be spoken of as readily if it does not occur as if it does occur. We can say "The sea battle we expected on 21 December" did not take place as if its (actual) occurrence were simply an additional feature, almost an optional extra. As if there are two broad classes of sea battles: those that do, and those that do not, occur.

It might be counterargued that the past-oriented assertion "There was a sea battle on such and such a date" also has general truth-makers. Any one of a broad class of events would make it true that a sea battle had occurred; so past and future battles are in a sense both general when we consider them as truth-makers. We need to dig a bit deeper.[23]

8.2.2.2 Events as tense tourists

> Events simply are or occur ... but they do not "advance" into a pre-existing frame called "time" ... An event does not move and neither do any of its relations.
>
> Grünbaum, "Relativity and the Atomicity of Becoming", 172

What I have argued so far is that the following propositions do not have the same referents:

(a) p_{future} – "There will be a sea battle tomorrow, 21 December" – uttered on 20 December.
(b) $p_{present}$ – "There is a sea battle going on today, 21 December" – uttered on 21 December.
(c) p_{past} – "There was a sea battle yesterday, 21 December" – uttered on 22 December.

More precisely, only p_{past} has a full-blown reference and $p_{present}$ is in the process of acquiring one. It is the incorrect belief that all three do have the same reference that justifies the claim that, if p_{past} turns out to be true, then p_{future} must have been true all the time and nothing could have stopped the battle that p_{future} referred to from happening. We can make this point in a way that touches more closely on traditional concerns about tensed time, by challenging the assumption that the three propositions refer to the same event: an event E which can be considered as being first in the future, then in the present and finally in the past. This way of thinking that sees events as "tense tourists" lies at the heart of the case for logical fatalism. For only if the event already exists in the future does p_{future} have a definite referent and one which is identical to that referred to by p_{past}. For the belief that future contingent propositions have truth values is based on the assumption that they have definite referents; that future events already have some kind of existence; that they set out from the future, enter the present and retire into the past.

The image of events as tense tourists is regarded as common sense, and seems to be passed on the nod by many philosophers. It is lucidly expressed by detenser Oaklander in a passage already quoted:

> Thus, for example, the inauguration of the fiftieth president of the United States is in the relatively distant future, but with the passage of time it will become less and less so and eventually will become present. And then, after its spotlight in the NOW, it will recede into the more and more distant past.[24]

Event E is first future, then present, and finally past; more precisely E_{future}, $E_{present}$ and E_{past} are the same entity; or that they are variant forms or phases of the identical item E. This is the other side of the notion that "E will happen", "E is happening", and "E has happened" have the same referents.

It is not only possible but necessary to separate belief in the reality of future and past, as well as the present, from the rather awkward idea that events have a prenatal existence in the future, waiting to be born, and a posthumous continuation after they have happened. In reality, a token event (and all events are token events) *will be* only once it *has been*. To put it aphoristically, "Call no event future until it is past".[25] To fail to observe this principle, and to assume that the reality of tensed time depends on events that occupy tenses and occupy them in turn, plays into the hands of the detensers, most notably McTaggart whose argument against the reality of tensed time (and via this for the unreality of time period) is worth a revisit.

If we believe in the reality of tensed or A-series time, McTaggart argues, we must hold that events that are future are also present and past.[26] But being future and present and past are incompatible states: the same thing cannot be "not-yet", "now" and "no-longer". The immediate response is that this would be a problem only if the event were past, present and future *at the same time.* While an event cannot be *simultaneously* future, present and past, it can be future, present and past at *different* times. An event which occurs on Wednesday can be future on Tuesday and past on Thursday.

McTaggart, of course, has anticipated this counterargument (he was a Cambridge man, after all and had Russell as a sparring partner) and thinks he can deal with it. Let us suppose that event E is present, then it is presently true that E is present, it was true in the past that it was future, and it will be true in the future that it will be past. This opens the way to a more complex argument[27] – to the effect that the defence of tensed events introduces a *second* A-series and this will run into the same problems as the first. This A-series has nine second-level predicates and, as time passes, each event – say the outbreak of the First World War in 1914 – falls under all of these predicates. Some of these predicates are incompatible with one another: "is past in the present" (which is true in 2014), "is present in the present" (true in 1914) and "is future in the present" (true in 1913). The response that events don't have all these second-level properties simultaneously, but have them successively, will prompt appeal to *third-level* predicates. It will be obvious that the problem will recur at this level and appeal to even higher-level predicates will not drive the problem away.

We can vary this argument by taking making explicit the fact, implicit in the above argument, that tenses are extended. Consider the future. There will be part of the future in which E is already past and part of the future in which E is present and part in which E is future. Supposing E takes place on 11 December and suppose also that today is 9 December. Tomorrow, 10 December, the event will be future – it won't yet have happened. In 3 days' time, 12 December, it will be in the past. So from the standpoint of 9 December, E is future (on 10 December), present (on 11 December) and past (on 12 December). 10 December, 11 December and 12 December are all part of the future. So E will be future *and* present *and* past in the future.

Every attempt to deal with McTaggart's argument leads back, he maintains, to this same problem: if we believe in the reality of tensed time, we require events to have incompatible tenses at the same time. He concludes from this that, given that the real is rational, or cannot be self-contradictory, tense must be unreal.

The discussion so far will, however, enable us to see what is wrong with McTaggart's starting point. It is a mistake to think of an event such as sea battle E as being *the same item* passing through three phases – phase 1 when it is E_{future}, phase 2 when it is $E_{present}$ and phase 3 when it is E_{past}. There is no such thing as an identical or unchanging E that has three lives in which it carries constitutive or monadic tensed properties – futurity, presence, and pastness – that (so McTaggart argues) are incompatible. We can see where McTaggart has gone wrong: he overlooks the fact that E_{future} is not the same as $E_{present}$ and $E_{present}$ is not the same as E_{past}. E_{future} is a mere *possibility*, more precisely a range of possibilities, the target of a proposition. It is a proposed item whose characteristics at the time of utterance (irrespective of whether the event subsequently actually takes place) are undetermined in the way that we have already discussed. $E_{present}$ is a combination of a determinate portion of an (ongoing) event E and possible continuations or completions. E_{past} is a complete, determinate, actual event. There is therefore nothing corresponding to a single item, a tense tourist E, visiting in succession future, present and past – never mind (to address McTaggart's concern) occupying them all at the same time and thus becoming self-contradictory. We could capture the difference between E_{future} and E_{past} by pointing out that the former could (say) be a sea battle lasting either 4 hours or 2 hours whereas the latter did last 2 hours and there is no possibility of its lasting 4 hours.

Given that this is pretty straightforward, why do some philosophers (and McTaggart is not alone) imagine that believing in the reality of tensed time requires subscribing to the belief that the same item (event E) can, indeed must, occupy three tenses, as a result of which it runs the risk of having to inhabit more than one tense at once? It is partly because we use the same kind of expression when we refer to an event in the future, in the present, and in the past; when we refer to an item as "a sea battle", irrespective of whether it does or does not take place. This similarity of referring expression in the two cases conceals the profound difference between them – between a mere possibility (*a* sea battle) whose character is dependent on how and in what detail it is entertained, described, or imagined, or anticipated, and is only an honorary event, and an actuality (*the* sea battle) whose content is out there in the real world, determinate in every detail, including those millions of details no-one has imagined or anticipated.

There are future possibilities – constrained to a greater or lesser extent by what is settled of the future in the present – but no future events. In philosophy, we should restrict the term "event" to something that has come to pass, is completed and is no longer ongoing – that is, in short, past. On 12 December we can see, in hindsight, that there was a sea battle that took place on 11 December, which had not yet happened on 10 December but (now we know) was going to happen the following day. We should not translate this into implying that there is a full-blown event already somehow in place on 10 December, heading towards the present, and, having passed through the present, ending up in the ever more distant past. It is only when an event is complete that we can say what *it* was that, before it happened, had "not yet" taken place. Events are in the future only when they have taken place; when, that is, they are seen (retrospectively) to have been in the future. We might strengthen our motto "*Call no event future until it is past*" to "*Call no event an event until it is past*". While it is true that something cannot be past until it has been present, it is only when it has actually occurred that we can be justified in judging that it had once been future.

This mustn't be taken as an attack on the reality of the future – after all we have described some of its furniture in the earlier sections of this chapter – only to affirm that it is not populated by events, except retrospectively, when they and it are no longer future. It is a truism that the future cannot exist before it comes into being – before it is past. It is entirely true that event E which took place at t_2 lay in the future at t_1 but it is equally true that that relationship "lying in the future" did not come into being until t_3 when the event is complete. At the very least, E_{future} is a set of possibilities whose range is constrained by probabilities, defined by laws and the ongoing processes and fixtures and fittings of the present. The closer the future in question, the more those probabilities approach to certainties. As I look at the objects that surround me in my room now, I can feel very confident that I am looking at the furniture of the immediate future (say, a second from now) but less confident that I am looking at the furniture of ten years hence and confident that I am not looking at the furniture of 1,000,000 years hence. My confidence regarding future *events*, however, will not conform to this scale.[28] Although I have a general sense of the probability of what will happen – I hear you walking up the stairs and anticipate that you will enter the room in a moment or two – my sense of what will happen will not reach down to a particular event. Your entry into the room will have many characteristics – the fall of light on your face, what you are saying as you enter, the position you assume – that are indeterminate. (And that's assuming that you do not change your mind and go back down the stairs before entering).

If I were a betting man, I might put a bet on there being a sea battle on a particular day. I would be mad to put a bet on the occurrence of the actual sea battle that occurs. As the bet becomes less spread, so the odds lengthen. When we reach an actual event, the odds are infinite. We could put this another way. There may be a 50/50 chance of their being a sea battle on a particular day. As we cone down on an actual battle, the chances of its happening diminish, until we reach a singular event with an infinite number of details, by which time the chances of the prediction being true will reach zero. So while we accept the reality of the future, we must not think of its reality as involving or even residing in a population of events ontologically equal to the material objects surrounding us in the present whose stability projects them unchanged into the near or even the middle future.

Some philosophers are (rightly) uncomfortable with the idea that an event can have three successive states: not-yet existing (and, possibly, never existing); coming into existence; and no-longer existing. They are particularly unhappy with the notion of a future event having a kind of existence before its time has come, before it occurs.

That it can be "in-waiting-to-happen" in a state in which it, as it were, ghost-happened, so actual happening at a particular time is almost an illusion. They have tried to get round this by suggesting that past and future events are the same as their present counterparts except that they are non-spatial and non-temporal. This is a desperate way of accommodating the idea that E can exist in a form in which it is not happening, not located at any particular part of space (defined by the object-substrate it is happening in).[29] It simply highlights the impossibility of assigning existence to an event that has not yet happened and may never do so.

It also exposes the dubiousness of thinking that event E's coming into being (future to present) and E's going out of being (present to past) are changes in the state of E – meta-events, as it were, that correspond to variations in a single event. It is as if E_{future} and E_{past} were essentially the same as $E_{present}$ (or ongoing) except for the small (!) details of not being in a state of occurring in the case of E_{past} and not occurring or existing in the case of E_{future}. A particular past pain and a future pain are not just variations of a present pain. A modification of a present pain would be a change in, for example, its intensity or location. Yesterday's toothache today is not a variant of today's toothache today. A lack of toothache isn't an item, in the way that a toothache is, nor even a lack of a particular toothache. The difference between today's present toothache and yesterday's (now absent) toothache is not a difference comparable to that between toothache and headache.

The notion that we are dealing with the same item, E, when it is future, present, and past is clearly connected with the idea we rejected in §5.2.2 that tenses are predicates or properties. It is this that leads us to a conception of E as a strange continuant that not only outlives its own occurrence but precedes it; as something that can pass into, and out of, existence with something fundamental – its identity – preserved. Tense tourism has an event travelling towards the time at which it occurs, towards itself (from its private future of not-yet-being – that is non-being) and then away from itself (into a private past of no-longer-being – that is non-being); an event seeking itself out, finding itself, and then retiring as an event emeritus in the past.

To affirm the reality of past events and deny that of future events when neither is in the process of becoming or occurring would suggest favouritism to the past over the future. The reason it is valid to separate the continuing reality from their continuing occurrence in the case of past but not in the case of future events is that the latter actually occurred and the former are putative. There is a fact that E occurred yesterday and no fact that E will occur tomorrow. "The fact that E has occurred" extends E's reality beyond its time of occurrence. When an event has occurred – so it has ceased "occurring" – it still remains "having occurred".[30]

8.2.2.3 Times and dates as tense tourists

> It seems manifest in our experience that time flows – from the past, to the present moment, and in the future.
>
> Savitt, *Time's Arrows Today*, 7

Events, then, are not tense tourists. And it is equally clear that they are not tenseless time tourists. An event that occurs over interval t_1-t_2 cannot also occur over interval t_2-t_3; nor can it be said in any sense to be happening at t_3. But is it legitimate to think of times as tense tourists?

It is easy to conflate the notion of events touring the tenses with that of times (and dates) doing the same. Here, again, is the passage from Oaklander:

> [W]e conceive of time as something that flows or passes from the future to the present and from the present to the past. Thus, for example, the inauguration of the fiftieth president of the United States is in the relatively distant future, but with the passage of time it will become less and less so and eventually will become present. And then, after its spotlight in the NOW, it will recede into the more and more distant past.[31]

The flow of times from the future to the past is merged with the passage of events along the same trajectory. It is easy to see why it is tempting to see times as tense tourists and then to imagine that events, that occur at times, hitch a ride and thus are able to tour the tenses.

Consider this. On 11 December, 12 December is future, on 12 December it is present, and on 13 December it is past. Days start off in the future, pass through the present, and end up in the past. What more could we ask of a tense tourist? Moreover, days form an orderly queue and there is no overtaking. 13 December will always be four days from 17 December. As for points in time, consider the successive moments t_1, t_2 and t_3. At t_1, t_2 is in the future; at t_2 it is present; and at t_3 it is past. Again, the tense tourism seems to be on the menu. What is more, neither days nor moments change character as they pass through tenses. "12 December" refers to the same item on 11 December, 12 December and 13 December. "t_2" remains unchanged from t_1 to t_3. We don't have the awkwardness of events somehow coming into and going out of being and still retaining an inviolate identity. This last point, however, betrays what is dubious about this line of reasoning. Dates and moments do not change – or perish – precisely because they lack the wherewithal to change.

It is difficult, nonetheless, to avoid the idea that times are kinds of *occurrences*. The temptation is particularly strong in the case of days or dates. Statements such as "Christmas Day always falls on 25 December" or "Easter Day is late this year" present these slices of time as happenings in themselves, quite apart from anything that takes place in or on them. And this is reinforced when we say (for example), "Christmas day is getting closer" as if the day were a kind of appointment. What we usually refer to as getting "closer" are certain planned activities – the kinds of things we or others do on Christmas day. In short, events. And, as we have discussed, future events do not progress in this way. The movement of events from the future to the present is only retrospective. Even so, it is difficult to avoid thinking of any day (including ones that have no traditional associated events) that it is "getting closer" – and at a certain speed. Every day gets closer at a rate of one day per 24 hours. During the course of a 2-hour train journey, every future time beyond the end of the journey gets 2 hours closer. So it is easy to be tempted to think of times – moments or days – in the way described by Oaklander as quasi-events that start in the future and end up in the past.

This is, of course, misleading. Real events occur at a time that is independent of them in the sense of not being fixed. In a non-deterministic universe, event E – say, my meeting up with you – can occur either on 10 December or 11 December. The event, its time of occurrence, and its duration are distinct. 10 December, however, can "occur" only on 10 December and it is obliged to last 24 hours. What is more, it cannot fail to occur on 10 December, though the events planned to occur in it may not transpire. Time interval t_1 can occur only at and during t_1 and must last as long as it. To think of times "taking place" at times, is clearly absurd if the times in question are themselves and impossible if another time. We can say that "my birth was at 6 p.m. on 10 October 1946" but not that "6 p.m. on 10 October 1946 took place at 6 p.m. 10 October 1946". It is even more absurd to think of dates and times as somehow outlasting themselves. As I get older, my birthdate recedes but that date does not get older.[32] And yet this would be necessary if times really began in the future and ended up in the past. The idea of 10 December journeying from the beginning of time to 10 December, passing through itself, and then journeying onward to the end of time, hardly commends itself. We would arrive at a situation in which all time and all dates somehow coexisted, with (say) 10 December and all its successors enjoying a prenatal existence on 9 December and a posthumous existence from 11 December onwards.

If moments and dates seem to pass unscathed through tenses – unlike events which are supposed to pass into and out of existence – and so seem to qualify as true tense tourists it is only because they have nothing to scathe. If they really were occurrences in themselves, then we would have, at any given time, the events that occur at or during that time *plus* the times "occurring" when the events occur. 10 December would be a meta-event, even a super-event, additional to all that happens "in" or "on" it. Dates, therefore, are not events or occurrences and they are even less qualified than events to be tense tourists. Times that are specified mathematically (and the calendar is essentially a mathematical series) are clearly not tensed. Something else is required to create the notion that 10 December is first future, then present, and finally past. That something is, of course the viewpoint of the utterer, defining the "now" – a collective utterer defining a common "now" and a common 10 December. And "now", "tomorrow", "yesterday" do not fasten on to dates and times without such a viewpoint. There is thus a double dissociation between times and tenses. The tenses are not intrinsic to the times any more than the times have times "at" which they "occur".

That dates do *not* travel is evident from the fact that it is as true to say that a particular day gets closer to the present as that the present closes in on a particular day. It makes no sense to try to adjudicate which is moving and hence to say of either of them that they are moving. While we colloquially say "At last the great day arrived" days do not arrive in the way that babies, buses, and guests arrive. The coming of Christmas is not an event. If it were, we would have to find some time – a day presumably – in which this arrival took place. There are no higher order days for days to occur in. We do not, therefore, have to imagine t_1 bravely stepping up to the plate (guess when?) at t_1 and becoming "Now"; or think of 25 December 2015 travelling to its rightful place, when it will dock into 25 December 2015, fitting smoothly into the space allocated to it.

Thus the absurd consequences of treating instants and stretches of time as quasi-occurrences and, additionally, imagining that those quasi-occurrences are on the temporal move. This view requires them, as with events, to have some kind of existence in a privately defined future or past; in short, to pre-exist and outlast themselves. The false image of times as quasi-occurrences is reinforced by the idea that, like events, they have temporal relations – even that they are (in some sense) like events in being "at" times. The relationship between t_1 and t_2 is not at all like the relationship between E_1 (that takes place at t_1) and t_1 or the relationship between E_1 (that takes place at t_1) and E_2 (that takes place at t_2). We can say of E_1 that it: (a) is at t_1; (b) takes place before t_2; and (c) is before E_2. We cannot say of t_1 that it is before a particular event, even when the event in question E_2 took place at t_2. And it cannot "take place" before t_2. Neither "take place" that is why they cannot be temporally related to one another in the way that events are. 12 December does not succeed 11 December in the way that the pudding succeeds the main course in a meal. A week is not a process.

Thinking of times as quasi-events or quasi-occurrents, is a crucial step towards the error of thinking that there is a passage of time analogous to, or even necessary for, the passage of events, or, indeed, for becoming. In passing, it is worth reiterating that resisting a dynamic account of time does not commit one to the opposite view that time is static. It is equally inappropriate to think of time as either frozen or flowing. Both dynamism and stasis are terms inappropriately transferred from the world of material objects and events.

8.2.2.4 Events and truth-makers

Our investigation of the status of future events and of propositions about future contingents invites us to explore the nature of truth, as it applies to declarative propositions asserting, or speculating about, matters of what may or may not subsequently turn out to be facts. It all seems very straightforward: the relevant propositions turn an event into a truth-maker and events make the relevant propositions true. The relationship between propositions, events, and truth-makers, however, is not as straightforward as it seems. Examining this relationship critically will help us to see how we seem obliged to pass from the empirically empty truism that "In future either p or not p" to "In future either p or not-p will happen" and from this to "One of p or not-p will happen by necessity".

The law of the excluded middle demands that there should or should not be a sea battle tomorrow, 12 December. On 11 December, it seems, a truth so general as to be empty (either p or not-p) delivers one that is highly specific (a sea battle at a particular time). In reality, that general truth does not specify any particular event, which is why it can be further generalized to "On 11 December, for *any* Event E, it either will or will not take place on 12 December". This is equally true, irrespective of the intrinsic probability or likelihood of the E in question. It is just as applicable if the E is a material impossibility such as "A man will leap to the moon unaided" or something highly likely, such as "Someone will walk on the face of the earth". Thus the profound disconnection between logical possibility and material probability. From the point of view of logic, however, p and not-p, Event E occurring and Event E not occurring, are simply two tines of a fork each marked by a proposition, and of equal standing.

We can look at this disconnection between logic and empirical reality another way by returning to the difference between that which makes a proposition true and that which constitutes an actual event. Consider the sea battle: any number or range of events could qualify as a sea battle. That which is common to all these events, counting as a truth-maker (a part of the world in virtue of which a proposition is true)[33] for the assertion "A sea battle took place on 12 December" – what we might call "a lowest common denominator" – is less than anything that would constitute an actual sea battle. As we discussed in §8.2.2.1, sea battles are not reducible to the criteria for their having taken place. Truth-makers, that is, fall short of events; or events (or states of affairs) exceed anything envisaged in a proposition, anything required to make it true.

To put this another way, an event that made a proposition true would also make many other propositions true since what makes only one proposition true would be insufficient to count as an event. An actual event has a "thisness" that (necessarily) exceeds any "whatness" envisaged in a proposition or any finite conjunction of propositions. What happens in the world are events, not truths – nor indeed falsehoods. The sea battle that takes place on 12 December is not simply a truth – "That a sea battle took on 12 December". Nor is it simply a falsehood – "That a sea battle did *not* take place on 12 December". Events, in short, do not merely fulfil propositions but, in order to do so, in order to be real events, they have to over-fulfil them; or rather the part or aspect that fulfils the proposition is only a minute part of any real event. Any actual event would be a truth-maker for the conjunction of a limitless number of propositions. No finite conjunction of propositions could exhaust an actual event.

Truth-makers would not be sufficient to populate an actual world of events, processes, objects and states of affairs. That in virtue of which events discharge the role of fulfilling the truth of propositions is not sufficient to make a whole event. Truth-makers do not amount to fully fledged states of affairs, etc.[34] A world of truth-makers would be ontologically flea-bitten, unable to stand on its own. Actual events are vehicles for truth-makers but must exceed them.

The future proposed in a proposition has as its existence condition that it should be entertained by individuals or by the community of minds: this is "the ancipator's share" we examined in §8.1.2.2. If that proposed future eventuates, what actually comes to pass must go beyond truth-makers, in the sense of being presupposed in, or required by, them. This has been expressed in the assertion that "truth supervenes on (at least partly) non-propositional being".[35] We have already (§6.2.3) seen this principle deployed to defend the reality of past events: if there are true (or false) things to be said about the latter, they must have some reality independent of the present.

The obverse of this is that future-oriented propositions ("There will/will not be a sea battle tomorrow") have only dummy referents, or placeholders for possible referents, that might fill them. Like tendrils waving in the air, they have nothing to contact. That is why, when a future-oriented assertion turns out to be true, we are not entitled to conclude that it was true all along because its truth-maker – embedded in an event that is its vehicle – had not yet come into existence. Likewise, if it turns out to be false, it hasn't been false all along because its falsity-maker has not come into existence. Until the event in question happened, there was nothing in the world to make it true. The truth relation requires both relata: a proposition makes an actual occurrence a maker of truth and an actual occurrence makes a proposition true.

One important driver to logical fatalism is the image of the future as a network of forks, delineated by propositions, with one branch of a fork being p and the other branch being not-p. Just how mistaken this is may be illustrated by an example that apparently fits the dichotomy model perfectly, allowing propositions to reach into the future beyond the merely logical p or not-p. There is a match tomorrow between Liverpool and Manchester United. It has been arranged that it will go on until one side achieves victory: a result is assured. Either Liverpool or Manchester United will therefore win. One of the following statements will therefore have proved to have been true: Manchester United will win or Liverpool will win. The logical structure of this dichotomy is that of an exclusive disjunction:

p: "Manchester United win the match."
q: "Liverpool win the match."
If p, not q.
If q, not p.

Irrespective of the outcome, there will be features of the victory that will go beyond the simply either/or p or q. A victory for either side will necessarily have an unlimited number of details that cannot be captured in a finite set of propositions, rather as we noted with the sea battle: not merely who scored what goals from what angle at what point in the game but all the other features of the contest, and, indeed, of the world into which it fits, which would include, for example, the journeys the crowd took to get to the ground and to contribute to the roar that egged on the players, or the colour of the sky. In short, any given journey down one side or other of the dichotomy is inseparable from a world that surrounds it and, in fact, will reach back to the present with which it is linked.

Let us return to our sea battle. An actual one has more details than can be accommodated by the "sea battle" of propositions asserting that it will happen. In fact, there are two profound differences: actual sea battles are not *just* sea battles; and proposed sea battles are classes of battles. The first point is relatively straightforward. A real sea battle will include A. B. Smith who has toothache, sea gulls flying overhead, and horses' heads on waves, none of which is in the specification of a battle. (It could be included, but there would always be something left out.) What is sufficient to make an actual event a truth maker of a proposition – so that the truth conditions of a proposition obtain at a particular time – is not sufficient to make an actual full-blooded event.

Let me approach this from another angle using a rather different example. Take the assertion "Raymond Tallis is a man". The things that have to be true for this to be true are not adequate for Raymond Tallis to exist, to make him a going concern. He doesn't have to be 5′ 10″ tall – as he happens to be – but he has to have some particular height, though no specific height is part of the definition of a man. And there are many other variables that have definite values in Raymond Tallis that are not part of the definition of a man but, even where the variables *are* necessary for him to count as a man (such as possessing XY chromosomes), the particular values they take are not prescribed so that they do not figure in those things that make the assertion true. Raymond Tallis, that is, has to have many other features additional to those which are necessary for him to qualify as a man in order to *be* an actual man; to *be* a man; to *be*. The qualifying conditions do not add up to an actual man walking the face of the earth. To generalize – and perhaps over-labour – the point: that which is sufficient for an item to qualify as a member of a class is not sufficient to make it an existent member of a class. An event stripped of everything but that within it which makes a proposition true would be like the Cheshire cat's cat-less smile. Truth-makers cannot be stand-alone.[36]

The second point – that the referent of a future contingent proposition is a *class* of events so that any individual truth-making event will not match what is proposed – is worth further attention. "Tomorrow's sea battle" encompasses everything from a desultory exchange of shots to an all-out scrimmage that leaves only a stain of blood and a few floating spars of wood. *Classes* of events do not occur – least of all at a particular time and place. Nor could they, if only because distinct members of the class cannot occupy the same time and place. A battle in which Smith was killed at 10 p.m. and one in which Smith was not killed at 10 p.m., though they might both answer to the description "sea battle tomorrow", are incompatible. The referent of past-oriented propositions by contrast is a token event which can occur; indeed, has occurred. It is only in Plato's heaven that classes can *be*; and then they are disconnected from any instantiation; and what is more they do not happen but simply, eternally, are.

We could summarize some of these points by saying that there are no complete descriptions of future events. Their indeterminacy is not comparable to the condition of an item that has a solid core and blurred edges: it goes all the way through. Future-oriented propositions cannot be genuinely referring given that they do not have a referent underwritten by a reality available at the time when the proposition is proposed and that which is proposed is in the future. It is only when the relevant event has occurred that the proposition has a real, rather than a dummy, referent. Hence the truth of Storrs McCall's observation:

> What is true today [regarding future contingent propositions] depends on what happens tomorrow, not the other way round. The set of true propositions in no way determines what the future is like. Instead, what the future is like determines the set of true propositions.[37]

An accurate prediction does not mandate what it predicts; rather, the occurrence of what it accurately predicts is what makes it an accurate prediction. We could put this more harshly by saying that future-oriented propositions steal their referents – and hence their truth-makers – from the events they only retrospectively seem to refer to. Given that nothing that exists is indeterminate – all existents are determinate – the referents that seem to be fulfilled by truth-makers are not events that actually happen. For nothing that really exists is either general or indeterminate. To say of a battle after it has occurred, that this is the battle I meant all along, is cheating.

8.2.2.5 A brief reflection on logic and existence

How did we arrive at the strange situation of having to defend the openness of the future against a threat from the law of the excluded middle? The relationship between logic and existence is – or should be – clear: there is none. After all, "Either p or not-p" is true in all possible worlds and so can have nothing to say about any actual one. The logical bounds of possibility do not prescribe anything. What then could make anyone believe on the basis of a logical argument that future dice are cast, even though no-one goes so far as to say that uttering propositions has cast them? We need to re-examine what has paved the journey from logical to material necessity, given that we regard the state of the universe at any one time to be logically independent of its states at any other point in time. We have hitherto focused on the error of conflating "Either p or not-p" with "Either such and such an event or not such and such an event", where the event in question is specified as, for example, a battle. But there are other sources of confusion.

The assumption of an equivalence between p and not-p

From the democratic standpoint of the logic of propositions, while the occurrence and the non-occurrence of a sea battle are opposite, they are equal. A sea battle occurring at t_1 confers the truth value T on the proposition p "A sea battle will occur at t_1" and the truth value F on the proposition not-p "A sea battle will not occur at t_1". The failure of a sea battle to occur at t_1 confers the truth value F on the proposition p "A sea battle will occur at t_1" and the truth value T on the proposition not-p "A sea battle will not occur at t_1". Appearances are, of course, deceptive. The truth-maker of p at least has some features (ships at sea, etc.) that would be required to make it true; whereas that of not-p has no features – or none specific to itself.[38] Anything other than a sea battle taking place tomorrow – including nothing of note at all – will be compatible with its being true. But what would make "there will be no sea battle tomorrow" true? It seems as if its truth is a kind of hole – a "sea battle tomorrow-shaped-hole" – clothing itself in anything that is not a sea battle. The asymmetry is telling. While, from the point of view of logic, p and not-p are not only opposite but equal, from the point of view of the actual world, they are ill-matched opposites because they are not equal. "No sea battle" is not simply the shadowy counterpart of an actual sea battle. There are no negative battles with defined territory, occupying a region of space and time as a battle does. To put this another way: it is not as if there is some real estate shared, equally or even unequally, between the truth-maker of p and of not-p: the latter, unlike the former, is not local. In short, while there is a logical opposite of p asserting that there will be a sea battle, there is no opposite of a sea battle in the world out there. There is the opposite of a proposition but not of an event. An absence of a sea battle is not a discrete state of affairs, though it may seem discrete when it borrows specificity from an increasingly precise specification of the battle that does not occur. Likewise, an increasingly imprecise specification would reduce the specificity of the truth-maker of not-p. If p were "There will be conflict in the next 1,000 years", the hole corresponding to not-p would be even more indefinable. It is p, in other words, that is wearing the trousers.

The fact that it is p calling the shots is evident when we consider confirmation. If I predict a sea battle in the next 1,000 years, my prediction will be confirmed as soon as a battle occurs. If I predict that there will not be a sea battle in the next 1,000 years, I have to wait for a 1,000 years to pass before my prediction is confirmed. Not-p is the dependent member of the pair – that is why it is marked, while p is unmarked. The sketch or outlines of possible worlds could be put together out of a collection of p's (in fact p is the sum total of possibility or proposable worlds) but not out of not-p's.

If we maintain that not-p's correspond to a reality equal to that proposed by p's, we would have to accept that not only do events tour tenses, moving towards the present from the future and ending up in the past, so too must all the non-events we can imagine; or more precisely the ontological potholes corresponding to non-occurrence of events. In short, we would be engulfed by a tide of non-happenings as well as of happenings. This over-generous realism would seem to give us a license to print, in virtue of uttering propositions, as many non-beings as we like. We could populate the world with entities that correspond to things that do not happen, so long as they are proposed. Such modal realism is a heavy price to pay for maintaining that the truth-makers of propositions and of their negatives are equally real.

Things get worse for "not-p". Unlike p, it can be dispensed with. Strictly, p covers the whole of the proposable world. We can translate negative propositions into positive ones. For, "There is no sea battle tomorrow" could be rephrased as "Peace between the nations continues to hold" or even "The phony war continues". Not-p exists only to contradict p. One could not imagine a discourse composed entirely of negative propositions but one could imagine one consisting of only positive ones. (Double negative propositions might deliver a possible world but they are positive propositions in disguise.) In short, p's have logical priority over not-p's.

In sum, while p and not-p are equal in the eyes of logic, they are not equal in terms of engagement with an actual world. The dichotomous nature of truth values, mapping on to p and not-p, deceives us into thinking otherwise. By defining the truth-makers of p and not-p in terms of each other, what happens can seem to be fitted into the tines of the fork "Either p or not-p"; in short, to be assimilated into the space of logic. p as the opposite of "not-p" – as "not-not-p" – crash diets what happens so it can fit into the place defined by a disjunction. Actual happenings are reduced to the negations of their negations, the progeny of logical operators. A sea battle could be regarded as a not-not-sea battle. This underlines that what the branches house is not events but the opposition between events and their opposites: pure opposition. The dichotomy is universally applicable precisely because it guarantees no specific content. Precisely because "p or not-p" is true in all possible worlds it does not specify anything about actual worlds.

Ignoring relative probability

Treating "p" and "not-p" as equivalent has another consequence: it ignores relative probability as the bridge between possibility and actuality. The two tines of the fork have equal weight. In reality, the probability of x happening or not happening varies as the time of the proposed event gets closer. The probability will also vary as the time scale and the nature of the content of the proposition varies.

Here are some examples:

(a) "There will/will not be a sea battle tomorrow between the Greeks and Romans" uttered in 2016.
(b) "There will/will not be a unicorn race next year."
(c) "There will/will not be changes somewhere in in the universe tomorrow."

In the case of (a) and (b), one tine ("p") will house an impossibility; in the case of (c) one tine ("p") will house a dead cert. Logical fatalism does not take account of the difference between the impossible, the improbable, the probable, and the inevitable. It allows only that one tine (which turns out to have been true) is inevitable and another tine (which turns out to be false) to be impossible. This underlines how logical fatalism works only by taking both tines of the fork together and arguing that, if one is true, the other must be false. It is about the zero probability of "p and not-p" and not about the probability of either p or not-p.

"Either p or not-p" is the openness of future, even though "Either p or not-p" is a dead cert. It is true whatever. It says nothing more than "anything can happen – or not happen".[39]

Necessity creep

We have already seen the step that permits "necessity creep" from the fork – "Either p or not-p" – to one or other of its tines; namely, that the contents of the tines seemed to be defined entirely by being the opposite of the other. "There is a sea battle tomorrow" is merely the opposite of "there is no sea battle tomorrow" and "there is no sea battle tomorrow" merely as the opposite of "there is a sea battle tomorrow". This is how "It is necessarily p or not-p" becomes "Either p or not-p is necessary".

So much for "necessity creep". There is another way of seeing how this happens; namely from the standpoint of generality. "Either p or not-p" must be true because the two tines encompass the totality of possibility and hence the totality of truth-makers and falsity-makers. Alternative possibilities – battle or no battle – may seem to be accommodated in and occupy all logical space: because they are seen as purely logical. If, however, they have any actual content – such as, for example, a sea battle tomorrow, then they fit with increasing difficulty in the tines.

We are distracted from this legerdemain by seeing the contents of the tines entirely in relationship to one another. If, however, they are allowed contents that go beyond logical opposition, then necessity withdraws from the tines to where it should be; namely the node in the fork. What is more, beyond the fork there is impossibility, because each tine contains an entire *class* of possibilities – for example "a sea battle tomorrow". The latter will contain an indefinite number of instantiations, which will be incompatible with one another. As we have already noted, p is compatible with A. B. Smith dying at 9 p.m. *and* not dying at 9 p.m. or shouting "Death to the enemy" at 10 p.m. *and* shouting "Death or glory at 10 p.m.", but it is caught up in contradiction given that it predicts a class that includes all 4 instantiations. The class of incompatible battles – or battles with incompatible details – will remain in play until an actual sea battle has taken place.

Events as stand-alone

The passage from logical to material necessity typically involves future contingents that are stand-alone. In reality, any given event such as a sea battle will have conditions, circumstances, and a causal ancestry that are not captured in the kind of p or not-p dichotomy that Aristotle invoked. The sea battle could not be necessary unless all that made it possible or likely – was also necessary and consequently already in place. In other words, even if a sequence of events gathered up in the idea of a sea battle could be accommodated in the tine of a fork, the events that made the fork carry a truth value themselves are inextricably caught up in a multitude of other events and states of affairs that seem to be independent of the necessity of the index event proposed in the "p or not-p" dichotomy.

To develop this a bit further: If the referent of "tomorrow's sea battle" were truly a material event, and not merely that part of a material event that counts as a truth-maker, its happening could not be a stand-alone fact. It will have conditions of material possibility which would also have to be in place if the battle were to happen. In short, the truth of the future contingent will be truly contingent on events and conditions between when the statement is uttered and the time of the proposed event. If all events are causally connected with all other contingents, the only way to save logical fatalism would be to make everything, including the assertions of the propositions "p" and "not-p", logically fated to happen. Logical fatalism requires the universality of material fatalism, which we shall discuss presently, though it would seem to make the laws, forces, and causes that underpin the case for material fatalism entirely redundant.

The upshot of this part of the discussion is that, while aspects of the future can be envisaged or described as p or not-p, any actual occurrent event (predicted or not) must be more than merely a naked tine in a fork. The apparent present truth value of the future contingent statements depends on borrowing, on account as it were, the ontological fullness of real – that is to say past or present – events. A future sea battle, unlike one that is occurring, or has occurred, is featureless – or is not sufficiently equipped with enough features to amount to a physical event. While the predictive proposition that there will be a sea battle may seem to have a qualitative, continuous, predicational generality and so seem to be richer and to be closer to having a genuine referent than an outcome prediction ("Manchester United will win not Liverpool") which may be dichotomous, the difference is illusory. Logical fatalism has the capacity only to guarantee – or to issue guarantees on – a future that lacks actual specific content or whose apparent content is derived from mere opposition between two opposites. In short it invokes possibilities that fall short of any actuality. The illusion that propositions about future contingents refer to singulars is based on retrospectively injecting into the referents of those propositions that turned out to be true the ontological fullness of events that actually took place, so making them seem to be about real, that is to say singular, items rather than general possibilities.

Łukasiewicz's idea that future contingent statements have a third truth value – "indeterminate" – needs to be replaced with this more accurate and less expensive idea: that to which they refer is indeterminate, not only in the sense of not having yet been, i.e. actualized, but also in the sense of having many determinables left open, and indeed over-flown by, future-oriented propositions. For an event to be a truth-maker, it has to have happened; and any event that has happened, any actual event, has to be more than what it is that makes it qualify as a truth-maker. But to speak of events as "realized possibilities" is to give too much retrospective specificity and hence weight to possibilities.[40]

The future that is predicted, even when predictions turn out to be true, lacks the ontological fullness of anything that actually takes place. All that the assertion of "p or not-p" does is to make our uncertainty about the future explicit. And the acuity of that uncertainty does not reach down to any actual event; only to general possibilities. "Tomorrow's sea battle" as referents of things that have not yet taken place, and may never do so, fall short of being fully characterized events. All bets on the future are spread. The apparent reference to an entity that has the singularity, and complete specification of an actual event, is due to a confusion between a definite entity referred to by a referring expression and an entire class of entities defined by entry criteria that may be satisfied but don't specify any actuality. Tomorrow's sea battle is only *a* or *any* sea battle until it takes place and then it is *the* sea battle that has taken place. If an anticipated sea battle seems to be identical with the sea battle it is because we look at the former from the viewpoint of a present in which it has already taken place, that is to say, in which it is complete, and hence past. The irreducible generality of what is referred to in a future-oriented proposition about nothing that yet exists is the other side of its intelligibility. That statements fall short in this way lies in the very nature of discourse – namely, that it is riddled with generality: otherwise, composed entirely of terms that refer to *hapax legomena*, it would be unintelligible. "Either p or not-p" is the supreme expression of this generality.

8.2.2.6 A wobbly viewpoint: tenseless and tensed views

We have discussed the reasons why logical fatalism has been taken seriously or why at least it has caused such headaches for philosophers who know that it is absurd. There is a further reason connected with something we discussed in §8.2.2.2: the idea of a tenseless core of tensed statements that seduces us into thinking that there is something preserved as an event passes from future, to the present, and to the past, and to overlook the ontological difference between a future possibility and a present or past actuality. This enables us to think of future events – which are only possibilities that have not yet happened – as if they were fundamentally the same as events that have happened and as if there were three variant forms of essentially the same event E, namely E_{future}, $E_{present}$ and E_{past}; or $E_{not-yet-happened}$, $E_{happening}$ and $E_{happened}$. We have already characterized the difference between statements about future events and statements about completed events as that between one that has a subject with a sense only and one that has both a sense and a reference. It is this imaginary tenseless core referent of propositions which can also deceive us into imagining that we know more about the future than we do.

We may highlight this indirectly via the "surprise exam" paradox. Susie has been warned that her knowledge of Latin will be tested in a surprise examination that could happen any time next week. The date of the exam is kept secret to prevent her from mugging up relevant stuff the night before and then forgetting it as soon as the exam is over. Now it seems obvious that she will not have the exam on Friday – the last day of the week – because it will be clear by the end of Thursday when the exam will take place and so it would not be a surprise. With Friday ruled out, the exam cannot be on Thursday because it would be obvious by end of play on Wednesday that Thursday is the only possibility. The same argument can be used to rule out Wednesday, Tuesday and Monday. Is the element of surprise therefore removed? Of course, it is not.

The paradox of the disappearing surprise depends on combining irreducibly different tensed viewpoints into a single overall, tenseless viewpoint. Susie's viewpoint is different (and her knowledge of the future less) on Monday than it is on Thursday. The apparent removal of surprise comes from ascribing to Monday the knowledge that comes only on Thursday; in short, retrospectively ascribing Thursday's superior knowledge to Monday and, indeed, ascribing to all the other days of the week the knowledge that is available only at the end of Thursday.

The key to this removal of surprise is conflating the anticipated occurrence of the exam (which is tensed – "The exam will happen") with the fact of the exam taking place on a particular day (which is tenseless). The element of surprise can be eliminated by allowing the possibility of what is an impossible viewpoint in which the series of days is taken as a whole and the viewpoint on Day 1 is granted, on account as it were, knowledge that is acquired only gradually – between Day 1 and Day 4. The examinee is allowed epistemic double vision, so that she knows on Monday not only what Monday knows but also what will become apparent when the whole series of days is complete. Monday is allowed to be both a point in the temporal series (from which the other days in the series are seen as opaque tomorrows) and as representing the series as a whole which has the knowledge that emerges as day succeeds day. This is clearly invalid, but it allows Monday to draw on what Thursday evening knows, when the odds of the examination happening tomorrow have narrowed to a certainty. We are tricked into thinking that the knowledge that emerges during the series of days – so that the odds are shortening as the week goes by – is apparently available to every day in the series by virtue of the timelessness of the factual truth about the day of the examination which is then back projected into time-sensitive knowledge. In short, the tense necessary for the surprise – future – is bundled into an "omnitense" viewpoint that spans all the days of the week and so renders Thursday as being as apparently visible from Monday as it is from Friday or Thursday itself. In reality, the viewpoint that disposes of the surprise would not be available to the candidate until the end of the week when there would be no surprise to be had. So Susie still has to study hard enough on Sunday to be able to retain information all the way to Friday in case that is when the examination is set.

Of course, the odds regarding which day the exam will take place will shorten as the days of the week pass; but they can only shorten as the candidate days disappear one by one. Thought cannot deliver what only time can show. That it appears to do so is due to the mental squint of looking at outcomes from a standpoint that oscillates between the tenses – future and past – because that outcome – as a fact – is tenseless. This mental squint is precisely what enables us to think of future events as if they were on all fours with past ones and propositions referring to them as having a true referent as do past-directed propositions.

8.2.2.7 Final thoughts against logical fatalism

The higher order, purely logical, truth that "'Either p or not-p' is true", cannot allow us to infer either that "p is true" or that "not-p is true". All that this says is that, of all possibilities – which can be encompassed by the sum total of all the disjunctions "p and not-p" – one must be true. The specified possibilities can be widened to cover all that is possible – as when we say "either something will happen in future or nothing will happen in future", which includes even the possibility that the universe may come to an end. The one of the pair "Either the sea battle will take place on 21 December or the sea battle will not take place on 21 December" that turns out to be true does not acquire its truth at the time it is postulated just because having become true, it is necessarily – and hence inescapably – true. Any necessity to be had lies in the disjunction – "Either p or not-p" – and not in one limb or the other of the disjunction. This is evident because either p or not-p could turn out to be true: which limb of the fork is realized is contingent, is open, otherwise we could not entertain both as being possible. The disjunction itself would be a logical impossibility. The logical truth or necessity lies in the conjunction that can be expressed in a contentless way as we have – "Either p or not-p"– and does not predict, even less mandate, any content. If the sea battle actually does take place on 21 December, then it can't also not take place on 21 December – and that is as far as "p or non-p" can take us. The rest is down to contingent reality. Even something as seemingly impossible as my being present at the battle and 100 miles away from it on the same day does not have its impossibility dictated by logic, if it is possible for me to get from one place to the other on the same day.

It seems unlikely that those who subscribe to logical fatalism believe in magic thinking. There is no suggestion that the future could be controlled or shaped by a machine that churned out billions of propositions a proportion of which (say, by chance, 50%) turned out to be true. Indeed, the fact that p or not-p could logically be true shows that neither is logically necessitated and that the mere act of asserting a particular truth will not bring it about. If either p or not-p mandated the state of affairs proposed in them, we would not have to wait for the future to become past. What (apparent) logical fatalism boils down to is the distinctly unalarming conclusion that "p is true" will correspond to the future only so long as "p is true".

In logic we have operations such as negation which can be applied to propositions. But negation cannot be applied to (material, actual) events. We can negate the assertion that "a sea battle took place on 21 December" but we cannot negate an actual sea battle. Projecting "either p or not-p" or "either p is true or p is false" into the material world is therefore a temptation to avoid. At the most superficial level, we note that the future when it is present does not have branches, some of which are occupied by actual events and some of which are left vacant – corresponding to "p" and "not-p".

Logic is about the general relationship between propositions and is valid not only in any possible version of this world and but also in any possible world; and so it cannot deliver particular truths about a particular world. While we may be inclined to apply the truth value T to "Not (p and not-p)" or "Either p or not-p", this is different from applying the truth value T to the assertion that the Battle of Hastings took place in 1066. In the former case, we should replace the word true with the word "valid".

It may still seem possible to unpack a hard-line version of logical fatalism from tautologies. An often cited example is, "If you are going to get killed in 1972, you are going to get killed, so there's no point in taking precautions." The mistake here is that of transposing the necessity from the relationship between the protasis ("If ...") and the apodosis ("then ...") to the protasis itself. Of course, there is no necessity in the protasis – and that is where the precautions can earn their keep – from which it follows that there is no necessity in the apodosis. The logical form of the argument is "If p, then p. p, therefore p". "What will be, will be" is a variant of this. It is the equivalent of "If A happens, then A happens". This then slides to "If A, then necessarily A". Again, the focus should be on the protasis. "If A, then necessarily A" applies only if A. In short, you get the necessity of A only if it has already been (contingently) delivered!

No more need to be said except to note that nothing follows from a truism or a *que sera, sera* logical shoulder shrug, irrespective of whether we are talking about what is happening, what has happened, or what will happen. From the logical argument, you get nothing more out than you put in.[41]

So propositional logic does not deliver constraints on the material realities that will come to be our future present. Is there something else that does this? Isn't the future foreclosed by other means than by assertions that turn out to be true and therefore (so it is argued) to have been true "all along". It is time to turn to material fatalism.

8.2.3 The predetermined future: material fatalism

> We ought ... to regard the present state of the universe as the effect of its anterior state and as the cause of the one which is to follow. Assume ... an intelligence which could know all the forces by which nature is animated, and the states at an instant of all the objects that compose it; ... for [this intelligence] nothing could be uncertain; and the future, as the past, would be present to its eyes.
>
> Laplace, *Philosophical Essay on Probabilities*,
> quoted in Popper, *The Open Universe*, xx

It never seemed remotely plausible that the future could be closed down simply in virtue of being obliged to honour the truth value of propositions made in advance. By contrast, the belief that the future is to a greater or less extent foreclosed in virtue of being determined by that which precedes it seems more plausible and to some (such as Laplace quoted above) self-evident. While we cannot shimmer from logical to material necessity, we may entertain the suspicion that the shape of the future of a world governed by laws, causes, or probabilities is already determined. This is a form of necessity that bears within it the sense of implacability that "either p or not-p" does not convey. Indeed, in the Laplacean universe there was never any space for either/or.

It is this which we will now address, though at considerably shorter length than we have discussed logical fatalism. This may seem lop-sided and you may even suspect me of filibustering over an unreal concern to postpone engaging with the real one. Why spend more time on an obvious falsehood than on something that contains obvious truths? For two reasons. First, as I promised, and hope have shown, the arguments around logical fatalism go beyond time itself to the relationship between language and the world, propositions and reality, events and facts. And secondly, anxieties about material fatalism reach deep into the question of the relationship between ourselves as more or less free agents and our condition as creatures in whom time is made explicit. These wider issues deserve more extended treatment which I will reserve for the final part of this book, in particular Chapter 12.

We believe we can shape the future while we cannot shape the past, though we may try to mitigate or limit its adverse effects, or build on it, in the future. The question is *to what extent* the future is open and, more particularly, open to manipulation. This is not a trivial question as every moment of our lives is future-oriented, and our individual and collective efforts are aimed at favouring one future, or one "outcome", over another. Without a future that is to some extent open, undecided, not preordained, our belief in the difference between actions and events, between a life that is led and a life that is merely passively suffered, between being an agent and being a material object, would be an inexplicable delusion.

There are, of course, benign and necessary limits to the openness of the future, if we think of it as the future of the world as anticipated by an individual person, or a group of people, or humanity. Each moment is furnished to a lesser or greater degree with a continuation of the furniture of the preceding moment, the preceding day, the preceding week and so on. We discussed that furniture in the first part of this chapter. Objects were the most obvious fixtures but there were also ongoing processes and (combining the stasis of objects and the dynamics of change) states of affairs: the platform from which futures grew out of the present, a necessary condition of a life that has any kind of continuity or controllability. If the world began anew every moment, life would be impossible. We are equally reliant on our own relative stability – sufficient to provide narrative continuity – and that of our fellow creatures. The joint enterprise that is communal life presupposes a multitude of stabilities, ranging from the sameness of our basic needs (for food, shelter, and acknowledgement) to the keeping of promises, delivering on commitments, and maintaining one's self in the kind of offices we fill. The very fact that we are positioned at a particular place on earth, location in society, point in our lives and in all the lives that intersect with our own, is a partial foreclosure of the future. Our future, in sum, is rooted in our material and social, personal and collective past. If each day, or each moment, were a blank sheet on which nothing was already written, our own nature, sharing this instability, would be such that there would be no specific way of engaging with whatever happens. There would be at best a torrent of disconnected experiences, helplessly endured, though it is more likely that there would be nothing that could sustain life or the organism and hence consciousness: no torrent, no experiences.

In short, while the various stabilities of the world, the endurance of objects and the probabilities of continuation, may limit the range of our actions and our realistic plans they are *enabling* constraints. And this is true at many levels. For example, we earn a living by respecting, or serving, others' wishes, by providing commodities and services. We cannot, therefore, have complete control of the future in accordance with our individual wishes because that would control, or set aside, others' wishes. To be free is to be something that, or rather someone who, continues engaging with a world that has stable objects, predictable habits of change, and with fellows who are themselves relatively stable.

There is, however, another way in which the future may be preordained, another aspect of stability that looks like an implacability that reveals us as helpless. The material universe in which we act out our future is shaped by the natural laws that have operated in the past and are operating in the present.[42] And that, of course, has its benign aspect. Without discernible, and seemingly unbreakable, habits in the material world, we would have no way of anticipating, never mind manipulating through purposeful action, what is about to happen. But this raises deep questions about whether we can really manipulate what happens or whether we and our seeming manipulations are simply expressions of the same laws that operate unbroken and unbreakable, without fear or favour, through pebbles, trees, and the bodies and brains or even minds of human beings. Whether, in short, the universe, of which we are a part, is following a path entirely specified by those laws, which we cannot deflect. If that were the case, the future, like the present, would be wholly determined by the past and, while it has not yet achieved existence, its determinate form is already fixed. What seem to us to be future possibilities or probabilities which we can take advantage of to shape the world according to our will are in fact certainties that will take place irrespective of any attention we pay to them.

Material fatalism gains plausibility when we swap our casual, everyday gaze for a scientific image of the world and the latter seems to progress towards a complete account of things. A hidden order is revealed in which a handful of hitherto unknown laws directs the passage of the world, including the human beings in it, from the present to the future. The replacement of causation seen at the macroscopic level by probabilities seen at the level of the quantum does not alter this. Firstly, we do not live, and actions are neither planned nor executed, at the subatomic level; and secondly, even if we did, this would be of little help since individual random quantum events conform to a set of fixed probabilities expressed in frequencies that are predefined to many more decimal points than are perceptible in everyday life. They would not give us any more elbow room than the most rigid causal connectedness. It seems difficult to avoid the conclusion that the realm of manipulable possibility and opportunity-bearing probabilities that we think we live in are themselves simply manifestations of a universe that unfolds through us (most obviously through our bodies) as much as it unfolds around us so that, undeflected, it bears us to its next phase. Future contingents are in fact inevitable; only our ignorance makes them seem contingent. They could be pre-empted only by a force greater than the laws of nature; by the kind of item people call "God".

If this were the whole story, the aspiration to freedom would be like wanting the universe to have incompatible properties. After all, it seems a bit rich to rely on the laws of nature defined with ever greater precision to ensure that our actions have their intended consequences while at the same time expecting them to be suspended to make space for genuine actions that truly deflect the natural course of events. The universal applicability of the laws of nature is a necessary condition of our living in a world where we can *do* anything; where our actions have consequences we expect and desire; and where our potency can be enhanced as we translate knowledge of the fundamental properties of matter into increasingly effective technologies. The very conditions of being an effective and reliable agent seem to render agency impossible. Are actions – if they are to be reliably efficacious – chimera, impossible events at once stitched into the very network of causes upon which they are supposed to operate and yet act upon them as if from the outside?

We have arrived, of course, at the standard problem of determinism and free will. The argument for determinism is readily summarized. The world is made up of material objects (including human bodies) that are subject to the laws of material nature.

Those material laws are made visible in the predictable, indeed inescapable, relationship between causes and effects. Every event has a prior cause and that cause is an effect of prior causes and soon we are headed towards some putative beginning when the Big Bang banged Being into existence. These events include human actions and all those things that we do to shape the future. So the material future is shaped by the material present which is shaped by the material past and we, and our actions, are just part of the unfolding of the material world which cannot be deflected by our intentions seen as independent points of departure. While we may be the causal ancestors of certain future events, we are equally causal descendants of a past that precedes us and indeed generated us. We are simply metaphysically undistinguished stretches of the many causal chains linking the pre-human past to the human and extra-human and post-human future. We can therefore no more bring about the future or the salient part of it – shape the bit we want to happen or prevent the bit we don't – than a pebble can arrange its own future, or than we or a pebble can bring about the past. The control we imagine we have over our individual or shared future is illusory.

This is entirely straightforward and entirely wrong. In order to see in what way it is wrong, we shall have to go back to the beginning of our inquiry and examine the nature of explicit time, in particular tensed time, and see how it liberates us – at least temporally – from the natural world which gave rise to, and succours us, and in which we have our being. This will be the theme of the last two chapters of this book.[43]

8.3 FINAL REFLECTIONS ON THE FUTURE

"Tomorrow never comes". Tell that to yesterday. Tomorrows, of course, cannot escape coming, but at the price of changing their status and becoming first today and then yesterday. It is the general tomorrow that remains out of reach: tomorrow is the day after whatever day it is today. To say "Tomorrow never comes" is really to say "The not-yet is not yet".

Even so, this truism makes the future seem somewhat insubstantial. Hence, of those philosophers who admit tensed time into their ontology, while most will accept the present, and quite a few accept the past, fewer will include the future. This may in part be because there are in truth no future events though, as we have discussed, the future is generously furnished by the enduring reality of what is already present in the present. This, however, is how we can assert both that the future is real and that, at the same time, it is not settled. Objects, ongoing processes, and laws and propensities form the already present general and particular background for a future whose event-contents are not yet real. What we might call the inertia of the world – the inertia of either stasis or of ongoing kinesis – underwrites the present reality of the future.

Those who see the future clearly know that any work it does is courtesy of the influence of the present idea of it on the present, not through events of its own.

Compared with the other side-panel of the triptych, the past, the future is further disadvantaged. Like the past, its existence is in some sense dependent on the present, but unlike the past it is not definite. There is a contrast between "what might have happened" which *is* trumped by what did happen, and "what might happen" which *is not* yet trumped by actuality.

This is one of the many reasons for rejecting the claim that the fixity of the past and the openness of the future are merely perspectival. The claim conflates the epistemic with the constitutive, or at least confuses the one with the other. My ignorance of the result of my blood sugar test – I have yet to ring up the doctor – is distinct from the indeterminacy of my blood sugar in the future. Its openness – and hence openness to change – is why the future is such a powerful and distinctive presence in our lives. Like the past it pervades our every moment, giving our hours their moment-by-moment momentum, but the nature of its influence is quite different.

The fact that it stretches before us in attenuating probabilities, to which there corresponds an ever-thinning reality-for-us – reflected in the way we discount the future the more remote it is – does not mean that it is unreal in the way that a fantasy is unreal: "tomorrows" have a higher ontological standing than goblins. As for the singular futures that concern us, they are underwritten by converging intentions, ideas, concerns shared by several or many individuals. A paradigm case would be an appointment to meet another person. The future is among other things a tightly woven nexus of shared promises, undertakings, cooperative enterprises, tethered to the objective system of times and dates, a high proportion of which will be actualized.

The relationship between the visible and the invisible future, analogous to that between the visible and the invisible past, is interesting and complex. There are circumstances, as we have noted, when we can literally see what is going to happen (two cars about to collide, you walking towards me, a stone falling to the ground) but these are a very small part of the future that preoccupies us. Indeed, we may be inclined to think of this literally visible future as part of the present, or at least as a "present future". For the most part, the future is out of sight – beginning with the invisibility of what we anticipate we might find under a stone, round a corner, or over a hill – and not only out of sight but unrelated to our sensory field. Tomorrow's appointment is not defined by its being close to or far from where I am standing now, even though my present location and the venue for the appointment may be thought of as spatially related.[44] Out of sight is into mind and into mind is to be gathered up into a space defined more by ideas and words and dates and times than by a relationship to the present moment as defined by the spatio-temporal coordinates of the body. So, while the future we foresee is rooted in the future we can see, it is also remote from it, because it belongs largely to a realm of facts and probabilities forged in the collective mind.

The presence of the future is inevitably patchy: its world is a pick-and-mix of *salient* possibilities. This is the sense in which it is true to say that the assumptions, anticipations, expectations, hopes, wishes, plans that reach into the future also construct it. Even our uncertainties belong more to ourselves than to it: we do not anticipate to what extent, or in what way, we may be wrong, though we accept that our anticipations are to a greater or lesser extent guesses. We think: "It could be A or B" and it turns out to be Z. We so order things – positioning ourselves, shaping the bits of the world that lie within our reach, co-opting others as individuals and groups, mobilizing the knowledge and power of the collectives to which we belong – as to maximize the chances of things turning out as we wish.

Though the future in the present – tomorrow's presence in today – may seem to be woven out of thoughts that evaporate as soon as they are thought, the flow of thought and the actions guided by them may be hardened into words as explicit undertakings and, by writing, into the million-strands of the many social contracts that bind us together. We are not alone in the task of being the stewards and midwives of our own future. The future is shared, upheld by clocks, diaries, and calendars.

Even when the expected happens, because expectation cannot assume the precise shape and three dimensional reality of actuality, what happens will be made up largely of components that are not expected, as we noted when we observed the contrast between future contingencies proposed in propositions and actual events. The fulfilment of expectation requires the correspondence only of the salient actualities to what is expected. When things go according to plan, most of what happens is unplanned, or not envisaged in the plan.[45]

At the same time, we know that the future is running out: we are heading blindfolded towards that tomorrow after which there will be no more tomorrows: the supply gives out. This body, currently sitting itself up, feeling warm and satisfyingly busy, underpinning its world, will cool, lose its identity with itself, and dissolve into the material stuff that once surrounded it, providing the infinitely varied theatres of its days. As the great poet Georg Trakl put it: "blind minute-hands / We climb towards midnight".[46] As the midnight hour strikes, our lives will have become a determinate, unalterable totality.

The present ordinary day is the unimaginable future of its own distant past. The maker of the hand axe could not conceive the world around the museum cabinet where the axe is displayed or the motives or conversations of those who, 400,000 years later, come to look at it. And my 10-year-old self could not imagine the sexagenarian typing these words or conceive of the world he lives in. The succession of days eats into, in the sense of diminishing, whatever future I will prove, when it comes to an end, to have had. We cannot say with 100 per cent certainty how much is left – "Call no life spanned until it is complete" – but there will come a time when we are done and dust; undone and a handful of dust. The future will give way to something disconnected itself, to a time that is not linked to a present or a past. What then? Will time, the inner secret of space, continue? Will there be a time beyond time?

It is time to consider eternity.[47]

CHAPTER 9

Beyond time: temporal thoughts on eternity

I hear the tortoise of time explode in the microwave of eternity.
Humphrey Lyttelton, "I'm Sorry I Haven't a Clue", BBC Radio 4

The English are not a very spiritual people, so they invented cricket to
give them some idea of eternity.   George Bernard Shaw[1]

9.1 THE IDEA OF ETERNITY

We may not know when our lives are going to end, but we can be certain that we are always approaching that end. The lengthening contrail of yesterdays warns us that the invisible store of tomorrows is depleting. Underlining this knowledge is a Grand Narrative of our lives captured in the idea of an arc: a phase of growth, maturation, and augmentation followed, after an interval, by a time of shrinkage, and diminution; of progressive empowerment succeeded by disempowerment; of becoming and then begoing. Gain – of friends, loved ones, possessions, CV, standing – is followed by loss. Personhood, attachment, potency, value, and ultimately our individual being, are taken from us. Everything in which we have invested ourselves will disinvest in us. On the way, bereavements – of those whom we love or merely like, of past selves and their worlds, and of our faculties – remind us of the final state in which we shall be deprived of ourselves.

And so we need consolation. One version (and by no means the only one) of that consolation is the idea of the continuing existence of ourselves, and all that we truly love and value, in a realm somehow outside of that temporal world in which we gained and lost everything to which we were attached. That realm has many guises but the one that is most relevant to our present inquiry goes under the name of eternity. Dying, so the not entirely reassuring story goes, is to exchange life in time for life, or at least existence, in eternity.

If the idea of eternity is complex and contradictory, this is because the need for consolation, while it may be the main reason for its presence in our thought about the world and ourselves, is not the only force shaping how it has been conceived. Given that the promise or hope of eternal life is central to many religious creeds, it has been subject to the vicissitudes to which any key term in a network of doctrines, themselves exposed to a multitude of historical, social, and political forces and accidents, might be expected to suffer. There are also important contributions from philosophy, mathematics, and even science. The axioms and theorems of mathematics and the laws of nature have been regarded as true for all time and hence in this sense eternal. But they are also seen as revealing that which is unchanging beneath change: A changes into B but, there is a permanent way defined by natural laws which determines what, or in what sense, things are conserved beneath apparent alteration. We have touched on this, in Part I *passim*, when we discussed the way the mathematical representation of change "freezes" it. It is a consequence of a totalizing vision, a view from no viewpoint (the secular equivalent of a "God's eye view"), in which time is represented spatially, merges with space in space–time, and the universe becomes an unchanging four-dimensional manifold. We shall return to this later in the present chapter.

In philosophy, the (literal and metaphorical) *locus classicus* of the idea of eternity is Plato's conception of an unchanging Heaven of timeless duration where reality – merely palely imaged in time as we experience it through our senses – is present in its perfect, real, self, as a Form or Idea, available to the intellect. The belief – or assumption, or intuition – that eternity may be accessed, or its nature revealed, through the intellect acting to free itself from the distortions arising out of embodiment, has its crucial source in Western philosophy in Parmenides.[2] To him we owe the most influential formulation of the argument that reality is timeless and unchanging and the deliverances of the senses that tell us quite otherwise are to be disregarded as illusions. And it has numerous descendants; its most notable manifestation in relatively recent philosophy being Kant's vision of a "noumenal" reality as eternal, undetermined by limitations of our ordinary experience, in particular by time.[3]

With such a mixed parentage and such a complex history, it is not surprising that the idea of eternity should be somewhat slippery. According to McTaggart, it has at least three facets:

(a) an unending extent or stretch of time – sempiternity or everlastingness;
(b) that which is entirely timeless – a state of existence independent of temporal conditions; and
(c) that which includes time but somehow also transcends it.[4]

McTaggart divides the second component – that which is timeless – into "the timelessness of truths and the timelessness of existences", though it is timeless truths that are supposed to reveal timeless existences. This was a good move, since the qualification for being a timeless truth can be quite unimpressive. While the toothache I had yesterday lasted only a few hours, the humble truth of the assertion that

"Raymond Tallis had an attack of toothache on 4 April 2016" is eternal. That may be why, beginning with Plato, the emphasis has been on timeless existences rather than timeless truths.

Such existence is usually reserved for ontological toffs. For Plato, Ideas or Forms such as Love, the Beautiful, and the Good were eternity's primary denizens. He couldn't, however, entirely exclude embarrassing ontological proles, such as hair and dirt, without being inconsistent. Platonist mathematicians – who (as we saw in §3.6) believe that their discipline unveils timeless realities – have populated eternity with menageries of mathematical objects such as the Circle, and the Square, integers, and more exotic beasts like pi or the square root of −1. And theologians have peopled eternity with the immortal souls of those who have lived sufficiently blameless lives. And then there is God, eternity's sovereign. The ontological diversity makes for a rather puzzling realm, in which humans co-exist with mathematical objects, and the living (after-living humans and living God) with lifeless abstractions, guaranteed immortality in virtue of never having been contaminated with life.

One might think that timelessness would guarantee everlastingness. Eternal truths and everlasting existences, given that they neither endure for a particular time or occur at a particular time, cannot pass into or out of existence. They no more begin in time than they end. They must have been, and will be, forever. Everlastingness is not, however, identical with timelessness. Even in a world without change, everlastingness presupposes duration – and hence time. Lasting takes time and everlasting takes more time: an infinite amount of it. The notion of something that has duration but no quantity of duration might seem to be self-contradictory.

One objection to this argument is that it is too rooted in an idea of duration connected with that of endurance contrasted with transience, and that this contrast can have no place in an eternal realm in which nothing changes, and there is nothing to clock the everlastingness of the everlasting. Responding in this way may, however, raise the question of whether time itself has any meaning in the absence of change or events that have a temporal order. "Sempiternity" sounds like a temporal vacuum. Is this possible? We will discuss this in §10.4.2 but it is worth noting for the present that where time cannot be measured – as in an unchanging universe which lacks all temporal markers – the assumption that it can still be said to have elapsed is contrary to Mach's verificationist principle (a guiding principle of twentieth-century physics) that that which cannot be measured cannot be said to be real. We may, however, entertain the possibility that eternity is not bound by such methodological constraints. Even so, everlastingness does not sit easily with unending time if we think of time not as a kind of autonomous stuff but as a relationship between changes.

Everlasting eternity may seem to be a composite notion, encompassing both a quasi-container ("an unending stretch of time", or "everlastingness") and its contents ("everlasting truths" and "everlasting existences").[5] The distinction we naturally make between on the one hand events that happen and objects that exist in time and on the other hand time itself is thus not so easy to sustain in eternity; in the distinction between unchanging items (truths, existences, laws or whatever) and the eternity in which they subsist.

As already noted, there is some overlap between the unchanging eternity of the theologian, the Parmenidean or Platonic philosopher, and that of the physicist, most clearly expressed in the block universe of special relativity, in which the time in which things happen is replaced by a four-dimensional manifold in which there is no happening. There are many ways of challenging this portrait of the universe as discussed in Chapter 3.[6] The shortest way of removing the threat of a frozen eternity from the "true" portrait of the world would be to argue that an account of the universe that sees "everything at the same time" (*totum simul*) would, merely by definition, preclude different contents emerging as we pass from time to time.

Indeed, *totum simul* is close to Boethius' definition of the eternity available to God:

> It is the common judgement, then, of all creatures that live by reason that God is eternal ... Eternity [for God] is the complete, simultaneous and perfect possession of everlasting life ... [I]t is one thing to progress like the world ... through everlasting life, and another thing to have embraced the whole of everlasting life in one simultaneous present.[7]

The reference to a universal "simultaneous present" may seem to be in direct opposition to the viewpoint of special relativity which holds that distant simultaneity is an illusion. But God, being everywhere, is never distant from anything. Simultaneity can therefore be a universal relation.

9.2 THE RELATIONSHIP BETWEEN TIME AND ETERNITY

Eternity thus seems to be a slippery concept. We have no way of adjudicating between everlastingness, unchangingness, timelessness, the office of being the home of timeless truths, and having all-at-once-ness, as to which is its prime characteristic. When we set aside the notion that time is unreal, or that the universe is an unchanging block – in short that all reality is eternal – then we encounter interesting challenges in addressing the relationship between time and eternity. And this remains even if we do not succumb to the temptation of thinking of eternity as enclosing time, rather as a day encloses a minute, so that time is simply a local stretch of eternity. The problems that have most exercised thinkers have been theological, prompted by the idea of God's special or episodic intervention in His Creation – most notably in human affairs. I will come to those in due course. But first let us look at the very idea that time and eternity might come into contact, such that time and timelessness might intersect.

9.2.1 Time and eternity: non-theological considerations

The contradictions inherent in any putative relationship between time and eternity could not be stated more clearly (though perhaps not intentionally) than in this passage from the *Timaeus*:

> Wherefore he [God] resolved to have a moving image of eternity, and when he set in order the heavens, he made this image eternal but moving according to number, while eternity itself rests in unity; and this image we call time.[8]

There are obvious problems. Firstly, if eternity is undifferentiated, it would be difficult to portray it even if by "time" Plato meant "the sum total of time" or "the sum total of what happens in time". In short, there could be no "image". Secondly, if such a portrait were possible, it would be difficult to see how time, seemingly inseparable from change, could portray something that is unchanging: how there could be "moving image" of that which is, by definition, at rest. And if eternity is "all at once" as Boethius (unknown of course to Plato) would have it, succession of events marking time would not be true to this. The abiding present of eternity – in which all and everything is co-present – could not be imaged in the transient denizens of time.

In sum: if our immersion in time were meant to give us an image of eternity, then it would be worse than a travesty. And this, of course, is Plato's most celebrated belief, informing the famous Allegory of the Cave, though things may be even less satisfactory than the allegory suggests. For Plato has no theory accounting for our access to, or interaction with the Forms whose "pale images" are all that are afforded to us by our sense experience.[9] (It is interesting to speculate how pallor – or some other attenuation – could facilitate the descent of Forms to Earth or to their engagement with the clay of our impermanent bodies.)

The passage just quoted suggests that, for Plato, the link between unchanging eternity and its moving image that is time is number. This invites a few highly speculative thoughts that I do not claim have any historical warrant. The succession of numbers – 1, 2, 3, etc. – is a series of frozen positions adding up to a flow activated by the counting of tokens. This moving series of unmoving quantitative abstractions might be an incomplete reconciliation between what Dantzig described as the legato of the music of the universe and the staccato of the symphony of numbers.[10] Numbers, perhaps, effect some rapprochement between eternity and time, but they do not reconcile the stasis of the former with the kinesis of temporal life. The mathematics of continuous change – an attempt to map continuous reality on to discontinuous numbers (or vice versa) – endeavours to bring what we might call punctuated stasis closer to a condition of genuine kinesis, and hence to let eternity into the temporal. There is a pertinent connection with Aristotle's attempt to capture time: "[T]ime is not movement, but only movement in so far as it admits enumeration. A proof of this: we discriminate the more or less by number".[11]

Plato's arresting and seemingly contradictory definition of the relation between eternity and time highlights a constant, profound, theme in Western philosophy. This is the problem of understanding the relationship between a reality that is often conceived or articulated as being undifferentiated (or relatively so) and unchanging (or relatively so), and a world of appearance that is highly heterogeneous and in constant flux. In Plato's case, this is manifest in the tension between the perfect, unchanging, Form of (say) the Good and actual manifestations of goodness, highly variable, unstable, and to a greater or lesser degree shabby or inferior.

The idea of eternity that has impinged most closely on our inquiry so far is connected with the various forms of mathematical realism discussed in §3.6. Behind mathematical realism is the assumption that the (unchanging) mathematical forms of objects, processes, and events are more truly real than anything encountered in everyday experience; or, more radically, that reality *is* the *form* these items exemplify (as in ontic structural realism); or, most radically of all, that (as Tegmark has argued) reality is made of mathematical objects. This elevation of mathematical truths to the status of being not only the real structure, but the very substance, of the world seen aright is a consequence of two dubious assumptions. The first is that (to use McTaggart's distinction) the existence of timeless truths implies that there are timeless existences; or, indeed, that the former are the latter. The second is the more obvious, and even more dubious, assumption that that which is timeless is most real, or that only that which is unchanging is truly real.

These forms of mathematical realism are extreme manifestations of the founding assumption of the Parmenidean–Platonic, or more broadly the rationalist, tradition in Western philosophy that privileges the intellect over the senses and the truths the intellect uncovers, or at least intuits and seeks, over transient perceptions rooted in sense experience. What truly is, is forever and unchanging.

A different expression of extreme Platonism (though he profoundly disagreed with Plato) is the account of the relationship between time and eternity developed by Kant in *The Critique of Pure Reason*. Reality – the noumenon – is inaccessible to sense experience. The latter imposes a spatio-temporal structure in the perception of the noumenon that permits it to appear as phenomena and consequently presents what is there as discrete objects occupying and moving in space, enduring and changing in time, and interacting causally. Sense experience, or "sensible intuition", is the link between the eternal, unchanging, undifferentiated noumenon or thing-in-itself and the transient, endlessly changing, and highly differentiated phenomena of appearances, ordered in time (as well as in space). The latter – the spatial array and time series – is unreal. Kant demonstrates to his own satisfaction the unreality of objective time (except as a form of sensible intuition) by showing that both arms of the antinomy – that the world does, and the world does not, have a beginning in time – are unintelligible. (This is discussed in §10.4.3.) Kant's own image of eternity is essentially blank – and for good reasons: to image eternity would be to project the phenomenal realm into the noumenal; the noumena are neither sensible nor knowable: "The concept of a noumenon is thus a merely *limiting concept*, the function of which is to curb the pretensions of sensibility; and it is therefore only of negative employment … It is bound up with the limitations of sensibility, though it cannot affirm anything positive beyond the field of sensibility".[12]

The most elaborate and protracted discussions of eternity in Western thought have revolved around human afterlife and the mode of God's existence. The belief that God is, or inhabits, eternity and that humans may, under certain circumstances in some sense, join Him put into high relief the problems around the intersection between time and eternity. I shall begin with humankind and then proceed to God.

9.2.2 Time and eternity: theological considerations 1: humans out of their element

I die after a blameless life in which I have shown my love of God by worship, faith and good deeds. Well qualified, I leave my (I hope) mourning relatives, and enter eternity where I enjoy my eternal life. Characterizing what happens in this way, suggests that I pass into eternity at a particular time, the day of my death – say (to be optimistic) 10 October 2035. Whereas this date makes sense in the world I have left, it hardly does so in eternity. 10 October 2035 makes even less sense in eternity than (to borrow Wittgenstein's example) that of 5 p.m. on the sun.[13] If we accept the notion that we came into the world from eternity – we were immortal souls before we were incarnated – then there is a time at which we exited eternity (in my case 10 October 1946) as well as a time in which we entered it. This flags up another problematic notion beyond that of the intersection between points in time and eternity – my birth and death; namely that of the relationship between intervals of time and eternity. In what way are those 88 years of virtuous life between my birth and my death represented in eternity?

We can approach the difficult issues of the temporal relationship between my life and eternity another way. We tend to think, or at least speak, of eternity as "an *after*life" because our tenancy begins after our life has ended. From which it follows that eternity, or my being in it, has a past; namely the future in which I anticipated, looked forward, or hoped for it. If we believe that life on earth precedes that in eternity, then we have to accept that life in eternity is afterlife on earth, given that "before" and "after" are symmetrical relations. It can get worse. If it is believed that souls entered life from (a prior) eternity, then there is a future tense of eternity: the temporal life that lay ahead of me before my conception. This not only encloses time within eternity – which may be doctrinally sound – but also threatens, by attaching eternity to a time series, to enclose eternity within time.

If time is not embedded in eternity nor eternity embedded in time, perhaps they are side by side. This doesn't seem to work either. If, having earned my afterlife in eternity, I am remembered by others, my afterlife will be located in their lives. I may not be aware of this but *they* will know that it was 2 days, or 4 months, or 6 years since I died, and that I have therefore spent a corresponding time in eternity. Two years after my death, you can think that I have spent two years in eternity. And my period in eternity, timed by the world's recollection of me, seems to be *simultaneous* with the time that has passed in your life since I passed on. But the idea of time and eternity parallel with one another – such that a moment of time might be simultaneous with a moment of eternity – clearly does not work since only events can be simultaneous with one another in virtue of happening at the same time. Times cannot be simultaneous with anything else.

There is, it would appear, a profound mismatch between my tenure of unchanging, timeless eternity and the duration you put on it; but so long as we think of eternity and the afterlife as connected – as when I pass from one to the other at birth or death – tenure of eternity cannot be separated from time. The distinction between my afterlife (my posthumous state) and after-time is a difficult one. If they are not entirely disentangled – and so long as I am remembered, or the world with its dates and times continues, it is not clear that they *can* be disentangled – the paradox of an eternal life (mine) that has a beginning in time, or that has a duration in a time that is parallel to eternity, cannot be escaped.

Which brings us to an existential mystery wider and deeper than the conceptual problems awoken by the seeming intersection of time and eternity. It seems more justified to characterize these instances of intersection as "eternized times" than "timeless moments", to think of the interpenetration of time and eternity as obliging eternity to enter time instead of the converse. At any rate, they are hosted by a human, that is to say temporal, being. The intersection is *an experience* that takes place at a specific time. The timing may be approximate, as in the case of Henry Vaughan, who "saw eternity the other night" with "round beneath it, Time in hours, days, years, / Driven by spheres / Like a vast shadow moved".[14]

Pascal is more precise, in his report of his glimpse of "everlasting joy":

> The year of grace 1654
> Monday, 23 November, feast of Saint Clement, Pope and Martyr, and of others in the Martyrology.
> Eve of Saint Chrysogonus, Martyr and others.
> From about half past ten in the evening until half past mid-night.[15]

There are homely, even humorous, aspects to this intersection. When Vaughan declares that he saw eternity "the other night" one has to resist wondering what he was doing when he had the vision and whether it was a weekday or a weekend. This is exploited by Kierkegaard when in *Either/Or* he talks ironically about "the aesthetics of marriage" where the partner, showing fidelity to eternal vows in a temporal and temporary life, is able to solve "the great riddle of living in eternity and hearing the hall clock strike".[16]

Irony is inherent in the endeavour to cultivate or court what is eternal in one's self, or to transcend one's self, to commune with the timeless while keeping an eye on the time. Anxiety, rather than a sense of irony, was the dominant feeling, when I was a school boy, hurrying to be on time for morning prayers, catching sight of the church clock and seeing that the hour of nine was only 10 minutes away. "My God, is that the time!?" Late, late, late – and, what is more, for communion with that which lies beyond time!

The very existence of a church clock seems paradoxical. How can the House of God, committed to communing with the timeless, the unchanging, with that which lies beyond or outside of seconds, minutes, hours and days, wear the time of the day so conspicuously on its sleeve, and broadcast that time to the time-torn populace by means of a time piece bathed in morning and evening light? This is not an oversight, of course; nor a mere opportunism that took advantage of the fact that churches are the tallest buildings to disseminate the time of the day to time-bound creatures largely without watches. Church bells, and the clocks to regulate them, were introduced to let everyone know when to perform a certain office of prayer; most importantly when to attend for the sacrament that permitted time to communicate with eternity.

Eternity was ultimately the loser as the summons by bells prepared the way for the summons by factory hooter; and the spread of clocks placed the grid, the meshes, of clocked time over the entirety of human life. Secular time marginalized intimations of eternity. As discussed in §4.6, our lives are minutely orchestrated. We are more driven, more impatient, more pulled this way and that by the many modes of the clock-face. Increasingly, consciousness bows down before the God of the Clock-time and the God of eternity pales in its daylight. Eternity is displaced by numbered time; timelessness by "physical" time without end. At any rate, the idea of eternity appears compromised by any imagined intersection with time because the intersection has to take place at particular moments in time – not least in order to be part of the history of time-bound individuals who experience them. It seems that on such occasions – as in church-going and the celebration of the Eucharist – that eternity gives up more of its identity in agreeing to the meeting than does time.

Something deeper in us keeps eternity at bay or in its (modest) place: our existential rootedness in being-with, in "us", in *mitsein*. Duty, solidarity, collegiality, anchor us, hold us down, imprison us even, in the complex networks of the temporal world. Notwithstanding Kierkegaard, eternity and the hall clock, the church bell and the anxious chorister, are at odds. The endeavour to make contact with eternity seems a kind of betrayal: the faraway look of one who tries to see his life under the aspect of eternity is an affirmation of a profound, irremediable solitude, against which the entirety of life, the lived assumptions of domestic life, and friendship, and community spirit, are ranged. The Sacrament by appointment – 11 a.m., don't be late! – has little chance of glowing with its putative meaning before a congregation steeped in daily life, aware of the formality and regularity of the occasion, and of each other, fixed in an unbroken framework of dailiness, the coordinated timetable of mundanity. The word "eternity", spoken as it must be at a particular time, is dropped into the unceasing chatter of the hour, the incandescent Now, losing its presence in the days and hours, glowing at best like a candle flame in broad daylight, or a solar roar reduced to a little brightness round the ankles of flowers.[17]

So much for eternity accessed from time. What about the very idea of living in eternity? We have already noted the problems associated with the fact that eternal life seems to be part of a time series in virtue of being subsequent to (the) time (of our lives). But the notion of life inside eternity is even more problematic.

In view of what happens to our bodies after our demise, resurrection of their flesh doesn't seem on the cards. The laws of nature would seem unlikely to re-constitute Raymond Tallis out of the confetti of his scattered ashes or reconstruct his once-smiling face from the faeces of creatures who have feasted on his deliquescent visage. Let us, however, permit ourselves to imagine that we are resurrected in the flesh after death. At what age would we be resurrected and to what circumstances might we be restored? At what point in the story of our life would we be resumed? Eternal life could scarcely be a matter of picking up the story as it has been left on our death bed.

If it were, it would be somewhat unattractive. An existence of everlasting vomiting would scarcely seem a reward worth struggling for. And the same questions apply to the most important part of our circumstances: those with whom we passed our lives. How old, in what state, should *they* be? And how will their resurrected state intermesh with ours?

But deeper, and more interesting, problems arise if we think of our sojourn in eternity not as a continuation of fleshly existence but in a discarnate, indeed disembodied state. This seems necessary because it is difficult to separate material existence, and *a fortiori* biological existence, from change. Life is permanent change, corrected by other changes – the "polyphasic dynamic equilibrium" that is organic existence. Eternity, construed as everlastingness, must imply no change of state, and hence no change. So what would life in eternity be like? Bodiless, and unchanging, we would be without specific needs. There would therefore be no agenda to give direction to the unfolding narrative that is inseparable from a self. Nothing would happen to us, not the least because, lacking spatial location, we would not be anywhere in particular, and not exposed to events. Consequently, no experience would be possible and no action necessary or meaningful even if it were possible. Continuation of life under such circumstances would seem like breathing in a vacuum; even less than a state of frozen expectation, or waiting-for-nothing, for waiting at least has the idea of a future and, irrespective of whether time is tenseless, existence inside eternity most certainly is without tenses.

Disembodiment would immunise us against causal vulnerability but only at the price of being denied any causal influence. If all you need for the afterlife is psychological continuation, then this is a potentially horrifying prospect. "So far from living in paradise" Paul Edwards argues, "a person deprived of his body and thus of his sense organs would, quite apart from many gruesome deprivations, be in a state of desperate loneliness and eventually come to prefer annihilation".[18] Beyond loss and tears, such an existence would also be without hope or joy. It would be even worse than relying on others to maintain your afterlife by recalling or commemorating you, even though such an afterlife would have a hollow centre; an emptiness at the heart of what is remembered – the first-person being that was "I". Posthumous fame or even affectionate recall – even if it were not confused and intermittent – would be entirely wasted on the dead.

The emptiness of eternal afterlife is not merely an unfortunate consequence of mislaying one's body or trying to soldier on without it. It is intrinsic to the very idea of eternity in which the mode of being is one of changelessness. Having nothing to do, to look back on, to look forward to, no emotions, wishes, desires, duties, needs, is a non-contingent feature of eternal life. Pure endurance lacks even the "And then … and then …" of one damn thing after another. It is storyless. There is no journeying or arrival; no process or event, only states – states that are undifferentiated and hence invulnerable to change.

Individual stasis in a boundless general stasis seems a strange continuation of, or even addendum to, a life whose essence is change in an ever-changing world. But absolute, framework-independent stasis seems necessary for immortality because a more than zero average rate of change will, extended over sufficient time – and there is sufficient time in eternity – result in the disappearance of the afterliver.

The continuation of a time-soaked creature such as a human being in a realm of pure duration is therefore deeply problematic. Time as the possibility of change and change as the possibility of experience seem necessary conditions of anything recognisable or imaginable or conceivable as life. The reports of those who have had and indeed enjoyed "timeless" experiences or "experiences of timelessness" are, necessarily, reports of individuals, such as Vaughan and Pascal, who have "returned" to time and are looking at their experiences from outside of timelessness. This hardly corresponds to the situation of the eternity-dweller.

The idea of life in eternity that is everlasting without having temporal magnitude or extent confronts us with the contestable notion of duration separated from other aspects of time, not to speak of stability in the absence of a contrast with transience. In earthly life we think of endurance or permanence as requiring a background of transience for its everlastingness to be captured; to be referenced to something that is ongoing, to informal or formal clocks that are changes which are quantitative markers of change.[19]

Ultimately, we may be forced to think of a timeless eternity, of pure duration, of mere everlastingness of contents, as a totality that has been summed – and should therefore be complete – and still somehow continuing and hence in some way being added to. And that is reflected in our image of life in eternity: of time somehow outside of time; of a life that continues after life comes to an end; of a story still ongoing when the stories are all told. It is a response to the feeling that death is an interruption; that our lives are never completed, only cut off. And it has at its heart a deep contradiction because we have to look at eternity from within a temporal standpoint, so that (for example) we see it as a future towards which we may be heading, from which (even more speculatively) we may have come, and which crosses with time at a point in time, as if dipping down from a parallel realm, simultaneous with that of the days of the week.[20]

9.2.3 Time and eternity: theological considerations 2: God in his element

The richest and (sometimes) the most tortured reflections on the idea of eternity and its intersection with time have been driven by theological questions, particularly those relating to God's interventions in human affairs. God and eternity are inseparable; for it seems that eternity, unlike the spatio-temporal manifold, cannot exist in-itself or by itself. It has to be witnessed, occupied. God is eternity's native, landlord, ruler and guarantor. He and eternity fit like a hand and a glove, a molecule and a receptor site: each needs the other; each makes sense of the other. And therein lies the source of our problems conceiving of Him and it.

If we think of eternity as the sum total of all things, then He cannot be offset from that sum-total but must be part of it: eternity cannot merely be the medium in which he has his Being. If he "dwelleth in eternity" (Psalm 8:1), then he and eternity cannot be one and the same, which makes the "in" problematic. This is a problem that is replicated in every facet of the idea of God. God is infinite, and yet is distinct from his creation, from which it follows that He must be less than the totality of things. I, this table, Liverpool, the sun and the billions of stars, are not God. If I am not God, then there is something that is not God; and so God is not boundless. God is omniscient and yet, in order for there to be anything in particular that he knows, there has to be a viewpoint from which he knows it: his knowledge has to be limited at any given moment. Or, if this is not accepted, there still has to be a distinction between the knower and the known, with the latter being a limit on the former.

And from his standpoint – which is that of one who is himself unchanging – it would be difficult to see how there could be registration of change. And the God who is supposed to change things – indeed be the author of all change, including the greatest of all changes, namely the Creation – it is difficult to see how he could cause things to change. He is obliged to do all he does do without the disturbance to his perfection that would be implicit in his lifting a finger.[21] God in changeless eternity would seem to be drained of all life; no more animate, sentient, active, personal, than the square root of minus one.

There is a particularly acute problem associated with the idea of special divine action, of intervention in the temporal realm, especially if this is thought to be triggered, occasioned, or justified, by a particular event or course of events, including the free actions of human beings. The personal God of the Abrahamic religions Who hearkens to prayers, takes historical events to heart, and intervenes in human life highlights the paradox of an Eternal One reaching out to the realm of time-soaked, time-swept, time-dissolved creatures like ourselves. It is entirely frivolous but irresistible to speculate that God's wrath, so evident in the Bible, may have been due to irritability arising out of a particularly acute form of jet lag owing to crossing not time zones but the border between time itself and eternity. More seriously, he would have to enter time in order to engage with the realm of events that take place in, and take, time. He could not continue to be a cause in the universe without descending from the timeless realm.

The eternity of physics and the eternity of theology overlap in the property of unchangingness. The unchangingness of the spatio-temporal manifold is, as we have seen, an unchangingness by definition – it is merely the sum total of the history of the universe seen from no particular viewpoint – whereas the unchangingness of God's eternity is a positive property, a profound existential tautology of perfected identity. Both physicists and theologians, however, seem to suspect that change is ultimately unreal, a suspicion that has haunted philosophy too, as we have noted, since Parmenides first argued that becoming was unthinkable, self-contradictory, and hence illusory.

God's interventions in human history, leaving aside their party political, partisan nature, seem demeaning for one who, being the author of the possibility of all possibilities, should be above the battle. There is a mismatch between a timeless Being and the time of human events, between No-Time (or All-Time) and a particular time. It also undermines His status as something that does not change: his response to events and the changes he brings about are at odds with his everlastingness and the eternity in which He is located. More specifically, the idea of intervention at a particular historical point that is separated by intervals of time from other interventions seems difficult to understand, given that there are no time markers or intervals in eternity.

It would seem, however, that there is no escape: God has to enter time in order to deflect the course of events. The supreme example of this is His giving his "only begotten" son to the world to redeem humanity: "Veiled in flesh the godhead see / Hail the incarnate deity".[22] The "incarnate deity" arrives at a time – 0 AD (or, more probably, 4 BCE) and departs 33 years later – and at a particular place – Palestine. How this is registered or mirrored in eternity is unclear. At any rate, this and other divine interventions, seem to depend on the assumption that time and eternity do indeed exist side-by-side – so that it is possible for an eternal God to alight on the world at a time, even if through the proxy of His Son, and then return whence he came.

If time and eternity are simultaneous, however, and eternity is timeless or all-at-once present, then – as Anthony Kenny has argued – all temporal events must be simultaneous with one another.[23] If E_1 is simultaneous with eternity and eternity is simultaneous with E_2, then E_1 and E_2 are simultaneous, even if they are respectively the birth of the earth and my pouring a cup of tea for a friend. A mapping of times – and temporal sequences – on to eternity in which there are no moments or sequences seems to be the ultimate mismatching.

It might be argued that from a God's eye view, there is no privileged temporal relationship between events: the universe is not merely tenseless but also lacks B-series time. The divine elimination of tensed and tenseless time would enable the temporal world consequently to align itself to God's eternity. In short, the universe seen *sub specie aeternis* becomes eternized. If God can visit the world – at a point in time (and space) – it is because, seen through his eyes (i.e. seen as it truly is) the world is like eternity. The problem is that this does not comfortably accommodate interventions at particular times that have (causal) consequences and send out ripples through a locality. What's more, if the world is in reality timeless or All-at-Once, then it is difficult to make sense of for example:

(a) the (necessary) temporal order between the prophecy of Christ's ministry on earth and his birth and between his birth and his life and death;

(b) the (necessary) temporal order between that ministry and its consequences such as the establishment of the Christian church.

In short, if the condition of an eternal God intervening in temporal (and spatial) affairs of humanity is that the temporal (and spatial) realm should be timeless and spaceless eternity, no sense is to be made of those interventions – either the need for them or any consequences they might have.

There are, as we have seen, God-free notions of eternity (permitted by general relativity) aligned with the world – such as "the sum total of time" (or space–time) or "the frame of reference that subsumes all frames of reference". Neither of these stands up to scrutiny. The "sum total" has to be summed and so requires something outside of it to do the summing. And a frame of reference, even one that subsumes all frames of reference, presupposes a viewpoint that gathers up all viewpoints and all frames of references.

We may be tempted at this stage to dismiss eternity as "just a word". What, however, could be the origin of this word: how did the intuition arise that gave us the idea of eternity?

9.3 WAS THE WORD IN THE BEGINNING?

From what has been said so far it seems that eternity, either as a destination for humankind or God's permanent dwelling, is the meeting place of rather many contradictions. This invites the conclusion that, while the word "eternity" has apparent meaning, it lacks a referent – particularly as it has to be spoken, written, heard, read or conceived at a particular time.[24] The question then arises as to how it entered human discourse and how it came to occupy such a prominent place in our thoughts and aspirations, not to speak of society and politics.

There are a couple of deflationary explanations we might set aside straightaway. The first is that we arrived at the notion of the Everlasting Eternal simply through conceiving of the opposite of the transient. There are three possible analogues here.

The first analogue is the notion of a Perfect Being which grows out of our sense of our own imperfections and the imperfections of all the beings – human and non-human – we encounter in life. The second is that the notion of the infinite – to which nothing could correspond (by definition) since it would be infinitely larger than anything we might conceive – arises out of our intuition that the concept of the "finite" must have an opposite. By this analogy, eternity is the product of the negation of a negation ("imperfect") or the negation of a limitation ("finite"). This deflation encounters several problems, irrespective of whether it is true to the cognitive origins of the concept. While we may reject Descartes' argument for the existence of a Perfect Being[25] – namely that we imperfect beings could not conceive of such an entity if it did not exist – there is an objection to this dismissive account of their genesis. It is that eternity as it is conceived has positive qualities – everlastingness, stability, supreme reality, the destination and reward of the righteous, the realm of God with His properties – that go beyond anything that could be generated by the mere negation of a negation.

This defence may also pre-empt a third deflationary claim: that eternity grows out of the negation of "mortality", as the accommodation suitable to house those who are lucky enough to be immortal. The latter does, however, suggest another source of the idea of eternity: consolation. Eternity is the place where all wrongs are righted, including the deepest wrong of the death sentence that is written on our birth certificate, where all sorrows are soothed, a realm where our tears might cease. Our preoccupation with eternity arises out of our status as the one type of being in the universe that knows its own transience. Our mortality – foretold in the bodies of our fellows who age before us, and in the fate of those who go first – is a giant fact that permeates every aspect of our life. Even so, the rich and complex idea of eternity is rather a lot to unpack from the anticipation of being undone.

What is more, as already discussed, imagined eternities seem to be ill-fitted to deliver the consolation we need. We take rather little trouble to fill out the general expectation or hope of bliss. This may be because the more precisely we imagine eternity, the less attractive it seems: cold, empty, and eventless, with little happening and nothing to be done. Consolation would seem ill-fitted to work synergistically with the negation of negation to deliver what we need from the idea of eternity. Of course, eternity – as a threat or a promise – has a major role in maintaining and regulating the (temporal) social order. But I shall refrain from humanist tub-thumping.

So, if its consolations are riven by contradictions, and it has not been generated simply by negation, how did the idea of eternity arise and come to have such a presence in our individual and collective lives and in shaping the course of history? I would like to suggest that it grew out of a master intuition that is rooted in a fundamental capacity that lies behind human language; namely of something enduring, transcendent and unchanging that is inherent in the words that we use. Without that permanence, it would not be possible to have intelligible communications – to transmit meant meanings.

Let me develop this idea at the risk of making it even more vulnerable. The notion of eternity, in opposition to time, is inspired by, the profound contrast between the tokens I utter on a particular occasion, at a particular time, and the types they instantiate. To be specific: a meaningful word is a point of intersection between an event in time – hearing a puff of air or glimpsing a splash of ink – and something that seems not to belong to the material world, but to an unchanging reality (or a reality usable only insofar as it is unchanging), namely a meaning or significance. This does not belong to any sensory field; rather, it is part of a nexus of significance that is not part of the physical space in which temporal events take place (and our bodies are located), but a semantic space. The contrast is most clearly developed in the case of individual words. As the words are joined up into sentences, their meaning takes on some of the temporality of their referents – states of affairs, or events. This is reinforced in their status as acts. A speech act is temporalized, occupying an interval of time, and being subordinated to a necessarily transient function.

The intersection between time and eternity, between change and permanence, is however reiterated at the (highest) level of language as a whole, the dialect of the tribe, which transcend the lives of individual speakers, belonging as it does to the quasi-immortal collective. Conversations start, stop and vanish, and lips come and go, but discourse, like the meanings it activates, which are collective, are there before us and outlive us. They have the hall marks of a permanence that transcends our lives and, to that extent, smacks of eternity. Our first words and our last link only one strand in the million-stranded, endless conversation humanity has with itself – the voice of our collective immortality.

Eternity is a place where there is meaning but no change; meaning that is not deferred; meaning that is not threatened with evaporating into emptiness; meaning that is not tethered to a moment of being meant. Here on earth, meaning is a present continuous: mean*ing*. It comes into being through unfolding, and it *is* through coming into being. In short, its being is becoming. That in virtue of which it blossoms, dooms it to fade. But that in virtue of which meaning is meant, is expressed, transcends the occasions of its use. The lips melt, the ink fades, but the meanings of words remain. We can examine this contrast at the level of more extended meaning in relation to stories that are handed down, and handed on, and become "timeless".

The story seems to be the most explicit and elaborate expression of unfolding meaning. Narrative holds us because it is steeped in a significance that is a journey towards meaning, or a journey from ignorance to knowledge. In the written story, the flow of meaning is also frozen; or rather the meaning that would travel from a beginning to a middle and thence to an end is co-present. This is an image of meaning with stability, of significance without change, of unfolding to future states without loss of past ones, which gives a hint of pure endurance without change. The fundamental property of narrative – a passage from beginning to end that at the same time holds the beginning and end together – is strengthened in writing, that lifts the tale from the volatility of the human body and the transience of exhaled air. Writing has repetition built into story-telling: that which is written can be re-read. But it is implicitly present in speech, in the individual words it employs. "Time" provides the paradigm case. Whoever says the word "time" thereby transcends time and, wittingly or not, invokes the idea of eternity. To speak "time" is to be ripe to think of eternity.

Which may be one of the reasons why St John was moved to open his narrative with "In the beginning was the Word" that goes beyond the idea of the Word as a covenant, a promise (fulfilled in the coming of Christ). It is narrative that creates the possibility of beginnings, and initiates the vector of a story, a line connecting an end and a beginning. And that beginning is highlighted even more with the word "beginning", especially when it is written down. In the beginning was the word "beginning", where *chairos* (God's time) irrupted into *chronos*. This is a local echo of something we shall discuss in §11.3.1: the irruption of viewpoint into a universe that has no privileged locations. But it also reflects the fact that at the (usually concealed) heart of language is an intersection between event and stasis, time and the timeless.

At any rate, the pursuit of a narrative reality, or reality through narrative, never reaches its goal: the story leaks away and we spend our lives chasing after it, passing through small, and large, climaxes to the ultimate anti-climax of death, where all meaning is cancelled. The story, however, remains, to be told again and again. It is once and future and past. This is particularly evident in the case of myths which are less narratives of something that once happened than the instantiation of something that took place before history, and hence before (and after) time. Herein lies the essential truth of Claude Lévi-Strauss' claim that the meaning of myths is the binary, or oppositional, structure to be found in them. Such structures are static and unchanging, making them "machines for the suppression of time".[26]

We have reached the wilder shores of speculation. Time therefore to retreat to something a little nearer and consider the more humble denizens of the realm of discourse – facts – using our well-worn example: the Battle of Hastings. The battle took place at a particular time and so did the events of which it was composed, such as the entry of the fatal and fateful arrow into Harold's eye. As we have already discussed in §5.2.3, *the fact that* the Battle occurred in 1066 and that Harold's eye was pierced by an arrow did not take place at a particular time. The statements that refer to it – that iterate Harold's eye-piercing as a fact – do of course occur at a time. The relationship between the event and the fact that asserts that it happened reflects something of the relationship between an entity occurring at a particular time, and temporally related to other such occurrents, and something that seems somehow to have been lifted out of, even above, time. Harold's ophthalmological disaster occurred at, say, 4 p.m. on 14 October 1066. *The fact that* his eye was pierced does not occur at any particular time; which is why it can be rehearsed at any time.

Sentences such as "Harold's eye was pierced at 4 p.m. on 14 October 1066" is what Quine called an eternal (or standing) sentence (to be contrasted with an "occasional" – occasion-dependent – sentence). Eternal sentences are those "whose truth is fixed once and for all, without regard to the passage of time, the varying of circumstances, and the speaker".[27] A contrasting occasional sentence would be "It is raining" which can be true or false depending on the temporal location of the utterance and the spatial location of the speaker. It might be objected that the fact is not truly eternal or entirely timeless for, while it does not have an end, and it does not last for a definite interval, it does have a beginning. Before 4 p.m. 14 October 1066, there was no such thing as "the fact that Harold was pierced in the eye at the Battle of Hastings". But once it is true, it is always true.[28] It is resistant to change.

There is therefore a permanence in the facts that are expressed in transient statements. Factual statements have something in them that is a humble reflection of the intersection between time and timelessness, transience and everlastingness. If a statement is true, we have two transients fused in something that is permanent:

- *Transient (occurrent)* 1: Harold having his eye pierced with an arrow – occurring at 4 p.m. 14 October 1066.
- *Transient (occurrent)* 2: RT stating that Harold had his eye pierced with an arrow at 4 p.m. 14 October 1066 at 5 p.m. on 5 February 2015.
- *Non-transient, non-occurrent fact*: "That Harold had his eye pierced with an arrow at 4 p.m. in 14 October 1066".[29]

A fact is not an occurrence though an occurrence is necessary to make an assertion a factual truth.[30] We seem to be getting eternity on the cheap: the eternity of unchanging facts doesn't seem to be the full dollar. Eternity is without beginning as well as without end. But, as we have noted, a fact is not a fact until the relevant event has occurred. The eternity of the fact thus seems a little lop-sided – certainly if we think of eternity as everlastingness; for everlastingness is not only without end but also without beginning; its extension is not merely into the future but also into the past.

Eternity has other, slightly more elevated, denizens than the eternal facts put into circulation by statements about transient events. They include the laws, theorems and entities of mathematics – such as geometrical figures, pi, and the square root of minus 1 – the rules of logic, and (perhaps) the laws of nature.[31] When, a mathematical proof is enacted, a timeless truth is materialized in an event – a statement – that takes place at a time and takes a certain amount of time. We have only one transient, because the referent of the steps in the proof is not transient, only its statement is. The obverse of this, however, is that such truths seem lacking in content, gathering apparent substance only when they are instantiated in items that come into being at a particular time – when, for example, the diagrammatic right-angled triangle that illustrates Pythagoras' theorem is traced on paper.

The hint of something eternal within discourse is profoundly suggestive and has, of course, been developed into the basis of an entire ontology, metaphysics, and epistemology in Plato. Plato's Forms, unchangeable, perfect, and truly and uniquely real, are the fountainhead of a river of thought leading via Plotinus and Philo of Alexander into early Christian theology. It might be argued that Plato's theory was the child of two intellectual vices. The first was the reification of the meanings of general terms – so that, for example, items that were referred to as "good" became a partial revelation of "the Good" – making it possible to build and populate a Heaven with "-Ness" monsters. Everlastingness and timelessness were higher-order Nesses, housing the unchanging Forms or Ideas. The second was the privileging of the intellect, accessing the realm of the intelligible, over the senses. In this latter respect, he was working within a Parmenidean framework that also privileged the unchanging over the changing and the intellect over the senses.[32] Perhaps more importantly – though this was almost certainly not his intention – Plato revealed the profundity of language and the extraordinary character of the speaking, writing, thinking, arguing, reflecting species to which he belonged.[33]

The Platonic eternity may seem to avoid some of the problems of the relationship between time and eternity that bedevils any notion of humanity or God commuting between the two. Unfortunately, it merely moves the bump in the carpet. For Plato making sense of the relationship between temporal beings and the eternal reality, was expressed in the technical problem of the "participation" of sensible objects in eternal Forms. In Kant, there is a similar problem of explaining how the eternal noumenon gives rise to minds which temporalize (and spatialize) that which is neither temporal nor spatial. It raises the question of the origin of transient unrealities such as phenomenal experiences and their objects out of that which is permanent and real, such as the denizens of the noumenal world.

Even so, the temptation to dismiss the Platonic heaven of eternal forms as merely the result of a misuse of language, or a misreading of its nature, should be resisted. It takes too much for granted, the extraordinary fact that we humans can intuit the idea of a stable, unchanging reality, underlying the flux of appearances, and the profundity of the Platonic response to this. That we can make so profound an error (if it were an error) says something very interesting about us; namely that this is yet another respect in which we are unlike anything else in the living, indeed material, world. It might be too much of a stretch to argue (pick 'n' mix Cartesianism, á la Descartes as it were) that a creature that can conceive of eternity must have something of the eternal in it, but it is not unreasonable to wonder "What manner of creature are we that can entertain the notion of eternity?" What does it say about us that, of all conscious beings, we alone imagine a life beyond our life, understand our lives as limited, look beyond those limits, and conceive of a state utterly different from those that characterize our lives? That we form the general conception of change and imagine an unchanging world. It is a particularly dramatic aspect of the fact – noted in Chapter 4 – that we alone, of all material beings unfolding in time, utter the word "time", have the concept "time", are aware of ourselves as being located in a dimension that we name and number, and of occupying a limited interval of it.

I have speculated that the notion of eternity may owe its origin to the sense of stable, permanent, everlasting meanings behind the linguistic tokens we use. However, the meanings still live only in tokens. Eternity does not break free from its origins. The word "eternity" – which can be spoken only at a particular time and exists only insofar as it is spoken – is the revenge of the token on the "eternist" pretentions of the type to be timeless. "Eternity" is formed and fades on our transient lips, enters and leaves our thoughts. It is a child of the moment. But what a moment! A moment that is more than a moment; that transcends itself in a manner that goes beyond even that transcendence we enjoy in our moment-to-moment present that is impregnated by a present past and present future.

If we are mindful of these extraordinary facts it is difficult to be entirely sure of a deflationary account of eternity. We might even turn Plato on his head and, instead of thinking of time as the moving (and comparatively unreal) image of eternity, conceive of eternity as the arrested image of time. Admittedly, the contradictions in the very idea of eternity seem to push us to the conclusion that it is somehow secondary: a shadow cast by the word "time" or even by our experience as creatures in time. But what a shadow! And what extraordinary beings we are that can conceive of such a shadow that points to a realm beyond darkness and light.

PART III
Finding time

CHAPTER 10

(What) is time?

Not many of us are perplexed about space. We can move around in it and it seems experientially obvious ... There are certainly subtleties about the nature of space, which go beyond the expectations of everyday thought, but they are nothing like as perplexing as those we encounter when we attempt to think about the nature of time.

Polkinghorne, "The Nature of Time", 278[1]

In Part I, I criticized the reduction of "time" in physical science to a naked quantity, little t, that had no reality independent of space or, perhaps, no reality at all. In Part II, human time was brought centre stage. I defended tensed time and examined the phenomenology of tensed experience and the mysteries, problems and experiences of present, past, and future tenses. Having, as it were, cleared the decks by removing some of the misunderstandings blocking our view of time, and brought lived time centre stage, I shall, in this final part of the book, try to see time as it really is. While this requires revisiting some of the topics already touched on, our investigation will take us beyond the theme of time narrowly construed to the nature of human consciousness and of the agency that is central to our lives. We shall find that time – more precisely tensed time – and freedom are closely connected.

10.1 DEFINING TIME: PRELIMINARY REFLECTIONS

The brackets round the first word in the title of this chapter are not a misprint. For it is reasonable to question what, if anything, remains of time, or is to be said about time itself, time in general, time as a whole, if we remove from it characterizations that seem to misrepresent it or fail the test of intelligibility, or, if they do make sense, are vacuous. While we have sought to rescue time from the jaws of physics, we have stripped it of other characteristics to the point perhaps where we may wonder whether it has any independent reality at all.

The idea that time has a direction results from representing it as a quasi-spatial line, nothwithstanding that a line-as-dimension cannot have a direction. Other characteristics are also directly at odds with the idea of time as a fourth dimension comparable to the three of space. These include the notion that time "flows" and that there is something called "the passage of time", whereas we are not in the slightest bit inclined to think of space flowing or passing, even less passing "away". As we saw in §2.3., it is not possible to give any coherent meaning to the passage of time, though there are many contemporary philosophers (such as Tim Maudlin and John Norton) who believe that we can. So what is left if we strip time of these characteristics or do not take them literally; if we deny that time "flows like a river", or "grows like a block" or behaves as "a moving spotlight" playing on the world (revealing an ever changing present)? What would an "aseptic" conception of time look like? Is there anything left of substance? Could it be that there is nothing corresponding to the word "time" other than confusions, misrepresentation, and illusions – or, to put it less harshly, metaphors?

Our exploration of the richness of tensed time was in part an answer to this question: of course there is more to time than borrowed clothes. What's more, if time were nothing in itself, we would still have much work to do explaining our time-aware, time-saturated, time-torn, lives; and there would be even more work to be done, if demonstrating the unreality of time required us (as for some thinkers it does) also to accept the unreality of change – of all happening, including the happenings involved in demonstrating that change is unreal. We shall return to the relationship between time and change in §10.4.

There is, however, a different kind of threat to our inquiry, hinted at by Augustine but developed by Wittgenstein and the battalions of philosophers influenced by him, arising from the observation that in everyday life we have no problem making sense of time, so long as we don't try to say what it is. Asking what time is and producing unsatisfactory answers seems a rather pointless activity, given that we operate unthinkingly and entirely effectively in our daily life with a common sense, if largely implicit, understanding of time. If you were to ask people what time it is, how long is available to finish a task, which of two events happened first, and how far such-and-such an event is in the future, they would have no trouble making sufficient sense of the questions to answer them satisfactorily if they had the pertinent information. Pretending to be puzzled by time, it is concluded, is the result of taking the relevant words out of context. The philosophical problems of time are examples of what happens when "language goes on holiday".[2]

The story so far suggests that the philosophy of time does not boil down merely to finding the solution to puzzles that should not puzzle us, to straightening out the turbulence in the flow of thought, to removing the cloudiness in our self-awareness arising out of misunderstanding what it is for a term such as "time" to have meaning, or to wasting time on healing self-inflicted intellectual injuries. There are real problems, interesting questions, and even mysteries hidden behind what may present as linguistic quibbles.

We may concede that the reality, and even the mystery, of time is incontrovertible but still argue that it is a mistake to try to gather up its manifestations and its presence throughout our ways of characterizing the world, and the role of the word "time" in a multitude of contexts, into a single concept or tightly defined set of concepts. The mistake can be characterized in different ways, most often as an "essentialism" that sees "time" corresponding to a natural kind, medium or even substance; and, corresponding to this, the delusion that one can pin down *the* meaning of the word as if that meaning were not distributed through a multitude of uses that are in some cases only tenuously connected with one another. There is, so this story goes, no distinct item corresponding to the word "time". The noun has a multitude of loosely connected meanings and uses that have evolved through history. In trying to pin down something called "time", we are following a trail of linguistic accidents in the mistaken belief that we are in pursuit of something common to all the uses of the word.[3]

I am sympathetic to this view but I am not persuaded by it. I no more think that the lexicographer has the last word on time than the physicist. I believe that the *philosophical* question "What Is Time?" is not vacuous. Whether pursuing the nature of time is a waste of, well, time is not, however, something that can be established in advance. The sceptical reader may wish to suspend judgement and decide on the basis of what follows whether we should give up trying to gain a perspicuous view of time, and abandon the very idea of a "philosophy of time" and the hope, which perhaps motivates more philosophers of time than are prepared to admit it, that by conceptualizing time, and seeing it as a whole, they may, if only momentarily, rise above it.

One thing is clear (and it is reinforced by the complexity and richness of the entry "time" in any substantive dictionary) is that the question "What Is Time?" is not simple. Indeed, it is the meeting point of a multiplicity of concerns, some of which we have touched on already, though they warrant revisiting. It may be useful to list them at the outset:

1. Even at the common-sense level, time has several aspects that are not easily reducible to each other:
   (i)   duration (periods, intervals – corresponding to the question "How long?");
   (ii) location (that range from points to dates, answering the question "When?");
   (iii) order (the A-series of past, present and future and B-series of before and after, corresponding to the question "In what sequence?").
   How do these relate to one another? (See §10.2.1.)
2. Are there *any* intrinsic properties of time additional to these, if we set aside flow or passage, growth, and directionality? And if there are not, then is time, after all, nothing? (See §10.2) What is the stuff of time? Is it punctate or continuous? If time is punctate, what are its points? Is it substantive? Does time have limits; more particularly, a beginning and an end? (See §10.3.)

3 How is time related to change? Does change take time or is time an aspect of change? Is time possible in the absence of change? Is the so-called "temporal vacuum possible? (See §10.3.1.) Is time inseparable from perception – either the perception of change or changing perception? Is change real? (See §10.4.)

4 What is the relationship between experienced and measured time, between subjective and objective time, between lived time and the time of physics? Which has priority? Is conscious humanity (and hence time consciousness) located in physical time or is physical time a derivative from perceived time or the perception of change? (See §10.5.)

It is this last question – essentially about the relationship between time and mind – that is perhaps the most important; at any rate, it is the one more than any other that has motivated the present inquiry. A satisfactory account of time would be able to unite, or at least connect or reconcile, time as something objectively measured (and as an objective feature of the physical universe) and time as subjectively experienced and assessed. This would include, but go deeper than, establishing an audit trail between, say, the immediate experience of the duration of events and their temporal order and the registers of time that structure our shared days and, ultimately, lie at the heart of scientific inquiry and the picture of the universe that has arisen from it. It would also examine the relationship between ourselves, seemingly very short-lived conscious and self-conscious creatures, and the stupendously long-lasting largely mindless universe in which we find ourselves. The last aspiration is couched partly in the subjunctive because it is also the theme of my work-in-stalled-progress entitled *Logos: The Mystery of the Sense-Making Animal*.

None of these lines of inquiry commits us in advance to the manifestly absurd notion that time is literally a stuff, a process, an event or a state of affairs. Time is not a stuff like the material of the chair I am sitting on, a process like the cooling of the coffee on my desk, an event like the sound of a letter struck on the keyboard, a state of affairs like the present condition of the room I am working in or, more broadly, the substrate in which the "ongoing" is going on. Nor is it, as Wittgenstein mockingly put it, "a *queer* medium"[4] analogous to the ether, perhaps. That it is none of these things does not mean that there is nothing left of it, that it is nothing. More generally: just because time isn't reducible or translatable into anything else, it doesn't follow that it isn't anything at all. At least, I hope so, though it would be something of a discovery to find towards the end of writing a very long book that I had been writing about nothing. There would, however, be some consolation in knowing that, if I am on a fool's errand, I have some distinguished company.

10.2 TIME IN ITSELF

Time is neither causation, motion, physicality, mentality, nor anything else. Time is time. Time is a series of items related by *primitive* and

irreducible relations of earlier, later and simultaneous and possessing
monadic properties of futurity, presentness or pastness.
Smith, "Absolute Simultaneity and the Infinity of Time", 140

I believe – as strongly as one can believe anything in science – that
... time will turn out to be the only aspect of our everyday experience
that *is* fundamental.
Smolin, *Time Reborn*, xxxi

In philosophy, time has always been an especially challenging topic.
At root, the problem is the quintessential difficulty that so often
motivates philosophical discussion: the problem of disentangling the
nature of the entity from the features that we happen to attribute to it.
Callender, *Oxford Handbook of the Philosophy of Time*, 2

At the heart of our common-sense way of conceptualizing time, and our talk of "flow"
and "passage", and "growing blocks" and "moving spotlight", is something we examined when we discussed "tense tourism"; namely the idea of time as a quasi-process,
and of intervals and moments of time as occurrents, as if they were quasi-events. It
is very difficult to resist thinking of "times" as items – "a series of items" according to
Quentin Smith in the quote at the head of this chapter – that happen, at a particular
time and over a particular time. This is most obvious in the case of labelled times,
stretches of time, such as Wednesday 27 July 2012. They appear to be located in time
in as much as they have temporal relations to other labelled stretches. It is not entirely
strained to say that Wednesday 27 July 2012 "occurs" – or at least "falls" – before
Thursday 28 July 2012 and after Tuesday 26 July 2012; or that it occupies the gap
between those two stretches of time. And this mode of thought can seduce us into
thinking of times themselves as being temporally related in the way that events are.

This appearance, however, evaporates as soon as we examine the facts about *when*
the times in question occur. Wednesday 27 July 2012 can occur only on Wednesday
27 July 2012 and it must last exactly 24 hours and is obliged to have the aforemen-
tioned relations to the other two days. Real events, by contrast, are not (apparently
at least) temporally fixed in this way. While the token event E that occurred at time t_1
could by being specified thus occur only then, there is no reason why an event identical in all respects should not occur at another time t_2. This follows from our belief
in the contingency of material events; and it must be true if we accept the reality of
agency, in virtue of which the course of events may be deflected. I can choose to go
shopping either on Wednesday or on Thursday; in contrast, t_1 is obliged to occur at
t_1; and, indeed, Wednesday 27 December cannot be headed off. While Event E_1 can
occur at any of a range of times (assuming we do not subscribe to material fatalism),
t_1 must occur before t_2 and be separated from it by a certain interval. E_1 is not obliged
to occur before E_2 or be separated from it by a certain interval – except in those cases
where the two events are causally related. (An interesting proviso which we shall
explore in Chapter 11). To look at this in a slightly different way, times are inevitable
while events are not: whatever happens, t_2 will follow t_1 and even if Christmas does

not turn out as planned 25 December has to turn up. And one final difference: mathematical time *per se* is homogeneous but no events or states of affairs are identical or can occur twice.

This little excursion may seem to make rather a meal of a truism but it is intended to highlight, and so expose, the notion, already discussed in §8.2.2.3, that times – instants and intervals – are kinds of occurrences and processes. It is present in our habit of speaking of times as "arriving": "And so the great day came"; "And suddenly Christmas was upon us"; "The morning passed"; "The long day came to an end" and so on. It is evident in a (not entirely serious) way of characterizing time (ascribed to Feynman) that "Time is what happens when nothing else happens".[5]

There is another reason why we might be tempted to think of times as quasi-events. We conflate the sense in which t_1 is earlier than t_2 with that in virtue of which E_1 (occurring at t_1) is earlier than E_2 (occurring at t_2). Even if we are not seduced by the ghost of a symmetry such that "If E_1 occurs at t_1, then t_1 must occur at E_1," it is difficult not to think of the intervals between times being comparable to the intervals between events. This is particularly difficult when the events in question are generated specifically to *mark* or *measure* time – as in the arrival of the hands at a point on the clock face. Our problem in getting entirely straight about this is in part due to the elusive nature of "at" discussed in §4.5 and §6.1.2.1. We think of events taking place *at* t_1 or 12:05 and this looks like a location. There are, however, two events involved when we time events by means of other events. It is this that makes "when" seems like a relationship between two events, as Einstein made clear in the already quoted passage in his 1905 relativity paper: "When I say, for example, 'The train arrives here at 7' that means that the passage of the little hand of my watch at the place marked 7 and the arrival of the train are simultaneous events."[6] Merging time with clock-time, at any rate, increases the tendency to make times quasi-occurrents ("the passage of the little hand of my watch at the place marked 7" *becomes* the time 7 p.m.) and to make the temporal relations between times seem like the temporal relations between events. So we may come more easily to think that two days separate Wednesday noon from Friday noon in the same way as two days separate Wednesday lunch from Friday lunch.

We have therefore to adopt an attitude of suspicion to the assumption that times have temporal order in the way that events have a temporal order. Clearly they do not. The order of times is not open to variation in the way that the order of events is. There is also a different kind of "at" when we say that an event occurs at a time earlier than another event compared with saying that a time occurs at a time earlier than another time. The relationship between event and time – as when we say that E_1 took place at t_1 – is not symmetrical. It would not be right to say that Wednesday took place at the sum total of Wednesday's events and it would be worse than vacuous to say "t_1 took place at t_1," because there is no "at" within t_1 to relate itself to itself in this way. (It would be better to admit that t_1 is implicitly "at t_1" but that the "at" is drawn out only in the explicit relationship between a time and an event.) And it is equally dubious to suggest that t_1 – which we connect with 12 noon Wednesday 12 December 2015 – has anything intrinsically "noon" about it, if only because noon does not have any properties, except insofar as we confuse time with clock-time and thus with the characteristic states of affairs (position of fingers on a dial, or of the sun in the sky) that mark clock-time. Notwithstanding Machian empiricism, time is not clock-time any more than space is ruler-space.

We shall discuss the question of whether there can be time – as quasi-unfolding or goings on – in the absence of events in §10.4. For the present, let us continue our critical examination of the idea that time in itself is a kind of process or seamless succession of events and note another reason why this is self-evidently wrong. It would imply that at any given moment, and any given place, there would be at least two events happening simultaneously: the material events (e.g. an object moving) and the time-events – the instants making up the interval during which the object was moving. The time-events would be suspect for another reason: they could not have a causal ancestry or descendants. If they did, there would be competing causal chains at every point in space–time. And, what is more, the notion of successive time-points being *caused* by their predecessors is very odd, particularly as they would have no specific characteristics.

Having reiterated the fact that time is not a process composed of successive quasi-occurrences that are times, let us remind ourselves of a fundamentally real feature of time: that it has several aspects that do not seem reducible to one another. These are:

(a) *location* (for example t_1 is at 12 noon on 6 February 2015);
(b) *order* (for example t_1 is before t_2);
(c) *duration* (t_{1-2} corresponds to, say, a period of two hours).

They map directly onto the temporal characteristics we ascribe to events: E_1 took place at 12 noon on 6 February 2015; E_1 occurred before E_2; and E_1 lasted two hours or was separated from E_2 by 2 hours. (But, for reasons just given, we must not be confused by this mapping to identify the time of events with time as events.)

The way we represent time and the temporal character of events often tends to conceal this irreducible complexity of location, duration, and order. We see the times set out in a graphical form that encompasses location, duration, and order. However, they can be fused only courtesy of an off-stage apparatus that permits the different aspects to be captured. The representation of temporal *location* requires the laying down of axes referred to an external frame of reference that translates positions on the graph to positions in actual time. Temporal *interval* requires the establishment of axes as scales. Only temporal *order* seems to be intrinsic – though special relativity feels obliged by the constancy of the measured speed of light (whatever that means see §3.5.3.1) to make this dependent on the frame of reference. While both order and interval will be inertial-frame dependent, they are still distinct.[7] We might be tempted to divorce duration (of, say, an event) from intervals (between events) but we could argue, against this, that intervals are just durations of other events, or of the sum total of others events – so the common sense interval between E_1 and E_2 is the duration of events E_3 to E_n that take place during that interval.

The point is that, even though times fall short of being events, there's something quite complex left over when time has been stripped bare of false attributes such as passage. This irreducible complexity gives credence to the notion that time truly is something-in-itself. We have no grounds, therefore, for concluding that time is nothing at all or for espousing a radically deflationary account of it.

Let us, however, look at some of these deflationary accounts of time.

A. Time is a hole or emptiness in the plenum of Being. It is nothing in itself but enables Becoming. For those of a Parmenidean persuasion, this means that time – "being other than Being" – is an illusion. To reiterate Parmenides' argument: what-is is what-it-is; that-which-is-not, is not; becoming which is the passage from that-which-is-not (the not yet) to what-is and thence to that-which-is-not (the no longer) must therefore be an illusion. Hence change is itself nothing, as is the time which it requires. This is not such a complete demolition job as it sounds because we can turn it on its head: this account of time, in accordance with which it opens possibility into actuality, makes nothing rather impressive, worthy perhaps of a capital letter: Nothing.[8]

B. Time is nothing more than a logical construction out of happenings – out of actions and events. This might be a plausible way of accounting for the doubtful notion of the passage of time; how we get unidirectional, smoothly flowing time by abstracting from in-all-directions, jumpy, discontinuous events and processes. And if it is asserted that time t_1 is, say, a set of events to which certain membership criteria apply, this does not deliver anything because it is necessary then to specify the membership criteria and we immediately run into circularity. The set of events constituting t_1 would be those events occurring at t_1. So we would arrive at the unhelpful conclusion that a time is a construction out of the set of the events that occur at that time. What's more, we would also be entitled to ask what the "at" corresponds to. If it has some substantive meaning, it would seem to mark a separation between the events and the time of their occurrence (just as when we say of an object it is at a particular place, the "at" marks an external relation between the object and the place). This would undermine the identification of the time with the events.

At any rate, it is too general a characterization to capture, even less to explain, the irreducible complexity we have discussed encompassing order, duration, interval, and tense. It also suggests that time is not something that is inherent in the material or natural world. Time as a "logical construction" would leave unexplained the seemingly inescapable *temporal* ordering of the world.[9] If we are plausibly to treat time in this way, we need to go the whole hog and argue that temporal order is itself mind-dependent. (This, of course, brings us to Kant's notion of time as a form of sensible intuition, which we shall discuss in §10.5.)

C. Another way of deflating time is to assert that time is a measurement, calibration, and referencing framework for change. There are two problems with this reduction. The first is that it does not explain what is distinctive about clocks and in virtue of what they serve whatever function it is that they serve; namely the (temporal) periodicity of the events they are designed to generate. Secondly (and more importantly), it leaves unstated the kind of measurements, calibrations, and referencing that are in question. Once these are specified – duration and order of events and the intervals between them – it is evident that time remains intact on the far side of the reduction of time to "what clocks measure".[10] For the duration, order and interval are *temporal* duration, *temporal* order, and *temporal* interval.

The deflating claim that time is what clocks measure not only reduces time to a measured quantity but is also circular: time is what clocks measure and a clock is something that measures time. At any rate, we should be suspicious, given that time is universal, and clocks are not.[11] To make ticks or tocks a privileged locus of time is clearly absurd: time is apparent everywhere in the clock (the gradual rusting of the mechanism) and everywhere around it – the lives being orchestrated by it and the material world those lives are lived in. There is a further problem with this definition: clocks (on their own) no more "tell the time" than thermometers (on their own) "tell the temperature". Measurements have to be *made* and the making of measurements is something that takes place in time, that takes time and is at a time.

D. A less obviously contentious account of time – because it leaves open the question of its objective reality – is one that sees it as the *form of change*. Unfortunately, this leaves us uncertain as to what is meant by "form" when it is applied to all objects, all states of affairs, all processes and all events. Narrowing the definition and describing time as "the order of events" (or the form of succession round a developing process) does not help. First, it is circular because "the order of events" must mean the *temporal* order (as opposed to, say, spatial order or order of magnitude). Secondly, it leaves out duration and location. The interval between two events is not the same as their order of occurrence and the connection between a time such as 12 noon on 12 December 2015 and an order of events is not clear. If there is a connection, it is long and winding.

Any attempt to identify time with change – however intimate their relationship (which we shall discuss in §10.4) – always runs into the difficulty of specifying in a non-circular way, the nature of the relationship between them, not the least because change has many non-temporal features – general, universal features such as spatiality, and features specific to individual changes. And to call time "the *temporal aspect* of change" would be circular.

E. There are those who would argue that time *is* what it *does*. This is close to the claim that time is an agent in its own right; that, indeed, it causes, or at least has a hand in, all change; that it brings to the unfolding of events something separate from, say, energy (transfer driving happening), matter (giving happening a substrate to happen in) or laws (keeping happening within certain bounds of possibility). There are several reasons for setting this aside, the most obvious being that if time were a cause, it would be difficult to see how it could cause Event A rather than Event B – in short how its input could be specific. Almost as obvious is the objection that if time *were* a universal cause, every event would be over-determined, each having its private cause (of which it was a specific effect) and having an additional universal cause in common with every other change. (For a further discussion of time as a cause see Addendum 2 to Chapter 11.)

F. There are other ways of specifying what time does: namely that it is permissive: it doesn't so much drive change as allow it to happen. The most succinct expression of this is that "time is the possibility of change". This is close to the truism that change takes time: no change can be instantaneous. More metaphysically, it might express the idea that time is a kind of meta-happening, creating a set of conditions that allows happenings to happen; more specifically that it allows the possible to be actualized, though this presupposes that possibilities are already in some sense there, as it were awaiting the call. There are two problems with this. First, if possibilities exist long enough to have a distinct reality, they must endure – that is, exist in time – before they are actualized. Secondly, it bypasses the question as to whether possibilities – that which might be rather than that which is – have any existence outside of a consciousness entertaining them.[12]

There is another aspect of the "permissiveness" of time: it allows change without contradiction.[13] Two apparently incompatible propositions "Object O is in position P_1" and "Object O is in position P_2", or "The wall is green all over" and "The wall is red all over", can both be true if we add "at time t_1" and "at time t_2" to the first and second members of the pair respectively. This permissiveness, however, does not capture the various aspects of time that we have noted (order, duration, location) nor does it identify other determinants of compatibility – such as the fact that the wall cannot be green all over and red all over unless someone repaints it, while it can be green all over and round all over. It isn't at any rate "generally" permissive not only because many things are not permitted (even beyond the constraints of logical contradiction) and, what is more, to be globally permissive would be to permit nothing in particular, which is not clearly different from permitting nothing. Worse still, it imports the logic of propositions ("not (p and not-p)") into the material world, including those parts of it (such as the universe prior to sentient beings – most of its history) that are innocent of logic, discourse, and consciousness.

It is not clear that this permissiveness means anything more than that changes take time and that time allows change without contradiction, by stopping (as the joke has it) "everything from happening at once" – or indeed everything being in all its states at once. It is obvious that everything could not happen at once, not only because some happenings are incompatible with, or cancel out, other happenings (moving to the left and moving to the right) but also because happenings require prior happenings either to bring them about or to create the conditions in which they are possible.

There is, however, a less vacuous aspect of the idea of time as permissiveness; namely that time makes it possible for *an agent to make things happen*. I will discuss this in Chapter 12, where I will argue that tensed time is the key to human agency. To justify this conclusion, we shall have first to revisit the relationship between time and causation, re-examining the so-called causal arrow (§11.2), and the claim that time is the causal dimension of space–time.[14]

The conclusion to which we are drawn is close to that set out by Quentin Smith in the first epigraph to this section and which bears reiterating: "Time is neither causation, motion, physicality, mentality, nor anything else. Time is time.

In other words, time is not only something real (with much remaining after it has been liberated from various unfortunate metaphors) but irreducible to anything else. As Plotinus pointed out, any endeavour to translate time into, say, motion results in circularity: "It comes to this: we ask 'What is Time?' and we are answered, 'Time is the extension of movement in time'"![15] The conclusion that "time is time" may seem a small prize at the end of a long journey. However, in the present context, the affirmation that, just because time is not something other than itself (something that flows or grows or moves, change or the form of change, etc.), it doesn't follow that it isn't anything at all, is worth making. Time is something – not of course in the sense of being a thing or a stuff. Just because we cannot define time does not mean that it does not have an existence in itself. The failure to define it or to separate it from other aspects of the universe is not an indirect proof that it is unreal.

We cannot nail down or pick up time; but we can circle round it. By this means, we shall, I hope get closer to ourselves, creatures of time who are owned by it and own it – and use and waste it – to ends not envisaged in the rest of the time-swept universe. Before we do that, however, there is more business to transact. First, we need to look a little bit more closely at what we might call the intrinsic properties of time (§10.3); then the relationship between time and change (§10.4); and thirdly the connection between, and relative priority of, subjective and objective time (§10.5). These items will form the agenda of the remainder of this chapter which will end with a few concluding remarks (§10.6) that will point us towards the final phases of our inquiry that will ultimately arrive at the relationship between time and freedom.

10.3 THE STUFF OF TIME

> "Time" as a substantive is terribly misleading.
> Wittgenstein, *Lectures on Philosophy*, §13

Notwithstanding that time is *sui generis* – which is why it resists definition – the question whether "time" indicates anything at all still haunts our inquiry. If we temporarily park up the idea that it is a kind of self-subsisting stuff – though we shall return to this notion in §10.3.3 – "time" remains as designating one of the most fundamental, and irreducible, modes of connectedness and separateness in our world, the other being space. But even then, when we try to specify what these modes of connectedness are, we drift towards a notion of time that is something more substantive than mere (relatively insubstantial) relations between things that are substantive, more than an aspect of the ordering of phenomena or physical events. The slightly less substantial notions of time as, say, the co-container, with space, of events and objects, the form of becoming, the form of the becoming of consciousness, the openness of the open, don't free us entirely from thinking about time as something with intrinsic properties. Nor should it. Time really seems to be "in itself", even if it is not a thing, a medium, or even a property like being coloured or having mass. So it does not seem vacuous to continue the quest for the nature of time.

In pursuit of this quest, we can briefly address four issues: temporal locations (§10.3.1); temporal instants and intervals (§10.3.2); relational and substantival views of time (and space) (§10.3.3); and whether time has a beginning (§10.3.4).

10.3.1 Temporal locations

Whatever happens does so at a time or over a particular stretch bounded by two times. The dog barked at 12 noon and its barking lasted between 12 noon and 12:05. We can of course specify these times by means of either a tensed or a tenseless description. We can say that "The dog barked between 12 and 12:05 on 16 August" or that "The dog barked between 24 hours ago and 23 hours and 55 minutes ago". While the relationship between the two modes of description is not at all straight-forward, they have the same truth-conditions if (and only if) the tensed statement is uttered at 12 noon on 17 August. Both statements are anchored in a time scheme – the tenseless statement directly and the tensed statement indirectly – in which that which is spoken of (the dog barking) and when it is spoken of are also anchored in that same time scheme. But while the way the two statements are connected with one another has been the focus of so much philosophical attention (Chapter 5), the very existence of time schemes has perhaps attracted less attention than it deserves. We perhaps take too much for granted how clock and calendar times enable any particular time to be connected with all other times by relationships of "before" and "after" or "by so much of", or "so long", a separation. As we noted in the dis-cussion of tensed time, "before" and "after" are as dependent on reference points as much as are "in the past" and "in the future". The journey towards objective time from "before" and "after" and from "in the past" and "in the future" to "at such and such a time", where such and such, is specified by some kind of number indicating a date (year, day, hour, and minute) is difficult to reconstruct. The time scheme is the product of a collective vision, of shared attention on a large (wide, long-stand-ing) scale, of a move from personal perception to collective knowledge and understanding.[16]

Locations in time are co-located in a single all-embracing time scheme. Times are nested in larger times: 12 noon is in the 24-hour cycle of day and night; Wednesday is the middle one-seventh of the week; December is the last one-twelfth of the year; 2012 belongs to the twenty-first century; and so on. Dates are primarily contain-ers not of events but of times which (as we have stressed) are not events. This is illustrated by the fact that it makes sense to think of events, but not times, as being causally related: what happened on 20 December may have caused something that happened on 21 December but there is no sense in which 20 December caused 21 December. So our most complete and accurate account of a date will be constructed solely of the times encompassed by it, the scheme or notational system to which it belongs.

Accepting that times are not events compounds the difficulty of relating lattices of temporal locations to the way that patterns of events are connected or co-located. When, that is, we try to determine the extent to which our time schemes are rooted in the way the universe unfolds. Some connection has been present from the beginning of explicit human time sense: the clock and the calendar originate in astronomical events that have the twin virtues of size (so they are visible to all: we are all cognitive brothers under the sun, moon and stars and astronomical events command global joint awareness) and of a perceptible or *prima facie* regularity. This latter is something to which we shall return when we consider the extent to which our time measures are objective.

10.3.2 Temporal instants and intervals

Things become even less straightforward when we move from the labels of temporal locations (such as 12 noon 24 December 2015) closer to the stuff of time itself: when we consider instants and intervals. They do not make sense even purely quantitatively; or, rather, one can make sense of instants only at the price of not being able to make sense of intervals.

Supposing we regard time as having as constitutive units durationless instants.[17] There are two ways of thinking of points in time: as non-extended; or extended but infinitesimally small. Non-extended points in time correspond neatly to numbers which, in themselves, are indivisible. The integer 1 marking a location is an absolutely precise marker: it does not have fuzzy edges: a determinate real number corresponds to an unextended (that is to say durationless) point. There is, however, a problem with this. If "1" marks a point of, or in, but not a stretch of, time, it does not have a location: nothing can have a location without laying claim to a part of that in which it is located so that it can establish a relation to a neighbourhood. (We argued this in §3.4.1, where the focus was on so-called spatial points.) It is this that places it next to, say, "2" and next but one to, say, "3" – or at least so long as the latter two also occupy time in order to be associated with one time rather than another. Time t cannot belong to, in the sense of being located in, 24 December 2015 without being an element of that day. Without each having a temporal occupancy, there can be no temporal relationship between instants or points of time. In order to be points *in* time, the points have to occupy some time; or to be located indirectly by some further relationship to places in time. They must have some basis for claiming their "at" as in "*at* 12 noon on 24 December 2015".

There is another, much-discussed, problem that we have also already touched on: if it consists purely of instants, how does time add up to stretches or intervals? The sum of any finite number of extensionless points is itself extensionless. What, after all, is the difference between a (by definition) unextended instant of time and no time? The answer is: no time. And since there is no other difference, the difference between an instant and nothing is – well, nothing. No matter how many instants you join, they will not amount to a second or even a nanosecond. The unextended sum of an indefinite number of temporally unextended points could not be inflated by inserting gaps between them since these gaps would be timeless. Invoking infinity would only multiply problems, even if we overlooked the awkward truth that there are no actual infinities in nature. An infinite division counteracted by a subsequent multiplication by infinity would always bring us back to our starting quantity, so the quantity has to be put in by hand as it were. Since every stretch of time contains the same number of instants, any interval put together out of an infinite number of instants will be the same interval. And what will that interval be? Mathematically, it will be whatever quantity you started with. Supposing we started with "1", this does not specify any definite interval. It fails to be a quantity of time because it does not specify what it is "1" of. Less obvious is the fact that the "1" that is generated by first dividing and then multiplying by infinity is not a stretch or interval: 1 is not the same as the interval between zero and 1. It is a widthless *border* separating 0.999 recurring and 1.000 (recurring) 1. The mathematics in short cannot generate substance.[18] The idea of more-than-zero intervals of time being made up of durationless instants seems like a fudge. The elements are deemed to be so minute that there would be no difference between granularity and the jointless continuity and smoothness of actual time. If, however, they are so minute, they would for reasons already given, fail to add up to a definite interval however small.

Given that instants (and points and "moments") are such slippery customers, and they cannot add up to intervals, how have they come to have such prominence in the philosophy of time? It may be because we are used to the pure, unsmeared "at" of times that are represented numerically. Noon on 24 December 2015 has no width; rather, any width that 12:00:00 does have is a contaminant. This is the sense in which "times" – except in colloquial usage – are unextended. Even though we cannot say whether t_1 is 12:42 or 12:43 we somehow feel that it is at a definite point somewhere between the two. Any uncertainty, we feel, lies within us and does not reflect an intrinsic blurring of t_1.[19] Times seem unextended in the way that numbers are unextended and there is a time corresponding to each number; and each number corresponds to a point in time.

The idea that time is made up of unextended, durationless or infinitesimal instants has more than one version. The most obvious divide is between those for whom punctate time is discrete and those for whom it is dense. In the former, every instant of time has a uniquely next or preceding instant. In the latter, there will always be another instant between any two instants. The difference between the latter and the notion of time as continuous is essentially mathematical. Continuous time is the time of Newton's differential equations representing change and dense time with difference equations representing change, as a parameter ranging over rational numbers.[20] No empirical consequences would follow from these putative micro-structural differences in the topology of time, as has been pointed out by Craig Callender:

> Time is usually assumed to be continuous. No doubt the reason for this is that science generally takes time to be continuous. But the reasons it does so are not directly empirical. That is, no experiment has been done to show

whether time is continuous, dense, or discrete. Rather time is considered to be continuous because our best theories of the universe say it is, but they do so mostly because it is much easier to write a theory using notions from calculus this way.[21]

This is particularly helpful because it suggests that the differences between continuous, dense, and discrete ideas of time are essentially matters of mathematical convenience. It exposes the vulnerability of the assumption that the mathematically most convenient way of conceiving the world is closest to reality (challenged in §3.6).[22] The durationless instant is not an element of time out of which temporal intervals have mysteriously to be constructed. They are simply the ideal limit of ever more precise timing; or, as Dummett has put it, "unattainable theoretical limits to the process of dissection" (of time).[23] Instants are not pre-mathematical primitives belonging to time itself but theoretical constructs, the product of taking the division of measurement to an ideal, that is to say purely mathematical, limit. And it is precisely because this limit is ideal rather than real, it is always possible to insert another instant between any pair of instants.

The notion of an instant of time is the product of conflation between a putative stuff of time, temporal boundaries (corresponding to ideal measurements that determine the absolute "when" of an event beginning and ending) and temporal locations. To refer to something said a little while back, we imagine that the "at", corresponding to the time when something happened, itself to have no duration. If we say that E took place from 12 noon to 12:05 p.m., we somehow imagine the "at" of those events mapped on to successions of instants whose first and last members corresponded to the beginning and end of the event. This fact that instants can be used *both* to define boundaries of intervals *and* constituents of intervals, and "at" as well as "during", should alert us to their status as constructs.[24]

Sorting out the relationship between instants and temporal intervals is not the only problem that arises if we propose that instants are the basic stuff of time. The question of their "occurrence", or their status as occurrents, returns. Are they themselves occurrences in time and do they occur at a particular location in time? We tend to think of instants as occurring in succession, one after the other, one before the other. This would imply that there would be a temporal relationship between them, as there is between events: that t_1 occurs before t_2 just as E_1 occurs before E_2. All of this is, of course, nonsense; even so it is difficult not to think of instants of time as being pseudo-events that have a location in a particular time and have temporal relationships, just as actual events are located in time (occurring at 12 noon and occurring before 13:00 and after 11:00) and consequently have temporal relationships. The difficulty is greater when we think of "times" that have labels. While we would not be inclined to say at 12 o'clock that "12 o'clock is occurring" as if this were an event additional to all those we observe occurring at 12 o'clock, we find the thought that "12:05 is 5 minutes after 12 o'clock" entirely acceptable, as if we can locate times *at* times (at the times they are) such they can have a temporal relationship to one another. But, to repeat an earlier point, if instants, and temporal locations, do not lay claim to their location by occupying time, then it is difficult to see how they can be temporally related to one another without the support of a macroscopic notational system. If, however, they are not real things in the world, then we should not expect then to lay claim to anything at all in any kind of space outside the logical space of a notational system. They do not have to assert or claim their own location.

Let us return to the temptation to think that if E_1 takes place at t_1, then t_1 must be simultaneous with E_1. But it is clear that t_1 cannot have this relationship with E_1 since simultaneity is a symmetrical relationship. We don't say that, if E_1 takes place at t_1, t_1 takes place at E_1. Likewise, we cannot say of E_1 that it takes place at E_1. In short, we can say that events take place at times but not that times take place at events, if only because events take place (at the very least in the literal sense of taking up a place) and times don't. Likewise, we can say that two events are simultaneous with each other but not that the time t_1 is simultaneous with either of the events, any more than t_1 is simultaneous with itself. This is another way of highlighting the fact that times are not events and t_1 has only a parasitic location as part of a notational system.

Behind these arguments lies a sense that t_1 unites all the events that take place at t_1 in a relationship of simultaneity, and in that sense rises above individual events. It is not an event or occurrence in itself but a time *at which* events occur. That is why, when we say that t_2 is after t_1 and before t_3, this is not analogous to saying that E_2 occurs after E_1 and before E_3. In the former case, we are not making an observation about the order of occurrences but about a way of labelling times. Not only is it true that times do not take place at events – for example, "Noon takes place at the beginning of my dinner" – it is also true that they do not take place at all. This is illustrated by the fact, to vary an argument made earlier, that if they were the kinds of things that "take place", they would be permitted to take place only at themselves.

This may meet some resistance. Surely, there are "earlier" and "later" times as well as "earlier" and "later" events – in other words times *do* have a temporal order – so that t_2 is a time *at* a time between t_1 and t_3. Yes, but this is simply an ordering of labels, as is evident from the fact that it could not be otherwise.

10.3.3 (Many) relations or (one) substance?

Some readers may worry that a discussion of "The Stuff of Time" that has largely considered time in, and by, itself, may seem like bad, or at least pre-relativistic and therefore primitive, physics. To accept the orthodox Minkowski position that space by themselves and time by themselves do not exist, however, would be to capitulate to the assumption that physics has the last word on time. This is a position which the present book rejects (and has, I hope, given sufficient reason for doing so.) The discussion that follows gives further grounds for not being too impressed by physics in this context: the unresolved and seemingly unresolvable argument about the way time (and space) should be treated.

A persistent controversy rages in the philosophy of space and time between those who claim that space–time ought to be taken as an entity which exists in its own right, and could exist even if there were no ordinary matter in the universe, and those who maintain that talk about space–time ought to be considered as nothing but a misleading way of representing the fact that there is ordinary matter and that there are spatio-temporal relations among material objects and happenings.[25]

The literature on the metaphysics of space and time is dominated by this debate between those who adopt Leibniz's view that they are relational (the total of all the relations between items "in" space and time) and those who accept the Newtonian view that space and time are substantive – existing in themselves, and thus provide an absolute reference frame in which events can be located.[26]

This substantivalist doctrine is the view that space–time has an existence independent of its contents, that the totality of space–time points is a substance that is logically capable of independent existence. In both cases, the question of whether time is singular or plural, appropriately referred to by mass or count nouns, jointless or composed of more-than-infinitesimal points, is often bypassed. The subject – of the stuff of time – is changed.

According to Newton: "Absolute, true and mathematical time, of itself, and from its own nature, flows equably without any relation to anything external and by another name is called duration."[27] For Leibniz, "space ... is something *merely relative*, as time is ... [it is] 'an *order of coexistences* as time is an *order of successions*.'"[28] Relativity theory seems at first to bring comfort to relationists and then to substantivalists.

Special relativity was in part inspired by Ernst Mach's rejection of the very idea of absolute space. He identified the remaining averaged out matter of the universe as the reference point that had hitherto provided a putative absolute space to differentiate states of motion and of rest. Acceleration in a particular zone was not with respect to space but with respect to the rest of the material universe. Behind this was the philosophical position that only the relationships between observable events and objects had any scientific or indeed any other meaning. Since spatial intervals do not have any meaning independently of observer-related measurements, space (or indeed space–time) is nothing in itself. It is therefore identified with the relations of items within it. As Einstein himself expressed it:

> I wished to show that space-time is not necessarily something to which one can ascribe a separate existence, independent of the actual objects of physical reality. Physical objects are not in space, but these objects are spatially extended. In this way, the concept of "empty space" loses its meaning.[29]

As of space, so of time. At the heart of special relativity is motion, which involves both space and time. Motion is the Machian displacement of bodies relative to each other, not to space itself. And the time of events – order of precedence and duration – is always relative to a frame of reference defined by other events, not by an external relationship to (absolute) time. Events do not have to carry the burden of sewing together a coherent, global time. General relativity, however, makes space (and time) somewhat more substantial. It is (to employ the usual phrase) "an active player" in the universe, rather than a nothing that nonetheless manages to separate things (a paradox that licensed Parmenides' challenge to the multiplicity of the Being). Its curvature is equivalent to gravitational force: a local gravitational field in the vicinity of a mass is a local curvature of space–time. What is more, matter, as seen through the gaze of quantum mechanics, loses those basic common-sense properties of impenetrability, continuity and locality, that make it the paradigm of a substance. It seems to melt into a field represented mathematically by the assignment of a real number to each point of space–time. Space and time firm up and matter becomes more ghost-like.[30] This substantivalist view is reinforced by one interpretation of quantum mechanics in which space–time points are real entities – in fact the basic stuff of physical theory.[31]

Confusion reigns: one could be forgiven for seeing space–time in general relativity as geometry or as its own geometry – which does not seem terribly substantive. This passage from Lawrence Sklar captures beautifully the confusing contribution of relativity to the debate:

> While Einstein was originally motivated to discover general relativity at least in part by the hope that he was coming up with a theory which was relationist in the Machian vein, further thought showed that this was not a very plausible reading of what it implied ... Indeed, on a surface reading, the general theory of relativity certainly has the appearance of a substantivalist account ... There is the geodesic structure of a curved space-time, a structure whose observable effects on the motion of material objects is plain.[32]

What is more, "in general relativity we need the geodesic structure and metric of space–time itself to explain the mechanical, optical, and metrical facts available to us in our empirical data".[33]

Part of the problem facing us when we try to decide what the physics tells us is that it is not always clear in what sense substantivalism and relativism are opposed. "Realism versus non-realism about space–time", "Stuff versus non-stuff" and "absolute versus non-absolute background" do not quite map on to each other – particularly as, when space and time are deemed "active players", the partition between background and events, stage and drama is broken down though it is not clear whether they count as causes or a geometrical non-causal explanation. What's more, the difference between substantivalism and relativism is not quite the same difference for space and for time. In the case of space, it is seemingly straightforward: motion is motion of bodies relative to each other, not to space itself. In the case of time, it is a matter of tim*ing* not being absolute.

The cast of characters may be augmented when we focus on *matter* and the question arises as to whether space–time exists in the absence of matter. If (as in general relativity), space–time is not clearly distinguished from matter, then it would be difficult to deny that space–time was substantive, without denying substance to matter. As Sklar has put it:

While not inevitable, a predictable relationist response ... will be to move ordinary matter into the same dispensable category as substantival space–time, accepting the substantivalists' claim that a consistent relationism ultimately results in a phenomenalistic approach to theories in general. [T]he consistent relationist will probably acknowledge that his antisubstantivalism vis-à-vis space–time must, to be coherent, be generalised to antirealism regarding ordinary matter as well.[34]

Alternatively, it breaks down the ontological hierarchy between the space–time manifold, the metric, and the matter field. Matter is upgraded or downgraded with space and time. Ultimately, it seems to melt into a field represented mathematically by the assignment of a real number to each point of space–time. It is both etherealized (because the reality of change is put into question) and frozen.

In short, general relativity seems to erode the terms in which the debate between the substantivalists and the relationists is conducted. When matter melts into something like space–time and space–time congeals into something like matter, we enter a conceptual soup on which the arguments don't seem to have any purchase. Just how bad things are is reflected in this observation by John Norton: "The metric field of relativity seems to defy easy characterization. We would like it to be exclusively part of space–time the container, or exclusively part of the matter contained. Yet it seems to be part of both."[35]

This is, as Sklar has pointed out, particularly difficult in the case of "geometrodynamic" theorizing "in which ordinary matter is *identified* with curved space–time itself, rather than as an autonomous 'inhabitant' of a space–time arena".[36] In the real world of everyday experience, there seems to be an ungainsayable contrast between space which is occupied and the items that occupy it – between the container and the contained. As for which is ontologically more basic and hence has superior reality, – matter or space–time – this remains uncertain, given that the field equations of general relativity have solutions even where space–time is devoid of matter, and given also that (under some interpretations) not only are space–time points real but they are the basic objects of physical theory.[37]

Let us stick with space for a moment. At the level of rather homely intuitions, it is difficult to separate matter and space. In the absence of matter, or energy, as the substrate of events, it is not possible to distinguish between "a lot of space" and "a small amount of space", even if we deny ourselves the common-sense intuition that empty space is nothing (and there is no difference between a lot of nothing and just a little nothing). Granted, without markers provided by something other than space – such as material objects – space does not have a definite extension (perhaps even any extension). On the other hand, without space to occupy – to be located and extended in – matter would not seem to be able to exist: after all, its primary, non-negotiable characteristic, the possibility of its having properties, would seem to be extensity.

There is an analogous discussion to be had about the separability of time from events, for which there is a significant philosophical literature, so we shall devote a separate discussion to it (in §10.4.2). But, to generalize the point just made, space–time existing above and beyond its material inhabitants seems to be necessary as the ground of possibility not only of extensity (including temporal extensity or duration and relations) but also of external relations and hence of relations period. Relations presuppose prior separation and hence something in virtue of which there is separation, even if that which separates is nothing but a mysteriously extended nothing, an uncontaminated extensity. If, at any rate, external relations *presuppose* space (and time), space cannot be those relations, or the sum of them. Even if, therefore, we do not require space to house matter, since the latter brings its own spatial housing with it, we require empty space to part material objects from one another, countable tokens from the mass of stuff. And, given that there is something fundamental common to empty and filled space – there is an important sense in which they are both "space" – it would seem as if, after all, growing or emerging matter would require space to emerge or grow into.

Another position, distinct from both relationism and substantivalism, has been suggested by James Ladyman. According to Ladyman, "Space–time is neither a substance, nor a set of relations between substances, but a structure in its own right".[38] This then raises the question: "Structure of what?". As we discussed in §3.6, Ladyman, and other subscribers to the doctrine of ontic structural realism believe that structure has (ontological) priority over content, relationships over relata, "real patterns" over things, so that space–time points can be upheld as real if "the facts about their identity and diversity [are] grounded in relations that they bear to each other".[39] "Space–time points do not have a primitive or stand-alone identity or self-identity: their individuality is secondary to the relational structures in which they are embedded". In the case of space–time, its reality lies in its *structure*, but the latter does not supervene on the reality of space–time points.

This (as we discussed in §3.6) seems to be less a tenable position than the *reductio ad absurdum* of the identification of reality with whatever can be grasped by mathematics, where relationships have (ontological) priority over items that are related and "every" (self-identical) "thing must go". The being of "1" is to be "less than 2" and "more than zero". Space–time points are handily unreal (lacking primitive or monadic identity) – or purely mathematical – for reasons we have already discussed while at the same time can act as guardians of the (structural) reality of space–time. But this cannot disguise the fact that reality according to ontic structural realism consists of items that borrow their existence from one another.[40]

It may not have escaped the reader that our attention keeps drifting from time to space – via space–time. This is an inevitable consequence of taking our cue from physics. It seems reasonable, in view of the confusing signals sent out by relativity, the part of physics most relevant to our topic, to look beyond this discipline, without denying the value of the operational definitions that have served science, and indeed science-based technology, and consequently many of our most pressing needs, well. Given that here, as elsewhere, physics seems to be in a metaphysical mess, a return to intuitions as a starting point for discussion is justified.[41] Consequently, treating time separately from space should not be regarded merely as the symptom of a failure to keep up with developments in natural science.

If we think of time as purely relational – that it is as a secondary or even an emergent characteristic of the network of events that are in some sense more fundamental – we run into a multitude of problems. The first and easiest to deal with is the challenge of making sense of temporal intervals – days, hours, etc. – which seem to have status independent of events, so that (for example) 25 December 2015 appears to be other than all the things that took place on it. This seems a problem only if we make the mistake (discussed already) of thinking of times, and *a fortiori* stretches of time as quasi-occurrences. The second is more serious: we cannot characterize temporal relations without appealing to the idea of time and running into the kind of circularity we have already noted, such that time is defined as "the temporal relationship between events". The third challenge is to take account of the fact that time has three aspects: location, duration, and relation. The duration of events, for example cannot easily be reduced to the relationship between events without dividing any given event into parts that are temporally related to each other.

This fact that time has several irreducible characteristics – location, interval or duration, and order – seems to be the most compelling case for ascribing substance to it – as well as for treating it (at least outside of physics) independently of space. As already noted, while the distinction between location and magnitude applies to both space and time, there is nothing in space corresponding to temporal order. Spatial order is not mandated from within space whereas temporal order is mandated from within time. We can visit locations in space in any order, whereas the order in which we visit locations in time is imposed. I can go to Paris before London or London before Paris but the order in which I find myself in (first) 12 and (then) 13 December is not elective. This is of course reflected in the fact that we do not visit times; if anything, times visit us (which is why we can choose *where* we are but not *when* we are) though putting it this way again risks the error of thinking of times as occurrences.

Let us, finally, return to what is for many the decisive argument for reducing time to (observer-dependent) relations between events: the denial of absolute measures of time. There is no universal "now" (though, as we discussed in §6.1, there is a "common now"). Against this argument, there is, however, the notion of "cosmic time" which measures the duration of the universe independent of all observers.[42] This idea of the universe itself as the ultimate clock, the final court of chronological appeal, is however deeply problematic. The most obvious difficulty arises from the fact that it eliminates the difference between the timer and the timed: the former is the sum total of everything. What meaning could we give to the idea of any measuring device that has nothing outside of it to measure? On the other hand, cosmic time is implicit in the idea that we can assign a date to the Big Bang with which the universe – at least in its present form – is supposed, according to the overwhelming consensus among physicists, to have originated. This is made clear by Unger:

> The view that the universe has a history... can be stated radically and comprehensively only if we accept that there is a preferred cosmic or global time. A simple description of what such time means is that everything that has happened or that will ever happen in the history of the universe, or in the

history of the universes that may have preceded the present universe, can in principle be placed on a single time line.[43]

This global time is "not simply a collection of local times" otherwise we would not be able to say that the universe is a certain age (i.e. is 13.8 billion years old). It not only transcends local times but also is at odds with the coexistence of past, present, and future of the block universe. The macroscopic sequence of events extending from the Big Bang, to the origin of the planets, to the origin of life, does not seem to be framework- and hence observer-dependent. And this is also pertinent to the question of the (ontological and perhaps logical) priority between time and events, time and change – which we shall discuss in §10.4.

For the present, we note that the question – to narrow it down to two possibilities – as to whether space and time are substantival or relational – or (as Katherine Hawley has expressed it) "space and time are entities in their own right, or whether they are mere abstractions from concrete objects and events"[44] – remains unresolved. Part of the uncertainty may lie in the incomplete overlap between on the one hand the idea of time as a stuff and on the other of time measures as absolute. Unpicking these two dimensions of substantivalism is not easy and we need to look more carefully at the relationship between time and events.[45]

Let us first begin at the beginning and examine the now standard claim that time was brought into being by a particular first event or process: the Big Bang.

10.3.4 Did time begin with a bang?

> So, we and everything we see, result out of quantum fluctuations in
> what is essentially nothingness near the beginning of time ...
> Krauss, *A Universe from Nothing*, Kindle location 1877

The question whether time has a beginning – even whether it is the kind of thing of which it can say it had a beginning – has wandered through Western thought, on the border between philosophy and theology, for millennia, and, notwithstanding the entry of cutting-edge science into the debate, no end seems to be in sight. The issue has been troubled by confusion and by the tendency of some writers to be too comfortable with paradoxes. Regarding confusion, questions are conflated: whether time had a beginning with whether the universe had a beginning; whether there was a first moment with whether there was a first event. As for paradox, the very notion of "a first moment" seems problematic. It invites us to entertain the idea of a moment that is like any other in all respects except one, namely that, while it has a successor moment, it has no predecessor moment. This is even more paradoxical than the number "1" which at least has the negative series to precede it and to mirror the series of its successors; and more puzzling even than zero, which is the hinge between the two series. The beginning of time has to be also a beginning in time in a sense which is best highlighted by a contrast with space. The beginning of space is either the time at which space began, or the point from which space expands, or the place from which a journey sets out. The uncertainty as to whether Moment 1 or Moment 0 is the beginning of time reflects this difficulty of deciding whether the beginning of time is part of time or something that leads into time; a moment with a successor but no predecessor or something that is not fully-fledged moment, straddling time and no time.[46]

A key contribution to the discussion in the Western philosophical tradition is in *The Critique of Pure Reason*. There Kant demonstrates to his own satisfaction that time cannot be something in the world out there, a property of things in themselves: on the contrary, he says, time is one of "the forms of sensible intuition" – an *a priori* form of inner sense – of the perceiving subject (the other being space). And he uses the question of whether the world has a beginning in time or – and this is a slither we must keep our eye on – whether time *itself* has a beginning to investigate this.[47] He shows that it is possible to prove both (a) that the world *must* have had a beginning in time and (b) that it *can't* have had a beginning in time. From this, he concludes that there is something wrong with the very idea of time as inherent in the universe. Instead, he argues, it is, along with space, a lens through which the in-itself, noumenal reality, is experienced by mind or minds (an important ambiguity) as a phenomenal world.

Kant's argument for the world having a beginning in time is short and to the point. If the world didn't begin at some moment in time, an infinite quantity of time – an "eternity", as Kant called it – would have already passed. This is not possible because no infinite series can be completed – a completed infinity is an absurd idea – even less added to as day succeeds day. (Assuming that there are no trans-finite quantities in nature – a safe assumption, I think.) If 12 December 2015 was located at an infinite period of time since the world began, it could not have been arrived at and there wouldn't be room for 13 December 2015.[48]

Kant's argument that the world *can't* have had a beginning in time is equally snappy. If the world began at time t_1, there must have been a period of worldless time before t_1. Nothing (least of all a whole world) can come into being in empty time, as there isn't anything to distinguish one moment in empty time from another. To put this another way: since successive moments of empty time are identical, there would not be a sufficient reason for one moment to give birth to the world, given that its predecessors are sterile.[49] It would be even more difficult to see how the first moment in time could arise – at a time.

The current orthodox response to Kant's antinomy of time is to say that the world *did* have a beginning. That beginning was at the Big Bang, 13.75 billion years, not an eternity, ago. But it was not preceded by already-existing empty time: time began with the beginning of the world. This solution echoes Augustine's assertion that "the world was made, not in time, but simultaneously with time"[50] Kant's first antinomy is therefore based on a false premise.

The theory that time and the world both began with the Big Bang 13.75 billion years ago includes two rather remarkable claims: that time began *at a particular time* – defined as $t_{present}$ minus 13.75 billion years; and that time and the world began *at the same time*. Let us look at these claims.

Since the Big Bang can be assigned a date, Something must have come out of Nothing at a particular moment. To assert this is to put Kant's worry in upper case: "What is special about one particular moment such that it is able to give birth to a world, given that the moment is not only empty of everything in addition to time but also empty of time itself?" becomes "What was special about a specific moment 13.8 billion years ago?" From the standpoint of the present, it is odd to think of a certain moment being metaphysically privileged – as Kant noted. Certain cosmologists say that there was *nothing* special about it: the universe is a random event that could have happened at any time because it happened for no reason. Even so, it is still necessary to explain or at least describe *what* happened at that not-special moment.

The fundamental problem for a physicist is that the creation – something out of nothing – requires a violation of the fundamental law of the conservation of mass-energy. The solution is to claim that quantum uncertainty permits this law to be suspended for a minute period. During this time, in which it seems there is no difference between existence and non-existence, virtual particles can pop into existence so long as they unpop within the quantum limits.

This, however, could be as good a mechanism for cancelling as for enacting the Creation. Something more is needed.[51] According to Krauss, the universe grew out of a false vacuum: a quantum field or "inflaton" which was temporarily stable but not in the lowest energy state. Random fluctuation (uncaused, as things are in the quantum world) sent the inflaton tumbling into a true vacuum.[52] This generated an equal amount of positive energy (matter) and negative energy (gravity): "On the scale of the entire universe, the positive energy of matter can be balanced by the negative gravitational energy, and so there is no restriction on the creation of entire universes. Because there is a law like gravity, the universe can and will create itself from nothing".[53] So the universe could be created from nothing because it adds up to nothing. The mass energy of all the constituents of a finite universe appears to be always equal in magnitude but opposite in sign to the total gravitational potential energies of those particles. By this means, the law of conservation is itself conserved when Nothing becomes Something because there is no net difference between Something and Nothing. The Big Bang with which the universe originated was simply a rearrangement of Nothing. It is the sound of one positive and one negative hand clapping. Unlike those who, hitherto, said "We would seek a sign!" to deliver the revelation of understanding, physicists-turned-theologians require two: a coexistent plus and minus sign.

Thus the story of the Creation spun as a tale of creative accounting. Since the net content of the universe amounts to nothing, and it takes (net) nothing to make nothing out of nothing, so there is nothing to be explained. So it is not at all surprising after all that it did come into existence. This account of the moment of creation has seemed to some to spare us having to confront questions of causation: the universe is neither (externally) caused by a creator nor self-caused.[54] An explanation that does not rely on causes is made to seem possible by an appeal to random instability: the universe was not propelled or fashioned into being but simply wobbled into itself.

One would not have to be particularly alert, however, to notice that the unstable quantum vacuum (the apotheosis of zero) in the starter pack is a bit more than nothing. Even more vulnerable is the idea that we can finesse a universe from nothing by a process that generates equal amounts of positive and negative energy, so that the universe has zero total energy. This seems to be somewhat literal-minded, taking the pluses and minuses in an equation for reality. Are we sure that notions such as positive and negative correspond to anything outside of the double entry book-keeping of the scientist? If they were real, and they added up to nothing, we would have to think of gravity as not merely nothing but *less than nothing*. It is difficult to see how this could make anything other than mathematical sense. And equally unexplained are the laws that are supposed to be in place to ensure that instabilities in the quantum field unfold into a universe. These include, centrally, quantum limits and short-enough times and the violations that are permitted in such times. The very notion that "nothing" could be unstable (or stable come to that) and that there could be a difference between a stable and an unstable nothing is – well, problematic.

The physicists' takeover of the theological question[55] of the creation has, it seems, resulted in the replacement of one question – "why is there something rather than nothing?" – by at least three questions. The most obvious is: "how did the quantum vacuum arise in the first place?" Even an ordinary vacuum, in the absence of anything else, seems dubious. Vacuums are vacuums *in*. They are defined by what they are not; by non-vacuous surroundings. They are, after all, the *ne plus ultra* of a hole. An entirely vacuous universe would be indistinguishable from nothing at all. The notion that it could have properties that are so fertile as to be able to generate a universe seems *prima facie* self-contradictory. Secondly: How does this vacuum generate two universes, one positive and one negative? And how do those universes, made up of huge number of parts, add themselves up to totals? And how do they live side by side or (given non-locality in the quantum world) together?

The notion that you can get nothing out of nothing if that nothing is the sum of negative and positive universes of equal size is reminiscent of the wilder shores of scholasticism. And if nothing is required to make a universe, we are entitled to Kantian surprise that the universe blasted itself into existence spontaneously at a particular point in time 13.8 billion years ago. The principle that "nothing shall come out of nothing" does not allow that the first nothing in the aphorism shall be the universe and the second nothing shall be nothing *tout court*.

That so many cosmologists should jettison this principle is due not only to uncritical acceptance of the apparent ontological implications of quantum weirdness but also to a confusion between theories and that of which they speak, of the map with any kind of extra-cartographic terrain. The first sentence of a paper by Hawking and Hertog says it all: "It seems likely that string theory contains a vast ensemble of stable and meta-stable vacua."[56] It is telling that we are informed that string theory "contains" rather than "postulates". The landscape of theories that is string theory becomes a landscape of possibilities, even probabilities, and then a landscape. Finally, how come there were already laws of nature to guide the emergence of opposing somethings out of nothing? Simply stating the notion that the laws of nature precede the existence of nature is enough to establish its absurdity. One could be forgiven for envisaging the laws hanging about on stand-by awaiting the call – of something or nothing.

This latter point is developed by Lawrence Kuhn in his brilliant critical essay.[57] He identifies no less than nine "levels of nothing" ranging from nothing as space and time that just happens to be totally empty of all visible objects to "no sets, no logic, no general principles, no universals, no possibilities of any kind". No physicist's account of the emergence of something from nothing even begins to match the sophistication of this kind of analysis.

Understandably, many cosmologists have given up on the idea that the Big Bang is at the beginning of time (and space) arguing that, rather, it is but a recent event in a much longer history. Instead of one Big Bang, there is a series of big bangs livening up a cosmos that has been around forever.[58] There is a causal connection – though one that may be weaker than causal connections evident within a single universe – between successive universes and they belong to the same temporal order. This, of course, only displaces the problem of the emergence of Something out of Nothing. Kant's paradox of an infinite amount of time having already passed returns, notwithstanding that that infinite amount is punctuated by the creation of a succession of universes.

There does seem to be something dubious about dating the beginning of time. Allocating a time to the beginning of time shares the problems of allocating a time (for it to be "at") to any moment in time, something which we have already discussed. Saying that the first moment in time t_1 took place at a time t_1 seems like a harmless tautology, but it is actively misleading, because it treats a moment in time as if it were itself a kind of *occurrence* (that "took place") – and an occurrence in time – as opposed to part of the framework within which things can occur. To say that time began at $t_{beginning}$ is to treat the beginning of time more like a kind of event. This impression is confirmed when a *value* is assigned to $t_{beginning}$ and it is asserted that it occurred 13.8 billion years ago.

Those who want to defend the notion of a beginning of time as a kind of occurrence might argue that we talk about the beginning of stretches of time. For example, there is nothing apparently wrong with saying that Wednesday began at midnight on Tuesday. The analogy is not valid, however. "Tuesday" or "Wednesday" are not time but divisions placed upon time, labels for stretches of pre-existing time. By contrast, the Big Bang is supposed to be both timeless and occur at a particular time: at the beginning of, and yet not part of, the series that it inaugurates.

The problem with saying that time began at a particular time is also highlighted by this obvious question: If it is perfectly valid to speak of 13.2, 13.3 and 13.8 billion years ago, why is it not valid to talk about 13.9, 13.81 or even 13.80001 billion years ago? There is something odd about assigning a metaphysically privileged status to a contingent, point in time. What is more, that first moment in time seems to have to fulfil several offices: being the beginning of the universe; being the beginning of time; and being the time when the universe entered time. The oddness is underlined by the fact that it can be looked back on, for example, from now, some 13.8 billion years on but it cannot be looked forward to say from 14.75 billion years ago.

Some have answered this objection by arguing that to talk of time before the Big Bang is like talking about points north of the North Pole. Once you have got to the North Pole, it makes no sense to talk about going any further north. The analogy does not work. As Lucas has pointed out, there is a deeper, astronomical meaning of north which allows a line pointing in that direction to be extended indefinitely.[59] North is a direction that has no terminus: you *can* be north of the North Pole. So the question still stands.

What about the second assumption: the supposed *simultaneity* of the beginning of the universe and the origin of time? How can we think of the start of time itself (as opposed to the time *of* some event) being also an event (and rather a large one – the creation of the universe)? There is no "at the same time as" until the universe has differentiated to the point where one event can be temporally related to other events via an observer. And there is a mismatch between a universe, whose coming-into-being is extended over time, and time itself, whose coming into being is presumably instantaneous, or at least not extended through time.

Kant's first antinomy therefore still haunts us. But we have good reason not to respond to the challenge it poses by embracing Kant's conclusion that time is therefore internal to the human mind. (This is something we shall discuss in §10.5, when we consider the significance of what Quentin Meillassoux has called "ancestrals" and his critique of "Kantian correlationism".) For the moment we note that our discussion of the question of whether or not the universe had a beginning in time may be rooted in a mode of thought that envisages the universe as a whole, as a single interconnected process so that it makes as much sense to apply the notion of beginning to it as it makes to apply it to an event or unfolding narrative within the universe. Perhaps the notion of beginning is inseparable from narrative. As we suggested in §9.3, in the beginning was the word – the word "beginning".[60] Only when such a word, or at least the concept behind it, is present, does t_1 count as "the first moment" rather than as t_0, the pre-moment that ushered in the series of moments.[61]

Perhaps, after all, our difficulties originate from the cosmological fallacy that Kant first noted, and Unger and Smolin discuss,[62] of extending the notion of "beginning" from localities – particular sequences, particular stories – to the totality of things. The questionability of this move is not allayed by the fact that the beginning was small – for example an infinitely dense, hot, infinitesimal, point. But if it were the form of succession of *all developing processes*, the idea of "beginning" would be difficult to attach to it. A series may have a beginning but the property of being a series does not. To say this, however, is to turn one's back on rather a lot of cosmology, which is not something a non-physicist should do lightly. See, however, Addendum 2 at the end of this chapter.

10.4 TIME AND CHANGE

The question of whether there was a first moment in time tends as we have noted to slither into the question of whether there was a first event in the history of the universe that may not only have inaugurated the cosmos but also fired the starting gun on time. At the point of origin, stuff and its capacity for change, happenings and their substrate, or the substrate and the propensity for happenings, including space and time, are created at the same time. The Big Bang is both the Prime Maker and the Prime Mover. This indirectly illuminates the way time and events are inextricably connected in our thinking. In this section, we shall explore the relationships between time and change: time permitting change; change measuring time; and change as a necessary condition of time.

10.4.1 The material universe

Some changes are used to measure time. That, at least, is the way it is usually expressed; and this way of putting it, reinforced by the transformations of time into "little t" in physical science, creates the impression that time is a kind of change or process in itself. The description of time as "what happens when nothing else does" – as happening uncontaminated by actual events – is amusing but not entirely vacuous. It brings it close to Newton's conception, mentioned earlier: "Absolute, true and mathematical time, *of itself, and from its own nature, flows equably without any relation to anything external* and by another name is called duration."[63] This is contrasted with its vulgar, everyday counterpart: "relative, apparent, and common time is some sensible and external (whether accurate or unequable) measure of duration by the means of motion, which is commonly used instead of true time: such as an hour, a month, a year".[64]

Newton's view is, it hardly needs to be said, one that has had a bad press since special relativity made temporal locations, relations, and durations observer-dependent, that is to say frame-dependent. Time is the relationship between events as observed from a frame of reference. The question whether time "is an absolute background stage on which events are played out or whether it is a secondary concept which derives from physical processes and hence affected by them"[65] is, as we saw in §10.3.3, unresolved in contemporary physics. Mach, who provided the philosophical background for so much of the physics of the last century, argued that "It is utterly beyond our power to measure the changes of things by time. Quite the contrary, time is an abstraction, at which we arrive by means of the changes of things".[66] We never measure the rate of change of anything by direct reference to the passage of time, it is argued, but by means of a motion that is deemed to measure time.

Leaving aside the arguments of the physicists, we may ask whether the notion of time as a pure, eventless succession can make sense. Would the group t_1, t_2, t_3, etc. count as a *series*, as a sequence, that has an inviolable order (such that t_2 is always later than t_1 and earlier than t_3) in the absence of change, of events (and hence of observers whose observations are events), at the very least as markers to tag them? And would time have to be granular – consisting of a sequence of discrete items – for it to be a *series*? What is more, could any sense be given to the apparently fundamental distinction between temporal relations ("before", "after"), temporal locations (e.g. "at t_1"), and temporal durations (e.g. 5 seconds) without time being a substrate for pre-existing events?

The joke that "time stops everything happening at once"– making time a condition for change without contradiction – seems yet another illustration of what so often happens when we try to grasp the essence of time: we enter a lexical circle. The notion of "something happen*ing*" presupposes a time when it happens; and "at once" is of course a temporal notion. The statement therefore unpacks to the assertion that "time stops everything happening at the same time". It is hardly necessary to point out that in the absence of time, simultaneity – or the threat of it – would be just as absent as succession. Without time, things could not be in a state of temporal competition any more than they could be kept temporally apart.

The joke is not, however, as vacuous as it might seem. It says more than "time stops the world being timeless". It seems to imply a profound difference between time as a relationship of simultaneity and time as a relationship of succession, almost suggesting that the former ("at once") is not really temporal whereas the latter is; or, to turn it on its head, time can exist in no quantity (there being only an "at once") which is nevertheless really time; as if a world without time would in fact be a world of "one time" ("at once") in which there were one kind of temporal relation (of simultaneity) but no temporal extensity. The joke, in short, jolts us into another insight into the slipperiness of time.

It is also a reminder that time is sometimes invoked as a way of avoiding a particular form of quasi-logical contradiction: it permits incompatible properties at the same place. In short, time is the possibility of change (of which more presently) such that the same entity may have more than one out of a range of mutually exclusive properties. So we have an interesting intersection between time and the scope of logical possibility.[67]

To reduce time to something in virtue of which change may be permitted, allowing particular items to have what would otherwise be incompatible properties, also reminds us that it is only against the background of (relative) stability that change is possible – for example movement requires a relatively unmoving frame of reference. But when this background is the object that is undergoing change, we seem to have the possibility of contradiction: Object O can remain Object O and still have property y *and* the property z, even though these are incompatible, if we are talking about different moments in time.

As we noted in §10.2, time as the possibility of change is permissive rather than being the primary motor. It is not comparable to energy (to drive change) or instability (to make it probable); nor does it as it were collude or cooperate with them.[68] After all, time does not *direct* change in the way that energy and inherent dispositions do; and change in no particular direction is no change.[69] Even less does time reverse changes: it does not heal wounds, only creates the possibility of wounds being healed;

they heal themselves though they "take time" to do so. Space, too, is the possibility of change: movement requires space as well as time. While there are changes in items (such as changes of colour) that do not involve their macroscopic movement all change requires spatial displacement at the atomic level, or a redistribution of mass-energy.[70]

If time is the possibility of change, a timeless world would be without happenings or the possibility of them. But time is also necessary for things to remain unchanged – or to count as such, as being stable. As the seventeenth-century natural philosopher and mathematician Isaac Barrow expresses it: "Time [denotes] … a certain capacity or possibility for a continuing of existence; just as space denotes a capacity for intervening length."[71] It is interesting that he concludes from this, however, that time is not, as it were, an added, independent ingredient in the world. The full quote is: "Time does not denote an actual existence but a certain capacity or possibility for a continuing of existence …". This definition of time as the possibility of "the continuation of anything in its own being" is less of a threat than might appear to the status of time as something in itself, as opposed to a property of (stable) objects, because there is a circularity. The "continuing" that is referred to is *temporal* continuity as opposed to, say, the kind of continuity that is expressed in the unbroken occupancy of space within its borders.

The fact that *both* change and the lack of it take time warrants further examination. There cannot be evident lack of change – explicit stability – without the passage of time. We need time for something to qualify as enduring. A notional timeless "instant" would not suffice to differentiate between stability and change. It could, however, be argued that the marker of time associated with the unchanging is outsourced to changes taking place elsewhere. Without change elsewhere in the universe, we have to ask, would something – an object or a sector of space – count as unchanging?

10.4.2 Temporal vacua

So change (and stability and the contrast between them) need time. Does this mean that time has to be in place first, in order that there can be change? Notwithstanding the "first", the priority would not, of course, be temporal: time cannot itself enter a temporal series as something before something else. No, the question is one that boils down to this: Can there be periods where time "passes" and yet nothing at all is happening in the entire universe? Or does time need change as much as change needs, or takes, time? Do events carry the burden of generating time, as perhaps extreme relationists believe. Shall we agree with Aristotle that "time does not exist without change"?[72] Or that time without change is the equivalent of dehydrated water? Or should we allow the possibility of "temporal vacua", stretches of time unoccupied by changes, analogous to vacua in space unoccupied by objects or fields? The question touches directly on Newton's idea of time "of itself and from its own nature" that "flows equably and without regards to anything external" – pure "duration".

A global temporal vacuum appears logically conceivable.[73] Thought experiments – such as those by Shoemaker and Newton-Smith – defend their conceivability by envisaging the temporal vacuum as a being achieved by stepwise "freezing" or "emptying" of the world, beginning with parts of the world separately evacuated.[74] This is a way of getting round the difficulty of the necessary disappearance of the observer (and consequently observations) in a wholly frozen universe. There must be an unfrozen outside to observe the frozen (part of) the world since (as is commonly believed) observations are the result of causal interactions between the observer and the observed. Shoemaker gets round this ingeniously.

Let us suppose the universe has three parts A, B, and C which take it in turns to freeze. Crucially, their freezing has different periodicity: A freezes for a year once every three years, B once every 4 years and C once every 5 years. There will be one year in 60 in which all three regions are frozen and the entire universe is changeless. While the wholly frozen universe cannot be observed, total freezing can be inferred. Whether, however, the inhabitants of this universe could conclude that once every 60 years there would be a total freeze would depend on the dubious assumption that a part of the universe could be *observed* to have frozen. Nothing could come out of or go into such a universe, so the interaction necessary for observation would not be possible without some change. So even the partial freezing that Shoemaker relies on is ruled out. There is an additional difficulty, raised by Ken Warmbrod: there would be nothing to restart a frozen total universe once it had stopped, so no freezing could be time-limited.[75]

Nevertheless, irrespective of whether the thought experiment is coherent, it is useful for thinking about whether time can be conceived independently of change or the possibility of it. We can address the question of temporal vacua in three ways:

(a) Can time that cannot be measured even in principle – because there are no changes in the universe – be said to have elapsed?
(b) Would time elapse in an eventless but still occupied universe?
(c) Could there be a temporal relation between a temporal vacuum and the time elapsing "before" and "after" it?

Let us consider each of these in turn.

Can time that cannot be measured even in principle be said to have elapsed?

The frozen universe would not merely be without clocks, and the possibility of clocks, but without the possibility of observations because the latter must ultimately be based on perceptions that are changes in observers. For relationists, it would follow that not only would there be no basis for any claim as to how much time had elapsed during the period that the world was unchanging – because temporal intervals are entirely frame-of-reference and observer dependent – but also there would simply be no meaning to the question "How long?". We need a succession of events to act as markers that would translate a succession of notional instants into an extended period of definite duration.

It might be argued that, even though the period of time that had elapsed strictly had no ("absolute") duration, there would be a gap between the last event before the universe froze and the first event after it started changing again. This interval, however, would have no definite duration nor would there be any way of assigning it a definite duration: it would be as arbitrary to think of it as an instant as to think of it as billions of years.[76] This must, surely, be fatal for the thought experiment since any physical parameter that truly exists must exist in a certain quantity, even if the measure of that quantity is observer-dependent rather than absolute. The idea of time elapsing in the frozen universe would seem therefore to be contradictory.

The conclusion holds up even if we do not capitulate to the Machian notion that time that is not, or cannot be, measured does not exist. It does however raise the possibility that the notion of a definite lapse of time in the absence of a human consciousness may be self-contradictory, something we shall address in the next section.

We must be careful not to drift towards the position this book is committed to rejecting; namely that if you take away measurement and remove number from time, there is nothing left; that the essence of time is to be found in the difference between (e.g.) x seconds and $2x$ seconds; that if you cannot say in principle *how much* time has passed, you cannot say that *any* time has elapsed. But it does seem that a period of time that has no definite extensity would not be a definite interval; hence not an interval; and no period of time.[77] There is a further consideration touching on the question of whether time would pass in the absence of observers or the possibility of observation. If it did not pass, we would have difficulty in explaining the necessary temporal order of events in the universe leading up to the emergence of sentient beings. We shall discuss this in §10.5.

Would time elapse in a frozen but still occupied universe?

In our thought experiment, the universe is brought to a halt: change is forbidden. But it is populated with static objects. Indeed, they could not go out of existence during the freeze because that would itself involve change. Won't time still elapse therefore because Isaac Barrow's criterion would be met: "a certain capacity or possibility for a continuing of existence"? And the occupants of the frozen universe would have "a continuing of [their] existence" because they would be there, ready for reanimation when the universe unfroze? Would this be enough to ensure the continuation of time across the freeze? Or does the time that reposes in continuation of objects require that endurance, stasis, should be manifest by contrast with a background of change? In the unfrozen world, experience of time involves both change and stasis: change located in (relatively) stable objects and states of affairs. This is most clearly evident in clocks where the moving finger requires the stillness of the clock-face.

If the universe were unoccupied – it was entirely void of objects and fields – there would be no possibility of change. Would time pass? Clearly not, if we were to define time as "the possibility of change". It would not even meet Barrow's minimalist definition for time: "a certain capacity or possibility for a continuing of existence". And Warmbrod's point – that a frozen universe would have no basis for restarting – would apply with even greater strength.

Could there be a temporal relation between a temporal vacuum and the time elapsing before and after it?

A spatial vacuum has a definite identity or existence only in virtue of its non-vacuous surroundings: a nothing requires encircling something to confer shape, and hence identity, upon it. *Omnis determinatio est negatio* even when the item in question is nothing. Vacua require their flasks. They are by being the negative of that which they are not. Would it be legitimate to consider temporal vacua without imagining them as having (presumably) temporal boundaries? Consider the universe grinding to halt at t_n and waking up at $t_n + x$. If we believe that, after all, no time passed in the frozen universe, the freeze must have begun at the same time as it ended. Not only is there no interval between t_n and $t_n + x$, but t_n and $t_n + x$ are the same moment in time – let us call it t.

If this were the case, we would have to assume that freezing and unfreezing both take place at t. This would seem to make t the temporal site of a contradiction. (The contradiction would be exacerbated if we deemed the cessation of change and the resumption of change as themselves being changes of a sort.) If there *were* a gap between the cessation and resumption of change, it would have to be a gap in time. In what sense would this gap in time – let us call it G – be related to time before (t_n) and after $(t_n + x)$ itself? It is natural to think that there is a sequence: t_n, G, $t_n + x$ corresponding to "active universe, frozen (timeless) universe, reactivated universe". The gap would be anomalous inasmuch as it had a temporal *location* (the freeze took place and ceased at the same time) but not a temporal *extensity*. It would fall foul of the paradox of mathematical points we discussed in §3.4.1: laying claim to a place without occupying a place. What's more, unlike the mathematical points discussed in §3.4.1, it would not have a coordinate frame of reference to borrow location from (except that of an imaginary external observer not permitted by the thought experiment).

The fact that these questions about temporal vacua seem unanswerable may itself be an indirect answer to the question whether time can be separated from change; whether time can be intelligibly said to continue in the universal absence of events and processes. The very notion of a temporal vacuum seems to be dubious, if only because it seems difficult to assign to it the boundaries a (finite) vacuum must have.

It is looking more likely that a world in which nothing happens but there is time may be a logical possibility but not a physical or even metaphysical one. However, the notion of time as "the *possibility* of change" seems at first to leave it undetermined that time may or may not be present in an unchanging universe. A possibility, after all, is a possibility not a necessity, certainty or an actuality. More precisely, a possibility of change implies the possibility of no change: time, to reiterate, is per-missive rather than coercive. If time *were* coercive, or (to put it more conventionally) had causal powers, we would find it difficult to conceive of a world, or even parts of the world, where nothing is happening.

So time without change is problematic, though change without stability is no less so. Change is change *in* or *of* that which is relatively stable. The leaves move back and forth but remain on the tree; the tree sheds the leaves but it remains; the tree dies but the wood remains; the woods decay and fall but the land remains. The face of the clock does not tick along with it. The Heraclitean notion of change in the absence of stability is therefore elusive. Heraclitus and Parmenides need each other.[78] When we conceive of the universe as a whole, we see local changes cancelling out: every exit (of mass or energy) is an entrance elsewhere. This is captured in the conservation of mass-energy. Even overall trends, such as the increase of entropy, or cosmic expan-sion, are offset: universal covariance or the preservation of structure in different frames of reference.

Whether or not time would stop if the universe stopped, it remains true that time is not in itself a change common to or additional to all the events and processes of the world. If it were either of these, it would be difficult to know what characteris-tics it had, given that it is equally present in all changes and, indeed, in stability and duration, as well as transience. The only plausible intrinsic characteristic – being fast or slow – is clearly a property of the events and processes that take time, not time itself; and, as we have seen, the notion of time passing fast or slow has time on both the numerator and denominator and on these grounds is to be discounted. If (a) we find it difficult to give a meaning to time in the absence of change (or the possibility of it)[79] and (b) we accept that change requires time, it is reasonable to conclude that we should not regard either time (moments, intervals) or change (events, processes) as having priority or being the more "fundamental". Plotinus' assertion that "Time is that in which all the rest (other than time) happens, in which all movements and rest exist smoothly side by side and under order"[80] should be regarded as a potent three-quarter truth, and certainly more sophisticated than "Time is what happens when nothing else does". Even so, we should not submit to the relationist imperative, not the least because reducing times to classes or sets of simultaneous events is to leave them in fact unreduced because "simultaneous" is a temporal concept. And the same applies to the reduction of time to the order in which events occur, because the order in question is a temporal order. Equally, events are clearly not reducible to the time they take, exemplify or measure. At any rate, while changes take time, it is very difficult to resist the notion that they also make it; that the time taken by an event is made by the sum of the other events. This brings us close to the relational view of time, and the time of special relativity where duration is inseparable from measure-ments located in particular frames of reference. However, relationism overlooks that in virtue of which events are brought into relation and there are frames of reference: the observer who makes time explicit and measures it.[81]

This is our cue to move on to discuss time and *the perception of change.*

10.4.3 The perceived world and temporal awareness

> Time does not exist without change; for when the state of our mind does not change at all, or we have not noticed its changing, we do not realise that time has elapsed.[82]
>
> Aristotle quoted in Gale, *The Philosophy of Time*, 11

We have so far examined the relationship between time and change by investigating whether it is valid to imagine time as passing, or at least continuing, in the absence of change in the material world. We have not yet properly considered a third party: the conscious subject in virtue of which time is perceived – experienced or known. How important the perceiver is to the metaphysics of time depends on the way we construe the relationship between time ("itself") and the time sense of sentient creatures, most importantly human beings. For some philosophers, the two are inseparable: time cannot be extricated from perception because it is our perception of change; more precisely our perception of the sequence of events. Change alone, unperceived change, would not be sufficient to generate time.

There are many problems with this analysis. The most obvious is that we would seem to have to jettison the idea that unperceived events are located at various points in time, have a certain temporal order, and have a certain duration. More generally, it would confine time to a universe in which there are conscious beings. As we shall discuss in the next section, this would not accommodate many facts we accept as incontrovertible; notably that the universe existed *before* there were sentient beings and that (for example) the formation of the earth, the beginning of life, and the emergence of conscious life had a certain temporal order and were separated by definite, real (very large) temporal intervals. Locating time within perception would turn on its head what most of us believe about the relationship between subjectively experienced and objective time, between human and physical time.

Before we can address this latter issue, however, we need to examine a little more carefully the relationship between our time sense – which must at the very least be the basis of our being creatures who measure time and who ultimately allocate (or discover) a temporal order to events in the material world – and our perception of the succession of events.

We touched on this theme at the beginning of the present volume when it was argued that explicit time, and our sense of temporal depth, was rooted in the visual sense which had a special relationship to the perception of change. To detect that something has changed, we have to be aware simultaneously of its changed state and the state from which it was changed. In Chapter 1, we considered seeing an object moving from position P_1 to position P_2. When the object reaches P_2, its earlier state is preserved in the continuing visibility of P_1. We can see both the present and the past position, so that the past is present in the present. To generalize: the sense that something has changed, that a happening has happened, requires co-awareness of initial and subsequent states. The alteration takes place against a relatively unchanging background or a relatively stable object which brings together the beginning and the end of the change. The co-presence of how things are "now" and how they were "before" is also the first step towards an apprehension of an interval of time between states and, ultimately, towards a sense of the *size* of the interval and the duration of the events bounding the interval – the "long" and "short" – that leads ultimately to time measurement. These pre-measurement senses of durations and intervals are of course read off from other happenings forming the background of the index events.

Much of the philosophical and psychological discussion of the relationship between our time sense and the perception of successive events has focused on rather simple, discrete examples.[83] The sequence of notes "do-re-mi" has played a starring role. The challenge has been seen as getting from a succession of experiences (or perceptions or feelings or sensations) to an experience (or perception or feeling or sensation) of succession – in response to the observation (particularly associated with William James) that "a succession of feelings, in and of itself, is not a feeling of succession".[84] If, as has been suggested, time is the form of succession round a developing process or series, the form has somehow to be abstracted from the succession.

The puzzle is standardly expressed as follows. Let us suppose "do" occurs at t_1, "re" at t_2, and "mi" at t_3. For the experience of succession to be extracted from the succession of experiences, "do" and "re" have somehow to be present in consciousness at t_3 as well as at t_1 and t_2 when they occur. It is only at t_3 that they have all occurred so they can amount to a series. After all, prior to t_3 there is no guarantee that they will occur at all. In what form are "do" and "re" present at t_3?[85] The solutions that are offered, often rooted in different theories regarding the structure of perceptions of composite experiences and their relationship to that which is perceived, all seem unsatisfactory. Let us look at a couple of solutions favoured by philosophers.

The first is to suggest that "do" is present either as an echo or reverberation of the perception when "mi" is present. The problem with this is that we might expect the echo and/or recollection experienced along with the perception to be experienced more like a chord than a succession; or worse, a mush of merged notes. Another attempt to explain how the successive experiences are turned into an experience of succession involves an appeal to the notion of "the specious present" (discussed in §6.1.2) which, as Hoerl defines it, is "a fairly limited maximum period of time that individual experiences can span".[86] "Do-re-mi" counts as a succession because they all belong to a single (extended) experience. Again, while this may explain how the three notes are brought together, it does not explain how they are kept tidily apart such that they are not experienced as a chord or as simultaneous.[87] Unless discrete events in the series are (a) separately registered, (b) registered as separate, *and* (c) registered as being connected, there would be no basis for the sense of succession. The co-presence of "do", "re" and "mi" as belonging to a succession cannot mean that they are somehow simultaneous for this additional reason: simultaneity is also a relation perceived between events and we cannot have a perceived relation that is at once "now" and "not now", "at the same time" and "not at the same time" in a single consciousness.

Behind this difficulty of getting an experience of a sequence out of a sequence of experiences, of making successive events belong to each other as members of a succession, of getting explicit "followed by" out of the experience of A followed by the experience of B, is a larger problem: that of understanding an experience that has to be at once unified and composite, so that the perception of "mi" at t_3 both is and is not combined with, or at least side by side with, the perception of "do" at t_1. They have to be both experienced together and experienced *as* distinct – both distinct in themselves and distinct in their temporal location. This problem also undermines the usual attempts to explain how we experience protracted events as extended in time. If, for example, the note "do" is sustained, I am aware of it as having a more distant beginning and a more remote ending. It is, as it were, a one note succession – of parts of notes.

The focus on sequences, a number of discrete items, rather than duration of any particular item overlooks a key element in the sense of the passage of time. Experienced time cannot be reduced to pure number: "How long?" is not just "How many?" (notes) but also "How (temporally) fat?" a note (or other event) is. To think of duration as essentially quantitative is retrospectively to read clock-time into our basic time sense. Counting would not generate sense of duration unless the duration of the intervals between items were already given. More fundamentally, as Mark Sacks has put it, "the mind could not first be equipped with temporal structure by observing the train of ideas, since to observe that passage already presupposes the ability to operate and detect a temporal structure".[88]

The example we have looked at is a sequence of discrete events. The difficulty of understanding where the feeling of succession comes from is at least in part due to the fact that the events are, by definition, distinct. In Chapter 1, time sense was derived from a process – movement – that was (a) continuous and (b) located in a visual field, in which past and present (and, indeed, future) locations were co-present. Spatial separation permitted the co-presence of non-simultaneous states of affairs: we can *see* the connection, the relationship *and* the relata. Some (but not all, as we shall see) of the problems associated with a sequence of sounds were, therefore, bypassed in appreciation of visual succession.

We might grade types of experiences according to how easily we might explain the sense of succession we expect them to generate, and an associated time sense. The most straightforward is continuous motion – movements of objects, including parts of one's own body.[89] Next is a succession of discrete sounds (as in a melody, or tapping) that are intrinsically connected and raise fulfillable expectations. Next up, there are: successions of discrete events that are not part of a series but are regularly even causally related (lightning and thunder); and discrete events that happen to occur in a temporal order but are not otherwise related (e.g. a bus passing by after someone sneezes). We could classify them as: (a) parts of the same process; (b) parts of the same series; (c) causally connected sequences of events; and (d) events that are related only in virtue of falling in the same perceiver's consciousness. There is a clear element of increasing discretion as to whether or not the observer connects them into a series, and experiences them as successive member of a sequence. Type (d) sequences, however, account for the vast majority of events in the real world that are, nonetheless, assigned their place in time. Many, perhaps the majority, of successive experiences do not deliver a direct experience of succession – if they are widely separated. For example, my having my lunch and, a couple of hours later, hearing a man sneeze do not belong to a series. My day is a succession of events but it is not an experienced succession because most events are lost to memory (as we discover when we write up our diaries). We shall return to this presently.

There is an element in sequences of events that we have not sufficiently noticed – as a result of focusing on sequences such as "do-re-mi" – that, while they are not entirely arbitrary, they are not tightly constrained. There is no prohibition on playing the notes in a different order. Many sequences of events – in particular those that matter to us – *are* intrinsically connected so that E_2 *makes sense* in relation to a prior E_1 and this remains true even if we do not accept that the direction of time is underpinned by the relationship between events that are causes and events that are effects. E_2 is made intelligible by E_1 and so carries the presence of E_1 within it. This is equally, or even more, evident in the cases of (apparently) continuously unfolding processes – for example an object or person moving towards me. Where he/it is now makes sense in the light of where he/it was just before. More broadly, the unfolding of the world, even where it takes the form of distinct, successive events, has an intelligibility that is not confined to a present moment separated from from the past, irrespective of whether the past is recalled or not. This is a development of the point made in our discussion of "the present" in Chapter 6 which is that it is not, nor does it grow out of, a mathematical instant. Intelligibility *presupposes* the co-presence of perceived states of the world that are not physically simultaneous or co-present. The world that makes sense to us is not a series of time slices that have somehow to be connected with one another. Intelligibility is not sliceable into, or experienced in, isolated moments.

There is another problem additional to that arising out of the disconnectedness between the events occurring in real stretches of time. It is that of scale. Our time sense extends beyond (say) a triplet of notes to an entire melody, to a long passage, to a whole symphony (we are aware that the scherzo was before the fourth movement) and beyond this to the programme to which the symphony contributed, the evening in which the concert was located – and that included getting to the concert hall, the drink in the bar, and meeting friends, as well as the experience of the music. In short, from small temporal sequences and ordinary intervals of time such as hours, mornings, weeks, seasons, years; the expansion of time sense from this moment to today, from moments to days. But something happens as we move from one to the other. When I listen to a symphony that lasts 40 minutes, I do not experience 40 minutes; or, rather, 40 minutes does not become an object of time experience. An experience that, according to the clock, lasts 40 minutes is not an experience *of* "40 minutes".[90] So the problem of time sense goes far beyond that of understanding how a moment of experience can contain experiences that are not currently happening and can retain the presence of past experiences without their being mistakenly thought of as being of present events. It goes beyond the succession of experiences amounting to an experience of succession mediated by a kind of unity limited by the constraints of a specious present which can straddle the actual present with a smidgeon of past, or episodes of perceptual experience that unfold over a period of clock-time.

Even so, it is worth dwelling for a little longer on the kind of sequences that have been so dominant in the philosophical treatment of temporal consciousness. A variety of ingenious solutions have been offered to the challenge of seeing how a succession of experiences could give rise to an experience of succession.[91] They have to be ingenious because they attempt to solve a problem that, as it is posed, is insoluble. Fortunately, the problem does not have to be solved as posed.

The apparent difficulty facing anyone who tries to explain how we hear the sequence "do-re-mi" is that the components must be presented *both* as temporally separated and co-present. Supposing "do" occurs at t_1, "re" occurs at t_2, and "mi" at t_3. The assumption is that the relevant experiences occur at, and do not outlast, t_1, t_2, t_3 respectively. How, therefore, can we experience the sequence "do-re-mi" at t_3, which must include experiencing "do" and "re" when, at t_3, they are no long occurring or (presumably) being experienced as present? The answer to the question is not to be found in ascribing to "do" and "re" a posthumous existence simultaneous with the real-time occurrence of "mi". This however is one of the most favoured explanations: the (past) experiences of "do" and "re" are "retained" along with the present experiences of "mi". It doesn't quite work because it doesn't deliver what is needed – namely, "do" and "re" as being both present (to mind) and as past; or being present-as-past. Clearly, if "do" and "re" were experienced simply as present, there would be no sense of succession.

This looks like an insuperable problem if the experience of (say) "do" is to be located both in objective time t_1 when it occurs and at objective time t_3 when it acquires its status as the first item in a three-item sequence that is now complete. This is *not*, however, how things are. The physical events that are the public musical notes are tied, restricted, to the physical times at which they occur. The private *experiences* of the notes are not tied to the physical times t_1, t_2, and t_3 in the same way. If this is difficult to apprehend, it is because the *relation* "at time t" which we (correctly) ascribe to the occurrence of the note or any physical event, is supplied by consciousness. It is the perceiver who makes of an event something that is explicitly connected with a time, such that the time is an external relationship of the event marked by "at". The "at time t" is a triadic relationship between an event, a perceiver, and a time forged by the perceiver. The event is "at present" when it is part of the present of a consciousness: the present moment of consciousness is not a mere moment because it is a consciousness of a present which, for reasons given in Chapter 6, is necessarily extended. More importantly, because of this asymmetry – which confers "at-t_1" on the event – the temporal location of the event is not mirrored in any supposed temporal location of the consciousness of the event. Even if each experience were confined to a momentary present, its meaningful (intentional) object would not be confined to a momentary present physical time "simultaneous with" the experience.

It would be absurd to say that the experience of the notes takes place at a different time from the time at which the notes occur. It is obviously (roughly) true that I hear the notes when they are played but the experience of the notes does not take its place in the same time frame as the notes themselves. The experiences are intentionally related to the notes. These experiences are not tied to the time at which they "occur" in the way that the notes are. So the experience of "do" is not confined to t_1 because it is not located in t_1; indeed, it is part of the consciousness (individual and collective) that locates the note, like other events, in a time frame. We could put this another way by saying that the experience of "do" is not simultaneous with the acoustic event "do" in the way that two notes occurring at the same time would be simultaneous with one another. Nor does it succeed "do" in the way that "re" and "mi" do. The simultaneity relation (and the relation of succession) is a connection between physical events, not between a physical event and the experience of it. While experiences of sequences of events may generate a sense of temporal structure in the world (hugely elaborated by means of clocks), the experiences are not themselves located in that temporal structure. The *experience* of event E-at-t_1 is not at-t_1 in the way that E is.

Overlooking the difference between on the one hand physical time t and physical events that take place at time t and on the other perceptions of events-at-time-t is another manifestation of the kind of thinking that leads to the erasure of the observer discussed in §3.5.3. Events and perceptions of events belong to a different order, opened up by intentionality (to be discussed in §12.2) and it reflects what late-nineteenth-century philosopher Alexis Meinong argued – that (as Dainton summarizes it) "the temporal properties of the objects we perceive need not coincide with the temporal properties of the presentations (or episodes of awareness) in which we apprehend" them.[92] We tend to overlook this difference because we as it were look through the presentations or the perceptions to the physical reality which is presented or perceived.

The separation between the two realms is what makes possible the everyday scandal of mental time travel, most evident in episodic memories that alight on token past events disconnected from the present, a phenomenon that has no basis in the world of t_1, t_2, and t_3 – a physical world which neither refers to itself (there is no "at t_1", etc.) nor locates its moments in a time scheme that lies outside of themselves – and it permits all the joys and sorrows of memory and anticipation. That is why Dainton's seemingly unexceptionable assertion "When we hear the clock strike twelve, our auditory experience also occurs at twelve (or at most a few moments later)"[93] glosses over the fact that it is only in virtue of our hearing the clock strike and interpreting it as a time marker that the physical event takes place "at 12"; that indeed it is "at". And this is why the time relationship of an event to the perception of the event is not the same as the simultaneity of one event with another or indeed of one perception with another.

Let E_1 and E_2 be two simultaneous events and P_1 and P_2 be the perception of those events. P_1's being about E_1 is not the same as being simultaneous with E_1 in the way that E_1 is simultaneous with E_2; nor is P_1 simultaneous with P_2 in the way that E_1 is simultaneous with E_2. To capture another aspect of this: "to be about E" is not the same as "to be simultaneous with P". (This relates to the fact that the physical world has no "now": to be present does not translate into "to be at such-and-such a t".) So it is not necessary, in order to see an event or process, or to register a succession, that takes place over the interval $t_1 - t_2$, to have an experience that is "at" all of $t_1 - t_2$

or at any of its moments, in particular the moment t_2. And this is why the past, in order to be present, does not have to give up its pastness. (This is the other side of the fact that "pastness" and "presentness" – or presence – are not physical features of events.) And why, in order to be experienced as a series, the experiences of the relevant events do not have to be simultaneous in the basic physical sense of occurring at the same time t (e.g. t_2). The moments of perception are not identical with the mutually exclusive moments of clock-time, which is why we can experience change and succession with phenomenal immediacy. "Now" is not t_1 (12 noon or whatever), though now may be "at-t_1". To think that it is, is to read clock-time, a late derivative of perception, back into immediate experience. Of course, an experience of an event will, if it is non-illusory, be temporally connected with that event and have a temporal duration corresponding to the part of the event that is experienced. But the temporal connection is not to be confused with identical clock-time, or the physical processes we use to "tell" the clock-time.

The error of conflating the temporal properties of the objects of experiences with the temporal properties of the experiences themselves is compounded if the contents of experiences are assumed to be identical with (rather than about) items in the physical world, with the properties described by physics. It is equivalent to thinking that the experience of blue is not only itself blue but that it has a certain spectral frequency. Such thinking is not merely a confusion between a vehicle and a content or between a representation and that which it represents – like expecting the word "red" to be red – as the representationalist theorists of perception would claim. It goes deeper than that.[94]

We have not so much offered an explanation of how a succession of experiences gives rise to an experience of succession as reconnected the question with the fundamental nature of consciousness. The diachronic unity in virtue of which events that occur at different times are brought together as co-present in consciousness without losing either their individual identity or their temporal separation is a manifestation of a more general characteristic of conscious experience: the unity-and-multiplicity of both the moment of consciousness and of consciousness over time. It is a ubiquitous characteristic and one that is not amenable to any explanation that draws on the properties of the physical world as seen through the eyes of physics.

The phenomenon of diachronic unity has taxed the wits of so many philosophers because it is assumed that the basic form of time is the physical time in which t_1 is not even sufficiently outside of itself to be "at t_1". There is then an attempt to find physical time in the operation of immediate time consciousness; to construct basic temporal experiences such as that of succession out of elements that belong to a world of events occurring "at-t_1" and are confined to it. The lack of spatio-temporal identity of its components in virtue of which they would themselves be "at" – and hence confined to – a point in space–time, sealed off from other components, is a universal feature of consciousness which is "about" that which is other than itself. The diachronic unity of distinct components of consciousness in the sensory field, extends beyond this to a conscious field or conscious moment that encompasses memories, emotions, and thoughts as well as sense experiences.

The weirdness of the entangled quantum world is normal for every-day, indeed every-moment, consciousness. The fact that experiences corresponding to successive events, that are therefore not simultaneous, are experienced together in consciousness without losing their separateness is no stranger than the fact that I can experience an array of sights and sounds and have a succession of thoughts all at once without them being confused. Experience is primordially joined up, with the joined items also retaining their distinct identity.

We progressively depart from this kind of unity when we move from immediate time consciousness and perception of change to indirect perception of change and to mediated, and ultimately objective, time consciousness. The difference is signalled at the most basic level in the gap between seeing a change – as when I watch a car moving along a road – and seeing *that* a change has occurred – as when I see a car at one place and then, looking up after an interval, see it in another place and only infer that it has occupied all the intervening positions.[95] Seeing *that* change has occurred in the absence of seeing (the process of) change accounts for most observation of change – not just very gradual ones such as a tree growing from a sapling to a mighty oak or a child maturing into an adult but relatively quick ones such as the passage of the sun across the sky and the evolution of the morning into afternoon. The difference is between perception and knowledge and the latter does not share any of the dynamism seen in directly perceived change. Of course, factual knowledge "that" does not have qualitative contents, just as it does not have a colour or a location.

Do seeing change occurring and seeing that change has occurred belong to the same building as ground floor and upper storeys? We can envisage bridges between the immediate perception-based time sense and knowledge-based time sense, as discussed in §7.2. The visual field may deliver time cues that are rooted in, but not constrained by, direct perception. A car that goes out of sight temporally may invite us to interpolate its intermediate positions so that an audit trail of succession is maintained, particularly if we can hear its progress. Indeed, the maintenance of continuity through one sense while there is an interruption in another, points to the beginning of a disconnection between (directly) seeing change and seeing *that* change has taken place, between perception of succession and knowledge of succession. This is elaborated and extended by all the modes of joint attention sustained by groups of humans – so that that which is out of sight may be maintained in mind. The visual field, which reveals that which is visibly hidden (under a stone, behind a tree, beyond the horizon), prepares us for the sense within us of that which exceeds experience but can be revealed indirectly by intelligence (from calls or gestures such as pointing) from others.

These bridges, however, seem to fall short of giving an adequate account of the process by which our sense of the temporal order of events is extended from successive experiences that are close enough to be directly connected to the allocation of events to a lattice of temporal locations, in which are connected:

(a) my lunch and my tea;
(b) my walk in the park yesterday and sitting at my desk today;

(c) a piece of litter being picked up the other day and a child going off to sleep "at last" this evening;

(d) the scheduled take off time of a plane and its time of arrival;

(e) a shooting in Alabama and a newspaper reader reading about it;

(f) a child's dreams of success and his adult career;

(g) the battles of Hastings, Agincourt and Waterloo;

(h) the birth of the solar system and the origin of the earth.

In short, direct perception delivers very little of the many strands of successions of events that we are aware of in ordinary life. And most items that are located in closely adjacent, as well as in widely separated, places in the temporal lattice are not experienced as parts of a succession. Indeed, it is impossible to experience most of the stretches of time we know of: they are beyond the capacity of our time sense. We cannot take in an hour in a single temporal glance. By the time evening has arrived, the morning has become a dappling of directly remembered experiences upheld by a lattice of facts attached, to different degrees, to the collectively sustained scaffolding of clock-times. The injunction to "live one day at a time" is more than a little ambitious. One whole hour at a time would be something of an achievement.

There is a particularly difficult challenge if we believe that time sense is entirely rooted in the individual perception of the sequence of events – even if we could see how a succession of feelings became a feeling of succession. It is this: seeing how time transcends these disorganized origins – a thread here, a thread there, a tangle of threads elsewhere. We need a loom on which the threads can be woven into the temporal fabric of our lives. The answer is, of course, that creating and maintaining the temporal lattice is not the work of a single consciousness, even less the direct awareness of that single consciousness. For the most part it is deposited in documents, objects, time-tabled behaviour and so on. We are immersed in public time. The sequence of notes is part of a symphony, to be enacted at an appointed time. Children are introduced to clock-time roughly in parallel with their direct sense of the temporal order of things. They learn to "tell the time" very early in their cognitive development: "at-t$_1$" unfolds in a multiplicity of formal and informal ways. Fragments of the lattice of clock-time, in short, encroach early on the infant, toddler, or pre-school sensorium. The nested frames of everyday, calendrical, political, historical, geological and other modes of time cast their confusing shadows on the consciousness of the growing child. This would be the subject of a rich seam of inquiry – for another time.

We may have thought we were making things easier for ourselves by choosing a simple, and artificially isolated, example – "do-re-mi" – that enables us to think of a distinct sequence of events mirrored in a distinct sequence of perceptions. But such an example is not true to our daily experience of time. Conscious experience is never confined to a single modality and it is not presented as individual atoms or threads of experience. Perceptions are inextricably parts of a field – a field not only of the particular modality to which they belong, but of the multi-modal consciousness that is experienced at any given moment, and which is permeated by memory, meaning, intelligibility, and purpose.

We began this section by examining the notion that "time is our perception of the sequence of events". This now seems vulnerable at many levels but it is worth reminding ourselves how this idea may have seemed attractive. It is motivated by the intuition that, while change (in the material world) is a *necessary* condition of there being time (given all the problems with temporal vacua), it is not a *sufficient* condition of it. For change to deliver time as something distinct and ultimately measurable it has to be perceived; more precisely the beginning and end of change have to be brought together by being co-perceived. It is not enough that Object O should be in State 1 and then State 2: the two states must be brought together so that the *transition* between them can be experienced, that is to say, brought into existence. It is the transition, not State 1 or State 2 of O, that is the change. Likewise – to move closer to the "do-re-mi" example – it is not sufficient that there should be a succession of events, E_1 followed by E_2, they must be brought together, to be co-present while at the same time being temporally distinct.

But as we dig deeper into the motivation for the idea of time being "our perception of the succession of events", we can see its insufficiency more clearly. The events that are perceived have not only to be perceived as set out in time but they have to *be* set out in time to justify their being perceived in this way; for "succession", of course, means *temporal* succession – and this is as true of successive perceptions as of successive perceived events. Without time already being inherent in the universe, events – and our perceptions of them – would not only fail to take their place in a temporal series but would not have duration, be separated by intervals, or be temporally related to events that do not belong to the series. "Do" must precede "re" and they both have to precede "mi" to justify the perceived order "do-re-mi".

There is a perhaps less radical, and hence less vulnerable, version of the theory that roots time in perception; namely that *the impression of the passage of time* is our perception of the succession of events. The temporally related events that constitute the succession are not in themselves united into a flow that is translated into a flow of the time that connects them. This may be closer to one sort of truth about time: that what the perception of the succession of events delivers is the beginning of an explicit time sense, which is (as discussed in Chapter 1) most easily understood in the case of the visual sense where the past is preserved in the present perception of a prior position occupied by a moving object. While all experiences are in time, so that there cannot be a specific experience or modulation of experience associated with time, time itself may be more explicit in some experiences.

A point made forcibly by Le Poidevin is that the *order* of events does not of itself have causal powers to generate perceptions (of their order), unlike, he believes the events themselves.[96] There are many reasons for this claim. One is that a gap between events – necessary to their being perceived as distinct and hence ordered – cannot have causal powers. It is not, as it were, a property of events. Another reason is that we cannot expect to have "two for the price of one" from (say) the note "do" – first, as generating the perception of "do", and second, as contributing to generating the perception of a series of notes "do-re-mi". Thus the succession of events does not have an independent power to cause the experience of succession. Mellor argues that the sense of succession is generated by the combination of the perceptions of individual notes and the causal effects of the memories of predecessor notes.[97] So, "mi" is experienced as the third member of a succession of notes because the perception of it is altered by the causal impact of the memories of "do" and "re" on the experience of "me". There is an obvious, surface reason for not accepting this view: the interaction between "do" and its successors would muddy the perception of the latter. But there are other reasons that go very deep indeed.

The most fundamental reason is a rejection of the causal theory of perception, and of memory of perceptions. As we shall discuss neither perceptions nor memories are mere effects. The intentionality of perceptions and the double intentionality of memories makes them something quite different. In that difference, we shall find the origin of tensed time and freedom and the clue to our liberation from the notion of time as entirely part of the causally closed world of the physical scientist. There is nothing in a causal relationship that can assign the cause to a past, even less to the private past of one of its effects. A causal relationship that causes us to see a succession in which we see what is present, its past, and the present as the future of that past, co-existing in the present, is some causal relationship! To this we shall return in Chapter 11.[98]

A putative causal relationship between a directly perceived succession of events – even if it were a reality – would hardly take us to clock-time, calendrical time, physical time, and astronomical time. For, even if perception did generate "before" and "after", "past" and "present", and possibly *more* past ("do") compared with *less* past ("re"), the jump to the lattice time of (say) 12 December compared with 11 December is unexplained. The sense of temporal order arising from "do-re-mi" does not even give the visible time of the day such "noon", "evening" – which is why we need to consult the clock, though we may make a rough guess from visual or other perceptual cues. Clock and calendar time lie beyond direct perception, particularly when they are subsumed into larger temporal orders – "tomorrow", "next week", "1983", "2,000 BC" – or temporal durations such as "10 minutes", "six weeks hence", "a hundred years ago".

This is but one expression of the chasm between perception (that takes place in one individual) and knowledge (that belongs to a community of minds): that the latter, but not the former, can relate them to objective time markers, to objective time schemata and (ultimately) to quantitative time schemata that in principle encompass the entire universe. Without a clear view of the nature of this gap – and an uncritical indeed naïve, assumption that the lived world of time and change is built up out of simple elements such as do-re-mi – we won't be able to think clearly about the relationship between subjective and objective time, the theme of §10.5.

At any rate, the connection between immediate time sense, clock-time, and the temporal order of the material world opens on to the wider questions of the relationships between individual experiences and the human and physical world as the latter is construed by the community of human minds (including that small but important subset the community of scientific minds). Physical events are not self-clocking even to the limited extent of flagging up the t at which they take place. Without the help of a clock, an experience of an event that lasts (say) 10 minutes does not register as an experience of 10 minutes (as well as of the event). The gap between temporalized experiences, timed experience, and timed time cannot be closed within immediate experience. It is not a gap to be measured objectively. As Dainton emphases:

> If my clock goes TICK-TICK-TICK I will hear TICK-TICK-TICK, with the order and temporal separation of the outer events being mirrored – in a generally faithful manner – by the order and temporal separation of the experiences (or their contents) reflecting the order of the relevant events.[99]

Amen to that, with the caveat that "mirrored" should be replaced by "experienced" in order to avoid a misleading representationalist metaphor. It does not follow from this (again to quote Dainton – who disagrees with the idea) *"that time represents itself"*.[100] This is no more the case than that natural clocks (and nature, as we have seen, is a nexus of clocks – from the subatomic to the sidereal – to the anthropomorphically inclined) "tell the time", or come to that hear themselves tick and adjust their mechanism accordingly. The mistake perhaps, is to think that among the secondary qualities that constitute experiences and which are not found in insentient nature, there is a primary quality – temporal order and duration – common to the physical world and the realm of conscious experience. In short, that physical time enters the mind unaltered.

One final – and crucial – point. Thinking of time as "our perception of the succession of events" makes the experience of time something of a spectator sport. In fact, time consciousness is woven into our agency in many ways. In Chapter 6, we observed that the intelligibility built into our actions – their "ongoingness" – contributes to the widening of our moment-to-moment awareness beyond its moments and beyond any "specious present". Our opportunities and responsibilities as agents magnify the scope of our time sense from directly perceived sequences to the kinds of things we plan, communicate about, and narrate. The timing built into our actions – from structuring straightforward actions such as walking out of the house, to washing the dishes or preparing a meal, to orchestrating our days, weeks and lives – extends, underlines, and gives existential reality to, stretches of time that extend beyond anything we could directly infer from, even less experience through, immediately observed sequences of events.

It is not possible to think adequately about actions without relating what is enacted to the agent; more specifically to the embodied subject, the self, as agent. The succession of experiences of embodied subject is not a succession of externally related items because they belong to an embodied subject that is identical with itself and with which it identifies. The identification is not a discovery, not something over which (at least in the overwhelming majority of cases) one could be mistaken. I suffer and enjoy this body, it is my location, and it is the proximate agent of my agency: these are aspects of the fact that I *am* it. Consequently its (or my) succession of experiences is referred to the same material item, are thereby connected, and hence are experienced *as* a succession. But succession is not focal and local: what this body experiences is a world; local successions are set against the background of successive world states. What ties the world state together is the embodied self who has a world as a whole. We would not experience "do-re-mi" as a succession were it not for the fact that I *am* the experience of successive states of a world disclosed to my senses and the theatre of my actions.

This background – that I am the successive experiences of a world – is necessary for my sense of temporal depth as it applies to a succession of notes or the successive positions of an object. In the case of the latter, the constancy of myself as a body maintained through elective change of place is the primordial example of "objecthood" that can be generalized to objects "out there". And the fact that the entire world changes and remains the same as I move, with the complex ballet of readjustments of relations that takes place throughout the visual field, validate the scaling up to an entire world.

This is another aspect of something we shall discuss in Chapter 12: that tensed time is a *sine qua non* of deliberate action. It is that in virtue of which we can operate on the material world from a virtual outside. We may imagine a virtuous circle in which tensed time makes agency possible and the operation of agency further extends the depth of tensed time, so that we deal not merely in what has just happened or is just about to happen, but in the remembered contents of days and weeks "ago" and the anticipated or planned contents of days and weeks "ahead".

10.4.4 The denial of change

In §10.4.2, we investigated whether or not it was possible to imagine time (flowing or not) in the absence of change. In the foregoing section, we have examined the claim that time, or our time sense (an important ambiguity to which we shall return), arises out of our perception of change – most explicitly in the form of a succession of discrete events. In the present section, we shall look at the origin of the belief that perhaps change itself is an illusion; that the events we perceive – that give time its ticks and tocks and are possibly the very substrate of time – are coinages of our minds.

A potent contemporary source of this belief is relativity theory and a classic statement of the denial of change is due to Hermann Weyl: "The objective world simply *is*, it does not *happen*. Only to the gaze of my consciousness, crawling upward along the lifeline of my body, does a section of this world come to life as a fleeting image in space which continually changes in time."[101] There is no "absolute" becoming, just as there are no absolute locations in space and time, or in space–time. Becoming is an illusion, the product of successive phases of the stream of consciousness. The philosopher David Gamez has suggested the origin of this illusion: "What we interpret [and presumably experience] as changes in [a] three-dimensional apple are, in fact, different perspectives on an unchanging four-dimensional apple."[102] This view is consistent with a conception of the space–time continuum as frozen. If there is no global "now", where it is all happening and "about to happen" passes into "having happened", then becoming seems to be ruled out.

Gamez's take on the apple makes clear that the shocking idea that nothing changes may not be as shocking as at first appears. In §3.5.3.1, we noted that folding the sum of its history into an object, by seeing it as four-dimensional entity, delivers the unstartling conclusion that the totality of what happens to an object cannot be further added to. And the same unstartling conclusion applies if the object in question is the entire universe. This casts a side-light on another source of the idea that change is unreal: the conflation of change, becoming, and time. All change is the emergence of one state from another. This can be made to seem impossible in two ways: (a) the Parmenidean route (*vide infra*) that becoming covers a transition from its private not-yet (or nothing) to something that is the case; and (b) the argument that becoming implies temporal becoming which, since time itself cannot change (there is nothing – and certainly no time – for it to change in), is not possible.

We can dismiss the second argument by pointing out that it is not necessary for time itself to change – to be on the move – for change to be possible. To think that it is necessary is to confuse the becoming of events with something corresponding to the becoming of time itself. What of the first argument? The idea of reality as an unchanging total touches on something that is valid: that the physicists' view of reality, in which time is a quasi-spatial dimension, has great difficulty accommodating change. Not only does it squeeze out tenses but, for some thinkers, it is obliged to squeeze out change – so that the frozen space–time continuum is a just image of reality. Change on this view is, as Weyl argues, a fiction dreamed up in the mind. Why it should be dreamed up in the mind and the assumption (evident also in the rejection of tense as unreal) embedded that that which is mind-dependent is unreal – is something we shall address presently.

The claim that becoming – and, equally, "begoing" – are unreal has a long history. It goes back to the very beginning of Greek philosophy – indeed to the greatest of the series of extraordinary beginnings grouped under the heading of "Presocratic philosophy": the brief poem by Parmenides called *On Nature*.[103] In this poem, Parmenides argued that change is unreal as follows. What-is is and what-is-not is not. Becoming requires what-is to come into being out of what-is-not; and begoing requires what-is to pass into what-is-not. But what-is-not is nothing at all; it therefore cannot be a womb for what-is, allowing it to come into being; nor can it be a tomb for what-is so that it can pass out of being. Our impression that there is change is therefore an illusion because it is self-contradictory. Movement, too, is unreal because moving objects require empty space to move into. But empty space cannot separate objects since empty space is nothing and objects separated by nothing must be contiguous, allowing no room for manoeuvre. Time is not real not only because it is inseparable from change but also because the past (not-any-longer) and the future (not-yet) are realms of what-is-not and what-is-not is not.

We could re-cast Parmenides' argument as follows. You can't speak of an event E coming into being (starting) or passing out of being (ending) because this would imply that it had three successive states: not-being-but-about-to-be; being; and not-being-but-having-been. Put in this way, it suggests that E in addition to its distinct existence while it is happening, has a private, ontological *en suite* within the realm of non-being – that from which it emerges into being – and a second *en suite* to which it returns when it has come to an end. This is evident nonsense as we discussed in

§8.2.2.2, when the idea of events as tense tourists implied that they both preceded and outlived their time of occurrence. As we shall see, however, it is the way their emergence and passing away is expressed that is nonsense rather than the idea that things/processes/events "become" and "be-go".

There are many problems with Parmenides' argument but the one that is most relevant here is that it merges existential and predicative senses of "is" (and "is-not"). There is a difference between that which comes to pass out of nothing (the most absolute form of becoming) which does indeed seem unoccasioned as Parmenides suggested and that which changes into something different, where the prior state of the substrate of change and the laws of change provide respectively the substrate and the guide of becoming. Absolute becoming looks like inexplicable emergence of being out of nothing, while ordinary becoming is merely the assumption of new predicates by beings.

This notwithstanding, the Parmenidean tendency to believe that what is real is something unchanging has hugely influenced Western science, though it has been expressed in many different ways. The most obvious is the rooting of the scientific account of reality in a physics founded on the notion of something that is conserved; for example, matter, atoms, momentum, or mass-energy. Notwithstanding the infinitely varied, endlessly changing world of our immediate experiences, reality boils down to something which is unchanged.

For much of the history of physics, matter was indestructible. Beneath the chemical reactions that produced our impression of an infinitely varied, changing world, was matter which was conserved. The equation that connected the before and after of a chemical reaction, such as $2H_2 + O_2 \rightarrow 2H_2O$, could be just as well expressed as $2H_2 + O_2 = 2H_2O$. The before and after were equal, in the sense that there was only a rearrangement of atoms and not a creation or destruction of them. When it was appreciated that matter could be turned into energy – captured in the most famous of all physical equations, $E = mc^2$ – the distinct laws of the conservation of matter and of the conservation of energy were replaced by the law of the conservation of mass-energy. Physics was poised on three fundamental conservation laws: energy, momentum, and angular momentum; or more fundamentally still a conservation of symmetry.

This principle of conservation extended to the laws of nature themselves. While Einstein's name is associated above all with the word "relativity", he should really be associated with the notion of "general covariance", describing what is necessary to conserve the laws of nature across all frames of reference; or to ensure that all inertial frames of reference are equivalent for the formulation of those laws. Yes, the temporal and spatial relationships between events could be defined by the inertial frame of reference from which they are observed, so there are no observer-independent "facts of the case" as to the nature of those relations. The "now" at which something happens is not global – and could indeed be as small as a single other reference event – and so the becoming of an event "at time t" is a local affair without a universal agreement as to the fact that it has occurred. "Happening" is a local matter, for all that "*the fact that* E occurred" does not seem to have spatio-temporal boundaries.

But this was only a first step. The aim was to find a description of space, time, motion, and gravity, which would ensure that the laws of nature were conserved across all inertial frames of reference, and that would preserve three invariants:

(a) the speed of light would be the same whatever the frame of reference from which it was measured;[104]
(b) the relationship of cause and effect between two events – a cause C and an effect E could not be reversed such that the thunder might cause the lightning; and
(c) space–time coincidence – so that two events that occur at the same point in space–time – would be preserved whatever the viewpoint of the observer. If two events were simultaneous *and* happened at the same place, they would be simultaneous with respect to every non-accelerating frame of reference.

These were aspects of his quest to find a way of describing the world in such a way as to ensure that the fundamental laws of physics were the same for all observers, by setting aside frames of reference; or by describing how they would alter the expression of the laws in observations while the laws themselves would be unchanged, and would form an immutable framework. The idea of space–time as a backdrop independent of observed phenomena is replaced by that of the unchanging framework of laws of nature. So the observer is transcended and observer-independence is restored to the laws of physics. General covariance seems to be an expression of the unchanging nature of reality. Or, to put it slightly differently, that which changes is not real in the sense of being fundamental. Thus there is "no privileged sense of motion, a sense in which things can be said to move or not, not just relative to this or that reference body, but 'truly'".[105] And motion (at the microscopic as well as the macroscopic level) is the basic change – or the basis of all change.

The relativistic bus could take us to a frozen universe by a different path. The true nature of events is that which is revealed to a view from nowhere. From this view, they would have only mathematical properties in turn defined in relation to a frame of reference, itself defined by other events. Changes would thus prove to be sets of eternal, unchanging mathematical relationships.[106] This is reflected in the slither between "events" and space–time points even though the latter, being dimensionless, lack substance and it is difficult to know what sense could be given to the idea that they occur, even less to any kind of "at" at which they occurred. At any rate, absolute universal stasis results when the mathematization of nature is completed by reducing events to space–time points, defined numerically with respect to coordinates, which cannot *occur* in time or be in space.

One doesn't of course have to go so far as to translate events into space–time points for change to be lost. If there is no definite time at which event E happens and is completed, there is no time at which we can say that it has happened or it is complete. The distinction between its being or not being does not lie within the event itself, any more than the distinction between its being present, or past, or (and this is dodgy of course) in the future. Everything has already happened, is happening, and has not yet happened, given that there is no privileged foliation of the space–time manifold at which the future becomes the past.

In view of this tendency of physics towards the notion that nothing fundamental changes, Weyl's claim that change is mind-dependent is unsurprising.[107] A relatively conservative interpretation of this mind-dependency is that consciousness is required to synthesize – bring together – successive phases of a process, as discussed in the previous section. And in this sense, the universe imagined in the absence of a conscious observer tends to freeze to a halt; to be a series of instants in which no change is possible. Everything is what-it-is and no more; it is not in addition that which it will be or was. There is no way of reaching out of the present (a present which itself is not "present" in the temporal sense of being "now" that we discussed in Chapter 6) to a future of about-to-be or a past of has-been. This is equally true of the universe viewed by the kind of observers that populate the textbooks of physics, who (or rather "which") are – as discussed in §3.5.3 – in effect virtual occupants of virtual viewpoints, ultimately reducible to pure mathematical points. The true observer, so far as physics is concerned, is someone for whom the world is a space–time continuum; but that someone would have to occupy a viewpoint that cannot be occupied because (a) it is a viewpoint on the whole – a view from nowhere in particular; and (b) it is a viewpoint that is additional to the whole which is a contradiction in terms. No wonder happening grinds to a halt. We need local observers and their localities to import change into the universe, as Weyl claimed. This viewless, mindless viewpoint would not only be a Nagelian "view from nowhere", but also "a view of everything", and hence "nothing in particular – in no particular time, place or state", and hence "a view of nothing". It would not only be inhospitable to tensed time but also to the tenseless time of "before" and "after", which is just as mind-dependent as "past", "present" and "future", as we discussed in Chapter 5. For no physical event is in itself "earlier than" or "later than" because these relations do not belong to the events themselves. An event may have a place in a time series but it does not have that place inherently or monadically. The place of event E_{575} – for example, "before E_{576}" and "after E_{574}" – is *conferred* just as are "before E_{2003}" and "after E_{22}". "Earlier" and "later" are relative terms – which is why a given event can be *both* "earlier" and "later"– and require observation and articulation to become determinate.[108]

The claim that whether or not E has occurred is entirely frame-dependent can be extended from events to beings. While space–time points are eternal, the items that occupy them are not. It is symmetry, not matter or energy, that is conserved through change. This can seem to lead to the scandalous conclusion that, since the time at which a being comes into being is frame-dependent, existence is relativized to frames. As Gödel said, "The concept of existence…cannot be relativized without destroying its meaning completely".[109] After all, the difference between a (stable) object capable of carrying changing predicates and the events that constitute those changes in predicates will also be frame-dependent: nothing is long-lasting or transient. Given that frames do not arise spontaneously in the physical world but are viewpoint-, and hence mind-, dependent, we are close to idealism, as Gödel pointed out.

It is worth looking a little more closely at the arguments against becoming or change as they are expressed by Weyl and Gamez in this light and examine the nature of the "mind" in question. Weyl, it will be recalled, spoke of "crawling upward along the lifeline of my body" as a result of which a section of the world would "come to life" as a "fleeting image". This is surely the language of the becoming and happening that is supposed to have been relativized out of monadic existence. Gamez ascribed our sense of changes in objects as being due to "different perspectives on an unchanging" object – presumably *changing* perspectives. How could successive perpectives be adopted in a frozen world? It is very odd to deny "real" changes in objects such as apples but allow real changes in perspectives (on objects). The inconsistency is hidden because we do not think of a perspective as a thing or a change in a perspective as an event. Unless, however, we think of perspectives as involving some kinds of events, and dependent on other events, it is difficult to see what they might be. Perspectives, or viewpoints, without embodied subjects are purely mathematical; that is to say neither viewpoints nor perspectives.

The questions have particular force when we consider the way mind is conceived in the world picture predominant among physicists and, indeed, many philosophers. According to the prevailing physicalism the mind is identical with physical activity in the brain. If there is no becoming in the material world, of which the brain is a part, why should there be becoming in the mind? What, moreover, is there in successive (material) brain states that enables them to synthesize themselves into states of succession, into a registration of becoming?

The standard explanation is as follows. $State_1$ stimulates a set of neurons N_1 at time t_1 shortly after it occurs and $State_2$ stimulates N_1 at time t_2 shortly after it occurs. The output from N_1 feeds into another set of neurons N_2 which registers the successive responses of N_1. But how would N_2 do this? If it simply added the outputs from N_1 the temporal separation of, and distinction between, the states would be lost in the addition sum, as the components of the sum would be present at the same time. If it did not add them up, they would be as separate in N_2 as they were in N_1. We are back with the problem discussed in the previous section of turning a succession of experiences into a (unified) succession, while keeping the members of the succession distinct. There is, it appears, no way of registering the temporal succession of the events in terms of brain activity – essentially because this requires that the two events should be fused and, at the same time, retain their distinct identity. They would have to be both separate ($State_1$ temporally separate and qualitatively distinct from $State_2$) and together as a related pair ($State_1$ related to $State_2$). The neural registration of happening, becoming, or of successive states would seem to be impossible.

Maintaining separateness and connectedness simultaneously – an insuperable problem for physicalist accounts of the mind – is a characteristic of every moment of consciousness, as when I look around me and see a world populated by more than one item.[110] This makes it even more surprising that the failure to develop a neural model of the experience of becoming is brushed off by some philosophers. Grünbaum, for example, has stated that he "cannot see why the states of awareness that make for becoming must have physical event counterparts that isomorphically become in their own right".[111] In other words, he cannot see why awareness of becoming must be underpinned by physical events that themselves are characterised by becoming – and in particular a becoming that broadcasts their dynamism through the co-presence of their phases. The fact that there does not appear to be anything corresponding to becoming in the piece of the material world that is the brain would not, he claims, stop the brain from registering becoming or, more precisely, for it from being that in virtue of which we have the impression of a world of becoming.

Far from solving the problem, this explanation, and the underlying assumption of an identity between the mind and the brain, simply highlights it. Whence the origin of the impression of a world of becoming in a universe that has no such property, of change in a universe that does not change? As Gale asks in his discussion of Grünbaum: "How can temporal becoming be intrinsic to mental events and not to the physical events (such as events in the brain) with which these mental events are correlated and upon which they are, for a naturalist, causally dependent?"[112] The neural explanation of experience of becoming presupposes real becoming in the brain such that the brain has successive, different states, that would register successive, different states in the world and (by some mysterious alchemy) register their succession. If becoming is not inherent in the material world at large, how could the interaction between the brain and the other bits of the material world give the impression of becoming? And why would it do so, anyway? Surely is it no part of the job description of an evolved organ like the brain to generate a globally erroneous image of the material world. More specific to the relativity argument, given that becoming is frame-dependent, how does the brain create that frame? As a set of material events, it looks more like an untended recording device (awaiting someone to read it) than a conscious observer. Or, (implausibly) does the neural activity in the brain become furnished with its own frame of reference to make sure that there is a "now" at which it can occur?

Grünbaum, in common with some others, argues that the idea of becoming is anthropocentric, even subjective. This hardly addresses the questions we have just asked. And, besides, if becoming were man-made, how did science, which has come from man, given us reason to deny the reality of becoming? How did we escape being centred on ourselves? We transcend ourselves individually in virtue of the collective; but how does the collective transcend itself to the point where it can arrive at such a global conclusion as that becoming is unreal? And what, by the way, is "mind" (as in "mind-dependent") such that it: (a) not only represents the physical world (according to the view that physical science gives us the strongest handle on reality); but also (b) *mis*represents it; and (c) creates the means (through science) to correct that misrepresentation?

Besides, there is nothing anthropocentric about the statements of change such as "The cat has walked next door" or "$F = ma$", even though the symbolic systems may be man-made. We should reserve the notion of "anthropocentricity" for our tendency to locate ourselves at the centre or top of things: the earth at the centre of the universe, our welfare as God's main concern; the notion that our meanings colonize the totality of what is; the suggestion that we are the summit of the Great Chain of Being. The idea that the universe is subject to change is hardly comparable to that kind of local or specific delusion. If our viewpoint were truly anthropocentric – to the point where it imprisoned us in an actually misleading image of the universe as riddled with becoming – how would we ever form the notion of "anthropocentricity" and criticize our collective viewpoint as "anthropocentric"? After all, chimpanzees do not rise above their own viewpoint to see that it is "chimpocentric".

If the notion of becoming *is* mind-dependent, is it dependent on the same mind as that which arrives at the conclusion that it is mind-dependent? How does one bit of the mind rise above the rest? It is possible to see how the community of minds might take individual minds – or individual sentient consciousnesses – to places where they would not otherwise go. It is not easy, however, to see how the community of minds – which is the receptacle of all higher order statements – could rise above itself to see (correctly or incorrectly) that it is "anthropocentric". It is, of course, a feature of mind in everyday life to observe that it has got some things wrong: to observe that it has drawn incorrect conclusions from observations. But this can hardly be globalized to the point where we discover that a universal feature of our experience – that there are happenings – proves to be wrong.

We can validly extrapolate local errors to the global *possibility* of error but not to the possibility of global error. There are several reasons for saying this: firstly, global error does not allow the contrast between getting things wrong and getting things right; secondly, it is difficult to know how we could wake out of global error, except into more of the same; and thirdly what makes us feel that we are able to articulate the error as it were from the outside? If language is that outside, then it is presumably *not* part of the world of becoming which seems strange given that all its manifestations (actual speech acts, moments of reading what has been written, etc.) are happenings.

Grünbaum's argument that, because physical science does without becoming, becoming is unreal, goes beyond the legitimate bounds of what science can tell us. Science cannot legislate over what is true or real at the level at which the very possibility of science is determined. The assumption that change is mind-dependent is a strange one for a physicalist for whom, presumably, the mind is brain activity – physical activity in this physical object. And what is more, it is one that is self-refuting. For the impression of becoming must be based upon experiences – and for a physicalist neural events – that come and go. Even if those experiences were indeed misleading, the fact that they exist proves that becoming is manifested somewhere in the universe. Becoming can no more be an illusion than consciousness can be an illusion.[113]

So we may conclude that the case for the unreality of happenings, of change, of becoming, is not made. The passage from this conclusion to understanding the relationship between change, perception and time, and between immediate time sense and physical time (in the double sense of time as it is measured in physics and time in the physical world), however, remains difficult and it has many diverticula. It is this that will form the substance of the next section.

10.5 OBJECTIVE AND SUBJECTIVE TIME

The writing of this book, as is the case with any long-term project, has been sustained by a variety of intentions, impulses, emotions, and goals. The most fundamental and constant motivation for writing *Of Time and Lamentation* has been a wish to address the sense of helplessness before what it seems impossible to resist calling "the passage of time". I began the book (at least in its final form) in my early sixties and I am now beyond my seventieth birthday and this feeling of helplessness is, if anything, stronger and more continuous. Marilynne Robinson's aphorism "Time is not on our side. Every minute more of it means one minute less of us"[114] is a bull's eye. It exposes the illusory nature of the hope that has motivated this book: that there may be a way of thinking about time that does not make our transience inevitable; and that counters the fact that our few decades of life are a minute part of a time span that out-spans us hundreds of millions of times over. Or more particularly, that we won't have to look forward to limitless time (beginning in my case in 20**), when the world will continue without us. One place to seek justification for this hope is in the relationship between "our" time and time itself, and to find a way of thinking about this relationship that will not see the former as a mist drop compared with the Atlantic Ocean.

The topic that I have labelled "Objective and Subjective Time" is really a tangle of topics. The tangle includes questions about the relationship between our immediate sense or (more often recollection) of the passage of time and what is reported on the clock. But these are rooted in deeper questions than the relative authority of (say) subjective assessment of the duration of, intervals between, and temporal order of events or experiences and objective measurements of them.

The gap between direct time experience (phenomenal time) and physical time (measured by clocks) raises several issues:

(a) The sense in which clocked time is purely an advance towards the reality of time compared with guessed-at duration.
(b) The extent to which clocks (and other devices for measuring time such as carbon dating) lose aspects of time, so that clocks are at a distance from time. This is the opposite of (a).
(c) The relative priority of lived and measured time: does the former grow out of the latter or the latter out of the former?

Thus the cloudiness at the heart of the question of the relative status of, and relationship between, subjective and objective time.

This can be illustrated by two stories of what we might call the genesis of the time sense:

(a) The first story begins with a mindless, material universe in which first life, and then sentient creatures, and then creatures with complex consciousnesses such as our own, emerge. Time is a fundamental feature of this universe, going back to its beginning. Time exists before any creature is aware of it, and certainly before anyone measures it. Though this story is dependent on clocks to be uncovered, time is not just what clocks measure because it is present in the universe prior to the (very recent) development of clocks. Let us call this "the priority of physical time" view.

(b) The second story begins with creatures like us that have an explicit sense of the succession of events and it argues that time is not fully itself until it has been measured by clocks with an arbitrarily determined level of sophistication. The temporal order of events that occur prior to the emergence of conscious creatures is only retrospectively assigned to them. Let us call this "the priority of lived time" view. "Experienced" here encompasses the sense of the duration and order of events and the existential experiences of urgency, patience, waiting, hurry, and boredom.

The central argument of Parts I and II of this book have constituted affirmative action for lived time over physical time reduced in the natural sciences (and the metaphysics uncritically based on them) to clock-time. Clocks sits rather awkwardly between a putative physical time and lived time. Clocks are not intrinsic parts of nature – as humans are required to create and consult devices that convert periodic events into measures of time – but the quantities and locations they deliver do not capture human time.

10.5.1 The priority of physical time

This seems the easier view to defend. The claim that time is mind-dependent does not stand up to the seemingly robust knowledge we have of the temporal order of things, according to which mind is a late entry in the universe. A temporal order of astronomical events was in place before geological time; and a temporal order of geological events was in place before historical or human time. The major philosophical resistance to this view over the last 200 or so years has been what Quentin Meillassoux has called "Kantian correlationism", which he characterizes as follows:

> By "correlation" we mean the idea according to which we only ever have access to the correlation between thinking and being and never to either term considered apart from the other. We will henceforth call correlationism any current of thought which maintains the unsurpassable character of the correlation so defined.[115]

The thinking subject and the "material" object are inseparable; each exists only as the correlate of the other. There is therefore no mind-independent reality-in-itself to which we can gain access; there is no world outside of our thinking of it. Or rather, all talk of the world outside of the correlation is itself immediately recuperated by the correlation.

How does this play out in relation to time? Kant argues that the notion of time as a property of a mind-independent physical world is fundamentally wrong. While time is presupposed in all human experience, this is not because it is inherent in a mind-independent material universe. Rather it is because it is one of the *a priori* "forms of sensible intuition" (the other being space) that structure the deliverance of the senses and make possible the experience of unified objects in a coherent world. Here is not the place to set out, or to evaluate, his case. I want instead to consider a particular argument anchored on the question of whether the world did or did not have a beginning in time. As we discussed in §10.3.4, the two possible answers to this question − "yes" and "no" − seem equally unsatisfactory. From this, Kant concludes that it is mistaken to think of time as a property of the physical world in itself. "Time is real with respect to all objects which could ever be given to our senses" but "Once we abstract from the subjective conditions of perception it is nothing at all and cannot be attributed to things in themselves". Neither space nor time exists in a mind-free world. Time (and space) are the forms of perception, the forms of the organization of my sensibility. Time is "the form of inner sense" and space "the form of outer sense", that in virtue of which objects appear as "outside" of, and hence independent of, me. While it is real "with respect to all objects that could ever be given to our senses", it is transcendentally ideal: "Once we abstract from the subjective conditions of perception it is nothing at all and cannot be attributed to things in themselves."[116]

Meillassoux argues that Kantian correlationism leads to conclusions that most rational individuals would reject. If there is no time in the mind-free world, what are we to think of the increasingly strong scientific evidence of events taking place, and what is more taking place in a certain temporal order, prior to the emergence of minds? Most of us accept that there was life on earth before there was mental life on earth; that the earth existed for billions of years before life on earth; that the solar system came into being before the earth was formed; and that there was a sequence of events prior to the solar system being formed which can be traced back to a putative Big Bang. It is not only an empirical fact that these events − which Meillassoux calls "ancestrals" − occurred in, and occupied, time; but it is (to make a point that Meillassoux did not make) a *logical* necessity that they should occur in a certain order. The solar system cannot form before the Big Bang created something from which it could be formed; the earth could not arise out of a solar system that had not yet come into being; life could not arise on earth before conditions such as those of temperature and hydration enabled certain molecules to arise and then develop into organisms; the emergence of sentient life presupposed the prior existence of life; and finally mind of the kind that could house (Kantian) forms of perception could not arise except out of sentient organisms. To deny the mind-independent reality of this temporal order would be to reject science and any basis for differentiating between the biblical and the astrophysical stories of the evolving universe, or between Darwinism and the "Young Earth Evolution", which claims that the universe is only a few thousand years old. All claims would be equally valid − or invalid.[117]

If the reality of ancestrals is accepted, then we should reject correlationism and accept that there are events, and a temporal order, location, and duration of events, that are independent of mind. Meillassoux is careful to distinguish ancestrals – which are unwitnessable because the sentient beings necessary to witness them have not evolved – from items that are merely unwitnessed. One can be a correlationist and still acknowledge that there are events and properties that lie outside of current experience. When I look at a material object – including my own body – I know that it has an inside that I cannot see or a back view that is currently concealed from me. And at any time, there are events nobody is witness to. Meillassoux's point is more radical. He is not talking about things that may be out of sight and consequently out of mind but things that are out of the possibility of being in mind: "the ancestral does not designate an absence *in* the given, and *for* givenness, but rather an absence *of* givenness as such ...".[118] The very possibility of the givenness of the "given" – or of Being as "the given" – appears to have had a time of origin. The existence of ancestrals prior to minds raises the question of the origin of minds in a mindless world:

> the problem of the arche-fossil [materials indicating the existence of an ancestral reality or event ... anterior to terrestrial life] is not the empirical problem of the birth of living organisms, but the ontological problem of the coming into being of givenness as such.[119]

Since there must have been events – in a temporal order – prior to the emergence of human or indeed any sentient life and that, furthermore, the emergence of life seems to have been the result of a vast number of temporally orchestrated processes, the conclusion that physical time has priority over lived time, never mind human time, seems inescapable. In short, the empirical reality of time is not its transcendental ideality – its being one of the *a priori* forms of sensible intuition – because it is real independentally of our empirical experience. The daunting idea that each of us is a brief episode in a reality of which we are a minute part seems to be upheld.

10.5.2 The priority of lived time

> [H]uman life does not happen in time but rather is time itself.
> Heidegger, *Being and Time*, 499, note iv

Let us look more critically at the assumption that there is a temporal order inherent in events prior to the emergence of human or any consciousness. Consider the claim that the earth came into being before there was life on that planet. Let us call the event of the formation of the earth E_1 and the emergence of life E_2 (clearly, it would be a countless series of events but let us simplify for the present). We are inclined to say that there is a temporal relationship between the two events: E_1 "occurred before" E_2, E_1 "was earlier than" E_2, E_1 "preceded" E_2, by such-and-such an interval. That is objectively true; but it is only a retrospective objective truth. Prior to the emergence of an advanced form of life (in fact very recent generations of *H. sapiens*) the relationship as such did not exist. It is obvious that it is not an intrinsic characteristic of E_1 to be "before E$_2$". After all, the emergence of life was not guaranteed after the formation of the earth. Things might have turned out differently. There is no intrinsic "before-the-formation-of-the-earth" – even less "before-the-birth-of-Raymond-Tallis" – in the Big Bang. It is less obvious, but no less true, that it is not an intrinsic characteristic of E$_2$ to be "after E$_1$". There is nothing at the time at which E$_2$ occurs to make it relate it to E$_1$; if there were, there would be grounds for saying that it is at the same time related to innumerable other events – trillions of discernible events – between E$_1$ and E$_2$. For the two events to be connected in a "before" and "after" relationship, they must be picked out. In other words, while the actual temporal order of events does not depend on the consciousness of recent generations of *H. sapiens*, that there is a temporal order, in which the events are connected, does so depend.

As we pointed out in §5.3, "before" and "after" and "earlier" and "later" are as mind-dependent as "past", "future" and "*x* years ago" and "*y* years hence". This may have been what motivated Mellor to argue that the earlier–later relation holds "between facts rather than between events and times"[120] There are, as we have discussed, problems with this: facts such as "The Battle of Hastings was fought in 1066" do not happen at a time, have locations in time, or have a temporal order. They do, however, require articulation and hence minds: they are events and states of affairs transformed into *that* such-and-such is the case. There is no "that" in the pre-sentient, indeed pre-human, world.

We could go further and argue that, if time is linked to explicit change, and there is no explicit change without consciousness, then time is even more closely connected with consciousness. This, however, is to go too far and to run into the danger of suggesting that change exists only insofar as it is made explicit and that the difference between State$_1$ and State$_2$ of the universe is real only insofar as the two states are brought together in a conscious synthesis. It is, however, difficult to imagine time in the absence of phenomenal appearance. Or rather we *can* imagine it: it is the little t of mechanics that is a pure quantity with no internal features.

10.5.3 Reflections on the antinomy

We have to take account of two fundamental facts, which point in opposite directions regarding the relative priority of subjective and objective time:

(a) On the one hand, there must be an intrinsic temporal order in the universe which was established before conscious beings, before there were subjects. It is, after all, a logical necessity, as well as an empirical fact, that a non-living universe must have preceded the emergence of life, and the Big Bang preceded the emergence of the earth. This ordering presupposes that time is an objective reality not dependent on consciousness.

(b) On the other hand, events do not intrinsically have the relationship "before" and "after" unless they are brought into that relationship by a consciousness that registers both, picks them out, and then assigns them to their temporal order. This would suggest that time is consciousness-dependent. (This is an argument that withstands the fact of the asymmetry of influence between prior causes and posterior effects, as we shall discuss in §11.4). In other words, without mind, time is rather featureless. There is for example, no differentiation between the order of, the interval between, and the durations of events.

The discussion as to whether time is mind-dependent – being for example a transcentally ideal "form of sensibility" – will remain confused so long as we are unclear as to what we mean by mind. This lack of clarity is strikingly (and instructively) evident in both Kant and Heidegger and it is important that we highlight this before we revisit the question of the relative authority of subjective and objective assessments of time.

When Kant talks about mind, it is not always clear whether he is talking about a token mind (an individual consciousness such as yours and mine) or mind-in-general – the mental aspect of what there is, unassigned to individuals. Each is equally unsatisfactory. It is perfectly obvious that the spatial and temporal "spectacles" as popularisations describe the forms of sensible intuition are not perched on the nose of individuals. None of us individually can construct the phenomenal world by means of our own consciousness. This universe of stable material objects connected in a unified space and of events connected in a unified time is not the work of one individual. On the other hand, the spectacles are not as it were a free-floating stuff detached from any individual subject, otherwise the individual spatial and temporal perspectives from which we experience the world, the unique streams of consciousness and life-histories, that we each have, would be inexplicable.

There is an analogous problem with Heidegger's *Dasein* – or "being there".[121] He argued that consciousness was not "inside the body" like something in a cabinet. It was out there: it did not reach out to the world; rather it was being-in-the-world. But is *Dasein* a category in which we all participate, in which case the fact that we experience being-in-the-world from the standpoint of our own bodies is inexplicable? Or is there one *Dasein* each, defined by the history of our bodies? If the latter, *Dasein* sounds very like a mind attached to, or caught up in, a body.

This is not a digression. If we are not clear what is meant by Kantian mind or Heideggerian *Dasein* then the argument over the priority between human and physical time – between time as a product of mind and mind as a product of time – will also lack clarity. It seems reasonable to accept that time perceived as a sequence of events – immediate time perception – is rooted in the individual mind. Here, too, we shall find boredom, hurry, waiting, impatience, enduring, and other emotional or more broadly existential, aspects of experienced time, though they also have one leg in what we might call "public time": the time of appointments, of responsibilities, of duty, of the small change of daily life. Public time is not interior to individual minds but a manifestation of the community of human minds. We may think of it as occupying a space between the time of immediate time sense, private to individuals, and physical time that seems to inhere in the material world.

For an individual, the journey from direct perception of temporal order, of intervals, and duration, to a sense of the temporal order of the world that reaches its highest expression in natural science, is accelerated by engagement with the public time of the clock and the calendar. The pre-school child is taught to tell what time it is; to fit her "now" into a lattice of hours, days, and ultimately dates, so that she can look forward to Christmas. Public time belongs to a mode of mindfulness that links the private and the communal mind; the viewpoint of me-here-now with an impersonal, unallocated viewpoint.[122]

Between subjective and objective time there is thus a third character, occupying a territory between indexical consciousness and deindexicalised science. This makes the comparison between two modes of time rather complex. The focus is usually on accuracy: the contrast between unreliable immediate judgements of (say) the duration of a time interval or how much time has "passed" and more reliable objective measurements. There seems to be a path of increasing authority from my unmediated estimate of how long something lasts to the report based on measurements from a caesium clock whose readings have been ultimately validated by the meshwork of laws of the utmost generality in which their settings are embedded. Subjective assessments of duration seem to be discredited by the fact that they vary from person to person and on the nature of the experience provided by the events whose duration is assessed. They are the paradigm of what science leaves behind on its path to truth. Subjective time seems to be objective time more or less traduced, as if the true portrait of time were revealed through measurement and the right way to experience time would be to estimate its quantity accurately, so that getting time right would seem to require getting ourselves out of the way.

It is in fact unclear what would constitute subjectively experiencing an hour as an hour or a day as a day. The experience of a length of time consists of looking back at (some of) the events that took place in it from the viewpoint of a time at or beyond the end of it – not, that is to say, experiencing as it happens. It is a matter of memory rather than perception and the experience of recollection will have a shorter duration than the time that is recollected. Remembering yesterday may reawaken headlines but will not give a sense of a 24-hour stretch of time. Intervals of time beyond a relatively short interval will be matters of knowledge, largely beyond the reach of immediate experience. The passage from the temporality built into sequences of events such as a run of musical notes to recalling a day, a year, a decade, "my youth" and so on is the passage largely from experience to "that x was experienced", "that x has taken place", "the fact that, etc." and it is supported by a publicly maintained scaffolding of days and dates.

Removing the subjective element from estimates of time empties it not only of fallible experiences but ultimately of the measurements that attempt to transcend those experiences and replace them with definite, universally true measures. The latter, of course, is seen to be naïve, overlooking the frame-dependency that special relativity is thought to have demonstrated to be inescapable. Describing time as susceptible to dilatation or contraction and space–time intervals as being allocated to space-like and time-like separations ultimately boils down to denying to time its measurement as an intrinsic property. Distant simultaneity, temporal order (except for that which is rooted in causal relations), a long time or a short time, are all denied constitutive reality. Eradicating the subject, with the ultimate refusal to privilege the viewpoint of one, any, observer, that leads to a mind-free time also results in time empty of any distinctive characteristics. We might call it time-free time. And this, of course, means time without the temporal order (of ancestrals) that we invoked to underpin the mind-independent nature of time.

There is thus a tension at the end-point of the journey from subjective time to objective time. There is a powerful story that global time – and the reality of time-in-itself – must be denied; while at the same time there is an equally powerful story that the universe has a history in which all its events are located on a single timeline, independent of all observers – so that it makes sense to say that the earth formed at a definite time before life on earth appeared.[123]

There is no place for mind in this view of the cosmos, though of course the totality signified by the idea of the "cosmos" can be brought together *as a multitudinous totality* only by mind. It is only in the discourse of (conscious, articulate) humans that rocks, stars, black holes, radiation, trees, laughter, add up to a universe. (Though it is equally true, as we shall discuss in §11.4, that it is the human mind, and the localities associated with them, that break up what might be regarded as a continuum – such as the putative single wave-function of the universe.).

To try to advance our understanding of the relationship between subjective and objective time, we need to return to thinking about the process of making time explicit and the relationship between immediately experienced time and clock-time – that ultimately gives rise to calendrical and historical time, and then modes of deep time ("geological" and "astronomical" time). It is clear that, say, clock-time does not just take immediately experienced time – the perceived order and durations of events and the intervals between them – and, as it were, count it and piece it together. Clocking time is not a matter of counting perceived or experienced time. Measuring time is not like enumerating pre-existent items such as sheep: time has to be re-presented in order to be countable. First, that which is "counted" is not out there, a pre-existing public object of potential joint attention in the way that sheep are. Explicit attention to time begins with shared, collective attention to, let us say, the global pulsation of light that divides time into portions called days, separated by portions called night. Time becomes more explicit with qualitative divisions into: "dawn", "morning", "evening". The next step is the transformation of those qualitative divisions into more precisely formalized temporal locations – for example those marked by the shadow of an obelisk moving over prepared ground. The locations are in turn divided into intervals corresponding to what are agreed to be equal intervals of time. It is at this point that such intervals are ripe to be transformed into numbers.

Time is thus made explicit as something in itself beyond the ground floor yielded by visual perception through being collectivized and, later, unitized. The intervals that can be recorded and quantified extend direct perception, beyond the specious present, or the minutes that have a tenuous hold on memory, to parts of days broken up into hours and days gathered up into years. This liberation of time sense from individual experience to anyone's experience and from anyone's experience to pure quantity sets humanity en route to the discovery of historical time and beyond this to transhuman – geological, astronomical – "deep" time.

Time extricated from sense experience and immediate time sense is as it were inserted or reinserted into the material world: it is transferred from perception to the objects of perception, to objects irrespective of whether or not they are perceived. Time becomes something that can be told by clocks; and the time they tell refers equally to events that are experienced by me, by you, by anyone, by no-one. Like the road sign that points the way for all and everyone and continues to point in the absence of anyone, the clock takes time experience out of the body or its sensorium. I can acquire knowledge about the temporal order of events I did not experience – E_1 I am told took place *at* the fourth hour and E_2 *at* the fifth hour and so I know that E_1 took place before E_2. The idea builds up of a temporal order that transcends any perceived sequence of events. The question of "When?" is one that can be settled by consulting others, clocks, or documents. The "at" also feed back into duration. Duration is an interval between two "ats". We cannot experience an hour directly, and certainly not a whole day, but we can see that it has "passed" as marked by the movement of the shadow. That is why the clock has an authority that over-rides any immediate impression of the duration of time and the latter seems to be merely a primitive or at least informal precursor of the former. Immediate time sense no longer qualifies, we are to believe, as a revelation of time itself: time is out there, in the keeping of instruments. "My God, is that the time?" Yes, it is, if that's what's on the clock and there is no evidence that it is running fast or slow. Quarrelling with clocks is a fool's game. There are locations in time we cannot guess at, orders of events we rely on reports or inferences from reports to establish, and durations (hours, days, years, centuries, millennia, and so on) we could not accommodate in experience.

We have an immediate time sense that does not reveal ourselves as creatures located in a vast framework of time. Indeed, from moment to moment, as we encounter a changing world and changes in ourselves, successive events, unfolding processes, we are to a considerable degree untimed timers. We have a core continuity that lifts us above, or at least sets us off from, the flux of the reality we encounter, and deal with. This succession of experiences does not belong to the world revealed by physical science, which is empty of phenomenal content and, ultimately, reduced to the relations between classes of events reduced to pure quantities. So ordinary time sense is demoted to something that is infravenient to the world revealed by natural laws. If natural laws were the whole story, there would not be the kinds of observations that ultimately result in natural laws, including those that lead to the discovery of that "deep" time in relation to which our lives are less than eye-blinks.

The passage to an ever expanding, evermore precisely measured, objective time is not therefore a straightforward revelation of the framework within which we pass our lives and the shedding of a subjective, localised, egocentric perspective. Turning the clock's gaze on ourselves, timing our own activities ("I took such-and-such a time to do so-and-so" – and noting declines and improvements, and personal bests and comparisons with the average for a reference group), being aware of having a certain life expectancy against an average length of life – is stranger than we customarily appreciate because we overlook the oddness of the passage from the subjective, or egocentric, perceptions that deliver the basic elements of an immediate time sense (the perception of a succession of events) to ever more accurate clock timing.

The passage from the implicit "now" of our experiences and of the events we are experiencing, to the explicit "now" of "now is noon", to "now" is 17 May 2015, "now" is 950 years after the Battle of Hastings, "now" is in the Anthropocene era, "now" is a moment in the 500 million year history of multi-cellular organisms, "now" is 4 billion years into the history of the earth, "now" is 13.8 billion years ABB ("after the Big Bang") is the widening of time awareness sense from experienced time to knowledge of time that lies beyond experience to time that lies beyond the possibility of experience.

The story of our progressive liberation or awakening from, or loss of, immediate time perception, has a couple of twists. The first is something I alluded to at the outset of this section: we – and more particularly our lifespan – become diminished in our own eyes. We shrink as we turn our expanding awareness on ourselves. Secondly, locating ourselves in an ever wider and deeper time was itself something that itself took place at particular times. Clock-time has a relatively short history and the advances in the measurement of time (increasing the range of time to be measured) itself has had a series of landmarks also located in time. We are confronted with the strange, reflexive notion of a time at which, or over which, a time sense emerged. A time during which time became ever more explicit.

From nipping into the kitchen to see what time it is now to locating that "now" in, say, astronomical time locates "now" ever further outside one's immediate sense of the present. However, it does not entirely shake off its roots in the primordial time sense. As Heidegger has put it: "Because the clock must be regulated by the 'natural' clock, even the use of clocks is grounded in the temporality of Da-sein that, with the disclosedness of the There, first makes possible a dating of time taken care of".[124] We cannot transcend that "temporality". When we check the clock or the calendar or look up an historical or astronomical fact we do so "now" for some now-related purpose. That the Big Bang happened 13.8 million years ago, or that it happened 4,000,000,000 years before the earth was formed, is a truth that exists only in the minds of individuals thinking about it at a "now". The thoughts of the thinker may escape the temporality of ordinary being-there but the thinking of them and the thinker do not. So the relations captured in astronomical timelines are no less rooted in the experience of individuals than relations such as "tomorrow". And this makes especially pertinent and (perhaps) consoling the fact that the time that seems to transcend – and indeed dwarf – the individual and even the collective human race itself comes into being at a certain time. The 13.8 billion-year sequence that is the timeline from the Big Bang to the present is something that has slowly emerged in the minds – or at least the discourse – of human beings.

To say this is not to relativize the truths of physical science but to underline how they grow out of, and never shake off, the temporality of lived time. Which is why it is equally valid to say that physical time came after human time because the mode of thinking and ordering things that is physics came into being only after human beings reached a certain level of sophistication as to say that human time has arisen only in a very recent phase of the physical world. To say that physics and the gathering of great stretches of time is a product of human consciousness is not idealism; the latter would be to say that the physical world is a product of human consciousness. The process of making time explicit began, as we discussed in Chapter 1, with the joint attention to successive positions of objects disclosed to vision. Time prior to human consciousness was not explicit and most certainly not ordered into the timelines that stories, history, and natural science has generated. The status of time-not-made-explicit is impossible to characterize, though we cannot deny its existence otherwise we would be back inside the Kantian cage.

The strangeness of the assumption that physical time and human time had a temporal order of appearance may be highlighted by reflecting a bit more on the fact that there was a time before time was timed. It is the process of timing itself that enables us to look back on, or at least to conceive of, a time before there was timing and a time before we or any other being in the universe had a time sense. Just how slippery things are hereabouts, consider the assertion that "The Big Bang took place 13.8 billion years ago". It is obvious that the tensed "ago" is a projection from our present temporal position and not inherent in the physical world.[125] What, however, are we to make of the units – of the 13.8 billion "years". Do they exist in the physical world, given that it is not naturally sliced in this way, and requires one part of the universe (apparent solar rotation) to clock another; and given that, before the universe was a year old, there were no years; indeed years had no basis until the arrival of that parvenu the Solar System? Thus the difficulties of determining what is left of time when it is not made explicit, not sensed, shared, or measured. What would be time in "death's dateless night" if there were no survivors to time the afterlife of the dead?

The phenomenal consciousness and self-consciousness in virtue of which time becomes explicit – that is to say distilled from change and unitized – has no presence in the world according to physical laws. This may have prompted a residue of idealist thinking in certain surprising quarters – for example Stephen Hawking's claim that "We create history by our observations, rather than history creating us".[126] Discussing the temporal order between physical time and the time that physical time was made explicit and ultimately measured by human beings who are, at least in some fundamental respects, part of the physical world, raises the spectre of a kind of Escher staircase where the top step flips into the bottom step. For Meillassoux, this kind of consideration lies at the origin of a reflexive, "speculative" metaphysics that breaks out of the prison of (Kantian) correlationism:

> Science reveals a time that not only does not need conscious time but that allows the latter to arise at a determinate point in its own flux. To think time is to think the status of a becoming which cannot be correlational because the correlation is in it, rather than being in the correlate. So the challenge is therefore the following: to understand how science can think a world wherein spatial-temporal givenness came into being within a time and a space which preceded every variety of givenness.[127]

We shall consider the "irruption" of givenness – in the form of viewpoints – in §11.3.1. For the present, we note only that we should hesitate before uncritically accepting a story that has the following distinct and successive steps:

(a) *Direct time sense.* Yielding a sense of the order of perceived events, a hint as to their duration (and, the obverse of this, of the size of the interval between them), arising from the proto-clock of the events surrounding them, including the events taking place in our own bodies.

(b) *Indirect time sense.* Progressing from observing change to seeing that change has taken place, corresponding to progress from direct perception of change to the indirect sense of change arising out of comparing a present state with a past one.

(c) *Natural clocks.* The first steps towards timing and the direct perception of time: day-timing that yields the (rough) location and (rough) duration of events mapped against the position of the sun and the angle and length of shadows. This is the beginning of public time mediated by joint attention to phenomena visible to all, expressed in and validated by meetings and coordinated activities.

(d) *Manufactured clocks.* Clock-time – giving more precise accounts of order, location and duration of events. The combination of (c) and (d) builds up yesterdays and tomorrows into "all our yesterdays" and "all our tomorrows".

(e) *Scientific or law-embedded time.* Time as little t, seen as a boundless quantity, opening the way to deep time.

Thus the simplistic story of the progressive self-revelation of the inherent properties of the material universe; of what would be seen if it had a viewpoint on itself. And hence of time as it is in the material universe: time in reality and the reality of time. Of course material objects don't have viewpoints on themselves, even less ones that reveal their intrinsic properties.

The ghost of Martin Escher returns: subjective experience of time gives rise to objective measures of time that locate subjective time as a comparatively short episode within itself. We are, it seems, born in the time that in a sense is born in us – a striking example of the "reciprocal containment" philosophers sometimes talk about. The question of the relationship between "subjective" and "objective" time is not merely one of a transition from unreliable estimates of time to reliable and valid measures. Rather it is more complex relationship between the time we are born into and the time that is born in us; of retrojecting time we experience and measure into places prior to or beyond the possibility of experiencing or measurement, where change could not be perceived.[128] It seems as if there are two journeys moving in opposite directions: a journey of the universe in a physical time to the generation of entities (ourselves) with a time sense; a journey of those entities from immediate perception of the sequence or duration of events to a scientific time sense that locates themselves at the end of the first journey. This two-phased journey is not entirely dissimilar to that taken by the material world towards pieces of matter – human beings

– that form the concept of the material world; in short the journey taken by matter and the universe such that they acquire inverted commas: "matter"; "universe".

Although the advertised topic of this section has just two players – objective and subjective time – there are at least four elements:

- the implicit temporality of the orchestrated activity of the insentient material world;
- the explicit time of human life;
- subjective time ("how long it feels" to experience and recollection); and
- objective time ("how long it was" to measurement).

The passage from immediate or subjective to objective measured time does not map on to that from implicit time in the material world to explicit time in human life. This slippage between implicit to explicit on the one hand and subjective (estimated) to objective measurement on the other is a marker of the complexity of the relationship between scientific and lived time, so that it is equally misleading to think of the latter embedded in the former as the former merely being an expression of, or in some sense internal to, the latter. I mention this to challenge the notion that clock-time somehow supersedes immediately experienced, clockless time. If our direct experiences are a poor guide to measurements, measurements are a poor guide to experiences. We must not think of clock-time as grown-up time and immediately perceived time as infantile time experience. The gain in accuracy is based, as we have said, on the loss of content. While lived time does not directly reveal clock-time, clock-time fails equally to reveal lived time. There is no right answer as to whether an interval on the clock should be experienced as, or indeed count as, a long or short time.

Both objective and subjective time are manifestations of time made explicit. It is true that time becomes explicit only when elementary particles are arranged in such a way as to constitute sophisticated sentient beings called human beings. In acknowledging that explicitness – or "givenness" to use Meillassoux's term – is a prior condition of both the subjective time of our lives and the objective time of the astrophysicist, we go some way towards a position that does justice to both lived time and the time of physics and the natural laws it uncovers.

10.6 CONCLUDING COMMENTS

Our attempt to answer the question "(What) is time?" has generated answers that are neither entirely simple nor entirely satisfactory. While there are certain accretions that we may remove from time – such as the ideas of "passage" and "flow" – something irreducible remains.

That irreducibility is highlighted by the fact that time has its several distinct features that cannot be translated without remainder into one another: location, order, and quantity. Of any event, we may say three quite distinct temporal things: that it happened at a particular time; that it happened before other events and after others; and that it took such and such a time to complete. We have discussed a multitude of definitions of time. Each seems to capture some important aspect without encompassing everything that is important.

One of the key arguments of this book – that time is more than the physicists' "little t" – is reinforced by the unsatisfactory nature of the mathematics of time, that seems unable to grasp even the relationship between instants and intervals. Twentieth-century physics that embraced a relational account of time seems to have ended by simultaneously losing time altogether and yet upgrading it to an "active player", along with space, in the universe. Contemporary astrophysics likewise proposes that time had definite beginning (in time? at a time?) while denying the global timeline that is implicit in the notion of the universe having a single history, beginning with the Big Bang.

Time, therefore, is complex and irreducible. But it is not stand-alone: purified time seems to have no characteristic except quantity. The attempt to separate time from change proves unsuccessful: a universal temporal vacuum would (if it were not simply a metaphysical impossibility) be timeless as well as changeless. The relationship between these inseparables, time and change, however, proves difficult to define; as does that between time and our perception of the sequence, duration, and temporal location of events. The tendency of relativistic physics to look at the world from the mathematical (imaginary or virtual) standpoint of the totality of events, leads to the denial of change and the reduction of time to one aspect of the space–time manifold in which nothing happens.

I hope enough has been established (particularly in the immediately preceding section) to challenge the assumption that fundamental, or real, time is the time measured by clocks, and ultimately the deep timeline of geology and astrophysics, and that human or lived time is secondary, mere froth on the river of process that extends from billions of years before sentient creatures emerged to an indefinite future, perhaps terminating, or pausing, in the Big Crunch. There seems to be no simple way of determining the priority between time as something we experience and time as it is constitutive of the order of the material world outside of consciousness. The passage from our ordinary time sense to ever more precise and repeatable quantifications of time is not a straightforward story of unpeeling the truth about time. Such a story bypasses too much, not the least the mysterious fact that we can assign a rough time (or date) to the transformation of time into something that is measured, and even the construction of pre-scientific, pre-historiographical times such as "noon", "yesterday" and "next year", and we know or believe on reasonable evidence that timing is very recent compared with the duration of the universe. It is predicated on a developed public consciousness, enacted in appointments to meet and coordinated activity, itself founded on joint attention, ultimately formalized in language. The notion of a universal time is an outgrowth of the world time of a society of intermeshing wills, duties, and rights; of a world which relies on punctuality to make it go round.

We may conclude from this that, in exploring "human time", we do not have to defer to the natural sciences or concede that what we are investigating is somehow secondary, metaphysically dubious. Urgency, hurry, regret, hope, and terror, bore-dom, and expectation are just as real manifestations of time as its expression in the laws of motion. The fact that physics has nothing to say about these things, or indeed tensed time – even denies their reality – is proof of the limitations of natural science, not of their unreality. The next two chapters will dig deeper into the nature of human time and how our time consciousness is related to our freedom and our capacity to be agents – something that would be inexplicable if we were entirely and solely children of physical time, as are rocks, trees, and most (perhaps all) animals.

Addendum
A note on the singularity

The idea of a definite beginning to the universe gained a certain amount of scientific respectability through the notion of the singularity. This is an original point in time and space; predicted – or retro-dicted – from the field equations of general relativity. It is the point of cosmic causal origin of all events. It seems to me to be a non-starter if only because, in the absence of space and time, this infinitely dense point cannot mark a locality from which the universe is unpacked. And if it is not localised, then the universe would seem to begin either nowhere or everywhere. To say this, how-ever, though it takes common sense to places where it has no right to be, exposes the singularity as a purely mathematical construct, but lacking coordinates to give it location. Or rather it takes a mathematical construct for a physical reality. (See §3.4.1).

At a more sophisticated level Unger and Smolin[129] object to the singularity for several reasons:

(a) If the universe has a process of coming into being, the laws of nature, how-ever stable, cannot have been immutable. We cannot, therefore, assume that the field equations hold up to the putative first moment.

(b) This vision of a singularity is a particularly gross example of the "cosmo-logical fallacy" (already referred to) in which laws that apply to parts of the universe are extrapolated to the universe as a whole and hence beyond their proper domain of application.

(c) It proposes something impossible; namely "a moment of simultaneity at which all physical quantities such as temperature, density, and strength of the gravitational field are infinite".[130] Mathematical infinities cannot cor-respond to physical realities: an infinity cannot (by definition) be realized because it must exceed any actual quantity.

Unger and Smolin conclude that the singularity is "the transmutation of a scientific enigma into an ontological fantasy".[131] To put it less harshly, singularity theorems, instead of revealing a surprising (and indeed contradictory) fact about time – that it had a beginning – mark a limit to the validity of general relativity.[132]

The problems multiply, of course, when attempts are made to reconcile quantum mechanics with relativity. Quantum theory does not allow time to reach all the way back to the beginning of the universe – to the beginning of time. The universe is a closed four-dimensional space for the first 10^{-43} seconds (the so-called Planck era) while it is less than 10^{-33} centimetres in diameter. Time emerges "gradually" from space. This account is full of contradictions, of course. What are we to make of a precisely defined period of time *before* time emerges? And of a temporal order in which time comes on the scene *after* space? Notwithstanding heroic attempts by philosophers such as Quentin Smith,[133] the self-contradiction stands and the idea of the singularity is in even more trouble when it tries to join itself up to the pre-relativistic Planck era of the universe.

I am therefore inclined to agree with Unger and Smolin, though they, too, have problems.[134] Their rejection of the Big Bang singularity seems to make way for a universe of infinite age. All in all, it does not seem as if physicists are yet able to fulfil the promise made by John Tyndall in 1874 that men of science would "wrest from theology the entire domain of cosmological theory".[135] Not that theologians have much to offer, either. But that is another story.[136]

CHAPTER 11

The onlooker: causation and explicit time

11.1 INTRODUCTION

Our inquiry so far has had three major aims. The first has been to rescue time from physics, where, reduced to a tenseless parameter little "t", it is in danger of disappearing altogether. Our approach was to expose the inadequacies of envisaging time as a pure quantity. The second has been to do justice to the richness of temporal experience by thick descriptions of time as it is lived, whether it is the tensed time of everyday life, or the after-image of time imagined in eternity. And, in the previous chapter, we have tried to determine what remains of time after we strip it of metaphors, such as those of passage, in which we clothe it in our everyday time talk.

Removing these accretions has not (unlike the search for the heart of an onion) left us with nothing. There seems to be something corresponding to "time in itself"; at any rate, we cannot remove time from our account of the world without that account being calamitously incomplete. We cannot translate "before" and "after", temporal location and temporal duration, "not yet", "now" and "no longer" into something other than time. They are part of the irreducible furniture of the world – just as hopeful anticipation, backward looking regret, expectation, recollection, hurry and calm, patience and impatience and countless other manifestations of our time-consciousness are ineradicable features of every moment of human life. Time, in other words, cannot be extruded from our changing world; nor, however, can it be extracted as a kind of juice from the ooze of process. In this respect, its existence is syncategorematic, as philosophers would say, though this makes it in no way inferior to space. Objects, after all cannot occupy or (if you are a relationist) sustain space without enduring through time. And entirely empty space, void of objects, not populated and triangulated by events, is as problematic as a temporal vacuum, even though the fact that we seem to see space directly and see time only indirectly, makes the idea of a spatial vacuum intuitively more acceptable: we can, that is to say, deceive ourselves over space more readily because we can visualize it.

This leaves us with a good deal of unfinished business. Behind it is a larger project of trying to get clearer about the relationship between what Sellars called the "manifest" and the "scientific" images of the world and which he identified as a key task for contemporary philosophy.[1] The manifest image is "the framework in which man came to be aware of himself as man-in-the-world" – which is the framework in which we normally encounter, observe, explain, and act in our world. Its key elements are persons and objects. The main players in the scientific image by contrast, are subatomic particles, force fields, wave packets subject to collapse and so on.

As Sellars has pointed out, the two images interact. After all, science is rooted in the inquiries of human beings, acting in a human world, and moderating their activities according to the expectations of the institutions in which they work. The intuitions that contribute to shaping the scientific image of the world, however counter-intuitive the latter, take their ultimate rise from everyday experience and the discourses of everyday life – hence the use of hapless, or at least problematic, notions such as "curved space" (see §3.5.2) that try to make phenomenal sense of what are essentially mathematical concepts. And, the traffic is, of course, two-way. There is no corner of everyday life or everyday consciousness making up the "manifest" image of the world, that has not been permeated by science; and what passes for common sense will have been influenced by the sciences, even if it takes time for this to happen and though in most cases the influence is mediated not through ideas as much as through the technology with which science enables us to furnish our everyday lives. As we have discussed, time as "t" has resulted in lives being timetabled and coordinated to an ever-closer degree, which may mean more precisely calibrated hurry, impatience, anticipation, pasts and futures of greater reach, and other modifications of our time-torn everyday world.

Tracing the connections between the scientific and manifest images of the world and attempting to reconcile them lies beyond the scope of this book. Besides, behind this final phase of our inquiry is a prejudice: a presumption in favour of the irreducible reality of certain phenomena that are marginalized by post-Galilean natural science. An exploration of the relationship between the "manifest" and "scientific" images of what there is should not start with the presumption that the former represents "mere" appearance and the latter reality. Quantitative natural science is inescapably associated with the disappearance of appearance[2] – of all those things that are evident to our sensoria – but this should not be interpreted as an awakening from cognitive slumber.

Armed with this prejudice I want to focus in the two final chapters on key aspects of our human life – centrally our agency and freedom, our *actively living* rather than merely undergoing our lives in time – that seem to be excluded from, even demonstrated to be impossible by, the scientific world picture. The standard argument against our freedom is that we are material objects in a material world and that every aspect of our lives (including our thoughts, intentions, decisions, etc.) is caught up in the causal net that has been unfolding since the universe began (if it had a beginning). Our lives are judged to be the effects of causes in which we had no say. This is, I believe, dangerous nonsense. To understand how it is that we are free, however, we have to understand the relationship between time and freedom. To address this issue, we need first to revisit the relationship between time and causation. This is the theme of the present chapter.

In order to conduct our investigation at the requisite depth, it will be necessary to return to the question, addressed in §2.3.5, of whether causation provides time with its direction (§11.2.1). Dealing with this issue will require us to take a more careful look at the nature of causation (§11.2.2). This will prompt an examination of the origin of the impression that the universe is a network of causes and effects and, more broadly, of the idea that what happens has somehow to be made to happen, though what makes it happen has no sense of agency. In §11.2.3, we shall revisit ideas of causation as other than a relationship between events. This will open the discussion on to the connection between causes and the (conscious) onlooker which will take us to a consideration of the irruption of viewpoint in a world that, according to physical science, is without viewpoint (§11.3.1). Finally, we shall examine the link between viewpoint and objectivity that ironically leads us on the path to the physical science which traduces time and allows no room for freedom and explicit time, more specifically temporal depth, and (explicit) causes (§11.3.2).

Readers following the arguments in this chapter may feel they have entered a major digression from the central theme of *Of Time and Lamentation*. What follows is, however, no more of a digression than was the extensive treatment of space in Chapter 3. Correctly understanding causation, and more broadly the connectedness and disconnectedness of our worlds, is a necessary step to a positive understanding of human time, not only in its relation to our specific freedoms, but to the wider truth of our existence; namely that we are able actively to *live* our lives rather than merely to suffer or undergo them, and to be creatures that have private and shared histories internalized as the great dramas and small change of our selves.

11.2 TIME AND CAUSATION

> If time is not a reality, causality [understood as the influence that a
> state of affairs exercises over what follows it] cannot be real.
> Unger & Smolin, *The Singular Universe and the Reality of Time*, 35

> Causal connection [is] a primitive feature of nature.
> Unger & Smolin, *The Singular Universe and the Reality of Time*, 221

Of all the candidates for the key to the connection between time and the order of the universe, the direction of causation seems to be the most compelling. That a cause must precede its effect(s) seems to lie at the heart of the temporality of the physical world. In relativity theory, insofar as happening is allowed, one event can influence another only if they have a time-like, as a opposed to a space-like, separation. This has led some philosophers – and a few physicists – to argue that time derives its directionality from the "asymmetry of influence" between cause and effect. In short, that the arrow of time is causal.

11.2.1 The causal arrow revisited

The sense that time has a direction – in the way that space (which is, after all, the sum of all directions) does not – has many sources. Among the most important are two. The first is the common pre-relativistic feeling that all "befores" and "afters" or "earliers" and "laters" in different localities and at different periods belong to a single order of succession, so that time is unified. The second is the equally strong feeling that how the world unfolds, reflected in universal trends and expressed ultimately in the narrative that links beginnings with ends, including the primordial beginning that is our birth with the primordial end that is our death, is non-negotiable. The reasons are not separate, of course; but they both seem to be satisfied by a story that links the directionality of time with the direction of causation. Causation has the virtue of appearing both universal (and so unifying time); and of seeming to underpin an irresistible forward push that corresponds to our sense that, in virtue of being born (or even of being a particular), we are boarded on a train we cannot get off: we are swept into and swept out of existence. Such intuitions seem incontrovertible, and not to be denigrated as part of the "folk physics" discredited by science.[3]

While Mellor (already discussed in §2.3.5) is not the only advocate of the idea that "Time is the causal dimension of space–time"[4] he is one of its clearest recent exponents. What is more, he does not espouse the erroneous claim (discussed in §10.2) that time itself has any causal efficacy. The intimate relationship between causal and temporal order is "not because time fixes causal order. It must be the other way round".[5] In looking for the basis of the directionality of time, he says, we need to identify a necessary ordering principle within happenings. (He will later argue that the happenings in question are not events but "facta", but we shall postpone discussion of this to §11.2.3.) This principle is provided by the relationship between cause and effect, a physical asymmetry that seems to deliver the asymmetry required to underpin the directionality of time. It apparently bypasses objections of the kind that Wittgenstein (whom we cited earlier) raised to the thermodynamic arrow of time: "It is not *a priori* that the world becomes more disorganised with time. It is a matter of experience that the disorganization comes at a later rather than an earlier time."[6]

The precedence of cause over effect seems to have that kind of *a priori* status: a cause *must* precede its effect and the reverse cannot be true. The idea of an effect bringing about its cause raises naïve questions about targeting. How would the thunder be able to seek out the lightning so that it could ensure that it was caused? And in the absence of any physical reason – lacking in the case of reverse causation – the choice of cause would be random. Clearly, an effect E could not bring about its own cause C unless it had already itself been brought about – by a preceding cause, namely *its* cause – presumably C. The relevant cause would have to be both before and after the effect..

This is more than a matter of definition or a truism. The respective roles of the causal event and its effect goes beyond a mere *logic* of causation or causal discourse: lightning causes thunder and not vice versa for good physical reasons. This is an empirical matter, rooted in the laws of material nature. Likewise, the fact that a pressure on a still object may set it in motion, a bang on a table will result in a sound, or a cloud passing across the sun will cause the land temporarily to darken. None of these pairings can be seen as having anything to do with logic.

Causation therefore entrains enough empirical content for the temporal priority of cause over effect to be more than a mere matter of definition. What is more, it is apparently directly visible and appears to be something we engage with every day, as well as explore and utilize in all physics – all the way down to the most fundamental level short of post-classical quantum mechanics, where causation gives way to probabilities. Even so, it is difficult to be entirely sure what Mellor and others (such as Michael Tooley) mean when they assert that time is the causal dimension of space–time. While the notion of time fixing causal order, dictating whether E_1 occurs before or after E_2, is unattractive, the alternative – causation fixing time order – is not readily intelligible.

It is clear that events that happen to be causes do not requisition their own precedence over events that happen to be effects. Consider E_1 causing E_2. It is hardly because of their respective causal relationships that E_1 occurs at t_1 prior to t_2 at which E_2 occurs. It would seem to be the other way round: *pace* Mellor it is their time order that puts E_1 in the running to cause E_2. While time order does not fix the causal order by prescribing the way events unfold, it does make certain causal relations possible. If E_1 is a necessary condition of E_2, its occurrence at t_1 is a necessary condition for E_2 occurring at some time after t_1. In other words, the time of occurrence of E_1 fixes, or limits, the possible times of occurrence of E_2. It is because E_1 occurs at t_1 and not, say, t_3 that E_2 can occur at t_2. If this is not time order fixing causal order, it is not causal order fixing time order, either. Neither option seems to do justice to reality. What is more, if the direction of causation were the basis of the direction of time, we could not distinguish between backwards and forwards causation, even to rule out the former, because whatever way causation went, that would be the forward movement of time, and hence forward causation

That might seem to be the end of that; however, it is worth exploring more widely the reasons why it is wrong to look to the causal order to furnish time with a direction. Ultimately it will lead to our understanding the connexion between explicit time and human freedom. Let us start with an objection that Mellor himself is aware of: that not everything that is in a relationship of "earlier-to-later-than" is in a causal relationship.

As I sit in a busy pub, I am aware of a buzz of activity around me. I can tease out a multitude of sequences of events that may be connected. Many of them, however, are disconnected. Even those that are connected are not connected in a strict causal relationship. I observe the successive steps of a man walking to the bar; someone picking up a glass, drinking from it, and putting it down; the succession of the sounds of his companion's voice travelling from the beginning to the end of a sentence; the rising and falling of the volume of sound generated by dozens of people talking at once. I see the picture on the television of runners on a track assuming their position at the start of the race connected with – but not inescapably connected – with the commentary to the effect that the race is about to start. I also overhear the piped music as I watch the sunlight through the window brightening on the swaying trees. This is simply what is available to my sensory field at present. I am aware that there is much else going on: there is traffic outside expressing the intentions of a succession of strangers. Overhead there are planes and clouds on the move in different ways for different reasons.

These events are in a temporal order of earlier and later. Even those that are apparently simultaneous will not be precisely so: they will overlap, with one a part of an event earlier than the corresponding part of another. Even so, we shall be hard put to find a "pure" causal sequence. The successive steps of the man going to the bar are not connected to one another in the way that his walking is causally connected with the sounds generated by his shoes. We might look to hidden causal connections between some construct such as "a motive" to buy a beer, or quench his thirst, and his trajectory or between the neural activity in his brain and spinal cord and the muscular contractions in his legs. These are rather ill-defined and in some ways competing. There may be other kinds of quasi-causal relations evident in the scene – such as between the utterance of a sentence by Person A and Person B making sense of it and stopping drinking in order that he might empty his mouth to reply. This is, however, all very fluffy.

The point is that, for the most part, the sequence of happenings going on around us at any particular time encompasses events that are temporally related ("before–after") but causally unrelated: there is no clear relationship between that person uttering a sentence and the clouds moving across the sky outside; between the man walking to the bar and the noise of the traffic outside; between the movements of two people walking on the opposite side of the pavement; between the contrail growing out of a plane and the imperceptible crumbling of the stonework of the buildings in the city below.

Mellor has anticipated this objection. "The time order of all facts can follow from the causal order of some of them", he argues. "The existence of times still enables us, despite the apparent shortage of causally related facts, to derive all time order from causal order".[7] Leaving aside for the present the slippage between causes (events) and "facts", it would seem to be a bald statement of faith that a subset of causally related events would establish a framework, a clock, to enable all events to be allocated their place in an overall temporal order. The idea that we would need only a subset of events to establish a temporal order rather as we need a subset of events (clock events) to quantify time wouldn't work because clocks measure primarily quantity of time and determine – in the sense not of fixing but only of recording – temporal order only secondarily. What is more, the successive events that make a clock – the successive ticks – while they may have a causally common origin are not related to each other as a succession of effects of a succession of causes. The extension of the source of a causal arrow from that which is actually causally connected to that which is merely *connectible*[8] via the clock of causal connections does not therefore seem to save the priority of the causal order over the temporal order.

An alternative defence of the causal arrow would be that the causal disconnectedness of the temporally related events that are taking place around us is only apparent. In reality, all events are the disparate children of common causal ancestors – or ancestor in the singular if one traces the genealogy to the putative Big Bang. Even if they are not parent and child they might be cousins ten times removed and it is only the narrowness of the spotlight of salience that conceals this. How far back you would have to go to find the common ancestor would depend on the events in question. So the causal origin of the successive steps of the man walking to the bar would have to be traced only to great-great-grand-events to find a common ancestor; but the steps of the man going to the bar and the flight overhead of the plane, would find us reaching perhaps to the origin of modern man; and the flight overhead of the plane and the movement of the clouds in the same sky would have us reaching back to the common processes that gave rise both to water and to conscious beings capable of making machines that exploit the laws of mechanics to their benefit – a long way back. Even so, this takes us far beyond the directly visible chains of causally connected events.[9]

Another extension of the population of causally connected events providing the necessary framework to establish a temporal order encompassing events that are not seemingly causally connected would seem to be provided by "coarse-grained" descriptions. An example would be "a breeze" which is a broad-front cause that connects clouds moving across the sky, trees waving, towels flapping on a washing line, and my getting annoyed that my papers are being blown away. These events may have a temporal order and a common causal ancestor but they are not directly causally connected and their temporal order has nothing to do with a causal relationship. The clouds moving swiftly across the sky and my getting annoyed are not causally related to one another.

Mellor's argument deserves more careful scrutiny and I offer a further examination in the Addendum to this chapter. In the meantime, we should perhaps give the last word to Poincaré:

> When a phenomenon appears to us as the cause of another, we regard it as anterior. It is therefore by cause that we define time; but most often when two facts appear to us to be bound by a constant relation, how do we recognise which is the cause and which is the effect? We assume that the anterior fact, the antecedent, is the cause of the other, the consequent. It is then by time that we define cause ... We say now *post hoc ergo propter hoc*; now *propter hoc ergo post hoc*; shall we escape from the vicious circle?[10]

The attempt to modify the idea that the direction of time is derived from the direction of causation to deal with the indubitable fact that most events that have a clear temporal relationship are not evidently causally related seems doomed. We cannot, however, leave it at that because there is manifestly an important relationship between temporal order and the direction of causation. It is not located where Mellor and other supporters of the idea of the causal arrow think it is. To pursue this, however, we need to examine the very idea of a cause more carefully and, indeed, the idea (stranger than is often thought) that what happens needs somehow to be made to happen – by for example a cause. This will eventually lead us to examine two linked facts not taken account of by the causal arrow: that directional time is time made explicit; and that causal connections require to be picked out to have this status.

There seems to be another source of temporal directionality in the causal arrow which connects with the thermodynamic arrow. This is the "arrow of increasing untidiness" in accordance with which a single cause has multiple effects. The asymmetry, however, is only apparent. The seeming singularity of "the" cause is deceptive. It is itself one of many effects of prior causes but it seems to be one (cause) with many (effects) because it has been picked out from a boundless population of fellow effects by its salience. It then takes on the character of a focal ancestor of spreading effects. The image of a point of origin – "the" Abrahamic cause – from which effects radiate is an artefact arising out of our choosing one event as an index. An origin is a resumption after an interruption, or a pause, and there are no such interruptions in the material world. The cause, what is more, is not intrinsically separate from its circumstances, so "its" (many) effects are not its work alone but also of the circumstances carried over from the time of the cause to that of the effect. The seeming solitude of the cause and the credit we give to it for a multitude of effects are both artefacts.[11]

The other aspect of the idea that time is the causal dimension of space–time is the claim that time itself has causal powers. What is relevant to the central argument connecting agency with the mode of our temporality is an understanding of causation, manipulation, and the relationship between them. The detailed discussion of the nature of causation that follows, therefore, is – notwithstanding appearances – not a digression.

11.2.2   On causes

> The law of causation ... is a relic of a bygone age, surviving, like the monarchy, only because it is erroneously supposed to do no harm.[12]
>
> Russell, "On the Notion of Cause", 171

It is easy to sympathize with those philosophers who have come to regard causes as – well, a lost cause.[13] The venerable idea that everything that happens is caused to happen by other, previous happenings – going right back to the first cause, the mysterious uncaused cause (God or Big Bang according to taste) that got happening to happen – has been under increasing attack for nearly quarter of a millennium. While it has fought back valiantly – mainly by redefining itself – things are looking pretty bad for the (efficient) cause.

There are many reasons for this. They include the fact that "cause" is a rather slippery concept that serves a multitude of explanatory needs.[14] (And this is true even if we confine ourselves to physical causes, bypassing questions about historical, social, or mental causation.) It draws on several overlapping inchoate notions, so that different theories of causation will address different issues, and they are not in competition for the same explanatory space. Among them is the idea of (material) necessity – that how things are is how they had to be – expressed most forthrightly in Leibniz's Principle of Sufficient Reason. Material (as opposed to logical) necessity has a rather complex and unhappy relationship with natural laws as they are usually conceived, not the least because those laws betray their stark contingency in the seemingly arbitrary values of fundamental constants built into and derived from them. While a higher-level law may seem to be an explanation of a lower-level one – so-called "nomological subsumption" – at any given level of generality, we still have an appeal to a naked uniformity: "Things happen like this because they always happen like this". Or the principle in accordance with which "Nature tends to repeat itself". If this repetition is not obvious – and the surface appearance of novelty seems to be the order of the day – this (it is assumed) is only because of our epistemic limitations that prevent us from looking through superficial differences to underlying similarity. Causation is woven into our idea of automatic *mechanisms* that ensure what happens shall inevitably happen. And the notion of a cause is also appealed to as that which has the *power* to bring things about. The fundamental attraction of the idea of causal efficacy is that it holds an explanatory promise in which powers and reasons, raw energy and intelligibility, converge. The boundary between causation and what we might call "becausation" is very ill-defined.

At any rate, there are numerous untidy intuitions behind the notion of causes as explanations. To get to the bottom of the very idea of causal explanation, we need to reflect on why events require explanations or, more generally, why we feel happening needs something else to compel it to happen, and why this something else should be prior happenings – in the last analysis, *immediately* prior happenings. By this means we shall uncover the origin of the felt need for causal explanation or at least the habit of cause-talk; namely that it lies in the relationship between conscious subjects and an opponent reality which we might call the physical world and the role of such subjects in creating localities in the latter which otherwise lack them. The idea of causation is, I will argue, an attempt to heal the fragmentation, indeed granulation, of the universe arising out of the irruption into it of explicit, enduring subjects with their points of view and their knowledge that partially transcends their individual points of view. Before we arrive at this conclusion, there is a good deal of ground to be covered. We shall, therefore, postpone consideration of it until §11.3.

11.2.2.1 Psychologizing causes

The most famous attack on the link between causes and effects as a necessary and universal connection and on the belief that causes are fundamental constituents of reality, intrinsic properties of the material world beyond the mind, was David Hume's reduction of the causal relationship to expectations:

> In reality, there is no part of matter that does ever, by its sensible quali-
> ties, discover any power or energy, or give us ground to imagine, that it
> could produce anything, or be followed by any other object, which we could
> denominate its effect.
>
> It appears, then, that this idea of a necessary connexion among events
> arises from a number of similar instances which occur of constant conjunc-
> tion of these events; nor can that idea ever be suggested by any one of these
> instance surveyed in all possible lights and positions. But there is nothing
> in the number of instances ... except only, that after a repetition of similar
> instances, the mind is carried by habit, upon the appearance of one event,
> to expect its usual attendant ... This connexion, therefore, which we feel in
> the mind, this customary transition of the imagination from one object to
> its usual attendant, is the sentiment or impression, from which we form the
> idea of power or necessary connexion.[15]

If we have observed that B has always followed A, he argues, we come to believe that
not only (i) B will in future always follow A but (ii) it must follow A because A causes
B such that, if A happens, B cannot help happening as it will be brought about by A.
It will also follow that, other things being equal, if A does not happen, neither will B.
Our experience, that exposes us to patterns of events in the universe, forges mental
habits that turn what is in fact a matter of the contingent succession of one thing after
another into something that feels like causal necessity. It may even feel like a rational
sequence: if A is always followed by B, then it is unthinkable that B will not follow A
and if it is unthinkable then the relationship of A and B feels necessary – irrespective
of whether it is – and has a sufficiency of reason. The reflection of the patterns of the
events to which we are exposed in our mental habits turns what is a mere matter of
the contingent succession of one thing after another into a universal law: if B in our
experience invariably follows A, we intuit that it will always follow A because the
latter has the power to bring B about. Causation becomes becausation.

There is, however, no basis in experience for extrapolating from experience hitherto – however extensive – to experience in the future. Only necessity could guarantee universality and there is nothing in experience to show that the way things turn
out is how they will always, how they must, turn out – "that the course of nature
continues always uniformly the same".[16]

There are problems with a theory that reduces (or upgrades) causes to mental
constructs. The most obvious is that it seemingly draws on the very thing that it
denies – a real causal relationship that cannot be assimilated into the mind, because
it is between the material world and the mind of the subject. Hume effectively presupposes the reality of a cause-and-effect relationship connecting the *experience* of
B-always-follows-A with the *idea* that B necessitates A: the stable pattern of events,
the constant concomitance of A-type and B-type events *causes* our sense of necessity. In other words, Hume sees our notion of causation as being itself a mandated
(mental) effect of a non-mental cause. What's more, since causal necessity is apparently universal – all human beings see it at work throughout the universe – this body-
mind causation is a manifestation of a (universal) causal law. We could summarize

this by saying that Hume is anti-realist about causes in the material world but realist about the causes of our causal sense.[17]

There is an additional difficulty: How do we ground the seemingly valid distinction between pairs of events that are causally related and those that are merely constantly associated, as would be the case if they were successive parts of the same process (as in stretches of the flight of a flying arrow) or if they were time-staggered effects of a common cause? More generally post hoc requires something more to justify being regarded as propter hoc. "B always follows A" is not sufficient to make A in our minds a sufficient reason of B. It is implausible that the difference between "one damn thing after another" and the relationship between a flash of lightning and a clap of thunder has no objective reality and is entirely cooked up in our minds. The painfully acquired methods, central to science, we have developed to distinguish causation from mere succession, however tightly correlated – and to expose seeming causal relationships as accidental associations – suggest that this difference is real; that there are justified and unjustified expectations and justified distinctions between propter hoc and mere post hoc.

What is more, whether or not law-like sequences of apparent causes and apparent effects may be challenged, it is perverse to deny that causal relationships are directly perceived between token events. It seems implausible to suggest that my belief that the stone hitting the window (cause) brought about the breaking of the glass (effect) corresponds to no extra-mental reality even if I may not be able to justify a general expectation, such that the sun, having risen every day of my life will rise forever. In short, there is a world of difference between the expectations that may project necessity into patterns of events and the direct observation of an undeniably causal relationship between one event and another.

Nevertheless, Hume's critique was profoundly challenging. It was a key element in the empirical tradition – unhappy with the idea of "hidden powers" – that he inspired. But it also provoked a different kind of reaction that led ultimately to Kantian idealism. Kant accepted that the idea of a necessary causal relationship between events could not be directly observed:

> The very concept of cause so obviously contains the concept of the necessity of the connection with an effect and a strict universality of the rule, that the concept [of cause] would be entirely lost if one pretended to derive it, as Hume did, from frequent association of that which happens with that which precedes, and [from] thereby arising custom (this a merely subjective necessity) of connection representations.[18]

Kant appreciated the profound significance of this and was stung into a radical response.

Yes, there was no justification within experience for imputing a necessary connexion between cause and effect; nor could there be. Mere observation of contingent associations between events that were (as Hume put it) "loose and separate" could not be an adequate basis for *universally* valid objective laws (extending beyond, necessarily local or limited, actual experience) and of true necessity linking events. Empirical rules of association would not provide the very cornerstone of our sense of a coherent world. Hume was therefore right in one respect: causation as a necessary connection was indeed contributed by our mind; but for Kant this was not a mere effect of experience on the mind. It was an aspect of the *a priori* intellectual structure of experience, of pure understanding: the necessary connection of perceptions was the very ground of possibility of experience, more generally, underpinning our sense of a coherent world. Causation was necessary for the unification of perceptions to deliver a sense of a unified world – the phenomenal world of both everyday experience and of science – populated by material objects and operating in accordance with physical laws. Subjective perceptions become objective knowledge by their "*necessary* unification" – the condition for there being experiences of an "outside" world accessible to all and everyone and ultimately disclosed to scientific investigation that would reveal it as a connected reality going under the name of the phenomenal world or Nature.[19]

In short, Kant was at one with Hume in the latter's view that the sense of causal necessity as "the cement of the universe" could not be justified in or by experience; but for Kant this was because it was that in virtue of which experience held together sufficiently for the very notion of justification to have any meaning.

Kant's view of causal necessity (and of space, time and substance) amounted to a world picture that many have found deeply unattractive. The noumenal reality hidden behind the veil of phenomenal appearance was unwelcome to the empirical spirit which Hume has done so much to foster in philosophy and beyond in the English-speaking world in the centuries since his death. Less costly ways of rescuing some aspects of the notion of causation – of seeing what it might mean, given that the idea of an intrinsic "power" or "necessary connexion" between events is seemingly untenable – have therefore been sought.

11.2.2.2 Causation and statistical probability

A more modest notion of causation is one in which A (the cause) does not make B (the effect) happen but simply increases its probability of happening. This is the interpretation that Mellor favours: a cause is something that raises the chances of an effect[20] – though for him causes and effects are facts or (somewhat obscurely) facta. (This is an important claim – though I believe it is confused, as I shall discuss presently). The strength and salience of A *qua* cause is reflected in the mathematical measure of the extent to which the probability of B's occurrence is raised by A's occurrence This is reflected in the strength of a statistical correlation between Type A and Type B events which is more or less resistant to changes in circumstances, helping to distinguish between causally related and causally unrelated sequences.

This mathematization of cause is a half-way stage to the complete replacement of causation by probability. The discarding of causation at the subatomic level entirely in favour of statistical probabilities has given this reduction of macroscopic causation a certain amount of *cachet*. The "smallist" assumption that the nature of the physical world is defined by the properties of its smallest components has meant to aficionados of scientism that causation, rejected by quantum mechanics, must also be entirely expelled from our picture of the world. All we have is the brute reality that nature has the habit of repeating herself. This is expressed not in a guaranteed definite (local) effect of a definite (local) cause but in a constant statistical distribution of data. If you measure the location of an electron orbiting, say, a hydrogen atom you will not get the same individual results each time but a spread of results that will remain constant over time.[21]

The image this gives is of a universe that is true to its habits – that, as Aristotle said, "what happens always happens for the most part" – without being *obligated* to this fidelity to itself by local causal pressures requiring B to follow A. Probabilities do not mandate events. There are many reasons why this image is unsatisfactory.[22] The one that is closest to our present concerns is doubt whether we can retain anything of the idea of a cause if we empty it of the idea of necessity located in a bond between one particular event and another. For at the heart of our intuitive sense of cause is something that goes beyond mere timeless or eternal habits of the material world: it is a kind of *pressure* that the past applies to the future; that what is now happening is obliged to do so by what has already happened, and what is happening now will oblige what will happen to happen next.

This sense of cause as a kind of *power*, and causation as the transmission of power, is missing (not always by oversight) from several alternative accounts. Let us look at one of these before we reflect on how it has come about that we think we need this, or something like it, to make sense of the unfolding of the universe.

11.2.2.3 Causes as counterfactuals

Consider what is possibly the current front-runner among philosophical accounts of causation in the analytical tradition: the idea of causes as counterfactuals, first suggested by David Hume and developed by J. S. Mill but most particularly associated in modern philosophy with David Lewis.[23] The theory has been developed with great sophistication but at its heart is the idea that event A is to be identified as the cause of event B if it is true that, if A had not happened, B would not have happened either: a cause is something that makes a (salient) difference to what happens. While the discussion of counterfactual theories of causation has tended to focus on token or singular events, rather than types of events, the patterns seen in types of events underpin the ascription of causal connections between singular events. We are justified in saying that A caused B if we can say with confidence, based on repeated observations, that "If A had not occurred, B would not have occurred": "It is generally observed that if A does not occur, B does not occur".

One of the difficulties facing the counterfactual theory is that of providing a secure basis for the difference between causes and conditions. It is accepted that causes as counterfactuals operate against a background field. If I had not been in London (A),

I would not have been knocked down by a London bus (B). It is perfectly obvious, however, that A, while it is a necessary or background condition of B, is not a sufficient condition of it, not a cause of B in the conventional sense. The vast majority of people in London are not being knocked down by London buses, even less being continually knocked down. Many events additional to A, or more precisely many existing states of affairs, are required to ensure that B happens. The counterfactual theory does not offer a satisfactory basis for singling out the event that counts as completing the prior or background conditions to make B inevitable. Not that this is a problem peculiar to the counterfactual theory. As Mill argued, "Nothing can better show the absence of any scientific ground for the distinction between the cause of a phenomenon and its conditions, than the capricious manner in which we select from among the conditions that which we choose to denominate the cause"[24] – a sentiment that has been echoed by many philosophers since. The translation of the difference between causes and conditions into occurrent events (causes) and standing circumstances (conditions) does not deliver the necessary contrast.

This, however, highlights the fundamental problem with counterfactual theories of causation. Conditions are, as it were, permissive rather than active – a mere platform, a stable background upon which the cause can stand, positioning the cause to bring about its effect. The failure to offer a satisfactory distinction between causes and conditions underlines how (permissive) counterfactual theories are rather negative. "If A had not happened, B would not have happened" is equally true where A is a static or stable background condition of my being knocked down by a London bus (such as my being in London) or something that looks like a cause (such as my colliding with the bus or walking across the road at the wrong time). To say of an event A that its absence may result in another event B not happening does not seem to capture the feeling, germane to the idea of a cause, and differentiating it from mere conditions, that it should be something that brings something about, makes something happen.

Strictly, the counterfactual theory has two aspects:

(a) Negative: if C had not occurred, then E would not have occurred,
(b) Positive: if C had occurred then E would have occurred.

The emphasis in the *counter*factual theory is on the negative side. For this reason, it seems too remote from the admittedly naïve – but nonetheless stubborn – intuitions upon which our idea of cause is based, those same intuitions which makes us protest against Hume's reduction of cause to our sense of causation and our sense of causation to mere mental habits. The counterfactual theory lacks what causes seem to bring to the party – namely the *oomph* to bring about events. Without this, the privileged, indeed intimate, relationship between a cause (as opposed to mere conditions, etc.) and an index event that is identified as its effect, seems to remain undefined. In short, various attempts to modify the counterfactual theory will seem unsatisfactory for a fundamental reason: that it is a *negative* definition of cause. If we set aside the idea of causes as *pressures*, or as local expressions of general powers, obliging their effects to occur – the necessity in the necessary connection between events – we may as well give up on the idea of cause entirely.[25]

This common sense intuition of causes as pressures is most readily realized in the notion of an impetus – energy, momentum, velocity – being imparted from one item to another, evident in the push-pull, moving-billiard-ball vision of the physical world, in which one object runs into another and donates something to it of its own motion. Object A collides with Object B (cause), and A slows down and deviates a bit (effect 1), and B is set in motion (effect 2). The movement of Object A seems to have within it the (causal) *power* to bring about the movement of Object B.[26] The expression of the causal power is an exchange of an (overall) conserved quantity of energy.

Where does this intuition come from? Why do we have the feeling that *an event is always made to happen by other events*; that happening *has to be made to happen by prior happening?* What is it that underpins our notion that the universe is, or has to be, *driven* by its own contents, so that what takes place at time t_1 shapes and/ or brings about what takes place at time t_{1+n}? Kant, as we have discussed, had his answer: it lay in the structures of understanding necessary for our perceptions to add up to a coherent, shared, public world. There are other possibilities. One of the most important is our sense of ourselves as actors in the world. Let us now look at this.

11.2.2.4 Causation and manipulability

A popular analysis of our intuition that there are causal powers driving the world forward acknowledges that it is deeply connected with our ability to make, or prevent, events from occurring, to bring things about, to make happening happen. We are allowed to think of A as the cause of B if an agent could bring about the occurrence of B, or at least increase its probability of its occurring, by bringing about the occurrence of A.[27]

Let us examine this theory as a half-way house between locating causation within ourselves (so that man is, as Lichtenberg dubbed us, "the cause-seeking creature"[28]) and the notion that the universe is self-driven, its contents at time t_1 shaping its contents at time t_{1+n}. This, the manipulability theory, sees causes as "handles" – for manipulating what happens or, more precisely, bringing about effects.

It has crisscrossing connections with the counterfactual theory.[29] For example, if A is the manipulation (I clap my hands) and B is the manipulated result (you wake up), then A is a cause of B (your waking at that moment) because, had A not occurred (counterfactual), B would not have occurred. Locating the basis for causal ascriptions in our powers of manipulation does, however, deal with one issue that the counterfactual theory does not seem to cope with; namely, defining what it is that separates causes from conditions or from other conditions – the viewpoint-dependent differentiation of foreground from background. According to the agency theory of causation, that which can be, or ought to have been, manipulated in order to bring about a desired event is the cause and the rest is background. The desired event or effect is the basis for picking out the cause. So clapping my hands stands out against the rest of the universe at the time at which this event takes place because it is linked to the result that is required and which is also singled out from the universe – namely your waking up. In other words, the desired effect singles out the cause by highlighting the set of events that can bring it about and by selecting, within that set of events, the ones that I can influence, and then by selecting within that subset the one that I have chosen.[30] Cause and effect single one another out: the desired effect confers salience on the cause and thus makes it count as *a* cause and indeed *the* cause.

This view of causation is attractive because it fits with our experience of making things happen, of seeming to necessitate them, of the work that has to be done to bring them about, and the resistance of the world that has to be overcome. It is also importantly connected with many things that are of the greatest importance in our lives; notably, the allocation of individual responsibility for significant events. It captures the intuitions we draw on when, for example, we consider issues of personal blame and legal liability. When we think of the reasons for a car crash, we tend to focus on circumstances that are unusual – such as a slippery road and poor visibility. But when we look for salient causes we pay particular attention to circumstances that are not only unusual but also avoidable so that they could or should have been avoided: failure to maintain the car or carelessness, drunkenness or sleepiness in the driver. This in turn reinforces the connection between the ideas of causation and of agency: causes are events we can and (if they are importantly desirable or undesirable) *should* bring about. That is why when I look for the cause of your waking up, I may focus on something that some*one* does or allows to happen, for example, not keeping the children quiet or forgetting to close the curtains. I cannot be blamed for the sun rising but I can be blamed for forgetting to prevent the sunlight streaming into the room.

The translation of causation into manipulability, however, is fraught with problems. The most obvious is that many events that count as causes are not *done* by anyone and perhaps could not be done. You might be woken up by the contractions of your bladder, not by something that I, or even you, might do.[31] We shall return to this but first let us look more closely at causes that I can exploit.

Supposing I bring about B (waking you up) by doing A (clapping my hands). How do I bring about A? Doesn't my clapping (A) itself have to be caused to happen? In other words, agent-related causation is not confined to the relationship between a manipulation and that which is manipulated. In order for me to clap my hands, certain neural discharges have to occur and I do not *do* those neural discharges. What is more, the connection between manipulator (hand clapping) and manipulated (you waking up) appears to have embedded in it many intermediate steps, with their own causal connections, which are hardly brought about by my agency. They tend to get overlooked, indeed are effectively invisible, because they are below the level at which the (causative, agentive) action and its intended effect are described. They are nonetheless just as real as the coarser-grained interaction between my hand-clap (seen as a single event) and your awakening (also seen as a single event). For the sound of my clapping to wake you up, the air between my hands and your ears has to vibrate and there has to be a certain kind of response in your brain. I *do* not do any of these things, either. The things we *do* are riddled with things that merely *happen*, that are themselves, so it seems, effects of causes. In other words, there is a large element of any manipulation that is not itself authored by agents – and indeed is unknown to them – even though they depend on the kind of certainty that we associate with causal connections.

What is more, agents rely on their actions having guaranteed consequences beyond the reach of their manipulations: I *do* A in order that B may happen so that C will happen. Agents can set things in train and beyond their intervention, unwilled mechanisms take over. The causative action controls only a limited part of its (desired) effects. Key to the agent's reliance on mere happening in his actions is the knowledge that the effect will be proportionate to the cause. This may be based upon the law of conservation of mass-energy or more generally a law that some quantity is conserved in the passage from cause to effect. Provision is made for the amplifying or damping effects of the conditions in which the cause is operating.[32] And where the effect is on a conscious individual (as when I wake you up) what follows this intended effect is related in a much more complicated way to the cause. My action had the desired effect of waking you up but this does not give me any control over the additional hours in which I advanced your return to wakefulness. These are the most intimate challenges to the manipulability theory.

The limited reach of manipulation, and the fact that the scope of manipulations falls short of the scope of what we usually consider to be causal relationships, is a powerful objection to the agency theory. It is difficult to resist thinking of causes operating outside the territory that is potentially exploitable for the purposes of controlling the way things unfold. While it is true that, if A causes B, I can (if the circumstances are right) bring about B by bringing about A or prevent B by preventing A, it seems odd that causes should be defined as, or restricted to, a distinct class or subset of material events that are defined by our powers (admittedly enhanced by our knowledge and knowledge-based technology) to change the world. Part of that oddness is that it makes the scope of causality dependent on the range of our powers.

More generally, merging causation with actual or potential agency seems to define the former rather anthropocentrically such that it could not be applied to, say, the interactions between planets prior to the emergence human of beings. (This is a variation of the argument from ancestrals discussed in §10.5.) Few of us would doubt that gravitational forces dependent on the relative positions of parts of the earth and the moon were causes of tides long before there was even the possibility of any agent being present to influence or exploit this. While it is not *logically* impossible to think of an agent having a manipulative role in the first billion years of the universe, it is a matter of fact that no agent could, as it were retrospectively, visit those years to shape what happened.[33] As Woodward has put it:

> If the only way in which we understand causation is by means of our prior grasp of agency, then it is hard to see what could justify us in extending the notion of causation to circumstances in which manipulation by human beings is not possible and the relevant experience of agency unavailable.[34]

Such extrapolation to the universe at large would seem to be a serious case of magic thinking on the part of the species *H. sapiens*, in particular philosophers, trying to tease out the origin of our causal sense.

There are many ways of dealing with this objection, the most popular being the so-called "interventionist" versions of manipulability theories, according to which an occurrence can count as an intervention, and hence as a cause, even if it does not involve human agency, action or intention. This does not, however, deliver what is needed: extending the scope of causation beyond consciousness and, in particular conscious agency. For an event to count as an intervention it would still have to have been picked out by another event which counts as its effect. But without the idea of human agency – or human wishes, needs, or aspirations – or, at the very least saliency, there would be no basis for picking out the relevant event.[35]

The most unsatisfactory aspect of the manipulability theory of causation is that it seems to give agency independence of, or priority over, physical causation. And this is assumed even though it is accepted that the operation of our freedom is limited, its limits being defined in part by the laws governing the interactions between our bodies as physical objects and the world as a physical system. It doesn't help us to understand how there could be a sub-group of events that are manipulated to bring about certain ends, a sub-group that in human beings has been expanded by the pooling of our powers either directly or indirectly via technology. It highlights, rather than dealing with, the philosophical puzzle that we can exercise agency at all; that we can re-direct the course of events, in what is frequently described as a "causally closed" world. How can we, or our wishes, alter anything – if it is given that we and they are the effects of causes whose origin lies beyond our very existence, never mind our control – unless whatever it is that occasions our actions is somehow sealed off from the causal net?

We can now turn the question on its head and anticipate a key argument in this part of the book. It is the thesis that our capacity for freedom not only requires that we can rely on a causally connected world – so that when we do A, the B we expect from previous experience *must* follow, other things (conditions at both ends of the cause–effect pair) being kept constant – but has the same source as our causal sense, our feeling that our freedom is constrained. I will argue that this sense of our freedom, as something limited or constrained, far from being the marker of a world closed against our manipulation, is the result of an opening up of the world of an embodied subject in the material universe; it arises ultimately out of the irruption of conscious selves into unconscious reality, and consequently of points of origin, of centres, and of localities in a reality that otherwise has none of these things. Causation and freedom, are not opponents, but partners in an opened-up world. Of this, more in Chapter 12.

11.2.2.5 Absences and non-happenings as causes

If the manipulability theory is more attractive than the counterfactual theory it is because the idea of a cause as a handle seems to make a cause something positive, even if the necessary "oomph" to bring things about seems to be shared between the agent and the material world: I throw the stone and the window-pane and stone can be left to bring about the unhappy consequences of their meeting. The counterfactual notion that A counts as the cause of B if the non-occurrence of A would result in the non-occurrence of B, or a reduction in its probability of occurring, is unattractively negative. What is more, the counterfactual theory shares the anthropocentricity of the manipulability theory. A counterfactual exists only as a *possibility* that is entertained – and rejected. This requires something – more precisely someone – to entertain that possibility. The being or existence of a counterfactual resides entirely in its being expected, anticipated, or in some way thought of. Counterfactuals are a specified non-happening whose only contribution to happening is not to stop it not happening and this seems doubly parasitic.

However, some particularly hospitable versions of the manipulability theory share the negativity of the counterfactual rival; for some have argued that non-actions may be causes. Here is an example. I (truthfully) tell you that your failure to turn up to our meeting made me cross. Does this mean that an event that does not happen, a mere nothing, has causal power? No. You are absent at many other times in my life when your being absent does not have the power to make me cross or indeed to experience any other emotion. The origin of my crossness lies elsewhere; with, for example the undertaking you made to meet me; the trouble I took to arrive at the venue in the reasonable expectation that you would be there; the time and effort it cost me to reschedule another meeting; in short, events that actually happened. Absences, like a vacuum, rely on their filled surroundings to have any identity and to have even the similitude of causal efficacy. The desperate suggestion that absences could operate as causes given the right circumstances only underlines the fact that absences, things that don't happen, borrow causal efficacy from presences, things that do happen. My failure to water the flowers in the last 24 hours does not cause them to wilt. The sun's heat – resulting in transpiration that exceeds the plant's ability to draw water from relatively dry ground – caused them to wilt. My failure to water them – an abstract singular idea, not an event or a negative event – only meant that they were not prevented from wilting. Causation by omission may have legal status – culpable negligence such as not watering the flowers is a punishable failure – but has no material reality. A universe that was composed entirely of absences – of non-events, of things that do not happen, of nothing – would not be very lively and manifestly not causally wired.

Absences, things that don't happen, have no material existence and consequently lack definite intrinsic character. Just try listing the characteristics of a failure to water the flowers. Here are some possibilities: my forgetfulness; my being out of the country; my not being in the garden; etc. There is no limit. Indeed, there is no reason why we should restrict the absences to my failure to water the flowers in the last 24 hours. I could cite an additional counterfactual for each second of the last 24 hours and for each person who might be considered as a potential candidate to water the flowers. (And defining the field of candidates would take us into very complex territory indeed regarding the notion of responsibility.) They are pure possibilities whose existence is entirely mental. There is no reason why we should think of any single one of these possibilities as *the* cause of something happening; and, given that there is no compelling reason for choosing one out of the millions of things that did not happen and could be thought of as salient, there would be an unresolvable conflict between those many things to count as the cause. In short, the wilting of the flowers would be crushingly over-determined by a tsunami of non-happenings. To think of any of them as causes – unmediated by, or independent of, an actual person who entertains them – is another instance of magic thinking.

There are equal difficulties with agent interventions that pre-empt events from happening; for example, my remembering to water the plants stops them dying. Something not happening should not be thought of as the other side – verso to recto – of its happening, its opposite but equal. The flowers not dying is not itself a specific state of the flowers and it does not take place at a particular time. More generally, negative events are not particulars; indeed, they are ghost-events, the shadows of actual events cast by their being entertained as possibilities that did not turn out to be true. They borrow their substance from actual events and (as we saw in §8.2.2.1) it is only in logic that they can seem to be the ontological peers of positive events. In reality, they lack the determinate properties of actual events. This raises difficulties. If I say event E did not happen at time t, then it would be true that E did not happen slowly at time t *and* that E did not happen quickly at time t which would seem to be a contradiction.[36]

11.2.2.6 Causes, discontinuity and oomph

The very idea of (necessitating) causation as that which keeps things going and on track is a response to a deeper sense that whatever happens is, indeed has to be, *made* to happen. This is implicit, after all, even in the reading of causes as counterfactuals, or at least when the counterfactual defines both the necessary and sufficient condition of the relevant event. The assumption is that if A did not make B happen, B would not have happened. The identification of non-happenings (my not watering the lawn) as causes, though contestable, inadvertently illuminates the origin of our belief in a universe whose unfolding can be described in the language of causes and effects (incorporating the subset of actions and consequences). The conviction that what happens has to be made to happen is, I want to argue, a response to a pulling apart of the world as a result of the emergence of conscious, specifically self-conscious beings who extract individual events (causes which have effects that are in turn causes) from the intrinsically undivided flow of becoming.

A key constituent of the image of a causally-propelled unfolding of nature is the differentiation of nature into standing conditions (a relatively static theatre) and occurrent events (the dynamic drama in the theatre). The latter are charged with carrying the story forward by exerting causal pressures and the former are merely the context in which those causal pressures can operate. While the standing conditions do of course change, they change more slowly than the succession of events: that is why they can provide the platform out of which events spring.

These, then, are the background assumptions behind the notion of causation as the work of discrete events providing the necessary oomph to make the occurrence of other discrete events seem to be sufficiently occasioned. Crucially for our argument, there are other possible ways of conceiving the material world that do not require us to invoke discrete causes of discrete effects. We may envisage the universe, as a continuous whole, unfolding seamlessly from its origin to the present. This view is consistent with one version of quantum mechanics in which the totality of "things" and "events" is in fact a single wave-function (as Ladyman argued in *Every Thing Must Go*). Any (classical) history that it has is, as it were, an unrolling four-dimensional carpet of states of affairs guaranteed by the initial conditions and the laws of nature that operate on them to generate subsequent conditions. The laws are not an independent force; they are at most railway lines or steering wheels rather than engines. And they are not even that, given that rails and steering wheels also operate through forces. They are simply the general shape of what in the broadest sense, and beneath immediate appearances to us, actually happens. The laws are simply the most capacious description of what is happening. It is worth looking at this a little more closely.

We may envisage something, analogous to a "vanishing point" in a perspectival painting, where scientific progress, by which individual laws are progressively subsumed under laws of ever greater generality reaches its terminus,[37] and we arrive at a terminus in which what is happening here and now is happening simply because this is how things happen everywhere and always. While the passage from a lower-order law to a higher-order law may seem like explanation – as when the behaviour of gases described in Boyle's law is revealed to be a manifestation of the laws of motion as applied to gaseous atoms – at the highest level we have simple brute fact: this is how things (most generally) are.

Thus the grand narrative of an unfolding universe, unified under laws or a law of the highest generality, not requiring further (causal) intervention, like an arrow in flight. At t_1 the arrow is at position P_1; at t_2 it is at P_2. Reaching P_2 at t_1 is not the *result* of anything happening at t_1: it is simply a continuation of what is happening at t_1. Of course, the movement of the arrow can be seen as the result of an event at t_0 when the bowstring sent it on its way. In the case of the universe as a whole, there is no distinct bowstring: the universe is not sent on its way by anything. The idea of a First Cause or Original Oomph would be an illegitimate backward extrapolation of the causes we identify in localities in the world. Indeed, as will be evident from the direction of the argument, the very idea of causation sits uneasily with the vision of the universe as an unfolding continuum so densely, or seamlessly, interconnected as to make the very idea of a connection between discrete parts redundant: there are no discrete parts to be connected.

Imagined against the background of a universe set going, continuously iterating the grand habits with which it was endowed, then any local action, with a circumscribed origin and destination, becomes a kind of deflection, not dissimilar to agency. The analogy would be with an arrow set in inertial motion that will continue in that motion unless acted on, and hence stopped or blown off course, by a force.

The global view implicit in the expectation that the world will unfold according to a fundamental law does without – indeed finds difficult to accommodate – the idea of the local oomph that prior events (causes) provide to ensure that posterior events (effects) come about. Successive states of the universe are not frogmarched into happening by their predecessors that have been similarly frogmarched. Once the universe is brought into being, once it is set unfolding according to its intrinsic properties, nothing more is needed to bring about the particular events, evident to a viewpoint, at t_2; certainly not specific causal powers operating at t_1.

The brutality of the brute mega-fact that "The universe is how the universe is" highlights how laws are ultimately descriptive rather than prescriptive. They do not have legislative power; even less *the power to bring about particular events*. Nevertheless, there is a residual sense that what happens *must* happen – even if this is only a pressure to conform to general laws of happening – but that the obligation applies only at the level of the highest generality. Particularity is underdetermined by general laws: something else is needed to make any actual event happen; or, indeed, for there to be particular manifestations of the law(s) of nature. Hence the continuing survival of the idea of cause. Causes take over at the point where laws give out, and the restlessness of the world resists translation into general principles described by numbers. This is evident where (individual) viewpoints create locations hosting particular happenings.

To understand the origin of our causal sense, therefore, we shall need to look at the nature and provenance of the conception of a granulated universe in which causation is invoked as a kind of cement between successive events in it or successive phases of it. While we think of science as the most sophisticated development of the causal sense en route to laws, the causal sense actually precedes anything corresponding to a scientific notion of a law of nature. It develops early in childhood and it is evident in pre-scientific cultures.

There are several supplementary observations in support of the claim that cause-and-effect pairings are not intrinsic to a material world conceived of as existing independent of or in the absence of conscious viewpoints. For a start, there is no intrinsic limit to the causal connectedness of any event. When we see or say that event A is caused by event B, both events are picked out by considerations of saliency. It is this that enables us to quarantine the pair from their limitless antecedents and their endless consequences and to separate them from background conditions. In the case of the example we have just discussed, clapping one's hands to wake someone up, the salient event is an individual waking up – of negligible importance in the universe but of great importance in our parish. This is the index event that triggers the search for causal ancestors and fixes its scope, determining where we should stop in tracing the chain of linked events. We have already noted that salience accounts for the apparent asymmetry between causes and effects; the fact that the consequences of a discrete event identified as a cause are far from discrete. Take a simple example: I drop a pebble in a pool. The splash, the ripples, the trembling of the reeds, etc. would exhaust any attempt at description. But this asymmetry is misleading: the causal ancestry of my dropping the pebble in the pool is as complex as its progeny and it, too, would defy complete description.[38] The closed system defined by a cause and its consequences has an asymmetry, and a tendency to increasing untidiness, that seems to be in line with the second law of thermodynamics; but the system is closed only by a description shaped by our individual interests, and their collectivization in the community of minds, creating an apparent starting point not inherent in the material world.

A final illustration of the salience-dependence of the identification of causes is in the relationship between causes and laws. The increased pressure applied to a gas causes a proportionate reduction of volume. The increased volume allocated to a fixed amount of gas causes a fall in pressure. Which is cause – increased pressure or decreased volume – and which is effect is intervention- or interest-dependent.

11.2.2.7 Causes, viewpoints and localities

First, a brief recap. We have two ways of imagining the evolving universe. The first is the expression through time of an unfolding of initial conditions in accordance with a multitude of laws that are ultimately expressions of a single law of the highest generality. This is a universe without interruptions, discrete events, or granulation: it is a continuum. The other is a universe in which there are discrete causes, acting locally (unlike laws) that bring about discrete effects (that have a local scope). What is it that distinguishes the two universes?[39]

This has been flagged already: the former is one in which there are no viewpoints, no localities. There is no here and there, no far and near, no centre or periphery, no "hidden" or "revealed", no knowledge or ignorance. The latter, the world of causation, by contrast, is one that is broken up into localities picked out by a *point of view* for which there is here and there, far and near, handy and out of reach, centre and periphery, the hidden and the revealed, knowledge and ignorance. The point of view, sustained by an embodied subject, places an interruption in the seamless unfolding of the universe (which latter has no points of view within itself as we discussed in Chapter 3). The present interests of the viewpoint identify a beginning and an end; or startings (causes) and endings (effects) – the index events which are of interest and endings that in some cases will be goals or fulfilled purposes.[40]

Is it valid to think of a material universe prior to conscious subjects whose unfolding would not be divided into causes and effects, into beginnings and ends? Self-evidently, the universe seen *sub specie aeternitatis* is not divided into *localities*. But without localities, it would not be differentiated into (prior, discrete) causes and into causes and contexts or circumstances; nor into relevant contexts and circumstances on the one hand and "the rest of" the universe ("outside") on the other. We may imagine the pre-conscious universe as an entirely connected whole, a fabric in which the connections are of infinite density and no connections are privileged. It is this that physics appears to aspire to recover in its "view-from-nowhere" theory of everything. This view of the world as a continuum, as we have already noted, is regarded as the most authoritative, or at least most powerful, account of the universe: that of quantum mechanics, according to which everything is entangled with everything else in a totality that is a single wave function.

The vision of the universe as a network of discrete causes and effects, of discrete events that need to be brought about by preceding events, in which happening doesn't just merely happen but is made to happen (or needs to be made to happen) by local causal oomph, is connected with our situation as embodied subjects operating in a locality in pursuit of our local needs. But this does not mean that causation is confined to those things we can, or could possibly, or could in principle, manipulate. Causation must be universal – not only within but also beyond our individual or collective grasp – once the seamless flow of events has been interrupted or broken open by a viewpoint, and the flow of events is confronted and manipulated from the localities created from which it is viewed. The oomph to resume the flow is required not universally but wherever we look: wherever the universe is broken up by the gaze (in the broadest sense) of an embodied subject. We must not confuse this with magic or anthropocentric thinking. Viewpoint picks out the events that are causally related but does not determine the nature of that relationship. That there is an *explicit* relationship between lightning and thunder is the product of viewpoint that picks them out as salient and therefore distinct events but the fact that the former causes the latter (and not the other way round) is not caused by our prayers or, more broadly, our sensorium.

I have dug beneath the rival theories of causation to see what motivates the very idea of cause. I have argued that it has its roots in something deeper than an endeavour to make a particular sense of the world. The causal sense arises out of the very fact that we are situated; that we have viewpoints which divide the world in complex ways. Out of this fundamental existential reality of conscious beings, originates a world granulated into events some of which have a characteristic that is preserved even in the most deflated account of cause: namely, saliency or privileged importance, foregrounded against a background of what is also happening. Behind saliency is the viewpoint of a subject whose existence is of concern to itself. This is a world in which there are stories, or threads, that have a beginning, a middle – and an end.

The idea that causal explanations are mobilized to bridge gaps opened up in a dis-tracted – that is to say pulled apart – world that is seen as composed of discrete events rather than seamlessly unfolding would be directly opposed by some philosophers. Wesley Salmon, for example, argues that causality is a property of spatio-temporally continuous processes rather than a relationship between discrete events.[41] This, however, does not do justice to our ordinary mode of thought. We think of (say) the distinct lightning causing the thunder rather than two phases of a single "thunderlightning process", even though as a matter of objective fact much of the interval between the two events is the result of the difference between the speed of light and the speed of sound, so that the rumble is a laggard compared with the flash. Nor do we think of a single event in causal terms – such that the first moments of the roll of thunder causes the succeeding moments. (We shall return to this issue in §11.2.3.) And the fact remains that, even for Salmon, there are distinct threads of becoming, even if his threads are continuous. Causation seems to answer to a need to reconnect items that are distinct. Causation, that is, is necessitated by interruption, which opens a space for beginnings, or constitutes endings. This in turn is the consequence of the irruption of consciousness. We shall bring this a little more into focus when we discuss "the onlooker".

11.2.2.8 Laws, causes and particular events

One way of viewing physical science is to see it as our most sustained endeavour to rise above the parochial viewpoints of embodied subjects. The most obvious fruits of this endeavour are general laws that purport to encompass ourselves and the material world we are in, not only things that matter to humans but also things that don't, within a single descriptive gaze. Despite their names, laws do not legislate or mandate what happens: they have no power. This is most evident when the laws are expressed in the form of an equation, for example, F = ma (force = mass × acceleration). There are no localities – in space or time – in these equations. The quantitative correlation between variables has no spatial or temporal direction or location. An increased force may result in an acceleration of a mass; and an accelerated mass may exert an increased force on anything it bumps into. Any directionality comes from the interests of an agent.

The retrospectively discovered pattern of what happens is not a constraint, even less an external or prior one, on what happens. The laws are not, as it were, continuous interventions. Nature's habit of repeating itself is not a *pressure* to repeat itself. Laws *are* the habits not something from without that necessitates those habits. Indeed, it is misleading even to think of nature in the absence of viewpoints repeating itself because this would imply that its unfolding was broken up into slices that are then observed to copy one another.

If laws nevertheless seem to legislate on what happens or is possible, this is only in relation to possibilities that *we* conceive and the intentions we form that can then be fulfilled or frustrated. It is our wishes and needs that translate the habits of the material world into an inevitability, into something implacable or ineluctable, into something we need to align ourselves with in order to achieve our goals or to pre-empt events we don't want to happen (something we shall discuss in §§12.4 *et seq.*). Outside of agency, the unfolding of states of the universe along certain lines seems simply that – an unfolding. (Our agency is expressed in a world that largely gets on with itself and indeed requires that world.) The universe does not disobey its own laws but it does not obey them either. Nature does not impose its own nature on itself.

Causes, on the other hand, seem to bring things about because they operate within localities that do have outsides. Once you have dropped the egg on the floor you cannot stop it smashing when it lands. The cause operates with the implacable law of gravity to bring about the effect. This inevitability is exploited in manipulability when we bring about a desired event by aligning the state of the universe with an invariable, or at least very frequent, predecessor of that event; or, less grandly, align the local state of affairs with the conditions that will make that event inevitable. Causes, unlike laws, do not operate at the level of generality. Even so, we may be tempted into thinking that they do so when we unpack the relationship between a particular cause and a particular effect and find laws "in operation". The laws, however, do not reach all the way down to singular events.

In the example just given, the laws in question are the laws of mechanics, not the laws of falling eggs. Question: why did Event A, a collision between Object 1 (the egg) and Object 2 (the floor), result in Event B, Object 2 changing its shape? Answer: because a static, rigid object such as a floor will apply a force to an object that collides with it and the force will translate into differential acceleration of parts of the egg in accordance with the general law $F = ma$. But the particular outcome of the event depends on the specific properties of the participants. Although these may be an expression of general laws (such as those that explain why an egg shell is fragile), they do not arrange the fateful meeting between the egg and the floor, sponsored by my carelessness.

We are tempted to see cause–effect sequences – which unfold in accordance with the general laws of nature – as an expression of the *power* of those laws to make things happen and in a certain way. By mobilizing explanations that straddle singular events and general laws, as when we give a scientific account of the relationship between a cause and an effect, we find a justification for our sense that things are made to happen, rather than just happening, and so satisfy our need to see what happens as having sufficient reason. We see the causes as expression of powers or of the powers of the laws they instantiate. This is misleading. Scientific, or even common sense, explanations connect not token individual events (this egg being dropped and this egg falling to the ground and being smashed) but types of event: causal *explanations* (as opposed to causal connections) are not token-token but type-type. It is this that makes them expressions of general laws and makes causes as expressions of those laws seem like explanations. But classes of events do not have causal power. Putative causal powers are exerted through tokens: it requires a particular moment of carelessness to end up with a smashed egg. No actual smashed eggs result from the general propensity of eggs to get smashed by a general fall to the ground. Classes of events – which are in the end only general descriptions awaiting instantiation – do not result in actual effects, actual happenings.[42]

So the seeming rationale conferred by the idea of causation is distant from the point where the causal power operates. The laws refer to the broadest classes of events but the powers are, can only be, exerted through individual events, though their individuality may be concealed by the necessarily general terms we use to describe them.

The powers that causes seem to have to shape or guarantee what happens are ultimately merely the shadowy presence of the general laws we intuit behind particular sequences of events, with causes being the local conduits for the expression of these laws. We are left ultimately with general patterns of happening that express (or can be made to look like an expression of) general laws. The fact that lower-level laws gradually converge on more general laws in an evermore unified scientific account of the world does not alter the situation that happenings happen merely because they happen. Relatively local laws (such as govern the fate of eggs) may seem to be explained by more general laws (such as $F = ma$ and the laws governing the effects of impacts on brittle objects) but ultimately we arrive at the most general possible laws, such as the field equations of general relativity or the Schrödinger wave equation, where explanation gives way to manifestly pure – and phenomenologically empty – description. Laws seem like explanations only from the standpoint of the lower-level laws looking up to them; but the explanatory satisfaction that the upward glance delivers is only the afterglow of our sense that events lit up by a viewpoint have particular explanations.[43]

Time, as we have noted throughout our investigation, is increasingly likely to get lost as natural science advances. However, it is not the only casualty. The ascent to generality is associated with loss of real space. The world of physics is not timeless but also placeless. Ultimately – as we discussed in Chapter 3 (especially §3.4.1) – events, space and time, shrivel to space–time points that are, effectively, numbers occupying time and place only parasitically or virtually through a frame of reference that is imposed on them. This asymptote of physical science is a restoration of the continuum of a world without viewpoint; a world devoid of phenomena because cleansed of viewpoints, a world viewed from nowhere. The terminus of the most powerful theories in physics – relativity theory and quantum mechanics – in pure number, without now or here, is exactly what one would expect. The network of discrete events which explanation reconnects by invoking causation is restored to the statue of a continuum before the irruption of viewpoint.

11.2.2.9 Localities, happening, and the apparent need for oomph: breaking and restarting the continuum of happening

Let us weave together the main strands of our discussion. Embodied subjects intro-duce viewpoints, localities, in the universe. In this world there are distinctions: between causes and effects; between features of events that are and features of events that are not causally relevant; between cause–effect pairs and the context and con-ditions in which causes may or may not lead to their effects; and between these contexts and conditions and the rest of the universe.

All of these distinct elements – locality, cause, contexts and conditions, and so on – of course have deep links with agency, since viewpoints are not merely pas-sive spectator points. Perception is inseparable from the possibilities opened up for "that being whose being is an issue for itself" as Martin Heidegger has put it; for a being-there that locates its own being in a "there" that is offset against a background elsewhere; for a "disclosedness" that reveals the world to itself – or a part of the universe to a part of itself.[44] They reveal objects as among other things "affordances" – possibilities for, obstructions to, or the background of, action. This is the nugget of deep truth in the manipulation theory of agency: that the reality of agency and the idea of causation have a shared origin in the irruption of locations in a location-less material world. The notion of agent causation is the recto to the verso of cause as (largely mindless) agency.

The opening up of locations – or worlds – around an embodied subject not only breaks up the seamless flow of happening into temporally and spatially discrete events – a coarse- or fine-grain granulation of that which is around the subject – but then requires that there shall be something that will restore the continuous flow of happening that, in reality, happens simply because it happens. Something additional appears to be required to explain, to give a hint of (sufficient) reason to, why events take place; why the flow continues despite the "inter-ruption" of consciousness. Singled out events – which of course share the implicit contingency of all happening – are explicitly contingent; consequently, more explanation is sought. That further explanation is not provided by natural laws (irrespective of whether they are contingent) since, as we have discussed, laws do not reach all the way down to the token events that are presented to conscious subjects (who live in token worlds). More seems to be required for them to happen. Hence the invocation of causal powers and the appeal to something carried over from earlier events to later ones making them the latter happen. Hence the idea that happening at time t_2 is mandated by happening at time t_1, through the combination of a quasi-inertial continuation of background conditions during the interval between t_1 and t_2 and the particular oomph that enables, within this background, certain events in t_1 to cause certain events in t_2.

There are accounts of causation that seem to occupy a middle ground between the continuum on the one hand and connections between distinct causes and effects such as that of Salmon mentioned earlier. These include seeing causes and effects as being necessarily contiguous (no spatio-temporal gap) or being phases of a single underlying process, in which each phase causes the next phase. Under such circumstances the passing on of oomph from cause to effect requires no material (only a descriptive) gap to be crossed and an unbroken flow of energy that passes through the cause and the effect or the continuation of the intrinsic momentum of a process. This will not, however, capture what is delivered by the idea of discrete causes bringing about discrete effects, an idea necessary to heal a primordially fragmented world resulting from the necessarily localised point of view of the subject irrupting into the continuum of what-is. This subject – herself embodied – is localised within that world and hence related to it in a multitude of ways, pertinent most immediately and pressingly to her bodily well-being and her survival. The irruption of the subject "dis-tracts" the putative wholeness of being into elements that are, or need to be, connected.

As will have been apparent, there is both coexistence and conflict between a cause-based and a law-based understanding of the physical world. Law-based explanations describe how things in general happen to happen, though they nonetheless seem to elevate the happening of individual events above brute contingency by describing them as regular instances of types, behaving just as all the members of their class behave. The law seems to say that what happened just now had to happen because it manifests a law that applies in all times and all places. The law – though it is itself contingent – redeems the token event from the appearance of pure contingency. If things are happening as they usually happen, things are happening as they should happen: God may not be in His Heaven but at least all is legal with the world. As we ascend to a view defined by laws of ever greater generality we eventually squeeze out locality, and causation connecting discrete events is replaced by process, by fields, and, finally, by frozen structures. At the level of, say, the field equations of general relativity, we have a manifold in which there is no sequence of events and therefore no need to invoke causes. At the most fundamental level of description, in quantum mechanics, there are no localities: force-fields give way to boundless continua marked by probability densities.

Physics, therefore, was always destined to abandon causes above a certain level of generality – though they are alive and well at the level at which most technologies work – because it progressively distances itself from the localities of everyday life in which token events occur in a particular order and require a local explanation to justify their occurrence. The appeal to laws of ever greater generality is the synchronic aspect of the diachronic notion that all token events (causes and their effects) have a common ancestry ultimately originating from (say) the Big Bang; simultaneous, non-interacting causal chains traceable backwards to a vanishing point, the singularity where time and change began. As embodied subjects, however, our gaze – and our interests – fall far short of that backward glance.

The loss of causation when we ascend above localities is expressed very well by Woodward. He asks us to consider this claim: "The State S_t of the entire universe at time t causes the State S_{t+d} of the entire universe at time t + d, where S_t and S_{t+d} are specifications in terms of some fundamental physical theory."[45] And he quotes Judaea Pearl who, argues that "If you include the whole universe in this model, causality disappears because interventions disappear – the manipulator and the manipulated lose their distinction."[46] He argues that "The systems of causal relationship that figure in common sense causal reasoning and in the biological, psychological, and social sciences" have the character of belonging to "small worlds" located in a larger environment. By contrast, "fundamental physical theories do not, at least when their domain is taken to be the entire universe".[47] In short, as locality is lost, so is causation. It is no coincidence that quantum mechanics that undermines the very idea of location also replaces causation with probability. The threat to location and to causation arose before quantum mechanics with the rise of fields and force fields and the convergence of mechanics and electrodynamics but quantum field theory took this trend in scientific thinking to its natural limit: the universe as a single wave function without localised objects or events.

While the account put forward in this section locates the origin of causation in consciousness, it does not do so in a way that is closer to Kant than to Hume.[48] The appeal to necessitating causes is rooted in the attempt to re-cement a world whose unfolding continuity has been broken up by a consciousness, a point of view that has irrupted into it. Seen in this way, universal causation is not of itself a constraint on agency but that in virtue of which there is agency. We should not speak of "a causally closed" world but of a world, opened by consciousness, stitched together, here and there by causal connectedness – a connectedness that is open for exploitation in manipulation. That world is one in which there is not only explicit time but more importantly tensed time, as we shall discuss in Chapter 12.

If there were no irruption of the conscious subject, and hence interruption, prising the world apart, then there would be no need to invoke the quasi-miraculous idea of causation, of a natural agency, as a universal restart button. The view of the world as a seamless unfolding process would do without causation altogether, except perhaps at a putative beginning. When an arrow is in flight, the successive phases of the trajectory are not *caused by* the preceding phases. The oomph is built in and inherited from moment to moment; the principle of inertia does not require anything – a boost or top up – to be transferred to the arrow. "Keeping going" is the default state. The world picture that does without causation would make processes all interconnected to the point where there are no connections as such, no bridges to be crossed, nothing to be transferred, no causal oomph required. Not only would the arrow's flight not be separated from other events in the world but the flight would not be separable from the movement of the bowstring that set it in flight. This would be an image of the world in which there are no localities, the origin would be a dimensionless point, prior to space, time and causation. It is an image familiar from standard cosmology.

The most familiar part of this image is reflected in Newton's first law of motion – that every body remains in a state of rest or uniform motion in a straight line unless acted upon by a force – and more generally in the idea of inertia: whatever is going on will continue going on (and "going on" includes stability) unless it is deflected by an outside force. The power of continuation or repetition, of habit, is intrinsic to the universe. Neither dynamic states – such as an arrow in flight – or a static state – such as an unchanging pebble – requires anything to ensure that their successive states are the same as the preceding ones unless there is something acting on them to destabilize what is happening. In the Newtonian world, first-order change – expressed in uniform motion in a straight line – is no different from stability. This stability – expressed in laws of classical physics such as the conservation of mass-energy – is evident as the viewpoint withdraws to an ever greater distance, localities are lost, and "outside" is pushed to the margins. Without the outside, there is nowhere from which causes may operate to disturb a system.

Effects outlive their causes. When I accidentally cause a tear in a cushion, it remains torn after the end of the cause. There is no magical self-healing and reversal. Likewise, the glass I knock off the table remains smashed. The challenge to the notion that causes and effects cannot be separated because a cause must be spatio-temporally contiguous with, indeed congruent with, its effect is most commonly illustrated by the ballistic phases of the motion of a projectile. When I throw a ball, we may think of the cause as the pressure my hand applies to the ball. When the ball leaves my hand, the pressure ceases but the effect continues in the absence of the cause.[49] It might be argued that we can redescribe these effects in such a way as to bring them back into the curtilage of the cause. If the effect of throwing was the increase in the velocity of the thrown missile from 0 to 60 mph, then the effect (reaching 60 mph) would be complete when the missile reached that speed. If the effect of dropping the wine glass was its actual fragmentation, then the continuation in this state would not count as a continuation of the effect of the dropping. These counter-arguments, however, rather than demonstrating that effects must be coterminous with causes, show that the division of the world into causes and effects is description-, interest-, and more generally viewpoint-dependent.

In summary, the endeavour to import a necessity into the singular, contingent events of the physical world, to making happening less happenstance, by inserting the sense of implacability originating from the law-like habits of that world into individual events, runs into all sorts of difficulties. "Causation" is an attempt to take explanation – "becausation" – down to the singularities of the actual world: to make general explanation bespoke to particular circumstances and to recruit brute forces to rational understanding, to unite energy and reason. The idea of causes as powers is close to being an anthropomorphization of happening, making events at time t_1 an agent that brings about events at time t_2.

The home territory for the idea of "powers" is the power we exert on the material or over each other, and the pushback against the exertion of such powers – the resistance we meet from the material and human world and our limited power over both. But the very notion of locally asserted powers is at odds with the wider assumption that the motor for change is built into the world – the Prime Maker (Big Bang or whatever) was the Prime Mover. In the context of this assumption, causes are not initiators, but merely conduits, for change. The activity of the universe is a great passivity, with the basic constituents of nature having no intrinsic only transmitted, no initiating only inherited, powers. Conservation laws (and their relevant manifestation in the law of proportionality of cause and effect) dictate that so-called causes bring nothing new – no additional oomph – to the unfolding of events. Bringing no powers, but riding or expressing the existing unfolding of things, they do not necessitate "their" effects.

This in no way gainsays the implacability of the material world. There has, after all, to be a necessity to be built into the world so that we can have a background of the taken for granted – ranging from the properties of our bodies getting on with themselves to the predictable unfolding of things – on which we can free wheel as we execute those niche inflections of happening that constitute free actions and shared enterprises, and maintain a space in which we live our lives rather than merely exist. This brings us to the theme of the next chapter. Before we address this, however, we have unfinished business with causation and the onlooker whose irruption into, a fragmentation of, the world underpins causal explanation or the need for it.

11.2.3 Causation: looking beyond event causation

Our examination of causation in this work is prompted by the claim that there is an intimate connection between the relationship between cause and effect and that between "before" and "after"; that the necessary temporal priority of cause to effect in causation supplies the basis of the supposed directionality of time. Our inquiry is further motivated by the suspicion that causation is invoked to glue together in an intelligible way a world sprung open by the irruption of viewpoint. Our inquiry into causation will, therefore, look beyond discrete events to other items in our fragmented world. There is nothing unconventional about this: the assumption that causes are necessarily relations between token events is disputed by many philosophers.

First let us return to the notion that causation furnishes time with directionality. A key interlocutor on this issue has been Mellor, whose commitment to the causal arrow of time is testified to by his other major publication *The Facts of Causation*, a rigorously argued analysis of what he believes to be the real nature of causation.[50] His analysis has two features. The first is an attempt to mediate between a conception of causes as having executive powers – making their effects happen – and an interpretation of causes that effectively replaces them by probabilistic patterns of sequences of events. Under the latter interpretation, causation is non-deterministic. The second is that what makes causal statements true is not events but facts (or "facta"). I shall deal with the first point briefly because it is less relevant to the fundamental argument I shall develop.

Mellor argues that causes are not straitjackets determining their effects but merely raise the latter's chances. This definition seems to avoid the Humean embarrassment associated with "causal necessity", as some kind of hidden force intrinsic to the material world, without reaching for Kantian clothes that make it internal to the world-making mind. More importantly, it captures different aspects of the complex notion of causation: the fact that causes may be means to ends (we do A to raise the chances of B); that they have an apparent explanatory force; and, given that you can't raise the chances of something that has already happened, that causes are prior to their effects. The definition also seems to straddle the notion of causes as having powers ("raising the chances") without that power mounting to material necessity. It is in tune with, though it does not entirely succumb to, the displacement of causation by probability in fundamental physics. The background conditions are the places at or contexts in which an E_{cause} can operate to produce something as specific as E_{effect} (cf. being in London is a necessary condition of seeing a friend in London). Factors (e.g. smoking as a factor in lung cancer) are half way between causes and correlations and (possibly) background conditions. Dispositions and states of affairs (the way objects and energies are disposed) are background conditions.

So far, so good. It is not clear, however, that it takes us any further in trying to define the difference between causes and conditions. Indeed, it pretty well completely breaks down the distinction between causes and conditions, except on the criteria of salience. After all, conditions also increase the probability of what are regarded as "effects". Consider lightning. This will increase the possibility of audible thunder, but it will do so only if there is air in the space between the lightning and ears of a potential auditor. Without lightning, there would be no thunder. Without air, there would be no thunder. Without conscious auditors, there would be no thunder. All of these "raise the chances" of a thunderclap being heard. Clearly, however, the lightning seems more qualified to count as a cause in our usual understanding than the other items. Even so, the lightning does not "raise the chances" to 100 per cent and the total deafness of potential auditors would lower the chances of a thunderclap being heard to 0 per cent. The difference between causes and conditions is to be found more in the matter of salience and the difference between standing conditions and occurrent events, a difference that makes the latter "stand out" – another aspect of salience. The hearing capacity of potential auditors normally goes without saying – or being noticed.

The discussion in the previous section would suggest that the difference lies not in the inherent properties of the causes and effects but in the way that happening is observed and from what viewpoint or for what reason. It is possible also that we might differentiate causes from conditions by seeing the former as relatively short-lived occurrents contrasted with longer-lasting standing states of affairs, between platforms and things that spring off from them.[51] Mellor, however, does not discuss this. The other problem is that the notion of "A raising the chances of B" could simply boil down to an expression of otherwise unexplained patterns of succession of events: this follows that because that is how things are. In other words, "raising the chances" does not bring anything specific to the party additional to the fact that events follow patterns. Its clearer application to agency – "If you want X to happen, then do Y" – rather narrows cause in a problematic way we discussed in §11.2.2.4.

Mellor argues that the fundamental kinds of causal statements concern facts (true propositions) rather than events. What makes causal statements true are fact-like genuine entities which he calls "facta".[52] This seems to go against our ordinary understanding of causal relations as being between token events: the bang on the table at t_1 and the noise emitted by it immediately afterwards. Before we examine this, it will be useful to look at other alternatives to token-events as the protagonists in the causal story.

We shall set aside the nearest alternative: that causation connects event-types. This is obviously vulnerable as event-types don't occur at any particular time while the manifestations of causation most certainly do. That's their job. The origin of this evident mistake is confusing actual causal *connections* with the wider notion of causal *explanations*. A particular bang on the table (E_{cause}) causes a particular noise (E_{effect}) but it does so because of the general properties of the table, of the item striking it, and the air between the table and the hearer's ears. In other words, a causal *explanation* will incorporate general observations and, beyond that, an appeal to the laws of physics. Locating causal explanation in the relationship between event-types arises out of what we might call "explanation-creep", shifting attention from a particular cause that accounts for a particular effect, to a general pattern of the linkages between causes and effects; from the reality of token interactions towards the intelligibility of types of interaction.

So much for event-types. More plausibly, we may regard *processes* as well as events as causes, but this is hardly surprising because (as we noted in §6.2.1.1) processes are only happenings seen from within, so they are ongoing. The same happenings seen from viewpoints that regard them as complete would count as events. In short, process-rooted causation is essentially event-based. Even so processes-as-causes are not without difficulty. Where processes causally interact (for example an ongoing rain-shower and the physical and social responses to it) we may find it difficult to define the limits of the cause–effect pair. The boundary between processes and the context or circumstances in which they act is fluid to the point of non-existence. Process causation may consequently result in an account of unfolding that is too thick-and-sticky-fingered for the clockwork of the universe. We could end up with a kind of process paste – which is hardly surprising given that the aggregation of events into processes is a step towards restoring the one-ness of a world previously fragmented into events, into smithereens of happening.

There have been other candidates for the offices of causes and effects. The weakest seem to be *properties*, with causation being relations between property instances, and properties being clusters of powers, typically located in objects or collections of objects. They do not seem to be adequate to amount to either causes or as effects, if only because they do not exist as stand-alone items. Properties, being general, seem to belong to the realm of possibility – defining the scope of possibility – rather than delivering actuality: they occupy a ground somewhere between dispositions and circumstantial conditions. Stephen Mumford and Rani Lill Anjum have argued that dispositions (of, say, material objects) are the source of causal power, being "more than contingent but less than purely necessary".[53] This does not, however, take us all the way down to individual events and token causation (i.e. actual causation) because dispositions require the right circumstances to be expressed. Those circumstances will include not only static background conditions but what we might call "a local ongoingness" in which they are expressed. Consider what is required for the brittleness of glass to translate into a pane of it becoming splinters of glass.

Even so, properties as causes cannot be so easily disposed of because they are a version of non-event causation that has had a major role in discussion of emergent properties, notably of mental items out of the material of the brain. A prominent example is John Searle's use of non-event causation to explain how neural activity can give rise to qualia.[54] Water, he says, is made of molecules of H_2O that are not in themselves shiny, slippery, or moist; however, there is no doubt that there is nothing more to water than molecules of H_2O. The sum of the microscopic entities causes the macroscopic appearance.[55] Something analogous applies to neural activity and consciousness.

This is not a persuasive example of non-event causation, for several reasons. Firstly, the cause ("molecules of H_2O") is identical with the effect (wet water). If the former is identical with the latter, then all the properties of the one should be shared with the other. In other words, the water should also be the cause of the effect "molecules of H_2O". The absence of directionality would seem to collapse the causal relationship and all we have is stuff – water, molecules of H_2O, call it what you like – being itself. The other objection is more directly relevant to our present concerns; namely that the supposed cause and the supposed effect are not separate in time: there is no ongoing water without (before or after) the ongoing molecules of H_2O. The notion that stuff such as water is something that is the cause of its own properties such that the latter are its effects is clearly absurd.

There is another version of non-event causation in which it is not mass-noun stuff but the count-noun *objects* composed of it that are self-causing. Mellor has argued that objects cause their successive states: that O at t_1 is the cause of O at t_2. It is part of his general principle of placing "the causation of stasis – a's being F at a later t because it is F at t – on a par with that of change".[56] Not only do things that happen have to be made to happen but the relative, local non-happening at the heart of the idea of a (stable) object also has to be made to not happen, so that objects retain their identity over time. This mode of object-causation would seem at least to preserve the temporal direction of causation: O at t_2 could not be the cause of O at t_1. But there is a lingering suspicion that O as cause and effect would have somehow to be its own cause (and effect).

There is the obvious concern that the notion of causation is being mobilized in circumstances where there is no happening, to ensure *no* change (though it may be required to resist macroscopic change in the face of a multitude of small changes – as in states of dynamic equilibrium). It is as if a seemingly idle object, doing nothing at all, is secretly madly busy about keeping itself in business. A cup must cup itself in order to remain a cup. More generally an object is something that does itself, not so much the referent of a noun as a standing verb. Such a view entirely merges causation with background conditions: O at t_1 is clearly the cardinal condition of O at t_2. More to the point, object-as-cause, securing its own continuity, would have no causal efficacy left over to act outside of itself. If the effect is proportionate to the cause, and both C and E are O, then there is no spare capacity for foreign engagement. And Mellor would seem to be committed to the notion that the more stable an object is, the more causally active it must be, more engaged in maintaining itself.[57] It would also imply that the object, busy about self-maintenance, would be quarantined from causes outside of it – unless they were invoked as part of a joint enterprise. However, though this is difficult, it is important for Mellor to maintain this in order, perhaps, to get the causal arrow to deliver duration of, as well as the succession of, states.[58]

The idea of objects causing (other) objects to materialize is a little awkward, if taken literally: it would make causation rather like 3D printing. On the other hand, the notion of objects being causes neither of themselves nor of other objects, but merely of events would seem to risk a disproportionality between cause and effect.[59] While, if the circumstances are right, there may be inequality between causes and subsequent (if not immediate) effects – as when I roll a stone down a hill that starts an avalanche which engulfs a village – the causation of an event by an object seems a different kind of disproportionality, not only in the sense of being damped rather than amplified but in the ontological difference between the parties on either side of the causal link. To put it another way, there is an odd asymmetry in a (whole) object bringing about a happening that was less than a whole object – simply a perturbation in part of it. Of course, if the entirety of the object was involved – in the sense of becoming an event-cause – it would lose its status as an object, which requires at least that it should have an unchanging core. Allowing an event to "set" as a noun phrase – "Raymond throwing the ball" – seems the best compromise, conferring upon it the apparent solidity (or at least stasis) of an object.

There is another mode of causation which might seem to be object-to-object which I would like to illustrate by a couple of examples. The first one is frequently cited: the see-saw. If we think of the see-saw as two distinct parts that are connected, then the entirety of the item to the left of the fulcrum is affected by the entirety of the item to the right of the fulcrum. This still does not, however, deliver object-object causation, for two main reasons. First, if we take each side of the see-saw as a whole, then the cause (one side goes down) and the effect (the other side goes up) are simultaneous. At the very least, they are sufficiently overlapping for any temporal order between them to be theoretical. Secondly, neither the cause nor the effect is an entire object. What we have is "one side going down" (event – as cause) and "the other side going up" (event – as effect). The see-saw example is unsatisfactory in other ways; notably, that the decision as to which of the events is cause and which effect is typically defined by the side at which an agent brings about the see-saw movement. In the absence of such an agent, we merely have not a succession of "seeings" causing "sawings" but an event, or a succession of events, or a process, called "the see-saw rocking". Another way of putting it is to describe it as "a rigid object rocking", all of whose parts are obliged to rock, without privileging one part. In short, the *separation* of the upward movement of one side and the downward movement of the other does not correspond to any physical reality.

The same considerations apply to another example: that of a train moving out of a station. Let us assume that the engine is in front and the carriages are securely connected to it and to one another. We could see the exit of the train as a single event or process driven by the engine; or we could see the movement of the engine as a cause with the movement of the first carriage as the effect which is in turn the cause of the movement of the second carriage which is in turn the cause of the movement of the third carriage – and so on. In other words, we may see the train pulling out as a single process or as a chain of causally related processes. There is no fact of this matter: the difference is entirely description-relative. Whether we detach the carriages in our account of the causal process(es) will be up to us and have nothing to do with what is intrinsically happening. This refers us back to the critique in the previous section of the notion of causes and effects as successive self-defining events, defined, that is, independently of anyone's interests, any criterion of saliency.

We could argue that these examples, in which the material involved in the cause and that involved in the effect are not clearly distinct, or are not considered separately,[60] are limiting cases illustrating something that is implicit in causation. Namely that the cause and the effect should necessarily be contiguous, at least at the moment at which the cause brings about the effect – a qualification that acknowledges the ballistic or inertial phase of effects when contact has been lost with the cause. This is evident in the causation of push-pull mechanics. Increasingly, however, physics has identified fields that permit "action at a distance" and hence the operation of causation over what appears to be gaps, though the fields are continuous. (This is an important step towards the "de-localization" of causes and the ultimate replacement of causation by probabilities seen in quantum mechanics.)

If no interval is allowed between cause and effect they have to be entirely overlapping throughout the period of causal action; in short they have not only to be congruent, but simultaneous. This was famously argued by Kant, giving the example of the depression caused in a cushion by an individual sitting on it.[61] Assuming perfect elasticity in the cushion, the pressure from Kant's bottom (the business end of the transaction) and the depression in the cushion must occupy the same period of time. This seems to be required by the principle of the proportionality of effect to cause; for example, the depression in the cushion should be proportional to (i.e. a direct translation of) the instantaneous pressure from the bottom. The kinetic energy is transformed into the energy required to overcome the resistance of the cushion. Under such circumstances, we might be inclined to give up on the separation between cause and effect, even as phases of a single process ("Kant's bottom depressing a cushion") because the overlap is complete. The proportionality principle could be extended further to support the claim that precise proportionality requires the cause to be identical with the effect in all respects and for the two to be in identical circumstances; in other words for the cause and effect to be the same token event. At the very least, this would require that the cause and effect should overlap completely: by the time the cause is complete, so too must the effect be.[62]

If this argument is decisive, then the notion of underpinning the direction of time with that of causation looks forlorn. However, the analysis of the relationship between the cushion and the bottom does not take account of real world slippage between causes and effects; or at least between the beginnings of causes (that take time) and the beginnings of effects (that endure) and the ends of causes and the ends of effects. While at the level of the (somewhat discredited) billiard ball atom, there has to be a notional instantaneous transmission from cause to effect, at a macroscopic level effects have to build up: sustained pushing as opposed to momentarily impacting. The depression in the cushion requires sustained pressure (at least over milliseconds) from Kant's bottom before it becomes macroscopically visible. We see hysteresis – delays in onset of and offset of effects compared with their causes – everywhere in everyday life. Beyond this, there are phenomena we have already touched on: the ballistic phases of effects and enduring consequences of momentary events. I knock a glass over. It is set in motion and continues moving beyond my period of contact with it – the first ballistic phase or continuation of the effect. Then it falls to the ground – a second ballistic phase of the effect. It strikes the ground and is shattered – an irreversible effect that will outlast the cause – in most cases forever.[63]

The thing that may strike anyone who considers the candidates for the relata connected in a causal relation is that they are all in some sense description-dependent or at least description-sensitive.[64] In §11.2.2, I argued that the notion of causation as a cementing of the universe presupposed that it had in some respect come apart so that its elements had in some sense to be put together again; more specifically, something had to ensure that it passed from one state to another; that a kind of continuous restart or reboot was necessary so that whatever happened had to be *made* to happen. The pulling apart was the result of the emergence of a conscious viewpoint that located things in relation to itself – as "near" and "far" and also as salient (foreground), salient (background) and irrelevant, invisible actuality assumed to be in some sense "there" but beyond the horizon of experience or, more broadly, concern. What is picked out could be most precisely identified as the referent of a noun phrase, either stand-alone or attached to a verb. Such an expression, added to the explicit or implicit assertion that it happened, would amount to a proposition. At this level, it is a matter of discretion whether causes are identified as token events, processes, properties, objects, or states of affair.

Consider a cat's yowling waking up a baby. It is equally valid to describe it as:

(a) The cat's yowling (event) caused the baby to wake up (event).
(b) There was a process of a baby being woken by a yowling cat.
(c) The noisiness of the cat (property) interrupted the sleepiness of the baby (property).
(d) The cat (object) woke the baby (object).
(e) The state of affairs in which the baby was awake was caused by the state of affairs in which the cat was yowling.

These are not, of course, equally good English but they are equally sound as analyses of the causal relationship and it illustrates how the pinning down of the relata involves linguistic choices. In most cases, what are identified as cause and effect are items that could not exist by themselves. This does not mean that the relationship itself is intra-linguistic or language dependent. There is a truth – "The cat woke the baby" – that is true irrespective of whether anyone says so. Or, rather, "The cat woke the baby" has an extra-linguistic truth maker, unlike (for example) "a baby is a young person" or "a cat is a member of the species *felis catus*".[65]

It is important to underline this in order to address the second, and for the present discussion more important, aspect of Mellor's analysis of causation: his identification of causes and effects as *facts*. This is how he puts it: "[C]auses and effects are first and foremost facts. Only derivatively, and then only in some cases, do they include particulars."[66] His reason for preferring facts is that while "*that* a particular exists" has chances, particulars do not: they merely happen, as opposed to having chances of happening.[67]

Before we criticize this aspect of Mellor's account of causation, it is worth reflecting on what it has going for it in addition to its responding to the necessary description-dependency of what count as causes and effects. The most striking benefit is that Mellor's identification of causes and effects as *facts* gives equal standing to positive and negative causes because these are equally facts. Consider the heat of the sun and my failure to water them as causes of the wilting of the flowers. As we have already discussed, it is difficult to see how something *not* happening, a non-event, could be a cause whereas both "Tallis watered the flowers" and "Tallis did not water the flowers" seem equally pukka as facts, and equally able to furnish propositions with truth values. This makes it easier to incorporate the counterfactual dimension into the idea of causation. This seems too generous: ascribing a kind of ghostly, energy-free, or honorary, even parasitic, causal power to things that do not happen. There are, however, other major problems with identifying causes and effects with facts and they take us to the heart of the connection between causes, events, and time.

The first is something that we have discussed already (especially in §5.2.3 "Reality as Tenseless Facts?"); namely that, while events occur at a definite time, facts do not; indeed, they do not occur at all. The Battle of Hastings took place in 1066. *The fact that* there was a Battle of Hastings, however, did not take place in 1066 and, *a fortiori*, the fact that there was a Battle of Hastings in 1066 did not take place in 1066 or, indeed, at any time. Facts – "the fact that x or y" – are not occurrents – this is why Mellor has selected them for his theory of causation in which causes raise the chances of effects. Causes and effects, however, take place at times – and it would be difficult for Mellor to deny this, given that he is relying on causation to provide criteria for allocating roles in the "before–after" relationship, and that he defines time as the causal dimension of space–time. Facts, what is more, are not located in space: the fact that the Battle of Hastings took place in 1066 is neither close to, nor far from, either the Battle of Agincourt or the fact that the Battle of Agincourt took place in 1415. So it is difficult to square "causes as facts" with the key feature of causation, that causes and effects are typically contiguous with one another or at least are directly or indirectly in communication.[68]

That facts are tenseless is another reason why detenser Mellor would wish to embrace them. But that which makes them tenseless also makes them timeless. Facts in this sense are eternal, perhaps only potentially so inasmuch, being true propositions or the referent of true propositions, they may have a beginning, though they do not have an end.[69] Since they concern the "done and dusted", they are beyond change. The Battle of Hastings came to an end but the fact that a battle took place at Hastings has no end – except in regimes (such as the former Soviet Union) where the past is as unpredictable and malleable as the future. Hence – to reiterate – having no time of occurrence they have no temporal relations.

The replacement of events by facts in Mellor's account of causation is at odds with his claim that the direction of time can be outsourced to the direction of causal relations and these latter are the relations between facts. Admittedly, facts, compared to transient events, seem stable, lasting from the events that make them true until the end of time. But are they out there in the physical world? Is his theory at least in part an over-reaction to an acknowledgement that causes and their effects are picked out linguistically? That they are not self-identifying, self-discriminating or self-bounding? Has this seduced him to the more radical notion that they are intra-linguistic, such that for him causes seem to be *de dicto* rather than *de re*? By making facts – something corresponding to verbal descriptions – stand in the place of events, he seems to risk drifting towards linguistic idealism. Facts are stubborn things but their stubbornness, relative after all only to lies and wishful thinking, does not go deep enough.

"Fact" after all is a profoundly ambiguous term. Are facts internal to descriptions or are they items "on the ground", "out there" as we would expect causes to be?[70] That they are not just items on the ground becomes clear when we ask ourselves the question: How many facts are there in this pub? It is not like asking "How many people are there in the pub?" or "How many barrels of beer are there in the cellar?" or "How many chairs are there inside the lounge bar?". Facts are description-dependent. It is a fact that there are more people in this pub than there are skyscrapers at the North Pole but this is not something located in either the pub nor the North Pole. Language and extra-linguistic reality are the inseparable recto and verso of facts. There are no facts without language but nor are there any without the relationship between language and extra-linguistic reality.

It might be argued that it is equally empty to ask how many (extra-linguistically defined) events are happening in the pub at a given time or how many events took place over a particular 20 minute period. There is, however, some way of specifying kinds of events to render them countable but this is not true of facts. For there is something about events that roots them outside of language: they are items on the ground, as for example, that man's journey to the bar at 8:30 p.m. Their description-dependency does not go "all the way down": they do not dissolve in language. This difference between facts and events can be highlighted by negative facts that have equal standing to positive ones. That the cat came into the room and that the cat did not come into the room are both facts but only one is an event. Yes, the fact that the cat did not come into the room had consequences – encouraging the mice to continue nibbling the cheese. But this is permissive rather than agentive and seems to acquire reality only in relation to the expectations of human beings which could in turn be reported equally as negative or positive facts. The "consequences" for the non-conscious material world are all negative; for example, that there were no pawmarks on the brand new carpet. There is no limit to the negative consequences we might unpack. But these are hardly effects of a cause. If they were, then we would have an infinity of negative effects of non-events. The fact that an elephant didn't come into the room would have even more impressive non-consequences, none of which needs spelling out. Indeed, there is a limitless number of things that do not happen at a given time, each with limitless describable consequences. The point is that they exist only insofar as they are thought up, envisaged and articulated – and are not on the ground. We can see this when we consider "the fact that nothing happened in the room between t_1 and t_2" is not an event or a set or succession of events. Facts are generated by our making things – non-happenings as well as happenings – explicit. Events, while they have to be made explicit in order that they should, as it were, be delineated, cannot be generated by statements of fact. In contrast, facts are made by statements of events. In short, Mellor's giving equal status to things that do not happen, as to things that do happen, in his account of causation, threatens to drag real events down to the level of things that did not happen. Linguistic idealism beckons.

Mellor's position, however, is perhaps not as vulnerable as the foregoing may suggest, especially when it is expressed as follows: "[Causes] relate not particulars but the entities, if any, whose existence makes true the sentences 'C' and 'E' entailed by a true 'E because C.'"[71] If we replaced "entities" or "existent entities" with occurrent events, with things that, unlike facts, actually happen at a particular time, it would be difficult to quarrel with this formulation.[72] However, to do so might not be possible to square with the other, seemingly unobjectionable, aspect of his account of causation: that causes raise the chances of effects. It is Mellor who argues that an event does not (in itself) have chances: it simply is. What has chances is "*That* it happens" or (more precisely, though Mellor does not say this), "*That* it might happen". In order to get from event E to "*that* E *happens*" or "*the fact that* E *happens*", or "*the chances* E *might happen*" several steps are necessary. The first is making E explicit as a discrete entity, cut out by a description. The second (another aspect of the first) is to see it as an example of a *class* of events of type E: events cut out by descriptions are classified. And the third is to locate Es in a world of possible events and to compare the frequency of their occurrence in the presence or absence of events of type C.

It is evident that Mellor has taken the notion of cause far from the common-sense idea of causation as an intrinsic necessity in the unfolding of the material world. He has rehoused the causal relation from the material world and actual events to the world of discourse and of possibilities that may or may not be realized. That is how events that do not happen – presented as negative facts – earn their place at the causal table. Outside of human life – with its plans and articulated expectations – things that do not happen carry no causal clout. If there are genuinely extra-linguistic items connected in his account of causal relations, they are not events but truth-makers. These, as we discussed in §8.2.2.4, fall short of particularity, and hence of reality or actuality. That which makes a proposition true is less than that which is sufficient to make an event. The irreducible generality of the referent of propositions is the trade-off for intelligibility.

In trying to understand why one thing follows another, we invoke general principles, laws, patterns, or mere habits. But that is not sufficient to deliver the oomph that seems to be necessary for causes to generate, or even render more probable, effects that can be ascribed to them. Without actual events located in space and time, there is no such oomph; and without transmission of oomph – the exchange of (overall) conserved quantity (of e.g. energy) – there is no causal relationship. The absence of the requirement for oomph in causal processes is the other side of Mellor's giving equal causal status to positive and negative facts – to omissions and absences (where nothing such as energy or momentum is transmitted) as well as commissions and presences. Even so, we can see a point where Mellor's theory of causation connects with the argument we presented earlier according to which causation belongs to a world made explicit in, by or to, a viewpoint that implants locations in the universe and springs it apart into things that are near or far, belonging to a foreground or a background, important or irrelevant. As Mellor has in my view rightly argued, causation cannot be separated from the "that" of "that such-and-such is the case". But he has embedded causation too deeply in an understanding of facts that assimilate them into language (or propositions) so that they cease to be occurrents, located at a particular point in time. Event E takes place at time t; but *that* E took place does not occur at any time. Facts, properly understood, straddle consciousness, language, and the material world. They are neither wholly mental, inside language, nor, though causality is an objective feature of the world, are causes "on the ground".

Mellor is right, therefore, in regarding causation as a relation in "thatter". His seeing language and the truth-makers of propositions as fundamental to causation reflects a realization that causes and effects do not pick themselves out: they are not entirely natural extra-linguistic kinds or indeed kinds to be found outside of any viewpoint.

They are the joint products of the viewpoint of the embodied subject and the reality it finds itself in.[73]

To take this discussion further, we need to consider the nature of viewpoints and look at the "onlooker".

11.3 THE ONLOOKER

11.3.1 The irruption of viewpoint

> The world is the dehiscence of the universe.   After Gabriel Marcel[74]

> If, then, the soul withdrew, sinking itself again into its primal unity, Time would disappear: the origin of Time, clearly, is to be traced to the first stir of the Soul's tendency towards the production of the sensible Universe...   Plotinus, quoted in Gale, *The Philosophy of Time*, 33

> The I am illuminates the world.   Aramaic John, book 1, verse 4

"The world", Wittgenstein said in the famous, oracular opening to the *Tractatus*, "is all that is the case".[75] We should clarify this: the human world is all that is the case. Outside of consciousness, and in particular the propositional awareness of human beings, there is no "is the case". Indeed, there is no "that".[76] And when Wittgenstein goes on to say, "The world is the totality of facts, not of things", he is not quite correct.[77] The human world is certainly one in which we have to take account of facts but it is also populated by things and events. It is human consciousness that turns these items – that they are (in the case of objects) and that they happen (in the case of events) – into facts, into what it is that makes true propositions true. But there is a more fundamental point, already made in §11.2.2, and most directly relevant to the present inquiry; namely, that the pre-human, or pre-conscious, universe in which the human world is located, is made up neither of discrete facts nor bounded things. Nor does it consist of little arias of causation set in a recitative of events that happen to be temporally (but not causally) related to one another.

It is tempting to envisage the universe prior to the irruption of viewpoints, as a homogeneous, continuous whole, unfolding through time – an unfolding that would presumably consist of pure continuity, as there is no differentiation to underpin change. Such a view, though strange would be consonant with the increasingly standard vision of the universe as seen through the lens of what is currently the most powerful scientific theory: quantum mechanics. Here, as we have noted, the totality is a single wave function and there are no individual objects and locations. In the pre-sentient world, it is not merely a case of the standard "entanglement" of items separately encountered: there is no prior disentanglement. These, along with spatial separation, heterogeneity, and distinct temporal locations arise in relation to sentience. Sentience illuminates and disentangles the universe, opening up a world and a viewpoint for which and from which it is illuminated. This point of view locates itself with respect to and within the world it illuminates.

Such a view of the world prior to sentience must by the nature of things outrun any possible evidence and the notion of the origin or generation of localised (and presumably embodied) viewpoints in an undifferentiated universe is, to say the least, problematical as anyone who has wrestled with Kant's *Critique of Pure Reason* will know only too well.[78] The causes we see operating in the world around us, and with which we operate, are at the very least description-dependent. More profoundly, they have to be "picked out" or individuated as unarticulated or articulated opportunities. More profoundly still, *events* are "picked out" linguistically or pre-linguistically. Salience is all: it directs what we pick out and also how fine-grained our attention is – whether we attend to or speak of the dog, of the dog's barking, of the dog's barking at that moment, of the dog's barking in that place at that moment, as the cause of the baby waking up. In short, our causal judgements are scale-relative because our event-perception is.

The point I am making has been expressed succinctly by Merleau-Ponty: "[events] are shapes cut out by a finite observer from the spatio-temporal totality of the objective world".[79] Donald Davidson's assertion that "events are identical if and only if they have exactly the same causes and effects"[80] links the observer-dependent individuation of events with the interest-dependent identification and individuation of causes and effects. There are particulars, and particular causal relations, only with respect to the perspectives of Lichtenberg's "cause-bearing animal". It is scarcely surprising therefore that as we shed perspective and ultimately mislay observers, particularity disappears – something we shall address in the next section.

To say this is not to indulge in magic thinking: events do not *occur* merely through being imagined or described. Real occurrent events do not become causes of (desired) effects simply because I deem or wish them to be so. The sincerity of my incantations does not make the world more biddable. If there is magic at work, it is the magic that gives the "onlooker" the privileged position in the world, a privilege that, as we shall see in the next chapter, enables true agency, even though the capacity to manipulate the world, to make it conform more closely to someone's desires, and to make it safer and more comfortable, has its limits. The privilege of the observer is not over other observers or over the physical world he encounters – illuminates and engages with – but the privilege of observing. The onlooker is the link between causation and the perception of the temporal order; between causation and agency and temporal depth; between the natural world as something given and that profoundly exceptional part of nature that is the human world.

In paying attention to onlookers, we are picking up an argument adumbrated in the first chapter, in which they were somewhat short-changed: (a) their consciousness was reduced to a literal single-sense viewpoint – vision; (b) the latter was supporting only explicit time and, important though this is, it is only one aspect of onlooking; and (c) they were spectators whereas onlookers are also active participants in a world that engulfs them through the embodiment that is the condition of their onlooking. The onlooker is a being who is (as Heidegger put it) "an issue for himself" and he is a "thrown being".[81] Onlookers are embarked on a voyage in part dictated by the sea from which they have emerged and in which they will without exception eventually drown.

We think of the world as illuminated by millions — more precisely billions — of pin-pricks of light whose particular kinds of need illuminate parts of it and leave others in the shade of inattention and irrelevance. It is not by accident we are attracted to this metaphor of a world being "illuminated" by the consciousness of an embodied subject. Vision has a unique capacity to enable the world to be experienced known, engaged with, and eventually foreseen, *from a distance*: the light that makes it possi-ble is relocated on the distant objects from which it arose or on which it was reflected. The light that comes from the glass is referred to the glass as the latter's visibility. The onlooker is separated from that which is revealed to her: there is touchless , non-reciprocated encounter. Telereception such as vision, which is a revelation of a world arrayed around an embodied subject, and is distinct from him, highlights the aboutness of experience.

The reason for my present focus on the subject as on*looker* is that vision is the sensory modality above all which highlights how, courtesy of intentionality, we can be in the heart of the (or our) material world (as we must, being living organisms) and yet off set from it. *Qua* onlookers, we are connected with and disconnected from that world. As our glance — the glance of an embodied subject not of a mere organ-ism as it were wired into its surroundings by stimuli triggering immediate reflex responses — pans round, so we connect and disconnect with different aspects of the world. We also *direct and choose* our experiences, most obviously when we posi-tion ourselves in order to have certain experiences. While non-human animals, too, position themselves — move to vantage points — to acquire perceptual information, in humans this capacity is vastly enlarged as we develop "extended intentionality" that draws not only on our individual capacities but also on the pooled experience of predecessors and contemporaries who have helped construct the community of minds — the *Lebenswelt* — to which we belong. It is on this basis that we come to *see* causes, rather than merely being a conduit for them as our causal sense would lead us to expect, and are able to *exploit* those causes as instruments to achieve envisaged ends. The viewpoint — more broadly an embodied subjectivity and objectivity — has, however, to be self-sustaining.

The onlooker is not a ghost requiring neither food, drink, warmth or shelter. She is inseparable from an organism whose continued existence is dependent on engage-ment with the world-as-environment as and when needs must. This explains why the universal unfolding into which viewpoint irrupts is not a connectedness of infinite density, in short a continuum. Instead, it is a rather patchy causal nexus. The latter is a location-dependent, subject-dependent salience that picks out events and sees them as potential causes related to effects we wish to bring about. "The cause-bearing animal" is also the location-bearing animal, situating and being situated.

Visual revelation is the paradigm of explicitness. What is *is* (in italics) when it is there before me, revealed: it is *that* (more italics) which is and that which it is. It is, and it happens, *for* a subject. The latter's objective location in the world as a body, which is nowhere in particular, is supplemented by a subjective location that is most definitely somewhere very particular – namely the moving centre of the universe, in relation to which things are near and far, touching on "me" closely, only slightly or not at all, of great interest, or little, or none. It is in relation to this most definite somewhere, occupied by an observer who lands in the world and arranges things around his immediate or remote interests, that the unfolding universe, envisaged as being in itself an unfolding plenum, exhibits discrete causes that seem to have to be linked to discrete effects by a necessitating mechanism.

The reader may worry that causation, the child of the irruption of viewpoints into the world, is now itself presented as in part an *effect* – of the impact of the revealed world on the (embodied) subject to whom it is revealed. In other words, that I am drifting to a position that causes, which I have claimed are not inherent in the viewpoint-free world are somehow implicated in conferring specific content on viewpoint. This suggests that they were there all along, in the absence of onlookers, ready to cause experiences of themselves.[82] This is more than a little local difficulty. It touches on deeper problems which I owe it to the reader to own up to, though I have no way of solving them.

Nor has anyone else. It is the mystery of the place of the mind, the subject, of first-person being in a universe that overwhelmingly seems mindless, subjectless and no-person:

(a) Idealism that incorporates that universe in the mind cannot deal with the fundamental fact that minds are inseparable from particular bodies, as their necessary condition, that share fundamental properties with the mindless universe. Embodiment, which is necessary for minds to be individuated, to occupy particular trajectories in space and time corresponding to their individual lives, is also a prerequisite for the *sharing* of lives that weaves the communal fabric of the human world. But this knowledge ultimately locates us in a universe that extends beyond our lives and makes our existence a minute product of a gigantic order of being that has largely got on without us.

(b) On the other hand, materialism cannot account for the distances opened up in the universe by minds, subjects, and persons: their worlds, the explicit distances within them, the knowledge they have, the "at" and "aboutness" that makes some parts of the world "here and now" and others "there and then" and yet others an "elsewhere" in part given over to the infinitely complex landscapes of memory, knowledge, and speculation.

(c) The most compelling attempts to escape this dilemma sometimes depend on ambivalence between mind as a category and minds as individuals. We discussed this in §10.5.3 with respect to a couple of examples from relatively recent Western philosophy: the explicit idealism of Kant; and the occult idealism of Heidegger.

The Kantian subject transcends the body; it is the bearer of, rather than located in, space and time. This may work if the bearer is a generic, eternal, locationless mind, which can ensure that space and time are shared, universal forms of experience (of "sensible intuition") so that you, I, that tree on a slope, the moon, and the distant stars belong together. Unfortunately, there is not simply one stuff called mind. There are minds in the plural – your mind and my mind – that address particular parts of space and time (and unite parts of the world through the perception of causes) and through their bodies are located with respect to them. The empirical selves of Mr Smith and Mrs Smith are tethered to the location and the fate of particular bodies located in particular parishes of space over specific stretches of time.

Heidegger hoped to cast aside the problems of a viewpoint located in a body by giving primacy to *Dasein* (being-there) as being-in-the-world. Bodies as items present-at-hand and minds that are aware of them are derivative. Unfortunately, for being-in-the-world to constitute the individual destiny of a *Dasein*, it is necessary for there to be awareness located in and localised by a particular body. Being-there implies being in a particular there, with different things to hand, and different concerns for "that being whose being is an issue for itself" – in short requires a being-here or being-in-a-particular-here. That role can be discharged not by a general category of *Dasein* but requires a plurality of individual *Daseins* that look suspiciously like embodied subjects. Any other view – that sees the world as both illuminated by and differentiated by a single category of *Dasein* – would be idealism.

This, perhaps the most compelling unfinished business of post-Kantian metaphysics, is not adequately addressed in this work; nor, to my knowledge, in any other. The image that lies closest to hand when we think of the irruption of viewpoint into the world is that of a pool of light. How those pools of light are themselves pooled to illuminate a single world, or a universe in which cohere all the worlds of self-conscious beings over history, remains entirely unclear.

11.3.2 Uncovering the universe and the path to objectivity

I have postulated a primordial universal connectedness prior to the emergence of, or in the absence of, conscious beings with viewpoints. We may think of this pre-conscious connectedness in terms of the continuity of matter and of the forces, and of the fields within which the forces operate, though in the pre-scientific era, the connectedness might be mediated through *logos* in which the entire world was intelligible to a higher being. The most recent scientific expression of this continuity includes the manifold of general relativity where masses, events, space and time are fused in mathematically described and variously curved space and variously dilated time. The alternative, also already discussed, is the universe as a single wave function. In neither case are there discrete entities – not even events – to be united through causal relations.

The connection between the irruption of an individual viewpoint which imports location (in space and time) and the causal sense becomes evident as science progresses to ever greater generality and distances itself from individual viewpoints. The gradual removal of the perspective, interest, and location of the observer by instruments that reveal ever more robust (location- and person-independent) objective, quantitative truth, replacing phenomenal reality by numbers, eventually leads to the loss of causation in favour of probability densities and, via the replacement of localised objects with continua that are force fields, loss of location. Causation linking particular, singular events is replaced by laws linking event-types and eventually by a manifold whose components are space–time points, defined by numbers that have no intrinsic location, or quantum fields in which everything is entangled with everything else and there are no discrete objects.

There is much that is deeply suspect in what I have just said. At the very least, with the undifferentiated continuum as a putative starting point, the origin of locality, of discrete, embodied, self-concerned subjects and their worlds of distinct objects and events, remains obscure. Man "the cause-bearing animal" is, if we are to believe the fossil record, a parvenu in the universe, a recent manifestation of life. He is the latest product of a series of processes: first, a lifeless universe giving rise to insentient life; next, insentient life acquiring smudges of awareness; then, pin-point sentient life giving rise to life with structured consciousness; and this in turn evolving to the self- and world-conscious existence of human beings. It requires a steely determination to think of each of these steps in non-causal terms; to think of "gives rise to" as simply an unfolding. This, however, is how we seem obliged to envisage the successive states of the universe leading up to, and hence in the absence of, self-interested viewpoints, of embodied subjects, such as ourselves.

The "world" of sub-human organisms is hardly a world in the way we understand it. Animals, as Heidegger said, are "world-poor".[83] Even less do such creatures exist in a universe, a putative infinity of space, time, and matter in which lived worlds are suspended. So there is a sense in which the putative starting point – the universe, envisaged as a continuous unfolding totality, encompassing all its spaces and its times – is brought into being with the emergence of the human viewpoint, the irruption of the full-blown onlooker.

This may seem close to philosophical idealism, or even a confusion of the epistemic givenness of the universe with its constitutive properties. This suspicion may be well-founded but let us stick for the present with the seemingly unexceptionable claim that the universe – as a unified totality extended over vast quantities of space rather than located at a particular place, and as enduring over vast quantities of time – does not exist in itself *as* a universe. This is no more radical than asserting that the space–time manifold cannot be accommodated at any space–time point. Or the part cannot enclose the whole. Or the whole cannot grasp the whole. The universe as an *extended* totality of something that has a multitude of parts *and* is a whole (hence the explicit extendedness) cannot exist except in relation to the viewpoint that irrupts into it and for which, eventually, it comes to be present in the form of knowledge that transcends the experience of the viewpoint.

This is the ultimate basis of the claim that the relationship between cause and effect cannot be understood independently of a deeper metaphysical inquiry into the nature of things and the place of humans in the universe at large. The reduction of "before-and-after" to "cause-and-effect" is therefore an extreme case of putting the cart before the horse. Chains of events connected in causal relationships are extracted from the general unfolding of the universe by an individual or collective consciousness and this will depend in turn on the position, the interests, the concerns and the potentialities of the individuals in question; in short a saliency that is rooted in an initial revelation of "what is *there*" to individuals in the aspect of what is before them that they have to take account of, modulated by where they are in their own lives, itself framed by certain – biological, historical, and social – characteristics of what it is to be human. This is why in the world around us only a minority of events are in an explicit causal relationship and that most of what is happening appears causally disconnected. This is not due simply to our short-sightedness. Even if we were aware of everything that was going on, the world would not appear to us as an infinitely dense mesh of causal chains. Causation would drop out as the universe was restored to an original unity.

Even so, there are truths about the world that do not appear to be interest- or even viewpoint-dependent. We are, or seem to be, in possession of objective truths of ever widening scope. The first phase of the path to objectivity – which involves shedding viewpoint-dependent local interests – is paved with material objects that can be reliably revisited and are there, what is more, for all others, friends and strangers, are sensed by dogs and cats, and deflect or arrest or propel other material objects. Among the latter is the privileged, special object that is the living, conscious body.[84]

Awakening out of mere sentience into a world of (discrete, stable, real, incompletely disclosed, independent) objects facing a subject is a crucial step in the discovery of the material continuum which was broken by the irruption of consciousness. A world of such objects is the folk ontological platform from which science takes its rise that, in the form of quantum mechanics and the four-dimensional continuous manifold, has recently arrived at a virtual, uninhabitable place in which there are no places, no localised objects, and no discrete events. The irruption of the subject lies at the start of a cognitive journey that ends wth the recovery of the universe uninhabited by itself. The gaze is key to this but let us start a little further back.

We may imagine a hierarchy of living creatures and the *umwelten* (to borrow the term of Jakob von Uexküll), the worlds, in which they live.[85] At the level of primitive (unicellular, parvocellular) organisms that world is an unsummed sum, an unobserved pattern, of exchanges of energy and materials across its boundary. Any world ascribed to such an organism is put together, or perceived by, another, much higher, organism – namely, a human being. The organism does not know the world it is at the centre of nor does it know the centre: it has no "at", "in", or "within", and does not have ownership of a world; it is not enworlded. From this we may trace a journey in which sentience develops into sense experience and, eventually, this yields a perceived – defined, explicit – world with an explicit, and explicitly environed, subject at its centre, which is both an ensemble of objects, events, spaces, times and persons, and a nexus of meanings.

The onlooker is at the centre of his world. The arrangement, however, is not straightforward: the concentric circles of near and far are not unchallenged. The ego at the centre of egocentric space is aware of other modes of organization of the world.

One of the most profound challenges comes from the acknowledgement of other egos sustaining spaces arranged around other centres. The onlooker is onlooked – by predators, authorities, family, friends, lovers. The emergent ontology subscribed to and lived by the subject will be crucially one that is had in common. The very idea of an object is of an entity that exists for other people and the very idea of space is of something that others occupy, are located in, and is had in common. We meet in a shared, continuous, unified space.

The onlooker is aware of objects arrayed around him and of himself as located among those objects. As an embodied subject he is a privileged object – that in virtue of which the objects are present – and as a body an object among objects. The path to objectivity is paved with intersubjective agreements between embodied subjects as to the nature of the space that is shared, agreements that are ultimately expressed in measurement that reduces space and the things that occupy it to pure quantities and seems to transcend even intersubjectivity. That this table is 1 metre wide and 2 metres away, or that the earth has a 25,000 miles circumference and that it is 240,000 miles away from the moon, is no longer a matter of agreement between you, me, and our community but seems to be inherent to the items in question.

Objective, quantitative space, does not, of course entirely erase egocentric space. The latter remains a continuous mode of our physical (as well as cultural) reality. The ways in which objective and subjective space intersect are many and various. Consider how navigating the streets interacts with reading the map of the streets. We alternate between scanning what is in front of us and moving our eyes over the map. Even the sat nav, taking its instructions from a coordinate system tethered to the stars, respects the ego of the driver: "Now turn to *your* left".

Our interaction with objects is dynamic. Even when they are not moving or in some other way changing, our experience of them is continually altering. I look at that chair and my gaze is constantly on the move, scanning it (indeed, an entirely static gaze on an entirely static object would fade).[86] This is how we build up, and maintain, awareness of an entire object, a table setting, a set table, a dining room. It is how a visual field, a visual setting, a context, a mini-world is constructed. The restlessness of the gaze is self-cancelling because the object (the chair) or array of objects (table setting, set table, dining room) it builds up is static. Central to this stasis is the sense that the objects exist in themselves: they are distinct from the flow of experience in which they are revealed. The beholder freezes items in the perceived world in order that they may be manipulated.

This is deeply mysterious: that the flow of happenings should be arrested; and that the unchanging laws of the unfolding universe should give rise to particular objects and, even more mysteriously, discrete events that precipitate out of continuous unfolding and then sink back into it. Both physically and psychologically I am an unceasing torrent. The reader may remember the beautiful analogy from Bergson of two trains moving in parallel at the same speed and passengers in each of them (in this case the embodied subject and the perceived object) being consequently able to reach out to each other and hold hands.[87] It seems particularly apt here, notwithstanding that we cannot begin to understand how the two trains maintain the same speed. How (to use Bergson's words) "fixity" can be extracted from "an ephemeral arrangement between mobilities" lies beyond our understanding.[88] Intelligibility will have a key role, as we shall discuss in Chapter 12. Free will would seem less distinctively problematic if it were appreciated that events are no less mysterious than actions. They are as dependent on the viewpoint – and indeed the stable and stabilizing viewpoint – of an embodied subject as are actions. (We see here an important link between focusing of attention and the exercise of freedom.)

Leaving aside the question of "How", the fact is that the world is arrested to the relatively unmoving framework of movement, the continuous relatively stable framework of occurrences, with the congruence of its successive moments, such that a background is established against which change, evolution, history, happening, may be experienced. This immediate background is set against a succession of ever-larger, ever more stable backgrounds: the chair is in the room, the room is in the house, the house is in the street, and so on. The background is extended further, and in different dimensions, by means of knowledge – propositional awareness of truths not attached to particular time – embodied in language. The vast semiosphere that extends beyond the biosphere of the human organism has a new kind of stability: that which belongs to items that are the referent of general terms.

Many consequences follow from this but two – which are linked – are of particular relevance to our present inquiry. The first is the sense that the world has an intrinsic reality that transcends our experience. This is a profound assault on the primary position of the sentient creature as being the continuing, and continually present, centre of an implicit world populated by intermittently present external objects. While the onlooker may be the necessary condition of his visual field and in some sense its ruler (so that he can cancel it by closing his eyes), his sovereignty is always being challenged: he is on the edge of a room, of a crowd, his position is eccentric. More fundamentally, because he is an embodied subject, identified with, or at least inseparable from his body, as an object among objects, it is evident that he occupies a rather small part of the world opened up to him by vision. The gaze that sees what is there sees also (a) that it is seen from a viewpoint and (b) that what is visible is only a part of what is there: there is much that is visibly invisible. The subject fills only a small part of a house, is a dwarf among trees, and a minute dot in a landscape or a city he has walked into being, though his preoccupations make this only an intermittent concern, a continuing low-grade uneasiness. It is both underlined by the various ways he has involuntarily to *be* the small body (and the small part of that body) which he is and at the same time concealed by the all-engulfing nature of being that body, most evident in effort, suffering or pleasure.[89] Toothache can occlude a mountain landscape.

Repositioning one's self to see more, to see the unseen but suspected, is the primordial form of inquiry, driven by the knowledge of the limits of one's own knowledge, or (in the case of closer scrutiny) the suspicion of error, by doubting one's own senses. The role of pointing in extending the sense of possibility, of that which is yet to be revealed, evident from other viewpoints, but those that are actually inhabited, is central, as the part it plays in infant development and in human life, makes plain.[90]

The gaze that knows where it is gazing from, that knows at least that it is gazing from somewhere in particular, is ripe to critique itself, to see itself as a mere version, as a perspective, as a subjective view on objects that have intrinsic properties that will always elude complete translation into experience.

The world opened up by and to our senses is, of course, not merely a coloured sphere or hemisphere of sense data. Our surroundings are (it hardly needs saying) intelligible. We see "chairs", "facial expressions", "dangerous situations", etc. Objects and states of affairs are "affordances" opening up possibilities for, and making demands on, us, as well as being permissive or obstructive backgrounds to our purposeful activity. To the extent that items are intelligible, though they occupy particular locations in space and time, they are instances of general classes, and as such are lifted above space and time. It is in the intelligible material world that the breathing space called "possibility" – that makes it seem necessary to invoke causes (and laws and the rest) to explain actuality – opens up. This is the origin of the modal realms of "might" and "must", of the sense of contingency (things might have been otherwise) that awakens the need for a corresponding principle that explains how they turned out as they did.

This intelligibility extends the freedom which we enjoy as onlookers, enabling us to access an ever wider world "out there" without exposing our bodies directly to it. Behind this is an extension of intentionality beyond, far beyond, its manifestation in the perception of objects, beyond the "aboutness" most marked in vision. It is here where the present apparent digression from our theme of time and causation will connect with our primary concerns about the nature of time and its place in our lives. Its purpose will become apparent in the next chapter.

It would be remiss not to round off this discussion with a brief further reflection on the suspicion raised earlier about the very nature of the inquiry we have just undertaken. We have sketched what we might call a genealogy of objectivity, a path from individual episodic sense experience to objective truths about the world. It is a path we may imagine being taken by organic matter as it evolves towards its masterpiece humanity and possibly recapitulated (with steps missed out or bypassed) by the developing infant acquiring everyday ontology. First, there were insentient beings who did not get it at all; then there were primitive sentient beings who experienced it but did not get it; and then there were more sophisticated beings who got more and more of it and got more and more of it right; and finally there were theorists of everything who got it all right.

The irony of "masterpiece" is intended to flag up some reservations about this Whiggish account of genetic epistemology. This story of consciousness is deeply peculiar. Its destination, its goal, its triumphant conclusion, is to rediscover the universe as it might look in the absence of consciousness. This is the continuum into which viewpoints emerged. So the story is one of a backward journey to the point of origin, to a primordial state before the original cognitive sin of the irruption of the onlooker, who turned the X of the universe into a seething tumult of "That x is the case", dis-tracting the world into elements that had then to be bound together and joined up into successive states each of which is made to happen by their predecessors as their causes. It is difficult to avoid the image of a building being completed in which the roof turns out to be the ground out of which the building grew. This ground is what is visible to the view that is seen from nowhere; a view that transcends all views and becomes no view at all. This story makes it less surprising that the end of all observations will be a completed objectivity in which the observer, who woke to an objective world, is erased and there are no subjects. It is analogous to, indeed a generalization of, the Escher staircase we noted in the relationship between subjective and objective time (§10.5), in which subjects seem to play a part in constructing the objective time that locates them as insignificantly brief episodes in a long history.

11.4 FINAL OBSERVATIONS ON TIME, CHANGE AND CAUSATION

Change takes time. Change requires time. These two statements don't mean exactly the same thing. The first merely asserts that change does not happen instantaneously, and so is extended over time. Whatever happens, happens at a certain (finite) rate. The second seems to imply something more: that time is a necessary ingredient of change; something, at least, that is needed for change to happen even if it does not cause it to happen, though behind it lurks the notion of time as creator and destroyer.

We have already looked briefly at the notion of time as the cause – or an auxiliary cause – of change. This is not a unitary idea. As Newton-Smith has pointed out, there is a distinction between "date causation" (with each moment in time bringing its distinctive causal contribution to the unfolding of events) from "duration causation" (with the causal contribution of time being a reflection of the quantity of time deployed).[91]

"Date causation" reflects the fact that certain times are propitious for the occurrence of certain events. However, this plausibly translates into the idea that certain *circumstances* (that happen to be prevailing at one time rather than another) predispose to certain events. We can cut out the middle man – time – in the causal chain. Event E occurs at time t not because time t requisitions it but because a state of affairs S at time t makes it probable. It is S not t that is relevant to determining what happens. It is darker towards midnight not because it is midnight but because of the relationship between the sun and the patch of earth on which we are located at that time. I celebrate my birthday on 10 October not because of the specific powers of 10 October to cause celebrations to happen but because that was the day in which I happened to be born.

Time as duration causation is less easily disposed of. Things take more time because they are improbable (we have to wait for them), they are against the general run of things, or they have to contend with a certain sluggishness in the states of affairs from which they arise. So, for example, it takes longer to get a heavy object moving from a state of apparent rest to a high speed than a light object to a modest speed. The difference is built into the relevant law of motion, $F = ma$, where a is acceleration – the rate of change of the rate of change of location. The equation, however, shows why we should not think of time as a cause proportional to its quantity. The work is being done on the left hand side of the equation – F, which produces the acceleration – not by t embedded in acceleration on the right hand side. On the right hand side, we have the substrate (mass) and the change in its motion (acceleration). The essence of the change is movement; time (which appears twice – first in its translation into velocity, and then in the translation of velocity into acceleration) is merely a quantitative descriptive of the movement. It is neither a movement nor an agency producing movement in its own right.

This may be challenged by pointing out that: (a) m is also a pure quantity, like the t that is hidden inside acceleration; and (b) the longer (time) F is sustained, the more acceleration results. Let us deal with the first point. m stands for the quantity of real physical stuff that has a stand-alone existence and can be seen and touched. Time does not seem stand-alone in this way. But what about the second point? If F is maintained for 10 seconds as opposed to 5 seconds, then the resultant acceleration of the relevant object will (assuming everything else is kept constant) be doubled. So can we not think of time as being as it were a co-cause acting "joint and severally" with F? The answer is no because we can increase the resultant acceleration by increasing the intensity of F – so a will double if F doubles – but there is no equivalent increase in the "intensity" of time. We can get more acceleration in a given time if we increase the force but we cannot get more acceleration in a given time if we vary the intensity of the time. That is why we speak of forces being increased (at a time) or sustained (over a longer time) and not of time being increased (at a time) or being sustained (over a given force).

That is the obvious reason why duration as a cause – and time more generally as a cause – must be set aside.

There is, however, a deeper reason. This is the other side of what we noted in the case of date causation: that events will not happen unless they have their causes and conditions in place. The other face of this principle is that time, being common to all events, and being itself homogeneous, would not have a role in bringing about one event rather than another. If time truly were something in itself independent of change – which is presupposed in the very idea of its having at least contributory causal powers – it would not have the power within itself to deflect the course of events in one direction rather than another. Changes bring about change and time being independent of change, or not being a specific kind of change, would not favour specific outcomes. It is fibroblasts, not time, that are the great healer of wounds.

What is more, if time had causal powers, every event would have two causes: first, the preceding local event or state of affairs and, secondly, time. Time as cause would seem to be the mother of all over-determination theories, at odds with the principle that no single event can have more than one sufficient cause at any given time. How the two – the apparent cause and time – would work together would remain obscure.

Denying the efficacy of time may seem to go against general relativity and other physical theories where time (and space) are seen as "active players" in the world. However, our discussion in §10.3.3 had led us to share the growing consensus that contemporary physics has left the metaphysics of space and time in total confusion allowing space and time to be: (a) purely relational, (b) substantial players in their own right, (c) simply parts of the geometry of the world, (d) all or (e) none of the above.

In sum, the fact that events require time does not mean that time is even a contributory cause of them. Where this leaves Mellor's claim that "time is the causal dimension of space–time"[92] unclear. Equally unclear is the relationship between the idea of time as an independent cause of events and its being the causal dimension of that in which events occur.

Let us end this discussion of the postulated causal powers of time by returning to the notion of time as *permissive* that we discussed in §10.2. There is, as it were, a proto-permissiveness: time as "the possibility of possibility". This, however, does not amount to anything near to a causal power. If we take the idea of cause seriously (and notwithstanding the discussion in this chapter it serves some function), it must at the very least have a role in making a particular event or state of affairs more probable. The possibility of possibility is remote from the greater (or lesser) probability of any actuality. A general opening of a universe-wide door to change does not deliver any traffic through the doors. The purely permissive is neither propulsive nor directive. It cannot even act synergistically with present circumstances, as it were allowing them a particular future different from the present. This is evident from the fact that time is equally present in that which is unchanging as in that which is changing; in a static as in a dynamic system. Notwithstanding the argument about temporal vacua, "nothing happening" is as time-consuming, indeed time-greedy, as "something happening".

The tenacity of the idea of time as a cause, as a force bringing things about, as bearing all her sons away, as healing wounds, and so on, is derived perhaps from our sense of the limited reach of our own agency; our sense of the universe getting on with itself, largely without our permission or intervention. More specifically, there is our tragic sense of life, our feeling that every day we are a day older, a day nearer our death, a feeling of helplessness. The succession of milestones between our birth and our death makes time seem an irresistible, propulsive, implacable force.[93]

Against this we pit our freedom – which brings us to the theme of the next chapter, and what is possibly the most important purpose of this exploration of time.

Addendum
Mellor on memory and the causal arrow of time

Mellor tries to maintain the connection between the direction of time and causation by assigning a key role to memory:

> In short, our experience of the direction of time demands nothing more than an accumulation of memories, of memories of memories, and so on. This, and the fact that memories are effects of what we remember, is what, on causal theory of time order, makes the flow of time seem to take us forward into the future rather than back into the past.[94]

That is to say, experiences are effects of events, memories are effects of experiences, and memories of memories are effects of memories, and so on. There is thus an objective causal arrow leading from perceptions to memories and thence to memories of memories. This is reflected in our experiences, giving us the sense of time flowing from the past (where the experiences and hence the events they are experiences of are located) to successive futures (memories, memories of memories) which provide a viewpoint from which experiences are seen to recede into the past.

There are many reasons why this view should be rejected. Firstly, the causal relationships between event and perception, and between earlier and later memory, are inferred rather than manifest – and there is something seriously amiss with thinking of causal relations in this context. More importantly, however, is something we have discussed already: namely that the causal relationship between a perception and the event it is about is not the same as the causal relationship between the perception and the memories of the event. Merging the two requires perception to work twice: once to be the objective basis for the direction of time (events must precede experiences, experiences must precede memories, and memories precede memories of memories); and a second time to provide the subjective experience of the direction of time. This is reflected in the fact that causation also has to work twice: once to underpin the relationship between experiences, memories and memories of memories; and a second to be the basis of the relation between experiences and the events in the experienced world that are supposed to cause them. This is the basis for getting "earlier-to-later" out of "cause-to-effect". Of course the events I am aware of must be prior to my experience of them and the experiences of those of events must be prior to the memories of those experiences. But that would seem to make the direction of time have priority over the direction of causality. Mellor, however, requires causation to determine the direction of time.

There are several other problems. The first is that, even if we accept the causal theory of perception and memory, there is clearly a rather dubious relationship between event-to-perception on the one hand and perception-to-memory on the other. The former is an interaction between a perceiving subject and the material world, and the latter is an interaction within the perceiving subject. The former does not seem to have the same kind of clear-cut temporal order as (say) the sequence leading from perception-to-memory to memory-of-memory. The first is implicit (or inferred as being a condition of a true perception, the warrant for its truth) and the latter is explicit, where the experience (or the experienced event) is clearly prior to the memory of the experience. Making things explicit is a back-tracking. It is, as we have discussed, counter-causal: the bounce-back of the embodied subject viewing the world from which he is receiving inputs. It retains the cause when the effect is in place – hence holding open the past.

Another problem with Mellor's attempt to derive the direction of time (in the material world) from the direction of causation is a wobble between time as something out there in the material world (such that there is a succession of events) and time as something perceived *as* the succession of events (including inner events such as memories). They are, however, different and this difference is highlighted when we think of time intervals versus the perception of time intervals. Consider a succession of events E_1, E_2, E_3. They give rise to three perceptions P_1, P_2, P_3. These three perceptions somehow come together, being remembered as a series or a sequence: $P_1 \rightarrow P_2 \rightarrow P_3$. The sequence, which is our perception of the sequence of events, is gathered up in a kind of super-percept that constitutes a perception of the time interval between P_1 and P_3: what we might call P_{time}. However, in arriving at P_{time}, we have gone beyond a causal sequence. Reaching back from the third to the first perception, is in the reverse direction of the causal sequence, rather as the individual percepts reach from themselves to their putative causes.

And this problem does not even take account of the fact that the notion of memories of perceptions or memories of memories of perception or memories of succession of perceptions or of successions of memories does not correspond to what is actually the case; namely that recalling memories is not a mere immediate effect of having a perception or a distant effect of having had a memory of a perception. It is often a voluntary act (auto-cueing) and is usually sporadically, even capriciously, prompted by our desire to make sense of the world. Connected with this is the fact that we can order memories as we like. I might recall today's breakfast at 10 a.m. and then recall a breakfast I had on holiday a few years ago at 10:05 a.m.

CHAPTER 12

Time and human freedom

12.1 INTRODUCTION

I have been more successful in saying what time is not than what it is. Perhaps this should not occasion surprise. The other side of the idea that time is real is the belief that it is *sui generis*, and consequently not analysable in terms of other things – as a quasi-spatial dimension, a succession of numbers, the direction of events, or pure change. All interpretations of time that do not translate it into something else turn out to be implicitly or explicitly circular; so that apparently satisfactory definitions turn out on closer inspection to be tautologies along the lines of "time is the temporal relationship between events" or "time is measurable duration". I shall be content to have arrived at the notion that time is fundamental or primitive – that time is time. There is, however, one final important job to be done, which concerns less what time is than what it does or rather what (human) time permits. In this final chapter, therefore, I want to examine the relationship between time and human freedom; more precisely between tensed time and agency.

(Voluntary) actions seem incompatible with the conventional idea of ourselves as a material part of a material universe, whose events express unfolding processes directed by fundamental physical laws established before we appeared on the scene and continuing after we have left. This vision of the world that brought us into being seems to be difficult to reconcile with the idea of free will, expressed in actions that are not traceable back to the Big Bang but originate with us, manifesting something that is unique to ourselves, deeds that redirect the course of events in accordance with our intentions. To see that this is possible, though perhaps not fully to understand *how* it is possible, we need to highlight phenomena that do not fit into the physicalist world picture. The items in question are intentionality, and its increasing elaboration in humans, and the temporal depth with which it interacts.

In the investigation that follows into how tensed time makes it possible for (conscious) humans to exercise freedom, I arrive at the fundamental purpose of this book:

to rescue the image of humanity from the increasingly common view that what the physical sciences say about the universe as a whole gives a complete and truthful portrait of what we humans are. That such scientism cannot accommodate intentionality or tensed time or find any basis for agency should suggest that the physical sciences are not, after all, moving towards a theory of (absolutely) everything; more specifically that they are seriously deficient when it comes to understanding human nature and the place of humankind in the cosmos. Unfortunately, the opposite conclusion has been drawn: namely that because science has no use for them, intentionality, tensed time, and agency are unreal or illusory; that it is our common-sense view of ourselves that is deficient.

In this, the final phase of the examination of time, therefore, I will bring together many themes of the previous chapters around the thought that temporal depth, rooted in the intentionality of human consciousness, and made explicit in tensed time, is the basis of human freedom. At the heart of this thought is the notion of explicit possibility – or of a space of possibility – which distances human beings from the material actuality of their condition. From this human "outside", they can act on their own behalf (operating directly or indirectly through the organism in which they are embodied), identifying, and using, largely material causes as the agents of their agency. Our might lies in "might" – in the entertainment of possibility.

Time opens up "usable possibility", only if it is available in a (tensed) form in which successive moments and their associated states of affairs are co-present. Through the lens of tensed time, the possibility of change can be discerned *as* possibility and actual events as the realization of possibilities. For agents, these possibilities correspond to goals, aims, wishes, fears, hopes and so on. Realized, they join the small but crucial sub-class of material events that are *brought about* rather than merely happening.

Ultimately, I shall argue, we owe our freedom to being creatures who are at once in time and, in virtue of our explicit awareness of time, also outside of it. At the root of this ability is the intentionality of human consciousness – the aboutness of perceptions, thought, memories, beliefs and such-like.

12.2 INTENTIONALITY, CAUSATION AND TENSED TIME

12.2.1 Intentionality: eliminating eliminativism

Let us begin at the ground floor.

I argued (in §11.3.2) that human beings, being uniquely developed as embodied subjects rather than mere organisms, are also unique in having fully developed sense of persisting objects distinct from themselves.[1] The human world is populated with, among other things, full-blown objects that are connected with subjects by the intentionality of perception. The object is experienced as being not only something other than the perceptions that reveal it but more than what is revealed. The object that the perception is "of" or "about" has a constancy – over time, across angles from which, and lights in which, it is perceived, and between persons. This constancy withstands change. This is most clearly evident in the case of a change of position: Object O at Position 1 at time t_1 is the same as Object O at position 2 at time t_2. In virtue of the continuing existence of Positions 1 and Positions 2, O becomes at t_2 the curator of its own past. By this means, it transcends not only the experiences that reveal it at any given time but, courtesy of those experiences and the constancy of the background against which it changes, it transcends its state at any particular time. That is implicit in our perceiving enduring objects rather than time-slices or disconnected states of objects.

Thus the intentionality of human consciousness at its most basic: the appearance of an object to a subject. Ultimately intentionality will unfold to create the vast "semi-osphere" – the realm of aboutness, of signs and meanings – that constitutes the individual, shared, and collective consciousness corresponding to the human world. Because it does not fit into the scientistic world picture, intentionality has attracted the hostile attention of philosophers committed to those various forms of physicalism that would assimilate the human world to the physical one. Let us first remind ourselves just what a difficult customer intentionality is.

At the most basic level, intentionality points, metaphorically speaking, in the opposite direction to causation. This is not, of course, reverse or backward causation or some kind of force emitted by perception. It is better to conceive of intentionality by thinking of perception reaching beyond itself to that which occasioned it and beyond that in turn to an object underlying, or implicated, in the immediate extra-cerebral, indeed extra-corporeal, cause of perception. In conventional understanding, seeing a cup has as its proximate cause the light reaching me from the cup, entering my eyes and ultimately triggering off nerve impulses in my visual cortex. Again in accordance with conventional understanding, the light that has been reflected from the surface of the cup – in virtue of which I see it, it appears to me – is causally upstream from the events in my brain. My seeing sees beyond myself and any bodily processes that are involved in seeing.

This is very awkward indeed for the materialist world picture. Just how awkward becomes apparent if we attempt to describe object perception as we have just done in the standard materialistic language of cause and effect. We have to envisage the effect (neural activity in my visual cortex) somehow being in contact with its own causal ancestry (the light from the cup), in order to "reach out to", "to be about" the cup and to relocate the light arising from the cup back on to it. To put this another way: the causal chain in virtue of which the light "gets in" (to the eye and the brain) fits comfortably inside the world picture of physicalism; while the gaze that "looks out" most certainly does not. This is underlined by the fact that what the gaze looks at is not the ever-changing pattern of light on the object but something that we see revealed by that light: an object with a back, and an underneath, and an inside, and a future, and a past, none of which are presently exposed by the light.

We may conclude from this that we should resist the idea that the appearance to a subject of a world of objects is the product of a causal interaction between objects – such as cups and brains – mediated in the case of vision by electromagnetic radiation. Causal interaction of the kind ascribed to the physical world does not explain perception because effects do not *face* their causes.

Another reason for being suspicious of the causal theory of perception (and, more broadly, of a causal theory of consciousness) is that, as we discussed in Chapter 11, the very idea of causation seems to presuppose consciousness. We might not agree with Hume's psychologizing reduction of causation to an association of ideas but other accounts – probabilistic, counterfactual, manipulative, and so on – also require consciousness for causes to be picked out. (The extent to which they have discrete existence independent of being picked out remains uncertain.)

There is an additional reason for rejecting a theory of perception that tries to assimilate the outgoing gaze to the causal consequences of the incoming light. It commits us to a causal theory of the perception of causes. Consider E_1 as a cause of E_2, its effect. That in virtue of which I am aware of E_1 and E_2 – the two perceptions P_1 and P_2 – and that in virtue of which I am aware of the causal relationship between E_1 and E_2 – let us call it P_3 – would be a causal relationship similar to that between E_1 and E_2. In this case, it would not be an event but a relationship between events that causes P_3. It is, however, clearly a different kind of process, a fact that can be highlighted by reminding ourselves that, in the causal relationship "E_1 causes E_2", E_2 does not refer back to, or establish an intentional relationship with E_1 – even less with the material objects in which the events E_1 and E_2 take place.

There is yet another problem with the causal theory of perception. We normally expect a proportionality between cause and effect, though circumstances may sometimes be such that the effect of a cause may be amplified. There is no imaginable proportionality between the putative cause of an experience and the experience itself. They belong to a different order. There is nothing in material events that would seem to make them able to have effects in virtue of which they have an appearance. Light in making itself visible, or in making the objects it illuminates visible, is nothing like the kinds of effects that we see in the physical world – for example photo-voltaic effects or the darkening of photo-sensitive pigments. The transformation of physical energy into (secondary) qualities they do not have in themselves – so that, for example, light looks bright or red – is another manifestation of the disproportionality, indeed incommensurability, between any physical cause ascribed to experience and the experience itself.

Questioning the causal theory of perception may seem to go counter to common sense. While perception does not typically perceive itself as being caused by its objects, this seems to be made manifest in ordinary experience. I pinch myself and feel pain or press my eyes and see sparkling lights: these appear to be examples of a conventional relationship between causes (the actions) and effects (the experiences). This is true; but these sensations lack intentionality: they are not about anything clearly distinct from the subject; or at least the embodied subject – in contrast to what is experienced in sight or hearing. But this might only open on to another question. Doesn't full-blown intentional perception also support the causal theory of perception? After all, I position myself to see a cup; or I switch on a light to see it more clearly. An object can be made to disappear by being covered up – or removed

– or by the subject closing his eyes or moving to another place. These, surely are examples of engaging with a causal chain to have experiences that are effects? They are indeed. And more generally, the world of perceptual experience is a world that physically impinges on me. But that is not the whole story.

The very idea of "impingement" – and, even more, being impinged upon by a "surrounding world" – needs to be examined critically. The perception that is made possible by positioning, or switching on a light, is not simply part of a single sequence of events originating in the light that (say) terminates in my brain. If the brain were the terminus, then there would be no difference between light being seen and light landing on a photo-sensitive surface or a mirror. In practice, neither the surface nor the mirror sees the light. Even less does either see the object from which the light arises. And even less does it see it as an enduring, independent "out there", kept at a literal or metaphorical distance as "other". That is why a mirror is not impinged upon – in the way that I am impinged upon – by a world that explicitly surrounds it. The moonlight that lands on a deserted pool is not referred by the pool to the moon as its origin. The moon is not revealed to the pool any more than the pool is revealed to the moon. Neither appears to the other.

Of course, when I see an object, there is a material connection mediated by light between the object and neural activity in the visual cortex. The intentional target of perception does, however, not stop at the neural activity in the brain or even retinal activity but reaches beyond this to the interaction between the light and the object made visible by it. This alone is sufficient to demonstrate that the sensory pathways and the perception they underpin are not simply means by which the conscious body is wired into a material world around it. Equally inexplicable, but less obviously so, is why the backward reach of perception stops at the object and does not continue up the causal ancestry in any of many directions: into the path the light has taken to the perceived object; into the process by which the object arrived at its present place, present state, or came into being; or even a notional point of convergence at a common causal ancestor of all these lineages, even perhaps the first (un)caused cause. It is as if the causal chain is bent back on itself as perception reaches out to its intentional object and intentionality is bent back on itself at the point where the embodied subject needs to engage with the world.

There is more to be said about the material events associated with consciousness seemingly reaching back to their own causal ancestors and the standing items that underpin them and we shall return to this.[2] But enough has been said, I hope, to explain why physicalists, particularly neurophilosophers, *hate* intentionality and are determined to eliminate it from philosophical discourse or wrap it up into the causal chain linking material events in the material world with material events in the material brain. Since it is going to have such an important role in our understanding of the possibility of free actions, it needs to be defended against those who, denying its reality, espouse a so-called "eliminativist" theory of mind, which replaces – or aims or claims to replace – talk of mental contents with talk of brain processes.

Writers such as Paul Churchland,[3] Patricia Churchland,[4] Stephen Stich[5] and Alex Rosenberg[6] have argued that those items to which intentionality is ascribed – which included propositional attitudes such as desires and beliefs as well as perceptions and memories – belong to a "folk psychology" which contemporary science (in particular neuroscience) cannot accommodate and that philosophy should no longer countenance. There is nothing, they argue, in the structure and the function of the brain that corresponds to (say) items that have intentionality. Since activity in the brain is identical with the mind, such items belong with angels, demons, and *élan vital*, in the ashcan of intellectual history.[7] In a scientifically grown up psychology, we are to believe, an ontology of perceptions, beliefs and desires will be replaced with an ontology of brain processes. The experience of the colour green is not something that is made possible by neural activity; it simply *is* a particular firing pattern in a colour space whose axes mark different frequencies and distributions of firing patterns. Green does not merely correlate with, or is caused by, this activity: it *is* this activity. It will be noted that the axes that define the space in which firing patterns take up their coordinate positions are smuggled in, as they are in general relativity (see §3.5.3.1).

Elminativists envisage "a post-intentional future in which we've given up trying to explain intentionality in scientific terms and instead abandon it altogether in favour of radically redescribing human nature exclusively in terms drawn from neuroscience, physics, chemistry, and the like".[8] The fundamental logic of this position is expressed most succinctly by Rosenberg: "Consciousness is just another physical process. If physical processes cannot by themselves have or convey propositional content [i.e. aboutness], then consciousness can't either."[9] Beliefs, thoughts, etc. don't map onto brain states from which it follows that beliefs, thoughts, and so on don't exist. The opposite (and obvious) conclusion – that since consciousness *is* intentional, it is not a physical process or not like those known to physics – seems to have been overlooked or rejected.

As many have pointed out, eliminativism is not only contrary to the overwhelming testimony of everyday experience, it is also self-contradictory or, more precisely, pragmatically self-refuting. Anyone who argues that intentional states and propositional attitudes are unreal is actually using language that has referents (in this case abstract ideas) as its (higher-level) intentional objects. What is more, they are expressing and asserting beliefs. What else other than beliefs are claims like these: "Intentional states do not exist", "You are wrong to think intentional states exist", "The claim that intentional states exist is false and based upon uncritical common sense", "The notion that there are intentional states must be false because scientists tell us they cannot find anything corresponding to them in the brain", etc.? In short, it is impossible to deny intentional states or to argue about the truth or falsehood of ideas without making assertions that, if they have any meaning, express higher-order intentional states which are, of course, rooted in a sea of perceptions "of" and other basic intentional items.[10] The subtitle of Stich's eliminativist polemic – *The Case Against Belief* – which sets out his beliefs about the nature of mind, (inadvertently) says all that is needed to be said.[11]

The causal theory of perception collapses the distance between subject and object and hence the space in which we individually and collectively live. Eliminativists have no basis for understanding how nerve fibres find meaning in their own activity. The cousin of the causal theory of perception, the causal theory of meaning, according to which meaning is the effect of material causes on a material body, squeezes out the semiosphere in which meaning is perceived and (what is more) is actively meant as well as passively received. The subject who is reduced to the necessary conditions of his or her existence – that is having a functioning brain and body – is entirely digested into the material world.[12]

12.2.2 Intentionality: intentional objects and temporal depth

With eliminativism eliminated, we may now proceed to examine intentionality at work. The fact that conscious contents are about, or reveal items, other than themselves – primordially, "solid" or "material" objects "out there" (whose nature was discussed in §11.3.2) – opens up the world. In the idea of an object, there is the intuition that there is something beyond the present experience. It is beyond it in various ways but the most important are: (a) it has hidden properties that are yet-to-be-revealed; (b) it is stable so that it will outlast the present moment; and (c) it is available to unselected others with whom we share the common space of our lives.[13]

The relevance of this to our overall inquiry is that all three aspects of the object that perception is "about" are significant for the establishment of temporal depth. While the future in this instance seems to dominate over the past – the not-yet over the no-longer – there will be other aspects of the object that clearly underwrite a (or its) past, most notably, in the case of a moving object (the same and not the same) its prior positions (as discussed in Chapter 1). What is more, the possibility opened up by the not-yet of "what might be there" (e.g. what might be revealed) is temporally bidirectional: extrapolation of the object into the future also projects it into its past, by drawing on the latter; temporal depth faces both ways. It is this that makes what is present capable of occupying "the (fat) present". Seen in this light, there is no relative priority of present over past and future. While the present defines what is past and what is future (by dividing the one from the other), the past and future highlight what is there as being that which is "presently" in the present, a presence that is not the sum total of presently available reality.

We will touch on how intentionality – and hence temporal depth – is elaborated shortly. For the moment, however, I want to focus on something key to our argument about freedom: the connection between the causal sense and temporal depth. To see an event as an *effect* of another event is to look past the present to the past, from the present event to the no longer present one. The backward glance, which gathers up the two items, reaches from the visible to the invisible or more broadly from the sensed to the unsensed. We have the basis (in consciousness) for explicit temporal order and for the cause to become "earlier" and the effect "later". When the pair is in place, the link between the two is bidirectional: the cause is prior to the effect and the effect is posterior to the cause. The backward glance causally upstream from what is present now to that which is identified as having caused it generates the bidirectional link, which does not privilege the backwards (present–past) over the forwards (present–future) direction. An index has been planted in the unfolding of things from which time points both ways. The observer holds both cause and effect together though neither material event knows the other. In the absence of the conscious observer neither transcends itself to be able to reach the other. There is nothing thundery in the lightning or luminous in the thunder. In the material world, everything is what it is and not something else.[14]

We have found the seed of temporal depth in the intentionality of the perceiving consciousness. However, the actual temporal depth of our moment-to-moment existence is much deeper than that – or indeed than any moment. Intentionality is elaborated through and in the community of minds upon which we draw and to which we contribute. Our "I" develops in the incubator of "we". Shared intentionality begins with joint attention – glancing at the same objects or processes, pointing out items to one another – and then is elaborated as we communicate through ever more complex sign systems culminating in our native languages, spoken and, recently, written. The impulse towards cognitive (and other) sharing is deeply rooted in humans and evident to a unique degree. Declarative pointing (not seen in other species) – whereby an infant shares what it has seen – appears even before speech; and explicit togetherness is underlined by incessant cross-bridging accomplished by communicating impressions. It is through joint attention and the trillion cognitive handshakes of communal life that intentionality extends its reach, its scope, and its depth. The intentionality of propositional attitudes – of beliefs, wishes, desires, and knowledge – that draw on an ever-deepening past and an ever-expanding future – is the most prominent and continuous manifestation of this. Thus intentionality is that in virtue of which we spin and inhabit webs of meaning and co-produce the human world. The boundless, densely woven fabric of the semiosphere and the technosphere will underpin, as we shall see, the widening gap between (voluntary) actions and mere happenings.

This highlights the error of atomistic accounts of the perceived, indeed experienced, world.[15] Individual objects are gathered up into our ongoing practical engagement with the world. They are loci of possibility belonging to an evolving location that is the field of our endeavours or an irrelevant background to conative energies that are addressed elsewhere – as when I am running en route to a distant goal, or in the case of the view racing past the window of a carriage as I follow a train of thought. Objects as stable, inert presences are isolated only for philosophical purposes by "rigid staring".[16] Nevertheless, they show clearly what is relevant to the present case: that intentionality appears to row back against the (temporally forward) tide of events.

We must not succumb to the temptation to see intentionality as contra-causal, as being backward causation, or even able to reverse it. Thinking of intentionality as a literal reaching back from an effect (say neural activity in my brain) to a causal ancestor (say the interference with the light on an object in what is seen to be a visual field), is a little misleading if only because picking out discrete events as discrete causes and discrete effects that they bring about is also the product of intentionality. Any causal chain has to be teased out from the continuum of happening, of the evolving universe. The important point is that intentionality rows against causality not in the sense of being counter-causal, even less magically annulling causes, but in the sense of being orthogonal to, or at least not aligned with, causation. There remains the puzzle we referred to earlier as to which intentionality stops at a particular target – namely the intentional object such as the screen I am presently looking at. We might invoke an evolutionary reason: that it is a good idea, from the point of view of survival, that I should see the object I need to use or the object that threatens me rather than, say, a rehearsal of the early history of the universe. Such explanations, however are ill-matched answers to metaphysical questions.[17] At best, they may offer an account why (if you already have intentional consciousness) it should be targeted like this but gives no hint as to how intentional consciousness arises and is successfully targeted in this way. It does not make intentionality any easier to fit into a materialist world picture, in particular its image of a causally closed universe in which human consciousness is claimed to be identical with material events in brains.

Let us return briefly to the elaboration of intentionality beyond a putative "ground floor" of material objects and events. At a certain level, objects and events are signs pointing beyond themselves, but some are more explicitly signs when they are seen to be traces of pasts and futures more generally and when, in creatures such as ourselves who not only consume meanings but produce them, who mean meanings, they are deliberately used to signify. This passage from "natural" signs to signs that signify by convention, which do not merely incidentally signify but are created in order to signify and whose power of signification depends on their belonging to a system of signs, is portentous. The use of sound energy to convey meanings vastly extends the scope of intentionality and correspondingly of its counter-causality. Memory and expectation implicit in the idea of causes pointing to future effects, effects pointing to past causes, objects whose stability implies previous and future states, and so on, may be elaborated into more complex propositional attitudes in explicit beliefs, desires, and plans. This takes us far beyond first-level intentionality exemplified particularly in the visual sense.

Even so, the gaze will prove particularly relevant to our search for agency via intentionality, if only because in vision we interact asymmetrically with the world. The seeing eye exposes a world while scarcely being exposed to it. It is connected with what is out there but keeps its distance and so is positioned to engage with it on terms that are its own. The gaze can consequently transcend its primary function as an early warning of a future that can be *fore*seen because it is seen, or as a foraging device, and become a means by which the grip of the material world may be progressively loosened. It is also uniquely amenable to collectivization: views are shared; glances are exchanged; the other's gaze is visible; and joint attention is solicited. Ears do not exchange the equivalent of glances; I cannot hear you hearing as I can see you seeing; and I cannot hear your "hear-point" as I can see your viewpoint, without cheating by looking; and joint hearing attention – directed by the "Listen!" – is rather further down the track than the joint attention to the visual world prompted by pointing.

Once, however, a common world is established through the shared space of vision, then the scene is set for intentionality to be extended boundlessly through signs that point into the no-longer and not-yet visible and through the meant meaning of intended signs that create an ever-growing sphere of possibility expanding into an abstract space of pasts and futures based upon them. The propositional awareness that we bring to and take from a limitless community of minds upheld by and drawing upon a trillion cognitive handshakes is the very stuff of human consciousness. It is here where we need to seek the roots, the possibility, of our agency. This is the soil from which our agency grows. The reference to propositional awareness[18] highlights three further dimensions of extended intentionality:

(a) intelligibility;
(b) truth and falsehood; and
(c) the non-spectatorial aspect of consciousness.

Propositional awareness is implicit in perception and even more in episodic memories but it is explicit in propositional attitudes such as thoughts, items of knowledge, beliefs, hopes and desires – those denizens of the mental world to which eliminativists are especially allergic. Their nature is best made visible by contrast with other modes of awareness. Compare the feeling of warmth as I enter the sunlight with my awareness *that* it is sunny or *that* the sun is out or my belief *that* it is warm because the sun is warming my arm. As we progress deeper into "that" so we move into a space of knowledge, expectation, and understanding. This is the realm of "because". Intelligibility, like perception, is not atomic: it is connected up in a realm of sense-making that reaches out of the present, drawing on the past to populate a future expectation. The intelligible world is not located at a point in time t: perceived, its events reach out of the moment of their occurrence to an outside-of-the-present that has no defined boundaries. In the form of facts, they leave time altogether, though they are brought back into time when they become part of the considerations guiding the present.

In the transition from a feeling of warmth on the arm to the belief that "it" is warm and "it is warm because the sun is shining and (judging from the clouds) it won't be warm for long", we move from sentience to realm of truth and falsehood. Even those who would imagine that sentience and even perception are products of the causal interactions between material brains and extra-cerebral material objects would presumably hesitate to think of truth and falsehood as being secreted out of the causal net or that both propositional awareness and that which makes it true or (in the case of desires, hopes, etc.) satisfies it are both products of a nexus of causes and effects. What is more, propositional awareness liberates the subject from locations in space and time. The knowledge of the knower is delocalised. (This is one of the reasons why knowledge can be shared, transmitted and taught.)

Intelligibility and truth – products of intentionality – are liberators from time, so that while physical time travel is impossible mental time travel is a constant feature of our being in time.[19] They are crucial to the development of the semiosphere by which our lives are liberated from the biosphere, the ecological niche, that confines other sentient creatures. Our daily existence is not a sequence of responses to impingements that are wired to one another through our bodies. Living in, and through, an intelligible world, our days – when they are on course – unfold not through causation but through becausation, and practical reason.

In the discussion of intentionality, I have focused on vision as it has a key role in creating a shared world and it seems to be the most liberated of the senses.[20] However, with this comes the possibility of exaggerating the spectatorial element of our being-in-the-world. From the moment we are born to the day of our death we are agents struggling with the stuff of the world (including our own bodies). It is time therefore to look at agency and the possibility of action in a world that seems from certain viewpoints to unfold in a way that cannot be deflected.

12.3 THE HUMAN AGENT

To live is to act. For this reason alone, the tendency to think of explicit time as something that is observed "out there" – in our perception of the succession of events or in clocks – is rather lop-sided. Time is inextricably caught up with embodiment and action. The time sense served up to us in our body clocks – heartbeats, breathing, the cycles of hunger and satiety, of wakefulness and sleep – permeates all of our activities and it is evident in the periodicity of rhythmic activities such as walking; but it is present also in the structure of actions, from the sequencing of motor components in quite basic acts such as reaching for an object, and more complex ones such as putting on a jacket, getting washed, preparing a meal, and in all the timetabled activity that fills our days. In such cases, the "succession" impregnates the elements composing it and the experience of those elements.[21]

When it comes to that small subset of events called actions, the permissive nature of time is absolutely central and the time in question is not the time of physics and the material world but explicit, tensed time. Tensed time, I shall argue, is the *sine qua non* of deliberate action and that in virtue of which, notwithstanding that we are in a crucial respect material objects subject to the laws of nature, we are able to operate on the material world as if from without. Tensed time not only makes action possible but the timing built into individual, joint or collective actions extends or underlines or gives greater reality to tensed time. A virtuous circle is set in motion.

The possibility of truly free or voluntary actions is of course denied by some. Indeed, determinism is for many thinkers so obvious as hardly to seem to need defending.

12.3.1 The impossibility of (free) action: traditional determinism

Let us first make clear what I mean by the free will that I am defending. Robert Kane's definition – "the power of agents to be the ultimate creators (or originators) and sustainers of their own ends and purposes"[22] – is a good start. Freedom of the will implies:

(a)   that we can truly say of at least some of our behaviour "the buck starts here";
(b)   that our actions have deflected the course of events;
(c)   that they express something within us that we can truly own; and
(d)   that what we have done is one of several possibilities genuinely open to us such that we could have done or chosen otherwise.

It does not require us to believe:

(a)   that *everything* an agent does is free;
(b)   that every part of a free action is explicitly done and freely executed; or
(c)   that the agent is free to do anything.

The traditional case against free will goes as follows: Actions are physical events. Every physical event has a prior physical cause which in turn has a prior cause. The causal chain that led up to "my" actions – which in theory could be traced back to the Big Bang – ultimately originates in events over which I have no control. Everything I (seemingly) do is thus the remote effect of happenings which I have not initiated. My actions are no more mine, in the sense of originating with me, than are their causal ancestors, most of which will have taken place before I was born. Actions (including their motivations) are part of the boundless causal nexus of the material universe. There is nothing outside this causally closed realm. A parallel argument could be made focusing on the (unbreakable) laws of nature that we touched on in §8.2.3. The combination of initial conditions and laws will determine the overall state of the universe (including ourselves) at any given time. Finally, my very existence – the necessary condition of my performing any actions at all – was not chosen by myself (nor could it have been) nor did I choose the general properties, and particular circumstances, of the body underpinning my existence (nor could I have done).

How, therefore, could we deflect the order of things, and initiate (initial conditions made into a verb), or be the *origin* of, events that we could count as our own? We shall find the answer to this question by challenging the assumptions underpinning determinism; notably, that the world of human agents is simply a parish of a causally closed physical universe whose unfolding is entirely prescribed by the laws of nature. The defence of tensed time in Chapter 5 and elsewhere in Part II, the exploration of causation in Chapter 11, and the reflections on intentionality earlier in the present chapter will give us the means to mount this challenge.

Let us first, however, examine some recent arguments from natural science to support the claim that free action is impossible.

12.3.2 The impossibility of free action: physics

The key role we shall assign to tensed time in human freedom is justified indirectly by the connection between determinism and the tenseless world picture thought to follow from special relativity. That its tenseless block universe implies determinism has been argued by many philosophers including, in recent decades, J. J. C. Smart, Hilary Putnam and Michael Lockwood. Lockwood's argument that "future events are simply already there and have already happened" is unequivocal and clear:

> To take the space-time view seriously is indeed to regard everything that ever exists, or ever happens, at any time or place as being just as real as the contents of the here and now. And this rules out any conception of free will that pictures human agents, through their choices, as selectively conferring actuality on what are initially only potentialities. Contrary to this common sense conception, the world [according to Minkowski] is, at all times and places, actuality through and through: a four-dimensional block universe.[23]

This renders entirely puzzling the status of the future in human life; namely that it presents itself as a set of possibilities some of which may not be actualized at all, many of which will be actualized to some degree, and none of which will be actualized in such a way as to fulfil (and fulfil only) certain (general) possibilities. In short, things that don't or might not, happen have no place in the physical world notwithstanding they are a huge presence in the human world. The world picture of physics (and of philosophers who take their cue from physics) is not able to accommodate possibilities – least of all those that are not realized – but also those that are realized to the (necessarily incomplete) degree to which possibilities are realized. Events are not past, present, or future in the world defined by Minkowski space–time. Where there is no future, and hence no "will" there can be no (free) will; indeed, where there is no "is" (present) or "was" (past) there is no space for voluntary actions to shape, or at least deflect, the course of events.

The denial of free will raises all sorts of immediate objections. The most obvious is that of trying to account for the apparent difference between events that are and events that are not product of agency: between a stone falling from the top of a mountain and a stone being thrown down a mountain; or more to the point, between events that happen without anyone intending them – the vast majority of events – and those that seem to have occurred because they have been intended.[24]

Among these – to anticipate later discussion – are events that could not have happened if they had not been envisaged in advance, that have many components that would not have come together had they not all been directed towards a particular goal. A relatively straightforward example from my own life would be the countless movements that are required to take a train to London and attend a meeting to make a case for impoved epilepsy services. Such events seem to exist only because they correspond to possibilities envisaged by someone who wants to achieve a certain goal. Determinism also makes the deployment of effort, the role of training and practice in perfecting skills, and careful planning – all those things evident in ordinary actions – seem inexplicable (if they are effective) or superfluous (if they are not). Even more redundant is envisaging the possibility of achieving a goal. In the case of a series of happenings such as an avalanche, the later phases do not come about because the final outcome of the avalanche is somehow envisaged by the stones busy with the earlier part of the avalanche. The co-presence of the earlier phase, the later phase, and the final destructive impact would be neither possible nor necessary. Actions, as we shall discuss, are events that happen because, and only because, they make sense to someone, serving an explicit purpose; other happenings just happen. Denial of free will would be not only to deny that our actions are free but to deny that there is a subset of happenings called actions.

The tenseless world picture of special relativity – and physics more generally – is often presented as being incompatible with free will because the future is there already, "waiting in the wings", not available to be shaped as we live our lives. Under this interpretation, the difference between a determinate state of the world, a state coming into being, and an envisaged possible state of affairs, would be lost. In fact, there would only be determinate states of affairs, without room for the becoming that is the present, and the possibilities that belong to the future. It would therefore be a mistake to interpret this as giving equal status and reality to the future: only the past would exist because whatever is real is necessarily determinate. The "block universe" may seem to allow for past, present, and future events and states of affairs to be side by side but in fact it privileges the past. The reason it does this is not hard to find and it is one we discussed in §10.4.4: the block universe is the universe seen from the standpoint of a gaze that sees it as a whole. This (imaginary or virtual) gaze, gathers up the sum of things into a (necessarily) completed whole: it is therefore past. If they are not (exclusively) past the same events would have to be past (determinate) *and* present (coming into being) *and* future (a mere possibility) at the same time – and indeed all the time. This would seem to involve contradiction: a given item cannot at the same time be a definite event with a definite time label, a general possibility, and undergoing the passage from being a general possibility to being a specific actuality.

The truth is that the tenseless universe of relativity does not, contrary to the way matters are usually discussed, allow for the coexistence of past, present and future – even less for an event as being not-yet, now, and no-longer – because there is no basis for the choice of coordinate systems to locate them in a tense. If these are not settled on, then events are not past, present, or future; and certainly not all three of them either at once or in succession. The viewpoint of relativity is a purely mathematical or virtual viewpoint. It is hardly surprising therefore that free will disappears; that a world without conscious observers is without free will. That a world without becoming is also one without becoming wrought by agents is even less surprising. The casualties of relativity include not only free actions but all events uniquely linked to specific times.

The link between free will and tensed time might tempt some to dismiss the former for another reason: that, like tensed time, it is "viewpoint-dependent" and therefore not entirely pukka. That, however, is exactly what free will ought to be: freedom should be the freedom of a being that has responsibilities, needs, wants and so on – and therefore a conscious being with a viewpoint. The notion of freedom is meaningless when not attached to such a creature. How could the universe as a whole be free? What would it be free of, from, or for?

For some, recent developments in physics have offered hope for rescuing the idea of free action in a deterministic universe. The replacement of causation by probability at the subatomic level investigated by quantum mechanics, according to which there is no linear dictation of particular events as a consequence of particular causes, does not however, really offer any support for the reality of agency. We do not live, and actions are not planned, or executed, at the subatomic level. Besides, individual random quantum events conform to a set of fixed probabilities expressed in frequencies that are predefined to many more decimal points than are perceptible in everyday life.

Equally, the observation that Laplacean prediction founders on the fact that minute changes in initial conditions can quickly result in vast differences in outcome so that complex systems are entirely unpredictable is not helpful. If unpredictability were sufficient for freedom, then weather systems (notoriously chaotic) would be some of the freest entities on earth. Hurricane Katrina would be responsible for the damage caused to New Orleans. What free will requires is not randomness or unpredictability in the material world but *control* of it. What's more, loosely textured laws would not widen the space for agency. We need nature to be utterly reliable if our actions are to have their intended consequences. If the laws were loose, not only would we have less control over the outcomes of our actions, so that they would take us closer to our goals, but we would not even be able to put complex actions together (and all actions are more complex than the names we give them would suggest).

12.3.3 The impossibility of free action: neurodeterminism

> Our belief in our freedom of will will fade and, moreover, our mastery
> over ourselves will gain most specifically from a greater and greater
> understanding of the physiological mechanism of our brain activity.
> Ivan Pavlov, quoted in Todes, *Ivan Pavlov*, 563

The assault on our belief in free will coming from science takes many other forms. I want to focus only on those that are directly connected with our investigation of time. Of particular relevance – because by default they highlight the true nature of action and the temporal depths and the tensed time they draw upon – are certain much-discussed neurophysiological studies that some have claimed have shown that actions are not truly voluntary and that in fact it is not we, but our brains, who are calling the shots when we act. The experiments of Benjamin Libet and his co-workers[25] and, more recently of John-Dylan Haynes's team[26] have generated results that have been interpreted as showing that free will is an illusion. Determinism has, it seems, been vindicated by evidence of *neuro*determinism.

The experiments carried out by the neurophysiologist Benjamin Libet in the 1980s and repeated and refined many times since then, have attracted lavish attention because they seem to show that our brain makes decisions to act before our conscious mind is aware of them, so they are not really *our* decisions at all. The neuroscientist and philosopher Patrick Haggard described the paper in which they were first reported as "one of the philosophically most challenging in modern scientific psychology".[27]

In a typical experiment, Libet's subjects are instructed to make a simple movement – to bend their right wrist or the fingers of their right hand – in their own time. Using an electro-encephalogram, the experimenter records activity in the brain that indicates a readiness to move. This so-called "readiness potential" (RP) is seen in the part of the cerebral cortex most closely associated with voluntary movement. The RP occurs about half a second before activity in the relevant muscles of the arm or hand, as recorded by an electromyogram. This is to be expected because it takes a certain amount of time for the neural activity in the cortex to translate into events in the relevant muscles. But Libet made another observation that seemed to raise serious questions. He asked his subjects to recall the position of a spot revolving round a clock face when they were first aware of their urge or intention to make a movement. To his surprise, he found that the RP occurred a consistent third of a second *before* the time at which the subjects reported being aware of a decision to move. Libet concluded from this that the *brain* (not the subject or the person) "decided" to initiate or at least to prepare to initiate the act before there was any reportable subjective awareness of a decision having been made. Generalizing wildly from this observation, commentators have concluded that the cerebral causes of our actions seem to occur *before* our conscious awareness of deciding to perform them and our actions have unconscious causes that begin before we think about the action.

These findings are open to a range of interpretations, as we shall see, but they cannot be dismissed as mere artefacts of the method of recording, though as has recently been shown we *infer* rather than perceive the moment we decided to act. Nor can the gap between the electrical signal of the initiation of action, the RP, and the awareness of the intention to perform the action be explained away as the interval between forming an intention and being sufficiently reflectively aware of the intention to allocate it to a particular time. The reason for this is that seemingly similar but more striking findings have been obtained in recent work, this time using an imaging technique called functional magnetic resonance imaging (fMRI). While electroencephalograph (EEG) scans can look at only limited brain activity, fMRI scans can survey the whole brain.

Haynes and colleagues carried out studies in which a succession of letters was displayed on a screen.[28] Subjects were asked to press a left or a right button at a moment of their own choosing and to note the letter which was being displayed at the time they felt that they were making a decision to press the button. The letter was a time marker. If the subject was going to press the right button (with the right hand), the left hemisphere would light up while pressing the left button would be associated with activity in the right hemisphere. Remarkably, the part of the cerebral cortex associated with voluntary movement lit up *a full 5 seconds* in the appropriate hemisphere before the individual was aware of having made a choice of left or right hand. Moreover, there were other areas in the frontal cortex (traditionally ascribed executive powers) that were active no less than *seven* seconds before awareness of the decision. If the delay in the response of the scanner detecting the activity was accounted for, the interval increased to *ten* seconds. Such a delay could not be due to the subject mistiming the intention to move – a possible explanation for Libet's original findings, as it is somewhat tricky to time one's own decisions. The authors concluded that there is a network of high level control areas "that begins to prepare an upcoming decision long before it enters awareness".[29] It looks like we don't know what we are doing until we have found that we have done it. Or, as Haggard put it, "We feel we choose but we don't."[30]

Libet's original interpretation of his experiments was that they demonstrated that we do not have free will: the brain "decides" to move, the brain "initiates" movement. As Libet put it later,: "If the 'act now' process is initiated unconsciously, then the conscious free will is not doing it."[31] We do, however, have "free *won't*": we can inhibit movements that are initiated by the brain. We don't quite initiate voluntary processes; rather we "select and control them", either by permitting the movement that arises out of an unconsciously initiated process or "by vetoing progress to actual motor activation". This has been expressed as our ability to "rubber stamp" decisions that have already been made by neural networks. It is, however, not very clear why the decisions should require rubber stamping. In the personless world of neuroscience, it makes no more sense for us to "rubber stamp" the decisions of our brain than for a falling pebble to endorse the gravitational field.

There have been many methodological challenges to the studies that appear to show that the brain makes a decision to act – to move the left or the right hand – before the agent is conscious of having selected the left or right side to move.[32] They are, however, beside our present concern. The real question is whether they have anything to say about the exercise of free will in the real world.

The answer is that they do not for two principal reasons:

(a) *The action in question is intrinsically meaningless.* What the experimenters required of their subjects was utterly trivial and had no significance outside of the experiment. The actions that Libet requested in response to an "urge" was, as von Wachter expressed it, closer to involuntary fidgets than voluntary actions.[33] The choice between left and right hand in Haynes's experiment was equally lacking in any kind of importance. Nothing was at stake and nothing of substance in the subject was engaged. Indeed, the "action" hardly counted as an action at all: a mere movement such as pressing a button. The button was not attached to anything such as an electronic device and the movement was not even trivially symbolic, such as pointing or thumbs up.

(b) *It was only a part-action that belonged to something bigger.* Any significance the movement had was as a component – and only a minute component – of something called "taking part in Dr Libet's experiment". This large-scale action began at least as far back as getting up in the morning to visit Dr Libet's laboratory (after, perhaps, setting the alarm to make sure one was not late); involved consenting to take part in a procedure whose nature and purpose and safety was fully understood; and it required (among many other things) listening to and understanding and agreeing to the instructions that were received – and *then* deciding to flex the wrist. In other words, the immediate prior intention, the psychological event timed by Libet, was not the whole or even a significant part story of the action. It was preceded by many other elements that were minutes, hours, perhaps days, before the hand movement in the lab. The real story is not just the flexing of the wrist but one of a sustained and complex resolve being maintained over a very long time. This includes many large items of behaviour – getting on and off buses, looking for the laboratory, cancelling or declining other commitments so as to be free to attend the lab, and so on – that have many thousands, perhaps hundreds of thousands, of motor components all orchestrated and subordinated to achieving a rather complex goal. None of this was, or needed to be, in play in the interval between the decision to move the finger and the actual movement. The decision to move was the decision it was only with respect to an enormous frame of reference surrounding the readiness potential and much of it was in place hours, perhaps days, before the experiment began.

Once this is appreciated, then the temporal relation in, say, Libet's experiment, between the last step – the wrist flexing, and the readiness potential seen in the lab – becomes unimportant. The decision to participate in the research, which alone gave the wrist flexion its meaning, began not milliseconds, seconds, or minutes, but hours before the wrist was flexed. Perhaps weeks, when the person decided to become a subject in the experiment and entertained the idea of "taking part in Dr Libet's experiment" which would itself be part of a greater intentional whole, such as "wanting to please Dr Libet" or "wanting to help those clever scientists understand the brain as it might one day help doctors to treat my child's brain injury more effectively". Libet and his subjects are engaged in a joint enterprise to find something out whose tentacular roots extend far and wide.

Libet's experiment inadvertently illustrates how the neurodeterminist case against freedom – seemingly demonstrating that we are our brains and our brains are calling the shots – is rooted in a shrivelled image of what constitutes an action in everyday life. If you want to make voluntary actions seem involuntary the first thing to do is to strip away their context – the self from which they originate, the nexus of meanings that is the world to which they are addressed – and then effectively break them down into their physical elements. This gets you well on the way to eliminating the difference between a fidget and a deliberate action and to make an action seem as if it could be explained by a burst of nerve impulses, embedded in a no-person neural reality, rather than in a first-person ("we" and "I") and second-person world where behaviour is not atomic but interconnected. The locus of free will is a *field* of intention, rooted in the self and its world that extends beyond the laboratory.[34] At the heart of all this is temporal depth and tensed time, to which we shall presently return. But first a quick observation on a broader assault from the neurosciences on the notion of human agency.

It has been observed that, in the case of learned behaviour, we perform better if we do not attend to what we are doing. Automatism without the intervention of the conscious will is the best strategy. While this is true, it is irrelevant to the question of free will. We can, in the case of learned skills, revisit them to see if we can improve our performance – as in the case of the golfer who decides to alter his swing or the pianist who decides to modify her technique – however practised and automatic they become. What is more, these practised and relatively mindless activities are performed within a frame of deliberate awareness. The pianist voluntarily, deliberately, consciously accepts the booking, makes her way to the piano on the stage, and waits for the conductor to raise the baton and give the nod to proceed. At a more homely level, we can anticipate and head off automatisms. A particularly striking example is the way we regulate our sleep. We rely on internal mechanisms or external events to wake up; however, we can over-ride these by setting the alarm before we go to sleep to rouse us at a certain time. The sleep-waking cycle is one of the most global expressions of our passivity and yet even here we can – and indeed must – assert our agency.

A seemingly more intimate assault on our capacity for truly voluntary action comes from unconscious influences on everyday activity. There are numerous examples from the psychological literature of how our behaviour can be modified by circumstances that we would not regard as relevant to the sort of choices we make. We may be more willing to give to a beggar if the recipient is sitting close to a bakery whose delicious emanations make us feel good. This seems to undermine the idea that we may have of ourselves that we act according to general moral principles rather than merely react to situations. However, the influence is brought to bear on behaviour that is regarded as discretionary and, what is more, requires an immediate response. I have a choice whether to give to a beggar and my giving or withholding generosity does not impinge on my more fundamental duties. This is not the same as deciding to turn up to run my clinic or not to do so, a decision that is woven into the very texture of my life and has a multitude of connections and consequences. Moreover, the encounter with the beggar is sudden, unplanned, and requires a rapid response – something close to a response to a stimulus.

The conclusion from these kinds of examples – and from the thousands of so-called "priming" experiments in which it has been shown that our perceptions and our preparedness to behave in a certain way may be influenced by subconscious stimuli – is only that immediate responses, relatively disconnected from temporally deep behavioural frameworks, are highly labile.[35] They do not warrant the conclusion that we are the 24/7 plaything of unconscious influences or that our belief that we are to an important degree captains of our souls, that we actively live our lives rather than merely suffer them, is a self-flattering illusion. The fundamental difference between sleep-walking and walking with a particular aim in mind, or between being the subject of an unexplained emotion (due to a subliminal stimulus with strong associations) and acting out our ordinary day's work, remains. And, as Merlin Donald, has pointed out "human beings do not normally wage war or build skyscrapers unconsciously".[36] The fact that we may sometimes, or often, be deceived that we are free or have acted freely, and be misled as to the scope of our freedom, does not prove that we have never been free. Just as the fact that we are sometimes mistaken, or prone to illusions, does not demonstrate that we always mistaken and that true perception and objective knowledge is not possible. Nor does the fact that, dreaming, I imagine that I am awake (because the dream is so vivid) prove that I am never awake. The very claim that you are less free under certain circumstances than you think you are presupposes that the idea of freedom has validity.

What most strikingly distinguishes actions from either reflexes or events taking place in the physical world independently of agents is not their components but the way the components are brought together. It is highly unlikely that all the elements that are combined when a subject takes part in Libet's experiment would occur simply as an expression of the laws or causal sequences observed by scientists in the natural world. The series of movements comprising Mrs Smith setting the alarm the night before, eating breakfast early, transporting herself to the laboratory, and then conforming to all the instructions given her by Libet would have a negligible chance of occurring without their being requisitioned by her sustained intention to act in a way that makes sense to herself.[37] And while none of the components of her actions breaks the law of physics – the dynamics of the trajectory of her body to the laboratory would be entirely in accordance with mechanical principles – their being brought together as a sequence has nothing to do with those laws. Each step that propels her to the laboratory depends on action and reaction being equal and opposite but that says nothing about the *sequence* of steps; whereas a pebble's fall from the top of a building would be exhaustively described by Newton's laws.[38]

We should be grateful therefore to Libet for involuntarily reminding us of the distinct nature of human actions: they are events, yes; but they are complex events whose components come together only because they add up to something that is significant. They are *requisitioned* by goals and, in the case of humans, those goals are frequently invisible though envisaged, distant, and abstract – as when I undertake the vast number of actions that is involved in my subscribing to, travelling to, and exercising in, a gym with the aim of postponing illness. It is our aims, not laws, that pick out and stitch together the events that make up actions.

12.3.4 Agency in practice

Human agency and the exercise of free will in shaping, or at least deflecting, the course of events seems problematic because we act through our bodies and the latter are part of the material world upon which we aspire to act. As material parts of the material world, it is difficult to conceive how we might seem to rise above, or extricate ourselves from, the laws of a causally closed world in order to utilize them to ends that are not evident in a material world without explicit ends. The Baron Munchausen challenge of lifting ourselves up by our hair seems especially daunting since we rely on unbreakable laws and a tight law-like relationship between events to make complex actions possible and to be sure that those actions will have their intended consequences. It seems impossible in theory and yet it happens, or seems to happen, in practice.

The answer to this conundrum lies in the intentionality of consciousness that prises open a material world that might seem otherwise causally closed, in the way we discussed in §12.2, and creates the possibility of an outside from which (conscious) agents may act. This outside is amplified by the knowledge, practices, and institutions of the community of minds that is the human world. A key dimension of this latter world, and of the participation of individuals in it is tensed time, the virtual time of the past and future in which possibilities are located, a time outside of physical time and the actualities of the material world. It is in this world that events are identified as causes and their law-governed relations with effects noted so that they can be exploited as means to being about certain ends.

This is a less radical position than the one adumbrated in §11.3, where the irruption of the "onlooker" into the continuum of the universe fragments it into discrete events that, being distinct, have their happening made intelligible by causal necessitation. It is, however, sufficient to provide at least the outline of a story in which agency far from being opposed to causation is in cahoots with it. Let us examine this relationship in a little more detail.

Material causes seem to be at once the opponents and the partners of agents. On the one hand, in the standard understanding of causation, it is material causes operating independently of agency that have brought us into being and will sweep us out of being. Agents cut a small figure in the spatial and temporal span of the universe: we are there to be made and unmade. Causation, expressed in physical laws and the sequence of individual events, seems to be the very implacability of the universe before which we are (ultimately) helpless. One manifestation of this is something we have noted already: the passage from cause to effect is associated with increasing untidiness, whereas the aims of agents are to tidy things up. Agency works with available energy – and works to make it available to serve our purposes – whereas the way of causation is to dissipate such energy and so to make it unavailable. Eventually, dissipated, we shall be part of the untidiness we tried during our lives to control.

On the other hand, agents necessarily operate through and with causes. Successful agency is based on exploiting associations between events that are more than mere associations, on the reliability of the fact that when the tree is shaken the fruit will fall to the ground. This principle – that we use causes to bring about effects – is evident in every moment of our lives, though the shaking and the fruit may get evermore complex, evermore mediated, and evermore abstract or general. When we travel by train to a destination, causation is in evidence in the relationship between our leg movements and the pavement when we walk to the ticket office, in the connection between movements of our vocal cords and the vibration of the air as we order a ticket, in the operation of the multitude of the components of the train as we are propelled to our destination. In short, all our actions must work with, or within, the patterns of material causation if they are (a) to be possible and (b) to have their desired effects.

Causation and agency therefore are unthinkable without each other. This raises the question as to how we can "take hold of" causes in order to turn them into handles. How it could be that an embodied subject – which may itself seem to be a set of effects of unchosen causes – can gain control, so as to be able to initiate, to originate, sufficient of what happens in her life as to make it true to say that she lived, rather than merely endured or suffered, it? Agency cannot be based on holidays from causation. The answer is to be found in the fact that causation and agency are inseparable: that in virtue of which events are picked out as causes of effects – desirable, undesirable, or irrelevant – is precisely that which makes agency possible. To say this is not to revert to the agency theory of causation (which we rejected in §11.2.2.4) but acknowledge that teasing the universe into strands of happening that are causally connected is a product of the viewpoint – that has no place in the world according to physics – that is concerned for itself, that feels itself to have needs and to be located in an environment that satisfies them or blocks their satisfaction. The causal sense – which picks events out of a continuum of happening – is driven by the sense of the possibility of agency, even though only a small subset of the events it picks out is a candidate to be a handle or a switch to deflect the course of events. The analogy would be with a light switched on to help us find a particular item, illuminates an entire room, including areas where the sought for item is not even likely to be found.

Highlighted causes (potential handles) give prominence to the background tapestry of potential causes or even strands of connected causes and effects. In some cases, the strands may be a nexus or even field of events – as when I see the effects of a gale: the clouds racing across the sky, the birds flying with difficulty against a headwind, trees shaking and flowers nodding, a goose-flesh of ripples on a pond, windows banging, papers blown across the road, and the coat of a long-haired dog being flattened. There is an entire world of handles and potential handles mixed with unfolding events-as-causes that are not even potential handles and may be obstacles to agency or even threats to our very existence as agents.

This profound partnership between the seemingly opposed causation and agency is rooted in the emergence of a vision of the world as a nexus of discrete events, some of which are causally related. To pick an event out is also to see it connected. (There are no explicit connections in a continuum or a plenum.) The connection is with what surrounds it but also (and central to our present discussion) what precedes it and what succeeds it. The glance, therefore, looks past what is to what has been and what will be. Events, for example, are seen as effects of what no longer is and as causes of what is not yet. The idea that Event X brings about or could bring about Event Y inspires the idea that *I* could bring about Event Y. The wind shakes the tree and the fruit falls off and this reveals the possibility that I might make the fruit fall off by shaking the tree.

There is another aspect of the link between agency and the causal sense: the level at which events are dissected or teased out. "The wind shaking the tree", "the fruit falling off", etc. are clearly that at which meaningful wholes in the form of *actions* are described – such as "my shaking the fruit off the tree". Nature – or what is out there – is carved by conscious subjects at agency-relevant joints which do not correspond to, say, the continuities and discontinuities of matter and/or energy. An afternoon is a nexus of such higher-level soft causal connections rather than the interactions of push–pull mechanics at the level of atoms.

It is here or hereabouts that we find the first step to the ultimate creation of a human environment that is overwhelmingly one of actual or potential agency, with most of the top-line events in our lives being actions (individual or group or communal) and the material landscape being packed wall-to-wall with artefacts, tools (including containers such as houses and transport), commodities, fixtures and fittings. We cannot stop uncontrolled causation seeping through the sides, of course, in the form of unintended consequences of our intended actions and unintended events. Hence the car horn that wakes the baby, the traffic accident, the traffic jam, the silent rusting of the metallic components of the vehicle. We put a good deal of effort into controlling the "spillover" of unplanned consequences of our actions.

Seeing events as causes that may be pointers to possible agency, exploits a directionality in the world. Thus the wind shaking the tree causes the fruit to fall off but the fruit falling off could not shake the tree nor the shaking tree make the wind blow. But within this overall pattern of unidirectionality there are foci of bidirectionality: action and reaction are equal and opposite. The tree causes turbulence in the wind, the shedding of the fruit allows branches to straighten out and so on. And at the microscopic level, there is near universal reversibility. However, at the level relevant to agency, back-tracking has near negligible probability. The directionality exploited by agents and the ordering of events, what is more, has a new basis. Agent causation creates an inviolate order between the means (which must be prior) and the end (which must be posterior).[39] Salience divides continuous processes into causes and effects as means and ends. The transfer of energy from one continuant to another – say from an ice cube to a drink that is too warm – is a single process which is divided into the melting (and warming) of the ice cube (the means) and the cooling of the drink (the end).

Hume's reduction of the relationship between cause and effect to mental connection between events that tend to occur together and the one seemingly invariably follows the other – such that the sense of causal necessity is in the eye of the beholder and not in the material world – does not take sufficient account of the facts of agency or the difference between science and pseudoscience. If causal connections were in the mind, it would be difficult to see the difference between mere associations and true causal relations. That this difference is real and that post hoc is truly different from propter hoc is evident from the variable results of trying to bring about events by means of bringing about the events that typically precede them. The most rigorous test of the difference between causation and mere association is the success or otherwise of agency, of using A to bring about B. If the relationship between A and B is only one of association, then trying to bring about B by bringing about A is mere rain-dancing or Cargo Cult Science.

The apparent requirement that whatever happens has to have been made to happen is a product, as we noted in §11.3.1 of the irruption of viewpoint in the world. The passage of the causal train, from immediate to distant consequences is established by the viewpoint that places the flag of here and now in the unfolding of the world. The origin of points of origination – the starting place and the restart button, the train of events having a beginning, somewhere where the buck starts – is in the laying down of place, of viewpoint. The emergence of a locality is an interruption. (It is rather analogous to what happens in rugby union when the player stops the flow of events by digging a mark in the ground, reorientates, and then resumes play with a drop kick.) This creates a point – a here-now – from which there appears to be widening circles of events that may be traced upstream and downstream.

This is the deepest level at which we can see how, far from being antagonistic, agency and causation are inseparable: the progeny of an interruption that opens up actuality to possibilities, they are brothers under the skin. Their common parent is intentionality which picks out events and then connects them – either merely seeing or actively exploiting their connection. If this makes discrete events no less mysterious than actions – causes no less mysterious than willings – it is because both seem to deflect the course of things from an inertial path or out of pathless inertia. We have the basis of an understanding of the relationship between agency and causation that does not make the former a *deus ex machina* and the latter the *machina*.

To operate as an agent, in this material world, embodied subjects cannot be above the fray. They cannot be free of the (by definition) unbreakable laws of nature, which includes a proportionality between cause and effect, expressed most generally in the conservation of mass-energy. They must get down and dirty: the object has to be lifted against gravity, the legs have to be moved and the feet have to exploit the friction of the pavement, the food has to be inserted in the mouth – all events that take place within the constraints imposed by the laws of mechanics and permitted by the laws of organic life – if aims are to be achieved. This is just as true when I am doing something as elevated as giving a lecture. And reliance on unsuspended laws of mechanical nature applies not only to the interactions of my body with the world, my visible behaviour, but also to the processes by which I acquired the skills that enabled me to find my way to a lecture hall, ascend a podium, and speak my speech. The closer we investigate the components of our behaviour, the more they clearly depend upon things that happen according to the laws of nature (inflected by a complex organism) rather than things I knowingly bring about. To take one particularly obvious example: the movements of the muscles of articulation associated with speech and some of the things that are necessary for me to choose words and order them rely on mechanisms of which I have little or no knowledge and certainly, as stroke patients know to their cost, couldn't "do" myself if the mechanisms broke down.

There is manifestly more work to be done in addressing the mystery of how we are able to operate on a material world, subject to the laws of nature, and shape it according to wishes that are unknown to the material world when we ourselves appear to be inescapably material objects also subject to the laws of nature. How, in short, are we able to operate material reality as if from the outside so that its events can become the agents of our agency? While we have broken down the direct opposition between causes and agency, and suggested a common origin, inasmuch as causes-of-effects and means-to-ends both owe their origin as discrete events to the irruption of viewpoints in the material world, this would not bring us nearer to ends if the physical world was still in business as usual.

To further our understanding of how it is possible to have actions in a world of mere events, and agents operating in a universe of material objects, fields, and forces, we need to examine a cluster of phenomena that ultimately owe their origin to intentionality. The latter will remain as the unexplained bedrock of the explanation as to how actions – which are complex ensembles of orchestrated events that would have had a near zero possibility of co-occurring by chance – are possible.

The key is that actions are occasioned by possibilities that are not, at the time they are envisaged, part of the material (that is to say actual) world, though they may subsequently be realized in it. They are entertained by creatures that can inhabit times outside of a physical present, in virtue of having a developed sense of tensed time – a future to which possibilities are related, a past that shapes the possibilities that are entertained, and a present that entertains and acts upon them. There is no place for tensed time in physics but if physics were the whole story, physicists would not be able to learn physics, or to travel to CERN, do their experiments, or open their lunch packs. Intentionality – orthogonal to causation – opens the "is" of the physical world to the triple-tensed reality of possibility and its realization as actuality. Our ability to use the might of "might" (as in "X might be the case") grows as the tenses, collectively curated by the communities of which each one of us is a part, deepen and our engagement with the material (and indeed the human) world becomes more mediated and indirect.

In the next two sections we shall examine the "outside" (§12.3.4.1) and the "distance" (§12.3.4.2) from which we are able to act in order to achieve freely envisaged goals before returning (in §12.3.5.1) to the question of the relationship between agency and causation.

12.3.4.1 Operating from without: ex and the machina

Our search for the outside – the *ex* from which we can act upon the material world which necessarily presents itself to us in the form of a closed causal nexus in order that we can rely on it – begins with intentionality, the aboutness of human consciousness, and its hugely amplified gaze. Our viewpoint is extended in our individual and collective memory. The sphere of our awareness expands in all directions, inflated by the sharing of experience, most spectacularly by language. Knowledge not only extends our intentional sphere but also reduces our exposure so that the relationship between ourselves, the knowers, and that which we know becomes even more asymmetrical. Most of my objects of knowledge are known without my being known by them or indeed exposed to them in any way.

The "outside" – outside of time made explicit as "now", outside of our physical position made explicit as "here", outside of the material world made explicit as something we face, take account of, and engage with – from which we can effect material changes in the material world (as well as less obviously material changes in a less obviously material world – the human world) grows as we mature and as the culture to which we belong evolves. Our sense of ourselves as the locus of this outside, as agents operating on a world, deepens with our sense of the past and future and our temporally deep selves contribute to further deepening the past (curated personally and collectively) and the future (again held individually and in common). It is this "outside" that I will focus on. And I want to switch the focus from causes (and effects) to laws (and instances).

One of the most striking aspects of the progress of our understanding of the physical world has been the gradual advance from observing specific associations between events, to observing associations between ever more general classes of events, thence to an intuition of laws expressed in these classes of causal connections, and from there to quantitative laws of ever wider generality. In the latter category are to be found principles such as that of least action, the conservation of inertia, of mass, of energy, of mass-energy, and ultimately equations such as the Schrödinger wave equation and the field equations of general relativity.

The laws are unbreakable: if they were genuinely broken – particularly if they were broken on a regular basis – they would be discredited and lose their status as laws. The ascent of science, therefore, seems to give an evermore complete description of what actually happens and what could happen. Its laws would seem to allow for no outside from which they could be exploited to serve ends not envisaged in the unconscious material world. Isn't our belief that we shape things – that we deflect the course of events – therefore a failure to recognize that it lies within our power only to bring about what would have happened anyway? In short, not to bring anything about?

To address this question, I want first to engage with an argument from John Stuart Mill, advanced in a paper published posthumously.[40] Mill was greatly exercised with trying to reconcile his materialism with his passion for liberty. How can there be free agents, when we are material parts of a material world and subject to the laws of nature? Mill argues that at any given juncture, there is more than one law of nature operating. By aligning ourselves with one law, we can use nature to achieve ends not envisaged in nature:

> Though we cannot emancipate ourselves from the laws of nature as a whole, we can escape from any particular law of nature if we are able to withdraw ourselves from the circumstances in which it acts. Though we can do nothing except through laws of nature, we can use one law to counteract another.[41]

It seems as if we utilize the laws of nature by aligning ourselves with the one that leads to our goal. We do this from a virtual outside-of-nature. Let me illustrate this with a trivial example: a child going to a park in order to enjoy slithering down a slide. The descent is courtesy of the laws of gravity but positioning ourselves to enjoy the descent is something else. Mummy has to agree and find the time. The trip to the park needs to be organized, other things have to be fitted around it, there is a journey to the park, to the playground, and thence to the slide, guided by know-how and know-that, and there is an ascent to the top of the slide. The slide itself has been erected as an expression of collective human will manifested in the Local Authority in order explicitly to utilize the laws of motion: it is a standing possibility of the joy of safely succumbing to the gravitational field – by appointment.

This trivial example illustrates how our ways of acting involve knowledge, as well as artefacts (which of course operate within the laws of nature) so that we can subordinate them to our own ends and can, as Mill said (quoting Francis Bacon), "obey nature so as to command her".[42] Our actions are not uncaused, extra-legal miracles: they go with the grain of causation and their material expression is entirely law-abiding. But we can step back into the great extra-natural space that is the human world and from there use material causes as handles or levers on the material world. Mill again:

> Every alteration of circumstances alters more or less the laws of nature under which we act; and by every choice we make either of ends or of means, we place ourselves to a greater or lesser extent under one set of laws instead of another.[43]

Another homely example may be helpful. Action and reaction are equal and opposite, something I exploit when I propel myself forward in walking. However, where there is a low coefficient of friction, my action may result not in propulsion but in the slithering of my feet. In order that the third law of motion will act in support of my aim, I roughen the surface on which I walk so as to increase its coefficient of friction.

Mill does not, however, take us all the way to explaining the possibility of voluntary action in a law-governed world or to resolving this paradox: that, as we discover or construct laws of increasing power and generality, we are ourselves increasingly empowered though those laws seem to encroach evermore closely on ourselves, seeming to define our material nature, and tightening the constraints of the material world on the possibilities open to us. We have yet to find the origin of the "outside" from which we can operate with (indeed exploit) the laws of nature and go with the grain of causation in order to achieve ends that are truly our own and not envisaged, or indeed envisageable within nature. The pursuit of this outside brings us back to the multiple worlds within worlds in which we pass our lives, woven ultimately out of the intentionality which is orthogonal to causation and to the law-governed interactions of the physical world.

This human world is a realm made possible by the special distance between the subject and the material world which has been amplified by the institutions, structures of cooperation and of power, subjects have worked together to create over human history. This public sphere, which is a dense network of signs of meant meanings, a semiosphere, whose most striking material expression is a "technosphere", in which we live and have our human being beyond the organic stuff of our body, is the outside from which we elucidate the laws of nature and get them to work on our behalf. This is where we use our pooled out-of-bodily being to mobilise our pooled strength to operate on the material world. And it is this that constitutes the outside into which we step back in order to operate on the material world in ultimately material ways and to shape it to our ends: the I-agent draws on the vast "we" of human agency. The stepping back is a huge collective stepping back into a space collectively created. Its ultimate origin, as we have argued, is in the sense of possibility arising out of the intentionality of experience that opens up the sense of (general) possibility.

The distinctive history of humanity within the universe is all the evidence we need of our power – individual and collective – to deflect the course of events as prescribed by natural laws; and the artefactscape within which we live is further eloquent testimony. Such is the scale of our influence on the course of events at least on our own planet that it has been suggested that the present era should be named the Anthropocene to acknowledge the impact of human activity on the earth's geology and ecosystems.

In recent centuries, the most obvious manifestation of our action *ex machina* has been our exploitation of the laws of nature in science-based technology, a supreme expression of accumulated knowledge that is the property of the great community of human minds. Technology has made the outside from which we operate on the natural world (including the part of the natural world that is our own bodies) into a rapidly expanding Space of Possibility, a first-person plural reality, constructed through the joined endeavours of vast ensembles of individuals present and absent, alive and dead, and amplified since the first hominids first awoke to their own existence.[44] Such conscious exploitation of causes and the laws of nature cannot itself be described in terms of material causes and material effects. Nor can it be reduced to the expression of biological tropisms or instincts or putative drives as proxy for intermediate material causes. The very notion of a "cause" is not itself an effect of a material cause, nor does any law of nature generate the notion of a law of nature.[45] To observe and use causes is to be something other than, more than, a mere set of effects and to seek out and exploit the laws of nature is to transcend them.

Of special relevance for this inquiry, is the fact that explicit causes, attributed causes, do not respect the kind of temporal order that we see in the material world. Most pertinently, in the ascription of, and prospective utilization of causes, we see the key role of tensed time in the production of voluntary action. There is a disruption of the linear succession of causes and effects in a future-oriented intention rooted in past experience which justifies a present action. The future possibility, or at least its being entertained, becomes the key "cause" of the present event. That is why it is absurd to think of the relationship between an intention and a truly voluntary action as being analogous to that between a prior cause and a posterior effect. Contrary to the presupposition implicit in the interpretation of Libet's experiments, true agency is not expressed in a train of atomic responses to a succession of immediately prior atomic intentions. This fact – that our willing arises out of a *field* of intentions and purposes and goals and meaning – is itself a manifestation of how our freedom is bound up with complex temporal relationships, of explicit tensed time, remote from the austerities of B-series physical time.[46]

That we overlook this is betrayed by the way we often think of actions:

intention (I) → action (A) → (desired) outcome (O)

so that it can be thought of as a causal chain in which

A is the effect of I and the cause of O

In fact, the way action typically works (if we are going to isolate a strand of action from a field of volition) is as follows:

O (as envisaged) → I → A → O (in reality)

In the case of real actions, it's more complex than this, with the agent leapfrogging back and forth, placing the future in advance of the present and calling on the past in order to do so. The envisaged future requisitions present actions in order to bring itself about. Agency, that is, reverses the usual order of things by beginning with the desired effect and looking for the cause that might realise it. Thus the upside-down, back-to-front, inside-out world created by intentionality. The asymmetry of influence in the physical world, in accordance with which earlier events influence later ones and not vice versa is reversed, with a later possible state bringing about an action that is earlier than it.

This reversal is particularly striking when we act upon our own future selves, as when Odysseus binds himself to the mast to head off the anticipated temptation to succumb to the Sirens' call. It would, of course, be strained to say the least to characterize Odysseus' future state as being a cause bringing about the effect of his present action of binding himself to the mast. It would be even more strained if I were to characterize more complex future-oriented actions activity – such as signing up to a gym in order to be able to take regular exercise – in terms of a physical state such as future good health or averted ill health as a single cause. But the fundamental idea of looping back and forth in time holds up.

And that is why we cannot think of an intention simply as a (prior) cause of an action. Causes as generally understood in the physical world are not future-oriented, elicited by and taking cognizance of a particular effect, envisaged on the basis of past experience. Actions by contrast, far from being part of a causally closed world which is identical with its present state, are openings in that world based on explicit identification and exploitation of causes and their effects. The future-oriented action relates to events that have not yet happened, and may not happen, and – in the case of pre-emptive action – are actually headed off.

This is a fundamental disruption in the causal chain teased out by a viewpoint. And there is another type of disruption. The relationship between envisaged outcomes, intentions and actions may be continuous or (and this is true in the case of most macroscopic actions) discontinuous. As I walk along a road to get to the shops, each step prepares the way for the next step. Where the goal is in sight, there is a direct connection between it and the succession of actions. If, however, I am driving to the shops, I may do many things – such as filling the car with petrol, taking the opportunity to clean the windscreen, etc. – that are only indirectly related to the trajectory that links the present with the goal and makes sense of what I am doing in the present.[47] There is less continuity still, when I am making preparations for something I want to take place or I want to avoid tomorrow, or next week, or a couple of years hence, or in my retirement a few decades hence. The discontinuity is evident when I break off from the actions relating to the future in question to do other things. Indeed, the journey towards the goal, and related preparations may be very intermittent.

Take the case of joining a pension scheme. I may visit an advisor one day, a few days later I get out the brochures he has given me and fall asleep over them, read them a few weeks later still, a month or so on discuss it with my partner, visit the advisor again and so on until a decision has been made, then sign the various forms when it is convenient, and subsequently continue paying the premium while all the time reviewing it to see whether it is adequate for my changing needs or my perception of them. There are clearly large gaps in the sequence of events that end up with my drawing an appropriate pension when I have retired. And in behaving this way, I am responding not to a (continuous) fear driving my actions but to a prudence – the feeling that I *ought* to fear the future – that stands in place of fear.

The future state that as it were backwardly influences my present actions – being a non-material pull rather than a material push – requisitions events that hold together only in the light of my goals. Their relationship has nothing to do with the kind of unbroken, law-shaped causal sequence that characterizes the unfolding of the material world. Nevertheless, when I shape my future I still have to *use*, and hence rely on, causal relations in the material world. How otherwise would I be able to walk to the pension adviser? How otherwise would I be able to see the documents when they are in front of me courtesy of the fluorescent lights in the office? How otherwise would my letter activating the payment of the pension reach the provider? But these causal sequences do not dictate that future; rather they are being used to shape it. And if they were to proceed entirely autonomously, sooner or later, like a driverless car, they would veer off course.

It will be evident from the examples just touched on, that free will is not expressed in actions narrowly construed as a linear succession of discrete events.[48] It is typically expressed through something broader: activity. Ordinary voluntary activity incorporates vast numbers of physical events arranged hierarchically with subordinate elements serving superordinate or over-arching purposes. These events are *requisitioned* as the means to bring about certain intermediate ends, themselves means to further ends. Seen in this light, it becomes even more clearly evident that an action is an event that would not have taken place unless it had a purpose explicitly entertained by an agent.

Let us revisit the commonplace example touched on earlier: a work-out in a gym. Travelling to the destination (walking, driving, walking), changing into appropriate kit, and engaging with treadmills and other devices (a privilege for which I have paid a subscription in advance, itself a process that also involves many steps) – all these intrinsically complex steps are linked together into an activity that itself is only part of a larger *programme* of activity that has the somewhat abstract aim of postponing the time when I might fall ill. If I am running away, it is not from a predator but from a possibility of illness – flagged up in my own case by a meta-analysis of research studies on dementia and exercise. Such a sequence of physical events (including those that are involved in taking out a subscription, such as making sure that one's credit card is up to date) would not have happened unless it had been assembled, and arranged in a certain order, itself dependent on a sustained and sustaining intention, a consciously envisaged goal, that makes them intelligible to the agent. The chances of the succession of events comprising an action such as going to the gym occurring spontaneously as an expression of unguided laws of nature would be negligible. The bespoke *sequence* of events could not be generated by the untutored *general* machinery of the laws of nature. It is tailored by an explicit, personal goal to which it is directed, such as fulfilling my target of going to the gym three times a week as recommended by the meta-analysis I have read.

Connected with this is the fact that we could not intelligibly represent these sequences of events in a format that the physicist would recognize. The interaction, the sequence, whereby one part of an action calls forth another, is not one that has any kind of counterpart in basic physics, even physics whose expression is modified in the context of complex organisms. It is events at the level I have described them that are requisitioned to deliver our ends: these are the handles by which we control – or at least attempt to control, and sometimes succeed – what happens in that part of the future of the universe that impinges on matters of interest to us. Such higher level events would be exemplied by items such as "ringing up a friend", "travelling to London", "booking a holiday" that are connected with one another through a shared participation in a journey to a goal and whose specification would not correspond to a particular set of material processes defined by a range of energy transfers.

The special status of the occasions for our actions may be highlighted by events that have both an immediate, physical or biological, effects and ones that are mediated by meaning, intelligibility, and purposes. Consider a command. You tell me to get on with something and your voice is so loud that the cat jumps. The feline jump is a relatively straightforward effect of a cause, operating at the level of a quasi-biological signal, a stimulus. My response to your command – to go to town to fetch something for you – is entirely different. It requires my understanding what you say, assenting to your authority, and then performing all the innumerable movements that getting to town, locating the object, taking hold of it, and bringing it back require, all of which will have to be shaped by my sense of doing the thing that I have agreed to. The succession of events, even in this relatively passive example, where I am obedient to the will of another, cannot be understood as a chain of causes and effects.

This difference may be illustrated by another example, rather simpler: the performance of a piece of music. I am playing a violin sonata. There is a clear causal relationship between the movement of my arm, the sound that comes out of the violin, and the fact that you can hear it. There is, however, a different kind of succession: the succession of the notes, where each chord as it were "requires" its successor in order to add up to the melody that is being played.[49] There are other kinds of connection: the way endless practice enables me to produce these chords in the right order, with the right pitch and so on; your journeying to the concert hall to hear me in order to experience the pleasurable effect you know the music will have on you; the relationship between that pleasurable effect and the place it has in your life; and so on.

We might be tempted to characterize the kind of distinction that is being made by saying that at a higher level causation gives way to reason but this is to insert too sharp a division between the material world and the world of human activity. Causes stick out, are isolated from the multi-dimensional flow of events that unfolds around and inside us, on the strength of their salience, their relevance to rational goals. Reasons isolate causes; and, at the same time, acting according to reasons, we can never be free of the material world of causation. Reason-pulled behaviour requires cause-pushed effects.

The level at which the unfolding of the universe is teased apart into a nexus of distinct causal chains, that are seen variously as handles, as foreground and background, as remote and near, and as controllable or uncontrollable, is also the level of our freedom. If we were not distanced from causal chains, we would not be able to exploit any of them, and there would be no distinction between that which can and that which cannot be exploited. The fact that we engage with the material world from a huge outside of shared consciousness, and that that world is shaped by being dissected in different ways by descriptions that express our evermore complex needs and evermore complex approaches to our needs, are manifestations of our agency and the way it is elaborated. It may say something about our nature outside of nature and (possibly) our future after our natural life has ended.

The most radical conclusion we may draw from this is that causation is description-dependent. This might tempt us to wonder whether causal pressures, the constraints of the material world, are ultimately dependent upon the way we view things. There is a kind of truth in this that falls short of full-blown magic thinking: the unfolding world breaks up into nexuses of causes only from the viewpoint of an individual that is aware of its needs. It is this that changes what happens spontaneously into handles to bring about what is made to happen by our conscious will. Failure to see this results in imagining that there is something called "material necessity" which brings the inescapable force of logic into the unfolding of actual events. "Material necessity" is a hybrid, making events the non-contingent consequences of contingent laws. The necessity, however, comes from our needs: it is this that turns the unfolding of things into that which provides or denies us what we need to remain alive. It is revealed to that (human) being that is uniquely aware of its necessities. It is not intrinsic to material objects, any more than "ought" is intrinsic to them.

It might be argued that contingency could fall by the same token. Contingency, after all, is a relationship between that which is conceived, entertained, proposed as a possibility and that which occurs, which makes possible the observation that that which occurs could just as well not have occurred. Alternatively, contingency may be understood as a reflection of our only partial knowledge of universe entirely predetermined by material necessity. If we knew the laws, and could do the calculations, nothing would seem contingent; nothing would take us by surprise: thus the Laplacean dream. But even the Laplacean picture – where contingency boils down to necessity concealed by our ignorance, our inability to see beyond our own viewpoint to the true nature of things – still requires us to be offset from the world to see it as shaped by wall-to-wall necessity and the flow of events as undeflectable. Indeed, the very notion of what is as "how things turned out to be" makes it the realization of an entertained possibility. The flow of events could not be conceived as either necessary or contingent if the what-is were not approached from an outside; from a viewpoint that establishes it as what-might-be (in the future) or what-might-have-been (in the past).

To summarize, we are true agents because we can operate on the law-governed, seemingly causally closed universe from outside. An agent is someone who uses events (causes-as-means) to bring about other events (effects). The very fact that we have the *idea* of causes, that we can identify individual causes for exploitation to bring about certain effects, that correspond to intended consequences, and that we are able to raise our gaze above individual sequences of events to discern law-like relations between types of events, reveals the extent to which we transcend the material world of which we are a part while at the same time being apart from it.[50] This lies at the heart of our distance from nature, enabling us to be agents originating actions that express what we individually are and deflecting the course of the events. The distance we maintain from the material world is, above all, a temporal distance, upheld by tensed time. We shall now examine this a little more closely.

12.3.4.2 *Action at a distance*: reculer pour mieux sauter

> Action on the move creates its own route; creates to a very great extent the conditions under which it is to be fulfilled and thus baffles all our calculations.
> Henri Bergson

We can be true agents because the vast majority of our actions are not mere reactions, responses to stimuli like the withdrawal of a limb from a hot surface, or the movement towards prey or a flight from a predator. Much of our activity has little to do with our immediate surroundings. While the here and now, centred on our bodily being, is the primary location or substrate of actions, what we are doing refers beyond it to a many-layered elsewhere that recedes from "just round the corner" and "in a moment or so" to another place, even continent, and hours, days, years, or even decades ahead. Much of our freedom comes from extending the depth of the tenses within which we exercise our capacity to act, the virtual time of the no longer and the not yet.

The distance of our distant goals takes many forms. Its commonest measure is an interval between that which occasions our actions and the actions themselves. Most importantly, this interval is not merely a matter of a delay in response to something that has (already) happened, though such delays are important. As Michael Gazzaniga has said, "much of what makes us human is not an ability to do more things, but an ability to inhibit automatic responses in favour of reasoned ones ... we may be the only species that engages in delayed gratification and impulse control".[51] Man is not only the doing animal but also the refraining animal. (He who hesitates is saved!). But there are also more significant delays where actions are intended but whose time is not yet ripe. To some extent, even refraining now can be future-oriented: it keeps a space clear for other actions. Often we lay down cues for ourselves aware that in the interval between the decision to act and the time appropriate for the action we may forget what we had intended to do. Man is the creature who not only knowingly acts in extended time frames but ambushes himself with reminders born out of awareness of his own capacity to forget. In these simple facts are extraordinarily complex relationships to time. Acting when I discover a knotted handkerchief in my pocket, I am responding to a command laid down in the past that anticipated the present moment when it was future. Individual freely chosen actions add up to a life that is actively lived rather than merely endured. This is ultimately rooted in the intentionality of perception, extended by the intentionality of signs that build up the shared world of the community of minds.

The remote future turns the present into a distant past from which we are able to manipulate that future. We come from far back in order that we may enhance our capacity to manipulate the world we live in: *reculer pour mieux sauter.* We increase our control over what happens on 25 December 2015 by beginning to act on its behalf in August of that year. Even where actions are responses to the events that just happen to or around us, they are embedded in ongoing activity that adds up to an agenda which has priority. Incidental encounters with persons, beasts, things, and happenings, are absorbed into the unfolding story of the morning's work, of the journey, of the relationship, of the construction of some object, institution, or document, of the daily round or the life-long project.

Actions, and their cognate spaces, are inserted into each like Russian dolls. I put one step in front of the other to get to the car; I drive to the station to catch the train; I catch the train in order to arrive at a particular destination in London; I go to London in order to contribute to a meeting; I contribute to the meeting in order to persuade others to support me in some project that, if all goes well, will be completed in 5 years' time. Our lives are woven out of a network of "in order tos". The successive "in order tos" presuppose futures of different scales. And at each level, there will be incidental happenings that will require to be negotiated: the ruck in the carpet or dogdirt on the pavement; the traffic jam to be negotiated; the seat to be found on the train; the other items on the agenda of the meeting and the greetings and ordinary courtesies of everyday intercourse. At any given time, there will be a multitude of planned and unexpected agenda items unfolding. Work, family, hobbies, passions, will weave in and out of the tissues of our hours.

Thus is the present suborned to a future whose, often remote, past it is. Thus are we ordinarily distanced from the situations in which we find ourselves; or rather our conception of our situation is vastly extended beyond our immediate surroundings.

We have to take account of those surroundings, of course. As I walk along the road to a meeting, consumed with thoughts about what lies ahead, planning my actions, I have still to avoid tripping over a hole in the pavement, bumping into someone else, or walking into a wall or a car travelling at speed; but these events that demand that I swerve do not blow me off course, away from an ongoing purpose which, in the vast majority of cases, is not located in my immediate surroundings. The latter are, at most, the intermediate substrates of the distant mediators of those actions that relate most immediately to my goals. No wonder we cannot usually infer what our fellow creatures are about as we encounter them in the streets. We need them to tell us what they are at and where this fits into the smaller, medium-sized, and larger purposes of their lives. By contrast, we see a herd of cows grazing and we know exactly what they are doing: they are grazing. We see a herd of humans rushing along a pavement but we do not know why they are rushing: every rush rushes towards a different bespoke goal not defined by the present physical location.

The future is my future – it is the place of my hopes, fears, and responsibilities – but it is also a shared, collective future.[52] I rely in part on borrowed, shared agency to get me to the right place when that future has become the present: the technologies that I use, the institutions that define and support me, the collective actions (team work of a multitude of teams), and the heritage – the shared past to inform the ideas, the norms, the duties and hopes of a shared future – are woven out of the joint attention that underpins our collective lives. The future is structured by timetables. It would be absurd to see the collaborative working – usually with chosen collabora- tors – that marks so much of our activity as an expression of material causal factors outside of our selves; to trace causal pathways in the formation of groups who choose to work together.

The distances opened up between stimulus and response and the extent to which actions are future driven is illustrated by learning. Animal learning is based largely on accidentally bumping into events and circumstances that supplement reflex responses with the shaping influence of the fruit of contingent experience. Human learning is increasingly actively sought out. We are taught, we practise, we rehearse in preparation for dealing with circumstances in which we might find ourselves, or to acquire the skills that may be required of us. Many actions are carried out for the sake of future performances when they will be required. They are dummy actions, divorced from any present function they may have, addressed to a future need.

Curricular learning is the most elaborate way of positioning ourselves not only to experience certain experiences – in pursuit of pain or pleasure – but also enable ourselves to act effectively. "Positioning" ourselves, being in a state of prepared- ness, taking precautions, anticipating possibilities (threats, opportunities that are currently invisible) that will prompt action *now* takes countless forms and may be extremely complex. It can encompass travelling to a city where we know there are better chances of employment, eating well to improve our future health, building up a well-equipped army in order to pre-empt a future attack, making membership of an insurance scheme compulsory so that no-one will be impoverished in old age. We lay down tracks that in part constrain the future; and in moving towards an envisaged and shaped future we progressively widen the gap between a life that is suffered, merely lived from moment to moment, in which we are tossed from episode to episode, and one that is led purposefully.[53]

We draw on increasing documentation of the past so that our anticipations of the future are more likely to be accurate at some level. This is both informal – as in individual recollection and collective recollection deposited in historical records – and formal as, in pursuit of knowledge of the most fundamental habits of the material world, we conduct scientific experiments whose findings are generalizable to a whole category of situations, past, present and future. We shape the future in our cooperative activity, in informal and statutory teams, that work to a common timetable mapping out a Not-yet that is an intricate meshwork of tabled time. (It would be possible to write an entire treatise on "The Power of the Appointment".) Most generally, we come at the future from an increasing temporal distance, either because it is being laid down in what is an evermore remote past or because we concern ourselves with an ever more distant future. The rich presence of the no-longer informs a complex and detailed sense of the not-yet.

An obvious example of this relates to the biological (but in humans utterly transformed) process of getting enough energy to keep ourselves alive. In common with all animals we eat what we come into contact with and not infrequently store it. Unlike animals, however, we cultivate, manufacture, process, and warehouse it. These future-oriented developments, securing our nutrition in days, weeks, and years to come, are themselves open to elaboration. We protect our stocks by building places to house them and ensuring they are secure. We share food through systems of exchange and dividing the labour required to grow, and later to manufacture, it. We anticipate year-on-year fluctuations in the food supply, holding some back, seeking new and different sources or different kinds of view. We discover and share new ways of conserving food. We develop laws regulating the sharing, pricing, storing, and quality controlling of food. Instead of reaching for a bumped-into banana, or raiding caches whose construction was programmed, I solve my problem of nutrition by earning a salary that requires me to have a certain set of skills which I have acquired in advance. The central narrative of many human lives is of years of preparation for a career and its unfolding – of a distant past reaching into a remote future. We thus arrive to a future already formatted in minute detail by actions taken in and informed by its many pasts. On this basis, we ensure that the future is as free as possible from hazard, illness, and want – freedoms that are the basis of all other freedoms.

In short, we create the conditions in which actions – long-range, non-emergency, non-cued actions – are possible. In creating these conditions, there will be different contributions from the individual, from the group with whom there is explicit collaboration (we all pull on the rope or we divide the task between us), and from the unlimited (and largely unsung) heritage given to us by our conspecifics who have created the environment, the technologies (artefacts, techniques and expertise), the rules and regulations governing collective behaviour, and so on, that have constructed the platform upon which our actions are possible and, indeed, make sense. Our agency is overwhelmingly "joint and several" and "the several" may range from a handful of partners to the many billions who have prepared the path for us. It is distributed not only over many steps but over many people, many generations, and many settings.

A propos positioning, we should note an important discrepancy between space and time. As discussed in §6.1.3, we are at liberty to choose our spatial location but not our temporal location: "here" is (within limits) discretionary – space travel is a ubiquitous feature of daily life; "now", by contrast, is mandated and time travel in the conventional sense is forbidden. If I want to make a difference to how things unfold in another town, I have somehow (in person, through proxies – other persons, instructions in print or by phone, etc.) to be present in that town. If I want to make a difference to what happens at a particular time, direct action requires that I wait until that time arrives. I can, however, get round this constraint on time travel by acting indirectly, creating conditions that will influence what will happen in due course, pulling levers that will eventually be attached to events happening in that future, lighting the blue touch paper and retiring, leaving a message to be opened and found at some time hence. In short, I can escape my confinement to "now" by exploiting the time delay built into the unfolding of events or prohibiting others' actions until a certain time: "Do not open this envelope until your birthday".

Discussions of free will often overlook the telling fact that some actions are easier than others; that there is a spectrum of difficulty between the automatic: as in the case of reflexes or learned skills, and the impossible, for example, lifting oneself up by one's hair or emailing one's body. If agency were a matter of breaking the laws of nature, all actions would be either insuperably difficult or there would be no limit to agency; everything would be equally possible or impossible; effortless or resistant to all effort. In reality, some actions are very easy, some are more difficult, and some are impossible. Quite rightly, we do not think of the events in a causally closed physical world as taking place with ease or requiring huge effort or not taking place because of failure of causes to bring about the effects they "aimed" at.

Before leaving this strand of our exploration of our freedom, let us go back to basics. The possibility of free action is dependent on the ability to respond not to some kind of causal push, or a sub-type of this applicable to living organisms such as "a stimulus", but to an envisaged possibility located in the future, whose content is informed by a past. We are free in proportion as the distance from which we act can be extended and the goal of our actions is not precisely located in space and time. The ground floor of the possibility of freedom is to be found in vision where we are in touch with the world without being touched by it, in which we see things that do not see us. The visual field is full of things that are present and visible, that carry within them the possibility of futures and evidence of a past, and reveal that there are hidden things – the insides of objects, items only part within the visual field, and things that are sensed as being beyond the horizon of the visible. What is more, it is possible to pan round a field, engaging with various strands of ongoing or possibility reality. A range of teased apart causal chains is highlighted by the pick-and-mix of attention, offering a multiplicity of opportunities for intervention. Some of these impinge directly upon us but most are "out there", allowing engagement to be elective.

It is on such a ground floor that our human world and the stage in which our freedom is exercised are built. The visibly invisible is the pathway to a realm of non-localised intelligibility: the individual and shared sense of what might (in general) be about to happen or what might have happened. The derivative intentionality of the semiosphere widens the range of possibilities, underlines their non-locality, and allows the distance from which we act to be widened indefinitely. The explicit no-longer and not-yet of the field expands into invisible yesterdays and tomorrows. The disconnection between the occasion for action and a physical cause or a bio-logical stimulus underwrites the freedom of that action. "Tomorrow" or an event explicitly located in it – to be brought about or pre-empted – is not a cause but a *be*cause; not a mindless transfer of energy but an event governed by a purpose. Making and honouring appointments is a paradigm instance of the "becausation" of present actions by a future invisible goal. Such bespoke invisible, indeed purely intelligible, goals are not seen outside of humanity. A chimp doesn't have a tomorrow; even less does it have the thousand tomorrows that are assumed in my plan for an event in 3 years' time.

12.3.4.3 Action, timing and temporality: the ratchet

The anticipation involved in hand-to-mouth coordination suggests that, at the very least, from early post-natal life onwards human (and most likely animal) movement involves an apparent timing that reflects an intrinsic or inherent temporality. I note the distinction between timing and temporality. Timing is something we can see and measure. Timing, however, can be accidental or merely coincidental. The fact of a more consistent timing, that the mouth almost always anticipates the hand, for example, suggests deeper temporal processes involved in bodily systems capable of such timing.[54]

We began in Chapter 1 by examining the conditions in which time became explicit. Because the sense most importantly involved in making time explicit was also the most spatial sense – namely vision – it was entirely predictable that explicit time should become quasi-spatial and, on this basis, time was at risk of being spatialized en route to being reduced to a pure quantity – little t. Vision is not only spatial but, of all the senses, the one that is most "out-of-the-body" – to the point where the seer can locate her own body in a visual field. Time, too, was therefore located out of the body, moving from pulses and breathing and footsteps to clockworks where it could be gathered up into a system of magnitudes, ranging from the homely – hours, days, and timetables – to the scientific, where time is assimilated into the meshes of the clockwork universe. The truth, however, is that time does not entirely leave the body because we are not merely spectators of our lives, or merely substrates of them, but active agents. Living is not a spectator sport and temporality is inseparable from agency.

Before addressing this, let us very briefly return to the conundrum that exercised us in §10.4.3: How does a succession of experiences deliver the experience of succession? The puzzle was exacerbated by the assumption that time was doled out in mathematical instants – a consequence of the reduction of temporality to a pure quantity. How could we escape the constraint of being in the moment to experience a succession of events that lies beyond the moment, and give present reality to events and their times of occurrence that are no longer or not yet? Once it is accepted that instants are constructs upon, rather than the basic constituents of, time, then the problem starts to look soluble, even artificial. It evaporates further when it is appreciated that, although it is possible to observe isolated sequences of events, our experience is of a more or less intelligible world whose meaning is no more confined to, or located in, successive instants of time, than it is located in points in space. Where there are discrete sequences that are brought together, they are bound by their belonging to an intelligible order that does not belong to elements individually. Indeed, as is so often the case, they are parts of instances of familiar wholes. "Do-re-mi" does not belong to t_1 when "do" occurs, nor to t_2 when "re" occurs, nor t_3 when "mi" occurs. The *intelligibility* of a recognized object or process is not located in, or confined to, the time at which it is experienced or occurs or is instantiated.

The other point we touched on in the discussion of the perception of sequences was one I want to develop now; namely that our experiences are not just those of a spectator. We are agents and there is a temporality in action, as highlighted in the quotation from Sean Gallagher at the head of this section. Deliberate action is intelligible to the agent such that every part of it, as a piece of "in process" or "en route", exists in a greater temporal whole than the moments in which it occurs. Agency in action is lived intelligibility.

This is expressed in different ways. Reaching for a glass involves timing of the initiation of the movement, of the ballistic phase in which the arm travels under its own momentum, the deceleration as the target is approached, the opening of the hand in preparation to enclose the glass, and then gripping it. Every step of a 100-yard journey belongs to that journey and is, as it were, magnified by being part of it. The action of getting dressed brings together a heterogeneous collection of actions, ranging from bending down to pull on a sock, to identifying a small drift of white as a shirt, to wandering around looking for cuff links, to going in an adjacent room to examine one's state of dress in a mirror. None of these elements is confined to the time in which it takes place because none of them has a complete stand-alone meaning: their intelligibility is part of something larger. These are small-scale actions. Tidying up the house, completing the day's correspondence, doing a ward round, preparing for an examination, going on holiday, bringing up a child – these are larger-scale actions whose elements transcend themselves in virtue of being part of, and making sense only in relation to, larger wholes. The main events that make them up are incorporated into an ongoing process whose extensity is made manifest by an explicit goal and an observed progress from a starting point. Our responsibilities to others or as individuals pursuing our own interests further extend the scope of our time sense, far beyond directly perceived successions of events, to the kinds of things we plan, communicate about, and narrate. The timing built into micro- and macro-actions gives existential reality to stretches of time are directly observed in sequences of events.

There is a ratcheting up process in which tensed times makes agency possible and the products of agency further extend the depth of tensed time, so that we deal not merely in what has just happened or is just about to happen, but in the remembered contents of days and weeks ago and the anticipated or planned contents of days and weeks ahead. The time that actions "take", or are envisaged to take, deepens our time sense which is underwritten by the communities of which we are a part.

The misleading focus on (passive) perception of time as opposed to action may be the result of the domination of our thinking about time by those extraordinary developments of observation, namely measurement, that reduces time to numbers. There is no activity in the mathematical world. This focus makes us think that a true sense of time is one which ends with numbers and that such numbers can be arrived at only by building up from fragments such as, for example, short sequences of events like "do-re-mi". Our lived experience of temporality is then denigrated as a primitive stage in our journey towards seconds, sidereal years, and the astronomers' millions of decades. This misrepresentation of time comes from the fact that time is made explicit, extra-corporeal, by the most spatial of senses, which is also the one that engages or immerse us least: vision. For vision, time is something that is primordially perceived rather than used. It is then used only indirectly in order to *time* events and its association with agency is assigned to the material world out there, where energy is agency without consciousness or ideas – or indeed experienced effort.

The constituents of actions have a temporal order that may or may not be mandated. The larger the actions, the less constraint there is on the order of the constituents, rather as grammar may dictate word order in a sentence but not how a conversation should go. We may pick things up and put them down, time-share between other activities, and urge ourselves to completion or indulge our tendency to prevarication. In all cases, the time stretch of the activity is further extended.

This, then, is a fundamental level of immediately experienced time in our lives: time realised in sequentially ordered actions, activities, and projects. It is not reducible to the spectator time that gives rise ultimately to clock-time. Lived time is indivisible far above the level of the moment understood as an extensionless mathematical instant. Of course, our agency can be, indeed often is, orchestrated by an external clock-time. We do things at certain clock-times, the clock tells us whether we need to hurry, it instructs as to whether we "have time" to do such and such. We carry out actions by appointment at agreed times and we make time for things we cannot do now. Such timing, however, is on the far side of human temporality. Clock timing is a relatively recent entry into the field of agency; and it is, what is more, a key respect in which human temporality as expressed in action is different from the time of even relatively complex behaviour of animals. Hand-to-mouth coordination, mating or fighting, in a chimp requires sequencing of actions just as it does in humans.

Let us return to the mutual ratcheting up of our tensed time sense and the complexity and scale of our actions. It is because I have a sense of the future, that I undertake actions that will deliver the goals that I seek in the future. But the scale of ongoing and completed actions itself holds open our sense of future. This is most clearly evident in collective actions. Huge cooperative enterprises whose completion dates are far into the future both draw upon and extend our sense of tensed time. Large scale projects populate ever more distant futures and draw on ever deeper pasts; and the sense of distant futures extended by the scale of actions and enterprises lies at the heart of the unfolding history of human consciousness. Its absence in non-human animals is due to a variety of factors. Among them is this: animals do not share their experiences and expertise, having little or no sense of each other's mental lives. Their sense of possibility is also more intimately limited, since their awareness of that which exists but is hidden from them is constricted. Our nearest primate kin, for example, have an attenuated sense of material objects existing independently of their awareness, and of those objects having intrinsic properties. Their sense of possibility, therefore, hardly gets off the ground floor.[55]

The extension of tensed time increases the size and kind of distances from which we operate on the world and directly and indirectly control the manner in which it operates on us. The distances are created and maintained collectively but are experienced and inflected and shaped individually, though very distant times – such as 2020 seen from 2016 – may seem pure numbers having only a public reality. The past that is operating when, for example, I travel to give a lecture is a past first of all that is one that I have had a significant role in shaping (choices, effort, training); so the "determination" is to a considerable degree "self-determination", not a condition of being under the thrall of an external force. The action expresses a vast number of things that are unique to myself and to my take on the world. (It is in virtue of this that I can also end up as the prisoner of my free choices, of commitments freely entered into.) This action that is expressive of a swath of my own, unique yesterdays, can be seen as originating within me, as that in myself which I have embraced as me. Agency draws on and draws together a lot of myself: acting freely is not only to act "whole-heartedly" but also cognitively and affectively large-heartedly, with many chambers beating in unison. This is in sharp contrast to an event such as an epileptic fit which has no relationship to my history, is hardly unique to me, and is an interruption to, rather than a part of, my biography.

Most importantly, and most pertinent to our thesis, the past that is present in this action is an explicit past that is also explicitly my past, though it is truly present, as it has to be in order to deliver what it has to deliver, namely, provide the unifying sense that occasions the components of the action, brings them together, and makes them an expression of my leading my life as opposed to merely experiencing it. At any given moment during an action, I am drawing on an explicit, uniquely personal past – my interests, my knowledge, my ambitions, my larger goals in life, the narrative of the self whose primary and overwhelmingly dominant narrator and interpreter is myself – as I move to an explicit personal future. Correspondingly, each stage in an action incorporates a multitude of dovetailing sense-making moments. As such, the action is entirely unlike an "effect" – either of the previous steps in the action or of some prior external cause or even an intention construed as a discrete internal cause. Material effects in themselves do not have temporal depth (they are what they are) and do not refer back to any antecedents causes, even less to reasons. What is more, they do not have the kind of spread, or openness, the field-like nature, of moments of deliberate action. Any relations observed between an action and antecedent causes or successor effects are external and are established by an external (human) viewpoint.

It is difficult to see, in the case of non-dramatic, daily life, the extent to which its actions are steeped in the past, in a visible and invisible (more generally, sensible and insensible) present, and reach into the future. It is because they are so familiar, they seem temporarily depthless and hence liable to be seen as events that are simply part of a physical sequence. The future orientation is particularly relevant to the difference between actions and other events because it is obvious that, since the aimed-at outcomes are only possibilities, they cannot be assimilated into the material world which is necessarily composed solely of actualities. The future that justifies a particular action, indeed *makes* the sense that occasions it, may be a matter of hours, days, years and even decades, hence. This is a measure of the extent to which at any given moment we are not identical with some (physical) state that can be accounted for in terms of prior and surrounding causes. We are internally connected to a past that is our own past via episodic memories that are hung with images and may be charged with feeling and linked also with a collective past presented to us as facts and other shared realities. And the future to which we are oriented is both a private future of what we see or imagine round the corner, of our specific tasks, commitments, or general goals and hopes, and a shared future of joint projects and enterprises and timetabled events. Thus we can retain, order, and learn from an ever deeper past. Informed by habits, immediate and mediated memories, by chronicles and institutions, our gaze towards the future penetrates further and we populate it more richly with more accurate expectations. The expectations that prompt and weld together our actions are not simply passive, mere anticipations of what is going to happen of its own accord. As individuals who lead our lives rather than merely experiencing them, or leading lives that are ours rather than acting out the biological script of a living organism, we are concerned that what happens should at least in part happen of *our* accord.

Of course, there are constraints arising from many directions – physical and biological constraints, cultural constraints originating from the characteristics of shared ways of life, the social and political and economic framework within which we operate, and the symmetrical or asymmetrical giving up of sovereignty, the particular duties, commitments, offices, we have to discharge, not to speak of the play of chance, accidents and the unexpected. But even within these constraints, there is a complex dialectic of activity and passivity, of the chosen and the unchosen. We may turn even our physical and biological givens into a source of recreation, of freely undertaken challenges. The social, political and economic framework confers meaning on our choices as well as limiting them: they are *enabling constraints*, like the grammar of language, and weave our moment-to-moment activities into a larger narrative, enabling us to participate, sometimes against other manifestations of our will, in a collective drama that is bigger than the trajectory of our own lives. We may freely choose to subordinate ourselves to others, to give meaning to our lives through service, and the very process of discharging duties, fulfilling an office, and honouring implicit standing commitments and explicit episodic promises, may add weight and depth to our sense of who we are.

The dialectic between activity and passivity, between working against and working with constraint, is seen at every moment of our lives. This is particularly evident in our pastimes, as when we go on holiday in order to experience the unknown, to open ourselves to whatever happens, *placet experiri*. The point, however, is that our openness to experience is always within controlled circumstances. We are like the child in the park who goes purposively to a special place – the slide – in order to allow herself to fall under the control of natural forces.

One aspect of our relationship to the future may seem trivial but in fact it is both of profound theoretical significance and wide practical importance: "tidying up".[56] Earlier we discussed the apparent asymmetry between causes and their effects. An index cause may have a multitude of effects and effects of their effects: it dissipates itself in successive generations of effects until its trillions of causal descendants fade into noise and that noise is lost in other noise. The succession of the elements of an action is not like that at all. Actions are counter to this natural dissipation: they are composed of a chain of events – or braided chains of events – that link a moment to a future goal and a past that makes sense of it. This is nothing like the way causal chains unfold in the material world. The latter may be disciplined by the laws of nature but this is different from being shaped by an explicit bespoke purpose, without which actions would disintegrate into at best random movements. In anticipation of the effect of the principle of untidiness and progressive loss of signal and control, we prepare the circumstances we shall encounter in the future by bringing together otherwise disparate and meaningless items into structures – ranging from clothes and meals to houses and cities – that will either directly obstruct our dissipation or (as in the case of artefacts such as tools) enable us to do so indirectly. When we leave places as we or others would like to find them, our actions row back against the usual direction of causation.

This, then, is the basis of our freedom to use present circumstances to bring about possible futures we wish to actualize. Because we are not mere effects, or the sites of entirely present events, but creatures extended in time that we ourselves make explicit, we stand to one side of the material world of cause and effect which is confined to the tenseless present – entering a world of "am" offset from the universe of "is", of subjects faced with objects, and yet engage with it at every level in our own actions; to return to our earlier claim, we can engage with it from the outside. This was foreshadowed in the onlooker, at once connected to and separated from the material world, who can foresee, partly on the basis of hindsight, and foreclose the range of possible futures. In this sense, we reverse the direction of causation, by making the future act on the present, which is its past. For example, my present expectation that it will rain in future prompts me to carry an umbrella now, so that when the anticipated rain comes, I will remain dry.

This is not, of course, backward causation because what is anticipated may not happen. For example, I want to avoid someone. I know he is planning to be at a meeting tomorrow. I therefore decide to avoid that meeting and give my apologies. It happens that he does not attend either. My actions today are influenced not by future *events* (there are, as we discussed in §8.2.2 no such things) but by future possibilities and they may be just as potent if they are realized or if they are not.

This is how it comes about that the self-as-agent is a point of departure, of origin, in a world that seems to have been unfolding without interruption since the Big Bang. The self is a field, increasingly self-sown, a realm that is inner in virtue of being a virtual outside of outsides, a place from which actions grow, sufficiently independent of the flow of the material world as to be able to break it up into causes that may be used as handles. The agenda of the self – rooted in a fidelity to its self over time – is most clearly expressed in the projects to which we commit ourselves, the principles that govern our actions, and the responsibility we take for them, the judgements we pass on ourselves, and the desire we have to think well of ourselves and to be thought well of.

Galen Strawson has argued against the possibility of free will on the grounds that we are not free since we are not self-caused, as nothing can be self-caused.[57] It is evident, however, that we *are* increasingly self-caused in the way that I have suggested. We are not ultimately self-caused in the sense of creating ourselves from nothing at all. Nor do we create ourselves abruptly from something unlike ourselves, so that we can take credit for being a member of the human species. But neither of these conditions is necessary for us to be free in any sense that truly matters – that is, sufficiently to guide our own lives to an important degree and to bear moral responsibility. But Strawson's criteria are not only impossible but also incoherent. He seems to think that we could not be or become free if we were any particular being that was in any respect unchosen, if we did not set out as a nothing that unfolded itself without assistance into a something. The obvious response to this impossible requirement for freedom is that we could not be free if we had nothing to be free for or on anyone's behalf. Without a starter pack, without givens – body, physical and cognitive capacities, date of birth, location in the physical and social world – there would be nothing to be free about. Strawson seems to think that a truly free act would have to be performed by someone who managed to be no-one and for no compelling reason. (This intuition lurks in the background of the existentialist cult of the utterly pointless *acte gratuit* as the most perfect expression of freedom.)

So we must accept that, as truly free agents with something to be free about, we have to be something that is not entirely self-caused. All of the self that is free – from the construction of a past and a future, and the frames of reference that make the present the wide sea of intelligibility that it is – is achieved in cooperation with those others whose culture we share. It does not, however, follow from this that we are dissolved in the collective; that we have been liberated from physical determinism only to become the passive expression or conduit of our culture. For we each enter, participate in, and leave a variety (indeed a unique mix) of cultures in unique ways. Our bodily trajectory through space and time commits us to a personal, individual take on the human worlds we find ourselves in. While, therefore, our participation in the collective expands the distance between ourselves and the material world opened by intentionality, and tensed time liberates us from physical determinism, our unique physical existence – such that *you* cannot literally occupy *my* world-line and the vicissitudes that come with it – liberates each of us from our culture. Our freedom, that is to say, has two sources: the individual and collective and each secures one aspect of our ability to be the source of our own actions.

12.3.5 Concluding thoughts on agency and causation

Let us gather up some stray threads of the complex network of ideas connecting agency and causation (some readers may feel the point has been made sufficiently and wish to omit this section).

- We may think of an action as an event that would not have happened if it did not serve the purposes of an agent and an agent as someone who uses causes as means to bring about effects or ends. This is preferable to characterizing the difference between happenings that are, those that are not, actions by asserting in the traditional fashion that the former are pulled by future goals and the latter are pushed by past events.
- An action, in other words, is a complex event requisitioned in the light of an envisaged future. Tailored to the needs of the individual whose future it is, it would have had zero or near zero probability of occurring without a future-oriented intention which might be very sustained. (Think of all the movements that are involved in teaching oneself French.) The way in which our actions are stitched together is quite different from the way in which causes are connected. The in-order-to has an entirely different mode of connectedness. Walking to the car to get to the railway station is nothing like a cause connected to an effect. The lightning does not flash *in order to* make the air thunder. This is apparent in many ways, but none more clearly than in the fact that walking to the car does not guarantee that I shall get to the station, not the least because I might change my mind about the advisability of going to the station. What is more, we not only entertain wishes but we reflect on them, and may critique them in the light of other, higher order wishes.
- The events that comprise the behaviour (movements of my body, for example) would not happen if I did not see their point. That is why the link between cause and effect is tighter than that between, and one part of, an action and the next. Proceeding from getting into my car and actually driving to the station has an element of discretion which is not evident in the succession of causally connected events such as thunder following lightning or a crash subsequent upon an object falling to the floor or indeed the movement of the engine and the movement of the car.
- The looseness of the link between successive steps of an action is even more evident when we think of the kind of complex cooperative action seen in everyday life – such as honouring appointments, running a school, or carrying out a scientific study. This is reflected in the distinctive impact of human action on the material world summarized in the concept of the "Anthropocene" to which we have already

referred. Irrespective of whether the universe is a "put-up job", the human world most certainly is.

- Agency must begin with the picking out of events as causes or potential causes. It is from the standpoint of an agent that event A is picked out as a cause and event B as an effect. Salience is all; and salience is what directs the countercausal arrow of intentionality to come to rest at one item rather than another. To identify an event-type as a type of cause of a type of effect is to stand outside at least part of a causal nexus and to be half-way to agency. This is the most intimate way in which causation and agency, far from being opponents, are inextricable.

- That in virtue of which the cause is picked out cannot be itself an effect of the cause: causes do not highlight themselves any more than they apply inverted commas to themselves as "causes".

- The picked-out event is taken as a whole. This does not mean that it cannot be broken down into parts or itself prove to be a part of a greater whole. Salience draws the boundaries that makes a whole of what is picked out. So it identifies "the car climbing the hill" – which has many components, including numerous rotations of the wheels and cycles of the engine – as a single item, even though it is only part of a bigger item "the drive to Cornwall". What we might call attentional (or descriptive) acuity identifies the beginning and end of an event and sets it off from other changes that overlap or are simultaneous with it.

- Identification of a cause is the identification of a beginning, or at least a starting point. It places a flag in the flow of events. Explicit localization generates "here" and "now" in relationship to which there is a future and past populated by different states of affairs. The cause–effect pairing – with the one coexistent with the other – requires that the cause is not lost into its effects but that the latter are seen as having a parentage in the former. To see events as the effects of causes is to see them as having an explicit past; a that-in-virtue-of-which they have happened. Making the cause as the explicit past of its effect opens up tensed time in both directions: the effect is the explicit future of the cause. In short, identification of causes is inseparable from experiencing temporal depth.

- As identified or suspected causes become more remote – or the causal chains are extended – and effects likewise, time becomes deeper. Everything that happens is seen as the consequence of prior happening reaching further and further back and the progenitor of subsequent happenings reaching further and further forward.

- The world opened up by tensed time is one in which actuality and possibility are co-present. True actions are not propelled into being by that which precedes them; rather, an explicit past informs our sense of what might happen and indeed the menu of possibility which we can select from. The past consequently infuses actions with meanings.

- Agency breaks the asymmetry of influence according to which the past determines the present and the future. It challenges the *vis a tergo* with an asymmetry pointing in the opposite direction. What I imagine or want to happen on Wednesday will shape how I order that part of the world I can manipulate on Tuesday. Agency is that in virtue of which the future shapes the past – the present in which the future is envisaged.

- On 10 October, I learn that a cold snap is due. This influences what I do that day: buy a new coat. It is a particularly compelling example of extended intentionality and our freeing ourselves from causal bonds: casting our minds back and forwards in time – which is commonplace – is entirely different from time travel that involves our bodies being transported by a time ship. In the case of anticipation, we are dealing with intentionality which is intrinsically countercausal.

- This makes it no less extraordinary that we can be invited or invite ourselves to recall specific events. I can remember what happened just now by direct recall. Such time travel is a dramatic illustration of how intentionality is independent of causation, even though causes are picked out as intentional objects. It is central to our agency.

- The power of possibility is a power unknown to the material world which is confined to what it is: it is what-is, and not what might be, will be, or has been.

- In classic causal connections in the material world, the cause is contiguous with or even continuous with its effect. Any distance between cause and effect is filled with intermediate effects-become-causes in their turn. In the case of agency, the action and the intended end may be separated very widely without any obvious connectivity between. I may shop in August for bargains that will be presents for Christmas. The causal gap is crossed by intention. Intentions are consequently not themselves causes in the way that we typically think of causes.

- The non-equivalence between causes and intentions is reflected in the notion of proportionality which applies to the former and not to the latter. Intention is rough, description-dependent – there are many ways of doing X – whereas cause is precise. The notion of proportionality could not therefore apply to the relationship between intentions and actions, even setting aside any (misconceived) problems about "mental causation".

- Even so, below the level of purpose and intention, there is a causal stitching together of the components of actions. I walk to the pub to meet you (agency) but my walking depends on a variety of causal mechanisms such as the connection between neural discharges and muscular contraction that enables ambulation – the movement of one leg in front of the other and the reflexes that maintain upright posture. Much of our agency consists of being a patient, relying on being carried to our goals and on material necessity that, for example, keeps our feet on the ground and ensures that the thrown ball maintains its motion after it has left our hand.

- Actions, what is more, remain physical events that consequently have unwilled physical consequences, quite independent of their goal; they are riddled with mere happening, which is why they can go off course. When I walk to the pub, there are many effects of my walking that I do not intend: the footprints left in the snow, the bird in the hedge, frightened by the noise of my approach, flying off. In most cases, they do not jeopardize the outcome we seek. Even so, we sometimes try to control them, as when, for example, I am leaving the house early in the morning, I creep down the stairs in order to avoid causing the stairs to creak and wake up the baby. Our actions, in short, always have unintended physical side-shoots but for the most part they are insignificant and are not contrary to our goals. The social and psychological consequences, however, may be more obtrusive. The domestic expressions of the laws of nature are easier to take account of than the expressions of the laws of human nature.

- The unwilled goes to the heart of the action; indeed, action would be impossible without it. There is the cooperation with the pavement propelling me along the road, there is the displaced air cooling my body and whispering in my ears, the physiological accompaniments of my actions (heart and respiratory changes, sweating), the wearing away of shoe leather, the susurrus of my clothes rubbing my moving parts — all things mixed with the emotions about the meeting I am about to have. Many of the unwilled accompaniments of the walking may themselves become a primary goal — as when I decide to walk to the pub because the physiological changes will be good for my heart.

- We do many things because we feel obliged to do them. Our activity is rule-, even conscience-, governed. This is profoundly different from mere habit understood as conditioned or unconditioned response, as is illustrated by the fact that we perform many actions not because we are presently motivated to do them but because we know that they will bring about the conditions in which it is possible to do those things that we are motivated to do or feel we ought to be — either out of duty or prudence. The "ought" that prompts me to contribute to a pension scheme is a far cry from the desires, fears, and calculations that shape my reactions to the items and possibilities I encounter in my actual surroundings or the adjacent possible to which those surroundings are a kind of anteroom. This is clearly not a kind of pressure from behind, even less a response to a stimulus.

- There are many ways in which selfhood and agency co-evolve — confirming the aphorism *ego ergo ago* ("I am an ego therefore I act"). Here are a few:

  - As we grow, we are increasingly defined by our choices. Such choices may sometimes imprison us with obligations against which we chafe — though our chafing is protracted by our choice to remain faithful to these choices and they are central to our self-definition.

  - As we mature, the bases of our actions reach further back in time, so that, for example, I may be acting out a plan conceived weeks, years, or decades before in a setting that has been constructed over weeks, years, or decades. This is most obvious in *projects* — such as training for a career, saving up for a house, or building up a collection — that stretch over long periods of time.

  - The implicit framework of our actions gets wider and deeper. The combination of temporal and spatial depth contributes to a handful of master narratives in according to which we are self-defined: "This is what I am", given definition not only by the shared world in which we find ourselves, but also by the personal world we have built inside it, and the embraced habits of taste, attention, sympathy and antipathy that (fine-)tune our interactions within it.

- In order that we shall count as having free will, it is not necessary to act from no platform, free of reason or motivation; only that we should act out of our self — a self whose elements have been those parts of our history we embrace and claim as our own and, indeed, as ourself. The significance of the accidents that promote or hinder that expression of freedom draws on those elements by which we identify ourselves. Individual freedom is thus inseparable from the interconnected, indeed nested, stories that we tell about ourselves.

- Freedom is not therefore a matter of choosing at any given moment between the branches of a fork – to turn left or right. It is exercised in a temporally deep, wide field – the self-world – of possibility which only occasionally crystallizes out into a binary choice between A and B. The tendency to see the operation of the free will as the capacity to choose between tines of a fork is a distorted reflection of the (correct) belief that true agency presupposed that one could have done other than one did in fact do; that there was a possible course B alternative to the course A one took.[58]

- It is arguable that if my freedom is an expression of myself – it consists in being true to my self – then I could *not* have done otherwise, or was less likely to do so, I am as it were the prisoner of what I have become. The argument does not stand up. Consider Luther's "Here I stand. I can do no other". "Here I stand" means I stand behind myself and the self I stand behind is the self that stands behind me in this moment. It is this kind of circularity which makes the self at any given moment: (a) not merely at that moment; (b) not the helpless inheritor of an imposed past; and (c) a new point of origin in the world. To choose is to choose the self that one is and to act in accordance with that self. Increasing freedom is in part expressed by being increasingly, the source of constraints on one's own actions. And to return to Luther, that which he chose to do was not simply to move his left hand or his right: it was to take a path whose meaning could not be understood without comprehending his relationship to 1,500 years of Christianity. His action was not a movement in physical space but the choice of a way of life for himself and for others who wished also to choose it.

- This underlines the extent to which freedom is neither fully expressed nor incubated in a linear series of binary decisions. Luther did not arrive at the place where he stood as a result of choosing between a succession of alternatives, journeying down a garden of forking paths. If he made binary decisions, they grew out of the field, the soil that was his self. The choices that faced him when he took his stand were choices that no-one else had had to confront. Where there are forks in the road, the road has been laid down in a territory formatted by prior choices at least in part made possible by preferences (for many aspects of life) cultivated, pursued, and fulfilled or frustrated.

- To act in accordance with our desires – as opposed merely to react or to be impulsive – is not the same as submitting to an inner cause that is the direct or indirect causal descendent of something that can be understood in biological, biochemical or other terms whose provenance is natural science. It is to reach into a future itself illuminated by our sense of who we are and then to reach back from that future to a present which will endeavour to fulfil that desire. A desire is not just a cause or a drive identical with a physiological state: desires narrate themselves; they are complex *propositional* attitudes.

- The margin of freedom – within which I actively live as opposed to merely suffer my life – is to be found in the space between the present in which I act and the past for which the context of, and need or motivation for, my action was a distant future; in the various ways in which I position and shape myself in order to enact my wishes; and in the human world which is the work of millions, indeed billions, of hands and minds, a boundless omnibus in which all may travel to places none could reach acting alone. It is this that is the great, the virtual, outside from which we act upon the material world of which we are a part and from which we are apart.[59]

- Many of the foregoing thoughts converge in or arise out of the notion of intelligibility – not merely a spectatorial intelligibility (which may be a relative latecomer, though it is a crucial element in the widening interval between means and ends, in *reculer pour mieux sauter*) but what we might call "existential" or "embodied" intelligibility of action. Like the possibilities they serve to bring about, the causes we mobilize in our actions are general and what they represent, although instantiated at a particular location in space and time, is not itself *at* such a location. They are part of a narrative which – as actions become more complex, and participate in projects and enterprises that are extended over increasing stretches of time ever more remote from the present – grows towards "a path in life", a CV, a biography. The key point is that intelligibility, opened up by intentionality, being general, is not tethered to time t, but belongs to a virtual time outside of time, evident to knowledge and enacted in agency. In the "aboutness" of understanding resides the basis for a limitless extension of what counts as the temporal theatre of our actions. At a very basic level, the temporal interval in which events are seen to be "now" and simultaneous widens with the belief that one has an active role in one or other of them.[60]

- This touches on a theme that has been present from the beginning in Western philosophy: the timelessness (and indeed spacelessness) of the intelligible realm. Plato accepted Parmenides' conclusion that reality was unchanging and that reality was accessed not through the senses but through the intellect. Parmenides argued that what-is is and what-is-not is not, so that becoming (from non-being into being) was impossible. He failed to notice what he was himself doing, namely thinking, and hence entertaining possibilities, and it is these that open up a new kind of space in the unified plenum of being. This is the space of tensed time, and not only of change but of agency.

- We can now see the connection between the apparent directionality of time and that of causation. Firstly, a cause is a *beginning*, an event in virtue of which ends are brought about and which in their turn define it as a beginning; an initial event that is also an initiating event. Secondly, causes are scissored out by salience, and hence are intelligible rather than atomic or purely material elements.

- Seeing cause through the lens of the agent's "because" and "in-order-to" highlights how the irruption of the subject, and the emergence of intentional relationships, turns the world inside out. Subjects make the universe their surroundings, the theatre of their active lives. The direction of time, such as it is, is a narrative direction and, insofar as it is aligned with the direction of causation, is so in virtue of causes being requisitioned beginnings to bring about ends. The deep connection between time and causation is the active onlooker who makes causes explicit and time deep.[61]

12.4 ASPECTS OF FREEDOM

12.4.1 Knowledge, reason and freedom

Man is "the uncoupled animal".[62] The basis of our freedom is to be found in our ability to stand outside the natural world of which we are a part. This is rooted in the intentionality of perception and is greatly enhanced by the joining of experience that makes us custodians of a shared past and future and the upholders of each other's distance from the present and hence the guardians of each other's freedom. Our most radical uncoupling from nature is courtesy of knowledge that is our greatest collective achievement, underpinning most of our other collective achievements. The empowerment, that comes from being privy to the world without reciprocally interacting with it, develops the asymmetry of the relationship between the embodied subject and his or her surroundings. The knowledge "That x is the case" transcends sentience, even telereception through sight and sound, and opens ever expanding realms of possibility, and virtual outsides from which it is possible to operate on the natural world and the artificial but still physical world of the human artefactscape. The realm of "thatter" comes to dominate over that of matter. I have discussed this at length elsewhere,[63] so I shall make only a few brief remarks here.

"That x is the case" – what I have called "propositional" (or, perhaps better, "propositionalized") awareness – is the universal marker of the distinctly human mode of encountering what is out there, where "out there" is without evident location or limit. There are, of course, direct collisions with objects and, in the case of vital activities such as eating and drinking, these are the necessary end-point of the pursuit of a chain of interlinked goals. A diet of pure "thatter" would be the recipe for starvation. Even so, our paths through the world are increasingly fact-guided. And the objects that surround us, line or pave or support or obstruct pathways connecting present with future states, the here and now with variably distant goals, are increasingly defined in propositional terms. Propositional knowledge is remote from any realm of causes and effects – though it may speak of them – and is exposed to tests of truth, and of validity. It is timeless, thus helping crucially to secure our place in virtual time, in an outside-of-time from which we may visit times.

Our human emotions that may transform the colour of the world from moment to moment are not simply physiological tempests. Leaving aside rare literal flights from, and fears directed towards, physical threats to life, emotions are *narrated* into and out of being and are sustained by signs and symbols, most notably language in the narrow sense. Consequently, much of our activity which in other creatures would require external prompts or pre-programmed instincts is driven by thought. Humans reflect upon events and respond after consideration; or they act in response not to actualities but to possibilities, which may be quite remote, served up on a platform of knowledge. The panic that attends my rush to an appointment for which I might be late grows out of considerations whose soil is words. The commitment to being courteous, the wish to impress, the determination to be "nicely" in time, are rooted in a consciousness that is as much as anything a stream of words flowing through banks of interconnected facts.

Thus the amplified intentionality that expands the world of everyday human life, a world that draws on a deep past (most explicit in the case of commitments, appointments and promises) and reaches into a deep future (again most obviously in the case of appointments, commitments and promises) and has an ever-widening horizon. This world is uncoupled from the immediate physical surroundings of the body, though the latter have to be engaged with (if only lightly as in the case of a phone call). To it belongs the context in which (say) we store up facts that might be useful; in which we bank beliefs to guide future actions; in which we decide to postpone decisions ("I'll sleep on it and let you know"), weigh pros and cons, puzzle out the puzzling, and mobilize reason in the service of the refrigerated passions implicit in the execution of our daily duties.

As for reason, this can seem to operate in a virtual outside-of-nature in two ways. First, in the form of reason*ing*, it is guided by a sense of validity that is not to be found in the material world. The succession of events in nature is neither consistent nor inconsistent, in the way that a succession of propositions in reasoning (however loose its operation, however close it is to mere reasonableness on the line drawn from pure logic to practical reasoning); nor is it true or false. There are regularities in nature – the basis for the laws – but there are no logical constraints. This is the other side of what we discussed in Chapter 8 – namely that logic cannot prescribe what actually comes to pass. The second is that (practical) reasoning deals with general possibilities, that might be directly and wordlessly envisaged but are also capable of being rehearsed in thought. "If I do this, this will happen ..." or "If I don't do this, then I will have to give up on this ..." are hardly pieces of the material world. "If–then" does not translate into "cause–effect".

This is one of the many considerations that show why it is wrong to think of reasons as *causes* of actions with the latter being understood as their effects. What is more, the action that I decide to do on the basis of reason is the realization of a general possibility. It has to meet certain criteria but these by themselves do not add up to an actual event which (as we have discussed in §8.2.2.4) has many other features than those which enable it to qualify as the desired action or outcome. There is an openness in goals as to how they might be realized. The relationship between my reason for seeing you (say, my concern about your health) and my driving to your home is hardly captured by (say) the law of conservation of mass-energy or of proportionality between cause and effect. The events that comprise a voluntary action simply have to meet a certain general specification and anything that does this will suffice – and hence (if my will is fulfilled) will happen.

The uncoupling that characterizes human freedom begins with intentionality, particularly as it is manifested in the visual sense. The one who looks is aware that there is more to the world than what she sees because she can see that she sees that world from a particular viewpoint whose multiple limitations are visible from that viewpoint. It is this – the sensing subject's insight into her subjectivity – that awakens the idea of an objective truth in objects beyond the senses. It is this, too, that prompts measurement. The mediated peering of measurement that uses tools created by other parties, and generates not an appearance but a number, goes further than peering, than scrutinizing from different angles. This is scrutiny from no angle at all en route to the view from nowhere and the subordination to a collective authority which deems that there is a wrong answer and a right one. This is a crucial development of intentionality in which the senses are replaced by something more purely active, and less prone to the hazards of the bio-sensor. The measurement does not dazzle with intense light and the thermometer does not feel the pain of the burned hand.

Whether *I* feel the stone to be more or less heavy than another stone is irrelevant once the objective truth has been established in the scales. This reduction of what is there to its mathematical skeleton is the ultimate submission to the collective in order to exploit the latter's collective strength. The space it opens up between ourselves and our own sense experience extends the distance between ourselves and the material world. This further uncoupling, is another step into freedom. It adds to the power of manipulation but does so at the price perhaps of losing something precious. To enable us to be uncoupled from the world and yet not to lose density of being, to be free and yet not emptied is, perhaps, one of the purposes of art – to which we shall now turn.

12.4.2 Some reflections on art, time and freedom

Anything one has to say about the large, sprawling, untidy topic, of "Art" is bound to be provisional and incomplete.[64] I am aware, for example, that the observations that follow will overlook the huge variety of purposes art has served in the history of humanity. The role of art in sacred rituals, religious worship, propping up the powerful, flattering the rich, providing erotic experiences, satisfying curiosity, promoting revolution and other political changes, in display and self-promotion, in mirroring society back to itself, and in providing escape and distraction, cannot be denied. I will focus, however, on those aspects that are closest to the preoccupations of this book.

Something common to all arts is the pursuit of experience for its own sake. We look at sights, listen to sounds, engage in or observe movements, or receive reports for the pleasure of looking, listening, moving, or attending to them. In a work of art, we are offered experiences freed of the context in which we are normally obliged to respond to objects and events. A portrait of a face does not require us to engage with the owner: there is no reciprocal exchange of glances. The landscape in a gallery does not have to be crossed, or acted upon, only looked at: it demands nothing of the onlooker except contemplation. The furniture of everyday life becomes something to be cherished for its phenomenal appearance and the memory of the experiences it evokes. We enjoy stories for their intrinsic interest and for the emotions they arouse, though they require no action of us. Let us look at those emotions.

Whitehead pointed out that humans were the only creatures who cultivated the emotions "for their own sake" – "apart from some imperious biological necessity".[65] And this is exemplified in our appetite for recreational fears, for making playthings of the feelings triggered by those things that terrify us most – such as the threat of violence, or of being engulfed by natural catastrophes, or of social disgrace. We entertain our fears – perhaps in a perfected form – that they might entertain us. Hence the popularity of the thriller and of the promised "appointment with fear". Hence the pleasure we derive from putting ourselves in the state of suspense similar to that which we might suffer if we were in reality being stalked by a human or animal predator, not knowing what the outcome might be.

This spectatorial pleasure connects closely with the source of our freedom: our ability to imagine possibilities. Stories enable us to observe threatening events without being helplessly caught up in emergency demands. With the assistance of proxies who undergo the dangers and ordeals we fear, we become able to spectate our own fears and even, perhaps, learn from reflecting on them, though the pursuit of pleasure is our primary aim. And we can walk away in the end, relieved that what we have gone through was only a dream voluntarily undergone. Most importantly, we have established a greater gap between stimulus and response: between that which makes us experience the emotion such as fear and any action we may have to take. (This is why the attempts by "neuroaestheticians" and others to understand the aesthetic experience as a biologically-based response to a stimulus fundamentally misunderstands it.)

Let us look more deeply at the connection between (great) art and the celebration of our freedom – our unique human agency. The key notion here is that of deep temporality and the co-presence of things that are usually encountered separately. An entire landscape is brought before us on a canvas, allowing us to wander it *ad libitem* without being exposed to other aspects of the depicted terrain. Our wandering eye is not itself situated in the remainder of the landscape: the latter becomes an eyeful. A novel brings a world before us, so that we have an expanded viewpoint that *encompasses* people, places, and times. Co-presence is evident in even the simplest story: it has a beginning that anticipates what follows and an end that connects across all that has intervened, something that is even more evident on rereading. The gathering together of times can be italicized by all sorts of techniques of internal stitching – echoes, recurrent motifs, narrative connections – that offer an enhanced temporal glance. In poetry, such techniques are exercised through the material presence – the very sound – of the words, italicized by internal and external rhymes, alliteration and assonance.

Of all the arts, the one most concerned with time is, of course, music. Repetitive rhythms enhance the sense of time "moving forward" and "standing still". In a melody, when simultaneous and successive notes are gathered up into chords and harmonies, time acquires a new form of depth in the parallel and cross-cutting presence of evolving sequences. Music is the ultimate journey that stands still, where departure

and arrival are one. The co-presence of all elements – actually or in prospect or retrospect – in form makes the work a *moving unmoved* as Aristotle characterized it.

In summary, we may think of works of art as devices for extending our temporal
depth, or at least for making explicit the temporal depth that is implicit in our being
in the world. This is further enhanced by the special experience of revisiting a painting, rereading a novel or a poem, listening to music become familiar, and connecting
the experiences with one another, with the experiences of other works of the same
artist, and with the worlds of different artists. The time over which we get to know,
to engage with, to understand, the works of an artist so that they become parts of
our lives, are bound together by the most profound internal stitching. The summer
of the first reading of *War and Peace*, the year of listening to a cycle of Mahler's sym-
phonies, acquire a unity that transcends all their necessary, and necessarily practical,
connectedness.

Lévi-Strauss described myths and music as "machines for the suppression of time".[66]
Myths are particularly prominent in societies that are not driven by a relentless striv-
ing for progress based on technological advance and ideas of, and for, political and
social reform. But in the accelerating, runaway, world we live in, such machines are
needed more than ever, even though the kind of myths Lévi-Strauss was concerned
with are now off the menu. We could just as well describe all arts as machines at
least for the compression of time, for helping us to escape from the gathering hurry,
by bringing together past, present, and future without their being collapsed simply
into a moving now. The raw succession (captured in "and then ... and then ... and
then") is synthesized into something corresponding to an enlarged consciousness
reaching further into the world to which it belongs, allowing actual experience to be
recovered, and possible experience to be imagined; bringing to the centre what lies
on and just beyond the horizon.

The most direct expression of freedom in art, in which experience is had, and
activity is performed for its own sake, is the way its elements and its successive
moments are connected. The essence of a free action, as we have seen, is one whose
components would not have been brought together without being requisitioned by
a sustained intention; an action is an event that occurs only because it is intelligible.
Art takes this further. Compare, as Paul Valéry did, walking and dancing: you walk
to get somewhere, whereas you dance for the sake of movement.[67] The successive
steps in a journey to a destination are subordinated to the usually quotidian need
that brought you to the destination – they would not have come together otherwise.
The freedom expressed through them is constrained. The successive movements in
a dance have no other aim than to realize a pattern.

Valéry used the analogy between walking and dancing to contrast prose and
poetry. In fact, we often talk in prose for no other reason than for the sake of talking
– much of our waking life is marked by sub-literary gassing – and prose literature
is frequently expression for its own sake, while poetry may be didactic. Even so,
there is an important truth, specific to literary art hereabouts. While in the case of
walking there is already a distance in the sequence of events – the steps – from the
chain of causes and effects, in dancing there is a second-order freedom because the

succession of movement is not tethered to any external aim or need. In literature this can be taken further. The distinct nature of the succession of events in speech makes them remote from the causal chain. First of all, it is obvious that a speech act, and the chaining together of its components, would not have occurred if it were not intelligible; more particularly, if it were not aimed at sharing intelligence and was thought by the utterer to be intelligible. The meaning of what is said is not tethered to the temporal location of the token utterance, the event of saying. Secondly, the succession of the elements of speech does not deliver a parallel succession of packets of sense. The sentence, or the paragraph, or the story, works as a whole and that whole is stitched together by links of anticipation and retrospection that run back and forth between the parts. It is not unusual for the meaning of the beginning of a sentence to become apparent only at the end. Thirdly, the speech act has a higher order intentionality that connects it with part of the world that may be absent, general, abstract, or all three. It is this high platform that enables literary art to take off even further from the material world, creating and expanding into, a new realm of freedom.

Consider, again, stories. The relationship between causation and narration is complex for a variety of reasons, the most obvious being that the unfolding events that are narrated are connected in a way that is different from the connection between the story-teller and the person to whom the story is told – whether it is the listeners round the camp fire or a critic in a library. What is more, both of these modes of connection are distinct from that in virtue of which the story is made audible (or visible) and intelligible, the material connections between the movements of the vocal cords and the reception of the uttered sounds that make up the story and the even more complex connections between the writing of the story and its being read. The elements of the story are held together by the promise of explanation – of the revelation of withheld facts, of linking what happened to Smith at time t_1 with what happened to Jones at time t_2, of progression from the beginning to the end of an important process, project, or relationship. It is a clear expression of *be*causation, going beyond picking out causal threads from the fabric or matt of process. There is not merely a succession of events but an unfolding of human sense bounded by beginnings and ends. The beginning, seeming to be inherent in the flow of events, is validated by the end to which it is attached and the journey that connects beginning and end. "The story begins" when and where the story begins. In the beginning was the word; and the beginning planted by the word is underwritten by the story that grows out of the word. In the beginning was the deed of declaring "In the beginning".[68]

The way in which the journey from concealment to revelation is managed, and how much world, how many worlds, or lights and shades of consciousness, are gathered en route is one key to the art of narrative. And the quality of the art determines whether rereading is as rewarding as, or more rewarding than, reading. The first reading, driven by the wish to find out what happens next is very much confined to each phase of the story; the (often greater) pleasure of rereading is motivated by enjoyment of the quality of the presentation of the happening, of seeing the same events illuminated from different viewpoints, and of light radiating outwards from viewpoints into the worlds illuminated by them. Most importantly, there is the connectedness between different phases of the story so that the later phases are co-present with the earlier phases, pregnant with what is to come. The opening sentence – "A man walked down a road" – however, banal, is charged with all that is to happen to the man and the world to which the road belongs.

This special mode of connectedness is something that Bergson identifies as central to our appreciation of art, which he illustrates with dance. The aesthetic pleasure, the inner joy, afforded by the grace of the dancer is not just a matter of fluency but of unity of successive elements:

> We [find] a superior grace in movements that were anticipated in present attitudes which seem to already indicate the following ones, as if they were somehow preformed. If sudden movements lack grace it is because each one is sufficient unto itself and does not announce those to come. If curved lines are more graceful than broken ones, it is because the curved line, which is always changing direction, turns in such a way that each new direction is already indicated in the preceding one. The perception of ease of motion is thus based on the pleasure we take in arresting the forward march of time and in holding the future in the present.[69]

And so we come back to music. While it may have arisen out of, or in close association with, dance, its mode of connectedness is even more completely liberated from that of the material world, and that of the body. There are many mediators of the experience of music: the written notes, the instrumentalists, and the conductor. The succession of notes traces disembodied shapes – the pure essence of dance, or of emotion remote from physiological need. While it has a significance, this is not only unconnected with any external purpose, it is free of any specific reference. This has been captured by Roger Scruton:

> Sounds ... can be identified without referring to any object which participates in them, and it is precisely this feature that is seized upon by music, and made into the template on which the art of music is built. Because sounds are pure events we can detach them, in thought and experience, from their causes, and impose upon them an order quite independent of any physical order in the world. This happens, I suggest, in the "acousmatic" experience of sound, when people focus on the sounds themselves and on what can be heard in them. What they then hear is not a succession of sounds, but a movement between tones, governed by a virtual causality that resides in the musical line.[70]

The sounds advance in a realm that is entirely liberated from the causal connectedness expressed in the making of notes by playing instruments or that is required in order to hear them by locating ourselves close by. The "virtual causality" of which Scruton speaks is a supreme expression of our liberation from material causation, where the unfolding of the sound is pure intelligibility untethered to the physical world. It is thereby a celebration of something expressed in art: of our freedom to act, and of the temporal depth that brings together chains of actions. And it takes to a higher level the liberation from sequential – tenseless – time that is implicit in voluntary actions.

In art, but above all music, time loops back on itself and in the experience of art we expand further beyond the moment into an imagined world to which that moment belongs. We are temporarily liberated from the elusive prison of the present tense.[71] If it is true (as it is true) that these escapes from time are located in time – the performance of the Beethoven symphony took place at a particular time and lasted a certain amount of time – if the flights from tabled time are themselves time-tabled, so be it. Yes, we make time dance and then are returned to the dance of time.

12.4.3 The limits of human freedom

We are and we are not material objects in the world in which we live our lives; more precisely we are, but we are not just, material objects. There are important and fundamental differences between us and pebbles, between us and all other forms of plant and animal life, between ourselves as adults and ourselves as new-born babies. While we are in an important sense self-caused – self-shaping, self-choosing, self-centredly acting – our capacity for being the origin of the events that define our biography has its limits. We are not responsible for that which made it possible for us to have a biography in the first place. I did not begin my life and, I guess, I will not be responsible for ending it. I had no hand in the processes that led up to my birth, and I can take neither blame nor credit for many aspects of my post-natal existence. I have lived – or, as we say, lived out – the life of a body which I had only a very marginal role in shaping. The health for which I am grateful and the illnesses I fear are for the most part outside of my control, though, with the aid of others, I might foster the former and avoid or at least postpone the latter. The many-layered world which I entered was neither shaped by me nor even (for the most part) tailored to me. I will end as I began – helpless, with as little ultimate control over my exit as I had over my entrance.

I have therefore written this book knowing (in that mode of knowledge that falls short of the depth of what it knows) that at any time its composition might be halted by an event as simple as an item dropping on my head which, if it does not terminate me entirely, may bring to an end the person capable of having thoughts like these or, indeed, any thoughts beyond fragmentary phrases floating in a sea of bewilderment. At any rate I know – again in that merely matter-of-fact way – that sooner or later the body that carries the name of the author of this work will become a material object with the absolute passivity of other material objects, initiating nothing, merely transmitting changes that pass through or engulf it. It will all be over with the agent Raymond Tallis.

You may think that there is no need to remind myself– even less you, my readers – that all living creatures are transient and humans are no exception. The reason for doing so is to head off the suspicion that the arguments in this and previous chapters have given credence to what under other circumstances would be regarded as magic thinking. We are free; we can shape our lives to some extent; but our freedom is limited; and the extent to which we shape our lives and choose ourselves is also limited. There are many constraints on our freedom: the body we have been given to live out, the circumstances – familial, social, geographical, cultural, and historical – in which we find ourselves, the accidents that impinge on us – these are only the most obvious. While we may to some extent co-author the story of our lives, the pen, the ink, the paper, and the script we use, to a considerable degree lie beyond our discretion. Even so, while the events that terminate our freedom may be shockingly simple – a brick on my head cancels all that decades of nurturing, training, learning, have made possible – this does not disprove the complexity and richness of our freedom.

If it is necessary to issue reminders of the obvious it is because it sometimes seems difficult to assert that we are truly agents, and affirm the reality of our freedom – to control aspects of our lives, to be the source of some events in the universe, where the buck starts, a new point of departure, a place where responsibility, credit and blame, can be justly lodged – without implying that we are somehow freed from the material world. The account we have given of agency is one which is inextricable from the laws of nature, from material causes and effects, if only because as agents we rely on a deterministic physical world. If the laws were purely discretionary, we would live in a realm of unpredictable chaos; indeed, we would not live in any world because the countless interlocking mechanisms of our bodies and the means to continuing their life would fall apart.

This said, the fact that I have rooted our freedom in a universal property of human consciousness – intentionality that prises open the tenseless plenum of the material world – may still seem to risk portraying conscious human beings as being omnipotent or at least having boundless freedom. The account of human freedom in Sartre's *Being and Nothingness*, that also locates it in the nature of consciousness, arrives at that point.[72] Whatever our circumstances, Sartre argues, we are no less than entirely free. If I am being tortured to betray my friends, I am no less free than when I do so spontaneously, out of the spirit of malice: it is I who decides the level of torture that should be sufficient to justify my giving away the secrets that may lead to their death. If I find that I cannot climb a mountain because I am tetraplegic, this discovery is not in itself a constraint on my freedom because it is I who have chosen the climbing of the mountain as a project which I am prevented from carrying out. My freedom is limited only in this respect: that I am not free to deny my freedom. To do so is bad faith – where I ascribe to circumstances outside of my own control my inability to behave in one way rather than another – which is itself an exercise of freedom.

It is perfectly obvious that freedom is not unlimited in this way. We recognize that there is a difference between the many contents of our biography that happen to us instead of being brought about by us; falling down the stairs versus descending the stairs in order to answer the door versus walking down the stairs as the first part of a journey to London to attend a meeting to make the case for improved services for people with epilepsy; between foreseeable and unforeseeable consequences of our actions, between things for which we can, and things for which we cannot, be blamed. It is an insufficiently remarked aspect of our freedom that some actions are easier than others; that there is an entire spectrum of difficulty between the automatic and the impossible, and that, while we can extend the bounds of possibility by means of effort, training, tactics, positioning, the use of tools, and cooperation with others, there are insuperable limits.

Sartre's view of freedom, however, is a corrective to the idea that whatever we do is simply the consequence of prior events which we have not willed or chosen; to the currently popular idea that "my brain made me do it".[73] It is a reminder that, just because freedom cannot be exercised by material objects governed by laws and causes, it does not follow that freedom cannot be exercised by human beings, even though they, too, are in one sense material objects. They are self-conscious beings and as such they are not identical with their bodies or with those properties of their bodies that are revealed by the natural sciences. It is, however, a necessary condition of that freedom that there should be a self-conscious agent and that that agent should have considerable temporal depth. The greater the temporal depth underpinning the action, the wider the territory of the self, the freer the action. There are circumstances – such as torture – which gradually remove our temporal depth, so that we become reduced to a present moment – with no outside – in which we are simply a site of pain and humiliation and the only value is the discontinuation of pain. This may be arrived at more slowly in the case of a paratrooper used to pain and physical endurance than, say, a doctor who has cultivated other aspects of his selfhood. As for the person with tetraplegia, while the inability to climb the mountain is relative to his wish to do so, it is easy to compare his present constraint compared with the lack of it when he climbed the same mountain before he was tetraplegic.

There are more common and intimate constraints on freedom. If I become demented or have a serious brain injury I may lose the clear aims, motives, values, inhibitions, ambitions that previously defined my freedom. That freedom is rooted in a capacity, requiring a functioning brain, to remember the past, understand the present, and entertain future possibilities and strive to actualize some. So long as I can at time t_2 entertain several possibilities for what might happen at time t_3 this says that the grip of time t_1 is not complete. The material world connects actuality to actuality and allows no room for possibility. But being a bearer of possibilities still depends on the bit of the material world that is my body and its brain. And if we go back in time, it is obvious that a new-born Raymond Tallis is less free than adolescent or adult Raymond Tallis. This follows from the link between freedom and the temporal depth and connectedness of consciousness. Sartre's Nothingness opening up the distance between Being and human being, enabling the latter to define itself in relation to and act upon the former, appears to have no temporal depth – or no basis for it. Indeed, it is difficult to see how it has a location; how it is individuated in bodies in which it is rooted. At any rate, Sartre's freedom seems to be all-or-nothing.

The inseparability between my body and myself as an agent is evident from two obvious considerations. Firstly, it is my body that provides the platform from which I operate as an agent (and, indeed, with its many material needs provides the ground floor of its agenda). Secondly, my body – and more particularly my body in working order – is the necessary (though not the sufficient) condition of my being an agent. This is the answer to those who fear that locating the granularity of the world in the irruption of consciousness, the origin of viewpoint, would seem to make the latter omnipotent to gloss "what is there" as it likes. We note that the viewpoint of the onlooker is that of an embodied subject dependent on an organic existence. His or her freedom is real but necessarily limited, not the least because that body (necessarily) has certain material properties. We are and we are not parts of the nature that generated our bodies. We had no freedom before we were born nor will we have any freedom after our death. We and our freedom are born and die together.

Agents, who have conscious purposes that requisition causes as handles, are, according to the now-standard world picture, recent arrivals in the universe. How we are to understand "recent" in this context, and the relative priority of subjective and objective, experienced and physical, explicit and implicit, time, remains unclear, as we discussed in §10.5. The idea of the irruption of consciousness, of the onlooker, into an insentient world is deeply problematic, as is the place of the mind in the cosmos. This is an unresolved knot at the heart of our inquiry, particularly one that upholds the reality of agency in a universe that is overwhelmingly insentient and has housed sentience for only a minute part of its 13.8 billion or so years of existence.

The reality of, and restrictions on, our freedom are, as we have argued, inseparable. This is true not merely at the level at which (say) rules may be "enabling constraints". It is true at two deeper levels. The first is that we rely on the law-governed relationship between events that limits our own activities to make any kind of activity possible. We could not walk without the friction and the inertia that demand energy of us in making locomotion possible. The "obstance" of objects (including our own body), their resistance and weightiness, which makes our life effortful also makes it controllable. The second is that without constraints there would be nothing to be free from, for or of. The cooperative activity in virtue of which we act collectively – through technology and institutions that enable and regulate our working together – enables us to advance our individual freedom. The levers we apply to our situation in order to shape it according to our wishes – our appetites, our interests, our sense of duty, our good and wicked motives – are greatly extended by the historical and geographical sources of magnification of our powers. This of course also increases our dependence on our fellow human beings as, with successive generations, they mediate more intimately and continuously in the interaction between our bodies and the world in which we and they must find our and their fortune. Increasingly our conspecifics, are the main influences, for good or ill, on our exercise of our freedom and our endeavour to flourish in accordance with our own idea of flourishing.

Ultimately, however, the natural world reasserts its sovereignty and the open future closes. All of us, generated by material processes over which we had no control, and maintained by such processes as enable our bodies to run themselves, will be obliterated by those very processes. Our span, and our real but limited freedom, will come to an end. The unfolding universe that brought us into being, and that small part of it the world in which we live, vastly outsizes and outlasts us and it will reclaim us.

Between the darkness of the womb and that of the tomb, our life arcs through the light, and we exercise our mysterious capacity to shape, define, and enact ourselves, as beings both inside and outside of time.

EPILOGUES
Personal and philosophical

PERSONAL EPILOGUE

> We look before and after,
> And pine for what is not …
> Percy Bysshe Shelley "To a Skylark"

Because the text of this book, though read in time, is set out in space, you, my much put-upon reader, can see that the end is in sight. Your predominant emotion may be one of relief. My own feelings are more mixed.

Of Time and Lamentation has been a dim possibility for as long as I have been thinking philosophically. I first seriously considered writing about time over 25 years ago. I was playing beach cricket with my (now grown-up) children on the last day of our summer holiday. The holiday had been perfect and I was consumed with anguish at the prospect of the coming scattering, our being dispersed after a wonderful fortnight together into our separate preoccupations, prefiguring the wider dispersal as our lives diverged. The nearest image of transience – of a handful of seeds thrown in the air, briefly together before parting to fall to our separate fates – was unbearable, if perhaps a little premature. I had therefore to take hold of time.

As originally conceived, *Of Time and Lamentation* was to be a collection of short pieces of what I hoped would be poetic prose. The idea was of something that would connect the puzzles with the epiphanies, the 2,500 years of argument and conversation, with the pangs felt when someone has said goodbye, another has died, a way of life has melted, or we have discovered that we have reached the age when there are more farewells than greetings, more last times than first. It would encompass the world new in a baby's first cry or a child's first day at school, old in a headstone whose letters are infilled with moss; the leaves fluttering in the sunlight and the rings of hoarded afternoons in the sawn log. Or the mystery of the determinate past of my footsteps in the snow and the indeterminate future of the unprinted fields ahead. Or unify the flower clock in the park with the atomic clock in the laboratory.

It will not have escaped your attention that this is not the book you have read. Someone else, perhaps, might write it. I turned to another genre. In the late 1990s *Of Time and Lamentation* became the name of a philosophical novel. Its hero was a vehicle – and too evidently so – designed to address some of the issues that have been examined in the present volume. The result was not good. At any rate, the 1,000-page manuscript has remained unread (including by its author) since it was finished. It is archived in my loft, where its pages are turning to peat. This was, however, the prompt a few years later – in 2007 or 2008 – to read more systematically in the philosophy of time and to start sketching early versions of the present volume.

Of Time and Lamentation version 3 grew in the interstices of the composition of my other books. I began it in earnest in 2009, finishing two drafts rather more quickly than was good for them. Since I began the third draft at the end of 2012, however, it has been my chief literary preoccupation.

If the champagne cork remains in the bottle as completion is in sight, this is in part because I have not appeased the anguish that motivated the writing of this book – notwithstanding the many delights of joining the philosophical conversation about the nature of time and the intense pleasure of approaching its mystery (and hence of our existence) through puzzles that provide hand-holds on its smooth surface. Delights and pleasure that I hope you, reader, have shared.

In the Preface (written several years ago) I estimated that I was somewhere between tea-time and midnight in my life's day. I am now significantly closer to midnight and to the process, quick or protracted, by which all that I am will be cancelled and my concern for all that I care for, love, or loath will end. Closer to a future that will not be able to look back on this present. While seeing our days as "numbered" and our lives as a quantity of time may seem to belong with the mathematization that has been rejected in this book, there is no escaping the fact that I have many more days behind, than ahead of, me. While writing the book has whiled away thousands of hours, it is equally true that those hours have whiled away me. My body has aged, underscoring the master-direction of my life from birth to death, preparing me to be skewered on the totality of things that gave rise to it. The smattering of mattering that has sustained my singular and utterly replaceable joys and sorrows, failures and successes, losses and gains, within the universe, is closer to dispersal. My world, like that of any 70-year-old, is not long for this world. Or not as long as he or it would like, whatever others might feel.

The many hundreds of days that have changed from tomorrows to yesterdays since I wrote the passage about tea-time and midnight in the Preface seem a loss more absolute for being so patchily recalled. The thousands of hours I have spent with my notebooks and laptop, turning tangled skeins of thought into something that approximates to an organized treatment of a definite topic divided into manageable themes, are all but forgotten. The succession of the seasons outside of my study window, and the lights and shades and customers in the Bollin Fee, the Cheadle Royal, the Victoria Arms, the Gateway, the King's Hall, and other favourite writing pubs, the counties slipping past the windows of countless train journeys, not to speak of Easters, solstices, autumns, Christmases – they have vanished as completely as the snows that chilled the bodies of Villon's ladies. All that remains, it seems to some backward gazes, are detached patches of light. The fact that I can remember so little of the hours of writing underlines the melancholy truth that, far from grasping time, I have slipped more closely into its grasp. The pages filled in those hours seem impoverished compared with the richness of the world around my writing self, and the harmony and disharmony of its phenomenal reality. The commitment to a project that would seem to conquer time by binding days, weeks, months, and years together, seems from the standpoint of the completed work to have made the loss more profound. I was always looking *away* – from the surrounding light to the thoughts within, symbolically captured in black ink. This book, like any other, is a graveyard of lost consciousness; or, if that seems too dramatic (and it is), a vast album of dead flowers, no less dead for being pressed.

This fact that I am nearer to extinction than when I began *Of Time and Lamentation* is not the kind of discovery that needs to be communicated to the Royal Society. The idea that it may be possible to think ourselves out of our condition of being transient, time-torn creatures has never looked remotely plausible. After all, reading, writing, speaking, and thinking – not to speak of breaking for a coffee or going to the library – are all time-consuming activities of an individual inseparable from – immersed in, orchestrated by, in a sense fashioned out of – time. The Platonic thought that thought itself is timeless is self-contradictory because all thoughts, including that one, must be *realized*, in tokens that occur in, and take, time whether one is thinking to one's self or communicating them to others. Thoughts are as much the children of Wednesdays as heartbeats. There is, moreover, no timeless "Archimedean standpoint" from which we may view time as beings who have escaped from it.[1] Though our thoughts are *about* time, they are incompletely extricated from it: they are located in time, located in our biographies as part of our passage from our beginning to our end. We cannot escape time by developing an atemporal view of time. As relativity theory shows, ascent to such a view, leaving nothing behind, would demonstrate the intransience of all we have loved only at the price of showing that nothing really happened in the first place.

And yet this is perhaps the deepest motive for the kind of philosophical inquiry conducted in this book: a longing to discover something about our condition that will make it less vulnerable, less ultimately tragic. There is a hope that even purely descriptive metaphysics will release an astonishment that will show the world in a new light and days will no longer seem a quotidian journey to a cancellation whose scale it cannot comprehend. That by careful attention to the way it coheres, it will be possible to pick the lock of a world where we sometimes seem to be in a prison, listening to the scaffold being built. But we know that it is all too easy to distance one's self from the fundamental truth of our lives for this to cut any ice when the blows fall.

It is a fundamental standard of intellectual honour not to subscribe to theories that we cannot wholeheartedly believe in when we are trying to sooth a crying infant, short of breath, consumed with anguish, or even running for a bus. Saying this is not to affirm a commitment to cognitive conservatism but an expression of an integrity that acknowledges that there is something fake about arguing one's self out of a way of understanding that has underpinned every step of one's path through the world. To demonstrate to one's own satisfaction that the difference between life and death is an illusion because nothing really changes when the heart stops beating would require a rejection of the fundamental premises that govern the life which one has shared with others. Nevertheless, even the project of rescuing time from scientistic world pictures, celebrating the reality of lived time, trying to make its mystery more clearly visible, keeps alive the ghost of a hope of rescuing humanity from the maws of the material world. And that hope is not entirely dishonourable.

An even more compelling reason for keeping the champagne in the bottle is my acute consciousness of unfinished business. While it is good that time has kept much of its mystery intact, that many of the problems, while given a new gloss, have remained unsolved, is less welcome. To some extent, this is beside the point: philosophy is only incidentally about solving problems and is more centrally about seeking questions that unpeel our thoughts and also connecting our thoughts more widely with one another. The philosopher as locksmith creating and cracking open paradoxes and *aporia* is also the celebrant of mysteries. This is some compensation for the knowledge that one can participate only in a small part of the Great Conversation, responding to the agenda, and often the methodological prejudices, of one's narrow slice of time.

There remains an inescapable sense, however, that there is "a heart of the matter" which has been overlooked; that all the trains of thought that have been pursued are a scattering or a network rather than a summation; an epiphany lost down a thousand footnotes. And equally inescapable is the feeling that the search for closure – evident at the level of the individual moment of thought, in the hurry to understand what one is saying to one's self, but also in the conflict between the potential openness of the processes of thought and the constraints of the idea of a work, a finished product – sweeps one away from the depths to an ever-expanding surface. This is how it is possible to spend decades thinking about time without drilling down to what it would mean to make adequate sense of it.

So I end with the feeling of a prospectus not honoured and of an inquiry abandoned rather than completed. Nevertheless, each writing, or rewriting, of *Of Time and Lamentation* prompted ways of thinking about time, themes, and ways of linking them, that were new to me if not necessarily to the discipline of philosophy. Every major philosophical topic, pursued at an appropriate depth, connects with every other major philosophical topic – as is entirely appropriate for a discipline that aspires to examine "how things in the widest sense hang together in the widest sense".[2] So this inquiry into the nature of time has touched on the philosophy of consciousness, of language, of science, on ontology, the theory of knowledge, the metaphysics of causation, first-person being and other topics that it naturally spreads into. But it has gone only so far into them. The incursions are confined not by natural limits but by an ill-defined idea of the shape of the inquiry in hand. But there is perhaps ultimately really only one philosophical inquiry and philosophy should dig deeper until it recovers its original unity. Another reason, then, for experiencing a sense of the incompleteness of this inquiry and for regarding this large volume as an interim report.

The aspect of the book that has approached nearest to completion is the critique of the claims of physics to be on the road to a theory of everything (including the physicist). The spirit behind this critique is echoed in this passage from Tim Maudlin:

> Unfortunately, physics has become infected with very low standards of clarity and precision on foundational questions. And physicists have become accustomed (and even encouraged) to just "shut up and calculate", to consciously refrain from asking for a clear understanding of the ontological import of their theories. This attitude has prevailed for so long that we easily lose sight of what a clear and precise account of physical reality even looks like.[3]

There could be no clearer statement of why philosophy should be (to use Roger Scruton's beautiful encapsulation) "the seamstress of the lebenswelt not the handmaiden of science".[4] Objective science does not, of course, cast light on the "who" but the "who" is not of marginal interest and, what is more, as Maudlin implies, physics hasn't got a grip on the "what" either.

As for the what, it seems to lie just outside of reach. Corresponding to this is the sense of having failed to deliver on an intuition, informing all that is central in my writing, I am unable to articulate. I would like to think that this corresponds to something to which Bergson referred: "[A] philosopher worthy of the name has never said more than a single thing: and even then it is something he has tried to say, rather than actually said".[5]

Anyone who cares about philosophical thought is haunted by the sense that they are not really thinking about the matter in hand, that the fingers that are trying to grip are numb. Sometimes it seems as if one is merely waiting and then pouncing too early, frightening away something heard in the undergrowth. And there is, finally, the suspicion that one is digging with a spade made of soft soil or trying to get one's head round one's head – an inevitable consequence of something mentioned at the outset: namely, having as one's object of thought something which is presupposed in any thought or indeed one's very existence.

PHILOSOPHICAL EPILOGUE

> The whole modern conception of the world is founded on the illusion that the so-called laws of nature are the explanations of natural phenomena.   Wittgenstein, *Tractatus Logico-Philosophicus*, §6.3.7.1

The unfinished business in *Of Time and Lamentation* could be expressed in many ways. The least unsatisfactory is how we should think of the place of conscious subjects in a world which is their world and a universe which, overwhelmingly, is not.

The challenge to do so has many provocations. Most importantly is the wish to heal a deep cognitive wound felt by secular humanists such as the author of this book. One of its best expressions is this by Ernest Gellner:

> The world in which men think seriously, and to which serious thought refers, is no longer identical with the world in which one lives one's daily life. The instability, contestability and often incomprehensibility of the serious, and respect-worthy kind of cognition, and hence of its object, make it and them altogether unsuitable to be the foundation of a stable, reliable social order, or to constitute the milieu of life.[6]

The classical expression of the specific task this presents for philosophy is by Wilfrid Sellars, whose "Philosophy and the Scientific Image of Man" we have visited from time to time. The aspiration should be to confront "these two conceptions, equally public, equally non-arbitrary, of man-in-the-world" and "attempt to see how they fall together, in one stereoscopic view".[7]

One much-noticed response to this has been E. O. Wilson's call for "consilience" and the pursuit of the deep laws that unite the sciences and the humanities.[8] Alas, Wilson's notion of "consilience" is very much of a marriage on terms acceptable to science. He illustrates his ambitions with barren examples of scientism such as "experimental epistemology" (unifying the theory of knowledge with neuroscience), "explaining consciousness and emotion in terms of brain activity", and "neurobiology of aesthetics". This is not encouraging: capitulation to science does not address the deep concern driving the wish for cognitive unity.

The urgency of the need to rescue ourselves from scientism is penetratingly expressed in an essay by W. T. Stace titled "Man Against Darkness".

> The founders of modern science – for instance, Galileo, Kepler, and Newton – were mostly pious men who did not doubt God's purposes. Nevertheless, they took the revolutionary step of consciously and deliberately expelling the idea of purpose as controlling nature from their new science of nature. They did this on the grounds that inquiry into purposes is useless for what science aims at: namely the prediction and control of events. To predict an eclipse, what you have to know is not its purpose but its causes. Hence science from the seventeenth century onwards became exclusively an inquiry into causes. The conception of purpose in the world was ignored and frowned on. This, though silent and almost unnoticed, was the greatest revolution in human history.[9]

It was important, as Galileo said, to separate the scientific project of understanding "how the heavens go" from the theological one of knowing "how to go to Heaven". Stace spells out the implications of this revolution – for ethics, politics, and the future of our species – and they are enormous. To some extent we are still free-wheeling on the assumptions of the pre-Galilean world-picture but this may not remain forever the case. The catastrophes of the twentieth century may be just a dress rehearsal.

Stuart Kauffman, exercised by the claims of reductionist scientists such as the physicist Steven Weinberg that "the more we know of the universe, the more meaningless it appears", notes that "Laplace's particles in motion allow only *happenings*. There are no meanings, no values, no doings".[10] Thus the post-Galilean universe in which events have only causes and no purposes. Kauffman argues that we need to "break the Galilean spell".

In order to do this, we need first of all to acknowledge that the Galilean spell has a lot going for it. The consequences of the seventeenth-century scientific revolution, for good or ill (mainly good), have been limitless. The pursuit of understanding though establishing causes instead of conjecturing purposes, "the disenchantment of the world", has accounted for much of the distance between effective science-based technologies and ineffective magic. The vision of a largely purposeless universe has so enhanced our ability to pursue our own purposes that it must have a profound validity, even if it leaves much out. Even so, the Galilean approach is, as we have discussed throughout, more impoverished than merely the setting aside of purposes. It is, as the historian E. A. Burtt describes it (in a passage already quoted) effectively *"the reading of man quite out of the real and primary realm"*.[11] Its view of nature is an exsanguinated one in which the phenomenal world, that of "secondary qualities", is set aside as less than fully real, in favour of a reality that is a "system of magnitudes". This leads ultimately to a vision of the world as a purely physical world and of the physical world as the world according to physics. Conscious subjects and ultimately objects are marginalized, even displaced, by measurements.

Human beings, measured by the measurements they have made, hardly measure up. Stephen Hawking's assertion that mankind is "the chemical scum on a moderate-sized planet, orbiting round a very average star in the outer suburb of one among a billion galaxies"[12] is only an extreme expression of a suspicion we are invited to entertain about ourselves in the wake of the scientific revolution.[13]

The challenge then, is understanding how we have an unprecedentedly successful approach to understanding reality, and manipulating it for our own purposes – making life longer and more bearable for so many – whose strength lies in bypassing purpose and key features of our conscious experience and in marginalizing, even squeezing out, ourselves as conscious subjects. This is clearly unsatisfactory, not just from the viewpoint of an arguably misplaced pride, but because it is pragmatically self-refuting. To take an example central to our discussion, general relativity excludes the observers, tensed time, and according to some interpretations, events taking place at definite times and hence actual becoming. The development of the theory, however, was by observers, living in tensed time, and experiencing events taken to be real and occurring at definite times in a definite order. So while post-Galilean science continues to give extraordinary gifts to the world in the form of theoretical understanding and practical technologies, the post-Galilean scientist loses his place in the world-picture of that science.

But the diagnosis of this as pragmatic self-refutation and the cry of "Gotcha!" is not enough. The contradiction at the heart of the scientific *episteme* demands that we should dig deeper. It should prompt inquiries into the place of the human mind in the cosmos – more profound and more radically questioning than are expressed either in a physicalism that identifies the mind with activity in that small part of the cosmos called the human brain, or in a panpsychism that sees mind everywhere, such that "the existence of every real concrete thing involves experiential being, even if it also involves non-experiential being".[14] We have dealt with physicalism explicitly in §12.2, and implicitly elsewhere. As for panpsychism, it seems something of a simplifying reaction to the discovery that consciousness cannot plausibly emerge even from the most promising bit of matter – the brain: the conclusion that it must already be present in some form in all of matter runs into many problems.[15] It seems unlikely that the proto-experiences of atoms and pebbles have much to do with experiences connected with, and ascribed to, subjects, that are the stuff of consciousness as we know it. The idea of atoms dimly experiencing themselves or their trajectories through space–time, or alternatively of the micro- or proto-experiences of the atoms of a body pooling themselves, to amount to the kind of macro-experiences that persons have, seem entirely implausible. The relationship between mind and cosmos is not a problem for objective, quantitative science to resolve if only because the latter both leaves out human consciousness and is a product of that consciousness.[16] Besides, even matter in itself remains beyond its scrutiny not least because science approaches matter from without and matter has no "outside of itself".

We are left, therefore, trying to make sense of the place of the conscious subject, of ourselves, in the subjectless reality described by quantitative science, and of a realm of qualities (not to speak of meanings and values) in a physical universe fruitfully reduced by effective science to a system of magnitudes. The master-question is that of the relationship between what is out there and what is in us (individually or collectively). The opposing positions that the mind is in the world and the world is in the mind – both entirely unsatisfactory – are reduplicated in the opposition between the idea that human time is located in, or reducible to, physical time and the contrary notion that physical time, via clock-time, has grown out of human time. And the notion, advanced in Chapter 11, that the world as we know it is the result of the irruption of consciousness into pre-existent unified Being may be more satisfactory than the idea that consciousness is a product of the world as known to physics but it leaves much unaccounted for and generates many problems of its own.

The inquiry therefore continues. It will soon be taken over by heads other than this one which, all too soon for its owner, will be thoughtless powder in a jar.

Notes

OVERTURE

1. Hitchens, *Hitch-22*, 4. This and the entire "Prologue with Premonitions" from which it is taken has a particular poignancy: it was published just before he was diagnosed with the cancer that killed him a year later. In his last book, written when he was, to use his characteristically witty inversion, being "battled by cancer", he reiterates this idea: "But, as with normal life, one finds that every passing day represents more and more relentlessly subtracting from less and less"; Hitchens, *Mortality*, 71.
2. Hammond, *Time Warped*. The chapter "Why Time Speeds Up As You Get Older" is a particularly astute account of attempts to understand this dismal phenomenon.
3. Mellor, *Real Time II*, 2.
4. Smith, *White Teeth*.
5. Every attempt to think about death turns our gaze back on life. See Tallis, *The Black Mirror*.
6. Huw Price makes this point in his indispensable *Time's Arrow and Archimedes' Point*, 3–4: "The most basic mistake … is that people who think about these problems – philosophers as well as physicists – often fail to pay adequate attention to the temporal character of the viewpoint we have on the world. We are creatures *in* time, and this has a very great effect on how we think *about* time and the temporal aspects of reality." Of course, no thought outside of time could have anything so vulgar as an occurrence, such that it could be had by anyone at any (particular) time.
7. I first encountered this observation about philosophy in Gabriel Marcel's *Being and Having*. It has recently been explored in depth by Barry Stroud in *Engagement and Metaphysical Dissatisfaction*.
8. Levinas developed his idea of ethics as the first philosophy in his first book *Totality and Infinity*.
9. Sellars, "Philosophy and the Scientific Image of Man".
10. Weinberg, *Dreams of a Final Theory*.
11. *Ibid.*, 132. This is almost precisely echoed by the chemist Peter Atkins: "I consider it a defensible proposition that no philosopher has helped to elucidate nature: philosophy is but a refinement of hindrance"; quoted in Hughes, "The Folly of Scientism".
12. Weinberg, *Dreams of a Final Theory*, 134.
13. Smolin, for example, has argued this in a string of books, beginning with *The Trouble with Physics*. This has culminated in his recent *magnum opus*, many years in the making, and co-authored with the philosopher Roberto Mangabeira Unger: *The Singular Universe and the Reality of Time*. Unger argues for the return of "natural philosophy" and their book in part exemplifies this.
14. Musser, "A Hole at the Heart of Physics".
15. Quoted in Musser, *ibid.*, 48.
16. Hawking & Mlodinow, *The Grand Design*, 13.
17. This is discussed in §10.3.4, "Did time begin with a bang?".

18. Weinberg, *Dreams of a Final Theory*, 133.

19. Putnam, "Time and Physical Geometry", 247.

20. For an exposition and critique of this view, see Tallis, *Aping Mankind*.

21. Ladyman & Ross, *Every Thing Must Go*. Ladyman, "An Apology for Naturalised Metaphysics" is strongly recommended as a brief, robust, and lucid clarification and defence of the approach developed in *Every Thing Must Go*.

22. Ladyman & Ross, *Every Thing Must Go*, 30.

23. See an excellent critical review by Cian Dorr in *Notre Dame Philosophical Reviews* 2010.06.61. A discussion between the author and James Ladyman is available on YouTube (*Adam's Opticks*, www.youtube.com/watch?v=j96Hls_-Ulc).

24. Interview with *Rational Sceptic*. This is an echo of the logical positivist's modest ambition to unify the sciences, reflected in Hans Reichenbach's assertion that "All the philosopher can do is to analyse the results of science, to construe their meaning, and stake out their validity" (quoted in Canales, *The Physicist and the Philosopher*, 154), adding that "There is no separate entrance to truth for philosophers: the path of the philosopher is indicated by that of the scientist" (quoted in Canales, *ibid.*, 155).

25. Of course, it would be absurd to suggest that the metaphysics of time had *nothing* to learn from (mathematical) physics, as we shall discuss in the Epilogue to Part I.

26. Maudlin, *The Metaphysics within Physics*, quoted in Richard Healey review of *The Metaphysics within Physics* in *Notre Dame Philosophical Reviews*, 2 April 2008

27. Quoted in Hey & Walters, *The Quantum Universe*, 6. The passage from which this sentence comes is worth quoting in full:

> There was a time when the newspapers said that only twelve men understood the theory of relativity. I do not believe there was ever such a time. There might have been a time when only one man did, because he was the only guy who caught on, before he wrote his paper. But after people read the paper a lot of people understood the theory of relativity in some way or other, certainly more than twelve. On the other hand, I think I can safely say that nobody understands quantum mechanics.

28. Al-Khalili, *Paradox*, 36.

29. Halvorson, "The Measure of All Things".

30. Mellor, *Real Time II*, 57.

31. Mermin discusses his responsibility (or otherwise) for this legendary rejoinder (to those who try to make sense of the Copenhagen interpretation(s) of quantum mechanics) in an entertaining little essay, "Could Feynman Have Said This?".

32. Dainton, *Time and Space*, 6.

33. See Tallis, *Aping Mankind*.

34. In this respect, we note that, while physics may advance as a result of departing ever further from our everyday experiences and intuitions, this should not be taken to imply that the latter were somehow primitive, folk beliefs we have grown out of. There is an interesting observation by R. Geroch:

> [I]t seems to be the case that physics, at least in its fundamental aspects, always moves in this one direction: fewer things making sense ... In quantum mechanics ... such notions as "the position of a particle" or "the speed of a particle" do not make sense. It may not be a bad rule of thumb to judge the importance of a new set of ideas in physics by the criterion of how many of the notions and relations that one feels to be necessary one is forced to give up.   (Quoted in Dainton, *Time and Space*, 200)

The importance in question is to the advance of physics not, or not necessarily, to our understanding of the physical world, even less ourselves.

35. Van Bendegem, "The Possibility of Discrete Time", 239.

36. This is a view often associated with Bergson.

37. Davies, *About Time*.

38. Tallis, *A Conversation with Martin Heidegger*.

39. Gale, *The Philosophy of Time*.

40. I interrupted *Of Time and Lamentation* to write a book devoted to that thought: *The Black Mirror: Fragments of an Obituary for Life*.

41. In the introduction to Moore, *George and Sam*.
42. Davies, "That Mysterious Flow", 17. Earlier, however, as already noted, he conceded that the failure of physics to accommodate tense might be a serious omission rather than a source of reassurance.
43. Bergson is widely quoted as having said this in an interview but I cannot find the original source.
44. Shakespeare, *Hamlet*, act 1, scene 2.
45. Peirce, "Some Consequences of Four Incapacities", 265.
46. For some philosophers, this has a kind of justice: "But where things have their origin, they must also pass away according to necessity; for they must pay the penalty and be judged for their injustice, accordance to the ordinance of time." Anaximander quoted in Heidegger, "The Anaximander Fragment", in *Early Greek Thinking*, 32–3.
47. Epicurus, as quoted in Porphyry, *To Marcella*, 31, translated in Long & Sedley, *The Hellenistic Philosophers*, 155.

CHAPTER 1

1. I emphasize this early on in response to an observation by Stan McDaniel, who read an earlier draft of this book: "If the sense of explicit time emerges in consciousness, it must come with the fully operative field of functions involved in the human sensory apparatus." We shall return to this in §§12.2–3 when we consider the extension of experienced temporal depth.
2. This is discussed at intervals throughout this book but most extensively in Chapter 12.
3. It is not entirely irrelevant that there are separate neural pathways associated with the perception of position and with the detection of motion. This separation underlies the illusion that, after we have looked at an object such as a waterfall in continuous motion, we look at another (still) object, it seems to move while not changing its position. See Gregory, *Eye and Brain*, 104–9.
4. P. F. Strawson made an analogous point in *Individuals*, 65, when he argued that we seem to assign spatial location to sounds – they seem "to come from right or left, from above or below, to come nearer and recede…on the strength of hearing alone" – only because we have a spatial schema established on the basis of other senses (vision, touch) that are intrinsically spatial. The intrinsic characteristics of sounds – timbre, pitch, loudness – are non-spatial. He concludes that "a purely auditory concept of space … is an impossibility" (*ibid.*, 65–6).
5. The contrast between vision and touch is revealed even at this level of, for example, manipulation or scratching. When I touch a line, I am literally in touch only with the part of the line at the tip of my finger. If, however, I watch my finger moving along the line, I can see where it has come from, where it is, and where it is going to, all at once. And even restricted areas such as my back are present as a unity only to my gaze, even though (as when I am shoving something) they are working as a whole. This does, however, raise the question of the kinaesthetic sense necessary to regulate movement. Again, the sense of the successive positions of one's fingers, or hand, or arm, would deliver a sense of temporal succession but not the co-presence of the components of the succession. As I move my arm, its position does not retain the ghost of its past position; nor is it infused with the presence of its future position. Even if there were a little bit of carry-over from earlier positions and anticipation of future ones – present in the sense of *movement* of one's arm – the particular positions it has passed through and it is about to reach would be muddled. Supposing I move my arm from position P_1 to P_2 to P_3 and so on to P_{20}. If, when it reached P_{10}, my arm retained a ghost of past positions and of future positions, it would be a very complex ghost indeed – particularly if the movement had the complexity of ordinary activities such as walking, running, or tying one's shoelaces. The only way the previous and future positions could be held in place would be if they were set out in space accessed directly – and that, of course, means visual space.

    Vision, therefore, remains crucial to that aspect of the sense of temporal depth that ultimately generates physical time as a fourth dimension. Temporal sense *per se* – as opposed to proto-clock-time – is built into complex actions and hence is present in our kinaesthetic sense, as we shall discuss in §12.3.2.3.

    Some may be unpersuaded that there is no auditory space equivalent to visual space. Jo Boswell (personal communication, for whom I am grateful for penetrating and thorough critique of this chapter), has argued as follows:

I sit with my eyes closed on a bench by the side of a road and can "at once" hear the calls of children in a playground to my left and the calls of birds in the trees to my right. When those birds are drowned out by the sound of an approaching car I may predict, and will soon be confirmed in my prediction, that the car will pass in front of me, from my right to my left, and proceed to drown out the playground instead. Is this simultaneous appreciation of successive positions of the car not adequate for an explicit sense of space (and hence time)?

This may be the case but auditory space is patchy and intermittent. While the elements may be spatially located and even located with respect to one another, they do not have the continuity and unity of a visual field – of which more presently.

6. The idea that vision is like touch inasmuch as a glance is a kind of probe is a suggestive metaphor but does not take account of the fact that foveal vision that focuses on part of the visual field is open to and explicitly surrounded by a wider peripheral field. In the case of touch, we do not palpate even the entirety of a single object, only those parts of it that are in contact with the fingers.

7. See also Sorensen, *Seeing Dark Things*.

8. See Rosar, "The Dimensionality of Visual Space".

9. The "over there" of the objects of the other distance sense – hearing – is quite different. This becomes evident when we consider an object that emits a sound – as when it is struck or when it roars. The sound is tethered to the object only if the object is visible; and the sound of the object is not inseparable from it in the way that the sight of it is. If I hear a lion, I may not know where it is. I cannot see a lion and not know where it is.

10. The relationship between (visual) object perception, objectivity, and objective knowledge, is examined in §11.3.2. For a brief discussion of the question of whether animal vision delivers a comparable sense of temporal depth see the addendum to this chapter.

11. There are important intermediate modes of temporality implicit in our bodily movements and deliberate actions such as reaching, grasping, and feeding one's self. The actions are timed, in order that (for example) coordination should be possible, but we do not (typically) time them. Anticipation, based on a sense of what remains to be achieved and what has been achieved so far, is implicit in ordinary learned, unreflecting, semi-automatic actions – most obviously in the succession of footsteps that have a deliberateness that heartbeats and (usually) breaths do not have (for a further discussion, see Ismael, "Temporal Experience"). It does not, however, fully locate time "out there".

12. Objects of course change in other ways than moving but they do not at the same time retain their unchanged state; or there is no marker of the state (analogous to the presence of a past position) from which they have changed. If a leaf goes from green to brown, there is nothing in the brown phase to tell us that it was once green: the green is not present in the brown. So our sense of its temporal depth has to come from elsewhere. Hence the centrality of motion and the ballet of revelation and concealment that is evident as we ourselves move through our visual field. There is nothing original in this thought, by the way. Isaac Barrow, a near-contemporary of Newton, asserted that "Without motion we would not perceive the passage of time" (quoted in Whitrow, *The Nature of Time*, 83). Without motion we would not conceive that we perceive the passage of time.

13. It is worth asking to what extent the relationships that I have described are culturally dependent rather than human universals and therefore have no place in a metaphysical exploration. Some readers, for example, may be aware that the Chinese do not "look back" to the past or "look forward" to the future. On the contrary, the past is ahead (it has already arrived) and the future is behind (it has not arrived – and the future is hidden behind today). This does not, of course, undermine the thesis that connects explicit time with a visuospatial sense. The opposition of "forward" and "back", and the connection with direction of gaze, remains.

14. See, for example, *Aping Mankind*, especially Chapter 6. An authoritative discussion by Thomas Suddendorf and Michael Corballis in "The Evolution of Foresight" concludes that "there is as yet no convincing evidence for time travel in non-human animals" (299). This conclusion has been questioned by Mathias Osvath in "Spontaneous Planning for Future Stone Throwing by a Male Chimpanzee" – on the basis of a single animal in captivity. The animal was seen to cache stones for future use. This is a rather slender database upon which to draw major conclusions about the time sense of nonhuman animals.

15. See Povinelli, *Folk Physics for Apes*.
16. This is particularly relevant to our concerns because causal sense is one of the lynch pins of our *sense* of the directionality of time, even though it does not confer an (intrinsic) arrow on time itself. This will be discussed in several places, notably §11.2.1.
17. See Tallis, *The Hand, I Am* and *The Knowing Animal*.
18. See Tallis, *The Kingdom of Infinite Space*. This is why the recently discovered anatomical differences in the organization of the primary visual cortex between human and nonhuman primates (Press & Coleman, "Human Specific Organization of Primary Visual Cortex") may be less important than it has been thought. The evolving folk ontology of humans is not driven from within the individual brain.

CHAPTER 2

1. Galileo, *The Assayer*. The full passage, as translated by Stillman Drake is: "Philosophy (i.e. physics) is written in this grand book – I mean the universe – which stands continually open to our gaze, but it cannot be understood unless one first learns to comprehend the language and interpret the characters in which it is written. It is written in the language of mathematics, and its characters are triangles, circles, and other geometrical figures, without which it is humanly impossible to understand a single word of it; without these, one is wandering around in a dark labyrinth" (ibid., 237–8).
2. The Presocratic philosopher Thales was reputed to have been able to determine the height of a pyramid by measuring the length of its shadow when his own shadow was equal to his height. This underlines one of the extraordinary leaps of the imagination behind "the peasant's clock"; namely, treating one's body as "anybody". It takes this further, treating one's body as "any object", commensurate with other objects such as pyramids. There is a sense in which we are all equal under the sun – you, I and that pyramid over there. Of course, there is a long history of using parts of one's body as measuring tools – hence the names of units such as "feet", "hands" and "cubits". For a thought-provoking discussion of the peasant's clock, see Heidegger, *Being and Time*, §80, "Time Taken Care of and Within-Timeness", esp. 378.
3. For a rich exploration of the spatial metaphors of time, see Carr, "Commentary on 'Placing the Past'", 501–5.
4. Wells, *The Time Machine*, 7 (italics in the original, but I would have added them if they weren't).
5. Einstein rejected the claim that general relativity was committed to spatialization of time. Unger's "The Inclusive Reality of Time" in Unger & Smolin, *The Singular Universe and the Reality of Time*, 189–90, quotes Einstein as admitting that there was "a tendency ... though often latent in the mind of the physicist" that was "real and profound, as is unequivocally shown by the extravagances of popularisers, and even of many scientists, in their exposition of relativity".
   There are areas of physics where time is unequivocally space-like. In the quantum cosmological setting of the Big Bang, "it is proposed that our ordinary concept of time is transcended ... and becomes like another dimension of space, so making three-plus-one dimensions of space and time into a four-dimensional space" (Barrow, *New Theories of Everything*, 89) and "as we approach the beginning, the conventional picture of time melts away and time becomes indistinguishable from space" (*ibid.*, 90). Somewhat confusingly this is further developed: "As we look back to that instant which we would have called the zero of time, the notion of time fades away and ultimately ceases to exist." This suggests that the completion of the spatialization of time is chronicidal.
6. This was famously challenged by Richard Taylor in his "Moving About in Time". Taylor's argument, however, does not alter the fundamental difference between passively going along with time, so that I have no choice about which day or even second I am in, and actively moving in space, such that I can, within limits, choose where to be. Nor does it capture the difference between the personal nature of my spatial location (the "here" which is uniquely occupied by me, voluntarily or involuntarily) and the "now" which is shared with others and which I do not choose. And there is no comparable contrast in time between objects in motion and objects at rest.
7. The domination of space over time is illustrated by recent developments. In the M version of string theory which requisitions 10 dimensions, there is still only one of time, the remaining dimensions being spatial.

8. It might be argued that spatial and temporal dimensions are interchangeable because, in relativity theory, the difference between space-like and time-like separations is simply one of sign: in space-like separations d² is positive and in time-like separations, it is negative. This, however, is quite a different kind of operation – one that takes place in mathematical space and not in the real world.

9. Raja Panjwani has pointed out (personal communication) that this is something that is reflected in the "coordinate transformation" whereby space is measured in radians, r, rather than in x, y, z coordinates. Space–time is then r, t. The mathematical transformation does not, however, override either our everyday experience or its representation in the overwhelming majority of classical physics. You still need the values of three dimensional variables to say where an object is and only one to say when it is.

10. On the difference between objects and events see §6.2.1, "What Is Present in the Present?".

11. It might be argued that it does because no other event can take place at the same time, given that distant simultaneity is an illusion. However, that physical fact does not preclude *the experience* of simultaneity. If it did, we would not be able to experience the complex, unified "nows" of everyday life, in which multitudes of events are part of the same conscious moment. This was one of the central issues in the dispute between Einstein and Bergson; see Canales, *The Physicist and the Philosopher*.

12. I am talking about *extrinsic* space – space occupied by an object that is seen with respect to a background space (for further discussion see §3.5.2, "Curved Space"). Once we take our leave of extrinsic space (and some would say of our senses) and enter the realm of *intrinsic* mathematical space, it may seem that almost anything is possible. For example, as Shahn Majid reminds us, while particles "all move *in* space–time … gravitons both move in space–time and *are* space–time" (Majid, *On Space and Time*, 68).

13. This may seem a rather naïve, not to speak uninformed, way of talking. One of the pillars of quantum mechanics is that, at the most fundamental level, there is no such thing as definite location or an item occupying a definite location existing independent of the item. This does not, however, alter the facts of everyday life. My belief in the difference between Fred and the room he is in cannot be dismissed as an error of an untutored mind, though there are some philosophers, as well as physicists, who maintain this. Ladyman holds that metaphysics should defer to physics and argues that there is no longer any reason to believe that there are real entities that have spatial location (see Ladyman & Ross, *Every Thing Must Go*). Fundamental particles are not fundamental as particles: they are properties of fields. From which it follows, if one subscribes to smallism – the belief that what is true of the very small is the real truth of the medium-sized and the very big, in short, of everything, or that all facts are determined by the facts about the smallest things – that physical objects with a particular size, localization and fixed dimensions must be excluded from a definitive account of what is real.

    This is deeply suspect for many reasons, exposed by the kind of examples that are offered to explain what is meant by the non-locality in question. Take this passage from a recent article:

    > [L]et us suppose you had a particle localised in your kitchen. Your friend, looking at your house from a passing car, might see the particle is spread out over the entire universe. What is localized for you is delocalized for your friend. Not only does the location of the particle depend on your point of view, so does the fact that the particle *has* location. In this case, it does not make sense to assume localized particles as basic entities.
    >
    > (Kuhlmann, "What is Real?", 36)

14. Newton, *Scholium to the Definitions in Philosophiae Naturalis Principia Mathematica*, book 1, 6 (quoted in Newton-Smith, *The Structure of Time*, 168). The idea of *mathematical* time flowing is even more obscure than that of ordinary time flowing. There is something intrinsically non-fluent in the mathematized world. This is discussed in §3.5.1.

15. See, for example, Kuchar, "The Problem of Time in Quantum Geometrodynamics".

16. Cf. Ernst Mach's critique of the "flow" of time in his *The Science of Mechanics*. Change, he argues, is more fundamental than the concept of time. Our talk about time "passing" really refers to the movements and changes around us. We shall develop this.

17. Not all philosophers are worried by the seeming vacuity of asserting that time flows and its speed of flow is (say) one second per second. Tim Maudlin ("The Passage of Time" in *The Metaphysics within*

Physics) is relaxed about the high cost of defending the "flow of time", arguing that "the passage of time entails only a preferred temporal direction and orientation". This is not so: if orientation gave passage so would spatial orientation. Indeed, one could put things the other way round: passage lays down or defines orientation.

Huw Price has pointed out that a ratio of a quantity to itself – e.g. one second per second – cannot be a rate ("The Flow of Time" in *Oxford Handbook of Philosophy of Time*). "One second per second" can be rescued from being a pure number only by invoking a hypertime or some other medium for time to flow in and to provide the markers to make sense of the rate of flow. A pure number is not a rate. If I said of you that your velocity was "1", you would be entitled to ask "1 what"? What's more, it could not be an empirical fact about time that it passes at one second per second: it is a logical necessity. Hence the vacuity of "time passes at one second per second".

18. It is interesting to reflect on what counts as the present moment in the river analogy. A river is a body of water – extending from the source to the mouth – moving at once, though at different speeds. But the most local candidate for a present moment is the water passing a particular point: a "here" that gives the basis for the "now". Otherwise it would be necessary to import the "now" from outside: it would be successive moments of the entire body of water. The role of the bank – not to speak of the observer on the bank – gets evermore complex and the river metaphor even more tenuous.

19. See, for example, Norton, "Time Really Passes", 23–34. Norton argues that if the passage of time were an illusion, then it would be very odd that it is "so universal, so solid and immutable"; in short, it does not have any of the distinguishing marks of an illusion, including the key characteristic of corrigibility. It is, moreover, rather strange that the physical world can induce this illusion in a part of itself – namely the physical brain. He argues that the only reason for claiming that the passage of time is an illusion is "the vanity that our physical theories have captured all the important facts of time" (*ibid.*, 30). I think there is more to it than that.

20. The transfer of becoming (and hence flow) from events to times (in this case stretches of time) is seen particularly clearly in the case of times of the day. As it gets darker, we say "the afternoon slipped away" or "the day got later". But we don't really think that the afternoon is passing at a rate of one afternoon per afternoon.

21. Plotinus explores the problems associated with the assumption that time is "Number, a Measure, belonging to Movement" (see "Time and Eternity", excerpts from *The Six Enneads* reprinted in Gale, *The Philosophy of Time*, 24–37).

22. Oaklander, *The Ontology of Time*, 17.

23. A classic expression of the belief that events are tense tourists – something to which we shall return in Chapter 8.

24. Dainton, *Time and Space*, 64. Maudlin, however, defends the passage of time while, at the same time, arguing that the tenseless B-series is fundamental and the A-series of tensed time secondary; that there can be temporal passage in a block universe. However, he reduces passage to "an asymmetry in the temporal structure of the world that has no spatial counterpart" which doesn't sound very fluid (see his "On the Passage of Time" in *The Metaphysics within Physics*). Eric Olson, by contrast, in "The Rate of Time's Passage", 3–9, argues that tensed time entails a dynamic view of time and, since the latter in turn entails the passage of time which must have a rate (a meaningless notion), time must be tenseless.

25. Tooley, *Time, Tense, and Causation*, 16.

26. The wobbling between the unfolding of events and the unfolding of time – the succession of times – helps to distract from the apparent fact that the sum total of all changes, which time must encompass, does not itself amount to an overall change. This is the basis for the static or "Block" account of the universe as a whole.

27. Mellor, *Real Time II*, 66.

28. *Ibid.*, 69.

29. *Ibid.* It is not entirely clear why this updating of particular, factual beliefs, of discrete cognitive items should translate into the sense of flow.

30. Broad, *Scientific Thought*.

31. *Ibid.*, 66.

32. It seems neither nonsensical nor evasive to say that time accrues at one day per day or more precisely one day's worth of added existences per day. But it doesn't say much.

33. "The growing block model [holds] … that physical reality consists of a space–time block of present and past *facts* but no future facts, and that the block grows" (Kutach, "The Asymmetry of Influence", 248; italics added).The standpoint from which this is judged will make the present seem like an advancing border at which tomorrows become todays. The sense of motion is deceptive, of course: our journey towards the end of the day, as a result of which another tomorrow will become a day, is not like walking home. And a morning passing is nothing like a bus passing. What is more, "days", (never mind "yesterdays" and "Wednesdays") are a long way from what we may regard as basic time: they seem derivative, belonging to an advanced version of explicit time that depends upon conscious, indeed highly socialized, human beings.

34. The growing block theory shares some of the problems associated with the (ungrowing) block universe of relativity theory. In the case of the latter, we have the difficulty of accounting for the evident distinction between past and present or, if that is an illusion, the origin of that illusion. In what sense do past events belong to the present total? The underlying difficulty is that of allocating events in the block to different points in time, while allowing them to *co*-exist. In the growing block, as in the self-totalling block, successive times are established by items that timelessly co-exist, though in the case of the growing block only past and present have to be accommodated. But coexistence means simultaneous existence and simultaneity can hardly be a timeless relation. What is more, we would have coexistence of states that are incompatible: the local corner shop would be always open and always closed and there would be no transition from being open to being closed. And it would be difficult to see what would underwrite the temporal world's order of "existences", their comparative duration, and the length of the intervals between them.

35. Barry Dainton (personal communication) has argued that while 25 and 26 December are not simultaneous, they *co-exist* tenselessly. But it seems to me that if two entities co-exist, they have to exist at the same time.

36. This does not touch on the nature of the "information" that "grows" with time. Information involves (as I shall discuss in §2.3.5) a relationship between what is the case and a conscious being: it is a correspondence relation. The increased total of events would have to be known to someone. There is nothing in the mere "accumulation" of days that would deliver increased knowledge or retain it as an accumulation. The mere increase of summed happening over time, would not of itself generate the sum, even less knowledge of the sum: there is no receptacle in which flowing time is captured and summed as a simultaneous volume.

37. Barry Dainton (personal communication) argues that this is not a sleight of hand. If time is purely relational, then successive momentary universe-states do equate to more times and if one adopts a substantivalist view, new phases of matter will come into existence as well. However, leaving aside the problems associated with both the relational and substantivalist accounts of space and time (discussed in §10.3.3), the summing of successive states to a growing total is still internal to a consciousness capable of doing the addition sum. It is clearly not performed by, nor its result contained in, any particular state of matter.

38. Since (we are told) the universe expands, surely spatial dimensions do indeed grow. The difference still remains, however. First, if space grows, it cannot do so one dimension at a time. So the similarity would apply only if time were not comparable to a single spatial dimension; namely length. Secondly – and of more significance – it is possible to think of non-growing space. Indeed, it is growth that we find difficult to understand except in terms of the increasing separation of items that are other than space; namely material objects.

   The expansion of space, however, remains a difficult notion. If it means that all the material elements of the universe are getting further apart and possibly more numerous, why not say that? Then it would seem to make sense to think of space as expanding, so long as its volume was defined by a boundary or hypersurface encompassing the sum of the objects, forces and fields of the universe. The idea of space being limited in this way, however, still raises the obvious questions – the ones that a child asks – about the difference between existent empty space between objects, forces and fields, and non-existent empty space beyond them. Why does emptiness inside the boundary count as space, while emptiness outside of it does not? In other words, while we can understand the idea of objects, etc. or their distribution being bounded we cannot apply this concept to space, unless we have a very strong substantivalist notion of space.

   Popularizing expositions such as "space is expanding and galaxies are being carried along for the ride" (Turner, "The Origin of the Universe", 38) do not help. What would space be expanding *into*?

By what means could it become more spacious? What does it mean, furthermore, to say that it is expanding at a certain rate? Velocity, after all, applies to the movement of things in space relative to other things in space; with respect to what would space be expanding? And how can empty space have the power other than mathematically to "drag" galaxies along?

Again, this view seems to make space something substantive, rather than a set of relations between objects; a stuff perilously like the ether, though the latter has made something of a comeback. As we shall discuss in §10.3.3, substantival accounts of space, having been discarded with special relativity seem to return with general relativity, though serious ambiguity remains. Even setting this aside, we can still ask how a physicist could allow space to be expanding separately from time (but, expanding at a finite rate, taking time to do so). What happened to Minkowski's assertion that space alone and time alone are ghosts?

Minkowski's assertion was, of course, mathematically based and the notion of expansion – either of space or of space–time – could be translated into the expansions of the geodesics or, more precisely, of co-moving test particles that represent geodesics. The mathematization helps, however, only so long as we do not think that there is a non-mathematical interpretation of the maths.

A recent paper – Francis *et al.*'s "Expanding Space" – is an excellent critique of the analogies used by those who explain the idea of expanding space in terms of dots on a balloon being blown up or raisins in rising dough. They conclude, first of all, that the universe does not expand into previously empty space; rather, it is expanding space. And, secondly, that the expansion of space should not be seen as a physical reality but as a teaching aid, helping one to visualize what is happening, when there is an increase over time of the distance between observers at rest with respect to cosmic fluid.

39. The notion of the successive states of the universe being represented by a line leads inevitably to the idea that if the universe reverts to an earlier state, this can be represented by a line curving back on itself.

40. Gödel quoted in Yourgrau, *The Disappearance of Time*, 24. It does, however, suggest something rather surprising, considering its source. Given that, according to relativity theory, distant simultaneity is an illusion, a universe in which all time was "now" would seem to have to be spatially compacted. There is an additional problem of clarifying the status of the "infinity" reality is supposed to consist of. There are, of course, no actual infinities. Infinity, by definition, exceeds all that is.

41. It has been argued by others that time *qua* passage is a local phenomenon tied to a world-line. This then raises the question of where the localities arise (something that we shall examine in Chapter 11).

42. Broad, *Scientific Thought*, 277. The moving spotlight seems more applicable to the past and future than the present. The spotlight alights on a past event and it is reawakened. In this case, the spotlight is not time itself but consciousness and, what is more, an individual consciousness. In the case of the future, the spotlight and the "spotlit" are internally connected, with the spotlight bringing its object into being as an envisaged possibility. In the case of the present, "happening" is not the displacement of the spotlight whereas in the case of recall and anticipation, it most certainly is. The moving spotlight theory has recently had a revival because it seems to reconcile one aspect of presentism – namely that the present is absolute and real – with permanentism – the belief that things exist forever (see Deasy, "The Moving Spot Theory"). Whether this is a recommendation (and I don't think it is) remains doubtful.

43. It is significant that any account of the moving spotlight theory is ambiguous between times and events; between making t_1 qualify as now and making what is there or happening at t_1 present, real, existing.

44. There are many other dynamic images of time in which what is on the move is not time itself but a timeless, unextended, "now" which picks out successive moments. These only multiply the problems of the dynamic idea of time. It separates "now" from time, in order that time-in-waiting can be picked out by it skipping along it.

45. See, for example, Skow, "Why Does Time Pass?".

46. "O God Our Help in Ages Past", hymn by Isaac Watts.

47. Quoted in Williams, "The Myth of Passage", 103, which appears in Richard Gale's edited volume *The Philosophy of Time*. The entire section on "Static versus Dynamic Temporal", along with Gale's excellent introduction, is worth reading – and re-reading.

48. Gale, *The Philosophy of Time*, 103.

49. *Ibid.*, 108.

50. Wittgenstein, *Philosophical Investigations*, para 464, 130e.
51. The very notion of "the passage of time" may imply the *becoming* of time itself: a succession of instants – t_1, t_2, etc. – coming into being. This treats time as if it were a kind of continuous occurrence. Occurrence, even less coming into being, is not "passage". We could of course narrow this difference between becoming and passage by analysing the passage of a car along the road as the successive comings-into-being of the car at the successive positions it occupies: car-at-P_1 is followed by car-at-P_2, etc. The noun phrases "car-at-P_1", etc. make the occupation of the succession positions the coming into being of entities. This seems rather desperate and not the slightest bit plausible.
52. It has been claimed by some philosophers that even time-symmetric laws of nature can generate an orientation corresponding to the difference between past and future. See, for example, Clarke, "Time in general relativity". This, however, as will be evident, is irrelevant to the arguments against "time's arrow".
53. This is also obviously linked with the fact that there is more than one degree of freedom in space: we can wander at will over a plane, or in a volume precisely *because* a plane or a volume does not have a prescribed direction.
54. And the even more doubtful idea of spatial points as occurrences that occur at particular points in time.
55. Interestingly, the concept of an arrow is the minimal way of getting a direction, by invoking two points separated by a distance; in this case marked by the "head" and the "tail".
56. Of course it is possible to have many kinds of highly structured states and objects that, nevertheless, give the impression of disorder. Take a normal household. What is more, as Ilya Prigogine has discovered, "*open systems in a state far from equilibrium* show no tendency towards increasing disorder even though they produce entropy" (quoted in Popper, *The Open Universe*, 173).
57. Eddington, *The Nature of the Physical World*. Eddington here refers to tensed time – "future" and "past" – which may not be appropriate for reasons we shall discuss in Part II. However, if we replace "past" with "earlier than time t" where time t is the point at which the observation is made and "future" with "later than time t", all will be well.
58. When thinking of irreversibility, we tend to focus on rather complex situations in which an explicit order is lost; for example the smashing of a cup or the diffusion of a gas. However, there are no situations that are truly reversible. When I move an object from A to B, the reverse movement from B to A does not restore the status quo. Small changes will have taken place during the course of the move that will not be reversed by macroscopic reversal and there will be changes around that movement that will also not be reversed. So the observation that most states of affairs *can* be reversed, in accordance with the reversibility of, say, the laws of motion, is apparent rather than real. We can never restore an earlier state without paying an extra price for reversal on top of the energy exchange involved in counteracting the movement that defines the change. This is a separate issue from the "tidiness" or "order" argument.
59. Callender, "There is No Puzzle about the Low Entropy Past" (accessed July 2013).
60. The argument is set out in Prigogine & Stengers, *Order Out of Chaos*.
61. As we shall discuss in Chapter 3, we lose "earlier" and "later" at the level of laws of nature – irrespective of whether they are or are not time-reversible – because they are timeless and are about classes of events that do not, of course, occur at any particular time. This would be contested by Unger & Smolin in *The Singular Universe and the Reality of Time*, in which they argue that the laws themselves evolve in time so that certain classes of events (those permitted by them) belong to a particular epoch.
62. It is important here to reiterate the distinction between token (and hence unique) events and events of a certain type. A token event cannot occur twice, because it would not be the same token event on both occurrences. If it were, it would occur both before and after itself and, of course (on both occasions) at the same time as itself. Likewise, if the universe reverts to a particular state, reversion is to the same type state not the same token state.

  What is more, a genuine recurrence would require not only that its context (the total state of the universe) should recur but also its predecessors and successors (and in the same order) so that the index event would have the same history and the same consequences. There are two reasons for this requirement: firstly causal connectedness or some other manifestation of the laws of nature demand it; and, secondly, in the absence of the same antecedents and consequences, it would not be the same state only the same disconnected instant. In short, for true (token) recurrence of S_1 the entire journey between S_1 and $S_{1\,recurrence}$ would have to be replicated. The odds against this happening would not be infinite but they would be much greater even than the Poincaré number.

Overlooking this requirement is the consequence of the incorrect assumption that time t_1 can be entirely defined by the states of the universe at time t_1, so that if the universe reverts to S_1 it has returned to an earlier t_1 or whatever. If, however, token t_1 really occurred twice, then it too would have to be both before and after itself. Such is the consequence of thinking that times are defined by (types of) states of affairs, or are indeed in some sense identical with them. Even if we allow a recurrence of S_1 that does not have the same history leading up to it (though what follows from it must also be identical, given the unchanging laws of nature – an interesting asymmetry), there is another concern, arising out of the identity of physical indiscernibles. If physics cannot distinguish two states of the universe, they are the same (token) state, at the same time. However, this assumption – which is a variation of Mach's principle (that which could not possibly be distinguished on the basis of experience must be identical) – makes too strong a claim for physics.

63. This is not a trivial point. We shall see that the arrow of increasing untidiness connects with an apparent asymmetry between singular cause and multiple effects. I say "apparent" because the cause is itself an effect picked out from a boundless population of effects. It is salience that makes an event, which is first an effect and then only subsequently a cause, a starting or reference point. This is one aspect of the fact that although we do not determine the order of most events, ordering them into "earlier" and "later" is connected with our picking them out; with the exercise of attention and freedom that inserts *Kairos* into *chronos* – a beginning into an unbroken unfolding of the material world (see in particular §11.2 *passim* and §12.3 *passim*). It is the picking out of an event that is the essential symmetry breaker.

64. Boltzmann quoted in Price, *Time's Arrow and Archimedes' Point*, 29. As Price himself expresses it, "the real puzzle of thermodynamics is not why entropy increases with time, but why it was ever so low in the first place" (*ibid.*, 79). Callender ("There is No Puzzle about the Low Entropy Past") does not think this is a problem but his argument is not persuasive. This low entropy may be seen as a property of a universe which is relatively undissipated (beginning with a dimensionless point of infinite density) but this merely displaces the improbability to the Big Bang which is, as Price points out, "the kind of collapse we should expect to get once every $10^{10^{123}}$ attempts" (*ibid.*). Price's book, to which I am indebted in this section, is an incomparable discussion of the whole issue of the physics of the directionality of time.

65. It raises another question: is the second law simply an expression of a truism; namely that the universe will most probably unfold from the less to the more probable state? It will be a truism if it is an *explanation* of what is observed. It makes it "stand to reason". But it is in fact more than a truism inasmuch as it both describes what we see and predicts what we might see.

66. Price *op cit.*, 42.

67. *Ibid.*, 86.

68. *Ibid.*, 44. He elaborates this point as follows: "At the root of this mistake [focusing on increased entropy as we look towards the "future" and not the entropy gradient as we look to the "past"] lies the failure to characterize the issue in sufficiently atemporal terms … [I]t has not been properly appreciated that we have no right to assume that it is an objective matter that entropy *increases* rather than *decreases*. What is objective is that there is an entropy gradient over time, not that the universe "moves" on this gradient in one direction rather than the other."

69. For a brief, lucid argument, to the effect that quantum mechanics is "kinder" to time than relativity see Lucas, "A Century of Time", 11. We shall return to this question in Chapter 3, especially §3.5.4.

70. Popper, "The Arrow of Time", cited in Price, *Time's Arrow and Archimedes' Point*, 51. This has been described as the natural preference for outgoing or "retarded" rather than incoming or "advanced" solutions of the equations governing "radiative" phenomena, whether they are waves in a pond or electromagnetic waves. Price's excellent discussion argues that "radiation is not intrinsically asymmetric, but 'just looks that way'" – in short, that it is an artefact of observation. The reality or otherwise of this and other asymmetries – is not relevant to our present concerns for reasons given.

71. *Ibid.*, 4.

72. The conflation – which we shall allow to pass for the present – is problematic, as we shall discuss in Chapter 3, especially §3.5.3.

73. There is a fascinating discussion of Einstein's progressive disenchantment with positivism in Weinberg, *Dreams of a Final Theory*, where he reports a conversation between Heisenberg and Einstein in Berlin in 1926, in which the latter argued that "every theory in fact contains unobserved quantities. The principle of employing only observed quantities cannot be consistently carried out":
    "And when I [Heisenberg] objected that in this I had merely been applying the type of philosophy that he, too, had made the basis of his special theory of relativity, he answered simply: 'Perhaps I did use such philosophy earlier, and also wrote it, but it is nonsense all the same' (*ibid.*, 143). And earlier in a lecture in 1922, Einstein had referred to Mach as "*un bon mécanicien*" but a "deplorable *philosophe*".

74. The time at which an experience occurs matters: it is part of the stream, even the narrative, of experience. The time at which a measurement takes place is not relevant – any more than the person who made it – apart from the issue of responsibility and quality control. Measurement is experience lifted out of time, out of experience.

75. See Meillassoux, *After Finitude*.

76. Another link between psychology and the direction of time is the link between "beforeness" and memory. For example, if A occurs before B, it is possible for me to be remembering A while I am experiencing B. Unfortunately this is too readily extended to the kind of world order of "before–after" that arrows are supposed to underpin or reflect. The fact that the origin of the earth was (an indeed must be) before the origin of life on earth is clearly not something that depends on memory to be underwritten.

77. Davies, "That Mysterious Flow", 27.

78. See the essay on "Information" in Tallis, *Why the Mind Is Not a Computer*.

79. Chalmers, *The Conscious Mind*, 297.

80. Wheeler, "It from Bit", in *At Home in the Universe*.

81. Davies, "That Mysterious Flow", 29.

82. The difference between "epistemic" and "constitutive" is clearly highly contested in quantum theory. What is more, the epistemic asymmetry between past and future would, it has been claimed, be lost in a classical Laplacean universe if the observer were also Laplacean. In a Laplacean universe, the initial conditions (and the initial materials) plus the laws of unfolding determine successive states of the universe. In this closed system, the future would be as determinate as the past, even though it had not happened. A Laplacean observer would be fully *au fait* with the laws governing the unfolding of the universe and could do the necessary mathematics to predict the future. The latter, therefore, would be as fully known to him as the past.

    This is of course only a thought experiment. More importantly, it is flawed because it does not do justice to the Laplacean observer who is a part of and yet outside the Laplacean universe. What is the status or standing of his knowledge? Even if his knowledge does not alter what happens – by, for example, prompting him to take steps to alter future events (because this would not be permitted by Laplacean determinism) – there are still fundamental problems. The most pressing is to characterize the kind of irruption the observer is into a universe such that the latter would be sufficiently other than him for him to have it as an object of knowledge. If he is not other than the universe but merely part of it and subject to its laws, how does he get an overview on it? How does he gain possession of the knowledge necessary for the unfolding of the universe to be gathered up into laws which can permit the future to be predicted? Knowledge somehow has to irrupt into a physical world that is unfolding on its own. As knowledge, or the knowing subject, irrupts, it divides time into past and present, into that which is remembered (in part) and that which is anticipated (in part). It is this irruption, not the Laplacean world into which it irrupts, that makes the thought experiment possible – and yet at the same time impossible or at least invalid.

    The failure to notice the problems associated with the knower is of a piece with the tendency to see information as being identical with states of the physical world, or with its passage over time from one state to another. This tendency overlooks something that is not part of the causal unfolding of the Laplacean world; namely the intentionality of consciousness that is present throughout perception but most developed in the pooling of perception in knowledge, and scientific facts and theories exemplified in Laplace's own monumental *Celestial Mechanics*. It is connected with a more general tendency in contemporary physics: to overlook the observer, even though in both relativity theory and quantum mechanics the observer appears to be brought into the very heart of physics (see §3.5.3)

83. I have also borrowed the second half of the heading above from the same essay by Kutach.
84. Mellor, *Real Time II*, 117. Mellor's position is rather more puzzling because he sees causes as "facts" and (as we shall discuss in Chapter 11) facts are not occurrences that take place at particular times. For other supporters of causal arrow see Grünbaum, *Philosophical Problems of Space and Time* and Le Poidevin, *Change, Cause and Contradiction*. See also Gale, *The Philosophy of Time*, 354: "We have learned from the theory of relativity that event sustain *time-like* separations from one another because of their *causal* interactions."
85. Mellor, *Real Time II*, 108. Time seems to be reduced to its orientation, to mere "before" and "after", and its quantity or location seem to be off-stage.
86. Actual causal relations are not logically necessitated, of course. The fact that the temporal order of lightning and thunder is contingent, howsoever general and profound the laws it instantiates, justifies the suspicion that this order (and of other causally linked material events) may not underpin the very basis of a temporal order. This is something to which we shall return in Chapter 11.
87. This last is a key theme of Chapters 11 and 12. The importance of the (often overlooked) issue of "picking out" index events as causes (and/or effects) is illustrated by the discussion of the causal arrow and the "asymmetry of influence" (which he rejects) by Price in *Time's Arrow*. The asymmetry he focuses on is that between the independence of those incoming influences that might raise the probability of an event E sufficiently for it to occur and the outcomes of E which are correlated. "[I]nterlocking systems are", he says, "uncorrelated before they interact" (*ibid.*, 263). Supposing I fall down in the street. A variety of factors (both standing conditions and occurrent events) might have together raised the probability of my falling down: (a) I was drunk; (b) the street was unlit; and (c) there was a bump in the pavement. These incoming influences are entirely uncorrelated. My fall might have several consequences: (a) I shout out; (b) I injure myself; (c) there is blood on the pavement; (d) several people rush to the spot. All of these, having in common the fact that their probability was raised by my fall, *are* correlated more highly than would be the case if they did not have a single cause.

    There seems therefore to be an important asymmetry, in which time and causality both participate, between the non-correlation of incoming influences and the correlation of outgoing influences. This asymmetry, however, is in a sense rigged, being dependent on picking out a (salient) index event such that a variety of probability-raising influences, innocent of each other, converge on a particular spot, and a variety of consequences, now correlated because they share a common causal ancestor, fanning out from that event. In reality, there are multitudes of ongoing processes – some correlated, some non-correlated – either side of the event, locally and beyond. The asymmetry is a product of a viewpoint centred on a particular event – as is the other asymmetry that the effects of an event seem untidier than the event that caused them.

    The correlation, incidentally, is evident even in the case of incoming influences on an index event – for example, my drunkenness might supply several connected inputs to my fall: unsteady gait, distracted attention, and a recklessness that makes me willing to walk down an unlit street. This correlation is lost in the coarse-grained description ("I was drunk") which clumps together many distinct but salient elements.
88. Dainton, *Time and Space*, 46 gives a very useful list of asymmetries thought to be relevant to the directionality of time.
89. Maudlin, "Remarks on the Passing of Time". This (laudable) refusal to reduce aspects of time to something non-temporal is reflected in the writings of many philosophers. Oaklander notes that: "Russell, (the early) C. D. Broad, myself, and others have maintained that temporal relations are primitive and unanalysable relations, and the difference between spatial and temporal relations is an irreducible qualitative difference"; Oaklander, *The Ontology of Time*, 131.
90. Price, "The Flow of Time", 292.
91. This, I think, is what is meant by this passage from John Earman (quoted by Price, *ibid.*, 284): "Assuming that space–time is temporally orientable, continuous time like transport takes precedence over any method (entropy and the like) of fixing a time direction".
92. The question of why space has (exactly) three dimensions has recently been investigated (inconclusively) in Webb, "Why Does Space Have Three Dimensions?". It is insufficient to reduce this to the convenience of representation because it simply moves the question on: why is the value of three variables necessary to define and hence represent a point in space? More to the point, why is space

cubic rather than planar or linear? These questions are pressing given that there is in physics ultimately no difference between up–down, side–side, and forward–back – for all that the untutored
mind feels that gravity underpins up–down. If there is no difference between them and yet they are
defined by contrast, they seem to have no intrinsic, only relational, identity. The final point is that,
according to many physical theories, there are more than three dimensions of space – perhaps up
to 9 in string theory.

93. The very idea of an arrow of time still contains the ghost of the passage of time – from the head to
the tail, even where the arrow is still.

94. This valid worry about the dynamism of events may, however, lead philosophers to draw invalid
conclusions; that, for example, the focus on events should be replaced by the focus on the "facts"
that are captured in descriptions of them. This may result in odd positions such as Mellor's view (in
The Facts of Causation) that we have referred to that it is facts not events that are causes. We shall
return to this in Chapter 11.

95. Imagine drawing a line from your birth to the present day, tracing all the movements you have made
hitherto. It would have to encompass many different kinds of lines, gathering up the movements
(say) associated with: tying a tie while you are walking from one room to another; engaging in a
phone call; attending a meeting convened to deal with a difficult colleague; completing a clinic or a
research project; or trying to get to Paris. There would be deviations, digressions, digressions from
digressions, self-embedded sub-routines, jumps from one kind of space to another; and so on. No
line, however elaborated, would capture any of it. The life-line, beloved by palmists, in which events
are displayed along a palmar crease, however, testifies to the power of the spatial analogy. On a
slightly more sophisticated level, is the notion of life as a journey. We shall return to the relationship
between narrative and the direction of time in Chapter 11.

96. Whitrow, *The Nature of Time*, 132.

97. Wells, *The Time Machine*, 7. There is a striking overlap with Hermann Weyl's claim that "The objective world simply *is*, it does not *happen*. Only to the gaze of my consciousness, crawling upward
along the lifeline of my body, does a section of this world come to life as a fleeting image in space
which continually changes in time" (*Philosophy of Mathematics and Natural Science*, 116).

98. Lewis, "The Paradoxes of Time Travel", 145. Lewis argues in this paper that the paradoxes of time
travel are mere "oddities" not "impossibilities". I hope that the arguments in this section will support
those like me who think they are in fact impossibilities not mere oddities.

99. There would be two ways of arriving at the target: travel first to Hastings and then go back in time;
or travel back in time to "No-particular-place" (in the light of our discussion about spatial locations
in the past) and then travel from "No-particular-place" to Hastings (which may itself have become
"No-particular-place").

100. This is analogous to Leibniz's thought experiment – advanced in support of a purely relational idea
of space – in which the entire universe is displaced by 2 feet. This would make no difference.

101. McTaggart, "Time" in *The Nature of Existence*, para 309.

102. *Ibid.*

103. But it usually doesn't because there are many butterflies and butterfly-sized events, and they have
different, self-cancelling consequences, and there are factors, more local to Puerto Rica which also
have their (usually conflicting) say. There are remote perturbations, nonetheless.

104. This would apply only to time travelling and not to discontinuities in time such as are postulated in
wormholes (see below).

105. Philip Dowe, echoing David Lewis, has argued that the constraints on the behaviour of the time
traveller at her destination are not fundamentally different from the context-dependent constraints
that operate in ordinary life; see Dowe, "The Case for Time Travel". This is not, of course, true
because the time traveller is constrained to the point of complete paralysis and even unconscious-
ness. *Everything* is forbidden. Dowe also argues that there is a difference between changing past
events (which he argues should be possible) and causing them (which he agrees should be impossible.) This is a distinction without a fundamental difference: changing an event is causing a new
event which would have different causal descendants and (what is more) doing this at a place where
everything is already done and dusted.

106. And there are other problems connected with the days *prior* to that on which the time traveller
landed. Supposing she made some trivial change in the state of her surroundings at 12 noon 14

October 1066 (the date of the Battle) – say, moved a drinking vessel from one side of a hut to another. That drinking vessel had arrived at its original position by means of the usual route. Now it is displaced. So the appropriate connections are broken; either there is a jump or the entire causal history accounting for the position of the cup (and everything else causally connected with it – in short everything else) has to be altered. We thus require (at least) two versions of all the days prior to the time traveller's arrival as well as of those after it.

107. Maudlin, *Philosophy of Physics*, 159. Returning to an event would presuppose that it was somehow continuing to happen, because there is an intrinsic dynamism – an unfoldingness – in events, or at least in the notion of them. Consider yesterday's breakfast. Returning to it would imply that it was still being eaten by me. So it would be both on the plate and in my stomach. What is more, it would have to have retained the context in which it took place – my having just got up, the radio playing (an interview with a politician being simultaneously perceived as happening and remembered as having happened), the bed cooling after my rising – none of which seems plausible. And I would have to alight at a particular moment in breakfast and, as it were, reactivate the meal from that moment on.

108. I am grateful to Barry Dainton for reminding me of this.

109. Yourgrau, *The Disappearance of Time*, 2–3.

110. The key idea here is that of "quantum jumping" from one time to another without passing through the intermediate temporal positions. This could be seen in theory in a wormhole – two black holes whose throats are connected by a tunnel. However, such tunnels are very unstable and would need to be stabilized by importation of negative energy. Until this has been shown to be technically possible, and relevant to the scale of macroscopic objects such as time travellers and their machines, extreme scepticism is in order. Other quantum-based approaches include appeal to the notion of the multiverse, in which individuals may visit earlier stages of their own lives but avoid conflict by locating the visit in a parallel universe. Given that the Many Worlds are, by definition, not in causal contact with each other – and hence not in communication – it is not at all clear how voluntary universe swapping would be possible. In short, the impossibility of time travel is not mitigated by the impossibility of inter-universe travel.

  Classical general relativity and semi-classical quantum gravity all raise the possibility of closed time-like curves (CTCs), where time loops back to earlier times. These are all highly contested. It is not clear whether the laws of nature would permit them as they might for example generate insoluble problems with poorly understood "negative energy" arising within wormholes. (I owe this point to Barry Dainton.) Some physicists, such as Stephen Hawking, have suggested that there must be additional laws – Hawking gathers them under the portmanteau term "the Chronological Protection Agency" – to prevent the paradoxes that would result from CTCs. (For excellent brief discussions, see Hunter, "Time Travel", and Earman *et al.*, "Time Machines" in *The Stanford Encyclopaedia of Philosophy*.)

111. A careful examination of what physics does and does not permit – Earman *et al.*, "Do the Laws of Physics Forbid the Operation of Time Machines?" – concludes only that "no result of a sufficient generality" from "classical general relativity, semi-classical quantum gravity, quantum field theory on curved spacetime and Euclidean quantum gravity" is adequate to rule out closed time-like curves, has been proved.

112. Arntzenius & Maudlin, "Time Travel and Modern Physics".

113. Shalamov, *Kolyma Tales*.

114. Penrose, "Causality, Quantum Theory and Cosmology", 143.

115. The very notion of "the speed of light" is problematic, given that it assumes the separation of space (or spatial intervals) located on the numerator and of time (or time intervals) located on the denominator though space and time are intrinsically inseparable according to special relativity. As Maudlin points out, "Once we abandon Newtonian absolute time and the persistence of points of Newtonian absolute space, there are no objective speeds, either of light or of anything else"; Maudlin, *The Philosophy of Physics*, 121. Maudlin argues that the speed of light is not something independent of, but folded into, space–time geometry. Others are not so accommodating. The physicist Léon Brillouin identified another numerator/denominator problem; namely that time and length were both defined using light waves: "The unit of length is based on the spectral line of krypton-86 … and the unit of time is based on the frequency of a spectral line of cesium … Hence the same physical phenomenon, a spectral line, is used for to different definitions: length and time" (quoted in Canales,

The Physicist and the Philosopher, 112–3). On this basis, it would appear that, as Canales interprets it, "any change in the velocity of light would go undetected because the changes would cancel out when length was divided by time". The confusions around the speed of light are endemic. As Roger Scruton (personal communication) has pointed out to me, there is an "elementary contradiction involved in the language of light years, and its cavalier use to tell us that the events we witness on galaxy Z occurred 20 million years ago, even though by the theory of relativity these are simultaneous with our observations of them according to the only criterion of simultaneity that we can apply". (See, however, §10.4.3 for a critique of the notion of the time relations between experiences and that which they perceive).

116. *Oxford English Dictionary*.
117. Quine, *Quiddities*, 196.
118. Churchland, *Matter and Consciousness*, 146–53.
119. Martin, "On the Need for Properties", 221–2.
120. It is important to avoid misunderstanding. I am not denying that there is an aspect of time that can be captured by treating it as a dimension in the physical or mathematical sense. Nor do I think it a simple error to represent it by a line in a graph or to mark a point in space–time by a set of four figures related to four axes. This has been a very potent way of thinking of change, and of the mechanical laws that govern change. The mistake is to think that this quasi-spatial representation captures time; to confuse a way of describing or representing time for time as it is experienced or time itself.

CHAPTER 3

1. Minkowski, "Space and Time", 37.
2. This is an appropriate juncture to acknowledge a thinker whom some readers may think not only covers much of the territory of this book but who has already arrived at some of its conclusions – namely, Henri Bergson. See the addendum to this chapter, where I discuss points of agreement and of difference. Whether the reduction of time to a line – making it ripe to be quantified and mapped on to a numerical sequence – is a human universal is a matter of considerable contention among anthropologists, particularly associated with a famous dispute between Edmund Leach (universalist) and his erstwhile pupil Anthony Gell.
3. In fact, it appears that the translation can go either way. Maudlin in "Time, Topology and Physical Geometry" argues that "relativity temporalizes space" with "before and after" being fundamental. He argues that a line – the shortest distance between two points – is defined by the shortest temporal distance within a light cone. If this (contested) view were true, it would not alter the fundamental concern that time has lost its intrinsic character by being married to space in space–time nor that space and time are both traduced and should form a victim support group.
4. Hawking & Mlodinow, *The Grand Design*, 131.
5. Raja Panjwani (personal communication) reminds me that Euclidean space can have any number of dimensions. What makes space Euclidean is not the number of dimensions but rather the way that vectors within the space relate to one another – as reflected, for example, in rules for multiplying them. The question as to why space is typically regarded as three-dimensional remains unanswered: it is deeply mysterious. Matthew Chalmers ("Seeing Triple") points out that "with a little tweaking relativity's mathematics works fine in any number of dimensions". Some can find it equally mysterious that the number of spatial dimensions, unlike nearly all constants in physics, is a whole number. It may be just a rock bottom fact, a point at which our digging is stopped and the spade is turned, "an unexplained explainer" as Callender (quoted by Chalmers, *ibid.*) describes it.
6. String theorists allow that there are real structures in space–time with zero thickness. They are however entirely the children of mathematics. Empirical sightings are sought, though expectation is not high. We could be in for a long wait.
7. The nature of visual space is extraordinarily complex. For a rich, nuanced discussed, see Rosar, "The Dimensionality of Visual Space". The intrinsic or natural geometry of visual space is addressed by Patrick Suppes in "Is Visual Space Euclidean?".

8. The transformation of shadows into the abstract representation of the form of objects is possible only for human beings who are embodied subjects as well as organisms and consequently see objects as items-in-themselves transcending their moment-to-moment experience of them. This is discussed in Tallis, *I Am*.

9. And, if we are partial to Just-So stories, we might succumb to the temptation to connect the places where geometry seemed to have originated – India, Egypt, Greece – to those places where the sun is brightest and the shadows sharpest. I would not have been the first to link the unique contribution of Greece to the development of geometry – taking it beyond empirical observation to a network of theorems – with the fact that it was in Greek culture that the hegemony of the visual as the guide to the real was most firmly established. See, for example, the editor's introduction in Levin, *Modernity and the Hegemony of Vision*. There are also the practical considerations that drove the development of geometry – "the measurement of land" evident in its title; namely, the need to settle disputes arising out of the periodic flooding of land by the Nile that eradicated the borders between property belonging to different owners.

10. The notion of "hodological" space was introduced by the gestalt psychologist Kurt Lewin to signify the space of possible action, the lived space arranged around us as the scene of our lives, the site of our journeys in which we inscribe customary paths. *Hodos* is the Greek for a "journey".

11. Dainton, *Time and Space*, 145.

12. One of the richest explorations of the contrast between scientific and science-dominated understanding of space is to be found in the writings of Lucien Lévy-Bruhl, whose comparison between the "primitive" or "pre-logical" mind with the "civilized" one, made him deeply unfashionable for a while. The relevance of his views to our present concern is summarized by Robert Jackson (personal communication) as follows:

> The "civilized" mind has a propensity to abstraction, whose products – concepts – are logically homogeneous, which permits of their combination. This is closely bound up with the homogeneous representation of space – and, indeed, of time. In contrast, the pre-logical mind imagines the various regions in space as differing in quality, as determined by their mystic participations with such and such groups of persons or objects ... The place [note the implied contrast of "place" with "space"] occupied by a person, an object, an image, is of paramount importance ... Each social group among the tribes of Central Australia, for instance, feels itself mystically bound up with the portion of ground it occupies or travels over... [E]ach locality with its characteristic aspect and form, its own peculiar rocks and trees, springs and sand-heaps, etc., is in mystic union with the visible or invisible beings who have revealed their presence there, or dwell there ... Between themselves and their locality there is reciprocal participation ...

The error, of course, by Lévy-Bruhl is to ascribe these two attitudes to space to, respectively, a "primitive" and a "civilized" mind. In reality, we all oscillate between what we might call the living experience and the geometrical reduction of space. (For a beautiful meditation on the tension between these two modes of grasping space, see the chapter "Walking in the City", in *The Practice of Everyday Life*).

Many anthropologists and some philosophers have mounted resistance to the sterilization of space. Notable among them is Henri Lefebvre (*The Production of Space*, 1), who sounds quite optimistic about regaining space for humanity:

> Not many years ago, the word 'space' had a strictly geometrical meaning: the idea it evoked was simply that of an empty area. In scholarly use it was generally accompanied by some such epithet as 'Euclidean', 'isotropic', or 'infinite', and the general feeling was that the concept of space was ultimately a mathematical one. To speak of 'social space', therefore, would have sounded strange.

It is hardly necessary to point out that *place* is an unmanageably complex concept. David Carr ("Commentary on 'Placing the Past'", 501) notes:

> [Using *place*] as the term for the original primary engagement with space that we never leave behind ... has the advantage of being more communal and less subjective and individual than the terms used by most previous phenomenologists. Space is at once more

humanized, even as it is less subjectivized, psychologized and individualized, by the concept of place.

At some level there has to be a deep connection between (mathematical) space and (lived) place. This is not only because mathematized space has proved central to the technological supports of daily life in lived place but also because there must be something like the continuous, boundless, homogeneous space for us to work together with each other and with the material world. In a beautifully argued, rich paper, Edward Slowik discusses how "providing a fundamental role to mathematical concepts in the analysis of place need not undercut the integrity of the lived-space approach" ("The Fate of Mathematical Place", 292).

This lies outside the already somewhat capacious scope of this book. It is relevant, however, to note that the assumption that lived-space must be more fundamental than physico-mathematical space raises all sorts of questions, such as how to counter a relativism about space that would give equal credence to (say) flat-earthers and round-earthers, or to geocentric and heliocentric accounts of the solar system.

13. This account of the origin of geometry does not take sides in an argument most closely associated with the French mathematician and philosopher of science Henri Poincaré. For Poincaré, the axioms of geometry were neither analytic judgements nor (as Kant had claimed) synthetic *a priori* judgements. They were conventions or "disguised definitions". But they were not *arbitrary* conventions as they were chosen by the criterion of economy and simplicity; it was this that justified the use of Euclidean geometry in Newtonian mechanics and (had he lived) Poincaré might have regarded as justifying the use of non-Euclidean geometry in formulating the field equations of the general theory of relativity.

14. Strictly, space in physics is a structure – characterized by a variety of features such as the ordering of points, the relationship between vectors and quantities, dimensions, etc. – but these boil down to numbers. (I owe this point to Raja Panjwani.)

15. The genealogy of Man the Measuring Animal, and of the necessary cognitive architecture that a creature who measures must have, is a fascinating area of inquiry. I have attempted to make sense of the origin of our distinctive human consciousness in a trilogy published by Edinburgh University Press, 2003–5. The most relevant volume is *The Hand* (2003).

16. Motion is central to the idea of nature developed in physical science – as is captured in the precept that "to be ignorant of motion is to be ignorant of nature" (quoted in Cohen, *The Birth of a New Physics*, 1). We arrive at the Galilean position that "The book of nature is written in the language of mathematics" as follows: the essence of motion is number, the essence of nature is motion, and consequently the essence of nature is number.

17. And was rewarded with exile – or perhaps even drowning at sea – for revealing the incommensurable magnitude or *alogos* at the very heart of the Pythagorean dream of discovering the true nature of the universe as mathematics. We shall return to this *alogos* when we discuss Zeno.

18. For physicists, of course, spaces with more than three dimensions are still spaces.

19. In part, we are inclined to allow negative numbers to slip beneath our guard because we oscillate between numbers as adjectives (as in "ten sheep") and numbers as nouns, as quasi-things (as in "ten"). A hundred sheep is the square of ten sheep, but it is the number of sheep that is squared not the sheep themselves. The existence of negative numbers should be enough in itself to throw into question the idea that numbers are the last word (!) on physical or even geometrical reality.

20. More on sheep. The passage from correspondence counting – with one symbol for each counted item – to numbers separated from the enumerated is crucial. Instead of writing 3 sheep symbols to signify 3 sheep, we have devised separate symbols for sheep and the number 3, which can be attached to sheep, goats, humans, and stars. See Martin, *Money*, 43 for the cultural importance of this step.

21. Mazur, *Imagining Numbers*, 10.

22. Leibniz, quoted in Dantzig, *Number, the Language of Science*, 204.

23. Jeans, *The Mysterious Universe*, 118 (quoted in Williams, "The Myth of Passage", 100). Or, as Einstein put it, "in order to give due prominence to [the relationship between the four-dimensional Minkowski continuum and the three-dimensional continuum of Euclidean geometrical space] we must replace the usual time coordinate t by an imaginary magnitude: $\sqrt{-1}.ct$ proportional to it" (Einstein, *Relativity*, 57).

24. Galileo, *The Assayer*, quoted in Burtt, *The Metaphysical Foundations of Modern Science.*
25. The distinction between primary qualities that are inseparable from, and belong to, material objects and secondary qualities which are manifested only in minds that encounter the objects was developed most clearly by John Locke in *Essay Concerning Human Understanding*, II, i.
26. Burtt, *The Metaphysical Foundations of Modern Science*, 89 (italics original).
27. For further discussion of this, see Tallis, *Aping Mankind.*
28. See *ibid.*, especially 140–5.
29. For a further development of some of the topics discussed here, from the viewpoint of human evolution, see "The Counting Hand" in Tallis, *The Hand.*
30. Newton, *Universal Arithmetic*, 2.
31. This is a term that appears in his early writings. It is discussed in Safranski, *Martin Heidegger*, 97.
32. See "Thatter" in Tallis, *The Knowing Animal.*
33. It is the opposite of "egocentric space" and because it is something that has to uphold invariance, when it is conjoined with time in the space–time manifold, it gives the impression of absolute stasis.
34. Aristotle, *Physics*, IV 219 b1–2.
35. Bergson in *Creative Evolution* deplored the fact that "the abstract time t attributed by science to a material object ...remains the same whatever the nature of the intervals between the correspondences" (quoted in Canales, *The Physicist and the Philosopher*, 220).
36. Webb, *Nothing*, 32.
37. *Ibid.*, 29.
38. As Bertrand Russell points out, idealized geometrical points "are qualitatively homogeneous; there is no inherent quality in a single point, as there is in a single colour, by which it can be qualitatively distinguished from another" (quoted in Rosar, "The Dimensionality of Visual Space", 12). One way of being qualitatively homogeneous is in virtue of a shared lack of qualities! Mathematical points do not, of course, have the capacity to house qualities: they are not big enough (say) to be blue rather than green.
39. Butterfield & Isham, "Emergence of Time in Quantum Gravity", 139. The full passage is of great interest:

> In short, the effect has been for matter now to play second fiddle to space and time. As these field theories, both classical and quantum, are presented to us, their basic objects seem to be just space-time points. All else – matter, fields, and even the metrical structure of space-time, the "chronogeometry" of the world are represented as mathematical structures defined on these points; in particular ... physical quantities for matter and fields are represented by structures defined point by point. And so it is natural to presume that all these are to be construed as properties of (and relations between) points, or higher-order properties and relations. In short, we arrive at the doctrine now called "substantivalism": that space-time points are genuine objects, indeed are the basic objects of physical theory.

The world-picture that is referred to here is one in which an event is a point in space–time or the basic elements of space–time are events specified by four real numbers in a coordinate system. The union of all points in space–time is a manifold and the intervals between the points are measured in units of distance. (We shall return to the journey from the relationism of special relativity to substantivalism of general relativity in §10.3.3.)

40. There are problems with this view, the most obvious being that, if space had to be built up of spatial points, and time of temporal points, or space–time of spatio-temporal points, then space would be unextended and time durationless. Slightly less vulnerable is the idea that the spatio-temporal manifold is a set of point-sized locations in space and time at which something could happen or be located.

  Even this is not acceptable to some. There is a significant "pointless" literature. Frank Arntzenius has argued in "Is Quantum Mechanics Pointless?" that in quantum field theory there are no operators defined at points in space–time, because of quantum smearing. Tim Maudlin has argued for a conception of geometrical space based on lines in "Time, Topology and Physical Geometry". A more fundamental assault on points comes from those who believe that geometry may be built without points, a view particularly associated with various Polish mathematicians and logicians, beginning with Alfred Tarski – see for example Gerla & Volpe, "Geometry without Points", which is for the most part above this reader's pay grade.

In Ladyman & Ross, *Every Thing Must Go*, Ladyman asserts that "space–time points are 'pseudo-scientific' and unknown to science" (14). There is an excellent discussion of the issue in Ladyman, "Structural Realism", §4.3. Ladyman here cites Carl Hoefer who argues that the problems for the idea that space–time is substantival as opposed to merely relational arises from "the ascription of primitive identity to space–time points". His view of space–time is neither substantivalist nor relationist in the conventional sense (see §10.3).

41. This is not to deny that there are real items that have a spatial location while not occupying, in the sense of taking up, and denying other items access to, space. Consider itches which do not stop anything else occupying the place we assign to them on our skin. While there is a sense in which it is true to say that the itch, the redness, and the pimple are in the same place – we could point to all three by pointing at any one of them, and scratch the itch, touch the redness and palpate the pimple with same finger – they do not occupy the place in the same way and they compete only with their own kind. The itch forbids another itch at the same place, the redness excludes another colour at that point, and a pimple will not allow room for another pimple in the place it occupies.

The case of shadows is apparently more difficult. They are clearly located in space and yet, being two-dimensional, do not occupy space. They do, however, mingle in the sense of adding up. One shadow overlaid with another makes for a darker shadow. Shadows, however, are clearly examples of items that borrow space: their location is stipulated by the objects casting them.

The relevance of this apparent digression is that spatial points – as examples of items that exist, and seem to exist, at a particular place, and yet occupy no space – are cousins of items such as (token) thoughts that are not (extended) things and yet are nothing, either. Is it possible that the projection into the physical world of entities that can be accessed only by thought (mathematical objects) is a reflection of our sense of our own nature as sentient, thinking creatures? The (visible) point is "endotted" just as the visible me is "embodied". We could speculate, not entirely wisely, that the point is a metaphor for the intermediate state of the "I" that is existentially here and yet is not physically located in the space corresponding to "here".

42. It is difficult to escape roundness when thinking of the fundamental constituents of space and time. There is something ontologically basic about a sphere, as the views of the Presocratic philosophers (notably Parmenides and the Atomists who responded to him), illustrate.

43. It is particularly handy that the numbers in question are "real numbers" that signal their exactitude by having infinitely many decimal places. (They include of course the integers where all the places after the decimal point are occupied by zeros.) They are as fine-grained as a space made of points. Space is seen as an ordered collection of points that can be put into one-to-one correlation with the system of real numbers.

44. Quoted in Rosar, "The Dimensionality of Visual Space", 14. We think of a dimension as the support for quantity of extension and direction of change. Of course the fact that space has three dimensions and the semi-circular canals regulating balance are also three is not perhaps a coincidence!

45. Notwithstanding the idea that general relativity, by liberating the description of states of motion and at rest from specific coordinate systems, seemed to reach out to reality. This is expressed with exceptional clarity by Dainton in a passage discussed later in this chapter:

> Using the tensor apparatus to represent the properties of space has a useful feature: the quantities this represented (if not the actual numbers employed) are independent of the system of coordinates used to refer to points in space. Coordinate independence (or "covariance") is a criterion of a quantity being physically real as opposed to an artefact of a particular mode of representation. The mass of a truck does not depend on whether it is measured in pounds or kilograms, and just as pounds and kilograms are interconvertible, so, too, are the tensor representations of geometrical quantities based on different systems of spatial coordinates. It was this property that led Einstein to seek out the tensor apparatus when formulating the general theory of relativity.
>
> (Dainton, *Time and Space*, 225)

However, the fact that the quantity is real in the sense of being invariant across frames of reference does not fasten it to a place. On the contrary, it liberates it from any actual place. It corresponds to an observation from no viewpoint.

46. What is more, creating volumes out of points, lines and surfaces requires the supplement of angles, so that spaces can be enclosed. Points do not have the wherewithal to establish the difference between extension and direction, because they have neither of these characteristics in themselves. They do not, therefore, have the means to close off, or to enclose, spaces.

47. There is another interesting side-light on the ambivalent relationship between mathematical entities and locations in the notion of parallel lines meeting at infinity, which is taken to be "the limit". If this really means something different from "parallel lines don't meet", then we have to think of "infinity" as a meeting place. It is a purely conceptual location: it does not, for example, have more than one realization to house the points of convergence of pairs of parallel lines that point in different directions – a pair that points up and down as opposed to a pair that points left and right.

48. Newton-Smith, *The Structure of Time*, 118. We could argue that the notion of the point corresponds to an ideal precision of measurement.

49. Prior, *Papers on Time and Tense*, 122–3.

50. Once we have separated spatial points from time, they are eternal; just as temporal points, if separable from space, would not have a spatial location.

51. An obvious consequence of this is that no finite collection of points could add up to an interval; but the more interesting one is that all infinite collections of points would add up to the same interval – as we shall discuss in §3.5.1 on Zeno's paradoxes of motion.

52. This examination of points should arm us against too-ready acceptance of the claim that the universe was unpacked from a "singularity", a dimensionless point of infinite pressure, density and curvature that appears instantaneously from nothing and immediately expands (though it has no space to expand into). This primordial point – which, given that it has no extension and yet has substance, is mathematically obliged to have infinite density – has an even more tenuous existence because there is nothing outside of it to give it location: it has nothing to parasitize.

53. Maudlin, "Time, Topology and Physical Geometry".

54. *Ibid.*; Maudlin gives lines priority.

55. The relationship between the notions of straightness and that of a line are wittily explored by Quine in his beautiful essay "Lines" in *Quiddities*.

56. See Mandelbrot, "How Long is the Coast of Britain?" For an excellent discussion, which places this paper in an appropriately wide context, see Gleick, *Chaos*, 94–6.

57. Dummett put it this way: "We can never, by measurement, identify any specific real number as giving the magnitude of the quantity [of anything] in terms of the assigned unit" (Dummett, "Is Time a Continuum of Instants?", 497).

58. Gleick, *Chaos*, 96.

59. See Smolin, *Time Reborn*, 7.

60. One consequence of this is to make physics more paradoxical than it need be. The confusion between measurements of, say, the length of the object and some putative intrinsic size generates the baffling suggestion that objects contract as they speed up. Analogously, the reduction of time to a length that is reported as clock-time generates the paradoxes of the twins that we shall discuss in §3.5.3.2. The conventional wisdom in physics that the length of a (rigid) object is dependent on its velocity relative to the frame of reference from which it is being observed merely places the final nail in the coffin in the idea that length is intrinsic to the object. There is only measured length, the outcome of a particular kind of interaction between the object, another designated to be a measuring rod, and an observer.

61. The nature of units, and their centrality to science, is a huge theme. For the present, this succinct remark from Max Born will have to suffice: "The foundation of every space and time measurement is laid by fixing the unit ... Thus we are always dealing with ratios, relative data concerning units which are themselves to a high degree arbitrary and are chosen for reason of their being easily reproduced, easily transported, durable and so forth" (Born, *Einstein's Theory of Relativity*, 1–2).

62. This is set out in his book *Space and Geometry in the Light of Physiological, Psychology and Physical Inquiry*.

63. As Leszek Kolakowski put it in *Positivist Philosophy*, 147, for Mach "there is no difference between ordinary experience accessible to any being endowed with a nervous system and scientifically organized experiment. There is no break in the continuity between science and spontaneous everyday behaviour."

64. Presented recently and accessibly (and thus vulnerably) in Krauss, *A Universe from Nothing*.
65. See "On Aristotle's Physics" in Cohen *et al.*, *Readings in Ancient Greek Philosophy*.
66. Cave, "With and Without End".
67. *Ibid.*, 117.
68. *Ibid.*, 119.
69. There have been attempts to deal with this difficulty (first articulated by the great nineteenth-century French mathematician Augustin-Louis Cauchy) by arguing, as Adolf Grünbaum does, that a line is an uncountable infinity of points plus a finite "distance function" which specifies how far apart the points are (see Huggett, "Zeno's Paradoxes"). This seems to be an ad hoc solution and one that bypasses rather than addresses Zeno's paradox. It is another expression of the tendency to mislocate the problem as an internal difficulty of mathematics rather than a misreading of the relationship between mathematics and the world.
70. Henri Bergson has made a similar point:

> [The arguments of Zeno] all confuse movement with the space covered or at least the conviction that one can treat [step-by-step] movement as one treats space, divide it without taking account of its articulations ... My course is a series of ... steps. You can distinguish its parts by the number of steps it involves. But you have not the right to disarticulate it according to another law or to suppose it articulated in another way. Movement, unlike space, is not indefinitely divisible. And space is indefinitely divisible when it is articulated according to empty number.   (*The Creative Mind*, 120)

71. *Ibid.*, 122.
72. *Ibid.*, 110.
73. Dantzig, *Number*, 176. We need, however, to be cautious over simple contrasts. Kant associated arithmetic with time and geometry with space. However, numbers can be "lined up" in space and the passage along a geometrical line can take time. As long ago as the early Pythagoreans, there was the theory of "figured numbers" in which geometrical figures were represented by counting stones (Kirk & Raven, *The Presocratic Philosophers*, 313–17). And W. Burkert (translated in *Lore and Science in Ancient Pythagoreanism*) referred to the origin of the identification of a unit with a point, of two with a line, of three with a plane, and of four with a solid pyramid from an early interpretation of Plato's *Timaeus*.
74. Unger & Smolin, *The Singular Universe and the Reality of Time*, 216.
75. In "The Perception of Change", lecture 2 (in *The Creative Mind*) Bergson argues that Zeno's paradoxes arise out of confusing indivisible movement with the space traversed by completed movement, adding that movement is continuous while "only in space is there a clear-cut distinction of parts external to one another". This is not quite right. The confusion is between continuous movement on the one hand and on the other a line purporting to represent that totality of the movement – with the beginning and end present simultaneously – that is open to endless division because it consists ultimately of points. For Bergson, the division between discontinuities and continuity is the difference between the intellect, which breaks up the unfolding of the world into frozen moments, and intuition that feels them from within as smooth and unbroken. He argues that "real time is duration without succession". As for space, it is arguably as continuous as time.
76. If we move at a constant velocity of 2 mph, the instantaneous velocity will be 2 mph. In reality, velocity will always vary, howsoever slightly, from moment to moment even when it is thought to be uniform. The more closely you look at it the more change you will see. And the shorter period of time over which it is observed, the more uniform the velocity because of the limits on the rate of acceleration or deceleration. We could imagine a velocity that is sustained roughly over an hour could be sustained more precisely over a minute, even more steadily over a second, even more over a millisecond, even more over a nanosecond. (There is less time to change velocity even in the case of accelerated motion.) So we are licensed to imagine an "instantaneous" velocity that is absolutely constant over a moment.

    The calculus was developed to deal with continuously changing variables – including velocity – where velocity over time is an average of velocities that are different however small the periods of time that are considered. The German mathematician Karl Weierstrass explained the effectiveness of the calculus (and its ability to deal with the problem of zero distances over zero time) by introducing the concept of the "limit" and arguing that what was being calculated was the value of dx/dt as d gets closer and closer to zero without actually reaching it.

77. As we shall discuss in Chapter 12, actions are not rooted in mathematical, punctate or even linear, time but in tensed time. The flying bus-chaser is not (entirely) *in* the moment she is *at*.

78. David Mermin denies that he said it and ascribes it to Richard Feynman in "Could Feynman Have Said This?", 10.

79. Anyone who thinks his/her intuitions are a safe guide to the laws of nature or physical reality should read Lewis Wolpert's *The Unnatural Nature of Science* and be chastened by seeing how science has advanced by disrespecting fundamental intuitions about the world around us.

80. Whitehead, *The Concept of Nature*, 2.

81. When we refer to the distance between two points, we implicitly mean the *shortest* distance and this must mean a distance without deviation. "Deviation" is defined with respect to the line connecting the two points. Where there is deviation from the line, the line connects more than the Euclidean ration of two points. This does not merely extend to the distance but, it is implied, adds something that does not belong to the *real* distance. Frequently, the shortest *feasible* distance is not the shortest distance. However, this is irrelevant to the fundamental notion of distance, which refers to the shortest possible journey by any item – a person, a crow, or an elementary particle, which does not have to choose a route.

   Unfortunately, tying the notion of real distance between reference points to that of the shortest distance does not restore the privileged status of straight lines. The shortest possible distance, or the shortest metric (invariant over frames of reference and therefore closest to one version of "reality"), may still be a curved line. To make a curved journey a logically mandated shortest route, it is necessary to curve space itself. Then the curvature of the trajectory will be distributed between the item and the space it is going through, so that we have a situation similar to that of a straight line in zero curvature space, where shortest distances are constrained, by definition, to be specified by straight lines.

82. Dainton, *Time and Space*, 225. Ensuring or preserving general covariance by bending space saves not only the phenomena but the many interlocking equations that survive testing against the phenomena. It is as Henri Poincaré would have put it (had he been alive then), a way of making the laws of physics as simple as possible.

83. Plotinus, "Time and Eternity" excerpts from *The Six Enneads*.

84. Quoted in Kurzweil, *How to Create a Mind*, 17.

85. Nagel, *Mind and Cosmos*, 81.

86. Barbour, "The Development of Machian Themes in the Twentieth Century", 83.

87. Mach quoted in Rosar, "The Dimensionality of Visual Space", 7.

88. See, for example, Davies, *The Ghost in the Atom*.

89. Jeans, *The Mysterious Universe*.

90. Frayn, *Copenhagen*, act 2.

91. Hawking & Mlodinow, *The Grand Design*.

92. J. A. Wheeler quoted in Smolin, *Time Reborn*, 293. This is, of course, a truism: a phenomenon is (etymologically) an "appearing" and that presupposes a conscious being to whom the appearance appears. Overlooking this truism, however, is central to the confusions teased out in this chapter.

93. Quoted in Rosar, "The Dimensionality of Visual Space", 25. It seems as though, if observers lose their particular places in the universe, they are uncaged and appear everywhere.

94. Quoted in Canales, *The Physicist and the Philosopher*, 236.

95. Schrödinger, "Mind and Matter", 119.

96. *Ibid.*, 122. This gives rise to a paradox "That all scientific knowledge is based on sense perception [though] the scientific views of natural processes formed in this way lack all sensual qualities and therefore cannot account for the latter. In the picture or model we form we usually forget about them..." (*ibid.*, 163).

97. Nagel, *The View from Nowhere*.

98. Quoted in Canales, *The Physicist and the Philosopher*, 316.

99. Quoted in Holmes, *The Age of Wonder*, 458.

100. The discussion that follows parallels and in places is indebted to chapter 27 of Canales, *The Physicist and the Philosopher*.

101. André Metz, quoted in Canales, *The Physicist and the Philosopher*, 315.
102. Whitrow, *The Natural Philosophy of Time*, 348. Italics added.
103. Russell, *ABC of Relativity*, quoted in Canales, *The Physicist and the Philosopher*, 315.
104. Sokal & Bricmont, *Intellectual Impostures*.
105. See Tallis, introduction to *Why the Mind is Not a Computer*.
106. Al-Khalili, *Paradox*, 122.
107. Even this has been challenged. Putnam says "if we allow all physical systems (even electromagnetic fields, etc.) as 'observers' (as why should we not?) and allow observers to use coordinate systems in which they are not at rest, then there are certainly 'enough observers'" to make the universe a physicist (Putnam, "Time and Physical Geometry", 247). The electromagnetic fields may be clothed in inverted commas but this does not seem to disqualify them from taking a peek at the world around them.
108. Maudlin, *Philosophy of Physics*, 109.
109. Einstein, "Autobiographical Notes", 59.
110. Maudlin, *Philosophy of Physics*, 106.
111. Dowden, "Time".
112. Savitt, "Being and Becoming in Modern Physics". There is a telling quotation from philosopher/physicist Howard Stein in the same article: "in Einstein–Minkowski space–time *an event's present is constituted by itself alone*". Stein argues this in order to fold his definitions of temporal concepts into the intrinsic geometric structure of space–time. The observer appears to be entirely superfluous to requirement.
113. Wikipedia, "Observer (Special Relativity)", https://en.wikipedia.org/wiki/Observer_(special_relativity).
114. Particularly a world from which phenomenal experiences have been drained.
115. Maudlin, *Philosophy of Physics*, 95.
116. This criticism does not depend on mistaking a coordinate system for a conscious field bounded by a sensory horizon. Rather, it underlines that there should be something corresponding to an observer for reference frames to be established.
117. Further problems arise if we try to think clearly about the brain's role in establishing points of view from which coordinates arise. In virtue of what does a material object come to locate itself at the origin or centre, the 0, 0, 0 of coordinatized space? The brain would have to transcend frameworks in order to specify the one in which it is located. For a physical object, privileging itself in this way is quite an achievement.
118. Arthur Eddington, quoted in Slowik, "The Fate of Mathematical Place", 24.
119. This is especially true of Big Science. The information acquired in CERN or from the FIDO space probe is delivered many years after the relevant experiments were planned. Many of the early participants in the project will be retired or dead.
120. Smart, "Spatialising Time", 163–8. A similar point was made by Quine (*Quiddities*, 197):

    When time is thus viewed [as one of four dimensions]… change is not thereby repudiated in favour of an eternal static reality, as some have supposed. Change is still there, with all its fresh surprises. It is merely incorporated. To speak of a body as changing is to say that its later stages differ from its earlier stages, just as its upper parts differ from its lower parts. Its later shape need be no more readily inferred from its earlier shape than its upper shape from its lower.

121. Or, more generally, the whole of which a change is part does not itself change.
122. Weyl, *The Philosophy of Mathematics and Natural Science*, 116.
123. Smolin, *Time Reborn*, 237.
124. However, as Unger & Smolin have pointed out: "the relation of general relativity to the idea of preferred cosmic time is more complicated and ambiguous than it may at first appear and cannot be described as a simple and insuperable contradiction" (*The Singular Universe and the Reality of Time*, 183). Among their reasons for saying this is that preferred cosmic time is implicit in the idea that the universe has a certain age, itself connected with the notion – derived from the general relativity – of the Big Bang taking place at a particular "ago". We shall return to this in Chapter 10.
125. *Ibid.*, 248 (italics added); just as simultaneity is necessary to identify the time of an event. As Einstein said in his 1905 paper, "When I say, for example, 'The train arrives here at 7', that means that the

passage of the little hand of my watch at the place marked 7 and the arrival of the train are simultaneous events"(quoted in Bernstein, *Einstein*, 55). The key – but overlooked – word is "at" – which we shall discuss in Chapter 4.

126. Lucas, "A Century of Time", 15.

127. We shall discuss this in Chapter 11, especially §11.3.1, "The Irruption of Viewpoint".

128. Halvorson, "The Measure of All Things", 139. The discussion that follows has been guided by Halvorson's beautiful exposition.

129. See for example Krips, "Measurement in Quantum Theory".

130. Halvorson, "The Measure of All Things", 147.

131. Quoted by Halvorson in an earlier version of his paper.

132. The many worlds interpretation amounts to what leading astrophysicist Paul Steinhardt (*Edge*, 13 January 2016) has cuttingly described as "A Theory of Anything" and such a theory is "*useless* because it does not rule out any possibility and *worthless* because it submits to no do-or-die tests". Such theories, he argues, should be retired. Unger & Smolin, *The Singular Universe and the Reality of Time*, 120, talk about "the massive underdetermination of reality by theory in some of the variants of particle physics now commanding the greatest respect". George Ellis and Joe Silk have argued in leading science journal *Nature* that they undermine the credibility of physics (Ellis & Silk, "Defend the Integrity of Physics"). Certainly, the idea that every one of the 10^{500} mathematically possible versions of string theory (a figure that exceeds the number of particles in our universe by 400 orders of magnitude) corresponds to a universe that actually exists would suggest to the unprejudiced mind that something had gone wrong. The criticism that the multi-universe is untestable has been challenged by the claim that the so-called WMAP (Wilkinson Microwave Anisotropy Probe) cold spot was empirical evidence for a parallel universe but this in turn has been refuted as the cold spot was found to be a statistical artefact.

133. Chalmers, "State of Mind", 34. QBism was invented by Christopher Fuchs and Rudiger Schack. There are two very accessible accounts by David Mermin: "Physics: QBism Puts the Scientist Back into Science" and "Why QBism is Not the Copenhagen Interpretation and What John Bell Might Have Thought of It".

134. See Tallis, *Aping Mankind* for a critique of the neural theory of mind and Tallis, *The Knowing Animal* for a more specific critique of the naturalization of knowledge.

135. The acknowledgement that the observer is not, after all, entirely part of the observed (physical) world is expressed by John Earman as follows: the default position is that "genuine changes in physical magnitude" – the basis of any quantitative change – "are not to be found in the world itself but only in a representation", which Earman accepts that many will view as "patently absurd". If there are no changes in the world while there are in representations of the world, the latter must be separate from the world, housed, presumably in observers who host representations (Earman, "Thoroughly Modern McTaggart", 14). Earman also gives a telling quote from Einstein: "the results of our measurings are nothing but the verifications of such meetings of material points of our measuring instruments with other material points, coincidences between the hands of a clock and points on the clock dial, and observed point-happenings at the same place and the same time" (*ibid.*, 12).

136. It is striking how varied and bitterly contested are the interpretations of the twin paradox. According to Peter Pesic ("Einstein and the Twin Paradox") even Einstein was uncertain of the exact place where it connected with relativity. Though it was alluded to in his 1905 paper, Einstein subsequently wobbled between (a) seeing the paradox as being explained by the relativity of simultaneity (that follows from special relativity) and (b) seeing it as the consequence of time dilation in accelerated frames of reference (and so linked to general relativity via the equivalence principle in which inertial and gravitational forces are identical). Those of us who have acquired frontal corrugations as a result of trying to think through the paradox may be comforted to know that it has tripped up some rather eminent names – at least if one accepts the authority of those who disagree with them. The most eminent scalp is that of none other than Richard Feynman. Maudlin quotes a long passage from Feynman explaining the paradox. He then adds: "Everything about this 'explanation' is wrong" (Maudlin, *Philosophy of Physics*, 81). It also gives comfort to anyone who feels that all explanations are going ultimately to be unsatisfactory because the metaphysical conclusions drawn from the thought experiment are specious.

137. I have recently discovered that some of the arguments in this section overlap with points made by Bergson in his dispute with Einstein. See Canales, *The Physicist and the Philosopher*; *passim*.

138. Greene, *The Elegant Universe*, 28 (italics added).
139. Savitt, "Time in the Special Theory of Relativity", 554.
140. Smeenk & Wutrich, "Time Travel and Time Machines", 577.
141. *Ibid.*, 578.
142. What follows ignores the problems discussed in note 116 for Chapter 2 above.
143. The calculations are set out in Davies, *About Time*, 55–67. There are countless expositions of the twin paradox, but Davies's account is particularly user-friendly for the non-physicist.
144. Davies discusses the compelling example of muons – which have a life expectancy of microseconds – and yet somehow manage to complete a journey from the upper atmosphere, where they are formed, to the earth, where they can be detected. That they can reach earth intact is possible not because they travel at greater than the speed of light but because, as they move at speeds close to that of light, time is stretched out by up to a thousand times. Their microsecond life is sufficient for them to get to earth because the microseconds last longer.
145. Davies, *ibid.*, 60. And it is important to appreciate that, as Davies reminds us, the twins will have travelled different relative distances. For the travelling twin, the distance of the star from earth will be 60 per cent of the distance as it will be for the earthbound twin. The distance will have shrunk by the same proportion as that by which time has expanded.
146. I am not making the dualist suggestion that the twins are (say) spirits inside their bodies. My claim is that they are not identical with their bodies in the way that the spaceship is identical with the material of the spaceship. The extraordinarily complex relationship between ourselves and our bodies – such that we are *embodied* subjects – is not matched in the non-conscious material world. A pebble is not *em*pebbled in the way that Raymond Tallis is *em*bodied. For an extensive discussion of this see Tallis, "Reports from Embodiment" in *I Am*.
147. Greene, *The Elegant Universe*, 41.
148. *Ibid.*, 42.
149. "Older" with reference to matter relates to material states, but in our case it has to be underpinned by the notion of having had more experience as well as being closer to the end of one's life in the sense of an increased possibility of death – in other words, it depends on a trajectory linking a beginning with an end – on a story (the fundamental story we shall argue in Chapter 10) that gives time a sense of direction. Interestingly, Greene (*ibid.*, 45) matches the duration or reach of the *memory* of space travellers to the time on their clock.
150. Savitt, "Time in the Special Theory of Relativity", 551 (italics added).
151. Einstein, "Autobiographical Notes", 59.
152. A position that is argued painstakingly in the *Six Enneads* (trans. Stephen McKenna), 7-13.
153. And "observables" become rather complex in fundamental physics. According to John Earman ("Thoroughly Modern McTaggart", 136), "Two different senses of the crucial notion of 'observable' have been put into play – that of Dirac (i.e. real valued functions of phase space variables that are constant along Dirac gauge orbits) and that of Bergmann (diffeomorphically invariant space–time quantities)." This is a long way from looking out of the window or even consulting a clock.
154. Plotinus, 13.
155. Hermann Bondi quoted in Lasky, "Time and the Twin Paradox".
156. Wells, *The Time Machine*, 7.
157. Weyl, *The Philosophy of Mathematics and Natural Science*, 122.
158. If the observer were identified with a coordinate frame of reference, there would be two problems in determining her extensity. If she were identical with an entire frame of reference, then she would be boundless, as the space indicated by the axes is open. If she were identified with e.g. 0, 0, 0 – the origin of the space – she would be unextended, sharp-edged, in the way that numbers are but observers cannot be.
159. Lucretius, *De Rerum Natura*, book III, 187. Also book V, 362.
160. Kolakowski, *Positivist Philosophy*, 147. This was connected with Mach's biologistic beliefs about the purpose of knowledge (promoting survival) and a consequent naturalistic account of the nature of knowledge.
161. Mach's "naturalization" of knowledge, which has been embraced by many subsequent philosophers, notably Quine, is discussed and criticized in Tallis, *The Knowing Animal*.
162. Whitrow, *The Natural Philosophy of Time*, 114.

163. Rovelli, "Forget Time", an essay written for the FQXi competition on the nature of time.
164. *Ibid.*, 1. Rovelli, however, puts forward a more complex position in "Analysis of the Distinct Meanings of the Notions of 'Time' in Different Physical Theories". Here, he identifies ten levels of increasing complexity of the notion of time – starting with the most complex (expectation versus memory, sense of the present, and directionality) and ending, via time as a pure parameter (as in coordinate time), with no time. Different physical theories retain notions of time with different levels of complexity. For example, he claims, thermodynamics has directionality in time which Newtonian mechanics lacks; while the time represented in classical general relativity is vulnerable in quantum theory because fluctuations of physical clocks and quantum superpositions of different metric structures "make the very notion of time fuzzy at the Planck scale" and time may be entirely absent in certain formulations of quantum gravity. His essential point is that "a single, pure and sacred notion of 'Time' does not exists in physics".
165. Halvorson, "Does Quantum Theory Kill Time?".
166. See Barbour, *The End of Time* for an account of a timeless world based on the Wheeler–DeWitt equation which generalizes quantum mechanics to the whole universe.
167. Moreva *et al*, "Time from Quantum Entanglement".
168. Kuchar, "The Problem of Time in Quantum Geometrodynamics", 169.
169. Lucas, "A Century of Time", 10. And he concludes, in the light of this, that "we no longer feel obliged to construe time in a non-temporal way in order to be truly scientific and philosophically respectable" (*ibid.*).
170. Maudlin argues that quantum mechanics cannot rescue tense lost by relativity because "the tenser merely trades one conflict with fundamental physics for another" as it gives a conflicting account of the order of some events. See Zimmerman, "Presentism and the Space–time Manifold", 236.
171. Penrose & Percival, "The Direction of Time".
172. Hilgevoord & Atkinson, "Time in a Quantum World".
173. *Ibid.*, 664.
174. *Ibid.*
175. *Ibid.*, 668.
176. *Ibid.*, 677.
177. Minkowski, "Space and Time", 37.
178. Albert Einstein, letter to Michele Besso's widow, quoted in Isaacson, *Einstein: His Life and Universe*, 540.
179. Popper, "Why I Reject Metaphysical Determinism", in *The Open Universe*, 90. It would be surprising, however, if Parmenides – who denied the existence of space – would have approved of Einstein's topology of space.
180. Price, *Time's Arrow and Archimedes' Point*, 12.
181. Earman, "Thoroughly Modern McTaggart", 24.
182. *Ibid.*, 17.
183. *Ibid.*, 14.
184. This trend is discussed in Tallis, *The Enduring Significance of Parmenides*. This is connected with Parmenides' privileging thought over the deliverance of the senses. We shall discuss this in an addendum to this chapter on "Intelligibility and Reality".
185. Smolin, *Time Reborn* and Unger & Smolin, *The Singular Universe and the Reality of Time* are the most important. While I, of course, agree with Smolin's defence of time I disagree with him in two important respects. First, he claims that "Time will turn out to be the only aspect of our everyday experience that *is* fundamental" (*Time Reborn*, xxxi). I believe that space is equally fundamental – and not something that is merely emergent as he argues in some detail. (See his chapter on "The Emergence of Space"). And there is a sense in which the manifest world of everyday experience is no less fundamental than the world as it is revealed to physics. And secondly, I do not support his belief that the physicist's assumption that the laws of nature are unchanging makes them "timeless" not only in the sense of being eternal but "timeless" in that they imply an unchanging universe, or at least, leach time out of the totality of things. If a physics based on unchanging, as opposed to evolving or emerging, laws results in a block universe, it is not because the laws are stable but because they are expressed mathematically and encompass both ends, and the middle, of change.
186. Smolin, *Time Reborn*, 8.

187. Smolin, *The Trouble with Physics*, 257.
188. For an excellent account of Bergson's critique of the scientific treatment of time – and a demolition of the claim by Ilya Prigogine that the science rediscovers time by discovering discovery of irreversible processes – see Szendrei, "Bergson, Prigogine and the Rediscovery of Time". See also Canales, *The Physicist and the Philosopher*, and the addendum to this chapter.
189. Musser, "A Hole at the Heart of Physics", 30.
190. Quoted in Martin, "On the Need for Properties", 221–2. Quine is famously associated with the indispensability argument for the reality of mathematical objects, in particular sets. His argument (discussed and critiqued in Colyvan, "Indispensability Arguments in the Philosophy of Mathematics") is that, if mathematical objects are indispensable in our best theories, then we have to accept their existence. This argument for Platonism with respect to mathematical entities thrives on being unclear about in virtue of what it is that "mathematical objects" earn their indispensability. Eternal, independent existence is only one way they might achieve it.
191. Whitehead, *The Concept of Nature*, 20.
192. The reason for this translating into quantitative science may be inadvertently revealed by Philolaus, the Pythagorean, who argued that "Everything that can be known has a number, for it is impossible to grasp anything with the mind or to recognise without this." See Addendum 2 to this chapter.
193. Aristotle, *Metaphysics*. Leonid Zhmud has advanced a powerful case – based on a close reading of the patchy and often indirect textual evidence – for doubting that the early Pythagoreans really did embrace the doctrine that "all is number" and for exempting Pythagoras himself from the charge of Pythagoreanism! He points out that they had nothing to say about number being the substance of the world. He argues that "it was not Pythagoreans who were responsible for [the doctrine of number as the essence of all things], and not even Plato. The 'Pythagorean' thesis 'Things are numbers' owes its birth to the disciples of Plato, and in the first place to Aristotle" (Zhmud, "'All is Number?', 279). From what Aristotle says about number, he further argues, "we can attribute to Pythagoras only the idea of similarity and correspondence of some notions with numbers". Zhmud identifies three levels of Pythagoreanism in Aristotle: (a) that things *are* numbers; (b) that things are *like* numbers; and (c) the *elements* of numbers are simultaneously the elements of things.
194. Bryce DeWitt, quoted in Kent, "Against Many-Worlds Interpretations". H. Everett III, the originator of the many worlds interpretation, was clearly a mathematical realist, arguing that "the graph of a state vector evolution … is a physical quantity" (quoted in Kent, *ibid.*, 10). So something exists twice: once as its happening; and once at the representation of its happening. Two for the price of one.
195. Kent, "Against Many-Worlds Interpretations", 8–9.
196. Ladyman & Ross, *Every Thing Must Go*, 158.
197. Russell, *An Outline of Philosophy*, This anticipates a view we shall discuss presently called "epistemic structural realism" – that all we can know is structure but there is more to the world than structures. There are individuals which are unknowable.
198. Think of the definition of "observables" in some version of quantum mechanics; see note 153.
199. And then there is the awkward matter (noted earlier) that the non-existence of absolute space and absolute time which makes the absolute, invariant speed of light seem a little puzzling. And it is, of course, only in the realm of science that the speed of light can exist independently of light itself.
200. Hamming, "The Unreasonable Effectiveness of Mathematics", 80.
201. Alexander Polyhistor, quoted and translated by F. M. Cornford, *Plato and Parmenides*, 3.
202. A thesis that is set out in detail in Tegmark, *Our Mathematical Universe*. A briefer account is available in the Wikipedia article "Mathematical Universe Hypothesis" and in Tegmark's "The Mathematical Universe".
203. Tegmark, *Our Mathematical Universe*, 279.
204. *Ibid*. It may seem unnecessary to state that no aspect of reality could be just an abstract point any more than David Hilbert is (or was) a set of points in Hilbert space. The discussion of points in §3.4.1 should I hope have made this clear. However, the reduction of light to numbers does deal with the embarrassing difficulty of assigning a definite speed to light. There is also the problem, of course, of separating space from time, to make one a numerator and the other a denominator, when there is only space–time. All of this raises questions about the seemingly metaphysically privileged status of light energy in the world picture of relativity.

205. *Ibid.*, 6. We are, it seems, numbers that blush. Even more absurdly, Tegmark claims that "all structures that exist mathematically exist physically as well" (321). The "as well" is difficult to explain if everything that there is is mathematical – that there is nothing in addition to mathematics.

206. We are "self-aware parts of a giant mathematical object", (*ibid.*, 6). The mathematical monism is somewhat spoiled by the fact that – as Wittgenstein pointed out – "Mathematics is a MOTLEY" (the English word and the capitals are Wittgenstein's own; quoted in Hacking, "What Mathematics Has Done to Some and Only Some Philosophers", 26). The Platonic heaven where mathematical objects are stored looks rather like a loft where things are piled up. Or, as Rovelli has said, mathematics "contains a lot of stuff", and "the traditional areas of classical mathematics geometry, arithmetic ... and algebra" are highly contingent (Rovelli, "Michelangelo's Stone", 1). What is more, mathematics at any point in the history of the subject, must be incomplete. So "the ensemble of all theorems that follow from all (non-contradictory) choice of axioms" – one definition of the platonic world of maths – will not only be extremely big but will "contain too much junk", or at any rate a good deal of material that is not in the slightest bit interesting. Rovelli concludes from this that "the claimed universality of mathematics is a parochial prejudice"; in short, "Which tiny piece of [mathematics] turns out to be interesting, which parts turn out to be 'mathematics' is far from obvious and universal. It is largely contingent" (*ibid.*). The idea that the mathematics that we find valuable forms a Platonic world *fully independent from us* is like the idea of an Entity that created the heavens and the earth and happens to resemble my grandfather. (I am grateful to Florindo Pirone for drawing this thought-provoking essay to my attention.)

207. Putnam, quoted by Jim Holt in "A Mathematical Romance", 29. This will not, of course, have been the first time that, as Hacking has put it, "the possibility of mathematical discovery provides an argument for the immortality of the soul" ("What Mathematics Has Done to Some and Only Some Philosophers", 8).

208. Martin, "On the Need for Properties", 228.

209. Tegmark, *Our Mathematical Universe*, 318.

210. It is not entirely unexpected that Tegmark (like many others for whom physical reality is mathematical) gives serious attention to the notion that the universe (and ourselves in it) could be unreal – namely a computer simulation – though he ultimately rejects this (see "Are We Living in a Computer Simulation?" in *Our Mathematical Universe*, 346–50). In a world that lacks substance, being only a mathematical structure, the difference between primary reality and computer simulation, or between particular actuality and general possibility, is lost. A world that is drained of phenomenal content and localities looks very much like a realm woven out of the (logical) abstractions generated by computers.

211. Kuhlmann, "What is Real?".

212. In writing and thinking about this topic I have been greatly assisted by Ladyman's excellent "Structural Realism".

213. Ladyman & Ross, *Every Thing Must Go*.

214. Ontic structural realism itself has several variants, identified by Peter Ainsworth ("What is Ontic Structural Realism?") as follows: (i) OSR 1, in which relations are ontologically primitive and objects and properties are not; (ii) OSR 2, in which objects and relations are ontologically primitive and properties are not; and (iii) OSR 3, in which properties and relations are ontologically primitive but objects are not. Ainsworth argues that OSR 3, but not the other two, are compatible with contemporary physics. Even the elementary particles look like mathematical objects (whose number must remain uncertain) mistaken for little things.

215. Ladyman & Ross, *Every Thing Must Go*.

216. It is not always clear whether (mathematical) structures are after all regarded as fundamental. On page 299 of *Every Thing Must Go*, Ladyman tells us that "structures describe real patterns" which later seems to have been promoted to ontological bedrock. We then have the problem of considering what the patterns are patterns *of*. Uncertainty is compounded by the assertion that "Mathematical structures are used for the *representation* of physical structure, and this kind of representation is ineliminable and irreducible in science" (*ibid.*, 159; italics added). To say of something that it can be represented mathematically is to imply that it is not itself mathematical. It is hardly surprising therefore that Ladyman refuses to engage with the question as to "what makes a structure physical

and not mathematical?". "In our view there is nothing more to be said about this that doesn't amount to empty words" (*ibid.*, 158). I would argue that there is much more to be said about this if the notion that the mathematical is the physical and/or vice versa is to be defended.

217.   The position is even more vulnerable given that gauge theory, according to Maudlin, contradicts the traditional dichotomies between monadic or intrinsic properties and relational ones, or between intrinsic and external relations (see Suaréz, "The Many Metaphysics within Physics").

218.   Ladyman, "Structural Realism", 15.

219.   Thus an extreme manifestation of the distance between daily experience, with its own ontology, and the most fundamental scientific account of what there is.

220.   This is a serious problem for an ontic structural realism rooted in quantum mechanics. Trying to make the desert of the mathematics of the ultra-small bloom into the objects of everyday life and to generate the variety of the manifest image of the world is an impossible task. The appeal to "emergence" is an attempt to explain something that has been made inexplicable; of explaining how, if Xs boil down to Ys, Ys boil up to Xs.

Equally forlorn is the invocation of "scale-relative ontology" – as when Ladyman asserts that "thinghood is scale-relative" or that "claims about what (really, mind-independently) exists should be relativized to (real, mind-independent) scales at which nature is measurable". It is a kind of magic thinking to imagine that scales (and observers) are built into the very fabric of the material world – that they are constitutive or monadic. If they were, then there would be a chaos of competing scales fighting it out in any piece of stuff. "Scale-relative" implies mode-of-measurement-relative and measurement presupposes a measurer or an observer: it cannot be mind-independent. The observer will, of course, be an embodied subject who necessarily has macroscopic thinghood, whatever scale he/she adopts in her measurements. This undermines Ladyman's claim that the ultimate reality is quantum reality.

Ladyman is not alone in this view or the explanation of how it is squared with the reality of everyday experience. Corey S. Powell in an article in *The Guardian* – "Is the Universe Smooth or Chunky?" – asserted that "For most of today's theorists, belief in the primacy of quantum mechanics runs deeper still. At a philosophical – epistemological – level they regard the large scale reality of classical physics as a kind of illusion, an approximation that emerges from the more 'true' aspect of the quantum world operating at an extremely small scale" (31). The absurdity of this position becomes apparent as soon as one questions how "truth", "aspects", "scales" and "illusions" could arise in a world that truly exists only at the quantum scale.

There are many other problems with ontic structural realism. Firstly, there are those it has in common with other structural theories. Foremost among these is that it is not clear what structure is preserved from theory to theory. If it is a purely mathematical structure, then it will have no extra-mathematical referent. And, secondly, ontic structural realism seems to be the progeny of two ill-matched parents: a meta-induction from the history of science; and a particular theory belonging to a particular phase in science – quantum field theory.

221.   Ladyman & Ross, *Every Thing Must Go*, 30.

222.   *Ibid.*, 28.

223.   Susan Stebbing was a brilliant champion in the 1930s of philosophy (against those who regarded it as rendered redundant by physics) and of the world against reduction to its representation in physics. In *Philosophy and the Physicists*, she highlighted a contrast. On the one hand there is "the world of physics" – which is the work of scientists and changes in accordance with the discoveries of experimentalists. On the other hand there is the physical world or Nature, which is what physics and other sciences are about. The latter does not change and there is no reason to suppose that *this* is created by physicists.

224.   As we shall discuss in Addendum 2.

225.   Putnam, *Philosophy in an Age of Science*, 55.

226.   Counting-as-aggregation is a paradigmatic example of the exploitation of a property of the visual field where we can see the many-as-one and the one-as-many, which enables (for example) six individual sheep to be seen as one herd. Counting *abstracts* from that aggregation. (It is no coincidence that "aggregation" originally meant the act of "flocking together", from *grex/gregis*, the Latin noun "flock".) This has a distant echo of the Presocratic definition of number as "a multitude composed of units" (quoted in Zhmud, "All is Number?", 285).

227. Here is another place where I dissent from Bergson. In *Time and Free Will* he argues that we count in space, not in time. When we enumerate, say, a flock of sheep, each new item is juxtaposed with all the previous items that have been counted. Sheep 2 is retained next to Sheep 1 and Sheep 3 next to Sheep 1 and 2 – and so on. Such juxtaposition, such simultaneity, can be located only in space. (I am indebted to Guerlac, *Thinking in Time*, 61–2 for this summary). In fact the "space" into which the sheep are gathered is an arithmetical realm whose elements are neither simultaneous nor successive. When I arrive at the sum total of "12" sheep, the numbers 1 through 12 do not exist side by side; nor do the sheep designated by them.
228. Wigner, "The Unreasonable Effectiveness of Mathematics in the Natural Sciences", 6.
229. Hamming, "The Unreasonable Effectiveness of Mathematics", 82.
230. Notwithstanding the difficulty of mapping staccato on to legato – see §3.5.1.
231. Wigner, "The Unreasonable Effectiveness of Mathematics in the Natural Sciences", 6.
232. Hamming, "The Unreasonable Effectiveness of Mathematics", 83.
233. Wigner, "The Unreasonable Effectiveness of Mathematics in the Natural Sciences", 7.
234. *Ibid.*, 4.
235. That is why the endeavour to give a mathematical account of why there is something rather than nothing is necessarily doomed. Smolin illustrates this with an anecdote about John Wheeler, who "used to write physics equations on the blackboard and say 'Now I'll clap my hands and a universe will spring into existence'" (Smolin, *Time Reborn*, 245). Mathematics, Smolin points out, always comes after nature: "It has no generative power" (*ibid.*, 246).
236. That "one" is an individual who brings light – whose invariant velocity of 186,000 miles per second is the cornerstone of relativity – to a halt as a seeming still patch or an illuminated scene bathed in apparently still brightness. Even where that "one" is endeavouring to become an "anyone" so general, so featureless, as to be indistinguishable from "no-one".
237. Especially since the mathematical "portrait" is featureless.
238. Unger & Smolin, *The Singular Universe and the Reality of Time*, 302.
239. Von Neumann & Goldstine, "Numerical Inverting of Matrices of High Order", 99, quoted in Popper, *The Open Universe*, 42. Popper connects this with his belief that theories are "human inventions – nets designed by us to catch the world".
240. Unger & Smolin, *The Singular Universe and the Reality of Time*, 332. This is another aspect of something suggested by Mark Steiner (quoted in Baker, "Science-Driven Mathematical Explanation", 248) that "if we dig below the surface of a given Mathematical Explanation in Science then we will always be able to find a 'pure' mathematical explanation at its core in which both the explanandum and the explanans are mathematical". This is a position which Baker himself questions.
241. Unger & Smolin, *The Singular Universe and the Reality of Time*, 317.
242. *Ibid.*, 240.
243. Einstein, *Geometry and Experience*, 1.
244. While it is equally necessarily true that 2 + 2 = 4 and 2 sheep + 2 sheep = 4 sheep, the necessity comes from the addition of the numbers not from the sheep. It is contingent that there are sheep and that there are 4 of them in 2 groups of 2.
245. The idea that the laws of nature are entirely mathematical is also fostered by the incorporation of various mathematical operations into many laws – even simple operations into basic laws. For example, the law of gravitational attraction involves multiplying the masses of the mutually attracted objects and inverting and squaring the distance between them.
246. Mill, *A System of Logic*, 328. The underdetermination of physics by empirical data is reflected at a higher level in the underdetermination of metaphysics by physics.
247. Landau, "A Confutation of Convergent Realism", 24.
248. Sklar, *Space, Time and Spacetime*, 1.
249. Hawking & Mlodinow, "The (Elusive) Theory of Everything", 1.
250. *Ibid.*, 92.
251. Hermann Weyl quoted in Smolin, *The Trouble with Physics*, 46.
252. Lectures quoted in Gleick, *Genius*, 436.
253. Feser, "Post-Intentional Depression". Intentionality will be central to the discussion in the final two chapters of the book.
254. Austin, *Sense and Sensibilia*, 62–77.

255. *Essai sur les donnees immediates de la conscience*, 52 [70], quoted in Guerlac, *Thinking in Time*, 57.
256. Bergson, *Time and Free Will*, 101.
257. Canales, *The Physicist and the Philosopher*, 6.
258. Guerlac, *Thinking in Time*.
259. Bergson, *Time and Free Will*, 95–99; Bergson, *Creative Evolution*, 172.
260. Discussed in Tallis, *The Enduring Significance of Parmenides*.
261. Quoted in Ladyman, "Structural Realism", 20.
262. Dainton, *Time and Space*, 225.
263. The German word for object *Gegenstande* is "that which has been brought to a halt".
264. Steven Weinberg quoted by Stuart Kauffman in "Breaking the Galilean Spell", 1.
265. We are, of course, willing to outsource intelligibility in proofs that no-one can grasp as a whole. Computer-generated proofs like that of the solution to the four-colour map problem "are completely beyond the human bounds of perspicuity, surveyability or Cartesian *intuitus*" (Hacking, "What Mathematics Has Done to Some and Only Some Philosophers", 3). We are in short, willing to settle for the mere ghost of intelligibility so long as it has been arrived at by the authorized means.
266. It might be argued that the scientific gaze actually jazzes up the material world, finding for example a secret ebullience even in a pebble whose constituent atoms are still in motion at all temperatures above absolute zero. But those movements are themselves gathered up into unmoving equations.
267. Kant, "Introduction", *Critique of Pure Reason*, 47. The understanding is pure because there is nothing – phenomenal qualities, secondary qualities, time, place, or even thinghood – left for the understand to understand.

CHAPTER 4

1. Yeats, "Under Ben Bulben".
2. Quoted by Robert Wicks, *Modern French Philosophy*, 75. See also my essay "You Chemical Scum, You" in *Reflections of a Metaphysical Flaneur and Other Essays*.
3. To some extent this is true even when our sense of time is "pre-clock"; as when I note that "It is late" or that "It is evening". But the distance between the time I note and the time at which I note it is not so clearly apparent as when time is measured – and particularly when measurements are being checked or challenged. I see *that* it is 4:30 on clock A and I check whether it really *is* 4:30 by consulting clock B.
4. Quoted in Bernstein, *Einstein*, 55.
5. Or as Martin Heidegger put it in his inimitable way, "Everyday, *circumspect* being-in-the-world needs *the possibility of sight*, that is brightness, if it is to take care of things at hand within what is objectively present … Day with its brightness gives it the possibility of sight, night takes it away" (*Being and Time*, 412). Thus astronomical and calendrical time-reckoning is not a matter of chance: "it has its existential and ontological necessity in the fundamental constitution of *Da-sein* as care" (*ibid.*, 412).
6. In the absence of anything at all – most notably conscious creatures – there is neither darkness nor light.
7. This is a heavenly piece of cheek, compounded by retro-engineering our timepieces into the creation itself and talking of a "clockwork universe" – a notion that the philosopher and physicist Georg Christoph Lichtenberg captured in his joking reference to "God, who winds up our sundials". An aphorism whose source I cannot trace.
8. Draggan, *A Walk Through Time*.
9. For a brief, very accessible account of how mechanical clocks generate events of equal periods that drive the indicators on the face at precisely controlled intervals, see Whipple, "Clock Watching".
10. The fact that time has been measured by cyclical events, beginning with solar and sidereal time, may also play into the ancient question of whether time is linear or cyclical and whether time itself ages or is endlessly renewed. The notion of time as cyclical is reinforced by the succession of the phases of the moon from nail pairing to crescent to gibbous to full, from full to gibbous, to crescent to nail paring; of the seasons from spring via summer, autumn and winter back to spring; from growth and increase, to harvest, and die-back and thence to growth and increase. That which is given is taken

away, and this is followed by a new time of gifts. The one-way passage from birth to death of an individual is punctuated by fresh starts represented by the rising generations who bring an endless succession of new beginnings to the world in which the old are fading.

11. This is analogous to language in which individual sounds corresponding to a particular word, count as identical, have the same semantic pay load, irrespective of minor acoustic differences from person to person, from moment to moment.

12. It has been suggested by Smolin that Galileo timed the movement of the pendulum by singing to himself. He claimed, by this means, to be able to measure time to a tenth of a pulse beat (Smolin, *Time Reborn*, 15).

13. As Whipple ("Clock Watching", 25) noted, "Even in the electrical age, the sundial had its place".

14. Poincaré ("The Measure of Time", 222) highlighted the challenge in getting from our direct perception of simultaneity, temporal order, and time intervals to objective measures. Indeed, there are two challenges, as Poincaré pointed out: transforming psychological time, which is qualitative, into quantitative time; and reducing facts which are experienced in different worlds to one and the same measure.

15. This example is highlighted by the eminent physicist and time sceptic Carlo Rovelli in his essay "Forget Time".

16. The relationship between casually observed time and astronomical time is not straightforward. Isaac Barrow, astronomer and contemporary of Newton, put this well: "[S]trictly speaking, the celestial bodies are not the first and original measures of time but rather those motions, which are observed around us by our senses, since we judge the regularity of celestial motion by the help of these" (quoted in Whitrow, *The Nature of Time*, 84).While the passage from explicit, subjectively judged, time to objective time is mediated by the universal, common experience of the cycling of astronomical phenomena, there is an iterative process of checking, confirmation and correlation. What is more, as increasing numbers of us participate in shared activities, for all sorts of different reasons, the scope, depth and density of intersubjective time agreement grows.

17. Rovelli, "Forget Time". This same point has been made by Newton-Smith: "If we need to appeal to a clock to justify that, say, one event lasts as long as another, and if some physical event serves as a clock only if the events it produces are isochronic [that, is of equal duration], how can we ever determine whether that assumption is warranted?" (*The Structure of Time*, 157).

18. Wigner quoted in Chapter 3 see note 106.

19. In "Science and Hypothesis", Poincaré pointed out that the curves we draw connecting points defined by two parameters – say time and acceleration – will always smooth out what has been observed. The curve will go above some points and below others. Curve-fitting is propelled by faith that the relationship between parameters is simple. This faith, which is justified, has enabled scientists to escape the limits of empirical precision.

Poincaré went further and argued that our measures are such as to make the laws of mechanics as simple as possible. The belief that, in this case, *simplex sigillum veri* is not merely a convenient excuse for making things easy for ourselves. The simplest laws will be the ones that encompass the maximum number of observations most economically and will consequently have the greatest predictive power. This clearly does not imply that physical laws are mere constructs; after all they are discovered on the basis of observation and subsequently tested against other observations. But it does throw into doubt a realism claiming that the laws of nature are entirely inherent in nature.

20. Sklar, "Time in Classical Dynamics", 572.

21. *Ibid.*, 574.

22. *Ibid.*, 575.

23. Newton-Smith, *The Structure of Time*, 160.

24. *Ibid.*

25. The story is almost certainly more complex than I have presented it. Yes, the laws of nature presuppose a greater precision of the relationship between observations than any actual or indeed possible observation. But something else is needed to choose between the laws that would be consistent with our observation. Connectedness between laws is one such thing but this relates to something even deeper, as already noted: the demand for simplicity. Laws are replaced either (a) because they prove wrong or (b) because they are subsumed under other laws of greater generality. It is not self-evident, however, that, an ideally successful explanation is one that provides the most economical way of

gathering up the facts of the universe. That simplicity is the mark of truth is an article of faith and it may have led us to overlook irreducible complexity.

26. Hermann Bondi quoted in Lasky, "Time and the Twin Paradox". There is a sense, explored in §3.4.2 in which length is created by the processes by which we measure it. This view, however, seems to be easier to uphold in the case of length than time because length is a single dimension and there are no single dimensions in the spatial world. Whatever exists is at least three-dimensional. Of course, time "in-itself" is problematic if space–time is fundamental and space and time are inseparable.

    In the hinterland of this argument is the notion – "Operationalism" – that all parameters are defined by the processes by which they are measured. Operationalism, however, is unsatisfactory not merely because it is anti-realist about science (and therefore does not justify the choice of operations that constitute measurement) but because all measurements involve movements that are not strictly relevant to the act of measurement. Getting to the laboratory, picking up the ruler when it has been dropped, or just picking up the ruler, and so on do not belong to the measurement. We therefore need a prior definition – or at least an intuition – of the parameter we are measuring that is independent of the operation of measurement.

27. Except in the important (and easily overlooked) sense that any observation stands outside of the space in which the observed event is located. This is clearly true even at the most basic level: vision is not part of the visual field, even though the (embodied) subject and his eye are thus located. If the latter were entirely immersed in that which is revealed by vision, vision would not be from a certain angle, would not be perspectival or vision *of*. This connects closely with the arguments in §3.5.3.

28. Thorndike, "The Nature, Purpose, and Measurement of Educational Products", 16.

29. Davies, *About Time*, 55–8. The habit of referring to naturally occurring periodic events as "clocks" irrespective of whether they are used as such goes deep and is spread wide. A particularly striking example is Louis de Broglie's idea that an electron has an internal clock – recently, it is claimed, experimentally confirmed (see Hestenes, "Electron Time, Mass and Zitter").

30. Any event or state of affairs may or may not be a sign depending on whether it signifies to someone. Clouds are clouds, that's all; they are *signs* of their likely effects – rain – only to an observer. This is the founding idea of semiotics: a sign signifies only in its being interpreted.

31. The reference to the network of laws to underpin the objective validity of time measurement distances horology from a merely coherence theory of the truth and points in the direction of a correspondence theory. It still, however, leaves the relationship between clocks and time incompletely characterized.

32. Carnap, "Intellectual Autobiography", 37.

33. Quoted in Bernstein, *Einstein*, 55.

34. See Chapter 12, especially §12.2.

35. Maudlin, *Philosophy of Physics*, 108.

36. The following passage from Heidegger is highly relevant: "Thus in *measuring time*, time gets *made public* in such a way that it is encountered in each case and at each time for everyone as 'now and now and now'. This time 'universally' accessible in clocks is found as an *objectively present multiplicity of nows* ..." (*Being and Time*, 383).

37. Pindar, "Clocking Off". Pindar has his tongue somewhat in his cheek, in part criticizing the standard story told by E. P. Thompson in his influential 1968 paper "Time, Work-Discipline and Industrial Capitalism".

38. See Glennie & Thrift, *Shaping the Day*. There is an excellent summary of their thesis by Ian Pindar in "Clocking Off".

39. For the ironies arising out of the intersection between time and eternity, see Chapter 9.

40. See Chapter 10, especially §10.5 for the quarrel between subjective and objective time. One of the best surveys of the scientific literature is Hammond, *Time Warped*.

41. This is reinforced by, and in its turn reinforces, the misleading idea of time as something in itself flowing independently of us from an indefinite invisible past to an indefinite invisible future. The moving finger stands for the flow of time that permits the unfolding of events. More pertinent to our present concern, the clock enables us to see round the kind of corners that are unimaginable to the unaided temporal eye.

42. We shall examine the passage – "out of sight and into mind" – from a visibly invisible to an invisible propositional or factual past in Chapter 7.

43. See "You Chemical Scum, You" in Tallis, *Reflections of a Metaphysical Flaneur and Other Essays*.
44. Unger & Smolin, *The Singular Universe*, 140.
45. Plotinus, *The Enneads*.
46. Russell, *An Outline of Philosophy*, 163.
47. Heidegger would not agree with this. He argues in *Being and Time* (§80, "Time Taken Care Of and Within-Timeness") that *Dasein*, being in the world and primordial time is "out there".
48. Quoted in Gale, *The Philosophy of Time*, 62.
49. Lucas, "A Century of Time", 15.

EPILOGUE TO PART I

1. Norton, "Time Really Passes", 30.
2. Hawley, "Metaphysics and Relativity".
3. Maudlin, *The Metaphysics within Physics*, quoted by Richard Healey in *Notre Dame Philosophical Reviews*, 28 February 2004.
4. Wittgenstein, *Philosophical Investigations*, para. 127.
5. Sellars, "Philosophy and the Scientific Image of Man", 35.
6. *Ibid.*, 38.
7. *Ibid.*, 42.
8. William Blake, from a poem inserted into a letter to Thomas Butts, 1802.
9. Sellars, "Philosophy and the Scientific Image of Man", 43.
10. Ladyman, for example, argues that our difficulties in accepting the world picture of quantum mechanics is that "proficiency in inferring the large-scale and small-scale structure of our immediate environment, or any features of parts of the universe distant from our ancestral stomping grounds, was of no relevance to our ancestors' reproductive fitness" (Ladyman & Ross, *Every Thing Must Go*, 2). Ladyman seemingly believes in the intrinsic reality of the kinds of causal or teleological influences unconsciously fixing the scope and limits of consciousness, and of the entities they operate on or within, and their environment, which we see in everyday life, even though they have no place in the reality of quantum physics. In short, Ladyman's meta-epistemological explanation of the difficulty we have in accepting or even conceiving the truth about what is real, actually presupposes the reality of the kind of items – medium-sized, self-identical human beings, who have knowledge derived from negotiating a world made of medium-sized self-identical objects – his ontology says are uneal. This strikes me as self-contradictory.
11. Strawson, "Intellectual Autobiography", 20.
12. Strawson, *Skepticism and Naturalism*, 23.
13. See Dorr, "Review of *Every Thing Must Go*" for an excellent summary of the attack on what Ladyman believes to be the intuition-driven metaphysics of analytical philosophy.
14. Newton-Smith, *The Structure of Time*, 4.
15. Wittgenstein, *Philosophical Investigations*, para 129.
16. Dunbar, "The Passage of Time", unpublished MS.
17. Mermin, "What's Bad About this Habit", 8.
18. Heidegger's definition of human *Dasein*. For further discussion, see Tallis, *A Conversation with Martin Heidegger*.

CHAPTER 5

1. Savitt, "Time in the Special Theory of Relativity", 551. Poincaré arrived at this conclusion before Einstein: "the qualitative problem of simultaneity is reduced to the quantitative problem of time measurement" (quoted in Torretti, "Relativity, Time Reckoning and Time Series", 68).
2. Savitt, "Time in the Special Theory of Relativity", 551.
3. Rovelli, "Analysis of the Distinct Meanings of the Notion of 'Time' in Different Physical Theories".
4. "For Einstein, their youth (just like their old age) and their birth (just like their death) were simply moments ... that they had not been able to see or foresee but that had always been there and that,

in the physical universe, had no particular importance" (Canales, *The Physicist and the Philosopher*, 339).

5. Smolin, "It's Time to Re-write Time", 30.

6. Smolin, *Time Reborn*, xxii.

7. There is another, related, source of the assumption that special relativity must exclude tensed time; something we have touched on already: namely, the way time is depicted. This is well expressed by John Taylor:

> Some of the psychological force of the claim that special relativity is incompatible with the tensed theory of time can be traced to the use of space-time diagrams in the presentation of the theory. We are presented with a picture in which events are spread out along a temporal dimension; the events are "all there at once", it seems. Future, present and past times are all alike; nothing within the picture picks out any moment as "the present", nor does the picture represent any process such as the transition of the (unreal) future into the (real) present and thence to the (fixed) past. On the contrary, the picture we are given of time is "static" and apparently excludes the possibility of this process of dynamic becoming. This picture has become known as the block universe.   (Taylor, "Time and Tense", 121).

8. Weyl, *The Philosophy of Mathematics and Natural Science*, 116.

9. See Hilgevoord & Atkinson, "Time in a Quantum World" (discussed in §3.5.4).

10. See Hartle, "The Physics of 'Now'". It is discussed very accessibly by Chown, "No Time Like the Present". Butterfield, "Seeing the Present", puts forward a similar argument. Living creatures need to believe that what is in fact "not quite now" is happening now. Their efficient sensory systems, particularly vision that has short lag times between events impinging on them and events being understood, combined with the relative stability of the world (with change happening much slower than the speed of light) make this belief good enough for survival purposes. Experiences are true (enough) of the events or states they report.

11. The inconsistency is very similar to that discussed in my critique of Ladyman's claim that "thing-hood" – not allowed by the quantum theory which he sees as capturing the fundamental truth of the universe – is a necessary illusion to ensure survival. See Epilogue Note 10 *supra*.

12. Hartle's argument also presupposes a directionality of time – an absolute before and after.

13. Carnap, "Intellectual Autobiography". Interestingly, Carnap goes on to say that "Einstein's thinking on this point involved a lack of distinction between experience and knowledge"; in other words, that "now" is a matter of experience and would quite properly be filtered out by science which, is a matter of knowledge and "in principle can say all that is to be said"! No comment necessary.

14. That is the force of Bergson's critique of the denial of distant simultaneity. He pointed out that the difference between the permitted simultaneity of events that were near to one another and non-permitted simultaneity of events that were widely separated in space lacked a real basis. There is no place in the space–time manifold for this gradual progression from the one to the other (see Canales, *The Physicist and the Philosopher*, 339). Behind this is the mystery of locality which cannot be accommodated by objective science as the latter is built on observations that require it (see §11.3.1). Without a conscious observer, there is no partitioning of the manifold into that which is distant (enough to cause simultaneity to vanish) and that which is near (enough to make simultaneity close to reality).

15. Zimmerman, "Presentism and the Space–time Manifold", 193. The principle that relativity regarding the order of precedence between events does not apply if they are causally connected is difficult to accommodate in the frozen spatio-temporal manifold, as we shall discuss in Chapter 11. Causation presupposes becoming.

16. William Lane Craig (quoted in Zimmerman, *ibid.*, 232) has suggested that "cosmic time" ("the fundamental frame of the cosmic expansion") "*contingently* coincides with metaphysical time" in which there is an "A-theoretically privileged foliation" – that is to say a temporal cut across the manifold that slices it all the way through corresponding to "now".

17. Bernard d'Espagnat quoted in Davies, *About Time*, 21.

18. Davies, "That Mysterious Flow", 18.

19. General relativity may be less hostile to tensed time, or at least to "now", than special relativity. Saunders (quoted in Zimmerman, "Presentism and the Space–time Manifold", 232) has suggested

that "for an important class of space–time models – *hyperbolically complete* spacetime … – there is a natural definition of global foliation … which is essentially unique". On the other hand, the space–time manifold does not seem terribly hospitable to tense, given that it finds even becoming embarrassing.

20. See Tallis, *The Enduring Significance of Parmenides*.

21. McTaggart, "The Unreality of Time".

22. Moore, "A Defence of Common Sense".

23. The central phenomenological tradition placed time at the very heart of human being. As Heidegger claimed "*Dasein* itself is *time*" (*History of the Concept of Time*, 197). Whether time is *Dasein* is another matter. We shall discuss the question of the priority of human and physical time in §10.5.

24. Some might defend themselves by arguing that time is absent from the quantum world of the very small but present in the cosmic world of the very large. This defence is not available to those (such as Rovelli) who believe that a theory of everything that brings together quantum theory and general relativity would dispense with time (see §3.5.4).

25. Mellor, *Real Time II*. See Grünbaum, *Philosophical Problems of Space and Time*; Le Poidevin, *Change, Cause and Contradiction* and Oaklander, "McTaggart's Paradox and Smith's Tensed Theory of Time" for other defences of detensed time.

26. McTaggart, *The Nature of Existence*, vol. 2, 10.

27. The notion of "truth-maker" is slippery and I shall return to it when we discuss logical fatalism in §8.2.

28. The argument that follows is directly opposed to the assertion by John Taylor that believing that the meeting begins at 12 o'clock is the same as believing at 12 o'clock that the meeting is beginning (Taylor, "Time and Tense", 28). Taylor's thesis is built on a sympathetic critique of Mellor's linguistic reduction of tense. His tense adverb theory holds that "tensed sentences … consist of root present tense sentences, which may be adverbially modified by tensed operators, such as "It was the case that" or "It will be the case that" to form past or future tensed sentences" (*ibid.*, 14). He argues that "tenses play that logical role of adverbs in qualifying root present tense sentences". The assumption that "future and past tensed sentences should be viewed as constructed from root present tense sentences" seems to imply that the present tense can be given a free pass and that, unlike the other two tenses, it is extra-linguistic. For this, and other reasons, the adverbial theory does not offer a satisfactory linguistic reduction of tensed to tenseless time.

29. They seem to belong to an "A+" or a "B-" series. They have the quantitative characteristics of the B-series and the indexicality of the A-series. We could, for example, explain why a wound had not healed because it was recent but not because it was "past". And there are signs of events being "soon" (or imminent) which is (somewhat) more precise than "future".

30. Quentin Smith offers a partial defence of this idea through the notion of "degree presentism": "The degree to which an item exists is proportional to its temporal distance from the present; the present, which has zero temporal distance from the present, has the highest (logically) possible degree of existence" (Smith, "Time and Degrees of Existence", 120). The idea of an event enjoying an increasingly ghostly existence as it recedes into the past is exceeded in questionability by the idea of a future event (that until it actually happens may or may not happen) acquiring increasing ontological muscle as it approaches the time appointed to it. The obvious challenge is to determine that in which the attenuated existence of the antenatal and posthumous event subsists. There is, as Oaklander points out, a blurring of "a subjective experience of the world with an objective characteristic of the world itself" ("Time and Existence", 153).

31. Mellor, *Real Time II*, 52.

32. Oaklander, *The Ontology of Time*, 17.

33. See Tallis, *The Enduring Significance of Parmenides*.

34. Savitt, "Being and Becoming in Modern Physics".

35. Not all philosophers accept this connection. Dainton warns that "we must not assume that the eternal dynamic dispute maps neatly on to the tensed tenseless dispute" (*Time and Space*, 64).

36. Oaklander, *The Ontology of Time*, 102.

37. Russell, "On the Experience of Time", 212.

38. This is the key thesis of Tooley, *Time, Tense and Causation*.

39. As we shall discuss in §11.2.3, Mellor argues that facts are causes; and, indeed, only facts are causes. We shall challenge this.

664 OF TIME AND LAMENTATION

40. See McTaggart, *The Nature of Existence*.

41. Wittgenstein, *Tractatus Logico-Philosophicus*, §1–1.1. The claim that the world is all that *is the case* is already open to challenge. That which is – or its sum the world – is not by itself and without assistance also "the case" or "that which is the case". It becomes "the case" only when it is articulated or in some other way made explicit. This may seem to be a pedantic point but overlooking it has many consequences, most directly a deflationary approach to truth. See Tallis, *The Knowing Animal*.

42. For a more detailed discussion on this, see Chapter 7 of Tallis, *Not Saussure*.

43. In his attack on what he calls the Myth of the Given, see Sellars, "Empiricism and the Philosophy of Mind". This may, in fact, be something Wittgenstein agrees with. In §1.13, he defines the world as "The facts in logical space".

44. It is important to highlight this because the great jump from experiencing something happening to reporting, thinking, asserting *that* it is taking place or did take place can be overlooked, consequently misleading us into thinking on the one hand that facts are states of affairs or occurrences; or on the other that they are purely assertions that happen to be true. The jump marked by *that* is huge and liberates humans uniquely from organic life to a human world made of a network of understanding. For a more detailed discussion see Tallis, *The Knowing Animal* where I discuss "that" and "thatter" and, in this work, Chapters 11 and 12 *passim*.

45. Another way of highlighting the difference between on the one hand events, objects, states of affairs, entities that are on the ground – items that *occur* or *endure* – and on the other facts is to note that the question "How many facts of a certain kind are there in this room?" is unanswerable, whereas "How many cats are there in this room?" can be answered. We shall discuss this in §11.2.3.

46. If we capture a change as a whole by naming it, referring to it by a noun or noun phrase, we remove the dynamic "ongoingness" from it. While the actual Battle of Hastings was a complex sequence of unfolding and interacting events, "The Battle of Hastings", which encompasses its beginning, middle, and end, is frozen. This is rather similar to what happens when we represent a journey by a line: beginning, middle, and end are co-present. The cosmos itself can be brought to a grinding halt by a gaze that encompasses its totality. This is the obverse of the claim made by Smart, to which we have already referred, that the apparently static universe of the general relativity, the space–time manifold, is simply the result of its encompassing the possibility of all events and is unchanging because it cannot be added to. Or, as Price has put it, the block universe "regards reality as a single entity of which time is an ingredient rather than as a changeable entity set in time" (Price, *Time's Arrow and Archimedes' Point*, 12). The embedding of time in the fabric of the material world also undermines the contrast between that which is unchanging and the changes that take place in it; between the enduring object and its ephemeral properties; or (even) between the person and her experiences.

47. *The fact that* I made that statement is also timeless because it will not change from day to day, even though the truth value of the assertion itself will change as time passes.

48. We shall discuss truth-makers in more detail in §8.2.2.4.

49. Prior, "Some Free Thinking about Time". A similar point is made by Saunders ("How Relativity Contradicts Presentism", 2): "*Pace* Mellor and others, it is equally possible to give tensed truth conditions for tenseless sentences as tenseless ones for tensed. Exercises in the philosophy of language do not seem to be settling anything."

50. Oaklander, *The Ontology of Time*, 245.

51. We do, of course, acknowledge differences within the tenses. We talk about "the recent past" and "the distant past", and we refer to "X's past" and "Y's past", where X and Y could be persons, places or things. Even so, the numbering of the calendric past and future does make the differences seem purely quantitative and consequently homogeneous. One day on the calendar is like another.

52. The marginalization of the conscious subject is widespread also in the humanities and even in philosophy – something not unconnected with their ambitions to be scientific. I discuss this in Tallis, *Enemies of Hope*. One chapter, "The Philosophies of Consciousness and the Philosophies of the Concept", describes the vicissitudes of consciousness in twentieth-century Western philosophy. I also discuss this in the critique of anti-psychologism in the Preface to *Why the Mind is Not a Computer*.

53. See Tallis, *I Am: A Philosophical Inquiry into Human Being, passim*.

54. Grünbaum, "The Status of Temporal Becoming", 337 (italics original).

55. Dainton, *Time and Space*, 36.
56. Merleau-Ponty, "The Primacy of Perception and its Philosophical Consequences". The central thesis is that "The perceived world is the always presupposed foundation of all rationality, all value, and all existence" (*ibid.*, 13). He adds that "This thesis does not destroy either rationality or the absolute. It only tries to bring them down to earth." Crucially for our considerations, he argues that "it is perceptual experience which gives us the passage from one moment to the next and thus realizes the unity of time".
57. Mellor, *Real Time II*, 15.
58. Kant, *Critique of Pure Reason*, 47.
59. Merleau-Ponty, *The Phenomenology of Perception*, 411.
60. The key reference here is Meillassoux, *After Finitude*, especially 10–22.
61. This is central to Heidegger's philosophy in *Being and Time*, see especially §69 "The Temporality of Being-in-the-World and the Problem of Transcendence of the World", 321–35. The relative priority of physical and lived time in relation to Heidegger's philosophy is discussed in Tallis, *A Conversation with Martin Heidegger*. It will be addressed in §10.5.
62. See Hammond, *Time Warped* for a comprehensive and entertaining account of the disconnection between objective measures and subjective experiences of time.
63. This is consistent with his claim that: "It is only by tensed statements that we can give the cash value of assertions that purport to be about 'time'" (Prior, *Past, Present and Future*, 198–9).
64. To say on 12 December "It was raining yesterday" does not seem to refer to anything that is more mind-dependent that saying on 12 December "It was raining on 11 December". In neither case is the tensed auxiliary "was" merely mind-dependent, except insofar as mind is required to make the relationship to a past explicit.
65. Nietzsche, "The Use and Abuse of History", 218–19.
66. Lucas, *A Treatise on Time and Space*, 280.
67. Nor should tensed time be compared with secondary qualities. Gale has rejected this notion because secondary qualities are often seen as the effects in the brain of the events that impinge on it:

> So far as I can make out, no defender of the mind-dependency thesis has advanced any-thing which is even remotely analogous to the … causal theory of perception (of secondary qualities). That they have not done so is not the result of laziness or oversight on their part, but rather due to a basic difference between A-determinations [assigning tenses] and secondary qualities which makes it possible to advance an analogous causal theory of the perception of becoming. The crucial difference is that A-determinations are not sensible properties, whereas secondary qualities are.   (Gale, *The Language of Time*, 228).

68. Lucas, "A Century of Time", 11.

CHAPTER 6

1. This is connected with the notion of the present as the one tense that is given free of charge, that comes with the material rations. This is wrong: "Matter" is not "present" because it is not presence. Bergson was surely wrong to say that "the material point, as mechanists understand it, remains in an eternal present" in contrast to the past which is "a reality [only] for conscious human beings" (*Essai sur les données immediate de la conscience*, cited and translated in Guerlac, *Thinking in Time*, 79). His ascription of an intrinsic present tense to material objects is clearly connected with the claim that consciousness is entirely memory. In fact, the material world is tenseless. After all, it is difficult to see how there could be a present tense without past and future to contrast it with.
2. Poincaré, "The Measure of Time".
3. Locke, *An Essay Concerning Human Understanding*, vol. 1, ch. XV, §11.
4. This veto need not be accepted of course. Einstein's key idea in special relativity that distance simul-taneity is defined by optical simultaneity (light signalling being the fastest mode of communication across space) is based upon Mach's verificationist principle that reality is limited to that which it is possible to observe (i.e. measure). This principle cannot itself be derived from experience. So the possibility arises that simultaneity may be something deeper than the observer-relative concept of standard physical theory. It might be something real in itself.

5. James, *The Principles of Psychology*, 609. He added that: "The practically cognized present is no knife-edge, but a saddle-back, with a certain breadth of its own, on which we sit perched, and from which we look in two directions into time".

6. This seems to be recognized by David Gamez in *What We Can Never Know* when he says that "The *now* ... is an instantaneous moment outside of time; an eternal moment without temporal extension" (105). Given that now is an instant which is outside of time, he has to reconnect time with now and does this by asserting that "Time is the relationship between the nows, the *becoming* of now, the bringing of a new now into existence".

7. Gödel quoted in Yourgrau, *The Disappearance of Time*, 164.

8. For an excellent discussion, see Dainton, "Time, Passage and Immediate Experience".

9. Ismael, "Temporal Experience", 462.

10. Brilliantly summarized in Spinney, "Once upon a Time".

11. A mathematical instant could not deliver a spatially extended experience or an experience referred to a location in space. Once we are freed from the logical constraint of the mathematical instant, a minute is no more a logical scandal than a second, nor a second more than a millisecond. All non-infinitesimal intervals are equally beyond the pale.

12. See Chapter 3, Addendum 2.

13. Hebb, "The Semi-Autonomous Process: Its Nature and Nurture".

14. "In each primal phase that originally constitutes the immanent content, we have retentions of the preceding phases and protentions of the coming phases of the future event as *about to happen*", Husserl, *On the Phenomenology of the Consciousness of Internal Consciousness of Time (1893–1917)*, §40.

15. This has the feeling of an ad hoc solution, invoking putative psychological contents to solve a theoretical problem.

16. Merleau-Ponty, *The Phenomenology of Perception*, 4.

17. Though, as Dainton has pointed out to me (personal communication), for Brentano, and Husserl at some periods, instantaneous phases of consciousness have rich contents that contain all of this. However, they are still left with the problem of extended time sense being carried by unextended moments of consciousness. The problem, as we shall see, can be avoided if we understand that the "intrinsic" time of conscious experiences is not to be conflated with the objective time of the physical world of which it is conscious.

18. Lotze quoted by Gallagher, "Sync-ing in the Stream of Experience".

19. See Dainton, "Time, Passage and Immediate Experience".

20. Husserl, *On the Phenomenology of the Consciousness of Internal Consciousness of Time (1893–1917)*, 345–6.

21. I have discussed the semiosphere in *Aping Mankind*; see especially "The Human World: A Trillion Cognitive Handshakes", 229–38.

22. Callender, "The Common Now", 7.

23. Mermin, "QBism as CBism".

24. Mellor, *Real Time II*, 9.

25. Savitt, "Being and Becoming in Modern Physics".

26. Callender, "The Common Now".

27. This is a small-scale reflection of the macroscopic truth that there is no change in the spatio-temporal manifold if it is seen from without – that is to say as a whole – because the latter is the sum of all changes and there is no space for change to add to the sum.

28. This may seem to some a simplification. Steward ("Processes, Continuants, and Individuals") challenges the idea that the difference between events and processes is that the former have temporal parts while the latter are continuants present in their entirety at each moment of their existence, though she defends the intuitions motivating this way of characterizing the difference. My own position does not locate the difference between events and processes in the intrinsic properties of the happenings in question. One can see a change as event-like or as process-like (cf. space-like and time-like as terms used in relativity) depending on the view point.

29. In a fascinating, carefully argued paper, Galton & Mitzoguchi – "The Water Falls but the Waterfall Does Not Fall" – argue that there *is* a fundamental difference between processes and events, suggesting, perhaps counter-intuitively, that processes are more basic: they are the stuff of events in

the way that matter is the stuff of objects. Intuitively, however, one might equally well think that processes are made of events. For this reason, I still feel that it is a question of viewpoint that determines the allocation of changes to either (ongoing) process or to (completed) event. Even so, the porosity of the boundary between processes and objects is particularly clear in the case of items such as waterfalls, which are processes (in virtue of the fact that they are given over entirely to change – the falling of water) and objects (the standing sheet of water which has definite edges, relatively fixed shape and even the stable location of fixtures like walls).

30. Cf. "[Events] are shapes cut out by a finite observer from the spatio-temporal totality of the objective world." Merleau-Ponty, *The Phenomenology of Perception*, 411. This is a point to which we shall return in Chapter 11.

31. Donald Davidson argues, persuasively I believe, that events are true particulars, that the problem of their individuation is no more difficult than that of objects, and that they are as ontologically robust and fundamental as the latter. As he puts it, "there is no reason to assign second rank to events" (Davidson, "The Individuation of Events", 175). It is understandable why we might feel inclined to do so. Giving events a stand-alone status might seem like including the Cheshire cat's smile, detached from the feline, in the register of real things.

32. Mellor, *Real Time II*, 89.

33. Davidson, "The Individuation of Events".

34. Russell, "The Ultimate Constituents of Matter", 124.

35. Mellor, *Real Time II*, 86.

36. The present, permitting something not only to come into and go out of being but also to settle or linger there has been a scandal for a long time in philosophy. It is evident as far back as the assertion of the first Western philosopher, Anaximander, at least according to Heidegger's brilliant exegesis, that whatever emerges must vanish because "lingering" in the present, which escapes both a coming to and a going away, is "out of joint". I discuss this in *The Enduring Significance of Parmenides*, 82–3.

37. Rainer Maria Rilke, *Duino Elegies*, Eighth Elegy.

38. Kundera, *The Art of the Novel*.

39. See, for example, Tallis & Spalding, *Summers of Discontent*.

40. The roll call of some philosophers who support presentism and their reasons for doing so can be found in Dowe's "Review of Craig Bourne's *A Future for Presentism*".

41. Bourne, *A Future for Presentism*.

42. Merricks argues that eternalism "merits an incredulous stare" (*Truth and Ontology*, 140).

43. Einstein, *Relativity*, 149.

44. For an excellent discussion of whether the geometry of space–time, which does not permit an absolute or frame-invariant idea of simultaneity, really does preclude the idea of a unique present, of *the* present, and consequently presentism, see Zimmerman, "Presentism and the Space–time Manifold". He concludes that "it is too early for presentists to begin hand-wringing" (*ibid.*, 233).

Saunders has argued – in "How Relativity Contradicts Presentism" – that presentists must claim that special relativity is incomplete. Readers will appreciate that rejecting special relativity as the *full* story about space–time would hardly count, to this author, against presentism. Nor need we accept that rejecting special relativity as the full story "tantamounts to rejecting special relativity" – just putting it in its proper place. The present may be *physically* undistinguished but this doesn't stop it from being *metaphysically* privileged. And it is of course true that very few physicists accept special relativity as the *full* story of space–time. General relativity has superseded special relativity, and the inconsistency of general relativity with quantum theory suggests that even general relativity is only a provisional story. The so-called theory of everything that unites gravity and quantum theory may restore the idea of a physically privileged foliation corresponding to the tense privileged by presentists and overthrow the relativistic democracy of inertial frames. Zimmerman ("Presentism and the Space–time Manifold", 226) notes that Maudlin has even suggested that it might be possible that a "quantum preferred foliation could be added on to an otherwise Minkowskian space–time". The jury seems to be out and they do not seem likely to return with their verdict any time soon. For the present we might observe that, given a choice between accepting that the present tense is unreal or that special relativity is seriously incomplete as an account of time, the latter seems a wiser choice to those not in thrall to the ideology of scientism.

45. Others have also worried about the truth value of statements about the future. I don't think this is a problem for presentism for reasons that will be evident in Chapter 8, especially §8.2.1.
46. See Mozersky, "Presentism", for a useful discussion of the grounding problem.
47. Bourne, *A Future for Presentism*, 59.
48. Lewis, "Tensed Quantifiers", 5.
49. We can conceive of a differentiated past without it being associated with an imagined future but equally we cannot imagine a differentiated future without a differentiated past to base it on.
50. Mozersky, "Presentism", 129.
51. Needless to say, presentists have looked to other ways of dealing with the grounding problem – see Davidson, "Presentism and Grounding Past Truths". One is the claim that there are presently past-directed properties as part of the world as a whole. This would include properties such as having included Socrates' baldness or (of the world) "being such that Socrates was snub-nosed". This appeal to the presence of properties that included pastness, has been described as "cheating" by some, such as Theodore Sider. It is worth noting another serious problem for presentism, arising from "cross-time relations". An example we have touched on is causal ancestry: the pavements are wet today because it rained two hours ago. The past rain must be real if the pavements are wet. Another is a generative relation. I am the grandson of my deceased grandfather. This true fact about me could not be true if my grandfather did not have some kind of reality sustaining my present relationship to him, though it is located in the past. The argument continues seemingly without end and, as the main text suggests, the defence against presentism should be directed elsewhere.
52. Abstract objects – such as economic trends – are also problematic for presentists. They clearly straddle past, present, and future, if you look at them at any point. They cannot be reduced to their effects at any given present.
53. Valberg, "The Temporal Present".
54. For a more detailed discussion of this, see Tallis, *Aping Mankind*, 103–11 and §12.2.
55. This must not be confused with the ancient view that the gaze was a quasi-material something coming out of the eyes – as if a glance or a glare were a kind of emission.
56. It is important to appreciate that there is nothing in material objects that is self-revealing: there are no appearances in the physical world though there are constraints on appearance. If there were such appearances intrinsic to, for example, pebbles, there would be a conflict as to which of their innumerable appearances – from front or back, from above or below, in good light or bad, from within or without – they would have. They clearly could not have them all at once but there would be no basis for choosing one over another.
57. Shakespeare, Sonnet 68.
58. Spencer, "Olive Trees". I always (incorrectly) remembered this as "the architect with his plans and the archaeologist with his spade".
59. And how complex those mediations could be, and what exotic intertwining! An example at random: in the nineteenth century, the oil from the sperm whale was extracted and transported many thousands of miles to light the streets and to lubricate the mechanisms inside watches.

CHAPTER 7

1. Bergson emphasised this in *Matter and Memory*, where he spoke of the past surviving in two ways – in "motor mechanisms" and "in independent memories"; see Guerlac, *Thinking in Time*, 124.
2. This fundamental distinction was first appreciated by Endel Tulving in *Elements of Episodic Memory*. It's more complicated since, of course, we may have episodic memories of the event in which we learned or were taught a fact.
3. It is for this reason that we might have reservations about using the term "memory" in this context. As I pointed out in a critique of Eric Kandel's work on memory using the sea slug *Aplysia* as a model, I don't think the past is explicitly present in the world of even the most seasoned sea slug. And we may be confident that the beast does not experience nostalgia (such as for the time before it met Professor Kandel and started having electric shocks applied to its nether parts). I have discussed this at some length in *Aping Mankind*, 123–32.
4. Memorization and auto-cueing of memories is discussed by Merlin Donald. For a brief account of his ideas, see Tallis, "On Being Thanked by a Paper Bag" in *The Mystery of Being Human*.

5. It is interesting that Hume differentiated between memories that were echoes of impressions, differing from them only in "degree of vivacity" and a full-blown idea that belonged to the imagination and had lost its vivacity. This is discussed in Sacks, *Objectivity and Insight*, 29 *et seq.*

6. Poincaré, "The Measure of Time", 222.

7. For more on this story see Tallis, *The Knowing Animal*.

8. True at the time of the first draft of this chapter. Several years on, it is no longer the case.

9. This applies to memories acquired by direct experience – such as witnessing an event – and not to what we know about the past through being informed by others. In the latter case, the authentication of the memory – which is, as it were, a proxy memory – is dependent on authentication of the source of information.

10. Dummett, "The Reality of the Past".

11. Meillassoux, *After Finitude*. See especially chapter 1, "Ancestrality".

12. Quine, "Two Dogmas of Empiricism".

13. Bergson, *Matter and Memory*, 150 quoted in Guerlac, *Thinking in Time*, 148.

14. I have not touched on the explicit, existential presence of *my* past in guilt, embarrassment, responsibility, pride in one's achievements, commitments and so on. This is not because it is unimportant but because it is too important to be dealt with only briefly.

15. We have focused on memory only as a spontaneously functioning faculty. But there is another important aspect of memory: memorization. Committing things – locations and routes, events, past experiences, facts – to memory may be fairly recent but it is a major aspect of our lives. The active laying down of memories for a purpose is temporally complex: I rehearse *now* what happened *then* in order that I shall be able to recall it in an explicit future that may have need of those memories. And, to compound the complexity, my active memorizing may itself be shaped by my recollection of the best way to remember things, itself assisted by my insight into the ways of my own memory.

16. Braude, "Memory without a Trace".

17. *Ibid.*, 193.

18. *Ibid.*, 187.

19. *Ibid.*, 188.

20. *Ibid.*, 193.

21. *Ibid.*, 195.

22. The commonest way of concealing the representation problem is to describe neural activity as "encoding" experiences as memories. Codes, after all, do not look like the encoded. This, however, only moves the problem on. Encoded experiences presumably require decoding for them to be re-experienced as memories. Given that it must be context-sensitive, decoding (even if it did not raise the spectre of a code-cracking homunculus) would require the memory to be remembered in order to guide the process.

23. Our troubles have hardly begun. Memories are not atomistic: like perceptions (only, perhaps, more so) they belong to interlocking fields – of experience, meaning, significance. Even so, they cannot be lost in the mass of past experience, like snow-flakes in a snow-drift. They have to be kept available for retrieval as distinct, singular items.

CHAPTER 8

1. See also §2.3.4 where I endeavour to discredit the idea of "the arrow of information". I highlight the ambiguity in the term "information" which is promiscuously applied to the resolution of indeterminate possibility into determinate actuality and to knowledge that is acquired.

2. I saw this on a poster on the tube; which only goes to show that philosophers are never off duty.

3. Smith, "Time and Degrees of Existence".

4. The example of "sakes" is from Daniel Dennett. I discuss this in "Naming Airy Nothings".

5. This touches on what Smolin has referred to as "closed box" characteristic of physics, such that it examines only parts of the world, sealed off against change. His argument that laws cannot be applied to the universe as a whole – developed in *Time Reborn* – is compelling and undermines the Laplacean notion of an ideal thinker predicting the future of the world from a knowledge of its initial state and the laws that apply to it.

6. Here are some examples drawn at random: (a) I reposition a cup so that no-one knocks it to the floor by accident. (b) We grow wheat in order to make bread which we shall sell and pay for other things we need such as clothes to keep us warm. (c) Techniques are developed that are aimed to strengthen our grip on the material world in future. These come from a long way off: we prepare charcoal to have a better fire to smelt iron to make a metal axe that will favour us in war or against predators, or to increase our power directly and indirectly through wealth. (d) We fight over territory that will enable one of us to have command over a vantage point that greatly extends our view of the world. (e) You agree to pay for our shared fence to be painted with preservative so that it and our neighbourly relations shall not rot as fast as they might do otherwise. (f) I study hard in order to avoid having to work in a dead-end job. (g) Collectively, we accept tax rises so that health care shall be provided free at the point of need for all of us. (h) Laws are passed to make the streets safer to walk down at night.
   We shall return to this in Chapter 12.

7. My wife, when she was looking forward to her retirement, cut out little numbered squares, one for each of the working days that remained, and placed them in a saucer on the left-hand side of the kitchen sink. As each day passed, she moved them over to the saucer on the right-hand side of the kitchen sink. Thus a literal metaphor of the passage of the remaining days of her pre-retirement life from future to past.

8. Perhaps we use "at" of times of the day – "See you at 4" – because they have no extensity. "At", of course, is a term charged with (largely overlooked) significance in the metaphysics of time, as we discussed in §4.5 and §6.1.2.1.

9. Both ways of putting it seem equally true, perhaps, because they are equally beside the mark. A third way of expressing it is that they *become* the present, a mid-way position between visiting and being visited.

10. The scope of that "in common" is variable. Those who share the same rain shower occupy a smaller part of the surface of the earth than those who live in the same time zone. Until relatively recently, time zone disparity was irrelevant and we all ran – or thought we ran – to the same solar clock.

11. Smart, "The Reality of the Future".

12. My understanding of this topic has been greatly enhanced by Hájek, "Interpretations of Probability".

13. *Ibid.*, 31.

14. Bourne, "Fatalism and the Future", 42.

15. Though I can order things so that I can influence what happens after my death; consequently, my present potency for good or ill may extend beyond my life.

16. There is nothing intrinsically possible about "future" events because I might entertain, as a possibility, something that is an impossibility.

17. Aristotle, *On Interpretation*, chapter 9.

18. *Ibid.*, §§18a–19b.

19. *Ibid.* Aristotle, however, clearly rules out magic thinking: "it is not because of the affirming or denying that it [e.g. the sea battle] will be or will not be the case". Jaakko Hintikka – in "The Once and Future Sea Fight" – questions whether Aristotle was concerned with propositions, in particular propositions whose truth is not context-dependent. However, the puzzle of logical fatalism in its modern and most interesting form is approached via uttered propositions.

20. Łukasiewicz, "On Three-Valued Logic". Łukasiewicz distinguished between the law of excluded middle (every sentence of the form "p or not-p" is true) and the principle of bivalence (every sentence is true or false). I don't think this distinction bears on the arguments for and against logical fatalism.

21. Ryle, *Dilemmas*, chapter II made a similar point when he asserted that "future tensed statements can convey only general information". More precisely, they can make only general assertions. This is echoed by Godfrey-Smith, "The Generality of Predictions" in his assertion that "one cannot name a wholly future entity", 18.

22. This is not just about the problem of description and of words failing to match "the exact curve of the thing" since it would then apply equally to statements about the past as about the future. Rather, it is about (Fregean) sense being deployed in the absence of a referent.

23. For some philosophers of language, the referents of propositions *are* real entities. As Richard Gaskell has pointed out: "Russellian propositions are meanings of declarative sentences, and are

composed in some way of *the worldly entities* introduced by the semantically significant parts of those sentences, centrally objects and properties" ("Proposition and World", 1; italics added). This would seem to raise many problems in relation to negative and conditional propositions. These highlight the unlikely nature of the claim that propositions which propose states of affairs somehow contain them or parts or aspects of them.

24. Oaklander, *The Ontology of Time*, 17.
25. There is a B-series equivalent: "Call no event 'before' until you have identified its 'after'", or even "Call no series B until you have picked out the series."
26. McTaggart, "The Unreality of Time".
27. I have closely followed Dainton's characteristically lucid exposition of the argument here. See *Time and Space*, 15–17.
28. From the standpoint of 12 December we can see that the event E on 11 December was going to happen. But it does not follow from this that there is a standpoint (any time before 11 December) from which we can have certain knowledge that E was going to happen; so that, from the Big Bang, it was "always" going to happen. If this were the case, there would be no change in the probability of E as we get closer to 11 December, because its probability would always be 100 per cent.
29. Zimmerman (cited in Dainton, *Time and Space*, 408) has identified philosophers such as Quentin Smith and Timothy Williamson who hold that when objects and events pass from future, to present, to past, they change from being non-spatial to being spatial and then to being non-spatial again.
30. There is another problem with events as tense tourists. They cannot be lone travellers. If they travel, they must travel with their circumstances, and the ancestors and descendants of those circumstances. The entire universe would thus be a tense tourist. Such a view, taken further, obliterates the distinction between the future, the present, and the past while at the same time maintaining that they exist as destinations for events.
    The becoming of events is often confused with tense tourism. In fact becoming takes place in one tense – the present. Take lunch. Its becoming is the passage from the starter to the dessert, not the passage of lunch from future to past.
31. Oaklander, *The Ontology of Time*, 17.
32. It is wrong to think of my birth and my birthdate as receding in the same way. It is another instance of the merging of times and events.
33. A definition with many problems. See the comprehensive review by McBride, "Truth-Makers". It will have to do for the present.
34. Behind the conflation of whatever it is that makes a proposition true and things that actually happen – which translates the world into a constellation of truth-makers – is (perhaps) the ghost of Tarski's semantic theory of truth – an empty notion of truth that seems to empty the world. "'Snow is white' is true if and only if snow is white." Yes; but any actual snow has to be more than just white and, what is more, it has to have fallen and in a particular place, and a particular quantity. The truth relation between p and the truth-maker of p does not occupy a place in the material world.
35. Merricks gives the thought that "truth depends on being" a run for its money in *Truth and Ontology*. He excludes negative truths, truths about the past (surprisingly), and true subjunctive conditionals – such as that I would have been unhappy if the Tories had been elected to power in 2005. We could develop this point by asserting that existence is not a predicate, not only because predication presupposes existence, but because no finite number of predicates could constitute a particular existent.
36. This has been well expressed by McBride, "Truth-Makers" (summarizing the views of Mulligan, Simons and Smith): "what is determined *a posteriori* to be a truth-maker may exhibit a complexity different from that of the statement it makes true". I would change "may exhibit" to "must exhibit".
37. McCall, *A Model of the Universe*, 14. He makes a similar point in "A Dynamic Model of Temporal Becoming", 176: "The notion of truth, so to speak, bakes no bread, it simply floats on top of whatever events occur or will occur, and in no way constrains or affects the possibility of them occurring." Or, more briefly, truth supervenes on being and not vice versa.
38. See McBride, "Truth-Makers", for a discussion of different views on the truth-makers of negative propositions.
39. We may distinguish between bound variables that are the names of (actual) objects that have an extra-propositional existence and propositional variables that do not.

40. This does not make them mere nothings. The entertaining of possibilities liberates us from the present moment and enables us to shape the future that will in future become present moments.

41. The trick is to move from "What will be will be" to "What will be cannot not be" to "What will be must be". This slip can be forestalled if we unpack the middle proposition as "What will be cannot not be, *if* it actually will be". The assertion "If E occurs, then E occurs" cannot be backdated to the time when it has not yet occurred and might not occur.

42. The necessity of the laws of nature – they are unbreakable by definition – does not extend to their empirical *form*. It may be speculated, however, that when the Theory of Everything is arrived at, the form of its laws will seem to have some kind of neccessity. This is most likely to be mathematical which offers, perhaps, the possibility of bringing material necessity closer to mathematical necessity. A fully mathematized account of the world would even bring the constants – which seem the most intractably contingent aspects of the physical world – into the realm of necessity. However, this would empty the world of specific content – a process that began with marginalizing secondary qualities. And we might end up with a single giant contingency – namely that there is something rather than nothing – with two daughter contingencies: that the something corresponds to some equations rather than none; and that the equations are realized in a universe.

    This is one of several reasons why we should be cautious in speaking of necessity in relation to the laws of nature. There is no necessitating pressure. The universe has habits, that's all. Indeed, the laws of nature are that which happens most naturally and which does not require to be enforced.

43. Relativity theory, when it does not dictate that nothing shall happen, may imply material fatalism. Putnam in "Time and Physical Geometry", 247, argues that "contingent statements about future events already have a truth value" because the events are already real. Not only are events fated to happen by prior states of affairs but also by, in some sense, having happened already! If we conclude on these grounds that there is no indeterminate future, we are also obliged to deny the existence of a determinate past. So "chronogeometrical determinism" – in which the world is close to being reduced to space–time points which neither come into nor pass out of being – is highly problematic.

44. In our arrangements, we treat space and time separately. They are variables that are set independently. I can arrange to meet you at this very spot where we are now in 2 months' time. Or I may arrange to meet you 200 miles away in London later today.

45. What is more, because our wishes, motives, drives, beliefs, urges, appetites and desires are not entirely transparent to us, we cannot be sure how we shall experience the future that conforms to and realizes them.

46. Trakl, "Decline", 114.

47. There is another variant of fatalism about the future that has exercised rather more of the human race than the logical or material varieties we have discussed: theo-logical fatalism. This is rooted in the belief that things will unfold in accordance with the will of God. There are insights even for infidels to be obtained from the extensive discussions by theologians of the extent to which the future would be constrained by God's foreknowledge, irrespective of whether it was propositional and subject to the principle of bivalence. (The remarks that follow have been provoked by David Kyle's excellent "God, Fatalism, and Temporal Ontology".)

    If the future is undetermined, then there is nothing definite for God to know. If God has foreknowledge, then the future is definite, settled, closed. There is no way that a future event could be known without already having been fixed; indeed, given that God's viewpoint is omnitemporal, without already having happened; there would be no "fore" in his "foreknowledge". If the future were settled by this means, there would be no difference between actions and other events. Indeed, agency would not be necessary to make anything – longed for, feared, or not even anticipated, being of no interest – happen. Events would require nothing of agents who could not, anyway, refrain from the action that God foresees. This is why the following attempt to make divine foreknowledge compatible with the ability to choose a course of action does not work:

> The past and future's existence does not entail that you do not have the power to refrain from performing action X at noon tomorrow. If you were to choose to refrain, your action of refraining would occur and the future would have existed in a different way and consequently God would have believed differently than he did.
>
> (Kyle, "God, Fatalism, and Temporal Ontology", 443)

CHAPTER 9

1. I haven't been able to track down the reference for this quotation. There is, however, general agreement that it was GBS who said it.
2. For further discussion of the relationship between Plato and Parmenides see Tallis, "Parmenides' Footnotes: Plato and Aristotle" in *The Enduring Significance of Parmenides*.
3. Kant, *Critique of Pure Reason*.
4. McTaggart, "The Relation of Time to Eternity". McTaggart asserts that the first sense of eternity as "unending time" is improper and he includes it only because of the frequency of its use.
5. I owe this formulation to Mackenzie, "Eternity", 403.
6. The most obvious is that it is riddled with contradiction. For the sum total that is the block universe has to be summed or totalled in something that is not part of the sum or of the total; namely some sort of viewpoint, that must look upon it from a without that does not have a (space–time) location.

   There are also objections from within physics. Eliot has argued ("Physics in the Real Universe") that the unchanging block universe misses out essential features of the time-irreversible macro-physical behaviour and the development of emergent complex systems, including life, which exist in the real universe. Smolin sees the timeless block universe as a product of the cosmological fallacy of applying to the whole what has been discovered in, and applies to, localities – "wrenching a theory beyond the limited domain where it can be compared to experiment"(*Time Reborn*, 155).
7. Boethius, *The Consolation of Philosophy*, V, VI. Augustine anticipates this view to some extent:

   > Furthermore, although you [meaning God] are before time, it is not in time that you precede it. If this were so, you would not be before all time. It is in eternity, which is supreme over time because it is a never-ending present, that you are at once before all past time and after all future time. For what is now the future, once it comes, will become the past, whereas you are unchanging, your years can never fail. Your years neither go nor come, but our years pass and others come after them, so that they may all come in their turn. Your years are completely present to you all at once, because they are at a permanent standstill … Your today is eternity.   (Augustine, *Confessions*, 263)

8. Plato, *Timaeus*, 37E6–38A6.
9. Recollection of Forms from prenatal life when our souls were united with them (as is suggested in *Meno*) or the sunlight of the supreme Form of the Good, shedding light on the other Forms, and so making it possible for us to apprehend them (*Republic*) seem more than a little ad hoc. Why, for example, should the Good be efficacious in this way? They exacerbate rather than solve the problem of the interaction between timeless Forms and time-bound beings such as ourselves.
10. See §3.5.1, where Dantzig's idea is discussed in relation to the tension within mathematics.
11. Aristotle, *Physics*, book IV, 218^a–24.
12. Kant, *Critique of Pure Reason*, A 272.
13. Wittgenstein, *Philosophical Investigations*, 111.
14. Vaughan, "The World".
15. Pascal, "A Memorial", in *Pensées*, 285.
16. Kierkegaard, *Either/Or*:"[The] married man, being a true conqueror, has not killed time but has saved it and preserved it in eternity … He solves the great riddle of living in eternity and yet hearing the hall clock strike, and hearing it in such a way that the stroke of the hour does not shorten but prolong his eternity".
17. It may seem to share this disabling characteristic with a word such as "universe" that is always spoken at a particular place and time within the universe but which nevertheless does not lose its meaning. Or "matter" that is uttered, and lifted on the wings of inverted commas, by a piece of matter but likewise retains its specific and yet very general meaning. Or, indeed, "time" whose tokens are emitted at particular times, without this making it unusable.
18. Edwards, *Immortality*, 194–9.
19. See §10.4 for a discussion as to whether there can be time in a universe evacuated of events.
20. McTaggart ("The Relation of Time to Eternity") has suggested another relationship. Development in time, he asserts, should be regarded as leading up to that which is timeless, so that each stage of the universe is closer to the realization of eternity. The latter, therefore, is located at the end of the

time series. This cheerful scenario harbours a paradox: time runs up to eternity but ceases "when" eternity is arrived at so that, while time is before eternity, eternity is not after time.

21. See Blumenfield, "On the Compossibility of the Divine Attributes".
22. The Christmas carol, "Hark, the Herald Angels Sing".
23. Kenny, *The God of the Philosophers*, 38–9.
24. There is a further twist in the tale of the intersection of time and eternity; namely that the idea of eternity seemed to have entered human history – or pre-history – at a particular time; that it evolved through history; and there were certain key moments such as Philo of Alexandria's realization that God is timeless.
25. Descartes' argument that a Perfect Being must exist because otherwise we, being imperfect, could not conceive of it falls victim to the counterargument that we might arrive at the notion of infinite simply by the operation of negation. This can be countered in its turn by arguing that the very notion of *im*perfection is defined with respect to its opposite. If imperfection is not prior to perfection, then the mystery of a finite creature thinking of some perfect being becomes the mystery of an imperfect being that can think of itself as imperfect and cook up the idea of a perfect being by contrast.
     The relevance of this argument and counterargument to our conception of eternity is that we have to step back and look at the very idea of a creature than can entertain this idea – to the extent that eternity can have a huge influence on the way he lives his life. The creature in question is *H. sapiens.*
26. See the chapter on "Machines for the Suppression of Time" in Leach, *Claude Lévi-Strauss.*
27. "Eternal Sentence", in Bunnin & Yun, *Blackwell Dictionary of Western Philosophy.*
28. We are, of course, in the vicinity here of the arguments around logical fatalism discussed in §8.2.2.
29. There is another transient component: the psychological experience of the person who is apprised of the fact.
30. The tendency to confuse facts with events – and to see facts as things that happen at a particular place and at a particular time – is discussed in Tallis, "Facts, Statements and the Correspondence Theory of Truth" in *Not Saussure.*
31. The laws may seem also to have had a beginning – even though the beginning may have been the Big Bang, the beginning *of* time, rather than a beginning *in* it. We shall discuss this question from different angles in §10.3.4. and §11.3.1.
32. A well-trodden path in intellectual history. I have discussed Plato as one of Parmenides' two major footnotes in *The Enduring Significance of Parmenides* (see especially, 132–48).
33. Just how deep is explored in the compelling writing of Merlin Donald. See, for example, his "Précis of *Origins of the Modern Mind*".

CHAPTER 10

1. It interesting that we are not inclined to ask – outside of technical discussions – (What) Is Space? The essence of space seems to be given immediately. And we are certainly not inclined to deny its reality on philosophical grounds. Physicists, however, variously promote it to "a player in its own right" (general relativity) or threaten to eliminate it (via delocalization in quantum field theory).
2. "Philosophical problems arise when language goes on holiday ... It is the engine idling"; Wittgenstein, *Philosophical Investigations*, §38.
3. This view that the question "What is time" is merely an (invalid) abstraction from a cluster of uses, and pursuing its essential natures leads us on a wild goose chase for illegitimate generalities is expressed by Wittgenstein's pupil Friedreich Waismann:

> Whoever is able to understand the word "time" in the various examples and to apply it, knows just "what time is" and no formulation can give him a better understanding of it. The question "What is time?" leads us astray, since it causes us to seek an answer of the form "Time is ...", and there is no such answer.
>
> (Waismann, *Introduction to Mathematical Thinking*, 117, quoted in Newton-Smith, *The Structure of Time*, 2; Newton-Smith does not support this view)

There is an interesting variation on this theme in Rovelli's, "Analysis of the Distinct Meanings of the Notion of Time, in Different Physical Theories", summarised in note 164 (page 653). In ordinary experience, time has tenses and a direction, there are uniquely defined intervals between events, and they have a definite order. Tense is absent in thermodynamics. Tense and direction disappear in Newtonian theory. Fixed intervals between events disappear in special relativity. In quantum gravity, all the attributes of time vanish. If "we observe Nature at progressively more fundamental levels, and we seek for laws of nature that hold in progressively more general contexts, then we discover that these laws require, or admit, a progressively weaker notion of time" (*ibid.*, 90). And Rovelli concludes that "*the 'higher level' characteristics of time are not present at the fundamental level, but 'emerge' as specific features of specific physical systems*" (ibid.; italics original). This does not undermine the reality of the "higher level" characteristics of time unless we think that the most general, most fundamental, is also the most real. It also leaves unexplained how it is that a physical system such as the brain (which Rovelli believes houses tensed time) could have these "emergent" properties. Unfortunately, he concludes that "the concept of time, with all its attributes, is not a fundamental concept in nature". Rather it is a "progressively more specialized concept that makes sense only for progressively more special systems" – a little local phenomenon – and even speculates that it might "disappear from the fundamental description of nature" as did the concept of colour or the concept of the centre of the universe. We could do without the latter but not so fast with colour (and other phenomenal aspects of the world) – or time!

4. "In our failure to understand the use of a word we take it as the expression of a queer process. So we think of time as a queer medium, of the mind as a queer kind of being"; Wittgenstein, *Philosophical Investigations*, §196.

5. Feynman, *The Feynman Lectures on Physics*, §5.2

6. Quoted in Bernstein, *Einstein*, 55.

7. Space has only two aspects: position and interval (magnitude). Order is not intrinsic – or not in the way it seems to be in the case of time. An event E_1 at position 1 may be noted before E_2 at position 2 but the apparent priority of the former over the latter has nothing to do with its spatial location. This is why we are free to travel in space – and to choose our here – but not in time – to choose our now.

8. This line of thought has persisted in Western philosophy. It had a relatively recent monumental expression in Sartre's *Being and Nothingness*. Sartre's Nothingness – rooted in the no-longer and the not-yet – seems to be pretty active, indeed muscular, for something that is nothing. The "ness" appears to have done wonders for its potency. It is tempting to think of "Nothingness" as "Nothing-on-steroids".

9. There are philosophers such as Bas van Fraassen for whom time is merely "a logical space", a mathematical construct, that brings together a variety of concepts. He goes further and argues that: "There would be no time were there no beings capable of reason … just as there would be no food were there no organisms, and no tea cups if there were no tea drinkers" (quoted in Dowden, "Time"). Van Fraassen's view shares a problem with the idealistic view of time namely that it would suggest that events that occur before conscious beings appear on the scene would have no temporal characteristics (order, interval, duration, location) – something we shall discuss in §10.3.4.

10. Putting time into clocks is consistent with the principle, to which we have referred, enunciated most influentially by Mach, that basic physical elements are identical with what can be, indeed is, measured. Half-way to this view is that of Dummett that "Time is the measure of change: its existence consists simply of there being functions giving the magnitudes of other quantities at different times" ("Is Time a Continuum of Instants?", 509). This seems to turn things upside down; rather as does the aphorism "to be is to be the value of a variable". In both cases, it inverts the actual order of things in which values, variables and functions supervene on existence.

11. These are comparable to one of the reasons we invoked in §2.2.3 for being suspicious at the idea that time flows – or flows uniformly – because flowing is a distinctive property of particular regions of the universe. You would not expect some parts of the world to be more "time-like" than others.

12. Such a view inherits all the problems of modal realism, not the least of which is ambiguity over whether or not possibilities have to be entertained in order to exist or whether it is sufficient that they should fall within a notional space of logical possibility.

13. Le Poidevin has argued this carefully in his *Change, Cause and Contradiction*. There is a sense in which two objects may occupy the same region of space at the same time. In my desk is a clay vase. It is two objects: a vase a few years old; and a piece of clay billions of years old. However, these two objects do not have properties that are in conflict – for example, being red and blue all over.

14. Bergson makes time more substantive, more muscular than anything I have suggested. It is an "energy" or "a creative force". This overlap may seem to overlap with the suggestion in general relativity that time is an active player in the world but in a key respect it is deeply alien to it. For in general relativity, space is just as active as time, whereas for Bergson, space is inertia and the spatializing gaze is deadening. And, of course, the truly active player in general relativity is not space nor time separately but space–time.

15. Plotinus, quoted in Gale, *The Philosophy of Time*, 27.

16. As we shall discuss in Chapter 12, it is a key element in, and a symptom of, our extraordinary ability to pool our individual distance from the net of organic stimulus and response. It is a key to our progressive freedom from the physical and indeed the biological destiny of other organisms.

17. I am leaving out of the discussion the equivocal testimony of quantum mechanics – that suggests that time is not infinitely divisible but that there is a minimal increment (the Planck time) – because I am not qualified to judge it.

18. There are, of course, at least two ways of interpreting a number such as "1". It could be seen as the precise mid-point between 0 and 2 and hence non-extended; or as an integer, an undivided numerical space between 0 and (the beginning of 2) and hence as quasi-extended. The former is more relevant to our present discussion because we are talking about points that are mapped on to the sequence of real numbers where there is no limit to interpolation. Between any two real numbers it is possible to insert another real number; between 1 and 2, insert 1.5; between 1.5 and 1.6, insert 1.55; and so on ad infinitum. The confusion between the two modes of understanding arises because numbers also have names and "one" does not clearly differentiate between the infinitely slim point-like number and the integer that spans the interval between "zero" and "two". The confusion is compounded by the use of numbers in quantification of stuff. "One gram" of stuff clearly encompasses all the quantities of stuff between zero stuff and a whole gram of stuff. But the totalled quantity has a definite edge; or at least for the relevant level of approximation.

19. "At" always requires smearing because it marks a relationship between a time and an event or an experience.

20. This discussion is deeply indebted to Newton-Smith's *The Structure of Time*, especially "The Topology of Time IV: The Micro-Aspects".

21. Callender, *Oxford Handbook of Philosophy of Time*, 4. This echoes Bergson: "*all change, all movement* [is] *absolutely indivisible*" (*The Creative Mind*, 118). Even in the case of stuttering events, we must assume that there is a continuity of invisible or background change that moves the process on from one stutter to the next. The question of whether time is discrete may be experimentally relevant to the endeavour to unify the general theory of relativity and quantum mechanics.

22. Another assumption – entangled with that belief that mathematics has a privileged relationship to reality – is that that which is smallest is most real, so that temporal instants are more real than, seconds, Wednesdays, or the time it takes to breathe in or walk to the shops. This smallism is analogous to the atomism that asserts that atoms are more real than chairs, neutrinos than people, and so on.

23. See Dummett, "Is Time a Continuum of Instants?", 515.

24. We haven't discussed the notion that time consists of discrete elements – so-called "chronons" which either individually or in small sets have greater than zero extension. Positing them is justified by the problems we have discussed arising out of conceiving of time as being made of durationless instants. An excellent, but necessarily inconclusive, discussion is van Bendegem, "The Possibility of Discrete Time".

25. The key arguments are accessibly summarized in Dainton, *Time and Space*, chapter 9.

26. Sklar, *Space, Time and Spacetime*, 8.

27. Newton, *Scholium to the Definitions in Philosophiae Naturalis Principia Mathematica*, book 1, 6 (quoted in Newton-Smith, *The Structure of Time*, 168). This highlights the connection between the substantivalist view of time and the idea of its passage.

28. Leibniz, "Third Letter to Clarke", paras 4 and 5.

29. Einstein, *Relativity*, 155.

30. This – which seems to assign causal powers even to a vacuum – is a step towards the notion of the quantum vacuum generating the universe, the cause of all causes.

31. However, see, for example, Kuchar, "The Problem of Time in Quantum Geometrodynamics", upon which I have depended in this paragraph. He warns against "taking as the basic objects of our

ontology ... those items that are presented as initial elements in a mathematical presentation of the theory" (*ibid.*, 139) because another formulation might begin with other elements. Amen to that. What is more, Kuchar adds, even if space–time points were real, the metric structure of space–time could be accessed only through material items such as rods and clocks, suggesting that "metric structure is not intrinsic to space–time, but rather a relational affair reflecting the nature both of space–time and matter" (*ibid.*, 140).

32. Sklar, *Space, Time and Spacetime*, 10.
33. *Ibid.*, 12.
34. *Ibid.*, 14.
35. Norton, "The Hole Argument". The contrast between container and contained is problematic, of course. What we might call spatial containers and temporal containers are also that which is contained in space and time respectively. Every (spatial) container for example encloses space, is located in it, and is a part of space.
36. Sklar, *Space, Time and Spacetime*, 14. The muddle is very deep indeed. Readers with long memories may recall the passage from Einstein quoted in the Preface: "I do not agree with the idea that the general theory of relativity is geometrizing physics or the gravitational field" (quoted in Unger & Smolin, *The Singular Universe and the Reality of Time*, 190).
37. There are also solutions to the field equations where the entire universe is rotating, which would make Mach rotate along with it in his grave.
38. Ladyman, "Structural Realism".
39. Ladyman & Ross, *Every Thing Must Go*, 144. There is an excellent discussion of the implications of relativity theory for the substantivalism versus relationism debate in the section "Individuality and Spacetime Physics" (141–4), which also gives the background to the case for ontic structural realism.
40. There is yet another approach to the debate. "The dynamical approach" (DA) starts from the place where physics began: the science of motion. It is discussed by Huggett & Hoefer in "Absolute and Relational Theories of Space and Motion". To some extent it was anticipated by Leibniz, for whom "true motion was not motion relative to absolute space, but the possession of quantity of forces, ontologically prior to any spatiotemporal quantities at all" (*ibid.*, 14). This is echoed by Sklar (quoted by Huggett & Hoefer, *ibid.*, 16) for whom "'true' acceleration is a primitive quantity not defined in terms of motion relative to anything, be it absolute space, a connection or other bodies".

It would seem, then, as if it were possible to be absolutist about motion – e.g. acceleration – and relativist about space – space–time. Hence the dynamical approach due to writers such as Harvey Brown, which "asserts that the space–time structure of our world is what it is *because of the laws of nature and their symmetries.* That is, the dynamical laws are fundamental and spacetime structure is derivative" (*ibid.*, 26). This seems, to say the least, perverse. To think of movement prior to space (prior to any "in" for there to be movement) or time (to think of time being taken) is very odd. It is even odder to think of the *laws* of motion as having priority: the laws cannot be formulated without reference to space and time. As Huggett & Hoefer put it "The DA advocate has to explain the sense in which dynamical laws that apparently presuppose spatio-temporal structures can be *true* of a world that lacks such structures intrinsically and then 'has' them only in a derivative, as-if sense" (*ibid.*, 28). You bet.
41. It may be argued that physics is not in a mess but is simply not equipped to answer questions it has gone beyond or shown to be empty or ill-formed. This has yet to be demonstrated.
42. Another way of putting this is to say that the truest measure of time is one that is most closely consonant with the weighted average of all the changes (in the case of mechanics, all the motions) in the universe. The weighted averages will be most accurately revealed by the most general, replicable laws, whose predictions are most precisely fulfilled.
43. Unger, "The Inclusive Reality of Time" in Unger & Smolin, *The Singular Universe and the Reality of Time*, 177. This restores an argument of Kant's that was supposed to be discredited by developments in mathematical physics since his time: "Different times are only parts of the same time". Times are all connected. We can imagine, Kant argues, time in which nothing is happening but not gaps in time. As pointed out above, global time may also be necessary for certain interpretations of quantum mechanics; or indeed for a consistent interpretation of quantum mechanics (see Rovelli, "Time in Quantum Gravity: An Hypothesis").
44. Hawley, "Metaphysics and Relativity".

45. Time as relation as opposed to substance seems less likely to be ascribed inappropriate properties such as "passage"!

46. This is faced head-on by Augustine, thinking about the Creator: "It is not in time that you [God] precede time. Otherwise you would not precede all times. In the sublimity of an eternity which is always in the present, you are before all things past and transcend all things future because they are to come" (*Confessions*, XI, xiii, 16).

47. Kant, *The Critique of Pure Reason*, 396–402. This is the first of his four "antinomies of pure reason" – philosophical problems with two contradictory but apparently necessary solutions – the others relating to atoms, freedom, and God.

48. Another way of thinking of this argument is that, if the universe did not have a beginning in time, it would be connected with the present by a negative "never" given that it could not be reached by backward travel. Since it never began, it never came into existence, and hence never existed. It is equally valid to translate "never came into existence" as "always already existing".

49. Kant uses a similar argument to demonstrate the fallacy of imagining one can make statements about the universe as a whole. This is echoed in Unger & Smolin's assault on what they call "the cosmological fallacy", which is "applying to the whole of the universe methods and ideas that can be successful only when applied to part of it", treating "the whole universe as if the whole were one more part" (*The Singular Universe and the Reality of Time*, 19).

50. Augustine, *Confessions*, XI, xiii. Since God brought the world and time into being together, the question of (say) what God was doing before the Creation does not arise.

51. It is telling that this Story of the Creation should begin with the very smallest – not just because the smallest is closest to nothing and so that is where we would start. It is also assumed that the universe began with "fundamental" processes, even though it eventually left them behind. In short that it began quantum and grew up to be classical and, eventually, matured into the Everyday. The transition from the quantum-fundamental to the classical and thence to the Everyday is entirely inexplicable. The embarrassment this should cause is suppressed by the implicit assumption that the upper layers are less real.

52. See Krauss, *A Universe from Nothing*.

53. Hawking & Mlodinow, *The Grand Design*, 227.

54. As we shall discuss in Chapter 11, it is a mistake to apply the notion of cause to the universe because causes act locally. (This is a point also made by Kant, but for a different reason.) This has not discouraged all philosophers, for example, Smith, "The Reason the Universe Exists is that it Caused Itself to Exist". There are, however, several reasons why the universe cannot be self-caused, apart from the fact that causes are local and cannot be applied to the entire universe, even less for the purposes of bringing itself into being. The most obvious is that a self-caused universe would have to be in place to bring itself about; in short, it would have to be before itself (as cause) and after itself (as effect). Even where there is overlap between cause and effect, the cause has to begin first. Secondly, what would be the origin of the "of" in "cause of" if the universe were the cause of itself? The "of" implies a separation between two elements but, given that the universe is both cause and effect, there is only one element. Smith's thesis is also criticized in Deltete, "Is the Universe Self-Caused?".

55. Philosopher of physics David Albert's critique of Krauss's "A Universe from Nothing" – "On the Origin of Everything" – is definitive.

56. Hawking & Hertog, "Populating the Landscape: A Top-Down Approach", 123527–1.

57. Lawrence Kuhn's dissection of different nothings (the different starter packs physicists allow themselves) in "Why This Universe?" is superb. It is an antidote to Krauss's scientifically sophisticated and metaphysically naïve arguments.

58. This is developed at length by Unger & Smolin, *The Singular Universe and the Reality of Time*. See also Addendum at the end of this chapter.

59. Lucas, "A Century of Time", 11.

60. There is a surprising point of contact with Stephen Hawking here. His claim (in Hawking & Mlodinow, *The Grand Design*, 179) that "We create history by our observation, rather than history creating us" is radically anthropocentric. This is at least in part connected with the belief that at the quantum level it is observation makes that which is there determinate, rather than mere probability amplitudes. It is questionable whether this observer-dependency actually applies at the macroscopic level of human history or indeed the history of the universe as a whole as revealed to science. If it does, we have many questions to answer. Who are "we" who created this history? How

did we come together? Are we together? What is the status of a shared illusion? What if (as we must assume) that illusion even encompasses science? Does it open the prospect of our falling down the rabbit hole of multiple, causally unconnected universes?

61. Hartle & Hawking, in "Wave Function of the Universe", suggested that time does not switch on suddenly but that, as we move backwards towards the Big Bang, time is increasingly space-like. Because of quantum effects this transition is blurred. So while there is no specific time at which time starts, time has not been present for all eternity. This attempt to avoid the seemingly insoluble conceptual problems around the idea of time beginning at a moment in time only multiplies difficulties. Leaving aside the opaque notion of time becoming "more space-like" we still have a (temporal) succession of decreasingly space-like states of time, implicit in a process being reprised in reverse as we move backwards – in time!

62. See note 48 above.

63. Newton, *Scholium to the Definitions in Philosophiae Naturalis Principia Mathematica*, book 1, 6.

64. *Ibid.*

65. Barrow, *New Theories of Everything*, 76. There are several confusions here. (a) Time as "a background stage" versus events: in real life stage and drama are made of the same stuff. (b) The alternative to being a background stage is not "merely a concept". (c) A *concept* isn't affected by the physical processes from which it "derives". And (d) what does "derives" mean here, anyway? However, the passage serves a purpose here.

66. Quoted in Barbour, "The Development of Machian Themes in the Twentieth Century", 91.

67. See Le Poidevin, *Change, Cause and Contradiction* for a detailed exploration. The necessity for time also applies to external properties: it is possible for the same object to be at two different places only at two different times. In this case, however, space is also involved.

68. Time is not like God as the very possibility of possibility but it is a broad permission for possibility.

69. Which is another reason why we should be cautious about accepting the idea, particularly associated with Mellor and Tooley, that time is the causal dimension of space–time (we shall discuss this in Chapter 11).

70. This doesn't take account of the post-classical deconstruction of location, movement, etc., at the quantum level. It may not be a bad thing.

71. Barrow, *The Geometrical Lectures of Isaac Barrow*, 35.

72. Aristotle, *Physics*, book IV, 218b 33.

73. There are solutions to the field equations of general relativity that describe a world that has a space–time structure, but is empty of matter and energy and hence (presumably) of change. Whether this proves anything is a matter of conjecture.

74. Shoemaker, "Time without Change". See also Newton-Smith, *The Structure of Time*, 19–28.

75. Warmbrod, "Temporal Vacua".

76. The preceding argument has in part been anticipated by Leibniz:

> If there were a vacuum in time, i.e. a duration without changes, it would be impossible to determine its length. Whence it comes that ... you cannot refute the one who would maintain that two worlds, one of which succeeds the other, touch as to duration, so that the one necessarily begins when the other ends without the possibility of an interval.
> (Quoted in Newton-Smith, *The Structure of Time*, 17)

As Newton-Smith points out, this argument presupposes that that which cannot be measured, does not truly exist; that time must be measurable, if only indirectly. Of course, even indirect measurement would be ruled out because the temporal vacuum would not be in any causal relationship with anything outside of it.

77. Warmbrod makes a similar point:

> The underlying difficulty [with the idea of the passage of time in a frozen universe] is implicit in the epistemology of claims about the observation of freezes. The observation and timing of a freeze requires there to be a timekeeper of some sort which is unfrozen and changing over the period of time in question.   (Warmbrod, "Temporal Vacua", 273)

In other words, there needs to be at least two changes. Of course, in an occupied universe, any single change will have universal consequences – a change in the part is a change in the whole – either through transmitted causation or through the change of external relations of all the other occupants to the occupant affected by the change. The multiple relational changes effected by one change would not, however, count as a clock because they would be causally consequential upon the change and would need to be related to it by a third party to turn the effect into a clock.

78. Bergson (*The Creative Mind*, 119) has argued that *all is mobility* and the appearance of stability is due to a matching of a dynamic, endlessly changing observer with a dynamic object: "fixity is only an ephemeral arrangement between mobilities". He illustrates this with a beautiful analogy of two trains moving in parallel at the same speed so that passengers in each of them can reach out to each other and hold hands. It seems strange, however, that he allows the idea of "the same speed" – or indeed "speed" – without allowing the idea of immobility. If there are different (absolute) speeds, there must be the possibility of zero speed.

79. If empty time were real and it had a duration which could be anything from zero to infinity, then it is possible that there are two infinities of time – one while the universe lay in the future, and another when it lay in the past – separated by the finite duration of the universe.

80. Plotinus in Gale, *The Philosophy of Time*, 35.

81. Mellor (*Real Time II*, 70) has argued that the identification of time with change *per se* is circular. We need events to identify points in space–time, so we cannot use time as the marker of a change that counts as an event.

82. This is connected with a view that raises alarm bells. Aristotle asks "whether, if soul (mind) did not exist, time would exist or not, a question which may be fairly asked; for if there cannot be someone to count, there cannot be anything that can be counted" (quoted in Gale, 465). He then went on to ask "whether time is the conscious numbering of movement or is instead the capability of movements being counted if there were consciousness". Little "t" here we come, perhaps.

83. An excellent recent discussion is Hoerl, "A Succession of Feelings, in and of Itself, is Not a Feeling of Succession". Dainton's "Temporal Consciousness" is a masterpiece of exposition, argument, and scholarship. In what follows, we focus on successions of discrete events, such as "do-re-mi". The problems arise just as acutely within a single unfolding or sustained event, where we distinguish its beginning from its end. Kant's observation that "Every apprehension of an event is ... a perception that follows upon another perception" is highly pertinent (quoted in Hoerl & McCormack, "Time in Cognitive Development", 449). Experience of any change has to retain earlier parts of change as the later parts are experienced. And experience of unchangingness must do so likewise. Any perception of an object – which is at least in part unchanging since its character as a thing resides in its stability – is likewise dependent on uniting successive perceptions.

84. James, *The Principles of Psychology*, 629.

85. The issues are teased out very helpfully in Le Poidevin, *Images of Time*, 97–120.

86. Hoerl, "A Succession of Feelings, in and of Itself, is Not a Feeling of Succession", 48. For James (*The Principles of Psychology*, 609), the specious present is the "unit of composition of our perception of time". The problem is even greater for a mind-brain identity theorist for whom perceptions and memories both correspond to (present) states of the perceiving brain. (See the discussion of the notion of "memory traces" in §7.4.)

87. This is a small-scale expression of "the binding problem" – that of explaining how contents of consciousness that are distinct are both brought together as part of the conscious field, the conscious moment, and at the same time kept tidily apart so that they are distinctly experienced and experienced as distinct. For the present, it is sufficient to note that neural explanations of "integrative mechanisms" that unify sequences fall foul of the fact that nerve impulses that take place at t_1 are confined to t_1.

88. Sacks, *Objectivity and Insight*, 13. This is part of a beautifully constructed and illuminating argument against the atomism derived from Locke and Hume rooted in the assumption that we build up our picture of the world on the basis of individual experiences glued together by association. Hume was particularly committed to the notion that "from the succession of ideas and impressions we form the idea of time" (cited in Sacks, *ibid.*, 33).

89. There is a particular interest in the perception of sequences of events that take place in one's own body, especially those that are periodic – such as breathing – and those that are periodic and typically regular – notably the heartbeat. They are for the most part private – breathing less so than the pulse – and, more importantly, not merely sensed or perceived but *lived*. It is this, beyond periodicity, that makes the heartbeat seem like a proto-clock and, because it engages us so intimately,

it has the world-tinting character of public time. The arch within a single breath – rising upwards and falling downwards of the chest wall in inspiration and expiration respectively – must be one of the most primordial sequences in the experienced world.

90. This is connected with the elusiveness of time in our lives, of our inability to experience, say, a day or even an hour, the way time seems to pass through our fingers, and the sense in which there is no difference between a long life and a short one (see Tallis, *The Black Mirror*).

91. Dainton, "Temporal Consciousness" is very helpful.

92. *Ibid.*

93. *Ibid.*

94. For a critique of representationalism, see Tallis, "David Chalmers' Unsuccessful Search for the Conscious Mind", in *Reflections of a Metaphysical Flaneur*.

95. A favourite example – used by C. D. Broad and Bertrand Russell (discussed in Hoerl, "A Succession of Feelings, in and of Itself, is Not a Feeling of Succession") – is the difference between directly seeing the second hand on a clock move and seeing *that* the hour hand has moved: "In the one case we are concerned with something that happens within a single sensible field; in the other we are concerned with a comparison between the contents of two different sensible fields" (Broad, *Scientific Thought*, 351).

96. Le Poidevin, *Images of Time*, 101–4.

97. Mellor, *Real Time II*, 114–15. Or as Le Poidevin (*Images of Time*, 130) puts it, "the causal influence of earlier perceptions on later ones gives rise to the experience of pure succession".

98. Consider a predictable sequence and an unpredictable one. If I hear "do", "re", "mi" it is possible that their relation of succession is something that unfolds concurrently with the experienced succession. If, however, I hear "do", "mi", "mi", "re", the succession will become apparent only after the series is completed. But any sense of succession of events – of "before" and "after" – will have to work just as well for random, as for ordered, series of events.

99. Dainton, "Temporal Consciousness". Of course, Machianism which identifies simultaneity with experience could not countenance the idea of simultaneity between an experienced event and the experience of it.

100. *Ibid.*

101. Weyl, *The Philosophy of Mathematics and Natural Science*, 116.

102. Gamez, *What We Can Never Know*, 115.

103. For a more detailed treatment of these arguments, see Tallis, *The Enduring Significance of Parmenides*.

104. We have already discussed the fact that the notion of "the speed light" is somewhat vulnerable. It relies on separating space from time in order to put the former on the numerator and the latter on the denominator. Maudlin has argued that the notion of the speed of light is Newtonian and what we ought to be talking about is light as part of the geometry of space–time. This seems highly unsatisfactory because it would make the assertion that the speed of light is faster than the speed of sound – hence the delay between seeing and hearing a distant cricketer strike a ball – difficult to comprehend. The freezing of light into geometry may be another – perhaps the supreme – example of how the notion of a four-dimensional universe seems to bring change to a halt and arrest becoming to being.

105. Huggett & Hoefer, "Absolute and Relational Theories of Space and Motion".

106. As we noted in §3.5.4, Einstein was happy to accept the title of "the Parmenidean" from Popper. It is perhaps misleading to describe the Parmenidean universe of the general theory as "frozen": it is neither frozen nor abuzz.

107. The *locus classicus* for the claim that temporal succession is within the mind is of course *The Critique of Pure Reason*. I am not going to discuss this here because it cuts deeper than the present issues and will be addressed in §10.5.

108. If the B-series is as mind-dependent as the A-series, does this mean that the temporal succession of events is something over which we have jurisdiction? No. Observation and articulation do not determine the relationship an event has to another event but only make it explicit. It is not just because I say so that my typing this page is correctly described as taking place over 700 years later than the event of King John applying his signature to the Magna Carta. But that relationship did not exist until I articulated it. (Cf. the facts have to be made – they are *facta* – but they are not made up.) Of this, more in Chapter 11.

109. Gödel, "A Remark about the Relationship Between Relativity and Idealistic Philosophy", 109.
110. For a detailed discussion, see Tallis, *Aping Mankind*, chapter 3, "A Castle Built on Sand".
111. Grünbaum, "The Status of Temporal Becoming", 344.
112. Gale, *The Philosophy of Time*, 300.
113. In a world without becoming there would presumably be no clocks, because clocks are devices that register time in virtue of changes in themselves. If there are no clocks there is no measure of time; there is, for example, no difference between a long time and a short time and a finite interval of time and no time at all. Therefore, physicists who (a) deny becoming (on the basis of general relativity) and (b) define time with respect to measurement (which is a key principle of relativity) are obliged to deny time.
114. I believe it was Marilynne Robinson who wrote this, but I am relying on memory and have been unable to verify the precise source.
115. Meillassoux, *After Finitude*, 5.
116. Kant, *Critique of Pure Reason*, 61, B44. I have here relied on the (to me exceptionally clear) translation of this passage by Stephan Körner (*Kant*, 38).
117. It is not entirely clear that this conclusion would follow from Kant. Roger Scruton has described Kant's view as follows: "The reality of time is presupposed in experience. And the reality of time presupposes the reality of an objective sequence. It is only by reference to that sequence, and to the enduring objects that structure it, that I can identify my own perception" (Scruton, *Kant*, 34). However, it does not follow from this that the reality of time is confined to experience; that time was born with the mind. While it is impossible to conceive of an experienced world without its contents being temporally ordered in the relations of succession and simultaneity, this is surely because the elements of the universe *are in fact* ordered in this way.
118. Meillassoux, *After Finitude*, 21.
119. *Ibid.*, 21.
120. Mellor, *Real Time II*, xiii.
121. Discussed in Tallis, *A Conversation with Martin Heidegger, passim*, especially 84–7 and 102 *et seq.*
122. The very idea of a common world or public realm presupposes a multitude of minds and hence (since there would be no agenda for these minds without bodies) a community of bodies.
123. See Unger & Smolin, *The Singular Universe and the Reality of Time*, 179.
124. Heidegger, *Being and Time*, 381.
125. This is consistent with Heidegger's position: "'Time' is neither objectively present in the 'subject' nor in the 'object', neither 'inside' nor 'outside' and it is prior to every 'subjectivity' and 'objectivity' because it presents the very possibility of this 'prior'" (*ibid.*, 419–20).
126. Hawking & Mlodinow, *The Grand Design*, 179. Admittedly he may have meant this in a more basic sense that, prior to observation, the (quantum) world is indeterminate.
127. Meillassoux, *After Finitude*, 22.
128. Our awareness of life "before man" and "after man" is a macroscopic version of our awareness of a world existing before and after our own individual lives.
129. See Unger & Smolin, *The Singular Universe and the Reality of Time*.
130. *Ibid.*, 145.
131. *Ibid.*, 160.
132. *Ibid.*
133. Smith, "The Ontological Interpretation of the Wave Function of the Universe".
134. It is interesting that recent developments in the endeavour to unify quantum mechanics and general relativity suggest that the universe, when traced backwards, may not after all have converged to a singularity (and hence to a beginning). See, for example, Ali & Saurya, "Cosmology from Quantum Potential".
135. John Tyndall, "Address to the British Association for the Advancement of Science, Belfast, 1874".
136. We have not discussed whether time has an end. Here the analogy with space seems closer than in the case of the beginning. Just as (contemporary physics notwithstanding) we cannot help imagining space continuing beyond any putative limit to space, so we cannot resist thinking that, after time has come to an end, there must be more time corresponding to that "after". In short, the notion that time lasts for a certain time, after which its time is (timelessly) up is baffling to say the least. However, anyone who is satisfied with this intuitive rejection of the end of time should read Earman,

"Till the End of Time" and be chastened. Earman also refers to the "pernicious" habit of separating space from time. Guilty as charged.

CHAPTER 11

1. Sellars, "Philosophy and the Scientific Image of Man".
2. See Tallis, *Aping Mankind*, especially, 140–5.
3. "We may make mistakes in perceiving spatial and temporal relations; illusions occur; but it is felt in the main these dimensions as given in perception directly reproduce the same dimensions as occur in physical reality. Naïve realism, defeated on the field of colour, remains upright on the plane of time and space." Treisman, "The Perception of Time: Philosophical Views and Psychological Evidence", 218. Long may it remain undefeated.
4. Mellor, *Real Time II*, 117. There is a hint of this idea in Kant, for whom "it is only the *a priori* concept of causality (requiring a necessary rule of connection between preceding and succeeding events) which can then transform a merely subjective temporal sequence into an objective one" (quoted in De Pierris & Friedman, "Kant and Hume on Causality", 31).
5. Mellor, *Real Time II*, 108. For Mellor (as also for most physicists) a time-like vector links two events that are causally connected and a space-like vector that links two events that are causally disconnected, being merely "side by side". This is consistent with special relativity that sees time-like vectors within a light cone and space-like vectors relating the inside and the outside of the light cone.
6. Wittgenstein, *Lectures on Philosophy*, §15.
7. Mellor, *Real Time II*, 113. The view that causation underpins the directionality of time is also explored in great depth and with considerable ingenuity by Michael Tooley.
8. In *Causation* (chapter 14, "Causation and the Direction of Time"), Tooley has also argued that it is necessary only that events should be connectible and not that they should be connected. But the concept of "connectible" is too vague.
9. The notion of common ancestry can also be extended to encompass processes that appear broken up into discrete components – for example the procession of drips out of a tap. The drips may all be the products of the sustained pressure of water in the pipes (and ultimately the tanks or reservoirs) to which the tap is attached. Even so, they may have separate causes and certainly can have distinct kinds of effects – as when something else intervenes. But they may also have conjoint effects, for example, wearing away a stone or adding themselves up to fill a bucket. In short there are occasions where there may be a causal convergence, at least descriptively.
10. Poincaré, "The Measure of Time", 5.
11. Price, in *Time's Arrow and Archimedes' Point*, has argued that there is a fundamental asymmetry between cause and effect. The incoming influences that generate a cause are independent of, not correlated with, one another whereas the outgoing events are connected, correlated. This, however, may be just another consequence of identifying an index event as a point of reference. The incoming events are not grouped with respect to a causal ancestor (the reference event) while the outgoing ones are. The contrast between the non-correlated input into the index cause and the correlated output is, in other words, an artefact of selecting a viewpoint from which the flow of happening is considered. In reality, there is coherence and correlation in the universe both before and after the index event but only afterwards is there a basis for picking out events to attach the title of "consequences" to. The incoming influences only seem to converge on the cause because they have been picked out by the index event that, collectively, they have made possible. Had the event not occurred, no relation would have been noticed between them. The correlation of the effects of the cause follows from their qualifying as effects.
12. Later (e.g. in *On Human Knowledge*) Russell was more sympathetic to the notion of cause.
13. I have engaged with the arguments about causation mainly as a result of thinking about time. The topic is therefore something of an away match for me. I am consequently indebted to the guidance not only of the standard sources but also of four review essays from the *Stanford Encyclopaedia of Philosophy*: De Pierris & Friedman, "Kant and Hume on Causality"; Dowe, "Causal Processes"; Schaffer, "The Metaphysics of Causation"; and Woodward, "Causation and Manipulability". These beautifully constructed, lucid surveys of the current state of philosophical thought on different

aspects of causation have provided a perfect springboard for investigating the philosophical litera-ture and for developing thoughts of my own. The acknowledgements in the text do not fully reflect the assistance I have received from them.

14. Skyrms describes our ordinary notion of causation as "an amiable confusion" (quoted in Healey, "Review of 'Asymmetries in Time'", 129). The amiable confusion is beautifully described by Sextus Empiricus:

> Some say that causes are bodies, others that they are incorporated. A cause would seem in general, according to them, to be that because of which, by being active, the effect comes about – as e.g. the sun or the heat of the sun is cause of the wax melting or of the melting of the wax. (On this point too they have been in dispute, some saying that causes are causes of nouns – e.g. of the melting – other that they are causes of predicates – e.g. of melting.) … Of these causes the majority hold that some are comprehensive, some co-operative, and some auxiliary.   (Sextus, *Outline of Scepticism*, 146–7)

15. Hume, *Enquiry into Human Understanding*, 64, 75.

16. Hume, *A Treatise of Human Nature*, 81.

17. Barry Stroud (quoted by Nagel in "Rain, Figaro and Metaphysics") makes a similar point about projectivism which builds on Humean theory when he says that it gives "a causal explanation of our causal beliefs without holding that there is anything in the independent world answering to their contents".

18. Kant quoted in De Pierris & Friedman, "Kant and Hume on Causality".

19. While the general principles of causality are *a priori*, particular causal laws are not. Even so, "Although we learn many laws through experience, they are only special determinations of still higher laws, and the highest of these, under which all others still stand, issue *a priori* from the under-standing itself" (Kant, *Critique of Pure Reason*, A126). For Kant, it is necessary that an appearance at any given time should be determined by the previous state: "I render my subjective synthesis of apprehension objective only by reference to a rule in accordance with which the appearances in their succession, that is as they happen, are determined by the preceding state. The experience of an event [i.e. of anything as *happening*] is itself possible only on this assumption" (*ibid.*, A195/B240).

20. Mellor, *The Facts of Causation*.

21. I owe this way of expressing the idea to Joe Boswell (personal communication).

22. See Tallis, "Could the Universe (Even) Give a Toss?" in *Epimethean Imaginings* for some additional reasons.

23. Lewis, "Causation".

24. Mill, *A System of Logic*, 198 (quoted in Schaffer, "The Metaphysics of Causation", 31). Trying to identify causes as necessary conditions and conditions as the circumstances that turn necessary into sufficient conditions is a lost cause. The standing (condition) occurrent (cause) contrast does not deliver a robust difference between cause and condition, either, because whether something is standing or occurrent depends on how it is described. This also applies to the distinction between primary and secondary cause or principle or subsidiary cause.

25. It could be argued (as we shall discuss presently) that the counterfactual theory, while setting aside the notion of a cause as an occult force, does not entirely dispose of causal "oomph". It but distracts from, displaces, or dissipates it, as is reflected in the fact that it breaks down the barrier between causes and conditions, protagonists and background players. The counterfactual theory of causa-tion is at least true to the asymmetry of certain causal patterns, such that while E may not always follow C, it is always true that E would not have occurred without C.

26. It is this model of causation that explained the initial resistance to the notion of fields of forces, and to so-called "action at a distance", exemplified in gravitational attraction, and the particular challenge presented to the mechanical world picture by electromagnetic fields. We are now used to thinking of fields as transmitters of causal influence in the material world. And we are comfortable with more exotic causes operating in everyday life: for example, a lifting of the rules on credit result-ing in a bank crash. Even here something of the fundamental intuition (but with a radically different balance between causes and conditions) survives, though the pushes and pressures are between abstractions sustained in the community of minds and mediated by the actions and expectations of individuals.

Hume points out that "the communication of motion" is something with which we are so familiar that we imagine we could have anticipated it *a priori* before we had any experience: "Such is the influence of custom, that, where it is strongest, it not only covers our natural ignorance, but even conceals itself, and seems to take place, merely because it is found in the highest degree" (Hume, *Enquiry into Human Understanding*, 28–9).This is why for a while it was believed that a fully trans-parent account even of social causation would find that it boiled down to the communication of motion by contact or impulse. The dream of becoming a Newton of the social world – and of a *principia* encompassing social "statics" and social dynamics – has possessed many thinkers and taken many forms over the last 250 years.

27. We could even turn things upside down by saying (as David Morey, personal communication, does) that "Matter or energy is agency without ideas".

28. "Man is a cause-seeking creature; in the spiritual order he could be called the cause-seeker. Other minds perhaps think things in other – to us inconceivable – categories" (quoted in Berlin, *The Age of Enlightenment*, 276).

29. Lucidly teased out in Woodward's excellent "Causation and Manipulability", to which I am greatly indebted.

30. We can put it this way: the desired outcome, B (your waking up) can occur as a result of many events, such as, for example (i) the sun rising and light coming in through the window, (ii) your full bladder contracting and sending arousing signals, (iii) my drawing the curtains and letting the light in, (iv) my clapping my hands. We may think of these as representing the set of conditions that could have woken you up. However, (iii) and (iv) belong to a subset of events that I can influence – events that lie within my power to change. And, finally, (iv) is the actual event that I bring about in order to wake you up.

31. Of course you might use this phenomenon to ensure that you do wake up early by deliberately not going to the toilet last thing at night, so you can count on a full bladder as your morning alarm. A high-risk strategy perhaps, but a striking reminder of the subtle ways we exploit the biological givens to our human ends.

32. This is one of the points of connection between the laws of nature and moral luck. At any rate, it is another way of highlighting the permeability of the barrier between causes (and effects) and condi-tions. The effect of a cause will be sensitive to the conditions in which it operates.

33. There is also the question of when we think of agency as coming into the universe. At what level of complexity of life does manipulation emerge? I am inclined to deny it to most organisms. Indeed, I am proudly anthropocentric in this regard. And this is connected with the plausible case that humans alone have a causal sense. See Tallis, "The Cause-Seeking Animal: Agency and the Causal Intuition" in *The Knowing Animal*.

34. Woodward, "Causation and Manipulability", 5.

35. Bergson makes the same point in *Matter and Memory* when he reminds us that the selection of the boundaries between entities in space (room, place setting, cup) and events in time (a gesture, a speech, a play) is determined by "the point where our possible action upon them ceases, where, consequently, they cease to interest our needs" (*ibid.*, 278).

36. My account of the range of possible metaphysical bases for causal connection and of the differences between sequences of events that are causally connected, and those that are not, is incomplete. Schaffer ("The Metaphysics of Causation") lists: nomological subsumption, statistical correlation, contiguous change, energy flow, physical processes, primitivism, and eliminativism, as well as the counterfactual dependence and agential manipulability we have touched on. These all have an impressive roll call of supporters. Schaffer organizes them into two main schools of thought: understanding the connection in terms of *probability* – causing is making more likely – and under-standing them in terms of process – causing is physical *producing*.

37. Always incomplete, of course, because science will never entirely shake off the pre-scientific con-sciousness, the interests, and the modes of imagining, and the language, of human beings. A more profound barrier to the ascent to utter generality is the scientist and her instruments, who in the guise of the observer fits very uncomfortably into the mathematical universe of objective science. The passage from Einstein we quoted in §3.5.3.1 highlights this:

> One is struck by the fact that the theory [relativity] … introduces two kinds of physical things, i.e. (1) measuring rods and clocks, (2) and all other things, e.g., the electromagnetic field, the material point, etc. This, in a certain sense, is inconsistent … strictly speaking, measuring rods and clocks would have to be represented as solutions of the basic equations (objects consisting of moving atomic configurations), not, as it were, theoretically self-sufficient entities.   (Einstein, "Autobiographical Notes", 59)

An analogous point is made by William Simpson (unpublished MPhil dissertation, University of Oxford, 2016) *vis-á-vis* the endeavour to reduce the universe to "the single wave function" of the microphysical interpretation of the universe: "Effective measuring devices are macroscopic objects without which the sciences would not advance but whose behaviours are not microphysically explicable." Simpson makes the point as part of a wider argument to the effect that the scientist's aspiration to advance beyond causation to laws formulated mathematically is pragmatically self-refuting as actions that depend on local causation, mediated through the properties of macroscopic objects not captured in microphysical science, are necessary to carry out effective science. This important point can be elaborated by noting that measurements involve many actions that have no place in the microphysical world; for example, travelling to CERN, carrying instruments from one room to another, setting up the experiment, looking at and transcribing the read-out from the instruments, not to speak of making sense of them and arguing over their significance. The journey from sensing to measuring does not at any stage leave ordinary sensing behind.

Smolin observes how physics falls short of addressing the entire universe: "Most of what we know about nature has come from experiments in which we artificially mark off and isolate a phenomenon from the continual whirl of the universe" (Smolin, *Time Reborn*, 38). He calls this "doing physics in a box". This box, it seems to me, is a half-way house between the parish of our consciousness and the putative view from nowhere corresponding to a complete theory of everything.

38. This is revealed in the principle, discussed by Price in *Time's Arrow and Archimedes' Point*, of "independence of incoming influences" (discussed in note 12 above).

39. We can get a hint of this contrast by thinking of an avalanche falling down the side of a mountain either as a unified process or as an ensemble of individual rocks that assume alternating roles of things acted upon and things acting upon other things; as being successively recipients and donors of inertial forces.

40. It is because it is self-conscious (and indeed self-interested) subjects, who pitch, and light up, individual and collective localities in a universe without intrinsic localities in which certain events are salient in virtue of being seen as immediate, or mediated handles, that the notion of causation as manipulability is so attractive despite its anthropomorphism.

41. See Salmon, *Scientific Explanation and the Causal Structure of the World*. Salmon's view that causality is a property of spatio-temporally continuous processes rather than a relationship between discrete events is consistent with the view advocated in this work of causation emerging out of a continuum, and it overlaps to a small degree with my more radical claim that it is the result of the irruption of consciousness into the world.

42. This is a point made by Wigner, "The Unreasonable Effectiveness of Mathematics in the Natural Sciences", which we have discussed in §3.6.

43. The ineliminable presence of manifestly contingent constants of nature – the gravitational constant, the energy state of the carbon nucleus – in the fundamental laws evident at this level underlines the passage from explanation to description. At the microphysical level of quantum mechanics, the ascent to the highest level of generality results in laws that correspond to quantitative descriptions of statistical probabilities based on what has already happened or, more precisely, been observed. A constrained randomness that results in a constant spread of observations reveals a universe that is probabilistic all the way down. It is constitutive, not merely epistemic, an expression of our incomplete knowledge, our uncertainty as to what is going to happen next arising out of our incomplete access to what has happened already and our imperfect ability to interpret, and hence extrapolate from it, to the future.

44. For more on this, the reader might want to consult Tallis, *A Conversation with Martin Heidegger*.

45. Woodward, "Causation and Manipulability", 21.

46. *Ibid.*, 22.

47. *Ibid.* Of course we may merge cause and effect, and so gather up the ballistic phase of the effect into the cause-effect relationship, by redescribing the process as "the ball being thrown" a cause whose effect does not begin until for example the process comes to a halt in the event "the window being broken".

48. If I am reluctant to confess to Kantian transcendental idealism, it is because – for the reasons given in §10.5.3 – there is a profound ambivalence in *Critique of Pure Reason* as to whether mind is mind-in-general or a set of individual consciousnesses. So, whereas I locate causation in a place deeper than that in which mere habits of expectation are formed (Hume) I am not ready to locate it in a putative place where an undifferentiated noumenal reality refracted through the mind gives rise to the phenomenal world of space, time, and distinct objects and events linked by causation (Kant).

49. There is a more animated view of the natural world as being "maintained", such that continuation or even mere preservation is continuous creation.

50. Mellor, *The Facts of Causation*; see especially Chapter 13.

51. In support of the claim that the boundary between causes and conditions is consequently arbitrary or conventional, one can think of standing causes, circumstances that are "active" – such as a gravitational field.

52. Mellor, *The Facts of Causation*, 61–2.

53. Mumford & Anjum, *Getting Causes from Powers*, 10.

54. See Searle, *Intentionality*.

55. The analogy fails spectacularly in its aim to reassure us that there is nothing special (and hence dodgy) about the idea of neural activity (analogous to water molecules) causing consciousness (analogous to shiny, slippery, moist water). The difference between molecules and ordinarily experienced water is the difference between water experienced at two (microscopic and macroscopic) levels. This explanation, however, bypasses precisely what has to be explained: namely the *origin* of these levels at which the water has different appearances: conscious viewpoints. It does not address the real question: how it is possible that anything (including neural activity) could give rise to appearances at all – irrespective of whether they are ordinary, unmediated appearances (water as I experience it directly) or appearances mediated by the theories, facts, and instruments of science (water as seen through the eyes of science). Searle seems to think that he can get his scale-relative ontologies – molecules of H_2O versus drops of water – in the absence of observers: water-in-itself is neither molecules nor drops, even less molecules causing drops. For a more detailed discussion of this example, see Tallis, *Aping Mankind*, 86–9.

56. Mellor, *Real Time II*, xiii. The idea that the identity of a physical object at different times can be defined by the notion of a "causal line", with earlier and later phases of the object belonging to the same causal line, is also associated with Russell, as we discussed in §6.2.1.1.

 Tooley takes this further in *Causation*, Chapter 14 ("Causation and the Direction of Time"), where he argues that, if one accepts a substantival view of space and time, space is an enduring entity, so that the idea that the later parts of space are causally dependent upon earlier ones is no stranger than the idea that any temporal stage of an object is dependent upon prior temporal stages. To extend causation to that in virtue of which there are successive stages of space is clearly to push causation into places where it has no right to be; for example, into a vacuum where nothing is happening. What is more, it still helps itself to "successive" phases of space that are connected and thus apparently gives temporal order priority over causal succession. Tooley's further claim that there can be causal relations "between space–time points, rather merely between events in space–time" (*ibid.*, 291) shows how far one has to go in order to give causation priority over temporality.

 Even these rather extravagant suggestions fail to deliver the necessary inversion of the priority between temporal order and causal succession. Space–time points, in order to engage in causal activity, would themselves have to have an order. What they would be ordered in and what would constitute these purely mathematical entities determining their own order is entirely unclear. Tooley's belief that "spatiotemporal regions themselves stand in causal relations to other spatio-temporal regions" permits him to conclude that "the direction of time is part of the very fabric of space–time itself" (*ibid.*, 261). To arrive at this obvious truth by such unintelligible means is an achievement of sorts.

57. This may make a kind of sense in which we think of the universe's default condition being a spontaneous restlessness that requires causal powers to resist. A stable object such as a cup may then be thought of as something digging its heels in against change.

58. There is a problem with Mellor's assertion that an object's State$_{n+1}$ is caused by its State$_n$. It would seem to be more plausible to think of an object's state as the (stable) background of any causal activity that involves it.

59. Of course, it is standard science that there can be a translation of a part of objects into pure events, as when matter becomes energy. But the rate of exchange – as when water changes phase and some of its substance is changed into energy – is not such as to challenge the ontology of everyday life, according to which objects are not just events. The supreme example of objects-as-effects and non-proportionality between cause and effect would be a first cause (such as instability in a quantum vacuum) giving rise to the universe: a fidgety Nothing bringing about the totality of Something, discussed in §10.3.3.

60. A similar reservation applies to considering (whole) states of affairs as causes and effects with the additional concern that (as with objects but even more clearly evident) there is a sense that states of affairs are things that have come to rest, pause or equilibrium, or they are a slice of the world, only through being viewed in a snapshot gaze that sees it as unchanging. What is more, if a state of affairs acts as one, its causal influences would seem to be transmitted block-to-block rather than through discrete chains that we typically think of in relation to causes. The model also seems to pre-empt any division into causes and background conditions: the platform from which causes operate (and the platform that makes the world susceptible to their effects) is lost. Given that there is no basis for slicing the world into successive states of affairs, we are close to the notion of a seamless unfolding that has been broken up by a viewpoint and which causation has been invoked to repair. (There are, for example, no built-in boundaries to the "now" at which causation operates.) This kind of block-to-block causation – in which the entire world at time t$_1$ is the cause of the entire world at time t$_2$ – could be seen as the *ne plus ultra* of joint causation.

61. The principle of proportionality between cause and immediate effect – which is prior to the operation of any conditions that permit amplification – is bound up with the notion that causation is the loss by a cause of what an effect gains – momentum, heat, or some transform of the donated energy.

62. Peter Cave (personal communication) has argued that, if a cause is truly sufficient to its effect, the latter should already be in place, so that causes and effects (and by extension all events) must happen simultaneously. If a cause is sufficient, it should be irresistible not even for a moment. This principle of immediacy and irresistibility should be particularly applicable if each stage of the cause is proportionate to each stage of the effect. This underlines the role of the idea of causation in repairing the undifferentiated continuity of the universe subjected to the irruption of viewpoint.

63. The players here are either objects (Kant's bottom, etc.) or causal continuants ("pressure from Kant's bottom") which do not "occur" (at a particular time) in the way events do and so do not naturally seem to fall into a temporal relationship.

64. This is evident even in the simplest of cases; for example, the standard collision between billiard balls. We think of the momentum exchange between the two billiard balls; or the sharing of the momentum of moving billiard ball A between itself and billiard ball B. We define the cause as the horizontal movement of A and the effect as the slowing of the horizontal movement of A and the increase in that of B. We marginalize other things that happen: the rotation of each billiard ball round its own axis, the interaction between the baize and the ball, and the depressions created in the baize by the movements of the balls. Even in this basic example, in short, there is a densely woven network of causally related events available to be unpicked with other noun phrases. We could of course divide what is happening into ever smaller cause-and-effect pairs, with causes acting over shorter and shorter periods of time until we arrive at causal relata that have no duration at all. Long before then, of course, we have left saliency behind.

65. It is important not to over-state the description-dependency of causal relationships. It does not "go all the way down". When I allocate blame for the window's being broken I could equally well characterize it as "I threw the ball" or "My throwing the ball". The transformation of a sentence with an active verb into a noun phrase does not impugn the causal power of that which is referred to or redistribute responsibility.

66. Mellor, "Causes as Facts", in *The Facts of Causation*. Mellor's players are transcendent entities (abstract and not located in space–time) rather than immanent ones such as events that are concrete and spatiotemporal. Given that there is no literal contact between facts, this may be why he calls them *facta* – the immanent truth-makers for true sentences or propositions. It is not the facts

but these truth-makers that do the pushing and shoving that causes seem to do to produce their effects. In this sense he is hedging his bets.

67. Here, and elsewhere in my discussion, I have found Rodriguez-Pereyra, "Mellor's Facts and Chances of Causation" very helpful.

68. If facts have a spatial location it is through proxies: documentation – presence on paper, on screens, in mouths, and in ears.

69. It was the observation that facts can never go out of existence or change which led McTaggart to argue against the reality of change. He confused facts and events. Calling events facts by making them noun-phrases preceded by "that" firms them up and gives them quasi-solidity, object-status – and a permanence that objects would envy.

70. For a discussion of this see Tallis, *Not Saussure*, Chapter 7. Among other things, this addresses the issue that Mellor does not make clear; namely the need to clarify, when speaking of facts (or *facta*, as Mellor does) whether one is speaking of items existing independently on the ground or requiring the help of mouths or pages.

71. Mellor, *The Facts of Causation*.

72. Vendler, "Effects, Results and Consequences", flags up the deep distinction in our use of "cause" and "effect" between occurrences of verb nominalizations that are fact-like or propositional and occurrences that are event-like.

73. We haven't discussed the relationship between fields of forces as causes and event-causes. A few observations are in order. Fields can seem like continuously acting, non-localised causes. The supreme example (before it was transformed into the geometry of space–time) was Newtonian gravity, which daringly suggested non-contiguous causation – action-at-a-distance. This opened the way for other fields, not the least being the electromagnetic field – whose magnetic aspect prompted Einstein's thrill when as a five-year-old he looked at a compass. The property of an object by which it continued to move at a fixed velocity in a straight line or remain in a state of rest was out-sourced to inertial forces – the averaged out influence of rest of the matter in the universe – operating at a distance. The transformation of gravitational and other forces into the geometry of space made the spatial separation of action-at-a-distance a matter of appearance only.

74. A variation on Gabriel Marcel's formulation in *Being and Having*: "The universe is the dehiscence of being" (diary entry for 1 November).

75. Wittgenstein, *Tractatus Logico-Philosophicus*, §1.

76. See Tallis, *The Knowing Animal* for a discussion of the "propositional awareness" distinctive to human consciousness.

77. Wittgenstein, *Tractatus Logico-Philosophicus*, §1.1.

78. And looking to quantum mechanics for support in metaphysical and ontological matters is hardly in tune with the anti-scientistic spirit of this book.

79. Merleau-Ponty, *The Phenomenology of Perception*, 411.

80. Davidson, "The Individuation of Events", 179.

81. See Heidegger, *Being and Time, passim*.

82. Our opposition to a causal theory of knowledge (of consciousness, perception, and memory discussed in §10.4.3) would also apply to knowledge of causes *qua* causes. An event E cannot *both* cause a perception and, in virtue of being the cause of the perception, make the latter (a) a perception of itself and (b) of the truth of the proposition *that* E occurred. Underlying this is a fundamental principle: that Being does not of itself generate truth about itself: x does not of itself make itself explicit as "That x is the case". That "truth supervenes on Being" implies that is not inherent in Being – or at least in the beings that are the subject of truth.

83. Heidegger, *The Fundamental Concepts of Metaphysics*.

84. It is difficult to resist Kant's claim that a full-blown object requires a full-blown subject: that the unity of the "I" and the unity of the "it" and indeed "the world" are codependent. Whether he would have approved of the suggestion that the path to objectivity is taken by sentient creatures evolving towards full subject-hood is another matter.

85. Von Uexküll, *Theoretical Biology*.

86. See Martinez-Conde *et al.*, "The Role of Fixational Eye Movements in Visual Perception". The authors discuss the paradox whereby "we must fix our gaze to inspect the minute details of our world, but if we were to fixate perfectly the entire world would fade from view".

87. See note 80 for Chapter 10, above.
88. This is true of senses other than vision – notably touch. The succession of tactile sensations adds up to an object revealed to touch. We create the stasis of a whole that exceeds the surface area of the palpitating fingers through the dynamics of touch.
89. See Tallis, "Auguries of Insignificance" in *The Black Mirror*.
90. On the significance of pointing, see Tallis, *Michelangelo's Finger*.
91. Newton-Smith, *The Structure of Time*, 28 *et seq*.
92. See Mellor, *Real Time II*, 84 and also Mellor, "Time" in *The Facts of Causation*.
93. The sense of approaching extinction is connected with the notion, referred to earlier as a disanalogy with space, that time is in a sense *used up*. Temporal positions do not endure: t_1 is available only at t_1 (though it is never itself "at" t_1). One expression of this is that we cannot go back to t_1 from any subsequent position (and we cannot avoid getting to t_1 from any antecedent position). The so-called time reversibility of physical changes is in fact a space-reversibility over time. (This is in fact probably just another way of saying that time passes and space doesn't.). We often refer to the wish that something that has happened would unhappen as "wanting to turn the clock back" – as if reversing events requires a reversal of the direction of time. If it did, nothing could be reversed. What has happened can be reversed; that it has happened cannot.
94. Mellor, *Real Time II*, 123.

CHAPTER 12

1. For a detailed discussion, see my *I Am* and *Aping Mankind*. It is because they lack a full-blown intentional relationship to objects and events perceived as things-in-themselves that non-human animals do not have a fully developed causal sense. Associative learning – which may be a cue for behaviour relevant to an effect, does not involve an explicit sense of causation. Conditioning of expectations and behaviour conflates mere association with true causation.
2. The problems with the causal theory of perception whereby effects are the registering of their causes are more nails in the coffin of the idea that time acquires its direction from the relationship between material causes and material effects.
3. Paul Churchland's most detailed account of his position is in *Matter and Consciousness*. It is succinctly summarised on page 67 of his "Eliminative Materialism and the Propositional Attitudes": "Eliminative materialism is the thesis that our common-sense conception of psychological phenomena constitutes a radically false theory, a theory so fundamentally defective that both the principle and the ontology of the theory will eventually be displaced, rather than smoothly reduced by, completed neuroscience."
4. Patricia Churchland's definitive account of her position is in her landmark *Neurophilosophy*.
5. Stich, *From Folk Psychology to Cognitive Science*. Stich has subsequently changed his mind; see "Do True Believers Exist?".
6. Rosenberg, "Eliminativism without Tears". Rosenberg bases some of his argument on research into the neurophysiology of memory by Eric Kandel and co-workers. Kandel discovered that the neural changes associated with acquisition of non-propositional know-how or conditioned reflexes were similar to those associated with the acquisition of explicit or propositional memories, though more synapses were involved. The obvious conclusion is not that non-propositional and explicit memory are essentially the same but that neurophysiology cannot register, even less explain, their obvious fundamental difference.
7. The assumption that what (quantitative) physical science cannot see or accommodate must be unreal will also extend to qualia and other contents of consciousness as physics and the biophysical sciences are drained of qualities and hence of phenomenal consciousness. The disconnect between neural activity and folk psychological contents is particular sharp in the case of items such as thoughts and beliefs. Token neural activity cannot carry the general meaning of a thought such as "Manchester United have had a poor season". The irreducible generality of its meaning is the necessary condition of its (shareable) intelligibility.
8. Feser, "Post-Intentional Depression".
9. Rosenberg, "Eliminativism without Tears", 13.

10. In *Intentionality*, Searle usefully distinguishes between original and derived intentionality, the former typically relating to perceptions and the latter to statements. The boundary is permeable, with original intentionality being affected by derived intentionality. What we see, even more what we notice, is deeply influenced by what we know.

11. Rosenberg ("Eliminativism without Tears") tries to escape the charge of self-refutation by stating that while intentionality is a myth, the brain is still chock full of "information". This information, however, is not "about" anything. It doesn't sound very informative information to me.

12. There are other reasons for rejecting the causal theory of perception upon which eliminativism depends. First, it requires the same event (or set of events) to be not only the cause of perception but also its content and a truth-maker making the perception it causes a truth about itself. (This is at odds with the post-Gettier recognition that the truth and justification of a belief come from different sources.) Secondly, the participants in the causal relationship are not clear because when I perceive an object, the putative cause is not the object (e.g. the glass I am seeing now) but the interaction between the object and the light and the interaction between this and the nervous system (or the sensory system). In the case of an event (e.g. seeing a car going down a road) the putative cause is even more complexly related to any perception. Thirdly, the event that is supposed to have caused the perception has to be picked out by an attentive consciousness. A conscious subject is not the passive effect of the energy that surrounds and hence impinges on her body.

13. There is a further question of how we know that objects are known by, or at least are in the worlds, of others. There are some obvious situations where this is revealed directly – as when we struggle to move an object together or compete over it when it is an object of desire. And we can also infer the reality of the object from the fact that another person steps round it, trips over it, disappears behind it, or manipulates it in our sight. But neither of these takes us all the way to a full appreciation that the things that surround us belong to a common world accessed by others.

14. The material world has no past or future tense and it borrows its present tense – the transformation of "is" into "*that* it is" and thus into the contents of "now" – from the subjects to whom it is present.

15. For excellent critiques see Merleau-Ponty, *The Phenomenology of Perception* (particularly directed against the atomism of Locke and Hume) and Sacks, *Objectivity and Insight*.

16. The perils of "rigid staring" and the failure to recognize that our being in the world is not merely a state of being surrounded by an array of objects that are merely "present at hand" as opposed to being immersed in a nexus of signification, are addressed in the discussion of Heidegger's *Being and Time* in Tallis, *A Conversation with Martin Heidegger*.

17. This view goes back to Locke and is succinctly summarized by Sacks as the idea that "our survival requires epistemic shortfall" (*Objectivity and Insight*, 17).

18. For a discussion of "propositional awareness" see Tallis, *The Knowing Animal*.

19. It is important not to take the phrase "mental time travel" too literally. We do not strictly travel to a token state of affairs obtaining at, or event occurring at, t_1 by means of a memory – a token event at time t_2. Even less do we travel, via a memory at t_2 to the actual time t_1.

20. When we scan the world, we can have some control over the order of our own experiences. Succession perceptions are not causally related: the top of a tree is no more the effect of the bottom of the tree than vice versa.

21. As discussed in §10.4.3, my sense of my own temporal depth and that of the world around me grow in parallel, each confirming and deepening the other. That the world around me has pasts and futures and that I have pasts and futures are mutually confirming or reinforcing intuitions. The successive positions or states of the object, the succession of experienced events, the successive states of the world, are internalized as consciousness of succession and consciousness of my consciousness as successive – as relating to a past that once was present and to a present that once was future.

22. Kane, *The Significance of Free Will*, 4. Roger Scruton (personal communication) has pointed out validly that this definition does not emphasize accountability and responsibility – concepts equally alien to no-person science – and other concepts under which we locate the manifestations of human agency. If I have focused my discussion where I have, this is because where the noisiest arguments are located.

23. Lockwood, *The Labyrinth of Time*, 68.

24. Those who deny freedom also owe us an explanation as to why certain actions appear to be more free than others. The notions of "wholeheartedness", of acting in accordance with one's deepest

needs, desires, convictions, etc., as opposed to acting impulsively or under duress, etc., behaving in response to conditioning as opposed to acting after a period of reflection, are distinctions that would have no meaning in a universe without the possibility of free action.

25. Libet *et al.*, "Time of Conscious Intention to Act in Relation to the Onset of Cerebral Activity (Readiness Potential)".

26. Soon *et al.*, "Unconscious Determinants of Free Decisions in the Human Brain".

27. Quoted in Smith, "Neuroscience vs Philosophy", 24.

28. Soon *et al.*, "Unconscious Determinants of Free Decisions in the Human Brain".

29. *Ibid.*, 543.

30. Quoted in Smith, "Neuroscience vs Philosophy", 24.

31. Libet, "Do We Have Free Will?", 47.

32. The most important – summarized in Ananthaswamy, "Brain Might Not Stand in the Way of Free Will" – has questioned the assumption that the Readiness Potential is the signature of the brain planning and deciding to move. It might just be a reflection of the random fluctuation of activity in the brain and, when it is a question of meaningless event such as wiggling a finger, we might be inclined to take the path of least resistance and move our finger when the brain force is, as it were, with us. This is particularly relevant given that subjects were asked to move on the basis of an "urge" to move. In short, the movement is triggered when the neural noise crosses a threshold; so the readiness potential was just the necessary prior conditions of making a decision when there is nothing else to drive it.

 This is a viewed shared by Merlin Donald in "Consciousness and the Freedom to Act", which sees the Readiness Potential as just a general state of anticipation, not specific to any particular movement. Von Wachter's demolition of Libet's claims in "Libet's Experiment Provides No Evidence against Strong Libertarian Free Will because Readiness Potentials Do Not Cause Our Actions" is definitive. His most important argument is based on experiments that demonstrate that the Readiness Potential does not cause the movements being investigated.

 The criticisms also apply to the experiments by Haynes *et al.* With respect to the latter, it is important to note that the scientists' ability to predict which finger the subject would wiggle was roughly 60 per cent correct and 40 per cent incorrect – not much more than chance. Haynes's more recent study still stayed with a simple task – where the choice was between adding or subtracting two numbers from a series being presented. More recently, Fried and colleagues have recorded directly from single neurons in patients undergoing neurosurgery and could predict with 80 per cent accuracy the timing of a decision just under a second before it was made (cited in Smith, "Neuroscience vs Philosophy", 25). The major barriers to drawing conclusion about free will from these experiments, to be discussed, still remain.

33. Von Wachter, "Libet's Experiment Provides No Evidence ...", 5.

34. Another problem with Libet's experiment is that it subscribes to a rather crude dualism. It assumes that there is an event called an intention that occurs at a particular time, corresponding to a subjective experience but not to brain events. The intention has to take place at a particular time but, being mental, does not occur at a particular place – which neurodeterminists who believe in physics as the last word must find rather awkward given that space and time are supposed to be inseparable.

35. The numerous experiments revealing the subtle changes in behaviour and awareness arising out of exposure to prior stimuli that the subject may be unaware of are summarized in Bargh & Ferguson, "Beyond Behaviourism".

36. Donald, "Consciousness and the Freedom to Act", 16. It is of course entirely proper that trivial decisions upon which little or nothing relevant to our long-term aims should be influenced by unregistered external influences, inner unconscious influences or caprice. If this were not the case, we would be paralysed, waiting for the arrival of a compelling reason to do A or B, turn right or turn left, or whatever. There has to be an extensive middle ground between on the one hand explicit, voluntary actions that are the product of deliberation and the kind of automatism that makes such action possible.

37. For a more detailed exposition of this point see Tallis, "How on Earth Can I be Free" in *The Mystery of Being Human* and below.

38. Just as the mechanical forces involved in falling down the stairs are not sufficient to account for descending with the intention of getting to the front door to start a journey to London.

39. It is possible that this is why writers such as Mellor are persuaded that causal order provides the basis for temporal order. The means-end ordering perhaps creates the impression of a clock inherent in cause-effect ordering. We cannot bring about the means by using the end – the shaking of the tree by the falling of the fruit. If my action X is to bring about intended goal Y, Y cannot precede X.

40. Mill, "Nature".

41. *Ibid.*, 152.

42. *Ibid.*

43. *Ibid.*, 152–3.

44. For reasons discussed in Tallis, *The Hand*, and its two successor volumes in the trilogy (*I Am* and *The Knowing Animal*).

45. Popper who describes scientific theories "as human inventions – nets designed by us to catch the world" (*The Open Universe*, 42) has made a similar point that theories are not part of the material world. One aspect of this is that theories are approximate while there is nothing in the material world that is approximate: it simply is. (Just as there is nothing in the material world that is either true or false; it simply is.)

46. This is clearly expressed by Shaun Gallagher: "[T]he question of freedom, or the free use of the will, is a matter that is most appropriately decided on the narrative time scale … and it is a mistake to think that it can be decided at the elementary scale (the scale of motor control)" ("Time in Action", 431).

47. Even this is a gross simplification. When one beast chases after another, there is an identity between the envisaged goal and an object in a certain place. But when I am walking to a pub, the goal will not be the building a certain number of yards away but the drinking, the conversation and the friendship it might foster. It would be odd to say that, because I am 20 yards from the pub, I am 20 yards away from my goal of cheering you up after the bad news I have learnt that you have just received.

48. Steward, "Processes, Continuants, and Individuals" is highly pertinent. She argues that processes, unlike events, are "entities which, like substances, are present in their entirety at each moment of their existence, rather than being composed, like events, of temporal parts" and suggests that this may be important for a better understanding of the nature of actions. We may think of complex actions (and which actions seen clearly are not complex?) as unified processes rather than chains of events. An action, being a process, is not merely an aggregate of its parts. The whole, in the keeping of the agent, dictates the parts in a way that an aggregation of events could not. In §6.2.1.1, we rather dismissed the boundary between events and processes as merely a matter of viewpoint. The Battle of Hastings seen from within while it is happening is a process; the Battle of Hastings referred from without by historians is an event. This difference is now more substantive. An action is, uniquely, something that can be seen from within, en route to its fulfilment or completion, a viewpoint particularly associated with that of the agent.

49. We shall return to this – and to Roger Scruton's notion of "virtual causality" in art – in §12.4.2.

50. The asymmetry between the agent who uses causes and the (material) world in which he or she operates is evident in the simplest action. Though, when I am sitting on a rock, there seems to be a kind of equality between the rock pushing up and my bottom pushing down, the process by which this interaction came into being was entirely different. Yes, rock and bottom level with one another as physical object to physical object, with action and reaction being equal and opposite; but the players arrived by different means. The arrival of the rock at my bottom could be explained in entirely physical terms, while an account of the arrival of my bottom at the rock would need to invoke my decision to sit down, having checked that the rock was safe, or that it was polite to do so, or that I had time to take a break before the job I had set myself. Thus the static or dynamic equilibrium of the action-reaction between me and the rock is profoundly asymmetrical: it was set in place by an initial genuine action: my coming up the hill, spotting the rock, and sitting down. This chain of happenings is quite different from the chain of happenings that brought the rock into being or the Newtonian dialogue between it and my bottom.

51. I have been unable to locate this quotation and if Gazzaniga did not say this, I shall proudly claim it as my own.

52. As Donald puts it, "Humanity's uniqueness lies in our collective cognitive systems, that is, in our cultures" ("Consciousness and the Freedom to Act", 15). The extension of our physical and cognitive capacities began before we were born – several million years ago, but most notably in recent

centuries. My capacity for moving over the surface of the earth has its roots in thousands of technological achievements reaching from the wheel to the petrol engine. Many of our actions are prepared by our ancestors whose agency we draw on.

53. Our control over the future is of course limited – by the bounds of our power, our incomplete knowledge, by forces impinging from outside the sphere that concerns us. And in willing a particular future, we do not bring about something that had no possibility of taking place in the absence of our intervention; rather we increase the probability of its happening. Our interventions are deflections in the field of possibility.

54. Gallagher, "Time in Action", 421.

55. See Povinelli, *Folk Physics for Apes*.

56. What follows may seem to say the opposite of what Price has claimed that "the asymmetry of causation is anthropocentric in origin. Roughly, it reflects the time-asymmetric perspective we occupy as *agents* in the world – the fact that we deliberate for the future on the basis of information about the past" (*Time's Arrow*, 10). As agents we are indeed time-asymmetric but we can turn the asymmetry on its head: we allow the future to influence the past so that the latter can influence the future.

57. Strawson, "The Impossibility of Moral Responsibility". I deal with this argument at greater length in *Aping Mankind*, 256–9.

58. Bergson criticized the notion that to act freely is merely to make a binary choice, arguing that the alternatives are "never really given as such in advance ... They are fictions invented after the fact in order to tell a story that has a beginning, a middle, and an end" (quoted in Guerlac, *Thinking in Time*, 83). There are no discrete alternatives, only a "multitude of different and successive states" (*ibid.*). To make the exercise of freedom a mere choice between equally justified forks in the road is making free will merely the exercise of caprice and emptying it of meaning.

59. Bergson, too, locates freedom in the (widening) interval between stimulus and response. Curiously, however, he locates the beginning of freedom in mere sensation which would oblige us to ascribe freedom to any sentient organism, including many that seem to have no freedom and certainly not freedom as we understand it. Our present argument locates the beginning of freedom not in sensation but in full-blown intentionality and the opening up of the plenum of being into a world of explicit objects and events that signify temporal depth – past, present, and future. Bergson, it seems to me, gets only half way to the right answer because the delay between stimulus and response is filled by cerebral events, by further material steps. The gap that we have identified is inseparable from intentionality prising open the material world and making way for tensed time and all that follows from that.

60. See Cunningham *et al.*, "Sensorimotor Adaptation to Violations of Temporal Contiguity".

61. The fact that the elements of an action are not atoms of movement located in an instant but fragments of an intelligible whole is connected with the argument we made in §3.5.1.

62. I discuss "The Uncoupled Animal" in *The Knowing Animal*.

63. Especially in *The Knowing Animal*.

64. Some of the arguments in this section are developed at greater length in Tallis & Spalding, *Summers of Discontent*.

65. Whitehead, "Religion in History", 21.

66. Lévi-Strauss, *Mythologiques I*, quoted in Leach, *Claude Lévi-Strauss*, 115.

67. Paul Valéry. I have quoted this frequently but cannot find where Valéry said it! If it is something I have made up, I shall be very pleased. There are, of course, many other activities undertaken for their own sake, most notably (and at present ubiquitously) sport. The reasons for not ranking sport with art as a fundamental liberation from the human condition are set out in chapter 6 of Tallis, *Theorrhoea and After*. One of the key reasons I offer is that sport is inseparable from the quantitative world – times, scores, rankings – and in this sense is subordinated to an outcome. Sport, in short, acquires a secondary quasi-utility through delivering victory. Art is only implicitly and accidentally competitive. One performance of Beethoven's piano sonatas may be better than another but that is not the key issue when we are listening to either performance. The victory at the end of the performance – if it is any good – is over the chains of time.

68. The scene in the first part of *Faust*, in which the eponymous hero struggles to translate the opening verse of the Gospel according to St John, is pertinent. He rejects "In the beginning was the word"

for "In the beginning was the deed". The word was a new kind of deed that inserted a beginning in the order of things; perhaps the insertion of *kairos* (the appointed time) into *chronos* (plain time).

69. Bergson, *Time and Free Will*, 9.
70. Scruton, *Understanding Music*, 5.
71. This is why attempts to give a biological explanation of art and to relate the aesthetic experience to the evolved properties of one organ in the organism – namely the brain – is to miss the point, indeed the fundamental nature, of art and the existential reality to which it belongs. In the creation and experience of art, humankind is most remote from (physical and biological) nature. I will spare the reader a reiteration of the arguments set out in Tallis & Spalding, *Summers of Discontent*.
72. Sartre, *Being and Nothingness*, where it is a theme that is developed over many hundreds of pages.
73. See Tallis, *Aping Mankind*.

EPILOGUES

1. I have borrowed this term from Huw Price (*Time's Arrow and Archimedes' Point*).
2. Sellars, "Philosophy and the Scientific Image of Man", 35.
3. Maudlin, *Philosophy of Physics*, xiv.
4. I have checked this beautiful phrase with Professor Scruton who acknowledges it as his own but cannot remember where he said it.
5. Address to the Fourth International Congress of Philosophy Bologna, 1911, quoted in Psillos, "Physics, Mathematics and Skepticism". Bergson adds that "[This single thing] being a thought which brings something new into the world … is of course obliged to manifest itself through the ready-made ideas it comes across and draws into its movement"; in my own case, as with Bergson, often through views with which I disagree.
6. Gellner, *Conditions of Liberty*, 95.
7. Sellars, "Philosophy and the Scientific Image of Man", 36. Mark Sacks in *Objectivity and Insight* has argued that "from the perspective of a sufficiently critical philosophy, the scientific image is merely the manifest image" (322). The former, like the latter, takes on "uncritical ontological commitments" in particular to the distinction between subjects or objects.
8. Wilson, *Consilience*.
9. Stace, "Man Against Darkness", 2. The indifference of the universe to each one of us is perhaps no more shocking than the indifference of some of us to all others and the indifference of all of us to most others. The universe does not know better – because it is not a knower.
10. Kauffman, "Breaking the Galilean Spell".
11. Burtt, *The Metaphysical Foundations of Modern Science*, 85; italics added.
12. Stephen Hawking on a US television show, *Reality on the Rocks: Beyond Our Ken*, 1995.
13. See, for example, Tallis, "You Chemical Scum, You".
14. Strawson *et al.*, *Consciousness and its Place in Nature*, 8.
15. See Strawson's critics in Strawson *et al.*, *ibid.*
16. That physics is the product of consciousness is not to be confused with the idealistic claim that the physical world is the product of consciousness.

References

Ainsworth, P. "What is Ontic Structural Realism?". *Studies in the History and Philosophy of Science. Part B: Studies in the History and Philosophy of Modern Physics* 41 (2010): 50–57.

Albert, D. "On the Origin of Everything". *New York Times* (25 March 2012).

Ali, A. F. & D. Saurya. "Cosmology from Quantum Potential". *Physics Letters B* 741 (2015): 276–9.

Al-Khalili, J. *Paradox: The Nine Greatest Enigmas in Science*. London: Bantam, 2012.

Ananthaswamy, A. "Brain Might Not Stand in the Way of Free Will". *New Scientist* (9 August 2012).

Aristotle. *Metaphysics*, W. D. Ross (trans.). In *The Works of Aristotle*, vol. 8, W. D. Ross (ed.). Oxford: Clarendon Press, 1928.

Aristotle. *On Interpretation*, E. M. Edgehill (trans.). In *The Works of Aristotle*, vol. 1, W. D. Ross (ed.). Oxford: Clarendon Press, 1928.

Aristotle. *Physics*, R. P. Hardie & R. K. Gaye (trans.). In *The Works of Aristotle*, vol. 2, W. D. Ross (ed.). Oxford: Clarendon Press, 1930.

Arntzenius, F. "Is Quantum Mechanics Pointless?". *Philosophy of Science* 70 (2003): 1444–57.

Arntzenius, F. & T. Maudlin. "Time Travel and Modern Physics". *The Stanford Encyclopedia of Philosophy* (winter 2013 edn), E. N. Zalta (ed.). Retrieved from http://plato.stanford.edu/archives/win2013/entries/time-travel-phys.

Auden, W. H. "In Time of War". In W. H. Auden & C. Isherwood, *Journey to a War*. London: Faber & Faber, 1939.

Augustine. *Confessions*, R. S. Pine-Coffin (trans.). London: Penguin, 1961.

Austin, J. L. *Sense and Sensibilia*. Reconstructed from manuscript notes by G. J. Warnock. Oxford: Oxford University Press, 1974.

Baker, A. "Science-Driven Mathematical Explanation". *Mind* 121(482) (2012): 243–67.

Barbour, J. "The Development of Machian Themes in the Twentieth Century". In J. Butterfield (ed.), *The Arguments of Time*, 83–111. Oxford: Oxford University Press, 1992.

Barbour, J. *The End of Time: The Next Revolution in our Understanding of the Universe*. Oxford: Oxford University Press, 1999.

Bargh, J. & M. Ferguson. "Beyond Behaviourism: On the Automaticity of Higher Mental Processes". *Psychological Bulletin* 126 (2000): 926–46.

Barrow, I. *The Geometrical Lectures of Isaac Barrow* (J. M. Child, trans.). Chicago, IL: Open Court, 1916.

Barrow, J. *New Theories of Everything*. Oxford: Oxford University Press, 2007.

Bergson, H. *Creative Evolution*, A. Mitchell (trans.). New York: Dover, 1998.

Bergson, H. *The Creative Mind: An Introduction to Metaphysics*, M. L. Andison (trans.). New York: Dover, [1946] 2007.

Bergson, H. *Matter and Memory*, N. M. Paul & W. S. Palmer (trans.). London: Allen & Unwin, 1911.

Bergson, H. *Time and Free Will: An Essay on the Immediate Data of Consciousness*, F. L. Pogson (trans.). New York: Dover, 2001.

Berlin, I. (ed.). *The Age of Enlightenment: The Eighteenth-Century Philosophers*. New York: Mentor, 1956.

Bernstein, J. *Einstein*. London: Fontana, 1973.

Blumenfield, D. "On the Compossibility of the Divine Attributes". *Philosophical Studies* 34 (1978): 91–103.

Boethius. *The Consolation of Philosophy*, V. E. Watts (trans.). London: Penguin, 1969.

Born, M. *Einstein's Theory of Relativity*. New York: Dover, 1962.

Bourne, C. "Fatalism and the Future". In C. Callender (ed.), *Oxford Handbook of Philosophy of Time*, 41–67. Oxford: Oxford University Press, 2011.

Bourne, C. *A Future for Presentism*. Oxford: Oxford University Press, 2006.

Braude, S. "Memory without a Trace". *Anti-Matter* 1 (2007): 91–106.

Broad, C. D. *Scientific Thought*. London: Routledge & Kegan Paul, 1923.

Bunnin, N. & J. Yu (eds). *Blackwell Dictionary of Western Philosophy*. Oxford: Blackwell, 2004.

Burkert, W. *Lore and Science in Ancient Pythagoreanism*. Cambridge, MA: Harvard University Press, 1972.

Burtt, E. A. *The Metaphysical Foundations of Modern Science*. Garden City, NY: Doubleday, 1954.

Butterfield, J. "Seeing the Present". *Mind* 93 (1984): 161–76.

Butterfield, J. & C. Isham. "Emergence of Time in Quantum Gravity". In J. Butterfield (ed.), *The Arguments of Time*, 111–169. Oxford: Oxford University Press, 1992.

Callender, C. "The Common Now". *Philosophical Issues* 18: 1 (2008): 339–61.

Callender, C. "Finding 'Real' Time in Quantum Mechanics". In W. L. Craig & Q. Smith (eds), *Einstein, Relativity and Absolute Simultaneity*, 50–72. Oxford: Oxford University Press, 2011.

Callender, C. (ed.). *Oxford Handbook of Philosophy of Time*. Oxford: Oxford University Press, 2011.

Callender, C. "There is No Puzzle about the Low Entropy Past". Retrieved from http://philosophyfaculty. ucsd.edu/faculty/ccallender/index_files/there%20is%20no%20puzzle%20about%20the%20low%20 entropy%20past.doc (accessed July 2016).

Canales, J. *The Physicist and the Philosopher: Einstein, Bergson, and the Debate that Changed our Understanding of Time*. Princeton, NJ: Princeton University Press, 2015.

Carnap, R. "Intellectual Autobiography". In P. A. Schillp (ed.), *The Philosophy of Rudolf Carnap*. LaSalle, IL: Open Court, 1963.

Carr, D. "Commentary on 'Placing the Past: Groundwork for a Spatial Theory of History'". *Rethinking History* 11(4) (2007): 501–5.

Carr, N. "Is Google Making Us Stupid? What the Internet is Doing to Our Brains". *The Atlantic* (July–August 2008).

Cave, P. "With and Without End". *Philosophical Investigations* 30 (2007): 105–24.

Chalmers, D. *The Conscious Mind: In Search of a Fundamental Theory*. Oxford: Oxford University Press, 1996.

Chalmers, D. & T. Bayne. "What Is the Unity of Consciousness?". In D. Chalmers (ed.), *The Character of Consciousness*, 497–541. Oxford: Oxford University Press, 2010.

Chalmers, M. "Seeing Triple". *New Scientist* (28 September 2013): 35–7.

Chalmers, M. "State of Mind". *New Scientist* (10 May 2014): 33–6.

Chown, M. "No Time Like the Present." In *The Never-Ending Days of Being Dead*. London: Faber, 2007.

Churchland, Patricia. *Neurophilosophy: Towards a Unified Science of the Mind/Brain*. Cambridge MA: MIT Press, 1986.

Churchland, Paul. "Eliminative Materialism and the Propositional Attitudes". *Journal of Philosophy* LXXVIII (1981): 67–90.

Churchland, Paul. *Matter and Consciousness*, 2nd edn. Cambridge, MA: MIT Press, 1988.

Clarke, C. J. S. "Time in General Relativity". In J. Earman, C. Glymour & J. Stachel (eds), *The Foundations of Space-Time Theories*. Minneapolis, MN: University of Minnesota Press, 1977.

Cohen, I. B. *The Birth of a New Physics*. London: Penguin, 1985.

Cohen, S., P. Curd & C. D. C. Reeve (eds). *Readings in Ancient Greek Philosophy: From Thales to Aristotle*. Indianapolis, IN: Hackett, 1995.

Colyvan, M. "Indispensability Arguments in the Philosophy of Mathematics". *The Stanford Encyclopedia of Philosophy* (spring 2015 edn), E. N. Zalta (ed.). Retrieved from http://plato.stanford.edu/archives/ spr2015/entries/mathphil-indis.

Cornford, F. M. *Plato and Parmenides.* London: Routledge & Kegan Paul, 1939.

Cunningham, D., B. Billock & B. Tsou "Sensorimotor Adaptation to Violations of Temporal Contiguity". 12 (2001): 532–5.

Currie, G. "Can There be a Literary Philosophy of Time?". In J. Butterfield (ed.), *The Arguments of Time*, 43–65. Oxford: Oxford University Press, 1992.

Dainton, B. "Temporal Consciousness". *The Stanford Encyclopedia of Philosophy* (winter 2016 edn), E. N. Zalta (ed.). Retrieved from http://plato.stanford.edu/archives/win2016/entries/consciousness-temporal.

Dainton, B. "Time, Passage and Immediate Experience". In C. Callender (ed.), *Oxford Handbook of the Philosophy of Time*, 382–419. Oxford: Oxford University Press, 2011.

Dainton, B. *Time and Space*, 2nd edn. Durham: Acumen, 2010.

Dantzig, T. *Number, the Language of Science: a Critical Survey Written for the Cultured Non-Mathematician.* London: Macmillan, 1930.

Davidson, D. "The Individuation of Events". In his *Essays on Actions and Events*, 163–80. Oxford: Clarendon Press, 1980.

Davidson, M. "Presentism and Grounding Past Truths". In R. Cuini *et al.* (eds), *New Papers on the Present Focus on Presentism.* Munich: Philosophia, 2013.

Davies, P. *About Time: Einstein's Unfinished Revolution.* London: Penguin, 2005.

Davies, P. *The Ghost in the Atom: A Discussion of the Mysteries of Quantum Physics.* Cambridge: Canto, 2003.

Davies, P. "That Mysterious Flow". *Scientific American* (February 2006): 40–47.

De Certeau, M. "Walking in the City". In *The Practice of Everyday Life.* Berkeley, CA: University of California Press, 2011.

De Pierris, G. & M. Friedman. "Kant and Hume on Causality". *The Stanford Encyclopedia of Philosophy* (winter 2013 edn), E. N. Zalta (ed.). Retrieved from http://plato.stanford.edu/archives/win2013/entries/kant-hume-causality.

Deasy, D. "The Moving Spotlight Theory". *Philosophical Studies* 72 (2015): 2073–89.

Deltete, R. J. "Is the Universe Self-Caused?". *Philosophy* 75 (2000): 599–603.

Donald, M. "Précis of *Origins of the Modern Mind: Three Stages in the Evolution of Culture and Cognition*". *Behavioural and Brain Sciences* 16: 4 (1993): 737–48.

Donald, M. "Consciousness and the Freedom to Act". In R. F. Baumeister *et al.* (eds), *Free Will and Consciousness: How Might they Work?* Oxford: Oxford University Press, 2010.

Dooley, M. *Roger Scruton: The Philosopher on Dover Beach.* London: Continuum, 2009.

Dorr, C. "Review of Ladyman & Ross: *Every Thing Must Go*". *Notre Dame Philosophical Reviews* (2010). Retrieved from http://philpapers.org/rec/DORROJ.

Dowden, B. "Time". *Internet Encyclopaedia of Philosophy.* Retrieved from www.iep.utm.edu/time.

Dowe, P. "The Case for Time Travel". *Philosophy* 75: 293 (2000): 441–51.

Dowe, P. "Causal Processes". *The Stanford Encyclopedia of Philosophy* (fall 2008 edn), E. N. Zalta (ed.). Retrieved from http://plato.stanford.edu/archives/fall2008/entries/causation-process.

Dowe, P. "Review of Craig Bourne's *A Future for Presentism*". *Mind* 118 (2009): 156–60.

Draggan, S. *A Walk Through Time: The Evolution of Time Measurement through the Ages.* Gaithersburg, MD: National Institute of Standards and Technology, 2011.

Dummett, M. "Is Time a Continuum of Instants?". *Philosophy* 75 (2000): 497–515.

Dummett, M. "The Reality of the Past". *Proceedings of the Aristotelian Society* new series 69 (1969): 239–58.

Dunbar, I. "The Passage of Time". Unpublished manuscript.

Earman, J. "Thoroughly Modern McTaggart: Or, What McTaggart Would Have said If He Had Read the General Theory of Relativity". *Philosopher's Imprint* 2(3) (2002).

Earman, J. "Till the End of Time". In J. Earman *et al.* (eds), *Minnesota Studies in the Philosophy of Science Volume VIII: Foundations of Space-Time Theories*, 109–13. Minneapolis, MN: University of Minnesota Press, 1977.

Earman, J., C. Smeenk & C. Wüthrich. "Do the Laws of Physics Forbid the Operation of Time Machines?". *Synthese* 169 (2009): 91–124.

Earman, J., C. Wüthrich & J. Manchak. "Time Machines". *The Stanford Encyclopedia of Philosophy* (summer 2016 edn), E. N. Zalta (ed.). Retrieved from http://plato.stanford.edu/archives/sum2016/entries/time-machine.

Eddington, A. S. *The Nature of the Physical World*. Cambridge: Cambridge University Press, 1930.

Edwards, P. (ed.). *Immortality*. Amherst, NY: Prometheus, 1997.

Einstein, A. "Autobiographical Notes". In P. A. Schilpp (ed.), *Albert Einstein: Philosopher Scientist*, vol. 1. LaSalle, IL: Open Court, 1949.

Einstein, A. *Geometry and Experience: A Lecture*. London: Methuen, 1922.

Einstein, A. *Relativity: The Special and General Theory*. London: Methuen, 1920.

Eliot, G. "Physics in the Real Universe: Time and Space-Time". *General Relativity and Gravitation* 12 (2006): 1797–824.

Ellis, G. & J. Silk. "Defend the Integrity of Physics". *Nature* 516 (2014): 321–3.

Feser, E. "Post-Intentional Depression". January 2015. Retrieved from http://edwardfeser.blogspot.com/2015/01/post-intentional-depression.html.

Feynman, R. *The Feynman Lectures on Physics*. Boston, MA: Addison-Wesley, 1963.

Francis, M. J. *et al.* "Expanding Space: The Root of all Evil?". *Publications of Astronomical Society of Australia* arXiv: 0707.0380.

Frayn, M. *Copenhagen*. London: Methuen, 1998.

Gale, R. *The Language of Time*. London: Routledge & Kegan Paul, 1968.

Gale, R. (ed.). *The Philosophy of Time: A Collection of Essays*. London: Macmillan, 1968.

Galileo, G. [1623] *The Assayer*. In *Discoveries and Opinions of Galileo*, S. Drake (trans.). Garden City, NY: Doubleday, 1957.

Gallagher, S. "Sync-ing in the Stream of Experience: Time-Consciousness in Broad, Husserl, and Dainton". *Psyche* 9(10) (2003).

Gallagher, S. "Time in Action". In C. Callender (ed.), *Oxford Handbook of Philosophy of Time*, 420–38. Oxford: Oxford University Press, 2011.

Galton, A. & R. Mitzoguchi. "The Water Falls but the Waterfall does not Fall: New Perspectives on Objects, Processes and Events". *Applied Ontology* 4 (2009): 71–107.

Gamez, D. *What We Can Never Know: Blindspots in Philosophy and Science*. London: Continuum, 2007.

Gaskell, R. "Proposition and World". In R. Gaskell (ed.), *Grammar in Early Twentieth-Century Philosophy*, 1–27. London: Routledge, 2001.

Gellner, E. *Conditions of Liberty: Civil Society and its Rivals*. London: Hamish Hamilton, 1994.

Gerla, G. & R. Volpe. "Geometry Without Points". *American Mathematical Monthly* 82 (10) (1985): 707–11.

Geroch, R. *General Relativity from A to B*. Chicago, IL: University of Chicago Press, 2013.

Gleick, J. *Chaos: Making a New Science*. London: Sphere, 1987.

Gleick, J. *Genius: Richard Feynman and Modern Physics*. New York: Little Brown, 1992.

Glennie, P. & N. Thrift. *Shaping the Day: A History of Timekeeping in England and Wales 1300–1800*. Oxford: Oxford University Press, 2009.

Gödel, K. "A Remark about the Relationship Between Relativity and Idealistic Philosophy". In P. A. Schilpp (ed.), *Albert Einstein: Philosopher-Scientist*, 557–62. La Salle, IL: Open Court, 1949.

Godfrey-Smith, W. "The Generality of Predictions". *American Philosophical Quarterly* 15 (1978): 15–25.

Greene, B. *The Elegant Universe: Superstrings, Hidden Dimensions, and the Quest for the Ultimate Theory*. London: Vintage, 2000.

Gregory, R. L. *Eye and Brain: The Psychology of Seeing*, 5th edn. Princeton, NJ: Princeton University Press, 2015.

Grünbaum, A. *Philosophical Problems of Space and Time*, 2nd edn. Dordrecht: Reidel, 1973.

Grünbaum, A. "Relativity and the Atomicity of Becoming". *Review of Metaphysics* 4(2) (1950): 143–86.

Grünbaum, A. "The Status of Temporal Becoming". In R. Gale (ed.), *The Philosophy of Time: A Collection of Essays*, 322–54. London: Macmillan, 1968.

Guerlac, S. *Thinking in Time: An Introduction to Henri Bergson*. Ithaca, NY: Cornell University Press, 2006.

Hacking, I. "What Mathematics Has Done to Some and Only Some Philosophers". Retrieved from www.cs.bham.ac.uk/research/projects/cogaff/misc/hacking-mathematics-1998.pdf.

Hájek, A. "Interpretations of Probability". *The Stanford Encyclopedia of Philosophy* (winter 2012 edn), E. N. Zalta (ed.). Retrieved from http://plato.stanford.edu/archives/win2012/entries/probability-interpret.

Halvorson, H. "Does Quantum Theory Kill Time?". 4 October 2010. Retrieved from Princton.edu/-halvorson/papers/notime pdf.

Halvorson, H. "The Measure of All Things: Quantum Mechanics and the Soul". In M. Baker & S. Goetz (eds), *The Soul Hypothesis: Investigations into the Existence of the Soul*, 138–163. London: Continuum, 2010.

Hamming, R. W. "The Unreasonable Effectiveness of Mathematics". *American Mathematical Monthly*, 87: 2 (1980): 81–90.

Hammond, C. *Time Warped: Unlocking the Mysteries of Time Perception*. Edinburgh: Canongate, 2013.

Hartle, J. "The Physics of 'Now'". *arXiv* (21 May 2004): gr-qc/0403001v2.

Hartle, J. B. & S. W. Hawking. "Wave Function of the Universe". *Physical Review D* 28 (1983): 2960–73.

Hawking, S. W. & T. Hertog. "Populating the Landscape: A Top-Down Approach". *Physical Reviews* D73123527 (2006).

Hawking, S. & L. Mlodinow. "The (Elusive) Theory of Everything". *Scientific American* 22(2) (2013): 90–93.

Hawking, S. & L. Mlodinow. *The Grand Design*. London: Transworld, 2010.

Hawley, K. "Metaphysics and Relativity". In R. Le Poidevin *et al.* (eds), *Routledge Companion to Metaphysics*, 507–16. London: Routledge, 2009.

Healey, R. "Review of *Asymmetries in Time: Problems in the Philosophy of Sciences*". *Philosophical Review* 100(1) (1991): 125–30.

Hebb, D. O. "The Semi-Autonomous Process: Its Nature and Nurture". *American Psychologist* 18 (1963): 16–27.

Heidegger, M. *Being and Time*, J. Stambaugh (trans.). New York: SUNY Press, 1996.

Heidegger, M. *Early Greek Thinking: The Dawn of Western Philosophy*. New York: Harper & Row, 1975.

Heidegger, M. *The Fundamental Concepts of Metaphysics: World, Finitude, Solitude*. Bloomington, IN: Indiana University Press, 2001.

Heidegger, M. *History of the Concept of Time*. Bloomington, IN: Indiana University Press, 2008.

Hestenes, D. "Electron Time, Mass and Zitter". FQXi Forum (December 2008). Retrieved from http://citeseerx.ist.psu.edu/viewdoc/summary?doi=10.1.1.169.7383.

Hey, T. & P. Walters. *The Quantum Universe*. Cambridge: Cambridge University Press, 1978.

Hilgevoord, J. & D. Atkinson. "Time in a Quantum World". In C. Callender (ed.), *Oxford Handbook of the Philosophy of Time*, 647–63. Oxford: Oxford University Press, 2011.

Hintikka, J. "The Once and Future Sea Fight: Aristotle's Discussion of Future Contingents in *De Interpretatione IX*". *Philosophical Review* 73(4) (1964): 461–92.

Hitchens, C. *Hitch-22: A Memoir*. London: Atlantic, 2010.

Hitchens, C. *Mortality*. London: Atlantic, 2012.

Hoerl, C. "A Succession of Feelings, in and of Itself, is Not a Feeling of Succession". *Mind* 122(488) (2013): 1233–78.

Hoerl, C. & T. McCormack. "Time in Cognitive Development". In C. Callender (ed.), *The Oxford Handbook of Philosophy of Time*, 439–59. Oxford: Oxford University Press, 2011.

Holmes, R. *The Age of Wonder*. London: Harper, 2008.

Holt, J. "A Mathematical Romance". *New York Review of Books* (5 December 2010).

Huggett, N. "Zeno's Paradoxes". *The Stanford Encyclopedia of Philosophy* (winter 2010 edn), E. N. Zalta (ed.). Retrieved from http://plato.stanford.edu/archives/win2010/entries/paradox-zeno.

Huggett, N. & C. Hoefer. "Absolute and Relational Theories of Space and Motion". *The Stanford Encyclopedia of Philosophy* (winter 2016 edn), E. N. Zalta (ed.). Retrieved from http://plato.stanford.edu/archives/win2016/entries/spacetime-theories.

Hughes, A. "The Folly of Scientism". *The New Atlantis* 37 (2012): 32–50.

Hume, D. *Enquiry into Human Understanding*, L. A. Selby-Bigge (ed.) with text revised by P. H. Nidditch. Oxford: Clarendon Press, 1975.

Hume, D. *A Treatise of Human Nature*. New York: Dolphin, 1961.

Hunter, J. "Time Travel". *The Internet Encyclopaedia of Philosophy*. Retrieved from www.iep.utm.edu/timetrav.

Husserl, E. *On the Phenomenology of the Consciousness of Internal Time (1893–1917)*, J. D. Brough (trans.). Dordrecht: Kluwer, 1991.

Isaacson, W. *Einstein: His Life and Universe*. New York: Simon & Schuster, 2007.

Ismael, J. "Temporal Experience". In C. Callender (ed.), *Oxford Handbook of Philosophy of Time*, 460–84. Oxford: Oxford University Press, 2011.

James, W. *The Principles of Psychology*. New York: Dover, [1890] 1950.

Jeans, J. *The Mysterious Universe*. Cambridge: Cambridge University Press, 1930.

Joyce, J. *Ulysses*. Paris: Sylvia Beach, 1922.

Kane, R. *The Significance of Free Will*. Oxford: Oxford University Press, 1998.

Kant, I. *Critique of Pure Reason*, N. Kemp Smith (trans.). London: Macmillan, 1964.

Kauffman, S. "Breaking the Galilean Spell". *Edge*. Excerpted from *Reinventing the Sacred: A New View of Science, Reason, and Religion*. New York: Basic Books, 2008.

Kenny, A. *The God of the Philosophers*. Oxford, Clarendon Press, 1979.

Kent, A. "Against Many-Worlds Interpretations". *International Journal of Modern Physics* A5 (1990): 1745–62. Accessed at arXiv:gr-qc/9703089v1 31 Mar 1997 1-31

Kierkegaard, S. *Either/Or: A Fragment of Life*, A. Hannay (trans.). London: Penguin, 1992.

Kirk, G. S. & J. E. Raven. *The Presocratic Philosophers*. Cambridge: Cambridge University Press, 1961.

Kolakowski, L. *Positivist Philosophy: From Hume to the Vienna Circle*, N. Guterman (trans.). London: Penguin, 1972.

Körner, S. *Kant*. London: Penguin, 1955.

Krauss, L. M. *A Universe from Nothing: Why there is Something Rather than Nothing*. New York: Simon & Schuster, 2012.

Krips, H. "Measurement in Quantum Theory: The End of Copenhagen Monocracy". In T. Metz (ed.), *Stanford Encyclopedia of Philosophy*, 6333–4. Retrieved from https://plato.stanford.edu/archives/sum2016/entries/qt-measurment/.

Kuchar, K. "The Problem of Time in Quantum Geometrodynamics". In J. Butterworth (ed.), *The Arguments of Time*, 169–97. Oxford: Oxford University Press, 1999.

Kuhlmann, M. "What is Real?". *Scientific American* (August 2013): 33–9.

Kuhn, R. L. "Why this Universe? Towards a Taxonomy of Possible Explanations". *Skeptic* 13 (2) (2007): 28–39.

Kundera, M. *The Art of the Novel*, L. Asher (trans.). London: Faber & Faber, 1988.

Kurzweil, R. *How to Create a Mind: The Secret of Human Thought Revealed*. London: Duckworth Overlook, 2013.

Kutach, D. "The Asymmetry of Influence". In C. Callender (ed.), *Oxford Handbook of Philosophy of Time*, 247–75. Oxford: Oxford University Press, 2011.

Kyle, D. "God, Fatalism, and Temporal Ontology". *Religious Studies* 45 (2009): 435–44.

Ladyman, J. "An Apology for Naturalised Metaphysics". In M. H. Slater & Z. Yudell (eds) *Metaphysics and the Philosophy of Science: New Essays*, 141–62. Oxford: Oxford University Press, 2017.

Ladyman, J. "Structural Realism". *The Stanford Encyclopedia of Philosophy* (winter 2016 edn), E. N. Zalta (ed.). Retrieved from http://plato.stanford.edu/archives/win2016/entries/structural-realism.

Ladyman, J. & D. Ross. *Every Thing Must Go: Metaphysics Naturalized*. Oxford: Oxford University Press, 2007.

Landau, L. "A Confutation of Convergent Realism". *Philosophy of Science* 48 (1) (1981): 19–49.

Laplace, M. *A Philosophical Essay on Probabilities*. New York: Dover, 1952.

Lasky, R. C. "Time and the Twin Paradox". *Scientific American* (17 January 2006).

Le Poidevin, R. *Change, Cause and Contradiction: A Defense of the Tenseless Theory of Time*. London: Macmillan, 1991.

Le Poidevin, R. *Images of Time*. Oxford: Oxford University Press, 2007.

Leach, E. *Claude Lévi-Strauss*. London: Fontana, 1970.

Lefebvre, H. *The Production of Space*. Oxford: Blackwell, 1991.

Levin, D. M. (ed.). *Modernity and the Hegemony of Vision*. Berkeley, CA: University of California Press, 1993.

Levinas, E. *Totality and Infinity: An Essay on Exteriority*. Pittsburgh, PA: Duquesne University Press, 1999.

Lewis, D. "Causation". *Journal of Philosophy* 70 (1973): 556–67.

Lewis, D. "The Paradoxes of Time Travel". *American Philosophical Quarterly* 13 (1976): 145–52.

Lewis, D. "Tensed Quantifiers" in *Oxford Studies in Metaphysics I* D. Zimmerman (ed.), 2004.

Libet, B. "Do We Have Free Will?". *Journal of Consciousness Studies* 6 (1996): 47–57.

Libet, B. *et al.* "Time of Conscious Intention to Act in Relation to the Onset of Cerebral Activity (Readiness Potential): The Unconscious Initiation of a Freely Voluntary Act". *Brain* 106 (1983): 623–64.

Locke, J. *An Essay Concerning Human Understanding*, vol. 1. Project Gutenberg EBook, [1690] 2004, retrieved from www.gutenberg.org/cache/epub/10615/pg10615.html.

Lockwood, M. *The Labyrinth of Time: Introducing the Universe*. Oxford: Oxford University Press, 2005.

Long, A. A. & D. N. Sedley. *The Hellenistic Philosophers*, vol. 1. Cambridge: Cambridge University Press, 1987.

Lucas, J. R. "A Century of Time". In J. Butterfield (ed.), *The Arguments of Time*, 1–21. Oxford: Oxford University Press, 1999.

Lucas, J. R. *The Future: An Essay on God, Temporality and Truth*. Oxford: Blackwell, 1989.

Lucas, J. R. *A Treatise on Time and Space*. London: Methuen, 1973.

Lucretius. *De Rerum Natura*, D. R. Slavitt (trans.). Berkeley, CA: University of California Press, 2008.

Łukasiewicz, J. ".On Three-Valued Logic". In S. McCall (ed.), *Polish Logic 1920–1939*. Oxford: Clarendon Press, [1920] 1967.

Mach, E. *The Science of Mechanics: A Critical and Historical Account of its Development*, T. J. McCormack (trans.). La Salle, IL: Open Court, 1960.

Mach, E. *Space and Geometry in the Light of Physiological, Psychology and Physical Inquiry*. Chicago, IL: Open Court, 1906.

Mackenzie, J. S. "Eternity". In J. Hastings (ed.), *Encyclopaedia of Religion and Ethics*, vol 10. Edinburgh: T. & T. Clark, 1914.

Majid, S. "Quantum Space-Time and Physical Reality". In S. Majid (ed.), *On Space and Time*, 56–140. Cambridge: Cambridge University Press, 2008.

Mandelbrot, B. "How Long is the Coast of Britain? Statistical Self-Similarity and Fractional Dimensions". *Science* 156 (1967): 636–8.

Marcel, G. *Being and Having*. Charleston, SC: Nabu Press.

Marcel, G. *Metaphysical Journal*, B. Wall (trans.). London: Rockliff, 1952.

Martin, C. B. "On the Need for Properties: The road to Pythagoreanism and Back". *Synthese* 112 (1997): 193–231.

Martin, F. *Money: The Unauthorised Biography*. London: Bodley Head, 2013.

Martinez-Conde, S., S. Mackinik & D. Hubel. "The Role of Fixational Eye Movements in Visual Perception". *Nature Reviews Neuroscience* 5 (2004): 229–40.

Maudlin. T. *The Metaphysics Within Physics*. Oxford: Oxford University Press, 2007.

Maudlin, T. *The Philosophy of Physics: Space and Time*. Princeton, NJ: Princeton University Press, 2012.

Maudlin, T. "Remarks on the Passing of Time". In *Proceedings of the Aristotelian Society* CII (Part 3) (2002): 237–52.

Maudlin, T. "Time, Topology and Physical Geometry". *Proceedings of the Aristotelian Society*, supp. vol. LXXXIV: 63–78.

Mazur, B. *Imagining Numbers (Particularly the Square Root of Minus Fifteen)*. London: Penguin, 2003.

McBride, F. "Truthmakers". *The Stanford Encyclopedia of Philosophy* (fall 2016 edn), E. N. Zalta (ed.). Retrieved from http://plato.stanford.edu/archives/fall2016/entries/truthmakers.

McCall, S. "A Dynamic Model of Temporal Becoming". *Analysis* 44 (1984): 172–76.

McCall, S. *A Model of the Universe: Space-Time, Probability, and Decision*. Oxford: Clarendon Press, 1994.

McFarlane, J. "Future Contingents and Relative Truth". *Philosophical Quarterly* 53 (2003): 321–36.

McTaggart, J. M. E. *The Nature of Existence*, vol 2. Cambridge: Cambridge University Press, 1927.

McTaggart, J. M. E. "The Relation of Time to Eternity". *Mind* 18 (71) (1909): 343–62.

McTaggart, J. M. E. "The Unreality of Time". *Mind* 18 (1908): 457–74.

Meillassoux, Q. *After Finitude: An Essay on the Necessity of Contingency*, R. Brassier (trans.). London: Continuum, 2007.

Mellor, D. H. *The Facts of Causation*. London: Routledge, 1995.

Mellor, D. H. *Real Time*. Cambridge: Cambridge University Press, 1981.

Mellor, D. H. *Real Time II*. London: Routledge, 1998.

Merleau-Ponty, M. *The Phenomenology of Perception*, C. Smith (trans.). London: Routledge & Kegan Paul, 1962.

Merleau-Ponty, M. "The Primacy of Perception and Its Philosophical Consequences". In his *The Primacy of Perception and Other Essays in Phenomenological Psychology, the Philosophy of Art, History and Politics*, J. M. Edie (trans.). Evanston, IL: Northwestern University Press, 1964.

Mermin, D. "Could Feynman Have Said This?". *Physics Today* (May 2004): 10.

Mermin, D. "What's Bad About this Habit?" *Physics Today*, May 2009: 8–9.

Mermin, D. "Physics: QBism Puts the Scientist Back into Science". *Nature* 507 (2014): 421–3.

Mermin, D. "QBism as CBism: Solving the Problem of 'Now'". *arXiv* (2013): 1312.7825.

Mermin, D. "Why QBism is Not the Copenhagen Interpretation and What John Bell Might Have Thought of It". In R. Bertlmann & A. Zeilinger (eds), *Quantum Unspeakables II*, 83–94. Berlin: Springer, 2015.

Merricks, T. *Truth and Ontology.* Oxford: Oxford University Press, 2007.

Metz, A. "Réplique de M. André Metz, *Revue de Philosophie* 31 (1924): 437–39.

Mill, J. S. "Nature". In H. D. Aiken (ed.), *The Age of Ideology: The Nineteenth-Century Philosophers*, 149–60. New York: Mentor, 1956.

Mill, J. S. *A System of Logic: Ratiocinative and Inductive, Being a Connected View of the Principles of Evidence and the Methods of Scientific Investigation.* New York: Longmans, Green & Co., 1900.

Minkowski, H. "Space and Time: Address to the 80th Assembly of German Natural Scientists and Physicists". 21 September 1908. In his *Space and Time: Minkowski's Papers on Relativity*, F. Lewerto & V. Petkov (trans.). Montreal: Minkowski Institute Press. Retrieved from http://rgs.vniims.ru/books/spacetime.pdf.

Moore, C. *George and Sam: Two Boys, One Family, and Autism.* New York: St Martin's Press, 2006.

Moore, G. E. "A Defence of Common Sense". Reprinted in *G. E. Moore: Philosophical Papers.* London: Routledge, 2002.

Moreva, E. *et al.* "Time from Quantum Entanglement: An Experimental Illustration". *arXiv* (2013): 1310.4691v1.

Mozersky, M. J. "Presentism". In C. Callender (ed.), *Oxford Handbook of Philosophy of Time*, 122–44. Oxford: Oxford University Press, 2011.

Mumford, S. & R. Anjum. *Getting Causes from Powers.* Oxford: Oxford University Press, 2011.

Musser, G. "A Hole at the Heart of Physics". In "A Matter of Time", special edition of *Scientific American* (February 2006).

Nagel, T. *Mind and Cosmos: Why the Materialist Neo-Darwinian Conception of Nature is Almost Certainly False.* Oxford: Oxford University Press, 2012.

Nagel, T. "Rain, Figaro and Metaphysics". *Times Literary Supplement* (30 August 2012).

Nagel, T. *The View from Nowhere.* Oxford: Oxford University Press, 1986.

Newton, I. *Scholium to the Definitions in Philosophiae Naturalis Principia Mathematica*, book 1, A. Motte (trans.) [1729], revised F. Cajori. Berkeley, CA: University of California Press, [1689] 1934.

Newton-Smith, W. *The Structure of Time.* London: Routledge & Kegan Paul, 1980.

Nietzsche, F. "The Use and Abuse of History". In G. Clive (ed.), *The Philosophy of Nietzsche*, 218–38. New York: Mentor, 1965.

Norton, J. D. "The Hole Argument". *The Stanford Encyclopedia of Philosophy* (fall 2015 edn), E. N. Zalta (ed.). Retrieved from http://plato.stanford.edu/archives/fall2015/entries/spacetime-holearg.

Norton, J. D. "Time Really Passes". *Humana Mente* 13 (2010): 23–34.

Oaklander, L. N. "McTaggart's Paradox and Smith's Tensed Theory of Time". *Synthese* 107 (1996): 205–21.

Oaklander, L. N. *The Ontology of Time.* Amherst, NY: Prometheus, 2004.

Oaklander, L. N. "Time and Existence: A Critique of 'Degree Presentism'". In M. E. Reicher (ed.), *States of Affairs*. Frankfurt: Ontos Verlag, 2009.

Oaklander, L. N. & Q. Smith (eds). *The New Theory of Time.* New Haven, CT: Yale University Press, 1994.

Olson, E. "The Rate of Time's Passage". *Analysis* 69 (1) (2009): 3–9.

Osvath, M. "Spontaneous Planning for Future Stone Throwing by a Male Chimpanzee". *Current Biology* 19(5) (2009): R190–1.

Pascal, B. *Pensées*, A. J. Krailsheimer (trans.), revised edn. London: Penguin, 1995.

Pearl, J. *Causality.* Cambridge: Cambridge University Press, 2000.

Peirce, C. S. "Some Consequences of Four Incapacities". In C. Hartshorne & P. Weiss (eds), *Collected Papers of Charles Sanders Peirce*, vol. 5. Cambridge, MA: Harvard University Press, [1868] 1931–5.

Penrose, I. R. "Causality, Quantum Theory and Cosmology". In S. Majid (ed.), *On Space and Time*, 141–95. Cambridge: Cambridge University Press, 2008.

Penrose, O. & J. C. Percival. "The Direction of Time". *Proceedings of the Physical Society* 79 (1962): 605–16.

Pesic, P. "Einstein and the Twin Paradox". *European Journal of Physics* 24 (2003): 585–90.

Petherbridge, D. *The Primacy of Drawing: Histories and Theories of Practice.* New Haven, CT: Yale University Press, 2010.

Pindar, I. "Clocking Off". *The Guardian* (14 March 2009).

Plato. *Timaeus*, B. Jowett (trans.). Retrieved from http://classics.mit.edu/Plato/timaeus.html.

Plotinus. *The Six Enneads*, S. McKenna (trans.). London: Faber & Faber, 1962.

Poincaré, H. "The Measure of Time". In his *The Foundations of Science: The Value of Science*, 222–34. New York: Science Press, 1913.

Poincaré, H. "Science and Hypothesis". In his *The Foundations of Science: The Value of Science*. New York: Science Press, 1913.

Polkinghorne, J. "The Nature of Time". In S. Majid (ed.), *On Space and Time*, 278–83. Cambridge: Cambridge University Press, 2008.

Popper, K. "The Arrow of Time". *Nature* 177 (17 March 1956): 538–9.

Popper, K. *The Open Universe: An Argument for Indeterminism*, W. W. Bartley (ed.). London: Routledge, 1988.

Povinelli, D. *Folk Physics for Apes: The Chimpanzee's Theory of How the World Works*. Oxford: Oxford University Press, 2003.

Powell, C. S. "Is the Universe Smooth or Chunky? Relativity versus Quantum Mechanics – The Battle for the Universe". *The Guardian* (4 November 2015).

Press, T. M. & G. Q. Coleman. "Human Specific Organization of Primary Visual Cortex". *Cerebral Cortex* 12 (2002): 672–91.

Price, H. "The Flow of Time". In C. Callender (ed.), *Oxford Handbook of Philosophy of Time*, 276–311. Oxford: Oxford University Press, 2011.

Price, H. *Time's Arrow and Archimedes' Point: New Directions for the Physics of Time*. Oxford: Oxford University Press, 1996.

Prigogine, I. "The Rediscovery of Time". A discourse originally prepared for the Isthmus Institute, presented to the American Academy of Religion, December 1983. Retrieved from http://dx.doi.org/10.1111/j.1467-9744.1984.tb00940.x.

Prigogine, I. & I. Stengers. *Order Out of Chaos*. London: Bantam, 1984.

Prior, A. N. *Past, Present and Future*. Oxford: Clarendon Press, 1967.

Prior, A. N. *Papers on Time and Tense*. Oxford: Oxford University Press, 1968.

Prior, A. N. "Some Free Thinking about Time". In B. J. Copeland (ed.), *Logic and Reality: Essays on the Legacy of Arthur Prior*. Oxford: Clarendon Press, 1996.

Psillos, S. "Physics, Mathematics and Skepticism: A Review of Hilary Putnam, *Philosophy in an Age of Science: Physics, Mathematics and Skepticism*". *Notre Dame Philosophical Reviews* (2013).

Putnam, H. *Philosophy in an Age of Science: Physics, Mathematics and Skepticism*, M. de Caro & D. Macaurthur (eds). Cambridge, MA: Harvard University Press, 2012.

Putnam, H. "Time and Physical Geometry". *Journal of Philosophy* 64(8) (1967): 240–7.

Quine, W. V. *Quiddities: An Intermittently Philosophical Dictionary*. London: Penguin, 1990.

Quine, W. V. "Two Dogmas of Empiricism". *Philosophical Review* 60 (1951): 20–43.

Quine, W. V. "Whither Physical Objects?" In R. S. Cohen, P. K. Feyerabend and M. W. Wartofsky (eds), *Essays in Memory of Imre Lakatos*. Boston, MA: Reidel, 1976.

Rodriguez-Pereyra, G. "Mellor's Facts and Chances of Causation". *Analysis* 58 (3) (1998): 175–81.

Rosar, W. H. "The Dimensionality of Visual Space". *Topoi* volume 35 (October 2016): 531–70.

Rosenberg, A. "Eliminativism without Tears: A Nihilistic Stance on the Theory of Mind". Unpublished manuscript.

Rovelli, C. "Analysis of the Distinct Meanings of the Notions of 'Time' in Different Physical Theories". *Il Nuovo Cimento* 110 (1) (1995): 81–93.

Rovelli, C. "Forget Time". *arXiv* (2009): 0903.3832v3.

Rovelli, C. "Michelangelo's Stone: An Argument against Platonism in Mathematics". arXiv (6 September 2015): 1508: 00001v2 [math. HO].

Rovelli, C. "Time in Quantum Gravity: An Hypothesis". *Physical Reviews D* 43(2) (1991): 442.

Russell, B. *ABC of Relativity*. London: Routledge Classics, 2009.

Russell, B. [1915]. "On the Experience of Time". In *The Collected Papers of Bertrand Russell*, vol. 7. London: Allen & Unwin, 1984.

Russell, B. "On the Notion of Cause". In his *Mysticism and Logic*. London: Pelican, 1953.

Russell, B. *An Outline of Philosophy*. London: Allen & Unwin, 1927.

Russell, B. "The Ultimate Constituents of Matter". In his *Mysticism and Logic*, 120–138. London: Pelican, 1953.

Ryle, G. *Dilemmas*. Cambridge: Cambridge University Press, 1954.

Sacks, M. *Objectivity and Insight.* Clarendon Press, Oxford, 2000.

Safranski, R. *Martin Heidegger: Between Good and Evil,* E. Osers (trans.). Cambridge, MA: Harvard University Press, 1998.

Salmon, W. *Scientific Explanation and the Causal Structure of the World.* Princeton, NJ: Princeton University Press, 1984.

Sartre, J.-P. *Being and Nothingness,* H. Barnes (trans.). London: Methuen, 1956.

Saunders, S. "How Relativity Contradicts Presentism". *Royal Institute of Philosophy Supplement* 50 (2002): 277–92.

Savitt, S. "Time in the Special Theory of Relativity". In C. Callender (ed.), *Oxford Handbook of the Philosophy of Time,* 456–70. Oxford: Oxford University Press, 2011.

Savitt, S. "Being and Becoming in Modern Physics". *The Stanford Encyclopedia of Philosophy* (summer 2014 edn), E. N. Zalta (ed.). Retrieved from http://plato.stanford.edu/archives/sum2014/entries/spacetime-bebecome.

Savitt, S. (ed.). *Time's Arrows Today.* Cambridge: Cambridge University Press, 1995.

Schaffer, J. "The Metaphysics of Causation". *Stanford Encyclopedia of Philosophy* (fall 2016 edn), E. N. Zalta (ed.). Retrieved from http://plato.stanford.edu/archives/fall2016/entries/causation-metaphysics.

Schrödinger, E. "Mind and Matter". In his *What is Life and Other Essays,* 93–164. Cambridge: Cambridge University Press, 1967.

Scruton, R. *Kant.* Oxford: Oxford University Press, 1981.

Scruton, R. *Understanding Music: Philosophy and Interpretation .* London: Bloomsbury Continuum, 2013.

Searle, J. *Intentionality: An Essay in the Philosophy of Mind.* Cambridge: Cambridge University Press, 1983.

Sellers, W. "Empiricism and the Philosophy of Mind". In H. Feigl & M. Scriven (eds), *Minnesota Studies in the Philosophy of Science,* vol. 1, 253–329. Minneapolis, MN: University of Minnesota Press, 1956.

Sellars, W. "Philosophy and the Scientific Image of Man". In R. Colodny (ed.), *Frontiers of Science and Philosophy,* 35–78. Pittsburgh, PA: University of Pittsburgh Press, 1962.

Sextus Empiricus. *Outlines of Scepticism,* J. Annas & J. Barnes (trans.). Cambridge: Cambridge University Press, 2000.

Shaffer, J. "The Metaphysics of Causation". In *Stanford Encyclopedia of Philosophy* (spring 2003 edn), E. N. Zalta (ed.). Retrieved from http://plato.stanford.edu/archives/spr2003/entries/causation-metaphysics.

Shalamov, V. *Kolyma Tales,* J. Glad (trans.). London: Penguin, 1994.

Shoemaker, S. "Time without Change". *Journal of Philosophy* LXVI (1969): 363–81.

Simpson, W. "Causal Powers of the Scientific Image". Unpublished MPhil dissertation, University of Oxford, 2016.

Sklar, L. *Space, Time and Spacetime.* Berkeley, CA: University of California Press, 1974.

Sklar, L. "Time in Classical Dynamics". In C. Callender (ed.), *Oxford Handbook of Philosophy of Time,* 571–6. Oxford: Oxford University Press, 2011.

Skow, B. "Why Does Time Pass?". *Nous* 46 (2012): 223–42.

Slowik, E. "The Fate of Mathematical Place: Objectivity and the Theory of Lived Space from Husserl to Casey". In V. Petkov (ed.), *Space, Time and Space-time: Physical and Philosophical Implications of Minkowski's Unification of Space and Time,* 291–311. Berlin: Springer, 2010.

Smart, J. J. C. "The Reality of the Future". *Philosophia* 10 (3–4) (1980): 141–50.

Smart, J. J. C. "Spatialising Time". In R. Gale (ed.), *The Philosophy of Time,* 163–8. London: Macmillan, 1968.

Smeenk, C. & C. Wütrich. "Time Travel and Time Machines". In C. Callender (ed.), *Oxford Handbook of Philosophy of Time,* 577–630. Oxford: Oxford University Press, 2011.

Smith, K. "Neuroscience vs Philosophy: Taking Aim at Free Will". *Nature* 477 (August 2011): 23–25.

Smith, Q. "Absolute Simultaneity and the Infinity of Time". In R. Le Poidevin (ed.), *Questions of Time and Tense,* 135–84. Oxford: Oxford University Press.

Smith, Q. "The Ontological Interpretation of the Wave Function of the Universe". *The Monist* 80 (1997): 160–85.

Smith, Q. "The Reason the Universe Exists is that it Caused Itself to Exist". *Philosophy* 74 (1999): 579–86.

Smith, Q. "Time and Degrees of Existence: A Theory of 'Degree Presentism'". *Royal Institute of Philosophy Supplement* (2002), 119–36.

Smith, Z. *White Teeth.* London: Penguin, 2001.

Smolin, L. "It's Time to Re-write Time". *New Scientist* 218 (2013): 30.

Smolin, L. *Time Reborn: From the Crisis of Physics to the Future of the Universe*. London: Allen Lane, 2013.

Smolin, L. *The Trouble with Physics: The Rise of String Theory, the Fall of a Science and What Comes Next*. London: Allen Lane, 2006.

Sokal, A. & J. Bricmont. *Intellectual Impostures*. London: Profile, 2003.

Soon, C. S. *et al.* "Unconscious Determinants of Free Decisions in the Human Brain". *Nature Neuroscience* 11 (2008): 543–46.

Sorensen, R. *Seeing Dark Things: The Philosophy of Shadows*. Oxford: Oxford University Press, 2008.

Spencer, B. "Olive Trees". In his *Complete Poetry*, P. Robinson (ed.). Newcastle: Bloodaxe, 2011.

Spinney, L. "Once upon a Time". *New Scientist* (10 January 2015): 28–31.

Stace, W. "Man Against Darkness". *Atlantic Monthly* (September 1948): 53–9.

Stebbing, L. S. *Philosophy and the Physicists*. London: Methuen, 1937.

Steward, H. "Processes, Continuants, and Individuals". *Mind* 122 (2013): 783–812.

Stich, S. "Do True Believers Exist?". *Aristotelian Society Supplement* 65 (1991): 229–44.

Stich, S. *From Folk Psychology to Cognitive Science: The Case Against Belief*. Cambridge, MA: MIT Press, 1983.

Strawson, G. "The Impossibility of Moral Responsibility". *Philosophical Studies* 75 (1994): 5–24.

Strawson, G. *et al. Consciousness and its Place in Nature*. Exeter: Imprint Academic, 2006.

Strawson, P. F. *Individuals: An Essay in Descriptive Metaphysics*. London: Methuen, 1965.

Strawson, P. F. "Intellectual Autobiography". In L. N. Hahn (ed.), *The Philosophy of P. F. Strawson*. La Salle, IL: Open Court, 1998.

Strawson, P. F. *Skepticism and Naturalism: Some Varieties*. London: Methuen, 1985.

Stroud, B. *Engagement and Metaphysical Dissatisfaction: Modality and Value*. Oxford: Oxford University Press, 2011.

Suaréz, M. "The Many Metaphysics within Physics". *Studies in History and Philosophy of Modern Physics* 40 (2009): 73–6.

Suddendorf, T. & M. Corballis. "The Evolution of Foresight: What is Mental Time Travel and is it Unique to Humans?". *Behavioural and Brain Sciences* 30 (2007): 299–351.

Suppes, P. "Is Visual Space Euclidean?". *Synthese* 35 (1977): 397–421.

Szendrei, E. V. "Bergson, Prigogine and the Rediscovery of Time". *Process Studies* 18 (2) (1989): 181–93.

Szymborska, W. "Three Oddest Words". In her *Poems: New and Collected*. New York: Houghton Mifflin, 1998.

Tallis, R. *Aping Mankind: Neuromania, Darwinitis and the Misrepresentation of Humanity*. Durham: Acumen, 2011 (reissued London: Routledge Classics, 2016).

Tallis, R. *The Black Mirror: Fragments of an Obituary for Life*. London: Atlantic, 2015.

Tallis, R. *A Conversation with Martin Heidegger*. Basingstoke: Palgrave Macmillan 2001.

Tallis, R. *The Enduring Significance of Parmenides: Unthinkable Thought*. London: Continuum, 2007.

Tallis, R. *Enemies of Hope*. Basingstoke: Palgrave Macmillan, 1997.

Tallis, R. *Epimethean Imaginings: Philosophical and Other Reflections on Everyday Light*. Durham: Acumen, 2014.

Tallis, R. *The Hand: A Philosophical Inquiry into Human Being*. Edinburgh: Edinburgh University Press, 2003.

Tallis, R. *I Am: A Philosophical Inquiry into First-Person Being*. Edinburgh: Edinburgh University Press, 2004.

Tallis, R. *The Kingdom of Infinite Space: A Fantastical Journey Around Your Head*. London: Atlantic, 2008.

Tallis, R. *The Knowing Animal: A Philosophical Inquiry into Knowledge and Truth*. Edinburgh: Edinburgh University Press, 2005.

Tallis, R. *Michelangelo's Finger: An Exploration of Everyday Transcendence*. London: Atlantic, 2010.

Tallis, R. *The Mystery of Being Human: God, Freedom, and the NHS*. London: Notting Hill Editions, 2016.

Tallis, R. "Naming Airy Nothings". *Philosophy Now* 104 (2013): 48–9.

Tallis, R. *Not Saussure: A Critique of Post-Saussurean Literary Theory*, 2nd edn. Basingstoke: Palgrave Macmillan, 1995.

Tallis, R. "Reality and Stability: From Parmenides to Einstein". *Philosophy Now* (Nov–Dec 2015): 49–50.

Tallis, R. *Reflections of a Metaphysical Flaneur*. Durham: Acumen, 2014.

Tallis, R. *Theorrhoea and After*. Basingstoke: Macmillan, 1999.

Tallis, R. *Why the Mind Is Not a Computer*. Exeter: Imprint Academic, 2004.

Tallis, R. "You Chemical Scum, You". *Philosophy Now* (May–June 2012): 48–9.

Tallis, R. & J. Spalding. *Summers of Discontent: The Purpose of the Arts Today*. London: Wilmington Square, 2014.

Taylor, J. "Time and Tense". Unpublished PhD thesis, University of Oxford, 1997.

Taylor, R. "Moving About in Time". *The Philosophical Quarterly* IX (1959): 289–301.

Tegmark, M. "The Mathematical Universe". *Foundations of Physics* 38 (2008): 101–50.

Tegmark, M. *Our Mathematical Universe: My Quest for the Ultimate Nature of Reality*. London: Allen Lane, 2014.

Thompson, E. P. "Time, Work-Discipline and Industrial Capitalism". *Past & Present* 38 (1967): 56–97.

Thorndike, E. L. "The Nature, Purpose, and Measurement of Educational Products". In G. M. Whipple (ed.), *Seventeenth Yearbook of the National Society for the Study of Education*, vol. 2, 16–24. Bloomington, IN: Public School Publishing, 1918.

Todes, D. *Ivan Pavlov: A Russian Life in Science*. Oxford: Oxford University Press, 2014.

Tooley, M. *Time, Tense, and Causation*. Oxford: Clarendon Press, 1997.

Torretti, R. "On Relativity, Time Reckoning and Time Series". In J. Butterfield (ed.), *The Arguments of Time*, 65–83. Oxford: Oxford University Press, 1999.

Trakl, G. "Decline". In M. Hamburger & C. Middleton (eds & trans.), *Modern German Poetry 1910–1960*. London: MacGibbon & Kee, 1962.

Treisman, M. "The Perception of Time: Philosophical Views and Psychological Evidence". In J. Butterfield (ed.), *The Arguments of Time*. Oxford: Oxford University Press, 1999.

Tulving, E. *Elements of Episodic Memory*. Oxford: Oxford University Press, 1983.

Turner, M. S. "The Origin of the Universe". *Scientific American* 22 (2) (2013): 36–43.

Tyndall, J. "Address to the British Association for the Advancement of Science, Belfast, 1874". Retrieved from www.victorianweb.org/science/science_texts/belfast.html.

Unger, R. B. & L. Smolin. *The Singular Universe and the Reality of Time*. Cambridge: Cambridge University Press, 2015.

Valberg, J. "The Temporal Present". *Philosophy* 88 (2013): 369–86.

Van Bendegem, J. P. "The Possibility of Discrete Time". In C. Callender (ed.), *Oxford Handbook of Philosophy of Time*, 145–61. Oxford: Oxford University Press, 2011.

Vaughan, H. "The World". In H. Gardner (ed.), *The New Oxford Book of English Verse*. Oxford: Clarendon Press, 1972.

Vendler, Z. "Effects, Results and Consequences". In R. J. Butler (ed.), *Analytic Philosophy*. New York: Barnes & Noble, 1962.

Von Neumann, J. & H. Goldstine. "Numerical Inverting of Matrices of High Order". *Bulletin of the American Mathematical Society* 53 (1947): 1022–99.

Von Uexkull, J. *Theoretical Biology*. New York: Harcourt Brace, 1926.

Von Wachter, D. "Libet's Experiment Provides No Evidence against Strong Libertarian Free Will because Readiness Potentials Do Not Cause Our Actions". Unpublished manuscript.

Waismann, F. *Introduction to Mathematical Thinking*. New York: Harper & Row, 1959.

Warmbrod, K. "Temporal Vacua". *Philosophical Quarterly* 54: 215 (2004): 266–87.

Webb, R. "From Zero to Hero". In J. Webb (ed.), *Nothing: From Absolute Zero to Cosmic Oblivion: Amazing Insights into Nothingness*, 25–33. London: Profile, 2013.

Webb, R. "Why Does Space Have Three Dimensions?" *New Scientist* (2 September 2015).

Weinberg, S. *Dreams of a Final Theory: The Search for the Fundamental Laws of Physics*. London: Hutchinson, 1993.

Wells, H. G. *The Time Machine*, R. Luckhurst (ed.). Oxford: Oxford University Press, [1895] 2017.

Weyl, H. *The Philosophy of Mathematics and Natural Science*. Princeton, NJ: Princeton University Press, 1949.

Wheeler, J. W. *At Home in the Universe*. Woodbury, NY: American Institute of Physics Press.

Whipple, T. "Clock Watching". *Eureka* (January 2012): 22–5.

Whitehead, A. N. *The Concept of Nature*. Cambridge: Cambridge University Press, 1920.

Whitehead, A. N. "Religion in History". The first in a series of lectures on "Religion in the Making", delivered at King's Chapel, Boston, 1926. Retrieved from http://theology.co.kr/whitehead/religion/1.html.

Whitrow, G. J. *The Natural Philosophy of Time*, 2nd edn. Oxford: Oxford University Press, 1980.

Whitrow, G. J. *The Nature of Time*. Harmondsworth: Penguin, 1975.

Wicks, R. *Modern French Philosophy: From Existentialism to Postmodernism*. Oxford: Oneworld, 2003.

Wigner, E. "The Unreasonable Effectiveness of Mathematics in the Natural Sciences". *Communications in Pure and Applied Mathematics* 13(1) (1960): 1–14.

Williams, D. C. "The Myth of Passage". In his *The Philosophy of Time: A Collection of Essays*, R. M. Gale (ed.). London: Macmillan, 1968.

Wilson, E. O. *Consilience: The Unity of Knowledge*. New York: Vintage, 1999.

Wittgenstein, L. *Lectures on Philosophy: 1932–5*, A. Ambrose (ed.). Oxford: Blackwell, 1979.

Wittgenstein, L. *Philosophical Investigations*, G. E. M. Anscombe (trans.). Oxford: Basil Blackwell, 1963.

Wittgenstein, L. *Tractatus Logico-Philosophicus*, D. F. Pears & B. F. McGuinness (trans.). London: Routledge & Kegan Paul, 1961.

Wolpert, L. *The Unnatural Nature of Science*. London: Faber & Faber, 1992.

Woodward, J. "Causation and Manipulability". *The Stanford Encyclopedia of Philosophy* (winter 2016 edn), E. N. Zalta (ed.). Retrieved from http://plato.stanford.edu/archives/win2016/entries/causation-mani.

Yeats, W. B. "Under Ben Bulben". In his *Last Poems, Last Plays*. London: Macmillan, 1939.

Yourgrau, P. *The Disappearance of Time: Kurt Gödel and the Idealistic Tradition in Philosophy*. Cambridge: Cambridge University Press, 1991.

Zhmud, L. "'All is Number?': 'Basic Doctrine' of Pythagoreanism Reconsidered". *Phronesis* XXXIV: 3 (1989): 270–92.

Zimmerman, D. "Presentism and the Space-Time Manifold". In C. Callender (ed.), *Oxford Handbook of Philosophy of Time*, 163–244. Oxford: Oxford University Press, 2011.

Index